YUAN'

Collins

Collins
Mandarin
Chinese
Dictionary

HarperCollins Publishers
Westerhill Road
Bishopbriggs
Glasgow
G64 2QT
Great Britain

First Edition 2007

Reprint 10 9 8 7 6 5 4 3 2 1 0

© HarperCollins Publishers 2007

ISBN 978-0-00-725999-1

Collins© and Bank of English©
are registered trademarks of
HarperCollins Publishers Limited

www.collinslanguage.com

A catalogue record for this book is
available from the British Library

Typeset by Thomas Callan

Printed in Italy by
Rotolito Lombarda S.p.A.

Acknowledgements
We would like to thank those authors
and publishers who kindly gave
permission for copyright material
to be used in the Collins Word Web.
We would also like to thank Times
Newspapers Ltd for providing
valuable data.

EDITORIAL COORDINATION
Gaëlle Amiot-Cadey
Marianne Noble

CONTRIBUTORS
顾越施
谢曦
孙有玲
李欣
Eugene Benoit
Daphne Day

目录   **CONTENTS**

商标说明
认为是商标的词语都相应
地注有商标符号。
无论加注或漏注商标符号都
不应被认作影响任何商标
的法律地位。

William Collins' dream of knowledge for all began with the publication of his first book in 1819. A self-educated mill worker, he not only enriched millions of lives, but also founded a flourishing publishing house. Today, staying true to this spirit, Collins books are packed with inspiration, innovation, and practical expertise. They place you at the centre of a world of possibility and give you exactly what you need to explore it.

Language is the key to this exploration, and at the heart of Collins Dictionaries is language as it is really used. New words, phrases, and meanings spring up every day, and all of them are captured and analysed by the Collins Word Web. Constantly updated, and with over 2.5 billion entries, this living language resource is unique to our dictionaries.

Words are tools for life. And a Collins Dictionary makes them work for you.

Collins. Do more .

INTRODUCTION

Learning Chinese is definitely a challenge. However, in some ways Chinese is not particularly complicated. Words do not change with gender, number or even tense, and there are not many complicated grammatical traps for the unwary. However, other things about it make it hard for native English speakers to learn.

CHINESE PRONUNCIATION

THE FOUR TONES
Chinese is a tonal language – the pitch of any syllable affects its meaning.

There are four tones: first tone (high, even pitch); second (rising pitch); third tone (falling and then rising) and fourth tone (falling pitch). There is also a fifth (or neutral) tone, which is pronounced so quietly and quickly that there is no discernible tone at all.

Tones are a very important part of the pronunciation – and wrong tones can cause real confusion.

EXAMPLES OF DIFFERENCES IN TONES:

First tone	Second tone	Third tone	Fourth tone	Neutral tone
mā	má	mǎ	mà	ma
妈	麻	马	骂	吗
mother	hemp	horse	curse; swear	[question particle]

It may seem unnatural to native speakers of English to have pitch so rigidly attached to words, but the tone is as fundamental a part of any syllable as are its vowels and consonants.

PINYIN
Pinyin, the Chinese phonetic alphabet, was first introduced to help children learn to write characters, and foreigners and speakers of non-Mandarin dialects to pronounce Standard Chinese correctly. It is also very useful for dictionaries, as it provides an alphabetical order

by which characters can be sorted. However, *pinyin* is not used much in China. Although signs in China are sometimes written in *pinyin*, do not expect people to understand *pinyin* as they would characters – in short, it should not be regarded as a substitute for learning Chinese characters. It is, however, a good, accurate guide to pronunciation.

CHINESE CHARACTERS

The Chinese script has a history that goes back at least three thousand years.

Although there are tens of thousands of known characters, a lot of these are archaic (some so old that even their meanings are unknown). An educated Chinese person will know roughly 4-6000 characters, and 2-3000 is considered sufficient for basic literacy (newspapers and the like).

Each character has to be learned individually – with the shape of the character, the sound of it and the meaning learned together as a unit.

There is no way of predicting the sound and meaning of an unknown Chinese character with any degree of accuracy. This does not mean, however, that there is no system behind the characters at all. All characters contain at least one of the component parts known as "radicals", and almost all radicals have an element of meaning; if you are familiar with these, not only will using a dictionary be much easier, it will also help you identify more of the building blocks of the characters you are trying to learn.

SIMPLIFIED AND COMPLEX CHARACTERS

In the 1950s and 60s the government of the People's Republic of China simplified the Chinese script, in an effort to improve the literacy rate by making characters easier to write. It is these simplified characters which are used in this dictionary.

CHINESE GRAMMAR

Compared to many languages, Chinese grammar is not particularly complicated.

Words do not change according to gender, number or case the way they do in many European languages. Sentence structure is generally straightforward, and there are not many exceptions to the grammatical rules (unlike English).

TALKING ABOUT TIME

It is sometimes said that Chinese has no tenses. This is not quite true, but speakers of Chinese talk about time in a way that is quite different from ours.

The English tense system is based on the idea of before and after the point of view of the narrator. Things that happened before the time in which we are talking take the past tense, those that are in the process of going on, the present, and things that have yet to take place, the future. This is shown by a change in the verbs. Chinese verbs, on the other hand, do not change with tense, but an aspect marker is placed before or after the verb. Some of the most common are 了 le (for completed actions – usually *but not always* in the past), 过 guò (for events that have already taken place), 要 yào (for things that are going to happen) and 在 zài (for things that are in the process of happening). These are no more than generalizations, however, and it is important not to use them indiscriminately as substitutes for English tenses, as that is not what they are for.

Adverbs of time are often used to show what time relation events have to each other, such as 已经 yǐjīng (already), 曾经 céngjīng (once), or specific times or dates.

明年我去中国。 Míngnián wǒ qù Zhōngguó.
(literally: Next year I go China). I'm going to China next year.

MEASURE WORDS

These are not unique to Chinese – you occasionally see something similar in English.

> a *gaggle* of geese
> a *piece* of fruit
> six *pints* of milk etc.

They do not occur very often in English. In Chinese, however, measure words are mandatory when giving a number of nouns. It is important to remember to put them in – and also to get them right, as there are a lot of measure words in Chinese.

一只青蛙	yī zhī qīngwā	one frog
三部电影	sān bù diànyǐng	three films
五封信	wǔ fēng xìn	five letters

Different measure words are used for different types of objects. 张 zhāng is used for flat things, such as tickets, sheets and tables. 条 tiáo is used to talk about long, thin things such as ribbons, or fish. The most common measure word is 个 gè, and it is a useful "default setting" for when you cannot remember the exact term you need.

WORD ORDER

Because of the less specific nature of the Chinese view of time, the tendency to avoid redundancy and the lack of cases to show a word's function in the sentence, word order is important in Chinese. It generally follows a subject-verb-object pattern, although there are certain particles or rhetorical constructions that change the order slightly. If the word order is wrong, it can be very hard to unscramble the sense of a phrase or sentence.

All this may seem a little intimidating to a beginner. However, the challenge of learning Chinese is in direct proportion to the pleasure of being able to use it. Not only is it an absorbing and intriguing language, which can express both brutal frankness and extreme delicacy, it also brings with it great opportunities to learn about a new and very different country and culture. And there could be no better time to begin that exploration than now, when China is taking a greater role in the world.

Esther Tyldesley, University of Edinburgh

HOW TO USE THE DICTIONARY

On the following pages you will find an outline of how information is presented in your Collins Chinese Dictionary. We hope that this will help you to get the most out of your dictionary, not simply from its comprehensive wordlist, but also from the information provided in each entry.

CHINESE-ENGLISH SIDE

HEAD ENTRIES

On the Chinese side, head entries are ordered traditionally, that is by single-character entries with multiple-character entries beginning with the same character nested below them.

标	biāo
标本	biāoběn
标点	biāodiǎn
标记	biāojì
标题	biāotí
标志	biāozhì
标准	biāozhǔn

表	biǎo
表达	biǎodá

Single character entries are ordered by pinyin, that is alphabetically and then by tone. In Chinese, there are four tones, each represented by a different mark above the relevant vowel:

‾	first tone	(flat tone)	mā
´	second tone	(rising tone)	má
ˇ	third tone	(falling rising tone)	mǎ
`	fourth tone	(falling tone)	mà
	light or no tone		ma

Where characters have the same pinyin and tone, they are ordered by the number of strokes in the character, with the smallest number of strokes first.

八	bā
巴	bā
芭	bā
疤	bā

Where characters have the same pinyin, tone, and number of strokes, they are ordered by the first stroke in the character, as follows:
一 丨 丿 、 ㇇

The multiple-character entries nested below single-character entries are similarly ordered by the pinyin (including tone), and then by the number of strokes.

蒸	zhēng
蒸气	zhēngqì
蒸汽	zhēngqì

Polyphones, that is characters with more than one pronunciation, are crossed-referred to the alternative pinyin.

斗 dǒu [名] 1 (指容器) cup 2 (斗状
物) ▸ 烟斗 yāndǒu pipe ▸ 漏斗
lòudǒu funnel
→ see also/另见 dòu

斗 dòu [动] 1 (打斗) fight ▸ 斗鸡
dòujī cock fighting 2 (战胜) beat
→ see also/另见 dǒu

RADICAL AND CHARACTER INDEX
If you do not know the pronunciation for the Chinese character that you are looking for, you can use the index before the start of the Chinese-English side. For further information on how to use the radical index, see the introduction to that section.

THE STRUCTURE OF ENTRIES

On the Chinese side there are two levels of entry (single-character entries and multiple-character entries), both of which have essentially the same entry structure. Pinyin romanization is given for both types of entry.

Parts of speech are given in square brackets after the pinyin. Where a word has more than one part of speech, Roman numerals are used. For a full list of all parts of speech used, see page xxii.

Where an entry has more than one meaning, it is divided into categories, which are shown by an Arabic numeral.

When expressing yourself in another language, it is important to be aware of when you can use certain words and expressions and with whom – you would communicate very differently with a business colleague than with a friend. To help you, we have labelled words and expressions appropriately throughout the dictionary.

A full list of field and register labels used in the dictionary is shown on page xxiii.

EXAMPLES

Word examples are preceded by a shaded arrow ▶. Fuller examples are preceded by an empty arrow ▷.

TRANSLATIONS

Translations are shown in normal roman type after the part of speech or indicator. In general, we have only given one translation per meaning, since we believe this is the most accurate and helpful approach.

In a few cases, there is no equivalent at all, and an explanation rather than a translation has to be given. In such cases it is shown in italics:

压岁钱 yāsuìqián [名] *traditional gifts of money given to children during the Spring Festival*

British and American English variants are shown where appropriate, and alternative parts of translations are preceded by 或 ('or'):

大学 dàxué [名] university (英) 或 college (美)

HEADWORDS

The words you look up in the dictionary – 'headwords' – are listed alphabetically. Homonyms (words which are written in the same way but have different pronunciations) are shown as separate headwords and differentiated by the use of superscript numbers. For example:

bow¹ [bəu] N [c] 1 (*knot*) 蝴蝶结 húdiéjié [个 gè] 2 (*weapon*) 弓 gōng [把 bǎ]
bow² [bau] I VI (*with head, body*) 鞠躬 jūgōng II VT [+ *head*] 低头 dītóu

American spellings of words are always shown, at the headword which is spelled in the British way:

axe, (*US*) **ax** [æks] N [c] 斧 fǔ [把 bǎ]

Irregular past tenses and plural forms are also shown as headwords in their alphabetical position and cross-referred to the base form. For example:

children ['tʃɪldrən] N PL *of* **child**

went [wɛnt] PT *of* **go**

Parts of speech are given in upper case after the phonetic spelling of the headword. We have used the notations C, U and S and PL in square brackets after each noun to show whether nouns are countable, uncountable, singular or plural. C means that the noun is countable, and has a plural form (eg *I'm reading a book; she's bought several books*). U means that the noun is not mormally counted, and is not used in the plural (eg *Lesley refused to give me more information*). S (*for singular noun*) means the noun is always singular, and is usually preceded by *a, an* or *the* (eg *We need to persuade people to repect the environment*). PL means the noun is always plural, and is used with plural verbs or pronouns (eg *These clothes are ready to wear*). For a full list of all parts of speech used, see page xxii.

hairdryer ['hɛədraɪəʳ] N [c] 吹风
机 chuīfēngjī [个 gè]

hair gel N [U] 发胶 fàjiāo

kick-off ['kɪkɔf] N [s] 开场时间
kāichǎng shíjiān

Where an entry has more than one meaning, it is divided into categories, which are shown by an Arabic numeral. You will often find information in round brackets and *italics* after the meaning category number. This information functions as a 'signpost' to help the user select the right translation when there is more than one to choose from. This 'signpost' or indicator may give a synonym of the headword, typical contexts in which the word might appear or a label indicating the subject field in which the word is used.

A full list of field and register labels used in the dictionary is shown on page xxiii.

link [lɪŋk] **I** N [c] **1** 联系 liánxì [种
zhǒng] **2** (*Comput*) (*also*: **hyperlink**)
超链接 chāoliànjiē [个 gè] **II** VT
1 [+ *places, objects*] 连接 liánjiē
2 [+ *people, situations*] 联系 liánxì

All phrases are given in bold and preceded by a shaded arrow ▶. For example:

half-time [hɑːfˈtaɪm] (*Sport*) N [U]
半场 bànchǎng ▶ **at half-time** 半
场时 bànchǎng shí

TRANSLATIONS
Translations are shown in normal roman type after the part of speech or indicator. In general, we have only given one translation per meaning, since we believe this is the most accurate and helpful approach. In a few cases, there is no equivalent at all, and an explanation rather than a translation has to be given.

au pair [ˈəuˈpɛəʳ] N [c] 为学习语言
而住在当地人家里并提供家政服务
的外国年轻人

PINYIN
Pinyin romanization is given for all translations, except where, as above, there is no real equivalent in Chinese and an explanation rather than a translation has been given.

MEASURE WORDS
Measure words are given after translations of nouns which are countable and take a measure word. They are given in square brackets, with their pinyin. For more information on measure words, see the introduction on page vii.

banknote [ˈbæŋknəut] N [c] 纸
币 zhǐbì [张 zhāng]

KEYWORDS
Certain commonly used words, such as have and do, have been treated in special depth because they constitute basic elements of English and have very many uses and meaning. We have given them

a special design to make it easier to find the meaning of construction you are looking for.

◯ **KEYWORD**

have [hæv] (*pt, pp* **had**) **I** vT **1** 有 yǒu ▶ **he has** *or* **he has got blue eyes/dark hair** 他长着蓝眼睛/黑头发 tā zhǎngzhe lán yǎnjīng/hēi tóufa ▶ **do you have** *or* **have you got a car/phone?** 你有车/电话吗? nǐ yǒu chē/diànhuà ma? ▶ **to**
...

LANGUAGE NOTES
Language notes have been given at certain entries on the Chinese side, for example, 盏 zhǎn and 捌 bā. These are intended to give learners more information about certain important aspects of the Chinese language.

CULTURAL NOTES
A number of entries include cultural notes, giving an insight into Chinese life and culture. These notes cover many subject areas including political institutions and systems, national festivals and Chinese traditions and customs.

接下来的几页概要地叙述本词典内容的组织方式。希望此说明能让使用者不但能通过广泛的选词而且还能通过每个词条中的信息最有效地使用本词典。

汉英部分

顺序
在汉语部分，词目按传统顺序排列，即单字词条下嵌入以相同汉字开头的多字词条。

标	**biāo**
标本	**biāoběn**
标点	**biāodiǎn**
标记	**biāojì**
标题	**biāotí**
标志	**biāozhì**
标准	**biāozhǔn**

表	**biǎo**
表达	**biǎodá**

单字词条按拼音字母顺序排序，再按声调顺序排序。注意，轻声排在四声之后。同音字按笔画的多寡排列，笔画少的在前，笔画多的在后。

八	**bā**
巴	**bā**
芭	**bā**
疤	**bā**

笔画相同的同音字按起笔笔画排列，顺序为：一丨丿丶一

单字词条下的多字词条也先按照拼音（包括声调），再按照笔画数进行排序。

蒸	zhēng
蒸气	zhēngqì
蒸汽	zhēngqì

多音字，即有一个以上发音的汉字，会标明"另见"，后接另一个发音。

斗 dǒu [名] **1**(指容器) cup **2**(斗状
物) ▶ 烟斗 yāndǒu pipe ▶ 漏斗
lòudǒu funnel
→ see also 另见 dòu

斗 dòu [动] **1**(打斗) fight ▶ 斗鸡
dòujī cock fighting **2**(战胜) beat
→ see also 另见 dǒu

部首与汉字索引
如果使用者不知道所使用汉字的发音，部首目录和检字表位于汉英部分之前。有关如何使用部首索引，参见部首和汉字索引的第一部分。

词目构成
汉语部分的词条有两个层次，单字词条和多字词条，但它们的构成方式基本相同。所有词条都标注汉语拼音。

词性在方括号中用中文标注，紧随拼音之后。如果有一个以上的词性，用罗马数字标识。词性列表参见第xxii页。

如果一个词条有一个以上的词义，则归入不同的意类，用阿拉伯数字标出。当一个词条有多种含义时，读者可以根据阿拉伯数字后圆括号中的信息找到相关的语境，进而查到正确的翻译。圆括号中的信息起到"路标"的功能，此"路标"标示了主词条的同义词或近义词，以及使用主词条的典型语境。

专业学科领域及修辞色彩缩略语列表见xxiii页。

例子

以词的形式出现的例子，前面用实心灰色箭头▶标出。更完整的例子，前面用空心箭头▷标出。

翻译

一般情况下，作为最精确、有效的办法，每个意义只提供一个翻译。 在某些情况下，如果根本没有相应的翻译对等语，则提供该词的解释，而不是翻译，用斜体表示。

压岁钱 yāsuìqián [名] *traditional gifts of money given to children during the Spring Festival*

以-s结尾的名词, 若用作复数, 则标注为pl, 若用作单数, 则标注为sg

奥林匹克运动会 Àolínpǐkè Yùndònghuì [名] Olympic Games (PL)

算术 suànshù [名] maths (SG) (英), math (美)

必要时, 同时给出英式英语和美式英语两种翻译, 可供选择的部分前标有"或":

大学 dàxué [名] university (英) 或 college (美)

英汉部分

同音异义词

书写相同但发音完全不同的单词作为单独的词条出现, 并且用数字上标加以区分:

bow¹ [bəu] N [c] **1** (*knot*) 蝴蝶结
húdiéjié [个 gè] **2** (*weapon*) 弓
gōng [把 bǎ]
bow² [bau] **I** VI (*with head, body*) 鞠
躬 jūgōng **II** VT [+ *head*] 低头 dītóu

如上所示，数字上标明确表明该单词的发音完全不同。

单词的拼写变化也作为单独的词条录入，并参见首先出现的拼
写形式，单词的美式拼写总是在括号中给出：

pajamas [pə'dʒɑːməz] (*US*) N PL
= **pyjamas**

axe, (*US*) **ax** [æks] N [c] 斧 fǔ
[把 bǎ]

不规则动词的时态变化和不规则名词的复数形式作为单独的词
条出现，并且指示参照原形：

children ['tʃɪldrən] N PL *of* **child**

went [wɛnt] PT *of* **go**

如果一个单词有一个以上的词义，则归入不同的意类，用阿拉
伯数字标出。进一步的词义区分在括号中用斜体表示。当一个
词条有多种含义时，读者可以根据阿拉伯数字后圆括号中的信
息找到相关的语境，进而查到正确的翻译。圆括号中的信息起
到"路标"的功能，此"路标"标示了主词条的同义词或近义
词，以及使用主词条的典型语境。

专业学科领域及修辞色彩缩略语列表见xxiii页。

link [lɪŋk] **I** N [c] **1** 联系 liánxì [种
zhǒng] **2** (*Comput*) (*also:* **hyperlink**)
超链接 chāoliànjiē [个 gè] **II** VT
1 [+ *places, objects*] 连接 liánjiē
2 [+ *people, situations*] 联系 liánxì

短语

短语用黑体表示，并跟在实心灰色箭头标志▶后。短语包括不同种类的固定结构，感叹语和其他语法结构：

to have a baby
in the background
to pack one's bags

例子

例句用斜体表示，并跟在空心箭头标志▷后。英语中最常用单词，都给出了大量的例子及在相应语境中的翻译，有助于读者在具体的语境中正确使用单词。

翻译

一般情况下，作为最精确、有效的办法，每个意义只提供一个翻译。 在某些情况下，如果根本没有相应的翻译对等语，则提供该词的解释，而不是翻译。

au pair [ˈəuˌpɛəʳ] N [c] 为学习语言而住在当地人家里并提供家政服务的外国年轻人

拼音

词条及动词词组翻译都标注有拼音。如果该词条没有相应的翻译，则给出相关的解释以帮助读者理解，并省略拼音。

量词

量词在可数名词的翻译之后，和拼音一起在方括号中。关于量词的详细信息请见序言中的XXX页。

banknote [ˈbæŋknəut] N [c] 纸币 zhǐbì [张 zhāng]

关键词

对于一些极其常用的词，例如have 和 do，我们给予了长篇的注释。这类词是构成英语的基本要素，语意众多，用法复杂。本词典对该类词作了特别的外观设计，便于读者查阅。

have [hæv] (*pt, pp* **had**) **I** VT **1** 有
yǒu ▸ **he has** *or* **he has got blue
eyes/dark hair** 他长着蓝眼睛/黑
头发 tā zhǎngzhe lán yǎnjīng/hēi
tóufa ▸ **do you have** *or* **have you
got a car/phone?** 你有车/电话
吗? nǐ yǒu chē/diànhuà ma? ▸ **to
...**

语言注释
为了帮助读者更加准确、熟练地掌握并运用英语，我们对一些
易混淆词进行了详细的比较说明。

文化注释
对于英语国家中特有的文化现象，我们都加注了说明和解释。

略语表/**REFERENCE LIST**

PARTS OF SPEECH   词性

abbreviation	*ABBR*	简
adjective	*ADJ*	形
adverb	*ADV*	副
auxiliary verb	*AUX VB*	助动
conjunction	*CONJ*	连
compound	*CPD*	复合词
definite article	*DEF ART*	定冠词
indefinite article	*INDEF ART*	不定冠词
interjection	*INT*	叹
noun	*N*	名
noun abbreviation	*N ABBR*	名词缩写
singular noun	*N SING*	单数名词
noun (plural)	*N(PL)*	名词
noun plural	*NPL*	复数名词
numeral	*NUM*	数
plural	*PL*	复数
plural adjective	*PL ADJ*	复数形容词
plural pronoun	*PL PRON*	复数代词
past participle	*PP*	过去分词
prefix	*PREFIX*	前缀
preposition	*PREP*	介
pres part	*PRES PART*	现在分词
pronoun	*PRON*	代
past tense	*PT*	过去时
suffix	*SUFFIX*	后缀
verb	*VB*	动
intransitive verb	*VI*	不及物动词
transitive verb	*VT*	及物动词
indicates that particle cannot be separated from the main verb	*VT FUS*	及物动词

SUBJECT FIELD LABELS 专业学科领域

Administration	*Admin*	行政
Agriculture	*Agr*	农
Anatomy	*Anat*	解剖
Architecture	*Archit*	建筑
Art		艺术
Astrology	*Astrol*	占星术
Astronomy	*Astron*	天文
Motoring	*Aut*	汽车
Aviation	*Aviat*	航空
Badminton		羽毛球
Baseball		棒球
Biology	*Bio*	生物
Bookkeeping		簿记
Botany	*Bot*	植物
Bowls		滚木球
Boxing		拳击
Cards		纸牌
Chemistry	*Chem*	化
Chess		国际象棋
Cinema	*Cine*	电影
Climbing		登山
Clothing		服饰
Commerce	*Comm*	商
Computing	*Comput*	计算机
Cricket		板球
Cooking	*Culin*	烹饪
Drawing		绘画
Drugs		药品
Economics	*Econ*	经济
Electricity	*Elec*	电子
Fencing		击剑
Finance	*Fin*	金融
Fishing		钓鱼
Football		足球

SUBJECT FIELD LABELS　　　　　　专业学科领域

Geography	*Geo*	地理
Geology	*Geol*	地质
Geometry	*Geom*	几何
Golf		高尔夫
Grammar	*Gram*	语法
History	*Hist*	历史
Industry	*Ind*	工业
Insurance		保险
Law		法
Linguistics	*Ling*	语言
Literature	*Liter*	文学
Mathematics	*Math*	数
Medicine	*Med*	医
Meteorology	*Met*	气象
Military	*Mil*	军
Mining	*Min*	矿
Music	*Mus*	音
Mythology	*Myth*	神
Nautical	*Naut*	航海
Parliament	*Parl*	议会
Philosophy	*Phil*	哲
Photography	*Phot*	摄影
Physics	*Phys*	物
Physiology	*Physiol*	生理
Politics	*Pol*	政治
Police		警察
Post office	*Post*	邮政
Psychology	*Psych*	心理
Publishing		出版
Radio	*Rad*	广播
Railways	*Rail*	铁路
Religion	*Rel*	宗
Rugby		橄榄球
Science	*Sci*	科学

School	*Scol*	教育
	Sewing	缝纫
Sociology	*Sociol*	社会
Space		宇航
Sport		体育
Technical usage	*Tech*	术语
Telecommunications	*Tel*	电信
Tennis		网球
Texting		手机短信
Theatre	*Theat*	戏剧
Television	*TV*	电视
University	*Univ*	大学
Zoology	*Zool*	动

REGISTER LABELS　　　　　　修辞色彩缩略语

dialect		方
euphemism		婉
formal	*frm*	正式
formerly		旧
humorous		诙谐
informal	*inf*	非正式
literary	*liter*	文
offensive		侮辱
old-fashioned	*o.f.*	过时
offensive	*inf!*	疑讳/讳
pejorative	*pej*	贬
humble		谦
respectful		敬
slang		俚
spoken language		口
written		书
polite		客套
literal	*lit*	字
figurative	*fig*	喻

英语发音指导/GUIDE TO ENGLISH PHONETICS

CONSONANTS/辅音

[b]	<u>b</u>aby
[t]	<u>t</u>ent
[d]	<u>d</u>addy
[k]	<u>c</u>ork <u>k</u>iss <u>ch</u>ord
[g]	<u>g</u>ag <u>g</u>uess
[s]	<u>s</u>o ri<u>c</u>e ki<u>ss</u>
[z]	cou<u>s</u>in bu<u>zz</u>
[ʃ]	<u>sh</u>eep <u>s</u>ugar
[ʒ]	plea<u>s</u>ure bei<u>g</u>e
[tʃ]	<u>ch</u>ur<u>ch</u>
[dʒ]	<u>j</u>udge <u>g</u>eneral
[f]	<u>f</u>arm ra<u>ff</u>le
[v]	<u>v</u>ery re<u>v</u>
[θ]	<u>th</u>in ma<u>th</u>s
[ð]	<u>th</u>at o<u>th</u>er
[l]	<u>l</u>ittle ba<u>ll</u>
[r]	<u>r</u>at <u>r</u>a<u>r</u>e
[m]	<u>m</u>u<u>mm</u>y co<u>mb</u>
[n]	<u>n</u>o ra<u>n</u>
[ŋ]	si<u>ng</u>ing ba<u>n</u>k
[h]	<u>h</u>at re<u>h</u>eat
[x]	lo<u>ch</u>

VOWELS/元音

[iː]	h<u>ee</u>l
[ɪ]	h<u>i</u>t p<u>i</u>ty
[ɛ]	s<u>e</u>t t<u>e</u>nt
[æ]	b<u>a</u>t <u>a</u>pple
[ɑː]	<u>a</u>fter c<u>a</u>r c<u>a</u>lm
[ʌ]	f<u>u</u>n c<u>ou</u>sin
[ə]	ov<u>e</u>r <u>a</u>bove
[əː]	<u>ur</u>n f<u>er</u>n w<u>or</u>k
[ɔ]	w<u>a</u>sh p<u>o</u>t
[ɔː]	b<u>or</u>n c<u>or</u>k
[u]	f<u>u</u>ll s<u>oo</u>t
[uː]	p<u>oo</u>l l<u>ew</u>d

DIPHTHONGS/双元音

[ɪə]	b<u>ee</u>r t<u>ie</u>r
[ɛə]	t<u>ea</u>r f<u>air</u> th<u>ere</u>
[eɪ]	d<u>a</u>te pl<u>ai</u>ce d<u>ay</u>
[aɪ]	l<u>i</u>fe b<u>uy</u> cr<u>y</u>
[au]	<u>ow</u>l f<u>ou</u>l n<u>ow</u>
[əu]	l<u>ow</u> n<u>o</u>
[ɔɪ]	b<u>oi</u>l b<u>oy</u> <u>oi</u>ly
[uə]	p<u>oo</u>r t<u>our</u>

SEMIVOWELS/半元音

[j]	<u>y</u>et
[w]	<u>w</u>et

不规则动词/ENGLISH IRREGULAR VERBS

PRESENT	PT	PP	PRESENT	PT	PP
arise	arose	arisen	**fight**	fought	fought
awake	awoke	awoken	**find**	found	found
be	was, were	been	**fling**	flung	flung
(am, is,			**fly**	flew	flown
are; being)			**forbid**	forbad(e)	forbidden
bear	bore	born(e)	**forecast**	forecast	forecast
beat	beat	beaten	**forget**	forgot	forgotten
begin	began	begun	**forgive**	forgave	forgiven
bend	bent	bent	**freeze**	froze	frozen
bet	bet,	bet,	**get**	got	got,
	betted	betted			(US) goten
bid (at	bid	bid	**give**	gave	given
auction)			**go** (goes)	went	gone
bind	bound	bound	**grind**	ground	ground
bite	bit	bitten	**grow**	grew	grown
bleed	bled	bled	**hang**	hung	hung
blow	blew	blown	**hang**	hanged	hanged
break	broke	broken	(execute)		
breed	bred	bred	**have**	had	had
bring	brought	brought	**hear**	heard	heard
build	built	built	**hide**	hid	hidden
burn	burnt,	burnt,	**hit**	hit	hit
	burned	burned	**hold**	held	held
burst	burst	burst	**hurt**	hurt	hurt
buy	bought	bought	**keep**	kept	kept
can	could	(been able)	**kneel**	knelt,	knelt,
cast	cast	cast		kneeled	kneeled
catch	caught	caught	**know**	knew	known
choose	chose	chosen	**lay**	laid	laid
cling	clung	clung	**lead**	led	led
come	came	come	**lean**	leant,	leant,
cost	cost	cost		leaned	leaned
creep	crept	crept	**leap**	leapt,	leapt,
cut	cut	cut		leaped	leaped
deal	dealt	dealt	**learn**	learnt,	learnt,
dig	dug	dug		learned	learned
do (does)	did	done	**leave**	left	left
draw	drew	drawn	**lend**	lent	lent
dream	dreamed,	dreamed,	**let**	let	let
	dreamt	dreamt	**lie** (lying)	lay	lain
drink	drank	drunk	**light**	lit,	lit,
drive	drove	driven		lighted	lighted
eat	ate	eaten	**lose**	lost	lost
fall	fell	fallen	**make**	made	made
feed	fed	fed	**may**	might	–
feel	felt	felt	**mean**	meant	meant

PRESENT	PT	PP	PRESENT	PT	PP
meet	met	met	**spell**	spelt,	spelt,
mistake	mistook	mistaken		spelled	spelled
mow	mowed	mown,	**spend**	spent	spent
		mowed	**spill**	spilt,	spilt,
must	(had to)	(had to)		spilled	spilled
pay	paid	paid	**spin**	spun	spun
put	put	put	**spit**	spat	spat
quit	quit,	quit,	**spoil**	spoiled,	spoiled,
	quitted	quitted		spoilt	spoilt
read	read	read	**spread**	spread	spread
rid	rid	rid	**spring**	sprang	sprung
ride	rode	ridden	**stand**	stood	stood
ring	rang	rung	**steal**	stole	stolen
rise	rose	risen	**stick**	stuck	stuck
run	ran	run	**sting**	stung	stung
saw	sawed	sawed,	**stink**	stank	stunk
		sawn	**stride**	strode	stridden
say	said	said	**strike**	struck	struck
see	saw	seen	**swear**	swore	sworn
sell	sold	sold	**sweep**	swept	swept
send	sent	sent	**swell**	swelled	swollen,
set	set	set			swelled
sew	sewed	sewn	**swim**	swam	swum
shake	shook	shaken	**swing**	swung	swung
shear	sheared	shorn,	**take**	took	taken
		sheared	**teach**	taught	taught
shed	shed	shed	**tear**	tore	torn
shine	shone	shone	**tell**	told	told
shoot	shot	shot	**think**	thought	thought
show	showed	shown	**throw**	threw	thrown
shrink	shrank	shrunk	**thrust**	thrust	thrust
shut	shut	shut	**tread**	trod	trodden
sing	sang	sung	**wake**	woke,	woken,
sink	sank	sunk		waked	waked
sit	sat	sat			
sleep	slept	slept	**wear**	wore	worn
slide	slid	slid	**weave**	wove	woven
sling	slung	slung	**weep**	wept	wept
slit	slit	slit	**win**	won	won
smell	smelt,	smelt,	**wind**	wound	wound
	smelled	smelled	**wring**	wrung	wrung
sow	sowed	sown,	**write**	wrote	written
		sowed			
speak	spoke	spoken			
speed	sped,	sped,			
	speeded	speeded			

数字/NUMBERS

CARDINAL NUMBERS/基数

nought (英), naught (美), zero	0	零 (líng)
one	1	一 (yī)
two	2	二 (èr)
three	3	三 (sān)
four	4	四 (sì)
five	5	五 (wǔ)
six	6	六 (liù)
seven	7	七 (qī)
eight	8	八 (bā)
nine	9	九 (jiǔ)
ten	10	十 (shí)
eleven	11	十一 (shíyī)
twelve	12	十二 (shí'èr)
thirteen	13	十三 (shísān)
fourteen	14	十四 (shísì)
fifteen	15	十五 (shíwǔ)
sixteen	16	十六 (shíliù)
seventeen	17	十七 (shíqī)
eighteen	18	十八 (shíbā)
nineteen	19	十九 (shíjiǔ)
twenty	20	二十 (èrshí)
twenty-one	21	二十一 (èrshíyī)
twenty-two	22	二十二 (èrshí'èr)
twenty-three	23	二十三 (èrshísān)
thirty	30	三十 (sānshí)
forty	40	四十 (sìshí)
fifty	50	五十 (wǔshí)
sixty	60	六十 (liùshí)
seventy	70	七十 (qīshí)
eighty	80	八十 (bāshí)
ninety	90	九十 (jiǔshí)
one hundred	100	一百 (yībǎi)

a hundred and one	101	一百零一 (yībǎi líng yī)
two hundred and twelve	212	二百一十二 (èrbǎi yīshí'èr)
one thousand	1,000	一千 (yīqiān)
one thousand and one	1,001	一千零一 (yīqiān líng yī)
two thousand five hundred	2,500	二千五百 (èrqiān wǔbǎi)
a hundred thousand	100,000	十万 (shíwàn)
one million	1,000,000	一百万 (yībǎi wàn)
one billion	1,000,000,000	十亿 (shíyì)

ORDINAL NUMBERS/序数

first	1st	第一 (dì-yī)
second	2nd	第二 (dì-èr)
third	3rd	第三 (dì-sān)
fourth	4th	第四 (dì-sì)
fifth	5th	第五 (dì-wǔ)
sixth	6th	第六 (dì-liù)
seventh	7th	第七 (dì-qī)
eighth	8th	第八 (dì-bā)
ninth	9th	第九 (dì-jiǔ)
tenth	10th	第十 (dì-shí)
hundredth	100th	第一百 (dì-yībǎi)
hundred and first	101st	第一百零一 (dì-yībǎi líng yī)
thousandth	1,000th	第一千 (dì-yīqián)

FRACTIONS AND PERCENTAGES/分数、小数和百分数

a half	½	二分之一 (èr fēn zhī yī)
a third	⅓	三分之一 (sān fēn zhī yī)
a quarter	¼	四分之一 (sì fēn zhī yī)
two-thirds	⅔	三分之二 (sān fēn zhī èr)
nought (英) *or* naught (美) point five	0.5	零点五 (líng diǎn wǔ)
six point eight nine	6.89	六点八九 (liù diǎn bājiǔ)
ten per cent	10%	百分之十 (bǎi fēn zhī shí)
one hundred per cent	100%	百分之百 (bǎi fēn zhī bǎi)

部 首 检 字 表
RADICAL INDEX

检字方法说明:

(1) 根据字的部首在部首目录中查到该部首所在检字表中的号码;

(2) 按此号码在检字表中找到该部首,并根据字的笔画(字的笔画数不含其部首)查到该字的汉语拼音。

How to use this index:

(1) Use pages 2 – 4 to identify the radical. Note the number preceding it.

(2) In the index on pages 5 – 45, use this number to find all the characters appearing in this dictionary which contain the radical. Characters are ordered according to the number of strokes. The pinyin given will lead you to the correct entry.

部 首 目 录

(75) 车	(101) 火	(122) 用	(144) 舟
(76) 戈	(102) 斗	(123) 鸟	(145) 衣
(77) 比	(103) 灬	(124) 疒	(146) 羊
(78) 瓦	(104) 户	(125) 立	(147) 米
(79) 止	(105) 礻	(126) 穴	(148) 艮
(80) 支	(106) 心	(127) 衤	(149) 羽
(81) 日	(107) 聿 (肀)	(128) 疋	(150) 糸
(82) 曰	(108) 毌 (毋	(129) 皮	
(83) 水	母)	(130) 矛	
(84) 贝			**7 strokes**
(85) 见			
(86) 牛 (牜)	**5 strokes**	**6 strokes**	(151) 走
(87) 手			(152) 赤
(88) 毛	(109) 示	(131) 耒	(153) 豆
(89) 气	(110) 石	(132) 老 (耂)	(154) 酉
(90) 攵	(111) 龙	(133) 耳	(155) 辰
(91) 片	(112) 业	(134) 西 (覀)	(156) 卤
(92) 斤	(113) 目	(135) 页	(157) 里
(93) 爪 (爫)	(114) 田	(136) 虍	(158) 足
(94) 父	(115) 罒	(137) 虫	(159) 身
(95) 月	(116) 皿	(138) 缶	(160) 釆
(96) 欠	(117) 钅	(139) 舌	(161) 谷
(97) 风	(118) 矢	(140) 竹 (竹)	(162) 豸
(98) 殳	(119) 禾	(141) 臼	(163) 角
(99) 文	(120) 白	(142) 自	(164) 言 (讠
(100) 方	(121) 瓜	(143) 血	

检 字 表

5 strokes		升	shēng	乖	guāi	丸	wán
师	shī	长	cháng	质	zhì	之	zhī
曲	qǔ		zhǎng	周	zhōu	**3 strokes**	
肉	ròu	币	bì	**8 strokes**		为	wéi;wèi
6 strokes		反	fǎn	拜	bài	**4 strokes**	
串	chuàn	乌	wū	重	chóng	主	zhǔ
7 strokes		**4 strokes**			zhòng	半	bàn
非	fēi	生	shēng	复	fù	头	tóu
畅	chàng	失	shī	**9 strokes**		**5 strokes**	
8 strokes		甩	shuǎi	乘	chéng	兴	xīng;xìng
临	lín	乐	lè;yuè	**11 strokes**		农	nóng
		5 strokes		甥	shēng	**6 strokes**	
(3)		年	nián	**13 strokes**		良	liáng
丿 部		丢	diū	舞	wǔ	**7 strokes**	
		乒	pīng	疑	yí	学	xué
1 stroke		向	xiàng	**14 strokes**		**8 strokes**	
九	jiǔ	后	hòu	靠	kào	举	jǔ
2 strokes		**6 strokes**					
千	qiān	我	wǒ	(4)		(5)	
川	chuān	每	měi	**、 部**		**乙(乚一**	
及	jí	龟	guī			**乛) 部**	
久	jiǔ	系	xì	**2 strokes**			
3 strokes		**7 strokes**		义	yì		
午	wǔ	垂	chuí				

1 stroke	亟 qì	**4 strokes**	**2 strokes**
了 le; liǎo		考 kǎo	厅 tīng
2 strokes	**(6)**	协 xié	历 lì
乞 qǐ	**二 部**	毕 bì	**3 strokes**
也 yě		华 huá	厉 lì
飞 fēi	二 èr	**5 strokes**	**4 strokes**
习 xí	**1 stroke**	克 kè	压 yā
乡 xiāng	亏 kuī	**6 strokes**	厌 yàn
3 strokes	**2 strokes**	直 zhí	**6 strokes**
尺 chǐ	元 yuán	丧 sāng; sàng	厕 cè
巴 bā	云 yún	卖 mài	**7 strokes**
孔 kǒng	**6 strokes**	**7 strokes**	厘 lí
书 shū	些 xiē	南 nán	厚 hòu
4 strokes		**8 strokes**	**8 strokes**
司 sī	**(7)**	真 zhēn	原 yuán
民 mín	**十 部**	**10 strokes**	**10 strokes**
5 strokes		博 bó	厨 chú
尽 jǐn; jìn	十 shí		厦 xià
买 mǎi	**2 strokes**	**(8)**	雁 yàn
6 strokes	支 zhī	**厂 部**	
乱 luàn	**3 strokes**		**(9)**
7 strokes	古 gǔ	厂 chǎng	**匚 部**
承 chéng			

2 strokes		删	shān	**(11)**		**1 stroke**
区	qū	判	pàn	**卜 部**		亿	yì

匹	pǐ	**6 strokes**		**2 strokes**
巨	jù	剌	cì	卜	bo	什	shén
4 strokes		到	dào			仇	chóu
		制	zhì	**3 strokes**		化	huà
5 strokes		刮	guā	卡	kǎ;qiǎ	仍	réng
医	yī	刹	shā	占	zhàn	仅	jǐn
		剁	duò	外	wài		
		刻	kè			**3 strokes**
(10)		刷	shuā	**6 strokes**		仨	sā
刂 部		**7 strokes**		卧	wò	代	dài
		削	xiāo			付	fù
		前	qián	**8 strokes**		仙	xiān
3 strokes		剃	tì	桌	zhuō	们	men
刊	kān					仪	yí
		8 strokes		**(12)**		他	tā
4 strokes		剔	tī	**冂 部**		仔	zǐ
刑	xíng	剥	bāo				
列	liè	剧	jù	**4 strokes**		**4 strokes**
划	huá;huà			同	tóng	伟	wěi
刚	gāng	**9 strokes**		网	wǎng	传	chuán
创	chuāng	副	fù			休	xiū
	chuàng	**10 strokes**		**(13)**		伍	wǔ
5 strokes		剩	shèng	**亻 部**		优	yōu
别	bié	割	gē			件	jiàn
利	lì						

任	rèn	佛	fó	倾	qīng	**14 strokes**	
伤	shāng	**6 strokes**		倒	dǎo; dào	儒	rú
价	jià	供	gōng	俱	jù		
伦	lún	使	shǐ	倡	chāng	**(14)**	
份	fèn	佰	bǎi	倍	bèi	**八 部**	
仰	yǎng	例	lì	健	jiàn		
仿	fǎng	侄	zhí	**9 strokes**		八	bā
伙	huǒ	侧	cè	做	zuò	**2 strokes**	
伪	wěi	佩	pèi	偿	cháng	分	fēn; fèn
似	sì	依	yī	偶	ǒu	公	gōng
5 strokes		**7 strokes**		偷	tōu	**3 strokes**	
估	gū	便	biàn; pián	停	tíng	只	zhī; zhǐ
体	tǐ	俩	liǎ	偏	piān	**4 strokes**	
何	hé	修	xiū	假	jiǎ; jià	共	gòng
但	dàn	保	bǎo	**10 strokes**		并	bìng
伸	shēn	促	cù	傲	ào	关	guān
作	zuò	俄	é	傍	bàng	**5 strokes**	
伯	bó	侮	wǔ	储	chǔ	兵	bīng
佣	yōng; yòng	俭	jiǎn	**11 strokes**		兑	duì
低	dī	俗	sú	催	cuī	弟	dì
你	nǐ	信	xìn	傻	shǎ	**6 strokes**	
住	zhù	侵	qīn	像	xiàng	其	qí
位	wèi	**8 strokes**		**12 strokes**		具	jù
伴	bàn	借	jiè	僧	sēng		
伺	cì	值	zhí				

典	diǎn	**2 strokes**	**10 strokes**	**2 strokes**

典　　　diǎn
卷　　　juǎn
单　　　dān

7 strokes

养　　　yǎng
首　　　shǒu

8 strokes

益　　　yì

9 strokes

黄　　　huáng
兽　　　shòu

10 strokes

普　　　pǔ
曾　　　céng

12 strokes

舆　　　yú

────────

(15)
人(入)部

人　　　rén
入　　　rù

1 stroke

个　　　gè

2 strokes

介　　　jiè
从　　　cóng
今　　　jīn
仓　　　cāng
以　　　yǐ

3 strokes

令　　　lìng

4 strokes

全　　　quán
会　huì; kuài
合　　　hé
企　　　qǐ
伞　　　sǎn

5 strokes

余　　　yú
含　　　hán

6 strokes

舍　　　shè
命　　　mìng

8 strokes

拿　　　ná

9 strokes

盒　　　hé

10 strokes

舒　　　shū

────────

(16)
勹 部

1 stroke

勺　　　sháo

2 strokes

勿　　　wù
匀　　　yún

3 strokes

句　　　jù
匆　　　cōng
包　　　bāo

9 strokes

够　　　gòu

────────

(17)
几 部

几　　jī; jǐ

1 stroke

凡　　　fán

2 strokes

4 strokes

朵　　　duǒ

5 strokes

壳　　　ké
秃　　　tū

6 strokes

凭　　　píng

12 strokes

凳　　　dèng

────────

(18)
儿 部

儿　　　ér

2 strokes

允　　　yǔn

3 strokes

兄　　　xiōng

4 strokes

光　　　guāng
先　　　xiān

8 strokes	7 strokes	(20)	10 strokes
党 dǎng	哀 āi	冫 部	寒 hán
9 strokes	亭 tíng		
兜 dōu	亮 liàng		(21)
	帝 dì	2 strokes	一 部
(19)	8 strokes	斗 dǒu; dòu	
亠 部	衰 shuāi	4 strokes	3 strokes
	高 gāo	冲 chōng	写 xiě
1 stroke	离 lí	chòng	4 strokes
亡 wáng	旁 páng	次 cì	军 jūn
2 strokes	9 strokes	决 jué	7 strokes
六 liù	毫 háo	冰 bīng	冠 guàn
3 strokes	商 shāng	5 strokes	8 strokes
市 shì	率 shuài	冻 dòng	冤 yuān
4 strokes	10 strokes	况 kuàng	10 strokes
交 jiāo	就 jiù	冷 lěng	幂 mì
产 chǎn	11 strokes	8 strokes	
充 chōng	禀 bǐng	准 zhǔn	(22)
6 strokes	12 strokes	凋 diāo	讠(言) 部
变 biàn	裹 guǒ	凉	
京 jīng	豪 háo	liáng; liàng	2 strokes
享 xiǎng	15 strokes	9 strokes	计 jì
夜 yè	赢 yíng	凑 còu	订 dìng
		减 jiǎn	

认	rèn	诘	jí
讥	jī	诚	chéng
3 strokes		话	huà
讨	tǎo	诞	dàn
让	ràng	询	xún
训	xùn	该	gāi
议	yì	详	xiáng
记	jì	**7 strokes**	
4 strokes		语	yǔ; yù
讲	jiǎng	误	wù
许	xǔ	诱	yòu
论	lùn	说	shuō
讽	fěng	**8 strokes**	
设	shè	请	qǐng
访	fǎng	读	dú
5 strokes		课	kè
证	zhèng	调	diào; tiáo
评	píng	谈	tán
诉	sù	谊	yì
词	cí	**9 strokes**	
译	yì	谋	móu
6 strokes		谎	huǎng
试	shì	谚	yàn
诗	shī	谜	mí

10 strokes

谢	xiè
谣	yáo
谦	qiān

(23)
卩 部

1 stroke

卫	wèi

3 strokes

印	yìn

4 strokes

危	wēi

5 strokes

却	què
即	jí

7 strokes

卸	xiè

(24)
阝(在左)部

2 strokes

队	duì

4 strokes

阵	zhèn
阳	yáng
阶	jiē
阴	yīn
防	fáng

5 strokes

陆	liù; lù
阿	ā
陈	chén
阻	zǔ
附	fù

6 strokes

陌	mò
降	jiàng
限	xiàn

7 strokes

陡	dǒu
除	chú
险	xiǎn
院	yuàn

8 strokes		6 strokes		2 strokes		3 strokes	
陶	táo	耶	yē	切	qiē	功	gōng
陷	xiàn	郁	yù			务	wù
陪	péi	郊	jiāo	**3 strokes**		加	jiā
9 strokes		郑	zhèng	召	zhào	**4 strokes**	
随	suí	**8 strokes**		**4 strokes**		动	dòng
隐	yǐn	都	dōu; dū	负	fù	劣	liè
10 strokes		部	bù	争	zhēng	**5 strokes**	
隔	gé			色	sè; shǎi	劳	láo
11 strokes		**(26)**		**5 strokes**		助	zhù
障	zhàng	**凵 部**		免	miǎn	男	nán
12 strokes				初	chū	努	nǔ
隧	suì	**2 strokes**		**6 strokes**		劲	jìn
		凶	xiōng	兔	tù	**6 strokes**	
(25)		**6 strokes**		**9 strokes**		势	shì
阝(在右)部		画	huà	象	xiàng	**7 strokes**	
		7 strokes		剪	jiǎn	勉	miǎn
4 strokes		幽	yōu			勇	yǒng
邪	xié			**(28)**		**11 strokes**	
那	nà	**(27)**		**力 部**		勤	qín
5 strokes		**刀 部**		力	lì	**(29)**	
邮	yóu	刀	dāo	**2 strokes**		**厶 部**	
邻	lín			办	bàn		

3 strokes		双	shuāng
去	qù	**3 strokes**	
台	tái	发	fā;fà
4 strokes		圣	shèng
牟	mù	对	duì
5 strokes		**4 strokes**	
县	xiàn	戏	xì
6 strokes		观	guān
叁	sān	欢	huān
参	cān	**5 strokes**	
	shēn	鸡	jī
8 strokes		**6 strokes**	
能	néng	取	qǔ
		叔	shū
(30)		受	shòu
又 部		艰	jiān
		7 strokes	
又	yòu	叙	xù
1 stroke		**8 strokes**	
叉	chā	难	nán
2 strokes		桑	sāng
友	yǒu	**11 strokes**	
劝	quàn	叠	dié

(31)	
廴 部	
4 strokes	
延	yán
6 strokes	
建	jiàn

(32)	
工 部	
工	gōng
2 strokes	
巧	qiǎo
左	zuǒ
3 strokes	
式	shì
巩	gǒng
4 strokes	
贡	gòng
攻	gōng
6 strokes	
项	xiàng

差	chā
	chà
	chāi

(33)	
土 部	
土	tǔ
3 strokes	
寺	sì
地	de;dì
场	chǎng
在	zài
至	zhì
尘	chén
4 strokes	
坛	tán
坏	huài
坟	fén
块	kuài
坚	jiān
坐	zuò
社	shè

5 strokes		10 strokes		10 strokes		扰	rǎo
坦	tǎn	填	tián	鼓	gǔ	拒	jù
垃	lā	塌	tā			找	zhǎo
幸	xìng	墓	mù	(35)		批	pī
坡	pō	塑	sù	扌 部		扯	chě
6 strokes		11 strokes				抄	chāo
型	xíng	墙	qiáng	1 stroke		折	shé
垮	kuǎ	12 strokes		扎	zhā		zhé
城	chéng	增	zēng	2 strokes		抓	zhuā
垫	diàn	墨	mò	打	dá; dǎ	抢	qiǎng
7 strokes		17 strokes		扑	pū	抑	yì
埋	mái			扔	rēng	抛	pāo
8 strokes		(34)		3 strokes		投	tóu
堵	dǔ	士 部		扛	káng	抗	kàng
域	yù			扣	kòu	抖	dǒu
堆	duī	4 strokes		托	tuō	护	hù
培	péi	声	shēng	执	zhí	扭	niǔ
基	jī	7 strokes		扩	kuò	把	bǎ
堂	táng	壶	hú	扪	mén	报	bào
堕	duò	9 strokes		扫	sǎo; sào	5 strokes	
9 strokes		喜	xǐ	4 strokes		抹	mā; mǒ
塔	da; tǎ	壹	yī	扶	fú	拓	tuò
堤	dī			技	jì	拔	bá
						拣	jiǎn
						担	dān; dàn

押	yā	挺	tǐng	捣	dǎo	搜	sōu
抽	chōu	括	kuò	挨	āi;ái	援	yuán
拐	guǎi	拾	shí	**8 strokes**		搀	chān
拖	tuō	挑	tiāo;tiǎo	捧	pěng	搁	gē
拍	pāi	指	zhǐ	措	cuò	搓	cuō
拆	chāi	挣	zhèng	描	miáo	搂	lǒu
拎	līn	挤	jǐ	捷	jié	搅	jiǎo
拥	yōng	拼	pīn	排	pái	握	wò
抵	dǐ	挖	wā	掉	diào	揉	róu
抱	bào	按	àn	捶	chuí	**10 strokes**	
拉	lā	挥	huī	推	tuī	摄	shè
拦	lán	挪	nuó	掀	xiān	摸	mō
拌	bàn	**7 strokes**		掏	tāo	摆	bǎi
拧	níng;nǐng	捞	lāo	掂	diān	携	xié
招	zhāo	捕	bǔ	掖	yè	搬	bān
披	pī	捂	wǔ	接	jiē	摇	yáo
拨	bō	振	zhèn	掸	dǎn	搞	gǎo
抬	tái	捉	zhuō	控	kòng	摊	tān
拇	mǔ	捆	kǔn	探	tàn	**11 strokes**	
6 strokes		损	sǔn	据	jū;jù	摘	zhāi
挂	guà	捌	bā	掺	chān	摔	shuāi
持	chí	捡	jiǎn	**9 strokes**		**12 strokes**	
拮	jié	挫	cuò	搭	dā	撕	sī
拷	kǎo	换	huàn	提	dī;tí	撒	sā;sǎ
挡	dǎng	挽	wǎn	插	chā	撑	chēng

撮	cuō	花	huā	获	huò	**11 strokes**
播	bō	苍	cāng	**8 strokes**	蔫	niān
撞	zhuàng	芭	bā	著	zhù	**12 strokes**
撤	chè	苏	sū	萝	luó	蔬	shū
13 strokes	**5 strokes**	菜	cài	**13 strokes**
操	cāo	茉	mò	菠	bō	薯	shǔ
擅	shàn	苦	kǔ	萤	yíng	薪	xīn
14 strokes	茂	mào	营	yíng	薄	báo; bò
擦	cā	苹	píng	**9 strokes**	**14 strokes**
16 strokes	苗	miáo	募	mù	藏	cáng
攒	zǎn	英	yīng	董	dǒng	**15 strokes**
	范	fàn	葡	pú	藕	ǒu
(36)	茄	qié	葱	cōng	藤	téng
艹 部	**6 strokes**	落	là; luò	**16 strokes**
	茬	chá	葵	kuí	蘑	mó
1 stroke	草	cǎo	**10 strokes**	
艺	yì	茶	chá	蒜	suàn	(37)
2 strokes	荒	huāng	蓝	lán	**寸 部**
艾	ài	荣	róng	幕	mù	
节	jié	荤	hūn	蒙	mēng	寸	cùn
3 strokes	荫	yīn		méng	**3 strokes**
芝	zhī	荔	lì		Měng	寻	xún
4 strokes	药	yào	蒸	zhēng	导	dǎo
芽	yá	**7 strokes**		
	莲	lián		

4 strokes

6 strokes

寿　　　shòu

6 strokes

封　　　fēng
耐　　　nài

7 strokes

射　　　shè

9 strokes

尊　　　zūn

(38)

弋部

6 strokes

贰　　　èr

(39)

廾(在下)部

3 strokes

异　　　yì

(40)

大部

大　　dà; dài

1 stroke

太　　　tài

3 strokes

夸　　　kuā
夺　　　duó
尖　　　jiān

5 strokes

奉　　　fèng
奇　　　qí
奋　　　fèn
态　　　tài

6 strokes

牵　　　qiān
美　　　měi
奖　　　jiǎng

7 strokes

套　　　tào

8 strokes

奢　　　shē

9 strokes

奥　　　ào

(41)

尢部

1 stroke

尤　　　yóu

2 strokes

龙　　　lóng

(42)

小部

小　　　xiǎo

1 stroke

少　　　shǎo
　　　　shào

3 strokes

当　　　dāng
　　　　dàng

6 strokes

省　　　shěng

尝　　　cháng

8 strokes

常　　　cháng

9 strokes

辉　　　huī
赏　　　shǎng
掌　　　zhǎng

17 strokes

耀　　　yào

(43)

口部

口　　　kǒu

2 strokes

右　　　yòu
叶　　　yè
叮　　　dīng
号　　　hào
叼　　　diāo
叫　　　jiào
另　　　lìng
叨　　　dāo
叹　　　tàn

3 strokes		吧	ba	7 strokes		10 strokes	
吐	tǔ; tù	**5 strokes**		唇	chún	嗷	áo
吓	xià	味	wèi	哲	zhé	嗜	shì
吊	diào	哎	āi	哮	xiào	嗝	gé
吃	chī	呼	hū	哨	shào	嗓	sǎng
吸	xī	呢	ne; ní	哭	kū	**11 strokes**	
吗	ma	咖	gā; kā	哦	ó; ò	嘛	ma
各	gè	知	zhī	唤	huàn	**12 strokes**	
名	míng	和	hé	啊	ā; á	噎	yē
4 strokes		**6 strokes**		**8 strokes**		嘲	cháo
吞	tūn	咸	xián	啦	lā; la	**13 strokes**	
否	fǒu	哄	hòng	唱	chàng	嘴	zuǐ
呆	dāi	哑	yǎ	唾	tuò	器	qì
呕	ǒu	虽	suī	啤	pí	噪	zào
吨	dūn	品	pǐn	售	shòu	**17 strokes**	
呀	yā	咽	yān; yàn	**9 strokes**		嚷	rǎng
吵	chǎo	咱	zán	喷	pēn		
员	yuán	响	xiǎng	喇	lǎ	(44)	
听	tīng	哈	hā	喊	hǎn	**囗 部**	
吩	fēn	哆	duō	喂	wèi		
吻	wěn	咬	yǎo	喉	hóu		
吹	chuī	咳	ké	喧	xuān	**2 strokes**	
告	gào	哪	nǎ	善	shàn	四	sì
吝	lìn	哟	yō				
启	qǐ	咨	zī				

3 strokes	4 strokes	岳　　yuè	7 strokes
因　　yīn	帐　　zhàng	6 strokes	徒　　tú
团　　tuán	希　　xī	炭　　tàn	8 strokes
回　　huí	5 strokes	峡　　xiá	得 dé;de;děi
4 strokes	帖　　tiě	8 strokes	9 strokes
园　　yuán	帘　　lián	崖　　yá	街　　jiē
围　　wéi	6 strokes	崭　　zhǎn	循　　xún
困　　kùn	帮　　bāng	崇　　chóng	10 strokes
5 strokes	带　　dài		微　　wēi
国　　guó	9 strokes	(47)	12 strokes
固　　gù	幅　　fú	彳 部	德　　dé
图　　tú	帽　　mào		
7 strokes		3 strokes	(48)
圆　　yuán	(46)	行 háng;xíng	彡 部
8 strokes	山 部	4 strokes	
圈　　quān		彻　　chè	
	山　　shān	5 strokes	4 strokes
(45)	3 strokes	征　　zhēng	形　　xíng
巾 部	岁　　suì	往　　wǎng	6 strokes
	4 strokes	6 strokes	须　　xū
2 strokes	岛　　dǎo	待 dāi;dài	8 strokes
布　　bù	5 strokes	律　　lǜ	彩　　cǎi
帅　　shuài	岸　　àn	很　　hěn	

12 strokes

影 yǐng

(49)
犭 部

2 strokes

犯 fàn

4 strokes

狂 kuáng
犹 yóu

5 strokes

狐 hú
狗 gǒu

6 strokes

狭 xiá
狮 shī
独 dú
狱 yù

7 strokes

狼 láng

8 strokes

猜 cāi
猪 zhū

猎 liè
猫 māo
猕 mí
猛 měng

9 strokes

猩 xīng
猴 hóu

10 strokes

猿 yuán

13 strokes

獭 tǎ

(50)
夕 部

夕 xī

3 strokes

多 duō

8 strokes

梦 mèng

(51)
夂 部

2 strokes

处 chǔ;chù
冬 dōng

4 strokes

麦 mài
条 tiáo

5 strokes

备 bèi

7 strokes

夏 xià

(52)
饣 部

2 strokes

饥 jī

4 strokes

饭 fàn
饮 yǐn

5 strokes

饰 shì
饱 bǎo
饲 sì

6 strokes

饺 jiǎo
饼 bǐng

7 strokes

饿 è

8 strokes

馄 hún
馅 xiàn

9 strokes

馋 chán

11 strokes

馒 mán

(53)
丬 部

4 strokes

状 zhuàng

6 strokes

将 jiāng

(54)
广 部

广	guǎng	**11 strokes**		恨	hèn	懊	ào
3 strokes		腐	fǔ	**7 strokes**		**13 strokes**	
庄	zhuāng	**15 strokes**		恭	gōng	懒	lǎn
庆	qìng	鹰	yīng	悄	qiāo		
4 strokes				**8 strokes**		(56)	
床	chuáng	(55)		情	qíng	**门 部**	
应	yīng;yìng	**忄 部**		惭	cán		
5 strokes				悼	dào	门	mén
店	diàn	**1 stroke**		惟	wéi	**2 strokes**	
庙	miào	忆	yì	惊	jīng	闪	shǎn
底	de;dǐ	**3 strokes**		惦	diàn	**3 strokes**	
废	fèi	忙	máng	惨	cǎn	问	wèn
6 strokes		**4 strokes**		惯	guàn	闯	chuǎng
度	dù	怀	huái	**9 strokes**		**4 strokes**	
庭	tíng	忧	yōu	愤	fèn	闲	xián
7 strokes		快	kuài	慌	huāng	间	jiān
席	xí	**5 strokes**		愉	yú	闷	mēn;mèn
座	zuò	性	xìng	**10 strokes**		**5 strokes**	
8 strokes		怕	pà	慎	shèn	闹	nào
廊	láng	怪	guài	**11 strokes**		**6 strokes**	
庸	yōng	**6 strokes**		慢	màn	闻	wén
康	kāng	恢	huī	慷	kāng	**7 strokes**	
鹿	lù	恰	qià	**12 strokes**		阅	yuè
				懂	dǒng		

9 strokes

阔　　　kuò

（57）

氵部

---

2 strokes

汇　　　huì
汉　　　hàn

3 strokes

汗　hán;hàn
污　　　wū
江　　jiāng
池　　　chí
汤　　　tāng

4 strokes

沙　　　shā
汽　　　qì
沟　　　gōu
没　méi;mò
沉　　　chén

5 strokes

沫　　　mò

浅　　　qiǎn
法　　　fǎ
泄　　　xiè
河　　　hé
泪　　　lèi
油　　　yóu
沿　　　yán
泡　　　pào
注　　　zhù
泳　　　yǒng
泥　　　ní
波　　　bō
治　　　zhì

6 strokes

洪　　　hóng
洒　　　sǎ
洞　　　dòng
测　　　cè
洗　　　xǐ
活　　　huó
派　　　pài
洋　　　yáng
浑　　　hún
浓　　　nóng

7 strokes

酒　　　jiǔ
涉　　　shè
消　　　xiāo
海　　　hǎi
涂　　　tú
浴　　　yù
浮　　　fú
流　　　liú
浪　　　làng
涨　　zhǎng
涩　　　sè

8 strokes

清　　　qīng
添　　　tiān
淋　　　lín
淹　　　yān
渠　　　qú
渐　　　jiàn
混　　　hùn
渊　　　yuān
渔　　　yú
淘　　　táo
液　　　yè
淡　　　dàn

深　　　shēn
渗　　　shèn

9 strokes

港　　　gǎng
湖　　　hú
湿　　　shī
温　　　wēn
渴　　　kě
滑　　　huá
湾　　　wān
渡　　　dù
游　　　yóu

10 strokes

满　　　mǎn
源　　　yuán
溪　　　xī
溜　　　liū
滚　　　gǔn

11 strokes

漱　　　shù
漂　piāo
　　　piào
漫　　　màn
滴　　　dī
演　　　yǎn

漏	lòu	**5 strokes**		密	mì
12 strokes		宝	bǎo	**9 strokes**	
潮	cháo	宗	zōng	富	fù
澳	ào	定	dìng	寓	yù
13 strokes		宠	chǒng	**10 strokes**	
激	jī	审	shěn	塞	sāi
17 strokes		官	guān	**11 strokes**	
灌	guàn	实	shí	赛	sài
		6 strokes		察	chá
(58)		宣	xuān	蜜	mì
宀 部		室	shì		
		宫	gōng	(59)	
		宪	xiàn	辶 部	
2 strokes		客	kè		
宁	nìng	**7 strokes**		**2 strokes**	
它	tā	害	hài	边	biān
3 strokes		宽	kuān	**3 strokes**	
宇	yǔ	家	jiā	达	dá
守	shǒu	宵	xiāo	迈	mài
安	ān	宴	yàn	过	guò
字	zì	宾	bīn	迅	xùn
4 strokes		**8 strokes**		巡	xún
完	wán	寄	jì		
灾	zāi	宿	sù		

4 strokes	
进	jìn
远	yuǎn
违	wéi
运	yùn
还	hái；huán
连	lián
近	jìn
返	fǎn
迎	yíng
这	zhè
迟	chí
5 strokes	
述	shù
迪	dí
迫	pò
6 strokes	
选	xuǎn
适	shì
追	zhuī
逃	táo
送	sòng
迷	mí
退	tuì
逊	xùn

7 strokes		遛	liù	**4 strokes**		己	jǐ
速	sù	**11 strokes**		层	céng	已	yǐ
逗	dòu	遭	zāo	屁	pì		
逐	zhú	**12 strokes**		尾	wěi	(63)	
逝	shì	遵	zūn	局	jú	**弓 部**	
逞	chěng	**13 strokes**		尿	niào		
造	zào	邀	yāo	**5 strokes**		**1 stroke**	
透	tòu	避	bì	居	jū	引	yǐn
途	tú			届	jiè	**4 strokes**	
逛	guàng	(60)		**6 strokes**		张	zhāng
逢	féng	**彐(彑)部**		屋	wū	**5 strokes**	
递	dì			屎	shǐ	弥	mí
通	tōng	**2 strokes**		**7 strokes**		弦	xián
8 strokes		归	guī	展	zhǎn	**6 strokes**	
逻	luó	**4 strokes**		**8 strokes**		弯	wān
逮	dǎi; dài	灵	líng	屠	tú	**7 strokes**	
9 strokes		**5 strokes**		**9 strokes**		弱	ruò
逼	bī	录	lù	犀	xī	**8 strokes**	
遇	yù			属	shǔ	弹	dàn; tán
遗	yí	(61)				**9 strokes**	
道	dào	**尸 部**		(62)		强	qiáng
遂	suí			**己(巳)部**			qiǎng
遍	biàn	尸	shī				
10 strokes							
遥	yáo						

(64) 子 部		3 strokes		姜	jiāng	3 strokes	
		如	rú	姿	zī	红	hóng
		妇	fù	娃	wá	纤	xiān
子	zǐ	她	tā	姥	lǎo	级	jí
		好	hǎo; hào	姨	yí	约	yuē
2 strokes		妈	mā			纪	jǐ; jì
孕	yùn	4 strokes		7 strokes			
		妥	tuǒ	娱	yú	4 strokes	
3 strokes		妩	wǔ			纬	wěi
存	cún	妙	miào	8 strokes		纯	chún
孙	sūn	妖	yāo	娶	qǔ	纱	shā
		妨	fáng	婴	yīng	纷	fēn
4 strokes				婚	hūn	纸	zhǐ
孝	xiào	5 strokes		婶	shěn	纺	fǎng
		妻	qī			纽	niǔ
5 strokes		委	wěi	9 strokes			
孤	gū	妹	mèi	媒	méi	5 strokes	
		姑	gū	嫂	sǎo	线	xiàn
6 strokes		姐	jiě	婿	xù	练	liàn
孩	hái	姓	xìng			组	zǔ
		始	shǐ	10 strokes		绅	shēn
(65) 女 部				媳	xí	细	xì
		6 strokes		嫌	xián	织	zhī
		要	yāo; yào			终	zhōng
				(66) 纟 部		绊	bàn
女	nǚ	威	wēi			经	jīng
2 strokes		耍	shuǎ	2 strokes			
奶	nǎi			纠	jiū		

6 strokes		缠	chán	8 strokes		1 stroke	
绑	bǎng	11 strokes		骑	qí	玉	yù
结	jiē; jié	缩	suō	9 strokes		3 strokes	
绕	rào			骗	piàn	玖	jiǔ
给	gěi	(67)		骚	sāo	4 strokes	
绝	jué	马 部				玩	wán
统	tǒng			(68)		环	huán
7 strokes		马	mǎ	幺 部		现	xiàn
绣	xiù	3 strokes				玫	méi
继	jì	驮	tuó	1 stroke		5 strokes	
8 strokes		驯	xùn	幻	huàn	珐	fà
绳	shéng	4 strokes		2 strokes		珊	shān
维	wéi	驴	lú	幼	yòu	玻	bō
绸	chóu	5 strokes				皇	huáng
综	zōng	驾	jià	(69)		6 strokes	
绿	lǜ	驼	tuó	巛 部		班	bān
9 strokes		6 strokes				7 strokes	
缅	miǎn	骂	mà	8 strokes		球	qiú
缆	lǎn	骄	jiāo	巢	cháo	理	lǐ
缎	duàn	骆	luò			望	wàng
缓	huǎn			(70)			
编	biān	7 strokes		王 部		8 strokes	
缘	yuán	验	yàn			琴	qín
10 strokes				王	wáng		
缝	féng; fèng						

(71)	杏	xìng	树	shù	桶	tǒng
韦 部	极	jí	亲	qīn	梭	suō
	权	chā	柴	qī	梨	lí
	4 strokes		染	rǎn	**8 strokes**	
8 strokes	林	lín	架	jià	棒	bàng
韩　　hán	枝	zhī	柔	róu	棋	qí
	杯	bēi	**6 strokes**		椰	yē
(72)	柜	guì	栽	zāi	植	zhí
木 部	板	bǎn	框	kuàng	森	sēn
	松	sōng	栖	xī	椅	yǐ
木　　mù	枪	qiāng	档	dàng	棵	kē
1 stroke	构	gòu	桥	qiáo	棍	gùn
本　　běn	枕	zhěn	桃	táo	棉	mián
术　　shù	果	guǒ	格	gé	椭	tuǒ
2 strokes	采	cǎi	校	xiào	集	jí
朴　　pǔ	**5 strokes**		核	hé	**9 strokes**	
机　　jī	某	mǒu	样	yàng	楼	lóu
权　　quán	标	biāo	根	gēn	概	gài
杀　　shā	查	chá	栗	lì	**10 strokes**	
杂　　zá	相	xiāng;xiàng	柴	chái	模	mó;mú
3 strokes	柳	liǔ	案	àn	榜	bǎng
杆　　gān	柿	shì	**7 strokes**		**11 strokes**	
材　　cái	栏	lán	检	jiǎn	横	héng
村　　cūn	柠	níng	梳	shū		hèng
			梯	tī		

樱	yīng	车	chē; jū	**2 strokes**	**6 strokes**
橡	xiàng	**1 stroke**		成 chéng	瓶 píng
12 strokes		轧	yà	**4 strokes**	瓷 cí
橱	chú	**2 strokes**		或 huò	
橙	chéng	轨	guǐ	**5 strokes**	**(79)**
橘	jú	**4 strokes**		战 zhàn	**止 部**
		转	zhuǎn	**8 strokes**	
(73)			zhuàn	裁 cái	止 zhǐ
犬 部		轮	lún	**13 strokes**	**2 strokes**
		软	ruǎn	戴 dài	此 cǐ
6 strokes		**5 strokes**		**14 strokes**	**3 strokes**
臭	chòu	轻	qīng	戳 chuō	步 bù
9 strokes		**6 strokes**			**4 strokes**
献	xiàn	较	jiào	**(77)**	武 wǔ
		7 strokes		**比 部**	肯 kěn
(74)		辅	fǔ		**6 strokes**
歹 部		辆	liàng	比 bǐ	耻 chǐ
		8 strokes			
2 strokes		缀	chuò	**(78)**	**(80)**
死	sǐ	**9 strokes**		**瓦 部**	**支 部**
5 strokes		输	shū		
残	cán			瓦 wǎ	**10 strokes**
(75)		**(76)**			敲 qiāo
车 部		**戈 部**			

（81）

日 部

日	rì

2 strokes

早	zǎo

3 strokes

旱	hàn
时	shí
旷	kuàng

4 strokes

旺	wàng
昆	kūn
明	míng
易	yì
昏	hūn

5 strokes

春	chūn
是	shì
显	xiǎn
星	xīng
昨	zuó
香	xiāng

6 strokes

晒	shài
晓	xiǎo
晃	huàng
晕	yūn; yùn

7 strokes

匙	chí
晨	chén
晚	wǎn

8 strokes

暂	zàn
晴	qíng
暑	shǔ
量	liǎng
	liàng
景	jǐng
晾	liàng
智	zhì

9 strokes

暖	nuǎn
暗	àn

11 strokes

暴	bào

15 strokes

曝	bào

（82）

曰 部

5 strokes

冒	mào

7 strokes

冕	miǎn

8 strokes

替	tì
最	zuì

（83）

水 部

水	shuǐ

1 stroke

永	yǒng

5 strokes

泉	quán

（84）

贝 部

3 strokes

财	cái

4 strokes

责	zé
败	bài
账	zhàng
贬	biǎn
购	gòu
货	huò
贪	tān
贫	pín
贯	guàn

5 strokes

贵	guì
贴	tiē
贷	dài
贸	mào
费	fèi
贺	hè

6 strokes

| 贿 | huì |
| 资 | zī |

8 strokes

| 赌 | dǔ |
| 赔 | péi |

10 strokes

| 赚 | zhuàn |

12 strokes

| 赠 | zèng |
| 赞 | zàn |

(85)
见 部

| 见 | jiàn |

4 strokes

| 规 | guī |

5 strokes

| 觉 | jué |

(86)
牛(牜) 部

| 牛 | niú |

4 strokes

| 牧 | mù |
| 物 | wù |

5 strokes

| 牲 | shēng |

6 strokes

| 特 | tè |
| 牺 | xī |

(87)
手 部

| 手 | shǒu |

6 strokes

| 拳 | quán |

11 strokes

| 摩 | mó |

15 strokes

| 攀 | pān |

(88)
毛 部

| 毛 | máo |

8 strokes

| 毯 | tǎn |

(89)
气 部

| 气 | qì |

6 strokes

| 氧 | yǎng |

(90)
攵 部

2 strokes

| 收 | shōu |

3 strokes

| 改 | gǎi |

5 strokes

| 政 | zhèng |
| 故 | gù |

6 strokes

| 敌 | dí |

| 效 | xiào |

7 strokes

教	jiāo;jiào
救	jiù
敏	mǐn
敢	gǎn

8 strokes

散	sǎn;sàn
敬	jìng
敞	chǎng

9 strokes

| 数 | shǔ;shù |

(91)
片 部

| 片 | piàn |

8 strokes

| 牌 | pái |

(92)
斤 部

斤	jīn	**4 strokes**		育	yù	脱	tuō
4 strokes		爸	bà	**5 strokes**		**8 strokes**	
欣	xīn			胡	hú	期	jī;qī
7 strokes		(95)		背	bēi;bèi	朝	cháo
断	duàn	**月 部**		胃	wèi	脾	pí
9 strokes				胆	dǎn	腋	yè
新	xīn	月	yuè	胜	shèng	腕	wàn
		2 strokes		胖	pàng	**9 strokes**	
(93)		有	yǒu	脉	mài	腻	nì
爪(⺥) 部		肌	jī	胎	tāi	腰	yāo
		肋	lèi	**6 strokes**		腥	xīng
4 strokes		**3 strokes**		胯	kuà	腮	sāi
爬	pá	肝	gān	脆	cuì	腺	xiàn
6 strokes		肚	dǔ	胸	xiōng	腿	tuǐ
舀	yǎo	肠	cháng	胳	gē	**10 strokes**	
爱	ài	**4 strokes**		脏	zāng	膜	mó
		肾	shèn	胶	jiāo	**11 strokes**	
(94)		肺	fèi	脑	nǎo	膝	xī
父 部		肿	zhǒng	脊	jǐ	**13 strokes**	
		服	fú;fù	朗	lǎng	臀	tún
父	fù	朋	péng	**7 strokes**			
2 strokes		股	gǔ	脚	jiǎo	(96)	
爷	yé	肮	āng	脖	bó	**欠 部**	
		肥	féi	脯	pú		
				脸	liǎn		

欠 qiàn	**5 strokes**	**5 strokes**	**4 strokes**
4 strokes	段 duàn	施 shī	炖 dùn
欧 ōu	**9 strokes**	**6 strokes**	炒 chǎo
7 strokes	毁 huǐ	旅 lǚ	炊 chuī
欲 yù	殿 diàn	**7 strokes**	炎 yán
8 strokes	**11 strokes**	旋	炉 lú
款 kuǎn	毅 yì	xuán; xuàn	**5 strokes**
欺 qī		**10 strokes**	炸 zhá; zhà
9 strokes	(99)	旗 qí	炮 pào
歇 xiē	**文 部**		烂 làn
10 strokes		(101)	**6 strokes**
歌 gē	文 wén	**火 部**	烤 kǎo
	2 strokes		烦 fán
(97)	齐 qí	火 huǒ	烧 shāo
风 部		**1 stroke**	烟 yān
	(100)	灭 miè	烫 tàng
风 fēng	**方 部**	**2 strokes**	**8 strokes**
11 strokes		灰 huī	焰 yàn
飘 piāo	方 fāng	灯 dēng	**9 strokes**
	4 strokes	**3 strokes**	煤 méi
(98)	放 fàng	灿 càn	**10 strokes**
殳 部	房 fáng		熄 xī

11 strokes	8 strokes	6 strokes	(106)
熨　　　yùn	煮　　　zhǔ	扇　　　shān	心 部
12 strokes	焦　　jiāo	shàn	
燃　　rán	然　　rán	8 strokes	心　　xīn
15 strokes	9 strokes	雇　　gù	1 stroke
爆　　bào	照　　zhào		必　　bì
	10 strokes	(105)	3 strokes
(102)	熬　　āo	礻 部	忘　　wàng
斗 部	熊　　xióng		忍　　rěn
	11 strokes	1 stroke	4 strokes
6 strokes	熟　　shú	礼　　lǐ	念　　niàn
料　　liào	12 strokes	4 strokes	忽　　hū
7 strokes	燕　　yàn	视　　shì	5 strokes
斜　　xié		5 strokes	思　　sī
	(104)	祖　　zǔ	怎　　zěn
(103)	户 部	神　　shén	急　　jí
灬 部		祝　　zhù	总　　zǒng
	户　　hù	7 strokes	怒　　nù
5 strokes	4 strokes	祸　　huò	6 strokes
点　　diǎn	所　　suǒ	9 strokes	恐　　kǒng
6 strokes	肩　　jiān	福　　fú	恶　　ě;è
烈　　liè	5 strokes		恋　　liàn
热　　rè	扁　　biǎn		

7 strokes			**3 strokes**		碳	tàn
悬	xuán	**(108)**	矿	kuàng	磁	cí
患	huàn	**毋(毋母)部**	码	mǎ	**10 strokes**	
悠	yōu		**4 strokes**		磕	kē
您	nín	**1 stroke**	研	yán	磅	bàng
8 strokes		母　　mǔ	砖	zhuān	**11 strokes**	
惹	rě	**5 strokes**	砚	yàn	磨	mó;mò
悲	bēi	毒　　dú	砍	kǎn		
惩	chéng		**5 strokes**		**(111)**	
9 strokes		**(109)**	砸	zá	**龙 部**	
想	xiǎng	**示 部**	破	pò		
感	gǎn		**6 strokes**		**6 strokes**	
愚	yú	示　　shì	硕	shuò	聋	lóng
愁	chóu	**6 strokes**	**7 strokes**		袭	xí
意	yì	票　　piào	硬	yìng		
慈	cí	**8 strokes**	确	què	**(112)**	
10 strokes		禁　　jìn	**8 strokes**		**业 部**	
愿	yuàn		碑	bēi		
		(110)	碎	suì	业　　yè	
(107)		**石 部**	碰	pèng		
聿(聿)部			碗	wǎn	**(113)**	
		石　　shí	碌	liù	**目 部**	
9 strokes			**9 strokes**			
肆	sì		碟	dié		

目	mù	**10 strokes**				shèng
2 strokes		瞒	mán	**(115)**	盘	pán
盯	dīng	瞎	xiā	**罒 部**	盖	gài
3 strokes		**11 strokes**			盗	dào
盲	máng	瞥	piē	**4 strokes**		
4 strokes		**12 strokes**		罚	fá	**(117)**
盼	pàn	瞧	qiáo	**8 strokes**		**钅 部**
看	kān;kàn	瞪	dèng	罪	zuì	
盾	dùn					**2 strokes**
眉	méi	**(114)**		**(116)**	针	zhēn
5 strokes		**田 部**		**皿 部**	钉	dīng
眠	mián					**3 strokes**
6 strokes		田	tián	**3 strokes**	钓	diào
眶	kuàng	**4 strokes**		盂	yú	金	jīn
睁	zhēng	界	jiè	**4 strokes**		**4 strokes**
眼	yǎn	**5 strokes**		盆	pén	钙	gài
8 strokes		留	liú	**5 strokes**	钝	dùn
睦	mù	畜	chù;xù	盏	zhǎn	钞	chāo
瞄	miáo	**6 strokes**		盐	yán	钢	gāng
睡	shuì	略	lüè	监	jiān	钥	yào
9 strokes		累	lěi;lèi	盎	àng	钩	gōu
瞅	chǒu	**7 strokes**		**6 strokes**		**5 strokes**
		番	fān	盔	kuī	钱	qián
				盛	chéng	钻	zuān

	zuàn	**10 strokes**	**4 strokes**	**9 strokes**
铁	tiě	镊 niè	秒 miǎo	稳 wěn
铃	líng	镇 zhèn	种 zhǒng	**11 strokes**
铅	qiān	镑 bàng	zhòng	穆 mù
6 strokes		**11 strokes**	秋 qiū	**12 strokes**
铝	lǚ	镜 jìng	科 kē	黏 nián
铜	tóng		**5 strokes**	
铲	chǎn	(118)	秤 chèng	(120)
银	yín	**矢 部**	租 zū	**白 部**
7 strokes			积 jī	
铺	pū		秩 zhì	白 bái
销	xiāo	**7 strokes**	称 chèn	**3 strokes**
锁	suǒ	短 duǎn	chēng	的 de; dí; dì
锅	guō	**8 strokes**	秘 mì	
锈	xiù	矮 ǎi	**6 strokes**	(121)
锋	fēng		移 yí	**瓜 部**
8 strokes		(119)	**7 strokes**	
错	cuò	**禾 部**	稍 shāo	瓜 guā
锚	máo		shào	**14 strokes**
锤	chuí		程 chéng	瓣 bàn
键	jiàn	**2 strokes**	稀 xī	
锯	jù	秀 xiù	税 shuì	(122)
9 strokes		私 sī	**8 strokes**	**用 部**
锻	duàn	**3 strokes**	稠 chóu	
		季 jì		

用	yòng		

（123）

鸟 部

鸟 niǎo

4 strokes

鸦 yā

5 strokes

鸭 yā
鸵 tuó
鸳 yuān

6 strokes

鸽 gē

7 strokes

鹅 é

8 strokes

鹌 ān

11 strokes

鹦 yīng

（124）

疒 部

4 strokes

疮 chuāng
疯 fēng
疫 yì
疤 bā

5 strokes

症 zhèng
病 bìng
疼 téng
疲 pí

6 strokes

痒 yǎng

7 strokes

痤 cuó
痛 tòng

8 strokes

痴 chī
痰 tán

9 strokes

瘦 shòu
猴 hóu

10 strokes

瘤 liú

瘫 tān

11 strokes

瘾 yǐn
瘸 qué

12 strokes

癌 ái

16 strokes

癫 diān

（125）

立 部

立 lì

4 strokes

竖 shù

5 strokes

站 zhàn
竞 jìng

6 strokes

章 zhāng

7 strokes

童 tóng

9 strokes

端 duān

（126）

穴 部

穴 xué

2 strokes

究 jiū
穷 qióng

3 strokes

空 kōng
   kòng

4 strokes

突 tū
穿 chuān
窃 qiè

5 strokes

窄 zhǎi
容 róng

7 strokes

窝 wō
窗 chuāng

(127) 衤 部	(128) 疋 部	(132) 老(耂) 部	(135) 页 部

(127) 衤 部

2 strokes
补　　　bǔ

3 strokes
衬　　　chèn

4 strokes
袄　　　ǎo

5 strokes
袜　　　wà
袖　　　xiù
被　　　bèi

7 strokes
裤　　　kù
裙　　　qún

8 strokes
褂　　　guà
裸　　　luǒ

9 strokes
褪　　　tuì

(128) 疋 部

6 strokes
蛋　　　dàn

(129) 皮 部

皮　　　pí

7 strokes

(130) 矛 部

矛　　　máo

(131) 耒 部

4 strokes
耕　　　gēng

(132) 老(耂) 部

老　　　lǎo

(133) 耳 部

耳　　　ěr

4 strokes
耽　　　dān

5 strokes
职　　　zhí
聊　　　liáo

6 strokes
联　　　lián

9 strokes
聪　　　cōng

(134) 西(覀) 部

西　　　xī

(135) 页 部

页　　　yè

2 strokes
顶　　　dǐng

3 strokes
顺　　　shùn

4 strokes
顽　　　wán
顾　　　gù
顿　　　dùn
预　　　yù

5 strokes
领　　　lǐng

7 strokes
频　　　pín

8 strokes
颗　　　kē

9 strokes
题　　　tí
颜　　　yán

额 é

10 strokes

颠 diān

13 strokes

颤 chàn

（136）

虍 部

2 strokes

虎 hǔ

5 strokes

虚 xū

（137）

虫 部

虫 chóng

2 strokes

虱 shī

3 strokes

虾 xiā

蚁 yǐ

蚂 mǎ;mà

4 strokes

蚕 cán

蚊 wén

5 strokes

蛇 shé

6 strokes

蛙 wā

7 strokes

蜗 wō

蛾 é

蜂 fēng

8 strokes

蜚 fēi

蜡 là

蝇 yíng

蜘 zhī

蝉 chán

9 strokes

蝶 dié

蝴 hú

蝎 xiē

蝙 biān

---

10 strokes

蟒 mǎng

11 strokes

螺 luó

13 strokes

蟹 xiè

15 strokes

蠢 chǔn

（138）

缶 部

3 strokes

缸 gāng

4 strokes

缺 quē

17 strokes

罐 guàn

（139）

舌 部

舌 shé

5 strokes

甜 tián

7 strokes

辞 cí

8 strokes

舔 tiǎn

（140）

⺮（竹）部

竹 zhú

3 strokes

竿 gān

4 strokes

笔 bǐ

笑 xiào

笋 sǔn

5 strokes

笨 bèn

笼 lóng

笛 dí

符 fú

第	dì	**7 strokes**		(145)		(147)	
6 strokes		舅	jiù	**衣 部**		**米 部**	
等	děng						
策	cè	(142)		衣	yī	米	mǐ
筒	tǒng	**自 部**		**5 strokes**		**3 strokes**	
答	dā; dá			袋	dài	类	lèi
7 strokes		自	zì	**6 strokes**		**4 strokes**	
签	qiān			裂	liè	粉	fěn
筷	kuài	(143)		装	zhuāng	**5 strokes**	
简	jiǎn	**血 部**				粘	zhān
8 strokes		血	xiě; xuè	(146)		粗	cū
算	suàn			**羊 部**		粒	lì
管	guǎn	(144)				**7 strokes**	
9 strokes		**舟 部**		羊	yáng	粮	liáng
箱	xiāng			**4 strokes**		**8 strokes**	
箭	jiàn	**4 strokes**		羞	xiū	精	jīng
篇	piān	舱	cāng	**5 strokes**		粽	zòng
10 strokes		航	háng	着	zháo	**9 strokes**	
篮	lán	**5 strokes**		**6 strokes**		糊	hú
		船	chuán	羡	xiàn	**10 strokes**	
(141)		**6 strokes**		**7 strokes**		糙	cāo
臼 部		艇	tǐng	群	qún	糖	táng
						糕	gāo

11 strokes

糟　　　zāo

---

(148)
艮 部

3 strokes

既　　　jì

---

(149)
羽 部

羽　　　yǔ

4 strokes

翅　　　chì

12 strokes

翻　　　fān

---

(150)
糸 部

4 strokes

素　　　sù
索　　　suǒ

紧　　　jǐn

6 strokes

紫　　　zǐ

11 strokes

繁　　　fán

---

(151)
走 部

走　　　zǒu

3 strokes

赶　　　gǎn
起　　　qǐ

5 strokes

越　　　yuè
趁　　　chèn
趋　　　qū
超　　　chāo

8 strokes

趣　　　qù
趟　　　tàng

---

(152)
赤 部

赤　　　chì

---

(153)
豆 部

豆　　　dòu

5 strokes

登　　　dēng

8 strokes

豌　　　wān

---

(154)
酉 部

3 strokes

配　　　pèi

4 strokes

酗　　　xù

---

6 strokes

酬　　　chóu
酱　　　jiàng

7 strokes

酸　　　suān

8 strokes

醋　　　cù
醉　　　zuì

9 strokes

醒　　　xǐng

---

(156)
卤 部

卤　　　lǔ

---

(157)
里 部

里　　　lǐ; li

4 strokes

野　　　yě

(158)		蹄	tí	**(162)**		12 strokes
足 部		**11 strokes**		**豸 部**		警 jǐng
		蹦	bèng			**13 strokes**
足	zú	**12 strokes**		**3 strokes**		譬 pì
4 strokes		蹲	dūn	豺 chái		
距	jù	蹭	cèng	豹 bào		**(165)**
跃	yuè	蹿	cuān	**7 strokes**		**辛 部**
5 strokes		蹬	dēng	貌 mào		
跌	diē					辛 xīn
跑	pǎo	**(159)**		**(163)**		**7 strokes**
6 strokes		**身 部**		**角 部**		辣 là
跨	kuà					**9 strokes**
跳	tiào	身	shēn	角 jiǎo		辨 biàn
跺	duò	**6 strokes**		**6 strokes**		辩 biàn
跪	guì	躲	duǒ	触 chù		**10 strokes**
路	lù	**8 strokes**		解 jiě		
跟	gēn	躺	tǎng			**(166)**
8 strokes				**(164)**		**青 部**
踢	tī	**(160)**		**言(訁见讠)部**		
踩	cǎi	**采 部**				青 qīng
踏	tà			言 yán		**6 strokes**
9 strokes		**5 strokes**		**7 strokes**		静 jìng
踹	chuài	释	shì	誓 shì		

（167） 雨 部	（168） 齿 部	4 strokes	8 strokes
		鱿　　　yóu	
雨　　　yǔ	齿　　　chǐ	6 strokes	9 strokes
3 strokes	6 strokes	鲜　　　xiān	鞭　　　biān
雪　　　xuě	龈　　　yín	7 strokes	（173） 骨 部
5 strokes		鲨　　　shā	
雷　　　léi	（169） 隹 部	9 strokes	
零　　　líng		鳄　　　è	骨　　　gǔ
雾　　　wù		12 strokes	
雹　　　báo	4 strokes	鳝　　　shàn	（174） 鬼 部
6 strokes	雄　　　xióng	鳞　　　lín	
需　　　xū	6 strokes		鬼　　　guǐ
7 strokes	雌　　　cí	（172） 革 部	4 strokes
霉　　　méi	8 strokes		魂　　　hún
9 strokes	雕　　　diāo	革　　　gé	魁　　　kuí
霜　　　shuāng		4 strokes	5 strokes
11 strokes	（171） 鱼 部	靴　　　xuē	魅　　　mèi
霭　　　ǎi		6 strokes	11 strokes
13 strokes	鱼　　　yú	鞋　　　xié	魔　　　mó
露　　lòu；lù		鞍　　　ān	

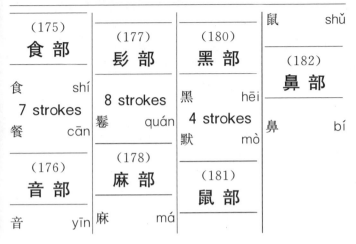

(175)

食 部

食   shí

7 strokes

餐   cān

(176)

音 部

音   yīn

(177)

髟 部

8 strokes

鬈   quán

(178)

麻 部

麻   má

(180)

黑 部

黑   hēi

4 strokes

默   mò

(181)

鼠 部

鼠   shǔ

(182)

鼻 部

鼻   bí

阿 ā [前缀] (方) ▶阿爸 ābà dad

阿拉伯 Ālābó [名] Arabia

阿拉伯数字 Ālābó shùzì [名] Arabic numerals (PL)

阿姨 āyí [名] (指年长妇女) auntie

啊 ā [叹] oh ▷啊！着火了！ Ā! Zháohuǒ le! Oh! It's caught fire!

哎 āi [叹] 1 (表示惊讶或不满) oh ▷哎！这么贵！ Āi! Zhème guì! Oh! It's so expensive! 2 (表示提醒) hey ▷哎！别踩了那朵花。 Āi! Bié cǎi le nà duǒ huā. Hey! Careful not to tread on that flower.

哎呀 āiyā [叹] oh ▷哎呀，这条路真难走！ Āiyā, zhè tiáo lù zhēn nán zǒu! Oh, this road is hard going!

哀 āi [形] (悲痛) sad

哀悼 āidào [动] mourn

挨 āi [动] 1 (靠近) be next to ▷两个孩子挨着门坐。 Liǎng gè háizi āi zhe mén zuò. The two children sat by the door. 2 (逐个) ▶挨个儿 āigèr one by one
→ see also/另见 ái

挨 ái [动] 1 (遭受) suffer ▶挨饿 ái'è suffer from hunger ▶挨骂 áimà get told off 2 (艰难度过) endure

挨打 áidǎ [动] be beaten up

癌 ái [名] cancer ▶癌症 áizhèng cancer

矮 ǎi [形] 1 (指人) short 2 (指物) low

艾 ài [名] (植) mugwort

艾滋病 àizībìng [名] AIDS

爱 ài [动] 1 (恋) love ▶爱人 àiren husband or wife, partner ▷我爱你。 Wǒ ài nǐ. I love you. 2 (喜欢) enjoy ▷爱上网 ài shàngwǎng enjoy surfing the net 3 (容易) ▷她爱晕车。 Tā ài yùnchē. She tends to get car sick.

爱好 àihào [动] be keen on ▷她有广泛的爱好。 Tā yǒu guǎngfàn de àihào. She has many hobbies.

爱护 àihù [动] take care of

爱情 àiqíng [名] love

安 ān I [形] 1 (安定) quiet ▶不安

bù'ān anxious **2**(平安) safe ▷治安 zhì'ān public order **II** [动] **1**(使安静) calm ▷安心 ānxīn calm the nerves **2**(安装) fit ▷门上安把锁 mén shàng ān bǎ suǒ fit a lock on the door

安定 āndìng **I** [形] stable **II** [动] stabilize ▷安定局面 āndìng júmiàn stabilize the situation

安家 ānjiā [动] **1**(also: 安置家庭) settle **2**(结婚) get married

安检 ānjiǎn [名] security check

安静 ānjìng [形] **1**(无声) quiet **2**(平静) peaceful

安乐死 ānlèsǐ [名] euthanasia

安排 ānpái [动] arrange

安全 ānquán [形] safe ▷注意安全。 Zhùyì ānquán. Be sure to take care. ▷人身安全 rénshēn ānquán personal safety

安全套 ānquántào [名] condom

安慰 ānwèi **I** [动] comfort **II** [形] reassured

安心 ānxīn [动] (形容心情) stop worrying

安装 ānzhuāng [动] install

鹌 ān see below/见下文

鹌鹑 ānchún [名] quail

鞍 ān [名] saddle ▷马鞍 mǎ'ān saddle

岸 àn [名] edge ▷河岸 hé'àn river bank ▷海岸 hǎi'àn seashore

按 àn **I** [动] **1**(用力压) press ▷按电钮 àn diànniǔ press a button ▷按门铃 àn ménlíng push a doorbell **2**(人) push ... down **3**(抑制) restrain ▷按不住心头怒火 àn bùzhù xīntóu nùhuǒ be unable to restrain one's fury **II** [介] (依照) according to ▷按制度办事 àn zhìdù bànshì do things by the book

按揭 ànjiē [名] mortgage

按摩 ànmó [动] massage

按照 ànzhào [介] according to ▷按照课本 ànzhào kèběn according to the text book

案 àn [名] (案件) case ▷案子 ànzi case

案件 ànjiàn [名] case

暗 àn **I** [形] (昏暗) dim ▷今晚月光很暗。 Jīnwǎn yuèguāng hěn àn. Tonight the moon is dim. **II** [副] secretly

暗号 ànhào [名] secret signal

暗杀 ànshā [动] assassinate

暗示 ànshì [动] hint

暗自 ànzì [副] secretly

肮 āng see below/见下文

肮脏 āngzāng [形] **1**(不干净) filthy **2**(喻) (不道德) vile

盎 àng [形] (书) abundant

盎司 àngsī [量] ounce

熬 áo [动] **1**(煮) stew ▷熬粥 áozhōu make porridge **2**(忍受) endure

熬夜 áoyè [动] stay up late

袄 ǎo [名] coat ▶棉袄 mián'ǎo padded jacket

傲 ào [形] proud
傲慢 àomàn [形] arrogant
傲气 àoqì [名] arrogance

奥 ào [形] profound
奥林匹克运动会 Àolínpǐkè Yùndònghuì [名] Olympic Games (PL)

澳 ào [名] bay
澳大利亚 Àodàlìyà [名] Australia

懊 ào [形] 1 (后悔) regretful 2 (恼怒) annoyed
懊悔 àohuǐ [动] regret

八 bā [数] eight ▶八月 bāyuè August

巴 bā [名] ▶下巴 xiàbā chin ▶尾巴 wěibā tail ▶嘴巴 zuǐbā mouth
巴士 bāshì [名] bus
巴掌 bāzhang [名] (手掌) palm

芭 bā [名] banana
芭蕾舞 bāléiwǔ [名] ballet

疤 bā [名] scar

捌 bā [数] eight
This is the complex character for eight, which is mainly used in banks, on receipts, etc.

拔 bá [动] 1 (抽出) pull ... up ▶拔草 bá...cǎo weed 2 (取下) pull ... out

▷拔牙 báyá pull out a tooth **3** (挑选) choose ▷选拔人才 xuǎnbá réncái select talented people **4** (超出) exceed ▷海拔 hǎibá height above sea level

把 bǎ **I** [动] **1** (握住) hold **2** (看守) guard **II** [名] (把手) handle **III** [量] **1** ▷一把刀 yī bǎ dāo a knife ▷一把剪子 yī bǎ jiǎnzi a pair of scissors

measure word, used for objects with a handle

2 handful ▷一把米 yī bǎ mǐ a handful of rice

measure word, used for the quantity of something that can be held in a hand

3 ▷两把花 liǎng bǎ huā two bunches of flowers

measure word, used for something that can be bundled together

IV [介] ▷把门关好 bǎ mén guān hǎo shut the door ▷把作业做完 bǎ zuòyè zuò wán finish doing one's homework ▷她把书放在桌子上了。 Tā bǎ shū fàngzài zhuōzi shàng le. She put the book on the table.

把 bǎ is used to alter the word order of a sentence, especially when the verb is a complex one. The normal word order of Subject + Verb + Object, becomes Subject + 把 + Object + Verb. It is very commonly used when the verb implies

a change of place, or when the verb is followed by certain complements. For instance, a word-for-word translation of the sentence, 我把书放在那儿。 Wǒ bǎ shū fàng zài nàr. (I put the book there) is 'I 把 book put there'.

把手 bǎshou [名] handle

把握 bǎwò **I** [动] grasp ▷把握时机 bǎwò shíjī seize the opportunity **II** [名] certainty ▷没把握 méi bǎwò there is no certainty

爸 bà [名] father

爸爸 bàba [名] dad

吧 ba [助] **1** (在句尾表示建议) ▷我们回家吧。 Wǒmen huíjiā ba. Let's go home. ▷吃吧! Chī ba! Eat! ▷再想想吧。 Zài xiǎngxiang ba. Think about it again. **2** (在句尾表示对推测的肯定) ▷你听说了吧? Nǐ tīngshuō le ba? You may have heard about this. ▷他明天走吧? Tā míngtiān zǒu ba? Is he leaving tomorrow?

Adding 吧 ba at the end of a sentence forms a suggestion, e.g. 我们走吧。 Wǒmen zǒu ba. (Let's go). But adding 吗 ma at the end of a sentence forms a question, e.g. 我们走吗? Wǒmen zǒu ma? (Shall we go?).

白 bái **I** [形] **1** (白色) white ▷白

糖 báitáng white sugar ▶白领 báilǐng white-collar **2** (明亮) bright ▶白天 báitiān daytime **3** (平淡) plain ▶白开水 bái kāishuǐ boiled water ▶白米饭 bái mǐfàn boiled rice **II** (副) (无结果) in vain ▶白费 báifèi waste ▶白等 báiděng wait in vain

白菜 báicài [名] Chinese cabbage

白酒 báijiǔ [名] clear spirit

白人 báirén [名] white people (PL)

百 bǎi [数] hundred

百分之百 bǎi fēn zhī bǎi absolutely

百万 bǎiwàn [数] million

佰 bǎi [名] hundred

This is the character for hundred which is used in banks, on receipts, cheques etc.

摆 bǎi [动] **1** (放置) arrange ▶摆放 bǎifàng place **2** (摇动) wave ▶摆动 bǎidòng sway ▶她向我摆手。 Tā xiàng wǒ bǎi shǒu. She waved her hand at me.

摆设 bǎishè [动] furnish and decorate

败 bài [动] (打败) defeat

败坏 bàihuài **I** [动] corrupt **II** [形] corrupt

拜 bài [动] (会见) pay a visit ▶拜访 bàifǎng visit

拜年 bàinián [动] pay a New Year call

拜托 bàituō [动] ▷拜托您给看会儿我女儿。 Bàituō nín gěi kān huǐr wǒ nǚr. Would you be kind enough to look after my daughter for a while?

班 bān **I** [名] **1** (班级) class ▶班长 bānzhǎng class monitor **2** (交通) scheduled trip ▶班机 bānjī scheduled flight ▶末班车 mòbānchē the last bus **3** (轮班) shift ▶上班 shàngbān go to work ▶下班 xiàbān finish work ▶晚班 wǎnbān night shift **4** (军) squad **II** [量] ▷下一班船 xià yī bān chuán the next boat ▷错过一班飞机 cuòguò yī bān fēijī miss a flight

measure word, used for scheduled transportations

班级 bānjí [名] classes (PL)

搬 bān [动] **1** (移动) take ... away ▷把这些东西搬走。 Bǎ zhèxiē dōngxi bān zǒu. Take these things away. **2** (迁移) move ▶搬家 bānjiā move house

板 bǎn **I** [名] (片状硬物) board **II** [动] put on a stern expression ▷板着脸 bǎn zhe liǎn pull a long face

办 bàn [动] **1** (处理) handle ▶办事 bànshì handle affairs ▷我们该怎么办？ Wǒmen gāi zěnme bàn? What should we do? **2** (创设) set ... up ▶办工厂 bàn gōngchǎng set up a factory **3** (经营) run ▶办学 bànxué run a school **4** (展览)

stage ▷办画展 bàn huàzhǎn stage an art exhibition

办法 bànfǎ [名] way ▷想办法 xiǎng bànfǎ find a way ▷联系办法 liánxì bànfǎ means of contact

办公 bàngōng [动] work

办理 bànlǐ [动] handle

半 bàn I [数] 1 (二分之一) half ▷半价 bàn jià half price ▷半年 bàn nián half a year 2 (在中间) middle ▷半夜 bànyè midnight II [副] partially ▷半新 bàn xīn almost new

半导体 bàndǎotǐ [名] 1 (指物质) semiconductor 2 (收音机) transistor radio

半岛 bàndǎo [名] peninsula

半径 bànjìng [名] radius

半球 bànqiú [名] hemisphere

半天 bàntiān [名] for quite a while ▷他等了半天。 Tā děng le bàntiān. He waited for quite a while.

伴 bàn [名] company ▷做伴 zuòbàn keep company

拌 bàn [动] (搅和) mix

绊 bàn [动] (使跌倒) trip

瓣 bàn I [名] (指花儿) petal II [量] ▷几瓣蒜 jǐ bàn suàn a few cloves of garlic ▷一瓣橘子 yī bàn júzi a segment of orange

measure word, used to describe flower petals and segments of fruits

帮 bāng [动] (帮助) help ▷我帮他买票。 Wǒ bāng tā mǎi piào. I helped him get the tickets.

帮忙 bāngmáng [动] help ▷请您帮我个忙。 Qǐng nín bāng wǒ ge máng. Please can you help me out?

帮助 bāngzhù [动] help ▷谢谢您的帮助。 Xièxie nín de bāngzhù. Thank you for your help.

绑 bǎng [动] tie up

榜 bǎng [名] list of names

榜样 bǎngyàng [名] model

棒 bàng I [名] (棍子) cudgel ▷棒子 bàngzi club II [形] (口) great ▷他英语说得很棒。 Tā Yīngyǔ shuō de hěn bàng. He speaks great English.

傍 bàng [动] be close to

傍晚 bàngwǎn [名] dusk

磅 bàng [量] pound

镑 bàng [名] pound

包 bāo I [动] 1 (包裹) wrap 2 (包含) include 3 (担保) guarantee 4 (约定专用) hire ▷包车 bāo chē hire a car ▷包飞机 bāo fēijī charter a plane II [名] 1 (包裹) parcel 2 (口袋) bag ▷背包 bēibāo backpack ▷钱包 qiánbāo wallet 3 (疙瘩) lump III [量] packet, bag ▷一包烟 yī bāo yān a packet of cigarettes ▷一包衣服 yī bāo yīfu a bag of clothes

measure word, used to describe things that are wrapped up

包含 bāohán[动] contain

包括 bāokuò[动] include

包子 bāozi[名] *steamed stuffed bun*

包子 bāozi

包子 bāozi are bigger than 饺子 jiǎozi. Shaped like buns, they are usually stuffed with meat or vegetable fillings, and are steamed rather than boiled.

剥 bāo[动] peel

雹 báo[名] hail ▶雹子 báozi hailstone

薄 báo[形] 1(不厚) thin 2(冷淡) cold ▶我对她不薄。 Wǒ duì tā bù báo. I treat her very well.

宝 bǎo I [名] treasure II [形] precious

宝贵 bǎoguì[形] valuable

饱 bǎo[形] full ▶我吃饱了。 Wǒ chī bǎo le. I am full.

保 bǎo[动] 1(保护) protect 2(保持) keep ▶保密 bǎomì keep ... secret ▶保鲜膜 bǎoxiān mó Clingfilm® (英), Saran wrap® (美) 3(保证) ensure

保安 bǎo'ān[名] security guard

保持 bǎochí[动] maintain ▶保持警惕 bǎochí jǐngtì stay vigilant

保存 bǎocún[动] preserve

保护 bǎohù[动] protect ▶保护环境 bǎohù huánjìng protect the environment

保龄球 bǎolíngqiú[名] (体育运动) bowling

保留 bǎoliú[动] 1(保存不变) preserve 2(意见) hold back ▶你可以保留自己的意见。 Nǐ kěyǐ bǎoliú zìjǐ de yìjiàn. You can keep your opinions to yourself.

保姆 bǎomǔ[名] 1(做家务的女工) domestic help 2(保育员) nanny

保守 bǎoshǒu[形] conservative

保卫 bǎowèi[动] defend

保险 bǎoxiǎn I [名] insurance II [形] safe

保证 bǎozhèng[动] guarantee

保重 bǎozhòng[动] take care of oneself

报 bào I [动] (告诉) report II [名] 1(报纸) newspaper ▶日报 rìbào daily ▶报社 bàoshè newspaper office 2(刊物) periodical ▶画报 huàbào glossy magazine

报仇 bàochóu[动] take revenge

报酬 bàochou[名] pay

报到 bàodào[动] register

报道 bàodào I [动] report ▶电视台报道了这条新闻。 Diànshì tái bàodào le zhè tiáo xīnwén. The television station reported this item of news. II [名] report ▶一篇关于克隆人的报道 yī piān guānyú kèlóng rén de bàodào a report about human cloning

报复 bàofù [动] retaliate

报告 bàogào I [动] report ▷向主管部门报告 xiàng zhǔguǎn bùmén bàogào report to the department in charge II [名] report ▷在大会上作报告 zài dàhuì shàng zuò bàogào give a talk at the conference

报关 bàoguān [动] declare

报刊 bàokān [名] newspapers and periodicals (PL)

报名 bàomíng [动] sign up

报失 bàoshī [动] report a loss

报销 bàoxiāo [动] (费用) claim for

报纸 bàozhǐ [名] newspaper

抱 bào [动] 1 (手臂围住) carry in one's arms 2 (领着) adopt 3 (心里存有) cherish ▷对某事抱幻想 duì mǒushì bào huànxiǎng have illusions about sth

抱歉 bàoqiàn I [形] sorry II [动] apologize

抱怨 bàoyuàn [动] complain

豹 bào [名] leopard

暴 bào [形] (猛烈) violent ▷暴雨 bàoyǔ rainstorm

爆 bào [动] 1 (猛然破裂) explode ▷爆炸 bàozhà explode 2 (突然发生) break out ▷爆发 bàofā break out

杯 bēi I [名] 1 (杯子) cup ▷玻璃杯 bōli bēi glass ▷酒杯 jiǔbēi wineglass ▷杯子 bēizi cup 2 (奖杯) cup ▷世界杯 Shìjièbēi World Cup II [量] cup, glass ▷一杯咖啡 yī bēi kāfēi a cup of coffee ▷两杯水 liǎng bēi shuǐ two glasses of water

背 bēi [动] 1 (驮) carry ... on one's back 2 (担负) take ... on ▷背起重任 bēi qǐ zhòngrèn take on great responsibility
→ see also/另见 bèi

悲 bēi [形] (悲伤) sad

悲惨 bēicǎn [形] miserable

悲观 bēiguān [形] pessimistic

悲伤 bēishāng [形] sad

碑 bēi [名] tablet ▷纪念碑 jìniànbēi monument

北 běi [名] north ▷北方 běifāng the North ▷北京 Běijīng Beijing ▷北部 běibù the north

北极 běijí [名] the North Pole

备 bèi [动] 1 (具备) have 2 (准备) prepare

备份 bèifèn [动] (计算机) keep a backup copy

备用 bèiyòng [动] backup ▷备用光盘 bèiyòng guāngpán backup CD

备注 bèizhù [名] (注解说明) notes (PL)

背 bèi I [名] 1 (指身体) back ▷背疼 bèiténg backache 2 (指反面) back ▷背面 bèimiàn reverse side 3 (指后面) behind ▷背后 bèihòu behind II [动] (背诵) recite
→ see also/另见 bēi

背景 bèijǐng [名] (指景物, 情况) background

背诵 bèisòng [动] recite

被 bèi I [名] quilt ▶被子 bèizi quilt II [介] ▷他被哥哥打了一顿。 Tā bèi gēge dǎ le yī dùn. He was beaten up by his elder brother. III [助] ▷他被跟踪了。 Tā bèi gēnzōng le. He was followed.

倍 bèi [名] times (PL) ▷这本书比那本书厚三倍。 Zhè běn shū bǐ nà běn shū hòu sānbèi. This book is three times thicker than that one. ▷物价涨了两倍。 Wùjià zhǎng le liǎngbèi. Prices have doubled.

本 běn I [名] 1 (本子) book ▶笔记本 bǐjìběn notebook 2 (版本) edition ▶手抄本 shǒuchāo běn hand-written copy II [形] 1 (自己的) one's own ▶本人 běnrén oneself 2 (现今) this ▶本月 běnyuè this month III [副] originally ▷我本想亲自去一趟。 Wǒ běn xiǎng qīnzì qù yītàng. I originally wanted to go myself. IV [量] ▷几本书 jǐ běn shū a few books

measure word, used for counting books, magazines, dictionaries, etc.

本地 běndì [名] locality ▷她是本地人。 Tā shì běndì rén. She is a native of this place.

本科 běnkē [名] undergraduate course ▷本科生 běnkē shēng undergraduate

本来 běnlái I [形] original ▷本来的打算 běnlái de dǎsuàn the original plan II [副] (原先) at first ▷我本来以为你已经走了。 Wǒ běnlái yǐwéi nǐ yǐjīng zǒu le. At first, I thought you had left.

本领 běnlǐng [名] skill

本身 běnshēn [名] itself

本事 běnshi [名] ability

本质 běnzhì [名] essence

笨 bèn [形] 1 (不聪明) stupid 2 (不灵巧) clumsy ▷他嘴很笨。 Tā zuǐ hěn bèn. He's quite inarticulate.

蹦 bèng [动] leap

逼 bī [动] 1 (强迫) force 2 (强取) press for ▶逼债 bīzhài press for repayment of a debt 3 (逼近) close in on

逼近 bījìn [动] close in on

逼迫 bīpò [动] force

鼻 bí [名] (鼻子) nose

鼻涕 bítì [名] mucus

鼻子 bízi [名] nose

比 bǐ I [动] 1 (比较) compare ▷比比过去, 现在的生活好多了。 Bǐbǐ guòqù, xiànzài de shēnghuó hǎo duō le. Life now is much better compared to the past. 2 (较量) compete ▷他们要比谁游得快。 Tāmen yào bǐbǐ shuí yóu de kuài. They are competing to see who swims the fastest. II [介] 1 (指得分) ▷零比零 líng bǐ líng nil-nil (英), no score (美) **2** (相对) ▷今年冬天比去年冷。 Jīnnián dōngtiān bǐ qùnián lěng. It is colder this winter than last winter.

比 bǐ is used to express comparisons: to say that X is taller than Y, simply say X 比 Y 高。 e.g. 上海比南京大。 Shànghǎi bǐ Nánjīng dà. (Shanghai is bigger than Nanjing).

比方 bǐfang [名] analogy ▷比方说 bǐfang shuō for example

比分 bǐfēn [名] score

比基尼 bǐjīní [名] bikini

比较 bǐjiào I [动] compare II [副] relatively ▷这里的水果比较新鲜。 Zhèlǐ de shuǐguǒ bǐjiào xīnxiān. The fruit here is relatively fresh.

比例 bǐlì [名] proportion

比率 bǐlǜ [名] ratio

比如 bǐrú [连] for instance

比赛 bǐsài [名] match

彼 bǐ [代] **1** (那个) that **2** (对方) the other side

彼此 bǐcǐ [代] (双方) both sides

笔 bǐ I [名] **1** (工具) pen ▶圆珠笔 yuánzhūbǐ ball-point pen **2** (笔画) brush stroke II [量] (款项) ▷一笔钱 yī bǐ qián a sum of money

measure word, used for money

笔记 bǐjì [名] (记录) note ▷记笔记 jì bǐjì take notes

笔记本电脑 bǐjìběn diànnǎo [名] laptop

币 bì [名] coin ▶货币 huòbì currency ▶外币 wàibì foreign currency

必 bì [副] **1** (必然) certainly **2** (必须) ▶必修课 bìxiūkè compulsory course

必然 bìrán I [形] inevitable II [名] necessity

必须 bìxū [副] ▷你们必须准时来上班。 Nǐmen bìxū zhǔnshí lái shàngbān. You must start work on time.

必要 bìyào [形] essential

毕 bì [动] finish

毕业 bìyè [动] graduate

避 bì [动] **1** (躲开) avoid ▶避风 bìfēng shelter from the wind **2** (防止) prevent

避免 bìmiǎn [动] avoid

避难 bìnàn [动] take refuge

避孕 bìyùn [动] use contraceptives ▷避孕药 bìyùn yào the pill

边 biān [名] **1** (边线) side ▷街两边 jiē liǎngbiān both sides of the street **2** (边缘) edge ▷路边 lù biān roadside **3** (边界) border **4** (旁边) side ▷在床边 zài chuáng biān by the bed

边…边… biān... biān... ▷边吃边谈 biān chī biān tán talk while eating

边疆 biānjiāng [名] border area

边界 biānjiè [名] border

边境 biānjìng [名] border

边缘 biānyuán [名] edge

编 biān [动] **1** (编辑) edit ▷编程 biānchéng program **2** (创作) write ▷编歌词 biān gēcí write lyrics **3** (捏造) fabricate ▷编谎话 biān huǎnghuà fabricate a lie

编辑 biānjí I [动] edit II [名] editor

蝙 biān *see below*/见下文

蝙蝠 biānfú [名] bat

鞭 biān I [名] **1** (鞭子) whip **2** (爆竹) firecracker

鞭炮 biānpào [名] firecracker

鞭炮 biānpào

Firecrackers are believed by the Chinese to scare off evil spirits and attract the god of good fortune to people's doorsteps, especially in the celebration of the Spring Festival and at weddings.

贬 biǎn [动] (降低) reduce ▷贬值 biǎnzhí depreciate

贬义词 biǎnyì cí [名] derogatory expression

扁 biǎn [形] flat ▷自行车胎扁了。 Zìxíngchē tāi biǎn le. The bicycle tyre is flat.

变 biàn [动] **1** (改变) change ▷小城的面貌变了。 Xiǎochéng de miànmào biàn le. The appearance of the town has changed. **2** (变成) become ▷他变成熟了。 Tā biàn chéngshú le. He's become quite grown up.

变化 biànhuà I [动] change II [名] change

便 biàn I [形] **1** (方便) convenient ▷轻便 qīngbiàn portable **2** (简单) simple ▷便饭 biànfàn simple meal II [动] excrete ▷小便 xiǎobiàn urinate ▷大便 dàbiàn defecate III [副] ▷稍等片刻演出便开始。 Shāoděng piànkè yǎnchū biàn kāishǐ. The performance is about to start in a moment.

→ *see also*/另见 pián

便利 biànlì I [形] convenient II [动] facilitate

便士 biànshì [量] pence

便条 biàntiáo [名] note

便携式 biànxiéshì [形] portable

便于 biànyú [动] be easy to ▷便于联系 biànyú liánxì be easy to contact

遍 biàn I [副] all over ▷找了个遍 zhǎo le ge biàn searched high and low II [量] ▷我说了两遍。 Wǒ shuō le liǎng biàn. I said it twice.

measure word, used for the number of times the same action takes place

辨 biàn [动] distinguish ▶辨别 biànbié distinguish

辨认 biànrèn [动] identify

辩 biàn [动] debate ▶辩论 biànlùn argue

标 biāo I [名] 1(记号) mark 2(标准) standard II [动] mark

标本 biāoběn [名] (样品) specimen

标点 biāodiǎn [名] punctuation

标记 biāojì [名] mark

标题 biāotí [名] 1(指文章, 书) title 2(指新闻) headline

标志 biāozhì [名] sign

标准 biāozhǔn I standard ▷道德标准 dàodé biāozhǔn moral standard II [形] standard ▷标准时间 biāozhǔn shíjiān standard time

表 biǎo [名] 1(计时器) watch ▶手表 shǒubiǎo wristwatch 2(计量器) meter ▶电表 diànbiǎo electricity meter 3(表格) form ▷火车时间表 huǒchē shíjiān biǎo train timetable ▷填申请表 tián shēnqǐng biǎo fill in the application form 4(指亲戚) cousin ▶表哥 biǎogē cousin

表达 biǎodá [动] express

表格 biǎogé [名] form

表面 biǎomiàn [名] surface

表明 biǎomíng [动] show

表示 biǎoshì I [动] (表达) express II [名] 1(言行或表情) gesture 2(意见) attitude

表现 biǎoxiàn I [动] (显出) show II [名] (指行为, 作风) performance

表演 biǎoyǎn I [动] (演出) perform II [名] performance

表扬 biǎoyáng [动] praise

别 bié I [形] (其他) other II [副] (不要) ▷别忘了关灯。 Bié wàng le guāndēng. Don't forget to turn off the light.

别人 biérén [名] other people

别墅 biéshù [名] villa

别针 biézhēn [名] safety pin

宾 bīn [名] guest

宾馆 bīnguǎn [名] hotel

冰 bīng I [名] ice II [动] 1(使感觉寒冷) be freezing ▷这水冰手。 Zhè shuǐ bīng shǒu. This water is freezing. 2(冰镇) cool ▶冰镇 bīngzhèn iced

冰淇淋 bīngqílín [名] ice cream

冰箱 bīngxiāng [名] fridge

兵 bīng [名] 1(军队) the army ▷当兵 dāng bīng join the army 2(士兵) soldier

饼 bǐng [名] (指面食) cake ▶月饼 yuèbǐng moon cake

饼干 bǐnggān [名] biscuit (英), cookie (美)

并 bìng I [动] 1(合并) merge 2(并拢) bring ... together ▷把脚并起来 bǎ jiǎo bìng qǐlái bring your feet together II [副] (表示强调) really ▷他今晚并不想出去。 Tā jīnwǎn bìng bù xiǎng chūqù. He really doesn't want to go out this evening. III [连] and ▷他会

说法语, 并在学习西班牙语。 Tā huì shuō Fǎ yǔ, bìng zài xuéxí Xībānyá yǔ He can speak French, and he is studying Spanish at the moment.

并且 bìngqiě [连] 1(和) and ▷她聪明并且用功。 Tā cōngmíng bìngqiě yònggōng. She is clever and diligent. 2(此外) also

病 bìng I [名] (疾病) disease ▷心脏病 xīnzàng bìng heart disease ▷生病 shēngbìng become ill ▷他去看病了。 Tā qù kànbìng le. He went to see a doctor. II [动] be ill ▷他病得不轻。 Tā bìng de bùqīng. He was seriously ill.

病毒 bìngdú [名] virus

病房 bìngfáng [名] ward

病菌 bìngjūn [名] bacteria

病人 bìngrén [名] 1(指医院里) patient 2(指家里) invalid

波 bō [名] (指水, 声音, 电) wave

拨 bō [动] 1(号码) dial ▷拨电话号 bō diànhuà hào dial the phone number 2(频道) change over to

玻 bō see below/见下文
玻璃 bōlí [名] glass

菠 bō see below/见下文
菠菜 bōcài [名] spinach
菠萝 bōluó [名] pineapple

播 bō [动] (电视, 收音机) broadcast ▶播放 bōfàng broadcast

伯 bó [名] (伯父) uncle

伯伯 bóbo [名] 1(伯父) uncle 2(用于称呼) uncle

脖 bó [名] neck ▶脖子 bózi neck

博 bó [形] abundant

博物馆 bówùguǎn [名] museum

补 bǔ [动] 1(衣服, 鞋, 车胎, 袜子) mend 2(牙) fill 3(增加) add

补充 bǔchōng I [动] add II [形] supplementary ▷补充说明 bǔchōng shuōmíng additional explanation

补考 bǔkǎo [动] resit

补习 bǔxí [动] take extra lessons

补助 bǔzhù [名] subsidy

捕 bǔ [动] catch

捕捉 bǔzhuō [动] 1(抓住) seize 2(捉拿) hunt down

不 bù [副] 1(用于否定句) not ▷不诚实 bù chéngshí dishonest ▷他不抽烟。 Tā bù chōuyān. He doesn't smoke. 2(用于否定回答) no ▷ "你累了吧？" "不，不累。" "Nǐ lèi le ba?" "Bù, bùlèi." "Are you tired?" — "No, I'm not." 3(客套) (不用) ▷不客气。 Bù kèqi. Please don't mention it. ▷不谢。 Bù xiè. You're welcome.

Negating sentences in Chinese is very straightforward: just use 不 bù before the verb. E.g. 我不喝酒。 Wǒ bù hējiǔ (I don't drink alcohol). The only exception is the verb 有 yǒu, to have, for which you must use 没 méi. E.g. 我没有钱。Wǒ méiyǒu qián. (I don't have any money). 不 bù is fourth tone unless it is followed by another fourth tone syllable, in which case it is usually pronounced as a second tone, eg. 不要 búyào. For more information on tones, please see the introduction.

不必 bùbì [副] ▷明天你们不必来了。Míngtiān nǐmen bùbì lái le. You don't have to come tomorrow.

不但 bùdàn [连] not only ▷这辆车的设计不但美观, 而且实用。Zhè liàng chē de shèjì bùdàn měiguān, ěrqiě shíyòng. The design of this car is not only beautiful, it's also practical.

不得了 bùdéliǎo [形] (表示程度) extreme ▷这孩子淘气得不得了。Zhè háizi táoqì de bùdéliǎo. This child is terribly naughty.

不断 bùduàn [副] continually ▷沙漠不断扩大。Shāmò bùduàn kuòdà. The desert is expanding all the time.

不敢 bùgǎn [动] not dare

不管 bùguǎn [连] ▷不管出什么事, 我们都要保持镇定。Bùguǎn chū shénme shì, wǒmen dōuyào bǎochí zhèndìng. Whatever happens, we must remain calm.

不过 bùguò I [副] 1 (仅仅) only ▷不过是点小伤。Bùguò shì diǎn xiǎoshāng. It's only a slight injury. 2 (非常) can't be better ▷这是最简单不过的方法。Zhè shì zuì jiǎndān bùguò de fāngfǎ. This is by far the easiest method. II [连] but ▷他很喜欢新学校, 不过离家太远了。Tā hěn xǐhuān xīn xuéxiào, bùguò lí jiā tài yuǎn le. He really likes his new school, but it's a very long way from home.

不仅 bùjǐn [副] 1 (不止) not just ▷这不仅是学校的问题。Zhè bùjǐn shì xuéxiào de wèntí. This is not just the school's problem. 2 (不但) not only ▷这地毯不仅质量好, 而且价格便宜。Zhè dìtǎn bùjǐn zhìliàng hǎo, ěrqiě jiàgé piányi. Not only is the carpet good quality, it's also cheap.

不久 bùjiǔ [名] ▶他们不久就要结婚了。Tāmen bùjiǔ jiùyào jiéhūn le. They are getting married soon.

不论 bùlùn [连] no matter ▷不论是谁, 都必须遵守法规。Bùlùn shì shuí, dōu bìxū zūnshǒu fǎguī. No matter who you are, you have to abide by the regulations.

不满 bùmǎn [形] dissatisfied

不免 bùmiǎn [副] inevitably

不然 bùrán [连] otherwise ▷多

谢你提醒我，不然我就忘了。Duōxiè nǐ tíxíng wǒ, bùrán wǒ jiù wàng le. Thanks very much for reminding me, or I would have forgotten about it.

不如 bùrú [动] not be as good as ▷城里太吵，不如住在郊区。Chénglǐ tài chǎo, bùrú zhùzài jiāoqū. The city is too noisy - it's better living in the suburbs.

不少 bùshǎo [形] a lot of ▷她有不少好朋友。 Tā yǒu bùshǎo hǎo péngyou. She has a lot of good friends.

不同 bùtóng [形] different

不幸 bùxìng I [形] 1 (不幸运) unhappy 2 (出人意料) unfortunate II [名] disaster

不要紧 bùyàojǐn [形] 1 (不严重) not serious ▷他的病不要紧。Tā de bìng bùyàojǐn. His illness is not serious. 2 (没关系) it doesn't matter

不一定 bùyīdìng [副] may not ▷她未必会回电话。 Tā wèibì huì huí diànhuà. She may not return your call.

不止 bùzhǐ [副] 1 (不停地) incessantly ▷大笑不止 dàxiào bùzhǐ laugh incessantly 2 (多于) more than ▷不止一次 bùzhǐ yīcì on more than one occasion

布 bù [名] cloth

布置 bùzhì [动] 1 (房间等) decorate 2 (任务, 作业) assign

步 bù [名] 1 (脚步) step ▶步伐

bùfá pace 2 (阶段) stage ▶步骤 bùzhòu step 3 (地步) situation

步行 bùxíng [动] go on foot

部 bù I [名] 1 (部分) part ▷东部 dōng bù the eastern part 2 (部门) department ▷总部 zǒngbù headquarters (PL) ▶部长 bùzhǎng department head ▷教育部 jiàoyù bù education department II [量] 1 一部电话 yī bù diànhuà a telephone ▷三部电影 sān bù diànyǐng three films measure word, used for films, phones, etc.

部队 bùduì [名] armed forces (PL)

部分 bùfen [名] part

部门 bùmén [名] department

部位 bùwèi [名] place

C

擦 cā [动] **1**(抹) wipe ... clean **2**(指用水) wash **3**(皮鞋) polish **4**(摩擦) rub **5**(涂) apply **6**(火柴) strike **7**(破) scrape ▶擦伤 cāshāng scrape **8**(挨着) brush **9**(瓜果) shred

猜 cāi [动] **1**(猜测) guess **2**(猜疑) suspect

猜测 cāicè I [动] speculate II [名] speculation

猜想 cāixiǎng [动] suppose

猜疑 cāiyí [动] have unfounded suspicions about

才 cái I [名] **1**(才能) ability ▶多才多艺 duōcái duōyì multi-talented **2**(人才) talent ▶奇才 qícái extraordinary talent II [副] **1**(刚) just ▷我才到家, 电话就响了。 Wǒ cái dào jiā, diànhuà jiù xiǎng le. Just as I arrived home, the phone rang. **2**(表示晚) not...until ▷我10点才到单位。 Wǒ shídiǎn cái dào dānwèi. I didn't arrive at work until ten o'clock. **3**(表示条件) only...if ▷学生只有用功, 才能取得好成绩。 Xuéshēng zhǐyǒu yònggōng, cái néng qǔdé hǎo chéngjì. Students will only be able to do well if they study hard. **4**(表示情况改变) only after ▷他解释后, 我才明白了他为什么那么难过。 Tā jiěshì hòu, wǒ cái míngbai tā wèishénme nàme nánguò. It was only after he explained that I understood why he was so sad. **5**(程度低) only ▷他才学会上网。 Tā cái xuéhuì shàngwǎng. He has only just learned how to use the Internet.

才华 cáihuá [名] talent

才能 cáinéng [名] ability

才子 cáizǐ [名] talented man

材 cái [名] (指物) material ▶教材 jiàocái teaching material

材料 cáiliào [名] **1**(原料) material **2**(资料) material **3**(人才) talent

财 cái [名] wealth

财富 cáifù [名] wealth

财政 cáizhèng [名] finance

裁 cái [动] **1**(衣服, 纸) cut **2**(减) cut ▶裁员 cáiyuán cut staff **3**(判断) decide

裁缝 cáifeng [名] **1** (指男装) tailor **2** (指女装) dressmaker

裁判 cáipàn **I** [名] judgment **II** [动] make a decision

采 cǎi [动] **1** (摘) pick **2** (选) choose **3** (开采) extract **4** (采集) gather

采访 cǎifǎng [动] interview

采购 cǎigòu **I** [动] purchase **II** [名] buyer

采取 cǎiqǔ [动] adopt

采用 cǎiyòng [动] adopt

彩 cǎi [名] (颜色) colour (英), color (美)

彩电 cǎidiàn [名] colour (英) 或 color (美) TV

彩卷 cǎijuǎn [名] colour (英) 或 color (美) film

彩排 cǎipái [动] rehearse

彩票 cǎipiào [名] lottery ticket

彩色 cǎisè [名] colour (英), color (美)

踩 cǎi [动] (脚) step on

菜 cài [名] **1** (植物) vegetable **2** (饭食) dish

菜单 càidān [名] menu

菜谱 càipǔ [名] **1** (菜单) menu **2** (指书) cookbook

参 cān [动] (加入) join ▶ 参军 cānjūn enlist
→ see also/另见 shēn

参观 cānguān [动] tour

参加 cānjiā [动] take part in ▷ 参加新年晚会 cānjiā xīnnián wǎnhuì attend a New Year's party ▷ 参加民主党 cānjiā Mínzhǔ Dǎng join the Democratic Party

参考 cānkǎo **I** [动] consult **II** [名] reference ▷ 参考书 cānkǎo shū reference book

参谋 cānmóu **I** [名] **1** (顾问) advisor **2** (指军职) staff officer **II** [动] give advice

参与 cānyù [动] participate in

餐 cān **I** [名] meal **II** [量] meal

餐车 cānchē [名] **1** (指推车) food trolley **2** (指车厢) buffet (英) 或 dining (美) car

餐巾 cānjīn [名] napkin

餐具 cānjù [名] eating utensils (PL)

餐厅 cāntīng [名] canteen

残 cán [形] **1** (指器物) defective **2** (指人或动物) disabled **3** (剩余) remaining

残废 cánfèi [动] be disabled

残疾 cánjí [名] disability ▷ 残疾人 cánjí rén people with disabilities

残酷 cánkù [形] brutal

残忍 cánrěn [形] cruel

蚕 cán [名] silkworm

惭 cán see below/见下文

惭愧 cánkuì [形] ashamed

惨 cǎn [形] (悲惨) tragic

灿 càn see below/见下文

灿烂 cànlàn [形] glorious

仓 cāng [名] store

仓库 cāngkù [名] storehouse

苍 cāng [形] (指鬓发) grey (英), gray (美)

苍白 cāngbái [形] 1(脸色) pale 2(文章，表演等) bland

苍蝇 cāngying [名] fly

舱 cāng [名] 1(用于载人) cabin ▶头等舱 tóuděngcāng first-class cabin 2(用于装物) hold ▶货舱 huòcāng cargo hold

藏 cáng [动] 1(隐藏) hide 2(储存) store 3(收集) collect ▶藏书 cángshū collect books
→ see also/另见 zàng

操 cāo [名] (体育活动) exercise

操场 cāochǎng [名] sports ground

操心 cāoxīn [动] concern

操作 cāozuò [动] operate

糙 cāo [形] poor

草 cǎo [名] 1(植物) grass ▶草地 cǎodì lawn, meadow 2(用作材料) straw

草稿 cǎogǎo [名] rough draft

草帽 cǎomào [名] straw hat

草莓 cǎoméi [名] strawberry

草率 cǎoshuài [形] rash

草原 cǎoyuán [名] grasslands (PL)

册 cè I [名] book ▶手册 shǒucè handbook ▶相册 xiàngcè photo album II [量] 1(指同一本书) copy 2(指不同本书) volume

厕 cè [名] toilet ▶公厕 gōngcè public toilet

厕所 cèsuǒ [名] toilet

侧 cè I [名] side ▶两侧 liǎngcè both sides II [动] turn ... away ▶我侧过脸去。 Wǒ cè guò liǎn qù. I turned my face away.

侧面 cèmiàn I [形] 1(非官方) unofficial 2(指方位) side II [名] side

测 cè [动] 1(测量) measure 2(推测) predict

测量 cèliáng I [动] measure II [名] survey

测试 cèshì I [动] test II [名] test

测验 cèyàn I [动] test II [名] test

策 cè [名] suggestion

策划 cèhuà I [动] design II [名] planning

策略 cèlüè I [名] strategy II [形] strategic

层 céng I [量] 1(指建筑物) floor 2(指覆盖物) layer 3(步) step 4(指含义) layer II [名] (指物，状态) layer

曾 céng [副] once

曾经 céngjīng [副] once

蹭 cèng [动] 1(摩擦) rub 2(沾上) smear 3(指速度) creep along

叉 chā [名] 1(器具) fork 2(餐具) fork 3(符号) cross

叉子 chāzi [名] 1(符号) cross 2(餐具) fork

差 chā [名] difference
→ see also/另见 chà, chāi

差别 chābié [名] difference

差错 chācuò [名] 1(错误) mistake 2(意外) accident

差距 chājù [名] difference

差异 chāyì [名] difference

插 chā [动] insert ▷我能不能插一句? Wǒ néng bùnéng chā yījù? Can I interrupt just a second?

插曲 chāqǔ [名] 1(音乐) incidental music 2(事件) interlude

插入 chārù [动] insert

插图 chātú [名] illustration

插销 chāxiāo [名] 1(闩) bolt 2(插头) electrical plug

插嘴 chāzuǐ [动] interrupt

插座 chāzuò [名] socket (英), outlet (美)

茶 chá [名] tea ▷红茶 hóngchá black tea ▷茶杯 chábēi teacup ▷茶壶 cháhú teapot ▷茶馆 cháguǎn teahouse ▷泡茶 pào chá make tea

茶具 chájù [名] tea set

茶叶 cháyè [名] tea leaves (PL)

查 chá [动] 1(检查) inspect 2(调查) investigate 3(字典, 词典) look ... up

查号台 cháhàotái [名] directory inquiries (SG) (英) 或 assistance (美)

查阅 cháyuè [动] look ... up

查找 cházhǎo [动] look for

察 chá [动] check ▷观察 guānchá observe

察觉 chájué [动] detect

杈 chà [名] branch

差 chà I [动] 1(不相同) be different from ▷你比他差远了。 Nǐ bǐ tā chà de yuǎn le. You are not nearly as good as him. 2(缺欠) be short of ▷差3个人 chà sān gè rén be three people short II [形] 1(错误) mistaken 2(不好) poor ▷质量差 zhìliàng chà poor quality
→ see also/另见 chā, chāi

差不多 chà bu duō I [形] very similar II [副] almost

拆 chāi [动] 1(打开) tear ... open 2(拆毁) dismantle

差 chāi [动] send ▷出差 chūchāi go on a business trip
→ see also/另见 chā, chà

差事 chāishi [名] 1(任务) assignment 2(差使) position

柴 chái [名] firewood

柴油 cháiyóu [名] diesel

豺 chái [名] jackal

掺 chān [动] mix

搀 chān 1(搀扶) support ... by the arm 2(混合) mix

馋 chán [形] greedy

缠 chán [动] 1(缠绕) twine 2(纠

缠) pester

蝉 chán [名] cicada

产 chǎn [动] 1 (生育) give birth to 2 (出产) produce

产量 chǎnliàng [名] yield

产品 chǎnpǐn [名] product

产权 chǎnquán [名] property rights (PL) ▷知识产权 zhīshi chǎnquán intellectual property

产生 chǎnshēng [动] produce

产业 chǎnyè [名] 1 (财产) property 2 (工业生产) industry

铲 chǎn I [名] shovel II [动] shovel

颤 chàn [动] tremble

颤抖 chàndǒu [动] shiver

长 cháng I [形] long II [名] (长度) length
→ see also/另见 zhǎng

长城 Chángchéng [名] the Great Wall

长城 Chángchéng

As one of the longest man-made mega structures in world, the Great Wall of China is nearly 4,000 miles in length, reaching from the border of Xinjiang province in the west to the eastern coast just north of Beijing. It is probably the most famous of China's landmarks, and was made a UNESCO World Heritage site in 1987. There are records of fortifications being built along the route which date from the 3rd century BC, although most of what remains today was built during the Ming dynasty (1368-1644). Built as a defence mechanism, its primary function was to withstand invasions by the northern tribes.

长处 chángchu [名] strong point

长度 chángdù [名] length

长江 Cháng Jiāng [名] the Yangtze

长久 chángjiǔ [形] long-term

长跑 chángpǎo [动] go long-distance running

长寿 chángshòu [形] long-lived ▷祝您长寿！ Zhù nín chángshòu! Here's to a long life!

长寿面 chángshòumiàn [名] long-life noodles (PL)

长寿面 chángshòumiàn

In the Chinese tradition, long-life noodles are eaten on one's birthday. They are very long, thin noodles symbolizing longevity.

长途 chángtú [形] long-distance ▷长途电话 chángtú diànhuà long-distance phone call ▷长途旅行 chángtú lǚxíng long journey

肠 cháng [名] intestines (PL)

肠子 chángzi [名] intestines (PL)

尝 cháng [动] taste ▶品尝 pǐncháng taste

尝试 chángshì [动] try

常 cháng I [形] 1 (平常) common 2 (经常) frequent ▶常客 chángkè regular guest II [副] often

常常 chángcháng [副] often

常识 chángshí [名] 1 (非专业知识) general knowledge 2 (生活经验) common sense

偿 cháng [动] 1 (归还) repay 2 (满足) fulfil ▶如愿以偿 rúyuànyǐcháng fulfil one's dreams

偿还 chánghuán [动] repay

厂 chǎng [名] (工厂) factory

场 chǎng I [名] 1 (地方) ground ▶排球场 páiqiúchǎng volleyball court ▶市场 shìchǎng market 2 (舞台) stage ▶上场 shàngchǎng go on stage 3 (戏剧片段) scene 4 (物) field II [量] 1 (比赛, 演出) ▷一场足球赛 yī chǎng zúqiú sài a football match ▷两场音乐会 liǎng chǎng yīnyuèhuì two concerts
  measure word, used for games and shows

2 (病) ▷一场重病 yī chǎng zhòngbìng a serious illness
  measure word, used for illnesses

3 (灾害, 战争, 事故) ▷一场火灾 yī chǎng huǒzāi a fire ▷一场战争 yī chǎng zhànzhēng a war ▷几场事故 jǐ chǎng shìgù several accidents
  measure word, used for afflictions, wars, accidents, etc.

场地 chǎngdì [名] space ▷运动场地 yùndòng chǎngdì sports area

场合 chǎnghé [名] occasion

场所 chǎngsuǒ [名] place ▷公共场所 gōnggòng chǎngsuǒ public place

敞 chǎng I [形] spacious ▶宽敞 kuānchǎng spacious II [动] be open ▷大门敞着。 Dàmén chǎng zhe. The main door is open.

畅 chàng I [形] 1 (无阻碍) smooth ▶畅通 chàngtōng unimpeded 2 (舒适) untroubled ▷他心情不畅。 Tā xīnqíng bùchàng. He's troubled by something. II [副] uninhibitedly ▶畅饮 chàngyǐn drink one's fill

畅快 chàngkuài [形] carefree

畅所欲言 chàng suǒ yù yán speak freely

畅通 chàngtōng [动] be open

畅销 chàngxiāo [动] have a ready market

倡 chàng [动] initiate

倡议 chàngyì [动] propose

唱 chàng [动] (发出乐音) sing ▶独唱 dúchàng solo ▶合唱 héchàng chorus

唱歌 chànggē [动] sing

唱戏 chàngxì [动] perform opera

抄 chāo [动] 1 (誊写) copy 2 (抄袭) plagiarize

　抄袭 chāoxí [动] (剽窃) plagiarize

钞 chāo [名] banknote

　钞票 chāopiào [名] banknote

超 chāo I [动] 1 (超过) exceed 2 (不受限制) transcend ▶超现实 chāoxiànshí surreal II [形] super ▷超低温 chāo dīwēn ultra-low temperature

　超级 chāojí [形] super ▷超级大国 chāojí dàguó superpower ▷超级市场 chāojí shìchǎng supermarket

　超人 chāorén [名] superman

　超市 chāoshì [名] supermarket

　超重 chāozhòng [动] 1 (超过载重量) overload 2 (超过标准量) be overweight

巢 cháo [名] nest

朝 cháo I [名] (朝代) dynasty II [动] face III [介] towards ▷他朝着我走过来。 Tā cháo zhe wǒ zǒu guòlai. He was walking towards me.

　朝鲜 Cháoxiǎn [名] North Korea

嘲 cháo [动] ridicule

　嘲笑 cháoxiào [动] laugh at

潮 cháo I [名] 1 (潮汐) tide 2 (社会运动) movement ▶工潮 gōngcháo labour (英) 或 labor (美) movement ▶思潮 sīcháo Zeitgeist II [形] damp

　潮流 cháoliú [名] 1 (水流) tide 2 (发展趋势) trend

　潮湿 cháoshī [形] damp

　潮水 cháoshuǐ [名] tidal waters (PL)

吵 chǎo I [动] 1 (发出噪音) make a racket 2 (争吵) squabble II [形] noisy

　吵架 chǎojià [动] quarrel

　吵闹 chǎonào [动] 1 (争吵) bicker 2 (打扰) disturb

　吵嘴 chǎozuǐ [动] bicker

炒 chǎo [动] 1 (烹调) stir-fry 2 (地皮, 外汇等) speculate ▶炒股 chǎogǔ speculate in stocks and shares 3 (方) (解雇) sack ▶炒鱿鱼 chǎo yóuyú be fired

车 chē [名] 1 (运输工具) vehicle ▶小汽车 xiǎoqìchē car ▶公共汽车 gōnggòngqìchē bus 2 (带轮的装置) wheel ▶风车 fēngchē windmill

　车费 chēfèi [名] fare

　车祸 chēhuò [名] traffic accident

　车间 chējiān [名] workshop

　车库 chēkù [名] garage

　车辆 chēliàng [名] vehicle

　车轮 chēlún [名] wheel

　车胎 chētāi [名] tyre (英), tire (美)

　车厢 chēxiāng [名] coach

　车站 chēzhàn [名] 1 (火车的) railway station 2 (汽车的) bus stop

扯 chě [动] (拉) pull

彻 chè [动] penetrate ▶彻夜
chèyè all night

彻底 chèdǐ [形] thorough

撤 chè [动] 1 (除去) take ... away
▶撤职 chèzhí dismiss from one's
job 2 (退) move away

撤退 chètuì [动] withdraw

撤销 chèxiāo [动] 1 (职务) dismiss
2 (计划) cancel 3 (法令) rescind

尘 chén [名] 1 (尘土) dirt ▶灰
尘 huīchén dust 2 (尘世) the
material world ▶尘世 chénshì
worldly affairs (PL)

尘土 chéntǔ [名] dust

沉 chén I [动] 1 (向下落) sink 2 (指
情绪) become grave II [形] 1 (指
程度深) deep ▶昨晚我睡得很
沉。 Zuówǎn wǒ shuì de hěn
chén. Last night I slept very
deeply. 2 (重) heavy 3 (不舒服)
heavy ▶我两条腿发沉。 Wǒ
liǎng tiáo tuǐ fāchén. My legs
feel heavy.

沉静 chénjìng [形] 1 (肃静) quiet
2 (指性格) placid

沉闷 chénmèn [形] 1 (天气，气氛)
depressing 2 (心情) depressed
3 (指性格) introverted

沉没 chénmò [动] sink

沉默 chénmò I [形] taciturn
II [动] be silent

沉痛 chéntòng [形] 1 (心情)
grieving 2 (教训) bitter

沉稳 chénwěn [形] 1 (稳重) steady、
2 (安稳) peaceful

沉重 chénzhòng [形] heavy

沉着 chénzhuó [形] calm

陈 chén [动] 1 (陈列) set ... out 2 (陈
述) state

陈旧 chénjiù [形] out-of-date

陈列 chénliè [动] display

陈述 chénshù [动] state

晨 chén [名] morning ▶早晨
zǎochén early morning

衬 chèn [名] lining ▶衬衫
chènshān shirt

衬托 chèntuō [动] set ... off

称 chèn [动] match ▶相称
xiāngchèn match ▶对称 duìchèn
be symmetrical
→ see also/另见 chēng

称心 chènxīn [动] be satisfactory

趁 chèn [介] ▶趁这个机会我讲
几句话。 Chèn zhè ge jīhuì wǒ
jiǎng jǐ jù huà. I would like to
take this opportunity to say a
few words.

称 chēng I [动] 1 (叫) call 2 (说) say
3 (测量) weigh II [名] name ▶简
称 jiǎnchēng short form
→ see also/另见 chèn

称呼 chēnghu I [动] call II [名]
form of address

称赞 chēngzàn [动] praise

撑 chēng [动] 1 (抵住) prop ... up
2 (船) punt 3 (坚持住) keep ... up
4 (张开) open 5 (容不下) fill to
bursting ▶少吃点吧，别撑着！
Shǎo chī diǎn ba, bié chēng zhe!

Don't eat so much, you'll burst!

成 chéng I [动] 1 (成功) accomplish ▷那件事成了。 Nà jiàn shì chéng le. The job is done. 2 (成为) become II [形] (可以) OK ▷成！就这么定了。 Chéng! Jiù zhème dìng le. OK – that's agreed.

成本 chéngběn [名] cost

成分 chéngfèn [名] 1 (组成部分) composition 2 (社会阶层) status

成功 chénggōng [动] succeed

成果 chéngguǒ [名] achievement

成绩 chéngjì [名] success

成就 chéngjiù I [名] achievement II [动] achieve

成立 chénglì [动] 1 (建立) found 2 (有根据) be tenable

成年 chéngnián [动] 1 (指动植物) mature 2 (指人) grow up

成人 chéngrén I [名] adult II [动] grow up

成熟 chéngshú [形] 1 (指果实) ripe 2 (指思想) mature 3 (指机会等) ripe

成为 chéngwéi [动] become

成问题 chéng wèntí [动] be a problem

成语 chéngyǔ [名] idiom

成员 chéngyuán [名] member

成长 chéngzhǎng [动] grow up

诚 chéng [形] honest ▷忠诚 zhōngchéng loyal ▷诚心 chéngxīn sincere

诚恳 chéngkěn [形] sincere

诚实 chéngshí [形] honest

承 chéng [动] 1 (承受) bear 2 (承担) undertake

承担 chéngdān [动] 1 (责任) bear 2 (工作) undertake 3 (费用) bear

承诺 chéngnuò I [动] undertake II [名] commitment

承认 chéngrèn [动] 1 (认可) acknowledge 2 (政权) recognize

承受 chéngshòu [动] 1 (禁受) bear 2 (经受) experience

城 chéng [名] 1 (城墙) city wall ▷城外 chéngwài outside the city 2 (城市) city ▷进城 jìnchéng go to town 3 (城镇) town

城堡 chéngbǎo [名] castle

城市 chéngshì [名] city

乘 chéng [动] 1 (搭坐) travel by ▷乘火车 chéng huǒchē travel by train 2 (利用) take advantage of 3 (几倍于) multiply ▷8乘5等于40。 Bā chéng wǔ děngyú sìshí. Eight times five is forty.

乘法 chéngfǎ [名] multiplication

乘方 chéngfāng [名] (数) power

乘客 chéngkè [名] passenger

乘务员 chéngwùyuán [名] conductor

盛 chéng [动] 1 (装) ladle ... out 2 (容纳) contain
→ see also/另见 shèng

程 chéng [名] 1 (规矩) rule ▷章程 zhāngchéng constitution 2 (程序) procedure ▷议程

yìchéng agenda ▶课程 kèchéng curriculum 3(距离) distance ▶路程 lùchéng journey 4(道路) journey

程度 chéngdù [名] 1(水平) level 2(限度) extent

程式 chéngshì [名] form

程序 chéngxù [名] 1(次序) procedure 2(计算机) program

惩 chéng [动] punish

惩罚 chéngfá [动] punish

橙 chéng see below/见下文

橙子 chéngzi [名] orange

逞 chěng [动] (夸耀) flaunt

逞能 chěngnéng [动] show off

秤 chèng [名] scales (PL)

吃 chī [动] 1(咀嚼吞咽) eat ▶吃药 chīyào take medicine 2(就餐) eat in 3(依靠) live off ▷吃劳保 chī láobǎo live off welfare 4(消灭) wipe ... out 5(耗费) withstand ▶吃力 chīlì strenuous 6(吸收) absorb

吃醋 chīcù [动] be jealous

吃惊 chījīng [动] surprise

吃苦 chīkǔ [动] put up with hardship

吃亏 chīkuī [动] 1(受损失) lose out 2(条件不利) be at a disadvantage

吃香 chīxiāng [形] (口) popular

痴 chī I [形] idiotic II [名] obsession

痴呆 chīdāi [形] idiotic

痴迷 chīmí [形] infatuated

池 chí [名] (池塘) pond ▶泳池 yǒngchí swimming pool

池塘 chítáng [名] pond

迟 chí [形] 1(慢) slow 2(晚) late

迟到 chídào [动] be late

迟钝 chídùn [形] (贬) slow

迟早 chízǎo [副] sooner or later

持 chí [动] 1(拿着) hold 2(支持) support ▶坚持 jiānchí maintain

持久 chíjiǔ [形] protracted

持续 chíxù [动] go on

匙 chí [名] spoon

尺 chǐ I [量] unit of length, equal to a third of a metre II [名] ruler ▶尺子 chǐzi ruler

尺寸 chǐcun [名] 1(长度) size 2(口) (分寸) sense of propriety

尺码 chǐmǎ [名] (尺寸) size

齿 chǐ [名] (器官) tooth ▶牙齿 yáchǐ tooth

耻 chǐ [名] 1(羞愧) shame 2(耻辱) disgrace

耻辱 chǐrǔ [名] disgrace

赤 chì [形] (红色) red

赤道 chìdào [名] the equator

赤裸裸 chìluǒluǒ [形] 1(光身子) stark naked 2(喻) (毫无掩饰) undisguised

翅 chì [名] 1(翅膀) wing 2(鳍) fin

翅膀 chìbǎng [名] wing

冲 chōng [动] 1 (向前闯) rush forward 2 (猛撞) clash ▶冲撞 chōngzhuàng collide 3 (浇) pour boiling water on 4 (冲洗) rinse 5 (指胶片) develop
→ see also/另见 chòng

冲刺 chōngcì [动] (字) sprint

冲动 chōngdòng [动] be impulsive

冲浪 chōnglàng [名] surf

冲突 chōngtū I [动] 1 (激烈争斗) conflict 2 (相抵触) clash II [名] (矛盾) conflict

冲洗 chōngxǐ [动] 1 (洗涤) wash 2 (指胶片) develop

充 chōng [动] 1 (满) fill ▶充电 chōngdiàn charge a battery 2 (担任) act as 3 (假装) pass ... off as

充当 chōngdāng [动] act as

充分 chōngfèn I [形] ample II [副] fully

充满 chōngmǎn [动] 1 (填满) fill 2 (有) brim with

充其量 chōngqíliàng [副] at best

充实 chōngshí I [形] rich II [动] enrich

充足 chōngzú [形] sufficient

虫 chóng [名] insect ▶虫子 chóngzi insect

重 chóng I [动] 1 (重复) repeat 2 (重叠) overlap II [副] again
→ see also/另见 zhòng

重叠 chóngdié [形] overlapping

重逢 chóngféng [动] reunite

重复 chóngfù [动] repeat

重新 chóngxīn [副] again

崇 chóng [形] high

崇拜 chóngbài [动] worship

崇高 chónggāo [形] lofty

宠 chǒng [动] spoil

宠爱 chǒng'ài [动] dote on

宠物 chǒngwù [名] pet

冲 chòng I [形] 1 (指气味刺鼻) pungent 2 (劲儿足) vigorous II [介] 1 (对着) at 2 (凭) because of III [动] (口) (正对) face
→ see also/另见 chōng

抽 chōu [动] 1 (取出) take ... out 2 (取出部分) take ▶抽时间 chōu shíjiān find time 3 (吸) inhale ▶抽烟 chōuyān smoke ▶抽血 chōuxiě take blood 4 (抽缩) shrink 5 (打) whip

抽搐 chōuchù [动] twitch

抽风 chōufēng [动] 1 (指疾病) have convulsions 2 (喻) (不合常理) lose the plot

抽奖 chōujiǎng [动] draw prizes

抽筋 chōujīn [动] (口) (肌肉痉挛) have cramp

抽空 chōukòng [动] find the time

抽签 chōuqiān [动] draw lots

抽水 chōushuǐ [动] 1 (吸水) pump water 2 (缩水) shrink

抽屉 chōuti [名] drawer

抽象 chōuxiàng [形] abstract

仇 chóu [名] 1 (仇敌) enemy 2 (仇恨) hatred ▶报仇 bàochóu avenge

仇恨 chóuhèn [动] hate

绸 chóu [名] silk ▶丝绸 sīchóu silk

酬 chóu [动] (报答) reward

酬金 chóujīn [名] remuneration

酬劳 chóuláo I [动] repay II [名] repayment

酬谢 chóuxiè [动] repay

稠 chóu [形] 1 (浓度大) thick 2 (稠密) dense

稠密 chóumì [形] dense

愁 chóu [动] be anxious ▶忧愁 yōuchóu be worried

丑 chǒu [形] 1 (丑陋) ugly 2 (令人厌恶) disgraceful

丑陋 chǒulòu [形] ugly

丑闻 chǒuwén [名] scandal

瞅 chǒu [动] (方) look at

臭 chòu [形] 1 (指气味) smelly 2 (惹人厌恶) disgusting 3 (拙劣) lousy

出 chū [动] 1 (与入相对) go out ▶出国 chūguó go abroad ▶出游 chūyóu go sightseeing 2 (来到) appear ▶出庭 chūtíng appear in court 3 (超出) exceed ▶出轨 chūguǐ derail 4 (给) give out 5 (产生) produce 6 (发生) occur ▶出事 chūshì have an accident 7 (发出) come out ▶出血 chūxiě bleed ▶出汗 chūhàn sweat 8 (显露) appear ▶出名 chūmíng become famous

出版 chūbǎn [动] publish

出差 chūchāi [动] go away on business

出发 chūfā [动] 1 (离开) set out 2 (表示着眼点) take ... as a starting point

出口 chūkǒu I [动] (指贸易) export II [名] exit

出路 chūlù [名] 1 (指道路) way out 2 (前途) prospects (PL) 3 (销路) market

出名 chūmíng [动] become famous

出勤 chūqín [动] (按时到) show up on time ▶出勤率 chūqínlǜ ratio of attendance

出色 chūsè [形] outstanding

出身 chūshēn I [动] come from II [名] background

出生 chūshēng [动] be born

出售 chūshòu [动] sell

出席 chūxí [动] attend

出现 chūxiàn [动] appear

出院 chūyuàn [动] leave hospital

出租 chūzū [动] let ▷有房出租 yǒu fáng chūzū room to let

出租汽车 chūzū qìchē [名] taxi

初 chū I [名] original II [形] 1 (第一) first ▶初恋 chūliàn first love 2 (最低) primary ▶初级 chūjí primary 3 (开始) early ▶初冬 chūdōng early winter

初步 chūbù [形] fundamental

初期 chūqī [名] initial stage

除 chú I [动] 1 (去掉) get rid of ▶开除 kāichú dismiss ▶去除 qùchú

remove 2(指算术) divide ▶除法 chúfǎ division ▷16除8等于2。 Shíliù chú bā děngyú èr. Sixteen divided by eight is two. **II**[介]**1**(表示不包括) except ▷除彼得外大家都来了。 Chú Bǐdé wài dàjiā dōu lái le. Everyone came except Peter. **2**(除此以外) apart from

除非 chúfēi **I**[连] unless ▷除非他要我去，否则我不去。 Chúfēi tā yào wǒ qù, fǒuzé wǒ bù qù. I won't go unless he wants me to. **II**[介] other than

除了 chúle [介]**1**(表示不包括) except ▷除了你其他人都参加了会议。 Chúle nǐ qítā rén dōu cānjiā le huìyì. Everyone else attended the meeting except you. **2**(除此以外) apart from ▷他除了学习英语，还学习日语。 Tā chúle xuéxí Yīngyǔ, hái xuéxí Rìyǔ. Apart from studying English, he also studies Japanese. **3**(表示非此即彼) apart from ... the only ... ▷他除了工作就是睡觉。 Tā chúle gōngzuò jiùshì shuìjiào. The only thing he does apart from work is sleep.

除夕 chúxī [名] New Year's Eve

厨 chú [名] **1**(厨房) kitchen ▶厨房 chúfáng kitchen **2**(厨师) cook

厨师 chúshī [名] cook

橱 chú [名] cabinet

橱窗 chúchuāng [名] **1**(指商店的展示窗) shop (英) 或 store (美)

window **2**(用于展览图片等) display case

处 chǔ [动] **1**(交往) get on with **2**(在) be in **3**(办理) deal with **4**(处罚) penalize
→ see also/另见 chù

处罚 chǔfá [动] punish

处方 chǔfāng [名] prescription

处分 chǔfèn **I**[动] punish **II**[名] punishment

处境 chǔjìng [名] situation

处理 chǔlǐ [动] **1**(解决) deal with **2**(减价) sell ... at a reduced price ▶处理品 chǔlǐ pǐn goods sold at a discount **3**(加工) treat

处于 chǔyú [动] be in a position ▶处于困境 chǔyú kùnjìng be in a difficult position

储 chǔ [动] store

储备 chǔbèi **I**[动] store ... up **II**[名] reserve

储藏 chǔcáng [动] **1**(保藏) store **2**(蕴藏) contain

储存 chǔcún [动] stockpile

储蓄 chǔxù **I**[动] save **II**[名] savings (PL)

处 chù [名] **1**(地方) place ▶益处 yìchù profit **2**(部门) department ▶人事处 rénshì chù human resources department
→ see also/另见 chǔ

畜 chù [名] livestock
→ see also/另见 xù

畜生 chùsheng [名] beast

触 chù [动] 1(接触) touch 2(触动) move

触犯 chùfàn [动] violate

触及 chùjí [动] touch

触摸 chùmō [动] touch

踹 chuài [动] (踢) kick

川 chuān [名] (河流) river

穿 chuān [动] 1(弄破纸等) pierce 2(谎言, 事实) expose 3(通过) pass through ▷穿过人群 chuān guò rénqún pass through the crowd ▷穿针 chuān zhēn thread a needle 4(串) piece ... together ▷穿珍珠 chuān zhēnzhū string pearls together 5(衣服, 鞋帽, 首饰等) wear 6(表示透彻) penetrate

穿着 chuānzhuó [名] outfit

传 chuán [动] 1(交给) hand ... down 2(传授) pass ... on 3(传播) spread 4(传导) conduct 5(表达) express ▷传情 chuánqíng express one's feelings 6(命令) summon 7(传染) infect
→ see also/另见 zhuàn

传播 chuánbō [动] disseminate

传达 chuándá I [动] pass ... on II [名] receptionist ▷传达室 chuándá shì reception room

传单 chuándān [名] leaflet

传媒 chuánméi [名] (传播媒介) media (PL)

传票 chuánpiào [名] (指法院) summons (SG)

传奇 chuánqí [形] legendary

传染 chuánrǎn [动] infect

传说 chuánshuō [名] legend

传统 chuántǒng I [名] tradition II [形] 1(世代相传) traditional 2(保守) conservative

传真 chuánzhēn [动] (指通讯方式) fax ▷给我发个传真吧。 Gěi wǒ fā ge chuánzhēn ba. Please send me a fax.

船 chuán [名] boat, ship

串 chuàn I [动] 1(连贯) string ... together 2(勾结) conspire 3(指信号) get mixed up 4(走动) drop by II [量] bunch ▷两串钥匙 liǎng chuàn yàoshi two bunches of keys ▷一串珍珠 yī chuàng zhēnzhū a string of pearls

创 chuāng [名] wound ▷创可贴 chuāngkětiē plaster (英), Band-Aid® (美)
→ see also/另见 chuàng

创伤 chuāngshāng [名] 1(指肉体) wound 2(指精神) trauma

疮 chuāng [名] (指疾病) ulcer ▷口疮 kǒuchuāng mouth ulcer ▷冻疮 dòngchuāng chilblain

窗 chuāng [名] window ▷窗子 chuāngzi window

窗户 chuānghu [名] window

窗口 chuāngkǒu [名] 1(字) window 2(喻) (渠道) vehicle 3(喻) (反映处) window

床 chuáng [名] bed ▷单人床 dānrénchuáng single bed ▷床

单 chuángdān bed sheet ▶上床 shàngchuáng go to bed

闯 chuǎng [动] 1 (冲) rush 2 (磨炼) steel oneself 3 (惹) stir ... up ▶闯祸 chuǎnghuò cause trouble

创 chuàng [动] create ▶独创 dúchuàng make an original creation → see also/另见 chuāng

创建 chuàngjiàn [动] establish

创立 chuànglì [动] establish

创业 chuàngyè [动] carve out a career

创意 chuàngyì [名] creativity

创造 chuàngzào [动] create

创作 chuàngzuò I [动] create II [名] work

吹 chuī [动] 1 (出气) blow ▶吹蜡烛 chuī làzhú blow out a candle 2 (演奏) play ▶吹口琴 chuī kǒuqín play the harmonica 3 (夸口) boast 4 (口) (破裂) fall through ▶我和女友吹了。 Wǒ hé nǚyǒu chuī le. I've broken up with my girlfriend.

吹风 chuīfēng [动] (吹干) blow-dry

吹牛 chuīniú [动] brag

吹捧 chuīpěng [动] flatter

吹嘘 chuīxū [动] boast

炊 chuī [动] cook ▶炊具 chuījù cooking utensil

垂 chuí [动] (一头向下) hang down

垂直 chuízhí [形] vertical

捶 chuí [动] pound

锤 chuí I [名] hammer II [动] hammer

春 chūn [名] (春季) spring

春节 Chūn Jié [名] Chinese New Year

春节 Chūn Jié

Chinese New Year, or Spring Festival, is the most important festival of the year and falls on the first day of the lunar calendar. Traditionally families gather together, children receive money in red envelopes, and in some parts of China everyone helps make and eat a festival feast. On greeting people over this festival it is traditional to wish them wealth and happiness, by saying 恭喜发财 gōngxǐ fācái.

春卷 chūnjuǎn [名] spring roll

春天 chūntiān [名] spring

纯 chún [形] 1 (纯净) pure 2 (纯熟) skilful (英), skillful (美)

纯粹 chúncuì I [形] pure II [副] purely

纯洁 chúnjié I [形] pure II [动] purify

纯净 chúnjìng [形] pure

唇 chún [名] lip

蠢 chǔn [形] 1 (愚蠢) stupid 2 (笨拙) clumsy

戳 chuō I [动] (穿过) poke II [名] seal

戳子 chuōzi [名] seal

辍 chuò [动] stop

辍学 chuòxué [动] give up one's studies

词 cí [名] 1 (语句) words (PL) ▶台词 táicí lines ▶闭幕词 bìmùcí closing speech 2 (指语言单位) word

词典 cídiǎn [名] dictionary

词汇 cíhuì [名] vocabulary

词语 cíyǔ [名] word

词组 cízǔ [名] phrase

瓷 cí [名] porcelain

辞 cí [动] 1 (辞职) resign 2 (辞退) dismiss

辞职 cízhí [动] resign

慈 cí [形] kind

慈爱 cí'ài [形] affectionate

慈善 císhàn [形] charitable

慈祥 cíxiáng [形] kind

磁 cí [名] (物) magnetism

磁场 cíchǎng [名] magnetic field

磁盘 cípán [名] disk

雌 cí [形] female ▶雌性 cíxìng female

此 cǐ [代] (这) this ▶此时此刻 cǐshí cǐkè right now

此外 cǐwài [连] apart from this

次 cì I [名] ranking ▶档次 dàngcì grade ▶名次 míngcì position II [形] 1 (第二) second ▶次日 cìrì next day 2 (差) inferior ▶次品 cìpǐn inferior product III [量] time ▶初次 chūcì first time ▶屡次 lǚcì repeatedly

次序 cìxù [名] order

次要 cìyào [形] secondary

刺 cì [名] sting

刺耳 cì'ěr [形] 1 (指声音) ear-piercing 2 (喻) (指言语) jarring

刺激 cìjī [动] 1 (指生物现象) stimulate 2 (推动) stimulate 3 (打击) provoke

刺猬 cìwei [名] hedgehog

匆 cōng [副] hastily

匆忙 cōngmáng [形] hurried

葱 cōng [名] spring onion

聪 cōng I [名] hearing II [形] 1 (指听力) acute 2 (聪明) clever

聪明 cōngmíng [形] clever

从 cóng I [动] 1 (跟随) follow 2 (顺从) comply with ▶服从 fúcóng obey 3 (从事) participate in II [名] follower III [形] (从属) subordinate ▶从犯 cóngfàn accessory IV [介] 1 (起于) from ▶从明天起 cóng míngtiān qǐ from tomorrow onwards 2 (经过) ▶飞机从我们头顶飞过。Fēijī cóng wǒmen tóudǐng fēiguò. The plane passed over our heads.

从此 cóngcǐ [副] after that

从而 cóng'ér [连] thus

从来 cónglái [副] ▷她从来未说过。 Tā cónglái wèi shuōguò. She never said it.

从前 cóngqián [名] 1 (过去) past ▷希望你比从前快乐。 Xīwàng nǐ bǐ cóngqián kuàilè. I hope you are happier than you were before. 2 (很久以前) once upon a time

从事 cóngshì [动] 1 (投身) undertake 2 (处理) deal with

凑 còu [动] 1 (聚集) gather ... together 2 (碰) encounter 3 (接近) approach

凑合 còuhe [动] 1 (聚集) gather ... together 2 (拼凑) improvise 3 (将就) get by

凑巧 còuqiǎo [形] lucky

粗 cū [形] 1 (横剖面大) thick 2 (颗粒大) coarse 3 (指声音) gruff 4 (糙) crude

粗暴 cūbào [形] rough

粗糙 cūcāo [形] 1 (不光滑) rough 2 (不细致) crude

粗话 cūhuà [名] obscene language

粗鲁 cūlǔ [形] crude

粗心 cūxīn [形] careless

粗野 cūyě [形] rough

促 cù I [形] urgent II [动] 1 (催) press 2 (靠近) be near

促进 cùjìn [动] promote

促使 cùshǐ [动] press for

醋 cù [名] (指调味品) vinegar

催 cuī [动] 1 (敦促) hurry ▶催促 cuīcù hurry 2 (加快) speed ... up ▶催眠 cuīmián hypnotize

脆 cuì [形] 1 (易碎) brittle 2 (指食物) crispy

脆弱 cuìruò [形] fragile

村 cūn [名] village ▶村子 cūnzi village

存 cún [动] 1 (存在) exist 2 (储存) store 3 (储蓄) save ▶存款 cúnkuǎn savings (PL) 4 (寄存) check ... in ▷存行李 cún xíngli check in one's bags 5 (保留) retain 6 (心里怀着) harbour (英), harbor (美)

存档 cúndàng [动] file

存放 cúnfàng [动] deposit

存心 cúnxīn [副] deliberately

存在 cúnzài [动] exist

存折 cúnzhé [名] passbook

寸 cùn [量] unit of length, approximately 3 cm

搓 cuō [动] rub

撮 cuō [动] (聚集) scoop ... up

痤 cuó see below/见下文

痤疮 cuóchuāng [名] acne

挫 cuò [动] (挫折) defeat ▶挫折 cuòzhé setback

措 cuò [动] 1 (安排) handle 2 (筹划) make plans

措施 cuòshī [名] measure

错 cuò I [形] (不正确) incorrect
II [动] (避开) miss III [名] fault
▷这是我的错。 Zhè shì wǒ de
cuò. This is my fault.

错过 cuòguò [动] miss ▷错过
机会 cuòguò jīhuì miss an
opportunity

错误 cuòwù I [形] wrong II [名]
mistake

搭 dā [动] 1 (建造) put ... up ▷搭帐
篷 dā zhàngpeng put up a tent
2 (挂) hang ▷我把大衣搭在胳
膊上。 Wǒ bǎ dàyī dā zài gēbo
shàng. I hung my overcoat over
my arm. 3 (坐) take ▷他每个月
搭飞机去上海。 Tā měi ge yuè
dā fēijī qù Shànghǎi. He takes the
plane to Shanghai every month.
▷搭便车 dā biànchē get a lift
4 (连接) join ▷搭伙 dāhuǒ join
forces ▷两家公司终于搭上了关
系。 Liǎng jiā gōngsī zhōngyú
dā shàng le guānxi. The two
companies finally joined forces.
5 (抬) carry

搭档 dādàng I [名] partner II [动]
team up

搭配 dāpèi [动] 1 (安排) combine 2 (配合) pair up 3 (指语言) collocate

答 dā [动] answer
→ see also/另见 dá

答理 dāli [动] 1 (理睬) bother 2 (打招呼) acknowledge

答应 dāying [动] 1 (回答) answer 2 (同意) agree 3 (承诺) promise

打 dá [量] dozen
→ see also/另见 dǎ

达 dá [动] 1 (数量, 目标) reach 2 (指时间) last 3 (通) ▷直达 zhídá non-stop journey 4 (表示) express ▷转达 chuándá convey

达到 dádào [动] 1 (要求, 水平, 目的) achieve ▷达到目的 dádào mùdì achieve an aim ▷达到要求 dádào yāoqiú satisfy requirements 2 (指过程) reach

答 dá [动] 1 (回答) answer 2 (还报) repay ▷报答 bàodá repay
→ see also/另见 dā

答案 dá'àn [名] answer

答复 dáfù [动] respond

答卷 dájuàn I [名] answer sheet II [动] answer exam questions

打 dǎ I [动] 1 (指暴力) hit ▷殴打 ōudǎ beat up ▷打人 dǎrén beat sb up 2 (敲) beat ▷打鼓 dǎ gǔ beat a drum 3 (破) break ▷我把暖瓶给打了。Wǒ bǎ nuǎnpíng gěi dǎ le. I broke the Thermos®. 4 (发出) send ▷打电话 dǎ diànhuà make a phone call ▷打手电 dǎ shǒudiàn shine a torch 5 (做游戏) play ▷打篮球 dǎ lánqiú play basketball 6 (表示动作) ▷打喷嚏 dǎpēntì sneeze ▷打滚 dǎgǔn roll about ▷打针 dǎzhēn have an injection 7 (建造) build ▷打基础 dǎ jīchǔ build the foundation 8 (涂抹) polish ▷打蜡 dǎlà wax 9 (交涉) deal with ▷打交道 dǎ jiāodao socialize ▷打官司 dǎ guānsi file a lawsuit 10 (制造) make ▷打家具 dǎ jiājù make furniture 11 (搅拌) beat ▷打两个鸡蛋 dǎ liǎng ge jīdàn beat two eggs 12 (编织) knit ▷打毛衣 dǎ máoyī knit a sweater 13 (捕捉) catch ▷打猎 dǎliè go hunting 14 (画) draw ▷打草稿 dǎ cǎogǎo draw up a draft 15 (举) hold ▷打伞 dǎsǎn hold an umbrella 16 (揭) open ▷打开 dǎkāi open 17 (穿凿) dig ▷打耳洞 dǎ ěrdòng pierce one's ears 18 (收割) gather ▷打柴 dǎchái gather firewood 19 (从事) do ▷打杂儿 dǎzár do odd jobs 20 (用) make ▷打比喻 dǎ bǐyù make a comparison 21 (捆) pack ▷打行李 dǎ xíngli pack one's bags 22 (拨动) flick ▷打字 dǎzì type ▷打字机 dǎzìjī typewriter II [介] from ▷打今儿起 dǎ jīnr qǐ from today
→ see also/另见 dá

打败 dǎbài [动] defeat

打扮 dǎban [动] make oneself up

打倒 dǎdǎo [动] 1 (击倒在地) knock down 2 (指口号) down with 3 (推翻) overthrow

打的 dǎ dī [动] take a taxi

打动 dǎdòng [动] move

打赌 dǎdǔ [动] bet

打发 dǎfa [动] 1 (时间) while away 2 (哄走) get rid of 3 (派) send

打工 dǎgōng [动] temp

打火机 dǎhuǒjī [名] lighter

打击 dǎjī I [动] crack down on II [名] (指精神上) blow

打架 dǎjià [动] have a fight

打开 dǎkāi [动] 1 (开启) open 2 (扩展) expand 3 (开) turn ... on

打气 dǎqì [动] (球, 轮胎) inflate

打扫 dǎsǎo [动] clean

打算 dǎsuan I [动] plan II [名] plan

打听 dǎting [动] ask about

打印机 dǎyìnjī [名] printer

打仗 dǎzhàng [动] fight a war

打招呼 dǎ zhāohu [动] (问好) greet

打折 dǎzhé [动] discount

大 dà [形] 1 (数量, 体积, 面积) big ▷大街 dàjiē street ▷一大批 yīdàpī a large amount of 2 (指力气) great ▷他劲儿真大！ Tā jìnr zhēn dà! He's so strong! 3 (重要) important 4 (强) strong ▷大风 dà fēng strong wind 5 (指声音) loud ▷大声 dàshēng loudly 6 (雨, 雪) heavy 7 (指年龄) old ▷你多大了？ Nǐ duōdà le? How old are you? ▷他比我大。 Tā bǐ wǒ dà. He's older than me. 8 (指程度) ▷大笑 dàxiào roar with

laughter 9 (老大) eldest ▷大姐 dà jiě eldest sister
→ see also/另见 dài

大胆 dàdǎn [形] bold

大地 dàdì [名] the land

大方 dàfang [形] 1 (慷慨) generous 2 (不拘束) natural 3 (不俗气) tasteful

大概 dàgài I [名] general idea II [形] approximate III [副] probably

大伙儿 dàhuǒr [代] everybody

大家 dàjiā [代] everybody

大款 dàkuǎn [名] (贬) moneybags (sg)

大量 dàliàng [形] (数量多) large amount of ▷大量资金 dàliàng zījīn a large investment ▷大量裁员 dàliàng cáiyuán lay off a large number of people

大陆 dàlù [名] 1 (指各大洲) continent 2 (指中国) the mainland ▷中国大陆 Zhōngguó dàlù mainland China

大米 dàmǐ [名] rice

大人 dàren [名] adult

大使 dàshǐ [名] ambassador

大使馆 dàshǐguǎn [名] embassy

大事 dàshì [名] important event

大提琴 dàtíqín [名] cello

大小 dàxiǎo [名] (尺寸) size

大写 dàxiě [名] (指字母) capital letter

大型 dàxíng [形] large-scale

大选 dàxuǎn [名] general election

大学 dàxué [名] university (英) 或 college (美)

大学生 dàxuéshēng [名] university (英) 或 college (美) student

大雪 dàxuě [名] heavy snow

大衣 dàyī [名] overcoat

大雨 dàyǔ [名] downpour

大约 dàyuē [副] 1 (指数量) approximately 2 (可能) probably

大众 dàzhòng [名] the people (PL)

大自然 dàzìrán [名] nature

呆 dāi I [形] 1 (傻) slow-witted 2 (发愣) blank ▶发呆 fādāi stare blankly II [动] stay ▷我在北京呆了一个星期。 Wǒ zài Běijīng dāi le yī ge xīngqī. I stayed in Beijing for a week.

待 dāi [动] stay ▷你再多待一会儿。 Nǐ zài duō dāi yīhuǐr. Do stay a little longer.
→ see also/另见 dài

逮 dǎi [动] catch
→ see also/另见 dài

大 dài see below/见下文

大夫 dàifu [名] doctor
→ see also/另见 dà

代 dài I [动] 1 (替) do ... on behalf of 2 (指问候) send regards to ▷你见到他时, 代我问好。 Nǐ jiàndào tā shí, dài wǒ wènhǎo. When you see him, say hello from me. 3 (代理) act as ▷代校长 dài xiàozhǎng acting headmaster II [名] 1 (时代) times (PL) ▶古

代 gǔdài ancient times 2 (辈分) generation 3 (朝代) dynasty ▷清代 Qīng dài Qing Dynasty

代表 dàibiǎo I [名] representative II [动] 1 (代替) stand in for 2 (委托) represent 3 (指意义, 概念) be representative of III [形] archetypal

代价 dàijià [名] cost

代理 dàilǐ [动] 1 (暂时替代) act on behalf of 2 (委托) represent

代理人 dàilǐrén [名] agent

代码 dàimǎ [名] code

代数 dàishù [名] algebra

代替 dàitì [动] substitute for

带 dài I [名] 1 (长条物) strap ▶皮带 pídài leather belt ▶磁带 cídài cassette ▶录像带 lùxiàngdài videotape 2 (轮胎) tyre (英) 或 tire (美) ▶车带 chēdài car tyre (英) 或 tire (美) 3 (区域) zone ▶热带 rèdài the tropics II [动] 1 (携带) take ▷别忘了带钱包! Bié wàng le dài qiánbāo! Don't forget to take your wallet! 2 (捎带) ▷你出去时带点牛奶回来, 好吗? Nǐ chūqù shí dài diǎn niúnǎi huílai, hǎo ma? Can you buy some milk when you're out? 3 (呈现) wear ▷面带笑容 miàn dài xiàoróng wear a smile on one's face 4 (含有) have 5 (连带) come with 6 (指导) direct 7 (领) lead 8 (养) bring ... up

带动 dàidòng [动] (指进步) drive

带领 dàilǐng [动] 1 (领着) guide

2 (指挥) lead

带头 dàitóu [动] take the initiative

待 dài [动] **1** (对待) treat **2** (招待) entertain **3** (等待) wait for
→ see also/另见 dāi

待业 dàiyè [动] be unemployed

待遇 dàiyù [名] pay

贷 dài I [动] **1** (指银行) lend **2** (指借钱方) take out a loan II [名] loan

贷款 dàikuǎn I [动] lend II [名] loan

袋 dài I [名] bag II [量] bag

袋鼠 dàishǔ [名] kangaroo

逮 dài [动] capture
→ see also/另见 dǎi

逮捕 dàibǔ [动] arrest

戴 dài [动] (眼镜, 帽子, 小装饰品等) wear

单 dān I [形] **1** (一个) single ▸单身 dānshēn single **2** (奇数) odd **3** (单独) solitary **4** (不复杂) simple **5** (薄弱) weak **6** (衣, 裤) thin II [副] only ▸成功不能单凭运气。 Chénggōng bùnéng dān píng yùnqi. To be successful you can't rely only on luck. III [名] **1** (单子) sheet ▸床单 chuángdān bed sheet **2** (列表) list ▸菜单 càidān menu

单程 dānchéng [名] single trip

单纯 dānchún I [形] simple II [副] merely

单词 dāncí [名] word

单单 dāndān [副] only

单调 dāndiào [形] monotonous

单独 dāndú [形] **1** (独自) alone **2** (独立) unaided

单位 dānwèi [名] **1** (指标准量) unit **2** (机构) unit

单元 dānyuán [名] unit ▸单元房 dānyuán fáng self-contained flat (英) 或 apartment (美)

单子 dānzi [名] **1** (指床上用品) sheet **2** (列表) list

担 dān [动] **1** (挑) carry ... on one's shoulder **2** (负) take ... on
→ see also/另见 dàn

担保 dānbǎo [动] guarantee

担当 dāndāng [动] take ... on

担架 dānjià [名] stretcher

担任 dānrèn [动] hold the post of

担心 dānxīn [动] worry

耽 dān see below/见下文

耽误 dānwu [动] delay

胆 dǎn [名] (胆量) courage

胆固醇 dǎngùchún [名] cholesterol

胆量 dǎnliàng [名] guts (PL)

胆子 dǎnzi [名] guts (PL)

掸 dǎn [动] brush

掸子 dǎnzi [名] duster

但 dàn I [连] but II [副] only ▸但愿 dànyuàn wish

但是 dànshì [连] but ▸虽然下雨, 但是不冷。 Suīrán xiàyǔ, dànshì bù lěng. Even though it's raining, it's not cold.

担 dàn [名] load
→ *see also*/另见 dān

担子 dànzi [名] (责任) responsibility

诞 dàn [动] be born

诞生 dànshēng [动] be born

淡 dàn [形] 1 (指味道浓淡) weak 2 (指咸淡) bland 3 (颜色浅) light 4 (稀薄) light 5 (不热情) indifferent 6 (不红火) slack

淡季 dànjì [名] low season

蛋 dàn [名] (卵) egg ▶鸡蛋 jīdàn egg

蛋白质 dànbáizhì [名] protein

蛋糕 dàngāo [名] cake

弹 dàn [名] (子弹) bullet ▶子弹 zǐdàn bullet ▶原子弹 yuánzǐdàn atomic bomb
→ *see also*/另见 tán

当 dāng I [介] 1 (向) in front of ▶当众 dāngzhòng in public ▶当着全班 dāng zhe quánbān in front of the whole class 2 (正在) ▶当我们到时，电影已开始了。Dāng wǒmen dào shí, diànyǐng yǐ kāishǐ le. When we arrived the film had already started. ▶当他在美国时，他爷爷去世了。Dāng tā zài Měiguó shí, tā yéye qùshì le. His grandfather passed away while he was in America. II [动] 1 (担任) act as ▶当经理 dāng jīnglǐ act as manager 2 (掌管) be in charge ▶当家 dāngjiā rule

the roost
→ *see also*/另见 dàng

当场 dāngchǎng [副] there and then

当初 dāngchū [名] those days

当代 dāngdài [名] the present ▶当代文学 dāngdài wénxué contemporary literature

当地 dāngdì [名] locality ▷当地风俗 dāngdì fēngsú local customs

当今 dāngjīn [名] the present

当面 dāngmiàn [动] do ... face to face

当年 dāngnián [名] those days

当前 dāngqián I [动] be faced with II [名] present ▷当前的目标 dāngqián de mùbiāo the present aim

当然 dāngrán I [副] of course II [形] natural

当时 dāngshí [名] ▷我当时高兴极了。Wǒ dāngshí gāoxìng jí le. I was ecstatic at the time.

当心 dāngxīn [动] be careful

挡 dǎng [动] (拦) keep off ▷别挡路! Bié dǎnglù! Keep off the road!

党 dǎng [名] (政党) party ▶党员 dǎngyuán party member

当 dàng I [形] appropriate ▶不当 bùdàng inappropriate II [动] 1 (作为) treat ... as 2 (认为) assume ▷我当你明白了。Wǒ dàng nǐ míngbai le. I assumed you'd understood. 3 (抵押) pawn 4 (指

时间和地点) ▶当天 dàngtiān that day ▶当场 dàngchǎng on the spot
→ see also/另见 dāng

当年 dàngnián [名] that same year

当铺 dàngpù [名] pawnshop

当作 dàngzuò [动] regard ... as

档 dàng [名] 1 (档案) file 2 (等级) grade

档案 dàng'àn [名] files (PL)

档次 dàngcì [名] grade

刀 dāo [名] (指工具) knife ▶刀子 dāozi knife

叨 dāo see below/见下文

叨唠 dāolao [动] prattle on

导 dǎo [动] 1 (引导) guide 2 (传导) conduct 3 (开导) give guidance 4 (导演) direct

导弹 dǎodàn [名] missile

导火线 dǎohuǒxiàn [名] 1 (字) fuse 2 (喻) trigger

导师 dǎoshī [名] 1 (字) tutor 2 (喻) mentor

导演 dǎoyǎn I [动] direct II [名] director

导游 dǎoyóu I [动] guide II [名] tour guide

导致 dǎozhì [动] lead to ▷粗心导致她没考好。 Cūxīn dǎozhì tā méi kǎo hǎo. Because of her carelessness she failed the exam.

岛 dǎo [名] island ▶岛国 dǎoguó

island nation ▶半岛 bàndǎo peninsula

倒 dǎo [动] 1 (横躺) fall ▶摔倒 shuāidǎo fall down ▶卧倒 wòdǎo lie down 2 (失败) fail ▶倒闭 dǎobì go bankrupt 3 (食欲) spoil ▷倒胃口 dǎo wèikǒu lose one's appetite 4 (换) change ▶倒班 dǎobān change shifts
→ see also/另见 dào

倒霉 dǎoméi [形] unlucky

倒塌 dǎotā [动] collapse

捣 dǎo [动] 1 (捶打) crush 2 (搅乱) make trouble

捣乱 dǎoluàn [动] 1 (扰乱) disturb 2 (制造麻烦) make trouble

到 dào [动] 1 (达到) arrive ▷火车到了。 Huǒchē dào le. The train has arrived. ▷到点了！ Dào diǎn le! Time is up! 2 (去) go ▷我到厦门旅游。 Wǒ dào Xiàmén lǚyóu. I'm going to Xiamen on a tour. 3 (用作动词的补语) ▷听到这个消息我很吃惊。 Tīngdào zhè ge xiāoxi wǒ hěn chījīng. When I heard the news I was very surprised. ▷你的要求我办不到。 Nǐ de yāoqiú wǒ bàn bù dào. I can't handle your demands.

到处 dàochù [名] all places (PL)

到达 dàodá [动] arrive

到底 dàodǐ I [动] ▷坚持到底 jiānchí dàodǐ keep going until the end II [副] 1 (究竟) ▷你到底在干什么？ Nǐ dàodǐ zài gàn shénme? What on earth are you up to? 2 (毕竟) after all 3 (终于) at last

倒 dào I [动] 1 (颠倒) ▶他把地图挂倒了。 Tā bǎ dìtú guà dào le. He hung the map up upside down. ▶姓和名写倒了。 Xìng hé míng xiě dào le. The first name and surname were written the wrong way round. 2 (后退) reverse ▶倒车 dàochē reverse a car 3 (倾倒) empty out ▶倒垃圾 dào lājī empty the rubbish out ▶倒杯茶 dào bēi chá pour a cup of tea II [副] 1 (表示意料之外) unexpectedly 2 (反而) instead 3 (表示让步) ▶这房子地段倒好，就是太小。 Zhè fángzi dìduàn dào hǎo, jiùshì tài xiǎo. Although the location of the house is good, it's still too small. 4 (表示转折) but 5 (表示不耐烦) ▶你倒是说呀！ Nǐ dào shì shuō ya! Can you get on with it please! 6 (表示责怪) ▶他说得倒漂亮。 Tā shuō de dào piàoliang. He's all talk.

→ see also/另见 dǎo

倒立 dàolì [动] 1 (物) be upside down 2 (人) do a handstand

倒计时 dàojìshí [动] count down

倒退 dàotuì [动] go back

倒影 dàoyǐng [名] reflection

悼 dào [动] mourn

悼念 dàoniàn [动] mourn

盗 dào I [动] rob ▶盗窃 dàoqiè steal II [名] robber ▶海盗 hǎidào pirate

盗版 dàobǎn I [动] pirate ▶盗版软件 dàobǎn ruǎnjiàn pirated software II [名] pirate copy

盗贼 dàozéi [名] thieves (PL)

道 dào I [名] 1 (路) road ▶近道 jìndào shortcut 2 (方法) way ▶生财之道 shēngcái zhī dào the road to riches 3 (技艺) art ▶茶道 chádào tea ceremony 4 (道教) the Tao 5 (线) line ▶横道儿 héngdàor horizontal line 6 (水流途径) channel ▶下水道 xiàshuǐdào sewer II [量] 1 ▶一道阳光 yī dào yángguāng a beam of sunlight ▶两道泪痕 liǎng dào lèihén two tear streaks

measure word, used for things in the shape of a long strip

2 ▶第二道门 dì'èr dào mén the second door ▶一道墙 yī dào qiáng a wall

measure word, used for doors, walls, etc.

3 ▶三道题 sān dào tí three questions ▶两道命令 liǎng dào mìnglìng two orders

measure word, used for orders, questions, procedures, etc.

4 (次) ▶我还要办一道手续。 Wǒ háiyào bàn yī dào shǒuxù I still need to complete one formality. ▶刷了两道漆 shuā le liǎng dào qī paint two coats 5 ▶五道菜 wǔ dào cài five dishes

measure word, used for dishes or courses of a meal

道德 dàodé [名] morals (PL)

道教 Dàojiào [名] Taoism

道理 dàoli [名] 1 (规律) principle 2 (情理) sense

道路 dàolù [名] path

道歉 dàoqiàn [动] apologize

得 dé I [动] 1 (得到) get ▷得奖 déjiǎng win a prize 2 (病) catch ▷他得了流感。 Tā dé le liúgǎn. He caught flu. 3 (计算) equal ▷四减二得二。 Sì jiǎn èr dé èr. Four minus two equals two. 4 (完成) be ready ▷晚饭得了。 Wǎnfàn dé le. Dinner is ready. 5 (适合) be suitable ▷得体 détǐ appropriate II [叹] 1 (表示同意，禁止) OK ▷得，就这么决定了。 Dé, jiù zhème juédìng le. OK, that's settled then. 2 (表示无可奈何) Oh no! ▷得，我又没考及格！ Dé, wǒ yòu méi kǎo jígé! Oh no, I failed again! III [助动] ▷版权所有，不得转载。 Bǎnquán suǒyǒu, bù dé zhuǎnzǎi. All rights reserved, copying not allowed.
→ see also/ 另见 de, děi

得到 dédào [动] get ▷得到帮助 dédào bāngzhù get help

得意 déyì [形] pleased with oneself

得罪 dézuì [动] offend

德 dé [名] 1 (品行) morality ▷品德 pǐndé moral character 2 (恩惠) kindness ▷恩德 ēndé kindness

3 (德国) Germany ▷德国 Déguó Germany ▷德语 Déyǔ German

地 de [助] ▷刻苦地学习 kèkǔ de xuéxí study hard ▷努力地工作 nǔlì de gōngzuò work hard
→ see also/ 另见 dì

Use 地 de after adjectives to form adverbs.

的 de [助] 1 (用于定语后) ▷昂贵的价格 ángguì de jiàgé high price ▷他的哥哥 tā de gēge his elder brother ▷经理的秘书 jīnglǐ de mìshū the manager's secretary 2 (名词化) ▷画画的 huàhuà de painter 3 (用于是…的强调结构) ▷我的嗓子是喊哑的。 Wǒ de sǎngzi shì hǎnyǎ de. My voice became hoarse from shouting.
→ see also/ 另见 dí, dì

Use 的 de to link descriptive words, phrases and clauses to the noun they describe, e.g. 她是一个很漂亮的女人。 Tā shì yīgè hěn piàoliàng de nǚrén. (She is a very beautiful woman.); 这是他昨天给我的书。 Zhè shì tā zuótiān gěi wǒ de shū. (This is the book which he gave me yesterday).

的话 dehuà [助] ▷见到她的话，替我问好。 Jiàndào tā de huà, tì wǒ wènhǎo. Please give her my regards if you see her.

得 de [助] 1 (用于动词后面) ▷这种野菜吃得。 Zhè zhǒng yěcài chī

de. This wild herb is edible. **2** [动词或补语中间] ▷她抬得动。 Tā tái de dòng. She can carry it. ▷我写得完。 Wǒ xiě de wán. I am able to finish writing it. **3** [动词和形容词后面] ▷他英语学得很快。 Tā Yīngyǔ xué de hěn kuài. He's learning English very quickly. ▷风大得很。 Fēng dà de hěn. The wind's very strong.

→ see also/另见 dé, děi

Most adverbial phrases follow the verb and are joined to it by 得 de. Such statements are often evaluations or judgements, and contain the idea of *to the extent of* or *to the degree that*, e.g. 她说得很流利。 Tā shuō de hěn liúlì. (She speaks very fluently.).

得 děi **I** [动] [口] (需要) need ▷买房得多少钱? Mǎifáng děi duōshao qián? How much money do you need to buy a house? **II** [动] [口] **1** (必要) must ▷我们得6点出发。 Wǒmen děi liùdiǎn chūfā. We have to leave at six. **2** (表示推测) will ▷快走, 电影得开始了。 Kuài zǒu, diànyǐng děi kāishǐ le. Get a move on, the film's just about to start.

→ see also/另见 dé, de

灯 dēng [名] light ▷台灯 táidēng desk lamp ▷红绿灯 hónglùdēng traffic lights (PL)

灯塔 dēngtǎ [名] lighthouse

登 dēng [动] **1** (由低到高) go up **2** (刊登) publish **3** (踩踏板) pedal **4** (踩) get up onto

登记 dēngjì [动] register

登录 dēnglù [动] log in ▷登录网站 dēnglù wǎngzhàn log in to a website

蹬 dēng [动] pedal

等 děng **I** [名] **1** (等级) grade ▷中等 zhōngděng medium ▷二等奖 èr děng jiǎng second prize **2** (类) kind **II** [动] **1** (相同) equal ▷等于 děngyú be equal to **2** (等待) wait ▷等车 děngchē wait for a bus **III** [连] (等到) when ▷等他来了, 我们再讨论。 Děng tā lái le, wǒmen zài tǎolùn. We'll talk about it when he comes. **IV** [助] **1** (列举未尽的) etc. **2** (煞尾的) namely

等待 děngdài [动] wait

等到 děngdào [连] when

等等 děngděng [助] and so on

等号 děnghào [名] (数) equals sign

等候 děnghòu [动] expect

等级 děngjí [名] grade

等于 děngyú [动] **1** (相等于) equal **2** (等同) be equivalent to

凳 dèng [名] stool ▷板凳 bǎndèng wooden stool ▷凳子 dèngzi stool

瞪 dèng [动] **1** (表示生气) glare at **2** (睁大) open one's eyes wide

低 dī I [形] 1 (指高度, 程度) low ▷他喜欢低声说话。 Tā xǐhuan dī shēng shuōhuà. He likes to speak quietly. 2 (指等级) junior ▷我比她低两届。 Wǒ bǐ tā dī liǎngjiè. I am two years below her. II [动] (头) bend

低潮 dīcháo [名] low ebb

低调 dīdiào [形] low-key

低级 dījí [形] 1 (不高级) inferior 2 (庸俗) vulgar

堤 dī [名] dyke

提 dī [动] carry
→ see also/另见 tí

提防 dīfáng [动] guard against

滴 dī I [动] drip II [名] drop ▷水滴 shuǐdī drop of water III [量] drop ▷几滴墨水 jǐ dī mòshuǐ a few drops of ink

的 dí see below/见下文
→ see also/另见 de, dì

的确 díquè [副] really

迪 dí [动] (书) enlighten

迪斯科 dísīkē [名] disco

敌 dí I [名] enemy II [动] oppose III [形] equal

敌人 dírén [名] enemy

笛 dí [名] 1 (音) flute 2 (警笛) siren

笛子 dízi [名] bamboo flute

底 dǐ [名] 1 (最下部分) bottom ▷鞋底 xiédǐ sole ▷底下 dǐxia under 2 (末尾) end ▷年底 niándǐ the end of the year

底层 dǐcéng [名] 1 (指建筑) ground floor 2 (最下部) bottom

抵 dǐ [动] 1 (支撑) support 2 (抵抗) resist 3 (补偿) compensate for 4 (抵押) mortgage 5 (抵消) offset 6 (代替) be equal to

抵达 dǐdá [动] reach

抵抗 dǐkàng [动] resist

抵押 dǐyā [动] mortgage

地 dì [名] 1 (地球) the Earth ▷地球 dìqiú the Earth 2 (陆地) land 3 (土地) fields (PL) 4 (地点) location ▷目的地 mùdìdì destination
→ see also/另见 de

地步 dìbù [名] 1 (处境) state, situation 2 (程度) extent

地带 dìdài [名] zone

地道 dìdào [名] tunnel

地道 dìdao [形] 1 (真正) genuine 2 (纯正) pure 3 (指质量) well done

地点 dìdiǎn [名] location

地方 dìfāng [名] locality ▷地方政府 dìfāng zhèngfǔ local government

地方 dìfang [名] 1 (区域) place ▷你是哪个地方的人？ Nǐ shì nǎ ge dìfang de rén? Where do you come from? 2 (空间) room 3 (身体部位) ▷我这个地方痛。 Wǒ zhè ge dìfang tòng. I ache here. 4 (部分) part ▷有不明白的地方吗？ Yǒu bù míngbai de dìfang ma? Are there any parts that are not clear?

地理 dìlǐ [名] geography

地面 dìmiàn [名] **1**(地表) the Earth's surface **2**(指房屋) floor

地球仪 dìqiúyí [名] globe

地区 dìqū [名] area

地摊 dìtān [名] stall

地毯 dìtǎn [名] carpet

地铁 dìtiě [名] **1**(also: 地下铁道) underground (英) 或 subway (美) **2**(列车) underground (英) 或 subway (美) train ▷坐地铁 zuò dìtiě take the underground (英) 或 subway (美)

地图 dìtú [名] map

地位 dìwèi [名] position ▷平等的地位 píngděng de dìwèi equal status ▷历史地位 lìshǐ dìwèi place in history

地下 dìxià [名] underground

地下室 dìxiàshì [名] basement

地震 dìzhèn [名] earthquake

地址 dìzhǐ [名] address ▷通信地址 tōngxìn dìzhǐ postal address

地址簿 dìzhǐbù [名] address book

地主 dìzhǔ [名] landlord

弟 dì [名] younger brother ▷表弟 biǎodì cousin ▷弟弟 dìdi younger brother

弟兄 dìxiong [名] brothers (PL)

弟子 dìzǐ [名] disciple

的 dì [名] target ▷目的 mùdì goal → see also/另见 de, dí

帝 dì [名] (君主) emperor

帝国 dìguó [名] empire

递 dì [动] (传送) pass

第 dì [名] ▷第三产业 dìsān chǎnyè tertiary industry ▷第三世界 dì sān shìjiè the Third World ▷第一次世界大战 dì yī cì shìjiè dàzhàn the First World War

第六感觉 dìliù gǎnjué [名] sixth sense

第一手 dìyīshǒu [形] first-hand

掂 diān [动] weigh in one's hand

颠 diān [动] **1**(颠簸) jolt **2**(跌落) fall

颠倒 diāndǎo [动] ▷这张照片上下颠倒了。 Zhè zhāng zhàopiàn shàngxià diāndǎo le. The photo is upside down.

典 diǎn [名] **1**(标准) standard **2**(书籍) standard work ▷词典 cídiǎn dictionary **3**(典故) allusion **4**(典礼) ceremony

典礼 diǎnlǐ [名] ceremony ▷毕业典礼 bìyè diǎnlǐ graduation ceremony

典型 diǎnxíng [形] (代表性) representative

点 diǎn I [名] **1**(时间单位) o'clock ▷早上8点 zǎoshang bā diǎn eight o'clock in the morning **2**(钟点) ▷到点了。 Dào diǎn le. It's time. **3**(小滴液体) drop ▷雨点 yǔdiǎn raindrops (PL) **4**(痕迹) stain **5**(指字, 画) dot **6**(指几何) point **7**(小数点) decimal point ▷五点六 wǔ diǎn liù five point six **8**(标志) point ▷终点 zhōngdiǎn end point **9**(方面) point ▶优点 yōudiǎn strong point ▶重点 zhòngdiǎn focal point **II** [动] **1**(画点) make a dot **2**(头) nod ▶点头 diǎntóu nod one's head **3**(药水等) apply ▶点眼药 diǎn yǎnyào apply eye drops **4**(查对) check ▶点名 diǎnmíng call the register **5**(指定) select ▶点菜 diǎncài order food **6**(灯，火，烟等) light ▷点烟 diǎn yān light a cigarette **7**(点缀) decorate **III** [量] **1**(少量) a little ▷有一点问题。 Yǒu yī diǎn wèntí. There is a bit of a problem. ▷她会说一点日语。 Tā huì shuō yī diǎn Rìyǔ. She can speak a little Japanese. **2**(事项) item ▷议事日程上有6点。 Yìshì rìchéng shàng yǒu liù diǎn. There are six items on the agenda. ▷我们有4点建议。 Wǒmen yǒu sì diǎn jiànyì. We have four recommendations.

点击 diǎnjī [动] click

点头 diǎntóu [动] nod

点心 diǎnxin [名] snack

点子 diǎnzi [名] **1**(关键部分) key point **2**(主意) idea

电 diàn **I** [名] **1**(能源) electricity ▶电能 diànnéng electric power ▶发电站 fādiànzhàn electric power station ▷停电了。 Tíng diàn le. There's been a power cut. **2**(电报) telegram **II** [动] **1**(触电) get an electric shock **2**(发电报) send a telegram ▶电贺 diànhè congratulate by telegram

电报 diànbào [名] telegram

电池 diànchí [名] battery

电动 diàndòng [形] electric

电话 diànhuà [名] **1**(电话机) telephone ▷办公室的电话占线。 Bàngōngshì de diànhuà zhànxiàn. The office phone is engaged (英) 或 busy (美). ▷别挂电话！ Bié guà diànhuà! Don't hang up! **2**(打，接，回) call ▶接电话 jiē diànhuà answer the phone

电话号码 diànhuà hàomǎ [名] phone number

电脑 diànnǎo [名] computer ▶手提电脑 shǒutí diànnǎo laptop

电器 diànqì [名] electrical appliance

电视 diànshì [名] television, TV ▷彩色电视 cǎisè diànshì colour (英) 或 color (美) television ▷看电视 kàn diànshì watch television

电台 diàntái [名] station

电影 diànyǐng [名] film (英) 或 movie (美)

电影院 diànyǐngyuàn [名] cinema

电子 diànzǐ [名] electron ▶电子表 diànzǐ biǎo digital watch ▶电子游戏 diànzǐ yóuxì electronic game ▶电子商务 diànzǐ shāngwù e-commerce ▶电子图书 diànzǐ túshū e-book ▶电子邮件 diànzǐ yóujiàn e-mail

店 diàn [名] **1**(商店) shop (英) 或 store (美) **2**(旅店) hotel

垫 diàn I [名] cushion ▶鞋垫 xiédiàn insole II [动] 1 (铺) insert 2 (付钱) pay

惦 diàn see below/见下文

惦记 diànjì [动] think about

殿 diàn [名] palace ▶宫殿 gōngdiàn palace

叼 diāo [动] have ... in one's mouth

凋 diāo [动] wither

凋谢 diāoxiè [动] wither

雕 diāo I [动] carve II [名] 1 (指艺术) sculpture ▶石雕 shídiāo stone sculpture 2 (鸟) vulture

雕刻 diāokè I [动] carve II [名] carving

雕塑 diāosù [名] sculpture

吊 diào [动] (悬挂) hang

钓 diào [动] fish ▶钓鱼 diàoyú go fishing

调 diào I [动] transfer II [名] 1 (口音) accent 2 (曲调) melody ▶走调 zǒudiào be out of tune 3 (音) key → see also/另见 tiáo

调查 diàochá [动] investigate

掉 diào [动] 1 (落下) fall 2 (落后) fall behind 3 (遗失) lose 4 (减少) reduce 5 (转回) turn ... round ▶把车头掉过来 bǎ chētóu diào guòlai turn the car round 6 (互换) swap ▶掉换 diàohuàn swap

跌 diē [动] fall down

叠 dié [动] 1 (叉加叉) pile ... up 2 (信, 纸, 衣, 被) fold

碟 dié see below/见下文

碟子 diézi [名] saucer

蝶 dié [名] butterfly ▶蝴蝶 húdié butterfly

叮 dīng [动] (蚊虫) bite

叮嘱 dīngzhǔ [动] warn

盯 dīng [动] stare at

钉 dīng [名] nail

顶 dǐng I [名] top ▶头顶 tóudǐng top of one's head ▶山顶 shāndǐng mountain top II [动] 1 (指用头) carry ... on one's head 2 (拱起) lift ... up 3 (支撑) prop ... up 4 (撞) butt 5 (迎着) face 6 (顶撞) be rude to 7 (承担) undertake 8 (相当) ▷他干活一个人能顶两个。 Tā gànhuó yī ge rén néng dǐng liǎng ge. He can do as much work as two people. 9 (顶替) take the place of III [量] ▷一顶帽子 yī dǐng màozi a hat ▷一顶蚊帐 yī dǐng wénzhàng a mosquito net

measure word, used for things with a pointy tip, such as caps and hats

IV [副] extremely ▷顶棒 dǐng bàng extremely good

顶点 dǐngdiǎn [名] (最高点) top

顶峰 dǐngfēng [名] summit

顶替 dǐngtì [动] 1 (替代) take the place of 2 (冒名) pose as

顶嘴 dǐngzuǐ [动] answer back

订 dìng [动] 1 (确立) draw ... up 2 (预订) order ▶订报 dìngbào subscribe to a newspaper 3 (校正) revise 4 (装订) fasten ... together

订单 dìngdān [名] order form

订购 dìnggòu [动] order

订婚 dìnghūn [动] get engaged

订货 dìnghuò [动] order goods

订金 dìngjīn [名] deposit

定 dìng I [形] 1 (平稳) calm 2 (不变的) settled ▶定论 dìnglùn final conclusion 3 (规定的) fixed ▶定义 dìngyì definition II [动] 1 (决定) decide ▷定计划 dìng jìhuà decide on a plan 2 (固定) settle 3 (预定) order III [副] definitely

定居 dìngjū [动] settle

定期 dìngqī I [动] set a date II [形] fixed III [副] regularly

丢 diū [动] 1 (遗失) lose 2 (扔掉) throw away 3 (投) toss

丢脸 diūliǎn [动] lose face

丢人 diūrén [动] lose face

东 dōng [名] 1 (方向) east ▶东南亚 Dōngnányà Southeast Asia 2 (主人) owner ▶股东 gǔdōng shareholder 3 (东道主) host

东道国 dōngdàoguó [名] host nation

东西 dōngxi [名] (物品) thing ▷今天他买了不少东西。 Jīntiān tā mǎi le bùshǎo dōngxi. He did quite a bit of shopping today.

冬 dōng [名] winter

冬眠 dōngmián [动] hibernate

冬天 dōngtiān [名] winter

董 dǒng [名] director

董事 dǒngshì [名] director

董事会 dǒngshìhuì [名] (指企业) board of directors

懂 dǒng [动] understand ▶懂得 dǒngdé understand

懂行 dǒngháng [动] (方) know the ropes

动 dòng [动] 1 (指改变位置) move ▷不许动! Bùxǔ dòng! Freeze! 2 (行动) act 3 (用作动补) ▷她太累了，走不动。 Tā tài lèi le, zǒu bù dòng. She's too tired – she can't go on. 4 (使用) use ▷我们得动脑筋。 Wǒmen děi dòng nǎojīn. We must use our brains. 5 (触动) affect 6 (感动) move ▶动人 dòngrén moving

动机 dòngjī [名] motive

动静 dòngjìng [名] 1 (声音) sound 2 (情况) movement

动力 dònglì [名] 1 (指机械) power 2 (力量) strength

动脉 dòngmài [名] artery

动身 dòngshēn [动] begin

动手 dòngshǒu [动] 1 (开始做) get to work 2 (用手摸) touch ▷只许看，不许动手。 Zhǐxǔ kàn, bùxǔ dòngshǒu. You can look, but don't touch. 3 (打人) strike a blow

动物 dòngwù [名] animal

动物园 dòngwùyuán [名] zoo

动员 dòngyuán [动] mobilize

动作 dòngzuò I [名] movement II [动] make a move

冻 dòng [动] freeze ▷冻死 dòngsǐ freeze to death

洞 dòng [名] 1(孔) hole 2(穴) cave

洞穴 dòngxué [名] cave

都 dōu [副] 1(全部) all ▷全体成员 quántǐ chéngyuán all the members 2(表示理由) all ▷都是他的错。 Dōu shì tā de cuò. It's all his fault. 3(甚至) even ▷老师待他比亲生父母都好。 Lǎoshī dài tā bǐ qīnshēng fùmǔ dōu hǎo. The teacher treated him even better than his parents. 4(已经) already ▷都到冬天了！ Dōu dào dōngtiān le! It's winter already!
→ see also/另见 dū

兜 dōu [名] 1(衣袋) pocket ▷裤兜 kùdōu trouser pocket 2(拎兜) bag ▷网兜 wǎngdōu string bag

兜风 dōufēng [动] (游逛) go for a spin

兜圈子 dōuquānzi [动] (喻) (拐弯抹角) beat about the bush

斗 dǒu [名] 1(指容器) cup 2(斗状物) ▷烟斗 yāndǒu pipe ▷漏斗 lòudǒu funnel
→ see also/另见 dòu

抖 dǒu [动] 1(颤抖) shiver 2(甩动) shake

陡 dǒu [形] steep

斗 dòu [动] 1(打斗) fight ▷斗鸡 dòujī cock fighting 2(战胜) beat
→ see also/另见 dǒu

斗争 dòuzhēng [动] 1(努力战胜) struggle 2(打击) combat 3(奋斗) fight for

豆 dòu [名] bean

豆子 dòuzi [名] (豆类作物) bean

逗 dòu [动] (引逗) tease

逗号 dòuhào [名] comma

逗留 dòuliú [动] stay

都 dū [名] (首都) capital
→ see also/另见 dōu

都市 dūshì [名] metropolis

毒 dú I [名] poison II [形] (有毒) poisonous

毒品 dúpǐn [名] drug

独 dú I [形] only ▷独生子 dúshēngzǐ only son ▷独生女 dúshēngnǚ only daughter II [副] 1(独自) alone 2(惟独) only

独裁 dúcái [动] dictate

独立 dúlì [动] 1(指国家) declare independence ▷独立宣言 dúlì xuānyán declaration of independence 2(指个人) be independent

独身 dúshēn [动] be single

独特 dútè [形] distinctive

独自 dúzì [副] alone

读 dú [动] 1 (朗读) read aloud 2 (阅读) read 3 (上学) go to school

读书 dúshū [动] 1 (阅读) read 2 (学习) study 3 (上学) go to school

读者 dúzhě [名] reader

堵 dǔ I [动] 1 (堵塞) block ▸堵车 dǔchē traffic jam 2 (发闷) suffocate II [量] ▷一堵墙 yī dǔ qiáng a wall
measure word, used for walls

堵塞 dǔsè [动] block up

赌 dǔ [动] 1 (赌博) gamble 2 (打赌) bet

赌博 dǔbó [动] gamble

赌注 dǔzhù [名] bet

肚 dù [名] belly

肚子 dùzi [名] (腹部) stomach

度 dù I [名] 1 (限度) limit 2 (气量) tolerance ▸大度 dàdù magnanimous 3 (考虑) consideration 4 (程度) degree ▸厚度 hòudù thickness II [量] 1 (指经度或纬度) degree ▸北纬42度 běiwěi sìshí'èr dù latitude 42 degrees north 2 (指电量) kilowatt-hour 3 (指温度) degree ▸零下十度 língxià shí dù minus ten degrees 4 (指弧度或角度) degree 5 (次) time III [动] spend

渡 dù [动] 1 (越过) cross 2 (指用船只) ferry 3 (喻) (通过) survive ▷渡难关 dù nánguān go through a difficult time

端 duān I [名] 1 (头) end 2 (开头) beginning ▸开端 kāiduān beginning II [动] carry

端午节 Duānwǔjié [名] Dragon Boat Festival

端午节 Duānwǔjié
Dragon Boat Festival is celebrated on the fifth day of the fifth month of the Chinese lunar calendar. The two main activities which take place at this time are dragon boat racing and eating 粽子 zòngzi.

端正 duānzhèng [形] 1 (不歪斜) upright 2 (正派) proper

短 duǎn I [形] short ▸短期 duǎnqī short-term II [动] owe III [名] weakness

短处 duǎnchu [名] weakness

短裤 duǎnkù [名] 1 (指女式内裤) pants (PL) 2 (指男式内裤) briefs (PL) 3 (指夏装) shorts (PL)

短缺 duǎnquē [动] lack

短信 duǎnxìn [名] text message

短暂 duǎnzàn [形] brief

段 duàn [量] 1 (用于长条物) ▷一段铁轨 yī duàn tiěguǐ a section of railway ▷一段木头 yī duàn mùtou a chunk of wood
measure word, used for a part of something that is thin and long
2 (指时间) period ▷一段时间

yī duàn shíjiān a period of time **3** (指路程) stretch **4** (部分) piece

断 duàn [动] **1** (分成段) break **2** (断绝) break ... off **3** (判断) decide

断定 duàndìng [动] determine

断言 duànyán [动] assert

缎 duàn [名] satin

锻 duàn [动] forge

锻炼 duànliàn [动] **1** (指身体) work out **2** (磨炼) toughen

堆 duī **I** [动] pile ▷别把垃圾堆在这里。Bié bǎ lājī duī zài zhèlǐ. Don't pile the rubbish up here. **II** [名] pile **III** [量] pile ▷一堆石头 yī duī shítou a pile of stones

队 duì [名] **1** (行列) line **2** (指集体) team ▶队长 duìzhǎng team leader ▶队员 duìyuán team member

队伍 duìwu [名] **1** (军队) troops (PL) **2** (指集体) contingent

对 duì **I** [动] **1** (回答) answer **2** (对待) treat **3** (朝着) face **4** (接触) come into contact with **5** (投合) suit ▷对脾气 duì píqi suit one's temperament ▷今天的菜很对他的胃口。Jīntiān de cài hěn duì tā de wèikǒu. Today's meal was definitely to his liking. **6** (调整) adjust **7** (核对) check ▷对表 duì biǎo set one's watch **8** (加进) add **II** [形] **1** (对面) opposite **2** (正确) correct **III** [介] **1** (朝) at **2** (对于) ▷吸烟对健康有害。Xīyān

duì jiànkāng yǒuhài. Smoking is harmful to your health. **IV** [量] pair ▷一对夫妻 yī duì fūqī a married couple

对比 duìbǐ [动] contrast ▶鲜明的对比 xiānmíng de duìbǐ marked contrast

对不起 duìbuqǐ [动] **1** (愧疚) be sorry ▷对不起，借过。Duìbuqǐ, jièguò. Excuse me-may I just get through?

对称 duìchèn [形] symmetrical

对待 duìdài [动] treat

对方 duìfāng [名] other side

对付 duìfu [动] **1** (应对) deal with **2** (将就) make do

对话 duìhuà **I** [名] dialogue **II** [动] hold talks

对立 duìlì [动] counter

对面 duìmiàn [名] **1** (对过) the opposite **2** (正前方) the front

对手 duìshǒu [名] **1** (指比赛) opponent **2** (指能力) match

对象 duìxiàng [名] **1** (目标) object **2** (指男女朋友) partner

对应 duìyìng [动] correspond

对于 duìyú [介] ▷对于这篇文章，大家理解不一。Duìyú zhè piān wénzhāng, dàjiā lǐjiě bù yī. Not everyone understands this article in the same way.

兑 duì [动] **1** (互换) exchange **2** (汇兑) cash

兑换 duìhuàn [动] convert

吨 dūn [量] ton

蹲 dūn [动] (弯腿) squat

炖 dùn [动] stew

钝 dùn [形] 1 (不锋利) blunt 2 (不灵活) dim

顿 dùn I [动] (停顿) pause II [量] ▷一顿饭 yī dùn fàn a meal ▷挨了一顿打 āi le yī dùn dǎ take a beating

measure word, used for meals

顿时 dùnshí [副] immediately

多 duō I [形] 1 (数量大) a lot of ▷很多书 hěn duō shū a lot of books 2 (相差大) more ▷我比你大多了。Wǒ bǐ nǐ dà duō le. I'm much older than you are. 3 (超出) too many ▷她喝多了。Tā hē duō le. She drank too much. 4 (过分) excessive ▷多疑 duōyí over-suspicious II [数] ▷2年多前 liǎngnián duō qián over two years ago III [动] be more than ▷多个人就多份力量。Duō ge rén jiù duō fèn lìliàng. The more people we have, the stronger we will be. IV [副] 1 (用在疑问句中) how ▷从北京到上海有多远？ Cóng Běijīng dào Shànghǎi yǒu duō yuǎn? How far is it from Beijing to Shanghai? ▷你儿子多大了？ Nǐ érzi duō dà le? How old is your son? 2 (表示感叹) how ▷多美的城市！ Duō měi de chéngshì! How beautiful this town is! 3 (表示任何一种程度) however ▷给我一把尺,多长都行。 Gěi wǒ yī bǎ chǐ, duō cháng dōu xíng. Give me a ruler – any length will do.

多媒体 duōméitǐ [名] multimedia

多么 duōme [副] 1 (用于询问程度) how ▷他到底有多么聪明？ Tā dàodǐ yǒu duōme cōngming? How clever is he really? 2 (用在感叹句) ▷多么蓝的天啊！ Duōme lán de tiān ya! What a clear day! 3 (表示程度深) no matter how

多少 duōshǎo [副] 1 (或多或少) somewhat ▷这笔买卖多少能赚点钱。 Zhè bǐ mǎimai duōshǎo néng zhuàn diǎn qián. We're bound to earn some money from this deal. 2 (稍微) slightly

多少 duōshao I [代] (用于询问数量) ▷这台电视机多少钱？Zhè tái diànshìjī duōshao qián? How much is this television? ▷今天有多少人到会？Jīntiān yǒu duōshao rén dàohuì? How many people attended the meeting today? II [数] ▷你们有多少我们要多少。 Nǐmen yǒu duōshao wǒmen yào duōshao. We want everything you've got.

多数 duōshù [名] the majority

多余 duōyú [形] 1 (超出需要量的) surplus 2 (不必要的) redundant

哆 duō see below/ 见下文

哆嗦 duōsuo [动] tremble

夺 duó [动] 1 (抢) seize 2 (争取) compete for 3 (剥夺) deprive 4 (决定) resolve

夺取 duóqǔ [动] 1 (武力强取) capture 2 (努力争取) strive for

朵 duǒ [量] ▷朵朵白云 duǒ duǒ báiyún white clouds ▷几朵玫瑰 jǐ duǒ méigui some roses measure word, used for clouds and flowers

躲 duǒ [动] 1 (隐藏) hide 2 (避让) avoid

躲避 duǒbì [动] 1 (回避) run away from 2 (躲藏) hide

躲藏 duǒcáng [动] hide

剁 duò [动] chop

堕 duò [动] fall

堕落 duòluò [动] go to the bad

堕胎 duòtāi [动] have an abortion

跺 duò [动] stamp

俄 é [名] (also: 俄罗斯 Éluósī) Russia ▶俄国 Éguó Russia

俄语 Éyǔ [名] Russian language

鹅 é [名] goose

蛾 é [名] moth ▶蛾子 ézi moth

额 é [名] forehead ▶额头 étóu forehead

恶 ě see below / 见下文
→ see also / 另见 è, wù

恶心 ěxin I [动] feel nauseous II [形] nauseating

恶 è I [名] evil II [形] 1 (凶恶) ferocious 2 (恶劣) evil
→ see also / 另见 ě, wù

恶劣 èliè [形] bad

恶梦 èmèng [名] nightmare

饿 è I [形] hungry ▷我很饿。Wǒ hěn è. I'm very hungry. II [动] starve

鳄 è [名] crocodile, alligator ▶鳄鱼 èyú crocodile, alligator

儿 ér [名] 1 (小孩子) child 2 (儿子) son ▶儿子 érzi son

儿女 érnǚ [名] children (PL)

儿童 értóng [名] child

而 ér [连] 1 (并且) and ▷美丽而聪明 měilì ér cōngming beautiful and clever 2 (但是) but ▷浓而不烈 nóng ér bù liè strong but not overpowering ▷她不是学生，而是老师。Tā bù shì xuéshēng, ér shì lǎoshī. She isn't a student, but a teacher.

而且 érqiě [连] and what's more ▷他会讲英语，而且讲得好。Tā huì jiǎng Yīngyǔ, érqiě jiǎng de hǎo. He can speak English, and what's more he speaks it very well.

耳 ěr [名] (耳朵) ear ▶耳朵 ěrduo ear

二 èr [数] two ▶二月 èryuè February ▷第二次 dì èr cì the second time

二十 èrshí [数] twenty

贰 èr [数] two
This is the complex character for two, which is mainly used in banks, on receipts, etc.

发 fā [动] 1 (送出) send ▷发工资 fā gōngzī pay wages 2 (发射) emit ▶发光 fāguāng shine 3 (产生) produce ▶发电 fādiàn generate electricity ▶发芽 fāyá sprout 4 (表达) express ▶发言 fāyán speak 5 (扩大) develop ▶发扬 fāyáng carry on 6 (兴旺) prosper ▶发家 fājiā make a family fortune 7 (使膨胀) ▶发面 fāmiàn leaven, dough 8 (散开) spread ▶发散 fāsàn diverge 9 (揭开) uncover ▶发掘 fājué unearth ▶揭发 jiēfā expose 10 (变得) become ▶发霉 fāméi go mouldy (英) 或 moldy (美) 11 (流露) ▶发愁 fāchóu worry ▷发脾气 fā píqi lose one's temper 12 (感到) feel 13 (起程) leave ▶出发 chūfā

set out
→ *see also*/另见 fà

发表 fābiǎo [动] 1(宣布)
announce 2(刊登) publish

发财 fācái [动] make a fortune

发出 fāchū [动] 1(发送) send out
2(散发) give out

发达 fādá I [形] developed II [动]
promote

发动 fādòng [动] 1(启动) start
2(发起) launch 3(鼓动) mobilize

发动机 fādòngjī [名] engine

发抖 fādǒu [动] 1(因恐惧等)
tremble 2(因寒冷等) shiver

发挥 fāhuī [动] 1(充分利用)
bring ... into play 2(详尽论述)
elaborate

发火 fāhuǒ [动] 1(着火) catch fire
2(爆炸) detonate 3(发脾气)
lose one's temper

发霉 fāméi [动] go mouldy (英) 或
moldy (美)

发明 fāmíng [动] invent

发票 fāpiào [名] 1(收据) receipt
2(发货清单) invoice

发烧 fāshāo [动] have a
temperature

发生 fāshēng [动] happen

发现 fāxiàn [动] discover

发言 fāyán [动] make a speech

发扬 fāyáng [动] carry on

发音 fāyīn [动] pronounce

发展 fāzhǎn [动] 1(变化) develop
2(扩大) expand

罚 fá [动] punish ▶罚款 fákuǎn
fine

罚款 fákuǎn I [动] fine II [名] fine

法 fǎ [名] 1(法律) law 2(方法)
method ▶用法 yòngfǎ use 3(标
准) model 4(佛理) Buddhism
5(法术) magic ▶戏法 xìfǎ
conjuring tricks

法国 Fǎguó [名] France

法律 fǎlǜ [名] law

法庭 fǎtíng [名] court

法语 Fǎyǔ [名] French

法院 fǎyuàn [名] court

发 fà [名] hair
→ *see also*/另见 fā

番 fān [量] ▶三番五次 sānfān-
wǔcì time and time again ▷经过
几番挫折他明白了许多道理。
Jīngguò jǐfān cuòzé tā míngbai
le xǔduō dàoli. After a few false
starts he picked up quite a lot.
measure word, used for
actions

番茄 fānqié [名] tomato

翻 fān [动] 1(换位置) turn over
2(寻找) rummage 3(推翻)
reverse 4(越过) get across 5(增
加) multiply 6(翻译) translate
7(翻脸) fall out

翻译 fānyì I [动] translate II [名]
translator

凡 fán I [名] 1(人世间) mortal
world 2(大概) approximation
II [形] ordinary III [副] (总共)

in all

烦 fán I [名] trouble II [动] (谦) trouble III [形] (厌烦) fed up

烦恼 fánnǎo [形] worried

繁 fán I [形] numerous II [动] propagate

繁华 fánhuá [形] bustling

繁忙 fánmáng [形] busy

繁荣 fánróng [形] flourishing

繁体字 fántǐzì [名] complex characters (PL)

繁体字 fántǐzì

Complex characters, also known as traditional Chinese characters, had been used as the Chinese script for centuries in all parts of China until 1956 when the government of the People's Republic of China carried out a programme of simplifying these characters in an effort to improve the literacy rate by making characters easier to write. Since then, 简体字 jiǎntǐzì 'simplified characters', have become the dominant form of the Chinese script. However, for various cultural and political reasons, many Chinese-speaking regions and communities did not accept these changes, and continue to use the old system. Hong Kong and Taiwan are among these regions.

繁殖 fánzhí [动] breed

反 fǎn I [名] 1(相反) opposite 2(造反) rebellion II [动] 1(转换) turn 2(回) return 3(反对) oppose 4(背叛) rebel III [形] opposite IV [副] 1(相反地) on the contrary 2(从反面) again ▶ 反思 fǎnsī review

反动 fǎndòng I [形] reactionary II [名] reaction

反对 fǎnduì [动] oppose

反复 fǎnfù [副] 1(重复) repeatedly 2(多变) capriciously

反抗 fǎnkàng [动] resist

反面 fǎnmiàn I [名] other side II [形] negative

反应 fǎnyìng [名] 1(反响) response 2(指机体) reaction 3(指物理, 化学) reaction

反映 fǎnyìng [动] 1(反照) reflect 2(汇报) report

反正 fǎnzhèng [副] anyway

返 fǎn [动] return

返回 fǎnhuí [动] come back

犯 fàn I [动] 1(违犯) violate 2(侵犯) attack 3(错误, 罪行等) commit II [名] criminal

犯法 fànfǎ [动] break the law

犯规 fànguī [动] break the rules

犯人 fànrén [名] prisoner

犯罪 fànzuì [动] commit a crime

饭 fàn [名] 1 (餐) meal ▶晚饭 wǎnfàn supper 2 (米饭) rice

饭店 fàndiàn [名] 1 (住宿) hotel 2 (吃饭) restaurant

饭馆 fànguǎn [名] restaurant

饭厅 fàntīng [名] dining room

范 fàn [名] 1 (模范) model ▶典范 diǎnfàn model 2 (范围) limit ▶规范 guīfàn standard 3 (模子) pattern

范围 fànwéi [名] limit

方 fāng I [名] 1 (方向) direction ▶南方 nánfāng the South 2 (方形) square ▶长方形 chángfāngxíng rectangle 3 (方面) side 4 (方法) method 5 (地方) place 6 (方子) prescription 7 (数) (乘方) power II [形] 1 (方形) square 2 (正直) honest

方案 fāng'àn [名] plan

方便 fāngbiàn [形] 1 (便利) convenient 2 (适宜) appropriate

方法 fāngfǎ [名] method

方面 fāngmiàn [名] 1 (指人) side 2 (指物) aspect

方式 fāngshì [名] way

方向 fāngxiàng [名] direction

方言 fāngyán [名] dialect

方针 fāngzhēn [名] policy

防 fáng I [动] 1 (防备) prevent 2 (防守) defend II [名] dyke

防止 fángzhǐ [动] prevent

妨 fáng [动] obstruct

妨碍 fáng'ài [动] obstruct

房 fáng [名] 1 (房子) house 2 (房间) room ▶书房 shūfáng study 3 (家族) ▷远房亲戚 yuǎnfáng qīnqi a distant relative

房东 fángdōng [名] landlord

房屋 fángwū [名] building

仿 fǎng [动] 1 (仿效) copy 2 (类似) be like

仿佛 fǎngfú I [连] as if II [形] similar

访 fǎng [动] 1 (访问) call on ▶访谈 fǎngtán call in for a chat 2 (调查) investigate

访问 fǎngwèn [动] visit

纺 fǎng I [动] spin II [名] silk

纺织 fǎngzhī [动] ▶纺织品 fǎngzhīpǐn textiles (PL)

放 fàng [动] 1 (使自由) release ▶解放 jiěfàng free 2 (暂时停止) ▷放学了。 fàngxué le. School is now over. 3 (放纵) let oneself go 4 (赶牲畜吃草) graze 5 (驱逐) expel ▶流放 liúfàng banish 6 (发出) send out ▶放炮 fàngpào fire a gun 7 (点燃) set ... off 8 (借出收息) lend 9 (扩展) ▷把照片放大 bǎ zhàopiàn fàngdà enlarge a photo 10 (花开) bloom 11 (搁置) put ... to one side 12 (弄倒) cut down 13 (使处于) put 14 (加进) add 15 (控制自己) ▷放严肃点 fàng yánsù diǎn become more serious 16 (放映) project 17 (保存) leave

放大 fàngdà [动] enlarge

放假 fàngjià [动] go on holiday (英) 或 vacation (美)

放弃 fàngqì [动] give ... up

放松 fàngsōng [动] relax

放心 fàngxīn [动] set one's mind at rest

放学 fàngxué [动] finish school

飞 fēi I [动] 1(鸟, 虫, 飞机) fly 2(空中游动) flutter 3(挥发) evaporate II [副] swiftly

飞机 fēijī [名] aeroplane (英), airplane (美)

飞行 fēixíng [动] fly

非 fēi I [名] 1(错误) wrong ▶是非 shìfēi right and wrong 2(also: 非洲 Fēizhōu) Africa II [动] 1(非议) blame 2(违反) run counter to ▶非法 fēifǎ illegal 3(不是) not be 4(强硬) insist on III [副] (必须) ▷我不让他去, 他非去不可。 wǒ bù ràng tā qù, tā fēi qù bù kě. I've tried to stop him, but he simply has to go.

非常 fēicháng I [形] exceptional II [副] very

非典 fēidiǎn [名] (非典型性肺炎) SARS

非法 fēifǎ [形] illegal

非洲 Fēizhōu [名] Africa

肥 féi I [名] fertilizer II [动] 1(使肥沃) fertilize 2(暴富) get rich III [形] 1(脂肪多) fat 2(肥沃) fertile 3(肥大) loose

肥胖 féipàng [形] fat

肥皂 féizào [名] soap

肺 fèi [名] lung

废 fèi I [动] abandon II [形] 1(不用的) waste 2(没用的) useless 3(残废的) disabled

费 fèi I [名] fee ▶车费 chēfèi bus fare II [形] expensive III [动] spend

费用 fèiyong [名] expense

分 fēn I [动] 1(分开) divide ▶分离 fēnlí separate ▶分裂 fēnliè split 2(分配) assign 3(辨别) distinguish II [名] 1(分支) branch 2(分数) fraction ▶分母 fēnmǔ denominator III [量] 1(分数) fraction ▷四分之三 sì fēn zhī sān three quarters 2(十分之一) one tenth 3(指货币) unit of Chinese currency, equal to a hundredth of a yuan 4(指时间) minute ▷5点过5分 wǔ diǎn guò wǔ fēn 5 minutes past 5 5(指弧度或角度) minute ▷36度20分角 sānshíliù dù èrshí fēn jiǎo 36 degrees 20 minutes 6(百分之一) per cent ▷月利1分 yuèlì yī fēn monthly interest of 1 per cent → see also/另见 fèn

分别 fēnbié I [动] 1(离别) split up 2(辨别) distinguish II [名] difference

分开 fēnkāi [动] separate

分配 fēnpèi [动] assign

分手 fēnshǒu [动] 1(告别) say goodbye 2(指男女关系) break up

分数 fēnshù [名] mark

分析 fēnxī [动] analyse (英), analyze (美)

吩 fēn *see below*/见下文

吩咐 fēnfù [动] instruct

纷 fēn [形] 1 (多) numerous ▶纷繁 fēnfán numerous 2 (乱) confused ▶纷扰 fēnrǎo confusion

纷纷 fēnfēn I [形] diverse II [副] one after another

坟 fén [名] grave

坟墓 fénmù [名] grave

粉 fěn I [名] 1 (粉末) powder 2 (粉丝) vermicelli II [动] 1 (成碎末) crumble ▶粉碎 fěnsuì crush 2 (变成粉状) pulverize III [形] 1 (白色) white 2 (粉红色) pink

粉笔 fěnbǐ [名] chalk

粉红 fěnhóng [形] pink

粉末 fěnmò [名] powder

分 fèn [名] 1 (成分) component 2 (限度) limit ▶过分 guòfèn excessive 3 (情分) feelings (PL) → *see also*/另见 fēn

分量 fènliàng [名] weight

份 fèn I [名] 1 (一部分) part ▶股份 gǔfèn share 2 (指划分单位) ▶年份 niánfèn year II [量] 1 (指食物) portion 2 (指报刊) copy

奋 fèn [动] 1 (振作) exert oneself ▶勤奋 qínfèn diligent 2 (举起) raise

奋斗 fèndòu [动] fight

愤 fèn [形] indignant ▶气愤 qìfèn indignant

愤怒 fènnù [形] angry

丰 fēng [形] 1 (丰富) abundant 2 (大) great

丰富 fēngfù I [形] abundant II [动] enrich

丰收 fēngshōu [动] have a good harvest

风 fēng I [名] 1 (指空气流动) wind 2 (风气) trend 3 (景象) scene ▶风光 fēngguāng scenery 4 (态度) manner ▶风度 fēngdù bearing 5 (消息) information II [形] rumoured (英), rumored (美) III [动] air ▶风干 fēnggān air-dry

风格 fēnggé [名] 1 (气度) manner 2 (特点) style

风景 fēngjǐng [名] scenery

风水 fēngshuǐ [名] feng shui

风俗 fēngsú [名] custom

风险 fēngxiǎn [名] risk

封 fēng I [动] (封闭) seal II [名] envelope III [量] ▷一封信 yī fēng xìn a letter

封建 fēngjiàn I [名] feudalism II [形] feudal

疯 fēng I [形] mad II [副] madly

疯子 fēngzi [名] lunatic

锋 fēng [名] 1 (尖端) point 2 (带头的) vanguard 3 (锋面) front

锋利 fēnglì [形] 1 (工具) sharp 2 (言论) cutting

蜂 fēng I [名] 1 (黄蜂) wasp 2 (蜜蜂) bee II [副] in swarms

蜂蜜 fēngmì [名] honey

逢 féng [动] come across

缝 féng [动] sew
→ see also/另见 fèng

讽 fěng [动] mock ▶讥讽 jīfěng satirize

讽刺 fěngcì [动] ridicule

奉 fèng [动] 1 (献给) present 2 (接受) receive 3 (尊重) respect 4 (信仰) believe in 5 (伺候) attend to

奉献 fèngxiàn [动] dedicate

缝 fèng [名] 1 (接合处) seam 2 (缝隙) crack
→ see also/另见 féng

缝隙 fèngxì [名] crack

佛 fó [名] 1 (佛教) Buddhism 2 (佛像) Buddha

佛教 fójiào [名] Buddhism

否 fǒu I [动] deny II [副] 1 (书) (不) no 2 (是, 能, 可) or not ▷他明天是否来参加聚会？ tā míngtiān shìfǒu lái cānjiā jùhuì? Is he coming to the party tomorrow or not?

否定 fǒudìng I [动] negate II [形] negative

否认 fǒurèn [动] deny

否则 fǒuzé [连] otherwise

夫 fū [名] 1 (丈夫) husband 2 (男子) man 3 (劳动者) manual worker

夫妇 fūfù [名] husband and wife

夫妻 fūqī [名] husband and wife

夫人 fūrén [名] Mrs

扶 fú [动] 1 (稳住) steady 2 (搀起) help up 3 (扶助) help

服 fú I [名] clothes (PL) II [动] 1 (吃) take ▶服药 fúyào take medicine 2 (担任) serve ▶服役 fúyì serve in the army 3 (服从) comply with 4 (使信服) convince 5 (适应) adapt
→ see also/另见 fù

服从 fúcóng [动] obey

服务 fúwù [动] serve

服务员 fúwùyuán [名] 1 (指商店里) attendant 2 (指饭馆里) waiter, waitress 3 (指宾馆里) room attendant

服装 fúzhuāng [名] clothing

浮 fú I [动] float II [形] 1 (表面上) superficial 2 (可移动) movable 3 (暂时) temporary 4 (轻浮) slapdash 5 (空虚) empty ▶浮夸 fúkuā exaggerated 6 (多余) surplus

浮肿 fúzhǒng [动] puff up

符 fú I [名] 1 (标记) mark 2 (图形) Daoist motif II [动] be in keeping with

符号 fúhào [名] mark

符合 fúhé [动] match

幅 fú I [名] 1 (指布) width 2 (泛指大小) size ▶幅度 fúdù range II [量] ▷一幅画 yī fú huà a painting ▷三幅书法 sān fú shūfǎ three calligraphies measure word, used for paintings, portraits and Chinese calligraphies

福 fú [名] good fortune

辅 fǔ [动] complement

辅导 fǔdǎo [动] coach

腐 fǔ I [形] rotten II [名] bean curd

腐败 fǔbài I [动] rot II [形] corrupt

父 fù [名] 1(父亲) father 2(指男性长辈) senior male relative ▶祖父 zǔfù grandfather

父母 fùmǔ [名] parents

父亲 fùqīn [名] father

付 fù [动] 1(事物) hand over ▶托付 tuōfù entrust 2(钱) pay ▶偿付 chángfù pay back

付账 fùzhàng [动] pay the bill

负 fù [动] 1(书)(背) carry on one's back ▶负重 fùzhòng carry a heavy load 2(担负) bear 3(遭受) suffer 4(享有) enjoy 5(拖欠) be in arrears 6(背弃) turn one's back on 7(失败) lose II [形] negative ▶负数 fùshù negative number

负担 fùdān I [动] bear II [名] burden

负责 fùzé I [动] be responsible II [形] conscientious

妇 fù [名] 1(妇女) woman ▶妇科 fùkē gynaecology (英), gynecology (美) 2(已婚妇女) married woman 3(妻) wife

妇女 fùnǚ [名] woman

附 fù [动] 1(附带) attach 2(靠近) get close to 3(依从) depend on

附近 fùjìn I [形] nearby II [名] vicinity

服 fù [量] dose
→ see also/另见 fú

复 fù I [形] 1(重复) duplicated ▶复制 fùzhì reproduce 2(繁复) complex II [动] 1(转) turn 2(回答) reply 3(恢复) recover 4(报复) take revenge III [副] again ▶复查 fùchá re-examine

复活节 Fùhuó Jié [名] (宗) Easter

复习 fùxí [动] revise

复印 fùyìn [动] photocopy

复杂 fùzá [形] complex

副 fù I [形] 1(辅助) deputy 2(附带) subsidiary ▶副业 fùyè subsidiary business II [名] assistant ▶大副 dàfù first mate III [动] correspond to IV [量] (套) pair ▷一副手套 yī fù shǒutào a pair of gloves ▷一副冷面孔 yī fù lěng miànkǒng a cold expression ▷一副笑脸 yī fù xiàoliǎn a smiling face

measure word, used for expressions

副作用 fùzuòyòng [名] side effect

富 fù I [形] 1(有钱) rich 2(丰富) abundant II [名] wealth III [动] enrich

富有 fùyǒu I [形] wealthy II [动] be full of

could be here.

改 gǎi [动] 1(改变) change 2(修改) alter 3(改正) correct

改变 gǎibiàn [动] change ▷我改变了主意。 Wǒ gǎibiàn le zhǔyi. I changed my mind.

改革 gǎigé [动] reform ▷改革开放 gǎigé kāifàng reform and opening up

改善 gǎishàn [动] improve

改正 gǎizhèng [动] correct ▷改正缺点 gǎizhèng quēdiǎn mend one's ways

钙 gài [名] (化) calcium

盖 gài I [名] (指器皿) cover ▷盖子 gàizi lid II [动] 1(蒙上) cover 2(遮掩) cover ... up 3(打上) stamp 4(压过) block ... out 5(建造) build

概 gài [名] (大略) outline

概括 gàikuò I [动] summarize II [形] brief

概念 gàiniàn [名] concept

咖 gā see below/见下文
→ see also/另见 kā

咖喱 gālí [名] curry

该 gāi I [动] 1(应当) ought to 2(轮到) be the turn of 3(活该) serve ... right ▷活该 huógāi serve ... right II [助动] 1(应该) should ▷工作明天该完成了。 Gōngzuò míngtiān gāi wánchéng le. The work should be finished by tomorrow. 2(表示推测) ▷再不吃的话，菜都该凉了。 Zài bù chī dehuà, cài dōu gāi liáng le. If we keep waiting the food is only going to get colder. 3(用于加强语气) ▷要是他能在这儿该多好啊！ Yàoshì tā néng zài zhèr gāi duō hǎo a! It would be great if he

干 gān I [动] have to do with ▷这不干我事。 Zhè bù gān wǒ shì. This has nothing to do with me. II [形] 1(无水) dry 2(不与水) dry ▷干洗 gānxǐ dry-clean 3(干涸) dried-up III [名] ▷豆腐干 dòufugān dried tofu ▷葡萄干 pútaogān raisin IV [副] (白白) in vain
→ see also/另见 gàn

干杯 gānbēi [动] drink a toast ▷"干杯！" "Gānbēi!" "Cheers!"

干脆 gāncuì [形] direct

干旱 gānhàn [形] arid

干净 gānjìng [形] **1** (无尘) clean **2** (一点不剩) complete ▷请把汤喝干净。Qǐng bǎ tāng hē gānjìng. Please finish your soup.

干扰 gānrǎo [动] disturb

干预 gānyù [动] interfere

干燥 gānzào [形] dry

杆 gān [名] post

肝 gān [名] liver

竿 gān [名] pole ▷竿子 gānzi pole

赶 gǎn [动] **1** (追) catch ▷赶公共汽车 gǎn gōnggòng qìchē catch a bus **2** (加快) rush ▷赶着回家 gǎn zhe huíjiā rush home **3** (驱赶) drive **4** (驱逐) drive ... out

赶紧 gǎnjǐn [副] quickly

赶快 gǎnkuài [副] at once ▷我们得赶快走了! Wǒmen děi gǎnkuài zǒu le! We must go at once!

赶上 gǎnshàng [动] catch up with

赶忙 gǎnmáng [副] hurriedly

敢 gǎn [动] **1** (有胆量) dare ▷敢于 gǎnyú dare to **2** (有把握) be sure

感 gǎn **I** [动] **1** (觉得) feel **2** (感动) move ▷感人 gǎnrén moving **II** [名] sense ▷成就感 chéngjiùgǎn a sense of achievement ▷方向感 fāngxiànggǎn a sense of direction

感到 gǎndào [动] feel ▷我感到幸运。Wǒ gǎndào xìngyùn. I feel lucky.

感动 gǎndòng [动] move ▷他容易被感动。Tā róngyì bèi gǎndòng. He's very easily moved.

感恩节 Gǎn'ēn Jié [名] Thanksgiving

感激 gǎnjī [动] appreciate

感觉 gǎnjué **I** [名] feeling **II** [动] **1** (感到) feel **2** (认为) sense

感冒 gǎnmào [动] catch a cold

感情 gǎnqíng [名] **1** (心理反应) emotion **2** (喜爱) feelings (PL)

感染 gǎnrǎn [动] (传染) infect

感想 gǎnxiǎng [名] thoughts (PL)

感谢 gǎnxiè [动] thank ▷感谢您的指导。Gǎnxiè nín de zhǐdǎo. Thank you for your guidance.

感兴趣 gǎn xìngqù [动] be interested in ▷他对绘画感兴趣。Tā duì huìhuà gǎn xìngqù. He's interested in painting.

干 gàn [动] **1** (做) do ▷干活 gànhuó work **2** (担任) act as ▷他干过队长。Tā gànguò duìzhǎng. He acted as team leader. → see also/另见 gān

干部 gànbù [名] cadre

刚 gāng **I** [形] strong **II** [副] **1** (恰好) just ▷水温刚好。Shuǐwēn gāng hǎo. The temperature of the water was just right. **2** (仅仅 just) ▷这儿刚够放一把椅子。Zhèr gāng gòu fàng yī bǎ yǐzi. There is just enough room for a chair. **3** (不久以前) only just ▷

宝宝刚会走路。Xiǎo bǎobao gāng huì zǒulù. The baby has only just started walking.

刚才 gāngcái [名] just now

刚刚 gānggāng [副] just

刚好 gānghǎo I [形] just right II [副] luckily

钢 gāng [名] steel ▶钢铁 gāngtiě steel

钢笔 gāngbǐ [名] fountain pen

钢琴 gāngqín [名] piano

缸 gāng [名] (器物) vat ▶鱼缸 yúgāng fish bowl

港 gǎng [名] 1 (港湾) harbour (英), harbor (美) 2 (香港) Hong Kong ▶香港 Xiānggǎng Hong Kong ▶港币 gǎngbì Hong Kong dollar

港口 gǎngkǒu [名] port

高 gāo [形] 1 (指高度) tall ▶高楼 gāolóu tall building 2 (指标准或程度) high ▶高标准 gāo biāozhǔn high standard 3 (指等级) senior ▶高中 gāozhōng senior school 4 (指声音) high-pitched 5 (指年龄) old 6 (指价格) high

高大 gāodà [形] (字) huge

高档 gāodàng [形] top quality

高等 gāoděng [形] higher ▶高等教育 gāoděng jiàoyù higher education

高级 gāojí [形] 1 (指级别) senior ▶高级法院 gāojí fǎyuàn high court 2 (超过一般) high-quality ▶高级英语 gāojí Yīngyǔ advanced English ▶高级宾馆 gāojí bīnguǎn luxury hotel

高考 gāokǎo [名] college entrance examination

高科技 gāokējì [形] hi-tech

高速 gāosù [形] rapid

高速公路 gāosù gōnglù [名] motorway (英), freeway (美)

高兴 gāoxìng I [形] happy II [动] enjoy

高原 gāoyuán [名] plateau

高中 gāozhōng [名] (also: 高级中学) senior school (英), high school (美)

糕 gāo [名] cake ▶蛋糕 dàngāo cake

搞 gǎo [动] 1 (干) do 2 (弄) get

告 gào [动] 1 (陈述) tell 2 (控诉) sue

告别 gàobié [动] say goodbye

告诉 gàosu [动] tell

告状 gàozhuàng [动] (抱怨) complain

哥 gē [名] 1 (哥哥) elder brother 2 (亲热称呼) brother

哥哥 gēge [名] elder brother

哥儿们 gērmen [名] (朋友) mate (英), buddy (美)

胳 gē see below/见下文

胳膊 gēbo [名] arm

鸽 gē [名] dove ▶鸽子 gēzi dove

搁 gē [动] 1 (放) put 2 (搁置) put aside

割 gē[动] cut

歌 gē I[名] song II[动] sing

歌剧 gējù[名] opera

歌曲 gēqǔ[名] song

歌手 gēshǒu[名] singer

革 gé I[名] leather II[动] (改变) change

革命 gémìng[动] revolutionize ▷工业革命 gōngyè gémìng industrial revolution

格 gé[名] (格子) check

格式 géshì[名] format

格外 géwài[副] 1(特别) especially 2(额外) additionally

隔 gé[动] 1(阻隔) separate 2(间隔) be apart

隔壁 gébì[名] next door ▷隔壁邻居 gébì línjū next-door neighbour(英) 或 neighbor(美)

嗝 gé[名] 1(饱嗝) burp ▷打饱嗝 dǎ bǎogé burp 2(冷嗝) hiccup ▷打冷嗝 dǎ lěnggé have a hiccup

个 gè I[名] (指身材或大小) size ▷个头儿 gètóur build II[量] (表示个数) ▷6个桃子 liù gè táozi six peaches ▷两个月 liǎng gè yuè two months

This is the most useful and common measure word, and can be used as the default measure word when you are unsure. It can be used for people, objects, fruits, countries, cities, companies, dates, weeks, months, ideas etc.

(表示动量) ▷开个会 kāi gè huì have a meeting ▷冲个澡 chōng gè zǎo have a shower

the most useful measure word, used for actions

个别 gèbié[形] 1(单个) individual 2(少数) a couple

个人 gèrén I[名] individual II[代] oneself ▷就他个人而言 jiù tā gèrén éryán as far as he's concerned ▷在我个人看来, 这是个好主意。 Zài wǒ gèrén kànlái, zhè shì gè hǎo zhǔyi. As far as I'm concerned this is a good idea.

个体 gètǐ[名] 1(指生物) individual 2(指经济形态) ▷个体经营 gètǐ jīngyíng private enterprise

个性 gèxìng[名] personality ▷他个性很强。 Tā gèxìng hěn qiáng. He has a very strong personality.

个子 gèzi[名] stature ▷高个子女人 gāo gèzi nǚrén a tall woman

各 gè I[代] each II[副] individually

各个 gègè I[代] each II[副] one by one

各种 gèzhǒng[代] all kinds

各自 gèzì[代] each

给 gěi I[动] 1(给予) give 2(让) let II[介] 1(为) for ▷我给妻子做早餐。 Wǒ gěi qīzi zuò zǎocān.

I made breakfast for my wife. **2** (向) to ▷留给他 liú gěi tā leave it to him ▷递给我 dì gěi wǒ pass it to me

根 gēn **I** [名] (指植物) root ▷祸根 huògēn the root of the problem **II** [量] ▷一根绳子 yī gēn shéngzi a rope ▷一根头发 yī gēn tóufa a hair

measure word, used for long thin objects, body parts and plants

根本 gēnběn **I** [名] root **II** [形] fundamental **III** [副] **1** (完全) at all **2** (彻底) thoroughly ▷根本转变态度 gēnběn zhuǎnbiàn tàidù completely change one's attitude

根据 gēnjù **I** [介] according to **II** [名] basis

根源 gēnyuán [名] cause

跟 gēn **I** [名] heel **II** [动] **1** (跟随) follow **2** (嫁) marry **III** [介] **1** (同) with ▷我跟朋友去公园了。 Wǒ gēn péngyou qù gōngyuán le. I went to the park with friends. **2** (向) ▷跟我说说这件事。 Gēn wǒ shuōshuo zhè jiàn shì. Tell me what happened. **3** (表示比较) as ▷他的教育背景跟我相似。 Tā de jiàoyù bèijǐng gēn wǒ xiāngsì. His educational background is similar to mine. **IV** [连] and

跟随 gēnsuí [动] follow

跟头 gēntou [名] **1** (跌倒) fall ▷翻跟头 fān gēntou do a somersault

跟踪 gēnzōng [动] tail

更 gēng [动] (改变) change ▷更正 gēngzhèng correct
→ see also/另见 gèng

更改 gēnggǎi [动] alter

更换 gēnghuàn [动] change

更替 gēngtì [动] replace

更新 gēngxīn [动] **1** (事物) replace ▷更新网站内容 gēngxīn wǎngzhàn nèiróng update web content **2** (森林) renew

更衣室 gēngyīshì [名] fitting room

耕 gēng [动] plough

耕地 gēngdì **I** [动] plough **II** [名] cultivated land

更 gèng [形] (更加) even more ▷天更黑了。 Tiān gèng hēi le. It's getting even darker.
→ see also/另见 gēng

更加 gèngjiā [副] even more

工 gōng [名] **1** (指人) worker ▷童工 tónggōng child labour **2** (指阶级) the working class **3** (工作或劳动) work **4** (工程) project **5** (工业) industry

工厂 gōngchǎng [名] factory

工程 gōngchéng [名] engineering project

工程师 gōngchéngshī [名] engineer

工夫 gōngfu [名] **1** (时间) time **2** (空闲) spare time

工具 gōngjù [名] **1** (器具) tool **2** (喻) instrument

工人 gōngrén[名]worker

工业 gōngyè[名]industry

工艺品 gōngyìpǐn[名]handicraft item

工资 gōngzī[名]pay

工作 gōngzuò[名]1(劳动)work 2(职业)job 3(业务)work

公 gōng I[形]1(非私有)public ▶公共 gōnggòng public 2(共识) general 3(公正)fair 4(雄性)male II[名]1(公务)official business 2(敬)(老先生)▶王公 Wáng gōng Mr Wang 3(丈夫的父亲) father-in-law ▶公公 gōnggong father-in-law

公安 gōng'ān[名]public security

公布 gōngbù[动]announce

公厕 gōngcè[名]public toilet

公尺 gōngchǐ[名]metre(英), meter(美)

公费 gōngfèi[名]public expense

公分 gōngfēn[名]centimetre (英), centimeter(美)

公共 gōnggòng[形]public

公共汽车 gōnggòng qìchē [名]bus

公共汽车站 gōnggòng qìchēzhàn [名]1(指总站)bus station 2(指路边站)bus stop

公斤 gōngjīn[名]kilogram

公开 gōngkāi I[形]public II[动] make public

公里 gōnglǐ[名]kilometre(英), kilometer(美)

公路 gōnglù[名]motorway

公民 gōngmín[名]citizen

公平 gōngpíng[形]fair

公社 gōngshè[名]commune

公司 gōngsī[名]company

公用 gōngyòng[形]public

公寓 gōngyù[名]1(旅馆) boarding house 2(楼房)flat (英), apartment(美)

公元 gōngyuán[名]A.D.

公园 gōngyuán[名]park

公正 gōngzhèng[形]impartial

公众 gōngzhòng[名]public

公主 gōngzhǔ[名]princess

功 gōng[名]1(功劳)contribution 2(成效)achievement

功夫 gōngfu[名]martial arts

功课 gōngkè[名]homework

功劳 gōngláo[名]contribution

功能 gōngnéng[名]function ▷多功能电话 duōgōngnéng diànhuà multi-functional telephone

攻 gōng[动](攻打)attack

攻击 gōngjī[动](进攻)attack

供 gōng[动]1(供应)supply 2(提供)provide

供给 gōngjǐ[动]supply

供求 gōngqiú[名]supply and demand

供应 gōngyìng[动]supply

宫 gōng[名](皇宫)palace ▶宫殿 gōngdiàn palace

恭 gōng[形]respectful

恭维 gōngwei [动] flatter

恭喜 gōngxǐ [动] congratulate

巩 gǒng see below/见下文

巩固 gǒnggù I [形] solid II [动] strengthen

共 gòng I [形] common II [动] share III [副] 1(一齐) together 2(总共) altogether IV [名] (also: 共产党) the communist party

共产党 gòngchǎndǎng [名] the communist party

共产主义 gòngchǎnzhǔyì [名] communism

共和国 gònghéguó [名] republic

共同 gòngtóng I [形] common II [副] together

贡 gòng [名] tribute

贡献 gòngxiàn I [动] devote II [名] contribution

沟 gōu [名] ditch

沟通 gōutōng [动] communicate

钩 gōu [名] 1(钩子) hook 2(符号) tick [动] 3(用钩子挂) hook 4(编织, 缝) crochet

狗 gǒu [名] dog

构 gòu I [动] 1(组成) compose 2(结成) form 3(建造) construct II [名] (结构) structure

构成 gòuchéng [动] 1(造成) constitute 2(组成) compose

构造 gòuzào [名] structure

购 gòu [动] buy

购买 gòumǎi [动] buy

购物 gòuwù [动] go shopping ▷她爱购物。 Tā ài gòuwù. She likes shopping.

够 gòu I [形] enough ▷5个就够了。 Wǔ gè jiù gòu le. Five is enough. II [动] reach

估 gū [动] guess

估计 gūjì [动] reckon

姑 gū [名] 1(姑母) aunt 2(丈夫的姐妹) sister-in-law

姑娘 gūniang [名] girl

姑姑 gūgu [名] aunt

孤 gū [形] (孤单) alone

孤单 gūdān [形] (寂寞) lonely

孤独 gūdú [形] solitary

孤儿 gū'ér [名] orphan

古 gǔ I [名] ancient times (PL) II [形] ancient

古代 gǔdài [名] antiquity

古典 gǔdiǎn I [名] classics (PL) II [形] classical

古董 gǔdǒng [名] (古代器物) antique

古迹 gǔjì [名] historic site

古老 gǔlǎo [形] ancient

股 gǔ I [名] 1(指绳或线) strand 2(股份) share II [量] (气体, 气味) whiff

股票 gǔpiào [名] share

股市 gǔshì [名] stock market

骨 gǔ [名] bone

骨头 gǔtou [名](字) bone

鼓 gǔ I [名] drum II [动] 1 ▶鼓掌 gǔzhǎng applaud 2 (凸起, 胀大) bulge ▷他鼓起嘴。Tā gǔ zhe zuǐ. He puffed his cheeks out. III [形] bulging ▷她的书包鼓鼓的。Tā de shūbāo gǔgǔ de. Her schoolbag was full to bursting.

鼓励 gǔlì [动] encourage

鼓舞 gǔwǔ I [动] inspire II [形] inspiring

固 gù I [形] strong ▶坚固 jiāngù solid ▶牢固 láogù firm II [副] (坚定) firmly

固定 gùdìng I [形] fixed II [动] fix

固体 gùtǐ [名] solid

固执 gùzhí [形] stubborn

故 gù [名] 1 (变故) incident 2 (原因) reason

故宫 gùgōng [名] the Forbidden City

故宫 gùgōng

As the largest collection of ancient wooden structures in the world, 故宫 gùgōng formed the imperial palaces of the Ming (1368-1644) and Qing (1644-1911) dynasties. It is located at what was once the exact centre of the old city of Beijing, just to the north of Tiananmen Square. It is now a major tourist attraction, both for the architecture of its 800-plus wooden buildings, and for the many artistic and cultural treasures which are housed within them. In 1987 it was declared a World Heritage Site by UNESCO.

故事 gùshi [名] story

故乡 gùxiāng [名] birthplace

故意 gùyì [副] deliberately

故障 gùzhàng [名] fault ▷这台机器出了故障。Zhè tái jīqì chū le gùzhàng. This machine is faulty.

顾 gù [动] 1 (看) look ▶回顾 huígù look back ▶环顾 huángù look around 2 (注意, 照管) attend to ▶照顾 zhàogù attend to

顾客 gùkè [名] customer

顾问 gùwèn [名] consultant

雇 gù [动] 1 (雇佣) employ 2 (租赁) hire

雇员 gùyuán [名] employee

雇主 gùzhǔ [名] employer

瓜 guā [名] (植) melon

刮 guā [动] 1 (指用刀) shave 2 (涂抹) smear 3 (风) blow

挂 guà [动] 1 (悬, 吊) hang 2 (中断电话) hang up

挂号 guàhào I [动] register II [形] registered ▷挂号信 guàhàoxìn registered mail

挂历 guàlì [名] calendar

褂 guà [名] gown ▶褂子 guàzi

gown

乖 guāi [形] (听话) well-behaved

拐 guǎi I [名] 1 (拐杖) walking stick 2 (拐角处) turning II [动] 1 (转变方向) turn ▷向左/右拐 xiàng zuǒ/yòu guǎi turn left 2 (拐骗) swindle

拐卖 guǎimài [动] abduct and sell

怪 guài I [形] strange II [动] 1 (觉得奇怪) be surprised 2 (责怪) blame III [副] (口) really IV [名] monster

怪不得 guàbude [连] no wonder

关 guān I [动] 1 (合拢) close 2 (圈起来) imprison 3 (停业) close down 4 (中断, 终止) turn... off ▷关灯 guān dēng turn off the light 5 (牵连) concern ▷这不关他的事。Zhè bù guān tā de shì. This matter does not concern him. II [名] 1 (守卫处所) pass 2 (出入境收税处) customs (PL) ▷海关 hǎiguān customs (PL) 3 (转折点) critical point 4 (关联部分) ▷关节 guānjié joint ▷关键 guānjiàn key

关闭 guānbì [动] 1 (合拢) close 2 (歇业或停办) close down

关怀 guānhuái [动] be concerned about

关税 guānshuì [名] customs duty

关系 guānxì I [名] (联系) relation II [动] impact on

关心 guānxīn [动] be concerned about

关于 guānyú [介] on

关照 guānzhào [动] (关心照顾) look after

关注 guānzhù [动] pay close attention to

观 guān I [动] look ▶围观 wéiguān gather round to watch ▶旁观 pángguān look on II [名] view

观察 guānchá [动] observe

观点 guāndiǎn [名] point of view

观看 guānkàn [动] watch

观念 guānniàn [名] concept

观众 guānzhòng [名] spectator

官 guān [名] 1 (公职人员) official 2 (器官) organ

官司 guānsi [名] lawsuit

官员 guānyuán [名] official

管 guǎn I [名] 1 (管子) pipe ▶水管 shuǐguǎn water pipe ▶管子 guǎnzi tube 2 (乐器) wind instrument ▶双簧管 shuānghuángguǎn oboe 3 (管状物) tube II [动] 1 (负责) be in charge of 2 (管辖) have jurisdiction over 3 (管教) discipline 4 (过问) interfere ▷这事不用你管。 Zhè shì bù yòng nǐ guǎn. It's no use you interfering in this. 5 (保证) guarantee ▶管保 guǎnbǎo guarantee 6 (提供) provide

管道 guǎndào [名] pipeline

管理 guǎnlǐ [动] 1 (负责) be in charge 2 (保管) take care of 3 (看管) keep guard over ▶企业管理 qǐyè guǎnlǐ business management

管用 guǎnyòng [形] effective

贯 guàn I [动] 1 (贯穿) pass through 2 (连贯) keep following II [名] ancestral home ▶籍贯 jíguàn place of origin

贯彻 guànchè [动] implement

贯穿 guànchuān [动] run through

冠 guàn I [动] crown II [名] crown

冠军 guànjūn [名] champion

惯 guàn [动] 1 (习惯) be used to ▶我吃西餐已经惯了。 Wǒ chī xīcān yǐjīng guàn le. I'm already used to Western food. 2 (纵容) spoil ▶惯孩子 guàn háizi spoil the children

灌 guàn [动] 1 (灌溉) irrigate 2 (注入) pour ... into

罐 guàn I [名] 1 (盛茶叶, 糖等) jar 2 (易拉罐) can 3 (煤气) cylinder ▶煤气罐 méiqìguàn gas cylinder II [量] can ▶两罐啤酒 liǎng guàn píjiǔ two cans of beer ▶五罐苏打水 wǔ guàn sūdǎshuǐ five cans of soda water

罐头 guàntou [名] tin ▶金枪鱼罐头 jīnqiāngyú guàntou tinned tuna fish

光 guāng I [名] 1 (指物质) light ▶月光 yuèguāng moonlight ▶阳光 yángguāng sunlight 2 (景物) scenery ▶风光 fēngguāng scenery 3 (荣誉) glory ▶增光 zēngguāng bring glory II [动] 1 (光大) glorify 2 (露出) bare

III [形] 1 (光滑) smooth ▶光滑 guānghuá smooth 2 (露着) bare ▶光脚 guāngjiǎo barefooted 3 (穷尽) used up ▶钱都用光了。 Qián dōu yòng guāng le. All the money's used up. IV [副] just ▶他光说不做。 Tā guāng shuō bù zuò. He's all talk.

光临 guānglín [动] be present

光明 guāngmíng I [名] light II [形] bright

光盘 guāngpán [名] CD

光荣 guāngróng [形] glorious

光线 guāngxiàn [名] light

广 guǎng [形] 1 (宽阔) broad 2 (多) numerous

广播 guǎngbō [动] broadcast

广场 guǎngchǎng [名] square

广大 guǎngdà [形] 1 (宽广) vast 2 (众多) numerous

广泛 guǎngfàn [形] wide-ranging ▶广泛开展活动 guǎngfàn kāizhǎn huódòng initiate a wide range of activities

广告 guǎnggào [名] advertisement

广阔 guǎngkuò [形] broad

逛 guàng [动] stroll

归 guī [动] 1 (返回, 还给) return 2 (合并) group ... together ▶归类 guīlèi categorise 3 (属于) be under the charge of ▶这本书归他所有。 Zhè běn shū guī tā suǒyǒu. This book belongs to him.

归功于 guīgōngyú[动] give credit to

归还 guīhuán[动] return

龟 guī[名] tortoise ▶乌龟 wūguī tortoise

规 guī[名] 1(工具) compasses (PL) 2(规则) rule

规定 guīdìng I[动] stipulate II[名] regulation

规范 guīfàn[名] standard ▶一定要规范市场秩序。 yīdìng yào guīfàn shìchǎng zhìxù We must standardize the market economy.

规矩 guīju I[名] norm II[形] well-behaved ▶他办事总是规矩。 Tā bànshì zǒngshì guīju. He always plays by the rules.

规律 guīlǜ[名] law

规模 guīmó[名] scale

规则 guīzé I[名] regulation II[形] orderly

规章 guīzhāng[名] regulations (PL)

轨 guǐ[名] (轨道) rail ▶轨道 guǐdào track

鬼 guǐ[名] 1(灵魂) ghost 2(勾当) dirty trick 3(不良行为者) ▶酒鬼 jiǔguǐ drunkard

鬼混 guǐhùn[动] hang around

鬼脸 guǐliǎn[名] grimace ▶做鬼脸 zuò guǐliǎn make a funny face

柜 guì[名] (柜子) cupboard ▶衣柜 yīguì wardrobe ▶保险柜 bǎoxiǎnguì safe

柜台 guìtái[名] counter

贵 guì[形] 1(指价格) expensive 2(值得珍视) valuable ▶贵宾 guìbīn VIP

贵重 guìzhòng[形] valuable

贵族 guìzú[名] aristocrat

跪 guì[动] kneel ▶跪下 guìxià kneel down

滚 gǔn I[动] 1(滚动) roll ▶滚动 gǔndòng roll 2(走开) get lost ▶滚烫 gǔntàng boiling hot II[形] 1(滚动的) rolling 2(沸腾的) boiling

棍 gùn[名] (棍子) stick ▶棍子 gùnzi stick

锅 guō[名] (指炊具) pot ▶炒菜锅 chǎocàiguō wok ▶火锅 huǒguō hotpot

国 guó I[名] country II[形] (国家) national ▶国徽 guóhuī national emblem ▶国歌 guógē national anthem ▶国旗 guóqí national flag

国产 guóchǎn[形] domestic

国画 guóhuà[名] traditional Chinese painting

国会 guóhuì[名] parliament

国籍 guójí[名] nationality

国际 guójì[形] international

国家 guójiā[名] state

国力 guólì[名] national strength

国民 guómín [名] citizen

国内 guónèi [形] domestic

国庆节 guóqìngjié [名] National Day

国庆节 guóqìngjié
国庆节 guóqìngjié (National Day) falls on 1 October, and commemorates the anniversary of the founding of the People's Republic of China in 1949. The PRC was declared by Chairman Mao Zedong, in Tiananmen Square in Beijing.

国王 guówáng [名] king

国务院 guówùyuàn [名] the State Council

国务院 guówùyuàn
国务院 guówùyuàn, the State Council, is the highest executive and administrative organ of the PRC government, headed by the Premier, and overseeing all the various ministries.

国营 guóyíng [形] state-run

果 guǒ [名] 1 (果子) fruit ▶果子 guǒzi fruit 2 (结局) outcome ▶效果 xiàoguǒ result ▶成果 chéngguǒ achievement

果断 guǒduàn [形] resolute

果然 guǒrán [副] really

果实 guǒshí [名] 1 (果子) fruit 2 (成果) fruits (PL)

果真 guǒzhēn [副] really

裹 guǒ [动] (缠绕) wrap

过 guò I [动] 1 (经过) pass through 2 (度过) spend ▷你假期怎么过的？ Nǐ jiàqī zěnme guò de? How did you spend your holiday? 3 (过去) pass 4 (超过) be more than ▷年过半百 nián guò bàn bǎi over fifty years old 5 (生活) live ▷我们过得很好。 Wǒmen guò de hěn hǎo. We live well. 6 (庆祝) celebrate ▷过生日 guò shēngrì celebrate a birthday II [名] fault III [介] past ▷现在是9点过8分。 Xiànzài shì jiǔ diǎn guò bā fēn. It is now eight minutes past nine.

When 过 guò is used as a verb suffix to indicate a past action, it often corresponds to the present perfect tense (e.g. 'I have done') in English, stressing that the subject has experienced something, e.g. 我去过中国三次 Wǒ qùguo Zhōngguó sān cì (I have been to China three times).

过程 guòchéng [名] process

过道 guòdào [名] corridor

过分 guòfèn [形] excessive

过后 guòhòu [副] later

过奖 guòjiǎng [动] flatter ▷您过奖了。 Nín guòjiǎng le. I'm flattered.

过来 guòlái [动] come over

过滤 guòlǜ [动] filter

过敏 guòmǐn [名] (医) allergy

过期 guòqī [动] expire

过年 guònián [动] celebrate the new year

过去 guòqù [名] the past

过去 guòqu [动] pass by

过日子 guò rìzi [动] live

过时 guòshí [形] outdated

过世 guòshì [动] pass away

过头 guòtóu [形] excessive

过瘾 guòyǐn [动] do to one's heart's content

过于 guòyú [副] too

哈 hā **I** [叹] aha **II** [拟] ha ha ▷哈哈大笑 hā hā dàxiào roar with laughter

还 hái [副] 1 (仍旧) still, yet ▷那家老饭店还很兴旺。 Nà jiā lǎo fàndiàn hái hěn xīngwàng. The old restaurant is still thriving. ▷她还没回来。 Tā hái méi huílái. She hasn't come back yet. 2 (更加) even more
→ see also/另见 huán

还是 háishì **I** [副] 1 (仍然) still 2 (最好) had better ▷你还是先完成作业吧。 Nǐ háishì xiān wánchéng zuòyè ba. You'd better finish your homework first. **II** [连] or ▷你是去巴黎还是去伦敦？ Nǐ shì qù Bālí háishì qù Lúndūn? Are you going to Paris or London?

孩 hái [名] child
孩子 háizi [名] child

海 hǎi [名] (海洋) ocean ▶地中海 Dìzhōnghǎi the Mediterranean Sea
海边 hǎibiān [名] coast
海拔 hǎibá [名] elevation
海报 hǎibào [名] poster
海滨 hǎibīn [名] seaside
海关 hǎiguān [名] customs (PL)
海军 hǎijūn [名] the navy
海绵 hǎimián [名] sponge
海滩 hǎitān [名] beach
海峡 hǎixiá [名] strait
海鲜 hǎixiān [名] seafood
海洋 hǎiyáng [名] ocean

害 hài I [动] 1 (损害) harm 2 (杀害) kill II [名] harm ▶害处 hàichu harm ▶灾害 zāihài disaster III [形] harmful ▶害虫 hàichóng pest
害怕 hàipà [动] be afraid
害羞 hàixiū [动] be shy

含 hán [动] 1 (用嘴) keep ... in the mouth 2 (包含) contain
含量 hánliàng [名] content
含义 hányì [名] meaning

寒 hán [形] (冷) cold ▶寒风 hánfēng chilly wind
寒假 hánjià [名] winter holiday
寒冷 hánlěng [形] cold

韩 hán [名] see below / 见下文
韩国 Hánguó [名] South Korea

喊 hǎn [动] 1 (大声叫) shout ▶喊叫 hǎnjiào cry out 2 (叫) call

汉 hàn [名] (汉族) the Han (PL) ▶汉人 Hànrén the Han people (PL)
汉语 Hànyǔ [名] Chinese
汉字 Hànzì [名] Chinese characters (PL)
汉族 Hànzú [名] the Han (PL)

汗 hàn [名] sweat ▶汗水 hànshuǐ sweat

旱 hàn [形] dry ▶旱灾 hànzāi drought

行 háng I [名] 1 (行列) row ▷第一行 dìyī háng first row 2 (行业) profession ▶同行 tóngháng people in the same profession II [量] line ▷一行字 yī háng zì a line of words
→ see also / 另见 xíng
行业 hángyè [名] industry

航 háng [动] 1 (指船) sail 2 (指飞机) fly
航班 hángbān [名] (指客机) scheduled flight
航空 hángkōng [动] fly ▷航空信 hángkōngxìn airmail ▷航空公司 hángkōng gōngsī airline

毫 háo [名] (千分之一) ▶毫米 háomǐ millimetre (英), millimeter (美) ▶毫升 háoshēng millilitre (英), milliliter (美)

毫不 háobù [副] not at all

毫无 háowú [副] without the slightest

豪 háo [形] grand ▶豪华 háohuá luxurious

好 hǎo I [形] 1 (令人满意) good ▷他脾气好。Tā píqi hǎo. He's good-natured. 2 (容易) easy ▷这事不好办。Zhè shì bù hǎo bàn. This won't be easy to manage. 3 (健康) well ▷你身体好吗？Nǐ shēntǐ hǎo ma? Are you keeping well? 4 (亲密) good ▷我们是好朋友。Wǒmen shì hǎo péngyou. We're good friends. 5 (表示问候) ▷你好！Nǐ hǎo! Hello! ▷大家好。Dàjiā hǎo. Hello everyone. 6 (表示完成) ▷工作找好了。Gōngzuò zhǎo hǎo le. I've found work. ▷衣服洗好了。Yīfu xǐ hǎo le. The clothes have been washed. 7 (表示答应, 结束等) ▷好，我们现在就去！Hǎo, wǒmen xiànzài jiù qù! OK, let's go then! II [副] 1 (强调多或久) very ▷我等了好久她才来。Wǒ děng le hǎo jiǔ tā cái lái. I'd waited for a long time before she arrived. 2 (表示程度深) ▷他话说得好快。Tā huà shuō de hǎo kuài. He speaks so quickly. III [名] (问候) regards (PL) ▷请代我向你太太问好。Qǐng dài wǒ xiàng nǐ tàitai wènhǎo. Please send my regards to your wife.
→ see also/另见 hào

好吃 hǎochī [形] delicious

好处 hǎochu [名] 1 (益处) benefit 2 (利益) profit

好久 hǎojiǔ [副] for a long time

好看 hǎokàn [形] 1 (漂亮) nice-looking 2 (精彩) good ▷这本书很好看。Zhè běn shū hěn hǎokàn. This book is very good.

好受 hǎoshòu [形] comfortable

好容易 hǎoróngyì [副] with great effort

好听 hǎotīng [形] 1 (指声音, 音乐) lovely 2 (指言语) nice

好玩儿 hǎowánr [形] fun

好像 hǎoxiàng [副] apparently

好笑 hǎoxiào [形] funny

好些 hǎoxiē [形] quite a great deal of

号 hào I [名] 1 (名称) name ▶外号 wàihào nickname 2 (商店) firm ▶商号 shānghào firm 3 (标记) sign ▶逗号 dòuhào comma 4 (次序) number 5 (日期) date ▷6月1号 liùyuè yī hào the first of June 6 (大小) size ▷大号 dàhào large-size 7 (乐器) brass instrument ▶小号 xiǎohào trumpet II [动] (脉) take ▶号脉 hàomài take a pulse

号码 hàomǎ [名] number

号召 hàozhào [动] appeal

好 hào [动] 1 (喜爱) like 2 (容易) be easy
→ see also/另见 hǎo

好奇 hàoqí [形] curious

喝 hē [动] drink

合 hé [动] **1**(闭) close **2**(合在一起) join ▶合资 hézī joint venture **3**(折合) be equal to **4**(符合) tally with

合并 hébìng [动] merge

合唱 héchàng [名] chorus

合法 héfǎ [形] legal

合格 hégé [形] qualified

合理 hélǐ [形] rational

合身 héshēn [形] fitted

合适 héshì [形] appropriate

合算 hésuàn [动] be worthwhile

合同 hétong [名] contract

合作 hézuò [动] cooperate

何 hé [代](什么) ▶何时 héshí when ▶何人 hérén who ▶何地 hédì where

和 hé **I**[连] and **II**[介] with ▷这事和你没关系。 Zhè shì hé nǐ méi guānxi. This has nothing to do with you. **III**[名](总数) total **IV**[动] draw ▷这场比赛和了。 Zhè chǎng bǐsài hé le. The match was a draw.

和蔼 hé'ǎi [形] affable

和好 héhǎo [动] reconcile

和睦 hémù [形] harmonious

和平 hépíng [名](指战争) peace

和气 héqi **I**[形] polite **II**[名] peace

和数 héshù [名] sum

河 hé [名](河) river

核 hé [名](指水果) stone

盒 hé [名] box

盒子 hézi [名] box

贺 hè [动] congratulate

贺卡 hèkǎ [名] greetings card

黑 hēi [形] **1**(指颜色) black ▶黑板 hēibǎn blackboard **2**(暗) dark **3**(秘密) secret ▶黑市 hēishì black market **4**(反动) ▶黑社会 hēishèhuì gangland ▶黑手党 hēishǒudǎng the Mafia

黑暗 hēi'àn [形] **1**(指光线) dark **2**(腐败) corrupt

黑人 hēirén [名] black person

很 hěn [副] very

恨 hèn [动] **1**(憎恶) hate **2**(后悔) regret

哼 hēng [动](唱) hum

横 héng **I**[名] horizontal **II**[形] **1**(梁, 线, 行) horizontal **2**(左右向) sideways ▶横躺 héngtǎng lie sideways **3**(指横截) across ▶人行横道 rénxíng héngdào zebra crossing **III**[动] turn ... lengthways

红 hóng **I**[形] **1**(指颜色) red ▶红旗 hóngqí red flag ▶红十字会 Hóngshízìhuì the Red Cross **2**(形容受欢迎) popular ▶走红 zǒuhóng be popular ▶红人 hóngrén rising star **3**(形容成功) successful ▶红运 hóngyùn lucky **II**[名](红利) bonus ▶分红 fēnhóng get a bonus

红茶 hóngchá [名] black tea

红绿灯 hónglǜdēng [名] traffic lights (PL)

红色 hóngsè [形] red

洪 hóng [名] (指洪水) flood ▶洪水 hóngshuǐ flood

喉 hóu [名] throat

喉咙 hóulong [名] throat

猴 hóu [名] monkey

猴子 hóuzi [名] monkey

后 hòu [名] 1 (背面) the back ▷房后有个车库。 Fánghòu yǒu gè chēkù. At the back of the house is a garage. 2 (指时间) ▶后天 hòutiān the day after tomorrow 3 (指次序) the last ▶后排 hòupái the last row

后边 hòubian [名] back

后代 hòudài [名] 1 (指时代) later generations (PL) 2 (子孙) offspring

后果 hòuguǒ [名] consequence

后悔 hòuhuǐ [动] regret

后来 hòulái [副] afterwards ▷我后来再也没有见过他。 Wǒ hòulái zài yě méi jiànguo tā. I didn't see him again after that.

后门 hòumén [名] back door

后面 hòumian I [名] back II [副] later

后年 hòunián [名] the year after next

后退 hòutuì [动] retreat

厚 hòu [形] 1 (书, 衣服, 脸皮) thick 2 (雪, 土) deep 3 (指感情) profound

厚道 hòudao [形] kind

呼 hū [动] 1 (排气) exhale 2 (喊) shout ▶呼喊 hūhǎn shout 3 (叫) call ▶呼叫 hūjiào call ▶呼救 hūjiù call for help

呼机 hūjī [名] pager

呼噜 hūlu [名] (口) snore

呼吸 hūxī [动] breathe

忽 hū [副] suddenly

忽然 hūrán [副] suddenly

忽视 hūshì [动] ignore

狐 hú see below/见下文

狐狸 húli [名] fox

胡 hú I [名] 1 (髭) moustache (英), mustache (美) 2 (长在下颚, 两腮) beard II [副] recklessly

胡乱 húluàn [副] 1 (随便) casually 2 (任意) wilfully

胡闹 húnào [动] play around

胡说 húshuō [动] talk nonsense

胡同 hútòng [名] lane

胡子 húzi [名] 1 (髭) moustache (英), mustache (美) 2 (指长在下颚, 两腮) beard

壶 hú [名] pot

湖 hú [名] lake

蝴 hú see below/见下文

蝴蝶 húdié [名] butterfly

糊 hú [动] paste

糊里糊涂 húlihútu confused

糊涂 hútu [形] 1 (不明白)

confused **2** (混乱) chaotic

虎 hǔ [名] tiger

互 hù [副] mutually

互联网 hùliánwǎng [名] the Internet

互相 hùxiāng [副] mutually

户 hù [名] **1** (门) door **2** (住户) family **3** (户头) bank account ▶账户 zhànghù account

户口 hùkǒu [名] (户籍) registered permanent residence

护 hù [动] (保护) protect

护理 hùlǐ [动] nurse

护士 hùshi [名] nurse

护照 hùzhào [名] passport

花 huā I [名] **1** (指植物) flower **2** (烟火) fireworks (PL) II [形] **1** (多彩) multi-coloured (英), multi-colored (美) **2** (有花的) floral ▶花篮 huālán flower basket **3** (模糊) blurred ▶头昏眼花 tóuyūn yǎnhuā muddle-headed and bleary-eyed **4** (虚假) superficial ▶花招 huāzhāo trick III [动] spend ▷花钱 huā qián spend money ▷花工夫 huā gōngfu put in effort

花费 huāfèi [动] spend ▶留学的花费很大。 liúxué de huāfèi hěn dà. It's very expensive to study abroad.

花生 huāshēng [名] peanut

花纹 huāwén [名] decorative design

花园 huāyuán [名] garden

花招 huāzhāo [名] trick

划 huá [动] **1** (拨水) row **2** (合算) be worthwhile ▷划不来 huábulái not worth it **3** (擦) scratch
→ see also/另见 huà

华 huá [名] (中国) China ▶华人 huárén Chinese person

华丽 huálì [形] resplendent

华侨 huáqiáo [名] overseas Chinese

华人 huárén [名] Chinese

滑 huá I [形] **1** (光滑) slippery **2** (油滑) crafty II [动] slip

滑冰 huábīng [动] ice skate

滑动 huádòng [动] slide

滑稽 huájī [形] comical

滑坡 huápō [动] **1** (字) slide **2** (喻) drop

滑雪 huáxuě [动] ski

化 huà I [名] chemistry ▶化肥 huàféi chemical fertilizer II [动] **1** (变化) change ▶化装 huàzhuāng disguise oneself **2** (消化) digest

化工 huàgōng [名] chemical industry

化石 huàshí [名] fossil

化学 huàxué [名] chemistry

化验 huàyàn [动] test

化妆 huàzhuāng [动] make oneself up

划 huà [动] **1** (划分) demarcate

▶划分 huàfēn divide **2** (划拨) transfer **3** (计划) plan
→ *see also*/另见 huá

画 huà **I** [动] **1** (用铅笔) draw **2** (用刷状) (笔画) paint **II** [名] **1** (用铅笔) drawing **2** (用刷状, 笔画) painting ▶油画 yóuhuà oil painting **3** (笔画) stroke **III** [形] painted

画报 huàbào [名] pictorial

画家 huàjiā [名] painter

画像 huàxiàng [名] portrait

画展 huàzhǎn [名] art exhibition

话 huà **I** [名] words (PL) ▶说话 shuōhuà talk ▶对话 duìhuà conversation ▶谎话 huǎnghuà lie **II** [动] talk about ▶话旧 huàjiù reminisce

话剧 huàjù [名] stage play

话题 huàtí [名] subject

怀 huái **I** [名] **1** (胸前) bosom **2** (胸怀) mind **II** [动] **1** (思念) think of **2** (存有) keep ... in mind **3** (有孕) become pregnant

怀念 huáiniàn [动] yearn for

怀疑 huáiyí [动] **1** (认为是真) suspect **2** (认为不可能) doubt

怀孕 huáiyùn [动] be pregnant

坏 huài **I** [形] **1** (不好) bad **2** (程度深) extreme **II** [动] go off ▶空调坏了。 Kōngtiáo huài le. The air-conditioning has broken down. **III** [名] dirty trick

坏处 huàichu [名] harm

坏蛋 huàidàn [名] (讳) bastard

坏话 huàihuà [名] (不利的话) bad words (PL)

欢 huān [形] **1** (快乐) happy **2** (活跃) vigorous

欢呼 huānhū [动] cheer

欢快 huānkuài [形] cheerful

欢乐 huānlè [形] joyful

欢心 huānxīn [名] favour (英), favor (美)

欢迎 huānyíng [动] welcome ▶欢迎来中国。 Huānyíng lái Zhōngguó. Welcome to China.

还 huán [动] **1** (回) return **2** (归还) return ▶还债 huánzhài repay a debt **3** (回报) repay ▶还价 huánjià haggle ▶还击 huánjī fight back
→ *see also*/另见 hái

环 huán **I** [名] **1** (圆圈) ring ▶耳环 ěrhuán earring **2** (环节) element ▶环节 huánjié element **II** [动] surround

环保 huánbǎo [名] (*also*: 环境保护 huánjìng bǎohù) environmental protection

环境 huánjìng [名] environment ▶生活环境 shēnghuó huánjìng living conditions (PL)

环绕 huánrào [动] surround

缓 huǎn **I** [形] **1** (慢) slow **2** (缓和) relaxed **II** [动] **1** (推迟) delay **2** (恢复) revive

缓慢 huǎnmàn [形] slow

幻 huàn [形] unreal

幻想 huànxiǎng I [动] dream II [名] fantasy

换 huàn [动] 1(交换) exchange 2(更换) replace

唤 huàn [名] summon

唤醒 huànxǐng [动] (叫醒) wake up

患 huàn I [动] 1(害) suffer from ▶患者 huànzhě sufferer 2(忧虑) worry II [名] trouble

荒 huāng [形] 1(荒芜) waste 2(荒凉) desolate 3(短缺) short 4(荒歉) famine

慌 huāng [形] nervous

慌忙 huāngmáng [形] hurried

慌张 huāngzhāng [形] nervous

皇 huáng [名] emperor ▶皇帝 huángdì emperor ▶皇后 huánghòu empress

皇宫 huánggōng [名] palace

黄 huáng I [形] 1(指颜色) yellow 2(色情) pornographic II [名] 1(蛋黄) yolk 2(黄金) gold

黄瓜 huángguā [名] cucumber

黄河 Huánghé [名] Yellow River

黄昏 huánghūn [名] dusk

黄金 huángjīn [名] gold

黄色 huángsè [名] 1(指颜色) yellow 2(色情) pornographic

黄油 huángyóu [名] butter

谎 huǎng [名] lie

谎言 huǎngyán [名] lie

晃 huàng [动] shake

晃动 huàngdòng [动] rock

灰 huī I [名] 1(灰烬) ash 2(尘土) dust 3(石灰) lime II [动] (消沉) be disheartened ▶灰暗 huī'àn gloomy

灰尘 huīchén [名] dust

灰色 huīsè [名] (指颜色) grey (英), gray (美)

灰心 huīxīn [动] lose heart

恢 huī [形] vast

恢复 huīfù [动] recover

挥 huī [动] 1(挥舞) wave 2(抹掉) wipe ... away 3(指挥) command 4(散出) scatter ▶挥发 huīfā evaporate

回 huí I [动] 1(旋转) circle 2(还) return 3(掉转) turn around ▶回头 huítóu turn one's head 4(答复) reply ▶回信 huíxìn reply to a letter II [量] 1(次数) time ▷ 我去过两回。 Wǒ qùguo liǎng huí. I have been there twice. 2(章) chapter

回报 huíbào [动] (报答) repay

回避 huíbì [动] avoid

回答 huídá [动] answer

回复 huífù [动] (答复) reply

回顾 huígù [动] look back

回合 huíhé [名] round

回话 huíhuà [动] reply

回扣 huíkòu [名] commission

回教 Huíjiào [名] Islam

回来 huílai [动] come back

回去 huíqu [动] go back

回声 huíshēng [名] echo

回收 huíshōu [动] 1 (再利用) recycle 2 (收回) retrieve

回信 huíxìn [动] write in reply

回忆 huíyì [动] recall

毁 huǐ [动] 1 (破坏) destroy 2 (诽谤) defame

毁坏 huǐhuài [动] destroy

汇 huì I [动] 1 (汇合) converge 2 (聚集) gather 3 (划拨) transfer II [名] 1 (外汇) foreign exchange 2 (聚集物) collection ▸词汇 cíhuì vocabulary

汇报 huìbào [动] report

汇集 huìjí [动] collect

汇率 huìlǜ [名] exchange rate

会 huì I [动] 1 (聚合) assemble 2 (见面) meet ▸会客 huìkè receive a guest 3 (理解) understand ▸领会 lǐnghuì understand 4 (通晓) be able to ▸会武术 huì wǔshù able to do martial arts II [助动] 1 (能做) can ▸我不会下象棋。 Wǒ bùhuì xià xiàngqí. I can't play chess. 2 (擅长) ▸会过日子 huì guò rìzi know how to economize 3 (可能) might ▸明天会更热。 Míngtiān huì gèng rè. Tomorrow might be hotter. III [名] 1 (集会) gathering 2 (团体) association ▸学生会 xuéshēnghuì student union 3 (城市) city ▸大都

会 dàdūhuì metropolis 4 (时机) opportunity ▸机会 jīhuì opportunity

→ see also/另见 kuài

Both 会 huì and 要 yào can be used to express the future tense. 会 huì is usually used to express a possible or probable outcome, e.g. 明天会下雨 míngtiān huì xiàyǔ (it might rain tomorrow); 要 yào refers to something definite, e.g. 我明天要上班 wǒ míngtiān yào shàngbān (I am going to work tomorrow). 会 huì, 能 néng, and 可以 kěyǐ can all be used to express ability and are sometimes used interchangeably. Strictly, 会 huì should express a learned ability, e.g. 我会说法语 wǒ huì shuō Fǎyǔ (I can speak French), while 能 néng should be used to express physical ability, e.g. 我能跑得很快 wǒ néng pǎo de hěn kuài (I can run very fast).

会话 huìhuà [动] converse

会见 huìjiàn [动] meet

会谈 huìtán [动] hold talks

会议 huìyì [名] 1 (集会) meeting 2 (机构) council

会员 huìyuán [名] member

贿 huì [名] bribe ▸贿赂 huìlù bribe

昏 hūn I [名] dusk II [形] 1 (黑暗) dark ▷ 昏暗 hūn'àn dim 2 (迷糊) muddled III [动] faint

昏迷 hūnmí [动] be unconscious

荤 hūn [名] meat

婚 hūn I [名] marriage II [动] marry

婚礼 hūnlǐ [名] wedding ceremony

婚姻 hūnyīn [名] marriage

浑 hún [形] 1 (浑浊) muddy 2 (糊涂) muddled

浑蛋 húndàn [名] (讳) bastard

浑身 húnshēn [副] from head to toe

浑浊 húnzhuó [形] murky

馄 hún see below/ 见下文

馄饨 húntún [名] wonton

馄饨 húntún

In Chinese cooking, 馄饨 húntún is a kind of dumpling filled with spiced minced meat and other ingredients such as chopped mushrooms, shrimps etc. It is usually served in the soup in which it is cooked. The English name for 馄饨 comes from the Cantonese pronunciation, wantan.

魂 hún [名] (灵魂) soul

混 hùn I [动] 1 (搀杂) mix 2 (蒙混) pass off ... as 3 (苟且生活) drift ▷ 混日子 hùn rìzi drift through the days II [副] aimlessly

混合 hùnhé [动] mix

混乱 hùnluàn [形] 1 (无秩序) chaotic 2 (无条理) disordered

混淆 hùnxiáo [动] confuse

活 huó I [动] 1 (生存) live 2 (使生存) keep ... alive II [形] 1 (有生命) alive 2 (不固定) flexible 3 (不死板) lively 4 (逼真) lifelike III [副] completely IV [名] 1 (工作) work 2 (产品) product

活动 huódòng I [动] 1 (运动) take exercise 2 (行动) operate 3 (动用关系) use connections II [名] activity III [形] movable

活该 huógāi [动] (口) serve ... right

活力 huólì [名] vitality

活泼 huópō [形] lively

活期 huóqī [形] current ▷ 活期账号 huóqī zhànghào current account

活跃 huóyuè [动] 1 (使有生气) invigorate 2 (积极从事) be active

火 huǒ I [名] 1 (火焰) fire 2 (枪支弹药) ammunition 3 (医) (指内火) internal heat 4 (喻) (愤怒) rage II [动] be in a rage III [形] 1 (红色) flaming red ▷ 火红 huǒhóng flaming red 2 (兴旺) prosperous

火柴 huǒchái [名] match

火车 huǒchē [名] train

火鸡 huǒjī [名] turkey

火警 huǒjǐng [名] fire alarm

火山 huǒshān [名] volcano

火腿 huǒtuǐ [名] ham

火焰 huǒyàn [名] flame

火药 huǒyào [名] gunpowder

火 huǒ **I** [名] **1**(同伴) companion **2**(指集体) partnership **3**(伙食) meals (PL) **II** [量] group

伙伴 huǒbàn [名] companion

伙食 huǒshí [名] meals (PL)

或 huò [连] or

或许 huòxǔ [副] perhaps

或者 huòzhě **I** [副] maybe **II** [连] or

货 huò [名] **1**(货币) currency **2**(货物) goods (PL) **3**(人) person ▶蠢货 chǔnhuò idiot

货币 huòbì [名] currency

货物 huòwù [名] goods (PL)

获 huò [动] **1**(捉住) capture **2**(得到) obtain **3**(收割) reap ▶收获 shōuhuò harvest

获得 huòdé [动] gain

祸 huò [名] **I** [名] misfortune **II** [动] harm

j

几 jī [名] small table ▶茶几 chájī tea table
→ see also / 另见 jǐ

几乎 jīhū [副] almost

讥 jī [动] mock

讥笑 jīxiào [动] jeer

饥 jī [形] hungry [名] famine

饥饿 jī'è [形] starving

机 jī **I** [名] **1**(机器) machine ▶发动机 fādòngjī engine **2**(飞机) aeroplane (英), airplane (美) ▶客机 kèjī airliner **3**(枢纽) pivot ▶转机 zhuǎnjī turning point **4**(机会) opportunity **5**(机能) ▶有机体 yǒujītǐ organism **II** [形] quick-witted ▶机智 jīzhì ingenious

机场 jīchǎng [名] airport

机关 jīguān [名] 1 (部门) department 2 (机械) mechanism

机会 jīhuì [名] opportunity

机灵 jīling [形] clever

机器 jīqì [名] machine

机械 jīxiè I [名] machinery II [形] rigid

机遇 jīyù [名] opportunity

肌 jī [名] muscle

肌肉 jīròu [名] muscle

鸡 jī [名] chicken ▶公鸡 gōngjī cock ▶母鸡 mǔjī hen

鸡蛋 jīdàn [名] egg

积 jī I [动] accumulate II [形] long-standing III [名] (数) product

积极 jījí [形] 1 (肯定的) positive 2 (热心的) active

积极性 jījíxìng [名] positive attitude

积累 jīlěi [动] accumulate

积蓄 jīxù I [动] save II [名] savings (PL)

基 jī I [名] base II [形] primary ▶基层 jīcéng grass roots

基本 jīběn I [形] 1 (根本) basic 2 (主要) essential 3 (基础) elementary II [副] basically

基础 jīchǔ I [名] foundation II [形] basic

基督教 Jīdūjiào [名] Christianity

基金 jījīn [名] fund

激 jī I [动] 1 (涌起) surge 2 (刺激)

catch a chill 3 (唤起) excite 4 (冰) chill II [形] violent

激动 jīdòng [动] excite ▶激动的孩子 jīdòng de háizi excited child ▶令人激动的电影 lìng rén jīdòng de diànyǐng exciting film

激光 jīguāng [名] laser

激烈 jīliè [形] intense

及 jí I [动] 1 (到达) reach 2 (比得上) be as good as 3 (赶上) be in time for II [连] and

及格 jígé [动] pass

及时 jíshí I [形] timely II [副] without delay

级 jí I [名] 1 (等级) level 2 (年级) year (英), grade (美) 3 (台阶) step II [量] step ▶100多级台阶 yībǎi duō jí táijiē a staircase of more than 100 steps

极 jí I [名] 1 (顶点) extreme 2 (指地球或磁体) pole ▶南极 nánjí the South Pole II [动] go to an extreme III [形] extreme ▶极限 jíxiàn limit IV [副] very

极其 jíqí [副] extremely

即 jí I [动] 1 (书) (就是) mean 2 (靠近) approach 3 (到) ▶即位 jíwèi ascend the throne 4 (就着) ▶即兴演唱 jíxìng yǎnchàng ad-lib II [形] present ▶即日 jírì this very day III [副] immediately

即将 jíjiāng [副] soon

即使 jíshǐ [连] even if

急 jí I [形] 1 (着急) anxious 2 (急躁) impatient 3 (猛烈) ▶水流很急。

shuǐliú hěn jí. There's a strong current. **4** (紧急) urgent **II** [名] priority **III** [动] worry

急救 jíjiù [动] give first-aid

急忙 jímáng [副] hurriedly

急诊 jízhěn [名] emergency treatment

集 jí **I** [动] gather **II** [名] **1** (集市) market ▶ 赶集 gǎnjí go to market **2** (集子) anthology ▶ 诗集 shījí an anthology of poems **3** (册) part

集合 jíhé [动] assemble

集体 jítǐ [名] collective

集团 jítuán [名] group

集中 jízhōng [动] concentrate

几 jǐ [数] **1** (用于疑问句) ▷ 昨天来了几位客人？ Zuótiān lái le jǐ wèi kèrén? How many customers came yesterday? **2** (用于陈述句) ▷ 几本书 jǐ běn shū several books ▷ 十几本书 shíjǐ běn shū more than ten books ▷ 几十本书 jǐshí běn shū several tens of books → see also/另见 jī

已 jǐ [名] self ▶ 自己 zìjǐ oneself

挤 jǐ [动] **1** (拥挤) crowd **2** (事情, 会议, 约会) be close **3** (推人) elbow one's way **4** (贬) (指社交) push one's way **5** (牙膏, 颜料) squeeze ... out ▶ 挤奶 jǐnǎi milk **6** (时间) make **7** (排斥) rob ... of

计 jì **I** [动] **1** (核算) calculate ▶ 共计 gòngjì total **2** (打算) plan **3** (考虑) bother **II** [名] **1** (计谋) strategy

2 (测量仪器) gauge ▶ 温度计 wēndùjì thermometer

计划 jìhuà **I** [名] plan **II** [动] plan

计算 jìsuàn [动] **1** (数) calculate **2** (筹划) plan **3** (暗算) scheme

计算机 jìsuànjī [名] computer

计算器 jìsuànqì [名] calculator

记 jì **I** [动] **1** (指往事) remember **2** (写) record **II** [名] **1** (指书或文章) record ▶ 游记 yóujì travel journal ▶ 日记 rìjì diary **2** (标志) mark **3** (指皮肤) birthmark

记得 jìde [动] remember

记号 jìhao [名] mark

记录 jìlù **I** [动] (写下) write ... down **II** [名] **1** (材料) record **2** (指人) secretary **3** (成绩) record

记忆 jìyì **I** [动] remember **II** [名] memory

记者 jìzhě [名] journalist

纪 jì **I** [名] **1** age ▶ 中世纪 zhōngshìjì the Middle Ages (PL) **2** (指地质) period ▶ 侏罗纪 zhūluójì the Jurassic period **3** (纪律) discipline **II** [动] record

纪律 jìlǜ [名] discipline

纪念 jìniàn **I** [动] commemorate **II** [名] memento

技 jì [名] **1** (技艺) skill ▶ 技能 jìnéng skill ▶ 技巧 jìqiǎo technique **2** (本领) ability ▶ 绝技 juéjì unique ability

技巧 jìqiǎo [名] technique

技术 jìshù [名] technology

技术员 jìshùyuán [名] technician

季 jì [名] season ▶春季 chūnjì spring ▶旺季 wàngjì busy season

季节 jìjié [名] season

既 jì I [副] already ▶既定 jìdìng fixed II [连] 1(表示兼而有之) ▶他既高又壮。 Tā jì gāo yòu zhuàng. He's tall and strong. 2(既然) since

既然 jìrán [连] since

继 jì I [副] 1(接续) continuously ▶继任 jìrèn succeed to a post 2(接连) successively ▶相继 xiāngjì one after another II [动] continue

继承 jìchéng [动] 1(遗产, 文化等) inherit 2(遗志, 未成事业) take ... on

继续 jìxù I [动] continue II [名] continuation

寄 jì [动] 1(邮递) post (英), mail (美) 2(付托) place 3(依附) depend on

加 jiā [动] 1(相加) ▷2加2等于4。 Èr jiā èr děngyú sì. Two plus two is four. 2(增加) increase 3(添加) add

加工 jiāgōng [动] 1(制作) process 2(完善) polish

加拿大 Jiānádà [名] Canada

加强 jiāqiáng [动] strengthen

加油 jiāyóu [动] 1(加燃料) refuel 2(加劲儿) make more effort ▷快, 加油! Kuài, jiāyóu! Come on, come on!

夹 jiā I [动] 1(钳) get hold of 2(携带) carry ... under one's arm 3(限制) ▷两边高楼夹着一条狭窄的街道。 Liǎngbiān gāolóu jiāzhe yī tiáo xiázhǎi de jiēdào. A narrow street hemmed in by tall buildings on either side. 4(带) mix ... with II [名] folder

家 jiā I [名] 1(家庭) family 2(住所) home 3(学派) school of thought 4(指人) ▶船家 chuánjiā boatman ▶农家 nóngjiā peasant ▶专家 zhuānjiā expert II [形] 1(饲养的) domestic ▶家畜 jiāchù domestic animal 2(嫡亲的) ▷家兄 jiāxiōng elder brother III [量] ▷一家公司 yī jiā gōngsī a company ▷两家人 liǎng jiā rén two families

measure word, used for families, companies, banks, factories, restaurants, hotels etc.

家伙 jiāhuo [名] 1(工具) tool 2(武器) weapon 3(人) guy

家具 jiājù [名] furniture

家庭 jiātíng [名] family

家务 jiāwù [名] housework

家乡 jiāxiāng [名] hometown

家长 jiāzhǎng [名] 1(一家之长) head of the family 2(父母) parent

假 jiǎ I [形] 1(虚伪) false 2(不真) artificial ▶假发 jiǎfà wig ▶假话 jiǎhuà lie II [连] if ▶假如 jiǎrú if

→ *see also*/另见 jià

假如 jiǎrú [连] if

假设 jiǎshè I [动] suppose II [名] hypothesis

假装 jiǎzhuāng [动] pretend

价 jià [名] **1** (价格) price ▸物价 wùjià price **2** (价值) value

价格 jiàgé [名] price

价钱 jiàqin [名] price

价值 jiàzhí [名] value

驾 jià I [动] **1** (驾驭) harness **2** (驾驶) drive II [代] (敬) ▸劳驾 láojià excuse me

驾驶 jiàshǐ [动] steer

驾照 jiàzhào [名] driving licence (英), driver's license (美)

架 jià I [名] **1** (架子) frame ▸书架 shūjià bookshelf ▸脚手架 jiǎoshǒujià scaffolding **2** (指行为) ▸吵架 chǎojià quarrel ▸打架 dǎjià fight II [动] **1** (撑起) support **2** (招架) ward ... off **3** (绑架) kidnap **4** (搀扶) support ... under the arm III [量] ▸5架飞机 wǔ jià fēijī five planes ▸一架钢琴 yī jià gāngqín a piano

　measure word, used for pianos, aircrafts, machines etc.

假 jià [名] holiday ▸暑假 shǔjià summer holiday ▸病假 bìngjià sick leave

→ *see also*/另见 jiǎ

假条 jiàtiáo [名] note

尖 jiān I [形] **1** (锐利) pointed **2** (指声音) shrill **3** (敏锐) sensitive **4** (吝啬) stingy **5** (尖刻) biting II [名] **1** (尖端) tip ▸笔尖 bǐjiān pen tip **2** (精华) the best

尖锐 jiānruì [形] **1** (锋利) sharp **2** (敏锐) penetrating **3** (刺耳) shrill

坚 jiān I [形] hard II [名] stronghold III [副] firmly ▸坚信 jiānxìn firmly believe

坚持 jiānchí [动] go on

坚定 jiāndìng [形] steadfast

坚决 jiānjué [副] resolutely

坚强 jiānqiáng [形] strong

坚硬 jiānyìng [形] hard

间 jiān I [介] between ▸课间 kèjiān between lessons II [名] **1** (范围) ▸晚间 wǎnjiān in the evening ▸田间 tiánjiān field **2** (屋子) room ▸房间 fángjiān room ▸洗手间 xǐshǒujiān toilet III [量] ▸两间客厅 liǎng jiān kètīng two living rooms ▸一间病房 yī jiān bìngfáng one ward

　measure word, used for rooms, lounges, hospital wards etc.

肩 jiān *see below*/见下文

肩膀 jiānbǎng [名] shoulder

艰 jiān [形] difficult ▸艰辛 jiānxīn hardship

艰巨 jiānjù [形] formidable

艰苦 jiānkǔ [形] harsh

艰难 jiānnán [形] hard

监 jiān I [动] supervise ▶监视 jiānshì keep watch II [名] 1 (监狱) prison ▶探监 tànjiān visit a prison 2 (负责人) inspector ▶总监 zǒngjiān chief-inspector

监督 jiāndū [动] supervise

监狱 jiānyù [名] prison

拣 jiǎn [动] choose

俭 jiǎn [形] frugal

俭朴 jiǎnpǔ [形] economical

捡 jiǎn [动] pick ... up

检 jiǎn [动] 1 (检查) examine ▶体检 tǐjiǎn medical examination 2 (检点) show restraint

检查 jiǎnchá I [动] examine II [名] self-criticism

减 jiǎn [动] 1 (减去) subtract 2 (减少) reduce 3 (降低) decrease ▶减退 jiǎntuì fail

减肥 jiǎnféi [动] slim

减轻 jiǎnqīng [动] reduce

减少 jiǎnshǎo [动] reduce

剪 jiǎn I [名] scissors (PL) II [动] 1 (铰) cut 2 (除去) eliminate

剪刀 jiǎndāo [名] scissors (PL)

简 jiǎn I [形] simple II [动] simplify ▶简化 jiǎnhuà simplify

简单 jiǎndān [形] 1 (不复杂) simple 2 (草率) casual 3 (平凡) ▷这孩子能说两门外语，真不简单。 Zhè háizi néng shuō liǎng mén wàiyǔ, zhēn bù jiǎndān. It is quite extraordinary that this child can speak two foreign languages.

简体字 jiǎntǐzì [名] simplified characters (PL)

简体字 jiǎntǐzì

简体字 jiǎntǐzì (simplified characters) are the type of Chinese characters used today throughout Mainland China, and mostly derive from the PRC government's efforts during the 1950s and 60s to make the script more accessible and improve literacy. The alternative and older form of the script, known as complex or traditional characters, 繁体字 fántǐzì, is used predominantly in Taiwan, Hong Kong and many overseas Chinese communities. The two systems are closely related and if you have learnt one then, with a little effort, the other form should not pose too many problems!

见 jiàn I [动] 1 (看到) see ▶罕见 hǎnjiàn rare 2 (接触) come into contact with ▷汽油见火就着。 Qìyóu jiàn huǒ jiù zháo. Petrol ignites on contact with a flame. 3 (看得出) be visible ▶见效 jiànxiào take effect 4 (参照) see ▷见上图 jiàn shàngtú see the above diagram 5 (会见)

meet ▸接见 jiējiàn receive **II** [名] opinion ▸偏见 piānjiàn prejudice **III** [助动] (书) ▷请见谅。 Qǐng jiànliàng. Please excuse me.

见面 jiànmiàn [动] meet

件 jiàn **I** [量] item ▷一件衣服 yī jiàn yīfu an item of clothing ▷两件事 liǎng jiàn shì two things **II** [名] correspondence ▷急件 jíjiàn urgent letter

建 jiàn [动] **1** (建造) build **2** (建立) found **3** (提出) propose ▸建议 jiànyì propose

建立 jiànlì [动] establish

建设 jiànshè [动] build

建议 jiànyì [动] propose

建筑 jiànzhù **I** [动] build **II** [名] building

建筑师 jiànzhùshī [名] architect

健 jiàn **I** [形] ▸强健 qiángjiàn strong and healthy ▸健全 jiànquán sound **II** [动] **1** (使强健) strengthen ▸健身 jiànshēn keep fit **2** (善于) be good at ▸健谈 jiàntán be good at small-talk

健康 jiànkāng [形] healthy

健忘 jiànwàng [形] forgetful

渐 jiàn [副] gradually

渐渐 jiànjiàn [副] gradually

键 jiàn [名] key

键盘 jiànpán [名] keyboard

箭 jiàn [名] arrow

江 jiāng [名] **1** (大河) river **2** (长江) Yangtze

将 jiāng **I** [副] ▷他将成为一名医生。 Tā jiāng chéngwéi yī míng yīshēng. He is going to become a doctor. **II** [动] **1** (下棋用语) check **2** (激) egg ... on **III** [介] with ▷请将车停在路边。 Qǐng jiāng chē tíng zài lùbiān. Please stop the car by the side of the road.

将军 jiāngjūn [名] general

将来 jiānglái [名] future

将要 jiāngyào [副] ▷她将要做妈妈了。 Tā jiāngyào zuò māma le. She is going to be a mother.

姜 jiāng [名] ginger

讲 jiǎng [动] **1** (说) speak **2** (解释) explain **3** (谈) discuss **4** (讲求) emphasize ▷讲卫生 jiǎng wèishēng pay attention to hygiene

讲话 jiǎnghuà [动] **1** (说话) speak **2** (发言) address

讲台 jiǎngtái [名] dais

讲座 jiǎngzuò [名] course of lectures

奖 jiǎng **I** [动] encourage ▸夸奖 kuājiǎng praise **II** [名] award

奖金 jiǎngjīn [名] bonus

奖励 jiǎnglì [动] encourage and reward

奖品 jiǎngpǐn [名] trophy

奖学金 jiǎngxuéjīn [名] scholarship

降 jiàng [动] **1** (落下) drop **2** (降低)

reduce ▶降价 jiàngjià reduce prices

降低 jiàngdī [动] reduce

降落 jiàngluò [动] land

酱 jiàng I [名] 1 (调味品) soya bean (英) 或 soybean (美) paste 2 (糊状食品) paste ▶果酱 guǒjiàng jam II [形] ▶酱肘子 jiàngzhǒuzi knuckle of pork in soy sauce

酱油 jiàngyóu [名] soy sauce

交 jiāo I [动] 1 (交出) hand ... in 2 (付给) pay 3 (托付) entrust 4 (结交) associate with ▶交友 jiāoyǒu make friends II [名] (交情) friendship ▶深交 shēnjiāo deep friendship

交叉 jiāochā I [动] 1 (相交) intersect 2 (穿插) alternate II [形] overlapping

交换 jiāohuàn [动] exchange

交际 jiāojì [动] socialize

交警 jiāojǐng [名] traffic police

交流 jiāoliú [动] exchange

交谈 jiāotán [动] talk

交通 jiāotōng [名] traffic

交往 jiāowǎng [动] have contact

交易 jiāoyì I [动] trade II [名] transaction

郊 jiāo [名] suburbs (PL) ▶郊外 jiāowài outskirts (PL)

郊区 jiāoqū [名] suburbs (PL)

骄 jiāo [形] 1 (骄傲) arrogant ▶骄气 jiāoqì arrogance 2 (书) (猛烈) fierce

骄傲 jiāo'ào I [形] 1 (傲慢) arrogant 2 (自豪) proud II [名] pride

胶 jiāo I [名] 1 (黏性物质) glue ▶万能胶 wànnéngjiāo all-purpose glue 2 (橡胶) rubber ▶胶鞋 jiāoxié rubber boots (PL) II [动] glue

胶卷 jiāojuǎn [名] film

胶囊 jiāonáng [名] capsule

教 jiāo [动] teach
→ see also/另见 jiào

焦 jiāo [形] 1 (成黄黑色) burnt 2 (着急) agitated ▶心焦 xīnjiāo feel agitated

焦急 jiāojí [形] anxious

角 jiǎo [名] 1 (指动物) horn 2 (军号) bugle 3 (数) angle ▶直角 zhíjiǎo right angle 4 (角落) corner ▶墙角 qiángjiǎo corner of a wall

角度 jiǎodù [名] 1 (数) angle 2 (视角) point of view

角落 jiǎoluò [名] corner

饺 jiǎo [名] Chinese dumpling ▶水饺 shuǐjiǎo Chinese dumpling

饺子 jiǎozi [名] dumpling

饺子 jiǎozi

Chinese dumplings, wrapped with a thin doughy skin, are usually filled with minced meat and mixed vegetables. They are normally steamed or boiled, and served with vinegar, soy sauce and other spices.

脚 jiǎo [名] **1** (指人, 动物) foot ▶脚印 jiǎoyìn footprint **2** (指物体) base ▶山脚 shānjiǎo foot of a mountain

搅 jiǎo [动] **1** (搅拌) stir **2** (混杂) mix **3** (搅扰) disturb

搅拌 jiǎobàn [动] stir

叫 jiào [动] **1** (喊叫) shout **2** (招呼) call **3** (菜, 车) order **4** (称为) be called **5** (吩咐) order

叫喊 jiàohǎn [动] yell

叫做 jiàozuò [动] be called

较 jiào [动] **1** (比较) compare ▶较量 jiàoliàng test one's strength **2** (书) (计较) dispute

教 jiào I [动] teach ▶教导 jiàodǎo instruct II [名] religion
→ see also/另见 jiāo

教材 jiàocái [名] teaching materials (PL)

教科书 jiàokēshū [名] textbook

教练 jiàoliàn [名] coach

教师 jiàoshī [名] teacher

教室 jiàoshì [名] classroom

教授 jiàoshòu I [名] professor II [动] lecture in

教学 jiàoxué [名] **1** (知识传授) teaching **2** (教与学) teaching and study

教训 jiàoxun I [名] lesson II [动] teach ... a lesson

教育 jiàoyù I [名] education II [动] educate

教员 jiàoyuán [名] teacher

阶 jiē [名] **1** (台阶) step **2** (官阶) rank

阶段 jiēduàn [名] stage

阶级 jiējí [名] class

结 jiē [动] bear ▶结果 jiéguǒ bear fruit
→ see also/另见 jié

结实 jiēshi [形] **1** (坚固耐用) sturdy **2** (健壮) strong

接 jiē [动] **1** (靠近) draw near **2** (连接) connect **3** (托住) catch **4** (接收) receive ▶接电话 jiē diànhuà answer the phone **5** (迎接) meet **6** (接替) take over

接触 jiēchù [动] (交往) come into contact with

接待 jiēdài [动] receive

接到 jiēdào [动] receive

接见 jiējiàn [动] have an interview with

接近 jiējìn I [动] approach II [形] approachable

接受 jiēshòu [动] accept

接着 jiēzhe [动] **1** (用手接) catch **2** (紧跟着) follow

街 jiē [名] **1** (街道) street **2** (方) (集市) market

街道 jiēdào [名] **1** (马路) street **2** (社区) neighbourhood (英), neighborhood (美)

节 jié I [名] **1** (连接处) joint **2** (段

落) paragraph **3** (节日) festival ▶圣诞节 Shèngdàn Jié Christmas **4** (事项) item ▶细节 xìjié details (PL) **5** (节操) moral fibre (英) 或 fiber (美) ▶气节 qìjié integrity **II** [动] **1** (节约) save **2** (删节) abridge **III** [量] **1** (指部分) section ▷一节管子 yī jié guǎnzi a length of pipe **2** ▷三节课 sān jié kè three classes ▷四节车厢 sì jié chēxiāng four carriages ▷两节电池 liǎng jié diànchí two batteries measure word, used for school classes, carriages, batteries etc.

节目 jiémù [名] programme (英), program (美)

节拍 jiépāi [名] beat

节日 jiérì [名] festival

节省 jiéshěng [动] conserve

节约 jiéyuē [动] save

结 jié **I** [动] **1** (编织) tie ▶结网 jiéwǎng weave a net **2** (结合) unite **3** (凝聚) freeze ▶结冰 jiébīng ice up **4** (了结) settle up ▶结账 jiézhàng settle up **II** [名] **1** (绳扣) knot ▶活结 huójié slip-knot **2** (字据) written undertaking **3** (生理) node → *see also*/另见 jiē

结构 jiégòu [名] composition

结果 jiéguǒ **I** [名] result **II** [副] in the end

结合 jiéhé [动] **1** (联系) combine **2** (结为夫妇) become husband and wife

结婚 jiéhūn [动] get married

结论 jiélùn [名] conclusion

结束 jiéshù [动] end

捷 jié **I** [形] quick ▶敏捷 mǐnjié nimble **II** [名] victory

捷径 jiéjìng [名] short cut

姐 jiě [名] elder sister

姐姐 jiějie [名] elder sister

姐妹 jiěmèi [名] sisters (PL)

解 jiě [动] **1** (分开) divide ▶解剖 jiěpōu dissect **2** (解开) untie **3** (解除) relieve **4** (解答) answer ▶解题 jiětí solve a problem **5** (理解) understand

解答 jiědá [动] answer

解放 jiěfàng [动] liberate

解雇 jiěgù [动] fire

解决 jiějué [动] **1** (处理) resolve **2** (消灭) annihilate

解释 jiěshì [动] explain

介 jiè [动] be situated between

介绍 jièshào [动] **1** (使相识) introduce **2** (推荐) sponsor **3** (使了解) give an introduction to

届 jiè **I** [动] fall due ▶届期 jièqī at the appointed time **II** [量] **1** (指开始上学的学年) year ▷82届毕业生 bā èr jiè bìyèshēng the class of '82 **2** (指大会, 首脑) ▷第10届奥运会 dì shí jiè Àoyùnhuì the tenth Olympic Games ▷第26届总统 dì èrshíliù jiè zǒngtǒng the twenty-sixth president

measure word, used for conferences, sports events, trade fairs, terms of office etc.

界 jiè [名] **1** (界限) boundary (PL) **2** (阶层) circles (PL) **3** (范围) range **4** (类别) category

借 jiè [动] **1** (借入) borrow **2** (借出) lend **3** (假托) use ... as a means of **4** (凭借) make use of

借口 jièkǒu I [动] use ... as an excuse II [名] excuse

借助 jièzhù [动] enlist the help of

斤 jīn [量] *unit of weight, equal to 500 grams*

今 jīn I [形] **1** (现在的) present **2** (当前的) current II [名] today

今后 jīnhòu [副] from now on

今年 jīnnián [名] this year

今天 jīntiān [名] today

金 jīn I [名] **1** (化) gold **2** (金属) metal ▷五金 wǔjīn hardware **3** (钱) money II [形] golden ▷金发 jīnfà blonde hair

金融 jīnróng [名] finance

金属 jīnshǔ [名] metal

金子 jīnzi [名] gold

仅 jǐn [副] only

仅仅 jǐnjǐn [副] just

尽 jǐn I [副] **1** (尽量) as far as possible ▷尽快 jǐnkuài as early as possible **2** (最) most **3** (表示继续) constantly II [动] **1** (不超过)

take no more than **2** (考虑在先) give priority to
→ *see also*/另见 jìn

尽管 jǐnguǎn I [副] without reserve ▷有话尽管说。 Yǒu huà jǐnguǎn shuō. If there's something you'd like to say please don't hold back. II [连] even though

尽量 jǐnliàng [副] to the best of one's ability

尽早 jǐnzǎo [副] as soon as possible

紧 jǐn I [形] **1** (不松) tight **2** (牢固) secure **3** (接近) close **4** (急迫) pressing **5** (严格) strict **6** (拮据) short of money II [动] tighten

紧急 jǐnjí [形] urgent

紧张 jǐnzhāng [形] **1** (激烈) intense **2** (不安) nervous **3** (不足) in short supply

尽 jìn I [动] **1** (完) exhaust **2** (达到极限) go to extremes **3** (充分发挥) use ... to the full **4** (努力完成) strive to accomplish II [形] complete
→ *see also*/另见 jǐn

尽力 jìnlì [动] try one's hardest

尽量 jìnliàng [动] do all one can

进 jìn [动] **1** (前进) advance **2** (进入) enter **3** (接纳) bring ... in ▷进货 jìnhuò stock up **4** (吃食) eat **5** (呈上) submit **6** (攻进) enter ▷进球 jìnqiú score a goal

进步 jìnbù I [动] improve II [形] advanced

进攻 jìngōng [动] attack

进化 jìnhuà [动] evolve

进口 jìnkǒu [动] import

近来 jìnlái [动] come in

进去 jìnqù [动] enter

进入 jìnrù [动] 1 (走进) enter 2 (到了) reach 3 (到位) get inside

进行 jìnxíng [动] carry ... out

进修 jìnxiū [动] take a refresher course

近 jìn [形] 1 (不远) near ▶近日 jìnrì recently 2 (接近) close 3 (亲近) close to

近来 jìnlái [副] recently

近视 jìnshì [形] short-sighted (英), near-sighted (美)

劲 jìn [名] 1 (力气) strength 2 (情绪) spirit 3 (态度) manner 4 (趣味) fun

禁 jìn I [动] 1 (禁止) forbid 2 (监禁) imprison ▶禁闭 jìnbì lock ... up II [名] taboo
→ see also / 另见 jīn

禁止 jìnzhǐ [动] forbid

京 jīng [名] 1 (首都) capital 2 (北京) Beijing

京剧 jīngjù [名] Beijing opera

京剧 jīngjù

京剧 jīngjù is a form of Chinese traditional opera which enjoys a history of over two hundred years, and is regarded as one of the most important Chinese cultural heritages. The performances combine singing, acting, music, dialogue, dancing and acrobatics. Different roles follow different patterns of acting, which are all rather symbolic, suggestive and exaggerated.

经 jīng I [名] 1 (经线) warp 2 (指中医) channels (PL) 3 (经度) longitude 4 (经典) scripture ▶佛经 fójīng Buddhist sutra II [动] 1 (经营) run ▶经商 jīngshāng be in business 2 (经受) endure 3 (经过) ▶途经西安 tújīng Xī'ān go via Xi'an III [形] regular

经常 jīngcháng I [形] day-to-day II [副] often

经过 jīngguò I [动] 1 (通过) pass 2 (延续) ▶经过3年的恋爱，他们终于结婚了。 Jīngguò sān nián de liàn'ài, tāmen zhōngyú jiéhūn le. Having been together for three years, they finally got married. 3 (经历) ▶企业经过裁员缩减了经费开支。 Qǐyè jīngguò cáiyuán suōjiǎn le jīngfèi kāizhī. Business expenditure was reduced through staff cutbacks. II [名] course

经济 jīngjì I [名] 1 (社会生产关系) economy 2 (个人财政状况) financial situation II [形] 1 (有关国民经济) economic 2 (实惠) economical ▶经济舱 jīngjìcāng economy-class cabin

经理 jīnglǐ [名] manager

经历 jīnglì [动] experience

经验 jīngyàn [名] experience

惊 jīng [动] **1** (紧张) start **2** (惊动) startle

惊奇 jīngqí [形] surprised

惊人 jīngrén [形] amazing

惊喜 jīngxǐ [动] be pleasantly surprised

惊讶 jīngyà [形] astonished

精 jīng I [形] **1** (经挑选的) refined ▶精兵 jīngbīng crack troops **2** (完美) excellent **3** (细密) precise **4** (心细) sharp ▶精明 jīngmíng shrewd **5** (精通) skilled II [名] **1** (精华) essence ▶酒精 jiǔjīng alcohol **2** (精力) energy III [副] (方) extremely

精彩 jīngcǎi [形] wonderful

精力 jīnglì [名] energy

精确 jīngquè [形] precise

精神 jīngshén [名] **1** (主观世界) mind **2** (宗旨) gist

精神 jīngshen [名] energy II [形] energetic

精通 jīngtōng [动] be proficient in

井 jǐng I [名] **1** (用于取水) well **2** (井状物) ▶天井 tiānjǐng skylight ▶矿井 kuàngjǐng mine shaft II [形] neat

景 jǐng I [名] **1** (风景) scenery **2** (情形) situation ▶背景 bèijǐng background **3** (布景) scene ▶外景 wàijǐng outdoor scene II [动] admire

景点 jǐngdiǎn [名] scenic spot

景色 jǐngsè [名] scenery

警 jǐng I [形] alert ▶警惕 jǐngtì on the alert II [动] **1** (使警觉) warn **2** (戒备) be on the alert III [名] **1** (危急) alarm ▶报警 bàojǐng raise the alarm **2** (警察) police ▶巡警 xúnjǐng an officer on the beat

警报 jǐngbào [名] alarm

警察 jǐngchá [名] police

警告 jǐnggào [动] warn

竞 jìng [动] compete

竞赛 jìngsài [名] competition

竞争 jìngzhēng [动] compete

敬 jìng I [动] **1** (尊重) respect **2** (恭敬地给) offer II [形] respectful

敬爱 jìng'ài [动] revere

敬礼 jìnglǐ [动] salute

静 jìng [形] **1** (不动) still **2** (无声) quiet

镜 jìng [名] **1** (镜子) mirror **2** (指光学器具) lens ▶眼镜 yǎnjìng glasses

镜子 jìngzi [名] mirror

纠 jiū [动] **1** (缠绕) entangle **2** (集合) assemble **3** (督察) supervise **4** (改正) correct

纠正 jiūzhèng [动] correct

究 jiū I [动] investigate II [副] actually

究竟 jiūjìng I [名] outcome II [副] actually

九 jiǔ [数] nine

九月 jiǔyuè [名] September

久 jiǔ [形] 1 (时间长) long 2 (时间长短) long

玖 jiǔ [数] nine
This is the complex character for 'nine', which is mainly used in banks, on receipts etc. to prevent mistakes and forgery.

酒 jiǔ [名] alcohol ▶葡萄酒 pútaojiǔ wine ▶敬酒 jìngjiǔ propose a toast

旧 jiù I [形] 1 (过时) old 2 (陈旧) used II [名] old friend

救 jiù [动] save
救护车 jiùhùchē [名] ambulance
救命 jiùmìng [动] save a life ▷救命啊！ Jiùmìng a! Help!

就 jiù I [动] 1 (靠近) move close to 2 (开始) take ... up 3 (完成) accomplish 4 (趁) take the opportunity 5 (搭配着吃) eat ... with II [副] 1 (强调时间短) shortly 2 (早已) already 3 (表示紧接着) as soon as 4 (表示条件关系) then 5 (强调数量多) as much as 6 (仅仅) only 7 (原本) already 8 (表示坚决) simply 9 (强调事实) exactly 10 (表示容忍) even though III [连] even if IV [介] on
就是 jiùshì I [副] 1 (表示赞同)

exactly 2 (表示坚决) still 3 (表示强调) really 4 (确定范围) only II [助] ▷你干就是了, 没人说你。 Nǐ gàn jiùshì le, méi rén shuō nǐ. Just go ahead and do it – no one will blame you! III [连] even if
就算 jiùsuàn [连] even if

舅 jiù [名] 1 (舅父) uncle 2 (妻子的弟兄) brother-in-law
舅舅 jiùjiu [名] uncle

居 jū I [动] 1 (住) live 2 (在) be II [名] house
居住 jūzhù [动] live

局 jú I [名] 1 (棋盘) chessboard 2 (次) game ▶平局 píngjú a draw 3 (形势) situation ▶时局 shíjú current political situation 4 (聚会) gathering ▶饭局 fànjú dinner party 5 (圈套) ruse ▶骗局 piànjú fraud 6 (部分) part 7 (机关部门) department 8 (业务机构) office II [量] set ▷我赢了这局棋。 Wǒ yíng le zhè jú qí. I won the chess game.
局长 júzhǎng [名] director

橘 jú [名] tangerine
橘子 júzi [名] orange ▷橘子汁 júzi zhī orange juice

举 jǔ I [动] 1 (往上托) raise ▶举重 jǔzhòng weightlifting 2 (兴起) mobilize ▶举兵 jǔbīng dispatch troops 3 (选举) elect 4 (提出) cite ▶举例 jǔlì cite an example II [名] act III [形] (书) whole

举办 jǔbàn [动] hold

举行 jǔxíng [动] hold

巨 jù [形] huge

巨大 jùdà [形] huge

巨人 jùrén [名] giant

句 jù I [名] sentence II [量] ▷ 说几句话 shuō jǐ jù huà say a few words ▷ 写两句诗 xiě liǎng jù shī write two lines of verse measure word, used for sentences, and lines in a speech, song or poem

句子 jùzi [名] sentence

拒 jù [动] 1 (抵抗) resist 2 (拒绝) refuse

拒绝 jùjué [动] refuse

具 jù I [动] have II [名] utensil ▶ 玩具 wánjù toy

具备 jùbèi [动] have

具体 jùtǐ [形] 1 (明确) detailed 2 (特定) particular

具有 jùyǒu [动] have

俱 jù [副] ▶ 面面俱到 miàn miàn jù dào attend to each and every aspect

俱乐部 jùlèbù [名] club

剧 jù I [名] drama ▶ 喜剧 xǐjù comedy II [形] severe ▶ 剧变 jùbiàn dramatic change

剧场 jùchǎng [名] theatre (英), theater (美)

剧烈 jùliè [形] severe

剧院 jùyuàn [名] 1 (剧场) theatre (英), theater (美) 2 (剧团) company

据 jù I [动] 1 (占据) occupy ▶ 盘据 pánjù forcibly occupy 2 (凭借) rely on ▶ 据点 jùdiǎn stronghold II [介] according to III [名] evidence ▶ 收据 shōujù receipt

据说 jùshuō [动] be said

距 jù [名] distance

距离 jùlí [动] be at a distance from

锯 jù I [名] saw II [动] saw

卷 juǎn I [动] 1 (裹成筒形) roll ... up 2 (撮起) sweep ... up 3 (喻) (牵涉) be swept up in II [名] roll III [量] roll ▷ 一卷卫生纸 yī juǎn wèishēngzhǐ a roll of toilet paper

决 jué I [动] 1 (决定) decide 2 (执行死刑) execute 3 (决口) burst 4 (定胜负) decide on a result ▶ 决战 juézhàn decisive battle II [副] under any circumstances III [形] decisive ▶ 果决 guǒjué resolute

决定 juédìng [动] 1 (打定主意) decide 2 (表示条件关系) determine

决心 juéxīn [名] determination

觉 jué I [动] 1 (感觉) feel 2 (觉悟) become aware of II [名] sense ▶ 知觉 zhījué consciousness

觉得 juéde [动] 1 (感到) feel 2 (认为) think

觉悟 juéwù [名] awareness

绝 jué I [动] 1 (断绝) cut ... off ▶ 隔绝 géjué isolate 2 (穷尽) exhaust

3 (无后代) have no descendants **4** (死) die **II** [形] **1** (不通) hopeless ▶绝路 juélù blind alley **2** (高超) superb **III** [副] **1** (最) extremely ▶绝密 juémì top secret **2** (绝对) absolutely

绝对 juéduì **I** [形] absolute **II** [副] absolutely

绝望 juéwàng [动] feel desperate

军 jūn **I** [名] **1** (军队) army ▶参军 cānjūn enlist **2** (指军队编制单位) regiment **3** (指集体) forces (PL) **II** [形] military ▶军费 jūnfèi military expenditure

军队 jūnduì [名] troops (PL)

军官 jūnguān [名] officer

军人 jūnrén [名] soldier

军事 jūnshì [名] military affairs (PL)

咖 kā see below/见下文
→ see also/另见 gā

咖啡 kāfēi [名] coffee ▷速溶咖啡 sùróng kāfēi instant coffee

卡 kǎ **I** [量] (卡路里) calorie **II** [名] (卡片) card

卡车 kǎchē [名] lorry (英), truck (美)

卡拉OK kǎlā'ōukèi [名] karaoke

卡通 kǎtōng [名] cartoon

开 kāi [动] **1** (打开) open ▶开门 kāimén open the door **2** (银行, 商店) be open **3** (绽放) bloom **4** (松开) come undone **5** (驾驶) drive ▶开汽车 kāi qìchē drive a car **6** (办) open ... up ▶开公司 kāi gōngsī start up a business

7(开始) start ▶开课 kāikè give a course ▶开学 kāixué start school ▶开演 kāiyǎn start the show **8**(举行) hold ▶开会 kāihuì have a meeting **9**(写出) write ... out **10**(灯, 电器, 煤气) turn on ▷开灯 kāi dēng turn on the light **11**(沸腾) boil ▷水刚开。 Shuǐ gāng kāi. The water was just boiled. **12**(饭) serve ▷开饭了。 Kāi fàn le. Dinner is ready.

开刀 kāidāo [动] operate on

开放 kāifàng [动] **1**(解禁) open ▷对外开放政策 duìwài kāifàng zhèngcè the opening-up policy **2**(开朗) be open-minded

开关 kāiguān [名] switch

开户 kāihù [动] open an account

开会 kāihuì [动] have a meeting

开课 kāikè [动] **1**(开学) start **2**(授课) teach a course

开朗 kāilǎng [形] (指性格) cheerful

开明 kāimíng [形] enlightened

开幕 kāimù [动] **1**(指演出) start **2**(指会) open

开辟 kāipì [动] **1**(开通) open ... up **2**(开发) develop

开始 kāishǐ **I**[动] start, begin **II**[名] beginning

开水 kāishuǐ [名] boiling water

开头 kāitóu **I**[动] begin **II**[名] beginning

开玩笑 kāi wánxiào [动] joke ▷别拿我开玩笑。 Bié ná wǒ kāi wánxiào. Don't make fun of me.

开心 kāixīn [形] happy

开展 kāizhǎn [动] launch

开支 kāizhī [动] spend

刊 kān **I**[动] (出版) publish **II**[名] periodical ▶报刊 bàokān the press

刊登 kāndēng [动] publish

刊物 kānwù [名] periodical

看 kān [动] **1**(照料) look after ▶看家 kānjiā look after the house **2**(看管) watch over
→ see also/另见 kàn

砍 kǎn [动] **1**(劈) chop **2**(减) cut

看 kàn [动] **1**(观看) look at ▶看到 kàndào see ▷看电视 kàn diànshì watch TV **2**(阅读) read **3**(认为) think ▶看成 kànchéng consider **4**(拜访) visit ▶看望 kànwàng visit **5**(照料) look after **6**(对待) treat **7**(诊治) treat ▶看病 kànbìng see a doctor **8**(取决于) depend on
→ see also/另见 kān

看不起 kàn bu qǐ [动] look down on

看待 kàndài [动] regard ▷当朋友看待 dāng péngyou kàndài regard as a friend

看法 kànfǎ [名] opinion

看好 kànhǎo [动] look good

看见 kànjiàn [动] see

看来 kànlái [动] seem

康 kāng [形] (健康) healthy ▶康复 kāngfù recover

慷 kāng *see below*/见下文

慷慨 kāngkǎi [形] (大方) generous

扛 káng [动] shoulder

抗 kàng [动] 1 (抵抗) resist 2 (抗拒) refuse

抗议 kàngyì [动] protest

考 kǎo [动] 1 (测试) have an exam ▶考上 kǎoshang pass the entrance exam 2 (检查) check ▶考察 kǎochá investigate

考虑 kǎolù [动] consider

考试 kǎoshì [动] sit an exam

考验 kǎoyàn [动] test

拷 kǎo [动] (拷贝) copy

烤 kǎo [动] 1 (指东西) roast ▶烤鸭 kǎoyā 2 (指人体) warm oneself ▶烤火 kǎohuǒ warm oneself by a fire

靠 kào [动] 1 (倚) lean 2 (近) keep to 3 (依赖) rely on 4 (信赖) trust

科 kē [名] 1 (指学术) discipline ▶文科 wénkē humanities (PL) 2 (指部门) department

科技 kējì [名] science and technology

科目 kēmù [名] subject

科学 kēxué I [名] science II [形] scientific

科学家 kēxuéjiā [名] scientist

科研 kēyán [名] scientific research

棵 kē [量] ▷一棵水仙 yī kē shuǐxiān a narcissus ▷三百棵

树 sānbǎi kē shù three hundred trees

measure word, used for plants, trees and vegetables

颗 kē [量] ▷一颗种子 yī kē zhǒngzi a seed ▷一颗汗珠 yī kē hànzhū a bead of sweat

measure word, used for small, round objects

磕 kē [动] bump

壳 ké [名] shell

咳 ké [动] cough

咳嗽 késou [动] cough

可 kě I [动] (同意) approve II [助动] 1 (可以) can 2 (值得) III [连] but

可爱 kě'ài [形] adorable

可悲 kěbēi [形] lamentable

可靠 kěkào [形] reliable

可乐 kělè [名] Coke®

可怜 kělián I [形] pitiful II [动] pity

可能 kěnéng I [形] possible II [副] maybe III [名] possibility ▶可能性 kěnéngxìng possibility

可怕 kěpà [形] frightening

可是 kěshì [连] but ▷这个小镇不大，可是很热闹。 Zhè gè xiǎozhèn bù dà, kěshì hěn rènào. This is a small town, but it's very lively.

可惜 kěxī I [形] regrettable II [副] regrettably

可笑 kěxiào [形] 1 (令人耻笑)

ridiculous **2**(引人发笑) funny

可以 kěyǐ I [助动] **1**(能够) can **2**(有权) may II [形] (不坏) not bad

可以 kěyǐ, 能 néng, and 会 huì can all be used to express ability and are sometimes used interchangeably. Both 可以 kěyǐ and 能 néng can express being able to do something because you have been granted permission, e.g. 你可以/能借我的照相机 nǐ kěyǐ/néng jiè wǒ de zhàoxiàngjī (you may/can borrow my camera). Strictly, 能 néng should be used to express physical ability, e.g. 我能跑得很快 wǒ néng pǎo de hěn kuài (I can run very fast), while 会 huì should express a learned ability, e.g. 我会说法语 wǒ huì shuō Fǎyǔ (I can speak French).

渴 kě I [形] thirsty ▶渴望 kěwàng long for II [副] eagerly

克 kè I [动] **1**(克制) restrain **2**(战胜) overcome II [量] gram

克服 kèfú [动] (战胜) overcome

克隆 kèlóng [动] clone

刻 kè I [动] engrave II [名] **1**(雕刻物品) engraving **2**(指十五分钟) quarter

刻苦 kèkǔ [形] hardworking

客 kè [名] **1**(客人) visitor ▶客厅 kètīng living room **2**(旅客) traveller (英), traveler (美) ▶客车 kèchē passenger train **3**(顾客) customer ▶客户 kèhù customer

客观 kèguān [形] objective

客气 kèqi I [形] polite II [动] be polite

客人 kèrén [名] guest

课 kè [名] **1**(学科) subject **2**(学时) class **3**(单元) lesson

课本 kèběn [名] textbook

课程 kèchéng [名] course ▶课程表 kèchéngbiǎo school timetable

课堂 kètáng [名] classroom

课题 kètí [名] (论题) topic

课文 kèwén [名] text

肯 kěn [助动] be willing

肯定 kěndìng I [动] confirm II [形] **1**(确定的) affirmative **2**(明确的) clear III [副] certainly

空 kōng I [形] empty ▶空虚 kōngxū empty II [名] sky ▶空中小姐 kōngzhōng xiǎojiě stewardess

→ see also/另见 kòng

空间 kōngjiān [名] space

空军 kōngjūn [名] air force

空调 kōngtiáo [名] air conditioner

空气 kōngqì [名] (大气) air

空前 kōngqián [形] unprecedented

孔 kǒng [名] hole

孔子 Kǒngzǐ [名] Confucius

孔子 Kǒngzǐ

孔子 Kǒngzǐ, Confucius, (trad. 551-479 BC) was a hugely influential thinker. A posthumous compilation of his sayings, 《论语》 Lúnyǔ, The Analects, is China's most important philosophical work, and was the key text on which much of the traditional Chinese education system was based.

恐 kǒng fear

恐怖 kǒngbù I [形] terrifying II [名] terror ▶恐怖主义 kǒngbù zhǔyì terrorism

恐龙 kǒnglóng [名] dinosaur

恐怕 kǒngpà [副] 1 (担心) fearfully 2 (大概) probably

空 kòng I [动] leave ... empty II [形] vacant ▶空白 kòngbái blank ▶空缺 kòngquē vacancy III [名] 1 (空间) space 2 (时间) free time ▶空儿 kòngr spare time ▶有空 yǒu kòng have free time
→ see also / 另见 kōng

控 kòng [动] 1 (控制) control 2 (控告) charge

控制 kòngzhì [动] control

口 kǒu I [名] 1 (嘴) mouth ▶口才 kǒucái eloquence ▶口吃 kǒuchī stammering ▶口红 kǒuhóng lipstick 2 (丁) ▶家口 jiākǒu family member ▶口味 kǒuwèi taste 3 (指容器) rim ▶瓶口 píngkǒu the mouth of a bottle 4 (指端口) ▶出口 chūkǒu exit ▶入口 rùkǒu entrance ▶窗口 chuāngkǒu window 5 (缝) split II [量] ▷我家有五口人。 Wǒ jiā yǒu wǔ kǒu rén. There are five people in my family.

measure word, used for the number of people in a family

口袋 kǒudài [名] bag

口号 kǒuhào [名] slogan

口气 kǒuqì [名] (语气) tone

口头 kǒutóu [名] 1 (嘴) word 2 (口语) ▷口头作文 kǒutóu zuòwén oral composition

口信 kǒuxìn [名] message

口音 kǒuyīn [名] (方音) accent

口语 kǒuyǔ [名] spoken language

扣 kòu I [动] 1 (拉紧) fasten 2 (朝下) put ... upside down 3 (抓) arrest ▶扣留 kòuliú arrest 4 (减) deduct ▶扣除 kòuchú II [名] button ▶扣子 kòuzi button

哭 kū [动] cry

苦 kǔ I [形] 1 (苦涩) bitter 2 (艰苦) hard II [动] (苦害) be hard on III [副] painstakingly ▶苦练 kǔliàn train hard IV [名] suffering ▶吃苦 chīkǔ bear hardships

苦难 kǔnàn I [名] hardship II [形] hard

苦恼 kǔnǎo [形] distressed

库存 kùcún [名] stock

裤 kù [名] trousers (PL) (英), pants (PL) (美) ▶裤子 kùzi trousers (PL) (英), pants (PL) (美)

夸 kuā [动] 1 (夸大) exaggerate 2 (夸奖) praise

夸奖 kuājiǎng [动] praise

夸张 kuāzhāng I [形] exaggerated II [名] hyperbole

垮 kuǎ [动] 1 (坍塌) collapse ▶垮台 kuǎtái collapse 2 (伤身) wear down

胯 kuà [名] hip

跨 kuà [动] 1 (迈步) step 2 (骑) mount 3 (超越) surpass ▶跨国 kuàguó transnational

会 kuài [名] accounting ▶财会 cáikuài finance and accounting → see also/另见 huì

会计 kuàijì [名] 1 (指工作) accounting 2 (指人员) accountant

块 kuài I [名] lump II [量] piece ▷一块蛋糕 yī kuài dàngāo a piece of cake ▷一块方糖 yī kuài fāngtáng a lump of sugar

快 kuài I [形] 1 (快速) 2 (赶快) 3 (灵敏) quick ▷他脑子快。 Tā nǎozi kuài. He's quick-witted. 4 (锋利) sharp 5 (直爽) straightforward ▶爽快 shuǎngkuài frank II [副] soon ▶快要 kuàiyào soon

快餐 kuàicān [名] fast food

快活 kuàihuo [形] delighted

快乐 kuàilè [形] happy

筷 kuài [名] chopsticks (PL) ▶筷子 kuàizi chopsticks (PL)

宽 kuān I [形] 1 (距离大) wide 2 (范围广) broad ▶宽敞 kuānchang spacious 3 (宽大) lenient ▶宽容 kuānróng tolerant II [名] width

宽带 kuāndài [名] broadband

款 kuǎn [名] 1 (项目) section 2 (钱) sum of money ▶现款 xiànkuǎn cash 3 (样式) style ▶款式 kuǎnshì style

狂 kuáng I [形] 1 (疯狂) crazy ▶发狂 fākuáng go crazy 2 (猛烈) violent ▶狂风 kuángfēng gale 3 (狂妄) arrogant 4 (狂热) wild II [副] wildly

旷 kuàng I [形] (空阔) spacious ▶旷野 kuàngyě wilderness II [动] neglect ▶旷课 kuàngkè play truant

况 kuàng [名] situation ▶状况 zhuàngkuàng condition

况且 kuàngqiě [连] besides

矿 kuàng [名] 1 (矿场) mine 2 (矿石) ore

框 kuàng I [名] 1 (框架) frame 2 (方框) box II [动] 1 (画圈) box 2 (口) (限制) limit

框架 kuàngjià [名] 1 (指建筑) frame 2 (指文书) framework

眶 kuàng [名] socket ▶眼眶

yǎnkuàng eye socket

亏 kuī I [动] 1 (亏损) lose 2 (欠缺) lack 3 (亏负) allow ... to suffer losses II [副] luckily ▷亏你把我叫醒，要不我就迟到了。 Kuī nǐ bǎ wǒ jiào xǐng, yào bù wǒ jiù chídào le. It's lucky you woke me up or I would have been late.

盔 kuī [名] helmet

葵 kuí see below/见下文

葵花 kuíhuā [名] sunflower

魁 kuí I [名] head ▷夺魁 duókuí win first place II [形] well-built ▷魁梧 kuíwú tall and sturdy

昆 kūn see below/见下文

昆虫 kūnchóng [名] insect

捆 kǔn I [动] tie ... up II [量] bundle ▷一捆书 yī kǔn shū a bundle of books

困 kùn I [动] 1 (困扰) be stricken 2 (限制) trap II [形] 1 (瞌睡) sleepy 2 (困难) difficult

困难 kùnnan [形] 1 (指事情) difficult ▷克服困难 kèfú kùnnan overcome difficulties 2 (指经济) poor

扩 kuò [动] expand

扩大 kuòdà [动] expand

括 kuò [动] 1 (包括) include 2 (加括号) bracket

括弧 kuòhú [名] bracket

阔 kuò [形] 1 (宽广) wide 2 (阔气) wealthy

垃 lā see below/见下文

垃圾 lājī [名] rubbish (英), garbage (美) ▷垃圾食品 lājī shípǐn junk food

拉 lā [动] 1 (用力移动) pull 2 (载运) transport ▷出租车司机拉我到了机场。 Chūzūchē sījī lā wǒ dào le jīchǎng. The taxi driver took me to the airport. 3 (演奏) play ▷拉小提琴 lā xiǎotíqín play the violin

喇 lǎ see below/见下文

喇叭 lǎba [名] 1 (管乐器) trumpet 2 (扩音器) loudspeaker

落 là [动] 1 (遗漏) be missing 2 (忘记) leave
→ see also/另见 luò

辣 là [形] (指味道) hot ▶辣酱 làjiàng chilli sauce ▶辣椒 làjiāo chillies

蜡 là [名] candle ▶蜡烛 làzhú candle

啦 la [助] ▶你回来啦！Nǐ huílai la! Hey – you're back!

来 lái I [动] 1 (来到) come ▶家里来了几个客人。Jiā lǐ lái le jǐ gè kèrén. Some guests came to the house. 2 (发生) happen ▶刚到家，麻烦来了。Gāng dào jiā, máfan lái le. As soon as I got home, the trouble started. 3 (泛指做事) ▶请来碗面条。Qǐng lái wǎn miàntiáo. A bowl of noodles, please. ▶你累了，让我来。Nǐ lèi le, ràng wǒ lái. You're tired – let me do it. 4 (表示要做) ▶请你来帮个忙。Qǐng nǐ lái bāng gè máng. Can you help me with this? 5 (表示目的) ▶我要想个法子来对付他。Wǒ yào xiǎng gè fǎzi lái duìfu ta. I must think of a way to deal with him. 6 (表示朝向) ▶服务员很快就把饭菜端了上来。Fúwùyuán hěnkuài jiù bǎ fàncài duān le shànglai. Soon the waiter had brought the food to the table. II [形] coming ▶来年 láinián the coming year III [助] 1 (表示持续) ▶近来 jìnlái lately ▶几年来 jǐ nián lái in the last few years 2 (表示概数) about ▶10来公斤重 shí lái gōngjīn zhòng about 10 kilos

来不及 láibùjí [动] lack sufficient time for

来得及 láidejí [动] have enough time for

来回 láihuí I [动] 1 (去了再来) make a round trip ▶从住宅小区到市中心来回有多远？Cóng zhùzhái xiǎoqū dào shìzhōngxīn láihuí yǒu duō yuǎn? How far is it from the residential area to town and back? 2 (来来去去) move back and forth II [名] round trip ▶我从学校到家一天跑两个来回。Wǒ cóng xuéxiào dào jiā yī tiān pǎo liǎng gè láihuí. I make the round trip from school to home twice a day.

来往 láiwǎng [动] have dealings with

来自 láizì [动] come from

拦 lán [动] stop

栏 lán [名] 1 (栏杆) fence ▶栏杆 lángān railing 2 (部分版面) column ▶栏目 lánmù column

蓝 lán [形] blue ▶蓝色 lánsè blue ▶蓝天 lántiān sky

篮 lán [名] (篮子) basket ▶篮子 lánzi basket

篮球 lánqiú [名] basketball

缆 lǎn [名] (似缆之物) cable

缆车 lǎnchē [名] cable car

懒 lǎn [形] 1 (懒惰) lazy 2 (疲倦) lethargic

懒得 lǎnde [动] not feel like ▶天

太热，我懒得出门。 Tiān tài rè, wǒ lǎn de chūmén. I don't feel like going out, it's too hot.

懒惰 lǎnduò [形] lazy

烂 làn I [形] 1 (破烂) worn-out 2 (头绪乱) messy ▶烂摊子 làn tānzi a shambles II [动] be rotten ▷西瓜烂了。 Xīguā làn le. The watermelon has gone off.

狼 láng [名] wolf

廊 láng [名] corridor ▶走廊 zǒuláng corridor

朗 lǎng [形] 1 (明亮) bright 2 (响亮) clear
朗读 lǎngdú [动] read ... aloud
朗诵 lǎngsòng [动] recite

浪 làng I [名] wave ▶浪潮 làngcháo tide II [形] wasteful ▶浪费 làngfèi squander
浪费 làngfèi [动] waste
浪漫 làngmàn [形] romantic

捞 lāo [动] (取) take ▶捕捞 bǔlāo fish for

劳 láo [动] 1 (劳动) work 2 (烦劳) trouble ▷劳您帮我看下行李。 Láo nín bāng wǒ kān xià xíngli. Would you mind keeping an eye on my luggage?
劳动 láodòng [名] labour (英), labor (美) ▷脑力劳动 nǎolì láodòng brain work
劳动力 láodònglì [名] 1 (劳动能力) labour (英), labor (美) 2 (人力) workforce

劳驾 láojià [动] (客套) excuse me

老 lǎo I [形] 1 (年岁大的) old 2 (有经验的) experienced ▶老手 lǎoshǒu veteran 3 (旧的) old ▷老同学 lǎo tóngxué old school friend 4 (火候大的) over-done II [名] (老人) old people III [副] 1 (经常) always 2 (长久) for a long time 3 (非常) very ▶老远 lǎoyuǎn very far

老百姓 lǎobǎixìng [名] ordinary people
老板 lǎobǎn [名] boss
老虎 lǎohǔ [名] tiger
老家 lǎojiā [名] home ▷我老家在上海。 Wǒ lǎojiā zài Shànghǎi. Shanghai is my hometown.
老练 lǎoliàn [形] experienced
老年 lǎonián [名] old age
老婆 lǎopo [名] (妻子) wife
老师 lǎoshī [名] teacher
老实 lǎoshi [形] 1 (诚实规矩) honest 2 (不聪明) naive
老鼠 lǎoshǔ [名] mouse
老外 lǎowài [名] foreigner

姥 lǎo see below/见下文
姥姥 lǎolao [名] (口) (母方的) granny
姥爷 lǎoye [名] (口) (母方的) grandpa

乐 lè I [形] happy II [动] 1 (乐于) take pleasure in 2 (笑) laugh → see also/另见 yuè
乐观 lèguān [形] optimistic

乐趣 lèqù [名] delight

乐意 lèyì [动] be willing to ▷他不乐意帮我们。 Tā bù lèyì bāng wǒmen. He's unwilling to help us.

了 le [助] **1** (表示动作或变化已完成) ▷他买了这本书。 Tā mǎi le zhè běn shū. He's bought this book. **2** (表示对未来的假设已完成) ▷下个月我考完了试回家。 Xià gè yuè wǒ kǎo wán le shì huíjiā. I'll go home next month once my exams are over. **3** (在句尾，表示出现变化) ▷下雨了。 Xiàyǔ le. It's raining. **4** (在句尾，表示提醒，劝告或催促) ▷该回家了。 Gāi huíjiā le. It's time to go home. ▷别喊了！ Bié hǎn le! Stop shouting!

→ see also/另见 liǎo

The usage of 了 le is one of the most complex parts of Chinese grammar, partly because it has two completely different functions. It can indicate completion of an action, e.g. 他喝了三杯啤酒 tā hē le sān bēi píjiǔ (he drank three glasses of beer). Sometimes, when placed at the end of a clause or a sentence, it usually indicates a change of some kind, e.g. 天黑了 tiān hēi le (it's gone dark).

雷 léi [名] (雷电) thunder ▷雷电

léidiàn thunder and lightning

累 lěi [动] (积累) accumulate ▶累积 lěijī accumulate
→ see also/另见 lèi

累计 lěijì [动] add up

肋 lèi [名] rib ▶肋骨 lèigǔ rib

泪 lèi [名] tear ▶眼泪 yǎnlèi tears (PL) ▷流泪 liúlèi shed tears

类 lèi I [名] kind ▶分类 fēilèi classify ▶类型 lèixíng type II [动] be similar to ▶类似 lèisì similar to

类别 lèibié [名] category

类似 lèisì [形] similar

累 lèi I [形] tired II [动] (使劳累) tire ▷别累着自己。 Bié lèizhe zìjǐ. Don't tire yourself out.
→ see also/另见 lěi

冷 lěng [形] **1** (温度低) cold **2** (不热情) frosty ▶冷淡 lěngdàn give the cold shoulder to

冷藏 lěngcáng [动] refrigerate

冷冻 lěngdòng [动] freeze ▶冷冻食品 lěngdòng shípǐn frozen food

冷静 lěngjìng [形] (沉着) cool-headed

冷饮 lěngyǐn [名] cold drink

厘 lí see below/见下文

厘米 límǐ [量] centimetre (英), centimeter (美)

离 lí [动] **1** (分离) leave **2** (距离) be far away from ▷我家离办公室不

太远。 Wǒ jiā lí bàngōngshì bù tài yuǎn. My home is quite near to the office.

离 lí is used to express separation of two things, or distance of one thing from another: to say that X is far away from Y, say "X 离 Y 远", e.g. 我家离火车站不远 wǒ jiā lí huǒchēzhàn bù yuǎn (my home is not far from the train station).

离婚 líhūn [动] divorce

离开 líkāi [动] depart

梨 lí [名] pear

礼 lǐ [名] 1 (仪式) ceremony 2 (表示尊敬) courtesy 3 (礼物) present

礼拜 lǐbài [名] (星期) week

礼貌 lǐmào [名] manners (PL)

礼堂 lǐtáng [名] hall

礼物 lǐwù [名] present

里 lǐ I [名] 1 (反面) inside 2 (里边) inner ▸里屋 lǐwū inner room II [介] in ▸屋子里 wūzi lǐ in the room III [副] ▸这里 zhèlǐ here ▸那里 nàlǐ there IV [量] lǐ, a Chinese unit of length, equal to 1/3 of a mile ▸英里 yīnglǐ mile

理 lǐ I [名] 1 (道理) reason ▸合理 hélǐ reasonable 2 (自然科学) natural science ▸理科 lǐkē science II [动] 1 (管理) manage ▸理财 lǐcái manage the finances 2 (整理) tidy ▸理发 lǐfà get a hair cut 3 (表示态度) acknowledge ▸理睬 lǐcǎi pay attention

理解 lǐjiě [动] understand

理论 lǐlùn [名] theory

理想 lǐxiǎng I [名] ideal II [形] ideal

理由 lǐyóu [名] reason

力 lì [名] 1 (物) force 2 (功能) strength 3 (体力) physical strength

力量 lìliang [名] 1 (力气) strength ▸这一拳力量很大。 Zhè yī quán lìliang hěndà. That was a very powerful punch. 2 (能力) power 3 (作用) strength ▸这种药的力量大。 Zhèzhǒng yào de lìliang dà. This medicine is very strong.

力气 lìqi [名] strength

历 lì [名] (经历) experience

历史 lìshǐ [名] history

厉 lì [形] 1 (严格) strict 2 (严肃) stern

厉害 lìhai [形] terrible ▸他口渴得厉害。 Tā kǒukě de lìhai. He was terribly thirsty.

立 lì I [动] 1 (站) stand 2 (竖立) stand ... up 3 (建立) ▸立功 lìgōng make contributions 4 (制定) set ... up ▸立法 lìfǎ legislate II [形] upright ▸立柜 lìguì wardrobe

立方 lìfāng I [名] cube II [量] cubic ▸立方米 lìfāngmǐ cubic metre (英) 或 meter (美)

立即 lìjí [副] immediately

立刻 lìkè [副] immediately

利 lì I [形] (锋利) sharp II [名] 1 (利

益) interest ▶利弊 lìbì pros and cons (PL) **2** (利润) profit and interest ▶暴利 bàolì staggering profits (PL) **III** [动] benefit

利害 lìhai [形] terrible ▷天冷得利害。 Tiān lěng de lìhai. It's terribly cold today.

利率 lìlǜ [名] interest rate

利润 lìrùn [名] profit

利息 lìxī [名] interest

利益 lìyì [名] benefit

利用 lìyòng [动] **1** (物) use **2** (人) exploit

例 lì [名] (例子) example ▶举例 jǔlì give an example

例如 lìrú [动] give an example ▷大商场货物齐全，例如服装，家电，食品等。 Dà shāngchǎng huòwù qíquán, lìrú fúzhuāng, jiādiàn, shípǐn děng. The big shopping centre sells all kinds of goods, for example, clothes, household appliances and food.

例外 lìwài [动] be an exception

例子 lìzi [名] example

荔 lì see below/见下文

荔枝 lìzhī [名] lychee

栗 lì [名] chestnut ▶栗子 lìzi chestnut

粒 lì [量] ▷一粒珍珠 yīlì zhēnzhū a pearl ▷三粒种子 sānlì zhǒngzi three seeds

measure word, used for small round objects, such as sand, grains, pills etc.

俩 liǎ [数] (口) (两个) two ▷我俩 wǒ liǎ the two of us

连 lián **I** [动] connect ▶连接 liánjiē link **II** [副] in succession ▷连看了几眼 lián kàn le jǐ yǎn glance at several times **III** [介] **1** (包括) including ▷连他4人 lián tā sì rén four people, including him **2** (甚至) even

连接 liánjiē [动] connect

连忙 liánmáng [副] at once

连续 liánxù [动] go on without stopping ▷他连续干了3天，觉都没睡。 Tā liánxù gàn le sān tiān, jiào dōu méi shuì. He worked for three days in a row without sleeping.

帘 lián [名] curtain (英), drape (美) ▶窗帘 chuānglián curtain (英), drape (美)

莲 lián [名] lotus ▶莲花 liánhuā lotus flower

联 lián [动] unite ▶联赛 liánsài league match

联合 liánhé **I** [动] (人) unite **II** [形] joint

联国 Liánhéguó [名] United Nations, UN

联络 liánluò [动] contact ▷联络方式 liánluò fāngshì ways to maintain contact

联系 liánxì [动] connect ▷理论联系实际 lǐlùn liánxì shíjì apply theory to practice ▶促进经济贸易联系 cùjìn jīngjì màoyì liánxì encourage economic and trade relations

脸 liǎn [名] **1** (面部) face **2** (前部) front ▶门脸 ménliǎn shop front (英), storefront (美) **3** (情面) face ▶脸面 liǎnmiàn face

脸色 liǎnsè [名] (气色) complexion

练 liàn I [动] practise (英), practice (美) ▶练武 liànwǔ practise martial arts II [形] experienced ▶熟练 shúliàn skilful (英), skillful (美)

练习 liànxí I [动] practise (英), practice (美) II [名] exercise

恋 liàn [动] **1** (恋爱) love ▶相恋 xiāngliàn fall in love with each other **2** (想念) miss ▶恋家 liànjiā be homesick

恋爱 liàn'ài [动] love ▶谈恋爱 tán liàn'ài be in love

恋人 liànrén [名] lover

良 liáng [形] good

良好 liánghǎo [形] good

良心 liángxīn [名] conscience

凉 liáng [形] (冷) cool → see also/另见 liàng

凉快 liángkuai [形] cool

量 liáng [动] (衡量) measure → see also/另见 liàng

粮 liáng [名] grain

粮食 liángshi [名] food

两 liǎng I [数] **1** (表示具体数目) two ▷两个小时 liǎng gè xiǎoshí two hours **2** (表示不定数目) a few ▷说两句 shuō liǎng jù say a few words II [量] liang, a Chinese unit of weight, equal to 50 grams

When citing numbers, including cardinal numbers, ordinal numbers, telephone numbers and serial numbers etc., 二 èr is used for the number two. However, when you want to talk about two things, you must use 两 liǎng and a measure word, e.g. 两个人 liǎng gè rén (2 people), 两杯茶 liǎng bēi chá (2 cups of tea) etc.

亮 liàng I [形] (光线) bright II [动] (发光) shine ▷灯还亮着。 Dēng hái liàng zhe. The lights are still lit.

凉 liàng [动] let ... cool → see also/另见 liáng

辆 liàng [量] ▷一辆汽车 yī liàng qìchē a car ▷两辆自行车 liǎngliàng zìxíngchē two bicycles measure word, used for vehicles and bicycles

量 liàng [名] **1** (限度) capacity **2** (数量) quantity → see also/另见 liáng

晾 liàng [动] **1** (弄干) dry **2** (晒干) air

聊 liáo [动] (口) chat ▶聊天室 liáotiānshì chat room

聊天儿 liáotiānr [动] (口) chat

了 liǎo [动] 1 (完毕) finish 2 (放在动词之后表示可能) ▷办不了 bàn bù liǎo not be able to handle ▷受得了 shòu de liǎo be able to bear → see also/另见 le

了不起 liǎobuqǐ [形] amazing

了解 liǎojiě [动] 1 (知道) understand 2 (打听) find ... out

料 liào [名] (材料) material ▶木料 mùliào timber

列 liè I [动] 1 (排列) set ... out 2 (安排) list ▶列举 lièjǔ list II [名] 1 (行列) rank 2 (类别) category

列车 lièchē [名] train

劣 liè [形] bad ▶恶劣 èliè bad

劣质 lièzhì [形] poor-quality

烈 liè [形] (强烈) strong ▶激烈 jīliè fierce ▶烈性酒 lièxìngjiǔ strong liquor

猎 liè [动] hunt ▶打猎 dǎliè go hunting

裂 liè [动] split ▶分裂 fēnliè split ▶破裂 pòliè break

裂口 lièkǒu [名] split

拎 līn [动] carry

邻 lín [名] neighbour (英), neighbor (美) ▶邻居 línjū neighbour

邻近 línjìn [动] be close to

邻居 línjū [名] neighbour (英), neighbor (美)

林 lín [名] 1 (树林) wood 2 (林业) forestry ▶林业 línyè forestry

临 lín [动] 1 (靠近) face ▶临危 línwēi face danger 2 (到达) reach ▶光临 guānglín presence 3 (将要) be about to ▶临产 línchǎn be in labour (英) 或 labor (美)

临近 línjìn [动] be close to ▷考试临近了。Kǎoshì línjìn le. The exams are approaching.

临时 línshí [副] temporarily

淋 lín [动] drench

淋浴 línyù [动] take a shower

鳞 lín [名] scale

吝 lìn [形] stingy ▶吝啬 lìnsè stingy

灵 líng I [形] 1 (灵敏) nimble ▶灵敏 língmǐn agile 2 (灵验) effective II [名] 1 (灵魂) soul 2 (神灵) deity ▶精灵 jīnglíng spirit

灵活 línghuó [形] 1 (敏捷的) agile 2 (机动的) flexible

铃 líng [名] 1 (响器) bell ▶铃铛 língdang small bell 2 (铃状物) ▶哑铃 yǎlíng dumb-bell

零 líng I [名] 1 (零数) zero 2 (零头) odd ▷她年纪七十有零。Tā niánjì qīshí yǒu líng. She's seventy-odd years old. II [形] 1 (零碎的) odd ▶零活 línghuó odd jobs (PL) ▶零钱 língqián small change 2 (部分的) spare ▶零件 língjiàn spare parts (PL) III [动] [连] ▷两年零三个月 liǎng nián líng sān gè yuè two years and three months ▷五元零二分 wǔ yuán líng èr fēn five yuan two fen

零钱 língqián [名] small change

零食 língshí [名] snack

零售 língshòu [动] retail

零用钱 língyòngqián [名] pocket money (英), allowance (美)

领 lǐng I [名] 1 (衣领) collar 2 (脖子) neck II [动] 1 (带领) lead 2 (占有) possess ▷占领 zhànlǐng occupy

领带 lǐngdài [名] tie

领导 lǐngdǎo I [动] lead ▷他领导有方。 Tā lǐngdǎo yǒufāng. He's an effective leader. II [名] leader

领土 lǐngtǔ [名] territory

领先 lǐngxiān [动] lead ▷他在比赛中遥遥领先。 Tā zài bǐsài zhōng yáoyáo lǐngxiān. He took a runaway lead in the competition.

领袖 lǐngxiù [名] leader

领养 lǐngyǎng [动] adopt

另 lìng I [代] another II [副] separately

另外 lìngwài I [代] other ▷我不喜欢这些衣服，我喜欢另外那些。 Wǒ bù xǐhuan zhèxiē yīfu, wǒ xǐhuan lìngwài nàxiē. I don't like these clothes – I like the others. II [副] in addition

令 lìng I [名] (命令) order II [动] 1 (令) order 2 (使) make

溜 liū [动] (走开) sneak off

溜达 liūda [动] go for a stroll

留 liú [动] 1 (不走) stay 2 (使留) keep ... back ▷挽留 wǎnliú persuade ... to stay 3 (留意) be careful ▷留神 liúshén be careful 4 (保留) keep 5 (积蓄) grow ▷留胡子 liú húzi grow a beard 6 (接受) accept 7 (遗留) leave ... behind 8 (留学) study abroad ▷留英 liú Yīng study in Britain

留步 liúbù [动] stop here

留念 liúniàn [动] keep as a souvenir

留神 liúshén [动] be on the alert

留心 liúxīn [动] take note

留学 liúxué [动] study abroad

留言 liúyán [动] leave a message

留意 liúyì [动] look ... out

流 liú I [动] (流动) flow ▷漂流 piāoliú drift II [名] 1 (水流) current ▷洪流 hóngliú torrent 2 (等级) grade ▷一流 yīliú first-class

流传 liúchuán [动] spread

流动 liúdòng [动] (移动) flow

流感 liúgǎn [名] the flu

流利 liúlì [形] fluent

流氓 liúmáng [名] 1 (下流) perversion 2 (歹徒) hooligan

流水 liúshuǐ [名] (流动水) running water

流行 liúxíng [动] be fashionable

瘤 liú [名] tumour (英), tumor

(美) ▶瘤子 liúzi tumour (英), tumor (美)

柳 liǔ [名] willow ▶柳树 liǔshù willow

六 liù [数] six

六月 liùyuè [名] June

陆 liù [数] six
→ see also/另见 lù

This is the complex character for "six", which is mainly used in banks, on receipts etc. to prevent mistakes and forgery.

遛 liù [动] 1 (指人) take a stroll 2 (指动物) walk ▶遛狗 liùgǒu walk the dog

龙 lóng [名] dragon

龙卷风 lóngjuǎnfēng [名] tornado

龙头 lóngtóu [名] tap (英), faucet (美)

聋 lóng [形] deaf

聋子 lóngzi [名] ▷他是个聋子。Tā shì gè lóngzi. He's deaf.

笼 lóng [名] (笼子) cage ▶笼子 lóngzi cage

楼 lóu [名] 1 (楼房) tall building ▷教学楼 jiàoxué lóu teaching block 2 (楼层) floor

楼房 lóufáng [名] multi-storey building

楼梯 lóutī [名] stairs (PL)

搂 lǒu [动] embrace

漏 lòu [动] 1 (雨, 水) leak 2 (消息, 风声) divulge 3 (词, 句) leave ... out

漏斗 lòudǒu [名] funnel

露 lòu [动] reveal
→ see also/另见 lù

露马脚 lòumǎjiǎo [动] give oneself away

炉 lú [名] stove

炉灶 lúzào [名] kitchen range

卤 lǔ I [名] 1 (盐卤) bittern 2 (卤汁) thick gravy II [动] stew ... in soy sauce

陆 lù [名] land
→ see also/另见 liù

陆地 lùdì [名] land

录 lù I [名] record II [动] 1 (记载) record ▶记录 jìlù take notes 2 (录音) tape-record

录取 lùqǔ [动] admit ▷她被剑桥大学录取了。 Tā bèi Jiànqiáo Dàxué lùqǔ le. She was given a place at the University of Cambridge.

录像 lùxiàng [动] video (英), videotape (美)

录音 lùyīn [动] record

鹿 lù [名] deer

路 lù [名] 1 (道路) road ▶路标 lùbiāo signpost 2 (路程) journey ▷一路平安 yī lù píng'ān have a safe journey 3 (门路) means ▶财路 cáilù a means of getting rich 4 (条理) sequence ▶思路 sīlù

train of thought 5 (路线) route
▶8路车 bālù chē No. 8 bus

路程 lùchéng [名] journey

路过 lùguò [动] pass through

路口 lùkǒu [名] crossing (英),
intersection (美)

路线 lùxiàn [名] 1 (指交通) route
2 (指思想) line

露 lù I [名] (水珠) dew II [动] reveal
▶暴露 bàolù expose
→ see also/另见 lòu

露天 lùtiān [名] the open air ▶露
天剧场 lùtiān jùchǎng open-air
theatre $ 或 theater $

露营 lùyíng [动] camp out

驴 lǘ [名] donkey

旅 lǚ [动] travel ▶差旅费 chāilǚfèi
travel expenses (PL)

旅馆 lǚguǎn [名] hotel

旅客 lǚkè [名] passenger

旅途 lǚtú [名] journey

旅行 lǚxíng [动] travel

旅游 lǚyóu [名] tour ▶旅游业
lǚyóu yè tourism ▶去国外旅游
qù guówài lǚyóu travel abroad

铝 lǚ [名] aluminium (英),
aluminum (美)

律 lǜ [名] law ▶纪律 jìlǜ discipline

律师 lǜshī [名] lawyer

绿 lǜ [形] green ▶绿灯 lǜdēng
green light

绿化 lǜhuà [动] make ... green
▶绿化荒山 lǜhuà huāngshān

plant trees on the mountains

绿卡 lǜkǎ [名] green card

绿洲 lǜzhōu [名] oasis

乱 luàn I [形] 1 (没有秩序的)
disorderly ▶杂乱 záluàn messy
2 (心绪不宁的) disturbed II [名]
(指冲突) chaos ▶战乱 zhànluàn
war chaos

乱哄哄 luànhōnghōng [形]
chaotic

乱七八糟 luànqībāzāo in a mess

略 lè I [名] 1 (简述) summary 2 (计
谋) plan ▶策略 cèlüè tactic
II [动] 1 (夺取) capture ▶侵略
qīnlüè invade 2 (简化) simplify
▶省略 shěnglüè omit

伦 lún [名] (人伦) human
relationships (PL)

伦敦 Lúndūn [名] London

伦理 lúnlǐ [名] ethics (SG)

轮 lún [名] 1 (轮子) wheel 2 (轮船)
steamship

轮船 lúnchuán [名] steamship

轮换 lúnhuàn [动] take turns

轮廓 lúnkuò [名] outline

轮流 lúnliú [副] in turns

轮椅 lúnyǐ [名] wheelchair

论 lùn I [名] 1 (文章) essay 2 (学
说) theory ▶相对论 xiāngduì
lùn theory of relativity II [动]
(分析) discuss ▶评论 pínglùn
comment on

论文 lùnwén [名] dissertation

萝 luó [名] trailing plant
　萝卜 luóbo [名] turnip ▶ 胡萝卜 húluóbo carrot

逻 luó [动] patrol
　逻辑 luóji [名] logic

螺 luó [名] (指动物) snail
　螺钉 luódīng [名] screw

裸 luǒ [动] expose
　裸体 luǒtǐ [形] naked

骆 luò see below/见下文
　骆驼 luòtuo [名] camel

落 luò [动] 1 (掉下) fall 2 (下降) go down ▶ 降落 jiàngluò descend 3 (降下) lower 4 (衰败) decline ▶ 衰落 shuāiluò wane 5 (落后) fall behind 6 (归属) fall to → see also/另见 là
　落后 luòhòu I [动] fall behind II [形] backward

妈 mā [名] (口) (母亲) mum (英), mom (美)
　妈妈 māma [名] (口) mum (英), mom (美)

抹 mā [动] (擦) wipe → see also/另见 mǒ
　抹布 mābù [名] cloth

麻 má I [名] (指植物) hemp II [形] (麻木) numb
　麻烦 máfan I [形] problematic II [名] trouble III [动] trouble ▶ 不好意思，麻烦您了。 Bùhǎo yìsi, máfan nín le. Sorry to trouble you.
　麻将 májiàng [名] mahjong

麻将 májiàng

　　The game of mahjong is usually played by four

people. 144 tiles appearing like dominoes and bearing various designs are drawn and discarded until one player has an entire hand of winning combinations. The game requires strategy as well as luck. In China, mahjong is also a popular gambling game.

麻醉 mázuì [动] (医) anaesthetize (英), anesthetize (美)

马 mǎ [名] horse

马达 mǎdá [名] motor

马虎 mǎhu [形] careless

马拉松 mǎlāsōng [名] marathon

马路 mǎlù [名] road

马上 mǎshàng [副] right away ▷他马上就到。 Tā mǎshàng jiù dào. He'll be here right away.

马戏 mǎxì [名] circus

码 mǎ [名] numeral ▷页码 yèmǎ page number

码头 mǎtou [名] pier

蚂 mǎ *see below*/见下文

蚂蚁 mǎyǐ [名] ant

骂 mà [动] 1(侮辱) insult 2(斥责) tell ... off

吗 ma [助] (表示疑问) ▷你去银行吗？ Nǐ qù yínháng ma? Are you going to the bank?

吗 ma is added to the end of any statement to turn it into a simple yes/no question, e.g. 你忙吗？ Nǐ máng ma? (Are you busy?), whereas 呢 ne is added to the end of a statement to form a tentative question, or to indicate that a response is expected, e.g. 你好吗？我很好，你呢？ Nǐ hǎo ma? Wǒ hěn hǎo, nǐ ne? (How are you? Fine, and you?).

嘛 ma [助] 1(表示显而易见) ▷事实就是这样嘛！ Shìshí jiùshì zhèyàng ma! That's just the way things are! 2(表示期望) ▷别不高兴嘛！ Bié bù gāoxìng ma! Please don't be unhappy.

埋 mái [动] 1(盖住) bury 2(隐藏) hide
→ *see also*/另见 mán

埋葬 máizàng [动] bury

买 mǎi [动] 1(购买) buy ▷不是每个人都买得起房。 Bùshì měigè rén dōu mǎideqǐ fáng. Not everyone can afford to buy a flat. ▷我去市场买东西。 Wǒ qù shìchǎng mǎi dōngxi. I'm going shopping in the market. 2(换取) win ... over ▷买通 mǎitōng buy ... off

买单 mǎidān [动] (方) pay a bill ▷买单！ Mǎidān! The bill, please!

买卖 mǎimai [名] 1(生意) business 2(商店) shop (英), store (美)

迈 mài [动] step ▶迈步 màibù stride

麦 mài [名] (麦类粮食) wheat ▶燕麦 yànmài oats (PL)

麦克风 màikèfēng [名] microphone, mike (口)

卖 mài [动] (出售) sell ▶书都卖完了。 Shū dōu mài wán le. The books are all sold out.

卖弄 màinong [动] show off

脉 mài [名] (脉搏) pulse ▶号脉 hàomài feel a pulse

脉搏 màibó [名] pulse

埋 mán see below/见下文 → see also/另见 mái

埋怨 mányuàn [动] 1(指责) blame 2(抱怨) complain

馒 mán see below/见下文

馒头 mántou [名] steamed bun

瞒 mán [动] hide the truth from ▶别瞒着我们! Bié mán zhe wǒmen! Don't keep us in the dark!

满 mǎn I [形] 1(充实) full 2(全) complete II [动] 1(使充满) fill 2(到) reach ▶孩子刚满六岁。 Háizi gāng mǎn liùsuì. The child has just turned six years old. III [副] fully

满意 mǎnyì [动] be satisfied

满足 mǎnzú [动] 1(感到满意) be satisfied 2(使满足) satisfy

漫 màn [动] overflow

漫长 màncháng [形] endless

漫画 mànhuà [名] comic strip

漫延 mànyán [动] spread

慢 màn I [形] (缓慢) slow II [动] slow ▶慢点儿! Màn diǎnr! Slow down! ▶钟慢了十分钟。 Zhōng màn le shí fēnzhōng. The clock is ten minutes slow.

忙 máng I [形] busy II [动] be busy with ▶你这一段忙什么呢? Nǐ zhè yīduàn máng shénme ne? What's been keeping you busy recently?

盲 máng [形] blind ▶文盲 wénmáng illiterate

盲目 mángmù [形] blind

盲文 mángwén [名] braille

蟒 mǎng [名] (动物) python

猫 māo [名] cat

猫儿眼 māoryǎn [名] spyhole

毛 máo I [名] 1(毛发) hair ▶羽毛 yǔmáo feather 2(指食物上) mould (英), mold (美) ▶面包上长毛了。 Miànbāo shàng zhǎng máo le. The bread is mouldy (英) 或 moldy (美). 3(指动物) fur ▶毛皮 máopí fur 4(羊毛) wool ▶毛衣 máoyī sweater 5(中国货币单位) mao unit of Chinese currency, 1/10 yuan II [形] (不纯) gross ▶毛重 máozhòng gross weight

毛笔 máobǐ [名] brush pen

毛病 máobìng [名] 1(故障) problem 2(缺点) shortcoming

3(疾病) illness

毛巾 máojīn [名] towel

毛孔 máokǒng [名] pore

矛 máo [名] spear

矛盾 máodùn **I** [名] **1**(相抵之处) conflict **2**(哲) contradiction **II** [形] uncertain

锚 máo [名] anchor

茂 mào [形] **1**(茂盛) luxuriant **2**(丰富) abundant

茂盛 màoshèng [形] flourishing

冒 mào [动] **1**(往外) give ... off ▷锅冒烟了。 Guō mào yān le. The wok is giving off smoke. **2**(不顾) risk ▷冒着生命危险 mào zhe shēngmìng wēixiǎn putting one's life at risk **3**(假充) pretend to be ▶冒牌 màopái bogus

冒充 màochōng [动] pass ... off as

冒牌 màopái [动] pirate ▷冒牌商品 màopái shāngpǐn pirated goods

冒险 màoxiǎn [动] take a risk

贸 mào [动] trade ▶外贸 wàimào foreign trade

贸易 màoyì [名] trade

帽 mào [名] (帽子) hat

帽子 màozi [名] (字) hat

貌 mào [名] (相貌, 外表) appearance

没 méi **I** [动] not have ▶没关系 méiguānxi it doesn't matter ▷屋子里没人。 Wūzi lǐ méi rén. There's no one in the room. **II** [副] not ▷他没看过大海。 Tā méi kànguò dàhǎi. He's never seen the sea before.

→ see also/另见 mò

Constructing negating sentences in Chinese is very straightforward: just use 不 bù before the verb, e.g. 我不喝酒。 Wǒ bù hējiǔ. (I don't drink alcohol). The only exception is the verb 有 yǒu, to have, for which you must use 没 méi, e.g. 我没有钱。 Wǒ méiyǒu qián. (I don't have any money).

没错儿 méicuòr [动] that's right

没劲 méijìn **I** [动] have no energy **II** [形] uninteresting

没门儿 méiménr [动] (不可能) be impossible

没事 méishì [动] **1**(有空) be free ▷我今晚没事。 Wǒ jīnwǎn méishì. I'm free tonight. **2**(不要紧) ▷没事。 Méishì. It doesn't matter.

没有 méiyǒu **I** [动] **1**(不具有) not have **2**(不存在) there is not **3**(全都不) ▷没有一个答案是正确的。 Méiyǒu yīgè dá'àn shì zhèngquè de. None of the answers are correct. **4**(不如) be not as ... as ... ▷他没有你努力。 Tā méiyǒu nǐ nǔlì. He's not as hard-working as you. **5**(不到) be less than ▷他们干了没有两个小时就休息了。 Tāmen gàn le méiyǒu liǎnggè xiǎoshí jiù xiūxi le. They had been working for less than two hours when they took a rest. **II** [副] **1** (尚未) not yet ▷ 他还没有到。 Tā hái méiyǒu dào. She hasn't arrived yet. **2** (未曾) never before ▷ 我没有吃过西餐。 Wǒ méiyǒu chīguò xīcān. I have never eaten Western food before.

没辙 méizhé [动] (方) not be able to do anything about

玫 méi *see below*/见下文

玫瑰 méigui [名] rose

眉 méi [名] (眉毛) eyebrow ▷ 眉毛 méimao eyebrow

媒 méi [名] **1** (媒人) matchmaker ▷ 做媒 zuòméi be a matchmaker **2** (媒介) intermediary

媒体 méitǐ [名] media

煤 méi [名] coal

煤气 méiqì [名] **1** (指燃料) gas **2** (指有毒气体) carbon monoxide ▷ 煤气中毒 méiqì zhòngdú carbon monoxide poisoning

霉 méi [动] **1** (指食物) mould (英), mold (美) **2** (指衣物) mildew

每 měi **I** [形] every, each ▷ 每次 měicì every time ▷ 每个晚上 měi gè wǎnshang every evening **II** [副] every time ▷ 每走一步, 他的脚都很疼。 Měi zǒu yī bù, tāde jiǎo dōu hěn téng. His feet ache with every step he takes.

美 měi **I** [形] **1** (美丽) beautiful **2** (好) good ▷ 我们的明天会更美。 Wǒmen de míngtiān huì gèng měi. Our future will be even better. **II** [名] **1** (美丽) beauty **2** (美洲) North and South America ▷ 南美 Nánměi South America ▷ 北美 Běiměi North America **3** (美国) the USA

美国 Měiguó [名] the US, the USA ▷ 美国人 Měiguórén American

美好 měihǎo [形] wonderful

美丽 měilì [形] beautiful

美满 měimǎn [形] perfectly satisfactory

美容 měiróng [动] make oneself more beautiful ▷ 美容店 měiróng diàn beauty salon ▷ 美容手术 měiróng shǒushù cosmetic surgery

美食 měishí [名] delicacy

美术 měishù [名] **1** (造型艺术) fine arts (PL) **2** (绘画) painting

美元 měiyuán [名] US dollar

妹 mèi [名] **1** (指同胞) younger sister **2** (指亲戚) ▷ 表妹 biǎomèi cousin

妹妹 mèimei (指同胞) younger sister

魅 mèi [名] demon

魅力 mèilì [名] charm

闷 mēn **I** [形] stuffy **II** [动] **1** (盖) cover ... tightly **2** (不出声) keep silent **3** (呆) shut oneself in
→ *see also*/另见 mèn

闷热 mēnrè [形] muggy

门 mén I [名] 1 (指出入口) door ▶门口 ménkǒu entrance 2 (指开关装置) switch ▶电门 diànmén switch II [量] ▷5门课 wǔ mén kè five courses ▷一门新技术 yī mén xīn jìshù a new technology measure word, used for academic subjects, courses and technology

门类 ménlèi [名] category

门卫 ménwèi [名] guard

门诊 ménzhěn [名] outpatient department

闷 mèn [形] 1 (烦) low 2 (无聊) bored
→ see also/另见 mēn

们 men [后缀] ▶我们 wǒmen we, us ▶你们 nǐmen you ▶他们 tāmen they, them

蒙 mēng [动] 1 (欺骗) deceive 2 (乱猜) make a wild guess
→ see also/另见 méng, Měng

蒙骗 mēngpiàn [动] deceive

蒙 méng I [动] 1 (遮盖) cover 2 (受到) receive II [形] ignorant ▶启蒙 qǐméng enlighten
→ see also/另见 mēng, Měng

蒙混 ménghùn [动] deceive ▷蒙混过关 ménghùn guòguān muddle through

猛 měng [形] 1 (凶猛) fierce [副] 2 (猛烈) fiercely 3 (忽然) suddenly

猛烈 měngliè [形] fierce

蒙 Měng [名] Mongolia ▶蒙古 Měnggǔ Mongolia ▶蒙古人 Měnggǔrén Mongolian ▶内蒙古 Nèiměnggǔ Inner Mongolia
→ see also/另见 mēng, méng

梦 mèng I [名] 1 (睡梦) dream ▶白日梦 báirìmèng daydream ▶做梦 zuòmèng have a dream 2 (幻想) illusion II [动] dream

梦话 mènghuà [名] 1 (字) ▷说梦话 shuō mènghuà talk in one's sleep 2 (喻) nonsense

梦想 mèngxiǎng [动] dream

弥 mí [动] fill

弥补 míbǔ [动] make ... up

迷 mí I [动] 1 (迷失) be lost ▶迷路 mílù lose one's way 2 (迷恋) become obsessed with 3 (迷惑) be deluded II [名] fan ▶球迷 qiúmí sports fan ▷足球迷 zúqiú mí football fan

迷你 mínǐ [形] mini ▷迷你裙 mínǐ qún mini-skirt

迷信 míxìn [动] 1 (鬼神) be superstitious about 2 (人或事) have blind faith in

猕 mí see below/见下文

猕猴桃 míhóutáo [名] kiwi fruit

谜 mí [名] 1 (谜语) riddle 2 (神秘) mystery

谜语 míyǔ [名] riddle

米 mǐ I [名] (稻米) rice ▶米饭 mǐfàn cooked rice II [量] metre (英), meter (美)

秘 mì I [形] secret II [动] keep ... secret III [名] secretary

秘密 mìmì [名] secret ▷一定要保守秘密！ Yīdìng yào bǎoshǒu mìmì! You must keep this a secret!

秘书 mìshū [名] secretary

密 mì [形] 1 (空隙小) dense 2 (关系近) close ▷亲密 qīnmì intimate 3 (精致) meticulous ▶精密 jīngmì precise 4 (秘密) secret ▶保密 bǎomì keep sth a secret

密度 mìdù [名] density

密封 mìfēng [动] seal ... tightly

密码 mìmǎ [名] 1 (口令) password 2 (符号系统) code

密切 mìqiè [形] close

幂 mì [名] (数) power

蜜 mì I [名] honey II [形] sweet

蜜蜂 mìfēng [名] bee

蜜月 mìyuè [名] honeymoon

眠 mián [动] 1 (睡) sleep ▶失眠 shīmián suffer from insomnia 2 (冬眠) hibernate

棉 mián [名] cotton

棉花 miánhua [名] (指植物) cotton

棉衣 miányī [名] cotton-padded clothing

免 miǎn [动] 1 (除去) exempt ▶免试 miǎnshì be exempt from an exam 2 (避免) avoid ▶免不了 miǎnbùliǎo be unavoidable 3 (不要) not be allowed ▷闲人免进 xiánrén miǎnjìn staff only

免费 miǎnfèi [动] be free of charge ▷注册一个免费电子邮箱 zhùcè yīgè miǎnfèi diànzǐ yǒuxiāng register for free e-mail

免疫 miǎnyì [名] immunity

勉 miǎn [动] 1 (努力) strive 2 (勉励) encourage 3 (勉强) force ... to carry on

勉强 miǎnqiǎng I [动] 1 (尽力) push oneself hard ▷做事不要太勉强。 Zuòshì bùyào tài miǎnqiǎng. Don't push yourself too hard. 2 (强迫) force ▷不要勉强孩子学钢琴。 Bùyào miǎnqiǎng háizi xué gāngqín. Don't force the child to study the piano. II [形] 1 (不情愿) reluctant ▷我让他帮忙，他勉强答应了。 Wǒ ràng tā bāngmáng, tā miǎnqiǎng dāyìng le. I asked him to help, and he reluctantly agreed. 2 (凑合) barely enough ▷他挣的钱勉强够自己花。 Tā zhèng de qián miǎnqiǎng gòu zìjǐ huā. The money he earned was barely enough to support himself. 3 (牵强) far-fetched ▷这个理论有点勉强。 Zhègè lǐlùn yǒudiǎn miǎnqiǎng. This theory is a bit far-fetched.

冕 miǎn [名] 1 (皇冠) crown ▶加冕 jiāmiǎn be crowned 2 (冠军头衔) title ▶卫冕 wèimiǎn defend one's title

缅 miǎn [形] (书) remote

缅甸 Miǎndiàn [名] Myanmar

面 miàn I [名] 1 (脸) face 2 (表面) surface 3 (方位) aspect ▷前面 qiánmiàn front 4 (情面) self-respect 5 (粉末) powder ▷辣椒面 làjiāomiàn chilli powder 6 (磨成粉的粮食) flour ▷面粉 miànfěn flour 7 (面条) noodles (PL) II [动] (朝) face III [量] 1 (用于扁平物) ▷一面墙 yī miàn qiáng a wall ▷两面镜子 liǎng miàn jìngzi two mirrors

measure word, used for objects with a flat surface, such as walls, mirrors, drums etc.

2 (指见面的次数) ▷我只见过她一面。 Wǒ zhǐ jiànguò tā yī miàn. I've only met her once before. ▷我们见过几面。 Wǒmen jiànguò jǐ miàn. We've met a few times.

measure word, used for encounters between two people

面包 miànbāo [名] bread ▷面包房 miànbāofáng bakery

面对 miànduì [动] face

面积 miànjī [名] area

面临 miànlín [动] face

面貌 miànmào [名] 1 (面容) features (PL) 2 (喻) appearance

面前 miànqián [名] ▷在困难面前 zài kùnnan miànqián in the face of difficulties

面试 miànshì [动] have an interview

面条 miàntiáo [名] noodles (PL) ▷意大利面条 Yìdàlì miàntiáo spaghetti

面子 miànzi [名] 1 (体面) face ▷丢面子 diū miànzi lose face 2 (情面) feelings (PL) ▷给我点面子，你就答应吧！ Gěi wǒ diǎn miànzi, nǐ jiù dāying ba! Show some respect for my feelings and say yes!

苗 miáo [名] (指植物) seedling ▷树苗 shùmiáo sapling

苗条 miáotiao [形] slim

描 miáo [动] 1 (画) trace 2 (涂抹) touch ... up

描述 miáoshù [动] describe

描写 miáoxiě [动] describe

瞄 miáo [动] fix one's eyes on

瞄准 miáozhǔn [动] (对准) take aim

秒 miǎo [量] (指时间) second ▷5秒 wǔ miǎo five seconds

妙 miào [形] 1 (好) wonderful 2 (巧妙) ingenious

庙 miào [名] temple

灭 miè [动] 1 (熄灭) go out 2 (使熄灭) extinguish ▷灭火器 mièhuǒqì fire extinguisher 3 (淹没) submerge 4 (消亡) perish 5 (消灭) kill

灭绝 mièjué [动] (消亡) become extinct

民 mín [名] 1 (人民) the people (PL) 2 (人) person ▶网民 wǎngmín Internet user 3 (民间) folk 4 (非军方) civilian

民歌 míngē [名] folk song

民间 mínjiān [名] 1 (百姓中间) folk ▶民间传说 mínjiān zǔzhī folklore 2 (非官方) ▶民间组织 mínjiān zǔzhī non-governmental organization

民警 mínjǐng [名] civil police

民主 mínzhǔ I [名] democracy II [形] democratic

民族 mínzú [名] nationality ▶少数民族 shǎoshù mínzú ethnic minority

敏 mǐn [形] 1 (快) quick ▶敏感 mǐngǎn sensitive 2 (聪明) clever ▶机敏 jīmǐn quick-witted

敏捷 mǐnjié [形] quick

名 míng I [名] 1 (名字) name ▶书名 shū míng book title 2 (名声) reputation II [形] famous ▶名著 míngzhù classics (PL) III [量] 1 (指人) ▶5名工人 wǔ míng gōngrén five workers ▶10名教师 shí míng jiàoshī ten teachers

measure word, used for people of any profession

2 (指名次) ▶期末考试她得了第一名。Qīmò kǎoshì tā dé le dìyī míng. She came first in the end-of-term exams.

measure word, used for rankings in competitions and exams

名称 míngchēng [名] name

名次 míngcì [名] ranking

名单 míngdān [名] list of names

名额 míng'é [名] quota

名牌 míngpái [名] famous name ▶名牌服装 míngpái fúzhuāng designer clothing

名片 míngpiàn [名] business card

名气 míngqi [名] fame

名人 míngrén [名] famous person

名声 míngshēng [名] reputation

名胜 míngshèng [名] tourist site

名字 míngzi [名] name ▶你叫什么名字？Nǐ jiào shénme míngzi? What's your name?

明 míng I [形] 1 (亮) bright 2 (清楚) clear 3 (公开) open II [名] 1 (视力) sight ▶失明 shīmíng lose one's eyesight 2 (光明) light III [动] 1 (懂) understand ▶明理 mínglǐ be understanding 2 (显示) show ▶表明 biǎomíng indicate

明白 míngbai I [形] 1 (清楚) clear 2 (聪明) sensible 3 (公开) explicit II [动] understand

明亮 míngliàng [形] 1 (亮堂) bright 2 (发亮) shining 3 (明白) clear

明确 míngquè I [形] clear-cut II [动] clarify

明显 míngxiǎn [形] obvious

明星 míngxīng [名] star

明智 míngzhì [形] sensible

命 mìng [名] 1 (性命) life 2 (命

运) fate **3** (寿命) lifespan **4** (命令) order

命令 mìnglìng [动] order

命名 mìngmíng [动] name

命运 mìngyùn [名] fate

摸 mō [动] **1** (触摸) stroke **2** (摸黑行动) feel one's way ▶摸索 mōsuǒ grope

模 mó **I** [名] model ▶模型 móxíng model **II** [动] imitate
→ *see also* /另见 mú

模范 mófàn [形] model

模仿 mófǎng [动] imitate

模糊 móhu [形] blurred

模拟 mónǐ [动] imitate ▶模拟考试 mónǐ kǎoshì mock exam

模式 móshì [名] pattern

模特儿 mótèr [名] model

模型 móxíng [名] **1** (样品) model **2** (模具) mould (英), mold (美)

膜 mó [名] (膜状物) film ▶保鲜膜 bǎoxiānmó clingfilm (英), plastic wrap (美)

摩 mó [动] (摩擦) rub ... together

摩擦 mócā **I** [动] rub **II** [名] **1** (阻力) friction **2** (冲突) conflict

摩托车 mótuōchē [名] motorbike

磨 mó [动] **1** (摩擦) rub **2** (指用磨料) grind ▶磨刀 módāo sharpen a knife **3** (折磨) wear ... down **4** (纠缠) pester **5** (拖延) dawdle
→ *see also* /另见 mò

磨擦 mócā [名] rub

磨蹭 móceng [形] sluggish

磨合 móhé [动] (适应) adapt to each other

磨炼 móliàn [动] steel

磨损 mósǔn [动] wear ... out

蘑 mó [名] mushroom

蘑菇 mógu [名] mushroom

魔 mó **I** [名] **1** (魔鬼) demon **2** (魔法) magic **II** [形] magic

魔法 mófǎ [名] magic

魔鬼 móguǐ [名] devil

魔术 móshù [名] magic

魔术师 móshùshī [名] magician

抹 mǒ [动] **1** (涂抹) apply **2** (擦) wipe **3** (去除) erase
→ *see also* /另见 mā

末 mò [名] (尾) end ▶世纪末 shìjì mò the end of the century

末尾 mòwěi [名] end

没 mò [动] **1** (沉没) sink **2** (漫过) overflow **3** (隐没) disappear ▶出没 chūmò appear and disappear
→ *see also* /另见 méi

没收 mòshōu [动] confiscate

沫 mò [名] foam ▶泡沫 pàomò bubble

茉 mò *see below* /见下文

茉莉 mòlì [名] jasmine

陌 mò [名] (书) footpath

陌生 mòshēng [形] unfamiliar

陌生人 mòshēngrén [名] stranger

墨 mò **I** [名] (墨汁) ink ▶墨汁

mòzhī ink II [形] dark ▶墨镜 mòjìng sunglasses

默 mò [动] 1 (不出声) do ... silently ▶默哀 mò'āi pay ... silent tribute 2 (默写) write ... from memory

磨 mò I [名] mill ▶磨坊 mòfáng mill II [动] grind → see also/另见 mó

谋 móu [名] plan ▶阴谋 yīnmóu plot

谋杀 móushā [动] murder

谋生 móushēng [动] make a living

某 mǒu [代] (指不确定的人或事) ▶某人 mǒurén somebody

模 mú [名] mould (英), mold (美) → see also/另见 mó

模样 múyàng [名] (相貌) looks (PL)

母 mǔ I [名] 1 (母亲) mother 2 (指长辈女子) ▶祖母 zǔmǔ grandmother 3 (喻) (基础) origin II [形] (雌性) female ▶母牛 mǔniú cow

母亲 mǔqīn [名] mother

拇 mǔ [名] see below/见下文

拇指 mǔzhǐ [名] 1 (指手) thumb 2 (指脚) big toe

木 mù I [名] 1 (树) tree 2 (木材) wood II [形] (僵) numb

木材 mùcái [名] timber

木匠 mùjiang [名] carpenter

木偶 mù'ǒu [名] puppet

木头 mùtou [名] wood

目 mù [名] 1 (眼睛) eye 2 (条目) item

目标 mùbiāo [名] 1 (对象) target 2 (目的) goal

目的 mùdì [名] 1 (指地点) destination 2 (结果) aim 3 (企图) intention

目光 mùguāng [名] 1 (视线) gaze 2 (眼神) look

目录 mùlù [名] 1 (指事物) catalogue (英), catalog (美) 2 (指书刊中) table of contents

目前 mùqián [名] present ▶到目前为止 dào mùqián wéizhǐ to date ▶我们目前的任务 wǒmen mùqián de rènwù our current tasks

牧 mù [动] herd

牧民 mùmín [名] herdsman

牧师 mùshi [名] priest

牧业 mùyè [名] animal husbandry

募 mù [动] (钱款) raise

募捐 mùjuān [动] collect donations

墓 mù [名] grave

墓碑 mùbēi [名] gravestone

墓地 mùdì [名] graveyard

幕 mù [名] (帷幔) curtain ▶银幕 yínmù the silver screen

睦 mù [动] get on ▶和睦 hémù harmonious

穆 mù [形] solemn

穆斯林 mùsīlín [名] Muslim

n

拿 ná [动] 1 (握) hold 2 (得) get

哪 nǎ [代] 1 (什么) which ▷你喜欢哪种音乐? nǐ xǐhuan nǎ zhǒng yīnyuè? What kind of music do you like? ▷哪个人是李先生? nǎ gè rén shì Lǐ Xiānshēng? Which one is Mr Li? 2 (任何一个) any ▷你哪天来都行。 nǐ nǎ tiān lái dōu xíng. You can come any day.

哪个 nǎge [代] which

哪里 nǎli [代] 1 (用于问处所) ▷你住在哪里? nǐ zhù zài nǎli? Where do you live? 2 (指某一地方) ▷我们应该在哪里见过。 wǒmen yīnggāi zài nǎli jiànguo. I'm sure we've met somewhere before. 3 (谦) ▷哪里,哪里,你过奖了。 nǎli, nǎli, nǐ guòjiǎng le.

No, no, it was nothing.

哪些 nǎxiē [代] which

那 nà I [代] that ▷那些人 nàxiē rén those people II [连] then ▷你想买, 那就买吧。 nǐ xiǎng mǎi, nà jiù mǎi ba. If you want to buy it, then buy it.

那边 nàbiān [名] that side

那个 nàge [代] (指代人, 事或物) that

那里 nàli [代] ▷我去过那里。 wǒ qùguo nàli. I've been there. ▷我也要去那里吗? wǒ yě yào qù nàli ma? Shall I go over there as well?

那么 nàme [代] 1 (表示程度) ▷你不该那么相信他。 nǐ bù gāi nàme xiāngxìn tā. You shouldn't trust him so much. 2 (表示方式) ▷你别那么想。 nǐ bié nàme xiǎng. Don't think in that way.

那些 nàxiē [代] those

那样 nàyàng [副] ▷我没有说过那样的话。 wǒ méiyǒu shuōguo nàyàng de huà. I never said anything like that.

奶 nǎi [名] milk ▶酸奶 suānnǎi yoghurt

奶酪 nǎilào [名] cheese

奶奶 nǎinai [名] (父方的) granny

耐 nài [动] 1 (指人) endure ▶耐性 nàixìng patience 2 (指材料) be resistant ▶耐用 nàiyòng enduring

耐力 nàilì [名] stamina

耐心 nàixīn [形] patient

男 nán [名] (男性) male

男孩子 nánháizi [名] boy

男朋友 nánpéngyou [名] boyfriend

男人 nánrén [名] man

南 nán [名] south ▶东南 dōngnán south-east ▶西南 xīnán south-west

南边 nánbiān [名] the south

南部 nánbù [名] southern part

南方 nánfāng [名] the South

南极 nánjí [名] South Pole

难 nán [形] 1 (困难) hard 2 (不好) bad, baffle

难道 nándào [副] ▷你难道还不明白吗? nǐ nándào hái bù míngbai ma? How can you not understand? ▷难道你就不累? nándào nǐ jiù bù lèi? Aren't you tired?

难过 nánguò I [动] have a hard time II [形] upset

难看 nánkàn [形] 1 (丑) ugly 2 (不体面) ashamed

难免 nánmiǎn [动] be unavoidable

难受 nánshòu [动] 1 (指身体) not feel well 2 (指心情) feel down

脑 nǎo [名] 1 (生理) brain 2 (脑筋) brain 3 (头部) head 4 (头领) leader ▶首脑 shǒunǎo head

脑袋 nǎodai [名] head

脑子 nǎozi [名] brain

闹 nào I [形] noisy II [动] 1 (吵闹) have a row ▷闹别扭 nào bièniu fall out 2 (病, 灾难) suffer from ▷闹肚子 nào dùzi have diarrhoea (英) 或 diarrhea (美)

闹钟 nàozhōng [名] alarm clock

呢 ne [助] 1 (表示疑问) ▷你们都走, 我呢? nǐmen dōu zǒu, wǒ ne? If you all go, what about me? ▷我到底错在哪儿呢? wǒ dàodǐ cuò zài nǎr ne? What did I actually do wrong? 2 (表示陈述) ▷离北京还远着呢。 lí Běijīng hái yuǎnzhe ne. Beijing is still quite far. 3 (表示持续) ▷老师还在办公室呢。 lǎoshī hái zài bàngōngshì ne. The teacher is still in the office.

→ see also/另见 ní

呢 ne is added to the end of a statement to form a tentative question, or to indicate that a response is expected, e.g. 你好吗? 我很好, 你呢? Nǐ hǎo ma? Wǒ hěn hǎo, nǐ ne? (How are you? Fine, and you?). It may also be used to stress continuity, e.g. 我还在吃饭呢 Wǒ hái zài chīfàn ne (I am still eating dinner), whereas 吗 ma is added to the end of any statement to turn it into a simple yes/no question, e.g. 你忙吗? Nǐ máng ma? (Are you busy?).

内 nèi [名] (里头) inside ▶室内 shìnèi indoor ▶内地 nèidì inland ▶他在一个月内完成了任务。 tā zài yī gè yuè nèi wánchéngle rènwu. He finished the task within a month.

内部 nèibù [形] internal

内服 nèifú [动] take orally

内行 nèiháng [名] expert

内科 nèikē [名] internal medicine

内容 nèiróng [名] content

内向 nèixiàng [形] introverted

能 néng I [名] 1 (能力) ability 2 (物) (能量) energy ▶能量 néngliàng energy II [形] capable III [助动] can

能 néng, 会 huì, and 可以 kěyǐ can all be used to express ability and are sometimes used interchangeably. Strictly, 能 néng should be used to express physical ability, e.g. 我能跑得很快 wǒ néng pǎo de hěn kuài (I can run very fast), while 会 huì should express a learned ability, e.g. 我会说法语 wǒ huì shuō Fǎyǔ (I can speak French). Both 能 néng and 可以 kěyǐ can express being able to do something because you have been granted permission, e.g. 你能/可以借我的照相机 nǐ néng/kěyǐ jiè wǒ de zhàoxiàngjī (You can/may borrow my camera).

能干 nénggàn [形] capable

能够 nénggòu [动] be able to

能力 nénglì [名] ability

能源 néngyuán [名] energy

呢 ní [名] woollen cloth
→ see also / 另见 ne

呢子 nízi [名] woollen cloth

泥 ní [名] (指土) mud

你 nǐ [代] 1 (称对方) you 2 (你的) your ▶你家有几口人？ nǐ jiā yǒu jǐ kǒu rén? How many people are there in your family?

你们 nǐmen [代] you (PL)

腻 nì [形] (太油) oily

蔫 niān [形] (枯萎) withered

年 nián I [名] 1 (时间单位) year 2 (元旦或春节) New Year 3 (岁数) age II [形] annual

年代 niándài [名] (时代) period

年级 niánjí [名] year (英), grade (美)

年纪 niánjì [名] age

年龄 niánlíng [名] age

年轻 niánqīng [形] young

黏 nián [形] sticky

念 niàn [动] 1 (读) read 2 (上学) study

念叨 niàndao [动] (唠叨) nag

念书 niànshū [动] study

念头 niàntou [名] idea

鸟 niǎo [名] bird

尿 niào I [名] urine ▶撒尿 sāniào urinate II [动] urinate

镊 niè [名] tweezers (PL) ▶镊子 nièzi tweezers (PL)

您 nín [代] you ▷您慢走！ nín màn zǒu! Mind how you go!

宁 níng [形] peaceful
→ see also/另见 nìng

拧 níng [动] 1 (毛巾, 衣服) wring 2 (皮肤) pinch

柠 níng see below/见下文

柠檬 níngméng [名] lemon

宁 nìng [副] ▶宁愿 nìngyuàn would rather
→ see also/另见 níng

牛 niú [名] 1 (指动物) cow ▶公牛 gōngniú bull 2 (指肉) beef ▶牛肉 niúròu beef

牛奶 niúnǎi [名] milk

牛仔裤 niúzǎikù [名] jeans (PL)

扭 niǔ [动] 1 (掉转) turn around 2 (拧) twist 3 (崴) sprain

纽 niǔ [名] (扣子) button ▶纽扣 niǔkòu button

纽约 Niǔyuē [名] New York

农 nóng [名] 1 (农业) agriculture 2 (农民) farmer

农场 nóngchǎng [名] farm

农村 nóngcūn [名] the countryside

农历 nónglì [名] lunar calendar

农民 nóngmín [名] farmer

农业 nóngyè [名] agriculture

浓 nóng [形] 1 (指气味, 味道) strong 2 (指烟雾) thick 3 (指兴趣) great ▷他对语言有很浓的兴趣。 tā duì yǔyán yǒu hěn nóng de xìngqù. He has a great interest in languages.

浓缩 nóngsuō I [动] condense II [形] condensed

弄 nòng [动] 1 (搞) make 2 (设法取得) get

努 nǔ [动] (劲儿) make an effort ▷我们再努把力。 wǒmen zài nǔ bǎ lì. Let's make one last effort.

努力 nǔlì [动] try hard ▷我会尽最大努力。 wǒ huì jìn zuìdà nǔlì. I'll try my very best.

怒 nù I [形] (生气) angry ▶恼怒 nǎonù furious II [名] anger ▶发怒 fānù lose one's temper

女 nǚ [名] 1 (女子) woman ▷女演员 nǚyǎnyuán actress 2 (女儿) daughter ▶子女 zǐnǚ children (PL)

女儿 nǚ'ér [名] daughter

女孩子 nǚháizi [名] girl

女朋友 nǚpéngyou [名] girlfriend

女人 nǚrén [名] woman

女士 nǚshì [名] 1 (指称呼) Ms. 2 (对妇女的尊称) lady

女婿 nǚxu [名] son-in-law

暖 nuǎn **I** [形] warm **II** [动] warm

暖和 nuǎnhuo **I** [形] warm **II** [动] warm up

暖气 nuǎnqì [名] heating

暖水瓶 nuǎnshuǐpíng [名] Thermos® flask

挪 nuó [动] move ▶挪动 nuódong move

哦 ó [叹] oh ▶哦, 他也来了。 Ó, tā yě láile. Oh, he's come too.
→ see also/另见 ò

哦 ò [叹] oh ▶哦, 我明白了。 Ò, wǒ míngbai le. Oh, now I understand.
→ see also/另见 ó

欧 ōu [名] (欧洲) Europe ▶欧洲 Ōuzhōu Europe

欧元 ōuyuán [名] euro

呕 ǒu [动] vomit

呕吐 ǒutù [动] vomit

偶 ǒu [名] **1** (人像) image ▶木偶 mù'ǒu puppet **2** (双数) even number ▶偶数 ǒushù even number

偶尔 ǒu'ěr [副] occasionally

偶然 ǒurán [形] chance

藕 ǒu [名] lotus root

爬 pá [动] 1 (前移) crawl 2 (上移) climb ▶ 爬山 páshān climb a mountain 3 (起床) get up 4 (升迁) be promoted

怕 pà [动] 1 (惧怕) fear 2 (担心) be afraid 3 (估计) may be

拍 pāi I [动] 1 (击打) beat 2 (拍摄) shoot 3 (发) send 4 (拍马屁) flatter II [名] 1 (用具) bat (英), paddle (美) 2 (节奏) beat

拍照 pāizhào [动] take a photograph

拍子 pāizi [名] 1 (用具) bat (英), paddle (美) ▷ 网球拍子 wǎngqiú pāizi tennis racket 2 (节奏) beat

排 pái I [动] 1 (摆放) put ... in

order 2(排演) rehearse 3(除去) drain II [名] 1(行列) row 2(指军队) platoon 3(指水运) raft III [量] row

排队 páiduì [动] queue (英), stand in line (美)

排球 páiqiú [名] volleyball

牌 pái [名] 1(标志板) board ▶门牌 ménpái house number ▶招牌 zhāopái shop sign 2(商标) brand

派 pài I [名] 1(帮派) group ▶学派 xuépài school of thought 2(风度) manner II [动] 1(分配) set 2(委派) send 3(安排) assign

派对 pàiduì [名] party

攀 pān [动] 1(向上爬) climb 2(指关系) seek friends in high places ▶高攀 gāopān be a social climber 3(拉扯) chat

攀登 pāndēng [动] scale

盘 pán I [名] 1(盘子) tray 2(盘状物) ▶棋盘 qípán chessboard 3(行情) quotation II [动] 1(绕) wind ▶盘旋 pánxuán wind 2(核查) examine ▶盘问 pánwèn interrogate 3(清点) make an inventory ▶盘货 pánhuò stocktake 4(转让) transfer III [量] 1(指物量) ▶三盘录像带 sān pán lùxiàngdài three videotapes 2(指动量) game measure word, used for videotapes, cassettes and board games

盘子 pánzi [名] plate

判 pàn I [动] 1(分辨) distinguish ▶判明 pànmíng ascertain 2(评定) judge 3(裁决) sentence ▶审判 shěnpàn try II [副] clearly

判断 pànduàn [动] judge

盼 pàn [动] 1(盼望) long 2(看) look ▶左顾右盼 zuǒgù-yòupàn look around

盼望 pànwàng [动] long

旁 páng I [名] side II [形] (口) other

旁边 pángbiān I [名] side II [副] beside

胖 pàng [形] fat

抛 pāo [动] 1(投掷) throw 2(丢下) leave ... behind 3(暴露) bare ▶抛头露面 pāotóu-lùmiàn appear in public 4(脱手) dispose of

抛弃 pāoqì [动] desert

跑 pǎo [动] 1(奔) run 2(逃) escape 3(奔波) run around 4(漏) leak

跑步 pǎobù [动] run

泡 pào I [名] 1(指气体) bubble 2(泡状物) ▶灯泡 dēngpào light bulb II [动] 1(浸) soak 2(消磨) dawdle 3(沏) infuse ▷泡茶 pào chá make tea

泡沫 pàomò [名] foam

炮 pào [名] 1(武器) cannon 2(爆竹) firecracker

陪 péi [动] 1(相伴) go with ▷我要陪母亲去医院。 wǒ yào péi mǔqīn qù yīyuàn I have to go to the hospital with my mother.

2(协助)assist

陪同 péitóng I[动]accompany II[名]guide

培 péi[动]foster

培训 péixùn[动]train

培养 péiyǎng[动]cultivate

培育 péiyù[动]1(培植养育) cultivate 2(培养教育)nurture

赔 péi[动]1(赔偿)make good 2(亏本)make a loss

赔偿 péicháng[动]compensate

佩 pèi[动]1(佩带)wear 2(佩服) admire ▶钦佩 qīnpèi esteem

佩服 pèifu[动]admire

配 pèi I[动]1(指两性)marry 2(指动物)mate 3(调和)mix ▶配药 pèiyào make up a prescription 4(分派)allocate ▶配售 pèishòu ration 5(衬托)match 6(符合)fit II[名]spouse

配合 pèihé I[动]cooperate II[形] complementary

喷 pēn[动]gush

喷泉 pēnquán[名]fountain

喷嚏 pēntì[名]sneeze

盆 pén[名]1(盛具)basin ▶脸盆 liǎnpén washbasin 2(盆状物) ▶骨盆 gǔpén pelvis

朋 péng[名]friend

朋友 péngyou[名]1(指友谊) friend 2(女友)girlfriend 3(男友) boyfriend

捧 pěng I[动]1(托)hold ... in both hands 2(奉承)flatter II[量] handful

碰 pèng[动]1(撞击)hit 2(遇见) bump into 3(试探)take a chance

碰见 pèngjiàn[动]encounter

碰巧 pèngqiǎo[副]by chance

批 pī I[动]1(批示)comment ▶批示 pīshì comment 2(批评) criticize II[名]wholesale III[量] 1(指人)group 2(指物)batch

批判 pīpàn[动]1(驳斥)repudiate 2(批评)criticize

批评 pīpíng[动]criticize

批准 pīzhǔn[动]approve

披 pī[动]1(搭)drape ... over one's shoulders 2(开裂)split

皮 pí I[名]1(表皮)skin 2(皮革)leather ▶漆皮 qīpí patent leather 3(外皮)covering 4(表面)surface 5(薄片)sheet ▶奶皮 nǎipí skin on the milk 6(指橡胶)rubber II[形]1(韧)thick-skinned 2(变韧的)rubbery 3(顽皮)naughty

皮包 píbāo[名]leather handbag

皮肤 pífū[名]skin

疲 pí[形]1(疲劳)tired 2(厌倦) tired of

疲倦 píjuàn[形]tired

疲劳 píláo[形]1(劳累)weary 2(衰退)weakened

啤 pí see below/见下文

啤酒 píjiǔ[名]beer

脾 pí [名] spleen

脾气 píqi [名] 1 (怒气) temper 2 (性情) temperament

匹 pǐ I [动] match II [量] 1 (指动物) ▷三匹马 sān pǐ mǎ three horses 2 (指布料) bolt

measure word, used for horses, mules, donkeys and bolts of silk

屁 pì I [名] wind ▷放屁 fàngpì fart II [形] meaningless

屁股 pìgu [名] 1 (指人) bottom 2 (指后部) rear

譬 pì [名] analogy ▷譬如 pìrú for example ▷譬喻 pìyù metaphor

譬如 pìrú [动] take ... for example

偏 piān [形] 1 (倾斜的) slanting 2 (不公的) biased

偏见 piānjiàn [名] prejudice

偏偏 piānpiān [副] 1 (表示主观) persistently 2 (表示客观) contrary to expectation 3 (表示范围) only

篇 piān I [名] 1 (文章) writing ▷篇章 piānzhāng sections (PL) 2 (单张纸) sheet ▷歌篇儿 gēpiānr song sheet II [量] ▷三篇文章 sān piān wénzhāng three articles

measure word, used for articles, essays etc.

便 pián see below/见下文
→ see also/另见 biàn

便便 piánpián [形] fat

便宜 piányi I [形] cheap II [名]

small gains (PL) III [动] let ... off lightly

片 piàn I [名] 1 (指薄度) piece ▷纸片 zhǐpiàn scraps of paper 2 (指地区) area II [动] slice III [形] 1 (不全) incomplete ▷片面 piànmiàn one-sided 2 (简短) brief IV [量] 1 (指片状) ▷两片药 liǎng piàn yào two tablets ▷几片树叶 jǐ piàn shùyè some leaves ▷一片面包 yī piàn miànbāo a slice of bread 2 (指大陆) stretch

measure word, used for thin flat objects

片面 piànmiàn I [名] one side II [形] one-sided

骗 piàn [动] 1 (欺骗) deceive 2 (骗得) swindle ▷骗钱 piànqián swindle

骗子 piànzi [名] swindler

漂 piāo [动] 1 (浮) float 2 (流动) drift
→ see also/另见 piào

飘 piāo [动] 1 (飞扬) flutter 2 (指腿、脚) wobble

飘扬 piāoyáng [动] flutter

票 piào [名] 1 (作凭证) ticket 2 (指钞票) note (英), bill (美) 3 (指戏曲) amateur performance

漂 piào see below/见下文
→ see also/另见 piāo

漂亮 piàoliang [形] 1 (好看) good-looking 2 (精彩) wonderful

拼 pīn [动] 1 (合) join together

2(竭尽全力) go all out ▸拼命 pīnmìng with all one's might **3**(字, 词) spell ▷你能拼一下这个词吗？ nǐ néng pīn yīxià zhègè cí ma? Can you spell this word?

拼命 pīnmìng [动] **1**(不要命) risk one's life **2**(努力) go all out

拼音 pīnyīn [名] Pinyin

贫 pín I [形] **1**(穷) poor ▸贫民 pínmín the poor **2**(少) deficient ▸贫血 pínxuè anaemia (英), anemia (美) II [动] (方) be a chatterbox

贫苦 pínkǔ [形] poverty-stricken

贫穷 pínqióng [形] poor

频 pín [副] frequently

频繁 pínfán [形] frequent

频率 pínlǜ [名] **1**(物) frequency **2**(指心脏) rate

品 pǐn I [名] **1**(物品) article ▸商品 shāngpǐn merchandise **2**(等级) grade ▸精品 jīngpǐn special product **3**(种类) type ▸品种 pǐnzhǒng variety **4**(品质) character ▸品德 pǐndé moral character II [动] taste

品尝 pǐncháng [动] savour (英), savor (美)

品德 pǐndé [名] moral character

品格 pǐngé [名] character

品质 pǐnzhì [名] **1**(品德) character **2**(质量) quality

品种 pǐnzhǒng [名] **1**(动) breed **2**(植) species **3**(指产品) kind

乒 pīng I [拟] bang II [名] (also: 乒乓球) table tennis

乒乓球 pīngpāngqiú [名] table tennis

平 píng I [形] **1**(平坦) flat ▸平原 píngyuán plain **2**(安定) calm **3**(普通) ordinary **4**(平均) even ▸平分 píngfēn fifty-fifty **5**(指比分) ▸平局 píngjú a draw II [动] **1**(夷平) level **2**(指成绩) equal **3**(镇压) suppress

平安 píng'ān [形] safe and sound

平常 píngcháng I [形] common II [副] usually

平等 píngděng [形] equal

平凡 píngfán [形] uneventful

平方 píngfāng [名] **1**(数) square **2**(平方米) square metre (英) 或 meter (美)

平衡 pínghéng [名] balance ▸平衡收支 pínghéng shōuzhī balance revenue and expenditure

平静 píngjìng [形] calm

平均 píngjūn [形] average

平时 píngshí [副] usually

平原 píngyuán [名] plain

评 píng [动] **1**(评论) criticize ▸批评 pīpíng criticize ▸书评 shūpíng book review **2**(评判) judge ▸评分 píngfēn mark **3**(选) select

评价 píngjià [动] evaluate

评论 pínglùn [动] review

苹 píng see below/见下文

苹果 píngguǒ [名] apple

凭 píng I [动] rely on II [名] evidence ▶凭据 píngjù credentials (PL) III [连] no matter

瓶 píng [名] bottle

瓶子 píngzi [名] bottle

坡 pō [名] slope ▶山坡 shānpō slope

迫 pò I [动] 1(逼迫) force 2(接近) approach II [形] urgent

迫切 pòqiè [形] pressing

破 pò I [形] 1(受损) broken 2(烂) lousy II [动] 1(受损) cut 2(破除) break ▶破例 pòlì make an exception 3(钱, 工夫) spend 4(揭穿) expose ▶破案 pò'àn solve a case 5(打败) defeat

破坏 pòhuài [动] 1(建筑, 环境, 文物, 公物) destroy 2(团结, 社会秩序) undermine 3(协定, 法规, 规章) violate 4(计划) bring ... down 5(名誉) damage

破裂 pòliè [动] 1(谈判) break down 2(感情) break up 3(外交关系) break off

扑 pū [动] 1(冲向) rush at 2(专注于) devote 3(扑打) swat 4(翅膀) beat

扑克 pūkè [名] poker

铺 pū [动] 1(摊开) spread 2(铺设) lay
→ see also/另见 pù

葡 pú see below/见下文

葡萄 pútao [名] grape

朴 pǔ see below/见下文

朴实 pǔshí [形] 1(简朴) simple 2(诚实) honest

朴素 pǔsù [形] 1(衣着) plain 2(生活) simple 3(语言) plain

普 pǔ [形] general

普遍 pǔbiàn I [形] common II [副] commonly

普通 pǔtōng [形] common

普通话 pǔtōnghuà [名] Mandarin

铺 pù [名] 1(商店) shop ▶杂货铺 záhuòpù general store 2(床) plank bed ▶卧铺 wòpù berth
→ see also/另见 pū

q

七 qī [数] seven

七月 qīyuè [名] July

妻 qī [名] wife ▶未婚妻 wèihūnqī fiancée

妻子 qīzǐ [名] wife

柒 qī [数] seven

This is the complex character for "seven", which is mainly used in banks, on receipts, etc. to prevent mistakes and forgery.

期 qī I [名] 1 (预定时间) time limit ▶到期 dàoqī expire 2 (一段时间) period of time ▶假期 jiàqī holiday II [量] 1 (指训练班) class 2 (指杂志, 报纸) edition III [动] expect

期待 qīdài [动] await

期间 qījiān [名] period of time

期望 qīwàng I [名] expectations (PL) II [动] expect

欺 qī [动] 1 (欺骗) deceive 2 (欺负) bully

欺负 qīfu [动] bully

欺骗 qīpiàn [动] deceive

齐 qí I [形] 1 (整齐) neat 2 (一致) joint 3 (完备) ready II [动] 1 (达到) reach 2 (取齐) level III [副] at the same time

其 qí [代] (书) 1 (他的) his 2 (她的) her 3 (它的) its 4 (他们的, 她们的, 它们的) their 5 (他) him 6 (她) her 7 (它) it 8 (他们, 她们, 它们) them 9 (那个) that

其次 qícì [代] 1 (下一个) next ▷其次要做的事是什么？ Qícì yào zuò de shì shì shénme? What are we going to do next? 2 (次要的) the second

其实 qíshí [副] actually

其他 qítā [代] other ▷我不知道，你问其他人吧。 Wǒ bù zhīdào, nǐ wèn qítā rén ba. I don't know, ask someone else. ▷还有其他事情没有？ Háiyǒu qítā shìqing méiyǒu? Is there anything else?

其余 qíyú [代] the rest

其中 qízhōng [名] among which ▷他有六套西服，其中两套是黑色的。 Tā yǒu liù tào xīfú, qízhōng liǎng tào shì hēisè de. He has six suits, of which two are black.

奇 qí I [形] 1 (非常少见的) strange ▶奇闻 qíwén fantastic story ▶奇事 qíshì miracle 2 (出人意料的) unexpected ▶奇袭 qíxí surprise attack ▶奇遇 qíyù lucky encounter II [动] surprise ▶惊奇 jīngqí surprise III [副] unusually

奇怪 qíguài [形] strange

奇迹 qíjì [名] miracle

骑 qí I [动] ride II [名] cavalry

棋 qí [名] chess ▶围棋 wéiqí go (board game)

旗 qí [名] flag ▶锦旗 jǐnqí silk banner

旗袍 qípáo [名] cheongsam (board game)

旗子 qízi [名] flag

乞 qǐ [动] beg ▶行乞 xíngqǐ go begging

乞丐 qǐgài [名] beggar

乞求 qǐqiú [动] beg

企 qǐ [动] look forward to

企图 qǐtú I [动] plan II [名] (贬) plan

企业 qǐyè [名] enterprise

启 qǐ [动] 1 (打开) open ▶开启 kāiqǐ open 2 (开导) enlighten 3 (开始) start

启发 qǐfā I [动] inspire II [名] inspiration

起 qǐ I [动] 1 (起来) rise ▶起立 qǐlì stand up 2 (取出) remove 3 (长出) form ▶脚上起泡 jiǎoshang qǐ pào form a blister on one's foot 4 (产生) become 5 (拟订) sketch out ▶起草 qǐcǎo draft 6 (建立) establish II [量] ▶一起交通事故 yī qǐ jiāotōng shìgù a traffic accident ▶一起火灾 yī qǐ huǒzāi a fire

measure word, used for accidents

起床 qǐchuáng [动] get up

起点 qǐdiǎn [名] starting point

起飞 qǐfēi [动] take off ▶飞机准时起飞。Fēijī zhǔnshí qǐfēi. The plane took off on time.

起来 qǐlái [动] 1 (站起或坐起) get up 2 (起床) get up

气 qì I [名] 1 (气体) gas ▶毒气 dúqì poison gas 2 (空气) air ▶球没气了。Zhè qiú méi qì le. This ball is deflated. 3 (气息) breath 4 (精神) mood 5 (气味) smell ▶臭气 chòuqì stink 6 (习气) manner ▶孩子气 háiziqì childishness 7 (怒气) anger 8 (医) qi II [动] 1 (生气) be angry 2 (使生气) provoke

气氛 qìfēn [名] atmosphere

气功 qìgōng [名] qigong

气候 qìhòu [名] climate

气温 qìwēn [名] temperature

气象 qìxiàng [名] 1 (大气现象) weather 2 (气象学) meteorology 3 (情景)

atmosphere

汽 qì [名] 1 (气体) vapour (英), vapor (美) 2 (蒸气) steam

汽车 qìchē [名] car ▶公共汽车 gōnggòng qìchē bus

汽水 qìshuǐ [名] fizzy drink

汽油 qìyóu [名] petrol (英), gasoline (美)

器 qì [名] 1 (器具) utensil ▶乐器 yuèqì musical instrument ▶瓷器 cíqì china 2 (器官) organ

器官 qìguān [名] organ

恰 qià [副] 1 (适当) appropriately 2 (刚好) exactly

恰当 qiàdàng [形] appropriate

恰好 qiàhǎo [副] luckily

千 qiān I [数] thousand II [形] many

千万 qiānwàn I [数] ten million II [副] ▷你千万别做傻事。 Nǐ qiānwàn bié zuò shǎshì. You absolutely mustn't do anything stupid.

牵 qiān [动] 1 (拉住) pull 2 (牵涉) involve

铅 qiān [名] (化) lead

铅笔 qiānbǐ [名] pencil

谦 qiān [形] modest

谦虚 qiānxū I [形] modest II [动] speak modestly

签 qiān I [动] 1 (名字) sign 2 (意见) endorse II [名] 1 (指占卜, 赌博, 比赛) lot 2 (标志) label ▶书

签 shūqiān bookmark 3 (细棍子) stick ▶牙签 yáqiān toothpick

签名 qiānmíng [动] sign

签证 qiānzhèng [名] visa

签字 qiānzì [动] sign one's name

前 qián I [形] 1 (正面的) front 2 (指次序) first 3 (从前的) former ▶前夫 qiánfū ex-husband 4 (未来的) future II [动] advance

前进 qiánjìn [动] 1 (向前走) advance 2 (发展) make progress

前面 qiánmian [副] in front

前年 qiánnián [名] the year before last

前天 qiántiān [名] the day before yesterday

前途 qiántú [名] future

前夕 qiánxī [名] eve

钱 qián [名] money

钱包 qiánbāo [名] 1 (女用) purse 2 (男用) wallet

浅 qiǎn [形] 1 (指深度) shallow 2 (指难度) easy 3 (指学识) lacking 4 (指颜色) light ▶浅蓝色 qiǎnlánsè light blue ▶浅绿色 qiǎnlǜsè pale green 5 (指时间) short

欠 qiàn [动] 1 (钱, 情) owe 2 (缺乏) lack 3 (移动) raise ... slightly

枪 qiāng [名] 1 (旧兵器) spear 2 (兵器) gun ▶手枪 shǒuqiāng pistol

强 qiáng I [形] 1 (力量大) strong 2 (程度高) able 3 (好) better 4 (略多于) extra ▷三分之一强 sān

fēn zhī yī qiáng a third extra
II [动] force
→ see also/另见 qiǎng

强大 qiángdà [形] powerful

强盗 qiángdào [名] robber

强调 qiángdiào [动] stress

强度 qiángdù [名] intensity

强奸 qiángjiān [动] rape

强烈 qiángliè [形] intense

墙 qiáng [名] wall

抢 qiǎng [动] 1 (抢劫) rob 2 (抢夺) grab 3 (抢先) forestall 4 (赶紧) rush

抢劫 qiǎngjié [动] rob

强 qiǎng [动] 1 (勉强) make an effort 2 (迫使) force
→ see also/另见 qiáng

强迫 qiǎngpò [动] force

悄 qiāo see below/见下文

悄悄 qiāoqiāo [副] 1 (悄然无声) quietly 2 (不让知道) stealthily

敲 qiāo [动] 1 (击) knock 2 (敲诈) blackmail

敲诈 qiāozhà [动] extort

桥 qiáo [名] bridge

桥梁 qiáoliáng [名] bridge

瞧 qiáo [动] look

巧 qiǎo [形] 1 (手、口) nimble 2 (有技能的) skilful (英), skillful (美) 3 (恰好) coincidental 4 (虚浮的) false

巧克力 qiǎokèlì [名] chocolate

巧妙 qiǎomiào [形] clever

切 qiē [动] cut

茄 qié [名] aubergine (英), eggplant (美)

茄子 qiézi [名] aubergine (英), eggplant (美)

窃 qiè **I** [动] steal **II** [副] surreptitiously

窃听 qiètīng [动] eavesdrop

窃贼 qièzéi [名] thief

侵 qīn [动] invade

侵略 qīnlüè [动] invade

亲 qīn **I** [名] 1 (父母) parent 2 (亲戚) relative 3 (婚姻) marriage ▶ 定亲 dìngqīn engagement 4 (新娘) bride **II** [形] 1 (指血缘近) blood 2 (指感情好) intimate **III** [副] personally **IV** [动] 1 (亲吻) kiss 2 (亲近) be close to

亲爱 qīn'ài [形] dear

亲近 qīnjìn [形] close

亲密 qīnmì [形] close ▷ 亲密朋友 qīnmì péngyǒu close friend ▶ 亲密无间 qīnmì wújiàn be as thick as thieves

亲戚 qīnqi [名] relative

亲切 qīnqiè [形] warm

亲热 qīnrè [形] affectionate

亲自 qīnzì [副] personally

琴 qín [名] ▶ 钢琴 gāngqín piano ▶ 小提琴 xiǎotíqín violin

勤 qín **I** [形] hard-working **II** [副] regularly **III** [名] 1 (勤务) duty

▶值勤 zhíqín be on duty **2**(到场) attendance ▶考勤 kǎoqín check attendance

勤奋 qínfèn [形] diligent

勤劳 qínláo [形] hard-working

青 qīng I[形] **1**(指绿色) green **2**(指伤痕) black **3**(指年纪) young ▶青年 qīngnián youth II[名] **1**(指青草) grass **2**(指庄稼) unripe crops (PL)

青年 qīngnián [名] youth

青少年 qīngshàonián [名] teenager

轻 qīng I[形] **1**(指重量) light **2**(指数量或程度) ▷他们年纪很轻。Tāmen niánjì hěnqīng. They are quite young. **3**(指无足轻重) not important **4**(指轻松愉快) relaxed ▶轻音乐 qīngyīnyuè light music II[副] **1**(指用力) gently **2**(轻率) rashly III[动] disparage

轻松 qīngsōng [形] relaxing

轻易 qīngyì [副] **1**(容易) easily **2**(随便) rashly

倾 qīng I[动] **1**(斜) lean **2**(塌) collapse **3**(倒出) empty out **4**(用尽) exhaust II[名] tendency

倾向 qīngxiàng I[动] incline to II[名] tendency

清 qīng I[形] **1**(纯净) clear **2**(寂静) quiet **3**(清楚) distinct ▶分清 fēnqīng distinguish **4**(完全) settled **5**(纯洁) pure II[动] **1**(清除) get rid of **2**(结清) settle **3**(清

点) check **4**(清理) put in order

清楚 qīngchu I[形] clear II[动] understand

清洁 qīngjié [形] clean

清静 qīngjìng [形] quiet

清明节 Qīngmíng Jié [名] Tomb Sweeping Festival

清明节 Qīngmíng Jié

清明节 Qīngmíng Jié, **Clear and Bright Festival** sometimes translated literally as **Tomb Sweeping Festival**, is celebrated on the 4th, 5th, or 6th of April. It is traditionally the time when Chinese families visit graves to honour their dead ancestors.

情 qíng [名] **1**(感情) feeling ▶热情 rèqíng warmth **2**(情面) kindness **3**(爱情) love **4**(情况) condition ▶实情 shíqíng true state of affairs

情节 qíngjié [名] **1**(内容) plot **2**(事实) circumstances (PL)

情景 qíngjǐng [名] sight

情况 qíngkuàng [名] **1**(状况) situation **2**(变化) military development

情侣 qínglǚ [名] lovers (PL)

情人节 Qíngrén Jié [名] Valentine's Day

情形 qíngxíng [名] situation

情绪 qíngxù [名] **1**(心理状态)

mood **2** (不很开心) moodiness

晴 qíng [形] fine

晴朗 qínglǎng [形] sunny

请 qǐng [动] **1** (请求) ask ▷请他进来。 Qǐng tā jìnlai. Ask him to come in. **2** (邀请) invite **3** (敬) ▷请这边走。 Qǐng zhèbiān zǒu. This way, please. ▷请大家安静一下。 Qǐng dàjiā ānjìng yīxià. Everyone quiet, please.

请假 qǐngjià [动] ask for leave

请教 qǐngjiào [动] consult

请客 qǐngkè [动] treat

请求 qǐngqiú [动] ask

请问 qǐngwèn [动] ▷请问怎么出去？ Qǐngwèn zěnme chūqù? Could you show me the way out, please?

请勿 qǐngwù [动] ▷请勿吸烟。 Qǐngwù xīyān. No smoking.

庆 qìng I [动] celebrate II [名] festival ▶国庆 guóqìng National Day

庆贺 qìnghè [动] celebrate

庆祝 qìngzhù [动] celebrate

穷 qióng I [形] poor II [名] limit III [副] **1** (彻底) thoroughly **2** (极端) extremely

秋 qiū [名] **1** (指季节) autumn (英), fall (美) **2** (指庄稼) harvest time **3** (指一年) year **4** (指厄运期) period

秋天 qiūtiān [名] autumn (英), fall (美)

求 qiú I [动] **1** (请求) request **2** (追求) strive II [名] demand

球 qiú [名] **1** (数) (球体) sphere **2** (指球状) ball ▶雪球 xuěqiú snowball **3** (指体育) ball ▶篮球 lánqiú basketball ▶足球 zúqiú football **4** (指比赛) ball game **5** (地球) the Earth ▶全球 quánqiú the whole world

球场 qiúchǎng [名] court

球迷 qiúmí [名] fan

区 qū I [动] distinguish II [名] **1** (地区) area **2** (指行政单位) region ▶自治区 zìzhìqū autonomous region

区别 qūbié [动] distinguish

区分 qūfēn [动] differentiate

区域 qūyù [名] area

趋 qū [动] **1** (走) hasten **2** (趋向) tend to become

趋势 qūshì [名] trend

趋向 qūxiàng I [动] tend to II [名] trend

渠 qú [名] ditch

渠道 qúdào [名] **1** (水道) irrigation ditch **2** (途径) channel

曲 qǔ [名] **1** (指歌曲) song **2** (指乐曲) music

曲子 qǔzi [名] tune

取 qǔ **1** (拿到) take **2** (得到) obtain **3** (采取) adopt **4** (选取) choose

取得 qǔdé [动] get

取消 qǔxiāo [动] cancel

娶 qǔ [动] marry

去 qù I [动] 1 (到) go 2 (除) get rid of 3 (距) be apart 4 (发) send II [形] past

去年 qùnián [名] last year

去世 qùshì [动] pass away

趣 qù I [名] interest ▸志趣 zhìqù interest II [形] interesting

趣味 qùwèi [名] taste

圈 quān I [名] 1 (环形物) circle ▸北极圈 Běijíquān Arctic Circle 2 (界) group II [动] circle

圈套 quāntào [名] trap

权 quán I [名] 1 (权力) power ▸当权 dāngquán be in power 2 (权利) right 3 (形势) ▸主动权 zhǔdòngquán initiative ▸控制权 kòngzhìquán control 4 (权宜) expediency II [副] for the time being

权力 quánlì [名] power

全 quán I [形] 1 (齐全) complete 2 (整个) whole II [副] entirely III [动] keep ... intact

全部 quánbù [形] whole

全面 quánmiàn [形] comprehensive

全体 quántǐ [名] everyone

泉 quán [名] spring ▸温泉 wēnquán hot spring

拳 quán [名] fist

拳头 quántou [名] fist

拳击 quánjī [名] boxing

鬈 quán [形] curly

劝 quàn [动] 1 (说服) advise 2 (勉励) encourage

劝告 quàngào [动] advise

缺 quē I [动] 1 (缺乏) lack 2 (残破) be incomplete 3 (缺席) be absent II [名] vacancy ▸补缺 bǔquē fill a vacancy

缺点 quēdiǎn [名] shortcoming

缺乏 quēfá [动] lack

缺口 quēkǒu [名] 1 (口子) gap 2 (缺额) shortfall

缺少 quēshǎo [动] lack

缺席 quēxí [动] be absent

缺陷 quēxiàn [名] defect

瘸 qué [动] be lame

却 què I [动] 1 (后退) step back 2 (使退却) drive ... back 3 (拒绝) decline ▸推却 tuīquè decline 4 (表示完成) ▸冷却 lěngquè cool off ▸忘却 wàngquè forget II [副] however

确 què I [副] 1 (确实地) really 2 (坚定地) firmly ▸确信 quèxìn firmly believe

确定 quèdìng I [动] determine II [形] definite

确实 quèshí I [形] true II [副] really

裙 qún [名] skirt

裙子 qúnzi [名] skirt

群 qún I [名] crowd II [量] 1 (指动物) herd, flock ▸一群绵羊 yī qún

miányáng a flock of sheep ▷一群
蜜蜂 yī qún mìfēng a swarm of
bees ▷一群奶牛 yī qún nǎiniú a
herd of cows 2 (指人) group ▷一
群学生 yī qún xuésheng a group
of students

群众 qúnzhòng [名] the masses
(PL)

然 rán [代] so

然而 rán'ér [连] however

然后 ránhòu [连] afterwards

燃 rán [动] 1 (燃烧) burn 2 (点
燃) light

燃料 ránliào [名] fuel

燃烧 ránshāo [动] burn

染 rǎn [动] 1 (着色) dye 2 (感染)
contract 3 (沾染) catch

嚷 rǎng [动] 1 (喊叫) howl 2 (吵闹)
make a racket

让 ràng I [动] 1 (退让) make
allowances 2 (允许) let 3 (转让)
transfer II [介] by

扰 rǎo [动] (搅扰) disturb ▶打扰

dǎrǎo disturb

绕 rào [动] 1(缠绕) wind 2(围绕) go round 3(迂回) make a detour

惹 rě [动] 1(引起) stir up 2(触动) provoke 3(招) make

热 rè I [名] 1(物) heat 2(高烧) fever ▶发热 fārè have a fever II [形] 1(温度高) hot 2(走俏) popular III [动] heat

热爱 rè'ài [动] love

热狗 règǒu [名] hot dog

热烈 rèliè [形] heated

热闹 rènao [形] lively

热情 rèqíng I [名] passion II [形] enthusiastic

热线 rèxiàn [名] 1(指电话或电报) hotline 2(指交通) busy route

热心 rèxīn [形] warm-hearted

人 rén [名] 1(人类) human being ▶人权 rénquán human rights (PL) 2(指某种人) person ▶军人 jūnrén soldier ▶中国人 Zhōngguórén a Chinese person/Chinese people 3(人手) manpower

人才 réncái [名] (指能人) talent

人工 réngōng [形] man-made

人口 rénkǒu [名] 1(地区人数) population 2(家庭人数) people

人类 rénlèi [名] mankind, humankind

人们 rénmen [名] people

人民 rénmín [名] the people

人民币 rénmínbì [名] Renminbi, RMB

人生 rénshēng [名] life

人体 réntǐ [名] the human body

人物 rénwù [名] 1(能人) figure 2(艺术形象) character

忍 rěn [动] (忍受) endure

忍耐 rěnnài [动] show restraint

忍受 rěnshòu [动] bear

认 rèn [动] 1(识) know 2(承认) admit

认得 rènde [动] be acquainted with

认识 rènshi I [动] know II [名] understanding

认为 rènwéi [动] think

认真 rènzhēn I [形] serious II [动] take ... seriously

任 rèn I [动] 1(聘) appoint ▶委任 wěirèn appoint 2(听凭) let II [名] (职责) responsibility

任何 rènhé [形] any ▷任何人都不能迟到。 Rènhé rén dōu bù néng chídào. No one can be late.

任务 rènwu [名] task

扔 rēng [动] 1(掷) throw 2(丢) throw ... away

仍 réng [副] still

仍然 réngrán [副] (表示继续) still

日 rì [名] 1(太阳) sun ▶日出 rìchū sunrise ▶日落 rìluò sunset 2(白天) daytime 3(天) day ▶明

日 míngrì tomorrow 4 (每天) every day ▶城市面貌日见改善。 Chéngshì miànmào rìjiàn gǎishàn. The city looks better and better every day. 5 (指某一天) day ▶生日 shēngrì birthday 6 (also: 日本) Japan

日报 rìbào [名] daily paper

日本 Rìběn [名] Japan

日常 rìcháng [形] everyday

日记 rìjì [名] diary

日历 rìlì [名] calendar

日期 rìqī [名] date

日用品 rìyòngpǐn [名] daily necessities

日语 Rìyǔ [名] Japanese

日元 Rìyuán [名] Japanese yen

日子 rìzi [名] 1 (日期) date 2 (时间) day 3 (生活) life

荣 róng [形] (光荣) glorious

荣幸 róngxìng [形] honoured (英), honored (美) ▶认识您,我感到非常荣幸。 Rènshi nín wǒ gǎndào fēicháng róngxìng. I feel honoured to know you.

荣誉 róngyù [名] (指名声) honour (英), honor (美)

容 róng I [动] 1 (容纳) fit ▶容纳 róngnà hold ▶容量 róngliàng capacity ▶容器 róngqì container 2 (容忍) tolerate ▶容忍 róngrěn tolerate 3 (允许) allow II [名] (相貌) appearance ▶容貌 róngmào features (PL)

容易 róngyì [形] 1 (简便) easy 2 (较

可能) likely

柔 róu [形] 1 (软) soft 2 (柔和) gentle

柔软 róuruǎn [形] soft

揉 róu [动] (搓) rub

肉 ròu [名] 1 (指人) flesh 2 (指动物) meat ▶猪肉 zhūròu pork 3 (指瓜果) flesh

如 rú [动] 1 (好似) be like 2 (比得上) be as good as ▶不如 bùrú not as good as 3 (例如)

如此 rúcǐ [代] so ▶他的态度竟如此恶劣。 Tā de tàidù jìng rúcǐ èliè. His attitude was so unpleasant.

如果 rúguǒ [连] if

如何 rúhé [代] ▶此事如何解决？ Cǐ shì rúhé jiějué? How are we going to sort this out? ▶你今后如何打算？ Nǐ jīnhòu rúhé dǎsuàn? What are your plans for the future?

儒 rú [名] (儒家) Confucianism ▶儒家 Rújiā Confucianism

入 rù [动] 1 (进入) enter ▶入场 rùchǎng enter 2 (参加) join ▶入学 rùxué enrol

入境 rùjìng [动] enter a country

入口 rùkǒu [名] (门) entrance

软 ruǎn [形] 1 (柔) soft ▶软和 ruǎnhuo soft 2 (温和) gentle 3 (柔弱) weak ▶软弱 ruǎnruò weak

软件 ruǎnjiàn [名] (计算机) software

软卧 ruǎnwò [名] light sleeper

软饮料 ruǎnyǐnliào [名] soft drink

弱 ruò [形] 1 (弱小) weak 2 (年幼) young 3 (软弱) weak

弱点 ruòdiǎn [名] weakness

仨 sā [数] (口) three ▶ 哥仨 gēsā three brothers

撒 sā [动] 1 (手, 网) let ... go 2 (贬) (疯, 野) lose control of oneself ▶ 撒野 sāyě have a tantrum → see also/另见 sǎ

撒谎 sāhuǎng [动] (口) lie

撒娇 sājiāo [动] behave like a spoiled child

撒气 sāqì [动] 1 (球, 车胎) get a puncture 2 (发泄怒气) take one's anger out on ▷ 别拿我撒气！ Bié ná wǒ sāqì! Don't take your anger out on me!

撒手 sāshǒu [动] (松手) let go

洒 sǎ [动] 1 (泼) sprinkle 2 (指不小心) spill

洒脱 sǎtuo [形] carefree

撒 sǎ [动] 1(散布) scatter 2(散落) spill
→ see also/另见 sā

腮 sāi [名] cheek

腮帮子 sāibāngzi [名] (口) cheek

塞 sāi I [动] stuff ... into II [名] cork

塞子 sāizi [名] cork

赛 sài I [名] match ▷演讲比赛 yǎnjiǎng bǐsài debating contest II [动] compete

赛车 sàichē I [动] race II [名] (指汽车) racing car

赛季 sàijì [名] season

赛跑 sàipǎo [动] race

三 sān [数] 1(指数目) three ▷三月 sānyuè March 2(表示序数) third 3(表示多数) several ▷三思 sānsī think twice

三角 sānjiǎo [名] triangle ▷三角恋爱 sānjiǎo liàn'ài love triangle

三明治 sānmíngzhì [名] sandwich

三围 sānwéi [名] vital statistics (PL)

三心二意 sān xīn èr yì half-hearted ▷他工作三心二意的。 Tā gōngzuò sān xīn èr yì de. He's half-hearted about his work.

叁 sān [数] three
This is the complex character for "three", which is mainly used in banks, on receipts, etc. to prevent mistakes and forgery.

伞 sǎn [名] umbrella

散 sǎn I [动] loosen II [形] loose
→ see also/另见 sàn

散漫 sǎnmàn [形] slack

散文 sǎnwén [名] prose

散 sàn [动] 1(分离) break up ▷乌云散了。 Wūyún sàn le. The dark clouds scattered. 2(散布) give ... out 3(排除) dispel
→ see also/另见 sǎn

散布 sànbù [动] 1(传单) distribute 2(谣言) spread

散步 sànbù [动] go for a stroll

丧 sāng [名] funeral
→ see also/另见 sàng

丧事 sāngshì [名] funeral arrangements (PL)

桑 sāng [名] mulberry

桑那浴 sāngnàyù [名] sauna

嗓 sǎng [名] 1(嗓子) throat 2(嗓音) voice

嗓门 sǎngmén [名] voice

嗓子 sǎngzi [名] 1(喉咙) throat 2(嗓音) voice

丧 sàng [动] lose
→ see also/另见 sāng

丧气 sàngqì [动] lose heart

丧失 sàngshī [动] lose

骚 sāo [动] disturb

骚扰 sāorǎo [动] harass ▶性骚扰 xìng sāorǎo sexual harassment

扫 sǎo [动] 1(打扫) sweep 2(除去)

clear ... away ►扫黄 sǎohuáng anti-pornography campaign
→ see also/另见 sào

扫除 sǎochú [动] 1(打扫) sweep ... up 2(除掉) eliminate

扫盲 sǎománg [动] eliminate illiteracy

扫描 sǎomiáo [动] scan

扫描仪 sǎomiáoyí [名] scanner

扫兴 sǎoxìng [形] disappointed

嫂 sǎo [名] (哥哥之妻) sister-in-law

嫂子 sǎozi [名] (口) sister-in-law

扫 sào see below/见下文
→ see also/另见 sǎo

扫帚 sàozhou [名] broom

色 sè [名] (颜色) colour (英), color (美)
→ see also/另见 shǎi

色彩 sècǎi [名] 1(颜色) colour (英), color (美) 2(指情调) tone

色盲 sèmáng [名] colour (英) 或 color (美) blindness

色情 sèqíng [形] pornographic

涩 sè [形] (味道) astringent

森 sēn [形] (形容树多) wooded

森林 sēnlín [名] forest

僧 sēng [名] Buddhist monk ►僧人 sēngrén Buddhist monk

杀 shā [动] 1(杀死) kill 2(战斗) fight 3(削弱) reduce

杀毒 shādú [动] get rid of a virus ►杀毒软件 shādú ruǎnjiàn anti-virus software

杀害 shāhài [动] murder

杀价 shājià [动] bargain ▷我很会杀价。 Wǒ hěn huì shājià. I'm a very good bargainer.

杀手 shāshǒu [名] killer

沙 shā [名] (石粒) sand

沙尘 shāchén [名] dust

沙尘暴 shāchénbào [名] sandstorm

沙发 shāfā [名] sofa

沙锅 shāguō [名] casserole

沙皇 shāhuáng [名] tsar

沙漠 shāmò [名] desert

沙滩 shātān [名] beach

沙哑 shāyǎ [形] hoarse

沙眼 shāyǎn [名] trachoma

沙子 shāzi [名] sand

纱 shā [名] (指织品) gauze

纱布 shābù [名] gauze

刹 shā [动] brake

刹车 shāchē I [动] 1(停止机器) brake 2(喻) (制止) put a stop to II [名] brake

鲨 shā [名] shark ►鲨鱼 shāyú shark

傻 shǎ [形] 1(蠢) stupid 2(死心眼) inflexible

傻瓜 shǎguā [名] fool

傻子 shǎzi [名] fool

厦 shà [名] tall building ▷摩天大厦 mótiān dàshà skyscraper

色 shǎi [名] colour (英), color (美)
→ see also/另见 sè

色子 shǎizi [名] dice

晒 shài [动] 1 (阳光照射) shine upon ▷他被晒黑了。 Tā bèi shài hēi le. He's tanned. 2 (吸收光热) lie in the sun ▷她在沙滩上晒太阳。 Tā zài shātān shàng shài tàiyang. She was sunbathing on the beach.

山 shān [名] (地质) mountain ▷小山 xiǎoshān hill

山村 shāncūn [名] mountain village

山洞 shāndòng [名] cave

山峰 shānfēng [名] peak

山谷 shāngǔ [名] valley

山脚 shānjiǎo [名] foothills (PL)

山林 shānlín [名] wooded hill

山脉 shānmài [名] mountain range

山坡 shānpō [名] mountainside

山区 shānqū [名] mountainous area

山水 shānshuǐ [名] 1 (风景) scenery 2 (画) landscape painting

山珍海味 shān zhēn hǎi wèi [名] exotic delicacies (PL)

删 shān [动] delete

删除 shānchú [动] delete

珊 shān see below/见下文

珊瑚 shānhú [名] coral

扇 shān [动] 1 (扇子) fan 2 (耳光) slap
→ see also/另见 shàn

闪 shǎn I [动] 1 (闪避) dodge 2 (受伤) sprain 3 (突然出现) flash 4 (闪耀) shine II [名] lightning ▷打闪了。 Dǎshǎn le. Lightning flashed.

闪电 shǎndiàn [名] lightning

闪动 shǎndòng [动] flash

闪烁 shǎnshuò [动] (忽明忽暗) twinkle

扇 shàn I [名] (扇子) fan II [量] ▷一扇窗 yī shàn chuāng a window ▷两扇门 liǎng shàn mén two doors

measure word, used for doors, windows, screens etc.

→ see also/另见 shān

善 shàn I [形] 1 (善良) kind 2 (良好) good ▷善事 shànshì good deeds 3 (友好) friendly II [动] 1 (擅长) be an expert at 2 (容易) be prone to ▷善忘 shànwàng forgetful

善良 shànliáng [形] kind-hearted

善于 shànyú [动] be good at

擅 shàn [动] be expert at

擅长 shàncháng [动] be skilled in

鳝 shàn [名] eel ▷鳝鱼 shànyú eel

伤 shāng I [动] 1 (身体部位) injure ▷扭伤 niǔshāng sprain 2 (感情) hurt II [名] injury

伤残 shāngcán [名] the disabled (PL)

伤风 shāngfēng [动] catch a cold

伤害 shānghài [动] 1 (感情) hurt 2 (身体) damage

伤痕 shānghén [名] scar

伤口 shāngkǒu [名] wound

伤心 shāngxīn [形] sad

商 shāng I [动] discuss ▷协商 xiéshāng negotiate II [名] 1 (商业) commerce ▷经商 jīngshāng trade 2 (商人) businessman, businesswoman 3 (数) quotient

商标 shāngbiāo [名] trademark

商场 shāngchǎng [名] shopping centre (英), mall (美)

商店 shāngdiàn [名] shop (英), store (美)

商量 shāngliáng [动] discuss

商品 shāngpǐn [名] commodity

商人 shāngrén [名] businessman, businesswoman

商谈 shāngtán [动] negotiate

商务 shāngwù [名] business ▷电子商务 diànzǐ shāngwù e-commerce

商业 shāngyè [名] commerce

赏 shǎng I [动] 1 (赏赐) award 2 (欣赏) admire 3 (赏识) appreciate II [名] reward

赏识 shǎngshí [动] think highly of

上 shàng I [名] 1 (指方位) upper part 2 (指等级, 质量) ▷上级 shàngjí higher authorities (PL) 3 (指时间, 次序) ▷上星期 shàng xīngqī last week ▷上半年 shàng bànnián the first half of the year II [动] 1 (向上) go up ▷上楼 shànglóu go upstairs 2 (按点前往) go ▷上学 shàngxué go to school ▷上班 shàngbān go to work 3 (去) go to ▷他上天津开会去了。 Tā shàng Tiānjīn kāihuì qù le. He went to Tianjin to attend a meeting. 4 (出场) make an entrance 5 (添补) fill ▷上货 shànghuò stock up 6 (饭, 菜) serve ▷上菜 shàng cài serve food 7 (安装) fix ▷上螺丝 shàng luósī fix a screw 8 (涂) apply ▷上涂料 shàng túliào apply paint 9 (登载) appear ▷上杂志 shàng zázhì appear in a magazine 10 (拧紧) tighten ▷我的表已上弦了。 Wǒde biǎo yǐ shàngxián le. I've wound up my watch. 11 (车, 船, 飞机) board 12 (表示达到目的) ▷当上老师 dāngshàng lǎoshī become a teacher III [介] 1 (在物体表面) on ▷椅子上 yǐzi shàng on the chair 2 (表示范围) in ▷报纸上 bàozhǐ shàng in the newspaper

上当 shàngdàng [动] be taken in

上等 shàngděng [形] first-class

上帝 Shàngdì [名] God

上吊 shàngdiào [动] hang oneself

上级 shàngjí [名] higher authorities (PL)

上来 shànglái [动] 1 (指动作趋向) ▷饭菜端上来了。 Fàncài

duān shànglái le. The meal was brought to the table. **2**(表示成功) ▷这个问题我答不上来。 Zhège wèntí wǒ dá bù shànglái. I can't answer this question.

上面 shàngmian [名] **1**(指位置高) ▷他住在我上面。 Tā zhùzài wǒ shàngmian. He lives above me. **2**(物体表面) ▷墙上面挂着相片。 Qiáng shàngmian guà zhe zhàopiàn. Photographs were hanging on the walls. **3**(以上的部分) ▷上面我们分析了各种可能性。 Shàngmian wǒmen fénxi le gèzhǒng kěnéngxìng. As can be seen above, we have made an analysis of all possibilities.

上年纪 shàng niánji [动] get old

上去 shàngqù [动] **1**(指由低到高) go up **2**(提高) improve

上身 shàngshēn [名] upper body

上升 shàngshēng [动] **1**(往高处移) ascend **2**(增加) increase

上市 shàngshì [动] appear on the market

上司 shàngsi [名] superior

上诉 shàngsù [动] appeal

上网 shàngwǎng [动] go online

上午 shàngwǔ [名] morning

上衣 shàngyī [名] top

上瘾 shàngyǐn [动] be addicted to

上涨 shàngzhǎng [动] rise

烧 shāo [动] **1**(着火) burn **2**(加热) heat ▷烧水 shāo shuǐ boil water **3**(烹) braise **4**(烤) roast ▷烧

鸡 shāojī roast chicken **5**(发烧) have a temperature

烧烤 shāokǎo [动] barbecue

稍 shāo [副] slightly
→ see also / 另见 shào

稍微 shāowēi [副] a little

勺 sháo [名] ladle

少 shǎo **I** [形] few ▷屋里家具太少。 Wū lǐ jiājù tài shǎo. There is very little furniture in the room. **II** [动] **1**(缺) lack ▷汤里少了葱。 Tāng lǐ shǎo le cōng. There is no onion in the soup. **2**(丢) be missing ▷她发现钱包里的钱少了一百块。 Tā fāxiàn qiánbāo lǐ de qián shǎo le yībǎi kuài. She discovered that one hundred kuai were missing from her purse.
→ see also / 另见 shào

少量 shǎoliàng [名] a little

少数 shǎoshù [名] minority

少数民族 shǎoshù mínzú [名] ethnic minorities (PL)

少数民族 shǎoshù mínzú

少数民族 shǎoshù mínzú refers to China's ethnic minorities. There are 56 distinct ethnic groups in China, of which the Han is by far the largest, accounting for over 90% of the population. The other 55 minorities are mainly located in the southwestern and northwestern provinces. Five regions have been set up as ethnic minorities autonomous regions.

少 shào [形] young ▶少女 shàonǚ young girl
→ *see also*/另见 shǎo

少年 shàonián [名] youth

哨 shào [名] (哨子) whistle

哨子 shàozi [名] whistle

稍 shào *see below*/见下文
→ *see also*/另见 shāo

稍息 shàoxī [动] stand at ease

奢 shē [形] extravagant

奢侈 shēchǐ [形] luxurious

舌 shé [名] tongue

舌头 shétou [名] tongue

折 shé [动] (折断) snap ▶他的腿折了。 Tāde tuǐ shé le. He broke his leg.
→ *see also*/另见 zhé

蛇 shé [名] snake

设 shè [动] 1 (摆) set ... up 2 (想) plan 3 (假定) suppose ▶设想 shèxiǎng envisage

设备 shèbèi [名] equipment

设计 shèjì [动] design ▶服装设计 fúzhuāng shèjì fashion design

设施 shèshī [名] facilities (PL)

社 shè [名] organization ▶旅行社 lǚxíngshè travel agent

社会 shèhuì [名] society ▷社会福利 shèhuì fúlì social welfare

社交 shèjiāo [名] social contact

社区 shèqū [名] community

舍 shè [名] house ▶宿舍 sùshè dormitory

射 shè [动] 1 (发) shoot 2 (喷) spout 3 (放出) emit ▶照射 zhàoshè shine

射击 shèjī I [动] fire II [名] shooting

射门 shèmén [动] shoot

射线 shèxiàn [名] (电磁波) ray

涉 shè [动] (牵涉) involve ▶涉嫌 shèxián be a suspect

涉及 shèjí [动] involve

摄 shè [动] 1 (吸取) absorb 2 (摄影) take a photo

摄像 shèxiàng [动] make a video

摄影 shèyǐng [动] 1 (照相) take a photo 2 (拍电影) shoot a film (英) 或 movie (美)

谁 shéi [代] 1 (表示问人) who ▷谁在门外? Shéi zài mén wài? Who's at the door? 2 (指任何一个人) whoever ▷谁先到谁买票。 Shéi xiān dào shéi mǎipiào. Whoever arrives first buys the tickets.

申 shēn [动] express

申请 shēnqǐng [动] apply ▷申请工作 shēnqǐng gōngzuò apply for a job

伸 shēn [动] stretch

伸手 shēnshǒu [动] (伸出手) hold out one's hand

身 shēn [名] 1 (身体) body 2 (生命) life 3 (自己) oneself

身材 shēncái [名] figure

身份 shēnfen [名] (地位) position

身份证 shēnfènzhèng [名] identity card

身体 shēntǐ [名] body

参 shēn [名] ginseng ▶人参 rénshēn ginseng
→ see also/另见 cān

绅 shēn [名] gentry

绅士 shēnshì [名] gentleman

深 shēn I [形] 1 (指深度) deep 2 (指距离) remote 3 (深奥) difficult 4 (深刻) deep ▶印象深 yìnxiàng shēn a deep impression 5 (密切) close 6 (浓重) dark ▶深蓝 shēnlán dark blue 7 (指时间久) late ▶深夜 shēnyè late at night II [名] depth III [副] very ▶深信 shēnxìn firmly believe

深奥 shēn'ào [形] profound

深度 shēndù I [名] depth II [形] extreme

深化 shēnhuà [动] deepen

深刻 shēnkè [形] deep

深入 shēnrù I [动] penetrate II [形] thorough

深远 shēnyuǎn [形] far-reaching

深造 shēnzào [动] pursue advanced studies

什 shén see below/见下文

什么 shénme [代] 1 (表示疑问) what ▷你要什么？ Nǐ yào shénme? What do you want? 2 (表示虚指) something ▷他们在商量着什么。 Tāmen zài shāngliàng zhe shénme. They are discussing something. 3 (表示任指) anything ▷我什么都不怕。 Wǒ shénme dōu bùpà. I'm not afraid of anything. 4 (表示惊讶，不满) what ▷什么！他拒绝出席会议！ Shénme! Tā jùjué chūxí huìyì! What! He refused to attend the meeting! 5 (表示责难) ▷你在胡说什么！ Nǐ zài húshuō shénme! What's that rubbish?

什么的 shénmede and so on [代] ▷餐桌上摆满了香蕉，李子，苹果什么的。 Cānzhuō shàng bǎimǎn le xiāngjiāo, lǐzi, píngguǒ shénme de. The dining table was loaded with bananas, plums, apples and so on.

神 shén I [名] 1 (宗) god 2 (精神) spirit ▶走神 zǒushén be absent-minded II [形] (高超) amazing ▶神奇 shénqí magical

神话 shénhuà [名] myth

神经 shénjīng [名] nerve

神秘 shénmì [形] mysterious

神气 shénqì I [名] manner II [形] 1 (精神) impressive 2 (得意) cocky

神圣 shénshèng [形] sacred

神态 shéntài [名] look

神仙 shénxiān [名] immortal

神学 shénxué [名] theology

审 shěn [动] 1 (审查) go over 2 (审讯) try ▷ 审案子 shěn ànzi try a case

审查 shěnchá [动] examine

审判 shěnpàn [动] try

审问 shěnwèn [动] interrogate

婶 shěn [名] aunt

肾 shèn [名] kidney

甚 shèn I [形] extreme II [副] very

甚至 shènzhì [副] even

渗 shèn [动] seep

慎 shèn [形] careful

慎重 shènzhòng [形] cautious

升 shēng I [动] 1 (由低往高) rise 2 (提升) promote ▷ 升职 shēngzhí be promoted II [量] litre (英), liter (美)

升级 shēngjí [动] 1 (升高年级) go up 2 (规模扩大) escalate 3 (指电脑) upgrade

升值 shēngzhí [动] appreciate

生 shēng I [动] 1 (生育) give birth to ▷ 生孩子 shēng háizi have a baby 2 (长) grow 3 (活) live ▷ 生死 shēngsǐ life and death 4 (患) get ▷ 生病 shēngbìng get ill 5 (点) light ▷ 生火 shēnghuǒ light a fire II [名] 1 (生命) life 2 (生平) life ▷ 今生 jīnshēng this life 3 (学生) student ▷ 新生 xīnshēng new student III [形] 1 (活的) living 2 (未熟的) unripe 3 (未煮的) raw

4 (生疏) unfamiliar

生产 shēngchǎn [动] 1 (制造) produce 2 (生孩子) give birth to

生存 shēngcún [动] survive

生动 shēngdòng [形] lively

生活 shēnghuó I [名] life II [动] 1 (居住) live 2 (生存) survive

生计 shēngjì [名] livelihood

生理 shēnglǐ [名] physiology

生命 shēngmìng [名] life

生命力 shēngmìnglì [名] vitality

生气 shēngqì [动] get angry

生人 shēngrén [名] stranger

生日 shēngrì [名] birthday

生态 shēngtài [名] ecology

生物 shēngwù [名] living things (PL)

生物学 shēngwùxué [名] biology

生肖 shēngxiào [名] animal of the Chinese zodiac

生效 shēngxiào [动] come into effect

生意 shēngyi [名] business

生育 shēngyù [动] give birth to

生长 shēngzhǎng [动] 1 (植物) grow 2 (生物) grow up

声 shēng [名] 1 (声音) sound 2 (名声) reputation ▷ 声誉 shēngyù fame 3 (声调) tone (of Chinese phonetics)

声波 shēngbō [名] sound wave

声调 shēngdiào [名] tone

声明 shēngmíng [动] state

声望 shēngwàng [名] prestige

声音 shēngyīn [名] 1 (指人) voice 2 (指物) sound

牲 shēng [名] (家畜) domestic animal

牲畜 shēngchù [名] livestock

甥 shēng [名] nephew ▶外甥 wàishēng nephew ▶外甥女 wàishēngnǚ niece

绳 shéng [名] rope

绳子 shéngzi [名] rope

省 shěng I [动] 1 (节约) save ▷省钱 shěng qián save money 2 (免掉) leave ... out II [名] province

省会 shěnghuì [名] provincial capital

省略 shěnglüè [动] leave ... out

省事 shěngshì [动] save trouble

省心 shěngxīn [动] save worry

圣 shèng I [形] holy ▶圣诞节 Shèngdàn Jié Christmas II [名] (圣人) sage

圣诞 Shèngdàn [名] Christmas

圣经 Shèngjīng [名] the Bible

胜 shèng [动] 1 (赢) win 2 (打败) defeat 3 (好于) be better than

胜利 shènglì [动] 1 (打败对方) be victorious 2 (获得成功) be successful

盛 shèng [形] 1 (兴盛) flourishing 2 (强烈) intense 3 (盛大) grand ▶盛宴 shèngyàn sumptuous dinner 4 (深厚) abundant ▶盛情 shèngqíng great kindness 5 (盛行) popular ▶盛行 shèngxíng be in fashion

→ see also/另见 chéng

盛大 shèngdà [形] magnificent

剩 shèng [动] be left ▶剩下 shèngxià remain

尸 shī [名] corpse

尸体 shītǐ [名] corpse

失 shī I [动] 1 (丢失) lose 2 (未得到) fail 3 (背弃) break II [名] mistake ▶过失 guòshī error

失败 shībài [动] fail

失眠 shīmián [动] be unable to sleep

失眠症 shīmiánzhèng [名] insomnia

失明 shīmíng [动] go blind

失望 shīwàng I [形] disappointed II [动] lose hope

失误 shīwù [动] slip up

失效 shīxiào [动] 1 (不起作用) stop working 2 (没有法力) be no longer valid

失信 shīxìn [动] go back on one's word

失业 shīyè [动] be unemployed, be out of work

失踪 shīzōng [动] be missing

师 shī [名] (老师) teacher

师傅 shīfu [名] (口) master

诗 shī [名] poetry

诗歌 shīgē [名] poetry

诗人 shīrén [名] poet

虱 shī [名] louse

狮 shī *see below*/见下文

狮子 shīzi [名] lion

施 shī [动] 1 (实行) carry ... out ▶施工 shīgōng construct 2 (给予) exert ▶施压 shīyā exert pressure 3 (肥料) apply ▶施肥 shīféi spread fertilizer

施行 shīxíng [动] (执行) implement

湿 shī [形] wet

湿润 shīrùn [形] moist

十 shí [名] ten ▶十月 shíyuè October ▶十一月 shíyīyuè November ▶十二月 shí'èryuè December

十分 shífēn [副] extremely

十字路口 shízì lùkǒu [名] crossroads (PL)

石 shí [名] stone

石油 shíyóu [名] oil

时 shí [名] 1 (指时间单位) hour 2 (指规定时间) time ▶准时 zhǔnshí on time 3 (时常) ▶不时 shíbùshí from time to time 4 (时尚) fashion ▶入时 rùshí fashionable ▶过时 guòshí out-of-date 5 (时候) time ▶当时 dāngshí at that time 6 (机会) opportunity 7 (语法) tense ▶过去时 guòqùshí past tense

时差 shíchā [名] time difference

时常 shícháng [副] often

时代 shídài [名] 1 (指时期) age

2 (指人生) period

时候 shíhou [名] time ▷你什么时候上班? Nǐ shénme shíhou shàngbān? What time do you go to work?

时机 shíjī [名] opportunity

时间 shíjiān [名] time ▷时间到了。 Shíjiān dào le. Time's up! ▷办公时间 bàngōng shíjiān working hours

时刻 shíkè I [名] moment II [副] constantly

时刻表 shíkèbiǎo [名] timetable (英), schedule (美)

时髦 shímáo [形] fashionable

时期 shíqī [名] period

时区 shíqū [名] time zone

时事 shíshì [名] current affairs (PL)

时装 shízhuāng [名] fashion

实 shí [形] 1 (实心) solid 2 (真实) true ▶实话 shíhuà truth

实际 shíjì I [名] reality II [形] 1 (实有的) real 2 (合乎事实的) practical

实践 shíjiàn I [动] practise (英), practice (美) II [名] practice

实力 shílì [名] strength

实情 shíqíng [名] actual state of affairs

实施 shíshī [动] implement

实习 shíxí [动] practise (英), practice (美)

实习生 shíxíshēng [名] trainee

实现 shíxiàn [动] realize

实行 shíxíng [动] put ... into practice

实验 shíyàn I [动] test II [名] experiment

实验室 shíyànshì [名] laboratory

实用 shíyòng [形] practical

实在 shízài I [形] honest II [副] really

拾 shí I [动] pick ... up II [数] ten This is the complex character for "ten", which is mainly used in banks, on receipts, etc. to prevent mistakes and forgery.

食 shí I [动] eat II [名] 1 (食物) food ▶主食 zhǔshí staple ▶狗食 gǒushí dog food 2 (指天体) eclipse ▶日食 rìshí solar eclipse

食品 shípǐn [名] food

食谱 shípǔ [名] recipe

食堂 shítáng [名] canteen

食物 shíwù [名] food

食欲 shíyù [名] appetite

史 shǐ [名] history

史诗 shǐshī [名] epic

史实 shǐshí [名] historical fact

使 shǐ I [动] 1 (使用) use 2 (让) make II [名] envoy ▶大使 dàshǐ ambassador

使馆 shǐguǎn [名] embassy

使用 shǐyòng [动] use ▶使用说明 shǐyòng shuōmíng operating instructions (PL)

始 shǐ [动] start

始终 shǐzhōng [副] all along

屎 shǐ [名] 1 (粪便) excrement 2 (眼, 耳) wax ▶耳屎 ěrshǐ ear wax

示 shì [动] show

示范 shìfàn [动] demonstrate

示威 shìwēi [动] demonstrate

世 shì [名] 1 (生) life ▶来世 láishì afterlife 2 (代) generation ▶世仇 shìchóu family feud 3 (时期) age 4 (世界) world ▶世上 shìshàng in this world

世纪 shìjì [名] century

世界 shìjiè [名] world

市 shì [名] 1 (城市) city 2 (市场) market

市场 shìchǎng [名] market

市民 shìmín [名] city residents (PL)

式 shì [名] 1 (样式) style 2 (典礼) ceremony 3 (式子) formula ▶公式 gōngshì formula

式样 shìyàng [名] style

事 shì [名] 1 (事情) thing ▶私事 sīshì private matter 2 (事故) accident ▶出事 chūshì have an accident 3 (事端) trouble ▶闹事 nàoshì make trouble 4 (责任) responsibility 5 (工作) job 6 (用于问答) problem ▷有事吗? 没事。 Yǒushì ma? Méishì. Are you OK? — I'm fine.

事故 shìgù [名] accident

事件 shìjiàn [名] event

事情 shìqíng [名] matter

事实 shìshí [名] fact ▷事实上 shìshí shàng in fact

事务 shìwù [名] work

事物 shìwù [名] thing

事业 shìyè [名] 1 (用于个人) undertaking 2 (用于社会) activity

势 shì [名] 1 (势力) force 2 (姿态) gesture 3 (趋势) tendency

势力 shìlì [名] power

势利 shìlì [形] snobbish

势利眼 shìlìyǎn [名] snob

势头 shìtóu [名] momentum

饰 shì I [动] 1 (装饰) decorate 2 (扮演) play II [名] ornament ▷首饰 shǒushì jewellery (英), jewelry (美)

饰物 shìwù [名] ornaments (PL)

饰演 shìyǎn [动] play

试 shì I [动] try ▷我可以试一下这双鞋吗？ Wǒ kěyǐ shì yīxià zhè shuāng xié ma? Can I try on this pair of shoes? II [名] examination

试卷 shìjuàn [名] exam paper

试题 shìtí [名] exam question

试验 shìyàn [动] test

试用 shìyòng [动] try ... out

试用期 shìyòngqī [名] probation

视 shì [动] 1 (看到) look at 2 (看待) look on

视觉 shìjué [名] vision

视力 shìlì [名] sight

柿 shì see below/见下文

柿子 shìzi [名] persimmon, sharon fruit

是 shì I [动] be ▷我是学生。 Wǒ shì xuésheng. I am a student. II [名] right ▷是非 shìfēi right and wrong III [副] yes

是 shì is the verb 'to be'. It is omitted when used with adjectives, e.g. 我很忙 wǒ hěn máng (I am very busy).

适 shì [形] 1 (适合) suitable 2 (恰好) right 3 (舒服) well

适当 shìdàng [形] appropriate

适合 shìhé [形] suitable

适应 shìyìng [动] adapt

室 shì [名] room ▷办公室 bàngōngshì office

室外 shìwài [形] outdoor

逝 shì [动] (人) die

逝世 shìshì [动] (书) pass away

释 shì [动] (解释) explain

释放 shìfàng [动] release

嗜 shì [动] be addicted to

嗜好 shìhào [名] hobby

誓 shì I [动] swear ▶发誓 fāshì vow II [名] vow

誓言 shìyán [名] oath

收 shōu [动] 1 (归拢) put ... away 2 (取回) take ... back 3 (接纳) accept 4 (结束) stop ▷收工 shōugōng stop work 5 (获得) gain ▷收入 shōurù income

收获 shōuhuò [动] 1 (指庄稼) harvest 2 (指成果) gain

收集 shōují [动] collect

收据 shōujù [名] receipt

收拾 shōushi [动] 1 (整顿) tidy 2 (修理) repair 3 (口) (惩罚) punish

收缩 shōusuō [动] 1 (指物理现象) contract 2 (紧缩) cut back

收听 shōutīng [动] listen to

收音机 shōuyīnjī [名] radio

手 shǒu [名] 1 (指人体) hand 2 (指人) expert ▷选手 xuǎnshǒu player

手表 shǒubiǎo [名] watch

手电筒 shǒudiàntǒng [名] torch (英), flashlight (美)

手段 shǒuduàn [名] 1 (方法) method 2 (贬) (花招) trick

手风琴 shǒufēngqín [名] accordion

手工 shǒugōng I [名] craft II [动] make ... by hand

手机 shǒujī [名] mobile phone (英), cell phone (美)

手绢 shǒujuàn [名] handkerchief

手铐 shǒukào [名] handcuffs (PL)

手枪 shǒuqiāng [名] pistol

手势 shǒushì [名] sign

手术 shǒushù I [名] operation II [动] operate

手套 shǒutào [名] glove ▷一副手套 yī fù shǒutào a pair of gloves

手腕 shǒuwàn [名] (指人体) wrist

手续 shǒuxù [名] procedure

手语 shǒuyǔ [名] sign language

手掌 shǒuzhǎng [名] palm

手纸 shǒuzhǐ [名] toilet paper

手指 shǒuzhǐ [名] finger

手镯 shǒuzhuó [名] bracelet

守 shǒu [动] 1 (防卫) guard 2 (遵循) observe ▶守法 shǒufǎ observe the law

守则 shǒuzé [名] regulation

首 shǒu I [名] 1 (脑袋) head 2 (头领) leader II [形] 1 (第一) first ▶首富 shǒufù the richest person 2 (最早) first III [量] ▷一首诗 yī shǒu shī one poem ▷两首歌 liǎng shǒu gē two songs

measure word, used for music, songs and poems

首都 shǒudū [名] capital

首领 shǒulǐng [名] chief

首脑 shǒunǎo [名] head of state

首饰 shǒushi [名] jewellery (英), jewelry (美)

首席 shǒuxí [形] chief

首先 shǒuxiān [副] 1 (最早) first 2 (第一) first

首相 shǒuxiàng [名] prime minister

首要 shǒuyào [形] primary

寿 shòu [名] (寿命) lifespan

寿命 shòumìng [名] life

受 shòu [动] 1 (接受) receive 2 (遭受) suffer 3 (忍受) bear

受罪 shòuzuì [动] 1(指苦难) suffer 2(指不愉快的事) have a hard time

兽 shòu [名] beast

兽医 shòuyī [名] vet

售 shòu [动] sell

售货员 shòuhuòyuán [名] shop assistant

瘦 shòu [形] 1(指人) thin 2(指食用肉) lean 3(指衣服, 鞋袜) tight

书 shū I [动] write ▶书写 shūxiě write II [名] 1(册子) book ▶书包 shūbāo school bag ▶书架 shūjià bookcase ▶书桌 shūzhuō desk ▶精装书 jīngzhuāngshū hardback 2(书)(信) letter ▶情书 qíngshū love letter 3(文件) document ▶申请书 shēnqǐngshū application documents (PL)

书店 shūdiàn [名] bookshop

书法 shūfǎ [名] calligraphy

书籍 shūjí [名] books (PL)

书记 shūjì [名] secretary

书面语 shūmiànyǔ [名] written language

书信 shūxìn [名] letter

书展 shūzhǎn [名] book fair

叔 shū [名] (指父亲的弟弟) uncle

叔叔 shūshu [名] (口) 1(指亲戚) uncle 2(指父辈男性) uncle

梳 shū I [名] comb ▶梳子 shūzi comb, brush II [动] comb

舒 shū [动] 1(指身体) stretch out

2(指心情) relax

舒服 shūfu [形] comfortable

舒适 shūshì [形] cosy (英), cozy (美)

输 shū [动] 1(运送) transport 2(失败) lose

输出 shūchū [动] (指从内到外) emit

输入 shūrù [动] (指从外到内) enter

输送 shūsòng [动] 1(物品) convey 2(人员) transfer

蔬 shū [名] vegetable

蔬菜 shūcài [名] vegetable

熟 shú [形] 1(指果实) ripe 2(指食物) cooked 3(熟悉) familiar ▷他对北京很熟。 Tā duì Běijīng hěn shú. He knows Beijing well. 4(熟练) skilled

熟练 shúliàn [形] skilled

熟人 shúrén [名] old acquaintance

熟食 shúshí [名] cooked food

熟悉 shúxī I [动] know well II [形] familiar

属 shǔ I [名] 1(生物) genus 2(家属) family member II [动] 1(隶属) be under 2(指属相) ▷你属什么? Nǐ shǔ shénme? What sign of the Chinese zodiac are you?

属相 shǔxiang [名] (口) sign of the Chinese zodiac

属于 shǔyú [动] belong to

暑 shǔ [名] 1(热) heat 2(盛夏)

midsummer

暑假 shǔjià [名] summer holidays (英) (PL), vacation (美)

鼠 shǔ [名] 1 (指家鼠) mouse ▶老鼠 lǎoshǔ mouse 2 (比家鼠大，尾巴长) rat

鼠标 shǔbiāo [名] mouse

数 shǔ [动] 1 (数目) count 2 (指名次) rank 3 (列举) list
→ see also / 另见 shù

薯 shǔ [名] potato ▶红薯 hóngshǔ sweet potato

术 shù [名] 1 (技艺) skill 2 (策略) tactic

术语 shùyǔ [名] terminology

束 shù I [动] 1 (捆) tie 2 (约束) restrain II [量] 1 (指花) bunch ▶一束鲜花 yī shù xiānhuā a bunch of flowers 2 (指光) ray ▶一束阳光 a ray of sunlight

束缚 shùfù [动] 1 (书) (捆绑) tie 2 (局限) restrain

述 shù [动] state

述说 shùshuō [动] give an account

树 shù I [名] tree II [动] (建立) establish

树立 shùlì [动] establish

树林 shùlín [名] wood

树木 shùmù [名] trees (PL)

树阴 shùyīn [名] shade

竖 shù I [形] vertical II [动] erect III [名] vertical stroke

数 shù [名] 1 (数目) number 2 (语法) ▶单数 dānshù singular ▶复数 fùshù plural
→ see also / 另见 shǔ

数据 shùjù [名] data (PL)

数据库 shùjùkù [名] database

数量 shùliàng [名] quantity

数码 shùmǎ I [名] numeral II [形] digital

数码相机 shùmǎ xiàngjī [名] digital camera

数目 shùmù [名] amount

数学 shùxué [名] mathematics (SG)

数字 shùzì [名] 1 (指系统) numeral 2 (数据) figure

漱 shù [动] gargle

漱口 shùkǒu [动] rinse one's mouth out

刷 shuā I [名] brush ▶牙刷 yáshuā toothbrush II [动] (清除) scrub

刷卡 shuākǎ [动] swipe a card

刷牙 shuāyá [动] brush one's teeth

刷子 shuāzi [名] brush

耍 shuǎ [动] 1 (方) (玩) play 2 (戏弄) mess ... around 3 (贬) (施展) play ▶别再耍小聪明了。 Bié zài shuǎ xiǎocōngming le. Don't play those petty tricks again.

耍花招 shuǎ huāzhāo [动] play tricks

衰 shuāi I [形] declining II [动] decline

衰老 shuāilǎo [形] ageing

衰弱 shuāiruò [形] weak

摔 shuāi [动] 1 (跌倒) fall 2 (下落) fall out ▷他从床上摔了下来。 Tā cóng chuáng shàng shuāi le xiàlái. He fell out of bed. 3 (跌坏) break

摔跤 shuāijiāo I [动] (摔倒) fall over II [名] wrestling

甩 shuǎi [动] 1 (抡) swing 2 (扔) fling 3 (抛开) throw ... off

甩卖 shuǎimài [动] sell at a reduced price

帅 shuài I [名] commander-in-chief II [形] handsome

率 shuài [动] command

率领 shuàilǐng [动] lead

双 shuāng I [形] 1 (两个) two 2 (偶数) even ▷双数 shuāngshù even number 3 (加倍) double II [量] pair ▷一双鞋 yī shuāng xié a pair of shoes ▷一双袜子 yī shuāng wàzi a pair of socks

双胞胎 shuāngbāotāi [名] twins (PL)

双方 shuāngfāng [名] both sides (PL)

双休日 shuāngxiūrì [名] the weekend

霜 shuāng [名] frost

谁 shuí [代] → shéi

水 shuǐ [名] 1 (物质) water 2 (指江河湖海) waters (PL) 3 (汁) liquid

▶消毒水 xiāodúshuǐ disinfectant

▶墨水 mòshuǐ ink

水彩 shuǐcǎi [名] 1 (指颜料) watercolour (英), watercolor (美) 2 (指画) watercolour (英), watercolor (美)

水果 shuǐguǒ [名] fruit

水晶 shuǐjīng [名] crystal

水库 shuǐkù [名] reservoir

水泥 shuǐní [名] cement

水平 shuǐpíng I [名] standard II [形] horizontal

水手 shuǐshǒu [名] sailor

水银 shuǐyín [名] mercury

水灾 shuǐzāi [名] flood

税 shuì [名] tax

税收 shuìshōu [名] tax revenue

税务局 shuìwùjú [名] tax office

睡 shuì [动] sleep

睡觉 shuìjiào [动] sleep

睡眠 shuìmián [名] sleep

顺 shùn I [介] 1 (指方向) with ▶顺时针 shùnshízhēn clockwise 2 (沿) along 3 (趁便) ▶顺便 shùnbiàn on the way II [动] 1 (朝同一方向) follow 2 (使有条理) put ... in order 3 (顺从) obey 4 (合意) be to one's liking ▶顺心 shùnxīn as one would wish III [形] successful ▷他找工作很顺。 Tā zhǎo gōngzuò hěn shùn. His job hunt has been very successful.

顺便 shùnbiàn [副] 1 (指乘方便)

on the way **2** (说, 问) by the way ▷顺便问一下, 他给你回电话了吗? Shùnbiàn wèn yīxià, tā gěi nǐ huí diànhuà le ma? By the way, did he call you back?

顺风 shùnfēng [动] (指祝福) ▶一路顺风! Yīlù shùnfēng! Bon voyage!

顺利 shùnlì [副] smoothly

顺序 shùnxù [名] order

说 shuō [动] **1** (用语言表达意思) say **2** (解释) explain **3** (责备) tell ... off

说服 shuōfú [动] persuade

说话 shuōhuà **I** [动] **1** (用语言表达意思) talk **2** (闲谈) chat **II** [副] (马上) any minute

说明 shuōmíng **I** [动] **1** (解释明白) explain **2** (证明) prove **II** [名] explanation ▷产品使用说明 chǎnpǐn shǐyòng shuōmíng instruction manual

硕 shuò [形] large

硕士 shuòshì [名] master's degree

司 sī [动] take charge of

司机 sījī [名] driver

丝 sī [名] **1** (指蚕) silk **2** (指像丝) thread ▶铁丝 tiěsī wire

丝绸 sīchóu [名] silk

私 sī [形] **1** (个人的) private ▶私事 sīshì private affairs **2** (自私的) selfish ▶无私 wúsī unselfish **3** (暗地里的) secret **4** (非法的) illegal

私人 sīrén [形] **1** (属于个人的) private **2** (人与人之间的) personal

私生活 sīshēnghuó [名] private life

私下 sīxià [副] privately

私营 sīyíng [动] run privately

私有 sīyǒu [形] private ▶私有化 sīyǒuhuà privatization

私自 sīzì [副] without permission

思 sī [名] thought ▶思路 sīlù train of thought

思考 sīkǎo [动] think

思念 sīniàn **I** [动] miss **II** [名] longing

思维 sīwéi [名] thinking

思想 sīxiǎng [名] **1** (指有体系) thought **2** (念头) idea

撕 sī [动] tear

死 sǐ **I** [动] die **II** [形] **1** (死亡的) dead **2** (不可调和的) implacable ▶死敌 sǐdí sworn enemy **3** (不能通过的) impassable ▶死胡同 sǐhútòng dead end **4** (确切的) fixed **5** (脑筋) slow-witted **6** (规定) rigid **7** (水) still **III** [副] **1** (拼死) to the death ▶死战 sǐzhàn fight to the death **2** (表示固执或坚决) stubbornly ▶死等 sǐ děng wait indefinitely **3** (表示到达极点) extremely ▶累死我了。 Lèi sǐ wǒ le. I'm completely exhausted.

死机 sǐjī [动] crash

死尸 sǐshī [名] corpse

死亡 sǐwáng [动] die

死刑 sǐxíng [名] death penalty

死者 sǐzhě [名] the deceased

四 sì [数] four

四季 sìjì [名] the four seasons (PL)

四声 sìshēng [名] *the four tones of Standard Chinese pronunciation*

四月 sìyuè [名] April

四肢 sìzhī [名] limbs (PL)

四周 sìzhōu [名] all sides

寺 sì [名] 1 (指佛教) temple, Tibetan Buddhist temple 2 (指伊斯兰教) mosque ▷清真寺 qīngzhēnsì mosque

似 sì I [动] (像) be like ▷他的脸似纸一样白。 Tā de liǎn sì zhǐ yīyàng bái. His face was as white as a sheet of paper. II [副] apparently

似乎 sìhū [副] apparently

饲 sì [动] raise ▷饲养 sìyǎng raise

饲料 sìliào [名] fodder

肆 sì [名] four

This is the complex character for "four", which is mainly used in banks, on receipts, etc. to prevent mistakes and forgery.

松 sōng I [名] (树) pine tree II [动] 1 (放开) relax 2 (鞋带, 腰带) loosen III [形] loose

松懈 sōngxiè [形] 1 (放松) relaxed 2 (松散) lax

送 sòng [动] 1 (信, 邮包, 外卖) deliver 2 (礼物) give ▷你准备送他什么结婚礼物？ Nǐ zhǔnbèi sòng tā shénme jiéhūn lǐwù? What are you going to give him as a wedding present? 3 (送行) see ... off ▷他把女朋友送到家。 Tā bǎ nǚpéngyou sòng dào jiā. He saw his girlfriend home.

送行 sòngxíng [动] see ... off

搜 sōu [动] search

搜查 sōuchá [动] search

搜集 sōují [动] gather

搜索 sōusuǒ [动] search for

搜索引擎 sōusuǒ yǐnqíng [名] search engine

苏 sū [动] revive

苏打 sūdá [名] soda

苏格兰 Sūgélán [名] Scotland ▷苏格兰短裙 Sūgélán duǎnqún kilt

俗 sú I [名] (风俗) custom ▷民俗 mínsú folk custom ▷入乡随俗 rùxiāng suísú when in Rome, do as the Romans do II [形] 1 (大众的) popular 2 (庸俗) vulgar

俗气 súqi [形] vulgar

俗语 súyǔ [名] common saying

诉 sù [动] 1 (说给人) tell ▷诉说 sùshuō tell 2 (倾吐) pour ... out ▷诉苦 sùkǔ complain 3 (控告) accuse ▷上诉 shàngsù appeal to a higher court

素 sù I [形] plain II [名] 1 (蔬菜, 瓜果等食物) vegetable 2 (有根本性质的) element ▷维生素 wéishēngsù vitamin

素描 sùmiáo [名] sketch

素食 sùshí [名] vegetarian food

素食者 sùshízhě [名] vegetarian

素质 sùzhì [名] character

速 sù I [名] speed II [形] quick ▷速算 sùsuàn quick calculation

速成 sùchéng [动] take a crash course

速递 sùdì [动] send by express delivery

速度 sùdù [名] speed

速溶 sùróng [动] dissolve quickly ▷速溶咖啡 sùróng kāfēi instant coffee

宿 sù [动] stay

宿舍 sùshè [名] dormitory

塑 sù I [动] model II [名] mould (英), mold (美)

塑料 sùliào [名] plastic

塑像 sùxiàng [名] statue

酸 suān I [形] 1 (指味道) sour 2 (伤心) sad 3 (迂腐) pedantic 4 (疼) sore II [名] acid

酸奶 suānnǎi [名] yoghurt

蒜 suàn [名] garlic

算 suàn [动] 1 (计算) calculate 2 (计算进去) count 3 (谋划) plan ▷暗算 ànsuàn plot against 4 (当作) be considered as 5 (由某人负责) blame 6 (算数) count 7 (作罢) ▷算了吧! Suàn le ba! Forget it! 8 (推测) suppose

算命 suànmìng [动] tell sb's fortune ▷算命先生 suànmìng xiānsheng fortune teller

算盘 suànpán [名] (计算用具) abacus

算术 suànshù [名] maths (英), math (美)

算账 suànzhàng [动] 1 (计算账目) work out accounts 2 (把事情扯平) get even with

虽 suī [连] although ▷他个子虽小，力气却很大。 Tā gèzi suī xiǎo, lìqi què hěn dà. Although he isn't big, he's very strong.

虽然 suīrán [连] although ▷虽然她很年轻，可是却很成熟。 Suīrán tā hěn niánqīng, kěshì què hěn chéngshú. Although she is very young, she is quite mature.

随 suí [动] 1 (跟随) follow 2 (顺从) go along with 3 (任凭) let ... do as they like ▷孩子大了，随他去吧。 Háizi dà le, suí tā qù ba. The child's grown up – let him do as he wishes.

随便 suíbiàn I [动] do as one wishes II [形] 1 (随意) casual 2 (欠考虑的) thoughtless III [副] ▷大家随便坐。 Dàjiā suíbiàn zuò. Everyone can sit where they like.

随和 suíhé [形] easygoing

随身 suíshēn [副] ▷随身行李 suíshēn xíngli hand luggage

随身听 suíshēntīng [名] Walkman®

随时 suíshí [副] at any time

随手 suíshǒu [副] on one's way ▷请随手关门。 Qǐng suíshǒu guānmén. Please close the door on your way.

随着 suízhe [动] follow

岁 suì [名] year ▷他20岁了。 Tā èrshí suì le. He's 20 years old.

岁数 suìshu [名] age

碎 suì I [动] 1 (破碎) break 2 (使粉碎) smash ▶碎纸机 suìzhǐjī shredder II [形] (不完整) broken

隧 suì [名] tunnel

隧道 suìdào [名] tunnel

孙 sūn [名] grandchild

孙女 sūnnǚ [名] granddaughter

孙子 sūnzi [名] grandson

损 sǔn [动] 1 (减少) decrease 2 (损害) harm 3 (损坏) damage

损害 sǔnhài [动] 1 (健康) damage 2 (利益) harm 3 (名誉) ruin 4 (关系) damage

损坏 sǔnhuài [动] damage

损失 sǔnshī I [动] lose II [名] loss

笋 sǔn [名] bamboo shoot

缩 suō [动] 1 (收缩) contract 2 (收回去) withdraw

缩减 suōjiǎn [动] 1 (经费) cut 2 (人员) reduce

缩水 suōshuǐ [动] shrink

缩写 suōxiě I [名] abbreviation II [动] abridge

所 suǒ I [名] 1 (处所) place 2 (用于机构名称) office ▶派出所 pàichūsuǒ local police station ▶诊所 zěnsuǒ clinic II [量] ▷三所医院 sān suǒ yīyuàn three hospitals ▷一所大学 yī suǒ dàxué a university

measure word, used for buildings, houses, hospitals, schools, universities, etc.

III [助] 1 (表示被动) ▷他被金钱所迷惑。 Tā bèi jīnqián suǒ míhuò. He's obsessed with money. 2 (表示强调) ▷这正是大家所不理解的。 Zhè zhèng shì dàjiā suǒ bù lǐjiě de. This is the bit that no-one understands.

所谓 suǒwèi [形] 1 (通常说的) what is known as ▷中医所谓 "上火" 不止是指嗓子疼一种症状。 Zhōngyī suǒwèi "shànghuǒ" bùzhǐ shì zhǐ sǎngzi téng yīzhǒng zhèngzhuàng. What is known in Chinese medicine as "excess internal heat" covers a lot more than sore throats and the like. 2 (形容不认可) so-called

所以 suǒyǐ [连] (表示结果) so ▷路上堵车，所以我迟到了。 Lù shàng dǔchē, suǒyǐ wǒ chídào le. There was a lot of traffic, so I am late.

所有 suǒyǒu I [动] own II [名] possession III [形] all

索 suǒ I [名] 1 (绳子) rope 2 (链子) chain II [动] 1 (找) search ▶探索 tànsuǒ explore 2 (要) request

索赔 suǒpéi [动] claim damages

索引 suǒyǐn [名] index

锁 suǒ I [名] lock II [动] (用锁锁住) lock

锁链 suǒliàn [名] chain

他 tā [代] (另一人) he ▷他的包 tā de bāo his bag ▷我还记得他。 Wǒ hái jìde tā. I still remember him.

他们 tāmen [代] they ▷他们的老师 tāmen de lǎoshī their teacher ▷我给他们写信。 Wǒ gěi tāmen xiěxìn. I wrote to them.

他人 tārén [名] others (PL)

它 tā [代] it

它们 tāmen [代] they

她 tā [代] she ▷她的帽子 tā de màozi her hat ▷我给她发了个短信。 Wǒ gěi tā fā le gè duǎnxìn. I sent her a text message.

塌 tā [动] (倒塌) collapse

塌实 tāshi [形] 1 (不浮躁) steady 2 (放心) at peace

塔 tǎ [名] 1 (指佛教建筑物) pagoda 2 (指塔形物) tower

塔楼 tǎlóu [名] tower block

獭 tǎ [名] otter ▶水獭 shuǐtǎ otter

踏 tà [动] (踩) step onto

胎 tāi [名] 1 (母体内的幼体) foetus (英), fetus (美) ▶怀胎 huáitāi be pregnant 2 (轮胎) tyre (英), tire (美)

胎儿 tāi'ér [名] foetus (英), fetus (美)

台 tái I [名] 1 (指建筑) tower ▶观测台 guāncètái observation tower 2 (指讲话, 表演) stage ▶舞台 wǔtái stage 3 (指作座子用) stand ▶蜡台 làtái candlestick 4 (台形物) ▶窗台 chuāngtái window sill ▶站台 zhàntái platform 5 (桌子或类似物) table ▶梳妆台 shūzhuāngtái dressing table ▶写字台 xiězìtái desk 6 (指电话服务) telephone service ▶查号台 cháhào tái directory inquiries (PL) 7 (指广播电视) station ▶电视台 diànshìtái television station 8 (also: 台湾) Taiwan II [量] 1 (指机器) ▷一台电脑 yī tái diànnǎo a computer ▷一百台电视 yībǎi tái diànshì one hundred TVs 2 (指戏剧, 戏曲) ▷两台京剧 liǎng tái Jīngjù two Beijing Opera performances ▷一台舞剧 yī tái wǔjù a ballet

measure word, used for machines, equipment, stage performances, etc.

台风 táifēng [名] typhoon

台阶 táijiē [名] (指建筑) step

台历 táilì [名] desk calendar

台球 táiqiú [名] 1 (指美式) pool 2 (指英式) billiards (SC)

抬 tái [动] 1 (举) raise 2 (搬) carry

抬头 táitóu [动] (昂头) raise one's head

太 tài I [形] 1 (高或大) highest 2 (指辈分高) senior ▶太爷爷 tài yéye great-grandfather II [副] 1 (指程度过分) too ▷这部电影太长。 Zhè bù diànyǐng tài cháng. This film is too long. 2 (指程度极高) so ▷我太高兴了。 Wǒ tài gāoxìng le. I am so happy.

太极拳 tàijíquán [名] Tai-chi

太空 tàikōng [名] space

太平洋 Tàipíngyáng [名] the Pacific Ocean

太太 tàitai [名] 1 (妻子) wife 2 (指对老年妇女) lady 3 (对已婚妇女) Mrs

太阳 tàiyáng [名] sun

态 tài [名] 1 (状态) state ▶常态 chángtài normality ▶体态 tǐtài posture 2 (语言) voice

态度 tàidu [名] 1 (举止神情) manner 2 (看法) attitude

贪 tān I [动] 1 (贪污) be corrupt 2 (不满足) crave 3 (好处, 便宜) covet II [形] greedy

贪吃 tānchī [动] be greedy

贪婪 tānlán [形] greedy

贪玩 tānwán [动] be too fond of a good time

贪污 tānwū [动] embezzle

贪心 tānxīn I [形] greedy II [名] greed

摊 tān I [动] 1 (摆开) spread ... out ▷摊开地图 tānkāi dìtú spread out a map 2 (指烹调) fry ▷他摊了个鸡蛋。 Tā tān le gè jīdàn. He fried an egg. 3 (分担) share II [名] stall

摊贩 tānfàn [名] street trader

瘫 tān I [名] paralysis II [形] paralysed (英), paralyzed (美)

瘫痪 tānhuàn I [名] paralysis II [动] be paralysed (英) 或 paralyzed (美)

坛 tán [名] 1 (土台) raised plot ▷花坛 huātán raised flower bed 2 (台子) platform ▷论坛 lùntán forum

谈 tán I [动] talk ▷谈生意 tán shēngyi discuss business II [名] talk

谈话 tánhuà [动] chat

谈论 tánlùn [动] discuss

谈判 tánpàn [动] negotiate

谈心 tánxīn [动] have a heart-to-heart talk

弹 tán [动] 1 (指弹性) spring ▷球弹不起来了。 Qiú tán bù qǐlái le. The ball doesn't bounce. 2 (棉花, 羊毛) fluff ... up 3 (土, 灰, 球) flick 4 (乐器) play ▷弹钢琴 tán gāngqín play the piano
→ see also/另见 dàn

弹簧 tánhuáng [名] spring

弹力 tánlì [名] elasticity

弹性 tánxìng [名] 1 (弹力) elasticity 2 (喻) flexibility ▷弹性工作制 tánxìng gōngzuò zhì flexible working system

痰 tán [名] phlegm

坦 tǎn [形] 1 (平整) flat ▷平坦 píngtǎn flat 2 (直率) candid 3 (心里安定) calm ▷坦然 tǎnrán composed

坦白 tǎnbái I [形] candid II [动] confess

坦率 tǎnshuài [形] frank

毯 tǎn [名] 1 (指地上) carpet ▷地毯 dìtǎn carpet 2 (指床上) blanket ▷毛毯 máotǎn wool blanket 3 (指墙上) tapestry ▷壁毯 bìtǎn tapestry

叹 tàn [动] (叹气) sigh

叹气 tànqì [动] sigh

炭 tàn [名] charcoal

探 tàn I [动] 1 (试图发现) explore ▷探险 tànxiǎn explore 2 (看望) visit ▷探亲 tànqīn visit one's relatives 3 (伸出去) stick ... out 4 (过问) inquire ▷打探 dǎtàn scout II [名] scout ▷侦探 zhēntàn detective

探测 tàncè [动] survey

探索 tànsuǒ [动] probe

探讨 tàntǎo [动] investigate

探望 tànwàng [动] (看望) visit

碳 tàn [名] carbon

汤 tāng [名] (指食物) soup

汤药 tāngyào [名] herbal medicine

堂 táng I [名] 1 (房屋) hall ▶礼堂 lǐtáng auditorium ▶课堂 kètáng classroom ▶教堂 jiàotáng church 2 (厅) hall II [量] ▷两堂课 liǎng táng kè two lessons
measure word, used for school lessons

糖 táng [名] 1 (指做饭) sugar 2 (糖果) sweet

躺 tǎng [动] lie

烫 tàng I [形] very hot ▷这汤真烫。 Zhè tāng zhēn tàng. This soup is boiling hot. II [动] 1 (人) scald 2 (加热) heat ... up 3 (熨) iron 4 (头发) perm

烫手 tàngshǒu [形] scalding

趟 tàng [量] 1 (指旅程) ▷我已经去了好几趟。 Wǒ yǐjīng qù le hǎo jǐ tàng. I've made several trips. 2 (指公车, 地铁等) ▷他错过了一趟车。 Tā cuòguò le yī tàng chē. He missed the bus.
measure word, used for journeys, visits, scheduled public transport, etc.

掏 tāo [动] 1 (拿出) take ... out 2 (挖) dig 3 (偷) steal

逃 táo [动] 1 (逃跑) run away 2 (逃避) flee

逃避 táobì [动] escape ▷逃避责任 táobì zérèn shirk responsibility ▷逃避关税 táobì guānshuì evade customs duties

逃跑 táopǎo [动] escape

桃 táo [名] peach ▶桃子 táozi peach

陶 táo [名] pottery

陶瓷 táocí [名] ceramics (PL)

陶器 táoqì [名] pottery

陶醉 táozuì [动] be intoxicated

淘 táo I [动] 1 (米) wash 2 (金子) pan for ▷淘金 táojīn pan for gold II [形] naughty

淘气 táoqì [形] naughty

淘汰 táotài [动] eliminate

讨 tǎo [动] 1 (债) demand 2 (饭, 钱) beg 3 (讨论) discuss

讨论 tǎolùn [动] discuss

讨厌 tǎoyàn I [形] 1 (可恶) disgusting 2 (指难办) nasty II [动] dislike

套 tào I [名] (套子) cover ▶手套 shǒutào glove ▶避孕套 bìyùntào condom II [动] (罩在外面) slip ... on III [量] set ▷一套西装 yī tào xīzhuāng a suit ▷两套邮票 liǎng tào yóupiào two sets of stamps
measure word, used for suits, collections of books, tools, etc.

套餐 tàocān [名] set meal

特 tè I [形] special II [副] 1 (特地)

especially **2** (非常) extremely

特别 tèbié **I** [形] peculiar **II** [副] **1** (格外) exceptionally **2** (特地) specially

特此 tècǐ [副] hereby

特地 tèdì [副] especially

特点 tèdiǎn [名] characteristic

特价 tèjià [名] bargain price ▷特价商品 tèjià shāngpǐn bargain

特例 tèlì [名] special case

特区 tèqū [名] special zone

特权 tèquán [名] privilege

特色 tèsè [名] characteristic

特殊 tèshū [形] special

特务 tèwu [名] special agent

特征 tèzhēng [名] characteristic

疼 téng **I** [形] sore ▷我牙疼。 Wǒ yá téng. I have toothache. **II** [动] love

藤 téng [名] vine ▶藤椅 téngyǐ cane chair

剔 tī [动] (牙, 指甲) pick

梯 tī [名] ladder ▷电梯 diàntī lift (英), elevator (美) ▶楼梯 lóutī stairs (PL)

踢 tī [动] kick ▷踢足球 tī zúqiú play football

提 tí [动] **1** (拿) carry **2** (升) raise ▶提拔 tíbá promote **3** (提前) bring forward **4** (提出) put ... forward ▷他提了个建议。 Tā tí le gè jiànyì. He put forward a proposal. **5** (提取) collect **6** (谈

起) mention ▷别再提那件事了。 Bié zài tí nà jiàn shì le. Don't mention that subject again.

提倡 tíchàng [动] promote

提出 tíchū [动] put ... forward

提纲 tígāng [名] synopsis

提高 tígāo [动] raise ▷提高效率 tígāo xiàolǜ increase efficiency

提供 tígōng [动] provide

提前 tíqián **I** [动] bring ... forward **II** [副] early

提问 tíwèn [动] ask a question

提醒 tíxǐng [动] remind

提议 tíyì **I** [动] propose **II** [名] proposal

题 tí **I** [名] subject ▶标题 biāotí title **II** [动] inscribe

题材 tícái [名] theme

题目 tímù [名] **1** (标题) title **2** (考题) question

蹄 tí [名] hoof

体 tǐ [名] **1** (身体) body ▶人体 réntǐ human body **2** (物体) substance ▶液体 yètǐ liquid

体操 tǐcāo [名] gymnastics (SG)

体会 tǐhuì **I** [动] come to understand **II** [名] understanding

体积 tǐjī [名] volume

体检 tǐjiǎn [名] physical examination

体力 tǐlì [名] physical strength

体贴 tǐtiē [动] show consideration for

体温 tǐwēn [名] temperature

体系 tǐxì [名] system

体现 tǐxiàn [动] embody

体型 tǐxíng [名] physique

体验 tǐyàn [动] learn from experience

体育 tǐyù [名] 1 (课程) P.E. 2 (运动) sport ▷体育比赛 tǐyù bǐsài sports event

体育场 tǐyùchǎng [名] stadium

体育馆 tǐyùguǎn [名] gym

体重 tǐzhòng [名] weight

剃 tì [动] shave

替 tì I [动] (代) replace II [介] for ▷别替他操心了。 Bié tì tā cāoxīn le. Don't worry about him.

替代 tìdài [动] replace

天 tiān I [名] 1 (天空) sky 2 (一昼夜) day ▷昨天 zuótiān yesterday 3 (一段时间) ▷天还早呢。 Tiān hái zǎo ne. It's still so early. 4 (季节) season ▷秋天 qiūtiān autumn (英), fall (美) 5 (天气) weather ▷阴天 yīntiān overcast weather ▷天很热。 Tiān hěn rè. It's a very hot day. 6 (自然) nature 7 (造物主) God ▷天知道！ Tiān zhīdao! God knows! 8 (神的住所) Heaven II [形] (指位于顶部的) overhead ▷天桥 tiānqiáo overhead walkway

天才 tiāncái [名] 1 (才能) talent 2 (人) genius

天鹅 tiān'é [名] swan

天空 tiānkōng [名] sky

天气 tiānqì [名] weather ▷天气预报 tiānqì yùbào weather forecast

天然 tiānrán [形] natural

天生 tiānshēng [形] inherent ▷这孩子天生聋哑。 Zhè háizi tiānshēng lóngyǎ. This child was born deaf-mute.

天使 tiānshǐ [名] angel

天堂 tiāntáng [名] Heaven

天下 tiānxià [名] the world

天线 tiānxiàn [名] aerial

天性 tiānxìng [名] nature

天真 tiānzhēn [形] innocent

添 tiān [动] (增加) add

田 tián [名] 1 (耕地) field 2 (开采地) field ▷油田 yóutián oilfield

田径 tiánjìng [名] track and field sports (PL)

田野 tiányě [名] open country

甜 tián [形] 1 (指味道) sweet 2 (指睡觉) sound

甜点 tiándiǎn [名] dessert

甜食 tiánshí [名] sweet

填 tián [动] 1 (塞满) fill 2 (填写) complete ▷填表格 tián biǎogé fill in a form

填充 tiánchōng [动] 1 (填上) stuff 2 (补足) fill ... in

填空 tiánkòng [动] (指考试) fill in the blanks

填写 tiánxiě [动] fill ... in

舔 tiǎn [动] lick

挑 tiāo [动] 1 (肩扛) carry ... on a carrying pole 2 (挑选) choose 3 (挑剔) nitpick
→ see also/另见 tiǎo

挑食 tiāoshí [动] be a fussy eater

挑剔 tiāotì [动] nitpick

挑选 tiāoxuǎn [动] select

条 tiáo I [名] 1 (细树枝) twig 2 (长条) strip 3 (层次) order 4 (分项) item 5 (律令) article 6 (短书信) note II [量] 1 (用于细长东西) ▷两条腿 liǎng tiáo tuǐ two legs ▷一条烟 yī tiáo yān a multipack of cigarettes 2 (指分事项的) ▷一条新闻 yī tiáo xīnwén an item of news 3 (指与人有关) ▷一条人命 yī tiáo rénmìng a life measure word, used for long thin things, news, human lives, etc.

条件 tiáojiàn [名] 1 (客观因素) condition 2 (要求) requirement 3 (状况) circumstances (PL)

条理 tiáolǐ [名] order

条约 tiáoyuē [名] treaty

调 tiáo [动] 1 (使和谐) harmonize ▶失调 shītiáo imbalance 2 (使均匀) blend ▷给钢琴调音 gěi gāngqín tiáo yīn tune a piano 3 (调解) mediate
→ see also/另见 diào

调节 tiáojié [动] adjust

调料 tiáoliào [名] seasoning

调皮 tiáopí [形] (顽皮) naughty

调整 tiáozhěng [动] adjust

挑 tiǎo [动] 1 (扯起一头) raise 2 (向上拨) prick
→ see also/另见 tiāo

挑战 tiǎozhàn [动] challenge ▷面临新挑战 miànlín xīn tiǎozhàn face a new challenge

跳 tiào [动] 1 (跃) jump ▷跳高 tiàogāo high jump ▷跳水 tiàoshuǐ diving ▷跳远 tiàoyuǎn long jump 2 (弹起) bounce 3 (起伏地动) beat ▷心跳 xīntiào heartbeat 4 (越过) jump over ▷跳过几页 tiàoguò jǐ yè skip a few pages

跳槽 tiàocáo [动] change jobs

跳舞 tiàowǔ [动] dance

跳跃 tiàoyuè [动] jump

贴 tiē I [动] 1 (粘) stick 2 (紧挨) be close to 3 (贴补) subsidize II [名] allowance

帖 tiě [名] 1 (请帖) invitation ▶请帖 qǐngtiě invitation 2 (小卡片) card

铁 tiě [名] (金属) iron

铁道 tiědào [名] railway (英), railroad (美)

铁路 tiělù [名] railway (英), railroad (美)

厅 tīng [名] 1 (大堂) hall ▶客厅 kètīng sitting room ▶餐厅 cāntīng canteen 2 (机关) office

听 tīng I [动] 1 (收听) listen to 2 (听从) obey ▷听老师的话 tīng lǎoshī de huà do as the teacher

says **II** [名] tin **III** [量] can ▷一听
啤酒 yī tīng píjiǔ a can of beer

听话 tīnghuà **I** [动] obey **II** [形]
obedient

听见 tīngjiàn [动] hear

听讲 tīngjiǎng [动] attend a
lecture

听说 tīngshuō [动] hear

听众 tīngzhòng [名] audience

亭 tíng [名] **1** (亭子) pavilion **2** (小
房子) kiosk ▶电话亭 diànhuàtíng
phone box (英), phone booth (美)

庭 tíng [名] **1** (书) (厅堂) hall **2** (院
子) courtyard **3** (法庭) law court

庭院 tíngyuàn [名] courtyard

停 tíng [动] **1** (止) stop **2** (停留)
stop off **3** (停放) park

停车场 tíngchēchǎng [名] car
park (英), car lot (美)

停顿 tíngdùn **I** [动] **1** (中止) halt
2 (指说话) pause **II** [名] pause

停止 tíngzhǐ [动] stop ▷停止营业
tíngzhǐ yíngyè cease trading

挺 tǐng [副] very

艇 tǐng [名] boat ▶游艇 yóutǐng
yacht ▶救生艇 jiùshēngtǐng
lifeboat

通 tōng **I** [动] **1** (连接) connect with
▶通商 tōngshāng have trade
relations with ▶通风 tōngfēng
ventilate **2** (使不堵) clear ... out
▷通下水道 tōng xiàshuǐdào clear
out a drain **3** (传达) inform ▶通信
tōngxìn correspond by letter ▷通

电话 tōng diànhuà communicate
by telephone **4** (通晓)
understand ▶精通 jīngtōng be
expert in **II** [名] expert ▷外语通
wàiyǔ tōng an expert in foreign
languages **III** [形] **1** (没有障碍)
open ▷电话打通了。 Diànhuà
dǎ tōng le. The call has been put
through. **2** (顺畅) workable **3** (通
顺) coherent **4** (普通) common
5 (整个) overall **IV** [副] **1** (全部)
completely **2** (一般) normally

通常 tōngcháng **I** [形] normal
II [名] normal circumstances
(PL) ▷我通常7点起床。 Wǒ
tōngcháng qīdiǎn qǐchuáng.
Under normal circumstances, I
get up at seven o'clock.

通道 tōngdào [名] (指出入)
passageway ▷地下通道 dìxià
tōngdào tunnel

通过 tōngguò **I** [动] **1** (经过)
pass ▷通过边境线 tōngguò
biānjìngxiàn cross the border
2 (同意) pass **II** [介] by means of

通俗 tōngsú [形] popular

通宵 tōngxiāo [名] all night

通信 tōngxìn [动] correspond

通讯 tōngxùn **I** [名] dispatch
II [动] communicate

通用 tōngyòng [动] be in common
use

同 tóng **I** [动] **1** (一样) be the same
▶不同 bùtóng be different **2** (共
同) do ... together ▶同居 tóngjū
cohabit **II** [介] **1** (跟) with **2** (指
比较) as

同伴 tóngbàn [名] companion

同等 tóngděng [形] of the same level

同类 tónglèi I [形] of the same kind II [名] the same kind

同盟 tóngméng [名] alliance

同情 tóngqíng [动] sympathize ▷表示同情 biǎoshì tóngqíng express sympathy

同时 tóngshí I [名] at the same time ▷同时发生 tóngshí fāshēng occur simultaneously II [连] besides

同事 tóngshì [名] colleague

同性恋 tóngxìngliàn [名] homosexuality

同学 tóngxué [名] 1 (指同校) fellow student 2 (指同班) classmate

同样 tóngyàng [形] 1 (一样) same 2 (情况类似) similar

同意 tóngyì [动] agree

同志 tóngzhì [名] comrade

铜 tóng [名] copper

铜牌 tóngpái [名] bronze medal

童 tóng [名] (小孩) child ▷神童 shéntóng child prodigy

童话 tónghuà [名] fairy tale

童年 tóngnián [名] childhood

统 tǒng I [名] ▷系统 xìtǒng system ▷血统 xuètǒng bloodline II [动] command III [副] all

统计 tǒngjì I [名] statistics (PL) ▷人口统计 rénkǒu tǒngjì census II [动] count

统统 tǒngtǒng [副] entirely

统一 tǒngyī I [动] 1 (使成一体) unite 2 (使一致) unify ▷统一思想 tǒngyī sīxiǎng reach a common understanding II [形] unified

统治 tǒngzhì [动] rule

桶 tǒng I [名] bucket ▷汽油桶 qìyóu tǒng petrol (英) 或 gasoline (美) drum ▷啤酒桶 píjiǔ tǒng beer barrel II [量] barrel ▷一桶柴油 yī tǒng cháiyóu a barrel of diesel oil ▷两桶牛奶 liǎng tǒng niúnǎi two churns of milk

筒 tǒng [名] 1 (竹管) bamboo tube 2 (粗管状物) ▷笔筒 bǐtǒng pen holder ▷邮筒 yóutǒng post box (英), mailbox (美) 3 (指衣服) ▷长筒袜 chángtǒngwà stockings (PL)

痛 tòng I [动] 1 (疼) ache ▷头痛 tóutòng have a headache ▷胃痛 wèitòng have a stomach ache 2 (悲伤) grieve ▷哀痛 āitòng sorrow II [副] deeply ▷痛打 tòngdǎ give a sound beating to

痛苦 tòngkǔ [形] painful

痛快 tòngkuài [形] 1 (高兴) joyful 2 (尽兴) to one's heart's content ▷玩个痛快 wán gè tòngkuài play to one's heart's content 3 (爽快) straightforward

偷 tōu I [动] (窃) steal II [副] stealthily

偷空 tōukòng [动] take time off

偷懒 tōulǎn [动] be lazy

偷窃 tōuqiè [动] steal

偷偷 tōutōu [副] secretly

头 tóu I [名] 1 (脑袋) head ▶点头 diǎntóu nod one's head 2 (头发) hair ▶分头 fēntóu parted hair ▶平头 píngtóu crew cut ▶梳头 shūtóu comb one's hair 3 (顶端) tip 4 (开始) beginning 5 (头目) head ▷谁是你们的头儿？ Shéi shì nǐmen de tóur? Who's your boss? II [形] 1 (第一) first ▶头奖 tóujiǎng first prize ▶头等 tóuděng first class 2 (领先) leading 3 (时间在前) first ▷头几年 tóu jǐ nián first few years III [量] 1 (指动物) ▷3头母牛 sān tóu mǔniú three cows 2 (指蒜) bulb ▷一头蒜 yī tóu suàn a bulb of garlic

measure word, used for cows, bulls, and vegetable bulbs

头发 tóufa [名] hair

头领 tóulǐng [名] leader

头脑 tóunǎo [名] brains (PL)

头衔 tóuxián [名] title

投 tóu [动] 1 (扔) throw 2 (放进去) put ... in 3 (跳下去) throw oneself 4 (投射) cast 5 (寄) post

投入 tóurù I [形] 1 (指专注) engrossed 2 (指逼真) realistic II [动] 1 (放入) put ... in 2 (参加) throw oneself into

投诉 tóusù I [动] lodge a complaint II [名] appeal

投降 tóuxiáng [动] surrender

投资 tóuzī I [动] invest II [名] investment

透 tòu I [动] 1 (渗透) penetrate 2 (泄露) leak out 3 (显露) appear II [形] 1 (透彻) thorough 2 (程度深) complete ▷我浑身都湿透了。 Wǒ húnshēn dōu shī tòu le. I'm soaked to the skin.

透彻 tòuchè [形] incisive

透露 tòulù [动] disclose

透明 tòumíng [形] transparent

秃 tū [形] 1 (指毛发) bald 2 (指山) barren 3 (指树) bare

秃顶 tūdǐng [动] be bald

秃子 tūzi [名] (口) baldy

突 tū [副] suddenly

突出 tūchū I [动] give prominence to ▷他从不突出自己。 Tā cóng bù tūchū zìjǐ. He never pushes himself forward. II [形] (明显) noticeable ▷突出的特点 tūchū de tèdiǎn prominent feature

突击 tūjī I [动] 1 (突然袭击) assault 2 (加快完成) do a rush job II [副] from nowhere

突破 tūpò [动] 1 (防线，界线) break through 2 (僵局，难关) make a breakthrough 3 (限额) surpass 4 (记录) break

突然 tūrán I [形] sudden II [副] suddenly

图 tú I [名] 1 (图画) picture 2 (地图) map 3 (计划) plan II [动] 1 (贪图) seek ▷图一时痛快 tú yīshí tòngkuai seek momentary gratification 2 (谋划) scheme

图案 tú'àn [名] design

图画 túhuà [名] picture

图书 túshū [名] books (PL)

图书馆 túshūguǎn [名] library

图像 túxiàng [名] image

图章 túzhāng [名] seal

徒 tú [名] (徒弟) apprentice ▶徒弟 túdì apprentice

途 tú [名] (途径) way ▶旅途 lǚtú journey ▶前途 qiántú prospect

途径 tújìng [名] channel

涂 tú [动] 1 (抹) spread ... on ▷涂油漆 tú yóuqī apply paint 2 (乱写乱画) scribble 3 (改动) cross ... out

涂改 túgǎi [动] alter

涂料 túliào [名] paint

屠 tú I [动] 1 (动物) slaughter 2 (人) massacre II [名] butcher

屠夫 túfū [名] (字) butcher

屠杀 túshā [动] massacre

土 tǔ I [名] 1 (泥) soil 2 (土地) land ▶领土 lǐngtǔ territory II [形] 1 (地方) local 2 (民间) folk 3 (不时髦) unfashionable

土地 tǔdì [名] 1 (田地) land 2 (疆域) territory

土豆 tǔdòu [名] potato

土话 tǔhuà [名] local dialect

土壤 tǔrǎng [名] soil

土著 tǔzhù [名] indigenous peoples (PL)

吐 tǔ [动] (排出口外) spit
→ see also/另见 tù

吐 tù [动] vomit
→ see also/另见 tǔ

吐沫 tùmo [名] saliva

兔 tù [名] 1 (野兔) hare 2 (家兔) rabbit

团 tuán I [名] 1 (球形物) ball 2 (组织) group ▶剧团 jùtuán drama company 3 (军) regiment II [动] 1 (聚合) unite ▶团聚 tuánjù reunite 2 (揉成球状) roll into a ball III [形] round IV [量] ▷一团面 yī tuán miàn a lump of dough ▷一团毛线 yī tuán máoxiàn a ball of wool

measure word, used for rolled up round things

团伙 tuánhuǒ [名] gang

团结 tuánjié [动] unite

团体 tuántǐ [名] organization

团圆 tuányuán [动] reunite

推 tuī [动] 1 (门、窗、车) push 2 (指用工具) scrape ▷他推了个光头。 Tā tuī le gè guāngtóu. He's shaved his head. 3 (录) push forward 4 (推断) deduce 5 (辞让) decline 6 (推诿) shift 7 (推迟) postpone 8 (举荐) elect

推测 tuīcè [动] infer

推辞 tuīcí [动] decline

推迟 tuīchí [动] put ... off

推出 tuīchū [动] bring ... out

推动 tuīdòng [动] promote

推广 tuīguǎng [动] popularize

推荐 tuījiàn [动] recommend

推销 tuīxiāo [动] promote

腿 tuǐ [名] 1 (下肢) leg ▶大腿 dàtuǐ thigh ▶小腿 xiǎotuǐ calf 2 (支撑物) leg

退 tuì [动] 1 (后移) retreat 2 (使后移) cause ... to withdraw 3 (退出) quit 4 (减退) recede 5 (减弱) fade 6 (退还) return 7 (撤销) cancel

退步 tuìbù I [动] 1 (落后) lag behind 2 (让步) give way II [名] leeway

退让 tuìràng [动] make a concession

退缩 tuìsuō [动] hold back

退休 tuìxiū [动] retire

褪 tuì [动] 1 (衣服) take ... off 2 (毛) shed 3 (颜色) fade

吞 tūn [动] 1 (整个咽下) swallow 2 (吞并) take over

吞并 tūnbìng [动] annex

吞没 tūnmò [动] 1 (据为己有) misappropriate 2 (淹没) engulf

臀 tún [名] buttock

托 tuō I [动] 1 (撑) support 2 (委托) entrust 3 (依赖) rely on II [名] tray

托儿所 tuō'érsuǒ [名] nursery

托福 tuōfú [名] TOEFL, Test of English as a Foreign Language

托付 tuōfù [动] entrust

托运 tuōyùn [动] ship

拖 tuō [动] 1 (拉) pull 2 (地板) mop 3 (下垂) trail 4 (拖延) delay

拖延 tuōyán [动] delay

脱 tuō [动] 1 (皮肤, 毛发) shed 2 (衣服, 鞋帽) take ... off 3 (摆脱) escape 4 (颜色) fade 5 (油脂) skim

脱臼 tuōjiù [动] dislocate

脱离 tuōlí [动] 1 (关系) break off 2 (危险) get away from

脱落 tuōluò [动] 1 (毛发, 牙齿) lose 2 (油漆, 墙皮) come off

脱水 tuōshuǐ [动] dehydrate

驮 tuó [动] carry on one's back

驼 tuó I [名] camel ▶骆驼 luòtuo camel II [形] hunchbacked ▶驼背 tuóbèi be hunchbacked

鸵 tuó see below/见下文

鸵鸟 tuóniǎo [名] ostrich

妥 tuǒ [形] 1 (适当) appropriate 2 (停当) ready

妥当 tuǒdang [形] appropriate

妥善 tuǒshàn [形] appropriate

妥协 tuǒxié [动] compromise

椭 tuǒ see below/见下文

椭圆 tuǒyuán [名] oval

拓 tuò [动] open ... up

拓展 tuòzhǎn [动] expand

唾 tuò I [名] saliva II [动] spit

唾沫 tuòmo [名] (口) saliva

W

挖 wā [动] 1(掘) dig ▶挖掘 wājué excavate 2(耳朵, 鼻子) pick

蛙 wā [名] frog
蛙泳 wāyǒng [名] breaststroke

娃 wá [名] (方) baby
娃娃 wáwa [名] 1(小孩) baby 2(玩具) doll

瓦 wǎ [名] tile
瓦斯 wǎsī [名] gas

袜 wà [名] sock ▶长筒袜 chángtǒngwà stocking
袜子 wàzi [名] sock

歪 wāi [形] (倾斜) slanting
歪斜 wāixié [形] crooked

外 wài I [名] 1(范围以外) outside ▶外边 wàibian outside 2(外国) foreign country II [形] 1(外国的) foreign 2(其他的) other ▶外人 wàirén outsider III [副] besides

外表 wàibiǎo [名] exterior

外地 wàidì [名] other parts of the country ▶外地人 wàidìrén person from another part of the country

外公 wàigōng [名] maternal grandfather

外国 wàiguó [名] foreign country

外国人 wàiguórén [名] foreign person

外号 wàihào [名] nickname

外汇 wàihuì [名] (外币) foreign currency

外交 wàijiāo [名] foreign affairs ▶外交部 wàijiāobù Ministry of Foreign Affairs

外交官 wàijiāoguān [名] diplomat

外科 wàikē [名] surgery ▶外科医生 wàikē yīshēng surgeon

外卖 wàimài [名] takeaway (英), takeout (美)

外贸 wàimào [名] foreign trade

外婆 wàipó [名] maternal grandmother

外企 wàiqǐ [名] foreign enterprise

外伤 wàishāng [名] injury

外商 wàishāng [名] foreign businessman

外甥 wàisheng [名] nephew

外孙 wàisūn [名] grandson

外套 wàitào [名] overcoat

外文 wàiwén [名] foreign language

外向 wàixiàng [形] (指性格) extrovert

外语 wàiyǔ [名] foreign language

弯 wān I [形] curved II [动] bend III [名] bend

湾 wān [名] bay

豌 wān see below/见下文

豌豆 wāndòu [名] pea

丸 wán I [名] (指药) pill ▷ 丸药 wányào pill II [量] pill ▷ 他服了一丸药。 Tā fú le yī wán yào. He took a pill.

完 wán I [形] whole II [动] 1 (完成) complete 2 (耗尽) run out 3 (了结) finish

完成 wánchéng [动] complete

完美 wánměi [形] perfect

完全 wánquán I [形] complete II [副] completely

完整 wánzhěng [形] complete

玩 wán [动] 1 (玩耍) play 2 (游玩) have a good time ▷ 我去泰国玩了一个星期。 Wǒ qù Tàiguó wán le yī gè xīngqī. I went to Thailand for a week's holiday. 3 (做客) visit 4 (表示祝愿) enjoy ▷ 玩得好！ Wán de hǎo! Enjoy yourself!

玩具 wánjù [名] toy

玩笑 wánxiào [名] joke ▷ 他喜欢跟人开玩笑。 Tā xǐhuan gēn rén kāi wánxiào. He likes to play jokes on people.

玩意儿 wányìr [名] (口) 1 (东西) thing 2 (玩具) toy 3 (器械) gadget

顽 wán [形] 1 (难以摆脱的) stubborn ▶ 顽固 wángù stubborn 2 (淘气) naughty ▶ 顽皮 wánpí mischievous

挽 wǎn [动] 1 (拉) hold 2 (卷起) roll ... up

晚 wǎn I [形] late ▶ 晚秋 wǎnqiū late autumn ▷ 我起晚了。 Wǒ qǐ wǎn le. I got up late. II [名] evening

晚安 wǎn'ān [形] good night

晚饭 wǎnfàn [名] dinner

晚会 wǎnhuì [名] party

晚年 wǎnnián [名] old age

晚上 wǎnshang [名] evening

碗 wǎn [名] bowl

万 wàn [数] ten thousand

万岁 wànsuì [叹] long live

万一 wànyī [连] if by any chance

腕 wàn [名] 1 (指手) wrist 2 (指脚) ankle

腕子 wànzi [名] 1 (指手) wrist 2 (指脚) ankle

亡 wáng [动] die ▶ 死亡 sǐwáng die

王 wáng [名] king

王国 wángguó [名] kingdom

王子 wángzǐ [名] prince

网 wǎng [名] 1 (工具) net 2 (网状

物) web 3 (系统) network ▸互联网 Hùliánwǎng the Internet

网吧 wǎngbā [名] Internet café

网络 wǎngluò [名] network

网民 wǎngmín [名] Internet user

网球 wǎngqiú [名] tennis ▸网球场 wǎngqiúchǎng tennis court

网页 wǎngyè [名] web page

网站 wǎngzhàn [名] website

网址 wǎngzhǐ [名] web address

往 wǎng I [介] to II [形] past ▸往事 wǎngshì past events (PL)

往往 wǎngwǎng [副] often

忘 wàng [动] forget

忘记 wàngjì [动] forget

旺 wàng [形] 1 (火) roaring 2 (人，生意) flourishing 3 (花) blooming

旺季 wàngjì [名] 1 (指生意) peak season 2 (指水果，蔬菜) season

旺盛 wàngshèng [形] 1 (精力，生命力) full of energy 2 (植物) thriving

望 wàng [动] 1 (向远处看) look into the distance 2 (察看) watch 3 (希望) hope

危 wēi I [形] dangerous II [动] endanger

危害 wēihài [动] harm

危机 wēijī [名] crisis

危险 wēixiǎn I [形] dangerous II [名] danger

威 wēi [名] power

威力 wēilì [名] power

威士忌 wēishìjì [名] whisky

威胁 wēixié [动] threaten

威信 wēixìn [名] prestige

威严 wēiyán I [形] dignified II [名] dignity

微 wēi I [形] tiny ▸微米 wēimǐ micron ▸微秒 wēimiǎo microsecond II [副] slightly

微波炉 wēibōlú [名] microwave oven

微风 wēifēng [名] gentle breeze

微量元素 wēiliàng yuánsù [名] trace element

微妙 wēimiào [形] delicate

微弱 wēiruò [形] faint

微生物 wēishēngwù [名] micro-organism

微小 wēixiǎo [形] tiny

微笑 wēixiào [动] smile

微型 wēixíng [形] mini

为 wéi I [动] 1 (是) be 2 (充当) act as II [介] by → see also/另见 wèi

为难 wéinán I [形] embarrassed II [动] make things difficult for

为期 wéiqī [动] be scheduled for

为生 wéishēng [动] make a living

为止 wéizhǐ [动] ▸到上周末为止 dào shàngzhōu mò wéizhǐ by the end of last week

违 wéi [动] break ▸违章 wéizhāng break regulations

违背 wéibèi [动] go against

违法 wéifǎ **I** [动] break the law **II** [形] illegal

违反 wéifǎn [动] go against

违犯 wéifàn [动] violate

围 wéi **I** [动] surround **II** [名] **1**(四周) all sides **2**(周长) measurement ▶三围 sānwéi vital statistics ▶胸围 xiōngwéi chest measurement

围棋 wéiqí [名] go (board game)

围棋 wéiqí

围棋 wéiqí is a popular strategic board game in China, Japan and other East-Asian countries. It originated in ancient China. It is known as go in Japan. It is played by two players alternately placing black and white round stone pieces on the intersections of a square grid on a square game board. To win, the player must control a larger area on the game board than his/her opponent.

围绕 wéirào [动] **1**(物体) revolve around **2**(话题) centre (英) 或 center (美) on

惟 wéi [副] **1**(单单) only **2**(书)(只是) but only

惟一 wéiyī [形] only

维 wéi **I** [动] **1**(连接) hold ... together **2**(保持) maintain **II** [名] dimension

维持 wéichí [动] **1**(保持) maintain **2**(资助) support

维护 wéihù [动] safeguard

维生素 wéishēngsù [名] vitamin

维修 wéixiū [动] maintain

伟 wěi [形] great

伟大 wěidà [形] great

伟哥 wěigē [名](医) Viagra®

伟人 wěirén [名] great man

伪 wěi [形] false

伪钞 wěichāo [名] counterfeit note (英) 或 bill (美)

伪君子 wěijūnzǐ [名] hypocrite

伪造 wěizào [动] forge

伪装 wěizhuāng **I** [动] disguise **II** [名] disguise

尾 wěi [名] **1**(尾巴) tail ▶尾巴 wěiba tail **2**(末端) end **3**(残余) remainder ▶扫尾 sǎowěi finish off

尾气 wěiqì [名] exhaust (英), tailpipe (美)

纬 wěi [名](地理) latitude ▶纬线 wěixiàn latitude

纬度 wěidù [名] latitude

委 wěi **I** [动] entrust **II** [名] **1**(委员) committee member ▶委员 wěiyuán committee member **2**(委员会) committee ▶委员会 wěiyuán huì committee

委屈 wěiqu [名] unjust treatment

委托 wěituō [动] entrust

委婉 wěiwǎn [形](指言词) tactful

卫 wèi [动] protect

卫生 wèishēng I [名] 1 (干净) hygiene 2 (扫除) clean-up II [形] hygienic

卫生间 wèishēngjiān [名] toilet (英), rest room (美)

卫生纸 wèishēngzhǐ [名] toilet paper (英) 或 tissue (美)

卫星 wèixīng [名] satellite

为 wèi [介] for ▷我真为你高兴! Wǒ zhēn wèi nǐ gāoxìng! I am really happy for you! → see also/另见 wéi

为了 wèile [介] in order to

为什么 wèishénme [副] why

未 wèi [副] not

未必 wèibì [副] not necessarily

未成年人 wèichéngniánrén [名] minor

未婚夫 wèihūnfū [名] fiancé

未婚妻 wèihūnqī [名] fiancée

未来 wèilái [名] future

位 wèi I [名] 1 (位置) location 2 (地位) position 3 (数学) digit ▷两位数 liǎng wèi shù two-digit number II [量] ▷两位教授 liǎng wèi jiàoshòu two professors ▷一位父亲 yī wèi fùqin a father measure word, used for people

位于 wèiyú [动] be located

位置 wèizhi [名] 1 (地点) location 2 (地位) place 3 (职位) position

位子 wèizi [名] 1 (座位) seat 2 (职位) position

味 wèi [名] 1 (滋味) taste 2 (气味) smell

味道 wèidao [名] (滋味) taste

味精 wèijīng [名] monosodium glutamate

胃 wèi [名] stomach

胃口 wèikǒu [名] 1 (食欲) appetite 2 (喜好) liking

喂 wèi I [动] feed ▷喂养 wèiyǎng raise II [叹] 1 (指打电话) hello 2 (指招呼) hey

温 wēn I [形] 1 (不冷不热) warm 2 (平和) mild II [动] (加热) warm ... up III [名] temperature

温度 wēndù [名] temperature

温和 wēnhé [形] 1 (指性情, 态度) mild 2 (指气候) temperate

温暖 wēnnuǎn [形] warm

温泉 wēnquán [名] hot spring

温柔 wēnróu [形] gentle

温室 wēnshì [名] greenhouse ▷温室效应 wēnshì xiàoyìng the greenhouse effect

文 wén [名] 1 (字) writing 2 (书面语) written language ▶中文 Zhōngwén the Chinese language 3 (文章) essay 4 (指社会产物) culture 5 (文科) humanities (PL)

文化 wénhuà [名] 1 (精神财富) culture 2 (知识) education

文件 wénjiàn [名] 1 (公文) document 2 (计算机) file

文具 wénjù [名] stationery

文科 wénkē [名] humanities (PL)

文盲 wénmáng [名] illiterate

文明 wénmíng I [名] civilization II [形] civilized

文凭 wénpíng [名] diploma

文物 wénwù [名] cultural relic

文学 wénxué [名] literature

文艺 wényì [名] 1 (文学艺术) art and literature 2 (文学) literature 3 (演艺) performing arts (PL)

文章 wénzhāng [名] (著作) essay

文字 wénzì [名] 1 (指符号) script 2 (指文章) writing

闻 wén I [动] (嗅) smell II [名] (消息) news (SG) ▶新闻 xīnwén news

蚊 wén [名] mosquito ▶蚊子 wénzi mosquito

吻 wěn I [名] kiss II [动] kiss

稳 wěn I [形] 1 (平稳) steady 2 (坚定) firm 3 (稳重) composed 4 (可靠) reliable 5 (肯定) sure II [动] keep calm

稳定 wěndìng I [形] steady II [动] settle

问 wèn I [动] 1 (提问) ask 2 (问候) send regards to 3 (干预) ask about II [名] question ▶疑问 yíwèn doubt

问候 wènhòu [动] send regards to

问题 wèntí [名] 1 (疑问) question 2 (困难) problem 3 (故障) fault 4 (分项) issue

窝 wō [名] (栖息地) nest

蜗 wō see below/见下文

蜗牛 wōniú [名] snail

我 wǒ [代] 1 (自己, 作主语) I 2 (自己, 作宾语) me

我们 wǒmen [代] 1 (作主语) we 2 (作宾语) us

卧 wò I [动] 1 (躺) lie 2 (趴伏) sit II [名] berth

卧铺 wòpù [名] berth

卧室 wòshì [名] bedroom

握 wò [动] 1 (抓) grasp 2 (掌握) master

握手 wòshǒu [动] shake hands

乌 wū I [名] crow ▶乌鸦 wūyā crow II [形] black ▶乌云 wūyún black cloud

乌龟 wūguī [名] tortoise

乌黑 wūhēi [形] jet-black

污 wū [形] 1 (肮脏) dirty 2 (腐败) corrupt ▶贪污 tānwū be corrupt

污染 wūrǎn [动] pollute

污辱 wūrǔ [动] (侮辱) insult

屋 wū [名] 1 (房子) house 2 (房间) room

屋顶 wūdǐng [名] roof

屋子 wūzi [名] room

无 wú I [动] (没有) not have ▶无效 wúxiào invalid ▶无形 wúxíng invisible II [副] not ▶无论如何 wúlùn rúhé in any case

无耻 wúchǐ [形] shameless

无辜 wúgū I [动] be innocent II [名] the innocent

无关 wúguān [动] have nothing to do with

无赖 wúlài [名] rascal

无论 wúlùn [连] no matter what

无情 wúqíng [形] 1 (指感情) heartless 2 (不留情) ruthless

无数 wúshù I [形] countless II [动] be uncertain

无所谓 wúsuǒwèi [动] 1 (谈不上) never mind 2 (不在乎) be indifferent

无限 wúxiàn [形] boundless

无线电 wúxiàndiàn [名] radio

无须 wúxū [副] needlessly

无知 wúzhī [形] ignorant

五 wǔ [名] five ▷ 五月 wǔyuè May ▷ 五分之一 wǔ fēn zhī yī one fifth

五官 wǔguān [名] the five sense organs

午 wǔ [名] noon

午饭 wǔfàn [名] lunch

午夜 wǔyè [名] midnight

伍 wǔ [名] (五) five

This is the complex character for "five", which is mainly used in banks, on receipts, etc. to prevent mistakes and forgery.

武 wǔ [形] 1 (军事的) military 2 (勇猛) valiant ▷ 威武 wēiwǔ powerful

武力 wǔlì [名] 1 (军事力量) military strength 2 (暴力) force

武器 wǔqì [名] weapon

武士 wǔshì [名] warrior

武术 wǔshù [名] martial arts circles (PL)

侮 wǔ [动] (侮辱) insult ▷ 侮辱 wǔrǔ insult

舞 wǔ I [名] dance II [动] (跳舞) dance

舞蹈 wǔdǎo [名] dance

舞台 wǔtái [名] stage

勿 wù [副] not ▷ 请勿吸烟 qǐng wù xīyān no smoking

务 wù I [名] business ▷ 任务 rènwù task II [副] without fail

务必 wùbì [副] without fail

物 wù [名] 1 (东西) thing ▷ 物体 wùtǐ body 2 (物产) produce ▷ 物产 wùchǎn produce 3 (动物) creature 4 (指哲学) matter

物价 wùjià [名] price

物理 wùlǐ [名] (指学科) physics (SG)

物业 wùyè [名] property

物质 wùzhì [名] 1 (哲) matter 2 (非精神) material things (PL)

物种 wùzhǒng [名] species (SG)

误 wù I [名] mistake II [形] 1 (不正确) erroneous ▷ 误会 wùhuì misunderstand 2 (非故意) accidental ▷ 误伤 wùshāng accidentally injure III [动] (耽误) miss ▷ 快点儿，别误了火车！

Kuàidiǎnr, bié wù le huǒchē!
Hurry up – we don't want to miss the train!

雾 wù [名] fog

夕 xī [名] 1 (傍晚) sunset ▶夕阳 xīyáng setting sun 2 (晚上) evening ▶除夕 chúxī New Year's Eve

西 xī [名] 1 (方向) west ▶西北 xīběi northwest ▶西南 xīnán southwest 2 (疆域) the West ▶西藏 Xīzàng Tibet

西班牙 Xībānyá [名] Spain ▷西班牙人 Xībānyárén Spaniard ▷西班牙语 Xībānyáyǔ the Spanish language

西餐 xīcān [名] Western food

西方 xīfāng [名] the West

西服 xīfú [名] Western clothes

西瓜 xīguā [名] watermelon

西红柿 xīhóngshì [名] tomato

西药 xīyào [名] Western medicine

西医 xīyī [名] (药品) Western medicine

吸 xī [动] 1 (气, 水等) draw ... in ▶吸烟 xīyān smoke cigarettes 2 (吸收) absorb 3 (吸引) attract

吸尘器 xīchénqì [名] vacuum cleaner

吸收 xīshōu [动] 1 (摄取) absorb 2 (接纳) recruit

吸引 xīyǐn [动] attract

希 xī [动] hope

希望 xīwàng I [动] hope II [名] hope

牺 xī see below/见下文

牺牲 xīshēng [动] 1 (献身) sacrifice oneself 2 (放弃) sacrifice

稀 xī [形] 1 (稀有) rare 2 (稀疏) sparse 3 (水多的) watery ▶稀饭 xīfàn rice porridge

稀少 xīshǎo [形] sparse

稀有 xīyǒu [形] rare

犀 xī [名] rhinoceros ▶犀牛 xīniú rhinoceros

溪 xī [名] brook

熄 xī [动] put ... out ▶熄灯 xīdēng put out the light

熄灭 xīmiè [动] put ... out

膝 xī [名] knee ▶膝盖 xīgài knee

习 xí I [动] 1 (学习) practise (英), practice (美) ▶习武 xíwǔ study martial arts 2 (熟悉) be used to ▶习以为常 xí yǐ wéi cháng become used to II [名] custom ▶习俗 xísú custom ▶习气 xíqì bad habit

习惯 xíguàn I [动] be used to II [名] habit

习性 xíxìng [名] habits (PL)

席 xí [名] 1 (编织物) mat ▶竹席 zhúxí bamboo mat 2 (座位) seat ▶席位 xíwèi seat ▶出席 chūxí be present 3 (宴席) feast ▶酒席 jiǔxí banquet

袭 xí [动] 1 (攻击) make a surprise attack ▶空袭 kōngxí air raid 2 (仿做) follow the pattern of ▶抄袭 chāoxí plagiarize

袭击 xíjī [动] attack

媳 xí [名] daughter-in-law

媳妇 xífù [名] 1 (儿子的妻子) daughter-in-law 2 (晚辈的妻子) wife

洗 xǐ [动] 1 (衣, 碗等) wash ▶洗衣店 xǐyīdiàn Launderette® (英), Laundromat® (美) 2 (胶卷) develop 3 (录音, 录像) wipe 4 (麻将, 扑克) shuffle

洗衣机 xǐyījī [名] washing machine

洗澡 xǐzǎo [动] have a bath

喜 xǐ I [形] 1 (高兴) happy 2 (可贺的) celebratory II [动] 1 (爱好) like ▶喜好 xǐhào like 2 (适宜) suit

喜爱 xǐ'ài [动] like

喜欢 xǐhuan [动] like

喜剧 xǐjù [名] comedy

戏 xì I [动] (嘲弄) joke ▶戏弄 xìnòng tease II [名] show ▶京戏 jīngxì Beijing Opera ▶马戏 mǎxì circus

戏法 xìfǎ [名] magic

戏剧 xìjù [名] theatre (英), theater (美)

戏曲 xìqǔ [名] Chinese opera

戏院 xìyuàn [名] theatre (英), theater (美)

系 xì I [名] 1 (系统) system 2 (部门) department II [动] (拴) tie → see also/ 另见 jì

系列 xìliè [名] series (sɢ)

系统 xìtǒng [名] system

细 xì I [形] 1 (绳, 线等) thin 2 (沙, 粮等) fine 3 (声, 语等) gentle 4 (节, 则等) detailed ▶细节 xìjié details (PL) II [副] minutely ▶细想 xìxiǎng consider carefully

细胞 xìbāo [名] cell

细菌 xìjūn [名] germ

细心 xìxīn [形] careful

细致 xìzhì [副] meticulously

虾 xiā [名] shrimp ▶龙虾 lóngxiā lobster ▶对虾 duìxiā prawn

瞎 xiā [形] (失明) blind

瞎话 xiāhuà [名] lie

峡 xiá [名] gorge ▶海峡 hǎixiá strait

峡谷 xiágǔ [名] canyon

狭 xiá [形] narrow ▶狭窄 xiázhǎi narrow

下 xià I [动] 1 (走下) go down ▶下山 xià shān go down the mountain ▶下楼 xià lóu go downstairs ▶下船 xià chuán disembark from a boat ▶下床 xià chuáng get out of bed 2 (落下) fall ▶下雨 xiàyǔ rain ▶下雪 xiàxuě snow 3 (传发) issue 4 (下锅煮) put ... in 5 (给出) give 6 (开始) begin ▶下笔 xiàbǐ start to write 7 (结束) finish ▶下班 xiàbān finish work ▶下课 xiàkè finish class 8 (生下) ▶下蛋 xià dàn lay an egg 9 (用于动词后, 表示脱离物体) ▶拧下灯泡 nǐng xià dēngpào unscrew a light bulb 10 (用于动词后, 表示动作完成) ▶记录下会议内容 jìlù xià huìyì nèiróng take the minutes at a meeting II [名] 1 (低) ▶下层 xiàcéng lower level 2 (另) ▶下次 xiàcì next time ▶下个星期 xià gè xīngqī next week 3 (指方位或时间) ▶楼下 lóuxià downstairs ▶树下 shù xià under the tree 4 (指范围, 情况, 条件) ▶在朋友的帮助下 zài péngyou de bāngzhù xià with help from friends ▶在压力下 zài yālì xià under pressure III [量] time ▶拍了几下 pāi le jǐ xià tapped a few times ▶拧了两下 nǐng le liǎng xià turned a couple of times

下岗 xiàgǎng [动] 1 (完工) leave one's post 2 (失业) be laid off

下海 xiàhǎi [动] (指经商) go into

business

下级 xiàjí [名] subordinate

下来 xiàlai [动] 1 (指由高到低) come down ▷我不上去了, 你下来吧。 Wǒ bù shàngqu le, nǐ xiàlai ba. I won't come up - you come down. 2 (指作物成熟) be harvested 3 (用于动词后, 指脱离物体) ▷他把眼镜摘了下来。 Tā bǎ yǎnjìng zhāi le xiàlai. He took off his glasses. 4 (用于动词后, 表示动作完成) ▷暴乱平息下来了。 Bàoluàn píngxī xiàlai le. The riot has calmed down. 5 (表示出现某种状态) ▷灯光暗了下来。 Dēngguāng àn le xiàlai. The light started to fade.

下流 xiàliú [形] dirty

下面 xiàmian I [副] 1 (指位置) underneath 2 (指次序) next II [名] lower levels (PL)

下去 xiàqu [动] 1 (指由高到低) go down 2 (指时间的延续) continue 3 (用于动词后, 指空间上) ▷从楼上跳下去 cóng lóu shàng tiào xiàqu jump from a building 4 (时间上的持续) ▷唱下去 chàng xiàqu keep singing 5 (指数量下降) ▷高烧已经退下去了。 Gāoshāo yǐjīng tuì xiàqu le. His temperature has already gone down. 6 (指程度深化) ▷天气有可能热下去。 Tiānqì yǒu kěnéng rè xiàqu. The weather will probably go on getting hotter.

下网 xiàwǎng (计算机) go offline

下午 xiàwǔ [名] afternoon

下载 xiàzǎi [动] download

吓 xià [动] frighten ▶吓人 xiàrén scary

吓唬 xiàhu [动] frighten

夏 xià [名] summer

夏令营 xiàlìngyíng [名] summer camp

夏天 xiàtiān [名] summer

仙 xiān [名] immortal ▶仙人 xiānrén immortal

先 xiān [形] (指时间) earlier ▶事先 shìxiān beforehand

先后 xiānhòu [副] successively

先进 xiānjìn [形] advanced

先生 xiānsheng [名] 1 (指男士) Mr 2 (老师) teacher 3 (丈夫) husband

纤 xiān [形] fine

纤维 xiānwéi [名] fibre

掀 xiān [动] lift

掀起 xiānqǐ [动] 1 (揭起) lift 2 (涌起) surge

鲜 xiān I [形] 1 (新鲜) fresh 2 (鲜美) delicious II [名] delicacy ▶海鲜 hǎixiān seafood

鲜艳 xiānyàn [形] brightly-coloured (英), brightly-colored (美)

闲 xián I [形] 1 (不忙) idle 2 (安静) quiet 3 (闲置) unused ▶闲房 xiánfáng empty house II [名] leisure

闲话 xiánhuà [名] **1**(流言) gossip **2**(废话) digression

闲事 xiánshì [名] other people's business

弦 xián [名] **1**(指乐器) string **2**(指钟表) spring

咸 xián [形] salted ▶咸菜 xiáncài pickled vegetables (PL)

嫌 xián [动] dislike ▷他嫌这儿吵，搬走了。Tā xián zhèr chǎo, bānzǒu le. He found it too noisy here and moved away.

嫌弃 xiánqì [动] cold-shoulder

嫌疑 xiányí [名] suspicion

显 xiǎn [动] **1**(表现) display **2**(呈现) be apparent

显然 xiǎnrán [副] obviously

显示 xiǎnshì [动] demonstrate

显眼 xiǎnyǎn [形] conspicuous

显著 xiǎnzhù [形] striking

险 xiǎn [形] **1**(险要) strategic **2**(危险) dangerous

县 xiàn [名] county

现 xiàn [形] **1**(现在) present ▶现状 xiànzhuàng present situation **2**(现有) ready ▶现金 xiànjīn cash

现场 xiànchǎng [名] scene ▶现场报道 xiànchǎng bàodào live report

现成 xiànchéng [形] ready-made

现代 xiàndài [名] modern times (PL)

现代化 xiàndàihuà [名] modernization

现实 xiànshí [名] reality

现象 xiànxiàng [名] phenomenon

现在 xiànzài [名] now

现状 xiànzhuàng [名] the current situation

限 xiàn **I** [动] limit **II** [名] limit

限期 xiànqī **I** [动] set a deadline **II** [名] deadline

限制 xiànzhì [动] restrict

线 xiàn [名] **1**(指细长物品) thread ▶电线 diànxiàn electric wire **2**(交通干线) line

线索 xiànsuǒ [名] clue

宪 xiàn [名] constitution

宪法 xiànfǎ [名] constitution

陷 xiàn **I** [名] **1**(书)(陷阱) trap **2**(过失) fault ▶缺陷 quēxiàn defect **II** [动] **1**(沉入) get bogged down **2**(凹进) sink **3**(卷入) get involved

陷害 xiànhài [动] frame

陷阱 xiànjǐng [名] trap

馅 xiàn [名] stuffing ▷饺子馅 jiǎozi xiàn *jiaozi* filling

羡 xiàn [动] admire

羡慕 xiànmù [动] envy

献 xiàn [动] **1**(给) give ▶献血 xiànxiě donate blood **2**(表演) show

腺 xiàn [名] gland

乡 xiāng [名] **1**(乡村) countryside **2**(家乡) home town

乡村 xiāngcūn [名] village

乡下 xiāngxia [名] countryside

相 xiāng [副] (互相) mutually ▶相差 xiāngchà differ
→ see also/另见 xiàng

相处 xiāngchǔ [动] get along

相当 xiāngdāng I [动] match II [形] appropriate III [副] quite

相对 xiāngduì I [动] be opposite II [形] 1 (非绝对的) relative 2 (比较的) comparative

相反 xiāngfǎn I [形] opposite II [连] on the contrary

相关 xiāngguān [动] be related

相互 xiānghù I [形] mutual II [副] ▶相互理解 xiānghù lǐjiě understand each other

相识 xiāngshí [动] be acquainted

相似 xiāngsì [形] similar

相同 xiāngtóng [形] identical

相像 xiāngxiàng [动] be alike

相信 xiāngxìn [动] believe

香 xiāng I [形] 1 (芬芳) fragrant 2 (美味) delicious 3 (睡得熟的) sound II [名] 1 (香料) spice 2 (烧的香) incense

香波 xiāngbō [名] shampoo

香肠 xiāngcháng [名] sausage

香港 Xiānggǎng [名] Hong Kong

香蕉 xiāngjiāo [名] banana

香料 xiāngliào [名] spice

香水 xiāngshuǐ [名] perfume

香烟 xiāngyān [名] (卷烟) cigarette

香皂 xiāngzào [名] soap

箱 xiāng [名] 1 (箱子) box 2 (箱状物) ▶信箱 xìnxiāng postbox (英), mailbox (美)

箱子 xiāngzi [名] box

详 xiáng [形] detailed

详情 xiángqíng [名] details (PL)

详细 xiángxì [形] detailed

享 xiǎng [动] enjoy

享受 xiǎngshòu [动] enjoy

响 xiǎng I [名] 1 (回声) echo 2 (声音) sound II [动] sound ▷手机响了。Shǒujī xiǎng le. The mobile (英) 或 cell (美) phone was ringing. III [形] loud

响亮 xiǎngliàng [形] loud and clear

响应 xiǎngyìng [动] respond

想 xiǎng [动] 1 (思考) think ▷想办法 xiǎng bànfǎ think of a way 2 (推测) reckon 3 (打算) want to 4 (想念) miss

In a positive sentence, both 想 xiǎng and 要 yào can be used to express "want to". To express "I don't want to", it is more common to use 不想 bù xiǎng, as the expression 不要 bù yào is stronger and indicates a definite decision, meaning "I shall not (under any circumstances)".

想法 xiǎngfǎ [名] opinion

想念 xiǎngniàn [动] miss

想像 xiǎngxiàng I [动] imagine II [名] imagination

向 xiàng I [名] direction II [动] 1(对着) face 2(偏袒) side with III [介] to ▷我向他表示了感谢。Wǒ xiàng tā biǎoshì le gǎnxiè. I expressed my thanks to him.

向导 xiàngdǎo [名] guide

向来 xiànglái [副] always

项 xiàng I [名] (项目) item ▶事项 shìxiàng item II [量] item ▷3项要求 sān xiàng yāoqiú three requirements ▷2项任务 liǎng xiàng rènwu two tasks

项链 xiàngliàn [名] necklace

项目 xiàngmù [名] 1(事项) item 2(指工程计划) project

巷 xiàng [名] lane

相 xiàng [名] 1(相貌) appearance 2(姿势) posture 3(官位) minister ▶外相 wàixiàng foreign minister 4(相片) photograph ▶照相 zhàoxiàng take a photograph → see also/另见 xiāng

相貌 xiàngmào [名] appearance

相片 xiàngpiàn [名] photograph

象 xiàng [名] 1(大象) elephant 2(样子) appearance

象棋 xiàngqí [名] Chinese chess

象棋 xiàngqí

象棋 xiàngqí is a very popular board game in China. It is a game of skill, played by two players on a board which imitates a battle field with a river in between two opposing sides. There are some similarities between the Chinese chess and international chess.

象牙 xiàngyá [名] ivory

象征 xiàngzhēng [动] symbolize

像 xiàng I [名] portrait ▶画像 huàxiàng paint portraits ▶雕像 diāoxiàng statue II [动] 1(相似) look like 2(比如) ▷像他这样的好孩子，谁不喜欢呢！Xiàng tā zhèyàng de hǎo háizi, shéi bù xǐhuan ne! Who doesn't like good children like this one! III [副] as if ▷像要下雪了。Xiàng yào xiàxuě le. It looks as if it might snow.

橡 xiàng [名] 1(橡树) oak 2(橡胶树) rubber tree

橡胶 xiàngjiāo [名] rubber

橡皮 xiàngpí [名] rubber (英), eraser (美)

削 xiāo [动] peel

消 xiāo [动] 1(消失) disappear 2(使消失) remove

消除 xiāochú [动] eliminate

消防 xiāofáng [名] fire fighting

消费 xiāofèi [动] consume

消耗 xiāohào [动] consume

消化 xiāohuà [动] digest

消极 xiāojí [形] 1(反面) negative

2(消沉) demoralized

消灭 xiāomiè [动] **1**(消失) die out **2**(除掉) eradicate

消失 xiāoshī [动] vanish

消息 xiāoxi [名] news (SG)

宵 xiāo [名] night ▷通宵 tōngxiāo all night

销 xiāo [动] **1**(熔化) melt **2**(除去) cancel **3**(销售) market **4**(消费) spend

销路 xiāolù [名] market

销售 xiāoshòu [动] sell

小 xiǎo [形] (不大) small ▷年龄小 niánlíng xiǎo young

小便 xiǎobiàn I [动] urinate II [名] urine

小吃 xiǎochī [名] **1**(非正餐) snack **2**(冷盘) cold dish

小丑 xiǎochǒu [名] (滑稽演员) clown

小儿科 xiǎo'érkē [名] (医) paediatrics (英) 或 pediatrics (美) department

小费 xiǎofèi [名] tip

小伙子 xiǎohuǒzi [名] lad

小姐 xiǎojie [名] **1**(称呼) Miss **2**(女子) young lady

小看 xiǎokàn [动] underestimate

小麦 xiǎomài [名] wheat

小名 xiǎomíng [名] pet name

小气 xiǎoqi [形] **1**(气量小) petty **2**(吝啬) stingy

小区 xiǎoqū [名] housing estate

小时 xiǎoshí [名] hour

小说 xiǎoshuō [名] novel

小提琴 xiǎotíqín [名] violin

小偷 xiǎotōu [名] thief

小心 xiǎoxīn I [动] be careful II [形] careful

小学 xiǎoxué [名] primary school (英), elementary school (美)

小学生 xiǎoxuéshēng [名] primary school pupil (英), elementary school student (美)

小组 xiǎozǔ [名] group

晓 xiǎo I [名] dawn II [动] **1**(知道) know **2**(使人知道) tell

晓得 xiǎode [动] know

孝 xiào I [动] be dutiful ▷孝子 xiàozǐ a filial son II [名] filial piety

孝顺 xiàoshùn I [动] show filial obedience II [形] filial

校 xiào [名] (学校) school

校长 xiàozhǎng [名] principal

哮 xiào I [名] wheezing II [动] wheeze

哮喘 xiàochuǎn [名] asthma

笑 xiào [动] **1**(欢笑) laugh **2**(嘲笑) laugh at

笑话 xiàohua I [名] joke II [动] laugh at

效 xiào I [名] effect II [动] **1**(仿效) imitate **2**(献出) devote ... to

效果 xiàoguǒ [名] **1**(结果) effect **2**(戏剧) effects (PL)

效率 xiàolù [名] efficiency

效益 xiàoyì [名] returns (PL)

些 xiē [量] 1 (不定量) some 2 (略微) a little

歇 xiē [动] (休息) rest

歇息 xiēxi [动] 1 (休息) have a rest 2 (睡觉) go to sleep

蝎 xiē [名] scorpion ▶蝎子 xiēzi scorpion

协 xié I [动] assist II [副] jointly ▶协议 xiéyì agree on

协会 xiéhuì [名] association

协调 xiétiáo I [动] coordinate II [形] coordinated

协议 xiéyì [名] agreement

协助 xiézhù [动] help

协作 xiézuò [动] collaborate

邪 xié [形] (不正当) evil

邪恶 xié'è [形] evil

斜 xié I [形] slanting II [动] slant

斜坡 xiépō [名] slope

携 xié [动] 1 (携带) carry 2 (拉着) hold

携带 xiédài [动] carry

鞋 xié [名] shoe

鞋匠 xiéjiàng [名] cobbler

写 xiě [动] 1 (书写) write 2 (写作) write 3 (描写) describe 4 (绘画) draw

写作 xiězuò [动] write

血 xiě [名] (口) blood
→ see also/另见 xuè

泄 xiè [动] (泄露) let ... out

泄露 xièlòu [动] let ... out

卸 xiè [动] 1 (搬下) unload ▶卸车 xièchē unload a vehicle 2 (除去) remove ▶卸妆 xièzhuāng remove one's makeup 3 (拆卸) strip 4 (解除) be relieved of ▶卸任 xièrèn step down

谢 xiè [动] 1 (感谢) thank ▷多谢! Duōxiè! Thanks a lot! 2 (认错) apologize 3 (拒绝) decline ▶谢绝 xièjué decline 4 (脱落) wither

谢谢 xièxie [动] thank you, thanks (口)

蟹 xiè [名] crab ▶螃蟹 pángxiè crab

心 xīn [名] 1 (心脏) heart 2 (思想) mind ▶用心 yòngxīn attentively ▶谈心 tánxīn heart-to-heart talk 3 (中心) centre (英), center (美)

心得 xīndé [名] what one has learned

心理 xīnlǐ [名] psychology

心灵 xīnlíng [名] mind

心情 xīnqíng [名] frame of mind

心愿 xīnyuàn [名] one's heart's desire

心脏 xīnzàng [名] heart

心脏病 xīnzàngbìng [名] heart disease

辛 xīn [形] 1 (辣) hot 2 (辛苦) laborious 3 (痛苦) bitter

辛苦 xīnkǔ I [形] laborious II [动] trouble ▷辛苦你了! Xīnkǔ nǐ le! Thanks for taking the trouble!

辛勤 xīnqín [形] hardworking

欣 xīn [形] glad

欣赏 xīnshǎng [动] 1(赏识) admire 2(享受) enjoy

新 xīn I [形] (跟旧相对) new II [副] newly

新潮 xīncháo I [形] fashionable II [名] new trend

新陈代谢 xīn chén dàixiè [名] metabolism

新郎 xīnláng [名] bridegroom

新年 xīnnián [名] 1(指一段时间) New Year 2(指元旦当天) New Year's Day

新娘 xīnniáng [名] bride

新闻 xīnwén [名] news (SG)

新鲜 xīnxiān [形] 1(指食物) fresh 2(指植物) tender 3(清新) fresh 4(新奇) novel

新颖 xīnyǐng [形] original

薪 xīn [名] (薪水) salary

薪水 xīnshui [名] salary

信 xìn I [动] 1(相信) believe ▶轻信 qīngxìn readily believe 2(信奉) believe in ▶信教 xìnjiào be religious II [名] 1(书信) letter ▶信箱 xìnxiāng letterbox (英), mailbox (美) 2(信息) information ▶口信 kǒuxìn verbal message 3(信用) trust ▶失信 shīxìn lose trust

信贷 xìndài [名] credit

信封 xìnfēng [名] envelope

信号 xìnhào [名] signal

信件 xìnjiàn [名] letter

信赖 xìnlài [动] trust

信任 xìnrèn [动] trust

信息 xìnxī [名] information

信心 xìnxīn [名] faith

信仰 xìnyǎng [动] believe in ▶他没有宗教信仰。 Tā méiyou zōngjiào xìnyǎng. He has no religious faith.

信用 xìnyòng [名] 1(指信任) word 2(指借贷) credit

信用卡 xìnyòngkǎ [名] credit card

信誉 xìnyù [名] reputation

兴 xīng [动] 1(旺盛) prosper 2(流行) be popular 3(使盛行) promote
→ see also/另见 xìng

兴奋 xīngfèn [动] be excited

兴盛 xīngshèng [形] prosperous

兴旺 xīngwàng [形] prosperous

星 xīng [名] 1(指天体) star ▶星星 xīngxing star 2(指名人) star ▶球星 qiúxīng football star

星期 xīngqī [名] 1(周) week 2(指某天) ▶星期天 xīngqītiān Sunday ▶星期三 xīngqīsān Wednesday ▷明天星期几? Míngtiān xīngqī jǐ? What day is it tomorrow?

猩 xīng [名] orang-utan ▶黑猩猩 hēixīngxing chimpanzee

腥 xīng [形] fishy

刑 xíng [名] (刑罚) punishment ▶死刑 sǐxíng the death penalty

行 xíng I [动] 1(走) walk ▶步行 bùxíng go on foot 2(流通) be current ▶发行 fāxíng issue 3(做) do ▶行医 xíngyī practise (英) 或 practice (美) medicine II [形] 1(可以) OK 2(能干) capable III [名] 1(旅行) travel 2(行为) conduct ▶暴行 bàoxíng act of cruelty
→ see also/另见 háng

行动 xíngdòng [动] 1(行走) move about 2(活动) take action

行李 xíngli [名] luggage

行人 xíngrén [名] pedestrian

行驶 xíngshǐ [动] travel

行为 xíngwéi [名] behaviour (英), behavior (美)

行走 xíngzǒu [动] walk

形 xíng [名] 1(形状) shape 2(形体) body

形成 xíngchéng [动] form

形容 xíngróng [动] describe

形式 xíngshì [名] form

形象 xíngxiàng [名] image

形状 xíngzhuàng [名] shape

型 xíng [名] type ▶体型 tǐxíng build ▶血型 xuèxíng blood group

型号 xínghào [名] model

醒 xǐng [动] 1(神志恢复) come to 2(睡醒) wake up 3(醒悟) become aware ▶提醒 tíxǐng remind

兴 xìng [名] excitement
→ see also/另见 xīng

兴趣 xìngqù [名] interest ▶他对

集邮有浓厚的兴趣。 Tā duì jíyóu yǒu nónghòu de xìngqù. He has a deep interest in stamp-collecting.

杏 xìng [名] apricot

幸 xìng I [形] lucky II [副] fortunately

幸福 xìngfú I [名] happiness II [形] happy

幸亏 xìngkuī [副] fortunately

幸运 xìngyùn I [名] good luck II [形] lucky

性 xìng [名] 1(性格) character ▶任性 rènxìng stubborn 2(性能) function ▶酸性 suānxìng acidity 3(性别) gender ▶男性 nánxìng male 4(情欲) sex 5(性质) ▶可靠性 kěkàoxìng reliability ▶实用性 shíyòngxìng utility 6(语法) gender ▶阳性 yángxìng masculine

性别 xìngbié [名] sex

性感 xìnggǎn [形] sexy

性格 xìnggé [名] personality

性质 xìngzhì [名] character

姓 xìng I [动] ▷我姓李。 Wǒ xìng Lǐ. My surname is Li. II [名] surname

姓名 xìngmíng [名] full name

凶 xiōng [形] 1(不幸的) unlucky 2(凶恶) ferocious ▶凶相 xiōngxiàng fierce look 3(厉害) terrible

凶狠 xiōnghěn [形] vicious

凶手 xiōngshǒu [名] murderer

兄 xiōng [名] brother

兄弟 xiōngdì [名] brother

胸 xiōng [名] 1 (胸部) chest 2 (心胸) heart

胸脯 xiōngpú [名] chest

雄 xióng [形] 1 (公的) male ▶雄性 xióngxìng male 2 (有气魄的) imposing 3 (强有力的) strong

熊 xióng [名] bear

熊猫 xióngmāo [名] panda

休 xiū [动] 1 (停止) stop 2 (休息) rest

休息 xiūxi [动] rest

休闲 xiūxián [动] (悠闲) be at leisure ▶休闲服装 xiūxián fúzhuāng casual clothes

修 xiū [动] 1 (修理) mend 2 (兴建) build 3 (剪) trim

修改 xiūgǎi [动] alter

修建 xiūjiàn [动] build

修理 xiūlǐ [动] repair

修饰 xiūshì [动] 1 (修整装饰) decorate 2 (修改润饰) polish

修养 xiūyǎng [名] 1 (水平) accomplishments (PL) 2 (指态度) gentility

羞 xiū [形] shy ▶害羞 hàixiū be shy

秀 xiù I [形] 1 (清秀) elegant 2 (优异) outstanding II [名] talent ▶新秀 xīnxiù new talent

秀气 xiùqi [形] 1 (清秀) delicate

2 (文雅) refined

袖 xiù [名] sleeve ▶袖子 xiùzi sleeve

袖珍 xiùzhēn [形] pocket-sized ▷袖珍收音机 xiùzhēn shōuyīnjī pocket radio

绣 xiù I [动] embroider II [名] embroidery

锈 xiù [名] rust ▶生锈 shēngxiù go rusty

须 xū I [副] ▶必须 bìxū must II [名] beard

须要 xūyào [动] need

须知 xūzhī [名] essentials (PL)

虚 xū [形] 1 (空着) empty 2 (胆怯) timid 3 (虚假) false 4 (虚心) modest 5 (弱) weak

虚构 xūgòu [动] fabricate

虚假 xūjiǎ [形] false

虚荣 xūróng [名] vanity

虚弱 xūruò [形] frail

虚伪 xūwěi [形] hypocritical

虚心 xūxīn [形] open-minded

需 xū I [动] need II [名] needs (PL) ▶军需 jūnxū military requirements (PL)

需求 xūqiú [名] demand

需要 xūyào I [动] need II [名] needs (PL) ▷日常生活需要 rìcháng shēnghuó xūyào necessities of life

许 xǔ [动] 1 (称赞) praise 2 (答应) promise 3 (允许) allow

许多 xǔduō [形] many ▷他养了许多金鱼。 Tā yǎng le xǔduō jīnyú. He keeps a lot of goldfish.

叙 xù [动] 1 (谈) chat 2 (记述) recount

叙事 xùshì [动] narrate

叙述 xùshù [动] recount

畜 xù [动] raise
→ see also/另见 chù

畜牧 xùmù [动] rear ▶畜牧业 xùmùyè animal husbandry

酗 xù see below/见下文

酗酒 xùjiǔ [动] get drunk

婿 xù [名] (女婿) son-in-law ▶女婿 nǚxù son-in-law

宣 xuān [动] 1 (宣布) announce 2 (疏导) lead ... off ▶宣泄 xuānxiè get ... off one's chest

宣布 xuānbù [动] announce

宣称 xuānchēng [动] announce

宣传 xuānchuán [动] disseminate ▶宣传工具 xuānchuán gōngjù means of dissemination

宣告 xuāngào [动] proclaim

宣誓 xuānshì [动] take an oath

宣言 xuānyán [名] declaration

宣扬 xuānyáng [动] advocate

宣战 xuānzhàn [动] declare war

喧 xuān [动] make a noise

喧哗 xuānhuá I [形] riotous II [动] create a disturbance

喧闹 xuānnào [形] rowdy

悬 xuán [动] 1 (挂) hang 2 (设想) imagine 3 (挂念) be concerned about 4 (未定) be unresolved

悬挂 xuánguà [动] hang

悬念 xuánniàn [名] suspense

悬崖 xuányá [名] precipice

旋 xuán I [动] 1 (旋转) revolve 2 (返回) return II [名] spiral
→ see also/另见 xuàn

旋律 xuánlǜ [名] melody

旋钮 xuánniǔ [名] knob

旋涡 xuánwō [名] whirlpool

旋转 xuánzhuǎn [动] revolve

选 xuǎn I [动] 1 (挑选) choose 2 (选举) vote II [名] 1 (指人) selection ▶人选 rénxuǎn selection of people 2 (作品集) collection ▶文选 wénxuǎn collected works (PL)

选拔 xuǎnbá [动] select

选举 xuǎnjǔ [动] elect

选民 xuǎnmín [名] electorate

选手 xuǎnshǒu [名] contestant

选修 xuǎnxiū [动] choose to study ▶选修课程 xuǎnxiū kèchéng optional course

选择 xuǎnzé [动] choose ▶别无选择 biéwú xuǎnzé have no choice

旋 xuàn [动] spin
→ see also/另见 xuán

旋风 xuànfēng [名] whirlwind

靴 xuē [名] boot

靴子 xuēzi [名] boot

穴 xué [名] 1 (洞) den 2 (穴位)

acupuncture point

穴位 xuéwèi [名] acupuncture point

学 xué I [动] 1 (学习) study ▷学英语 xué Yīngyǔ learn English 2 (模仿) imitate II [名] 1 (学问) learning ▶博学 bóxué erudition 2 (学科) science ▶生物学 shēngwùxué biology 3 (学校) school ▶大学 dàxué university ▶中学 zhōngxué senior school (英), high school (美) ▶小学 xiǎoxué primary school (英), elementary school (美)

学费 xuéfèi [名] tuition fee

学科 xuékē [名] subject

学历 xuélì [名] educational background

学生 xuésheng [名] student

学士 xuéshì [名] (指学位) bachelor's degree

学术 xuéshù [名] learning

学说 xuéshuō [名] theory

学位 xuéwèi [名] degree

学问 xuéwen [名] learning

学习 xuéxí [动] study

学校 xuéxiào [名] school

学业 xuéyè [名] studies (PL)

学者 xuézhě [名] scholar

雪 xuě [名] snow ▶下雪 xiàxuě to snow

雪花 xuěhuā [名] snowflake

血 xuè [名] (血液) blood

→ see also/另见 xiě

血统 xuètǒng [名] blood relation

血型 xuèxíng [名] blood type

血压 xuèyā [名] blood pressure

血液 xuèyè [名] 1 (血) blood 2 (主要力量) lifeblood

血缘 xuèyuán [名] blood relation

熏 xūn [动] 1 (烟气接触物体) blacken 2 (熏制) smoke ▶熏肉 xūnròu smoked meat

---

寻 xún [动] search

寻常 xúncháng [形] usual

寻求 xúnqiú [动] seek

寻找 xúnzhǎo [动] look for

巡 xún [动] patrol

巡逻 xúnluó [动] patrol

询 xún [动] inquire

询问 xúnwèn [动] ask

循 xún [动] abide by

循环 xúnhuán [动] circulate

训 xùn I [动] 1 (教导) teach 2 (训练) train II [名] rule

训练 xùnliàn [动] train

迅 xùn [形] swift

迅速 xùnsù [形] swift

驯 xùn I [形] tame II [动] tame

驯服 xùnfú I [形] tame II [动] tame

Y

压 yā I [动] 1 (施力) press 2 (超越) outdo 3 (使稳定) control 4 (压制) suppress 5 (积压) put ... off II [名] pressure

压力 yālì [名] 1 (物) pressure 2 (指对人) pressure 3 (负担) burden

压迫 yāpò [动] 1 (压制) oppress 2 (挤压) put pressure on

压岁钱 yāsuìqián [名] *traditional gifts of money given to children during the Spring Festival*

压抑 yāyì [动] suppress

呀 yā [叹] (表示惊异) oh ▷呀！已经12点了！ Yā! Yǐjīng shí'èr diǎn le! Oh! It's 12 o'clock already!

押 yā [动] (抵押) leave ... as a security

押金 yājīn [名] deposit

鸦 yā [名] crow

鸦片 yāpiàn [名] opium

鸭 yā [名] duck

牙 yá [名] (牙齿) tooth

牙齿 yáchǐ [名] tooth

牙床 yáchuáng [名] gum

牙膏 yágāo [名] toothpaste

牙签 yáqiān [名] toothpick

牙刷 yáshuā [名] toothbrush

牙痛 yátòng [名] toothache

牙医 yáyī [名] dentist

芽 yá [名] (指植物) sprout

崖 yá [名] cliff

哑 yǎ [形] 1 (不能说话) mute 2 (不说话) speechless 3 (嘶哑) hoarse

哑巴 yǎba [名] mute

哑铃 yǎlíng [名] dumbbell

哑语 yǎyǔ [名] sign language

轧 yà [动] (碾) roll

亚 yà I [形] inferior ▶亚军 yàjūn runner-up II [名] Asia

亚洲 Yàzhōu [名] Asia ▶她是亚洲人。 Tā shì Yàzhōurén. She's Asian.

咽 yān [名] pharynx
→ *see also*/另见 yàn

咽喉 yānhóu [名] (字) throat

烟 yān [名] 1 (指气体) smoke 2 (烟草) tobacco ▶香烟 xiāngyān cigarette

烟草 yāncǎo [名] 1 (指植物) tobacco plant 2 (烟草制品) tobacco

烟花 yānhuā [名] firework

烟灰缸 yānhuīgāng [名] ashtray

烟民 yānmín [名] smokers (PL)

淹 yān [动] (淹没) flood

淹没 yānmò [动] 1 (漫过) submerge 2 (喻) drown ... out

延 yán [动] 1 (延长) extend 2 (推迟) delay

延长 yáncháng [动] extend

延迟 yánchí [动] delay

严 yán [形] 1 (严密) tight 2 (严格) strict

严格 yángé [形] strict

严谨 yánjǐn [形] (严密谨慎) meticulous

严厉 yánlì [形] severe

严肃 yánsù [形] 1 (庄重) solemn 2 (严格认真) severe

严重 yánzhòng [形] serious

言 yán I [动] speak II [名] 1 (话) speech 2 (字) words (PL)

言论 yánlùn [名] speech ▷言论自由 yánlùn zìyóu freedom of speech

言情片 yánqíngpiān [名] romantic film (英) 或 movie (美)

言语 yányǔ [名] language

岩 yán [名] rock

炎 yán I [形] scorching II [名] (炎症) inflammation

炎黄子孙 Yán-Huáng zǐsūn [名] Chinese people

炎热 yánrè [形] scorching hot

炎症 yánzhèng [名] inflammation

沿 yán I [介] along II [动] (依照) follow III [名] edge

沿岸 yán'àn [名] bank

沿海 yánhǎi [名] coast

研 yán [动] (研究) research ▶研究院 yánjiūyuàn research institute ▶研究生 yánjiūshēng postgraduate student

研究 yánjiū [动] 1 (探求) research 2 (商讨) discuss

盐 yán [名] salt

颜 yán [名] 1 (字) face 2 (颜色) colour (英), color (美)

颜料 yánliào [名] colouring (英), coloring (美)

颜色 yánsè [名] (色彩) colour (英), color (美)

眼 yǎn [名] 1 (眼睛) eye 2 (小洞) small hole

眼光 yǎnguāng [名] 1 (视线) gaze 2 (观察能力) vision 3 (观点) perspective

眼红 yǎnhóng [动] be jealous

眼界 yǎnjiè [名] horizons (PL)

眼睛 yǎnjing [名] eye

眼镜 yǎnjìng [名] glasses (PL)

眼泪 yǎnlèi [名] tear

眼力 yǎnlì [名] 1 (视力) eyesight 2 (鉴别能力) judgement

眼神 yǎnshén [名] 1(指神态) expression 2(方)(视力) eyesight

演 yǎn [动] (表演) perform

演出 yǎnchū [动] perform

演讲 yǎnjiǎng [动] make a speech

演示 yǎnshì [动] demonstrate

演说 yǎnshuō [动] make a speech

演员 yǎnyuán [名] performer

演奏 yǎnzòu [动] perform

厌 yàn [动] (厌恶) detest

厌烦 yànfán [动] be sick of

厌恶 yànwù [动] loathe

砚 yàn [名] ink stone ▶砚台 yàntai ink stone

咽 yàn [动] swallow
→ see also/另见 yān

宴 yàn [动] host a dinner ▶宴请 yànqǐng invite ... to dinner

宴会 yànhuì [名] banquet

验 yàn [动] (检查) test

验光 yànguāng [动] have an eye test

验血 yànxiě [动] have a blood test

谚 yàn [名] saying ▶谚语 yànyǔ proverb

雁 yàn [名] wild goose

焰 yàn [名] flame

燕 yàn [名] swallow

燕麦 yànmài [名] oats (PL)

燕尾服 yànwěifú [名] tailcoat

羊 yáng [名] sheep ▶山羊

shānyáng goat

羊毛 yángmáo [名] wool

羊绒衫 yángróngshān [名] cashmere

阳 yáng [名] 1(阴的对立面) Yang (from Yin and Yang) 2(太阳) sun ▶阳光 yángguāng sunlight

阳台 yángtái [名] balcony

阳性 yángxìng [名] 1(医) positive 2(语言) masculine

洋 yáng I [名] (海洋) ocean II [形] (外国的) foreign

洋白菜 yángbáicài [名] cabbage

洋葱 yángcōng [名] onion

仰 yǎng [动] (脸向上) look up

仰望 yǎngwàng [动] look up

养 yǎng I [动] 1(供给) provide for 2(饲养) keep ▷我爱养花。 Wǒ ài yǎng huā. I like growing flowers. 3(生育) give birth to 4(培养) form ▷养成习惯 yǎng chéng xíguàn form a habit II [形] foster ▶养母 yǎngmǔ foster mother ▶养子 yǎngzǐ adopted son

养活 yǎnghuo [动] (口) 1(提供生活费用) support 2(饲养) raise 3(生育抚养) give birth to

养料 yǎngliào [名] nourishment

养育 yǎngyù [动] bring up

养殖 yǎngzhí [动] breed

氧 yǎng [名] oxygen ▶氧气 yǎngqì oxygen

痒 yǎng [动] itch

样 yàng I [名] 1 (模样) style 2 (标准物) sample II [量] type ▷样水果 sān yàng shuǐguǒ three types of fruit

样品 yàngpǐn [名] sample

样式 yàngshì [名] style

样子 yàngzi [名] 1 (模样) appearance 2 (神情) expression

妖 yāo [名] evil spirit

妖精 yāojing [名] (妖怪) demon

要 yāo [动] 1 (求) ask 2 (邀请) invite → see also / 另见 yào

Both 要 yào and 会 huì can be used to express the future tense. 要 yào refers to something definite, e.g. 我明天要上班 wǒ míngtiān yào shàngbān (I am going to work tomorrow); 会 huì is usually used to express a possible, or probable outcome, e.g. 明天会下雨 míngtiān huì xiàyǔ (It might rain tomorrow).

要求 yāoqiú I [动] demand II [名] request

腰 yāo [名] 1 (身体中部) waist 2 (裤腰) waist

腰包 yāobāo [名] wallet

腰带 yāodài [名] belt

腰果 yāoguǒ [名] cashew nut

腰围 yāowéi [名] waistline

腰子 yāozi [名] kidney

邀 yāo [动] (邀请) invite

邀请 yāoqǐng [动] invite

谣 yáo [名] 1 (歌谣) folk song ▶歌谣 gēyáo folk song 2 (谣言) rumour (英), rumor (美) ▶谣言 yáoyán hearsay

谣传 yáochuán I [动] be rumoured (英) 或 rumored (美) II [名] rumour (英), rumor (美)

摇 yáo [动] shake

摇动 yáodòng [动] 1 (摇东西) wave 2 (晃) shake

摇滚乐 yáogǔnyuè [名] rock and roll

摇晃 yáohuàng [动] shake

摇篮 yáolán [名] cradle

遥 yáo [形] distant ▶遥控器 yáokòngqì remote control

遥控 yáokòng [动] operate by remote control

遥远 yáoyuǎn [形] 1 (指距离) distant 2 (指时间) far-off

咬 yǎo [动] 1 (指用嘴) bite 2 (夹住) grip

舀 yǎo [动] ladle

药 yào [名] 1 (指治病) medicine 2 (指化学物品) chemical

药材 yàocái [名] herbal medicine

药方 yàofāng [名] prescription

药物 yàowù [名] medicine

要 yào I [形] important II [动] 1 (想得到) want ▷我女儿要一个新书包。 Wǒ nǚ'ér yào yī gè xīn shūbāo. My daughter wants a new schoolbag. **2** (要求) ask ▷老师要我们安静。 Lǎoshī yào wǒmen ānjìng. The teacher asked us to be quiet. **III** [助动] **1** (应该) should ▷饭前要洗手。 Fàn qián yào xǐshǒu. You should wash your hands before you eat. **2** (需要) need ▷我要上厕所。 Wǒ yào shàng cèsuǒ. I need the toilet. **3** (表示意志) want ▷我要学开车。 Wǒ yào xué kāichē. I want to learn to drive. **4** (将要) be about to ▷我们要放暑假了。 Wǒmen yào fàng shǔjià le. We're about to break for summer vacation. **IV** [连] (如果) if ▷你要碰见他，替我问声好。 Nǐ yào pèngjiàn tā, tì wǒ wèn shēng hǎo. If you meet him, say hello from me.

→ see also/另见 yāo

In a positive sentence, both 要 yào and 想 xiǎng can be used to express "want to". To express "I don't want to", it is more common to use 不想 bù xiǎng, as the expression 不要 bù yào is stronger and indicates a definite decision, meaning "I shall not (under any circumstances)".

要不 yàobù [连] **1** (否则) otherwise ▷快点走，要不你要迟到了。 Kuàidiǎn zǒu, yào bù nǐ yào chídào le. Go quickly, otherwise you'll be late. **2** (表示选择) either ... or ▷我们要不

去看电影，要不去咖啡厅，你说呢？ Wǒmen yàobù qù kàn diànyǐng, yàobù qù kāfēitīng, nǐ shuō ne? We can either go to see a film or go to a coffee shop – which would you prefer?

要紧 yàojǐn [形] **1** (重要) important **2** (严重) serious

要领 yàolǐng [名] **1** (要点) gist **2** (基本要求) main points (PL)

要么 yàome [连] either ... or ▷你要么学文，要么学理。 Nǐ yàome xué wén, yàome xué lǐ. You either study arts or science.

要是 yàoshi [连] if ▷要是你不满意，可以随时退货。 Yàoshi nǐ bù mǎnyì, kěyǐ suíshí tuìhuò. If you're not satisfied, you can return the goods at any time.

钥 yào see below/见下文

钥匙 yàoshi [名] key

耀 yào [动] (照射) shine

耶 yē see below/见下文

耶稣 Yēsū [名] Jesus

椰 yē [名] coconut

椰子 yēzi [名] **1** (树) coconut tree **2** (果实) coconut

噎 yē [动] (堵塞) choke

爷 yé [名] (祖父) (paternal) grandfather

爷爷 yéye [名] (口) (祖父) (paternal) granddad

也 yě [副] **1** (同样) also ▷他也去过中国。 Tā yě qùguò Zhōngguó.

He's been to China too. **2**(表示转折) still ▷即使他来了，也帮不上忙。 Jíshǐ tā lái le, yě bāng bù shàng máng. Even if he comes, it still won't be of any use.

也许 yěxǔ[副] perhaps

野 yě **I**[名](野外) open country ▷野餐 yěcān picnic **II**[形] **1**(野生) wild ▷野菜 yěcài wild herbs (PL) **2**(蛮横) rude ▷粗野 cūyě rough **3**(无约束) unruly

野餐 yěcān[动] have a picnic

野蛮 yěmán[形] **1**(蒙昧) uncivilized **2**(残暴) brutal

野生 yěshēng[形] wild

野兽 yěshòu[名] wild animal

野外 yěwài[名] open country

野心 yěxīn[名] ambition

野营 yěyíng[名] camp

业 yè[名] **1**(行业) industry ▷饮食业 yǐnshí yè the food and drink industry **2**(职业) job ▷就业 jiùyè obtain employment ▷失业 shīyè be unemployed **3**(学业) studies (PL) ▷毕业 bìyè graduate **4**(产业) property ▷家业 jiāyè family property

业务 yèwù[名] profession

业余 yèyú **I**[名] spare time **II**[形] amateurish

业主 yèzhǔ[名] owner

叶 yè[名](叶子) leaf

页 yè **I**[名] page **II**[量] page

页码 yèmǎ[名] page number

夜 yè[名] night

夜班 yèbān[名] night shift

夜猫子 yèmāozi[名](方)**1**(猫头鹰) owl **2**(喻)(晚睡者) night owl

夜生活 yèshēnghuó[名] nightlife

夜市 yèshì[名] night market

夜宵 yèxiāo[名] late-night snack

夜总会 yèzǒnghuì[名] nightclub

液 yè[名] liquid

液体 yètǐ[名] liquid

腋 yè[名](夹肢窝) armpit ▷腋毛 yèmáo underarm hair

一 yī[数] **1**(指数目) one ▷一辈子 yībèizi a lifetime **2**(相同) ▷一类人 yī lèi rén the same sort of people **3**(全) ▷一屋子烟 yī wūzi yān full of smoke

一 yī is pronounced as 1st tone when it is used by itself to mean the number one, for example in telephone numbers etc. When it is followed by another syllable it changes its tone depending on the tone of the subsequent syllable. If the subsequent syllable is 1st, 2nd or 3rd tone then it is pronounced as 4th tone yì. If the subsequent syllable is a 4th tone, then it is pronounced as a 2nd tone yí. For consistency, changes of tone in pinyin are not shown in this book.

一般 yībān [形] 1(一样) same ▷他们俩一般大。 Tāmen liǎ yībān dà. The two of them are the same age. 2(普通) ordinary

一半 yībàn [名] half

一边 yībiān I [名] (一面) side II [副] at the same time

一道 yīdào [副] together

一点儿 yīdiǎnr [量] 1(一些) some ▷你行李太多，我帮你提一点儿吧。 Nǐ xíngli tàiduō, wǒ bāng nǐ tí yīdiǎnr ba. You've got so much luggage - let me help you with some of it. 2(很少) a little ▷这件事我一点儿都不知道。 Zhè jiàn shì wǒ yīdiǎnr dōu bù zhīdào. I know nothing about this.

一定 yīdìng I [形] 1(规定的) definite 2(固定的) fixed 3(相当) certain 4(特定) given II [副] definitely ▷放心，我一定去机场接你。 Fàngxīn, wǒ yīdìng qù jīchǎng jiē nǐ. Don't worry, I'll definitely pick you up at the airport.

一共 yīgòng [副] altogether ▷这套书一共多少本？ Zhè tào shū yīgòng duōshao běn? How many books are there in this set?

一…就… yī...jiù... [副] as soon as ▷我一到家就给你打电话。 Wǒ yī dào jiā jiù gěi nǐ dǎ diànhuà. I'll call you as soon as I get home.

一连 yīlián [副] on end ▷一连下了几个月的雨。 Yīlián xià le jǐ

gè yuè de yǔ. It's been raining for months on end.

一路 yīlù [名] 1(行程) journey ▷一路顺利吗？ Yīlù shùnlì ma? Did you have a good journey? 2(一起) the same way ▷咱俩是一路。 Zán liǎ shì yīlù. We're going the same way.

一面 yīmiàn I [名] aspect ▷积极的一面 jījí de yīmiàn a positive aspect II [副] at the same time ▷她一面听音乐，一面看小说。 Tā yīmiàn tīng yīnyuè, yīmiàn kàn xiǎoshuō. She was listening to music and reading a novel at the same time.

一齐 yīqí [副] simultaneously

一起 yīqǐ I [名] the same place II [副] together

一切 yīqiè [代] 1(全部) all 2(全部事物) everything

一时 yīshí I [名] 1(一个时期) time 2(短暂时间) moment II [副] 1(临时) for the moment 2(时而) sometimes

一同 yītóng [副] together

一下 yīxià I [量] ▷我去问一下。 Wǒ qù wèn yīxià. I'll just go and ask.

measure word, used after verbs to indicate one's attempts to do something

II [副] at once ▷天一下就冷了。 Tiān yīxià jiù lěng le. All at once the weather turned cold.

一向 yīxiàng [副] always

一些 yīxiē [量] 1(部分) some 2(几

个) a few **3** (略微) a little ▷她感觉好一些了。 Tā gǎnjué hǎo yīxiē le. She feels a little better.

一样 yīyàng [形] same ▷他俩爱好一样。 Tā liǎ àihǎo yīyàng. They have the same hobbies.

一再 yīzài [副] repeatedly

一直 yīzhí [副] **1** (不变向) straight **2** (不间断) always ▷大风一直刮了两天两夜。 Dàfēng yīzhí guā le liǎng tiān liǎng yè. The gale blew for two days and two nights. **3** (指一定范围) all the way ▷从南一直到北 cóng nán yīzhí dào běi from the north all way to the south

一致 yīzhì I [形] unanimous II [副] unanimously

衣 yī [名] (衣服) clothing ▶衣裳 yīshang clothes (PL)

衣服 yīfu [名] clothes (PL)

医 yī I [名] **1** (医生) doctor **2** (医) medicine ▶中医 zhōngyī Chinese traditional medicine II [动] treat

医疗 yīliáo [动] treat ▶免费医疗制度 miǎnfèi yīliáo zhìdù system of free medical care

医生 yīshēng [名] doctor

医术 yīshù [名] medical skill

医务室 yīwùshì [名] clinic

医学 yīxué [名] medicine

医药 yīyào [名] medicine

医院 yīyuàn [名] hospital

医治 yīzhì [动] cure

依 yī [动] **1** (依靠) depend on **2** (依从) comply with

依旧 yījiù [副] still

依据 yījù I [动] go by II [名] basis

依靠 yīkào I [动] rely on II [名] support

依赖 yīlài [动] depend on

依然 yīrán [副] still

依照 yīzhào [介] according to

壹 yī [数] one

This is the complex character for "one", which is mainly used in banks, on receipts, etc. to prevent mistakes and forgery.

仪 yí [名] **1** (外表) appearance **2** (礼节) ceremony **3** (仪器) meter

仪器 yíqì [名] meter

仪式 yíshì [名] ceremony

姨 yí [名] **1** (母亲的姐妹) aunt **2** (妻子的姐妹) sister-in-law

移 yí [动] **1** (移动) move **2** (改变) change

移动 yídòng [动] move

移民 yímín I [动] emigrate II [名] immigrant

遗 yí [动] **1** (遗失) lose **2** (留下) leave ... behind

遗产 yíchǎn [名] legacy

遗传 yíchuán [动] inherit

遗憾 yíhàn I [名] regret II [动] be a pity

遗弃 yíqì [动] **1** (车, 船等) abandon **2** (妻, 子等) desert

遗书 yíshū [名] (书面遗言) last letter (of dying man)

遗体 yítǐ [名] remains (PL)

遗忘 yíwàng [动] forget

遗址 yízhǐ [名] ruins (PL)

遗嘱 yízhǔ [名] will

疑 yí [动] doubt

疑难 yínán [形] knotty

疑问 yíwèn [名] question

疑心 yíxīn I [名] suspicion II [动] suspect

已 yǐ [副] already

已经 yǐjīng [副] already

以 yǐ (书) I [动] use ▶以强凌弱 yǐ qiáng líng ruò use one's strength to humiliate the weak II [介] 1 (依照) by 2 (因为) for 3 (表示界限) ▶以内 yǐnèi within ▶以南 yǐnán to the south III [连] ▷我们要改进技术，以提高生产效率。Wǒmen yào gǎijìn jìshù, yǐ tígāo shēngchǎn xiàolù. We should improve the technology so as to increase production.

以便 yǐbiàn [连] in order that

以后 yǐhòu [名] ▷两年以后 liǎng nián yǐhòu two years later ▷以后我们去看电影。Yǐhòu wǒmen qù kàn diànyǐng. Afterwards we're going to see a film.

以及 yǐjí [连] as well as

以来 yǐlái [名] ▷入冬以来 rù dōng yǐlái since the beginning of the winter

以免 yǐmiǎn [连] in case

以前 yǐqián [名] ▷10年以前 shí nián yǐqián ten years ago ▷她以前是老师。Tā yǐqián shì lǎoshī. She was a teacher before.

以为 yǐwéi [动] think

以下 yǐxià [名] (低于某点) ▷30岁以下 sānshí suì yǐxià under thirty

以致 yǐzhì [连] so that

蚁 yǐ [名] ant ▶蚂蚁 mǎyǐ ant

椅 yǐ [名] chair

椅子 yǐzi [名] chair

亿 yì [数] hundred million

义 yì I [名] 1 (正义) righteousness 2 (情谊) human relationship 3 (意义) meaning II [形] 1 (正义的) just 2 (拜认的) adopted ▶义父 yìfù adoptive father

义卖 yìmài [动] sell ... for charity

义气 yìqi I [名] loyalty II [形] loyal

义务 yìwù I [名] duty II [形] compulsory

艺 yì [名] 1 (技能) skill ▶手艺 shǒuyì craftsmanship 2 (艺术) art

艺人 yìrén [名] (演员) performer

艺术 yìshù I [名] 1 (文艺) art 2 (方法) skill ▷管理艺术 guǎnlǐ yìshù management skills II [形] artistic

艺术家 yìshùjiā [名] artist

忆 yì [动] remember ▶记忆 jìyì memory

议 yì I [名] opinion ▶建议 jiànyì propose II [动] discuss ▶商议 shāngyì discuss

议程 yìchéng [名] agenda

议会 yìhuì [名] parliament

议论 yìlùn I [动] discuss II [名] talk

议题 yìtí [名] topic

议员 yìyuán [名] MP (英), congressman, congresswoman (美)

异 yì I [形] 1 (不同) different ▶差异 chāyì difference 2 (奇异) strange 3 (另外) other ▶异国 yìguó foreign country II [动] separate ▶离异 líyì separate

异常 yìcháng [形] unusual

异性 yìxìng [名] (指性别) the opposite sex

译 yì [动] translate

译文 yìwén [名] translation

译者 yìzhě [名] translator

译制 yìzhì [动] dub

抑 yì [动] repress

抑郁 yìyù [形] depressed

抑制 yìzhì [动] 1 (生理) inhibit 2 (控制) control

易 yì [形] (容易) easy ▷易传染 yì chuánrǎn easily transmissible

易拉罐 yìlāguàn [名] can

疫 yì [名] epidemic

疫苗 yìmiáo [名] inoculation

益 yì I [名] benefit II [形] beneficial III [动] increase IV [副] increasingly

益处 yìchù [名] benefit

谊 yì [名] friendship ▶友谊 yǒuyì friendship

意 yì [名] 1 (意思) meaning 2 (心愿) wish ▶好意 hǎoyì good intention

意见 yìjiàn [名] 1 (看法) opinion 2 (不满) objection

意识 yìshí I [名] consciousness II [动] realize

意思 yìsi [名] 1 (意义) meaning 2 (意见) idea 3 (愿望) wish 4 (趣味) interest ▶有意思 yǒu yìsi interesting ▷没意思 méi yìsi boring 5 (心意) token

意图 yìtú [名] intention

意外 yìwài I [名] accident II [形] unexpected

意义 yìyì [名] 1 (含义) meaning 2 (作用) significance

毅 yì [形] resolute

毅力 yìlì [名] perseverance

因 yīn I [连] because II [介] because of ▷昨天他因病缺课。Zuótiān tā yīn bìng quēkè. He missed a class yesterday because of illness. III [名] cause ▶病因 bìngyīn cause of the illness

因此 yīncǐ [连] so

因而 yīn'ér [连] therefore

因素 yīnsù [名] 1 (成分) element 2 (原因) factor

因特网 Yīntèwǎng [名] the Internet

因为 yīnwei [连] because

阴 yīn I [形] 1 (指天气) overcast 2 (阴险的) insidious ▶阴谋 yīnmóu plot 3 (物) negative ▶阴性 yīnxìng negative II [名] 1 (阳的对立面) Yin (from Yin and Yang) 2 (指月亮) the moon ▶阴历 yīnlì lunar calendar 3 (阴凉处) shade ▶树阴 shùyīn the shade

阴暗 yīn'àn [形] gloomy

阴部 yīnbù [名] private parts (PL)

阴凉 yīnliáng [形] shady and cool

音 yīn [名] 1 (声音) sound 2 (消息) news (SG)

音量 yīnliàng [名] volume

音响 yīnxiǎng [名] (指设备) acoustics (PL)

音像 yīnxiàng [名] audio and video

音乐 yīnyuè [名] music

音乐会 yīnyuèhuì [名] concert

银 yín I [名] 1 (指) (金属) silver 2 (指) (货币) money ▶收银台 shōuyíntái cashier's desk II [形] silver

银行 yínháng [名] bank

银河 yínhé [名] the Milky Way

银幕 yínmù [名] screen

银牌 yínpái [名] silver medal

龈 yín [名] gum ▶牙龈 yáyín gum

引 yǐn [动] 1 (牵引) draw 2 (引导) lead ▶引路 yǐnlù lead the way

3 (引起) cause 4 (引用) cite

引导 yǐndǎo [动] 1 (带领) lead 2 (启发诱导) guide

引进 yǐnjìn [动] 1 (人) recommend 2 (物) import

引力 yǐnlì [名] gravitation

引起 yǐnqǐ [动] cause

引擎 yǐnqíng [名] engine

引用 yǐnyòng [动] (引述) quote

引诱 yǐnyòu [动] 1 (诱导) induce 2 (诱惑) tempt

饮 yǐn I [动] drink II [名] drink

饮料 yǐnliào [名] drink

饮食 yǐnshí [名] food and drink

饮用水 yǐnyòngshuǐ [名] drinking water

隐 yǐn [动] conceal

隐藏 yǐncáng [动] conceal

隐瞒 yǐnmán [动] cover ... up

隐私 yǐnsī [名] private matters (PL)

瘾 yǐn [名] (嗜好) addiction ▶上瘾 shàngyǐn be addicted to

印 yìn I [名] 1 (图章) stamp 2 (痕迹) print II [动] (留下痕迹) print

印刷 yìnshuā [动] print

印象 yìnxiàng [名] impression

印章 yìnzhāng [名] seal

荫 yìn [形] shady

荫凉 yìnliáng [形] shady and cool

应 yīng I [动] 1 (答应) answer 2 (应允) agree II [助动] should

→ *see also*/另见 yìng

应当 yīngdāng [助动] should

应该 yīnggāi [助动] should

应允 yīngyǔn [动] consent

英 yīng [名] 1 (才能出众者) hero ▷精英 jīngyīng elite 2 (英国) Britain

英镑 yīngbàng [名] pound sterling

英国 Yīngguó [名] Great Britain ▷英国的 Yīngguó de British

英国人 Yīngguórén [名] the British

英俊 yīngjùn [形] (漂亮的) handsome

英雄 yīngxióng I [名] hero II [形] heroic

英勇 yīngyǒng [形] brave

英语 yīngyǔ [名] English

婴 yīng [名] baby

婴儿 yīng'ér [名] baby

樱 yīng [名] 1 (樱桃) cherry ▷樱桃 yīngtáo cherry 2 (樱花) cherry blossom ▷樱花 yīnghuā cherry blossom

鹦 yīng *see below*/见下文

鹦鹉 yīngwǔ [名] parrot

鹰 yīng [名] eagle

迎 yíng [动] 1 (迎接) welcome 2 (对着) meet

迎合 yínghé [动] cater to

迎接 yíngjiē [动] welcome

萤 yíng [名] firefly ▷萤火虫 yínghuǒchóng firefly

营 yíng I [动] (经营) operate II [名] 1 (军队驻地) barracks (PL) 2 (军队编制) battalion 3 (营地) camp ▷营地 yíngdì camp

营救 yíngjiù [动] rescue

营销 yíngxiāo [动] sell

营养 yíngyǎng [名] nourishment

营业 yíngyè [动] do business

蝇 yíng [名] fly ▷苍蝇 cāngyíng fly

赢 yíng [动] 1 (胜) win 2 (获利) gain

赢利 yínglì [名] gain

影 yǐng [名] 1 (影子) shadow 2 (照片) photograph 3 (电影) film (英), movie (美)

影片 yǐngpiàn [名] 1 (胶片) film 2 (电影) film (英), movie (美)

影响 yǐngxiǎng I [动] affect II [名] influence

影印 yǐngyìn [动] photocopy

应 yìng [动] 1 (回答) answer ▷回应 huíyìng answer 2 (满足) respond to 3 (顺应) comply with 4 (应付) handle ▷应急 yìngjí handle an emergency

→ *see also*/另见 yīng

应酬 yìngchou I [动] socialize with II [名] social engagement

应付 yìngfu [动] 1 (采取办法) handle 2 (敷衍) do half-heartedly 3 (将就) make do with

应聘 yìngpìn [动] accept an offer

应用 yìngyòng I [动] apply II [形]

applied

硬 yìng I [形] 1(坚固) hard 2(刚强) firm 3(能干的) strong II [副] obstinately

硬币 yìngbì [名] coin

硬件 yìngjiàn [名] 1(计算机) hardware 2(设备) equipment

硬盘 yìngpán [名] hard disk

哟 yō [叹] (表示轻微的惊异或赞叹) oh

佣 yōng I [动] hire II [名] servant ▶佣人 yōngrén servant
→ see also/另见 yòng

拥 yōng [动] 1(抱) embrace 2(围着) gather round 3(拥挤) swarm 4(拥护) support

拥抱 yōngbào [动] embrace

拥护 yōnghù [动] support

拥挤 yōngjǐ I [形] crowded II [动] crowd

拥有 yōngyǒu [动] have

庸 yōng [形] (不高明) mediocre

庸俗 yōngsú [形] vulgar

永 yǒng I [形] (书) everlasting II [副] forever

永恒 yǒnghéng [形] everlasting

永久 yǒngjiǔ [形] eternal

永远 yǒngyuǎn [副] eternally

泳 yǒng [名] swim ▶蛙泳 wāyǒng breaststroke

泳道 yǒngdào [名] lane

勇 yǒng [形] brave

勇敢 yǒnggǎn [形] brave

勇气 yǒngqì [名] courage

用 yòng I [动] 1(使用) use 2(需要) need 3(消费) consume ▶用餐 yòngcān have a meal II [名] 1(费用) expense ▶家用 jiāyòng household expenses (PL) 2(用处) use ▶没用 méiyòng useless

用处 yòngchu [名] use

用功 yònggōng I [形] hardworking II [动] work hard

用户 yònghù [名] user ▷网络用户 wǎngluò yònghù internet user

用具 yòngjù [名] tool

用力 yònglì [动] exert oneself

用品 yòngpǐn [名] goods (PL)

用途 yòngtú [名] use

佣 yòng see below/见下文
→ see also/另见 yōng

佣金 yòngjīn [名] commission

优 yōu [形] (优良) excellent

优点 yōudiǎn [名] strong point

优良 yōuliáng [形] fine

优美 yōuměi [形] elegant

优势 yōushì [名] advantage

优先 yōuxiān [动] have priority

优秀 yōuxiù [形] outstanding

优越 yōuyuè [形] superior

忧 yōu I [形] anxious II [动] worry III [名] anxiety

忧伤 yōushāng [形] sad

忧郁 yōuyù [形] depressed

幽 yōu [形] (暗) dim ▶幽暗 yōu'àn

gloomy

幽默 yōumò [形] humorous

悠 yōu [形] **1** (久远) remote **2** (闲适) leisurely

悠久 yōujiǔ [形] long-standing

悠闲 yōuxián [形] leisurely

尤 yóu [副] especially

尤其 yóuqí [副] especially

由 yóu I [动] **1** (听凭) give in to **2** (经过) go through II [介] **1** (归) by **2** (根据) ▷ 由此可见… yóu cǐ kě jiàn… from this we can see… **3** (从) from **4** (由于) due to III [名] cause ▷ 理由 lǐyóu reason

由于 yóuyú [介] as a result of

邮 yóu I [动] post (英), mail (美) II [名] **1** (邮务) post (英), mail (美) **2** (邮票) stamp

邮递 yóudì [动] send … by post (英) 或 mail (美)

邮电 yóudiàn [名] post and telecommunications

邮寄 yóujì [动] post (英), mail (美)

邮件 yóujiàn [名] post (英), mail (美)

邮局 yóujú [名] post office

邮票 yóupiào [名] stamp

邮政 yóuzhèng [名] postal service

邮资 yóuzī [名] postage

犹 yóu [副] still

犹豫 yóuyù [形] hesitant

油 yóu I [名] oil II [形] oily

油滑 yóuhuá [形] slippery

油腻 yóunì I [形] greasy II [名] greasy food

油漆 yóuqī I [名] varnish II [动] varnish

鱿 yóu [名] squid

鱿鱼 yóuyú [名] squid

游 yóu [动] **1** (游泳) swim **2** (游览) tour

游客 yóukè [名] tourist

游览 yóulǎn [动] tour

游牧 yóumù [动] live a nomadic life

游说 yóushuì [动] lobby

游戏 yóuxì I [名] game II [动] play

游行 yóuxíng [动] march

游泳 yóuyǒng I [动] swim II [名] swimming

游泳池 yóuyǒngchí [名] swimming pool

友 yǒu I [名] friend ▷ 男友 nányǒu boyfriend II [形] friendly ▷ 友好 yǒuhǎo friendly

友爱 yǒu'ài [形] affectionate

友情 yǒuqíng [名] friendship

友人 yǒurén [名] friend

友谊 yǒuyì [名] friendship

有 yǒu [动] **1** (具有) have **2** (存在) ▷ 院子里有一棵大树。 Yuànzi li yǒu yī kē dàshù. There's a big tree in the courtyard. **3** (发生) occur ▷ 我的生活有了一些变化。 Wǒ de shēnghuó yǒu le yīxiē biànhuà. A few changes have occurred in my life. **4** (表

示程度) have ▷他特别有学
问。 Tā tèbié yǒu xuéwèn. He's
extremely knowledgeable. **5**(某)
▷有时候 yǒushíhou sometimes
▷有一次，他得了冠军。 Yǒu
yī cì, tā dé le guànjūn. He won a
prize once.

有的 yǒude [名] some ▷展出
的作品，有的来自本土，有
的来自海外。 Zhǎnchū de
zuòpǐn, yǒude láizì běntǔ, yǒude
láizì hǎiwài. Of the articles on
display, some are local, others
are from overseas.

有关 yǒuguān [动] **1**(有关系) be
relevant **2**(涉及到) be about

有利 yǒulì [形] favourable (英),
favorable (美)

有趣 yǒuqù [形] interesting

有限 yǒuxiàn [形] limited

有限公司 yǒuxiàn gōngsī [名]
limited company

有线电视 yǒuxiàn diànshì [名]
cable TV

有幸 yǒuxìng [形] fortunate

有意思 yǒuyìsi I [形] **1**(有意
义) significant **2**(有趣味)
interesting II [动] be interested
in

又 yòu [副] **1**(重复) again **2**(同
时) ▷她是一个好教师，又是
一个好妈妈。 Tā shì yī gè hǎo
jiàoshī, yòu shì yī gè hǎo māma.
She's both a good teacher and a
great mother. **3**(也) too **4**(另外)
another **5**(再加上) and ▷一又三

分之二 yī yòu sān fēn zhī èr one
and two thirds **6**(可是) but

右 yòu [名] **1**(右边) right ▷右边
yòubian right side ▷请向右转。
Qǐng xiàng yòu zhuǎn. Please
turn right. **2**(右翼) the Right

幼 yòu I [形] young II [名] child
▷幼儿园 yòu'éryuán nursery
school (英), kindergarten (美)

幼儿 yòu'ér [名] small child

幼年 yòunián [名] infancy

幼小 yòuxiǎo [形] young

幼稚 yòuzhì [形] **1**(书)(年龄很小)
young **2**(头脑简单) naive

诱 yòu [动] **1**(诱导) guide **2**(引
诱) entice

诱饵 yòu'ěr [名] bait

诱惑 yòuhuò [动] **1**(引诱) entice
2(吸引) attract

于 yú [介] **1**(在) in **2**(向) from **3**(对)
to **4**(从) from **5**(比) than ▷大于
dàyú bigger than

于是 yúshì [连] so

余 yú [名] **1**(零头) ▷500余人
wǔbǎi yú rén more than five
hundred people **2**(指时间) ▷课
余 kèyú extra-curricular

余地 yúdì [名] room

盂 yú [名] jar ▷痰盂 tányú
spittoon (英), cuspidor (美)

鱼 yú [名] fish ▷鱼肉 yúròu fish

娱 yú I [动] amuse II [名]
amusement

娱乐 yúlè I [动] have fun II [名] entertainment

渔 yú [动] (捕鱼) fish ▶渔业 yúyè fisheries

愉 yú [形] happy

愉快 yúkuài [形] happy ▷祝你旅行愉快！ Zhù nǐ lǚxíng yúkuài! Have a pleasant journey!

愚 yú I [形] foolish ▶愚蠢 yúchǔn foolish II [动] fool

愚昧 yúmèi [形] ignorant

舆 yú [形] popular

舆论 yúlùn [名] public opinion

与 yǔ I [介] with II [连] and

宇 yǔ [名] 1(房屋) house 2(四方) the universe

宇航 yǔháng I [动] travel through space II [名] space travel

宇航员 yǔhángyuán [名] astronaut

宇宙 yǔzhòu [名] universe

羽 yǔ [名] 1(羽毛) feather 2(翅膀) wing

羽毛 yǔmáo [名] feather

羽毛球 yǔmáoqiú [名] 1(指运动) badminton 2(指球体) shuttlecock

雨 yǔ [名] rain ▶下雨 xiàyǔ to rain

雨具 yǔjù [名] waterproofs (PL)

雨水 yǔshuǐ [名] (降水) rain

语 yǔ I [名] (语言) language ▶手语 shǒuyǔ sign language II [动] talk

语调 yǔdiào [名] tone

语法 yǔfǎ [名] grammar

语句 yǔjù [名] sentence

语气 yǔqì [名] 1(口气) tone of voice 2(语法) mood

语文 yǔwén [名] 1(语言文字) language 2(中文) Chinese 3(语言与文学) language and literature

语言 yǔyán [名] language

语音 yǔyīn [名] pronunciation

语音信箱 yǔyīn xìnxiāng [名] voice mail

语种 yǔzhǒng [名] language

玉 yù [名] (玉石) jade

玉米 yùmǐ [名] (指植物) maize (英), corn (美)

郁 yù [形] (烦闷) gloomy

郁闷 yùmèn [形] melancholy

育 yù I [动] 1(生育) give birth to 2(养活) raise ▶养育 yǎngyù bring up II [名] education ▶教育 jiàoyù education

狱 yù [名] (监狱) prison ▶监狱 jiānyù prison

浴 yù [动] wash

浴盆 yùpén [名] bath

浴室 yùshì [名] bathroom

预 yù [副] in advance

预报 yùbào [动] predict ▶天气预报 tiānqì yùbào weather forecast

预备 yùbèi [动] prepare

预测 yùcè [动] predict

预防 yùfáng [动] prevent

预感 yùgǎn [动] have a premonition

预计 yùjì [动] estimate

预见 yùjiàn [动] foresee

预科 yùkē [名] foundation course

预料 yùliào [动] predict

预算 yùsuàn [名] budget

预习 yùxí [动] prepare for lessons

预言 yùyán [动] predict

域 yù [名] region ▶领域 lǐngyù realm

欲 yù [名] desire

欲望 yùwàng [名] desire

遇 yù I [动] meet ▶遇到 yùdào meet II [名] 1 (待遇) treatment 2 (机会) opportunity

寓 yù I [动] 1 (居住) live 2 (寄托) imply II [名] residence ▶公寓 gōngyù flat (英), apartment (美)

寓言 yùyán [名] fable

鸳 yuān [名] mandarin duck

鸳鸯 yuānyang [名] (指鸟) mandarin duck

冤 yuān [名] 1 (冤枉) injustice ▶冤枉 yuānwang treat unfairly 2 (冤仇) enmity

元 yuán I [名] 1 (始) first 2 (首) chief ▶元首 yuánshǒu head of state 3 (主) fundamental ▶元素 yuánsù element 4 (整体) component ▶单元 dānyuán unit 5 (圆形货币) coin ▶金元 jīnyuán gold coin II [量] yuan ▶5元钱 wǔ yuán qián five yuan

元旦 Yuándàn [名] New Year's Day

元件 yuánjiàn [名] part

元帅 yuánshuài [名] commander-in-chief

元宵 yuánxiāo [名] *sweet round dumplings made of glutinous rice, usually eaten with the broth in which they are cooked*

元宵节 Yuánxiāo Jié [名] the Lantern Festival

元宵节 Yuánxiāo Jié

The Lantern Festival is celebrated on the 15th day of the Lunar Chinese New Year. The traditional food which is eaten at this festival is called 元宵 yuánxiāo or 汤圆 tāngyuán, a traditional sweet dumpling made of glutinous rice, with various sweet fillings.

园 yuán [名] 1 (指菜地或果林) garden 2 (指游乐场所) park

园丁 yuándīng [名] (园艺工人) gardener

园林 yuánlín [名] garden

园艺 yuányì [名] gardening

员 yuán [名] 1 (指工作或学习的人) ▶理发员 lǐfàyuán hairdresser 2 (成员) member

员工 yuángōng [名] staff (PL)

原 yuán [形] 1 (本来的) original 2 (未加工的) raw ▶原油 yuányóu crude oil

原来 yuánlái I [形] original II [副] 1 (起初) originally 2 (其实) all along

原理 yuánlǐ [名] principle

原谅 yuánliàng [动] forgive

原料 yuánliào [名] (指烹饪) ingredient

原始 yuánshǐ [形] 1 (古老) primitive 2 (最初) original

原先 yuánxiān I [形] original II [副] originally

原因 yuányīn [名] reason

原则 yuánzé [名] principle

原著 yuánzhù [名] the original

原子 yuánzǐ [名] atom

圆 yuán I [形] 1 (圆形的) round ▶圆圈 yuánquān circle 2 (球形的) spherical 3 (圆满的) satisfactory II [名] (数) (圆周) circle

圆规 yuánguī [名] compasses (PL)

圆满 yuánmǎn [形] satisfactory

圆舞曲 yuánwǔqǔ [名] waltz

援 yuán [动] (援助) help ▶支援 zhīyuán support

援救 yuánjiù [动] rescue

援助 yuánzhù [动] help

缘 yuán [名] 1 (缘故) cause 2 (缘分) fate 3 (边缘) edge

缘分 yuánfèn [名] fate

缘故 yuángù [名] cause

猿 yuán [名] ape

猿猴 yuánhóu [名] apes and monkeys (PL)

猿人 yuánrén [名] ape-man

源 yuán [名] source ▶水源 shuǐyuán source

远 yuǎn [形] 1 (指距离) far ▶远程 yuǎnchéng long-distance 2 (指血统) distant 3 (程度高) far

远大 yuǎndà [形] far-reaching

远方 yuǎnfāng [名] afar

远见 yuǎnjiàn [名] foresight

远亲 yuǎnqīn [名] distant relative

远视 yuǎnshì [名] (医) long sightedness

远足 yuǎnzú [动] hike

院 yuàn [名] 1 (院落) courtyard ▶院子 yuànzi yard 2 (指机关或处所) ▶电影院 diànyǐngyuàn cinema (英), movie theater (美) 3 (学院) college 4 (医院) hospital

愿 yuàn I [名] (愿望) wish II [助动] ▶我不愿说。 Wǒ bù yuàn shuō. I don't want to say anything.

愿望 yuànwàng [名] wish

愿意 yuànyì [动] 1 (同意) be willing to 2 (希望) wish

约 yuē I [动] 1 (束缚) restrict 2 (商定) arrange 3 (邀请) invite II [形] brief ▶简约 jiǎnyuē brief III [副] about

约会 yuēhuì [名] 1 (指工作) appointment 2 (指恋人) date

约束 yuēshù [动] bind

月 yuè [名] 1 (月球) the moon ▸满月 mǎnyuè full moon 2 (月份) month ▸三月 sānyuè March 3 (每月) monthly ▸月薪 yuèxīn monthly salary

月饼 yuèbing [名] mooncake

月饼 yuèbing

Mooncakes, the traditional festival food for 中秋节 Zhōngqiū Jié (the Mid-Autumn Festival), are round cakes made of a variety of sweet fillings including beanpaste, egg and peanut.

月份 yuèfèn [名] month

月光 yuèguāng [名] moonlight

月经 yuèjīng [名] (例假) period

月亮 yuèliang [名] the moon

月票 yuèpiào [名] monthly ticket

乐 yuè [名] music ▸器乐 qìyuè instrumental music ▸民乐 mínyuè folk music
→ see also/另见 lè

乐队 yuèduì [名] band

乐器 yuèqì [名] musical instrument

乐曲 yuèqǔ [名] music

乐团 yuètuán [名] philharmonic orchestra

岳 yuè [名] 1 (高山) mountain 2 (妻子的父母) parents-in-law (PL)

岳父 yuèfù [名] father-in-law

岳母 yuèmǔ [名] mother-in-law

阅 yuè [动] 1 (看) read 2 (检阅) inspect 3 (经历) experience

阅读 yuèdú [动] read

阅览 yuèlǎn [动] read

阅历 yuèlì [动] experience

跃 yuè [动] leap ▸跳跃 tiàoyuè jump

越 yuè I [动] 1 (跨过) jump over 2 (超过) exceed II [副] ▸越发 yuèfā increasingly

越来越 yuèláiyuè [副] more and more ▸天气越来越暖和了。 Tiānqì yuèláiyuè nuǎnhuo le. The weather is getting warmer and warmer.

越野 yuèyě [动] go cross-country

越⋯越⋯ yuè…yuè… [副] the more … the more … ▸越早越好 yuè zǎo yuè hǎo the earlier the better

晕 yūn [动] 1 (晕眩) feel dizzy 2 (昏迷) faint ▸她晕过去了。 Tā yūn guòqu le. She passed out.
→ see also/另见 yùn

云 yún [名] cloud

云彩 yúncai [名] cloud

匀 yún I [形] even II [动] 1 (使均匀) even … out 2 (分) apportion

匀称 yúnchèn [形] well-proportioned

允 yǔn [动] allow

允许 yǔnxǔ [动] allow

孕 yùn I [动] be pregnant ▸怀

孕 huáiyùn be pregnant **II** [名] pregnancy

运 yùn **I** [动] **1** (运动) move **2** (搬运) transport **3** (运用) use **II** [名] luck ▶好运 hǎoyùn good luck

运动 yùndòng **I** [动] (物) move **II** [名] **1** (体育活动) sport **2** (大规模) movement

运动鞋 yùndòngxié [名] trainer

运动员 yùndòngyuán [名] athlete

运河 yùnhé [名] canal

运气 yùnqi [名] luck

运输 yùnshū [动] transport

运算 yùnsuàn [动] calculate

运行 yùnxíng [动] move

运用 yùnyòng [动] make use of

运转 yùnzhuǎn [动] (指机器) run

运作 yùnzuò [动] operate

晕 yùn [动] feel giddy ▶晕机 yùnjī be airsick ▶晕车 yùnchē be carsick ▶晕船 yùnchuán be seasick
→ see also/另见 yūn

熨 yùn [动] iron

熨斗 yùndǒu [名] iron

杂 zá **I** [形] miscellaneous ▶复杂 fùzá complicated **II** [动] mix

杂货 záhuò [名] groceries (PL)

杂技 zájì [名] acrobatics (PL)

杂志 zázhì [名] magazine

砸 zá [动] **1** (撞击) pound **2** (打破) break ▷杯子砸坏了。 Bēizi záhuài le. The cup was broken.

灾 zāi [名] **1** (灾害) disaster ▶水灾 shuǐzāi flood **2** (不幸) misfortune

灾害 zāihài [名] disaster

灾难 zāinàn [名] disaster

栽 zāi [动] **1** (种) plant ▶栽花 zāi huā grow flowers **2** (摔倒) tumble

再 zài [副] **1** (又) again ▷你再说一遍。 Nǐ zài shuō yī biàn. Say that again. **2** (更) more ▷请把音量放得再大些。 Qǐng bǎ yīnliàng fàngde zài dàxiē. Please turn the volume up a bit. **3** (继续) ▷我不能再等了。 Wǒ bùnéng zài děng le. I can't wait any longer. **4** (接着) then ▷你做完功课再看小说。 Nǐ zuòwán gōngkè zài kàn xiǎoshuō. You can read your book when you've finished your homework. **5** (另外) ▷再说 zàishuō besides

再见 zàijiàn [动] say goodbye ▷再见! Zàijiàn! Goodbye!

再三 zàisān [副] again and again

在 zài **I** [动] **1** (存在) live **2** (处于) be ▷你的书在桌子上。 Nǐ de shū zài zhuōzi shang. Your book is on the table. ▷我父母在纽约。 Wǒ fùmǔ zài Niǔyuē. My parents are in New York. **3** (在于) rest with **II** [副] ▷情况在改变。 Qíngkuàng zài gǎibiàn. Things are changing. ▷他们在看电视。 Tāmen zài kàn diànshì. They're watching TV. **III** [介] at ▷在机场等候 zài jīchǎng děnghòu wait at the airport ▷在历史上 zài lìshǐ shang in history

在乎 zàihu [动] care

在于 zàiyú [动] **1** (存在) lie in **2** (取决于) depend on

咱 zán [代] **1** (咱们) we **2** (方) (我) I

咱们 zánmen [代] **1** (我们) we **2** (方) (我) I

攒 zǎn [动] save

暂 zàn **I** [形] brief **II** [副] temporarily

暂时 zànshí [名] ▷暂时的需要 zànshí de xūyào temporary need

赞 zàn [动] **1** (帮助) assist ▷赞助 zànzhù assistance **2** (称颂) commend ▷赞赏 zànshǎng admire

赞成 zànchéng [动] approve

赞美 zànměi [动] praise

赞同 zàntóng [动] approve of

赞扬 zànyáng [动] pay tribute to

脏 zāng [形] dirty ▷脏话 zānghuà dirty word

遭 zāo [动] meet with ▷遭殃 zāoyāng suffer

遭到 zāodào [动] encounter

遭受 zāoshòu [动] suffer

糟 zāo **I** [名] dregs (PL) **II** [动] **1** (浪费) waste ▷糟蹋 zāotà spoil **2** (腌制) flavour (英) 或 flavor (美) with alcohol **III** [形] **1** (腐烂) rotten **2** (弄坏) messy

糟糕 zāogāo [形] terrible ▷真糟糕, 我的钥匙丢了。 Zhēn zāogāo, wǒ de yàoshi diū le. Oh no, I've lost my key!

早 zǎo **I** [名] morning **II** [副] a long time ago **III** [形] early

早安 zǎo'ān [名] ▷早安! Zǎo'ān! Good morning!

早餐 zǎocān [名] breakfast

早晨 zǎochen [名] morning

早饭 zǎofàn [名] breakfast

早晚 zǎowǎn **I** [名] morning and evening **II** [副] **1**(迟早) sooner or later **2**(方)(将来) some day

早上 zǎoshang [名] morning

造 zào [动] **1**(制作) make **2**(瞎编) concoct ▶造谣 zàoyáo start a rumour (英) 或 rumor (美)

造成 zàochéng [动] cause

造反 zàofǎn [动] rebel

造型 zàoxíng [名] model

噪 zào [动](嚷) clamour (英), clamor (美) ▶噪音 zàoyīn noise

责 zé **I** [名] responsibility ▶负责 fùzé be responsible for **II** [动] (责备) blame ▶指责 zhǐzé censure

责备 zébèi [动] blame

责任 zérèn [名] responsibility

怎 zěn [代](方) ▷你怎能相信他的话？ Nǐ zěn néng xiāngxìn tā de huà? How can you believe him?

怎么 zěnme **I** [代] ▷你看这事我该怎么办？ Nǐ kàn zhè shì wǒ gāi zěnme bàn? What do you think I should do about this? ▷你昨天怎么没来上课？ Nǐ zuótiān zěnme méi lái shàngkè? Why weren't you in class yesterday? **II** [副](泛指方式) ▷我是怎么想就怎么说。 Wǒ shì zěnme xiǎng jiù zěnme shuō. I say whatever I think. ▷他最近怎么样？ Tā zuìjìn zěnme yàng? How has he been doing?

怎样 zěnyàng [副] how

增 zēng [动] increase

增加 zēngjiā [动] increase

增长 zēngzhǎng [动] increase

赠 zèng [动] present ▶捐赠 juānzèng donate

赠品 zèngpǐn [名] gift

扎 zhā [动] **1**(刺) prick **2**(住下) set up camp **3**(钻进) plunge into

扎实 zhāshi [形] **1**(结实) sturdy **2**(实在) solid

炸 zhá [动] fry
→ see also/另见 zhà

炸 zhà [动] **1**(爆破) blow ... up **2**(破裂) explode **3**(逃离) run scared
→ see also/另见 zhá

炸弹 zhàdàn [名] bomb

炸药 zhàyào [名] explosive

摘 zhāi [动] **1**(取) pick **2**(选) select **3**(借) borrow

窄 zhǎi [形] **1**(不宽敞) narrow **2**(气量小) narrow-minded **3**(不宽裕) hard up

粘 zhān [动] stick

盏 zhǎn **I** [名] small cup **II** [量] ▷一盏灯 yī zhǎn dēng a lamp measure word, used for lamps and lights

展 zhǎn **I** [动] **1**(进行) develop **2**(施展) give free rein to **3**(暂缓) postpone **II** [名] exhibition

展出 zhǎnchū [动] exhibit

展开 zhǎnkāi [动] **1**(张开) spread **2**(进行) develop

展览 zhǎnlǎn [名] exhibition

展品 zhǎnpǐn [名] exhibit

崭 zhǎn *see below*/见下文

崭新 zhǎnxīn [形] brand-new

占 zhàn [动] (占用) occupy

战 zhàn I [名] war II [动] 1 (战斗) fight 2 (发抖) shiver

战斗 zhàndòu [动] fight

战胜 zhànshèng [动] overcome

战士 zhànshì [名] soldier

战争 zhànzhēng [名] war

站 zhàn I [动] 1 (站立) stand 2 (停下) stop II [名] 1 (停车地点) stop ▷公共汽车站 gōnggòng qìchēzhàn bus stop 2 (服务机构) centre (英), center (美)

张 zhāng I [动] 1 (打开) open 2 (展开) extend ▷扩张 kuòzhāng stretch 3 (夸大) exaggerate ▶夸张 kuāzhāng exaggerate 4 (看) look 5 (开业) open for business 6 (陈设) lay ... on II [量] 1 (指平的物体) ▷一张海报 yī zhāng hǎibào a poster ▷一张书桌 yī zhāng shūzhuō a desk 2 (指嘴或脸) ▷一张大嘴 yī zhāng dà zuǐ a big mouth ▷一张脸 yī zhāng liǎn a face

measure word, used for flat objects such as newspaper, maps, paintings, cards, tickets, pancakes; furniture such as beds, desks, sofas; mouths and faces

章 zhāng [名] 1 (作品) article ▶文章 wénzhāng article 2 (章节) chapter 3 (条理) order 4 (章程) regulation ▶宪章 xiànzhāng charter 5 (图章) seal 6 (标志) badge (英), button (美)

长 zhǎng I [形] 1 (大) older ▷他年长我3岁。 Tā niánzhǎng wǒ sān suì. He's three years older than me. 2 (排行第一) oldest ▶长兄 zhǎngxiōng oldest brother II [名] 1 (年长者) ▶兄长 xiōngzhǎng elder brother 2 (头领) head ▶校长 xiàozhǎng head teacher III [动] 1 (生) form 2 (发育) grow 3 (增加) acquire
→ *see also*/另见 cháng

涨 zhǎng [动] increase

掌 zhǎng I [名] 1 (手掌) palm 2 (人的脚掌) sole 3 (动物的脚掌) foot 4 (掌形物) ▶仙人掌 xiānrénzhǎng cactus 5 (U型铁) horseshoe 6 (鞋掌) sole II [动] 1 (打) slap 2 (钉) sole 3 (主持) be in charge of

掌握 zhǎngwò [动] control

丈 zhàng [名] (长度单位) *Chinese unit of length, equal to 3.3 metres*

丈夫 zhàngfu [名] husband

帐 zhàng [名] curtain ▶蚊帐 wénzhàng mosquito net

帐篷 zhàngpeng [名] tent

账 zhàng [名] 1 (账目) accounts (PL) 2 (账簿) ledger 3 (债务) credit ▶赊账 shēzhàng buy on credit

账单 zhàngdān [名] bill

账号 zhànghào [名] account number

障 zhàng I [名] barrier II [动] hinder

障碍 zhàng'ài I [动] hinder II [名] obstacle

招 zhāo I [动] 1 (挥动) beckon 2 (招收) recruit 3 (引来) attract 4 (惹怒) provoke 5 (坦白) confess II [名] 1 (计谋) trick 2 (指下棋) move

招待 zhāodài [动] entertain ▶招待会 zhāodàihuì reception

招呼 zhāohu [动] 1 (呼唤) call 2 (问候) greet 3 (吩咐) tell

着 zháo [动] 1 (挨) touch 2 (受到) be affected by 3 (燃烧) be lit 4 (入睡) fall asleep

着急 zháojí [形] worried

找 zhǎo [动] 1 (寻找) look for 2 (退余额) give change ▶找钱 zhǎoqián give change 3 (求见) call on

召 zhào [动] summon

召开 zhàokāi [动] hold

照 zhào I [动] 1 (照射) light up 2 (映现) reflect 3 (拍摄) take a photograph 4 (照料) look after 5 (对照) contrast 6 (遵照) refer to ▶参照 cānzhào consult 7 (明白) understand II [名] 1 (照片) photograph 2 (执照) licence (英), license (美) III [介] 1 (按照) according to 2 (向着) in the direction of

照常 zhàocháng [副] as usual

照顾 zhàogu [动] 1 (照料) look after 2 (考虑) consider

照看 zhàokàn [动] look after

照料 zhàoliào [动] take care of

照片 zhàopiàn [名] photograph

照相 zhàoxiàng [动] take a picture

照相机 zhàoxiàngjī [名] camera

折 zhé I [动] 1 (折断) break 2 (损失) lose 3 (弯曲) wind 4 (回转) turn back 5 (使信服) convince 6 (折合) convert ... into 7 (折叠) fold II [名] 1 (折子) notebook ▶存折 cúnzhé bank book 2 (折扣) discount → see also/另见 shé

折叠 zhédié [动] fold

折扣 zhékòu [名] discount

折磨 zhémó [动] torment

哲 zhé I [形] wise II [名] sage

哲学 zhéxué [名] philosophy

这 zhè [代] (指人或事物) this

这边 zhèbian [副] here

这个 zhège [代] this ▷这个可比那个好多了。 Zhège kě bǐ nàge hǎo duō le. This one is much better than that one.

这么 zhème [代] 1 (指程度) so ▷今天这么热。 Jīntiān zhème rè. It's so hot today. 2 (指方式) such ▷我看就应该这么做。 Wǒ kàn jiù yīnggāi zhème zuò. I think it should be done this way.

这儿 zhèr [副] here

这些 zhèxiē [代] these (PL)

这样 zhèyàng[代] 1(指程度) so ▷乡村的风景这样美。 Xiāngcūn de fēngjǐng zhèyàng měi. The scenery in the countryside is so beautiful. 2(指状态) such ▷再这样下去可不行。 Zài zhèyàng xiàqù kě bùxíng. It really won't do to carry on like this.

针 zhēn[名] 1(工具) needle 2(针状物) ▷表针 biǎozhēn hand (on watch) ▷别针 biézhēn safety pin 3(针剂) injection 4(缝合) stitch

针对 zhēnduì[动] 1(对准) be aimed at 2(按照) have ... in mind

真 zhēn I[形] true ▷真话 zhēnhuà truth ▷真品 zhēnpǐn genuine product II[副] really ▷他真勇敢。 Tā zhēn yǒnggǎn. He is really brave.

真理 zhēnlǐ[名] truth

真实 zhēnshí[形] true

真正 zhēnzhèng[形] true

枕 zhěn I[名] pillow II[动] rest one's head on

枕头 zhěntou[名] pillow

阵 zhèn[名] 1(军)(阵形) battle formation 2(军)(阵地) position 3(时间) a while

振 zhèn[动] 1(振动) vibrate 2(振作) boost

振动 zhèndòng[动] vibrate

镇 zhèn I[名] 1(城镇) town 2(重地) garrison II[动] 1(抑制) suppress 2(守卫) guard 3(安定) calm 4(冷却) cool III[形] calm ▷镇静 zhènjìng calm

镇定 zhèndìng[形] calm

正 zhēng see below/见下文 → see also/另见 zhèng

正月 zhēngyuè[名] first month of the lunar year

争 zhēng[动] 1(争夺) contend 2(争论) argue

争论 zhēnglùn[动] argue

争取 zhēngqǔ[动] strive for

征 zhēng I[动] 1(征讨) mount a military expedition 2(召集) draft ▷征兵 zhēngbīng conscript 3(征收) levy ▷征税 zhēngshuì levy taxes 4(征求) solicit ▷征订 zhēngdìng solicit subscriptions II[名] 1(征程) journey ▷长征 chángzhēng the Long March 2(迹象) sign ▷特征 tèzhēng feature

征服 zhēngfú[动] conquer

征求 zhēngqiú[动] solicit

征兆 zhēngzhào[名] sign

睁 zhēng[动] open

蒸 zhēng[动] 1(指烹饪方法) steam 2(蒸发) evaporate

蒸气 zhēngqì[名] vapour (英), vapor (美)

蒸汽 zhēngqì[名] steam

整 zhěng I[形] 1(完整) whole 2(规整) tidy II[动] 1(整理) sort ... out 2(修理) repair 3(刁难) punish

整个 zhěnggè [形] whole

整理 zhěnglǐ [动] sort ... out

整齐 zhěngqí [形] 1 (有序的) orderly 2 (均匀的) even

正 zhèng I [形] 1 (不偏不斜) straight ▷正前方 zhèng qiánfāng directly ahead ▷这照片挂得不正。 Zhè zhàopiàn guà de bù zhèng. This photograph is not hung straight. 2 (居中的) main 3 (正面) right 4 (正直) upright ▷公正 gōngzhèng just 5 (正当) right ▷正轨 zhèngguǐ the right track 6 (纯正) pure ▷这道菜的味儿不正。 Zhè dào cài de wèir bù zhèng. This dish does not taste authentic. 7 (规范的) regular 8 (主要的) principal ▷正餐 zhèngcān main meal 9 (指图形) regular 10 (物) positive 11 (数) (大于零的) positive ▷正数 zhèngshù positive number II [动] 1 (使不歪) straighten 2 (改正) put ... right III [副] 1 (恰好) just 2 (正在) right now ▷天正刮着风。 Tiān zhèng guā zhe fēng. It's windy right now.
  → see also/另见 zhēng

正常 zhèngcháng [形] normal

正当 zhèngdāng [形] legitimate

正确 zhèngquè [形] correct

正式 zhèngshì [形] official

正在 zhèngzài [副] right now

证 zhèng I [动] prove II [名] 1 (证据) evidence ▷物证 wùzhèng material evidence 2 (证件) ▷身份证 shēnfènzhèng identity card

证明 zhèngmíng I [动] prove II [名] certificate

政 zhèng [名] 1 (政治) politics (SG) 2 (事务) affairs (PL)

政策 zhèngcè [名] policy

政党 zhèngdǎng [名] political party

政府 zhèngfǔ [名] government

政权 zhèngquán [名] political power

政治 zhèngzhì [名] politics (SG)

挣 zhèng [动] 1 (赚得) earn ▷挣钱 zhèngqián earn money 2 (摆脱) break free

之 zhī [助] (的) ▷父母之爱 fùmǔ zhī ài parental love

之后 zhīhòu [介] after

之间 zhījiān [介] 1 (指两者) between 2 (指三者或三者以上) among

之前 zhīqián [介] before

之上 zhīshàng [介] above

之下 zhīxià [介] below

之一 zhīyī [代] one of

之中 zhīzhōng [介] amid

支 zhī I [动] 1 (支撑) prop ... up 2 (伸出) raise 3 (支持) bear 4 (调度) send 5 (付出) pay ... out 6 (领取) get II [量] 1 (指乐曲) ▷一支钢琴曲 yī zhī gāngqín qǔ a piano tune 2 (指细长物) ▷一支钢笔 yī zhī gāngbǐ a pen 3 (指队伍) ▷一支部队 yī zhī bùduì an army unit

measure word, used for songs, tunes, troops, and stick-like objects

支持 zhīchí [动] 1(鼓励) support 2(支撑) hold out

支出 zhīchū I [动] spend II [名] expenditure

支付 zhīfù [动] pay

支票 zhīpiào [名] cheque (英), check (美) ▷把支票兑付成现金 bǎ zhīpiào duìhuàn chéng xiànjīn cash a cheque

支援 zhīyuán [动] help

只 zhī [量] ▷一只拖鞋 yī zhī tuōxié a slipper ▷两只小船 liǎng zhī xiǎochuán two boats ▷三只小鸟 sān zhī xiǎo niǎo three birds → see also/另见 zhǐ

measure word, used for one of a pair such as gloves, eyes, feet; also used for animals, insects, birds and boats

芝 zhī see below/见下文

芝麻 zhīma [名] sesame

枝 zhī [名] branch

知 zhī I [动] 1(知道) know 2(使知道) inform II [名] knowledge

知道 zhīdao [动] know ▷这事我可不知道。 Zhè shì wǒ kě bù zhīdao. I really know nothing about this.

知识 zhīshi [名] knowledge

织 zhī [动] knit

蜘 zhī see below/见下文

蜘蛛 zhīzhū [名] spider

执 zhí I [动] 1(拿着) hold 2(执掌) take charge of 3(坚持) stick to 4(执行) carry out II [名] written acknowledgment ▷回执 huízhí receipt

执行 zhíxíng [动] carry out

执照 zhízhào [名] licence (英), license (美)

直 zhí I [形] 1(不弯曲) straight 2(竖的) vertical 3(公正) upstanding 4(直爽) candid II [动] straighten III [副] 1(直接) straight 2(不断地) continuously 3(简直) simply

直到 zhídào [介] until

直接 zhíjiē [形] direct

直升机 zhíshēngjī [名] helicopter

侄 zhí [名] nephew

侄女 zhínǚ [名] niece

侄子 zhízi [名] nephew

值 zhí I [名] 1(价值) value 2(数) value II [动] 1(值得) be worth 2(碰上) just happen to be 3(轮到) be on duty

值班 zhíbān [动] be on duty

值得 zhíde [动] be worth ▷这书值得买。 Zhè shū zhíde mǎi. This book is worth buying.

职 zhí [名] 1(职位) post 2(职责) duty

职工 zhígōng [名] 1(员工) staff 2(工人) blue-collar worker

职业 zhíyè [名] occupation

职员 zhíyuán [名] member of staff

植 zhí [动] 1(栽种) plant 2(树立) establish

植物 zhíwù [名] plant ▷ 草本植物 cǎoběn zhíwù herbs

止 zhǐ I [动] 1(停止) stop 2(截止) end II [副] only

只 zhǐ [副] only ▷ 我只在周末有时间。 Wǒ zhǐ zài zhōumò yǒu shíjiān. I only have time at the weekend.
→ see also/另见 zhī

只好 zhǐhǎo [副] have to

只是 zhǐshì I [副] merely II [连] but

只要 zhǐyào [连] so long as

只有 zhǐyǒu [副] only

纸 zhǐ [名] paper

纸币 zhǐbì [名] note (英), bill (美)

指 zhǐ I [名] finger ▷ 中指 zhōngzhǐ middle finger ▷ 无名指 wúmíngzhǐ ring finger II [动] 1(对着) point to 2(点明) point ... out 3(针对) refer to 4(依靠) rely on

指出 zhǐchū [动] point ... out

指导 zhǐdǎo [动] instruct

指挥 zhǐhuī I [动] command II [名] 1(指挥官) commander 2(乐队指挥) conductor

指南针 zhǐnánzhēn [名] compass

指示 zhǐshì [动] instruct

指责 zhǐzé [动] criticize

至 zhì I [动] arrive II [介] to ▷ 从东至西 cóng dōng zhì xī from east to west III [副] 1(至于) ▷ 至于 zhìyú as to 2(最) extremely ▷ 至少 zhìshǎo at least

至今 zhìjīn [副] so far

至少 zhìshǎo [副] at least

至于 zhìyú [介] as to

制 zhì I [动] 1(制造) make 2(拟订) work ... out 3(约束) restrict II [名] system

制订 zhìdìng [动] work ... out

制定 zhìdìng [动] draw ... up

制度 zhìdù [名] system

制造 zhìzào [动] 1(物品) manufacture 2(气氛, 局势) create

制作 zhìzuò [动] make ▷ 制作网页 zhìzuò wǎngyè create a web page ▶ 制作商 zhìzuòshāng manufacturer

质 zhì I [名] 1(性质) nature ▶ 本质 běnzhì nature 2(质量) quality 3(物质) matter 4(抵押品) pledge ▶ 人质 rénzhì hostage II [形] simple III [动] question ▶ 质疑 zhìyí cast doubt on

质量 zhìliàng [名] 1(物) mass 2(优劣) quality

治 zhì [动] 1(治理) control 2(医治) cure 3(消灭) exterminate 4(惩办) punish 5(研究) research

治安 zhì'ān [名] security ▷ 社会治安 shèhuì zhì'ān public order

治疗 zhìliáo [动] cure

秩 zhì [名] order

秩序 zhìxù [名] sequence

智 zhì I [形] wise II [名] wisdom

智慧 zhìhuì [名] intelligence

智力 zhìlì [名] intelligence

智商 zhìshāng [名] IQ

中 zhōng I [名] 1 (中心) centre (英), center (美) ▸中央 zhōngyāng central 2 (中国) China ▸中餐 zhōngcān Chinese food 3 (两端之间的) the middle ▸中层 zhōngcéng mid-level 4 (不偏不倚) impartial ▸适中 shìzhōng moderate 5 (在过程里的) course II [动] be suitable for

中国 Zhōngguó [名] China

中国人 Zhōngguórén [名] Chinese person

中华人民共和国 Zhōnghuá Rénmín Gònghéguó [名] People's Republic of China

中华人民共和国 Zhōnghuá Rénmín Gònghéguó

The People's Republic of China was declared in Tiananmen Square on October 1st 1949 by Chairman Mao Zedong.

中华 Zhōnghuá [名] China

中间 zhōngjiān [名] 1 (中心) middle 2 (之间) ▷我站在他俩中间。 Wǒ zhàn zài tā liǎ zhōngjiān. I was standing in between the both of them.

中介 zhōngjiè [名] agency ▷房产

中介 fángchǎn zhōngjiè estate agent

中年 zhōngnián [名] middle age

中秋节 Zhōngqiū Jié [名] Mid-Autumn Festival

中秋节 Zhōngqiū Jié

The Mid-Autumn Festival is celebrated on the 15th day of the 8th month of the Chinese lunar calendar. Traditionally families gather to observe the moon and eat 月饼 yuèbǐng, mooncakes. The roundness of both the full moon and the cakes symbolize the unity of the family.

中文 Zhōngwén [名] Chinese

中午 zhōngwǔ [名] noon

中心 zhōngxīn [名] centre (英), center (美)

中学 zhōngxué [名] high school (英), senior school (美)

中旬 zhōngxún [名] *the middle ten days of a month*

中央 zhōngyāng [名] 1 (中心地) centre (英), center (美) 2 (最高机构) central government

中药 zhōngyào [名] Chinese medicine

中医 zhōngyī [名] 1 (医学) traditional Chinese medicine 2 (医生) doctor of traditional Chinese medicine

终 zhōng I [动] die II [副] in the

end **III** [形] all ▶终身 zhōngshēn all one's life

终点 zhōngdiǎn [名] **1** (尽头) terminus **2** (体育) finish

终于 zhōngyú [副] finally

终止 zhōngzhǐ [动] stop

钟 zhōng [名] **1** (响器) bell **2** (记时器) clock **3** (指时间) ▷5点钟 wǔ diǎnzhōng five o'clock

钟表 zhōngbiǎo [名] clocks and watches

钟头 zhōngtóu [名] hour

肿 zhǒng [动] swell

种 zhǒng **I** [名] **1** (物种) species (SG) **2** (人种) race **3** (种子) seed **4** (胆量) courage **II** [量] kind, type ▷各种商品 gè zhǒng shāngpǐn all kinds of commodities ▷3种选择 sān zhǒng xuǎnzé three choices → see also/另见 zhòng

种子 zhǒngzi [名] seed

种族 zhǒngzú [名] race

种 zhòng [动] sow ▶种田 zhòngtián farm ▶种痘 zhòngdòu vaccinate → see also/另见 zhǒng

重 zhòng **I** [名] weight **II** [形] **1** (重量大) heavy **2** (程度深) strong **3** (重要) important ▶重任 zhòngrèn important task **4** (不轻率) serious ▶稳重 wěnzhòng staid **III** [动] stress ▶注重 zhùzhòng pay attention to → see also/另见 chóng

重大 zhòngdà [形] major

重点 zhòngdiǎn [名] key point

重量 zhòngliàng [名] weight

重视 zhòngshì [动] attach importance to

重要 zhòngyào [形] important

周 zhōu **I** [名] **1** (圈子) circle **2** (星期) week **II** [动] **1** (环绕) circle **2** (接济) give ... financial help **III** [形] **1** (普遍) widespread **2** (完备) thorough

周到 zhōudào [形] thorough

周末 zhōumò [名] weekend

周围 zhōuwéi [名] the vicinity

猪 zhū [名] pig

猪肉 zhūròu [名] pork

竹 zhú [名] bamboo

竹子 zhúzi [名] bamboo

逐 zhú **I** [动] **1** (追赶) chase **2** (驱逐) drive ... away **II** [副] one after another

逐步 zhúbù [副] step by step

逐渐 zhújiàn [副] gradually

主 zhǔ **I** [名] **1** (接待者) host ▶东道主 dōngdàozhǔ host **2** (所有者) owner ▶房主 fángzhǔ home-owner **3** (当事人) person concerned **4** (主见) idea **5** (上帝) God **II** [形] main **III** [动] **1** (主持) take charge **2** (主办) take charge of **2** (主张) be in favour (英) 或 favor (美) of **3** (从自身出发) look at ... subjectively ▶主观 zhǔguān subjective

主动 zhǔdòng [形] voluntary

主观 zhǔguān [形] subjective

主人 zhǔrén [名] **1**(接待者) host **2**(雇佣者) master ▶女主人 nǚzhǔrén mistress **3**(所有者) owner

主任 zhǔrèn [名] director

主席 zhǔxí [名] chairman, chairwoman

主要 zhǔyào [形] major

主义 zhǔyì [名] doctrine ▶社会主义 shèhuì zhǔyì socialism ▶浪漫主义 làngmàn zhǔyì romanticism

主意 zhǔyi [名] **1**(办法) idea **2**(主见) opinion

主张 zhǔzhāng I [动] advocate II [名] standpoint

煮 zhǔ [动] boil

助 zhù [动] help

助手 zhùshǒu [名] assistant

住 zhù [动] **1**(居住) live **2**(停住) stop **3**(用作动词补语)

住宿 zhùsù [动] stay

住院 zhùyuàn [动] be hospitalized

住宅 zhùzhái [名] house

住址 zhùzhǐ [名] address

注 zhù I [动] **1**(灌入) pour ▶注射 zhùshè inject **2**(集中) concentrate **3**(解释) explain II [名] **1**(记载) record ▶注册 zhùcè enrol (英), enroll (美) **2**(赌注) bet

注意 zhùyì [动] be careful

祝 zhù [动] wish

祝贺 zhùhè [动] congratulate

著 zhù I [形] marked II [动] **1**(显出) show **2**(写作) write III [名] work

著名 zhùmíng [形] famous

著作 zhùzuò [名] writings (PL)

抓 zhuā [动] **1**(拿住) grab **2**(划过) scratch **3**(捉拿) catch **4**(着重) take control of **5**(吸引) attract **6**(把握住) seize

抓紧 zhuājǐn [动] make the most of

专 zhuān [动] **1**(集中) concentrate **2**(独占) dominate ▶专卖 zhuānmài monopoly

专家 zhuānjiā [名] expert

专门 zhuānmén I [形] specialized II [副] especially

专心 zhuānxīn [形] single-minded

专业 zhuānyè [名] special field of study

砖 zhuān [名] brick

转 zhuǎn [动] **1**(改换) turn ▶转弯 zhuǎnwān turn a corner ▶转学 zhuǎnxué change schools **2**(传送) pass ... on ▶转送 zhuǎnsòng deliver
→ see also/另见 zhuàn

转变 zhuǎnbiàn [动] transform

转告 zhuǎngào [动] pass on

转 zhuàn [动] turn
→ see also/另见 zhuǎn

赚 zhuàn [动] **1**(获得利润) make a profit **2**(挣钱) earn

庄 zhuāng [名] **1**(指村庄) village

2(指土地) manor ▶庄园 zhuāngyuán manor **3**(指商店) ▶茶庄 cházhuāng teahouse ▶饭庄 fànzhuāng restaurant

庄稼 zhuāngjia [名] crops (PL)

庄严 zhuāngyán [形] solemn

装 zhuāng I [动] **1**(修饰) dress up ▶装饰 zhuāngshì decorate **2**(假装) pretend **3**(装载) load **4**(装配) install II [名] (服装) clothing ▶套装 tàozhuāng matching outfit

状 zhuàng [名] **1**(形状) shape **2**(情况) state ▶症状 zhèngzhuàng symptom **3**(诉状) complaint ▶告状 gàozhuàng bring a case **4**(证书) certificate ▶奖状 jiǎngzhuàng certificate

状况 zhuàngkuàng [名] condition

状态 zhuàngtài [名] condition

撞 zhuàng [动] **1**(碰撞) collide **2**(碰见) bump into **3**(试探) try **4**(闯) dash

撞车 zhuàngchē [动] **1**(车辆相撞) collide **2**(发生分歧) clash

追 zhuī [动] **1**(追赶) chase **2**(追究) investigate **3**(追求) seek **4**(回溯) reminisce

追捕 zhuībǔ [动] pursue and capture

追求 zhuīqiú [动] **1**(争取) seek **2**(求爱) chase after

准 zhǔn I [动] **1**(准许) allow ▶批准 pīzhǔn ratify **2**(依据) be in accord with II [名] standard III [形] **1**(准确) accurate ▶准时 zhǔnshí

punctual **2**(类似) quasi

准备 zhǔnbèi [动] **1**(筹划) prepare **2**(打算) plan

准确 zhǔnquè [形] accurate

准时 zhǔnshí [形] punctual

捉 zhuō [动] **1**(握住) clutch **2**(捕捉) catch

桌 zhuō I [名] table ▶书桌 shūzhuō desk II [量] table ▷一桌菜 yī zhuō cài a table covered in dishes

桌子 zhuōzi [名] table

咨 zī [动] consult

咨询 zīxún [动] seek advice from

姿 zī [名] **1**(容貌) looks (PL) **2**(姿势) posture

姿势 zīshì [名] posture

资 zī I [名] **1**(钱财) money ▶外资 wàizī foreign capital ▶邮资 yóuzī postage **2**(资质) ability ▶天资 tiānzī natural ability **3**(资格) qualifications (PL) ▶资历 zīlì record of service II [动] **1**(资助) aid ... financially **2**(提供) provide

资本 zīběn [名] (本钱) capital

资格 zīgé [名] **1**(条件) qualifications (PL) **2**(身份) seniority

资金 zījīn [名] funds (PL)

资料 zīliào [名] **1**(必需品) means (PL) **2**(材料) material

资源 zīyuán [名] resources (PL)

子 zǐ I [名] **1**(儿子) son ▶母子 mǔzǐ mother and son **2**(人) person

▶男子 nánzǐ man **3** (种子) seed ▶瓜子 guāzǐ melon seed **4** (卵) egg ▶鱼子 yúzǐ fish roe **5** (粒状物) ▶棋子 qízǐ chess piece **6** (铜子) coin **II** [形] **1** (幼小) young **2** (附属) affiliated

子女 zǐnǚ [名] children

仔 zǐ [形] young

仔细 zǐxì [形] **1** (细心) thorough **2** (小心) careful

紫 zǐ [形] purple

自 zì **I** [代] oneself **II** [副] certainly **III** [介] from

自从 zìcóng [介] since

自动 zìdòng [形] **1** (主动的) voluntary **2** (机械的) automatic

自动取款机 zìdòng qǔkuǎnjī [名] cashpoint (英), ATM (美)

自费 zìfèi [形] self-funded

自己 zìjǐ **I** [代] oneself **II** [形] our

自觉 zìjué **I** [动] be aware of **II** [形] conscientious

自来水 zìláishuǐ [名] tap water

自然 zìrán **I** [名] nature **II** [形] natural **III** [副] naturally

自杀 zìshā [动] commit suicide

自私 zìsī [形] selfish

自我 zìwǒ [代] self

自信 zìxìn [形] self-confident

自行车 zìxíngchē [名] bicycle

自学 zìxué [动] teach oneself

自由 zìyóu **I** [名] freedom **II** [形] free

自愿 zìyuàn [动] volunteer

自助餐 zìzhùcān [名] self-service buffet

字 zì [名] **1** (文字) character **2** (字音) pronunciation **3** (书法作品) calligraphy ▶字画 zìhuà painting and calligraphy **4** (字体) script **5** (字据) written pledge

字典 zìdiǎn [名] dictionary

字母 zìmǔ [名] letter

宗 zōng [名] **1** (祖宗) ancestor **2** (家族) clan **3** (宗派) school ▶正宗 zhèngzōng orthodox school **4** (宗旨) purpose

宗教 zōngjiào [名] religion

综 zōng [动] summarize ▶综述 zōngshù sum ... up

综合 zōnghé **I** [动] synthesize **II** [形] comprehensive

总 zǒng **I** [动] gather ▶总括 zǒngkuò sum ... up **II** [形] **1** (全部的) total **2** (为首的) chief ▶总部 zǒngbù headquarters (PL) **III** [副] **1** (一直) always **2** (毕竟) after all

总理 zǒnglǐ [名] premier

总是 zǒngshì [副] always

总算 zǒngsuàn [副] **1** (最终) finally **2** (大体上) all things considered

总统 zǒngtǒng [名] president

粽 zòng [名] *see below*/见下文

粽子 zòngzi [名] *glutinous rice dumplings*

粽子 zòngzi

The traditional festival food for the Dragon

Boat Festival are large pyramid-shaped glutinous rice dumplings wrapped in reed or bamboo leaves, often with sweet or meat fillings.

走 zǒu [动] 1 (行走) walk ▶走路 zǒulù walk ▷出去走走 chūqu zǒuzǒu go out for a walk 2 (跑动) run 3 (运行) move 4 (离开) leave ▷我先走。 Wǒ xiān zǒu. I'll be off. 5 (来往) visit 6 (通过) go through 7 (漏出) leak 8 (改变) depart from 9 (去世) die

走道 zǒudào [名] path

走动 zǒudòng [动] 1 (行走) walk about 2 (来往) visit each other

走后门 zǒu hòumén use one's connections

走廊 zǒuláng [名] corridor

租 zū I [动] 1 (租用) (房屋) rent 2 (租用) (汽车, 自行车, 录像带) rent (英), hire (美) 3 (出租) rent out II [名] rent ▶房租 fángzū rent

足 zú I [名] foot ▶足迹 zújì footprint II [形] ample ▶充足 chōngzú adequate III [副] 1 (达到某种程度) as much as 2 (足以) enough

足够 zúgòu [动] be enough

足球 zúqiú [名] football

阻 zǔ [动] block

阻止 zǔzhǐ [动] stop

组 zǔ I [动] form II [名] group

组成 zǔchéng [动] form

组织 zǔzhī I [动] organize II [名] 1 (集体) organization 2 (指器官) tissue 3 (指纱线) weave

祖 zǔ [名] 1 (祖辈) grandparent 2 (祖宗) ancestor 3 (首创者) founder

祖父 zǔfù [名] grandfather

祖国 zǔguó [名] motherland

祖母 zǔmǔ [名] grandmother

祖先 zǔxiān [名] ancestors (PL)

钻 zuān [动] 1 (打洞) drill 2 (穿过) go through 3 (钻研) bury one's head in
   → see also/另见 zuàn

钻研 zuānyán [动] study ... intensively

钻 zuàn [名] 1 (工具) drill 2 (钻石) diamond
   → see also/另见 zuān

钻石 zuànshí [名] 1 (金刚石) diamond 2 (宝石) jewel

嘴 zuǐ [名] 1 (口) mouth 2 (嘴状物) ▷茶壶嘴 cháhú zuǐ spout of a teapot 3 (话) words (PL) ▶插嘴 chāzuǐ interrupt

最 zuì [副] most ▷最难忘的海外之旅 zuì nánwàng de hǎiwài zhī lǚ the most unforgettable trip abroad ▷这家饭店服务最好。 Zhè jiā fàndiàn fúwù zuì hǎo. The service at this restaurant is the best.

最初 zuìchū I [形] initial II [副] at first

最好 zuìhǎo I [形] best II [副] had better

最后 zuìhòu I [形] final II [副] at last

最近 zuìjìn [形] recent

罪 zuì I [名] 1 (恶行) crime ▶犯罪 fànzuì commit a crime 2 (过失) blame 3 (苦难) hardship 4 (刑罚) punishment ▶死罪 sǐzuì death sentence II [动] blame

罪犯 zuìfàn [名] criminal

醉 zuì I [形] 1 (饮酒过量的) drunk ▶醉鬼 zuìguǐ drunk 2 (用酒泡制的) steeped in wine II [动] drink too much

尊 zūn I [形] senior II [动] respect

尊敬 zūnjìng [动] respect

尊重 zūnzhòng I [动] respect II [形] serious ▷放尊重些! Fàng zūnzhòng xiē! Behave yourself!

遵 zūn [动] follow

遵守 zūnshǒu [动] observe

昨 zuó [名] 1 (昨天) yesterday ▶昨日 zuórì yesterday 2 (过去) the past

昨天 zuótiān [名] yesterday

左 zuǒ I [名] left ▶左边 zuǒbian the left II [形] 1 (相反的) conflicting 2 (进步的) leftist ▶左派 zuǒpài left-wing

左边 zuǒbian [名] the left side

左右 zuǒyòu I [名] 1 (左和右) left and right 2 (跟随者) attendants

(PL) 3 (上下) ▷他身高1点75米左右。 Tā shēngāo yī diǎn qī wǔ mǐ zuǒyòu. He is about 1.75 metres tall. II [动] control

作 zuò I [动] 1 (起) rise 2 (写) write ▶作家 zuòjiā writer ▶作曲 zuòqǔ compose music 3 (装) pretend 4 (犯) do 5 (当) take ... as ▶作废 zuòfèi become invalid 6 (发作) feel II [名] work ▶杰作 jiézuò masterpiece

作罢 zuòbà [动] drop

作家 zuòjiā [名] writer

作品 zuòpǐn [名] work

作为 zuòwéi I [名] 1 (行为) action 2 (成绩) accomplishment 3 (干头儿) scope II [动] (当作) regard ... as

作文 zuòwén [动] write an essay

作业 zuòyè I [名] work II [动] do work

作用 zuòyòng I [动] affect II [名] 1 (影响) effect 2 (活动) action

作者 zuòzhě [名] author

坐 zuò [动] 1 (坐下) sit ▷坐在窗口 zuò zài chuāngkǒu sit by the window 2 (乘坐) travel by ▷坐飞机 zuò fēijī travel by plane

座 zuò I [名] 1 (坐位) seat ▶座号 zuòhào seat number 2 (垫子) stand 3 (星座) constellation ▷双子座 Shuāngzǐ Zuò Gemini II [量] ▷一座山 yī zuò shān a mountain ▷三座桥 sān zuò qiáo three bridges ▷五座办公楼 wǔ zuò bàngōnglóu five office buildings measure word, used for mountains, buildings, bridges, etc.

座谈 zuòtán [动] discuss

座位 zuòwèi [名] seat

做 zuò [动] 1 (制造) make 2 (写作) write 3 (从事) do ▷做生意 zuò shēngyi do business 4 (举行) hold ▷做寿 zuòshòu hold a birthday party 5 (充当) be ▷做大会主席 zuò dàhuì zhǔxí chair a meeting 6 (用作) be used as 7 (结成) become ▷做朋友 zuò péngyou be friends

做法 zuòfǎ [名] method

做客 zuòkè [动] be a guest

做梦 zuòmèng [动] dream

A & E (Brit) N ABBR (= **accident and emergency**) 急诊室 jízhěnshì

abbey ['æbɪ] N [c] 大修道院 dà xiūdàoyuàn [座 zuò]

abbreviation [əbriːvɪ'eɪʃən] N [c] 缩写 suōxiě [个 gè]

ability [ə'bɪlɪtɪ] N [s] ▸ **ability (to do sth)** (做某事的)能力 (zuò mǒushì de) nénglì

able ['eɪbl] ADJ ▸ **to be able to do sth** (have skill, ability) 能够做某事 nénggòu zuò mǒushì; (have opportunity) 可以做某事 kěyǐ zuò mǒushì

abolish [ə'bɔlɪʃ] VT [+ system, practice] 废止 fèizhǐ

abortion [ə'bɔːʃən] (Med) N [c/u] 流产 liúchǎn [次 cì] ▸ **to have an abortion** 流产 liúchǎn

KEYWORD

a [eɪ, ə] (before vowel or silent h: **an**) INDEF ART **1** (article) 一个 yīgè ▸ **a man** 一个男人 yīgè nánrén ▸ **a girl** 一个女孩 yīgè nǚhái ▸ **an elephant** 一只大象 yīzhī dàxiàng ▸ **she's a doctor** 她是一名医生 tā shì yīmíng yīshēng ▸ **they haven't got a television** 他们没有电视 tāmen méiyǒu diànshì
2 (one) 一 yī ▸ **a year ago** 一年前 yīnián qián
3 (expressing ratios, prices etc) ▸ **five hours a day/week** 一天/一周5个小时 yītiān/yīzhōu wǔgè xiǎoshí ▸ **100 km an hour** 每小时100公里 měi xiǎoshí yībǎi gōnglǐ

KEYWORD

about [ə'baut] I PREP (relating to) 关于 guānyú ▸ **a book about London** 关于伦敦的一本书 guānyú Lúndūn de yīběn shū ▸ **what's it about?** 这是关于什么的? zhèshì guānyú shénme de? ▸ **we talked about it** 我们谈到了这事 wǒmen tándào le zhèshì ▸ **to be sorry/pleased/angry about sth** 对某事感到抱歉/开心/生气 duì mǒushì gǎndào bàoqiàn/kāixīn/shēngqì ▸ **what** or **how about eating out?** 出去吃怎么样? chūqù chī zěnmeyàng?
II ADV **1** (approximately) 大约 dàyuē ▸ **about a hundred/thousand people** 大约

100/1000人 dàyuē yībǎi/yīqiān rén 2 (*place*) 在 zài ▶ **to leave things lying about** 把东西到处乱放 bǎ dōngxi dàochù luànfàng ▶ **to be about to do sth** 正要做某事 zhèng yào zuò mǒushì

above [ə'bʌv] I PREP (*higher than*) 在⋯上面 zài...shàngmian II ADV (*in position*) 在上面 zài shàngmian III ADJ ▶ **the above address** 上述地址 shàngshù dìzhǐ ▶ **above all** 首先 shǒuxiān

abroad [ə'brɔːd] ADV 1 (*be*) 在国外 zài guówài 2 (*go*) 到国外 dào guówài

absence ['æbsəns] N 1 [c/u] [*of person*] 缺席 quēxí [次 cì] 2 [s] [*of thing*] 缺乏 quēfá

absent ['æbsənt] ADJ 缺席的 quēxí de ▶ **to be absent** 不在 bùzài

absolutely [æbsə'luːtlɪ] ADV (*utterly*) 绝对地 juéduì de

absorbent cotton [əb'zɔːbənt-] (*US*) N [u] 脱脂棉 tuōzhīmián

abuse [*n* ə'bjuːs, *vb* ə'bjuːz] I N 1 [u] (*insults*) 辱骂 rǔmà 2 [u] (*ill-treatment: physical*) 虐待 nüèdài; (*sexual*) 猥亵 wěixiè 3 [c/u] (*misuse: of power, alcohol, drug*) 滥用 lànyòng [种 zhǒng] II VT 1 (*ill-treat: physically*) 虐待 nüèdài 2 (*sexually*) [+ *child*] 摧残 cuīcán

academic [ækə'dɛmɪk] I ADJ 学术的 xuéshù de II N 大学教师 dàxué jiàoshī

academy [ə'kædəmɪ] N [c] 1 学会 xuéhuì [个 gè] 2 (*school, college*) 学院 xuéyuàn [个 gè]

accelerate [æk'sɛləreɪt] VI (*Aut*) 加速 jiāsù

accelerator [æk'sɛləreɪtəʳ] (*Aut*) N [c] 加速器 jiāsùqì [个 gè]

accent ['æksɛnt] N [c] 口音 kǒuyīn [种 zhǒng] ▶ **to speak with an (Irish/French) accent** 讲话带 (爱尔兰/法国) 口音 jiǎnghuà dài (Ài'ěrlán/Fǎguó) kǒuyīn

accept [ək'sɛpt] VT 接受 jiēshòu

access ['æksɛs] I N [u] ▶ **access (to sth)** (*to building, room*) 进入 (某物) jìnrù (mǒuwù); (*to information, papers*) (某物的) 使用权 (mǒuwù de) shǐyòngquán II VT (*Comput*) 存取 cúnqǔ

accident ['æksɪdənt] N [c] 1 (*involving vehicle*) 事故 shìgù [个 gè] 2 (*mishap*) 意外 yìwài [个 gè] ▶ **to have an accident** 出事故 chū shìgù ▶ **by accident** (*unintentionally*) 无意中 wúyì zhōng; (*by chance*) 偶然 ǒurán

accidental [æksɪ'dɛntl] ADJ 意外的 yìwài de

accident and emergency (*Brit*) N [c] 急诊室 jízhěnshì [个 gè]

accommodation [əkɔmə'deɪʃən] I N [u] 住处 zhùchù II **accommodations** (*US*) NPL = **accommodation**

accompany [ə'kʌmpənɪ] VT 1 (*frm: escort*) 陪伴 péibàn 2 (*Mus*) 为⋯伴奏 wèi...bànzòu

according [ə'kɔːdɪŋ] ▶ **according to** PREP [+ *person*] 据⋯所说 jù...suǒshuō; [+ *account, information*] 根据 gēnjù

account [əˈkaunt] N [c] **1** (*with bank, at shop*) 账户 zhànghù [个 gè] **2** (*report*) 描述 miáoshù [番 fān] ▶**to take sth into account, take account of sth** 考虑到某事 kǎolǜ dào mǒushì

accountant [əˈkauntənt] N [c] 会计师 kuàijìshī [位 wèi]

accuracy [ˈækjurəsɪ] N [u] **1** [*of information, measurements*] 准确 zhǔnquè **2** [*of person, device*] 精确 jīngquè

accurate [ˈækjurɪt] ADJ [+ *information, measurement, instrument*] 精确的 jīngquè de; [+ *description, account, person, aim*] 准确的 zhǔnquè de

accuse [əˈkjuːz] VT **1** ▶**to accuse sb of (doing) sth** 指责某人(做)某事 zhǐzé mǒurén (zuò) mǒushì **2** ▶**to be accused of sth** (*of crime*) 被指控某事 bèi zhǐkòng mǒushì

ache [eɪk] I VI 痛 tòng II N [c] 疼痛 téngtòng [种 zhǒng] ▶**I've got (a) stomach/toothache** 我胃/牙痛 wǒ wèi/yá tòng

achieve [əˈtʃiːv] VT [+ *victory, success, result*] 取得 qǔdé

achievement [əˈtʃiːvmənt] N [c] 成就 chéngjiù [个 gè]

acid [ˈæsɪd] N [c/u] (*Chem*) 酸 suān [种 zhǒng]

across [əˈkrɒs] I PREP **1** (*moving from one side to the other of*) 穿过 chuānguò **2** (*situated on the other side of*) 在···对面 zài···duìmiàn **3** (*extending from one side to the other of*) 跨越 kuàyuè II ADV **1** (*from one side to the other*) 从一边到另一边

cóng yībiān dào lìngyībiān **2** ▶**across from** (*opposite*) 在···对面 zài···duìmiàn **3** ▶**across at/to** (*towards*) 朝向 cháoxiàng **4** (*in width*) 宽 kuān

act [ækt] VI **1** (*take action*) 行动 xíngdòng **2** (*behave*) 举止 jǔzhǐ ▷*They were acting suspiciously.* 他们举止可疑。tāmen jǔzhǐ kěyí. **3** (*in play, film*) 演戏 yǎnxì ▶**acts of sabotage** 破坏行动 pòhuài xíngdòng

action [ˈækʃən] N **1** [u] (*steps, measures*) 行动 xíngdòng **2** [c] (*deed*) 行为 xíngwéi [种 zhǒng] ▶**to take action** 采取行动 cǎiqǔ xíngdòng

active [ˈæktɪv] ADJ **1** 活跃的 huóyuè de **2** [+ *volcano*] 活的 huó de

activity [ækˈtɪvɪtɪ] I N [c] 活动 huódòng [项 xiàng] II **activities** NPL 活动 huódòng

actor [ˈæktər] N [c] 演员 yǎnyuán [个 gè]

actress [ˈæktrɪs] N [c] 女演员 nǚ yǎnyuán [个 gè]

actual [ˈæktjuəl] ADJ 真实的 zhēnshí de

actually [ˈæktjuəlɪ] ADV **1** 实际地 shíjì de **2** (*in fact*) 事实上 shìshíshang ▶**actually, we have the same opinion** 实际上我们有同样的观点 shíjì shàng wǒmen yǒu tóngyàng de guāndiǎn

AD ADV ABBR (= **Anno Domini**) 公元 gōngyuán

ad [æd] (*inf*) N (*advertisement*) 广告 guǎnggào

adapt [ə'dæpt] I VT 使适合 shǐ shìhé II VI ▸ **to adapt (to)** 适 应 shìyìng

adaptor [ə'dæptəʳ] (Elec) N [c] 转 接器 zhuǎnjiēqì [个 gè]

add [æd] VT 1 (put in, put on) 加 入 jiārù 2 ▸ **to add (together)** (calculate total of) 加(起来) jiā (qǐlái)

addict ['ædɪkt] N [c] ▸ **drug/ heroin addict** 吸毒/海洛因成瘾 的人 xīdú/hǎiluòyīn chéngyǐn de rén [个 gè]

addicted [ə'dɪktɪd] ADJ ▸ **to be addicted to sth** 对某事上瘾 duì mǒushì shàngyǐn

addition [ə'dɪʃən] N [U] (Math) 加 法 jiāfǎ ▸ **in addition to** 除…之外 chú…zhīwài

address [ə'drɛs] N [c] 地址 dìzhǐ [个 gè]

adjective ['ædʒɛktɪv] N [c] 形容 词 xíngróngcí [个 gè]

adjust [ə'dʒʌst] VT [+ device, position, setting] 校准 jiàozhǔn

adjustable [ə'dʒʌstəbl] ADJ 可调 节的 kě tiáojié de

admire [əd'maɪəʳ] VT 钦佩 qīnpèi

admit [əd'mɪt] VT 1 (confess) 承 认 chéngrèn 2 (accept) [+ defeat, responsibility] 接受 jiēshòu ▸ **he admits that…** 他承认… tā chéngrèn… ▸ **to be admitted to hospital** 住进医院 zhùjìn yīyuàn

adolescent [ædəʊ'lɛsnt] N [c] 青 少年 qīngshàonián [个 gè]

adopt [ə'dɔpt] VT 1 [+ plan, approach, attitude] 采用 cǎiyòng 2 [+ child] 收养 shōuyǎng

adopted [ə'dɔptɪd] ADJ 被收养的 bèi shōuyǎng de

adoption [ə'dɔpʃən] N [c/U] [of child] 收养 shōuyǎng

adult ['ædʌlt] I N [c] 成年人 chéngniánrén [个 gè] II ADJ (grown-up) 成年的 chéngnián de

advance [əd'vɑ:ns] [+ notice, warning] 预先的 yùxiān de ▸ **in advance** (book, prepare, plan) 提 前 tíqián

advanced [əd'vɑ:nst] ADJ 1 (highly developed) 先进的 xiānjìn de 2 (Scol) [+ student, pupil] 高年级的 gāoniánjí de; [+ course, work] 高等 的 gāoděng de

advantage [əd'vɑ:ntɪdʒ] N [c] 1 (benefit) 好处 hǎochù [种 zhǒng] 2 (favourable factor) 有利因素 yǒulì yīnsù [个 gè] ▸ **to take advantage of** [+ person] 利用 lìyòng; [+ opportunity] 利用 lìyòng

adventure [əd'vɛntʃəʳ] N [c] 冒险 活动 màoxiǎn huódòng [次 cì]

adverb ['ædvə:b] N [c] 副词 fùcí [个 gè]

advert ['ædvə:t] (Brit) N 广告 guǎnggào

advertise ['ædvətaɪz] I VI 做广 告 zuò guǎnggào II VT 1 [+ product, event] 为…做广告 wèi…zuò guǎnggào 2 [+ job] 刊登 kāndēng

advertisement [əd'və:tɪsmənt] (Comm) N [c] 广告 guǎnggào [则 zé]

advice [əd'vaɪs] N [U] 忠告 zhōnggào ▸ **a piece of advice** 一 条建议 yītiáo jiànyì

advise [əd'vaɪz] VT ▸ **to advise**

sb to do sth 劝某人做某事 quàn mǒurén zuò mǒushì

aerial[ˈɛərɪəl] (*Brit*) N [C] 天线 tiānxiàn [根 gēn]

aerobics[ɛəˈrəubɪks] N [U] 有氧健身操 yǒuyǎng jiànshēncāo

aeroplane[ˈɛərəpleɪn] (*Brit*) N [C] 飞机 fēijī [架 jià]

affair[əˈfɛər] I N 1[S] (*matter, business*) 事情 shìqing 2[C] (*romance*) 风流韵事 fēngliú yùnshì [桩 zhuāng] II **affairs** NPL 1(*matters*) 事务 shìwù 2(*personal concerns*) 私事 sīshì ▶**to have an affair (with sb)** (和某人)发生暧昧关系 (hé mǒurén) fāshēng àimèi guānxi

affect[əˈfɛkt] VT 影响 yǐngxiǎng

afford[əˈfɔːd] VT ▶ **to be able to afford (to buy/pay) sth** 买/支付得起某物 mǎi/zhīfùdeqǐ mǒuwù

afraid[əˈfreɪd] ADJ (*frightened*) 害怕的 hàipà de ▶**to be afraid of sb/sth** 害怕某人/某物 hàipà mǒurén/mǒuwù ▶**to be afraid to do sth/of doing sth** 怕做某事 pà zuò mǒushì ▶**to be afraid that...** (*worry, fear*) 担心… dānxīn…; (*expressing apology, disagreement*) 恐怕… kǒngpà… ▶**I'm afraid so/not** 恐怕是/不是的 kǒngpà shì/bùshì de

Africa[ˈæfrɪkə] N 非洲 Fēizhōu

African[ˈæfrɪkən] I ADJ 非洲的 Fēizhōu de II N [C] (*person*) 非洲人 Fēizhōurén [个 gè]

after[ˈɑːftər] I PREP 1(*in time*) 在…以后 zài…yǐhòu 2(*in place, order*) 在…后面 zài…hòumiàn II ADV (*afterwards*) 以后 yǐhòu III CONJ (*once*) 在…以后 zài…yǐhòu ▶**the day after tomorrow** 后天 hòutiān ▶**it's ten after eight** (*US*) 现在是8点过10分 xiànzài shì bādiǎn guò shífēn ▶**after all** 毕竟 bìjìng ▶**after doing sth** 做完某事后 zuòwán mǒushì hòu

after, afterwards 和 **later** 用于表示某事发生在说话的时间，或者某个特定事情之后。**after** 可以和 **not long**, **shortly** 等连用。*After dinner she spoke to him…Shortly after, she called me.* 在无须指明某个特定时间或事件时，可以用 **afterwards**。*Afterwards we went to a night club…You'd better come and see me later.* **afterwards** 可以和 **soon**, **shortly** 等连用。*Soon afterwards, he came to the clinic.* **later** 表示某事发生在说话之后，可以和 **a little**, **much** 或 **not much** 等连用。*A little later, the lights went out… I learned all this much later.* 可以用 **after, afterwards** 和 **later** 后跟表示时间段的词语，表示某事发生的时间。*… five years after his death…She wrote about it six years later/afterwards.*

afternoon[ˈɑːftəˈnuːn] N [C/U] 下午 xiàwǔ [个 gè] ▶**this afternoon** 今天下午 jīntiān xiàwǔ ▶**tomorrow/yesterday**

afternoon 明天/昨天下午 míngtiān/zuótiān xiàwǔ ▶**(good) afternoon!** (hello) 下午好! xiàwǔ hǎo!

after-shave (lotion) ['ɑːftə ʃeɪv-] N [U] 须后(润肤)水 xūhòu (rùnfū) shuǐ

afterwards ['ɑːftəwədz], (US) **afterward** ['ɑːftəwəd] ADV 以后 yǐhòu

again [ə'gɛn] ADV 又一次地 yòu yīcì de ▶**again and again/time and again** 一再 yīzài

against [ə'gɛnst] PREP 1 (leaning on, touching) 紧靠在 jǐnkào zài 2 (opposed to) 反对 fǎnduì 3 (in game or competition) 同…对抗 tóng…duìkàng 4 ▶**to protect against sth** 保护免受某种伤害 bǎohù miǎnshòu mǒuzhǒng shānghài ▶**they'll be playing against Australia** 他们将在比赛中同澳大利亚队对抗 tāmen jiāng zài bǐsài zhōng tóng Àodàlìyà duì duìkàng ▶**against the law/rules** 违反法律/规则 wéifǎn fǎlǜ/guīzé ▶**against one's will** 违背自己的意愿 wéibèi zìjǐ de yìyuàn

age [eɪdʒ] N 1 [C/U] 年龄 niánlíng 2 [C] (period in history) 时代 shídài [个 gè] ▶**what age is he?** 他多大了? tā duōdà le? ▶**at the age of 20** 20岁时 èrshí suì shí ▶**an age, ages** (inf) 很长时间 hěncháng shíjiān ▶**the Stone/Bronze/Iron Age** 石器/铜器/铁器时代 shíqì/tóngqì/tiěqì shídài

aged[1] ['eɪdʒd] ADJ ▶**aged 10** 10岁 shí suì

aged[2] ['eɪdʒɪd] NPL ▶**the aged** 老人 lǎorén

agent ['eɪdʒənt] N [C] 代理人 dàilǐrén [个 gè]

aggressive [ə'grɛsɪv] ADJ 好斗的 hàodòu de

ago [ə'gəu] ADV ▶**2 days ago** 两天前 liǎngtiān qián ▶**long ago/a long time ago** 很久以前 hěnjiǔ yǐqián ▶**how long ago?** 多久以前? duōjiǔ yǐqián?

agony ['ægənɪ] N [C/U] 痛苦 tòngkǔ [种 zhǒng]

agree [ə'griː] VI 1 (have same opinion) 同意 tóngyì 2 ▶**to agree to sth/to do sth** 同意某事/做事 tóngyì mǒushì/zuò mǒushì ▶**to agree with sb about sth** 关于某事赞成某人的看法 guānyú mǒushì zànchéng mǒurén de kànfǎ ▶**to agree on sth** [+ price, arrangement] 商定某事 shāngdìng mǒushì

agreement [ə'griːmənt] N 1 [C] ▶**an agreement (on sth)** (decision, arrangement) (关于某事的)协议 (guānyú mǒushì de) xiéyì [个 gè] 2 [U] (consent) 同意 tóngyì

agricultural [ˌægrɪ'kʌltʃərəl] ADJ 农业的 nóngyè de

agriculture ['ægrɪkʌltʃəʳ] N [U] 农业 nóngyè

ahead [ə'hɛd] ADV 1 (in front) 在前地 zàiqián de 2 (in work, achievements) 提前地 tíqián de 3 (in competition) 领先地 lǐngxiān de 4 (in the future) 在未来 zài wèilái ▶**the days/months ahead** 今后几天/几个月 jīnhòu jǐtiān/jǐgè yuè ▶**ahead of time/schedule**

提前 tíqián ▶**right** or **straight ahead** 笔直向前 bǐzhí xiàngqián ▶**go ahead!** (giving permission) 干吧！gànba!

aid [eɪd] N [U] 援助 yuánzhù

AIDS [eɪdz] N ABBR (= **acquired immune deficiency syndrome**) 艾滋病 àizībìng

aim [eɪm] I VT ▶ **to aim sth (at sb/sth)** [+ gun, camera] 将某物瞄准 (某人/某物) jiāng mǒuwù miáozhǔn (mǒurén/mǒuwù) II VI (with weapon) 瞄准 miáozhǔn III N [c] (objective) 目标 mùbiāo [个 gè] ▶**to aim at sth** (with weapon) 瞄准某物 miáozhǔn mǒuwù ▶**to aim to do sth** 打算做某事 dǎsuàn zuò mǒushì

air [ɛəʳ] I N [U] 空气 kōngqì II CPD [+ travel] 乘飞机 chéng fēijī; [+ fare] 飞机 fēijī ▶**in/into/ through the air** 在/进入/穿过天空 zài/jìnrù/chuānguò tiānkōng ▶**by air** (flying) 乘飞机 chéng fēijī

air-conditioned [ˈɛəkənˈdɪʃənd] ADJ 装有空调的 zhuāngyǒu kōngtiáo de

air conditioning [-kənˈdɪʃənɪŋ] N [U] 空气调节 kōngqì tiáojié

air force N [c] 空军 kōngjūn [支 zhī]

air hostess (Brit) N [c] 空中小姐 kōngzhōng xiǎojiě [位 wèi]

airline [ˈɛəlaɪn] N [c] 航空公司 hángkōng gōngsī [家 jiā]

airmail [ˈɛəmeɪl] N [U] ▶ **by airmail** 航空邮寄 hángkōng yóujì

airplane [ˈɛəpleɪn] (US) N [c] 飞机 fēijī [架 jià]

airport [ˈɛəpɔːt] N [c] 飞机场 fēijīchǎng [个 gè]

aisle [aɪl] N [c] 过道 guòdào [条 tiáo] ▶**aisle seat** (on plane) 靠过道的座位 kào guòdào de zuòwèi

alarm [əˈlɑːm] N 1 [c] (warning device) 警报 jǐngbào [个 gè] 2 [c] (on clock) 闹钟 nàozhōng [个 gè]

alarm clock N [c] 闹钟 nàozhōng [个 gè]

Albania [ælˈbeɪnɪə] N 阿尔巴尼亚 Ā'ěrbānníyà

album [ˈælbəm] N [c] 1 册子 cèzi [本 běn] 2 (LP) 唱片 chàngpiàn [张 zhāng]

alcohol [ˈælkəhɒl] N [U] 酒 jiǔ

alcoholic [ælkəˈhɒlɪk] I N [c] 酒鬼 jiǔguǐ [个 gè] II ADJ [+ drink] 含酒精的 hán jiǔjīng de

alert [əˈlɜːt] N [c] (situation) ▶ **a security alert** 安全警戒 ānquán jǐngjiè [个 gè]

A level (Brit) N [c/U] 中学中高级考试 zhōngxué zhōnggāojí kǎoshì

Algeria [ælˈdʒɪərɪə] N 阿尔及利亚 Ā'ěrjílìyà

alike [əˈlaɪk] ADJ ▶ **to be/look alike** 是/看起来相似的 shì/ kànqǐlái xiāngsì de

alive [əˈlaɪv] ADJ (living) ▶ **to be alive** 活着的 huózhe de ▶**alive and well** 安然无恙的 ānrán wúyàng de

◯ KEYWORD

all [ɔːl] I ADJ 所有的 suǒyǒu de ▶**all day/night** 整日/夜 zhěngrì/ yè ▶**all big cities** 所有的大城市

suǒyǒu de dàchéngshì
II PRON **1** 全部 quánbù ▶**all I
could do was apologize** 我所能
做的全部就是道歉 wǒ suǒ néng
zuò de quánbù jiùshì dàoqiàn ▶**I
ate it all, I ate all of it** 我把它全都
吃了 wǒ bǎ tā quán dōu chīle ▶**all
of us** 我们中的所有人 wǒmen
zhōng de suǒyǒu rén ▶**we all sat
down** 我们都坐下了 wǒmen dōu
zuòxià le ▶**is that all?** 那就是全部
吗？ nà jiùshì quánbù ma?
2 (*in expressions*) ▶**after all**
(*considering*) 毕竟 bìjìng ▶**in all**
总共 zǒnggòng ▶**best of all** 最好
不过的是 zuìhǎo bùguò de shì
III ADV **1** (*emphatic*) 完全 wánquán
▶**he was doing it all by himself**
他完全是自己做的 tā wánquán shì
zìjǐ zuò de ▶**all alone** 孤零零的
gūlínglíng de
2 (*in scores*) ▶**the score is 2 all** 比
分2比2平 bǐfēn èr bǐ èr píng

allergic [ə'lə:dʒɪk] ADJ [+ *reaction,
response*] 过敏的 guòmǐn de ▶**to
be allergic to sth** 对某物过敏 duì
mǒuwù guòmǐn

allergy ['ælədʒɪ] (*Med*) N [c/u] 过
敏症 guòmǐnzhèng [种 zhǒng]
▶**to have an allergy to sth** 对
某物有过敏症 duì mǒuwù yǒu
guòmǐnzhèng

allow [ə'lau] VT **1** (*permit*) 允许
yǔnxǔ **2** [+ *sum, time, amount*] 留
出 liúchū ▶**to allow sb to do sth**
允许某人做某事 yǔnxǔ mǒurén
zuò mǒushì

all right I ADJ ▶**to be all right**

(*satisfactory*) 还不错的 hái bùcuò
de; (*well, safe*) 安然无恙的 ānrán
wúyàng de II ADV **1** 顺利地 shùnlì
de **2** 没问题地 méi wèntí de **3** (*as
answer*) 可以 kěyǐ

almond ['ɑːmənd] N [c/u] (*nut*)
杏仁 xìngrén [颗 kē]

almost ['ɔːlməust] ADV 差不多
chàbùduō

alone [ə'ləun] I ADJ 独自的
dúzì de II ADV (*unaided*) 独自地
dúzì de ▶**to leave sb/sth alone**
(*undisturbed*) 不要打扰某人/某物
bùyào dǎrǎo mǒurén/mǒuwù

along [ə'lɒŋ] I PREP **1** 沿着
yánzhe **2** [+ *road, corridor, river*] 沿
着 yánzhe II ADV 沿着 yánzhe
▶**along with** (*together with*)
与…一起 yǔ…yìqǐ

alphabet ['ælfəbet] N ▶**the
alphabet** 字母表 zìmǔbiǎo

already [ɔːl'redɪ] ADV 已经 yǐjīng
▶**I have already started making
dinner** 我已经开始做晚餐了 wǒ
yǐjīng kāishǐ zuò wǎncān le ▶**is it
five o'clock already?** (*expressing
surprise*) 已经到5点了吗？ yǐjīng
dào wǔdiǎn le ma?

also ['ɔːlsəu] ADV **1** (*too*) 也 yě
2 (*moreover*) 同样 tóngyàng

alternate [ɔl'tə:nɪt] ADJ **1** 交替的
jiāotì de **2** (*US: alternative*) 供替换
的 gōng tìhuàn de

alternative [ɔl'tə:nətɪv] I ADJ
1 (*Brit*) 另外的 lìngwài de
2 (*non-conventional*) 非常规的
fēi chángguī de II N [c] ▶(**an**)
alternative (**to**) …的替代
…de tìdài [个 gè] ▶**to have no**

alternative (but to) （除…外）别无选择 (chú…wài) biéwú xuǎnzé

alternatively [ɔl'tə:nətɪvlɪ] ADV 或者 huòzhě

although [ɔ:l'ðəu] CONJ 1 尽管 jǐnguǎn 2 (but) 但是 dànshì

altogether [ɔ:ltə'gɛðər] ADV 1 (completely) 完全 wánquán 2 (in total) 总共 zǒnggòng ▶how much is that altogether? 总共多少钱？zǒnggòng duōshǎo qián?

aluminium [ælju'mɪnɪəm], (US) **aluminum** [ə'lu:mɪnəm] N [U] 铝 lǚ

always ['ɔ:lweɪz] ADV 总是 zǒngshì ▶He's always late 他总是迟到 tā zǒngshì chídào

am [æm] VB see **be**

a.m. ADV ABBR (= ante meridiem) 上午 shàngwǔ

amateur ['æmətər] N [c] 业余爱好者 yèyú àihàozhě [个 gè]

amaze [ə'meɪz] VT 使惊讶 shǐ jīngyà ▶to be amazed (at/by/that...) （对/被…）惊讶 (duì/bèi…) jīngyà

amazing [ə'meɪzɪŋ] ADJ 令人惊讶的 lìng rén jīngyà de

ambassador [æm'bæsədər] N [c] 大使 dàshǐ [位 wèi]

ambition [æm'bɪʃən] N [c] ▶an ambition (to do sth) （做某事的）志向 (zuò mǒushì de) zhìxiàng [个 gè] ▶to achieve one's ambition 实现自己的抱负 shíxiàn zìjǐ de bàofu

ambitious [æm'bɪʃəs] ADJ 雄心勃勃的 xióngxīn bóbó de

ambulance ['æmbjuləns] N [c] 救护车 jiùhùchē [辆 liàng]

America [ə'mɛrɪkə] N 美洲 Měizhōu

American [ə'mɛrɪkən] I ADJ 美国的 Měiguó de II N [c] (person) 美国人 Měiguórén [个 gè]

among(st) [ə'mʌŋ(st)] PREP 在…当中 zài…dāngzhōng

如果指两个以上的人或物，用 **among** 或 **amongst**。如果只指两个人或物，用 **between**。...an area between Mars and Jupiter...an opportunity to discuss these issues amongst themselves. **amongst** 是有些过时的表达方式。注意，如果你 **between** 某些东西或某些人，他们在你的两侧。如果你 **among** 或 **amongst** 某些东西或某些人，他们在你的周围。...the bag standing on the floor between us...the sound of a pigeon among the trees...

amount [ə'maunt] N [c/U] (quantity) 数量 shùliàng; [of money] 数额 shù'é [个 gè]; [of work] 总量 zǒngliàng [个 gè]

amp ['æmp] N [c] 安培 ānpéi

amplifier ['æmplɪfaɪər] N [c] 扬声器 yángshēngqì [个 gè]

amuse [ə'mju:z] VT (distract, entertain) 给…消遣 gěi…xiāoqiǎn ▶to be amused at/by sth 被某事逗乐 bèi mǒushì dòulè

amusement arcade N [c] 游乐场 yóulèchǎng [个 gè]

an [æn, ən] DEF ART see **a**

anaesthetic, (US) **anesthetic**
[ænɪs'θɛtɪk] N [c/u] 麻醉
剂 mázuìjì [种 zhǒng] ▶**local
anaesthetic** 局部麻醉 júbù
mázuì ▶**general anaesthetic** 全
身麻醉 quánshēn mázuì

analyse, (US) **analyze** ['ænəlaɪz]
VT 分析 fēnxī

analysis [ə'næləsɪs] (pl **analyses**
[ə'næləsi:z]) N [c/u] 分析 fēnxī
[种 zhǒng]

analyze ['ænəlaɪz] (US) VT =
analyse

ancestor ['ænsɪstəʳ] N [c] 祖先
zǔxiān [位 wèi]

ancient ['eɪnʃənt] ADJ 1 [+ Greece,
Rome, monument] 古代的 gǔdài de
2 (very old) 古老的 gǔlǎo de

and [ænd] CONJ 和 hé ▶**men and
women** 男人和女人 nánrén hé
nǚrén ▶**better and better** 越来
越好 yuè lái yuè hǎo ▶**to try and
do sth** 试着做某事 shìzhe zuò
mǒushì

anesthetic [ænɪs'θɛtɪk] (US) =
anaesthetic

anger ['æŋgəʳ] N [u] 生气 shēngqì

angry ['æŋgrɪ] ADJ 生气的
shēngqì de ▶**to be angry with
sb/about sth** 对某人/某事生气
duì mǒurén/mǒushì shēngqì ▶**to
make sb angry** 使某人生气 shǐ
mǒurén shēngqì

animal ['ænɪməl] N [c] 动物
dòngwù [只 zhī]

ankle ['æŋkl] (Anat) N [c] 踝 huái
[个 gè]

anniversary [ænɪ'və:sərɪ] N
[c] 1 ▶**anniversary (of sth)** （某

事的) 周年纪念 (mǒushì de)
zhōunián jìniàn [个 gè] 2 (also:
wedding anniversary) 结婚周年
纪念 jiéhūn zhōunián jìniàn [个 gè]

announce [ə'nauns] VT 宣布
xuānbù ▶**the government has
announced that...** 政府宣称…
zhèngfǔ xuānchēng…

announcement [ə'naunsmənt]
N [c] 1 宣布 xuānbù 2 (at airport or
station) 通告 tōnggào [个 gè] ▶**to
make an announcement** 发表声
明 fābiǎo shēngmíng

annoy [ə'nɔɪ] VT 使烦恼 shǐ
fánnǎo

annoyed [ə'nɔɪd] ADJ 厌烦的
yànfán de ▶**to be annoyed at
sth/with sb** 对某事/某人感到厌
烦 duì mǒushì/mǒurén gǎndào
yànfán

annoying [ə'nɔɪɪŋ] ADJ [+ noise,
habit, person] 讨厌的 tǎoyàn de

annual ['ænjuəl] ADJ 1 [+ meeting,
report] 每年的 měinián de
2 [+ sales, income, rate] 年度的
niándù de

anorak ['ænəræk] N [c] 连帽防
风夹克 liánmào fángfēng jiákè
[件 jiàn]

another [ə'nʌðəʳ] I ADJ 1
▶**another book** (one more) 另一本
书 lìng yī běn shū 2 (a different one)
另外的 lìngwài de 3 ▶**another 5
years/miles/kilos** 再有5年/英
里/公斤 zài yǒu wǔ nián/yīnglǐ/
gōngjīn II PRON 1 (one more) 再一
个 zài yī gè 2 (a different one) 不
同的一个 bùtóng de yīgè ▶**one
another** 相互 xiānghù

answer ['ɑ:nsər] I N [c] 1 (reply) 回答 huídá [个 gè]; (to letter) 回信 huíxìn [封 fēng] 2 (solution) 答案 dá'an [个 gè] II VI (reply) 回答 huídá; (to telephone ringing, knock at door) 应答 yìngdá III VT [+ person] 答复 dáfù; [+ question] 回答 huídá; [+ letter] 回复 huífù ▶to answer the phone 接听电话 jiētīng diànhuà

answering machine ['ɑ:nsərɪŋ-] N [c] 电话答录机 diànhuà dálùjī [台 tái]

Antarctic [ænt'ɑ:ktɪk] N ▶the Antarctic 南极 Nánjí

anthem ['ænθəm] N [c] 赞美诗 zànměishī [首 shǒu]

antibiotic ['æntɪbaɪ'ɔtɪk] N [c] 抗生素 kàngshēngsù [种 zhǒng]

antique [æn'ti:k] N [c] 古董 gǔdǒng [件 jiàn]

antiseptic [æntɪ'sɛptɪk] N [c/u] 杀菌剂 shājùnjì [种 zhǒng]

anxious ['æŋkʃəs] ADJ 忧虑的 yōulù de

○ **KEYWORD**

any ['ɛnɪ] I ADJ 1 (in negatives, in questions) 一些的 yīxiē de ▶I haven't any chocolate/sweets 我没有巧克力/糖了 wǒ méiyǒu qiǎokèlì/táng le ▶there was hardly any food 几乎没有食物了 jīhū méiyǒu shíwù le ▶have you got any chocolate/sweets? 你有巧克力/糖吗？ nǐ yǒu qiǎokèlì/táng ma? 2 (in "if" clauses) 任何的 rènhé de ▶if there are any tickets left 如果有票剩下的话 rúguǒ yǒu piào shèngxia de huà 3 (no matter which) 任意的 rènyì de ▶take any card you like 拿你喜欢的任意一张卡 ná nǐ xǐhuan de rènyì yī zhāng kǎ 4 (in expressions) ▶any day now 从现在起的任何一天 cóng xiànzài qǐ de rènhé yītiān ▶(at) any moment (在)任何时候 (zài) rènhé shíhou ▶any time (whenever) 不论何时 bùlùn héshí; (also: at any time) 在任何时候 zài rènhé shíhou II PRON 1 (in negatives) 一些 yīxiē ▶I didn't eat any (of it) 我(这)点也没吃 wǒ (zhè) yīdiǎn yě méi chī ▶I haven't any (of them) 我一个也没有 wǒ yīgè yě méiyǒu 2 (in questions) 一些 yīxiē ▶have you got any? 你有吗？ nǐ yǒu ma? 3 (in "if" clauses) 任何 rènhé ▶if any of you would like to take part, ... 如果你们中任何人想参加的话，… rúguǒ nǐmen zhōng rènhé rén xiǎng cānjiā de huà, … 4 (no matter which ones) 无论哪一个 wúlùn nǎ yīgè ▶help yourself to any of the books 无论哪本书你随便拿 wúlùn nǎběn shū nǐ suíbiàn ná III ADV 1 (with negative) 丝毫 sīháo ▶I don't play tennis any more 我不再打网球了 wǒ bùzài dǎ wǎngqiú le ▶don't wait any longer 不再等了 bùzài děng le 2 (in questions) …一点 …yīdiǎn

▶**do you want any more soup/ sandwiches?** 你还想再要点汤/三明治吗？ nǐ hái xiǎng zài yào diǎn tāng/sānmíngzhì ma?

anybody ['ɛnɪbɔdɪ] PRON = **anyone**

anyhow ['ɛnɪhau] ADV = **anyway**

anyone ['ɛnɪwʌn] PRON 1 (in negatives, "if" clauses) 任何人 rènhé rén 2 (in questions) 任何一个人 rènhé yīgè rén ▶**I can't see anyone** 我见不到任何人 wǒ jiànbùdào rènhé rén ▶**did anyone see you?** 有人看到你吗？ yǒurén kàndào nǐ ma? ▶**anyone could do it** 任何人都能做到 rènhé rén dōunéng zuòdào

anything ['ɛnɪθɪŋ] PRON (in negatives, questions, "if" clauses) 任何事 rènhé shì ▶**I can't see anything** 我什么也看不见 wǒ shénme yě kànbùjiàn ▶**hardly anything** 几乎没有任何东西 jīhū méiyǒu rènhé dōngxi ▶**did you find anything?** 你找到些什么吗？ nǐ zhǎodào xiē shénme ma? ▶**if anything happens to me...** 如果任何事情发生在我身上… rúguǒ rènhé shìqíng fāshēng zài wǒ shēnshàng… ▶**you can say anything you like** 你可以畅所欲言 nǐ kěyǐ chàng suǒ yù yán

anyway ['ɛnɪweɪ] ADV 1 (besides) 无论如何 wúlùn rúhé 2 (all the same) 还是 háishì 3 (in short) 总之 zǒngzhī ▶**I shall go anyway** 不论如何我要走了 bùlùn rúhé wǒ yào zǒu le

anywhere ['ɛnɪwɛəʳ] ADV (in negatives, questions, "if" clauses) 任何地方 rènhé dìfāng ▶**I can't see him anywhere** 我哪里都见不到他 wǒ nǎlǐ dōu jiànbùdào tā

apart [ə'pɑːt] ADV [couple, family] 分开 fēnkāi ▶**to take sth apart** 拆卸某物 chāixiè mǒuwù ▶**apart from** (excepting) 除去 chúqù

apartment [ə'pɑːtmənt] N [c] (US) 公寓 gōngyù [处 chù]

apologize [ə'pɔlədʒaɪz] VI 道歉 dàoqiàn ▶**to apologize to sb (for sth)** 向某人（为某事）道歉 xiàng mǒurén (wèi mǒushì) dàoqiàn

apology [ə'pɔlədʒɪ] N [c/u] 道歉 dàoqiàn [个 gè]

apostrophe [ə'pɔstrəfɪ] N [c] 撇号 piěhào [个 gè]

apparently [ə'pærəntlɪ] ADV 表面看来 biǎomiàn kànlái

appear [ə'pɪəʳ] VI 1 (seem) 看起来 kànqǐlái 2 (come into view, begin to develop) 出现 chūxiàn ▶**to appear to be/have** 看起来是/有 kànqǐlái shì/yǒu

appendicitis [əpendɪ'saɪtɪs] N [u] 阑尾炎 lánwěiyán

appetite ['æpɪtaɪt] N [c/u] 食欲 shíyù

applause [ə'plɔːz] N [u] 掌声 zhǎngshēng

apple ['æpl] N [c] 苹果 píngguǒ [个 gè]

appliance [ə'plaɪəns] (frm) N [c] 器具 qìjù [件 jiàn]

applicant ['æplɪkənt] N [c] 申请人 shēnqǐngrén [个 gè]

application [æplɪ'keɪʃən] N 1

[c] 申请 shēnqǐng [份 fèn] **2** [c] (*Comput: program*) 应用程序 yìngyòng chéngxù [个 gè]

application form N [c] 申请表格 shēnqǐng biǎogé [份 fèn]

apply [ə'plaɪ] VI (*make application*) 提出申请 tíchū shēnqǐng ▸**to apply for sth** [+ *job, grant, membership*] 申请某事 shēnqǐng mǒushì

appointment [ə'pɔɪntmənt] N [c] (*arranged meeting*) 约会 yuēhuì [个 gè]; (*with hairdresser, dentist, doctor*) 预约 yùyuē [个 gè] ▸**to make an appointment (with sb)** (*to see hairdresser, dentist, doctor*) (和某人) 预约 (hé mǒurén) yùyuē

appreciate [ə'priːʃɪeɪt] VT (*be grateful for*) 感谢 gǎnxiè ▸**I (really) appreciate your help** 我 (十分) 感谢你的帮助 wǒ (shífēn) gǎnxiè nǐde bāngzhù

approach [ə'prəʊtʃ] I VI [*person, car*] 走近 zǒu jìn; [*event, time*] 临近 línjìn II VT **1** (*draw near to*) 向…靠近 xiàng…kàojìn **2** [+ *situation, problem*] 处理 chǔlǐ III N [c] (*to a problem, situation*) 方式 fāngshì [种 zhǒng]

approval [ə'pruːvəl] N [u] 批准 pīzhǔn

approve [ə'pruːv] VI 赞成 zànchéng

approximate [ə'prɒksɪmɪt] ADJ 近似的 jìnsì de

apricot ['eɪprɪkɒt] N [c/u] 杏子 xìngzi [个 gè]

April ['eɪprəl] N [c/u] 四月 sìyuè; *see also* **July**

apron ['eɪprən] N [c] 围裙 wéiqún [条 tiáo]

Aquarius [ə'kwɛərɪəs] N [u] (*sign*) 宝瓶座 Bǎopíng Zuò gè

Arab ['ærəb] I ADJ 阿拉伯的 Ālābó de II N [c] 阿拉伯人 Ālābórén [个 gè]

Arabic ['ærəbɪk] N [u] (*language*) 阿拉伯语 Ālābóyǔ

arch [ɑːtʃ] N [c] 拱 gǒng [个 gè]

archaeology [ɑːkɪ'ɔlədʒɪ] N [u] 考古学 kǎogǔxué

archeology [ɑːkɪ'ɔlədʒɪ] (*US*) = **archaeology**

architect ['ɑːkɪtɛkt] N [c] 建筑师 jiànzhùshī [位 wèi]

architecture ['ɑːkɪtɛktʃəʳ] N [u] 建筑学 jiànzhùxué

Arctic ['ɑːktɪk] N ▸**the Arctic** 北极 Běijí

are [ɑːʳ] VB *see* **be**

area ['ɛərɪə] N **1** [c] (*region, zone*) 地区 dìqū [个 gè] **2** [c] (*of room, building etc*) 区 qū [个 gè] **3** [c/u] (*Math, Geom*) 面积 miànjī [个 gè] **4** [c] (*part*) 部分 bùfen [个 gè] ▸**in the London area** 在伦敦周边地区 zài Lúndūn zhōubiān dìqū

area code (*esp US*) N [c] 区号 qūhào [个 gè]

Argentina [ɑːdʒən'tiːnə] N 阿根廷 Āgēntíng

argue ['ɑːgjuː] VI (*quarrel*) ▸**to argue (with sb) (about sth)** (为某事) (和某人) 争吵 (wèi mǒushì) (hé mǒurén) zhēngchǎo

argument ['ɑːgjumənt] N [c/u] (*quarrel*) 争吵 zhēngchǎo [阵 zhèn] ▸**an argument for/against sth**

赞成/反对某事的论据 zànchéng/
fǎnduì mǒushì de lùnjù

Aries ['ɛərɪz] N [U] (*sign*) 白羊座
Báiyáng Zuò

arithmetic [ə'rɪθmətɪk] N [U]
(*Math*) 算术 suànshù

arm [ɑːm] I N [c] 1 胳膊 gēbo
[条 tiáo] 2 [*of jacket, shirt etc*] 袖
子 xiùzi [只 zhī] II **arms** NPL
(*weapons*) 武器 wǔqì

armchair ['ɑːmtʃɛəʳ] N [c] 扶手椅
fúshǒuyǐ [把 bǎ]

armed [ɑːmd] ADJ 武装的
wǔzhuāng de

army ['ɑːmɪ] N ▶ **the army** 军
队 jūnduì

around [ə'raund] I ADV (*about*) 到
处 dàochù II PREP 1 (*encircling*) 围
绕 wéirào 2 (*near*) 在附近 zài fùjìn
3 大约 dàyuē

arrange [ə'reɪndʒ] I VT 1 (*organize*)
安排 ānpái 2 (*put in order*) 整理
zhěnglǐ II VI ▶ **to arrange to do
sth** 安排做某事 ānpái zuò mǒushì

arrangement [ə'reɪndʒmənt] I N
[c] 1 (*agreement*) 约定 yuēdìng [个
gè] 2 (*grouping, layout*) 布置 bùzhì
[种 zhǒng] II **arrangements** NPL
(*plans, preparations*) 安排 ānpái

arrest [ə'rɛst] VT 逮捕 dàibǔ ▶ **to
be under arrest** 被逮捕 bèi dàibǔ

arrival [ə'raɪvl] N [c/u] 到达 dàodá

arrive [ə'raɪv] VI 1 到 dào 2 [*letter,
meal*] 来 lái

arrow ['ærəu] N [c] 1 (*weapon*)
箭 jiàn [支 zhī] 2 (*sign*) 箭头标志
jiàntóu biāozhì [个 gè]

art [ɑːt] I N 1 [U] 艺术 yìshù 2 [U]
(*activity of drawing, painting etc*) 美

术 měishù 3 [c] (*skill*) 技艺 jìyì [项
xiàng] II **arts** NPL ▶ **the arts** 艺
术活动 yìshù huódòng III CPD
▶ **arts** [+ *graduate, student, course*]
文科 wénkē ▶ **work of art** 艺术
品 yìshùpǐn

art gallery N [c] 美术馆
měishùguǎn [个 gè]

article ['ɑːtɪkl] N [c] 1 物品 wùpǐn
[件 jiàn] 2 (*in newspaper*) 文章
wénzhāng [篇 piān] 3 (*Ling*) 冠词
guàncí [个 gè]

artificial [ɑːtɪ'fɪʃəl] ADJ 人造的
rénzào de

artist ['ɑːtɪst] N [c] 画家 huàjiā
[位 wèi]

KEYWORD

as [æz, əz] I CONJ 1 (*referring to
time*) 当…时 dāng…shí ▶ **he
came in as I was leaving** 我离开
时他进来了 wǒ líkāi shí tā jìnlai le
2 (*since, because*) 因为 yīnwèi ▶ **as
you can't come, I'll go on my
own** 既然你不能来，我就自己去
jìrán nǐ bùnéng lái, wǒ jiù zìjǐ qù
3 (*referring to manner, way*) 像…一
样 xiàng…yīyàng ▶ **as you can
see** 如你所见到的 rú nǐ suǒ
jiàndào de ▶ **it's on the left as
you go in** 在你进入时的左侧 zài
nǐ jìnrù shí de zuǒcè
II PREP 1 (*in the capacity of*) 作为
zuòwéi ▶ **he works as a salesman**
他做推销员的工作 tā zuò
tuīxiāoyuán de gōngzuò
2 (*when*) 在…时 zài…shí ▶ **he was
very energetic as a child** 他小时

候精力很旺盛 tā xiǎoshíhou jīnglì hěn wàngshèng
III ADV 1 (in comparisons) ▶ **as big/good/easy** etc **as...** 像…一样大/好/容易{等} xiàng…yīyàng dà/hǎo/róngyì {děng} ▶ **you're as tall as he is** or **as him** 你和他一样高 nǐ hé tā yīyàng gāo ▶ **as soon as** 一…就… yī…jiù… 2 (in expressions) ▶ **as if** or **though** 好像 hǎoxiàng

ash [æʃ] N [U] 灰末 huīmò
ashamed [əˈʃeɪmd] ADJ ▶ **to be/feel ashamed** 感到羞愧 gǎndào xiūkuì ▶ **to be ashamed of sb/sth** 对某人/某事感到羞愧 duì mǒurén/mǒushì gǎndào xiūkuì
ashtray [ˈæʃtreɪ] N [C] 烟灰缸 yānhuīgāng [个 gè]
Asia [ˈeɪʃə] N 亚洲 Yàzhōu
Asian [ˈeɪʃən] I ADJ 亚洲的 Yàzhōu de II N [C] (person) 亚洲人 Yàzhōurén [个 gè]
ask [ɑːsk] I VT 1 ▶ **to ask (sb) a question** 问 (某人) 一个问题 wèn (mǒurén) yīgè wèntí 2 (invite) 邀请 yāoqǐng II VI 问 wèn ▶ **to ask (sb) whether/why...** 问 (某人) 是否/为什么… wèn (mǒurén) shìfǒu/wèishénme… ▶ **to ask sb to do sth** 请求某人做某事 qǐngqiú mǒurén zuò mǒushì ▶ **to ask to do sth** 要求做某事 yāoqiú zuò mǒushì ▶ **to ask sb the time** 向某人询问时间 xiàng mǒurén xúnwèn shíjiān ▶ **to ask sb about sth** 向某人打听某事 xiàng mǒurén dǎtīng mǒushì ▶ **I asked**

him his name 我问他叫什么 wǒ wèn tā jiào shénme
▶ **ask for** VT FUS 1 [+ thing] 要 yào 2 [+ person] 找 zhǎo
asleep [əˈsliːp] ADJ 睡着的 shuìzháo de ▶ **to be asleep** 睡着了 shuìzháo le ▶ **to fall asleep** 入睡 rùshuì
aspirin [ˈæsprɪn] N [C] (tablet) 阿司匹林药片 āsīpǐlín yàopiàn [片 piàn]
assemble [əˈsɛmbl] I VT [+ machinery, object] 装配 zhuāngpèi II VI (gather) 聚集 jùjí
assembly [əˈsɛmblɪ] N 1 [C] (meeting) 集会 jíhuì [个 gè] 2 [U] 装配 zhuāngpèi
assignment [əˈsaɪnmənt] N [C] 任务 rènwù [项 xiàng]; (for student) 作业 zuòyè [个 gè]
assistance [əˈsɪstəns] N [U] 帮助 bāngzhù
assistant [əˈsɪstənt] N [C] 1 (helper) 助手 zhùshǒu [个 gè] 2 (Brit: in shop) 营业员 yíngyèyuán [个 gè]
assortment [əˈsɔːtmənt] N [C] ▶ **an assortment of sth** 各种各样的某物 gèzhǒng gèyàng de mǒuwù [件 jiàn]
assume [əˈsjuːm] VT 假设 jiǎshè
assure [əˈʃuəʳ] VT 使确信 shǐ quèxìn
asterisk [ˈæstərɪsk] N [C] 星号 xīnghào [个 gè]
asthma [ˈæsmə] N [U] 哮喘 xiàochuǎn
astonishing [əˈstɔnɪʃɪŋ] ADJ 惊人的 jīngrén de

astronaut['æstrənɔːt] N [C] 宇航员 yǔhángyuán [位 wèi]

astronomy[əs'trɒnəmɪ] N [U] 天文学 tiānwénxué

⬤ KEYWORD

at[æt] PREP 1(*position, time, age*) 在 zài ▶**we had dinner at a restaurant** 我们在一家饭店吃了饭 wǒmen zài yìjiā fàndiàn chī le fàn ▶**at home** 在家 zàijiā ▶**at work** 在工作 zài gōngzuò ▶**to be sitting at a table/desk** 坐在桌边/书桌边 zuòzài zhuōbiān/shūzhuōbiān ▶**there's someone at the door** 门口有人 ménkǒu yǒurén; (*towards*) ▶**to throw sth at sb** 向某人扔某物 xiàng mǒurén rēng mǒuwù ▶**at four o'clock** 在4点钟 zài sìdiǎn zhōng ▶**at Christmas** 在圣诞节 zài Shèngdànjié

2(*referring to price, speed*) 以 yǐ ▶**apples at £2 a kilo** 苹果每公斤两镑 píngguǒ měi gōngjīn liǎngbàng ▶**at 50 km/h** 以每小时50公里的速度 yǐ měi xiǎoshí wǔshí gōnglǐ de sùdù

3(*in expressions*) ▶**not at all** (*in answer to question*) 一点也不 yìdiǎn yě bù; (*in answer to thanks*) 别客气 bié kèqi

ate[eɪt] PT *of* **eat**

athlete['æθliːt] N [C] 运动员 yùndòngyuán [名 míng]

athletics[æθ'letɪks] N [U] 田径运动 tiánjìng yùndòng

Atlantic[ət'læntɪk] I ADJ 大西洋的 Dàxīyáng de II N ▶**the Atlantic (Ocean)** 大西洋 Dàxīyáng

atlas['ætləs] N [C] 地图册 dìtúcè [本 běn]

atmosphere['ætməsfɪər] N 1[C] [*of planet*] 大气层 dàqìcéng [个 gè] 2[S] 气氛 qìfēn

attach[ə'tætʃ] VT 附上 fùshàng

attachment[ə'tætʃmənt] N [C] [*of tool, computer file*] 附件 fùjiàn [个 gè]

attack[ə'tæk] I VT 1[+ *person*] 袭击 xíjī 2[+ *place, troops*] 攻击 gōngjī 3(*criticise*) 抨击 pēngjī II VI (*Mil, Sport*) 进攻 jìngōng III N 1[C/U] (*on person*) 袭击 xíjī [次 cì] 2[C/U] (*military assault*) 攻击 gōngjī [次 cì] 3[C/U] [*of illness*] 发作 fāzuò [阵 zhèn] ▶**an attack on sb** (*assault*) 袭击某人 xíjī mǒurén; (*criticism*) 抨击某人 pēngjī mǒurén

attempt[ə'tɛmpt] I N [C] (*try*) 尝试 chángshì [个 gè] II VI ▶**to attempt to do sth** 试图做某事 shìtú zuò mǒushì ▶**an attempt to do sth** 做某事的企图 zuò mǒushì de qìtú

attend[ə'tɛnd] VT 1[+ *school, church, course*] 上 shàng 2[+ *lecture, conference*] 参加 cānjiā

attention[ə'tɛnʃən] N [U] 1(*concentration*) 注意 zhùyì 2(*care*) 照料 zhàoliào ▶**to pay attention (to sth/sb)** 关注 (某事/某人) guānzhù (mǒushì/mǒurén)

attitude['ætɪtjuːd] N [C/U] 看法 kànfǎ [个 gè]

attorney[ə'tɜːnɪ] (US) N [c]
(lawyer) 律师 lǜshī [位 wèi]

attract[ə'trækt] VT 吸引 xīyǐn

attraction[ə'trækʃən] I N [U]
(charm, appeal) 吸引力 xīyǐnlì
II **attractions** NPL (also: **tourist
attractions**) (amusements) 游览胜
地 yóulǎn shèngdì

attractive[ə'træktɪv] ADJ [+ man,
woman] 有魅力的 yǒu mèilì de;
[+ thing, place] 吸引人的 xīyǐn rén
de ▶**he was very attractive to
women** 他对女人很有吸引力 tā
duì nǚrén hěnyǒu xīyǐnlì

auburn['ɔːbən] ADJ 赤褐色的
chìhèsè de

auction['ɔːkʃən] I N [c] 拍卖
pāimài [次 cì] II VT 拍卖 pāimài

audience['ɔːdɪəns] N [c] 1(in
theatre) 观众 guānzhòng [位
wèi] 2(Rad, TV) 听众 tīngzhòng
[位 wèi]

August['ɔːgəst] N [c/U] 八月
bāyuè; see also **July**

aunt[ɑːnt] N [c] (father's sister) 姑
母 gūmǔ [位 wèi]; (father's older
brother's wife) 伯母 bómǔ [位
wèi]; (father's younger brother's
wife) 婶母 shěnmǔ [位 wèi];
(mother's sister) 姨母 yímǔ [位
wèi]; (mother's brother's wife) 舅母
jiùmǔ [位 wèi]

auntie, aunty['ɑːntɪ] (inf) N
= **aunt**

au pair['əu'pɛər] N [c] 为学习语言
而住在当地人家里并提供家政服务
的外国年轻人

Australia[ɔs'treɪlɪə] N 澳大利
亚 Àodàlìyà

Australian[ɔs'treɪlɪən] I ADJ 澳
大利亚的 Àodàlìyà de II N [c]
(person) 澳大利亚人 Àodàlìyàrén
[个 gè]

Austria['ɔstrɪə] N 奥地利 Àodìlì

author['ɔːθər] N [c] (writer: of
novel) 作家 zuòjiā [位 wèi]; [of text]
作者 zuòzhě [个 gè]

autobiography[ɔːtəbaɪ'ɔgrəfɪ]
N [c] 自传 zìzhuàn [部 bù]

automatic[ɔːtə'mætɪk] I ADJ 自
动的 zìdòng de II N [c] (car) 自动
挡 zìdòngdǎng [个 gè]

automatically[ɔːtə'mætɪklɪ]
ADV 1(by itself) 自动地 zìdòng de
2(without thinking) 无意识地 wú
yìshi de 3(as a matter of course) 自
然而然地 zìrán'érrán de

automobile['ɔːtəməbiːl] (US) N
[c] 汽车 qìchē [辆 liàng]

autumn['ɔːtəm] (Brit) N [c/U] 秋
季 qiūjì [个 gè] ▶**in (the) autumn**
在秋季 zài qiūjì

available[ə'veɪləbl] ADJ 1 可用
的 kě yòng de 2[+ person] 有空的
yǒukòng de

avalanche['ævəlɑːnʃ] N [c] 雪崩
xuěbēng [次 cì]

average['ævərɪdʒ] I N [c] 1(Math:
mean) 平均数 píngjūnshù [个 gè]
2 ▶ **the average (for sth/sb)** (某
物/某人的)平均水平 (mǒuwù/
mǒurén de) píngjūn shuǐpíng
[个 gè] II ADJ (ordinary) 普通的
pǔtōng de ▶**on average** 平均
píngjūn ▶**above/below (the)
average** 高于/低于平均水平
gāoyú/dīyú píngjūn shuǐpíng

avoid[ə'vɔɪd] VT 1[+ person,

obstacle] 避免 bìmiǎn **2** [+ *trouble,
danger*] 防止 fángzhǐ ▶**to avoid
doing sth** 避免做某事 bìmiǎn
zuò mǒushì

awake [ə'weɪk] (*pt* **awoke**, *pp*
awoken *or* **awakened**) ADJ ▶**to
be awake** 醒着的 xǐngzhe de

award [ə'wɔːd] I N [c] (*prize*) 奖
jiǎng [个 gè] II VT [+ *prize*] 授予
shòuyǔ

aware [ə'wɛəʳ] ADJ ▶**to be aware
of sth** (*know about*) 意识到某事
yìshí dào mǒushì; (*be conscious of*)
觉察到某事 chájué dào mǒushì
▶**to be aware that...** 知道…
zhīdào…

away [ə'weɪ] I ADV **1** (*move, walk*)
…开 …kāi **2** (*not present*) 不在
bùzài II ADJ [+ *match, game*] 客场
的 kèchǎng de ▶**a week/month
away** 还有一个星期/月 háiyǒu
yīgè xīngqī/yuè ▶**two kilometres
away** 离这里两公里远 lí zhèlǐ
liǎng gōnglǐ yuǎn

awful ['ɔːfəl] I ADJ **1** 糟糕的
zāogāo de **2** [+ *shock, crime*] 可怕
的 kěpà de **3** ▶**to look/feel awful**
(*ill*) 看起来/感觉很糟糕的 kàn
qǐlái/gǎnjué hěn zāogāo de II ADV
(*US: inf: very*) 十分地 shífēn de
▶**an awful lot (of)** (*amount*) 大量
的 dàliàng de; (*number*) 非常多的
fēicháng duō de

awkward ['ɔːkwəd] ADJ
1 [+ *movement*] 笨拙的 bènzhuó
de **2** [+ *time, question*] 令人尴尬的
lìng rén gāngà de

axe, (*US*) **ax** [æks] N [c] 斧 fǔ
[把 bǎ]

baby ['beɪbɪ] N [c] 婴儿 yīng'ér
[个 gè] ▶**to have a baby** 生孩子
shēng háizi

baby carriage (*US*) N [c] 婴儿车
yīng'ér chē [辆 liàng]

babysit ['beɪbɪsɪt] (*pt, pp* **babysat**)
VI 代人照看孩子 dài rén zhàokàn
háizi

babysitter ['beɪbɪsɪtəʳ] N [c] 代
人照看孩子的人 dài rén zhàokàn
háizi de rén [个 gè]

bachelor ['bætʃələʳ] N [c]
1 (*unmarried man*) 单身汉
dānshēnhàn [个 gè] **2** ▶ **Bachelor
of Arts/Science** 文/理科学士学
位 wén/lǐkē xuéshì xuéwèi [个 gè]

back [bæk] I N [c] **1** 背部 bèibù
[个 gè] **2** 背面 bèimiàn [个 gè]; [*of
house, door, book*] 后面 hòumiàn

[个 gè]; [of car] 后部 hòubù [个 gè] **II** VT **1** (support) 支持 zhīchí; (financially) 资助 zīzhù **2** (reverse) 倒 dào **III** ADJ [+ garden, door, room, wheels] 后面的 hòumiàn de **IV** ADV **1** (not forward) 向后 xiàng hòu **2** (returned) 回 huí ▶ **to be back** 回来 huílái ▶ **can I have it back?** 我能要回它吗？wǒ néng yàohuí tā ma?
▶ **back down** VI 做出让步 zuòchū ràngbù
▶ **back out** VI (withdraw) 退出 tuìchū
▶ **back up** VT **1** [+ statement, theory] 证实 zhèngshí **2** (Comput) [+ disk] 备份 bèifèn

backache ['bækeɪk] N [c/u] 背痛 bèitòng [阵 zhèn]

background ['bækgraund] N **1** [c] [of picture, scene, events] 背景 bèijǐng [个 gè] **2** [c/u] [of person: origins] 出身 chūshēn [种 zhǒng]; (experience) 经验 jīngyàn [种 zhǒng] ▶ **in the background** 在背后 zài bèihòu

backing ['bækɪŋ] N [U] (support) 支持 zhīchí; (financial) 资助 zīzhù

backpack ['bækpæk] N [c] 双肩背包 shuāngjiān bēibāo [个 gè]

backpacker ['bækpækəʳ] N [c] 背包旅行者 bēibāo lǚxíngzhě [名 míng]

> ● **BACKPACKER**
> ●
> ● **backpacker** 一词指预算紧
> ● 张的青年旅行者。他们把全
> ● 部的随身物品放在一个背包

里，尽可能地节俭开支，为
的是能延长旅行时间多了解
一个地区，多看一些地方。

backstroke ['bækstrəuk] N [U] (also: **the backstroke**) 仰泳 yǎngyǒng

backup ['bækʌp] **I** ADJ (Comput) [+ copy, file, disk] 备份的 bèifèn de **II** N [U] (support) 支持 zhīchí

backward ['bækwəd] ADV (esp US) = **backwards**

backwards ['bækwədz] ADV 向后地 xiàng hòu de

backyard [bæk'jɑːd] N [c] 后院 hòuyuàn [个 gè]

bacon ['beɪkən] N [U] 腌猪肉 yān zhūròu

bad [bæd] ADJ **1** [+ weather, health, conditions, temper] 坏的 huài de; [+ actor, driver] 不胜任的 bù shèngrèn de; [+ behaviour, habit] 不良的 bùliáng de **2** (wicked) 恶的 è de **3** (naughty) 不听话的 bù tīnghuà de **4** [+ mistake, accident, headache] 严重的 yánzhòng de **5** [+ back, arm] 有病的 yǒubìng de **6** (rotten) 腐烂的 fǔlàn de ▶ **to be bad for sth/sb** 对某事/某物有害 duì mǒushì/mǒuwù yǒuhài ▶ **not bad** 不错 bùcuò

badge [bædʒ] N [c] (Brit) 徽章 huīzhāng [个 gè]

badly ['bædlɪ] ADV **1** (poorly) 不令人满意地 bù lìng rén mǎnyì de **2** (damaged, injured) 严重地 yánzhòng de

badminton ['bædmɪntən] N [U] 羽毛球 yǔmáoqiú

bad-tempered ['bæd'tɛmpəd]
ADJ 脾气坏的 píqi huài de

bag [bæg] N [c] **1** 袋 dài [个 gè]
2 (suitcase) 行李箱 xínglǐxiāng [个
gè] **3** (handbag) 手袋 shǒudài [个
gè] ▸ **to pack one's bags** 准备离
开 zhǔnbèi líkāi

baggage ['bægɪdʒ] N [U] 行
李 xíngli

baggage (re)claim N [U] 行李领
取 xíngli lǐngqǔ

bake [beɪk] VT 烤 kǎo

baker ['beɪkəʳ] N [c] (also:
baker's) 面包店 miànbāodiàn
[家 jiā]

bakery ['beɪkərɪ] N [c] 面包房
miànbāofáng [个 gè]

balance ['bæləns] N **1** [U] 平衡
pínghéng **2** [c] (in bank account) 余
额 yú'é [笔 bǐ] **3** [s] (remainder to
be paid) 余欠之数 yúqiàn zhī shù
▸ **to keep/lose one's balance**
保持/失去平衡 bǎochí/shīqù
pínghéng

balcony ['bælkənɪ] N [c] 露
台 lùtái [个 gè]; (covered) 阳台
yángtái [个 gè]

bald [bɔːld] ADJ 秃的 tū de ▸ **to go
bald** 变秃 biàntū

ball [bɔːl] N [c] 球 qiú [个 gè]

ballet ['bæleɪ, US bæ'leɪ] N [U] 芭
蕾舞 bālěiwǔ

ballet dancer N [c] 芭蕾舞演员
bālěiwǔ yǎnyuán [位 wèi]

balloon [bə'luːn] N [c] 气球 qìqiú
[只 zhī]

ballpoint (pen) ['bɔːlpɔɪnt(-)] N
[c] 圆珠笔 yuánzhūbǐ [支 zhī]

ban [bæn] I N [c] 禁止 jìnzhǐ [种

zhǒng] II VT 禁止 jìnzhǐ

banana [bə'nɑːnə] N [c] 香蕉
xiāngjiāo [只 zhī]

band [bænd] N [c] **1** (group) 群 qún
2 (Mus) 乐队 yuèduì [个 gè]

bandage ['bændɪdʒ] N [c] 绷带
bēngdài [条 tiáo]

Band-Aid® ['bændeɪd] (US) N [c]
邦迪创可贴 Bāngdí chuàngkětiē
[贴 tiē]

bang [bæŋ] I N [c] **1** (noise) 砰的
一声 pēng de yīshēng; [of gun,
exhaust] 爆炸声 bàozhà shēng [阵
zhèn] **2** (blow) 撞击 zhuàngjī [下
xià] II VT [+ one's head, elbow] 撞
zhuàng III **bangs** NPL (US: fringe)
刘海 liúhǎi ▸ **to bang into sth/sb**
猛撞某物/某人 měngzhuàng
mǒuwù/mǒurén

Bangladesh [bæŋglə'dɛʃ] N 孟加
拉国 Mèngjiālāguó

bank [bæŋk] N [c] **1** (Fin) 银行
yínháng [家 jiā] **2** [of river, lake] 岸
àn [个 gè]

bank account N [c] 银行账户
yínháng zhànghù [个 gè]

bank card N [c] **1** (Brit: for cash
machine) 银行卡 yínhángkǎ [张
zhāng] **2** (US: credit card) 行信用
卡 yínháng xìnyòngkǎ [张 zhāng]

bank holiday (Brit) N [c] 法定假
期 fǎdìng jiàqī [个 gè]

banknote ['bæŋknəut] N [c] 纸
币 zhǐbì [张 zhāng]

bar [bɑːʳ] N [c] **1** 酒吧 jiǔbā [个 gè]
2 (counter) 吧台 bātái [个 gè] **3** 条
tiáo **4** (tablet: of soap, chocolate)
块 kuài

barbecue ['bɑːbɪkjuː] N [c] 烧烤

聚会 shāokǎo jùhuì [次 cì]

barefoot(ed) [ˈbɛəfut(ɪd)] ADV 赤脚地 chìjiǎo de

barely [ˈbɛəlɪ] ADV 几乎不 jīhū bù

bargain [ˈbaːgɪn] N [c] 1 (good buy) 廉价品 liánjiàpǐn [件 jiàn] 2 (deal, agreement) 协议 xiéyì [个 gè]

barge [baːdʒ] N [c] 驳船 bóchuán [艘 sōu]

bark [baːk] VI (dog) 叫 jiào

barmaid [ˈbaːmeɪd] (esp Brit) N [c] 酒吧女侍 jiǔbā nǚshì [个 gè]

barman [ˈbaːmən] (pl **barmen**) (esp Brit) N [c] 酒吧男侍 jiǔbā nánshì [个 gè]

barrel [ˈbærəl] N [c] 桶 tǒng [个 gè]

barrier [ˈbærɪəʳ] N [c] 关口 guānkǒu [个 gè]

bartender [ˈbaːtɛndəʳ] (US) N [c] 酒吧侍者 jiǔbā shìzhě [个 gè]

base [beɪs] N [c] 1 (bottom) 底部 dǐbù [个 gè] 2 (basis) 根基 gēnjī [个 gè] 3 基地 jīdì [个 gè]; (for individual, organization) 总部 zǒngbù [个 gè] ▶**to be based on sth** 以某物为根据 yǐ mǒuwù wéi gēnjù ▶**I'm based in London** 我长驻伦敦 wǒ chángzhù Lúndūn

baseball [ˈbeɪsbɔːl] N [U] 棒球 bàngqiú

basement [ˈbeɪsmənt] N [c] 地下室 dìxiàshì [间 jiān]

basic [ˈbeɪsɪk] ADJ 基本的 jīběn de; see also **basics**

basically [ˈbeɪsɪklɪ] ADV 1 (fundamentally) 基本上 jīběnshang 2 (in fact, put simply) 简而言之 jiǎn ér yán zhī

basics [ˈbeɪsɪks] NPL ▶**the basics** 基本点 jīběndiǎn

basin [ˈbeɪsn] N [c] 1 (bowl) 盆 pén [个 gè] 2 (also: **wash basin**) 洗脸盆 xǐliǎnpén [个 gè] 3 (of river, lake) 流域 liúyù [个 gè]

basket [ˈbaːskɪt] N [c] 筐 kuāng [个 gè]

basketball [ˈbaːskɪtbɔːl] N [U] 篮球 lánqiú

bat [bæt] N [c] 1 (animal) 蝙蝠 biānfú [只 zhī] 2 (for cricket, baseball) 球板/棒 qiúbǎn/bàng [只 zhī] 3 (Brit: for table tennis) 球拍 qiúpāi [只 zhī]

bath [baːθ] N [c] 1 (Brit: bathtub) 浴缸 yùgāng [个 gè] 2 (act of bathing) 洗澡 xǐzǎo [次 cì] ▶**to have** or **take a bath** 洗澡 xǐzǎo

bathe [beɪð] VI (esp Brit) 戏水 xìshuǐ 2 (esp US: have a bath) 洗澡 xǐzǎo

bathroom [ˈbaːθrum] N [c] 1 卫生间 wèishēngjiān [个 gè] 2 (US: toilet) 厕所 cèsuǒ [处 chù] ▶**to go to the bathroom** (US) 去卫生间 qù wèishēngjiān

bathtub [ˈbaːθtʌb] (US) N [c] 浴缸 yùgāng [个 gè]

battery [ˈbætərɪ] N [c] 1 电池 diànchí [块 kuài] 2 (in car) 电瓶 diànpíng [个 gè]

battle [ˈbætl] N [c] 1 (Mil) 战役 zhànyì [场 chǎng] 2 (fig: struggle) 斗争 dòuzhēng [场 chǎng]

bay [beɪ] N [c] 湾 wān [个 gè]

BC ADV ABBR (= **before Christ**) 公

元前 gōngyuán qián

◯ **KEYWORD**

be [biː] (pt **was, were**, pp **been**)

I VI **1** (with complement) 是 shì
▶**I'm English/Chinese** 我是英
国人/中国人 wǒ shì Yīngguórén/
Zhōngguórén ▶**she's tall/pretty**
她长得高/漂亮 tā zhǎngde gāo/
piàoliàng ▶**this is my mother** 这
是我妈妈 zhèshì wǒ māma ▶**who
is it?** 是谁啊? shì shuí a? ▶**be
careful/quiet!** 当心/安静!
dāngxīn/ānjìng!

2 (referring to time, date) 是 shì
▶**it's 5 o'clock** 现在是5点钟
xiànzài shì wǔdiǎnzhōng

3 (describing weather) ▶**it's hot/
cold** 天热/冷 tiān rè/lěng

4 (talking about health) ▶**how are
you?** 你身体怎么样? nǐ shēntǐ
zěnmeyàng?

5 (talking about age) 有 yǒu ▶**how
old are you?** 你多大了? nǐ
duōdà le?

6 (talking about place) 在 zài
▶**Madrid is in Spain** 马德里在
西班牙 Mǎdélǐ zài Xībānyá ▶**the
supermarket isn't far from
here** 超市离这儿不远 chāoshì lí
zhè'er bùyuǎn ▶**I won't be here
tomorrow** 我明天不在这儿 wǒ
míngtiān bùzài zhè'er ▶**have you
been to Beijing?** 你去过北京吗?
nǐ qùguò Běijīng ma? ▶**we've
been here for ages** 我们已经在这
里好久了 wǒmen yǐjīng zài zhèlǐ
hǎojiǔ le ▶**the meeting will be in**

the canteen 会议将在食堂举行
huìyì jiāng zài shítáng jǔxíng

7 (referring to distance) 有 yǒu ▶**it's
10 km to the village** 这儿离村庄
有10公里 zhè'er lí cūnzhuāng yǒu
shí gōnglǐ

8 (cost) 花 huā ▶**how much was
the meal?** 这顿饭花了多少钱?
zhèdùn fàn huāle duōshǎo qián?
▶**that'll be £5 please** 请付5英镑
qǐngfù wǔyīngbàng

9 (linking clauses) 是 shì ▶**the
problem is that ...** 问题是…
wèntí shì…

II AUX VB **1** (forming continuous
tenses) ▶**what are you doing?** 你
在干什么? nǐ zài gàn shénme?
▶**they're coming tomorrow** 他
们明天来 tāmen míngtiān lái

2 (forming passives) ▶**to be
murdered** 被谋杀 bèi móushā
▶**he was killed in a car crash** 他
在一场车祸中丧生 tā zài yīchǎng
chēhuò zhōng sàngshēng

3 (in tag questions) ▶**it was
fun, wasn't it?** 有意思,是不
是? yǒu yìsi, shì bù shì? ▶**he's
good-looking, isn't he?** 他长得不
错,是不是? tā zhǎngde bùcuò,
shìbùshì?

beach [biːtʃ] N [c] 海滩 hǎitān
[片 piàn]

beads [biːdz] NPL (necklace) 项链
xiàngliàn

beam [biːm] N [c] (of wood, metal)
梁 liáng [根 gēn]

bean [biːn] N [c] 豆 dòu [粒 lì]
▶**coffee/cocoa beans** 咖啡/可可

豆 kāfēi/kěkě dòu

bear [bɛə^r] (*pt* **bore**, *pp* **borne**)
I N [c] 熊 xióng [头 tóu] II VT
1 (*tolerate*) 容忍 róngrěn 2 (*endure*)
忍受 rěnshòu

beard [bɪəd] N [c] 胡须 húxū
[根 gēn]

beat [bi:t] (*pt* **beat**, *pp* **beaten**) VT
[+ *opponent, record*] 击败 jībài

beaten [ˈbi:tn] PP *of* **beat**

beautiful [ˈbju:tɪful] ADJ 1 美丽的
měilì de 2 [+ *shot, performance*] 精
彩的 jīngcǎi de

beautifully [ˈbju:tɪflɪ] ADV 极好
地 jíhǎo de

beauty [ˈbju:tɪ] N [U] 美 měi

became [bɪˈkeɪm] PT *of* **become**

because [bɪˈkɔz] CONJ 因为
yīnwéi ▶**because of** 因为 yīnwéi
我们在解释一件事发生
的原因时，可以使用
because, **as** 或 **since**。
because 最为常用，并且
是唯一可以回答 **why**
提出的问题。'Why can't
you come?' — 'Because I'm
too busy.' 在引出含有原因
的从句时，尤其是在书面
语中，我们可以用 **as** 或
since 代替 **because**。
I was rather nervous, as I
hadn't seen her for a long
time...Since the juice is quite
strong, you should always
dilute it.

become [bɪˈkʌm] (*pt* **became**,
pp **become**) VI 1 (+ *noun*) 成为
chéngwéi 2 (+ *adj*) 变 biàn

bed [bɛd] N [c] 床 chuáng [张
zhāng] ▶**to go to bed** 去睡觉 qù

shuìjiào

bed and breakfast N [U] 住宿加
早餐 zhùsù jiā zǎocān

bedding [ˈbɛdɪŋ] N [U] 床上用品
chuángshang yòngpǐn

bedroom [ˈbɛdrum] N [c] 卧室
wòshì [间 jiān]

bee [bi:] N [c] 蜜蜂 mìfēng [只 zhī]

beef [bi:f] N [U] 牛肉 niúròu
▶**roast beef** 烤牛肉 kǎo niúròu

beefburger [ˈbi:fbə:gə^r] (*Brit*)
[c] 牛肉汉堡包 niúròu hànbǎobāo
[个 gè]

been [bi:n] PP *of* **be**

beer [bɪə^r] N [U] 啤酒 píjiǔ
▶**would you like a beer?** 你想喝
一瓶啤酒吗? nǐ xiǎng hē yīpíng
píjiǔ ma?

beet [bi:t] N [c] (*US: red vegetable*)
甜菜根 tiáncàigēn [根 gēn]

beetle [ˈbi:tl] N [c] 甲虫 jiǎchóng
[只 zhī]

beetroot [ˈbi:tru:t] (*Brit*) N [c/u]
甜菜根 tiáncàigēn [根 gēn]

before [bɪˈfɔ:^{r}] I PREP 之
前 zhīqián II CONJ 在…之前
zài...zhīqián III ADV 以前 yǐqián
▶**before doing sth** 在做某事之
前 zài zuò mǒushì zhīqián ▶**I've
never seen it before** 我以前从没
见过 wǒ yǐqián cóngméi jiànguò

beg [bɛg] VI [*beggar*] 乞讨 qǐtǎo ▶**I
beg your pardon** (*apologizing*) 对
不起 duìbùqǐ; (*not hearing*) 请再说
一遍 qǐng zàishuō yībiàn

began [bɪˈgæn] PT *of* **begin**

beggar [ˈbɛgə^r] N [c] 乞丐 qǐgài
[个 gè]

begin [bɪˈgɪn] (*pt* **began**, *pp*

begun) I VT 开始 kāishǐ II VI 开始 kāishǐ ▸to begin doing or to do sth 开始做某事 kāishǐ zuò mǒushì

beginner [bɪ'gɪnə^r] N [c] 初学者 chūxuézhě [位 wèi]

beginning [bɪ'gɪnɪŋ] N [c] 开始 kāishǐ [个 gè] ▸at the beginning 开始时 kāishǐ shí

begun [bɪ'gʌn] PP of **begin**

behave [bɪ'heɪv] VI 表现 biǎoxiàn

behaviour , (US) **behavior** [bɪ'heɪvjə^r] N [U] 举止 jǔzhǐ

behind [bɪ'haɪnd] I PREP 在…后面 zài…hòumian II ADV (at/towards the back) 在/向后面 zài/xiàng hòumian ▸to be behind (schedule) 落后于(计划) luòhòu yú (jìhuà) ▸to leave sth behind (forget) 落下 luòxià

beige [beɪʒ] ADJ 灰棕色的 huīzōngsè de

Beijing ['beɪ'dʒɪŋ] N 北京 Běijīng

Belgian ['bɛldʒən] I ADJ 比利时的 Bǐlìshí de II N [c] (person) 比利时人 Bǐlìshírén [个 gè]

Belgium ['bɛldʒəm] N 比利时 Bǐlìshí

believe [bɪ'liːv] VT 相信 xiāngxìn ▸to believe that ... 认为… rènwéi…

bell [bɛl] N [c] (on door) 门铃 ménlíng [个 gè]

belong [bɪ'lɔŋ] VI ▸to belong to [+ person] 属于 shǔyú; [+ club, society] 是…的成员 shì…de chéngyuán

belongings [bɪ'lɔŋɪŋz] NPL 所有物 suǒyǒuwù

below [bɪ'ləu] I PREP 1 (beneath) 在…之下 zài…zhīxià 2 (less than) 低于 dīyú II ADV 1 (beneath) 下面 xiàmian 2 (less) 以下 yǐxià ▸below zero 零度以下 língdù yǐxià ▸temperatures below normal or average 低于正常{或}平均温度 dīyú zhèngcháng (huò) píngjūn wēndù

belt [bɛlt] N [c] 腰带 yāodài [条 tiáo]

bench [bɛntʃ] N [c] 长椅 chángyǐ [条 tiáo]

bend [bɛnd] (pt, pp bent) I VT 使弯曲 shǐ wānqū II VI 1 屈身 qūshēn 2 [road, river] 转弯 zhuǎnwān III N [c] (in road, river) 弯 wān [个 gè] ▸bend down VI 弯腰 wānyāo

beneath [bɪ'niːθ] I PREP 在…之下 zài…zhīxià II ADV 在下面 zài xiàmian

benefit ['bɛnɪfɪt] I N [c/u] 好处 hǎochù [个 gè] II VI ▸to benefit from sth 从某事中获益 cóng mǒushì zhōng huòyì

bent [bɛnt] I PT, PP of **bend** II ADJ 弯曲的 wānqū de

berth [bə:θ] N [c] 卧铺 wòpù [张 zhāng]

beside [bɪ'saɪd] PREP 在…旁边 zài…pángbiān; see also **besides**

besides [bɪ'saɪdz] I ADV (also: beside) (in addition) 另外 lìngwài II PREP (also: beside) (in addition to, as well as) 除…之外 chú…zhīwài

> **besides** 引出的事物包括在我们所谈及的事情之内。She is very intelligent besides being very beautiful.

不过，当我们说 **the only person besides** 另外某人时，或 **the only thing besides** 另外某物时，我们指在某一特定场合或上下文中的惟一其他人或物。*There was only one person besides me who knew where the money was hidden.* 介词 **except** 后面通常跟我们的陈述中惟独不包括的那些物，人，事的名词或代词形式。*She spoke to everyone except me.* **except** 也可作连词，引导从句或副词短语。*There was nothing more to do now except wait.* **except** 还可以引出由连词 **that**，**when** 或 **if** 引导的从句。*The house stayed empty, except when we came for the holidays.* **except for** 是用在名词前的介词短语，用来引出某人或某物，说明要不是有某人或某物，所陈述的便为全部事实。*Everyone was late except for Richard.*

best [bɛst] I ADJ 最好的 zuìhǎo de II ADV 最 zuì III N ▸ **the best** 最好的事物 zuìhǎo de shìwù ▸ **the best thing to do is …** 最好是… zuìhǎo shì… ▸ **to do** or **try one's best** 尽某人最大的努力 jìn mǒurén zuìdà de nǔlì

bet [bɛt] (pt, pp bet or betted) I N [c] 赌注 dǔzhù [个 gè] II VT1 ▸ **to bet sb 100 pounds that…** 就…和某人赌100英镑 jiù…hé mǒurén

dǔ yībǎi yīngbàng 2 (expect, guess) ▸ **to bet (that)** 断定 duàndìng III VI ▸ **to bet on** [+ horse, result] 下赌注于 xià dǔzhù yú

better ['bɛtər] I ADJ 1 (comparative of good) 更好的 gènghǎo de 2 (after an illness or injury) 好转的 hǎozhuǎn de II ADV (comparative of well) 更好地 gènghǎo de ▸ **to get better** (improve) 变得更好 biànde gènghǎo; [sick person] 渐愈 jiànyù ▸ **to feel better** 感觉好一些 gǎnjué hǎo yīxiē ▸ **I'd better go** or **I had better go** 我得走了 wǒ děi zǒule

between [bɪ'twiːn] I PREP 1 (in space) 在…中间 zài…zhōngjiān 2 (in time) 介于…之间 jièyú…zhījiān 3 (in amount, age) 介于…之间 jièyú…zhījiān II ADV ▸ **in between** (in space) 在…中间 zài…zhōngjiān; (in time) 期间 qījiān ▸ **to choose between** 从中选一个 cóngzhōng xuǎn yīgè ▸ **to be shared/divided between people** 由大家一起分享/分用 yóu dàjiā yīqǐ fēnxiǎng/fēnyòng

beyond [bɪ'jɔnd] I PREP 1 在…的另一边 zài…de lìng yībiān 2 [+ time, date, age] 迟于 chíyú II ADV 1 (in space) 在另一边 zài lìng yībiān 2 (in time) 在…之后 zài…zhīhòu

Bible ['baɪbl] (Rel) N [c] ▸ **the Bible** 圣经 Shèngjīng [部 bù]

bicycle ['baɪsɪkl] N [c] 自行车 zìxíngchē [辆 liàng] ▸ **to ride a bicycle** 骑自行车 qí zìxíngchē

big [bɪg] ADJ 1 大的 dà de

2 [+ *change, increase, problem*] 大的 dà de

bike [baɪk] N [c] **1** (*bicycle*) 自行车 zìxíngchē [辆 liàng] **2** (*motorcycle*) 摩托车 mótuōchē [部 bù]

bikini [bɪ'ki:nɪ] N [c] 比基尼 bǐjīní [套 tào]

bill [bɪl] N [c] **1** (*requesting payment*) 账单 zhàngdān [个 gè] **2** (*Brit: in restaurant*) 账单 zhàngdān [个 gè] **3** (*US: banknote*) 钞票 chāopiào [张 zhāng]

billfold ['bɪlfəuld] (*US*) N [c] 钱夹 qiánjiā [个 gè]

billion ['bɪljən] N [c] 十亿 shíyì

bin [bɪn] N [c] (*Brit*) 垃圾箱 lājīxiāng [个 gè]

binoculars [bɪ'nɔkjuləz] NPL 双筒望远镜 shuāngtǒng wàngyuǎnjìng

biochemistry [baɪə'kɛmɪstrɪ] N [U] 生物化学 shēngwù huàxué

biography [baɪ'ɔgrəfɪ] N [c] 传记 zhuànjì [部 bù]

biology [baɪ'ɔlədʒɪ] N [U] 生物学 shēngwùxué

bird [bə:d] N [c] 鸟 niǎo [只 zhī]

Biro® ['baɪərəu] (*Brit*) N [c] 圆珠笔 yuánzhūbǐ [支 zhī]

birth [bə:θ] N [c/U] 出生 chūshēng

birth certificate N [c] 出生证明 chūshēng zhèngmíng [个 gè]

birth control N [U] 节育 jiéyù

birthday ['bə:θdeɪ] I N [c] 生日 shēngrì [个 gè] II CPD [+ *cake, card, present*] 生日 shēngrì

biscuit ['bɪskɪt] N [c] **1** (*Brit*) 饼干 bǐnggān [片 piàn] **2** (*US*) 小圆饼 xiǎoyuánbǐng [张 zhāng]

bishop ['bɪʃəp] N [c] 主教 zhǔjiào [位 wèi]

bit [bɪt] I PT *of* **bite** II N [c] **1** (*esp Brit: piece*) 少许 shǎoxǔ **2** (*esp Brit: part*) 部分 bùfen [个 gè] **3** (*Comput*) 比特 bǐtè [个 gè] ▸ **a bit mad/dangerous** 有点疯狂/危险 yǒudiǎn fēngkuáng/wēixiǎn ▸ **for a bit** (*inf*) 一会儿 yīhuǐr ▸ **quite a bit** 不少 bùshǎo

bite [baɪt] (*pt* **bit**, *pp* **bitten** ['bɪtn]) I VT 咬 yǎo II N [c] **1** (*mouthful*) 口 kǒu **2** (*from dog*) 咬伤 yǎoshāng [处 chù] **3** (*from snake, mosquito*) 咬痕 yǎohén [个 gè] ▸ **to bite one's nails** 咬指甲 yǎo zhǐjia

bitter ['bɪtəʳ] ADJ [+ *taste*] 苦的 kǔ de

black [blæk] I ADJ **1** 黑色的 hēisè de **2** [+ *person*] 黑人的 hēirén de **3** [+ *tea, coffee*] 不加牛奶的 bù jiā niúnǎi de II N [U] 黑色 hēisè ▸ **black out** VI (*faint*) 暂时失去知觉 zànshí shīqù zhījué

blackboard ['blækbɔ:d] N [c] 黑板 hēibǎn [个 gè]

blackmail ['blækmeɪl] I N [U] 敲诈 qiāozhà II VT 敲诈 qiāozhà

blade [bleɪd] N [c] 刃 rèn

blame [bleɪm] I N [U] (*for mistake, crime*) 责备 zébèi II VT ▸ **to blame sb for sth** 为某事责备某人 wèi mǒushì zébèi mǒurén ▸ **to be to blame (for sth)** 该 (为某事) 负责任 gāi (wèi mǒushì) fù zérèn ▸ **to blame sth on sb** 把某事归咎于某人 bǎ mǒushì guījiù yú mǒurén

blank [blæŋk] ADJ 空白的 kòngbái de

blanket ['blæŋkɪt] N [c] 毛毯 máotǎn [床 chuáng]

blast [blɑːst] N [c] (explosion) 爆炸 bàozhà [次 cì]

blaze [bleɪz] I N [c] 大火 dàhuǒ [场 chǎng] II VI (fire) 熊熊燃烧 xióngxióng ránshāo

blazer ['bleɪzər] N [c] 上装 shàngzhuāng [件 jiàn]

bleed [bliːd] (pt, pp **bled** [blɛd]) VI 流血 liúxuè ▶**my nose is bleeding** 我流鼻血了 wǒ liú bíxuè le

blender ['blɛndər] N [c] 搅拌器 jiǎobànqì [个 gè]

bless [blɛs] VT (Rel) 赐福 cìfú ▶**bless you!** (after sneeze) 上帝保佑! shàngdì bǎoyòu!

blew [bluː] PT of **blow**

blind [blaɪnd] I ADJ 失明的 shīmíng de II (for window) 向上卷的帘子 xiàng shàng juǎn de liánzi III the blind NPL (blind people) 盲人 mángrén ▶**to go blind** 失明 shīmíng

blink [blɪŋk] VI 眨眼睛 zhǎ yǎnjīng

blister ['blɪstər] N [c] 水泡 shuǐpào [个 gè]

blizzard ['blɪzəd] N [c] 暴风雪 bàofēngxuě [场 chǎng]

block [blɔk] I N [c] 1 街区 jiēqū [个 gè] 2 (of stone, wood, ice) 块 kuài II VT [+ entrance, road] 堵塞 dǔsè ▶**block of flats** or (US) **apartment block** 公寓楼 gōngyùlóu ▶**3 blocks from here** 离这里有3个街区那么远 lí zhèlǐ yǒu sāngè jiēqū nàme yuǎn

blond(e) [blɔnd] ADJ 1 [+ hair] 金色的 jīnsè de 2 [+ person] 金发的人 jīnfà de rén

blood [blʌd] N [U] 血液 xuèyè

blood pressure N [U] 血压 xuèyā ▶**to have high/low blood pressure** 有高/低血压 yǒu gāo/dī xuèyā ▶**to take sb's blood pressure** 量某人的血压 liáng mǒurén de xuèyā

blood test N [c] 验血 yànxuè [次 cì] ▶**to have a blood test** 验血 yànxuè

blouse [blauz, US blaus] N [c] 女士衬衫 nǚshì chènshān [件 jiàn]

blow [bləu] (pt **blew**, pp **blown**) I N [c] 1 (punch) 拳打 quándǎ [顿 dùn] 2 打击 dǎjī [个 gè] II VI 1 [wind, sand, dust etc] 吹 chuī 2 [person] 吹气 chuīqì III VT [wind] 吹 chuī ▶**to blow one's nose** 擤鼻子 xǐng bízi ▶**blow away** I VT 吹走 chuīzǒu II VI 刮跑 guāpǎo ▶**blow down** VT [+ tree, house] 刮倒 guādǎo ▶**blow out** VT [+ flame, candle] 吹灭 chuīmiè ▶**blow up** I VI (explode) 爆炸 bàozhà II VT 1 (destroy) 使爆炸 shǐ bàozhà 2 (inflate) 冲气 chōngqì

blow-dry ['bləudraɪ] N [c] 吹风定型 chuīfēng dìngxíng

blown [bləun] PP of **blow**

blue [bluː] I ADJ 蓝色的 lánsè de II N [U] 蓝色 lánsè III blues NPL (Mus) ▶**the blues** 蓝调 lándiào

blunt [blʌnt] ADJ 1 (not sharp) 钝的 dùn de 2 [+ person, remark] 直率的 zhíshuài de

blush [blʌʃ] VI 脸红 liǎnhóng

board [bɔːd] I N 1 [c] (*piece of wood*) 木板 mùbǎn [块 kuài] 2 [c] (*also:* **noticeboard**) 公告板 gōnggàobǎn [块 kuài] 3 [c] (*also:* **blackboard**) 黑板 hēibǎn [个 gè] 4 [c] (*for chess*) 盘 pán 5 [U] (*at hotel*) 膳食 shànshí II VT [+ *ship, train, plane*] 上 shàng III VI (*frm: on ship, train, plane*) 登上 dēngshang
▶**board and lodging** 食宿 shísù
▶**on board** 在船/车/飞机上 zài chuán/chē/fēijī shàng

boarding card ['bɔːdɪŋ-] N [c] 登机卡 dēngjīkǎ [张 zhāng]

boarding school N [c/U] 寄宿学校 jìsù xuéxiào [个 gè]

boast [bəust] I VI ▶**to boast (about** *or* **of)** 说(关于某事的)大话 shuō (guānyú mǒushì de) dàhuà II N [c] 自夸 zìkuā [种 zhǒng]

boat [bəut] N [c] 1 (*small vessel*) 船 chuán [艘 sōu] 2 (*ship*) 轮船 lúnchuán [艘 sōu] ▶**to go by boat** 乘船去 chéngchuán qù

body ['bɔdɪ] N 1 [c] 身体 shēntǐ [个 gè] 2 [c] (*corpse*) 尸体 shītǐ [具 jù]

bodybuilding ['bɔdɪ'bɪldɪŋ] N [U] 健身 jiànshēn

bodyguard ['bɔdɪgɑːd] N [c] 保镖 bǎobiāo [个 gè]

boil [bɔɪl] I VT 1 [+ *water*] 烧开 shāokāi 2 [+ *eggs, potatoes*] 煮 zhǔ II VI [*liquid*] 沸腾 fèiténg III N (*Med*) 疖子 jiēzi ▶**to boil a kettle** 烧开水 shāo kāishuǐ

boiler ['bɔɪləʳ] N [c] (*device*) 锅炉 guōlú [个 gè]

boiling (hot) ['bɔɪlɪŋ-] (*inf*) ADJ
▶**I'm boiling (hot)** 我太热了 wǒ tài rè le

bolt [bəult] N [c] 1 (*to lock door*) 插销 chāxiāo [个 gè] 2 (*used with nut*) 螺钉 luódīng [颗 kē]

bomb [bɔm] I N [c] 炸弹 zhàdàn [颗 kē] II VT 轰炸 hōngzhà

bomber ['bɔməʳ] N [c] 1 (*Aviat*) 轰炸机 hōngzhàjī [架 jià] 2 (*terrorist*) 投放炸弹的人 tóufàng zhàdàn de rén [个 gè]

bombing ['bɔmɪŋ] N [c/U] 轰炸 hōngzhà [阵 zhèn]

bone [bəun] N 1 [c/U] 骨头 gǔtou [根 gēn] 2 [c] (*in fish*) 刺 cì [根 gēn]

bonfire ['bɔnfaɪəʳ] N [c] 1 (*as part of a celebration*) 篝火 gōuhuǒ [堆 duī] 2 (*to burn rubbish*) 火堆 huǒduī [个 gè]

bonnet ['bɔnɪt] N [c] (*Brit: of car*) 引擎罩 yǐnqíngzhào [个 gè]

bonus ['bəunəs] N [c] 1 (*extra payment*) 红利 hónglì [份 fèn] 2 (*additional benefit*) 额外收获 éwài shōuhuò [份 fèn]

book [buk] I N [c] 1 (*novel etc*) 书 shū [本 běn] 2 [*of stamps, tickets*] 册 cè II VT [+ *ticket, table, seat, room*] 预订 yùdìng ▶**fully booked** 预订一空 yùdìng yīkōng
▶**book into** (*Brit*) VT FUS [+ *hotel*] 登记入住 dēngjì rùzhù

bookcase ['bukkeɪs] N [c] 书橱 shūchú [个 gè]

booklet ['buklɪt] N [c] 小册子 xiǎocèzi [本 běn]

bookshelf ['bukʃɛlf] N [c] 书架 shūjià [个 gè]

bookshop ['bʊkʃɔp] (*Brit*) N [c] 书
店 shūdiàn [家 jiā]
bookstore ['bʊkstɔːʳ] (*esp US*) N =
bookshop
boot [buːt] N [c] 1 靴子 xuēzi [双
shuāng]; (*for football, walking*) 鞋
xié [双 shuāng] 2 (*Brit: of car*) 车后
行李箱 chē hòu xínglǐxiāng [个 gè]
▶ **boot up** (*Comput*) I VT 使运行
shǐ yùnxíng II VI 开始运行 kāishǐ
yùnxíng
border ['bɔːdəʳ] N [c] 边界 biānjiè
[条 tiáo]
bore [bɔːʳ] I PT *of* **bear** II VT
1 [+ *hole*] 钻 zuàn 2 [+ *oil well,
tunnel*] 开凿 kāizáo 3 [+ *person*]
使厌烦 shǐ yànfán ▶ **to be bored
(with sth)** (对某事) 不感兴趣 (duì
mǒushì) bùgǎn xìngqù
boring ['bɔːrɪŋ] ADJ 乏味的
fáwèi de
born [bɔːn] ADJ ▶ **to be born**
[*baby*] 出生 chūshēng
borrow ['bɔrəʊ] VT 借 jiè
boss [bɔs] N [c] 1 (*employer*) 老板
lǎobǎn [个 gè] 2 (*inf: leader*) 领导
lǐngdǎo [位 wèi]
both [bəʊθ] I ADJ 两者都 liǎngzhě
dōu II PRON 1 (*things*) 两者
liǎngzhě 2 (*people*) 两个 liǎnggè
III CONJ ▶ **both A and B** A和B两者
都 A hé B liǎngzhě dōu ▶ **both of
us went** *or* **we both went** 我们两
个都去了 wǒmen liǎnggè dōuqù le
bother ['bɔðəʳ] I VT 1 (*worry*) 烦
扰 fánrǎo 2 (*disturb*) 打扰 dǎrǎo
II VI 在乎 zàihu III N [U] (*trouble*)
麻烦 máfan ▶ **don't bother** 不用
了 bùyòng le

bottle ['bɔtl] N [c] 1 瓶子 píngzi
[个 gè] 2 [c] (*amount contained*) 瓶
píng 3 [c] (*baby's*) 奶瓶 nǎipíng [个
gè] ▶ **a bottle of wine/milk** 一瓶
葡萄酒/牛奶 yīpíng pútáojiǔ/
niúnǎi
bottle opener N [c] 开瓶器
kāipíngqì [个 gè]
bottom ['bɔtəm] I N 1 [c] [*of
container, sea*] 底部 dǐbù [个 gè]
2 [c] [*of page, list*] 下端 xiàduān
[个 gè] 3 [U/s] [*of class, league*] 最
后一名 zuìhòu yīmíng 4 [c] [*of hill,
tree, stairs*] 最底部 zuìdǐbù [个 gè]
5 [c] (*buttocks*) 臀部 túnbù [个
gè] II ADJ (*lowest*) 最下面的 zuì
xiàmiàn de ▶ **at the bottom of**
在…的底部 zài…de dǐbù
bought [bɔːt] PT, PP *of* **buy**
bound [baʊnd] ADJ ▶ **to be
bound to do sth** (*certain*) 一定做
某事 yīdìng zuò mǒushì
boundary ['baʊndrɪ] N [c] 边界
biānjiè [个 gè]
bow¹ [bəʊ] N [c] 1 (*knot*) 蝴蝶结
húdiéjié [个 gè] 2 (*weapon*) 弓
gōng [把 bǎ]
bow² [baʊ] I VI (*with head, body*) 鞠
躬 jūgōng II VT [+ *head*] 低头 dītóu
bowl [bəʊl] N [c] 1 碗 wǎn [个 gè]
2 (*contents*) 一碗的量 yī wǎn de
liàng 3 (*for washing clothes/dishes*)
盆 pén [个 gè]
bowling ['bəʊlɪŋ] N [U] 保龄球
bǎolíngqiú ▶ **to go bowling** 打保
龄球 dǎ bǎolíngqiú
bow tie [bəʊ-] N [c] 蝶形领结
diéxíng lǐngjié [个 gè]
box [bɔks] I N [c] 1 (*container*) 盒

子 hézi [个 gè] **2** (*contents*) 盒
hé **3** (*also*: **cardboard box**) 纸箱
zhǐxiāng [个 gè] **4** (*crate*) 箱 xiāng
II VI (*Sport*) 拳击 quánjī

boxer ['bɒksər] N [c] (*Sport*) 拳击运动员
quánjī yùndòngyuán [位 wèi]

boxer shorts, boxers NPL 平角
裤 píngjiǎokù

boxing ['bɒksɪŋ] (*Sport*) N [U] 拳
击 quánjī

Boxing Day (*Brit*) N [c/U] 圣诞节
后的第一天，是公共假日

boy [bɔɪ] N [c] **1** (*male child*) 男孩
nánhái [个 gè] **2** (*young man*) 男青
年 nán qīngnián [个 gè]

boyfriend ['bɔɪfrɛnd] N [c] 男朋
友 nánpéngyou [个 gè]

bra [brɑː] N [c] 胸罩 xiōngzhào
[件 jiàn]

bracelet ['breɪslɪt] N [c] 手镯
shǒuzhuó [只 zhī]

braid [breɪd] N [c] (*US*: **plait**) 辫子
biànzi [条 tiáo]

brain [breɪn] N [c] 脑 nǎo [个 gè]

brainy ['breɪnɪ] ADJ (*inf*) 聪明的
cōngming de

brake [breɪk] **I** N [c] (*Aut*) 刹车
shāchē [个 gè] **II** VI (*driver, vehicle*)
刹车 shāchē

branch [brɑːntʃ] N [c] **1** (*of tree*) 树
枝 shùzhī [条 tiáo] **2** (*of shop*) 分店
fēndiàn [家 jiā]; (*of bank, company*)
分支机构 fēnzhī jīgòu [个 gè]

brand [brænd] N [c] 牌子 páizi
[块 kuài]

brand-new ['brænd'njuː] ADJ 全
新的 quánxīn de

brandy ['brændɪ] N [c/U] 白兰地
酒 báilándìjiǔ [瓶 píng]

brass [brɑːs] N [U] 铜 tóng

brave [breɪv] ADJ **1** 勇敢的
yǒnggǎn de **2** [+ *attempt, smile,
action*] 英勇的 yīngyǒng de

Brazil [brə'zɪl] N 巴西 Bāxī

bread [brɛd] N [U] 面包 miànbāo

break [breɪk] (*pt* **broke**, *pp*
broken) **I** VT **1** 打碎 dǎsuì **2** [+ *leg,
arm*] 弄断 nòngduàn **3** [+ *promise,
contract*] 违背 wéibèi **4** [+ *law,
rule*] 违反 wéifǎn **5** [+ *record*] 打
破 dǎpò **II** VI 破碎 pòsuì **III** N **1** [c]
(*rest*) 休息 xiūxi [次 cì] **2** [c] (*pause,
interval*) 间歇 jiànxiē [个 gè] **3** [c]
(*fracture*) 骨折 gǔzhé [次 cì] **4** [c]
(*holiday*) 休假 xiūjià [次 cì] ▸ **to
break the news to sb** 委婉地向
某人透露消息 wěiwǎn de xiàng
mǒurén tòulù xiāoxi ▸ **to take a
break** (*for a few minutes*) 休息一下
xiūxi yīxià ▸ **without a break** 连
续不断 liánxù bùduàn

▸ **break down** VI 坏掉 huàidiào

▸ **break in** VI [*burglar*] 破门而入
pòmén ér rù

▸ **break into** VT FUS [+ *house*] 强
行进入 qiángxíng jìnrù

▸ **break off** VT **1** [+ *branch, piece
of chocolate*] 折断 zhéduàn
2 [+ *engagement, relationship*] 断
绝 duànjué

▸ **break out** VI **1** (*begin*) 爆发
bàofā **2** (*escape*) 逃脱 táotuō

▸ **break up I** VI **1** [*couple, marriage*]
破裂 pòliè **2** [*meeting, party*] 纷
纷离去 fēnfēn líqù **II** VT **1** [+ *fight*]
调停 tiáotíng **2** [+ *meeting,
demonstration*] 驱散 qūsàn ▸ **to
break up with sb** 同某人分手

tóng mǒurén fēnshǒu

breakdown ['breɪkdaun] N [C]
1 (Aut) 故障 gùzhàng [个 gè] 2 [of
system, talks] 中断 zhōngduàn
[次 cì] 3 [of marriage] 破裂 pòliè
[个 gè] 4 (Med) (also: **nervous
breakdown**) 精神崩溃 jīngshén
bēngkuì [阵 zhèn] ▶**to have a
breakdown** 精神崩溃 jīngshén
bēngkuì

breakfast ['brɛkfəst] N [C/U] 早
餐 zǎocān [顿 dùn]

break-in ['breɪkɪn] N [C] 闯入
chuǎngrù

breast [brɛst] N 1 [C] [of woman]
乳房 rǔfáng [个 gè] 2 [C/U] 胸脯肉
xiōngpúròu [块 kuài]

breath [brɛθ] N 1 [C/U] (intake of
air) 呼吸 hūxī [下 xià] 2 [U] (air
from mouth) 口气 kǒuqì ▶out of
breath 上气不接下气 shàngqì
bùjiē xiàqì ▶bad breath 口臭
kǒuchòu ▶to get one's breath
back (Brit) 恢复正常呼吸 huīfù
zhèngcháng hūxī ▶to hold one's
breath 屏住呼吸 bǐngzhù hūxī

breathe [briːð] I VT [+ air] 呼吸
hūxī II VI 呼吸 hūxī
▶ **breathe in** VI 吸入 xīrù
▶ **breathe out** VI 呼出 hūchū

breed [briːd] (pt, pp **bred** [brɛd])
I VT [+ animals] 繁殖 fánzhí II N [C]
品种 pǐnzhǒng [个 gè]

breeze [briːz] N [C] 微风 wēifēng
[阵 zhèn]

brewery ['bruːərɪ] N [C] 啤酒厂
píjiǔchǎng [家 jiā]

bribe [braɪb] I N [C] 贿赂 huìlù [种
zhǒng] II VT 行贿 xínghuì ▶to

bribe sb to do sth 贿赂某人去做
某事 huìlù mǒurén qù zuò mǒushì

brick [brɪk] N [C/U] 砖 zhuān
[块 kuài]

bride [braɪd] N [C] 新娘 xīnniáng
[个 gè]

bridegroom ['braɪdgruːm] N [C]
新郎 xīnláng [个 gè]

bridesmaid ['braɪdzmeɪd] N [C]
伴娘 bànniáng [个 gè]

bridge [brɪdʒ] N 1 [C] 桥 qiáo [座
zuò] 2 [U] (Cards) 桥牌 qiáopái

brief [briːf] I ADJ 1 短暂的
duǎnzàn de 2 [+ description, speech]
简短的 jiǎnduǎn de II **briefs** NPL
1 (for men) 男式三角内裤 nánshì
sānjiǎo nèikù 2 (for women) 女式
三角内裤 nǔshì sānjiǎo nèikù

briefcase ['briːfkeɪs] N [C] 公事包
gōngshìbāo [个 gè]

briefly ['briːflɪ] ADV 简短地
jiǎnduǎn de

bright [braɪt] ADJ 1 [+ light] 亮
的 liàng de 2 [+ person] 聪明的
cōngming de; [+ idea] 巧妙的
qiǎomiào de 3 [+ colour] 鲜亮的
xiānliàng de

brilliant ['brɪljənt] ADJ 1 [+ person,
mind] 才华横溢的 cáihuá héngyì
de 2 [+ idea, performance] 出色的
chūsè de 3 (esp Brit: inf: wonderful)
棒极了的 bàngjíle de

bring [brɪŋ] (pt, pp **brought**) VT
(with you) 带来 dàilái; (to sb) 拿
来 nálái
▶ **bring along** VT 随身携带
suíshēn xiédài
▶ **bring back** VT (return) 带回来
dài huílái

▶ **bring forward** VT [+ *meeting*] 提前 tíqián

▶ **bring round** VT [+ *unconscious person*] 使苏醒 shǐ sūxǐng

▶ **bring up** VT 1 [+ *child*] 抚养 fǔyǎng 2 [+ *question, subject*] 提出 tíchū

Britain ['brɪtən] N (*also*: **Great Britain**) 英国 Yīngguó ▶**in Britain** 在英国 zài Yīngguó

- **BRITAIN**
-
- **Britain** 或 **Great Britain**
- 由英格兰, 威尔士, 苏格兰和
- 北爱尔兰组成。如指整个
- 不列颠, 应慎用 **England**
- 和 **English**, 以免引起苏
- 格兰和北爱尔兰人的不满。
- **United Kingdom** 作为王国
- 的官方称谓, 常简略为 **the**
- **UK**, 覆盖大不列颠及北爱
- 尔兰。**British Isles** 包括大
- 不列颠, 北爱尔兰, 爱尔兰共
- 和国 (不隶属 **the UK**) 和四
- 周岛屿。

British ['brɪtɪʃ] I ADJ 英国的 Yīngguó de II NPL ▶ **the British** 英国人 Yīngguórén

broad [brɔːd] ADJ 宽的 kuān de ▶**in broad daylight** 光天化日之下 guāng tiān huà rì zhīxià

broadband ['brɔːdbænd] N (*Comput*) 宽带 kuāndài

broadcast ['brɔːdkɑːst] (*pt, pp* **broadcast**) I N [c] 广播 guǎngbō [段 duàn] II VT 播送 bōsòng

broccoli ['brɒkəlɪ] N [U] 花椰菜 huāyēcài

brochure ['brəʊʃjʊər, US brəʊ'ʃʌr] N [c] 小册子 xiǎocèzi [本 běn]

broil [brɔɪl] (*US*) VT 烤 kǎo

broke [brəʊk] I PT *of* **break** II ADJ (*inf*: *penniless*) 身无分文的 shēn wú fēnwén de

broken ['brəʊkn] I PP *of* **break** II ADJ 1 破碎的 pòsuì de 2 [+ *machine*] 坏损的 huàisǔn de ▶**a broken leg** 折断的腿 zhéduàn de tuǐ

bronchitis [brɒŋ'kaɪtɪs] N [U] 支气管炎 zhīqìguǎnyán

bronze [brɒnz] N 1 [U] (*metal*) 青铜 qīngtóng 2 [c] (*Sport*) (*also*: **bronze medal**) 铜牌 tóngpái [块 kuài]

brooch [brəʊtʃ] N [c] 胸针 xiōngzhēn [枚 méi]

brother ['brʌðər] N [c] 兄弟 xiōngdì [个 gè]; (*elder*) 哥哥 gēge [个 gè]; (*younger*) 弟弟 dìdi [个 gè]

brother-in-law ['brʌðərɪnlɔː] N [c] (*older sister's husband*) 姐夫 jiěfu [个 gè]; (*younger sister's husband*) 妹夫 mèifu [个 gè]; (*husband's older brother*) 大伯子 dàbǎizi [个 gè]; (*husband's younger brother*) 小叔子 xiǎoshūzi [个 gè]; (*wife's older brother*) 内兄 nèixiōng [个 gè]; (*wife's younger brother*) 内弟 nèidì [个 gè]

brought [brɔːt] PT, PP *of* **bring**

brown [braʊn] I ADJ 1 褐色的 hèsè de; [+ *hair, eyes*] 棕色的 zōngsè de 2 (*tanned*) 晒黑的 shàihēi de II N [U] (*colour*) 褐色 hèsè

browse [brauz] VI (*on the internet*) 浏览 liúlǎn

bruise [bru:z] N [C] 青瘀 qīngyū [块 kuài]

brush [brʌʃ] I N [C] 刷子 shuāzi [把 bǎ]; (*for hair*) 发刷 fàshuā [把 bǎ]; [*artist's*] 画笔 huàbǐ [支 zhī] II VT 1 [+ *carpet etc*] 刷 shuā 2 [+ *hair*] 梳 shū ▶**to brush one's teeth** 刷牙 shuāyá

Brussels sprout [ˈbrʌslz-] N [C] 芽甘蓝 yágānlán [个 gè]

bubble [ˈbʌbl] N [C] 泡 pào [个 gè]

bubble gum N [U] 泡泡糖 pàopàotáng

bucket [ˈbʌkɪt] N [C] 1 (*pail*) 桶 tǒng [个 gè] 2 (*contents*) 一桶 yītǒng

buckle [ˈbʌkl] I N [C] (*on shoe, belt*) 扣环 kòuhuán [个 gè] II VT [+ *shoe, belt*] 扣住 kòuzhù

Buddhism [ˈbudɪzəm] N [U] 佛教 Fójiào

Buddhist [ˈbudɪst] I ADJ 佛教的 Fójiào de II N [C] 佛教徒 Fójiàotú [个 gè]

buffet [ˈbufeɪ, *US* buˈfeɪ] N [C] 1 (*in station*) 餐厅 cāntīng [个 gè] 2 (*food*) 自助餐 zìzhùcān [顿 dùn]

bug [bʌg] N [C] 1 (*esp US: insect*) 虫子 chóngzi [只 zhī] 2 (*Comput: in program*) 病毒 bìngdú [种 zhǒng] 3 (*inf: virus*) 病菌 bìngjūn [种 zhǒng]

build [bɪld] (*pt, pp* **built**) I N [C/U] (*of person*) 体格 tǐgé [种 zhǒng] II VT [+ *house, machine*] 建造 jiànzào

▶ **build up** VI (*accumulate*) 积

聚 jījù

builder [ˈbɪldəʳ] N [C] (*worker*) 建筑工人 jiànzhù gōngrén [位 wèi]

building [ˈbɪldɪŋ] N [C] 建筑物 jiànzhùwù [座 zuò]

built [bɪlt] I PT, PP *of* **build** II ADJ ▶ **well-/heavily-built** [+ *person*] 体态优美/粗笨的 tǐtài yōuměi/cūbèn de

bulb [bʌlb] N [C] 1 (*Elec*) 电灯泡 diàndēngpào [个 gè] 2 (*Bot*) 球茎 qiújīng [个 gè]

Bulgaria [bʌlˈgɛərɪə] N 保加利亚 Bǎojiālìyà

bull [bul] N [C] 公牛 gōngniú [头 tóu]

bullet [ˈbulɪt] N [C] 子弹 zǐdàn [发 fā]

bulletin [ˈbulɪtɪn] N [C] 公告 gōnggào [个 gè]

bulletin board C 1 (*Comput*) 公共留言板 gōnggòng liúyánbǎn 2 (*US: noticeboard*) 布告栏 bùgàolán

bully [ˈbulɪ] I N [C] 恃强凌弱者 shìqiáng língruò zhě [个 gè] II VT 欺侮 qīwǔ

bum [bʌm] (*inf*) N [C] 1 (*Brit: backside*) 屁股 pìgu 2 (*esp US: tramp*) 流浪汉 liúlànghàn [个 gè]

bump [bʌmp] I N [C] 1 肿包 zhǒngbāo [个 gè] 2 (*on road*) 隆起物 lóngqǐwù [个 gè] II VT (*strike*) 碰 pèng

▶ **bump into** VT FUS 1 [+ *obstacle, person*] 撞到 zhuàngdào 2 (*inf: meet*) 碰见 pèngjiàn

bumpy [ˈbʌmpɪ] ADJ 崎岖不平的 qíqū bùpíng de

bunch [bʌntʃ] N [c] **1** [of flowers] 束 shù **2** [of keys, bananas, grapes] 串 chuàn

bungalow ['bʌŋgələu] N [c] 平房 píngfáng [间 jiān]

bunk [bʌŋk] N [c] 铺位 pùwèi [个 gè]

burger ['bəːgəʳ] N [c] 汉堡包 hànbǎobāo [个 gè]

burglar ['bəːgləʳ] N [c] 窃贼 qièzéi [个 gè]

burglary ['bəːgləri] N **1** [c] (act) 盗窃 dàoqiè [次 cì] **2** [U] (crime) 盗窃罪 dàoqièzuì

burn [bəːn] (pt, pp **burned** or (Brit) **burnt**) I VT **1** 焚烧 fénshāo **2** [+ fuel] 燃烧 ránshāo II VI **1** [fire, flame] 燃烧 ránshāo **2** [house, car] 烧着 shāozháo III N [c] 烧伤 shāoshāng [次 cì] ▶**I've burnt myself!** 我把自己烫伤了！ wǒ bǎ zìjǐ tàngshāng le! ▶**burn down** VI [house] 烧毁 shāohuǐ

burnt [bəːnt] PT, PP of **burn**

burst [bəːst] (pt, pp **burst**) VI [pipe, tyre] 爆裂 bàoliè ▶**to burst into flames** 突然着火 tūrán zháohuǒ ▶**to burst into tears** 突然大哭起来 tūrán dàkū qǐlái ▶**to burst out laughing** 突然大笑起来 tūrán dàxiào qǐlái

bury ['bɛri] VT **1** 掩埋 yǎnmái **2** [+ dead person] 埋葬 máizàng

bus [bʌs] N [c] 公共汽车 gōnggòng qìchē [辆 liàng]

bus driver N [c] 公共汽车司机 gōnggòng qìchē sījī [位 wèi]

bush [buʃ] N [c] 灌木 guànmù [棵 kē]

business ['bɪznɪs] N **1** [c] (firm) 公司 gōngsī [家 jiā] **2** [U] (occupation) 商业 shāngyè **3** [U] (trade) 生意 shēngyì ▶**to be away on business** 出差 chūchāi ▶**to do business with sb** 和某人做生意 hé mǒurén zuò shēngyì

businessman ['bɪznɪsmən] (pl **businessmen**) N [c] 商人 shāngrén [个 gè]

businesswoman ['bɪznɪswumən] (pl **businesswomen**) N [c] 女商人 nǚ shāngrén [个 gè]

bus station N [c] 公共汽车车站 gōnggòng qìchē chēzhàn [个 gè]

bus stop N [c] 公共汽车站 gōnggòng qìchē zhàn [个 gè]

bust [bʌst] N [c] 胸部 xiōngbù

busy ['bɪzi] ADJ **1** 忙的 máng de **2** [+ shop, street] 繁忙的 fánmáng de **3** [+ schedule, time, day] 忙碌的 mánglù de **4** (esp US) (Tel) 占线的 zhànxiàn de ▶**I'm busy** 我正忙着呢 wǒ zhèng mángzhe ne

KEYWORD

but [bʌt] CONJ (yet, however) 但是 dànshì ▶**I'd love to come, but I'm busy** 我想来，但是有事 wǒ xiǎnglái, dànshì yǒushì ▶**not only ... but also** 不但…而且 bùdàn…érqiě

butcher ['butʃəʳ] N [c] **1** 肉商 ròushāng [个 gè] **2** (shop) (also: **butcher's**) 肉铺 ròupù [个 gè]

butter ['bʌtəʳ] N [U] 黄油

huángyóu
butterfly [ˈbʌtəflaɪ] N [c] 蝴蝶
húdié [只 zhī]
button [ˈbʌtn] N [c] **1** (on clothes)
钮扣 niǔkòu [颗 kē] **2** (on machine)
按钮 ànniǔ [个 gè] **3** (US: badge) 徽
章 huīzhāng [个 gè]
buy [baɪ] (pt, pp bought) I VT 买
mǎi II N [c] (purchase) 所买之物
suǒ mǎi zhī wù [件 jiàn] ▶to buy
sb sth 给某人买某物 gěi mǒurén
mǎi mǒuwù ▶to buy sth off or
from sb 从某人处购买某物 cóng
mǒurén chù gòumǎi mǒuwù
buzz [bʌz] VI [insect, machine] 发出
嗡嗡声 fāchū wēngwēngshēng

○ **KEYWORD**

by [baɪ] I PREP **1** (referring to cause,
agent) 被 bèi ▶a painting by
Picasso 毕加索的画 Bìjiāsuǒ de
huà ▶surrounded by a fence 由
篱笆围着 yóu líba wéizhe
2 (referring to method, manner,
means) ▶by bus/car/train 乘
公共汽车/汽车/火车 chéng
gōnggòng qìchē/qìchē/huǒchē
▶to pay by cheque 以支票支付
yǐ zhīpiào zhīfù ▶by moonlight/
candlelight 借助月光/烛光 jièzhù
yuèguāng/zhúguāng
3 (via, through) 经由 jīngyóu ▶he
came in by the back door 他从后
门进来 tā cóng hòumén jìnlai
4 (close to, beside) 靠近 kào jìn
▶he was standing by the door
他正站在门边 tā zhèng zhànzài
ménbiān ▶the house by the river

河边的房子 hébiān de fángzi
5 (with times, dates, years) 以前
yǐqián ▶by 4 o'clock 4点以前
sìdiǎn yǐqián ▶by April 7 4月7号
以前 sìà yuè qī hào yǐqián ▶by
now/then 到如今/那时 dào
rújīn/nàshí
6 (during) ▶by day/night 在白
天/晚上 zài báitiān/wǎnshang
7 (specifying degree of change) 相差
xiāngchā ▶crime has increased
by 10 per cent 犯罪率上升了
10% fànzuìlù shàngshēng le bǎi
fēn zhī shí
8 (in measurements) ▶a room 3
metres by 4 一间长3米宽4米的房
间 yī jiān cháng sān mǐ kuān sì mǐ
de fángjiān
9 (Math) ▶to divide/multiply by
3 被3除/乘 bèi sān chú/chéng
10 ▶by myself/himself etc
(unaided) 我/他{等}自己 wǒ/tā
{děng} zìjǐ; (alone) 我/他{等}单独
wǒ/tā {děng} dāndú
II ADV see **go by, pass by** etc

如果你说 I'll be home by ten
o'clock, 你的意思是你要
在10点或10点以前到家，
但绝不会晚于10点。如果
你说 I'll be home before ten
o'clock, 你的意思是10点
是你到家的最晚时间，你
可能9点以前就到家了。如
果你说 I'll be at home until
ten o'clock, 你的意思是
10点以前你会在家里，但
10点以后就不在了。当我
们谈论某人写了一本书或
剧本，导演了一部电影，作

了一部乐曲或画了一幅画时，我们说一部作品是 **by** 那个人或是 **written by** 那个人。*a collection of piano pieces by Mozart* 当我们谈到某人给你写信或留言时，我们说信或留言是 **from** 那个人。*He received a letter from his brother.*

bye(-bye) ['baɪ('baɪ)] (*inf*) INT 再见 zàijiàn

cab [kæb] N [c] 出租车 chūzūchē [辆 liàng]

cabbage ['kæbɪdʒ] N [c/u] 卷心菜 juǎnxīncài [头 tóu]

cabin ['kæbɪn] N [c] **1** (*on ship*) 船舱 chuáncāng [个 gè] **2** (*on plane*) 机舱 jīcāng [个 gè]

cable ['keɪbl] N **1** [c/u] (*rope*) 缆绳 lǎnshéng [根 gēn] **2** [c/u] (*Elec*) 电缆 diànlǎn [根 gēn]

cable television N [u] 有线电视 yǒuxiàn diànshì

cactus ['kæktəs] (*pl* **cactuses** or **cacti** ['kæktaɪ]) N [c] 仙人掌 xiānrénzhǎng [棵 kē]

cafeteria [kæfɪ'tɪərɪə] N [c] 自助餐厅 zìzhù cāntīng [个 gè]

cage [keɪdʒ] N [c] 笼子 lóngzi [个 gè]

cagoule [kə'guːl] N [c] 连帽防雨
长夹克衫 liánmào fángyǔ cháng
jiákèshān [件 jiàn]

cake [keɪk] N [c/U] 蛋糕 dàngāo
[块 kuài]; (small) 糕点 gāodiǎn
[块 kuài]

calculate ['kælkjuleɪt] VT 计
算 jìsuàn

calculation [kælkju'leɪʃən] N
[c/U] (Math) 计算 jìsuàn

calculator ['kælkjuleɪtər] N [c]
计算器 jìsuànqì [个 gè]

calendar ['kæləndər] N [c] 日历
rìlì [本 běn]

calf [kɑːf] (pl **calves**) N [c] 1 小
牛 xiǎoníu [头 tóu] 2 (Anat) 腿肚
tuǐdù [个 gè]

call [kɔːl] I VT 1 (name) 为⋯取名
wèi…qǔmíng 2 (address as) 称
呼 chēnghū 3 (describe as) 说成
是 shuōchéng shì 4 (shout) 喊
hǎn 5 (Tel) 打电话 dǎ diànhuà
6 (summon) 召唤 zhāohuàn II VI
(telephone) 打电话 dǎ diànhuà
III N 1 [c] (shout) 大喊 dà hǎn 2
[c] (Tel) 电话 diànhuà [次 cì] 3 [c]
(visit) 探访 tànfǎng [次 cì] ▸ **to
be called sth** [person] 被叫某
名 bèijiào mǒumíng; [object] 被
称为某物 bèi chēngwéi mǒuwù
▸ **who's calling?** (Tel) 请问是谁?
qǐngwèn shìshuí? ▸ **to make a
phone call** 打电话 dǎ diànhuà
▸ **to give sb a call** 打电话给某人
dǎ diànhuà gěi mǒurén
▸ **call back** I VI (Tel) 再打电话 zài
dǎ diànhuà II VT (Tel) 给⋯回电话
gěi…huí diànhuà
▸ **call off** VT 取消 qǔxiāo

call centre, (US) **call center**
N [c] (Tel) 电话中心 diànhuà
zhōngxīn [个 gè]

calm [kɑːm] ADJ 1 冷静的 lěngjìng
de 2 [+ sea] 平静的 píngjìng de
▸ **calm down** I VT [+ person,
animal] 使平静 shǐ píngjìng II VI
[person] 平静下来 píngjìng xiàlái

calorie ['kælərɪ] N [c] 卡路里
kǎlùlǐ

calves [kɑːvz] NPL of **calf**

Cambodia [kæm'bəudɪə] N 柬埔
寨 Jiǎnpǔzhài

camcorder ['kæmkɔːdər] N [c]
摄像放像机 shèxiàng fàngxiàng
jī [部 bù]

came [keɪm] PT of **come**

camel ['kæməl] N [c] 骆驼 luòtuo
[头 tóu]

camera ['kæmərə] N [c] 1 (Phot)
照相机 zhàoxiàngjī [架 jià] 2 (Cine,
TV) 摄影机 shèyǐngjī [部 bù]

cameraman ['kæmərəmæn]
(pl **cameramen**) N [c] 摄影师
shèyǐngshī [位 wèi]

camp [kæmp] I N [c] (for refugees,
prisoners, soldiers) 营 yíng II VI 扎
营 zhāyíng ▸ **to go camping** 外出
露营 wàichū lùyíng

campaign [kæm'peɪn] N [c] 运动
yùndòng [场 chǎng]

camper ['kæmpər] N [c] 1 (person)
野营者 yěyíngzhě [个 gè] 2 (also:
camper van) 野营车 yěyíngchē
[辆 liàng]

camping ['kæmpɪŋ] N [U] 野
营 yěyíng

campsite ['kæmpsaɪt] N [c] 营地
yíngdì [个 gè]

campus ['kæmpəs] N [c] 校园 xiàoyuán [个 gè]

can¹ [kæn] N [c] **1** (*for food, drinks*) 罐头 guàntou [个 gè]; (*for petrol, oil*) 罐 guàn [个 gè] **2** (*contents*) 一听所装的量 yītīng suǒ zhuāng de liàng [听 tīng] **3** (*contents and container*) 一罐 yīguàn

KEYWORD

can² [kæn] (*negative* **cannot, can't**, *conditional, pt* **could**) AUX VB **1** (*be able to*) 能 néng ▸ **can I help you?** (*in shop*) 您要买点儿什么？nín yào mǎidiǎn'r shénme?; (*in general*) 我能帮你吗？wǒ néng bāngnǐ ma? ▸ **you can do it if you try** 如果试试的话你是能做的 rúguǒ shìshì de huà nǐ shì néng zuò de ▸ **I can't hear/see anything** 我什么也听/看不见 wǒ shénme yě tīng/kàn bùjiàn **2** (*know how to*) 会 huì ▸ **I can swim/drive** 我会游泳/开车 wǒ huì yóuyǒng/kāichē **3** (*permission, requests*) 可以 kěyǐ ▸ **can I use your phone?** 我可以用你的电话吗？wǒ kěyǐ yòng nǐde diànhuà ma? ▸ **can you help me?** 你可以帮我一下吗？nǐ kěyǐ bāng wǒ yīxià ma? **4** (*possibility*) 可能 kěnéng ▸ **he can be very unpleasant** 他有时会非常不高兴 tā yǒushí huì fēicháng bù gāoxìng

can, could 和 **be able to** 都是用来表示某人有能力做某事，后接原形动词。**can** 或 **be able to** 的现在式都可以指现在，但 **can** 更为常用。*They can all read and write...The snake is able to catch small mammals.* **could** 或 **be able to** 的过去式可用来指过去。**will** 或 **shall** 加 **be able to** 则用于表示将来。指在某一特定时间能够做某事，用 **be able to**。*After treatment he was able to return to work.* **can** 和 **could** 用于表示可能性。**could** 指的是某个特定情况下的可能性，而 **can** 则表示一般情况下的可能性。*Many jobs could be lost...Too much salt can be harmful.* 在谈论过去的时候，使用 **could have** 加过去分词形式。*It could have been much worse.* 在谈论规则或表示许可的时候，用 **can** 表示现在，用 **could** 表示过去。*They can leave at any time.* 注意，当表示请求时，**can** 和 **could** 两者都可。*Can I have a drink?...Could we put the fire on?* 但表示建议时只能使用 **could**。*You could phone her and ask.*

Canada ['kænədə] N 加拿大 Jiānádà

Canadian [kə'neɪdɪən] I ADJ 加拿大的 Jiānádà de II N [c] (*person*) 加拿大人 Jiānádàrén [个 gè]

canal [kə'næl] N [c] 运河 yùnhé

[条 tiáo]

cancel ['kænsəl] VT 取消 qǔxiāo

cancer ['kænsəʳ] N 1 [c/u] (Med) 癌症 áizhèng [种 zhǒng] 2 (Astrol) ▶**Cancer** [u] (sign) 巨蟹座 Jùxiè Zuò

candidate ['kændɪdeɪt] N [c] 1 (for job) 候选人 hòuxuǎnrén [位 wèi] 2 (in exam) 报考者 bàokǎozhě [个 gè]

candle ['kændl] N [c] 蜡烛 làzhú [根 gēn]

candy ['kændɪ] (US) N [c/u] 糖果 tángguǒ [块 kuài]

canned [kænd] ADJ 罐装的 guànzhuāng de

cannot ['kænɔt] = **can not**

canoe [kə'nu:] N [c] 独木船 dúmùchuán [艘 sōu]

canoeing [kə'nu:ɪŋ] N [u] 划独木船 huá dúmùchuán

can opener [-'əupnəʳ] N [c] 开罐器 kāi guànqì [个 gè]

can't [kɑ:nt] = **can not**

canteen [kæn'ti:n] N [c] 食堂 shítáng [个 gè]

canvas ['kænvəs] N [u] 帆布 fānbū

cap [kæp] N [c] 帽 mào [顶 dǐng]

capable ['keɪpəbl] ADJ 有能力的 yǒu nénglì de ▶**to be capable of doing sth** 有做某事的能力 yǒu zuò mǒushì de nénglì

capacity [kə'pæsɪtɪ] N [s] [of container, ship] 容量 róngliàng; [of stadium, theatre] 可容纳人数 kě róngnà rénshù

capital ['kæpɪtl] N 1 [c] (city) 首都 shǒudū [个 gè] 2 [u] (money)

资本 zīběn 3 [c] (also: **capital letter**) 大写字母 dàxiě zìmǔ [个 gè] ▶**capital R/L** etc 大写字母 R/L{等} dàxiě zìmǔ R/L {děng}

capitalism ['kæpɪtəlɪzəm] N [u] 资本主义 zīběn zhǔyì

Capricorn ['kæprɪkɔ:n] N [u] (sign) 摩羯座 Mójié Zuò

captain ['kæptɪn] N [c] 1 [of ship] 船长 chuánzhǎng [位 wèi] 2 [of plane] 机长 jīzhǎng [位 wèi] 3 [of team] 队长 duìzhǎng [个 gè]

capture ['kæptʃəʳ] VT [+ animal] 捕获 bǔhuò; [+ person] 俘虏 fúlǔ

car [kɑ:ʳ] N [c] 1 (Aut) 汽车 qìchē [辆 liàng] 2 (US) (Rail) 车厢 chēxiāng [节 jié] ▶**by car** 乘汽车 chéng qìchē

caravan ['kærəvæn] N [c] (Brit) 活动住房 huódòng zhùfáng [处 chù]

card [kɑ:d] N 1 [c] 卡片 kǎpiàn [张 zhāng] 2 [c] (also: **playing card**) 扑克牌 pūkèpái [张 zhāng] 3 [c] (greetings card) 贺卡 hèkǎ [张 zhāng] 4 [c] (also: **business card**) 名片 míngpiàn [张 zhāng] 5 [c] (bank card, credit card) 信用卡 xìnyòngkǎ [张 zhāng] ▶**to play cards** 打牌 dǎpái

cardigan ['kɑ:dɪgən] N [c] 开襟毛衣 kāijīn máoyī [件 jiàn]

care [kɛəʳ] I N [u] 照顾 zhàogù II VI 关心 guānxīn ▶**with care** 小心 xiǎoxīn ▶**take care!** (saying goodbye) 慢走! mànzǒu! ▶**to take care of sb** 照顾某人 zhàogù mǒurén ▶**to take care of sth** [+ possession, clothes] 保管某

物 bǎoguǎn mǒuwù; [+ *problem, situation*] 处理某物 chǔlǐ mǒuwù
▶**I don't care** 我不在乎 wǒ bù zàihu
▶**care about** VT FUS [+ *person, thing, idea*] 关心 guānxīn
▶**care for** VT FUS 照顾 zhàogù

career [kə'rɪər] N [c] **1** (*job, profession*) 事业 shìyè [项 xiàng]
2 (*working life*) 生涯 shēngyá [个 gè]

careful ['kɛəful] ADJ **1** 小心的 xiǎoxīn de **2** [+ *work, thought, analysis*] 仔细的 zǐxì de ▶**(be) careful!** 小心！xiǎoxīn! ▶**to be careful with sth** [+ *money*] 谨慎地使用某物 jǐnshèn de shǐyòng mǒuwù; [+ *fragile object*] 小心对待某物 xiǎoxīn duìdài mǒuwù

carefully ['kɛəfəlɪ] ADV **1** (*cautiously*) 小心地 xiǎoxīn de **2** (*methodically*) 用心地 yòngxīn de

careless ['kɛəlɪs] ADJ [+ *person, worker*] 粗心的 cūxīn de; [+ *driving*] 疏忽的 shūhu de; [+ *mistake*] 疏忽造成的 shūhu zàochéng de ▶**it was careless of him to let the dog out** 他真不当心，把狗放了出去 tā zhēn bù dāngxīn, bǎ gǒu fàng le chūqù

caretaker ['kɛəteɪkər] N [c] (*Brit*) 看门人 kānménrén [个 gè]

car ferry N [c] 汽车渡轮 qìchē dùlún [艘 sōu]

cargo ['kɑːgəʊ] (*pl* **cargoes**) N [c/u] 货物 huòwù [批 pī]

car hire N (*Brit*) N [u] 汽车出租 qìchē chūzū

Caribbean [kærɪ'biːən] N ▶**the Caribbean (Sea)** 加勒比海 Jiālèbǐhǎi

carnival ['kɑːnɪvl] N **1** [c/u] (*festival*) 狂欢节 kuánghuānjié [个 gè] **2** [c] (*US*) 游艺团 yóuyìtuán [个 gè]

car park N [c] (*Brit*) 停车场 tíngchēchǎng [处 chù]

carpenter ['kɑːpɪntər] N [c] 木匠 mùjiàng [个 gè]

carpet ['kɑːpɪt] N [c] (*fitted*) 地毯 dìtǎn [条 tiáo]; (*rug*) 小地毯 xiǎo dìtǎn [块 kuài]

car rental N [u] 汽车出租 qìchē chūzū

carriage ['kærɪdʒ] N [c] (*Brit*) (*Rail*) 车厢 chēxiāng [节 jié]

carrier bag (*Brit*) N [c] 购物袋 gòuwùdài [个 gè]

carrot ['kærət] N [c/u] 胡萝卜 húluóbo [根 gēn]

carry ['kærɪ] VT **1** [+ *person*] 抱 bào; (*by hand with the arm down*) 提 tí; (*on one's back*) 背 bēi; (*by hand*) 拿 ná **2** (*transport*) [*ship, plane*] 运载 yùnzài
▶**carry on** I VI 继续 jìxù II VT (*continue*) [+ *work, tradition*] ▶**carry on with sth** 继续做某事 jìxù zuò mǒushì ▶**to carry on doing sth** 继续做某事 jìxù zuò mǒushì
▶**carry out** VT [+ *order, instruction*] 执行 zhíxíng

cart [kɑːt] N [c] **1** 大车 dàchē [辆 liàng] **2** (*US*) (*also*: **shopping cart**) 手推车 shǒutuīchē [辆 liàng]

carton ['kɑːtən] N [c] **1** (*esp US*)

cardboard box) 纸箱 zhǐxiāng [个 gè] **2** [*of milk, juice, yoghurt*] 容器 róngqì [个 gè]

cartoon [kɑː'tuːn] N [c] **1** (*drawing*) 漫画 mànhuà [幅 fú] **2** (*Brit: comic strip*) 系列幽默画 xìliè yōumò huà [套 tào] **3** (*animated*) 卡通片 kǎtōngpiàn [部 bù]

cartridge ['kɑːtrɪdʒ] N [c] **1** (*for gun*) 弹壳 dànké [个 gè] **2** (*for printer*) 墨盒 mòhé [个 gè]

case [keɪs] N **1** [c] **1** (*instance*) 情况 qíngkuàng [种 zhǒng] **2** [c] (*container*) 盒子 hézi [个 gè] **3** [c] (*Brit*) (*also:* **suitcase**) 行李箱 xínglixiāng [个 gè] ►**lower/upper case** 小/大写 xiǎo/dàxiě ►**in case he comes** 以防万一他会来 yǐfáng wànyī tā huì lái ►**in any case** 无论如何 wúlùn rúhé ►**just in case** 以防万一 yǐfáng wànyī ►**in that case** 既然是那样 jìrán shì nàyàng

cash [kæʃ] I N [u] **1** (*notes and coins*) 现金 xiànjīn **2** (*money*) 现款 xiànkuǎn II VT 兑现 duìxiàn ►**to pay (in) cash** 付现金 fù xiànjīn

cashew [kæ'ʃuː] N [c] (*also:* **cashew nut**) 腰果 yāoguǒ [颗 kē]

cashier [kæ'ʃɪəʳ] N [c] 出纳员 chūnàyuán [个 gè]

casino [kə'siːnəu] N [c] 赌场 dǔchǎng [个 gè]

cassette [kæ'sɛt] N [c] 磁带 cídài [盘 pán]

cast [kɑːst] (*pt, pp* **cast**) N [c] (*Theat*) 演员表 yǎnyuánbiǎo [份 fèn]

castle ['kɑːsl] N [c] 城堡

chéngbǎo [座 zuò]

casual ['kæʒjul] ADJ **1** (*chance*) 漫不经心的 màn bù jīngxīn de **2** (*unconcerned*) 随便的 suíbiàn de **3** (*informal*) 非正式的 fēizhèngshì de

casualty ['kæʒjultɪ] N **1** [c] (*of war, accident: injured*) 伤病员 shāngbìngyuán [个 gè]; (*dead*) 伤亡人员 shāngwáng rényuán [批 pī] **2** [u] (*Brit: in hospital*) 急诊室 jízhěnshì

cat [kæt] N [c] 猫 māo [只 zhī]

catalogue, (*US*) **catalog** ['kætəlɔg] N [c] **1** (*for mail order*) 目录 mùlù [个 gè] **2** (*of exhibition*) 目录 mùlù [个 gè] **3** (*of library*) 书目 shūmù [个 gè]

catastrophe [kə'tæstrəfɪ] N [c] 大灾难 dàzāinàn [场 chǎng]

catch [kætʃ] (*pt, pp* **caught**) VT **1** [+ *animal, fish*] 捕获 bǔhuò; [+ *thief, criminal*] 抓获 zhuāhuò **2** [+ *ball*] 接 jiē **3** [+ *bus, train, plane*] 赶上 gǎnshang **4** (*discover*) [+ *person*] 发现 fāxiàn **5** [+ *flu, illness*] 染上 rǎnshang ►**to catch sb doing sth** 撞见某人做某事 zhuàngjiàn mǒurén zuò mǒushì ► **catch up** VI 追上 zhuīshang

category ['kætɪgərɪ] N [c] 种类 zhǒnglèi [个 gè]

catering ['keɪtərɪŋ] N [u] 饮食业 yǐnshíyè

cathedral [kə'θiːdrəl] N [c] 大教堂 dàjiàotáng [个 gè]

Catholic ['kæθəlɪk] I ADJ 天主教的 Tiānzhǔjiào de II N [c] 天主教徒 Tiānzhǔjiào tú [个 gè]

cattle ['kætl] NPL 牛 niú

caught [kɔːt] PT, PP of **catch**

cauliflower ['kɔlɪflaʊəʳ] N [c/u] 菜花 càihuā [头 tóu]

cause [kɔːz] I N [c] 起因 qǐyīn [个 gè] II VT 导致 dǎozhì ▶to cause sb to do sth 促使某人做某事 cùshǐ mǒurén zuò mǒushì ▶to cause sth to happen 导致某事发生 dǎozhì mǒushì fāshēng

cautious ['kɔːʃəs] ADJ 谨慎的 jǐnshèn de

cave [keɪv] N [c] 山洞 shāndòng [个 gè]

CD N ABBR (= **compact disc**) 激光唱片 jīguāng chàngpiàn

CD player N [c] 激光唱机 jīguāng chàngjī [部 bù]

CD-ROM [si:di:'rɔm] N ABBR (= **compact disc read-only memory**) 光盘只读存储器 guāngpán zhǐdú cúnchǔ qì ▶on CD-ROM 光盘版 guāngpán bǎn

ceiling ['si:lɪŋ] N [c] 天花板 tiānhuābǎn [块 kuài]

celebrate ['sɛlɪbreɪt] VT 庆祝 qìngzhù

celebrity [sɪ'lɛbrɪtɪ] N [c] 名人 míngrén [位 wèi]

cell [sɛl] N [c] 1 (Bio) 细胞 xìbāo [个 gè] 2 (in prison) 牢房 láofáng [间 jiān]

cellar ['sɛləʳ] N [c] 地下室 dìxiàshì [间 jiān]; (for wine) 酒窖 jiǔjiào [个 gè]

cello ['tʃɛləʊ] N [c] 大提琴 dàtíqín [把 bǎ]

cement [sə'mɛnt] N [u] (concrete) 水泥 shuǐní

cemetery ['sɛmɪtrɪ] N [c] 墓地 mùdì [处 chù]

cent [sɛnt] N [c] 分 fēn

center ['sɛntəʳ] (US) N = **centre**

centigrade ['sɛntɪgreɪd] ADJ 摄氏的 Shèshì de

centimetre, (US) **centimeter** ['sɛntɪmi:təʳ] N [c] 厘米 límǐ

central ['sɛntrəl] ADJ 中心的 zhōngxīn de

central heating N [u] 中央供暖系统 zhōngyāng gōngnuǎn xìtǒng

centre, (US) **center** ['sɛntəʳ] N 1 [c] 中心 zhōngxīn [个 gè] 2 [c] (building) 中心 zhōngxīn [个 gè] ▶to be at the centre of sth 是某事的关键 shì mǒushì de guānjiàn ▶to centre or be centred on (focus on) 集中于 jízhōng yú

century ['sɛntjʊrɪ] N [c] 世纪 shìjì [个 gè] ▶the 21st century 21世纪 èrshíyī shìjì ▶in the twenty-first century 在21世纪 zài èrshíyī shìjì

cereal ['si:rɪəl] N 1 [c] (plant, crop) 谷类植物 gǔlèi zhíwù [种 zhǒng] 2 [c/u] (also: **breakfast cereal**) 谷类食品 gǔlèi shípǐn [种 zhǒng]

ceremony ['sɛrɪmənɪ] N [c] 典礼 diǎnlǐ [个 gè]

certain ['sə:tən] ADJ 1 (sure) 肯定的 kěndìng de 2 (some) 某些 mǒuxiē ▶to be certain that... 肯定… kěndìng… ▶to make certain that... 证实… zhèngshí… ▶to be certain of 肯定 kěndìng ▶a certain amount of sth 一定量的某物 yīdìngliàng de mǒuwù ▶to know sth for certain 确定某事

quèdìng mǒushì

certainly ['sə:tənlɪ] ADV
1 (undoubtedly) 无疑地 wúyí
de **2** (of course) 当然 dāngrán
▶**certainly not** 绝对不行 juéduì
bùxíng

certificate [sə'tɪfɪkɪt] N [c] **1** [of
birth, marriage] 证 zhèng [张
zhāng] **2** (diploma) 结业证书 jiéyè
zhèngshū [个 gè]

chain [tʃeɪn] N **1** [c/u] 链条
liàntiáo [根 gēn] **2** [c] (jewellery) 链
子 liànzi [条 tiáo]

chair [tʃeəʳ] N [c] 椅子 yǐzi [把 bǎ];
(armchair) 扶手椅 fúshǒuyǐ [把 bǎ]

chairman ['tʃeəmən] (pl
chairmen) N [c] 主席 zhǔxí
[位 wèi]

chalk [tʃɔ:k] N [c/u] (for writing) 粉
笔 fěnbǐ [支 zhī]

challenge ['tʃælɪndʒ] I N [c/u]
1 (hard task) 挑战 tiǎozhàn [个
gè] **2** (to rival, competitor) 挑
战 tiǎozhàn [个 gè] II VT
[+ rival, competitor] 向…挑战
xiàng…tiǎozhàn ▶**to challenge
sb to a fight/game** 挑战某人
打架/比赛 tiǎnzhàn mǒurén
dǎjià/bǐsài

champagne [ʃæm'peɪn] N [c/u]
香槟酒 xiāngbīn jiǔ [瓶 píng]

champion ['tʃæmpɪən] N [c] 冠
军 guànjūn [位 wèi]

championship ['tʃæmpɪənʃɪp] N
[c] 锦标赛 jǐnbiāo sài [届 jiè]

chance [tʃɑːns] I N **1** [c/u]
(likelihood, possibility) 可能
性 kěnéngxìng [种 zhǒng] **2** [s]
(opportunity) 机会 jīhuì **3** [u]

(luck) 运气 yùnqì II ADJ [+ meeting,
discovery] 偶然的 ǒurán de ▶**he
hasn't much chance of winning**
他赢的机会不大 tā yíng de jīhuì
bùdà ▶**the chance to do sth** 做某
事的机会 zuò mǒushì de jīhuì ▶**by
chance** 偶然 ǒurán

change [tʃeɪndʒ] I VT **1** 改变
gǎibiàn **2** [+ wheel, battery] 换
huàn **3** [+ trains, buses] 换 huàn
4 [+ clothes] 换 huàn **5** [+ job,
address] 更改 gēnggǎi **6** [+ nappy]
换 huàn **7** [+ money] 兑换 duìhuàn
II VI **1** 变化 biànhuà **2** (change
clothes) 换衣 huànyī **3** (on bus,
train) 换车 huànchē III N **1** [c/u]
(alteration) 转变 zhuǎnbiàn [种
zhǒng] **2** [s] (novelty) 变化 biànhuà
3 [u] 零钱 língqián; (money
returned) 找头 zhǎotou ▶**to
change one's mind** 改变主意
gǎibiàn zhǔyì ▶**for a change** 为了
改变一下 wèile gǎibiàn yīxià ▶**a
change of clothes/underwear**
一套换洗的衣服/内衣 yītào
huànxǐ de yīfu/nèiyī ▶**small
change** 零钱 língqián ▶**to give
sb change for** or **of 10 pounds** 给
某人10英镑的零钱 gěi mǒurén
shí yīngbàng de língqián ▶**keep
the change!** 不用找了！ bùyòng
zhǎole!

changing room (Brit) N [c] **1** (in
shop) 试衣室 shìyīshì [间 jiān]
2 (Sport) 更衣室 gēngyīshì [间
jiān]

channel ['tʃænl] N [c] **1** (TV) 频
道 píndào [个 gè] **2** (for water) 沟
渠 gōuqú [条 tiáo] ▶**the (English)**

Channel 英吉利海峡 Yīngjílì hǎixiá

chaos ['keɪɔs] N [U] 混乱 hùnluàn

chapel ['tʃæpl] N [c] (in hospital, prison, school) 附属教堂 fùshǔ jiàotáng [个 gè]

chapter ['tʃæptə^r] N [c] 章 zhāng

character ['kærɪktə^r] N 1 [c] 特性 tèxìng [种 zhǒng] 2 [c] (in novel, film) 角色 juésè [个 gè] 3 [c] (letter, symbol) 字母 zìmǔ [个 gè]

characteristic [kærɪktə'rɪstɪk] N [c] 特征 tèzhēng [个 gè] ▶ to be characteristic of sb/sth 反映某人/某物的特性 fǎnyìng mǒurén/mǒuwù de tèxìng

charge [tʃɑ:dʒ] I N [c] 费用 fèiyòng [笔 bǐ] II VT 1 [+ sum of money] 要价 yàojià; [+ customer, client] 收费 shōufèi 2 (also: **charge up**) [+ battery] 使充电 shǐ chōngdiàn III **charges** NPL 费费 fèi ▶ **free of charge** 免费 miǎnfèi ▶ **to be in charge of sth/sb)** (of person, machine) 主管(某事/某人) zhǔguǎn (mǒushì/mǒurén) ▶ **how much do you charge?** 你收费多少? nǐ shōufèi duōshǎo? ▶ **to charge sb £20 for sth** 因某物收某人20英镑 yīn mǒuwù shōu mǒurén èrshí yīngbàng

charity ['tʃærɪtɪ] N [c] (organization) 慈善机构 císhàn jīgòu [个 gè] ▶ **to give money to charity** 把钱捐给慈善团体 bǎ qián juāngěi císhàn tuántǐ

charm [tʃɑ:m] N [c/U] [of place, thing] 魅力 mèilì [种 zhǒng]; [of person] 迷人的特性 mírén de

tèxìng [个 gè]

charming ['tʃɑ:mɪŋ] ADJ [+ person] 迷人的 mírén de; [+ place, custom] 吸引人的 xīyǐn rén de

chart [tʃɑ:t] N [c] 图表 túbiǎo [个 gè]

charter flight N [c] 包机 bāojī [架 jià]

chase [tʃeɪs] VT 追赶 zhuīgǎn

chat [tʃæt] I VI (also: **have a chat**) 聊天 liáotiān II N [c] (conversation) 聊天 liáotiān [次 cì]

chatroom (Comput) N [c] 聊天室 liáotiānshì [个 gè]

chat show (Brit) N [c] 访谈节目 fǎngtán jiémù [个 gè]

chauvinist ['ʃəuvɪnɪst] N [c] (also: **male chauvinist**) 大男子主义者 dànánzǐzhǔyìzhě [个 gè]

cheap [tʃi:p] ADJ 1 便宜的 piányi de 2 [+ ticket] 降价的 jiàngjià de; [+ fare, rate] 廉价的 liánjià de

cheat [tʃi:t] I VI 作弊 zuòbì II VT 欺骗 qīpiàn III N [c] (in games, exams) 作弊者 zuòbìzhě [个 gè] ▶ **cheat on** (inf) VT FUS 不忠实于 bù zhōngshí yú

check [tʃɛk] I VT 1 核对 héduì; [+ passport, ticket] 检查 jiǎnchá 2 (also: **check in**) [+ luggage] 托运 tuōyùn II VI (investigate) 检查 jiǎnchá III N [c] 1 (inspection) 检查 jiǎnchá [次 cì] 2 (US: in restaurant) 账单 zhàngdān [张 zhāng] 3 (US) = **cheque** 4 (pattern: gen pl) 图案 tú'àn [个 gè] 5 (US: mark) 勾号 gōuhào [个 gè] IV ADJ (also: **checked**) [+ pattern, cloth] 方格图案的 fānggé tú'àn de ▶ **to**

check sth against sth 将某物与某物相比较 jiāng mǒuwù yǔ mǒuwù xiāng bǐjiào ▸**to check with sb** 向某人证实 xiàng mǒurén zhèngshí ▸**to keep a check on sb/sth** (watch) 监视某人/某物 jiānshì mǒurén/mǒuwù

▸ **check in** VI (at hotel, clinic) 登记 dēngjì; (at airport) 办理登机手续 bànlǐ dēngjì shǒuxù

▸ **check into** VT 登记入住 dēngjì rùzhù

▸ **check out** VI (of hotel) 结账离开 jiézhàng líkāi

checkbook ['tʃɛkbuk] (US) N = **cheque book**

checked [tʃɛkt] ADJ see **check**

checkers ['tʃɛkəz] (US) NPL 西洋跳棋 xīyáng tiàoqí

check-in ['tʃɛkɪn] (also: **check-in desk**) N [c] 旅客验票台 lǔkè yànpiào tái [个 gè]

checkout ['tʃɛkaut] N [c] 付款台 fùkuǎntái [个 gè]

check-up ['tʃɛkʌp] N [c] (by doctor) 体检 tǐjiǎn [次 cì]; (by dentist) 牙科检查 yákē jiǎnchá [次 cì]

cheek [tʃiːk] N 1 [c] 面颊 miànjiá [个 gè] 2 [U] 厚颜无耻 hòuyánwúchǐ ▸**to have the cheek to do sth** 居然有脸做某事 jūrán yǒuliǎn zuò mǒushì

cheeky ['tʃiːkɪ] (esp Brit) ADJ 恬不知耻的 tián bù zhī chǐ de

cheer [tʃɪəʳ] I VI 欢呼 huānhū II N [c] 喝彩 hècǎi [阵 zhèn] ▸**cheers!** (esp Brit: toast) 干杯! gānbēi!

▸ **cheer up** VI 振作起来 zhènzuò qǐlái

cheerful ['tʃɪəful] ADJ 兴高采烈的 xìnggāocǎiliè de

cheese [tʃiːz] N [c/U] 干酪 gānlào [块 kuài]

chef [ʃɛf] N [c] 厨师 chúshī [位 wèi]

chemical ['kɛmɪkl] N [c] 化学剂 huàxué jì [种 zhǒng]

chemist ['kɛmɪst] N [c] 1 (Brit) (also: **chemist's**) 药商 yàoshāng [个 gè] 2 (scientist) 化学家 huàxuéjiā [位 wèi]

chemistry ['kɛmɪstrɪ] N [U] 化学 huàxué

cheque, (US) **check** [tʃɛk] N [c] 支票 zhīpiào [张 zhāng] ▸**to pay by cheque** 用支票付款 yòng zhīpiào fùkuǎn

cheque book, (US) **checkbook** ['tʃɛkbuk] N [c] 支票簿 zhīpiào bù [本 běn]

cherry ['tʃɛrɪ] N [c] 1 (fruit) 樱桃 yīngtáo [颗 kē] 2 (also: **cherry tree**) 樱桃树 yīngtáo shù [棵 kē]

chess [tʃɛs] N [U] 象棋 xiàngqí

chest [tʃɛst] N [c] 1 胸部 xiōngbù 2 (box) 箱子 xiāngzi [个 gè]

chestnut ['tʃɛsnʌt] N [c] 栗子 lìzi [颗 kē]

chew [tʃuː] VT 嚼 jiáo

chewing gum ['tʃuːɪŋ-] N [U] 口香糖 kǒuxiāngtáng

chick [tʃɪk] N [c] 小鸟 xiǎoniǎo [只 zhī]

chicken ['tʃɪkɪn] N 1 [c] 鸡 jī [只 zhī] 2 [c/U] (meat) 鸡肉 jīròu [块 kuài]

chickenpox ['tʃɪkɪnpɔks] N [U] 水痘 shuǐdòu

chief [tʃiːf] I N [c] 首领 shǒulǐng [个 gè] II ADJ 首要的 shǒuyào de

child [tʃaɪld] (pl **children**) N [c] **1** 儿童 értóng [个 gè] **2** (son, daughter) 孩子 háizi [个 gè] ▸**she's just had her second child** 她刚生了第二个孩子 tā gāng shēng le dì'èr gè háizi

child minder (Brit) N [c] 保姆 bǎomǔ [个 gè]

children ['tʃɪldrən] N PL of **child**

Chile ['tʃɪlɪ] N 智利 Zhìlì

chill [tʃɪl] VT [+ food, drinks] 使冷冻 shǐ lěngdòng ▸**to catch a chill** 着凉 zháoliáng

chilli, (US) **chili** ['tʃɪlɪ] N [c/u] 辣椒 làjiāo [个 gè]

chilly ['tʃɪlɪ] ADJ 相当冷的 xiāngdāng lěng de

chimney ['tʃɪmnɪ] N [c] 烟囱 yāncōng [节 jié]

chin [tʃɪn] N [c] 下巴 xiàba [个 gè]

China ['tʃaɪnə] N 中国 Zhōngguó

china ['tʃaɪnə] N [u] (crockery) 瓷器 cíqì

Chinese [tʃaɪ'niːz] (pl **Chinese**) I ADJ 中国的 Zhōngguó de II N **1** [c] (person) 中国人 Zhōngguórén [个 gè] **2** [u] (language) 汉语 Hànyǔ

chip [tʃɪp] N [c] **1** (Brit) 薯条 shǔtiáo [根 gēn] **2** (US: snack) 薯片 shǔpiàn [片 piàn] **3** (Comput) (also: **microchip**) 集成电路片 jíchéng diànlù piàn [块 kuài]

chiropodist [kɪ'rɒpədɪst] (Brit) N [c] 足医 zúyī [位 wèi]

chocolate ['tʃɒklɪt] I N **1** [u] 巧克力 qiǎokèlì **2** [c/u] (drinking chocolate) 巧克力饮料 qiǎokèlì yǐnliào [瓶 píng] **3** [c] (piece of confectionery) 巧克力糖 qiǎokèlì táng [块 kuài] II CPD [+ cake, pudding, mousse] 巧克力 qiǎokèlì ▸**bar of chocolate** 巧克力条 qiǎokèlì tiáo ▸**piece of chocolate** 一块巧克力 yīkuài qiǎokèlì

choice [tʃɔɪs] N **1** [c/u] (between items) 选择 xuǎnzé [个 gè] **2** [c] (option) 选择 xuǎnzé [个 gè] ▸**a wide choice** 多种多样 duōzhǒng duōyàng ▸**to have no/little choice** 没有/没有太多选择 méiyǒu/méiyǒu tàiduō xuǎnzé

choir ['kwaɪər] N [c] 合唱团 héchàngtuán [个 gè]

choke [tʃəuk] VI (on food, drink) 噎住 yēzhù; (with smoke, dust) 呛 qiàng ▸**to choke on sth** 被某物噎了 bèi mǒuwù yēle

choose [tʃuːz] (pt **chose**, pp **chosen**) I VT 挑选 tiāoxuǎn II VI ▸**to choose between** 在…之间作出选择 zài…zhījiān zuòchū xuǎnzé ▸**to choose to do sth** 选择做某事 xuǎnzé zuò mǒushì

chop [tʃɒp] I VT [+ vegetables, fruit, meat] 切 qiē II N [c] (Culin) 排骨 páigǔ [根 gēn]
▸**chop down** VT [+ tree] 砍倒 kǎndǎo
▸**chop up** VT 切 qiē

chopsticks ['tʃɒpstɪks] N PL 筷子 kuàizi

chose [tʃəuz] PT of **choose**

chosen ['tʃəuzn] PP of **choose**

Christ [kraɪst] N 耶稣 Yēsū

christening ['krɪsnɪŋ] N [c] 洗

礼 xǐlǐ [次 cì]

Christian ['krɪstɪən] **I** ADJ 基督教的 Jīdūjiào de **II** N [c] 基督徒 Jīdūtú [个 gè]

Christian name N [c] 教名 jiàomíng [个 gè]

Christmas ['krɪsməs] N [c/u] **1** 圣诞节 Shèngdàn Jié [个 gè] **2** (period) 圣诞节期间 Shèngdàn Jié qījiān ▸**Happy** or **Merry Christmas!** 圣诞快乐! Shèngdàn Kuàilè! ▸**at Christmas** 在圣诞节 zài Shèngdànjié ▸**for Christmas** 为了圣诞节 wèile Shèngdànjié

Christmas Eve N [c/u] 圣诞夜 Shèngdàn Yè [个 gè]

Christmas tree N [c] 圣诞树 Shèngdàn shù [棵 kē]

church [tʃɜːtʃ] N [c/u] 教堂 jiàotáng [座 zuò]

cider ['saɪdər] N [c/u] **1** (Brit: alcoholic) 苹果酒 píngguǒ jiǔ [瓶 píng] **2** (US: non-alcoholic) 苹果汁 píngguǒ zhī [瓶 píng]

cigar [sɪ'gɑːr] N [c] 雪茄烟 xuějiā yān [支 zhī]

cigarette [sɪgə'rɛt] N [c] 香烟 xiāngyān [支 zhī]

cinema ['sɪnəmə] N [c] (Brit) 电影院 diànyǐng yuàn [个 gè]

circle ['sɜːkl] N [c] 圆圈 yuánquān [个 gè]

circular ['sɜːkjʊlər] N [c] (letter) 供传阅的函件 gōng chuányuè de hánjiàn [封 fēng]

circumstances ['sɜːkəmstənsɪz] NPL 情况 qíngkuàng ▸**in** or **under the circumstances** 在这种情况下 zài zhèzhǒng qíngkuàng xià

circus ['sɜːkəs] N [c] 马戏团 mǎxì tuán [个 gè]

citizen ['sɪtɪzn] N [c] 公民 gōngmín [个 gè]

citizenship ['sɪtɪznʃɪp] N [u] 公民身份 gōngmín shēnfèn

city ['sɪtɪ] N [c] 城市 chéngshì [座 zuò] ▸**the City** (Brit) (Fin) 英国伦敦商业区 Yīngguó Lúndūn shāngyèqū

○ **THE CITY**
○
● **the City** (伦敦商业区)是伦
● 敦的一部分, 位于市中心的
● 东部。很多重要的金融机构
● 都将总部设在这里, 譬如英
● 格兰银行, 伦敦证券交易所和
● 其他几个主要银行。这些金
● 融机构的所在地通常统称为
● **the City**。在历史上, 这个地
● 区是伦敦的心脏, 有自己的
● 市长和警力。

city centre (esp Brit) N [c] 市中心 shì zhōngxīn [个 gè]

civilization [sɪvɪlaɪ'zeɪʃən] N [c/u] 文明 wénmíng [种 zhǒng]

civilized ['sɪvɪlaɪzd] ADJ [+ society, people] 文明的 wénmíng de

civil war N [c/u] 内战 nèizhàn [场 chǎng]

claim [kleɪm] **I** VT **1** [+ expenses, rights, inheritance] 要求 yāoqiú **2** [+ compensation, damages, benefit] 索取 suǒqǔ **II** VI (for insurance) 提出索赔 tíchū suǒpéi **III** N

[c] 索赔 suǒpéi [项 xiàng] ▶to claim or make a claim on one's insurance 提出保险索赔的要求 tíchū bǎoxiǎn suǒpéi de yāoqiú ▶insurance claim 保险索赔要求 bǎoxiǎn suǒpéi yāoqiú

clap [klæp] VI 鼓掌 gǔzhǎng

clarinet [klærɪ'nɛt] (Mus) N [c] 单簧管 dānhuángguǎn [根 gēn]

class [klɑːs] I N 1 [c] (Scol: group of pupils) 班级 bānjí [个 gè]; (lesson) 课 kè [堂 táng] 2 [c/u] (social) 阶级 jiējí [个 gè] II VT (categorize) ▶to class sb/sth as 将某人/某物分类为 jiāng mǒurén/mǒuwù fēnlèi wéi

classic ['klæsɪk] N [c] 经典 jīngdiǎn [种 zhǒng]

classical ['klæsɪkl] ADJ 1 (traditional) 传统的 chuántǒng de 2 (Mus) 古典的 gǔdiǎn de

classmate ['klɑːsmeɪt] N [c] 同学 tóngxué [位 wèi]

classroom ['klɑːsrʊm] N [c] 教室 jiàoshì [间 jiān]

claw [klɔː] N [c] 爪子 zhuǎzi [只 zhī]

clay [kleɪ] N [u] 黏土 niántǔ

clean [kliːn] I ADJ 1 干净的 gānjìng de; [+ water] 清洁的 qīngjié de II VT [+ car, cooker] 弄干净 nòng gānjìng; [+ room] 打扫 dǎsǎo ▶a clean driving licence or (US) record 未有违章记录的驾照 wèiyǒu wéizhāng jìlù de jiàzhào ▶to clean one's teeth (Brit) 刷牙 shuāyá ▶ clean up [+ room, place] 打扫干净 dǎsǎo gānjìng; [+ mess] 整理 zhěnglǐ

cleaner ['kliːnər] N [c] (person) 清洁工 qīngjié gōng [位 wèi]

clear [klɪər] I ADJ 1 [+ explanation, account] 明确的 míngquè de 2 (visible) 清晰的 qīngxī de 3 (audible) 清晰的 qīngxī de 4 (obvious) 无疑的 wúyí de 5 (transparent) 透明的 tòumíng de 6 (unobstructed) 畅通的 chàngtōng de II VT [+ place, room] 清空 qīngkōng III VI [weather, sky] 变晴 biànqíng; [fog, smoke] 消散 xiāosàn ▶to be clear about sth 很明确某事 hěn míngquè mǒushì ▶to make o.s. clear 表达清楚 biǎodá qīngchǔ ▶to clear the table 收拾饭桌 shōushi fànzhuō ▶ clear away 清除 qīngchú ▶ clear off (inf) VI (leave) 走开 zǒukāi ▶ clear up I VT 1 [+ room, mess] 清理 qīnglǐ 2 [+ mystery, problem] 澄清 chéngqīng II VI (tidy up) 清理 qīnglǐ

clearly ['klɪəlɪ] ADV 1 明确地 míngquè de; (think) 清醒地 qīngxǐng de; (see) 清楚地 qīngchu de; (speak, hear) 清晰地 qīngxī de 2 (visible, audible) 清楚地 qīngchu de 3 (obviously) 显然 xiǎnrán

clever ['klɛvər] ADJ 1 聪明的 cōngmíng de 2 (sly, crafty) 要小聪明的 shuǎ xiǎocōngmíng de 3 [+ device, arrangement] 巧妙的 qiǎomiào de

click [klɪk] N [c] (Comput) ▶ with a click of one's mouse 按一下鼠标 àn yīxià shǔbiāo [下 xià] ▶to click on sth (Comput) 点击某处

diǎnjī mǒuchù

client ['klaɪənt] N [c] (of lawyer) 委托人 wěituōrén [个 gè]; (of company, restaurant, shop) 顾客 gùkè [位 wèi]

cliff [klɪf] N [c] 悬崖 xuányá [个 gè]

climate ['klaɪmɪt] N [c/u] 气候 qìhòu [种 zhǒng]

climb [klaɪm] I VT (also: **climb up**) [+ tree] 爬 pá; [+ mountain, hill] 攀登 pāndēng; [+ ladder] 登 dēng; [+ stairs, steps] 上 shàng II VI [person] 攀爬 pānpá III N [c] 攀登 pāndēng [次 cì] ▶**to go climbing** 去爬山 qù páshān

climber ['klaɪmə˞] N [c] 登山者 dēngshānzhě [个 gè]

climbing ['klaɪmɪŋ] N [u] 攀登 pāndēng

clingfilm ['klɪŋfɪlm] (Brit) N [u] 保鲜纸 bǎoxiān zhǐ

clinic ['klɪnɪk] (Med) N [c] 诊所 zhěnsuǒ [家 jiā]

cloakroom ['kləukrum] N [c] 1 (for coats) 衣帽间 yīmàojiān [个 gè] 2 (Brit: bathroom) 厕所 cèsuǒ [处 chù]

clock [klɒk] N [c] 钟 zhōng [个 gè] ▶**around the clock** (work, guard) 日夜不停 rìyè bùtíng ▶**clock in** VI (for work) 打卡上班 dǎkǎ shàngbān ▶**clock off** VI (from work) 打卡下班 dǎkǎ xiàbān ▶**clock on** VI = **clock in** ▶**clock out** VI = **clock off**

close¹ [kləus] I ADJ 1 近的 jìn de 2 [+ relative] 直系的 zhíxì de

3 [+ contest] 势均力敌的 shìjūnlìdí de II ADV (near) 紧紧地 jǐnjǐn de ▶**close to** (near) 近 jìn ▶**a close friend** 一位密友 yīwèi mìyǒu ▶**close by, close at hand** 在近旁 zài jìnpáng

close² [kləuz] I VT 1 关 guān 2 [+ shop, factory] 关闭 guānbì II VI 1 关 guān 2 [shop, library] 关门 guānmén ▶**close down** VI [factory, business] 关闭 guānbì

closed [kləuzd] ADJ [+ door, window] 关着的 guānzhe de; [+ shop, library] 关着门的 guānzhe mén de; [+ road] 封锁着的 fēngsuǒzhe de

closely ['kləuslɪ] ADV 1 (examine, watch) 仔细地 zǐxì de 2 (connected) 密切地 mìqiè de

closet ['klɒzɪt] N [c] (US) 壁橱 bìchú [个 gè]

cloth [klɒθ] N 1 [c/u] (fabric) 布料 bùliào [块 kuài] 2 [c] (for cleaning, dusting) 布 bù [块 kuài] 3 [c] (tablecloth) 桌布 zhuōbù [块 kuài]

clothes [kləuðz] NPL 衣服 yīfu ▶**to take one's clothes off** 脱衣服 tuō yīfu

cloud [klaud] N 1 [c/u] 云 yún [片 piàn] 2 [c] [of smoke, dust] 雾 wù [团 tuán] ▶**cloud over** VI 阴云密布 yīnyún mìbù

cloudy ['klaudɪ] ADJ 多云的 duōyún de ▶**it's cloudy** 天阴 tiānyīn

clown [klaun] N [c] 小丑 xiǎochǒu [个 gè]

club [klʌb] N [c] **1** 俱乐部 jùlèbù [个 gè] **2** (*Sport*) 俱乐部 jùlèbù [个 gè] **3** (*nightclub*) 夜总会 yèzǒnghuì [家 jiā]

clue [klu:] N [c] **1** (*in investigation*) 线索 xiànsuǒ [条 tiáo] **2** (*in crossword, game*) 提示 tíshì [个 gè] ▶**I haven't a clue** (*inf*) 我一无所知 wǒ yī wú suǒ zhī

clumsy [ˈklʌmzɪ] ADJ 笨手笨脚的 bènshǒubènjiǎo de

clutch [klʌtʃ] N [c] (*Aut*) 离合器 líhéqì [个 gè]

coach [kəʊtʃ] I N [c] **1** (*Brit*) 长途汽车 chángtú qìchē [辆 liàng] **2** (*Sport*) 教练 jiàoliàn [位 wèi] II VT (*Sport*) 训练 xùnliàn

coal [kəʊl] N [u] 煤 méi

coast [kəʊst] N [c] 海岸 hǎi'àn [个 gè]

coat [kəʊt] N [c] **1** (*overcoat*) 外套 wàitào [件 jiàn] **2** (*of animal*) 皮毛 pímáo [层 céng]

coat hanger N [c] 衣架 yījià [个 gè]

cocaine [kəˈkeɪn] N [u] 可卡因 kěkǎyīn

cock [kɔk] N [c] (*Brit*) 公鸡 gōngjī [只 zhī]

cocoa [ˈkəʊkəʊ] N [u] 可可 kěkě

coconut [ˈkəʊkənʌt] N [c] (*nut*) 椰子 yēzi [个 gè]

cod [kɔd] (*pl* cod *or* cods) N [c] (*fish*) 鳕鱼 xuěyú [条 tiáo]

code [kəʊd] N **1** [c] (*cipher*) 密码 mìmǎ [个 gè] **2** (*Tel*) 区号 qūhào [个 gè] **3** [c/u] (*Comput, Sci*) 编码 biānmǎ [个 gè]

coffee [ˈkɔfɪ] N **1** [u] 咖啡 kāfēi **2** [c] (*cup of coffee*) 一杯咖啡 yībēi kāfēi [杯 bēi] ▶**black coffee** 黑咖啡 hēi kāfēi ▶**white coffee** 牛奶咖啡 niúnǎi kāfēi

coffin [ˈkɔfɪn] N [c] 棺材 guāncai [口 kǒu]

coin [kɔɪn] N [c] 硬币 yìngbì [枚 méi]

coincidence [kəʊˈɪnsɪdəns] N [c/u] 巧合 qiǎohé [种 zhǒng]

Coke® [kəʊk] N [u] (*drink*) 可口可乐 Kěkǒu Kělè

cold [kəʊld] I ADJ [+ *water, object*] 凉的 liáng de; [+ *weather, room, meat*] 冷的 lěng de II N **1** [u] (*weather*) ▶**the cold** 寒冷天气 hánlěng tiānqì **2** [c] (*illness*) 感冒 gǎnmào [次 cì] ▶**it's cold** 天气寒冷 tiānqì hánlěng ▶**to be** *or* **feel cold** [*person*] 感到冷 gǎndào lěng ▶**to catch (a) cold** 患感冒 huàn gǎnmào

collapse [kəˈlæps] VI 倒坍 dǎotān; [*person*] 倒下 dǎoxià

collar [ˈkɔləʳ] N [c] 领子 lǐngzi [个 gè]

collarbone [ˈkɔləbəʊn] N [c] 锁骨 suǒgǔ [根 gēn]

colleague [ˈkɔliːg] N [c] 同事 tóngshì [个 gè]

collect [kəˈlɛkt] VT **1** 采集 cǎijí **2** (*as hobby*) 收集 shōují **3** (*Brit: fetch*) [+ *person*] 接 jiē; [+ *object*] 取 qǔ **4** [+ *money, donations*] 募捐 mùjuān ▶**to call collect, make a collect call** (*US*) (*Tel*) 打对方付款的电话 dǎ duìfāng fùkuǎn de diànhuà

collection [kəˈlɛkʃən] N **1** [c] [*of*

art, stamps] 收藏品 shōucáng pǐn [件 jiàn] **2** [c] (for charity, gift) 募捐 mùjuān [次 cì]

collector [kəˈlɛktəʳ] N [c] 收藏家 shōucáng jiā [位 wèi]

college [ˈkɔlɪdʒ] N **1** [c/u] (for further education) 学院 xuéyuàn [个 gè] **2** [c] (of university) 学院 xuéyuàn [个 gè] ▶**to go to college** 上大学 shàng dàxué

collide [kəˈlaɪd] VI 碰撞 pèngzhuàng ▶**to collide with sth/sb** 与某物/某人碰撞 yǔ mǒuwù/mǒurén pèngzhuàng

collision [kəˈlɪʒən] N [c/u] (of vehicles) 碰撞 pèngzhuàng [下 xià]

colonel [ˈkəːnl] N [c] 上校 shàngxiào [位 wèi]

color etc [ˈkʌləʳ] (US) = **colour** etc

colour, (US) **color** [ˈkʌləʳ] I N **1** [c] 颜色 yánsè [种 zhǒng] **2** [c] (skin colour) 肤色 fūsè [种 zhǒng] II VT 给…着色 gěi…zhuósè III CPD [+ film, photograph, television] 彩色 cǎisè ▶**in colour** [+ film, illustrations] 彩色 cǎisè

colourful, (US) **colorful** [ˈkʌləful] ADJ 色泽鲜艳的 sèzé xiānyàn de

colour television, (US) **color television** N [c/u] 彩色电视 cǎisè diànshì [台 tái]

column [ˈkɔləm] N [c] (Archit) 支柱 zhīzhù [个 gè]

comb [kəum] I N [c] 梳子 shūzi [把 bǎ] II VT 梳理 shūlǐ

combination [kɔmbɪˈneɪʃən] N [c] 混合 hùnhé [种 zhǒng]

combine [kəmˈbaɪn] I VT ▶**to**

combine sth with sth 将某物与某物结合起来 jiāng mǒuwù yǔ mǒuwù jiéhé qǐlái II VI [qualities, situations] 结合 jiéhé; [people, groups] 组合 zǔhé ▶**a combined effort** 协力 xiélì

KEYWORD

come [kʌm] (pt **came**, pp **come**) VI **1** 来 lái ▶**come here!** 到这儿来! dào zhèʳ lái! ▶**can I come too?** 我也能来吗? wǒ yěnéng láima? ▶**come with me** 跟我来 gēn wǒ lái ▶**a girl came into the room** 一个女孩进了房间 yīgè nǚhái jìnle fángjiān ▶**why don't you come to lunch on Saturday?** 何不星期六过来吃午饭呢? hébù xīngqīliù guòlái chī wǔfàn ne? ▶**he's come here to work** 他已经到了这儿工作 tā yǐjīng dàole zhèʳ gōngzuò **2** ▶**to come to** (reach) 到达 dàodá; (amount to) 达到 dàdào ▶**to come to a decision** 做出决定 zuòchū juédìng ▶**the bill came to £40** 账单共计40英镑 zhàngdān gòngjì sìshí yīngbàng **3** (be, become) ▶**to come first/second/last** etc (in series) 排在第一/第二/最后{等} páizài dìyī/dì'èr/zuìhòu{děng}; (in competition, race) 位居第一/第二/最后{等} wèijū dìyī/dì'èr/zuìhòu{děng}

▶**come across** VT FUS 偶然发现 ǒurán fāxiàn

▶**come apart** VI 裂成碎片 lièchéng suìpiàn

▶**come back** VI (return) 回来

huílái

▶ **come down** VI 1 [*price*] 降低 jiàngdī

2 [*plane*] 坠落 zhuìluò

3 (*descend*) 降下 jiàngxià

▶ **come forward** VI (*volunteer*) 自告奋勇 zìgàofènyǒng

▶ **come from** VT FUS 来自 láizì ▶ I **come from London** 我来自伦敦 wǒ láizì Lúndūn ▶ **where do you come from?** 你是哪里人？nǐ shì nǎlǐ rén?

▶ **come in** VI 进入 jìnrù ▶ **come in!** 进来！jìnlai!

▶ **come off** VI [*button, handle*] 脱落 tuōluò

▶ **come on** VI (*progress*) 进展 jìnzhǎn ▶ **come on!** (*giving encouragement*) 来！lái!; (*hurry up*) 快一点！kuàiyìdiǎn!

▶ **come out** VI 1 [*person*] 出去 chūqù

2 [*sun*] 出现 chūxiàn

3 [*book*] 出版 chūbǎn; [*film*] 上映 shàngyìng

▶ **come through** VT FUS (*survive*) 经历…而幸存 jīnglì…ér xìngcún

▶ **come to** VI (*regain consciousness*) 苏醒 sūxǐng

▶ **come up** VI 1 (*approach*) 走近 zǒujìn

2 [*problem, opportunity*] 突然出现 tūrán chūxiàn

▶ **come up to** VT FUS 1 (*approach*) 走近 zǒujìn

2 (*meet*) ▶ **the film didn't come up to our expectations** 电影没有我们预期的那么好 diànyǐng méiyǒu wǒmen yùqī de nàme hǎo

comedian [kə'miːdɪən] (*Theat, TV*) N [c] 喜剧演员 xǐjù yǎnyuán [个 gè]

comedy ['kɒmɪdɪ] N 1 [U] (*humour*) 幽默 yōumò 2 [c] (*play, film*) 喜剧 xǐjù [部 bù]

comfortable ['kʌmfətəbl] ADJ 1 [*person*] ▶ **to be comfortable** 舒服的 shūfu de 2 [+ *furniture, room, clothes*] 使人舒服的 shǐ rén shūfu de ▶ **to make o.s. comfortable** 自在点 zìzài diǎn

comma ['kɒmə] N [c] 逗号 dòuhào [个 gè]

command [kə'mɑːnd] N 1 [c] (*order*) 命令 mìnglìng [项 xiàng] 2 [c] (*Comput*) 指令 zhǐlìng [个 gè]

comment ['kɒment] I N [c/U] 评论 pínglùn [种 zhǒng] II VI ▶ **to comment (on sth)** (对某事) 发表意见 (duì mǒushì) fābiǎo yìjiàn ▶ **"no comment"** "无可奉告" "wú kě fèng gào"

commentary ['kɒməntərɪ] N [c/U] 实况报道 shíkuàng bàodào [段 duàn]

commentator ['kɒmənteɪtər] N [c] 解说员 jiěshuōyuán [位 wèi]

commercial [kə'məːʃəl] I ADJ [+ *success, failure*] 从盈利角度出发 cóng yínglì jiǎodù chūfā; [+ *television, radio*] 商业性的 shāngyè xìng de II N [c] (*advertisement*) 广告 guǎnggào [则 zé]

commit [kə'mɪt] VT 犯 fàn ▶ **to commit suicide** 自杀 zìshā

committee [kə'mɪtɪ] N [c] 委员会 wěiyuánhuì [个 gè]

common [ˈkɔmən] ADJ 常见的 chángjiàn de ▸**to have sth in common** [+ people] 有某些共同点 yǒu mǒuxiē gòngtóngdiǎn; [things] 有共同的某特征 yǒu gòngtóng de mǒutèzhēng ▸**to have sth in common with sb/sth** 与某人/某物有某共同点 yǔ mǒurén/mǒuwù yǒu mǒu gòngtóngdiǎn

common sense N [U] 常识 chángshí

communicate [kəˈmjuːnɪkeɪt] VI 联络 liánluò

communication [kəmjuːnɪˈkeɪʃən] I N [U] 交流 jiāoliú II **communications** NPL 通讯 tōngxùn

communism [ˈkɔmjunɪzəm] N [U] 共产主义 gòngchǎnzhǔyì

community [kəˈmjuːnɪtɪ] N [c] 社区 shèqū [个 gè]

commute [kəˈmjuːt] VI 乘车上下班 chéngchē shàngxiàbān ▸**to commute to/from London/Brighton** 去/从伦敦/布赖顿乘车上下班 qù/cóng Lúndūn/Bùlàidùn chéngchē shàngxià bān

compact disc N [c] 激光唱片 jīguāng chàngpiàn [张 zhāng]

company [ˈkʌmpənɪ] N 1 [c] (firm) 公司 gōngsī [个 gè] 2 [U] (companionship) 交往 jiāowǎng ▸**to keep sb company** 陪伴某人 péibàn mǒurén

comparatively [kəmˈpærətɪvlɪ] ADV [+ easy, safe, peaceful] 相对地 xiāngduì de

compare [kəmˈpɛəʳ] I VT 比

较 bǐjiào II VI ▸**to compare favourably/unfavourably (with sth/sb)** 比得上/比不上(某物/某人) bǐdeshang/bǐbùshang (mǒuwù/mǒurén) ▸**to compare sb/sth to** 把某人/某物比作 bǎ mǒurén/mǒuwù bǐzuò ▸**compared with** or **to** 与…相比 yǔ…xiāngbǐ ▸**how does he compare with his predecessor?** 和他前任比起来他怎么样? hé tā qiánrèn bǐ qǐlái tā zěnmeyàng?

comparison [kəmˈpærɪsn] N [c/U] 比较 bǐjiào [种 zhǒng] ▸**in** or **by comparison (with)** (与…)比较起来 (yǔ…) bǐjiào qǐlái

compartment [kəmˈpɑːtmənt] N [c] (Rail) 隔间 géjiān [个 gè]

compass [ˈkʌmpəs] N [c] 指南针 zhǐnánzhēn [个 gè]

compatible [kəmˈpætɪbl] ADJ [+ people] 意气相投的 yìqì xiāngtóu de; (Comput) 兼容的 jiānróng de ▸**to be compatible with sth** (Comput) 与某物兼容 yǔ mǒuwù jiānróng

compensation [kɔmpənˈseɪʃən] N [U] 赔偿金 péicháng jīn ▸**compensation for sth** 因某事而获得的赔偿金 yīn mǒushì ér huòdé de péichángjīn

compete [kəmˈpiːt] VI [companies, rivals] 竞争 jìngzhēng; (in contest, game) 比赛 bǐsài ▸**to compete for sth** [companies, rivals] 争夺某物 zhēngduó mǒuwù; (in contest, game) 争夺某物 zhēngduó móuwù ▸**to compete with sb/sth (for sth)** [companies, rivals] 与某

人/某物竞争(以得到某物) yǔ mǒurén/mǒuwù jìngzhēng (yǐ dédào mǒuwù); (in contest, game) 与某人/某物竞争(以获得某奖项) yǔ mǒurén/mǒuwù jìngzhēng (yǐ huòdé jiǎngxiàng)

competent ['kɔmpɪtənt] ADJ 称职的 chènzhí de; [+ piece of work] 合格的 hégé de

competition [kɔmpɪ'tɪʃən] N 1 [U] (rivalry) 竞争 jìngzhēng 2 [c] (contest) 竞赛 jìngsài [项 xiàng] ▶in competition with 与…竞争 yǔ…jìngzhēng

competitive [kəm'pɛtɪtɪv] ADJ 1 [+ industry, society] 竞争性的 jìngzhēngxìng de 2 [+ person] 求胜心切的 qiúshèngxīnqiè de

competitor [kəm'pɛtɪtəʳ] N [c] 1 (in business) 竞争对手 jìngzhēng duìshǒu [个 gè] 2 (participant) 参赛者 cānsàizhě [个 gè]

complain [kəm'pleɪn] VI ▶to complain (about sth) (就某事)投诉 (jiù mǒushì) tóusù; (grumble) (就某事)诉苦 (jiù mǒushì) sùkǔ ▶to complain to sb (about sth) (就某事)向某人投诉 (jiù mǒushì) xiàng mǒurén tóusù

complaint [kəm'pleɪnt] N [c] 抱怨 bàoyuàn [个 gè] ▶to make a complaint (to sb) (向某人)投诉 (xiàng mǒurén) tóusù

complete [kəm'pliːt] I ADJ 1 完全的 wánquán de 2 (whole) 完整的 wánzhěng de 3 (finished) 完成的 wánchéng de II VT 1 完成 wánchéng 2 [+ form, coupon] 填写 tiánxiě ▶complete with 附

带 fùdài

completely [kəm'pliːtlɪ] ADV (different, satisfied, untrue) 完全 wánquán; (forget, destroy) 彻底 chèdǐ

complexion [kəm'plɛkʃən] N [c] 面色 miànsè [种 zhǒng]

complicated ['kɔmplɪkeɪtɪd] ADJ 复杂的 fùzá de

compliment [n 'kɔmplɪmənt, vb 'kɔmplɪmɛnt] I N [c] 赞美 zànměi [种 zhǒng] II VT 赞美 zànměi ▶to pay sb a compliment 赞美某人 zànměi mǒurén ▶to compliment sb on sth 为某事赞美某人 wèi mǒushì zànměi mǒurén

composer [kəm'pəuzəʳ] N [c] 作曲家 zuòqǔjiā [位 wèi]

comprehension [kɔmprɪ'hɛnʃən] N 1 [U] (understanding) 理解 lǐjiě 2 [c/U] (Scol) 理解力练习 lǐjiělì liànxí [项 xiàng]

comprehensive [kɔmprɪ'hɛnsɪv] I ADJ 1 [+ review, list] 全面的 quánmiàn de 2 (of insurance) 综合的 zōnghé de II N [c] (Brit) (also: **comprehensive school**) 综合性中学 zōnghéxìng zhōngxué [所 suǒ]

compulsory [kəm'pʌlsərɪ] ADJ 必须的 bìxū de; [+ course] 必修的 bìxiū de

computer [kəm'pjuːtəʳ] I N [c] 计算机 jìsuànjī [台 tái] II CPD [+ language, program, system, technology etc] 电脑 diànnǎo

computer game N [c] 电脑游戏 diànnǎo yóuxì [局 jú]

computer programmer

N [C] 电脑编程员 diànnǎo biānchéngyuán [位 wèi]

computer science N [U] 计算机科学 jìsuànjī kēxué

computing [kəm'pjuːtɪŋ] I N [U] 计算机运用 jìsuànjī yùnyòng; (also: **computing studies**) 计算机学 jìsuànjīxué II CPD [+ course, skills] 电脑 diànnǎo

concentrate ['kɒnsəntreɪt] VI 集中精力 jízhōng jīnglì ▶to **concentrate on sth** (keep attention on) 全神贯注于某事 quán shén guàn zhù yú mǒushì; (focus on) 集中注意力于某事 jízhōng zhùyìlì yú mǒushì

concentration [kɒnsən'treɪʃən] N [U] 专心 zhuānxīn

concern [kən'sɜːn] I N [U] (anxiety) 担忧 dānyōu II VT (worry) 使担忧 shǐ dānyōu ▶**concern for sb** 为某人担心 wèi mǒurén dānxīn ▶**as far as I'm concerned** 据我看来 jù wǒ kànlái ▶**the people concerned** (in question) 有关人士 yǒuguān rénshì

concerned [kən'sɜːnd] ADJ (worried) 担心的 dānxīn de ▶to **be concerned about sb/sth** 担心某人/某事 dānxīn mǒurén/mǒushì

concerning [kən'sɜːnɪŋ] PREP 关于 guānyú

concert ['kɒnsət] N [C] 音乐会 yīnyuèhuì [个 gè]

concert hall N [C] 音乐厅 yīnyuètīng [个 gè]

conclusion [kən'kluːʒən] N 1 [S] (end) 结尾 jiéwěi 2 [C] (deduction) 结论 jiélùn [个 gè] ▶to **come to**

the **conclusion that...** 得出的结论是… déchū de jiélùn shì...

concrete ['kɒŋkriːt] I N [U] 混凝土 hùnníngtǔ II ADJ 1 [+ block, floor] 混凝土的 hùnníngtǔ de 2 [+ proposal, evidence] 确实的 quèshí de

condemn [kən'dɛm] VT (denounce) 谴责 qiǎnzé

condition [kən'dɪʃən] I N 1 [S] (state) 状态 zhuàngtài 2 [C] (stipulation) 条件 tiáojiàn [个 gè] II **conditions** NPL 环境 huánjìng ▶**in good/poor condition** 状况良好/不好 zhuàngkuàng liánghǎo/bùhǎo ▶**weather conditions** 天气形势 tiānqì xíngshì ▶**on condition that...** 在…条件下 zài...tiáojiàn xià

conditional [kən'dɪʃənl] I ADJ 有条件的 yǒu tiáojiàn de II N (Ling) ▶**the conditional** 条件从句 tiáojiàn cóngjù

conditioner [kən'dɪʃənər] N [C/U] 护发素 hùfàsù [种 zhǒng]

condom ['kɒndəm] N [C] 安全套 ānquán tào [只 zhī]

conduct [kən'dʌkt] VT [+ orchestra, choir] 指挥 zhǐhuī

conductor [kən'dʌktər] N [C] 1 (of orchestra) 指挥家 zhǐhuījiā [位 wèi] 2 (US: on train) 列车员 lièchēyuán [位 wèi] 3 (on bus) 售票员 shòupiàoyuán [位 wèi]

cone [kəun] N [C] 1 (shape) 圆锥体 yuánzhuītǐ [个 gè] 2 (also: **ice cream cone**) 锥形蛋卷冰淇淋 zhuīxíng dànjuǎn bīngqílín [个 gè]

conference ['kɒnfərəns] N [C] 会

议 huìyì [次 cì]

confess [kən'fɛs] VI 坦白 tǎnbái
▶**to confess to sth/to doing sth**
承认某事/做了某事 chéngrèn
mǒushì/zuòle mǒushì

confession [kən'fɛʃən] N [C/U]
(admission) 坦白 tǎnbái [种 zhǒng]
▶**to make a confession** 坦白
tǎnbái

confidence ['kɔnfɪdns] N **1**
[U] (faith) 信赖 xìnlài **2** [U]
(self-assurance) 自信 zìxìn ▶**in
confidence** 秘密地 mìmì de

confident ['kɔnfɪdənt] ADJ (self-
assured) 自信的 zìxìn de ▶**to be
confident that...** 有信心… yǒu
xìnxīn…

confidential [kɔnfɪ'dɛnʃəl] ADJ
机密的 jīmì de

confirm [kən'fə:m] VT 肯定
kěndìng; [+ appointment, date] 确
认 quèrèn

confiscate ['kɔnfɪskeɪt] VT 没
收 mòshōu ▶**to confiscate sth
from sb** 没收某人的某物 mòshōu
mǒurén de mǒuwù

confuse [kən'fju:z] VT **1** (perplex)
把…弄糊涂 bǎ...nòng hútu **2** (mix
up) 混淆 hùnxiáo

confused [kən'fju:zd] ADJ 困惑
的 kùnhuò de

confusing [kən'fju:zɪŋ] ADJ 含混
不清的 hánhùn bùqīng de

confusion [kən'fju:ʒən] N **1** [C/U]
(uncertainty) 惶惑 huánghuò [种
zhǒng] **2** [U] (mix-up) 混淆 hùnxiáo

congratulate [kən'grætjuleɪt]
VT 祝贺 zhùhè ▶**to congratulate
sb on sth/on doing sth** 祝贺某

人某事/做某事 zhùhè mǒurén
mǒushì/zuò mǒushì

congratulations
[kəngrætju'leɪʃənz] NPL 祝贺
zhùhè ▶**congratulations on your
engagement!** 祝贺你订婚了!
zhùhè nǐ dìnghūn le!

Congress ['kɔngrɛs] N (US)
▶ **Congress** 国会 guóhuì

congressman ['kɔngrɛsmən] (pl
congressmen) (US) N [c] 国会议
员 guóhuì yìyuán [位 wèi]

congresswoman
['kɔngrɛswumən] (pl
congresswomen) (US) N [c] 女国
会议员 nǔ guóhuì yìyuán [位 wèi]

connection [kə'nɛkʃən] N **1** [C/U]
(link) 联系 liánxì [种 zhǒng] **2**
[c] (Elec) 接头 jiētóu [个 gè] **3**
[c] (train, plane) 联运 liányùn [种
zhǒng] ▶**what is the connection
between them?** 他们之间有什么
关系? tāmen zhījiān yǒu shénme
guānxì?

conscience ['kɔnʃəns] N [c] 是非
感 shìfēi gǎn [种 zhǒng] ▶**to have
a guilty/clear conscience** 感到
内疚/问心无愧 gǎndào nèijiù/wèn
xīn wú kuì

conscientious [kɔnʃɪ'ɛnʃəs] ADJ
认真的 rènzhēn de

conscious ['kɔnʃəs] ADJ **1** (awake)
清醒的 qīngxǐng de **2** [+ decision,
effort] 蓄意的 xùyì de ▶**to be
conscious of sth** 意识到某事
yìshí dào mǒushì

consciousness ['kɔnʃəsnɪs] N
[U] (Med) 知觉 zhījué ▶**to lose
consciousness** 失去知觉 shīqù

zhījué

consequence [ˈkɔnsɪkwəns] N [c] 后果 hòuguǒ [种 zhǒng]

consequently [ˈkɔnsɪkwəntlɪ] ADV 所以 suǒyǐ

conservation [kɔnsəˈveɪʃən] N [U] [of environment] 环保 huánbǎo; [of energy] 节约 jiéyuē

conservative [kənˈsəːvətɪv] I ADJ 1 (traditional) 保守的 bǎoshǒu de 2 (Brit)(Pol) ▶ **Conservative** 保守党 bǎoshǒudǎng II N [c] (Brit) (Pol) ▶ **Conservative** 保守党人士 bǎoshǒudǎng rénshì [名 míng]

conservatory [kənˈsəːvətrɪ] N [c] 暖房 nuǎnfáng [间 jiān]

consider [kənˈsɪdər] VT 1 (think about) 考虑 kǎolǜ 2 (take into account) 考虑到 kǎolǜ dào

considerate [kənˈsɪdərɪt] ADJ 体贴的 tǐtiē de

considering [kənˈsɪdərɪŋ] I PREP 考虑到 kǎolǜ dào II CONJ ▶ **considering (that)...** 考虑到… kǎolǜ dào…

consist [kənˈsɪst] VI ▶ **to consist of** 由…组成 yóu…zǔchéng

consonant [ˈkɔnsənənt] N [c] 辅音 fǔyīn [个 gè]

constant [ˈkɔnstənt] ADJ 1 [+ threat, pressure, pain, reminder] 不断的 bùduàn de 2 [+ interruptions, demands] 重复的 chóngfù de 3 [+ temperature, speed] 恒定的 héngdìng de

constantly [ˈkɔnstəntlɪ] ADV 1 (repeatedly) 不断地 bùduàn de 2 (uninterruptedly) 持续地 chíxù de

constipated [ˈkɔnstɪpeɪtɪd] ADJ

便秘的 biànmì de

construct [kənˈstrʌkt] VT 建造 jiànzào

construction [kənˈstrʌkʃən] N 1 [U] [of building, road, machine] 建造 jiànzào 2 [c] (structure) 建筑 jiànzhù [座 zuò]

consult [kənˈsʌlt] VT [+ doctor, lawyer, friend] 咨询 zīxún; [+ book, map] 查阅 cháyuè

consumer [kənˈsjuːmər] N [c] [of goods, services] 消费者 xiāofèizhě [个 gè]; [of resources] 使用者 shǐyòngzhě [个 gè]

contact [ˈkɔntækt] I N 1 [c/u] (communication) 联络 liánluò [种 zhǒng] 2 [c] (person) 熟人 shúrén [个 gè] II VT 联系 liánxì ▶ **to be in contact with sb** 与某人有联络 yǔ mǒurén yǒu liánluò

contact lenses NPL 隐形眼镜 yǐnxíng yǎnjìng

contain [kənˈteɪn] VT [+ objects] 装有 zhuāngyǒu; [+ component, ingredient] 含有 hányǒu

container [kənˈteɪnər] N [c] 1 (box, jar etc) 容器 róngqì [个 gè] 2 (for transport) 集装箱 jízhuāngxiāng [个 gè]

content¹ [ˈkɔntɛnt] I N [U] 内容 nèiróng II **contents** NPL [of bottle, packet] 所含之物 suǒhán zhī wù

content² [kənˈtɛnt] ADJ 满足的 mǎnzú de

contest [ˈkɔntɛst] N [c] 比赛 bǐsài [项 xiàng]

contestant [kənˈtɛstənt] N [c] 参赛者 cānsàizhě [位 wèi]

context [ˈkɔntɛkst] N [c/u] [of

word, phrase] 上下文 shàngxiàwén [个 gè]

continent ['kɒntɪnənt] N [c] 大陆 dàlù [个 gè] ▶on the Continent (Brit) 在欧洲大陆 zài Ōuzhōu dàlù

continental breakfast N [c] 欧洲大陆式早餐 Ōuzhōu dàlù shì zǎocān [顿 dùn]

continue [kən'tɪnju:] VI 1 继续 jìxù 2 [speaker] 继续说 jìxù shuō ▶to continue to do sth or doing sth 持续做某事 chíxù zuò mǒushì ▶to continue with sth 继续某事 jìxù mǒushì

continuous [kən'tɪnjuəs] ADJ 连续不停的 liánxù bù tíng de

contraception [kɒntrə'sɛpʃən] N [U] 避孕 bìyùn

contraceptive [kɒntrə'sɛptɪv] N [c] (drug) 避孕药 bìyùn yào [片 piàn]; (device) 避孕工具 bìyùn gōngjù [种 zhǒng]

contract ['kɒntrækt] N [c] 合同 hétong [份 fèn]

contradict [kɒntrə'dɪkt] VT 驳斥 bóchì

contradiction [kɒntrə'dɪkʃən] N [c/U] 矛盾 máodùn [种 zhǒng]

contrary ['kɒntrərɪ] N [c/U] ▶the contrary 相反 xiāngfǎn ▶on the contrary 正相反 zhèng xiāngfǎn

contrast [n 'kɒntrɑːst, vb kən'trɑːst] I N [c/U] 1 明显的差异 míngxiǎn de chāyì [种 zhǒng] 2 ▶to be a contrast to sth 与某物截然不同 yǔ mǒuwù jiérán bùtóng [个 gè] II VI ▶to contrast

with sth 与某事形成对照 yǔ mǒushì xíngchéng duìzhào ▶to contrast sth with sth 将某物与某物进行对比 jiāng mǒuwù yǔ mǒuwù jìnxíng duìbǐ

contribute [kən'trɪbju:t] I VI ▶to contribute (to sth) (with money) (给某事) 捐助 (gěi mǒushì) juānzhù II VT ▶to contribute 10 pounds (to sth) (给某事) 捐献10英镑 (gěi mǒushì) juānxiàn shí yīngbàng

contribution [kɒntrɪ'bju:ʃən] N [c] 捐献 juānxiàn [次 cì]

control [kən'trəul] I VT [+ country, organization] 统治 tǒngzhì; [+ person, emotion, disease, fire] 控制 kòngzhì II N [U] [of country, organization] 控制权 kòngzhì quán III controls NPL [of vehicle, machine, TV] 操纵装置 cāozòng zhuāngzhì ▶to control o.s. 克制自己 kèzhì zìjǐ ▶to be in control (of sth) (of situation, car) 控制着 (某事) kòngzhì zhe (mǒushì) ▶to be under control [fire, situation] 处于控制之下 chǔyú kòngzhì zhīxià ▶circumstances beyond our control 不在我们控制之中的情况 bùzài wǒmen kòngzhì zhīzhōng de qíngkuàng

controversial [kɒntrə'və:ʃl] ADJ 有争议的 yǒu zhēngyì de; [+ book, film] 引起争论的 yǐnqǐ zhēnglùn de

convenient [kən'vi:nɪənt] ADJ [+ method, system, time] 方便的 fāngbiàn de; [+ place] 近便的 jìnbiàn de

conventional [kən'vɛnʃənl] ADJ 符合习俗的 fúhé xísú de; [+ *method, product*] 传统的 chuántǒng de

conversation [kɔnvə'seɪʃən] N [C/U] 交谈 jiāotán [次 cì] ▶**to have a conversation (about sth/with sb)** (和某人)谈(某事) (hé mǒurén) tán (mǒushì)

convert [kən'vɜːt] VT (*transform*) [+ *substance*] 使转化 shǐ zhuǎnhuà; [+ *building*] 改建 gǎijiàn ▶**to convert sth into sth** [+ *substance*] 将某物转化成某物 jiāng mǒuwù zhuǎnhuà chéng mǒuwù; [+ *building*] 将某建筑改建成某建筑 jiāng mǒujiànzhù gǎijiàn chéng mǒujiànzhù

convince [kən'vɪns] VT 1 (*cause to believe*) 使信服 shǐ xìnfú 2 说服 shuōfú ▶**to convince sb to do sth** 说服某人去做某事 shuōfú mǒurén qù zuò mǒushì

cook [kuk] I VT [+ *food, meat, vegetables*] 烹调 pēngtiáo; [+ *meal*] 做 zuò II VI 1 [*person*] 做饭 zuòfàn 2 [*food*] 烧 shāo III N [C] 厨师 chúshī [位 wèi] ▶**a good cook** 会做饭的人 huì zuòfàn de rén

cooker ['kukə^r] (*Brit*) N [C] 厨灶 chúzào [个 gè]

cookie ['kukɪ] N [C] 1 (*US: for eating*) 小甜饼 xiǎotiánbǐng [块 kuài] 2 (*Comput*) 记忆块 jìyì kuài [个 gè]

cooking ['kukɪŋ] N [U] 烹调 pēngtiáo

cool [kuːl] I ADJ 1 凉的 liáng de 2 (*calm, unemotional*) 冷静的 lěngjìng de 3 (*inf: good*) 顶呱呱的 dǐngguāguā de; (*fashionable*) 酷的 kù de II VT 使变凉 shǐ biànliáng III VI 冷下来 lěngxiàlái IV N ▶**to keep/lose one's cool** (*inf*) 保持冷静/失去自制而激动起来 bǎochí lěngjìng/shīqù zìzhì ér jīdòng qǐlái ▶**to keep sth cool** 保持某物的凉度 bǎochí mǒuwù de liángdù
▶ **cool down** VI 变凉 biànliáng

co-operate [kəu'ɔpəreɪt] VI 1 (*collaborate*) 合作 hézuò 2 (*be helpful*) 配合 pèihé

cope [kəup] VI 对付 duìfù

copper ['kɔpə^r] N [U] 铜 tóng

copy ['kɔpɪ] I N 1 [C] 复制品 fùzhìpǐn [件 jiàn] 2 [C] 本/张/份 běn/zhāng/fèn II VT 模仿 mófǎng ▶**to make a copy of sth** 复印某物 fùyìn mǒuwù

cork [kɔːk] N [C] 瓶塞 píngsāi [个 gè]

corkscrew ['kɔːkskruː] N [C] 瓶塞钻 píngsāizuàn [个 gè]

corn [kɔːn] N 1 [U] (*Brit: cereal crop*) 谷物 gǔwù 2 [U] (*US: maize*) 玉米 yùmǐ ▶**corn on the cob** 玉米(棒子) yùmǐ (bàngzi)

corner ['kɔːnə^r] N [C] 1 角落 jiǎoluò [个 gè] 2 [*of road*] 街角 jiējiǎo [个 gè]

corpse [kɔːps] N [C] 死尸 sǐshī [具 jù]

correct [kə'rɛkt] I ADJ 正确的 zhèngquè de; [+ *decision, means, procedure*] 适当的 shìdàng de II VT [+ *mistake, fault, person*] 纠

正 jiūzhèng

correction [kəˈrɛkʃən] N [c] 修改 xiūgǎi [次 cì]

corridor [ˈkɔrɪdɔːʳ] N [c] (*in house, building*) 走廊 zǒuláng [条 tiáo]; (*on train*) 车厢过道 chēxiāng guòdào [个 gè]

corruption [kəˈrʌpʃən] N [U] 贪赃舞弊 tānzāng wǔbì

cosmetics [kɔzˈmɛtɪks] NPL (*beauty products*) 化妆品 huàzhuāng pǐn

cost [kɔst] (*pt, pp* cost) I N [c] 价格 jiàgé [种 zhǒng] II VT 价格为 jiàgé wéi ▸**how much does it cost?** 这多少钱? zhè duōshǎo qián? ▸**it costs 5 pounds/too much** 价格为5英镑/太高 jiàgé wéi wǔ yīngbàng/tàigāo ▸**the cost of living** 生活费用 shēnghuó fèiyòng

costume [ˈkɔstjuːm] N [c/U] 戏装 xìzhuāng [套 tào]

cot [kɔt] N [c] 1 (*Brit: child's*) 幼儿床 yòu'ér chuáng [张 zhāng] 2 (*US: bed*) 帆布床 fānbù chuáng [张 zhāng]

cottage [ˈkɔtɪdʒ] N [c] 村舍 cūnshè [个 gè]

cotton [ˈkɔtn] I N [U] 1 (*fabric*) 棉布 miánbù 2 (*thread*) 棉线 miánxiàn II CPD [+ *dress, sheets*] 棉布 miánbù

cotton wool (*Brit*) N [U] 脱脂棉 tuōzhī mián

couch [kautʃ] N [c] 长沙发 cháng shāfā [个 gè]

cough [kɔf] I VI 咳嗽 késou II N [c] 咳嗽 késou [阵 zhèn] ▸**to**

have a cough 咳嗽 késou

KEYWORD

could [kud] AUX VB 1 (*referring to past*) ▸**we couldn't go to the party** 我们没能去参加聚会 wǒmen méi néng qù cānjiā jùhuì ▸**he couldn't read or write** 他不会读也不会写 tā búhuì dú yě búhuì xiě

2 (*possibility*) 他可能在图书馆 tā kěnéng zài túshūguǎn ▸**you could have been killed!** 可能你连命都没了! kěnéng nǐ lián mìng dōu méile!

3 (*in conditionals with "if"*) ▸**if we had more time, I could finish this** 如果有更多时间, 我能够完成的 rúguǒ yǒu gèngduō shíjiān, wǒ nénggòu wánchéng de ▸**we'd have a holiday, if we could afford it** 如果能支付得起的话, 我们就去度假了 rúguǒ néng zhīfù de qǐ de huà, wǒmen jiù qù dùjià le

4 (*in offers, suggestions, requests*) 可以 kěyǐ ▸**I could call a doctor** 我可以叫个医生 wǒ kěyǐ jiào gè yīshēng ▸**could I borrow the car?** 我可以借一下车吗? wǒ kěyǐ jiè yīxià chē ma? ▸**he asked if he could make a phone call** 他问是否可以打个电话 tā wèn shìfǒu kěyǐ dǎgè diànhuà

council [ˈkaunsl] N [c] 议会 yìhuì [个 gè]

count [kaunt] I VT 1 (*also:* **count**

up) 数 shǔ **2** (include) 把…计算在内 bǎ…jìsuàn zàinèi **II** vi **1** 数 shǔ **2** (matter) 有价值 yǒu jiàzhí ▶**to count (up) to 10** 数到10 shǔdào shí

▶ **count on** vт FUS [+ support, help] 指望 zhǐwàng; [+ person] 依靠 yīkào

counter ['kauntəʳ] N [c] 柜台 guìtái [个 gè]

country ['kʌntrɪ] N **1** [c] (nation) 国家 guójiā [个 gè] **2** (countryside) ▶**the country** 乡下 xiāngxià [个 gè] **3** [c] (native land) 家乡 jiāxiāng [个 gè]

countryside ['kʌntrɪsaɪd] N [U] 农村 nóngcūn

couple ['kʌpl] N [c] **1** (married) 夫妻 fūqī [对 duì]; (living together) 情侣 qínglǚ [对 duì] **2** ▶ **a couple of** (two) 两个 liǎnggè

courage ['kʌrɪdʒ] N [U] 勇气 yǒngqì

courier ['kurɪəʳ] N [c] **1** (messenger) 信使 xìnshǐ [个 gè] **2** (rep) 旅游团的服务员 lǚyóutuán de fúwùyuán [个 gè]

course [kɔːs] N **1** [c] 课程 kèchéng [个 gè] **2** (of meal) ▶**first/next/last course** 第一/下一/最后一道菜 dìyī/xiàyī/zuìhòu yīdào cài [道 dào] **3** [c] (for golf, horse-racing) 场 chǎng ▶**of course** (naturally) 自然 zìrán; (certainly) 当然 dāngrán

▶**of course!** 没问题！ méi wèntí!

▶**of course not!** 当然不行！ dāngrán bùxíng!

court [kɔːt] N [c] **1** (Law) 法庭 fǎtíng [个 gè] **2** (for tennis, badminton) 球场 qiúchǎng [个 gè].

courthouse ['kɔːthaus] (US) N [c] 法院 fǎyuàn [个 gè]

courtyard ['kɔːtjɑːd] N [c] 庭院 tíngyuàn [个 gè]

cousin ['kʌzn] N [c] (older male on father's side) 堂兄 tángxiōng [个 gè]; (younger male on father's side) 堂弟 tángdì [个 gè]; (older female on father's side) 堂姐 tángjiě [个 gè]; (younger female on father's side) 堂妹 tángmèi [个 gè]; (older male on mother's side) 表兄 biǎoxiōng [个 gè]; (younger male on mother's side) 表弟 biǎodì [个 gè]; (older female on mother's side) 表姐 biǎojiě [个 gè]; (younger female on mother's side) 表妹 biǎomèi [个 gè]

cover ['kʌvəʳ] **I** vт **1** ▶**to cover sth (with sth)** (用某物)盖着某物 (yòng mǒuwù) gàizhe mǒuwù **2** (in insurance) ▶**to cover sb (against sth)** 给某人保(某事的)险 gěi mǒurén bǎo (mǒushì de) xiǎn **II** N **1** [c] 套子 tàozi [个 gè] **2** [c] 封面 fēngmiàn [个 gè] **3** [U] (insurance) 保险 bǎoxiǎn **III covers** NPL (on bed) 铺盖 pūgai ▶**to be covered in** or **with sth** 被某物覆盖 bèi mǒuwù fùgài

▶ **cover up** vт [+ facts, feelings, mistakes] (用某事)掩饰某事 (yòng mǒushì) yǎnshì mǒushì

cow [kau] N [c] 奶牛 nǎiniú [头 tóu]

coward ['kauəd] N [c] 胆小鬼 dǎnxiǎoguǐ [个 gè]

cowboy ['kaubɔɪ] N [c] 牛仔 niúzǎi [个 gè]

crab [kræb] N 1 [c] (*creature*) 螃蟹 pángxiè [只 zhī] 2 [U] (*meat*) 蟹肉 xièròu

crack [kræk] N [c] 裂缝 lièfèng [条 tiáo]
▶ **crack down on** VT FUS 对…严惩不贷 duì…yánchéng bùdài

cracked [krækt] ADJ 破裂的 pòliè de

cracker ['krækə^r] N [c] (*biscuit*) 薄脆饼干 báocuì bǐnggān [块 kuài]

cradle ['kreɪdl] N [c] 摇篮 yáolán [个 gè]

craft [krɑːft] N [c] (*weaving, pottery etc*) 工艺 gōngyì [道 dào]

cramp [kræmp] N [c/u] 抽筋 chōujīn [阵 zhèn]

crane [kreɪn] N [c] 起重机 qǐzhòngjī [部 bù]

crash [kræʃ] I N [c] 1 (*of car*) 撞击 zhuàngjī [下 xià]; (*of plane*) 坠机 zhuìjī [次 cì] 2 (*noise*) 哗啦声 huālā shēng [声 shēng] II VT [+ *car, plane*] 使撞毁 shǐ zhuànghuǐ III VI 1 [*car, driver*] 撞击 zhuàngjī; [*plane*] 坠毁 zhuìhuǐ 2 (*Comput*) 死机 sǐjī ▶ **a car/plane crash** 撞车/飞机失事 zhuàngchē/fēijī shīshì ▶ **to crash into sth** 猛地撞上某物 měngde zhuàngshàng mǒuwù

crawl [krɔːl] VI 爬 pá

crazy ['kreɪzɪ] (*inf*) ADJ 发疯的 fāfēng de ▶ **to go crazy** 发疯 fāfēng

cream [kriːm] I N 1 (*dairy cream*) 奶油 nǎiyóu 2 [c/u] (*for skin*) 乳霜 rǔshuāng [瓶 píng] II ADJ (*in colour*) 乳白色的 rǔbáisè de

crease [kriːs] N [c] (*in cloth, paper: fold*) 折痕 zhéhén [道 dào]; (*wrinkle*) 皱纹 zhòuwén [条 tiáo]

create [kriːˈeɪt] VT 创造 chuàngzào

creative [kriːˈeɪtɪv] ADJ 有创造力的 yǒu chuàngzàolì de

creature ['kriːtʃə^r] N [c] 动物 dòngwù [种 zhǒng]

crèche [krɛʃ] (*Brit*) N [c] 儿所 tuō'érsuǒ [个 gè]

credit ['krɛdɪt] N 1 [U] (*financial*) 贷款 dàikuǎn 2 [U] (*recognition*) 赞扬 zànyáng 3 [c] (*Scol, Univ*) 学分 xuéfēn [个 gè] ▶ **on credit** 赊账 shēzhàng

credit card N [c] 信用卡 xìnyòng kǎ [张 zhāng]

crew [kruː] N 1 [c] 全体工作人员 quántǐ gōngzuò rényuán 2 [c] (*TV*) 组 zǔ [个 gè]

crib [krɪb] N [c] (*US*) 有围栏的童床 yǒu wéilán de tóngchuáng [张 zhāng]

cricket ['krɪkɪt] N [U] (*sport*) 板球 bǎnqiú

○ **CRICKET**

○ 在大英帝国时代，**cricket** (板球) 做为一种夏季运动引入印度、巴基斯坦和澳大利亚等国。如今，板球在这些国家依然十分盛行。两队各11名队员，通常为男性。队员通常穿传统的白色运动服。板球的规则以复杂著称。两队轮流击球。击球的队尽力争取最多次数的 **run**

● （跑垒），其打击手在两组称
● 为 **stump**（三门柱）的柱子
● 间跑。另一队争取在击球手
● 跑到门柱前用球击中门柱，
● 还可以在球触地前接住球将
● 该击球手淘汰出局。

crime [kraɪm] N 1 [c] (illegal act)
罪行 zuìxíng [种 zhǒng] 2 [U]
(illegal activities) 犯罪活动 fànzuì
huódòng

criminal ['krɪmɪnl] N [c] 罪犯
zuìfàn [个 gè]

crisis ['kraɪsɪs] (pl **crises** ['kraɪsiːz])
N [c/U] 危机 wēijī [种 zhǒng]

crisp [krɪsp] N [c] (Brit: potato
crisp) 薯片 shǔpiàn [片 piàn]

critical ['krɪtɪkl] ADJ 1 (crucial) 关
键的 guānjiàn de 2 (serious) 危急
的 wēijí de

criticism ['krɪtɪsɪzəm] N 1
[U] (censure) 批评 pīpíng 2 [c]
(complaint) 指责 zhǐzé [种 zhǒng]

criticize ['krɪtɪsaɪz] VT 批评
pīpíng

Croatia [krəʊ'eɪʃə] N 克罗地亚
Kèluódìyà

crocodile ['krɔkədaɪl] N [c] 鳄鱼
èyú [只 zhǐ]

crooked ['krukɪd] ADJ (off-centre)
歪的 wāi de

crop [krɔp] N 1 [c] (plants) 庄稼
zhuāngjia [种 zhǒng] 2 [c] (amount
produced) 收成 shōuchéng [个 gè]

cross [krɔs] I N [c] 1 (x shape) 交
叉符号 jiāochā fúhào [个 gè];
(showing disagreement) 叉号
chāhào [个 gè] 2 (crucifix shape)
十字 shízì [个 gè] 3 (Rel) 十字架

shízìjià [个 gè] II VT [+ street, room]
横穿 héngchuān III VI [roads, lines]
相交 xiāngjiāo IV ADJ (angry) 生气
的 shēngqì de

▶ **cross out** VT (delete) 取消
qǔxiāo

▶ **cross over** VI (cross the street) 过
马路 guò mǎlù

crossing ['krɔsɪŋ] N [c] 1 (voyage)
横渡 héngdù [次 cì] 2 (Brit) (also:
pedestrian crossing) 人行横道
rénxíng héngdào [个 gè]

crossroads ['krɔsrəʊdz] (pl
crossroads) N [c] 十字路口 shízì
lùkǒu [个 gè]

crosswalk ['krɔswɔ:k] (US) N [c]
人行横道 rénxíng héngdào [个 gè]

crossword ['krɔswə:d] N [c] (also:
crossword puzzle) 填字游戏
tiánzì yóuxì [个 gè]

crowd [kraud] N [c] 人群 rénqún
[个 gè] ▶ **crowds of people** 大批
人群 dàpī rénqún

crowded ['kraudɪd] ADJ 拥挤的
yōngjǐ de

crown [kraun] N [c] 皇冠
huángguān [个 gè]

cruel ['kruəl] ADJ 残忍的 cánrěn
de; [+ treatment, behaviour] 恶毒的
èdú de ▶ **to be cruel to sb** 残酷地
对待某人 cánkù de duìdài mǒurén

cruelty ['kruəltɪ] N [U] 残忍
cánrěn

cruise [kru:z] N [c] 游船
yóuchuán [艘 sōu] ▶ **to be/go
on a cruise** 乘游船旅行 chéng
yóuchuán lǚxíng

crush [krʌʃ] VT 1 [+ garlic] 压碎
yāsuì 2 [+ person] 使挤在一起 shǐ

jǐzài yīqǐ

cry [kraɪ] vɪ (*weep*) 哭 kū ▶**what are you crying about?** 你哭什么? nǐ kū shénme?

cub [kʌb] N [c] **1** 幼兽 yòushòu [只 zhī] **2** (*also*: **cub scout**) 幼童军 yòutóngjūn [名 míng]

cube [kju:b] N [c] 立方体 lìfāngtǐ [个 gè]

cucumber ['kju:kʌmbər] N [c/u] 黄瓜 huángguā [根 gēn]

cuddle ['kʌdl] I vт, vɪ 搂抱 lǒubào II N [c] 拥抱 yōngbào [个 gè]

cultural ['kʌltʃərəl] ADJ 文化的 wénhuà de

culture ['kʌltʃər] N [c/u] 文化 wénhuà [种 zhǒng]

cunning ['kʌnɪŋ] ADJ 狡猾的 jiǎohuá de

cup [kʌp] N [c] **1** (*for drinking*) 杯子 bēizi [个 gè] **2** (*trophy*) 奖杯 jiǎngbēi [个 gè] ▶**a cup of tea** 一杯茶 yībēi chá

cupboard ['kʌbəd] N [c] 柜子 guìzi [个 gè]

curb [kə:b] N [c] (*US*) = **kerb**

cure [kjuər] I vт (*Med*) 治好 zhìhǎo; [+ *patient*] 治愈 zhìyù II N [c] (*Med*) 疗法 liáofǎ [种 zhǒng]

curious ['kjuərɪəs] ADJ 好奇的 hàoqí de ▶**to be curious about sb/sth** 对某人/某物感到好奇 duì mǒurén/mǒuwu gǎndào hàoqí

curl [kə:l] N [c] 卷发 juǎnfà [头 tóu]

curly ['kə:lɪ] ADJ 卷曲的 juǎnqū de

currant ['kʌrnt] N [c] 无子葡萄干 wúzǐ pútao gān [粒 lì]

currency ['kʌrnsɪ] N [c/u] 货币 huòbì [种 zhǒng]

current ['kʌrnt] I N [c] **1** (*of air, water*) 流 liú [股 gǔ] **2** (*Elec*) 电流 diànliú [股 gǔ] II ADJ [+ *situation, tendency, policy*] 目前的 mùqián de

current affairs NPL 时事 shíshì ▶**a current affairs programme** 时事讨论节目 shíshì tǎolùn jiémù

curriculum [kə'rɪkjuləm] (*pl* **curriculums** *or* **curricula** [kə'rɪkjulə]) N [c] **1** 全部课程 quánbù kèchéng **2** (*for particular subject*) 课程 kèchéng [门 mén]

curriculum vitae [-'vi:taɪ] (*esp Brit*) N [c] 简历 jiǎnlì [份 fèn]

curry ['kʌrɪ] N [c/u] (*dish*) 咖喱 gālí [种 zhǒng]

cursor ['kə:sər] (*Comput*) N [c] 光标 guāngbiāo [个 gè]

curtain ['kə:tn] N [c] (*esp Brit*) 窗帘 chuānglián [幅 fú] ▶**to draw the curtains** (*together*) 拉上窗帘 lāshàng chuānglián; (*apart*) 拉开窗帘 lākāi chuānglián

cushion ['kuʃən] N [c] 靠垫 kàodiàn [个 gè]

custom ['kʌstəm] I N **1** [c/u] (*tradition*) 传统 chuántǒng [个 gè] **2** [c/u] (*convention*) 惯例 guànlì [个 gè] II **customs** NPL 海关 hǎiguān ▶**to go through customs** 过海关 guò hǎiguān

customer ['kʌstəmər] N [c] 顾客 gùkè [位 wèi]

customs officer N [c] 海关官员 hǎiguān guānyuán [位 wèi]

cut [kʌt] (*pt, pp* **cut**) I vт **1** 切 qiē **2** (*injure*) ▶**to cut one's**

hand/knee 割破手/膝盖 gēpò shǒu/xīgài **3** [+ *grass, hair, nails*] 修剪 xiūjiǎn **4** [+ *scene, episode, paragraph*] 删剪 shānjiǎn **5** [+ *prices, spending*] 削减 xiāojiǎn **II** N **1** [c] (*injury*) 伤口 shāngkǒu [个 gè] **2** [c] (*reduction*) 削减 xuējiǎn [次 cì] ▶**to cut sth in half** 将某物切成两半 jiāng mǒuwù qiēchéng liǎngbàn ▶**to cut o.s.** 割破自己 gēpò zìjǐ ▶**to get** *or* **have one's hair cut** 剪发 jiǎnfà ▶**a cut and blow-dry** 剪发吹干 jiǎnfà chuīgān

▶**cut down** VT **1** [+ *tree*] 砍倒 kǎndǎo **2** (*reduce*) 减少 jiǎnshǎo
▶**cut down on** VT FUS [+ *alcohol, coffee, cigarettes*] 减少 jiǎnshǎo
▶**cut off** VT [+ *part of sth*] 切掉 qiēdiào; [+ *supply*] 停止供应 tíngzhǐ gōngyìng
▶**cut up** VT 切碎 qiēsuì

cute [kjuːt] ADJ **1** (*inf*) [+ *child, dog, house*] 可爱的 kě'ài de **2** (*esp US: inf: attractive*) 迷人的 mírén de

cutlery ['kʌtlərɪ] (*Brit*) N [U] 餐具 cānjù

CV N ABBR (= **curriculum vitae**) 简历 jiǎnlì

cybercafé ['saɪbəkæfeɪ] N [c] 网吧 wǎngbā [家 jiā]

cycle ['saɪkl] **I** N [c] 自行车 zìxíngchē [辆 liàng] **II** VI 骑自行车 qí zìxíngchē **III** CPD [+ *shop, helmet, ride*] 自行车 zìxíngchē ▶**to go cycling** 骑自行车 qí zìxíngchē

cycle lane N [c] 自行车道 zìxíngchēdào [条 tiáo]

cycling ['saɪklɪŋ] N [U] 骑自行车

qí zìxíngchē

cyclist ['saɪklɪst] N [c] 骑自行车的人 qí zìxíngchē de rén [个 gè]

cylinder ['sɪlɪndə'] N [c] [*of gas*] 罐 guàn [个 gè]

cynical ['sɪnɪkl] ADJ 愤世嫉俗的 fènshìjísú de

Cyprus ['saɪprəs] N 塞浦路斯 Sàipǔlùsī

Czech Republic N ▶**the Czech Republic** 捷克共和国 Jiékègònghéguó

dad [dæd] (*inf*) N [C] 爸爸 bàba
[个 gè]

daffodil ['dæfədɪl] N [C] 黄水仙
huángshuǐxiān [支 zhī]

daily ['deɪlɪ] I ADJ 每日的 měirì de
II ADV 每日 měirì

daisy ['deɪzɪ] N [C] 雏菊 chújú
[朵 duǒ]

dam [dæm] N [C] 水坝 shuǐbà
[个 gè]

damage ['dæmɪdʒ] I N [U] 1 损坏
sǔnhuài 2 (*dents, scratches*) 损伤
sǔnshāng II VT 毁坏 huǐhuài

damp [dæmp] ADJ 潮湿的
cháoshī de

dance [dɑːns] I N 1 [C] (*waltz,
tango*) 舞蹈 wǔdǎo [曲 qǔ] 2 [C]
(*social event*) 舞会 wǔhuì [个 gè]
II VI 跳舞 tiàowǔ

dancer ['dɑːnsər] N [C] 舞蹈演员
wǔdǎo yǎnyuán [位 wèi]

dancing ['dɑːnsɪŋ] N [U] 跳舞
tiàowǔ

dandruff ['dændrəf] N [U] 头皮
屑 tóupíxiè

danger ['deɪndʒər] N 1 [U] (*unsafe
situation*) 危险 wēixiǎn 2 [C]
(*hazard, risk*) 威胁 wēixié [个 gè]
▶**there is a danger of/that...**
有…的危险 yǒu...de wēixiǎn ▶**to
be in danger of doing sth** 有…的
危险 yǒu...de wēixiǎn

dangerous ['deɪndʒrəs] ADJ 危
险的 wēixiǎn de ▶**it's dangerous
to...** …是危险的 ...shì wēixiǎn de

Danish ['deɪnɪʃ] I ADJ 丹麦的
Dānmài de II N [U] (*language*) 丹麦
语 Dānmàiyǔ

dare [dɛər] I VT ▶**to dare sb to
do sth** 激某人做某事 jī mǒurén
zuò mǒushì II VI ▶**to dare (to) do
sth** 敢做某事 gǎn zuò mǒushì ▶**I
daren't tell him** (*Brit*) 我不敢告诉
他 wǒ bùgǎn gàosù tā ▶**I dare say**
(*I suppose*) 我相信 wǒ xiāngxìn
▶**how dare you!** 你怎敢！nǐ
zěngǎn!

daring ['dɛərɪŋ] ADJ 勇敢的
yǒnggǎn de

dark [dɑːk] I ADJ 1 [+ *room, night*]
黑暗的 hēi'àn de 2 [+ *eyes, hair,
skin*] 黑色的 hēisè de; [+ *person*]
头发和皮肤深色的 tóufa hé pífū
shēnsè de 3 [+ *suit, fabric*] 深色
的 shēnsè de II N ▶**the dark** 黑
暗 hēi'àn ▶**dark blue/green** 深蓝
色/绿色 shēnlán sè/lǜsè ▶**it is/is
getting dark** 天黑了 tiān hēile

darling ['dɑːlɪŋ] N 亲爱的 qīn'àide

dart [dɑːt]: **darts** NPL 投镖游戏 tóubiāo yóuxì

data ['deɪtə] NPL 数据 shùjù

database ['deɪtəbeɪs] N [c] 数据库 shùjùkù [个 gè]

date [deɪt] I N [c] 1 日期 rìqī [个 gè] 2 (*meeting with friend*) 约会 yuēhuì [个 gè] 3 (*fruit*) 海枣 hǎizǎo [颗 kē] II VT [+ *letter, cheque*] 给…注明日期 gěi…zhùmíng rìqī ▶**what's today's date?, what's today's date?** 今天几号？ jīntiān jǐhào? ▶**date of birth** 出生日期 chūshēng rìqī ▶**to be out of date** (*old-fashioned*) 落伍 luòwǔ; (*expired*) 过期 guòqī ▶**to be up to date** (*modern*) 时新 shíxīn

daughter ['dɔːtər] N [c] 女儿 nǚ'ér [个 gè]

daughter-in-law ['dɔːtərɪnlɔː] (*pl* **daughters-in-law**) N [c] 媳妇 xífu [个 gè]

dawn [dɔːn] N [c/u] 黎明 límíng [个 gè]

day [deɪ] N 1 [c] 天 tiān 2 [c/u] (*daylight hours*) 白天 báitiān [个 gè] ▶**during the day** 在白天 zài báitiān ▶**the day before/after** 前/后一天 qián/hòu yītiān ▶**the day after tomorrow** 后天 hòutiān ▶**these days** (*nowadays*) 现在 xiànzài ▶**the following day** 第二天 dì'èrtiān ▶**one day/some day/one of these days** 有一天 yǒu yītiān ▶**by day** 在白天 zài báitiān ▶**all day (long)** 一天到晚 yītiān dàowǎn ▶**to work an 8**

hour day 每天工作8小时 měitiān gōngzuò bā xiǎoshí

daylight ['deɪlaɪt] N [u] 白昼 báizòu

dead [dɛd] ADJ 1 死的 sǐ de 2 [+ *battery*] 不能再用的 bùnéng zài yòng de ▶**over my dead body!** (*inf*) 绝对不行！ juéduì bùxíng!

deadline ['dɛdlaɪn] N [c] 截止日期 jiézhǐ rìqī [个 gè] ▶**to meet a deadline** 如期 rúqī

deaf [dɛf] ADJ 聋的 lóng de; (*partially*) 耳背的 ěrbèi de

deafening ['dɛfnɪŋ] ADJ [+ *noise*] 震耳欲聋的 zhèn ěr yù lóng de

deal [diːl] (*pt, pp* **dealt**) N [c] 协议 xiéyì [个 gè] ▶**to do/make/strike a deal with sb** 和某人做买卖 hé mǒurén zuò mǎimài ▶**it's a deal!** (*inf*) 成交！ chéngjiāo! ▶**a good** *or* **great deal (of)** 大量(的…) dàliàng(de…) ▶ **deal with** VT FUS [+ *problem*] 处理 chǔlǐ

dealer ['diːlər] N [c] 1 商人 shāngrén [个 gè] 2 (*in drugs*) 毒品贩子 dúpǐn fànzi [个 gè]

dealt [dɛlt] PT, PP *of* **deal**

dear [dɪər] I ADJ 1 亲爱的 qīn'ài de 2 (*esp Brit: expensive*) 昂贵的 ángguì de II N ▶ **(my) dear** 亲爱的 qīn'ài de III INT ▶ **oh dear/dear dear/dear me!** 呵/哎呀！ hè/āiyā! ▶ **Dear Sir/Madam** (*in letter*) 亲爱的先生/女士 qīn'ài de xiānshēng/nǚshì ▶ **Dear Peter/Jane** 亲爱的彼得/简 qīn'ài de Bǐdé/Jiǎn

death [dɛθ] N [c/u] 死亡 sǐwáng

[个 gè] ▶(a matter of) life and death 生死攸关(的事情) shēngsǐ yōuguān (de shìqíng) ▶to scare/ bore sb to death 吓死某人/使某人感到无聊之极 xiàsǐ mǒurén/shǐ mǒurén gǎndào wúliáo zhī jí

death penalty N ▶the death penalty 死刑 sǐxíng

debate [dɪ'beɪt] N [c/u] 讨论 tǎolùn [次 cì]

debt [dɛt] N 1 [c] (sum of money owed) 债务 zhàiwù [笔 bǐ] 2 [u] (state of owing money) 欠债 qiànzhài ▶to be in/get into debt 负债 fùzhài

decade ['dɛkeɪd] N [c] 十年 shínián [个 gè]

decaffeinated [dɪ'kæfɪneɪtɪd] ADJ 不含咖啡因的 bù hán kāfēiyīn de

deceive [dɪ'siːv] VT 欺骗 qīpiàn

December [dɪ'sɛmbəʳ] N [c/u] 十二月 shíèryuè; see also **July**

decent ['diːsənt] ADJ [+ person] 受尊重的 shòu zūnzhòng de

decide [dɪ'saɪd] I VT [+ question, argument] 解决 jiějué II VI 决定 juédìng ▶to decide to do sth 决定做某事 juédìng zuò mǒushì ▶I can't decide whether... 我无法决定是否… wǒ wúfǎ juédìng shìfǒu...

decimal ['dɛsɪməl] I ADJ [+ system, currency] 十进位的 shíjìnwèi de II N [c] 小数 xiǎoshù [个 gè]

decision [dɪ'sɪʒən] N [c] 决定 juédìng [个 gè] ▶to make a decision 作出决定 zuòchū juédìng

deck [dɛk] N [c] 甲板 jiǎbǎn [个 gè]

deckchair ['dɛktʃɛəʳ] N [c] 折叠式躺椅 zhédiéshì tǎngyǐ [把 bǎ]

declare [dɪ'klɛəʳ] VT 1 [+ intention, attitude] 宣布 xuānbù; [+ support] 表明 biǎomíng 2 (at customs) 报关 bàoguān ▶to declare war (on sb) (向某人)宣战 (xiàng mǒurén) xuānzhàn

decorate ['dɛkəreɪt] VT 1 ▶to decorate (with) (用…)装饰 (yòng…) zhuāngshì 2 (paint etc) 装潢 zhuānghuáng

decoration [dɛkə'reɪʃən] N [c/u] 装饰 zhuāngshì [种 zhǒng]

decrease [n 'diːkriːs, vb diː'kriːs] I N [c] ▶decrease (in sth) (某物的)减少 (mǒuwù de) jiǎnshǎo II VT, VI 减少 jiǎnshǎo

deduct [dɪ'dʌkt] VT ▶to deduct sth (from sth) (从某物中)减去某物 (cóng mǒuwùzhōng) jiǎnqù mǒuwù

deep [diːp] I ADJ 1 深的 shēn de 2 [+ voice, sound] 低沉的 dīchén de 3 [+ sleep] 酣睡的 hānshuì de II ADV 深 shēn ▶it is 1 m deep 它有1米深 tā yǒu yīmǐ shēn ▶to take a deep breath 深呼吸 shēn hūxī

deeply ['diːplɪ] ADV 1 (breathe, sigh) 深深地 shēnshēn de 2 (sleep) 沉沉地 chénchén de

deer [dɪəʳ] (pl deer) N [c] 鹿 lù [头 tóu]

defeat [dɪ'fiːt] I N [c/u] 1 [of army] 战败 zhànbài [次 cì] 2 [of team] 击败 jībài [次 cì] II VT 1 [+ enemy,

opposition] 战胜 zhànshèng
2 [+ team] 击败 jībài

defect ['di:fɛkt] N [c] 缺点
quēdiǎn [个 gè]

defence, (US) **defense**
[dɪ'fɛns] N 1 [U] (protection) 防御 fángyù 2
[U] (Mil) 国防措施 guófáng cuòshī
▶**the Ministry of Defence**, (US)
the Department of Defense 国
防部 Guófángbù

defend [dɪ'fɛnd] VT 防御 fángyù
▶**to defend o.s.** 自卫 zìwèi

defender [dɪ'fɛndəʳ] N [c] (in team) 防守队员 fángshǒu duìyuán
[个 gè]

defense [dɪ'fɛns] (US) N =
defence

definite ['dɛfɪnɪt] ADJ 1 [+ plan, answer, views] 明确的 míngquè
de 2 [+ improvement, possibility, advantage] 肯定的 kěndìng de
▶**is that definite?** 肯定吗?
kěndìng ma?

definitely ['dɛfɪnɪtlɪ] ADV 确定地
quèdìng de

defy [dɪ'faɪ] VT [+ law, ban] 蔑视
miǎoshì

degree [dɪ'gri:] N [c] 1 ▶**degree
(of sth)** (level) (某事的) 程度
(mǒushì de) chéngdù [种 zhǒng]
2 (measure of temperature, angle, latitude) 度 dù 3 (at university) 学
位 xuéwèi [个 gè] ▶**to some
degree/a certain degree** 从
某种/一定程度上来说 cóng
mǒuzhǒng/yīdìng chéngdù shàng
lái shuō ▶**10 degrees below
(zero)** 零下10度 língxià shídù
▶**a degree in maths** 数学学位

shùxué xuéwèi

delay [dɪ'leɪ] I VT 1 [+ decision, ceremony] 推迟 tuīchí 2 [+ person]
耽搁 dānge; [+ plane, train] 延
误 yánwù II VI 耽搁 dānge III N
[c/U] 延误 yánwù [个 gè] ▶**to be
delayed** [person, flight, departure]
被耽搁了 bèi dānge le ▶**without
delay** 立即 lìjí

delete [dɪ'li:t] VT 删除 shānchú

deliberate [dɪ'lɪbərɪt] ADJ 故意的
gùyì de ▶**it wasn't deliberate** 那
不是故意的 nà bùshì gùyì de

deliberately [dɪ'lɪbərɪtlɪ] ADV 故
意地 gùyì de

delicate ['dɛlɪkɪt] ADJ 1 (fragile)
易碎的 yìsuì de 2 [+ problem, situation, issue] 微妙的 wēimiào
de 3 [+ colour, flavour, smell] 清淡可
口的 qīngdàn kěkǒu de

delicious [dɪ'lɪʃəs] ADJ 美味的
měiwèi de

delight [dɪ'laɪt] N [U] 快乐 kuàilè

delighted [dɪ'laɪtɪd] ADJ
▶**delighted (at or with sth)** (对某
事) 感到高兴 (duì mǒushì) gǎndào
gāoxìng ▶**to be delighted to do
sth** 乐意做某事 lèyì zuò mǒushì

deliver [dɪ'lɪvəʳ] VT 1 [+ letter, parcel] 传送 chuánsòng 2 [+ baby]
接生 jiēshēng

delivery [dɪ'lɪvərɪ] N 1 [U] 传送
chuánsòng 2 [c] (consignment)
递送的货物 dìsòng de huòwù
[件 jiàn]

demand [dɪ'mɑ:nd] I VT
[+ apology, explanation, pay rise] 要
求 yāoqiú II N 1 [c] (request) 要求
yāoqiú [个 gè] 2 [U] (for product)

需求量 xūqiúliàng ▶to make demands on sb/sth 对某人/某事提出要求 duì mǒurén/mǒushì tíchū yāoqiú ▶to be in demand 受欢迎 shòu huānyíng

democracy [dɪ'mɔkrəsɪ] N **1** [U] (*system*) 民主 mínzhǔ **2** [c] (*country*) 民主国 mínzhǔ guó [个 gè]

democratic [dɛmə'krætɪk] ADJ 民主的 mínzhǔ de

demolish [dɪ'mɔlɪʃ] VT 拆毁 chāihuǐ

demonstrate ['dɛmənstreɪt] I VT [+ *skill, appliance*] 演示 yǎnshì II VI ▶to demonstrate (for/against sth) 示威(支持/反对某事) shìwēi (zhīchí/fǎnduì mǒushì) ▶to demonstrate how to do sth 演示如何做某事 yǎnshì rúhé zuò mǒushì

demonstration [dɛmən'streɪʃən] N [c] **1** 示威 shìwēi [次 cì] **2** [of appliance, cooking] 演示 yǎnshì [个 gè]

demonstrator ['dɛmənstreɪtər] N [c] 示威者 shìwēizhě [个 gè]

denim ['dɛnɪm] N [U] 斜纹粗棉布 xiéwén cū miánbù

Denmark ['dɛnmaːk] N 丹麦 Dānmài

dent [dɛnt] N [c] 凹部 āobù [个 gè]

dental ['dɛntl] ADJ 牙齿的 yáchǐ de

dentist ['dɛntɪst] N [c] **1** (*person*) 牙医 yáyī [位 wèi] **2** ▶ **the dentist('s)** 牙医诊所 yáyī zhěnsuǒ [家 jiā]

deny [dɪ'naɪ] VT 否定 fǒudìng

deodorant [diː'əudərənt] N [c/U] 除臭剂 chúchòujì [种 zhǒng]

depart [dɪ'paːt] VI ▶to depart (from/for somewhere) (从某地)出发/出发(赶往某地) (cóng mǒudì) chūfā/chūfā (gǎnwǎng mǒudì)

department [dɪ'paːtmənt] N [c] **1** (*in shop*) 部 bù [个 gè] **2** (*in school or college*) 系 xì [个 gè]

department store N [c] 百货商店 bǎihuò shāngdiàn [家 jiā]

departure [dɪ'paːtʃər] N [c/U] 出发 chūfā

departure lounge N [c] 候机厅 hòujītīng [个 gè]

depend [dɪ'pɛnd] VI **1** ▶to depend on sth 依某物而定 yī mǒuwù ér dìng **2** ▶you can depend on me/him (rely on, trust) 你可以信赖我/他 nǐ kěyǐ xìnlài wǒ/tā **3** ▶to depend on sb/sth (for survival) 依靠某人/某物为生 yīkào mǒurén/mǒuwù wéishēng ▶it (all) depends 要看情况而定 yào kàn qíngkuàng érdìng

deposit [dɪ'pɔzɪt] N [c] 储蓄 chǔxù [笔 bǐ]; (on house, bottle, when hiring) 押金 yājīn [份 fèn] ▶to put down a deposit of 50 pounds 支付50英镑的保证金 zhīfù wǔshí yīngbàng de bǎozhèngjīn

depressed [dɪ'prɛst] ADJ 沮丧的 jǔsàng de

depressing [dɪ'prɛsɪŋ] ADJ 令人沮丧的 lìng rén jǔsàng de

deprive [dɪ'praɪv] VT ▶to deprive

sb of sth 剥夺某人某物 bōduó mǒurén mǒuwù

depth [dɛpθ] N [c/u] 深 shēn ▶**at/to/from a depth of 3 metres** 在/到/从3米深处 zài/dào/cóng sānmǐ shēnchù ▶**to study/ analyse sth in depth** 深入研究/分析某事 shēnrù yánjiū/fēnxī mǒushì

descend [dɪ'sɛnd] VI (frm) 下来 xiàlai ▶**to be descended from** 是…的后裔 shì…de hòuyì

describe [dɪs'kraɪb] VT 描述 miáoshù

description [dɪs'krɪpʃən] N [c/u] 描述 miáoshù [种 zhǒng]

desert ['dɛzət] N 1 [c/u] (Geo) 沙漠 shāmò [片 piàn] 2 [c] (fig: wasteland) 荒地 huāngdì [片 piàn]

deserve [dɪ'zəːv] VT 应受 yīngshòu ▶**to deserve to do sth** 应该获得某事 yīnggāi huòdé mǒuwù

design [dɪ'zaɪn] I N 1 [u] (art, process, layout, shape) 设计 shèjì 2 [c] (pattern) 图案 tú'àn [种 zhǒng] II VT 设计 shèjì ▶**to be designed for sb/to do sth** 专门为某人/做某事设计 zhuānmén wèi mǒurén/zuò mǒushì shèjì

designer [dɪ'zaɪnə'] I N [c] 设计者 shèjìzhě [位 wèi] II CPD [+ clothes, label, jeans] 名师设计的 míngshī shèjì de

desk [dɛsk] N [c] 1 (in office) 办公桌 bàngōngzhuō [张 zhāng] 2 (for pupil) 书桌 shūzhuō [张 zhāng] 3 (in hotel, at airport, hospital) 服务台 fúwùtái [个 gè]

desk clerk (US) N [c] 接待员 jiēdàiyuán [位 wèi]

despair [dɪs'pɛə'] N [u] 绝望 juéwàng ▶**in despair** 绝望地 juéwàng de

desperate ['dɛspərɪt] ADJ 1 [+ person] 绝望的 juéwàng de 2 [+ attempt, effort] 铤而走险的 tǐng ér zǒu xiǎn de 3 [+ situation] 危急的 wēijí de

desperately ['dɛspərɪtlɪ] ADV 拼命地 pīnmìng de

despise [dɪs'paɪz] VT 鄙视 bǐshì

despite [dɪs'paɪt] PREP 尽管 jǐnguǎn

dessert [dɪ'zəːt] N [c/u] 饭后甜点 fànhòu tiándiǎn [份 fèn]

destination [dɛstɪ'neɪʃən] N [c] 目的地 mùdìdì [个 gè]

destroy [dɪs'trɔɪ] VT 破坏 pòhuài

destruction [dɪs'trʌkʃən] N [u] 破坏 pòhuài

detail ['diːteɪl] I N [c] 细节 xìjié [个 gè] II **details** NPL 详情 xiángqíng ▶**in detail** 详细地 xiángxì de

detailed ['diːteɪld] ADJ 详细的 xiángxì de

detective [dɪ'tɛktɪv] N [c] 侦探 zhēntàn [个 gè]

detective story, detective novel N [c] 侦探小说 zhēntàn xiǎoshuō [部 bù]

detergent [dɪ'təːdʒənt] N [c/u] 清洁剂 qīngjiéjì [种 zhǒng]

determined [dɪ'təːmɪnd] ADJ 坚定的 jiāndìng de ▶**to be determined to do sth** 决心做某事 juéxīn zuò mǒushì

detour ['diːtuə'] N [c] 1 ▶**to make**

a detour 绕道 ràodào [次 cì]
2 (US: on road) 绕行道路 ràoxíng dàolù [条 tiáo]

develop [dɪ'vɛləp] **I** VT
1 [+ business, idea, relationship] 发展 fāzhǎn; [+ land, resource] 开发 kāifā **2** [+ product, weapon] 开发 kāifā **3** (Phot) 冲洗 chōngxǐ
II VI [person] 成长 chéngzhǎng; [country, situation, friendship, skill] 发展 fāzhǎn

development [dɪ'vɛləpmənt] N
1 [U] (growth) 成长 chéngzhǎng; (political, economic) 发展 fāzhǎn
2 [C] (event) 新形势 xīn xíngshì [种 zhǒng]

devil ['dɛvl] N ▶ **the Devil** 撒旦 Sādàn [个 gè]

devoted [dɪ'vəutɪd] ADJ
1 [+ husband, daughter] 忠诚的 zhōngchéng de **2** ▶ **devoted to sth** (specialising in) 致力于某事的 zhìlì yú mǒushì de

diabetes [daɪə'biːtiːz] N [U] 糖尿病 tángniàobìng

diabetic [daɪə'bɛtɪk] N [C] 糖尿病患者 tángniàobìng huànzhě [个 gè]

diagonal [daɪ'ægənl] ADJ 斜的 xié de

diagram ['daɪəgræm] N [C] 图解 tújiě [个 gè]

dial ['daɪəl] **I** N [C] (on clock or meter) 标度盘 biāodùpán [个 gè]
II VT [+ number] 拨 bō **III** VI 拨号 bōhào

dialling code ['daɪəlɪŋ-] (Brit) N [C] 电话区号 diànhuà qūhào [个 gè]

dialogue, (US) **dialog** ['daɪələɡ] N [c/u] (conversation) 对话 duìhuà [次 cì]

diamond ['daɪəmənd] N [C] 钻石 zuànshí [颗 kē]

diaper ['daɪəpəʳ] (US) N [C] 尿布 niàobù [块 kuài]

diarrhoea, (US) **diarrhea** [daɪə'riːə] N [U] 腹泻 fùxiè ▶ **to have diarrhoea** 腹泻 fùxiè

diary ['daɪərɪ] N [C] **1** 日记簿 rìjìbù [个 gè] **2** (daily account) 日记 rìjì [篇 piān]

dice [daɪs] (pl **dice**) N [C] 骰子 shǎizi [个 gè]

dictation [dɪk'teɪʃən] N [c/u] (at school, college) 听写 tīngxiě [次 cì]

dictionary ['dɪkʃənrɪ] N [C] 词典 cídiǎn [本 běn]

did [dɪd] PT of **do**

die [daɪ] VI 死 sǐ ▶ **to die of** or **from sth** 死于某事 sǐyú mǒushì ▶ **to be dying** 奄奄一息 yǎn yǎn yī xī ▶ **to be dying for sth/to do sth** 渴望某事/做某事 kěwàng mǒushì/zuò mǒushì
▶ **die out** VI **1** [custom, way of life] 灭亡 mièwáng **2** [species] 灭绝 mièjué

diesel ['diːzl] N **1** [U] (also: **diesel oil**) 柴油 cháiyóu **2** [C] (vehicle) 柴油机驱动的车辆 cháiyóujī qūdòng de chēliàng [辆 liàng]

diet ['daɪət] **I** N **1** [c/u] 饮食 yǐnshí [种 zhǒng] **2** [C] (slimming) 减肥饮食 jiǎnféi yǐnshí [份 fèn] **II** VI 节食 jiéshí ▶ **to be on a diet** 实行减肥节食 shíxíng jiǎnféi jiéshí

difference ['dɪfrəns] N [C] 差异

chāyì [种 zhǒng] ▶**the difference in size/colour** 尺寸/颜色上的差异 chǐcùn/yánsè shàng de chāyì ▶**to make a/no difference (to sb/sth)** (对某人/某事)有/无影响 (duì mǒurén/mǒushì) yǒu/wú yǐngxiǎng

different ['dɪfrənt] ADJ 不同的 bùtóng de

difficult ['dɪfɪkəlt] ADJ 1 困难的 kùnnán de 2 [+ person, child] 执拗的 zhíniù de ▶**it is difficult for us to understand her** 我们很难理解她 wǒmen hěnnán lǐjiě tā

difficulty ['dɪfɪkəltɪ] N [c] 困难 kùnnán [个 gè] ▶**to have difficulty/difficulties** 有困难 yǒu kùnnán

dig [dɪg] (pt, pp dug) I VT 1 [+ hole] 挖 wā 2 [+ garden] 掘土 juétǔ II VI (with spade) 挖掘 wājué
▶**dig up** VT [+ plant, body] 挖出 wāchū

digital ['dɪdʒɪtl] ADJ 1 [+ clock, watch] 数字的 shùzì de 2 [+ recording, technology] 数码的 shùmǎ de

digital camera N [c] 数码相机 shùmǎ xiàngjī [台 tái]

digital television N [u] 数字电视 shùzì diànshì

dim [dɪm] ADJ 1 暗淡的 àndàn de 2 (inf: stupid) 迟钝的 chídùn de

dime [daɪm] (US) N [c] 一角银币 yījiǎo yínbì [枚 méi]

dimension [daɪˈmɛnʃən] I N [c] (aspect) 方面 fāngmiàn [个 gè] II **dimensions** NPL (measurements) 面积 miànjī

diner ['daɪnər] N [c] (US: restaurant) 廉价餐馆 liánjià cānguǎn [家 jiā]

dinghy ['dɪŋgɪ] N [c] (also: rubber dinghy) 橡皮筏 xiàngpífá [个 gè]

dining room N [c] 1 (in house) 饭厅 fàntīng [个 gè] 2 (in hotel) 餐厅 cāntīng [个 gè]

dinner ['dɪnər] N 1 [c/u] 晚餐 wǎncān [顿 dùn] 2 [c] (formal meal) 正餐 zhèngcān [顿 dùn]

dinner party N [c] 宴会 yànhuì [个 gè]

dinner time N [c/u] 晚饭时间 wǎnfàn shíjiān [段 duàn]

dinosaur ['daɪnəsɔːr] N [c] 恐龙 kǒnglóng [只 zhī]

dip [dɪp] VT 蘸 zhàn

diploma [dɪˈpləumə] N [c] 毕业文凭 bìyè wénpíng [张 zhāng]

direct [daɪˈrɛkt] I ADJ 直达的 zhídá de II VT 1 (show) 给…指路 gěi…zhǐlù 2 (manage) 管理 guǎnlǐ 3 [+ play, film, programme] 导演 dǎoyǎn III ADV 直接地 zhíjiē de

direction [dɪˈrɛkʃən] I N [c] 方向 fāngxiàng [个 gè] II **directions** NPL 1 (to get somewhere) 指路说明 zhǐlù shuōmíng 2 (for doing something) 用法说明 yòngfǎ shuōmíng ▶**in the direction of** 朝 cháo

director [dɪˈrɛktər] N [c] 1 [of company] 经理 jīnglǐ [位 wèi] 2 [of organization, public authority] 主任 zhǔrèn [位 wèi] 3 [of play, film] 导演 dǎoyǎn [位 wèi]

directory [dɪˈrɛktərɪ] N [c] 1 电话号码簿 diànhuà hàomǎbù [个 gè]

2 (*on computer*) 文件名录 wénjiàn mínglù [个 gè]

dirt [dəːt] N [U] 污物 wūwù

dirty ['dəːtɪ] ADJ 脏的 zāng de

disabled [dɪs'eɪbld] ADJ **1** 伤残 的 shāngcán de **2** (*mentally*) 残疾 的 cánjí de

disadvantage [dɪsəd'vɑːntɪdʒ] N [c/U] (*drawback*) 不利 búlì [种 zhǒng]

disagree [dɪsə'griː] VI ▶ **to disagree (with sb)** 不同意 (某 人的观点) bù tóngyì (mǒurén de guāndiǎn) ▶ **to disagree (with sth)** (对某事表示) 不同意 (duì mǒushì biǎoshì) bù tóngyì

disagreement [dɪsə'griːmənt] N [c] (*argument*) 争执 zhēngzhí [个 gè]

disappear [dɪsə'pɪəʳ] VI **1** (*from view*) 消失 xiāoshī **2** (*go missing*) 失踪 shīzōng **3** (*cease to exist*) 消 失 xiāoshī

disappearance [dɪsə'pɪərəns] N [c/U] [*of person*] 失踪 shīzōng [次 cì]

disappoint [dɪsə'pɔɪnt] VT [+ *person*] 使失望 shǐ shīwàng

disappointed [dɪsə'pɔɪntɪd] ADJ 失望的 shīwàng de

disappointment
[dɪsə'pɔɪntmənt] N **1** [U] (*emotion*) 失望 shīwàng **2** [c] (*cause*) 令人 失望的人/事 lìng rén shīwàng de rén/shì [个/件 gè/jiàn]

disapprove [dɪsə'pruːv] VI ▶ **to disapprove (of sb/sth)** 不同意 (某人/某事) bù tóngyì (mǒurén/ mǒushì)

disaster [dɪ'zɑːstəʳ] N [c/U] **1** (*earthquake, flood*) 灾难 zāinàn [次 cì] **2** (*accident, crash etc*) 灾祸 zāihuò [场 chǎng] **3** (*fiasco*) 惨败 cǎnbài [次 cì] **4** (*serious situation*) 灾难 zāinàn [个 gè]

disastrous [dɪ'zɑːstrəs] ADJ **1** (*catastrophic*) 灾难性的 zāinànxing de **2** (*unsuccessful*) 惨 败的 cǎnbài de

disc [dɪsk] N [c] **1** 圆盘 yuánpán [个 gè] **2** (*Comput*) = **disk**

discipline ['dɪsɪplɪn] N [U] 纪 律 jìlü

disc jockey N [c] 简称为DJ，意为 广播电台或迪斯科舞厅流行音乐唱 片播放及介绍人

disco ['dɪskəu] N (*event*) 迪斯 科 dísīkē

disconnect [dɪskə'nɛkt] VT **1** [+ *pipe, tap, hose*] 拆开 chāikāi **2** [+ *computer, cooker, TV*] 断开 duànkāi

discount ['dɪskaunt] N [c/U] 折扣 zhékòu [个 gè]

discourage [dɪs'kʌrɪdʒ] VT 使泄 气 shǐ xièqì

discover [dɪs'kʌvəʳ] VT 发现 fāxiàn

discovery [dɪs'kʌvərɪ] N **1** [c/U] [*of treasure, cure*] 发现 **2** [c] (*thing found*) 被发现的事物 bèi fāxiàn de shìwù [个 gè]

discrimination [dɪskrɪmɪ'neɪʃən] N [U] 歧视 qíshì ▶ **racial/sexual discrimination** 种族/性别歧视 zhǒngzú/xìngbié qíshì

discuss [dɪs'kʌs] VT 讨论 tǎolùn

discussion [dɪs'kʌʃən] N [c/U] 讨

论 tǎolùn [次 cì]

disease [dɪ'ziːz] N [C/U] (illness) 病 bìng [场 chǎng]

disgraceful [dɪs'greɪsful] ADJ 可 耻的 kěchǐ de

disguise [dɪs'gaɪz] I N [C] 伪装 品 wěizhuāngpǐn [件 jiàn] II VT ▸ **(to be) disguised (as sth/sb)** [+ person] 假扮成 (某物/某人) jiǎbànchéng (mǒuwù/mǒurén) ▸ **in disguise** 乔装着 qiáozhuāng zhe

disgusted [dɪs'gʌstɪd] ADJ 感到 厌恶的 gǎndào yànwù de

disgusting [dɪs'gʌstɪŋ] ADJ 1 [+ food, habit] 令人作呕的 lìng rén zuò'ǒu de 2 [+ behaviour, situation] 讨厌的 tǎoyàn de

dish [dɪʃ] I N [C] 1 盘 pán [个 gè]; (for eating) 碟 dié [个 gè] 2 (recipe, food) 一道菜 yī dào cài [道 dào] 3 (also: **satellite dish**) 盘形物 pánxíngwù [个 gè] II **dishes** NPL 碗碟 wǎndié ▸ **to do** or **wash the dishes** 刷洗碗碟 shuāxǐ wǎndié

dishonest [dɪs'ɒnɪst] ADJ 1 不诚实的 bù chéngshí de 2 [+ behaviour] 不正直的 bù zhèngzhí de

dishwasher ['dɪʃwɒʃəʳ] N [C] 洗碗 机 xǐwǎnjī [台 tái]

dishwashing liquid ['dɪʃwɒʃɪŋ-] (US) N [U] 洗洁剂 xǐjiéjì

disinfectant [dɪsɪn'fɛktənt] N [C/U] 消毒剂 xiāodújì [种 zhǒng]

disk [dɪsk] N [C] (Comput: hard) 硬 盘 yìngpán [个 gè]; (floppy) 软盘 ruǎnpán [张 zhāng]

dislike [dɪs'laɪk] VT 不喜欢 bù

xǐhuān ▸ **one's likes and dislikes** 某人的爱好和厌恶 mǒurén de àihào hé yànwù

dismiss [dɪs'mɪs] VT 解雇 jiěgù

disobedient [dɪsə'biːdɪənt] ADJ 不服从的 bù fúcóng de

disobey [dɪsə'beɪ] VT 1 不顺从 bù shùncóng 2 [+ order] 不服从 bù fúcóng

display [dɪs'pleɪ] I N 1 [C] (in shop, at exhibition) 陈列 chénliè [种 zhǒng] 2 [C] (information on screen) 显示 xiǎnshì [个 gè] 3 [C] (screen) 显示屏 xiǎnshìpíng [个 gè] II VT 1 [+ exhibits] 陈列 chénliè 2 [+ results, information] 显 示 xiǎnshì

disposable [dɪs'pəuzəbl] ADJ 一 次性的 yīcìxìng de

dispute [dɪs'pjuːt] (industrial) 争 执 zhēngzhí

disqualify [dɪs'kwɒlɪfaɪ] VT 取 消…的资格 qǔxiāoellipherede zīgé

disrupt [dɪs'rʌpt] VT 1 [+ conversation, meeting] 扰 乱 rǎoluàn 2 [+ plan, process] 妨 碍 fáng'ài

dissolve [dɪ'zɒlv] VT (in liquid) 溶 解 róngjiě

distance ['dɪstns] N [C/U] 距 离 jùlí [个 gè] ▸ **within walking distance** 步行可到 bùxíng kě dào

distinct [dɪs'tɪŋkt] ADJ [+ advantage, change] 明确的 míngquè de

distinguish [dɪs'tɪŋgwɪʃ] VT ▸ **to distinguish one thing from another** 将一事物与另一事物

区别开来 jiāng yīshìwù yǔ lìngyī shìwù qūbié kāilái

distract [dɪsˈtrækt] VT [+ *person*] 使分心 shǐ fēnxīn ▸**to distract sb's attention** 分散某人的注意力 fēnsàn mǒurén de zhùyìlì

distribute [dɪsˈtrɪbjuːt] VT 1 (*hand out*) 分发 fēnfā 2 (*share out*) 分配 fēnpèi

district [ˈdɪstrɪkt] N [c] 地区 dìqū [个 gè]

disturb [dɪsˈtəːb] VT (*interrupt*) 打扰 dǎrǎo

disturbing [dɪsˈtəːbɪŋ] ADJ 令人不安的 lìng rén bù'ān de

ditch [dɪtʃ] N [c] 沟 gōu [条 tiáo]

dive [daɪv] VI (*into water*) 跳水 tiàoshuǐ; (*under water*) 潜水 qiánshuǐ

diver [ˈdaɪvər] N [c] 潜水员 qiánshuǐyuán [位 wèi]

diversion [daɪˈvəːʃən] N [c] (*Brit*) 临时改道 línshí gǎidào [次 cì]

divide [dɪˈvaɪd] I VT 1 ▸**to divide (up)** 划分 huàfēn 2 (*in maths*) 除 chú 3 ▸**to divide sth between/among sb/sth** (*share*) 在两个/两个以上的人/物之间分配某物 zài liǎnggè/sāngè yǐshàng de rén/wù zhījiān fēnpèi mǒuwù II VI (*into groups*) 分开 fēnkāi ▸**to divide sth in half** 将某物一分为二 jiāng mǒuwù yī fēn wéi èr ▸**40 divided by 5** 40除以5 sìshí chúyǐ wǔ

diving [ˈdaɪvɪŋ] N [U] 1 (*underwater*) 潜水 qiánshuǐ 2 (*from board*) 跳水 tiàoshuǐ

division [dɪˈvɪʒən] N 1 [U] (*Math*) 除法 chúfǎ 2 [U] (*sharing out: of*

labour, resources) 分配 fēnpèi

divorce [dɪˈvɔːs] I N [c/U] 离婚 líhūn [次 cì] II VT [+ *spouse*] 与…离婚 yǔ…líhūn III VI 离婚 líhūn

divorced [dɪˈvɔːst] ADJ 离异的 líyì de ▸**to get divorced** 离婚 líhūn

DIY (*Brit*) N ABBR (= **do-it-yourself**) 自己动手的活计 zìjǐ dòngshǒu de huójì ▸**to do DIY** 自己动手做 zìjǐ dòngshǒu zuò

- **DIY**
-
-
- 英国人对 **DIY** 很上瘾,有
- 时幽默地称其为一种全民
- 性消遣。**DIY** 意为 **do-it-**
- **yourself**,是指自己动手制
- 作和修理东西,尤其是在家
- 里。房主不雇佣专业的建筑
- 工人,木匠或油漆匠,这样不
- 仅省钱,也能从自己动手改
- 进家里的设备,环境中得到莫
- 大的满足感。专门的 **DIY** 商
- 店销售工具,油漆和其他能满
- 足 **DIY** 爱好者嗜好的用品。

dizzy [ˈdɪzɪ] ADJ ▸**to feel dizzy** 感到头晕 gǎndào tóuyūn

DJ N ABBR (= **disc jockey**) 简称为 DJ,意为广播电台或迪斯科舞厅流行音乐唱片播放及介绍人

KEYWORD

do [duː] (*pt* **did**, *pp* **done**) I VT 1 做 zuò ▸**what are you doing?** 你在做什么呢? nǐ zài zuò shénme ne? ▸**are you doing anything tomorrow evening?** 你明晚有什

么打算？ nǐ míngwǎn yǒu shénme dǎsuàn? ▸**what did you do with the money?** (how did you spend it) 你怎么用这笔钱的？ nǐ zěnme yòng zhèbǐ qián de? ▸**what are you going to do about this?** 你打算对此怎么办？ nǐ dǎsuàn duìcǐ zěnmebàn?

2 (for a living) ▸**what do you do?** 你做什么工作？ nǐ zuò shénme gōngzuò?

3 (with noun) ▸**to do the cooking** 做饭 zuòfàn

4 (referring to speed, distance) ▸**the car was doing 100** 汽车以100英里的时速行进 qìchē yǐ yìbǎi yīnglǐ de shísù xíngjìn ▸**we've done 200 km already** 我们的时速已达到了200公里 wǒmen de shísù yǐjīng dádào le èrbǎi yīnglǐ

5 (cause) ▸**the explosion did a lot of damage** 爆炸造成了很大损失 bàozhà zàochéng le hěndà sǔnshī ▸**a holiday will do you good** 休次假会对你有好处 xiū cì jià huì duì nǐ yǒu hǎochù

II VI **1** (act, behave) 做 zuò ▸**do as I tell you** 按我告诉你的做 àn wǒ gàosù nǐ de zuò

2 (get on) 进展 jìnzhǎn ▸**he's doing well/badly at school** 他的学习成绩很好/很差 tāde xuéxí chéngjī hěnhǎo/hěnchà ▸**"how do you do?" — "how do you do?"** "你好" "你好" "nǐhǎo" "nǐhǎo"

3 (suit) 行 xíng ▸**will it do?** 行吗？ xíngma?

4 (be sufficient) 足够 zúgòu ▸**will £15 do?** 15镑够吗？ shíwǔ bàng

gòuma?

III AUX VB **1** (in negative constructions) ▸**I don't understand** 我不懂 wǒ bùdǒng ▸**she doesn't want it** 她不想要这个 tā bùxiǎng yào zhège ▸**don't be silly!** 别傻了！ bié shǎ le!

2 (to form questions) ▸**do you like jazz?** 你喜欢爵士乐吗？ nǐ xǐhuān juéshìyè ma? ▸**what do you think?** 你怎么想？ nǐ zěnme xiǎng? ▸**why didn't you come?** 你为什么没来？ nǐ wèishénme méilái?

3 (for emphasis, in polite expressions) ▸**do sit down/help yourself** 赶快坐啊/千万别客气 gǎnkuài zuò a/qiānwàn bié kèqi

4 (used to avoid repeating vb) 用于避免动词的重复 ▸**they say they don't care, but they do** 他们说不在乎，但实际是在乎的 tāmen shuō bù zàihu, dàn shíjì shì zàihu de ▸**(and) so do I** 我也是 wǒ yěshì ▸**and neither did we** 我们也不 wǒmen yěbù ▸**"who made this mess?" — "I did"** "是谁弄乱七八糟的？" "是我" "shì shuí nòngde luàn qī bā zāo de" "shì wǒ"

5 (in question tags) ▸**I don't know him, do I?** 我不认识他，是吗？ wǒ bù rènshi tā, shìma? ▸**she lives in London, doesn't she?** 她住在伦敦，不是吗？ tā zhùzài Lúndūn, bùshì ma?

▸**do up** VT FUS **1** [+ laces] 系紧 jìjǐn; [+ dress, coat, buttons] 扣上 kòu shàng

2 (esp Brit) [+ room, house] 装修

zhuāngxiū

▶ **do with** VT FUS **1** (*need*) ▶ **I could do with a drink/some help** 我想喝一杯/需要帮助 wǒ xiǎng hē yìbēi/xūyào bāngzhù
2 (*be connected*) ▶ **to have to do with** 与…有关 yǔ…yǒuguān
▶ **what has it got to do with you?** 这跟你有什么关系? zhè gēn nǐ yǒu shénme guānxi?
▶ **do without** VT FUS 没有…也行 méiyǒu…yě xíng

dock [dɔk] N [c] (*Naut*) 船坞 chuánwù [个 gè]

doctor ['dɔktə^r] N [c] **1** 医生 yīshēng [位 wèi] **2** ▶ **the doctor's** 诊所 zhěnsuǒ [家 jiā]

document ['dɔkjumənt] N [c] **1** 文件 wénjiàn [份 fèn] **2** (*Comput*) 文档 wéndàng [个 gè]

documentary [dɔkju'mɛntərɪ] N [c] 纪录片 jìlùpiàn [部 bù]

does [dʌz] VB *see* **do**

doesn't ['dʌznt] = **does not**

dog [dɔg] N [c] **1** 狗 gǒu [只 zhī] **2** (*male*) 雄兽 xióngshòu [头 tóu]

do-it-yourself ['du:ɪtjɔː'sɛlf] I N [U] 自己动手的活计 zìjǐ dòngshǒu de huójì II ADJ [+ *store*] 出售供购买者自行装配物品的 chūshòu gòng gòumǎizhě zìxíng zhuāngpèi wùpǐn de

dole [dəul] (*inf*) N [U] (*Brit*) ▶ **(the) dole** (*payment*) 失业救济金 shīyè jiùjìjīn ▶ **(to be) on the dole** (*Brit*) 靠失业救济金生活 kào shīyè jiùjìjīn shēnghuó

doll [dɔl] N [c] 娃娃 wáwa [个 gè]

dollar ['dɔlə^r] N [c] 元 yuán

dolphin ['dɔlfɪn] N [c] 海豚 hǎitún [只 zhī]

dominoes ['dɔmɪnəuz] N [U] 多米诺骨牌游戏 duōmǐnuò gǔpái yóuxì

donate [də'neɪt] VT **1** ▶ **to donate (to sb)** [+ *money, clothes*] 捐赠 (给某人) juānzèng (gěi mǒurén) **2** [+ *blood, organs*] 捐献 juānxiàn

done [dʌn] PP *of* **do**

donkey ['dɔŋkɪ] N [c] 驴 lú [头 tóu]

don't [dəunt] = **do not**

donut ['dəunʌt] (*US*) N = **doughnut**

door [dɔː^r] N [c] 门 mén [扇 shàn] ▶ **to answer the door** 应门 yìngmén

doorbell ['dɔːbɛl] N [c] 门铃 ménlíng [个 gè]

dormitory ['dɔːmɪtrɪ] N [c] **1** (*room*) 宿舍 sùshè [间 jiān] **2** (*US: building*) 宿舍楼 sùshèlóu [座 zuò]

dose [dəus] N [c] 一剂 yíjì

dot [dɔt] N [c] 圆点 yuándiǎn [个 gè] ▶ **on the dot** (*punctually*) 准时地 zhǔnshí de

dot-com [dɔt'kɔm] N [c] 网络公司 wǎngluò gōngsī [家 jiā]

double ['dʌbl] I ADJ 双份的 shuāngfèn de II VI [*population, size*] 变成两倍 biànchéng liǎngbèi
▶ **it's spelt with a double "M"** 它的拼写中有两个 "M" tāde pīnxiě zhōng yǒu liǎnggè "M"
▶ **double the size/number (of sth)** (是某物)大小/数量的两倍 (shì mǒuwù) dàxiǎo/shùliàng de

liǎngbèi

double bass N [c/u] 低音提琴 dīyīn tíqín [把 bǎ]

double-click ['dʌbl'klɪk] VI 双击 shuāngjī

double-decker ['dʌbl'dɛkəʳ] (*esp Brit*) N [c] (*bus*) 双层公共汽车 shuāngcéng gōnggòng qìchē [辆 liàng]

double glazing [-'gleɪzɪŋ] (*Brit*) N [u] 双层玻璃 shuāngcéng bōlí

double room N [c] 双人房 shuāngrénfáng

doubt [daut] I N [c/u] (*uncertainty*) 怀疑 huáiyí [种 zhǒng] II VT [+ *person's word*] 不信 bùxìn ▶to **doubt if** *or* **whether...** 拿不准是否… nábùzhǔn shìfǒu… ▶I **doubt it (very much)** 我(很)怀疑 wǒ (hěn) huáiyí

doubtful ['dautful] ADJ 1 (*questionable*) ▶it **is doubtful that/whether...** 不能确定…/是否… bùnéng quèdìng…/shìfǒu… 2 (*unconvinced*) ▶to **be doubtful that/whether...** 怀疑…/是否… huáiyí…/shìfǒu… ▶to **be doubtful about sth** 对某事有怀疑 duì mǒushì yǒu huáiyí

doughnut, (*US*) **donut** ['dəunʌt] N [c] 炸面饼圈 zhá miànbǐngquān [个 gè]

down [daun] I ADV 1 (*downwards*) 向下 xiàngxià 2 (*in a lower place*) 在下面 zài xiàmian II PREP 1 (*towards lower level*) 沿着…往下 yánzhe…wǎng xià 2 (*at lower part of*) 在下面 zài xiàmian 3 (*along*) 沿着 yánzhe ▶she **looked down**

她向下看 tā xiàngxià kàn ▶he **walked down the road** 他沿街走去 tā yánjiē zǒuqù ▶**down there** 在那儿 zài nàr ▶**England are two goals down** (*behind*) 英格兰落后两球 Yīnggélán luòhòu liǎngqiú

download ['daunləud] VT 下载 xiàzǎi

downstairs ['daun'stɛəz] ADV 1 (*on or to floor below*) 楼下 lóuxià 2 (*on or to ground level*) 在义 zài yī céng

downtown ['daun'taun] (*US*) I ADV 1 (*be, work*) 在市中心 zài shì zhōngxīn 2 (*go*) 去市中心 qù shì zhōngxīn II ADJ ▶**downtown Chicago** 芝加哥的市中心 Zhījiāgē de shì zhōngxīn

dozen ['dʌzn] N [c] 一打 yīdá ▶**two dozen eggs** 两打鸡蛋 liǎngdá jīdàn ▶**dozens of** 许多 xǔduō

draft [drɑːft] N 1 [c] (*first version*) 草稿 cǎogǎo 2 [c] (*bank draft*) 汇票 huìpiào [张 zhāng]; *see also* **draught**

drag [dræg] VT (*pull*) [+ *large object, body*] 拖 tuō

dragon ['drægn] N [c] 龙 lóng [条 tiáo]

drain [dreɪn] I N [c] (*in street*) 排水沟 páishuǐgōu [条 tiáo] II VT [+ *vegetables*] 使…流干 shǐ…liúgān III VI [*liquid*] 流入 liúrù

drama ['drɑːmə] N 1 [u] (*theatre*) 戏剧 xìjù 2 [c] (*play*) 一出戏剧 yīchū xìjù [幕 mù] 3 [c/u] (*excitement*) 戏剧性 xìjùxìng [种 zhǒng]

dramatic [drə'mætɪk] ADJ
1 (marked, sudden) 戏剧性的
xìjùxìng de 2 (exciting, impressive)
激动人心的 jīdòng rénxīn de
3 (theatrical) 戏剧的 xìjù de

drank [dræŋk] PT of **drink**

drapes [dreɪps] (US) NPL 窗帘
chuānglián

draught, (US) **draft** [drɑːft] N [c]
气流 qìliú [股 gǔ]

draughts [drɑːfts] (Brit) N [U] 西
洋跳棋 xīyáng tiàoqí

draw [drɔː] (pt **drew**, pp **drawn**)
I VT 1 画 huà 2 [+ curtains, blinds]
(close) 拉上 lāshang; (open) 拉
开 lākāi II VI 1 (with pen, pencil
etc) 画画 huàhuà 2 ▸ to draw
(with/against sb) (esp Brit: Sport)
(与某人) 打成平局 (yǔ mǒurén)
dǎ chéng píngjú III N [c] 1 (esp
Brit: Sport) 平局 píngjú [个 gè]
2 (lottery) 抽奖 chōujiǎng [次 cì]
▸ draw up VT [+ document, plan]
草拟 cǎonǐ

drawback ['drɔːbæk] N [c] 欠缺
qiànquē [个 gè]

drawer [drɔːr] N [c] 抽屉 chōuti
[个 gè]

drawing ['drɔːɪŋ] N 1 [c] (picture)
素描 sùmiáo [幅 fú] 2 [U] (skill,
discipline) 绘画 huìhuà

drawing pin (Brit) N [c] 图钉
túdīng [枚 méi]

drawn [drɔːn] PP of **draw**

dread [drɛd] VT (fear) 惧怕 jùpà

dreadful ['drɛdful] ADJ 糟透的
zāotòu de

dream [driːm] (pt, pp **dreamed**
or **dreamt**) I N [c] 1 梦 mèng

[场 chǎng] 2 (ambition) 梦想
mèngxiǎng [个 gè] II VI ▸ to
dream about (when asleep) 梦到
mèngdào

dreamt [drɛmt] PT, PP of **dream**

drench [drɛntʃ] VT (soak) 使湿透
shǐ shītòu

dress [drɛs] I N [c] 连衣裙
liányīqún [条 tiáo] II VT 1 [+ child]
给…穿衣 gěi…chuān yī 2 [+ salad]
拌 bàn III VI 穿衣 chuān yī ▸ to
dress o.s., get dressed 穿好衣服
chuānhǎo yīfu
▸ **dress up** VI 1 (wear best
clothes) 穿上盛装 chuānshang
shèngzhuāng 2 ▸ to dress up as
化装成 huàzhuāng chéng

dresser ['drɛsər] N [c] 1 (Brit:
cupboard) 碗橱 wǎnchú [个 gè]
2 (US: chest of drawers) 梳妆台
shūzhuāngtái [个 gè]

dressing gown N [c] 晨衣 chényī
[套 tào]

dressing table N [c] 梳妆台
shūzhuāngtái [个 gè]

drew [druː] PT of **draw**

dried [draɪd] ADJ [+ fruit, herbs] 干
的 gān de; [+ eggs, milk] 粉状的
fěnzhuàng de

drier ['draɪər] N = **dryer**

drill [drɪl] I N [c] 钻 zuàn [个 gè];
[of dentist] 钻头 zuàntóu [个 gè]
II VT 在…上钻孔 zài…shang
zuānkǒng

drink [drɪŋk] (pt **drank**, pp **drunk**)
I N 1 [c] (tea, water etc) 饮料 yǐnliào
[种 zhǒng] 2 [c] (alcoholic) 酒 jiǔ
[瓶 píng] II VT 喝 hē III VI (drink
alcohol) 喝酒 hējiǔ ▸ to have a

drink 喝一杯 hē yībēi; (*alcoholic*) 喝酒 hējiǔ

drive [draɪv] (*pt* **drove**, *pp* **driven**) I N 1 [c] (*journey*) 车程 chēchéng [段 duàn] 2 [c] (*also:* **driveway**) 私家车道 sījiā chēdào [条 tiáo] 3 [c] (*also:* **CD ROM/disk drive**) 驱动器 qūdòngqì [个 gè] II VT 1 [+ *vehicle*] 驾驶 jiàshǐ 2 ▶ **to drive sb to the station/airport** 驱车送某人去车站/飞机场 qūchē sòng mǒurén qù chēzhàn/fēijīchǎng III VI 开车 kāichē ▶ **to go for a drive** 开车兜风 kāichē dōufēng ▶ **it's a 3-hour drive from London** 到伦敦要3个小时的车程 dào Lúndūn yào sāngè xiǎoshí de chēchéng ▶ **to drive sb mad/to desperation** 逼得某人发疯/绝望 bīde mǒurén fāfēng/juéwàng ▶ **to drive at 50 km an hour** 以每小时50公里的速度驾车 yǐ měi xiǎoshí wǔshí gōnglǐ de sùdù jiàchē

driver ['draɪvəʳ] N [c] 1 [*of own car*] 驾驶员 jiàshǐyuán [位 wèi] 2 [*of taxi, bus, lorry, train*] 司机 sījī [位 wèi]

driver's license ['draɪvəz-] (US) N [c] 驾驶执照 jiàshǐ zhízhào [本 běn]

driveway ['draɪvweɪ] N [c] 车道 chēdào [条 tiáo]

driving instructor N [c] 驾驶教练 jiàshǐ jiàoliàn [位 wèi]

driving licence (*Brit*) N [c] 驾驶执照 jiàshǐ zhízhào [本 běn]

driving test N [c] 驾驶执照考试 jiàshǐ zhízhào kǎoshì [次 cì]

drizzle ['drɪzl] VI ▶ **it is drizzling** 下着毛毛雨 xiàzhe máomáoyǔ

drop [drɔp] I N 1 [c] [*of liquid*] 滴 dī 2 (*reduction*) ▶ **a drop in sth** 某物的下降 mǒuwù de xiàjiàng II VT 1 (*lose hold of*) 失手落下 shīshǒu luòxià 2 (*deliberately*) 放 fàng 2 将…送到 jiāng…sòng dào III VI [*amount, level*] 下降 xiàjiàng; [*object*] 落下 luòxià

▶ **drop in** (*inf*) VI ▶ **to drop in (on sb)** 顺便拜访(某人) shùnbiàn bàifǎng (mǒurén)

▶ **drop off** I VI (*fall asleep*) 睡着 shuìzháo II VT [+ *passenger*] 将…送到 jiāng…sòng dào

▶ **drop out** VI (*of college, university*) 辍学 chuòxué

drought [draut] N [c/u] 旱灾 hànzāi [场 chǎng]

drove [drəuv] PT *of* **drive**

drown [draun] I VT ▶ **to be drowned** 被淹死 bèi yānsǐ II VI [*person, animal*] 溺死 nìsǐ

drug [drʌg] N [c] 1 (*prescribed*) 药 yào [片 piàn] 2 (*recreational*) 毒品 dúpǐn [种 zhǒng] ▶ **to take drugs** 吸毒 xīdú ▶ **hard/soft drugs** 硬/软毒品 yìng/ruǎn dúpǐn

drug addict N [c] 吸毒成瘾者 xīdú chéngyǐnzhě [个 gè]

drug dealer N [c] 毒品贩子 dúpǐn fànzi

druggist ['drʌgɪst] (US) N [c] 1 药剂师 yàojìshī [位 wèi] 2 ▶ **druggist('s)** (*shop*) 药店 yàodiàn [家 jiā]

drugstore ['drʌgstɔːʳ] (US) N [c] 杂货店 záhuòdiàn [家 jiā]

drum [drʌm] I N [c] 鼓 gǔ [面

miàn] II **drums** NPL (*kit*) 鼓 gǔ

drummer ['drʌmə^r] N [c] 鼓手 gǔshǒu [位 wèi]

drunk [drʌŋk] I PP *of* **drink** II ADJ 醉的 zuì de ▶**to get drunk** 喝醉了 hēzuì le

dry [draɪ] I ADJ 1 干的 gān de 2 [+ *climate, weather, day*] 干燥的 gānzào de II VT 把…弄干 bǎ…nòng gān III VI [*paint, washing*] 变干 biàn gān ▶**to dry one's hands/hair** 擦干手/头发 cāgān shǒu/tóufa

dry-cleaner ['draɪ'kliːnə^r] N [c] (*also*: **dry cleaner's**) 干洗店 gānxǐdiàn [家 jiā]

dryer ['draɪə^r] N [c] 1 (*tumble dryer, spin-dryer*) 干衣机 gānyījī [台 tái] 2 (*hair dryer*) 吹风机 chuīfēngjī [个 gè]

duck [dʌk] N 1 [c] (*bird*) 鸭 yā [只 zhī] 2 [U] (*as food*) 鸭肉 yāròu

due [djuː] I ADJ ▶**to be due** [*person, train, bus*] 应到 yīng dào; [*baby*] 预期 yùqī; [*rent, payment*] 应支付 yīng zhīfù II ADV ▶**due north/south** 正北方/南方 zhèng běifāng/nánfāng ▶**due to…** (*because of*) 由于… yóuyú…

dug [dʌg] PT, PP *of* **dig**

dull [dʌl] ADJ 1 [+ *weather, day*] 阴沉的 yīnchén de 2 (*boring*) 单调乏味的 dāndiào fáwèi de

dumb [dʌm] ADJ 1 哑的 yǎ de 2 (*pej: stupid, foolish*) 愚蠢的 yúchǔn de

dump [dʌmp] I N [c] 垃圾场 lājīchǎng [个 gè] II VT 1 (*get rid of*) 倾倒 qīngdào 2 [+ *computer data*]

转储 zhuǎn chǔ

Dumpster® ['dʌmpstə^r] (*US*) N [c] （用以装运工地废料的无盖）废料筒 (yòngyǐ zhuāngyùn gōngdì fèiliào de wú gài)fèiliàotǒng [个 gè]

during ['djuərɪŋ] PREP 1 在…期间 zài…qījiān 2 (*at some point in*) 在…时候 zài…shíhou

dusk [dʌsk] N [U] 黄昏 huánghūn ▶**at dusk** 黄昏时刻 huánghūn shíkè

dust [dʌst] N [U] (*dirt: outdoors*) 尘土 chéntǔ; (*: indoors*) 灰尘 huīchén

dustbin ['dʌstbɪn] (*Brit*) N [c] 垃圾箱 lājīxiāng [个 gè]

dustman ['dʌstmən] (*Brit*) (*pl* **dustmen**) N [c] 清洁工 qīngjiégōng [位 wèi]

dusty ['dʌstɪ] ADJ 满是尘土的 mǎn shì chéntǔ de

Dutch [dʌtʃ] I ADJ 荷兰的 Hélán de II N [U] (*language*) 荷兰语 Hélányǔ III **the Dutch** NPL (*people*) 荷兰人 Hélánrén

duty ['djuːtɪ] I N [c/U] 1 (*responsibility*) 责任 zérèn [个 gè] 2 (*tax*) 税 shuì [种 zhǒng] II **duties** NPL (*tasks*) 任务 rènwù

duty-free ['djuːtɪ'friː] ADJ [+ *drink, cigarettes*] 免税的 miǎnshuì de ▶**duty-free shop** 免税商店 miǎnshuì shāngdiàn

duvet ['duːveɪ] (*Brit*) N [c] 羽绒被 yǔróngbèi [床 chuáng]

DVD player N [c] DVD播放器 DVD bōfàngqì [台 tái]

dye [daɪ] I N [c/U] 染料 rǎnliào [种 zhǒng] II VT 染色 rǎnsè

dynamic [daɪ'næmɪk] ADJ 生气勃勃的 shēngqì bóbó de

dyslexia [dɪs'lɛksɪə] N [U] 诵读困难 sòngdú kùnnan

dyslexic [dɪs'lɛksɪk] ADJ 诵读有困难的 sòngdú yǒu kùnnan de

each [i:tʃ] I ADJ 每 měi II PRON (*each one*) 每个 měigè ▶**each one of them** 他们中的每一个 tāmen zhōngde měiyīgè ▶**each other** 互相 hùxiāng ▶**they have 2 books each** 他们每人有两本书 tāmen měirén yǒu liǎngběnshū ▶**they cost 5 pounds each** 每个售价5镑 měigè shòujià wǔbàng

> **each** 表示一个群体中的每一个人或物，强调的是每一个个体。**every** 指由两个以上的个体组成的群体中的所有的人或物，强调的是整体。 *He listened to every news bulletin...an equal chance for every child...* 注意 **each** 指两个当中的任何一个。*Each apartment has two bedrooms...We each*

carried a suitcase. **each** 和 **every** 后面都只能跟名词单数形式。

ear [ɪəʳ] N [c] 耳朵 ěrduo [只 zhī]

earache ['ɪəreɪk] N [c/u] 耳朵痛 ěrduo tòng

earlier ['əːlɪəʳ] I ADJ [+ date, time] 较早的 jiàozǎo de II ADV (leave, go) 提早 tízǎo ▶**earlier this year** 本年初 běnnián chū

early ['əːlɪ] I ADV 1 (in day, month) 在初期 zài chūqī 2 (before usual time: get up, go to bed, arrive, leave) 早 zǎo II ADJ [+ stage, career] 早期的 zǎoqī de ▶**I usually get up early** 我通常早起床 wǒ tōngcháng zǎo qǐchuáng ▶**early this morning** 今天一大早 jīntiān yīdàzǎo ▶**early in the morning** 清早 qīngzǎo ▶**you're early!** 你怎么这么早! nǐ zěnme zhème zǎo!

earn [əːn] VT 挣得 zhèngdé ▶**to earn one's** or **a living** 谋生 móushēng

earnings ['əːnɪŋz] NPL 收入 shōurù

earphones ['ɪəfəunz] NPL 耳机 ěrjī

earring ['ɪərɪŋ] N [c] 耳环 ěrhuán [只 zhī]

earth [əːθ] N 1 [u/s] (also: **the Earth**) 地球 dìqiú 2 [u] (land surface) 陆地 lùdì 3 [u] (soil) 泥土 nítǔ

earthquake ['əːθkweɪk] N [c] 地震 dìzhèn [次 cì]

easily ['iːzɪlɪ] ADV 不费力地 bù fèilì de

east [iːst] I N 1 [s/u] 东方

dōngfāng 2 ▶**the East** (the Orient) 东方国家 dōngfāng guójiā II ADJ 东部的 dōngbù de III ADV 向东方 xiàng dōngfāng ▶**the east of Spain** 西班牙东部 Xībānyá dōngbù ▶**to the east** 以东 yǐdōng ▶**east of ...** …以东 …yǐdōng

Easter ['iːstəʳ] N [u] 复活节 Fùhuó Jié ▶**the Easter holidays** 复活节假期 Fùhuó Jié jiàqī

eastern ['iːstən] ADJ 1 (Geo) 东部的 dōngbù de 2 ▶**Eastern** (oriental) 东方的 Dōngfāng de

easy ['iːzɪ] ADJ 1 容易的 róngyì de 2 [+ life, time] 安逸的 ānyì de ▶**dogs are easy to train** 狗很容易训练 gǒu hěn róngyì xùnliàn ▶**it's easy to train dogs** 训狗是容易的 xùngǒu shì róngyì de

eat [iːt] (pt **ate**, pp **eaten** ['iːtn]) I VT 吃 chī II VI 1 吃 chī 2 (have a meal) 吃饭 chīfàn

eaten ['iːtn] PP of **eat**

echo ['ɛkəu] (pl **echoes**) N [c] 回音 huíyīn [个 gè]

ecology [ɪ'kɔlədʒɪ] N [u] 1 (environment) 生态 shēngtài 2 (subject) 生态学 shēngtàixué

economic [iːkə'nɔmɪk] ADJ 1 经济的 jīngjì de 2 (profitable) 有利可图的 yǒulì kětú de

economical [iːkə'nɔmɪkl] ADJ 节约的 jiéyuē de

economics [iːkə'nɔmɪks] N [u] 经济学 jīngjìxué

economy [ɪ'kɔnəmɪ] N 1 [c] 经济 jīngjì [种 zhǒng] 2 [u] (thrift) 节约 jiéyuē

eczema ['ɛksɪmə] N [u] 湿疹

shīzhěn

edge [ɛdʒ] N [c] 1 边缘 biānyuán
[个 gè] 2 (of table, chair) 棱 léng

editor ['ɛdɪtəʳ] N [c] 编辑 biānjí
[个 gè]

educate ['ɛdjukeɪt] VT 教育
jiàoyù

education [ɛdju'keɪʃən] N [U/s]
教育 jiàoyù

effect [ɪ'fɛkt] I N [c/u] 影响
yǐngxiǎng [个 gè] II effects NPL
(Cine) 特别效果 tèbié xiàoguǒ
▶to take effect [drug] 见效
jiànxiào ▶to have an effect on
sb/sth 对某人/某事产生影响
duì mǒurén/mǒushì chǎnshēng
yǐngxiǎng

effective [ɪ'fɛktɪv] ADJ 有效的
yǒuxiào de

efficiency [ɪ'fɪʃənsɪ] N [U] 效
率 xiàolǜ

efficient [ɪ'fɪʃənt] ADJ 效率高的
xiàolǜ gāo de

effort ['ɛfət] N 1 [U] 努力 nǔlì 2 [c]
(attempt) 尝试 chángshì [个 gè] [2
U/s] ▶to make an effort to do sth
努力做某事 nǔlì zuò mǒushì

e.g. ADV ABBR (= exempli gratia)
(for example) 举例来说 jǔlì lái shuō

egg [ɛg] N [c] 蛋 dàn [个 gè]

eggplant ['ɛgplɑːnt] (US) N [c/u]
茄子 qiézi [个 gè]

Egypt ['iːdʒɪpt] N 埃及 Āijí

eight [eɪt] NUM 八 bā; see also five

eighteen [eɪ'tiːn] NUM 十八
shíbā; see also fifteen

eighteenth [eɪ'tiːnθ] NUM 第十
八 dì shíbā; see also fifth

eighth [eɪtθ] NUM 1 第八 dì bā

2 (fraction) 八分之一 bā fēn zhī yī;
see also **fifth**

eighty ['eɪtɪ] NUM 八十 bāshí; see
also **fifty**

Eire ['ɛərə] N 爱尔兰共和国
Àiʼěrlán Gònghéguó

either ['aɪðəʳ] I ADJ 1 (one or other)
两者任一的 liǎngzhě rènyī de
2 (both, each) 两者中每一方的
liǎngzhě zhōng měiyīfāng de ▶on
either side 在两边 zài liǎngbiān
II PRON 1 (after negative) 两者之中
任何一个 liǎngzhě zhī zhōng rènhé
yīgè ▶I don't like either of them
两个我都不喜欢 liǎnggè wǒ dōu
bù xǐhuān 2 (after interrogative)
两者之中任何一个 liǎngzhě zhī
zhōng rènhé yīgè III ADV (in
negative statements) 也 yě IV CONJ
▶ either... or... 要么…要么…
yàome...yàome... ▶no, I don't
either 不，我也不 bù, wǒ yě bù

elastic [ɪ'læstɪk] N [U] 橡皮
xiàngpí

elastic band (Brit) N [c] 橡皮筋
xiàngpíjīn [根 gēn]

elbow ['ɛlbəʊ] N [c] (Anat) 肘
zhǒu [个 gè]

elder ['ɛldəʳ] ADJ [+ brother, sister]
年龄较大的 niánlíng jiào dà de

elderly ['ɛldəlɪ] I ADJ 年长的
niánzhǎng de II NPL ▶the elderly
老人家 lǎorénjiā

eldest ['ɛldɪst] I ADJ 年龄最大的
niánlíng zuìdà de II N [s/PL] 年龄
最大的孩子 niánlíng zuìdà de háizi

elect [ɪ'lɛkt] VT 选举 xuǎnjǔ

election [ɪ'lɛkʃən] N [c] 选
举 xuǎnjǔ [次 cì] ▶to hold an

election 举行选举 jǔxíng xuǎnjǔ

electric [ɪ'lɛktrɪk] ADJ 1 电动的 diàndòng de 2 [+ current, charge, socket] 电的 diàn de

electrical [ɪ'lɛktrɪkl] ADJ 电动的 diàndòng de

electric guitar N [c/u] 电吉他 diànjítā [把 bǎ]

electrician [ɪlɛk'trɪʃən] N [c] 电工 diàngōng [个 gè]

electricity [ɪlɛk'trɪsɪtɪ] N [u] 1 (energy) 电 diàn 2 (supply) 供电 gòngdiàn

electric shock N [c] 触电 chùdiàn [次 cì]

electronic [ɪlɛk'trɒnɪk] ADJ 电子的 diànzǐ de

electronics [ɪlɛk'trɒnɪks] N [u] 电子学 diànzǐxué

elegant ['ɛlɪgənt] ADJ 优雅的 yōuyǎ de

elementary school (US) N [c/u] 小学 xiǎoxué

elephant ['ɛlɪfənt] N [c] 大象 dàxiàng [头 tóu]

elevator ['ɛlɪveɪtər] (US) N [c] 电梯 diàntī [部 bù]

eleven [ɪ'lɛvn] NUM 十一 shíyī; see also **five**

eleventh [ɪ'lɛvnθ] NUM 第十一 dì shíyī; see also **fifth**

eliminate [ɪ'lɪmɪneɪt] VT 1 [+ poverty] 消除 xiāochú 2 [+ team, contestant, candidate] 淘汰 táotài

else [ɛls] ADV ▶ **or else** (otherwise) 否则 fǒuzé; (threatening) 要不然 yàobùrán ▷ Don't talk to me like that again, or else! 别这么跟我说

话，要不够你受的！ bié zhème gēn wǒ shuōhuà,yàobù gòu nǐ shòu de! ▶ **something else** 其他东西 qítā dōngxi ▶ **anything else** 任何其他东西 rènhé qítā dōngxi ▶ **what else?** 其他什么? qítā shénme ▶ **everywhere else** 其他任何地方 qítā rènhé dìfāng ▶ **everyone else** 其他人 qítā rén ▶ **nobody else** 没有其他人 méiyǒu qítā rén

elsewhere [ɛls'wɛər] ADV 1 (be) 在别处 zài biéchù 2 (go) 到别处 dào biéchù

e-mail ['i:meɪl] I N [c/u] 电子邮件 diànzǐ yóujiàn [封 fēng] II VT 1 [+ person] 给…发电子邮件 gěi...fā diànzǐ yóujiàn 2 [+ file, document] 用电子邮件寄 yòng diànzǐ yóujiàn jì

e-mail account N [c] 电子邮件账号 diànzǐ yóujiàn zhànghào [个 gè]

e-mail address N [c] 电子邮件地址 diànzǐ yóujiàn dìzhǐ [个 gè]

embarrassed [ɪm'bærəst] ADJ ▶ **to be embarrassed** 不好意思的 bùhǎo yìsi de

embarrassing [ɪm'bærəsɪŋ] ADJ 令人尴尬的 lìng rén gāngà de

embassy ['ɛmbəsɪ] N [c] 大使馆 dàshǐguǎn [个 gè]

emergency [ɪ'mə:dʒənsɪ] N [c] (crisis) 紧急情况 jǐnjí qíngkuàng [个 gè] ▶ **in an emergency** 在紧急情况下 zài jǐnjí qíngkuàng xià

emergency room (US) N [c] 急诊室 jízhěnshì [个 gè]

emigrate ['ɛmɪgreɪt] VI 移居外国 yíjū wàiguó

emotion [ɪ'məʊʃən] N [c/u] 感情 gǎnqíng [种 zhǒng]

emotional [ɪ'məʊʃənl] ADJ 易动 感情的 yì dòng gǎnqíng de

emperor ['ɛmpərər] N [c] 皇帝 huángdì [个 gè]

emphasize ['ɛmfəsaɪz] VT 强调 qiángdiào

empire ['ɛmpaɪər] N [c] 帝国 dìguó [个 gè]

employ [ɪm'plɔɪ] VT 雇用 gùyòng ▶**he was employed as a technician** 他受雇做技师 tā shòugù zuò jìshī

employee [ɪmplɔɪ'iː] N [c] 雇员 gùyuán [个 gè]

employer [ɪm'plɔɪər] N [c] 雇主 gùzhǔ [个 gè]

employment [ɪm'plɔɪmənt] N [U] 工作 gōngzuò

empty ['ɛmptɪ] I ADJ 空的 kōng de II VT 倒空 dào kōng

encourage [ɪn'kʌrɪdʒ] VT 1 [+ person] 鼓励 gǔlì 2 [+ activity, attitude] 支持 zhīchí 3 [+ growth, industry] 助长 zhùzhǎng ▶**to encourage sb to do sth** 鼓励某 人去做某事 gǔlì mǒurén qùzuò mǒushì

encouragement [ɪn'kʌrɪdʒmənt] N [U] 鼓励 gǔlì

encyclop(a)edia [ɛnsaɪkləu'piːdɪə] N [c] 百科全书 bǎikē quánshū

end [ɛnd] I N 1 [s] [of period, event] 末期 mòqī 2 [s] [of film, book] 末尾 mòwěi 3 [c] [of street, queue, rope, table] 尽头 jìntóu [个 gè] 4 [c] [of town] 端 duān II VT (finish, stop)

终止 zhōngzhǐ III VI [meeting, film, book] 结束 jiéshù ▶**at the end of August** 在8月末 zài bāyuè mò ▶**to come to an end** 完结 wánjié ▶**in the end** 最终 zuìzhōng ▶ **end up** VI ▶**to end up in/at** [+ place] 最终到了 zuìzhōng dào le

ending ['ɛndɪŋ] N [c] 结局 jiéjú [个 gè] ▶**a happy ending** 美满结 局 měimǎn jiéjú

enemy ['ɛnəmɪ] N [c] 敌人 dírén [个 gè]

energetic [ɛnə'dʒɛtɪk] ADJ 1 精 力充沛的 jīnglì chōngpèi de 2 [+ activity] 生机勃勃的 shēngjī bóbó de

energy ['ɛnədʒɪ] N [U] 能源 néngyuán

engaged [ɪn'geɪdʒd] ADJ 1 (to be married) 已订婚的 yǐ dìnghūn de 2 (Brit: Tel) 被占用的 bèi zhànyòng de 3 (Brit) [+ toilet] 被 占用的 bèi zhànyòng de ▶**to get engaged (to)** (与…) 订婚 (yǔ…) dìnghūn

engagement [ɪn'geɪdʒmənt] N [c] (to marry) 婚约 hūnyuē [个 gè]

engagement ring N [c] 订婚戒 指 dìnghūn jièzhǐ [枚 méi]

engine ['ɛndʒɪn] N [c] 1 (Aut) 发 动机 fādòngjī [台 tái] 2 (Rail) 机车 jīchē [部 bù]

engineer [ɛndʒɪ'nɪər] N [c] 1 (who designs machines, bridges) 工程 师 gōngchéngshī [位 wèi] 2 (who repairs machines, phones etc) 机械 师 jīxièshī [位 wèi]

engineering [ɛndʒɪ'nɪərɪŋ] N [U] 1 工程 gōngchéng 2 (science) 工程

学 gōngchéngxué

England ['ɪŋglənd] N 英格兰 Yīnggélán

English ['ɪŋglɪʃ] I ADJ 英国的 Yīngguó de II N (*language*) 英语 Yīngyǔ III **the English** NPL (*people*) 英国人 Yīngguórén ▶**an English speaker** 一个讲英语的人 yīgè jiǎng yīngyǔ de rén

Englishman ['ɪŋglɪʃmən] (*pl* **Englishmen**) N [c] 英格兰男人 Yīnggélán nánrén [个 gè]

Englishwoman ['ɪŋglɪʃwumən] (*pl* **Englishwomen**) N [c] 英格兰 女人 Yīnggélán nǚrén [个 gè]

enjoy [ɪn'dʒɔɪ] VT (*take pleasure in*) 享受…的乐趣 xiǎngshòu...de lèqù ▶**to enjoy doing sth** 喜欢做某事 xǐhuān zuò mǒushì ▶**to enjoy o.s.** 过得快活 guòde kuàihuó ▶**enjoy your meal!** 吃好! chīhǎo!

enjoyable [ɪn'dʒɔɪəbl] ADJ 有乐 趣的 yǒu lèqù de

enormous [ɪ'nɔːməs] ADJ **1** 庞大 的 pángdà de **2** [+ *pleasure, success, disappointment*] 巨大的 jùdà de

enough [ɪ'nʌf] I ADJ [+ *time, books, people*] 足够的 zúgòu de II PRON (*sufficient, more than desired*) 足够 的东西 zúgòu de dōngxi III ADV ▶**big/old/tall enough** 足够大/到 年龄了/足够高 zúgòu dà/ dào niánlíng le/ zúgòu gāo ▶**enough time/money to do sth** 有足够 的时间/金钱去做某事 yǒu zúgòu de shíjiān/jīnqián qùzuò mǒushì ▶**have you got enough?** 你够 吗? nǐ gòuma ▶**enough to eat** 够吃 gòuchī ▶**will 5 be enough?** 5个够吗? wǔgè gòuma ▶**l've had enough!** 我受够了! wǒ shòugòu le ▶**that's enough, thanks** 足 已, 谢谢 zúyǐ, xièxiè

enquiry [ɪn'kwaɪərɪ] N = **inquiry**

enrol, (*US*) **enroll** [ɪn'rəul] I VT **1** 招…入学 zhāo...rùxué **2** (*on course, in club*) 注册 zhùcè II VI (*at school, university, on course, in club*) 注 册 zhùcè

en suite ['ɔnswiːt] (*Brit*) ADJ [+ *bathroom*] 接连的 jiēlián de

ensure [ɪn'ʃuər] (*frm*) VT 保证 bǎozhèng

enter ['ɛntər] I VT **1** [+ *room, building*] 进入 jìnrù **2** [+ *race, competition*] 参加 cānjiā **3** (*Comput*) [+ *data*] 输入 shūrù II VI 进来 jìnlái

entertain [ɛntə'teɪn] VT **1** (*amuse*) 给…娱乐 gěi...yúlè **2** (*invite*) [+ *guest*] 招待 zhāodài

entertainment [ɛntə'teɪnmənt] N [U] 娱乐活动 yúlè huódòng

enthusiasm [ɪn'θuːzɪæzəm] N [U] 热情 rèqíng ▶**enthusiasm for sth** 对某事的热情 duì mǒushì de rèqíng

enthusiastic [ɪnθuːzɪ'æstɪk] ADJ 极感兴趣的 jí gǎn xìngqù de; [+ *response, reception*] 热情的 rèqíng de ▶**to be enthusiastic about sth** 对某事满怀热情 duì mǒushì mǎnhuái rèqíng

entire [ɪn'taɪər] ADJ 整个的 zhěnggè de

entirely [ɪn'taɪəlɪ] ADV 完全地 wánquán de

entrance ['ɛntrns] N [c] 入口

rùkǒu [个 gè] ▶**the entrance to sth** 某处的入口 mǒuchù de rùkǒu

entry ['ɛntrɪ] N 1 [c] (*way in*) 入口 rùkǒu [个 gè] 2 [c] (*in competition*) 登记 dēngjì [个 gè] 3 [c] (*item: in diary*) 项目 xiàngmù [个 gè]; (: *Comput*) 输入 shūrù [项 xiàng] ▶**"no entry"** (*to land, room*) "禁止入内" jìnzhǐ rùnèi; (*Aut*) "禁止通行" jìnzhǐ tōngxíng

envelope ['ɛnvələup] N [c] 信封 xìnfēng [个 gè]

environment [ɪn'vaɪərnmənt] N [c/u] 环境 huánjìng [个 gè] ▶**the environment** (*natural world*) 自然环境 zìrán huánjìng

environmental [ɪnvaɪərn'mɛntl] ADJ 环境保护的 huánjìng bǎohù de

environmentally friendly [ɪnvaɪərn'mɛntəlɪ-] ADJ 不污染环境的 bù wūrǎn huánjìng de

envy ['ɛnvɪ] I N [u] 羡慕 xiànmù II VT (*be jealous of*) 羡慕 xiànmù ▶**to envy sb sth** 羡慕某人的某物 xiànmù mǒurén de mǒuwù

epilepsy ['ɛpɪlɛpsɪ] N [u] 癫痫 diānxián

episode ['ɛpɪsəud] N [c] (*TV, Rad*) 集 jí

equal ['i:kwl] I ADJ 1 相等的 xiāngděng de 2 [+ *intensity, importance*] 同样的 tóngyàng de II VT 1 [+ *number, amount*] 等于 děngyú 2 (*match, rival*) 比得上 bǐdéshàng ▶**they are roughly equal in size** 它们大小差不多 tāmen dàxiǎo chàbùduō ▶**to be equal to** (*the same as*) 与…相

同 yǔ…xiāngtóng ▶**79 minus 14 equals 65** 79减14等于65 qīshíjiǔ jiǎn shísì děngyú liùshíwǔ

equality [i:'kwɔlɪtɪ] N [u] 平等 píngděng

equally ['i:kwəlɪ] ADV 1 (*share, divide*) 平等地 píngděng de 2 (*good, important*) 同样地 tóngyàng de

equator [ɪ'kweɪtər] N ▶**the equator** 赤道 chìdào

equipment [ɪ'kwɪpmənt] N [u] 设备 shèbèi

equivalent [ɪ'kwɪvələnt] I ADJ 相同的 xiāngtóng de II N [c] 相当的人/物 xiāngdāng de rén/wù [个 gè]

ER N ABBR (*US: Med*: = **emergency room**) 急诊室 jízhěnshì [个 gè]

eraser [ɪ'reɪzər] (*esp US*) N [c] 橡皮 xiàngpí [块 kuài]

error ['ɛrər] N [c/u] 差错 chācuò [个 gè] ▶**to make an error** 犯错误 fàn cuòwù

escalator ['ɛskəleɪtər] N [c] 自动扶梯 zìdòng fútī [部 bù]

escape [ɪs'keɪp] I VI 1 (*get away*) 逃走 táozǒu 2 (*from jail*) 逃跑 táopǎo 3 (*from accident*) ▶**to escape unhurt** 安然逃脱 ānrán táotuō II VT [+ *injury*] 避免 bìmiǎn ▶**to escape from** [+ *place*] 从…逃跑 cóng…táopǎo; [+ *person*] 避开 bìkāi

especially [ɪs'pɛʃlɪ] ADV 尤其 yóuqí

essay ['ɛseɪ] N (*Scol*) 论文 lùnwén

essential [ɪ'sɛnʃl] I ADJ 1 (*necessary, vital*) 必要的 bìyào

de 2 (*basic*) 基本的 jīběn de
II **essentials** NPL (*necessities*) 必
需品 bìxūpǐn ►**it is essential to...**
必须… bìxū...

estate [ɪsˈteɪt] N [c] 1 (*land*) 庄
园 zhuāngyuán [个 gè] 2 (*Brit*)
(*also*: **housing estate**) 住宅区
zhùzháiqū

estate agent (*Brit*) N [c] 房地
产经纪人 fángdìchǎn jīngjìrén
[个 gè]

estimate [*n* ˈɛstɪmət, *vb*
ˈɛstɪmeɪt] I N [c] 估计 gūjì [种
zhǒng] II VT (*reckon, calculate*)
估计 gūjì ►**the damage was
estimated at 300 million pounds**
估计损失为3亿英镑 gūjì sǔnshī
wéi sānyì yīngbàng

etc, (*esp US*) **etc.** ABBR (= *et
cetera*) 等等 děngděng

Ethiopia [iːˈθɪəpɪə] N 埃塞俄比
亚 Āisài'ébǐyà

ethnic [ˈɛθnɪk] ADJ 种族的
zhǒngzú de

EU N ABBR (= **European Union**)
►**the EU** 欧洲联盟 Ōuzhōu
Liánméng

euro [ˈjuərəu] (*pl* **euros**) N [c] 欧元
Ōuyuán [个 gè]

Europe [ˈjuərəp] N 欧洲 Ōuzhōu

European [juərəˈpiːən] I ADJ 欧
洲的 Ōuzhōu de II N [c] (*person*) 欧
洲人 Ōuzhōurén [个 gè]

European Union N ►**the
European Union** 欧洲联盟
Ōuzhōu Liánméng

evacuate [ɪˈvækjueɪt] VT
1 [+ *people*] 疏散 shūsàn 2 [+ *place*]
撤离 chèlí

evaluate [ɪˈvæljueɪt] VT 评估
pínggū

even [ˈiːvn] I ADV 甚至 shènzhì
II ADJ 1 (*flat*) 平坦的 píngtǎn de
2 [+ *number*] 偶数的 ǒushù de
►**he didn't even hear what I
said** 他甚至根本没听见我的话 tā
shènzhì gēnběn méi tīngjiàn wǒ
de huà ►**even more** 甚至更多
shènzhì gèngduō ►**even if** 即使
jíshǐ ►**even though** 尽管 jǐnguǎn
►**not even** 连…也不 lián...yěbù
►**even on Sundays** 甚至星期天
shènzhì xīngqītiān

evening [ˈiːvnɪŋ] N [c/u] 1 (*early*)
傍晚 bàngwǎn [个 gè] 2 (*late*) 晚
上 wǎnshang [个 gè] 3 (*whole
period, event*) 晚上 wǎnshang [个
gè] ►**in the evening** 在晚上 zài
wǎnshang ►**this evening** 今晚
jīnwǎn ►**tomorrow/yesterday
evening** 明/昨晚 míng/zuówǎn

evening class N [c] 夜校 yèxiào
[个 gè]

event [ɪˈvɛnt] N [c] 事件 shìjiàn
[个 gè]

eventually [ɪˈvɛntʃuəlɪ]
ADV 1 (*finally*) 终于 zhōngyú
2 (*ultimately*) 最终 zuìzhōng

请勿将 **eventually** 和
finally 混淆。如果某事拖
延了很久，或者经历了相
当复杂的过程后终于发生
了，可以说它 **eventually**
发生了，*Eventually, they
got to the hospital... I found
Victoria Avenue eventually.*
eventually 还可以表示
发生的一系列事情中的最

后一件事 ， 通常这最后的一件事是前面一系列事情的结果。， *Eventually, they were forced to return to England.* 在经历了长期等待或期盼后，某事终于发生了，可以说它 **finally** 发生了。 *Finally, I went to bed... The heat of the sun finally became too much for me.* **finally** 还可以表示发生的一系列事情当中最后的一件事。 *The sky turned red, then purple, and finally black.*

ever [ˈɛvəʳ] ADV 从来 cónglái ▶**have you ever seen it/been there** *etc*? 你曾经见过它/去过那儿｛等｝吗？ nǐ céngjīng jiànguò tā/qùguò nà'er (děng) ma? ▶**ever since** (*adv*) 从…以来 cóng... yǐlái ▶*We have been friends ever since.* 我们从那时以来一直是朋友。 wǒmen cóng nàshí yǐlái yīzhí shì péngyǒu; (*conj*) 自从 zìcóng ▶*Jack has loved trains ever since he was a boy.* 杰克自小就喜爱火车。 Jiékè zìxiǎo jiù xǐ'ài huǒchē ▶**the best ever** 迄今最佳 qìjīn zuìjiā ▶**hardly ever** 几乎从不 jīhū cóngbù

KEYWORD

every [ˈɛvrɪ] ADJ **1** (*each*) 每个 měigè ▶**every village should have a post office** 每个村庄都应该有一个邮局 měigè cūnzhuāng dōu yīnggāi yǒu yīgè yóujú **2** (*all possible*) 一切可能的 yīqiè

kěnéng de ▶**recipes for every occasion** 各个场合均适用的菜谱 gègè chǎnghé jūn shìyòng de càipǔ **3** (*with time words*) 每 měi ▶**every day/week** 每天/周 měitiān/zhōu ▶**every Sunday** 每个星期天 měigè xīngqītiān ▶**every now and then** *or* **again** 不时地 bùshí de

everybody [ˈɛvrɪbɔdɪ] PRON 每人 měirén ▶**everybody knows about it** 谁都知道 shuí dōu zhīdào ▶**everybody else** 其他所有人 qítā suǒyǒurén

everyone [ˈɛvrɪwʌn] PRON = **everybody**

请勿将 **everyone** 和 **every one** 混淆。 **everyone** 总是指人，并且用作单数名词。*Everyone likes him...On behalf of everyone in the school, I'd like to thank you.* 在短语 **every one** 中，**one** 是代词，在不同的上下文当中，它能够指代任何人或事物。其后经常紧随单词 **of**，*We've saved seeds from every one of our plants...Every one of them phoned me.* 在这些例子当中，**every one** 是表达 **all** 的含义，而且语气更强烈。

everything [ˈɛvrɪθɪŋ] PRON 所有事物 suǒyǒu shìwù ▶**is everything OK?** 都还好吧？ dōu hái hǎo ba ▶**everything is ready**

所有都准备就绪 suǒyǒu dōu zhǔnbèi jiùxù ▶he did everything possible 他尽了最大努力 tā jìnle zuìdà nǔlì

everywhere ['ɛvrɪwɛəʳ] I ADV 各处 gèchù II PRON 所有地方 suǒyǒu dìfang ▶there's rubbish everywhere 到处都是垃圾 dàochù dōushì lājī ▶everywhere you go 无论你去哪里 wúlùn nǐ qù nǎlǐ

evidence ['ɛvɪdns] N [U] 1 (proof) 根据 gēnjù 2 (signs, indications) 迹象 jìxiàng

evil ['iːvl] ADJ 邪恶的 xié'è de

ex- [ɛks] PREFIX [+ husband, president etc] 前 qián ▶my ex-wife 我的前妻 wǒde qiánqī

exact [ɪg'zækt] ADJ 确切的 quèqiè de

exactly [ɪg'zæktlɪ] ADV 1 (precisely) 确切地 quèqiè de 2 (indicating agreement) 一点不错 yīdiǎn bùcuò ▶at 5 o'clock exactly 在5点整时 zài wǔdiǎnzhěng shí ▶not exactly 不完全是 bù wánquán shì

exaggerate [ɪg'zædʒəreɪt] I VI 夸张 kuāzhāng II VT (overemphasize) 夸大 kuādà

exam [ɪg'zæm] N 测验 cèyàn

pass an exam 表示考试通过，若没通过，则说 **fail an exam**。参加考试，用动词 **take**，在英式英语中则用 **sit an exam**。

examination [ɪgzæmɪ'neɪʃən] N 1 [c] (frm: Scol, Univ) 考试 kǎoshì [次 cì] 2 [c/u] (Med) 体检 tǐjiǎn

examine [ɪg'zæmɪn] VT 1 (inspect) 检查 jiǎnchá 2 (Scol, Univ) 对…进行测验 duì…jìnxíng cèyàn 3 (Med) 检查 jiǎnchá

example [ɪg'zɑːmpl] N [c] 例子 lìzi [个 gè] ▶for example 例如 lìrú ▶an example of sth 某物的例子 mǒuwù de lìzi

excellence ['ɛksələns] N [U] 卓越 zhuōyuè

excellent ['ɛksələnt] I ADJ 极好的 jíhǎo de II INT ▶excellent! 太好了! tài hǎo le!

except [ɪk'sɛpt] PREP 除了 chúle ▶except for 除了…外 chúle…wài ▶except if/when …时例外 …shí lìwài

exception [ɪk'sɛpʃən] N [c] 例外 lìwài [个 gè]

exchange [ɪks'tʃeɪndʒ] I VT 1 [+ gifts, addresses] 交换 jiāohuàn 2 ▶to exchange sth (for sth) [+ goods] 用某物交换（某物）yòng mǒuwù jiāohuàn (mǒuwù) II N [c/u] [of students, sportspeople] 交流 jiāoliú [次 cì] ▶in exchange (for) 作为（对…的）交换 zuòwéi (duì…de) jiāohuàn

exchange rate N [c] 汇率 huìlǜ [个 gè]

excited [ɪk'saɪtɪd] ADJ 兴奋的 xīngfèn de ▶to be excited about sth/about doing sth 对某事/做某事感到激动 duì mǒushì/zuò mǒushì gǎndào jīdòng ▶to get excited 激动兴奋 jīdòng xīngfèn

excitement [ɪk'saɪtmənt] N [U] 兴奋 xīngfèn

exciting [ɪkˈsaɪtɪŋ] ADJ 令人兴奋的 lìng rén xīngfèn de

exclamation mark (Brit), **exclamation point** (US) N [C] 感叹号 gǎntànhào [个 gè]

excluding [ɪksˈkluːdɪŋ] PREP 不包括 bù bāokuò

excuse [n ɪksˈkjuːs, vb ɪksˈkjuːz] I N [C/U] 借口 jièkǒu [个 gè] II VT 1 (justify) 是…的正当理由 shì...de zhèngdàng lǐyóu 2 (forgive) 原谅 yuánliàng ▶to make an excuse 找借口 zhǎo jièkǒu ▶excuse me! (attracting attention) 劳驾! láojià; (as apology) 对不起! duìbùqǐ ▶excuse me, please 请原谅 qǐng yuánliàng ▶excuse me? (US) 对不起，你说什么? duìbùqie, nǐ shuō shénme?

exercise [ˈɛksəsaɪz] I N 1 [U] (physical exertion) 运动 yùndòng 2 [C] (series of movements) 练习 liànxí [个 gè] 3 [C] (Scol, Mus) 练习 liànxí [个 gè] II VT [+ muscles] 锻炼 duànliàn; [+ mind] 运用 yùnyòng III VI (person) 锻炼 duànliàn ▶to take or get exercise 做健身活动 zuò jiànshēn huódòng ▶to do exercises (Sport) 锻炼身体 duànliàn shēntǐ

exhaust [ɪgˈzɔːst] N (esp Brit) 1 [C] (also: **exhaust pipe**) 排气管 páiqìguǎn [根 gēn] 2 [U] (fumes) 废气 fèiqì

exhausted [ɪgˈzɔːstɪd] ADJ 精疲力竭的 jīng pí lì jié de

exhibition [ɛksɪˈbɪʃən] N [C] 展览会 zhǎnlǎnhuì [个 gè]

exist [ɪgˈzɪst] VI 1 (be present) 存在 cúnzài 2 (live, subsist) 生存 shēngcún

exit [ˈɛksɪt] I N [C] 出口 chūkǒu [个 gè] II VT (Comput) 退出 tuìchū ▶to exit from sth [+ room, motorway] 离开某处 líkāi mǒuchù

expect [ɪksˈpɛkt] I VT 1 (anticipate) 预料 yùliào 2 (await) 期待 qīdài 3 [+ baby] 怀有 huáiyǒu 4 (suppose) 料想 liàoxiǎng II VI ▶to be expecting (be pregnant) 怀孕 huáiyùn ▶to expect sth to happen 预期某事将发生 yùqī mǒushì jiāng fāshēng ▶I expect so 我想会的 wǒ xiǎng huìde

expense [ɪksˈpɛns] I N [C/U] 费用 fèiyòng [笔 bǐ] II **expenses** NPL 经费 jīngfèi

expensive [ɪksˈpɛnsɪv] ADJ 1 昂贵的 ángguì de 2 [+ mistake] 代价高的 dàijià gāo de

experience [ɪksˈpɪərɪəns] I N 1 [U] (in job) 经验 jīngyàn 2 [U] (of life) 阅历 yuèlì 3 [C] (individual event) 经历 jīnglì II VT [+ feeling, problem] 体验 tǐyàn

experienced [ɪksˈpɪərɪənst] ADJ 有经验的 yǒu jīngyàn de

experiment [n ɪksˈpɛrɪmənt, vb ɪksˈpɛrɪmɛnt] I N [C] 1 (Sci) 实验 shíyàn [个 gè] 2 (trial) 试用 shìyòng [次 cì] II VI 试验 shìyàn ▶to perform or conduct or carry out an experiment 做实验 zuò shíyàn

expert [ˈɛkspəːt] I N [C] 专家 zhuānjiā [位 wèi] II ADJ [+ opinion, help, advice] 专家的 zhuānjiā de ▶an expert on sth 某事的专家

mǒushì de zhuānjiā

expertise [ɛkspəːˈtiːz] N [U] 专门知识 zhuānmén zhīshí

expire [ɪksˈpaɪəʳ] VI [passport, licence] 过期 guòqī

explain [ɪksˈpleɪn] VT 1 [+ situation, contract] 解释 jiěshì 2 [+ decision, actions] 阐明 chǎnmíng ▶ to explain why/how etc 解释为什么/如何〔等〕jiěshì wèishénme/rúhé(děng) ▶ to explain sth to sb 向某人解释某事 xiàng mǒurén jiěshì mǒushì

explanation [ɛkspləˈneɪʃən] N 1 [c/u] (reason) （对…的）解释 (duì...de) jiěshì [个 gè] 2 [c] (description) ▶ explanation (of) （…的）说明 (...de) shuōmíng [个 gè]

explode [ɪksˈpləʊd] I VI 爆炸 bàozhà II VT [+ bomb, tank] 使爆炸 shǐ bàozhà

exploit [ɪksˈplɔɪt] VT [+ resources] 开发 kāifā; [+ person, idea] 剥削 bōxuē

explore [ɪksˈplɔːʳ] I VT 探索 tànsuǒ II VI 探险 tànxiǎn

explosion [ɪksˈpləʊʒən] N [c] 1 爆炸 bàozhà [个 gè] 2 激增 jīzēng [个 gè]

export [vb ɛksˈpɔːt, n ˈɛkspɔːt] I VT 输出 shūchū II N 1 [U] (process) 出口 chūkǒu 2 [c] (product) 出口物 chūkǒuwù [宗 zōng]

express [ɪksˈprɛs] VT 表达 biǎodá; [+ service, mail] 特快的 tèkuài de ▶ to express o.s. 表达自己的意思 biǎodá zìjǐ de yìsi

expression [ɪksˈprɛʃən] N 1 [c]

(word, phrase) 言辞 yáncí [种 zhǒng] 2 [c/u] (on face) 表情 biǎoqíng [种 zhǒng]

extension [ɪksˈtɛnʃən] N [c] 1 [of building] 扩建部分 kuòjiàn bùfen [个 gè] 2 [of contract, visa] 延期 yánqī [次 cì] 3 (Tel) 分机 fēnjī [部 bù] ▶ extension 3718 (Tel) 3718分机

extent [ɪksˈtɛnt] N [U/s] [of problem, damage] 程度 chéngdù ▶ to a certain extent 在一定程度上 zài yīdìng chéngdù shàng

extinct [ɪksˈtɪŋkt] ADJ [+ animal, plant] 灭绝的 mièjué de

extra [ˈɛkstrə] I ADJ 额外的 éwài de II ADV (in addition) 额外地 éwài de III N [c] 1 (luxury) 额外的事物 éwài de shìwù [件 jiàn] 2 (surcharge) 另外的收费 lìngwài de shōufèi [项 xiàng] ▶ wine will cost extra 酒另外收钱 jiǔ lìngwài shōuqián

extraordinary [ɪksˈtrɔːdnrɪ] ADJ 非凡的 fēifán de

extreme [ɪksˈtriːm] ADJ 1 极度的 jídù de 2 [+ opinions, methods] 极端的 jíduān de

extremely [ɪksˈtriːmlɪ] ADV 非常 fēicháng

extremist [ɪksˈtriːmɪst] N [c] 过激分子 guòjī fènzǐ [个 gè]

eye [aɪ] N [c] (Anat) 眼睛 yǎnjing [只 zhī] ▶ to keep an eye on sb/sth 密切注意某人/某事 mìqiè zhùyì mǒurén/mǒushì

eyebrow [ˈaɪbrau] N [c] 眉毛 méimao [个 gè]

eyelash [ˈaɪlæʃ] N [c] 眼睫毛

yǎnjiémáo [根 gēn]

eyelid ['aɪlɪd] N [c] 眼皮 yǎnpí
[个 gè]

eyeliner ['aɪlaɪnəʳ] N [c/u] 眼线
笔 yǎnxiànbǐ

eyeshadow ['aɪʃædəu] N [c/u] 眼
影 yǎnyǐng

eyesight ['aɪsaɪt] N [u] 视力 shìlì

fabric ['fæbrɪk] N [c/u] 织物
zhīwù [件 jiàn]

fabulous ['fæbjuləs] ADJ (inf) 极
好的 jíhǎo de

face [feɪs] I N 1 [c] (Anat) 脸 liǎn
[张 zhāng] 2 [c] (expression) 表情
biǎoqíng [个 gè] II VT 1 [+ direction]
面向 miànxiàng 2 [+ unpleasant
situation] 面对 miànduì ▶ I can't
or **couldn't face it** 我应付不了 wǒ
yìngfù bùliǎo ▶ to come **face to
face with** [+ person] 与…面对面
yǔ…miàn duì miàn
▶ face up to VT FUS
1 [+ truth, facts] 接受 jiēshòu
2 [+ responsibilities, duties] 承担
chéngdān

face cloth (Brit) N [c] 洗脸毛巾
xǐliǎn máojīn [条 tiáo]

facility [fə'sɪlɪtɪ] N [c] (service) 设施 shèshī [种 zhǒng]

fact [fækt] N [c] 真相 zhēnxiàng [个 gè] ▶in (actual) fact, as a matter of fact (for emphasis) 实际上 shíjì shàng ▶facts and figures 精确的资料 jīngquè de zīliào

factory ['fæktərɪ] N [c] 工厂 gōngchǎng [家 jiā]

fail [feɪl] I vт [+ exam, test] 没有通过 méiyǒu tōngguò II vi 1 [candidate] 没通过 méi tōngguò 2 [attempt, plan, remedy] 失败 shībài ▶to fail to do sth 未能做某事 wèinéng zuò mǒushì

failure ['feɪljər] N 1 [c/u] (lack of success) 失败 shībài [次 cì] 2 [c] ▶failure to do sth 没有做某事 méiyǒu zuò mǒushì

faint [feɪnt] I ADJ 1 [+ sound, light, smell, hope] 微弱的 wēiruò de 2 [+ mark, trace] 隐约的 yǐnyuē de II vi 晕倒 yūndǎo ▶to feel faint 感到眩晕 gǎndào xuànyūn

fair [feər] I ADJ 1 (just, right) 公平的 gōngpíng de 2 (quite large) 相当的 xiāngdāng de 3 (quite good) 大体的 dàtǐ de 4 [+ skin, complexion] 白皙的 báixī de; [+ hair] 金色的 jīnsè de II N [c] 1 (trade fair) 交易会 jiāoyìhuì [届 jiè] 2 (Brit: also: funfair) 游乐场 yóulèchǎng [座 zuò] ▶it's not fair! 太不公平了! tài bù gōngpíng le!

fairground ['fɛəɡraʊnd] N [c] 游乐场 yóulèchǎng [座 zuò]

fairly ['fɛəlɪ] ADV 1 (justly) 公平地 gōngpíng de 2 (quite) 相当 xiāngdāng

faith [feɪθ] N 1 [u] (trust) 信任 xìnrèn 2 [u] (religious belief) 信仰 xìnyǎng ▶to have faith in sb/sth 相信某人/某事 xiāngxìn mǒurén/mǒushì

faithful ['feɪθful] ADJ 忠实的 zhōngshí de

faithfully ['feɪθfəlɪ] ADV ▶Yours faithfully (Brit) 您忠实的 nín zhōngshí de

fake [feɪk] I N [c] 赝品 yànpǐn [件 jiàn] II ADJ 假的 jiǎ de

fall [fɔːl] (pt fell, pp fallen) I vi 1 掉 diào 2 [snow, rain] 下 xià 3 [price, temperature, currency] 下降 xiàjiàng II N 1 [c] [of person] 摔倒 shuāidǎo [次 cì] 2 [c] (in price, temperature) 下降 xiàjiàng [次 cì] 3 [c/u] (US: autumn) 秋天 qiūtiān [个 gè] ▶to fall in love (with sb/sth) 爱上 (某人/某事) àishàng (mǒurén/mǒushì)

▶fall down vi 1 [person] 摔倒 shuāidǎo 2 [building] 倒塌 dǎotā

▶fall off vi [person, object] 掉下 diàoxià

▶fall over vi [person, object] 跌倒 diēdǎo

▶fall through vi [plan] 落空 luòkōng

fallen ['fɔːlən] PP of **fall**

false [fɔːls] ADJ 假的 jiǎ de

fame [feɪm] N [u] 声誉 shēngyù

familiar [fə'mɪlɪər] ADJ 熟悉的 shúxī de ▶to be familiar with 对…熟悉 duì…shúxī

family ['fæmɪlɪ] N [c] 1 (relations) 家庭 jiātíng [个 gè] 2 (children) 孩子 háizi [个 gè]

famine ['fæmɪn] N [c/u] 饥荒 jīhuāng [阵 zhèn]

famous ['feɪməs] ADJ 著名的 zhùmíng de

fan [fæn] N [c] 1 [of pop star] 迷 mí [个 gè]; (Sport) 球迷 qiúmí [个 gè] 2 (Elec) 风扇 fēngshàn [台 tái] 3 (handheld) 扇子 shànzi [把 bǎ]

fanatic [fə'nætɪk] N [c] 狂热者 kuángrè zhě [名 míng]

fancy-dress party ['fænsɪdrɛs-] N [c] 化装舞会 huàzhuāng wǔhuì [个 gè]

fantastic [fæn'tæstɪk] ADJ 1 极好 的 jíhǎo de 2 [+ sum, amount, profit] 巨大的 jùdà de

FAQ N ABBR (= frequently asked question) 常见问题 chángjiàn wèntí

far [fɑːʳ] I ADJ 1 远的 yuǎn de 2 ▶ the far end/side 尽头的 jìntóu de II ADV 1 远 yuǎn; (in time) 久远地 jiǔyuǎn de 2 (much, greatly) …得多 de duō ▶ as far as I know 据我所知 jùwǒ suǒzhī ▶ by far …得多 …de duō ▶ so far 迄今为止 qìjīn wéizhǐ ▶ it's not far from here 离这里不远 lí zhèlǐ bùyuǎn ▶ how far? 多 远？ duōyuǎn? ▶ far away 遥 远 yáoyuǎn ▶ far better 好得多 hǎodeduō

fare [fɛəʳ] N [c] 票价 piàojià [种 zhǒng]; (in taxi) 乘客 chéngkè [位 wèi] ▶ half/full fare 半/全价 bàn/quánjià

Far East N ▶ the Far East 远东 Yuǎndōng

farm [fɑːm] N [c] 农场 nóngchǎng

[个 gè]

farmer ['fɑːməʳ] N [c] 农民 nóngmín [个 gè]

farming ['fɑːmɪŋ] N [u] 农业 nóngyè

fascinating ['fæsɪneɪtɪŋ] ADJ 迷 人的 mírén de

fashion ['fæʃən] N [u/s] 流行的式 样 liúxíng de shìyàng ▶ in fashion 流行 liúxíng

fashionable ['fæʃnəbl] ADJ 流行 的 liúxíng de

fast [fɑːst] I ADJ 快的 kuài de II ADV 快 kuài ▶ my watch is 5 minutes fast 我的表快5分 钟 wǒde biǎo kuài wǔfēnzhōng ▶ fast asleep 酣睡 hānshuì

fasten ['fɑːsn] VT [+ coat, jacket, belt] 系 jì

fast food N [u] 快餐 kuàicān

fat [fæt] I ADJ 肥胖的 féipàng de; [+ animal] 肥的 féi de II N 1 [u] (on person, animal, meat) 脂肪 zhīfáng 2 [c/u] (for cooking) 食用油 shíyòng yóu [桶 tǒng]

用 **fat** 形容某人胖，显 得过于直接，甚至有些 粗鲁。比较礼貌而又含 蓄的说法是 **plump** 或 **chubby**，后者更为正式。 **overweight** 和 **obese** 暗 示某人因为肥胖而有健康 问题。**obese** 是医学术 语，表示某人极度肥胖或 超重。一般而言，应尽量 避免当面使用任何表示肥 胖的词汇。

fatal ['feɪtl] ADJ 1 致命的 zhìmìng de 2 [+ mistake] 严重的

yánzhòng de

father ['fɑ:ðəʳ] N [c] 父亲 fùqīn [位 wèi]

Father Christmas (Brit) N 圣诞老人 Shèngdàn lǎorén

father-in-law ['fɑ:ðərənlɔ:] (pl **fathers-in-law**) N [c] [of woman] 公公 gōnggong [位 wèi]; [of man] 岳父 yuèfù [位 wèi]

faucet ['fɔ:sɪt] (US) N [c] 水龙头 shuǐlóngtou [个 gè]

fault [fɔ:lt] N 1 [s] 错误 cuòwù 2 [c] (defect: in person) 缺点 quēdiǎn [个 gè]; (: in machine) 故障 gùzhàng [个 gè] ▸ **it's my fault** 是我的错 shì wǒde cuò

fava bean ['fɑ:və-] (US) N [c] 蚕豆 cándòu [颗 kē]

favour, (US) **favor** ['feɪvəʳ] N [c] 恩惠 ēnhuì [种 zhǒng] ▸ **to do sb a favour** 帮某人的忙 bāng mǒurén de máng ▸ **to be in favour of sth/doing sth** 赞成某事/做某事 zànchéng mǒushì/zuò mǒushì

favourite, (US) **favorite** ['feɪvrɪt] I ADJ 最喜欢的 zuì xǐhuan de II N [c] 偏爱 piān'ài [种 zhǒng]

fax [fæks] I N [c] 1 传真 chuánzhēn [份 fèn] 2 (also: **fax machine**) 传真机 chuánzhēnjī [台 tái] II VT [+ document] 用传真发送 yòng chuánzhēn fāsòng

fear [fɪəʳ] N 1 [c/u] (terror) 害怕 hàipà [种 zhǒng] 2 [c/u] (anxiety) 焦虑 jiāolù [种 zhǒng]

feather ['fɛðəʳ] N [c] 羽毛 yǔmáo [根 gēn]

feature ['fi:tʃəʳ] N [c] 特点 tèdiǎn [个 gè]

February ['fɛbruərɪ] N [c/u] 二月 èryuè; see also **July**

fed [fɛd] PT, PP of **feed**

fed up (inf) ADJ ▸ **to be fed up** 厌倦 yànjuàn

fee [fi:] N [c] 费 fèi [种 zhǒng]; [+ of doctor, lawyer] 费用 fèiyòng [项 xiàng]

feeble ['fi:bl] ADJ 1 虚弱的 xūruò de 2 [+ attempt, excuse, argument] 无力的 wúlì de

feed [fi:d] (pt, pp fed) VT 喂 wèi

feel [fi:l] (pt, pp felt) VT 1 (touch) [+ object, face] 摸 mō 2 [+ pain] 感到 gǎndào 3 (think, believe) 认为 rènwéi ▸ **to feel that...** 感到… gǎndào… ▸ **to feel hungry** 觉得饿 juéde è ▸ **to feel cold** 觉得冷 juéde lěng ▸ **to feel lonely/better** 感到孤独/感觉好多了 gǎndào gūdú/gǎnjué hǎo duō le ▸ **I don't feel well** 我觉得身体不适 wǒ juéde shēntǐ bùshì ▸ **to feel sorry for sb** 同情某人 tóngqíng mǒurén ▸ **to feel like** (want) 想要 xiǎng yào

feeling ['fi:lɪŋ] I N 1 [c] (emotion) 感受 gǎnshòu [种 zhǒng] 2 [c] (physical sensation) 感觉 gǎnjué [种 zhǒng] 3 [s] (impression) 感觉 gǎnjué II **feelings** NPL 1 (attitude) 看法 kànfǎ 2 (emotions) 情感 qínggǎn ▸ **I have a feeling that...** 我有种感觉… wǒ yǒuzhǒng gǎnjué… ▸ **to hurt sb's feelings** 伤害某人的感情 shānghài mǒurén de gǎnqíng

feet [fi:t] NPL of **foot**

fell [fɛl] PT of **fall**

felt [fɛlt] PT, PP of **feel**

felt-tip pen, felt-tip ['fɛlttɪp-] N [c] 毡头墨水笔 zhāntóu mòshuǐbǐ [支 zhī]

female ['fiːmeɪl] I N [c] 1 (Zool) 雌兽 císhòu [头 tóu] 2 (woman) 女性 nǚxìng [位 wèi] II ADJ 1 (Zool) 雌性的 cíxìng de 2 (relating to women) 妇女的 fùnǚ de ▶**male and female students** 男女学生 nánnǚ xuéshēng

feminine ['fɛmɪnɪn] ADJ 1 女性的 nǚxìng de 2 (Ling) 阴性的 yīnxìng de

feminist ['fɛmɪnɪst] N [c] 女权主义者 nǚquán zhǔyìzhě [位 wèi]

fence [fɛns] N [c] 篱笆 líba [道 dào]

fencing ['fɛnsɪŋ] N [U] (Sport) 击剑 jījiàn

ferry ['fɛrɪ] N [c] (small) 摆渡 bǎidù [个 gè]; (large: also: **ferryboat**) 渡船 dùchuán [艘 sōu]

festival ['fɛstɪvəl] N [c] 1 (Rel) 节日 jiérì [个 gè] 2 (Theat, Mus) 艺术节 yìshù jié [届 jiè]

fetch [fɛtʃ] VT 去拿来 qù nálai ▶**to fetch sth for sb, fetch sb sth** 去给某人拿来某物 qù gěi mǒurén nálai mǒuwù

fever ['fiːvər] N [c/U] (Med) 发烧 fāshāo [次 cì]

few [fjuː] I ADJ 1 (not many) 少数的 shǎoshù de 2 ▶**a few** (some) 几个 jǐge II PRON 1 ▶**a few** (some) 几个 jǐge 2 ▶**in the next few days** 在接下来的几天里 zài jiēxiàlái de jǐtiān lǐ ▶**in the past few days** 在过去的几天里 zài guòqù de jǐtiān

lǐ ▶**a few of us/them** 我们/他们中的几个 wǒmen/tāmen zhōng de jǐge ▶**a few more** 再多几个 zài duō jǐge ▶**very few survive** 极少幸存 jíshǎo xìngcún

fewer ['fjuːər] ADJ 较少的 jiàoshǎo de ▶**no fewer than** 不少于 bù shǎoyú

fiancé [fɪˈɔnseɪ] N [c] 未婚夫 wèihūnfū [个 gè]

fiancée [fɪˈɔnseɪ] N [c] 未婚妻 wèihūnqī [个 gè]

fiction ['fɪkʃən] N [U] 小说 xiǎoshuō

field [fiːld] N [c] 1 (grassland) 草地 cǎodì [块 kuài] 2 (cultivated) 田地 tiándì [片 piàn] 3 (Sport) 场地 chǎngdì [个 gè] 4 (subject, area of interest) 领域 lǐngyù [个 gè]

fierce [fɪəs] ADJ 1 凶猛的 xiōngměng de 2 [+ loyalty, resistance, competition] 强烈的 qiángliè de

fifteen [fɪfˈtiːn] NUM 十五 shíwǔ ▶**she's fifteen (years old)** 她15岁了 tā shíwǔ suì le

fifteenth [fɪfˈtiːnθ] NUM 第十五 dì shíwǔ; see also **fifth**

fifth [fɪfθ] NUM 1 (in series) 第五 dìwǔ 2 (fraction) 五分之一 wǔfēnzhīyī ▶**on July fifth, on the fifth of July** 在7月5日 zài qīyuè wǔrì

fifty ['fɪftɪ] NUM 五十 wǔshí ▶**he's in his fifties** 他50多岁 tā wǔshí duō suì

fight [faɪt] (pt, pp **fought**) I N [c] 1 斗殴 dòuōu [场 chǎng] 2 斗争 dòuzhēng [场 chǎng] II VT

figure   336

与…对打 yǔ…duìdǎ **III** VI **1** 战斗 zhàndòu **2** (*struggle*) 奋斗 fèndòu ▶**to fight for/against sth** 为支持/反对某事而斗争 wèi zhīchí/fǎnduì mǒushì ér dòuzhēng

figure ['fɪgə'] **I** N [c] **1** (*number, statistic*) 统计数字 tǒngjì shùzì [个 gè] **2** (*digit*) 数字 shùzì [个 gè] **3** (*body, shape*) 身材 shēncái [种 zhǒng] **II** VT (*esp US: inf: reckon*) 估计 gūjì ▶**that figures** (*inf*) 那不足为怪 nà bùzú wéiguài

file [faɪl] **I** N [c] **1** (*dossier*) 档案 dàng'àn [份 fèn] **2** (*folder*) 文件夹 wénjiànjiā [个 gè] **3** (*Comput*) 文件 wénjiàn [份 fèn] **II** VT **1** (*also:* **file away**) [+ *papers, document*] 把…归档 bǎ...guīdàng **2** [+ *wood, metal, fingernails*] 把…锉平 bǎ...cuòpíng

fill [fɪl] VT **1** [+ *container*] 装满 zhuāngmǎn **2** [+ *space, area*] 占满 zhànmǎn **3** [+ *tooth*] 补 bǔ ▶**to fill sth with sth** 用某物填满某物 yòng mǒuwù tiánmǎn mǒuwù
▶ **fill in** VT (*esp Brit*) [+ *form, name*] 填写 tiánxiě
▶ **fill out** VT [+ *form*] 填写 tiánxiě

filling ['fɪlɪŋ] N [c] (*in tooth*) 填补物 tiánbǔ wù [种 zhǒng]

film [fɪlm] **I** N **1** [c] (*esp Brit*) 影片 yǐngpiàn [部 bù] **2** [c/u] (*Phot*) 胶卷 jiāojuǎn [卷 juǎn] **II** VT 把…拍成影片 bǎ...pāichéng yǐngpiàn

film star N [c] (*esp Brit*) 影星 yǐngxīng [位 wèi]

filthy ['fɪlθɪ] ADJ 污秽的 wūhuì de

final ['faɪnl] **I** ADJ **1** 最后的 zuìhòu de **2** [+ *decision, offer*] 不可变更的 bùkě biàngēng de **II** N [c] (*Sport*) 决赛 juésài [场 chǎng]

finally ['faɪnəlɪ] ADV **1** (*eventually*) 终于 zhōngyú **2** (*lastly*) 最后 zuìhòu **3** (*in conclusion*) 总之 zǒngzhī

find [faɪnd] (*pt, pp* **found**) VT **1** [+ *person, object, exit*] 找到 zhǎodào; [+ *lost object*] 找回 zhǎohuí **2** (*discover*) [+ *answer, solution*] 找出 zhǎochū; [+ *object, person*] 发现 fāxiàn **3** [+ *work, job*] 得到 dédào; [+ *time*] 有空 yǒukòng ▶**to find sb guilty/not guilty** 判决某人有罪/无罪 pànjué mǒurén yǒuzuì/wúzuì ▶**to find one's way** 认得路 rènde lù
▶ **find out I** VT [+ *fact, truth*] 查明 chámíng **II** VI ▶ **to find out about sth** (*deliberately*) 获知某事 huòzhī mǒushì; (*by chance*) 偶然发现某物 ǒurán fāxiàn mǒuwù

fine [faɪn] **I** ADJ **1** (*satisfactory*) 还不错的 hái bùcuò de **2** (*excellent*) 好的 hǎo de **3** (*in texture*) 细的 xì de **4** [+ *weather, day*] 晴朗的 qínglǎng de **II** ADV (*well*) 不错地 bùcuò de **III** N [c] (*Law*) 罚款 fákuǎn [笔 bǐ] **IV** VT (*Law*) 处…以罚金 chǔ...yǐ fájīn ▶**(I'm) fine** (我)很好 (wǒ) hěnhǎo ▶**(that's) fine** (那)好吧 (nà) hǎoba ▶**you're doing fine** 你做得很好 nǐ zuòde hěnhǎo

finger ['fɪŋgə'] N [c] 手指 shǒuzhǐ [根 gēn]

finish ['fɪnɪʃ] **I** N **1** [s] (*end*) 结束 jiéshù **2** [c] (*Sport*) 终点 zhōngdiǎn [个 gè] **II** VT [+ *work*] 结束

jiéshù; [+ *task, report, book*] 完成 wánchéng III VI 1 [*course, event*] 结束 jiéshù 2 [*person*] 说完 shuōwán ▶**to finish doing sth** 做完某事 zuòwán mǒushì

Finland ['fɪnlənd] N 芬兰 Fēnlán

fir [fəːʳ] N [c] (*also*: **fir tree**) 冷杉 lěngshān [棵 kē]

fire ['faɪəʳ] I N 1 [U] (*flames*) 火 huǒ 2 [c] (*in fireplace, hearth*) 炉火 lúhuǒ [团 tuán] 3 [c/U] (*accidental*) 火灾 huǒzāi [场 chǎng] II VT 1 (*shoot*) 射出 shèchū 2 (*inf*: *dismiss*) 解雇 jiěgù III VI (*shoot*) 开火 kāihuǒ ▶**on fire** 起火 qǐhuǒ ▶**to catch fire** 着火 zháohuǒ

fire alarm N [c] 火警警报 huǒjǐng jǐngbào [个 gè]

fire brigade N [c] 消防队 xiāofáng duì [支 zhī]

fire engine (*Brit*) N [c] 救火车 jiùhuǒchē [辆 liàng]

firefighter ['faɪəfaɪtəʳ] N [c] 消防队员 xiāofáng duìyuán [位 wèi]

fireman ['faɪəmən] (*pl* **firemen**) N [c] 消防队员 xiāofáng duìyuán [位 wèi]

fire station N [c] 消防站 xiāofángzhàn [个 gè]

fire truck (*US*) N [c] 救火车 jiùhuǒchē [辆 liàng]

firework ['faɪəwəːk] I N [c] 烟火 yānhuǒ [团 tuán] II **fireworks** N PL (*display*) 烟火表演 yānhuǒ biǎoyǎn

firm [fəːm] I ADJ 1 [+ *mattress, ground*] 硬实的 yìngshí de 2 [+ *person*] 坚定的 jiāndìng de II N [c] 公司 gōngsī [家 jiā]

first [fəːst] I ADJ 1 (*in series*) 第一的 dìyī de 2 [+ *reaction, impression*] 最初的 zuìchū de 3 [+ *prize, division*] 头等的 tóuděng de II ADV 1 (*before anyone else*) 首先 shǒuxiān 2 (*before other things*) 首先 shǒuxiān 3 (*when listing reasons*) 第一 dìyī 4 (*for the first time*) 第一次 dìyīcì 5 (*in race, competition*: *come, finish*) 第一名 dìyīmíng ▶**at first** 起先 qǐxiān ▶**the first of January** 1月1号 yīyuè yīhào

first aid N [U] 急救 jíjiù

first-class [fəːstˈklɑːs] I ADJ 1 (*excellent*) 第一流的 dìyīliú de 2 [+ *carriage, ticket, stamp*] 一类的 yīlèi de II ADV (*travel, send*) 作为一类 zuòwéi yīlèi

firstly ['fəːstlɪ] ADV 首先 shǒuxiān

first name N [c] 名 míng [个 gè]

fish [fɪʃ] I N 1 [c] 鱼 yú [条 tiáo] 2 [U] (*food*) 鱼肉 yúròu II VI (*commercially*) 捕鱼 bǔyú; (*as sport, hobby*) 钓鱼 diàoyú ▶**to go fishing** 去钓鱼 qù diàoyú

fisherman ['fɪʃəmən] (*pl* **fishermen**) N [c] 渔民 yúmín [位 wèi]

fishing ['fɪʃɪŋ] N [U] 钓鱼 diàoyú

fishing boat N [c] 渔船 yúchuán [条 tiáo]

fist [fɪst] N [c] 拳 quán [个 gè]

fit [fɪt] I ADJ 1 (*healthy*) 健康的 jiànkāng de II VI 1 [*clothes, shoes*] 合身 héshēn 2 (*in space, gap*) 适合 shìhé ▶**to keep fit** 保持健康 bǎochí jiànkāng ▶**to have a fit** (*Med*) 癫痫病发作 diānxiánbìng fāzuò ▸**to be a good fit** 很合身 hěn héshēn

▸**fit in I** VI (lit) 容纳 róngnà **II** VT [+ appointment, visitor] 定时间于 dìng shíjiān yú

fitness ['fɪtnɪs] N [U] 健康 jiànkāng

five [faɪv] NUM 五 wǔ ▸**that will be five pounds, please** 请付 5镑 qǐng fù wǔbàng ▸**she's five (years old)** 她5岁了 tā wǔsuì le ▸**it's five o'clock** 5点了 wǔdiǎn le

fix [fɪks] VT 1 [+ date, price, meeting] 确定 quèdìng 2 (mend) 修理 xiūlǐ 3 [+ problem] 解决 jiějué

fizzy ['fɪzɪ] (Brit) ADJ 带气的 dàiqì de

flag [flæg] N [c] 旗 qí [面 miàn]

flame [fleɪm] N [c/U] 火焰 huǒyàn [团 tuán] ▸**in flames** 燃烧着 ránshāo zhe

flash [flæʃ] I VI 闪光 shǎnguāng **II** N [c] 1 闪光 shǎnguāng [阵 zhèn] 2 (Phot) 闪光灯 shǎnguāngdēng [个 gè] ▸**to flash one's headlights** 亮起车头灯 liàngqǐ chētóudēng

flashlight ['flæʃlaɪt] (esp US) N [c] 手电筒 shǒudiàn tǒng [个 gè]

flask [flɑːsk] N [c] (also: **vacuum flask**) 保温瓶 bǎowēnpíng [个 gè]

flat [flæt] I ADJ 1 平的 píng de 2 [+ tyre, ball] 气不足的 qì bùzú de 3 (Brit) [+ battery] 没电的 méidiàn de II N [c] (Brit) 公寓 gōngyù [套 tào]

flatter ['flætə'] VT 奉承 fèngchéng

flavour, (US) **flavor** ['fleɪvə']

I N [c/U] 味 wèi [种 zhǒng] II VT 给…调味 gěi…tiáowèi

flea [fliː] N [c] 跳蚤 tiàozao [只 zhī]

flew [fluː] PT of **fly**

flexible ['flɛksəbl] ADJ 1 柔韧的 róurèn de 2 [+ person, schedule] 机动的 jīdòng de

flight [flaɪt] N 1 [c] 航班 hángbān [个 gè] 2 [c] (also: **flight of stairs, flight of steps**) 一段楼梯 yīduàn lóutī [段 duàn]

flight attendant N [c] (male) 男空服人员 nán kōngfú rényuán [位 wèi]; (female) 空姐 kōngjiě [位 wèi]

float [fləut] VI 1 漂浮 piāofú 2 (stay afloat) 浮着 fúzhe

flock [flɔk] N [c] 群 qún

flood [flʌd] I N [c/U] 洪水 hóngshuǐ [次 cì] II VT 淹没 yānmò

floor [flɔːʳ] N 1 [c] 地板 dìbǎn [块 kuài] 2 [c] (storey) 楼层 lóucéng [个 gè] ▸**on the floor** 在地板上 zài dìbǎn shàng ▸**ground floor** (Brit) 一楼 yīlóu ▸**first floor** (Brit) 二楼 ; (US) 一楼

在英式英语中，建筑的 **ground floor** 是指紧贴地面的那个楼层。它上面的一层叫 **first floor**。在美式英语中，**first floor** 是指紧贴地面的楼层，它上面的一层是 **second floor**。

floppy ['flɔpɪ] N [c] (also: **floppy disk**) 软盘 ruǎnpán [张 zhāng]

florist ['flɔrɪst] N [c] 1 花商 huāshāng [个 gè] 2 (also: **florist's**)

花店 huādiàn [家 jiā]

flour ['flauə^r] N [U] 面粉 miànfěn

flow [fləu] I VI 流动 liúdòng II N [C/U] 1 流动 liúdòng 2 [of traffic] 川流不息 chuānliú bùxī

flower ['flauə^r] I N [C] 花 huā [朵 duǒ] II VI 开花 kāihuā ▸ in flower 正开着花 zhèng kāizhe huā

flown [fləun] PP of fly

flu [fluː] N [U] 流感 liúgǎn

fluent ['fluːənt] ADJ [+ speech, reading, writing] 流畅的 liúchàng de ▸ to speak fluent French, be fluent in French 讲流利的法语 jiǎng liúlì de Fǎyǔ

flush [flʌʃ] VT ▸ to flush the toilet 冲厕所 chōng cèsuǒ

flute [fluːt] N [C] 长笛 chángdí [支 zhī]

fly [flaɪ] (pt **flew**, pp **flown**) I VT [+ plane] 驾驶 jiàshǐ II VI 1 [bird, insect, plane] 飞 fēi 2 [passengers] 乘飞机 chéng fēijī III N [C] (insect) 苍蝇 cāngying [只 zhī] ▸ fly away VI 飞走 fēizǒu

focus ['fəukəs] (pl **focuses**) I N 1 [U] (Phot) 聚焦 jùjiāo 2 [c] 重点 zhòngdiǎn [个 gè] II VI ▸ to focus (on) (with camera) 聚焦（于）jùjiāo (yú) 集中 (于) jízhōng (yú) ▸ in focus/out of focus 焦点对准/没对准 jiǎodiǎn duìzhǔn/méi duìzhǔn ▸ to be the focus of attention 为关注的焦点 wéi guānzhù de jiāodiǎn

fog [fɒg] N [C/U] 雾 wù [场 chǎng]

foggy ['fɒgɪ] ADJ [+ day, climate] 有雾的 yǒuwù de ▸ it's foggy 今天有雾 jīntiān yǒu wù

fold [fəuld] VT (also: **fold up**) 折叠 zhédié

folder ['fəuldə^r] N [c] 文件夹 wénjiàn jiā [个 gè]

follow ['fɒləu] VT 1 跟随 gēnsuí 2 [+ example, advice, instructions] 遵循 zūnxún 3 [+ route, path] 沿着…行进 yánzhe…xíngjìn ▸ I don't quite follow you 我不太理解你的意思 wǒ bùtài lǐjiě nǐde yìsi ▸ as follows (when listing) 如下 rúxià; (in this way) 按如下方式 àn rúxià fāngshì ▸ followed by 接着是 jiēzhe shì

following ['fɒləuɪŋ] I PREP (after) 在…之后 zàiellipherezhīhòu II ADJ 1 [+ day, week] 接着的 jiēzhe de 2 (next-mentioned) 下述的 xiàshù de

fond [fɒnd] ADJ ▸ to be fond of [+ person] 喜爱 xǐ'ài; [+ food, walking] 喜欢 xǐhuan

food [fuːd] N [C/U] 食物 shíwù [种 zhǒng]

fool [fuːl] I N [C] 白痴 báichī [个 gè] II VT (deceive) 欺骗 qīpiàn

foot [fut] (pl **feet**) N 1 [c] (measure) 英尺 yīngchǐ 2 [c] [of person] 脚 jiǎo [只 zhī] ▸ on foot 步行 bùxíng

football ['futbɔːl] N 1 [c] (ball) 足球 zúqiú [只 zhī] 2 [U] (sport) (Brit) 足球 zúqiú; (US) 美式足球 měishì zúqiú

footballer ['futbɔːlə^r] (Brit) N [c] 足球运动员 zúqiú yùndòngyuán [位 wèi]

footpath ['futpɑːθ] N [c] 人行小径 rénxíng xiǎojìng [条 tiáo]

footprint ['futprɪnt] N [c] 足迹

zújì [个 gè]

○ KEYWORD

for [fɔːʳ] PREP 1 为 wèi ▶**is this for me?** 这是为我准备的吗？ zhèshì wèi wǒ zhǔnbèi de ma? ▶**a table for two** 供两人用的桌子 gòng liǎngrén yòng de zhuōzi
2 (*purpose*) 为了 wèile ▶**what's it for?** 它有什么用途？ tā yǒu shénme yòngtú ▶**it's time for lunch** 该吃午饭了 gāi chī wǔfàn le ▶**what for?** 为什么呢？ wèi shénme ne? ▶**a knife for chopping vegetables** 用于切菜的刀 yòngyú qiēcài de dāo
3 (*time*) ▶**he was away for two years** 他离开两年了 tā líkāi liǎngnián le ▶**it hasn't rained for three weeks** 已经有3周没下雨了 yǐjīng yǒu sānzhōu méi xiàyǔ le ▶**the trip is scheduled for June 5** 旅行安排在6月5日 lǚxíng ānpái zài liùyuè wǔrì
4 (*in exchange for*) ▶**I sold it for £50** 我以50镑卖掉了它 wǒ yǐ wǔshí bàng màidiào le tā ▶**to pay 50 pence for a ticket** 花50便士买张票 huā wǔshí biànshì mǎi zhāng piào
5 (*reason*) 因为 yīnwèi
6 (*on behalf of, representing*) 为 wèi ▶**he works for a local firm** 他为一家当地公司工作 tā wèi yījiā dāngdì gōngsī gōngzuò ▶**G for George** George中的G George zhōng de G
7 (*destination*) 前往 qiánwǎng

▶**he left for Rome** 他前往罗马 tā qiánwǎng Luómǎ
8 (*with infinitive clause*) ▶**it is not for me to decide** 这不是由我来决定的 zhè bùshì yóu wǒ lái juédìng de ▶**there is still time for you to do it** 你还有时间去做 nǐ hái yǒu shíjiān qù zuò
9 (*in favour of*) 赞成 zànchéng
10 (*referring to distance*) 达 dá ▶**there are roadworks for 50 km** 长跑练习长达50公里 chángpǎo liànxí chángdá wǔshí gōnglǐ

for 和 **to** 都可用于表示某人的目的，但后接不同的语言结构。**for** 用于表示目的时，后面必须跟名词。*Occasionally I go to the pub for a drink.* **for** 通常不用在动词前面。不能说 *I go to the pub for to have a drink.* **for** 用在 **-ing** 形式前表示某物的用途。*...a small machine for weighing the letters...* 与动词连用时，不定式前不加 **for**。*She went off to fetch help.*

forbid [fəˈbɪd] (*pt* **forbade** [fəˈbæd], *pp* **forbidden**) VT 禁止 jìnzhǐ ▶**to forbid sb to do sth** 禁止某人做某事 jìnzhǐ mǒurén zuò mǒushì
forbidden [fəˈbɪdn] PP *of* **forbid**
force [fɔːs] I N 1 [U] (*violence*) 武力 wǔlì 2 [U] (*strength*) 力量 lìliàng II VT 强迫 qiángpò III **forces** NPL (*Mil*) 部队 bùduì ▶**to force sb to do sth** 强迫某人做某事 qiángpò

mǒurén zuò mǒushì

forecast ['fɔːkɑːst] (pt, pp **forecast** or **forecasted**) I N [c] 预报 yùbào [个 gè] II vt (predict) 预测 yùcè

forehead ['fɔrɪd] N [c] 额 é [个 gè]

foreign ['fɔrɪn] ADJ 外国的 wàiguó de

foreigner ['fɔrɪnə^r] N [c] 外国人 wàiguórén [个 gè]

forest ['fɔrɪst] N [c/u] 森林 sēnlín [片 piàn]

forever [fə'rɛvə^r] ADV 永远 yǒngyuǎn

forgave [fə'geɪv] PT of **forgive**

forge [fɔːdʒ] vt [+ signature, banknote] 伪造 wěizào

forget [fə'gɛt] (pt **forgot**, pp **forgotten**) I vt 1 忘记 wàngjì 2 (leave behind) [+ object] 忘带 wàng dài II vi (fail to remember) 忘记 wàngjì ▶to forget to do sth 忘记做某事 wàngjì zuò mǒushì ▶to forget that... 忘记… wàngjì…

forgive [fə'gɪv] (pt **forgave**, pp **forgiven** [fə'gɪvn]) vt 原谅 yuánliàng ▶to forgive sb for sth 原谅某人某事 yuánliàng mǒurén mǒushì

forgot [fə'gɔt] PT of **forget**

forgotten [fə'gɔtn] PP of **forget**

fork [fɔːk] N [c] 1 餐叉 cānchā [把 bǎ] 2 (in road, river, railway) 岔路 chàlù [条 tiáo]

form [fɔːm] I N 1 [c] (type) 类型 lèixíng [种 zhǒng] 2 [c] (Brit: Scol: class) 年级 niánjí [个 gè] 3 [c] (document) 表格 biǎogé

[张 zhāng] II vt 1 (make) 组成 zǔchéng 2 (create) [+ group, organization, company] 成立 chénglì ▶in the form of 通过…方式 tōngguò…fāngshì

formal ['fɔːməl] ADJ 正式的 zhèngshì de

former ['fɔːmə^r] ADJ 前任的 qiánrèn de ▶in former times/years 以前 yǐqián

fortnight ['fɔːtnaɪt] (Brit) N [c] 两星期 liǎng xīngqī

fortunate ['fɔːtʃənɪt] ADJ 幸运的 xìngyùn de

fortunately ['fɔːtʃənɪtlɪ] ADV 幸运的是 xìngyùn de shì

fortune ['fɔːtʃən] N [c] 大笔钱 dàbǐqián ▶to make a fortune 发大财 fā dàcái

forty ['fɔːtɪ] NUM 四十 sìshí

forward ['fɔːwəd] ADV = **forwards**

forwards ['fɔːwədz] ADV 向前 xiàngqián

fought [fɔːt] PT, PP of **fight**

found [faund] I PT, PP of **find** II vt [+ organization, company] 创办 chuàngbàn

fountain ['fauntɪn] N [c] 喷泉 pēnquán [个 gè]

four [fɔː^r] NUM 四 sì; see also **five**

fourteen ['fɔː'tiːn] NUM 十四 shísì; see also **five**

fourteenth ['fɔː'tiːnθ] NUM 第十四 di shísì; see also **fifth**

fourth ['fɔːθ] NUM 1 第四 dìsì 2 (US: quarter) 四分之一 sìfēnzhīyī; see also **fifth**

fox [fɔks] N [c] 狐狸 húli [只 zhī]

fragile ['frædʒaɪl] ADJ 易损的

yìsǔn de

frame [freɪm] N [c] **1** 框 kuàng [个 gè] **2** (*also*: **frames**) [*of spectacles*] 眼镜架 yǎnjìngjià [副 fù]

France [frɑːns] N 法国 Fǎguó

fraud [frɔːd] N [c/u] 诈骗 zhàpiàn [种 zhǒng]

freckle ['frɛkl] N [c] 雀斑 quèbān [个 gè]

free [friː] ADJ **1** (*costing nothing*) 免费的 miǎnfèi de **2** [+ *person*] 自由的 zìyóu de **3** [+ *time*] 空闲的 kòngxián de **4** [+ *seat, table*] 空余的 kòngyú de ▶**free (of charge), for free** 免费 miǎnfèi ▶**to be free of** *or* **from sth** 没有某物 méiyǒu mǒuwù ▶**to be free to do sth** 随意做某事 suíyì zuò mǒushì

freedom ['friːdəm] N [u] 自由 zìyóu

freeway ['friːweɪ] (US) N [c] 高速公路 gāosù gōnglù [条 tiáo]

freeze [friːz] (*pt* **froze**, *pp* **frozen**) I VI **1** [*liquid, weather*] 结冰 jiébīng **2** [*pipe*] 冻住 dòngzhù II VT [+ *food*] 冷冻 lěngdòng

freezer ['friːzər] N [c] 冰柜 bīngguì [个 gè]

freezing ['friːzɪŋ] ADJ (*also*: **freezing cold**) [+ *day, weather*] 极冷的 jílěng de; [+ *person, hands*] 冰凉的 bīngliáng de ▶**I'm freezing** 冻死我了 dòngsǐ wǒ le

French [frɛntʃ] I ADJ 法国的 Fǎguó de II N [u] (*language*) 法语 Fǎyǔ III **the French** NPL (*people*) 法国人 Fǎguórén

French fries [-fraɪz] (*esp US*) NPL 炸薯条 zhá shǔtiáo

Frenchman ['frɛntʃmən] (*pl* **Frenchmen**) N [c] 法国男人 Fǎguó nánrén [个 gè]

Frenchwoman ['frɛntʃwumən] (*pl* **Frenchwomen**) N [c] 法国女人 Fǎguó nǚrén [个 gè]

frequent ['friːkwənt] ADJ 频繁的 pínfán de

fresh [frɛʃ] ADJ **1** 新鲜的 xīnxiān de **2** [+ *approach, way*] 新颖的 xīnyǐng de ▶**fresh air** 新鲜空气 xīnxiān kōngqì

Friday ['fraɪdɪ] N [c/u] 星期五 xīngqīwǔ [个 gè]; *see also* **Tuesday**

fridge [frɪdʒ] (*Brit*) N [c] 冰箱 bīngxiāng [台 tái]

fried [fraɪd] I PT, PP *of* **fry** II ADJ [+ *food*] 炒的 chǎo de

friend [frɛnd] N [c] 朋友 péngyou [个 gè] ▶**to make friends with sb** 与某人交朋友 yǔ mǒurén jiāo péngyou

friendly ['frɛndlɪ] ADJ 友善的 yǒushàn de ▶**to be friendly with** 跟…友好 gēn…yǒuhǎo

friendship ['frɛndʃɪp] N [c] 友情 yǒuqíng [种 zhǒng]

fright [fraɪt] N [c] 惊吓 jīngxià [个 gè] ▶**to give sb a fright** 吓唬某人一下 xiàhu mǒurén yīxià

frighten ['fraɪtn] VT 使惊恐 shǐ jīngkǒng

frightened ['fraɪtnd] ADJ ▶**to be frightened** 被吓倒 bèi xiàdǎo ▶**to be frightened of sth/of doing sth** *or* **to do sth** 害怕某事/做某事 hàipà mǒushì/zuò mǒushì

frightening ['fraɪtnɪŋ] ADJ 令人

恐惧的 lìngrén kǒngjù de
frog [frɔg] (Zool) N [c] 青蛙
qīngwā [只 zhī]

KEYWORD

from [frɔm] PREP 1 (indicating
starting place) 来自 láizì ▶**where
are you from?** 你来自哪里？
nǐ láizì nǎlǐ? 2 **from London to
Glasgow** 从伦敦到格拉斯哥 cóng
Lúndūn dào Gélāsīgē
2 (indicating origin) 来自 láizì ▶**a
present/telephone call/letter
from sb** 来自某人的礼物/电话/信
láizì mǒurén de lǐwù/diànhuà/xìn
3 (with time, distance, price,
numbers) 从 cóng ▶**from one
o'clock to** or **until two** 从1点直到
2点 cóng yīdiǎn zhídào liǎngdiǎn
▶**it's 1 km from the beach** 从海
滩到这儿有1公里 cóng hǎitān dào
zhèr yǒu yī gōnglǐ

front [frʌnt] I N [c] (of house, dress)
前面 qiánmiàn; (of coach, train, car)
前部 qiánbù [个 gè] II ADJ 前面
的 qiánmiàn de ▶**in front** 在前面
zài qiánmiàn ▶**in front of** (facing)
在…前面 zài…qiánmiàn; (in the
presence of) 在…面前
front door N [c] 前门 qiánmén
[个 gè]
frontier ['frʌntɪəʳ] N [c] (Brit) 国
界 guójiè [个 gè]
front page N [c] (Publishing) 头版
tóubǎn [个 gè]
frost [frɔst] N [c] [c] 霜 shuāng
[次 cì]

frosty ['frɔstɪ] ADJ 有霜冻的 yǒu
shuāngdòng de
froze [frəuz] PT of **freeze**
frozen ['frəuzn] I PP of **freeze**
II ADJ 1 [+ food] 冷冻的 lěngdòng
de; [+ ground, lake] 结冰的 jiébīng
de 2 [+ person, fingers] 冰冷的
bīnglěng de
fruit [fruːt] (pl **fruit** or **fruits**) N
[c/u] 水果 shuǐguǒ [种 zhǒng]
frustrated [frʌs'treɪtɪd] ADJ 泄气
的 xièqì de
fry [fraɪ] (pt, pp **fried**) I VT 油
煎 yóujiān II **fries** NPL (Culin) =
French fries
frying pan ['fraɪɪŋ-] N [c] 平底煎
锅 píngdǐ jiānguō [个 gè]
fuel ['fjuəl] N [c/u] 燃料 ránliào
[种 zhǒng]
full [ful] ADJ 1 满的 mǎn de;
[+ cinema, car, restaurant] 满
的 mǎn de 2 [+ details] 全部的
quánbù de; [+ information, name]
完全的 wánquán de ▶**I'm full (up)**
我吃饱了 wǒ chībǎo le ▶**full of** 充
满 chōngmǎn
full stop (Brit) N [c] 句号 jù hào
[个 gè]
full-time ['ful'taɪm] I ADJ
[+ work, study] 全职的 quánzhí
de; [+ student, staff] 全日制的
quánrìzhì de II ADV (work, study)
全日地 quánrì de
fully ['fulɪ] ADV 完全地 wánquán
de
fumes [fjuːmz] NPL 浓烈的烟气
nóngliè de yānqì
fun [fʌn] N [u] 乐趣 lèqù ▶**to
have fun** 玩得开心 wánde kāixīn

▶**to do sth for fun** 为找乐而做某事 wèi zhǎolè zuò ěr mǒushì ▶**to make fun of sb/sth** 取笑某人/某物 qǔxiào mǒurén/mǒushì

fund [fʌnd] I N [c] 基金 jījīn [项 xiàng] II **funds** NPL (*money*) 资金 zījīn

funeral [ˈfjuːnərəl] N [c] 葬礼 zànglǐ [个 gè]

funfair [ˈfʌnfɛəʳ] (*Brit*) N [c] 露天游乐场 lùtiān yóulèchǎng [个 gè]

funny [ˈfʌnɪ] ADJ 1 (*amusing*) 可笑的 kěxiào de 2 (*strange*) 奇怪的 qíguài de

fur [fəːʳ] N [c/u] 毛 máo [根 gēn]

furious [ˈfjuərɪəs] ADJ 大发雷霆的 dà fā léitíng de

furniture [ˈfəːnɪtʃəʳ] N [u] 家具 jiājù ▶**a piece of furniture** 一件家具 yījiàn jiājù

further [ˈfəːðəʳ] ADV 更远地 gèngyuǎn de ▶**how much further is it?** 还有多远? háiyǒu duōyuǎn?

further education N [u] 继续教育 jìxù jiàoyù

fuse, (*US*) **fuze** [fjuːz] N [c] 保险丝 bǎoxiǎnsī [根 gēn] ▶**a fuse has blown** 保险丝烧断了 bǎoxiǎnsī shāoduàn le

fuss [fʌs] N [s/u] 大惊小怪 dàjīng xiǎoguài ▶**to make** *or* **kick up a fuss (about sth)** (对某事)小题大做 (duì mǒushì) xiǎo tí dà zuò

future [ˈfjuːtʃəʳ] I ADJ 将来的 jiānglái de II N 1 ▶**the future** 未来 wèilái 2 (*Ling: also:* **future tense**) ▶**the future** 将来时 jiāngláishí ▶**in (the) future** (*from now on*) 从今以后 cóngjīn yǐhòu

▶**in the near/foreseeable future** 在不久/可预见的未来 zài bùjiǔ/kě yùjiàn de wèilái

fuze [fjuːz] (*US*) N [c] VT, VI = **fuse**

gallery ['gælərɪ] N [c] (also: **art gallery**) 美术馆 měishùguǎn [个 gè]

gamble ['gæmbl] I VI 1 (bet) 赌博 dǔbó 2 (take a risk) 投机 tóujī II N [c] (risk) 冒险 màoxiǎn [次 cì] ▶**to gamble on sth** 对某事打赌 duì mǒushì dǎdǔ; [+ success, outcome] 对某事冒险 duì mǒushì màoxiǎn

gambling ['gæmblɪŋ] N [U] 赌博 dǔbó

game [geɪm] N 1 [c] (sport) 运动 yùndòng [项 xiàng] 2 [c] (activity: children's) 游戏 yóuxì [个 gè] 3 [c] (also: **board game**) 棋盘游戏 qípán yóuxì [项 xiàng]; (also: **computer game**) 电脑游戏 diànnǎo yóuxì [项 xiàng] 4 [c] (match) 比赛 bǐsài [场 chǎng] ▶**a game of football/tennis** 一场足球/网球赛 yīchǎng zúqiú/wǎngqiú sài

gang [gæŋ] N [c] 一帮 yī bāng

gangster ['gæŋstər] N [c] 歹徒 dǎitú [个 gè]

gap [gæp] N [c] 缝隙 fèngxī [个 gè]

gap year (Brit) N [c] 高中和大学之间的空隙年

○ **GAP YEAR**

○
○ 在高中毕业以后，进入大学继
○ 续接受高等教育之前，学生
○ 可以休息一年，这一年被称
○ 为 **gap year**。在 **gap year**
○ 其间，很多人选择去旅游或
○ 去国外生活，也有人更愿意
○ 工作。无论如何选择，他们
○ 都能从学校学习生活之外获
○ 得宝贵的生活经验。

garage ['gærɑːʒ] N [c] 1 (of private house) 车库 chēkù [个 gè] 2 (for car repairs) 汽车修理厂 qìchē xiūlǐchǎng [个 gè] 3 (Brit: petrol station) 加油站 jiāyóuzhàn [个 gè]

garbage ['gɑːbɪdʒ] N [U] 1 (esp US: rubbish) 垃圾 lājī 2 (nonsense) 废话 fèihuà

garbage can (US) N [c] 垃圾箱 lājīxiāng [个 gè]

garbage man (pl **garbage men**) (US) N [c] 清洁工 qīngjiégōng [位 wèi]

garden ['gɑːdn] N [c] 花园 huāyuán [个 gè]

gardener ['gɑːdnəʳ] N [c]
(professional) 园丁 yuándīng
[位 wèi]; (amateur) 园艺爱好者
yuányì àihàozhě [个 gè]

gardening ['gɑːdnɪŋ] N [U] 园
艺 yuányì

garlic ['gɑːlɪk] N [U] 大蒜 dàsuàn

gas [gæs] N 1 [U] (for cooking,
heating) 煤气 méiqì 2 [U] (US: also:
gasoline) 汽油 qìyóu

gasoline ['gæsəliːn] (US) N [U] 汽
油 qìyóu

gas station (US) N [c] 加油站
jiāyóuzhàn [个 gè]

gate [geɪt] N [c] 1 门 mén [个 gè];
(of building) 大门 dàmén [个 gè]
2 (at airport) 登机口 dēngjīkǒu
[个 gè]

gather ['gæðəʳ] I VT (understand)
▶ **to gather (that)...** 获悉…
huòxī… II VI 聚集 jùjí

gave [geɪv] PT of **give**

gay [geɪ] I ADJ 同性恋的
tóngxìngliàn de II N [c] 同性恋
tóngxìngliàn [个 gè]

GCSE (Brit) N ABBR (= **General
Certificate of Secondary
Education**) 普通中等教育证
书 Pǔtōng Zhōngděng Jiàoyù
Zhèngshū

gear [gɪəʳ] N 1 [c] (of car, bicycle)
排挡 páidǎng [个 gè] 2 [U]
(equipment) 装备 zhuāngbèi 3
[U] (clothing) 服装 fúzhuāng ▶ **to
change** or (US) **shift gear** 换挡
huàndǎng

geese [giːs] NPL of **goose**

gel [dʒɛl] N [c/U] 啫 zhēlí [瓶 píng]
▶ **bath/shower gel** 浴液 yùyè

Gemini ['dʒɛmɪnaɪ] N [U] (sign) 双
子座 Shuāngzǐ Zuò

general ['dʒɛnərl] ADJ 1 (overall)
[+ situation] 总的 zǒng de;
[+ decline, standard] 一般的 yībān
de 2 [+ terms, outline, idea] 笼统的
lǒngtǒng de

general election N [c] (in Britain,
United States) 大选 dàxuǎn [届 jiè]

generally ['dʒɛnrəlɪ] ADV 1 (on
the whole) 大体上 dàtǐshang
2 (usually) 通常 tōngcháng

generation [dʒɛnə'reɪʃən] N [c]
一代人 yīdàirén [代 dài]

generous ['dʒɛnərəs] ADJ 大方的
dàfāng de

genius ['dʒiːnɪəs] N [c] 天才
tiāncái [位 wèi]

gentle ['dʒɛntl] ADJ 温和的
wēnhé de

gentleman ['dʒɛntlmən] (pl
gentlemen) N [c] 先生 xiānsheng
[位 wèi]

gents [dʒɛnts] N ▶ **the gents**
(Brit: inf) 男厕 náncè

genuine ['dʒɛnjuɪn] ADJ (real) 真
正的 zhēnzhèng de; [+ emotion,
interest] 实实在在的 shíshí
zàizài de

geography [dʒɪ'ɔgrəfɪ] N [U] 1 地
理 dìlǐ 2 (school/university subject)
地理学 dìlǐxué

germ [dʒəːm] (Bio) N [c] 细菌
xìjūn [种 zhǒng]

German ['dʒəːmən] I ADJ 德国的
Déguó de II N 1 [c] (person) 德国人
Déguórén [个 gè] 2 [U] (language)
德语 Déyǔ

Germany ['dʒəːmənɪ] N 德国

Déguó

 KEYWORD

get [gɛt] (*pt, pp* **got**, (*US*) *pp*
gotten) **I** VT 1 ▸ **to have got** *see
also* **have, got**
2 [+ *money, permission, results,
information*] 获得 huòdé; [+ *job,
flat, room*] 得到 dédào ▸ **he got
a job in London** 他在伦敦得到一
份工作 tā zài Lúndūn dédào yīfèn
gōngzuò
3 (*fetch*) 去拿 qùná ▸ **to get
sth for sb** 为某人去拿某物 wèi
mǒurén qù ná mǒuwù ▸ **can I get
you a coffee?** 要我给你拿杯咖啡
吗？ yào wǒ gěi nǐ ná bēi kāfēi
ma？ ▸ **I'll come and get you** 我会
来接你的 wǒ huì lái jiē nǐ de
4 [+ *present, letter, prize, TV channel*]
收到 shōudào ▸ **what did you get
for your birthday?** 你生日时得到
了什么礼物？ nǐ shēngrìshí dédào
le shénme lǐwù？
5 [+ *plane, bus*] 乘坐 chéngzuò
▸ **I'll get the bus** 我会乘坐公共
汽车 wǒ huì chéngzuò gōnggòng
qìchē
6 (*cause to be/become*) ▸ **to get
sth/sb ready** 使某事/某人准备
就绪 shǐ mǒurén/mǒushì zhǔnbèi
jiùxù
7 (*take, move*) 把…送到
bǎ…sòngdào ▸ **we must get him
to hospital** 我们必须把他送到
医院 wǒmen bìxū bǎ tā sòngdào
yīyuàn
8 (*buy*) 买 mǎi; (*regularly*) 买

到 mǎidào ▸ **I'll get some milk
from the supermarket** 我要去
超市买牛奶 wǒ yào qù chāoshì
mǎi niúnǎi
9 (*be infected by*) [+ *cold, measles*] 染
上 rǎnshang ▸ **you'll get a cold** 你
会得感冒的 nǐ huì dé gǎnmào de
10 [+ *time, opportunity*] 有 yǒu
11 ▸ **to get sth done** (*do oneself*)
做某事 zuò mǒushì; (*have done*) 完
成某事 wánchéng mǒushì ▸ **to get
one's hair cut** 理发 lǐfà ▸ **to get
sb to do sth** 让某人做某事 ràng
mǒurén zuò mǒushì
II VI 1 (*become, be: +adj*) 变得
biàn de ▸ **to get old/tired/cold/
dirty** 变老/变得疲倦/变冷/变脏
biànlǎo/biànde píjuàn/biànlěng/
biànzāng ▸ **to get drunk** 喝醉
了 hēzuì le
2 (*go*) ▸ **to get to work/the
airport/Beijing** *etc* 到办公
室/到达机场/到达北京 {等} dào
bàngōngshì/dàodá jīchǎng/dàodá
Běijīng {děng} ▸ **how did you get
here?** 你是怎么到这儿的？ nǐ shì
zěnme dào zhèr de？ ▸ **he didn't
get home till 10pm** 他直到晚上
10点才到家 tā zhídào wǎnshàng
shídiǎn cái dàojiā ▸ **how long
does it take to get from London
to Paris?** 从伦敦到巴黎需要多
久？ cóng Lúndūn dào Bālí xūyào
duōjiǔ？
3 (*begin*) ▸ **to get to know sb** 开
始了解某人 kāishǐ liǎojiě mǒurén
▸ **let's get going** *or* **started!** 开始
吧！ kāishǐ ba！
III AUX VB 1 ▸ **to have got to** *see*

also **have, got**

2 (*passive use*) 作为构成被动语态的助动词 ▸ **to get killed** 被杀 bèishā

▸ **get away** VI 逃跑 táopǎo

▸ **get back** I VI (*return*) 回来 huílái II VT (*reclaim*) 重新得到 chóngxīn dédào

▸ **get back to** VT FUS (*return to*) [+ *activity, work*] 回到 huídào; [+ *subject*] 重新回到 chóngxīn huídào ▸ **to get back to sleep** 重又睡着 chóng yòu shuìzháo

▸ **get in** VI **1** [*train, bus, plane*] 抵达 dǐdá

2 (*arrive home*) 到家 dàojiā

▸ **get into** VT FUS [+ *vehicle*] 乘坐 chéngzuò

▸ **get off** I VI (*from train, bus*) 下车 xiàchē II VT (*as holiday*) 放假 fàngjià

▸ **we get three days off at Christmas** 圣诞节时我们放了3天假 Shèngdànjié shí wǒmen fàngle sāntiānjià III VT FUS [+ *train, bus*] 从…下来 cóng…xiàlái

▸ **get on** I VI **1** (*be friends*) 和睦相处 hémù xiāngchǔ ▸ **to get on well with sb** 与某人相处融洽 yǔ mǒurén xiāngchǔ róngqià **2** (*progress*) 进展 jìnzhǎn ▸ **how are you getting on?** 你过得怎么样? nǐ guòde zěnmeyàng? II VT FUS [+ *bus, train*] 上 shàng

▸ **get on with** VT FUS (*continue, start*) 开始继续做 kāishǐ jìxù zuò

▸ **get out** I VI (*of vehicle*) 下车 xiàchē II VT (*take out*) 拿出 náchū

▸ **get out of** VT FUS [+ *vehicle*] 从…下来 cóng…xiàlái

▸ **get over** VT FUS [+ *illness, shock*] 从…中恢复过来 cóng…zhōng huīfù guòlái

▸ **get through** I VI (*Tel*) 接通 jiētōng II VT FUS [+ *work, book*] 完成 wánchéng

▸ **get together** VI [*people*] 聚在一起 jùzài yīqǐ

▸ **get up** VI 站起来 zhànqǐlái; (*out of bed*) 起床 qǐchuáng

ghost [gəust] N [C] 鬼神 guǐshén [种 zhǒng]

giant ['dʒaɪənt] I N [C] 巨人 jùrén [个 gè] II ADJ (*huge*) 巨大的 jùdà de

gift [gɪft] N [C] **1** 礼物 lǐwù [件 jiàn] **2** (*talent*) 天赋 tiānfù [种 zhǒng]

gin [dʒɪn] N [U] 杜松子酒 dùsōngzǐjiǔ

ginger ['dʒɪndʒəʳ] I N [U] (*spice*) 姜 jiāng II ADJ (*colour*) 姜色的 jiāngsè de

girl [gəːl] N [C] **1** (*child*) 女孩 nǚhái [个 gè]; (*young woman, woman*) 姑娘 gūniang [个 gè] **2** (*daughter*) 女儿 nǚ'ér [个 gè]

girlfriend ['gəːlfrɛnd] N **1** [C] [(*of girl*)] 女性朋友 nǚxìng péngyǒu [个 gè] **2** [(*of boy*)] 女朋友 nǚ péngyǒu [个 gè]

KEYWORD

give [gɪv] (*pt* **gave**, *pp* **given**) VT

1 ▶**to give sb sth, give sth to sb** 给某人某物 gěi mǒurén mǒuwù; (as gift) 送给某人某物 sònggěi mǒurén mǒuwù ▶**I gave David the book, I gave the book to David** 我把这本书送给了戴维 wǒ bǎ zhèběn shū sònggěi le Dàiwéi ▶**give it to him** 把它送给他 bǎ tā sònggěi tā

2 [+ advice, details] 提供 tígōng ▶**to give sb sth** [+ opportunity, surprise, shock, job] 给某人某物 gěi mǒurén mǒuwù

3 (deliver) ▶**to give a speech/a lecture** 做演讲/讲座 zuò yǎnjiǎng/jiǎngzuò

4 (organize) ▶**to give a party/ dinner party** etc 做东办一个聚会/宴会﹝等﹞ zuòdōng bàn yī gè jùhuì/yànhuì ﹝děng﹞

▶ **give back** VT 交还 jiāohuán
▶**to give sth back to sb** 把某物交还给某人 bǎ mǒuwù jiāohuán gěi mǒurén
▶ **give in** VI (yield) 屈服 qūfú
▶ **give up** I VI 放弃 fàngqì II VT [+ job] 辞掉 cídiào ▶**to give up smoking** 戒烟 jièyān

glad [glæd] ADJ 高兴的 gāoxìng de ▶**I'd be glad to help you** 我很愿意帮你你 wǒ hěn yuànyì bāngzhù nǐ

glamorous ['glæmərəs] ADJ 富有魅力的 fùyǒu mèilì de

glass [glɑːs] I N 1 [U] (substance) 玻璃 bōlí 2 [c] (container) 玻璃杯 bōlibēi ﹝个 gè﹞ 3 [c] (glassful) 一杯 yī bēi II **glasses** NPL (spectacles)

眼镜 yǎnjìng ▶**a pair of glasses** 一副眼镜 yīfù yǎnjìng

global ['gləubl] ADJ 全球的 quánqiú de

global warming [-'wɔːmɪŋ] N [U] 全球变暖 quánqiú biànnuǎn

glove [glʌv] N [c] 手套 shǒutào [副 fù] ▶**a pair of gloves** 一副手套 yīfù shǒutào

glue [gluː] N [c/u] 胶 jiāo [种 zhǒng]

⭕ KEYWORD

go [gəu] (pt **went**, pp **gone**, pl **goes**) I VI 1 去 qù ▶**he's going to New York** 他要去纽约 tā yào qù Niǔyuē ▶**where's he gone?** 他去哪儿了？ tā qù nǎr le? ▶**shall we go by car or train?** 我们开车去还是坐火车去？ wǒmen kāichē qù háishì zuò huǒchē qù?

2 (depart) 离开 líkāi ▶**let's go** 我们走吧 wǒmen zǒuba ▶**I must be going** 我必须得走了 wǒ bìxū děi zǒu le ▶**our plane goes at 11pm** 我们的飞机晚上11点起飞 wǒmen de fēijī wǎnshàng shíyīdiǎn qǐfēi

3 (disappear) 消失 xiāoshī ▶**all her jewellery had gone** 她所有的珠宝首饰都不见了 tā suǒyǒu de zhūbǎo shǒushì dōu bùjiàn le

4 (attend) ▶**to go to school/ university** 上学/上大学 shàngxué/shàng dàxué

5 (with activity) ▶**to go for a walk** 去散步 qù sànbù ▶**to go on a trip** 去旅行 qù lǚxíng

6 (work) 运转 yùnzhuàn

7 (*become*) ▶**to go pale/mouldy/ bald** 变得苍白/发霉/秃顶 biàn de cāngbái/fāméi/tūdǐng

8 (*be about to, intend to*) ▶**are you going to come?** 你要来吗? nǐ yào lái ma? ▶**I think it's going to rain** 我想天要下雨了 wǒxiǎng tiān yào xiàyǔ le

9 (*progress*) 进行 jìnxíng ▶**how did it go?** 这事进展如何? zhèshì jìnzhǎn rúhé?

10 (*lead*) [*road, path*] 通向 tōngxiàng

11 (*in other expressions*) ▶**there's still a week to go before the exams** 考试前还有一个星期的时间 kǎoshì qián háiyǒu yī gè xīngqī de shíjiān ▶**to keep going** 继续下去 jìxù xiàqù

II N 1 [c] (*try*) 尝试 chángshì [次 cì] ▶**to have a go (at sth/at doing sth)** 试一下 (某事/做某事) shì yīxià (mǒushì/zuò mǒushì)

2 [c] (*turn*) 轮流 lúnliú [次 cì] ▶**whose go is it?** 轮到谁了? lúndào shuí le?

▶**go ahead** VI **1** [*event*] 发生 fāshēng

2 (*press on*) ▶**to go ahead with sth** 着手做某事 zhuóshǒu zuò mǒushì ▶**go ahead!** (*encouraging*) 干吧! gànba!

▶**go around** VI **1** [*news, rumour*] 传播 chuánbō

2 (*revolve*) 转动 zhuàndòng

▶**go away** VI **1** (*leave*) 离开 líkāi

2 (*on holiday*) 外出 wàichū

▶**go back** VI 返回 fǎnhuí

▶**go back to** VT FUS [+ *activity,*

work, school] 回到 huídào

▶**go down** VI **1** [*price, level, amount*] 下降 xiàjiàng

2 [*sun*] 落下 luòxià

3 [*computer*] 死机 sǐjī

II VT FUS [+ *stairs, ladder*] 从···下来 cóng...xiàlái

▶**go for** VT FUS (*fetch*) 去取 qùqǔ

▶**go in** VI 进去 jìnqù

▶**go in for** VT FUS [+ *competition*] 参加 cānjiā

▶**go into** VT FUS (*enter*) 进入 jìnrù

▶**go off** VI **1** (*leave*) 离去 líqù

▶**he's gone off to work** 他已经去 上班了 tā yǐjīng qù shàngbān le

2 (*explode*) 爆炸 bàozhà

3 [*alarm*] 响起 xiǎngqǐ

4 [*lights*] 熄灭 xīmiè

▶**go on** VI **1** (*continue*) 继续 jìxù

▶**to go on with one's work** 继续 自己的工作 jìxù zìjǐ de gōngzuò

▶**to go on doing sth** 继续做某事 jìxù zuò mǒushì

2 (*happen*) 发生 fāshēng ▶**what's going on here?** 这里发生什么事 了? zhèlǐ fāshēng shénme shì le?

▶**go out** VI **1** [*person*] 离开 líkāi; (*to party, club*) 出去消遣 chūqù xiāoqiǎn ▶**are you going out tonight?** 你今晚出去吗? nǐ jīnwǎn chūqù ma?

2 [*couple*] 和···交往 hé...jiāowǎng

▶**to go out with sb** 和某人交往 hé mǒurén jiāowǎng

3 [*light, fire*] 熄灭 xīmiè

▶**go over** VI 过去 guòqù

▶**go round** VI = **go around**

▶**go through** VT FUS [+ *place, town*] 路过 lùguò

▶**go up** VI 1 [*price, level, value*] 上涨 shàngzhǎng 2 (*go upstairs*) 上楼 shànglóu

▶**go up to** VT FUS 向…走过去 xiàng…zǒuguòqù

▶**go with** VT FUS (*accompany*) 与…相共存 yǔ…xiāngbàn gòngcún

▶**go without** VT FUS [+ *food, treats*] 没有 méiyǒu…

goal [gəul] N [C] 1 (*Sport*) 进球得分 jìnqiú défēn [次 cì] 2 (*aim*) 目标 mùbiāo [个 gè] ▶**to score a goal** 进一球 jìn yīqiú

goalkeeper [ˈgəulkiːpəʳ] N [C] 守门员 shǒuményuán [个 gè]

goat [gəut] N [C] 山羊 shānyáng [只 zhī]

God [gɔd] N 上帝 Shàngdì

goggles [ˈgɔglz] NPL 护目镜 hùmùjìng

gold [gəuld] I N [U] (*metal*) 黄金 huángjīn II ADJ [+ *ring, watch, tooth*] 金的 jīn de

golf [gɔlf] N [U] 高尔夫球 gāoˈěrfúqiú ▶**to play golf** 打高尔夫球 dǎ gāoˈěrfúqiú

golf course N [C] 高尔夫球场 gāoˈěrfúqiúchǎng [个 gè]

gone [gɔn] I PP of **go** II ADJ 离去的 líqù de III PREP (*Brit: inf: after*) 过 guò ▶**the food's all gone** 食物都没了 shíwù dōu méi le

good [gud] I ADJ 1 (*pleasant*) 令人愉快的 lìng rén yúkuài de 2 [+ *food, school, job*] 好的 hǎo de 3 (*well-behaved*) 乖的 guāi de 4 [+ *idea, reason, advice*] 好的 hǎode 5 (*skilful*) 好的 hǎode 6 [+ *news, luck, example*] 好的 hǎo de 7 (*morally correct*) 公正的 gōngzhèng de II N [U] (*right*) 善 shàn ▶**good!** 好！hǎo! ▶**to be good at (doing) sth** 精于（做）某事 jīngyú (zuò) mǒushì ▶**to be no good at (doing) sth** 不擅长（做）某事 bù shàncháng (zuò) mǒushì ▶**it's no good doing...** 做…没有用 zuò…méiyǒu yòng ▶**it's good for you** 对你有益 duì nǐ yǒuyì ▶**it's good to see you** 很高兴见到你 hěn gāoxìng jiàndào nǐ ▶**good morning/afternoon!** 早上/下午好！zǎoshàng/xiàwǔ hǎo! ▶**good night!** (*before going home*) 再见！zàijiàn!; (*before going to bed*) 晚安！wǎnˈān! ▶**for good** (*forever*) 永久地 yǒngjiǔ de; *see also* **goods**

goodbye [gudˈbaɪ] INT 再见 zàijiàn ▶**to say goodbye** 告别 gàobié

good-looking [ˈgudˈlukɪŋ] ADJ 好看的 hǎokàn de

goods [gudz] NPL 商品 shāngpǐn

goose [guːs] (*pl* **geese**) N [C] 鹅 é [只 zhī]

gorgeous [ˈgɔːdʒəs] ADJ [+ *weather, day*] 宜人的 yírén de

gossip [ˈgɔsɪp] I N [U] (*rumours*) 流言蜚语 liúyán fēiyǔ II VI (*chat*) 闲谈 xiántán

got [gɔt] PT, PP of **get** ▶**have you got your umbrella?** 你有伞吗？nǐ yǒu sǎn ma? ▶**he has got to accept the situation** 他只得接受现状 tā zhǐdé jiēshòu xiànzhuàng

gotten ['gɔtn] (*US*) PP *of* **get**

government ['gʌvnmənt] N [c] (*institution*) 政府 zhèngfǔ [届 jiè]

GP N ABBR [c] (= **general practitioner**) 家庭医生 jiātíng yīshēng [位 wèi]

graceful ['greɪsful] ADJ 优美的 yōuměi de

grade [greɪd] N [c] 1 (*school mark*) 分数 fēnshù [个 gè] 2 (*US: school class*) 年级 niánjí [个 gè]

grade crossing (*US*) N [c] 铁路线 与公路交叉处

grade school (*US*) N [c/u] 小学 xiǎoxué [座 zuò]

gradual ['grædjuəl] ADJ 逐渐的 zhújiàn de

gradually ['grædjuəlɪ] ADV 逐渐 地 zhújiàn de

gram [græm] N [c] 克 kè

grammar ['græmər] N [u] 语 法 yǔfǎ

gramme [græm] (*Brit*) N = **gram**

grand [grænd] ADJ 壮丽的 zhuànglì de

grandchild ['grænt∫aɪld] (*pl* **grandchildren**) N [c] (*male on father's side*) 孙子 sūnzi [个 gè]; (*female on father's side*) 孙女 sūnnǚ [个 gè]; (*male on mother's side*) 外 孙 wàisūn [个 gè]; (*female on mother's side*) 外孙女 wàisūnnǚ [个 gè]

grandfather ['grændfɑːðər] N [c] (*on mother's side*) 外公 wàigōng [位 wèi]; (*on father's side*) 爷爷 yéye [位 wèi]

grandmother ['grænmʌðər] N [c] (*on father's side*) 外婆 wàipó [位

wèi]; (*on father's side*) 奶奶 nǎinai [位 wèi]

grandson ['grænsʌn] N [c] (*on father's side*) 孙子 sūnzi [个 gè]; (*on mother's side*) 外孙 wàisūn [个 gè]

grape [greɪp] N [c] 葡萄 pútáo [串 chuàn] ▶**a bunch of grapes** 一串 葡萄 yīchuàn pútáo

grapefruit ['greɪpfruːt] **grapefruit** *or* **grapefruits**) N [c/u] 葡萄柚 pútáo yòu [个 gè]

graph [grɑːf] N [c] 图表 túbiǎo [幅 fú]

graphics ['græfɪks] I N [u] (*design*) 制图学 zhìtúxué II NPL (*images*) 图 形 túxíng

grass [grɑːs] N [c/u] (*Bot*) 草 cǎo [株 zhū] ▶**the grass** (*the lawn*) 草 坪 cǎopíng

grate [greɪt] VT [+ *food*] 磨碎 mósuì

grateful ['greɪtful] ADJ 感激的 gǎnjī de ▶**to be grateful to sb for sth** 为某事感激某人 wèi mǒushì gǎnjī mǒurén

grave [greɪv] N [c] 坟墓 fénmù [座 zuò]

graveyard ['greɪvjɑːd] N [c] 墓地 mùdì [块 kuài]

gray [greɪ] (*US*) ADJ = **grey**

greasy ['griːsɪ] ADJ 1 [+ *food*] 油腻 的 yóunì de 2 [+ *skin, hair*] 多油脂 的 duō yóuzhīde

great [greɪt] I ADJ 1 (*large*) 巨大的 jùdà de 2 [+ *success, achievement*] 重大的 zhòngdà de; [+ *pleasure, difficulty, value*] 极大的 jídà de; [+ *risk*] 超乎寻常的 chāohū xúncháng de 3 [+ *city, person, work* *of art*] 伟大的 wěidà de **4** (*terrific*) [+ *person, place*] 好极了的 hǎojíle de; [+ *idea*] 棒极了的 bàngjíle de **II** INT ▶**great!** 太好了！tàihǎole! ▶**we had a great time** 我们玩得很快活 wǒmen wánde hěn kuàihuo

Great Britain N 大不列颠 Dàbùlièdiān

Greece [griːs] N 希腊 Xīlà

greedy [ˈɡriːdɪ] ADJ 贪心的 tānxīn de

Greek [ɡriːk] **I** ADJ 希腊的 Xīlà de **II** N **1** [c] (*person*) 希腊人 Xīlàrén [个 gè] **2** [U] (*modern language*) 希腊语 Xīlàyǔ

green [ɡriːn] **I** ADJ **1** 绿色的 lǜsè de **2** (*environmental*) 环保的 huánbǎo de **II** N [c/u] 绿色 lǜsè [抹 mǒ]

greengrocer [ˈɡriːnɡrəʊsəʳ] (*esp Brit*) N [c] (*shop*) (*also:* **greengrocer's**) 果蔬店 guǒshūdiàn [家 jiā]

greenhouse [ˈɡriːnhaʊs] **I** N [c] 暖房 nuǎnfáng [间 jiān] **II** CPD [+ *gas, emissions*] 温室 wēnshì

grew [ɡruː] PT *of* **grow**

grey, (*US*) **gray** [ɡreɪ] **I** ADJ **1** 灰色的 huīsè de; [+ *hair*] 灰白的 huībái de **2** [+ *weather, day*] 阴沉的 yīnchén de **II** N [c/u] 灰色 huīsè [种 zhǒng]

grey-haired [ɡreɪˈhɛəd] ADJ 灰白头发的 huībái tóufa de

grief [ɡriːf] N [U] 悲痛 bēitòng

grill [ɡrɪl] VT (*Brit*) [+ *food*] 烤 kǎo

grit [ɡrɪt] N [U] 沙粒 shālì

groan [ɡrəʊn] VI 呻吟 shēnyín

grocer [ˈɡrəʊsəʳ] N [c] **1** (*person*) 食品杂货商 shípǐn záhuòshāng [个 gè] **2** (*shop: also:* **grocer's**) 食品杂货店 shípǐn záhuòdiàn [家 jiā]

grocery [ˈɡrəʊsərɪ] **I** N [c] (*also:* **grocery shop** (*Brit*), **grocery store** (*esp US*)) 食品杂货店 shípǐn záhuòdiàn [家 jiā] **II groceries** NPL (*provisions*) 食品杂货 shípǐn záhuò

groom [ɡruːm] N [c] (*also:* **bridegroom**) 新郎 xīnláng [位 wèi]

ground [ɡraʊnd] **I** PT, PP *of* **grind** **II** N **1** (*floor*) ▶**the ground** 地面 dìmiàn **2** (*earth, soil, land*) ▶**the ground** 土地 tǔdì **3** [c] (*Sport*) 场 chǎng ▶**on the ground** 在地面上 zài dìmiàn shàng

ground floor N [c] 一楼 yīlóu [层 céng]

group [ɡruːp] N [c] **1** 组 zǔ [个 gè] **2** (*also:* **pop group, rock group**) 组合 zǔhé [个 gè] ▶**in groups** 成组地 chéngzǔ de

grow [ɡrəʊ] (*pt* **grew**, *pp* **grown**) **I** VI **1** [*plant, tree*] 生长 shēngzhǎng; [*person, animal*] 长大 zhǎngdà **2** [*amount, feeling, problem*] 扩大 kuòdà **II** VT [+ *flowers, vegetables*] 栽种 zāizhòng ▶**to grow by 10%** 增长 10% zēngzhǎng bǎi fēn zhī shí ▶ **grow up** VI (*be brought up*) 长大 zhǎngdà; (*be mature*) 成熟 chéngshú

grown [ɡrəʊn] PP *of* **grow**

grown-up [ɡrəʊnˈʌp] N [c] 成年人 chéngniánrén [个 gè]

growth [grəʊθ] N 1 [U/S] [*of economy, industry*] 发展 fāzhǎn 2 [U] [*of child, animal, plant*] 生长 shēngzhǎng ▸**a growth in sth** 某方面的发展 mǒu fāngmiàn de fāzhǎn

grumble ['grʌmbl] VI (*complain*) 抱怨 bàoyuàn

guarantee [gærən'tiː] N [C] (*Comm: warranty*) 质保承诺 zhìbǎo chéngnuò [个 gè]

guard [gɑːd] I N [C] (*sentry*) 警卫 jǐngwèi [个 gè] II VT [+ *building, entrance, door*] 守卫 shǒuwèi; [+ *person*] 保护 bǎohù ▸**to be on one's guard (against)** 提防 dīfáng

guess [gɛs] I VT, VI (*conjecture*) 猜测 cāicè II N [C] 猜测 cāicè [种 zhǒng] ▸**I guess so** 我想是吧 wǒxiǎng shìba?

guest [gɛst] N [C] (*at home*) 客人 kèrén [位 wèi]; (*at special event*) 宾客 bīnkè [位 wèi]; (*in hotel*) 房客 fángkè [位 wèi]

guide [gaɪd] I N [C] 1 (*tour guide*) 导游 dǎoyóu [位 wèi] 2 (*local guide*) 向导 xiàngdǎo [位 wèi] 3 (*also:* **guide book**) 指南 zhǐnán [本 běn] II VT 1 (*round city, museum*) 给…导游 gěi…dǎoyóu 2 (*lead*) 给…领路 gěi…lǐnglù

guidebook ['gaɪdbuk] N [C] 旅游指南 lǚyóu zhǐnán [本 běn]

guided tour ['gaɪdɪd-] N [C] 有导游的游览 yǒu dǎoyóu de yóulǎn [次 cì]

guilty ['gɪltɪ] ADJ 1 [+ *person, feelings*] 内疚的 nèijiù de 2 [+ *secret, conscience*] 自知有过错的 zìzhī yǒu guòcuò de 3 (*responsible*) 有过失的 yǒu guòshī de 4 (*Law*) 有罪的 yǒuzuì de ▸**guilty of murder/ manslaughter** 谋杀/误杀罪 móushā/wùshā zuì

guitar [gɪ'tɑːʳ] N [C] 吉他 jítā [把 bǎ]

gum [gʌm] N 1 [C] (*Anat*) 牙床 yáchuáng [个 gè] 2 [U] (*also:* **chewing gum/bubblegum**) 口香糖 kǒuxiāngtáng

gun [gʌn] N [C] (*small, medium-sized*) 枪 qiāng [支 zhī]; (*large*) 炮 pào [架 jià]

guy [gaɪ] N [C] (*man*) 家伙 jiāhuo [个 gè] ▸**(you) guys** 伙计们 huǒjìmen

gym [dʒɪm] N 1 [C] (*also:* **gymnasium**) 健身房 jiànshēnfáng [个 gè] 2 [U] (*also:* **gymnastics**) 体操 tǐcāo

gymnast ['dʒɪmnæst] N [C] 体操运动员 tǐcāo yùndòngyuán [位 wèi]

gymnastics [dʒɪm'næstɪks] N [U] 体操 tǐcāo

gypsy ['dʒɪpsɪ] N [C] 吉卜赛人 Jípǔsàirén [个 gè]

habit [ˈhæbɪt] N [c/u] 习惯 xíguàn [个 gè] ▶**to be in the habit of doing sth** 有做某事的习惯 yǒu zuò mǒushì de xíguàn ▶**a bad habit** 坏习惯 huài xíguàn

hacker [ˈhækəʳ] (*Comput*) N [c] 黑客 hēikè

had [hæd] PT, PP *of* **have**

hadn't [ˈhædnt] = **had not**

hail [heɪl] I N [u] 冰雹 bīngbáo II VI 下雹 xiàbáo

hair [hɛəʳ] N [u] 头发 tóufa [c] (*single strand*) 毛发 máofa [根 gēn] ▶**to do one's hair** 梳头 shūtóu ▶**to have** *or* **get one's hair cut** 剪头发 jiǎn tóufa

hairbrush [ˈhɛəbrʌʃ] N [c] 发刷 fàshuā [把 bǎ]

haircut [ˈhɛəkʌt] N [c] 1 理发 lǐfà [次 cì] 2 (*hairstyle*) 发型 fàxíng [种 zhǒng] ▶**to have** *or* **get a haircut** 剪头发 jiǎn tóufa

hairdresser [ˈhɛədrɛsəʳ] N [c] 1 美发师 měifàshī [位 wèi] 2 (*also:* **hairdresser's**) 发廊 fàláng [个 gè]

hairdryer [ˈhɛədraɪəʳ] N [c] 吹风机 chuīfēngjī [个 gè]

hair gel N [u] 发胶 fàjiāo

hairspray [ˈhɛəspreɪ] N [u] 喷发定型剂 pēnfà dìngxíngjì

hairstyle [ˈhɛəstaɪl] N [c] 发型 fàxíng [种 zhǒng]

half [hɑːf] (*pl* **halves**) I N, PRON [c] 1 一半 yībàn 2 (*Brit: child's ticket*) 半票 bànpiào [张 zhāng] II ADJ [+ *bottle*] 一半的 yībàn de III ADV (*empty, closed, open, asleep*) 半 bàn ▶**to cut sth in half** 把某物切成两半 bǎ mǒuwù qiēchéng liǎngbàn ▶**two/three** *etc* **and a half** 二/三 {等} 点五 èr/sān (děng) diǎn wǔ ▶**half a pound/kilo/mile** 半磅/公斤/英里 bànbàng/gōngjīn/yīnglǐ ▶**a day/week/pound** *etc* **and a half** 一天/星期/磅 {等} 半 yītiān/xīngqī/bàng (děng) bàn ▶**half an hour** 半小时 bàn xiǎoshí ▶**half past three/four** *etc* 三/四 {等} 点半 sān/sì (děng) diǎn bàn

half-hour [hɑːfauəʳ] N [c] 半小时 bàn xiǎoshí [个 gè]

half price [ˈhɑːfpraɪs] I ADJ 半价的 bànjià de II ADV 半价地 bànjià de

half-term [hɑːftəːm] (*Brit: Scol*) N [c/u] 期中假 qīzhōng jià [段 duàn] ▶**at half-term** 期中假时 qīzhōng jià shí

half-time [ˈhɑːfˈtaɪm] (*Sport*) N [U] 半场 bànchǎng ▸**at half-time** 半场时 bànchǎng shí

halfway [ˈhɑːfˈweɪ] ADV (*between two points*) 到一半 dào yībàn ▸**halfway through sth** 在某事过了一半时 zài mǒushì guòle yībàn shí

hall [hɔːl] N 1 [c] (*esp Brit: entrance*) 门厅 méntīng [个 gè] 2 [c] (*room*) 礼堂 lǐtáng [个 gè]

ham [hæm] I N [c] 火腿 huǒtuǐ II CPD [+ *sandwich, roll, salad*] 火腿 huǒtuǐ

hamburger [ˈhæmbəːɡəʳ] N [c] 汉堡包 hànbǎobāo [个 gè]

hammer [ˈhæməʳ] N [c] 锤子 chuízi [把 bǎ]

hand [hænd] I N 1 [c] 手 shǒu [双 shuāng] 2 [c] (*of clock*) 指针 zhǐzhēn [个 gè] II VT 递 dì ▸**to do sth by hand** 手工制作 shǒugōng zhìzuò ▸**to give** *or* **lend sb a hand (with sth)** 帮某人 (做某事) bāng mǒurén (zuò mǒushì) ▸**on the one hand..., on the other hand...** 一方面…，另一方面… yī fāngmiàn…, lìngyī fāngmiàn…
▸**hand in** VT 上交 shàngjiāo
▸**hand out** VT 分配 fēnpèi
▸**hand over** VT 交给 jiāogěi

handbag [ˈhændbæg] (*Brit*) N [c] 手包 shǒubāo [个 gè]

handcuffs [ˈhændkʌfs] NPL 手铐 shǒukào ▸**in handcuffs** 带手铐 dài shǒukào

handkerchief [ˈhæŋkətʃɪf] N [c] 手帕 shǒupà [条 tiáo]

handle [ˈhændl] I N [c] (*of bag*) 把手 bǎshǒu [个 gè]; [*of cup, knife, paintbrush, broom, spade*] 柄 bǐng [个 gè]; [*of door, window*] 拉手 lāshǒu [个 gè] II VT [+ *problem, job, responsibility*] 处理 chǔlǐ

handlebars [ˈhændlbɑː(z)] NPL 把手 bǎshǒu

handmade [ˈhændˈmeɪd] ADJ 手工制作的 shǒugōng zhìzuò de

handsome [ˈhænsəm] ADJ 英俊的 yīngjùn de

handwriting [ˈhændraɪtɪŋ] N [U] 笔迹 bǐjì

handy [ˈhændɪ] ADJ 1 (*useful*) 方便的 fāngbiàn de 2 (*close at hand*) 手边的 shǒubiān de

hang [hæŋ] (*pt, pp* **hung**) I VT 挂 guà II VI (*be suspended*) 悬挂 xuánguà
▸**hang about** VI = **hang around**
▸**hang around** (*inf*) VI 闲荡 xiándàng
▸**hang on** VI (*wait*) 稍等 shāoděng
▸**hang round** (*Brit*) VI = **hang around**
▸**hang up** I VI (*Tel*) 挂断电话 guàduàn diànhuà II VT [+ *coat, hat, clothes*] 挂起 guàqǐ

hanger [ˈhæŋəʳ] N [c] (*also*: **coat hanger**) 衣架 yījià [个 gè]

hangover [ˈhæŋəʊvəʳ] N [c] 宿醉 sùzuì [次 cì]

happen [ˈhæpən] VI 发生 fāshēng ▸**what will happen if...?** 如果…会怎么样？ rúguǒ…huì zěnmeyàng? ▸**tell me what happened** 告诉我发生了什么事 gàosù wǒ fāshēng le shénme shì

happiness [ˈhæpɪnɪs] N [U] 幸福 xìngfú

happy [ˈhæpɪ] ADJ 1 高兴的 gāoxìng de 2 [+ *life, childhood, marriage, place*] 美满的 měimǎn de ▶**to be happy with sth** (*satisfied*) 对某事满意 duì mǒushì mǎnyì ▶**to be happy to do sth** (*willing*) 乐意做某事 lèyì zuò mǒushì ▶**happy birthday!** 生日快乐！shēngrì kuàilè! ▶**happy Christmas!** 圣诞快乐！Shèngdàn kuàilè!

harassment [ˈhærəsmənt] N [U] 骚扰 sāorǎo

harbour, (*US*) **harbor** [ˈhɑːbəʳ] N [c] 港口 gǎngkǒu [个 gè]

hard [hɑːd] I ADJ 1 [+ *surface, object*] 硬的 yìng de 2 [+ *question, problem*] 困难的 kùnnan de; [+ *work*] 费力的 fèilì de 3 [+ *push, punch, kick*] 用力的 yònglì de II ADV 1 [*work, try, think*] 努力地 nǔlì de 2 用力地 yònglì de ▶**it's hard to tell/say/know** 很难讲/说/知道 hěnnán jiǎng/shuō/zhīdào ▶**such events are hard to understand** 这种事很难理解 zhèzhǒng shì hěnnán lǐjiě ▶**it's hard work serving in a shop** 商店工作很难做 shāngdiàn gōngzuò hěnnán zuò

hard disk (*Comput*) N [c] 硬盘 yìngpán [个 gè]

hardly [ˈhɑːdlɪ] ADV 1 (*scarcely*) 几乎不 jīhū bù 2 (*no sooner*) ▶**he had hardly sat down when the door burst open** 他一坐下门就被猛地打开了 tā yī zuòxià mén jiù bèi měng de dǎkāi le ▶**hardly ever/any/anyone** 几乎从不/没有/没有任何人 jīhū cóngbù/méiyǒu/méiyǒu rènhé rén ▶**I can hardly believe it** 我简直不能相信 wǒ jiǎnzhí bùnéng xiāngxìn

hardware [ˈhɑːdwɛəʳ] N [U] (*Comput*) 硬件 yìngjiàn

hardworking [hɑːdˈwəːkɪŋ] ADJ 勤奋的 qínfèn de

harm [hɑːm] VT 1 (*damage*) 损坏 sǔnhuài 2 (*injure*) 伤害 shānghài

harmful [ˈhɑːmful] ADJ 有害的 yǒuhài de

harp [hɑːp] N [c] (*Mus*) 竖琴 shùqín [架 jià]

harvest [ˈhɑːvɪst] N 1 [c/U] (*harvest time*) 收获 shōuhuò [种 zhǒng] 2 [c] (*crop*) 收成 shōucheng [个 gè]

has [hæz] VB *see* **have**

hasn't [ˈhæznt] = **has not**

hat [hæt] N [c] 帽子 màozi [顶 dǐng]

hate [heɪt] VT [+ *person*] 恨 hèn; [+ *food, activity, sensation*] 讨厌 tǎoyàn ▶**to hate doing/to do sth** 不喜欢做某事 bù xǐhuān zuò mǒushì

hatred [ˈheɪtrɪd] N [U] 仇恨 chóuhèn

○ KEYWORD

have [hæv] (*pt, pp* **had**) I VT 1 有 yǒu ▶**he has** *or* **he has got blue eyes/dark hair** 他长着蓝眼睛/黑头发 tā zhǎngzhe lán yǎnjīng/hēi tóufa ▶**do you have** *or* **have you**

got a car/phone? 你有车/电话吗? nǐ yǒu chē/diànhuà ma? ▶**to have** or **have got sth to do** 有必须得做的事 yǒu bìxū děi zuò de shì ▶**she had her eyes closed** 她闭上了眼睛 tā bìshàng le yǎnjīng **2** ▶**to have breakfast** 吃早饭 chī zǎofàn ▶**to have a drink/a cigarette** 喝一杯/抽支烟 hē yìbēi/chōu zhī yān **3** ▶**to have a swim/bath** 游泳/洗澡 yóuyǒng/xǐzǎo ▶**to have a meeting/party** 开会/开派对 kāihuì/kāi pàiduì **4** (receive, obtain) 得到 dédào ▶**can I have your address?** 能告诉我你的地址吗? néng gàosù wǒ nǐde dìzhǐ ma? ▶**you can have it for £5** 付5英磅它就是你的了 fù wǔ yīngbàng tā jiùshì nǐde le **5** ▶**to have a baby** 生孩子 shēng háizi **6** ▶**to have sth done** 指使/安排做某事 zhǐshǐ/ānpái zuò mǒushì ▶**to have one's hair cut** 理发 lǐfà **7** ▶**to have a headache** 头痛 tóutòng ▶**to have an operation** 动手术 dòng shǒushù **II** AUX VB **1** ▶**to have arrived/gone** 已到了/走了 yǐ dàole/zǒule ▶**has he told you?** 他已经告诉你了吗? tā yǐjīng gàosù nǐ le ma? ▶**when she had dressed, she went downstairs** 穿好衣服后, 她下了楼 chuānhǎo yīfu hòu, tā xiàle lóu ▶**I haven't seen him for ages/since July** 我已经很久/自7月以来就没见过他了 wǒ yǐjīng hěnjiǔ/zì qīyuè yǐlái jiù méi

jiànguò tā le **2** (in tag questions) ▶**you've done it, haven't you?** 你已经做了, 是不是? nǐ yǐjīng zuò le, shì bùshì? **3** (in short answers and questions) ▶**yes, I have** 是的, 我有/已做了 shìde, wǒ yǒu/yǐzuò le ▶**no I haven't!** 不, 我还没有/没做呢! bù, wǒ hái méiyǒu/méizuò ne! ▶**so have I!** 我也一样! wǒ yě yīyàng! ▶**neither have I** 我也没有过 wǒ yě méiyǒu guò ▶**I've finished, have you?** 我已经完成了, 你呢? wǒ yǐjīng wánchéng le, nǐne? **4** (be obliged) ▶**to have (got) to do sth** 不得不做某事 bùdébù zuò mǒushì ▶**she has (got) to do it** 她必须得这么做 tā bìxū děi zhème zuò

▶**have on** VT [+ clothes] 穿着 chuānzhe ▶**he didn't have anything on** 他什么都没穿 tā shénme dōu méi chuān

haven't ['hævnt] = **have not**
hay fever N [U] 花粉病 huāfěnbìng
hazel ['heɪzl] ADJ [+ eyes] 淡褐色的 dàn hèsè de
he [hi:] PRON 他 tā
head [hɛd] **I** N [c] **1** 头 tóu [个 gè] **2** [of company, organization, department] 领导 lǐngdǎo [个 gè] **3** (Brit: head teacher) 校长 xiàozhǎng [位 wèi] **II** VT **1** [+ list, group] 以…打头 yǐ…dǎtóu **2** (Football) [+ ball] 用头顶 yòng tóu dǐng ▶**10 pounds a** or **per**

head 每人10英镑 měirén shí yīngbàng ▶**from head to foot** or **toe** 从头到脚 cóng tóu dào jiǎo ▶**heads or tails?** 正面还是反面? zhèngmiàn háishì fǎnmiàn?
▶ **head for** VT FUS 前往 qiánwǎng
▶**to be heading** or **headed for Glasgow** 正前往格拉斯哥 zhèng qiánwǎng Gélāsīgē

headache ['hɛdeɪk] N [C] 头痛 tóutòng [阵 zhèn] ▶**to have a headache** 头痛 tóutòng

headlight ['hɛdlaɪt] N [C] 前灯 qiándēng [个 gè]

headline ['hɛdlaɪn] N [C] 标题 biāotí [个 gè] ▶**the headlines** (Publishing) 头条新闻 tóutiáo xīnwén; (TV, Rad) 内容提要 nèiróng tíyào

headmaster [hɛd'mɑːstəʳ] (Brit) N [C] 校长 xiàozhǎng [位 wèi]

headmistress [hɛd'mɪstrɪs] (Brit) N [C] 女校长 nǚ xiàozhǎng [位 wèi]

head office N [C/U] [of company] 总部 zǒngbù

headphones ['hɛdfəʊnz] NPL 耳机 ěrjī

headquarters ['hɛdkwɔːtəz] NPL 总部 zǒngbù

heal [hiːl] VI 痊愈 quányù

health [hɛlθ] N [U] 健康 jiànkāng
▶**to be good/bad for one's health** 对某人的健康有益/不利 duì mǒurén de jiànkāng yǒuyì/búlì
▶**to drink (to) sb's health** 举杯祝某人健康 jǔbēi zhù mǒurén jiànkāng

healthy ['hɛlθɪ] ADJ 1 健康的

jiànkāng de 2 [+ diet, lifestyle] 对健康有益的 duì jiànkāng yǒuyì de

heap [hiːp] N [C] 堆 duī [个 gè]

hear [hɪəʳ] (pt, pp **heard** [həːd]) VT 1 听见 tīngjiàn 2 [+ news, lecture, concert] 听 tīng ▶**to hear sb doing sth** 听见某人做某事 tīngjiàn mǒurén zuò mǒushì ▶**to hear that...** 听说… tīngshuō…
▶**to hear about sth/sb** 听说某事/某人 tīngshuō mǒushì/mǒurén
▶**to hear from sb** 得到某人的消息 dédào mǒurén de xiāoxi ▶**I've never heard of him** 我从来没听说过他 wǒ cónglái méi tīngshuō guò tā

heart [hɑːt] N 1 [C] 心脏 xīnzàng [颗 kē] 2 [C] (emotions) 感情 gǎnqíng [种 zhǒng] 3 [C] (shape) 心形物 xīnxíng wù [个 gè] ▶**to learn/know sth (off) by heart** 背诵某事 bèisòng mǒushì; () ▶**to break sb's heart** 使某人伤心 shǐ mǒurén shāngxīn

heart attack N [C] 心脏病发作 xīnzàngbìng fāzuò [阵 zhèn] ▶**to have a heart attack** 心脏病发作 xīnzàngbìng fāzuò

heat [hiːt] I N 1 [U] 热 rè 2 [U] (temperature) 热度 rèdù 3 [C] (Sport) (also: **qualifying heat**) 预赛 yùsài [场 chǎng] II VT [+ water, food] 加热 jiārè; [+ room, house] 取暖 qǔnuǎn ▶**I find the heat unbearable** 热得我实在受不了了 rède wǒ shízài shòubùliǎo
▶ **heat up** VT [+ food] 加热 jiārè

heater ['hiːtəʳ] N [C] (electric heater, gas heater) 供暖装置 gōngnuǎn zhuāngzhì [个 gè]; (in car) 暖气设备 nuǎnqì shèbèi [套 tào]

heating ['hi:tɪŋ] N [U] (system) 暖气 nuǎnqì

heatwave ['hi:tweɪv] N [C] 酷暑时期 kùshǔ shíqī [段 duàn]

heaven ['hɛvn] N [U] 天堂 tiāntáng

heavy ['hɛvɪ] ADJ 1 重的 zhòng de 2 [+ traffic] 拥挤的 yōngjǐ de; [+ fine, penalty, sentence] 重的 zhòng de; [+ drinking, smoking, gambling] 过度的 guòdù de; [+ rain, snow] 大的 dà de ▶ how heavy are you/is it? 你/它有多重? nǐ/tā yǒu duōzhòng?

he'd [hi:d] = **he would, he had**

hedge [hɛdʒ] N [C] 树篱 shùlí [道 dào]

heel [hi:l] N [C] 1 [of foot] 脚后跟 jiǎohòugēn [个 gè] 2 [of shoe] 鞋跟 xiégēn [个 gè]

height [haɪt] N 1 [C/U] 高度 gāodù [个 gè] 2 [C] (altitude) 高处 gāochù ▶ of average/medium height 平均/中等高度 píngjūn/zhōngděng gāodù

held [hɛld] PT, PP of **hold**

helicopter ['hɛlɪkɔptər] N [C] 直升飞机 zhíshēng fēijī [架 jià]

hell [hɛl] I N [U] 地狱 dìyù II INT (inf!) 天啊 tiān a ▶ it was hell (inf) 糟糕极了 zāogāo jíle

he'll [hi:l] = **he will, he shall**

hello [hə'ləu] INT (as greeting) 你好 nǐhǎo; (Tel) 喂 wèi; (to attract attention) 劳驾 láojià

helmet ['hɛlmɪt] N [C] 头盔 tóukuī [个 gè]; [of soldier, policeman, fireman] 钢盔 gāngkuī [个 gè]

help [hɛlp] I N [U] 帮助 bāngzhù II VT [+ person] 帮助 bāngzhù III VI 1 (assist) 帮忙 bāngmáng 2 (be useful) 有用 yǒuyòng ▶ thanks, you've been a great help 谢谢, 你帮了很大忙 xièxiè, nǐ bāngle hěndà máng ▶ I helped him (to) fix his car 我帮助他修了他的车 wǒ bāngzhù tā xiūle tāde chē ▶ help! 救命! jiùmìng! ▶ can I help you? (in shop) 我能为您效劳吗? wǒ néng wèi nín xiàoláo ma? ▶ I can't help feeling sorry for him 我情不自禁地同情他 wǒ qíng bù zì jīn de tóngqíng tā ▶ it can't be helped 没办法 méi bànfǎ

helpful ['hɛlpful] ADJ 有用的 yǒuyòng de; [+ advice, suggestion] 有建设性的 yǒu jiànshèxìng de

helping ['hɛlpɪŋ] N [C] [of food] 一份 yīfèn

helpless ['hɛlplɪs] ADJ 无依无靠的 wúyīwúkào de

hen [hɛn] N [C] 母鸡 mǔjī [只 zhī]

her [həːr] I PRON 她 tā II ADJ 她的 tā de ▶ I haven't seen her 我还没见到她。 wǒ hái méi jiàndào tā ▶ they gave her the job 他们给了她那份工作 tāmen gěile tā nàfèn gōngzuò ▶ her face was very red 她的脸很红 tāde liǎn hěnhóng

herb [həːb], US əːrb] N [C] 草本植物 cǎoběn zhíwù [株 zhū]

herd [həːd] N [C] 牧群 mùqún [群 qún]

here [hɪər] ADV 1 (in/to this place) 在这里 zài zhèlǐ 2 (near me) 到这

里 dào zhèlǐ ▶**here's my phone number** 这是我的电话号码 zhèshì wǒde diànhuà hàomǎ ▶**here he is** 他到了 tā dào le ▶**here you are** (take this) 给你 gěi nǐ ▶**here and there** 各处 gèchù

hero ['hɪərəu] (pl **heroes**) N [c] **1** 男主人公 nán zhǔréngōng [个 gè] **2** [of battle, struggle] 英雄 yīngxióng [位 wèi]

heroin ['hɛrəuɪn] N [U] 海洛因 hǎiluòyīn

heroine ['hɛrəuɪn] N [c] **1** 女 主人公 nǚ zhǔréngōng [个 gè] **2** (of battle, struggle) 女英雄 nǚ yīngxióng [位 wèi]

hers [həːz] PRON 她的 tā de ▶**this is hers** 这是她的。 zhèshì tāde ▶**a friend of hers** 她的一个朋友 tāde yīgè péngyou

herself [həː'sɛlf] PRON **1** 她自 己 tā zìjǐ **2** (emphatic) 她本人 tā běnrén ▶**she hurt herself** 她伤 了自己 tā shāngle zìjǐ ▶**she made the dress herself** 这件连衣裙 tā zìjǐ zuòde zhèjiàn liányīqún ▶**she lives by herself** 她独自一人住 tā dúzì yīrén zhù

he's [hiːz] = **he is, he has**

hesitate ['hɛzɪteɪt] VI 犹豫 yóuyù ▶**he did not hesitate to take action** 他毫不迟疑地采取 了行动 tā háobù chíyí de cǎiqǔ le xíngdòng ▶**don't hesitate to contact me** 请务必和我联系 qǐng wùbì héwǒ liánxì

heterosexual ['hɛtərəu'sɛksjuə l] N [c] 异性恋者 yìxìngliànzhě [个 gè]

hi [haɪ] INT (as greeting) 嘿 hēi; (in e-mail) 你好 nǐhǎo

hiccup ['hɪkʌp] **hiccups** NPL ▶**to have/get (the) hiccups** 打 嗝 dǎgé

hidden ['hɪdn] PP of **hide**

hide [haɪd] (pt **hid**, pp **hidden**) **I** VT 隐藏 yǐncáng; [+ feeling, information] 隐瞒 yǐnmán **II** VI 藏 起来 cáng qǐlái ▶**to hide from sb** 躲着某人 duǒzhe mǒurén

hi-fi ['haɪfaɪ] N [c] 高保真音响设 备 gāobǎozhēn yīnxiǎng shèbèi [套 tào]

high [haɪ] **I** ADJ 高的 gāo de **II** ADV (reach, throw) 高高地 gāogāo de; (fly, climb) 高 gāo ▶**it is 20 m high** 有20米高 yǒu èrshímǐ gāo ▶**foods that are high in fat** 脂肪含量高的食品 zhīfáng hánliàng gāo de shípǐn ▶**safety has always been our highest priority** 安全一直是我们最重视的 问题 ānquán yīzhí shì wǒmen zuì zhòngshì de wèntí ▶**high up** 离地 面高的 lí dìmiàn gāo de

high 不能用于描写人，动 物和植物，而应用 **tall**。 She was rather tall for a woman. **tall** 还可以用来 描写建筑物，如摩天大 楼等，以及其他高度大 于宽度的东西。...tall pine trees...a tall glass vase...

higher education ['haɪə^r-] N [U] 高等教育 gāoděng jiàoyù

high-rise ['haɪraɪz] ADJ 高层的 gāocéng de

high school N [c/U] 中学

zhōngxué [所 suǒ]

hijack ['haɪdʒæk] VT 劫持 jiéchí

hijacker ['haɪdʒækə'] N [c] 劫持者 jiéchízhě [个 gè]

hike [haɪk] I VI 步行 bùxíng II N [c] (walk) 徒步旅行 túbù lǚxíng [次 cì] ▶**to go hiking** 做徒步旅行 zuò túbù lǚxíng

hiking ['haɪkɪŋ] N [u] 步行 bùxíng

hill [hɪl] N [c] 小山 xiǎoshān [座 zuò]; (slope) 坡 pō [个 gè]

him [hɪm] PRON 他 tā ▶**I haven't seen him** 我还没看见他 wǒ hái méi kànjiàn tā ▶**they gave him the job** 他们给了他那份工作 tāmen gěile tā nàfèn gōngzuò

himself [hɪm'sɛlf] PRON 1 他自己 tā zìjǐ 2 (emphatic) 他本人 tā běnrén ▶**he hurt himself** 他伤了自己 tā shāngle zìjǐ ▶**he prepared the supper himself** 他自己准备了晚餐 tā zìjǐ zhǔnbèi le wǎncān ▶**he lives by himself** 他独自一人住。 tā dúzì yīrén zhù

Hindu ['hɪndu:] I N [c] 印度教信徒 Yìndùjiào xìntú [位 wèi] II ADJ 与印度教有关的 yǔ Yìndùjiào yǒuguān de

hip [hɪp] N [c] 髋部 kuānbù [个 gè]

hippie ['hɪpɪ] N [c] 嬉皮士 xīpíshì [个 gè]

hire ['haɪə'] I VT (esp Brit) 租用 zūyòng; (+ worker) 雇用 gùyòng II N [u] (Brit: of car, hall) 租用 zūyòng

hire car (Brit) N [c] 租的车 zū de chē

his [hɪz] I ADJ 他的 tā de II PRON 他的 tā de ▶**his face was very red**

他的脸很红 tāde liǎn hěnhóng ▶**these are his** 这些是他的 zhèxiē shì tāde ▶**a friend of his** 他的一个朋友 tāde yīgè péngyǒu

history ['hɪstərɪ] N [u] 历史 lìshǐ

hit [hɪt] (pt, pp hit) I VT 1 (strike) 打 dǎ 2 (collide with) 碰撞 pèngzhuàng 3 [+ target] 击中 jīzhòng II N [c] 1 (on website) 点击 diǎnjī [次 cì] 2 (hit song) 成功而风行一时的事物 chénggōng ér fēngxíng yīshí de shìwù [个 gè]

hitchhike ['hɪtʃhaɪk] VI 搭便车旅行 dā biànchē lǚxíng

hitchhiker ['hɪtʃhaɪkə'] N [c] 搭便车旅行者 dā biànchē lǚxíngzhě [个 gè]

HIV N ABBR (= **human immunodeficiency virus**) 艾滋病病毒 àizībìng bìngdú

hoarse [hɔ:s] ADJ 嘶哑的 sīyǎ de

hobby ['hɔbɪ] N [c] 爱好 àihào [种 zhǒng]

hockey ['hɔkɪ] N [u] 1 (Brit) 曲棍球 qūgùnqiú 2 (US: on ice) 冰球 bīngqiú

hold [həʊld] (pt, pp held) I VT 1 拿 ná 2 (contain) 容纳 róngnà II VI (Tel) 等着 děngzhe III N [c] [of ship, plane] 货舱 huòcāng [个 gè] ▶**hold the line!** (Tel) 别挂线！ bié guàxiàn! ▶**to hold sb prisoner/hostage** 扣留某人作为囚犯/人质 kòuliú mǒurén zuòwéi qiúfàn/rénzhì ▶**to get/grab/take hold of sb/sth** 紧紧拿着/抓着/握着某人/某物 jǐnjǐn názhe/zhuāzhe/wòzhe mǒurén/mǒuwù ▶**I need to get hold of Bob** 我需要找到鲍勃

wǒ xǔyào zhǎodào Bàobó

▶ **hold on** VI 1 (keep hold) 抓牢 zhuāláo 2 等一会儿 děng yīhuìr

▶ **hold up** VT 1 (lift up) 举起 jǔqǐ 2 (delay) 阻碍 zǔ'ài

hold-up ['həuldʌp] N [C] 1 (robbery) 持械抢劫 chíxiè qiǎngjié [次 cì] 2 (delay) 延搁 yángē [次 cì]; (in traffic) 交通阻塞 jiāotōng zǔsè [阵 zhèn]

hole [həul] N [C] 1 (space, gap) 洞 dòng [个 gè] 2 (tear) 破洞 pòdòng [个 gè]

holiday ['hɔlɪdeɪ] (Brit) N [C/U] 假期 jiàqī [个 gè] ▶ **public holiday** 公共假期 gōnggòng jiàqī ▶ **the school/summer/Christmas holidays** (Brit: Scol) 学校/暑/圣诞假期 xuéxiào/shǔ/Shèngdàn jiàqī ▶ **to be on holiday** 在度假 zài dùjià

Holland ['hɔlənd] N 荷兰 Hélán

hollow ['hɔləu] ADJ (not solid) 空的 kōng de

holy ['həulɪ] ADJ 神圣的 shénshèng de

home [həum] I N 1 [C/U] (house) 家 jiā [个 gè] 2 [C/U] (country, area) 家乡 jiāxiāng [个 gè] 3 [C] (institution) 收容院 shōuróngyuàn [个 gè] II ADV (be, go, get etc) 在家 zàijiā ▶ **at home** (in house) 在家 zàijiā

homeless ['həumlɪs] I ADJ 无家可归的 wújiā kěguī de II NPL ▶ **the homeless** 无家可归的人 wújiā kěguī de rén

homepage ['həumpeɪdʒ] N [C] 主页 zhǔyè [个 gè]

homesick ['həumsɪk] ADJ 想家的 xiǎngjiā de

homework ['həumwəːk] N [U] 家庭作业 jiātíng zuòyè

homosexual [hɔmə'sɛksjuəl] I ADJ 同性恋的 tóngxìngliàn de II N [C] 同性恋者 tóngxìngliànzhě [个 gè]

honest ['ɔnɪst] ADJ 诚实的 chéngshí de ▶ **to be honest,...** 说实话，… shuō shíhuà, ...

honesty ['ɔnɪstɪ] N [U] 诚实 chéngshí

honey ['hʌnɪ] N [U] 蜂蜜 fēngmì

honeymoon ['hʌnɪmuːn] N [C] 蜜月 mìyuè [个 gè]

Hong Kong ['hɔŋ'kɔŋ] N 香港 Xiānggǎng

hood [hud] N [C] 1 兜帽 dōumào [个 gè] 2 (US) (Aut) 发动机罩 fādòngjī zhào [个 gè]

hoof [huːf] (pl hooves) N 蹄 tí

hook [huk] N [C] 钩 gōu [个 gè] ▶ **to take the phone off the hook** 不把电话听筒挂上 bùbǎ diànhuà tīngtǒng guàshàng

hooray [huː'reɪ] INT 好哇 hǎo wa

Hoover® ['huːvər] (Brit) I N [C] 吸尘器 xīchénqì [台 tái] II VT [+ carpet] 用吸尘器吸 yòng xīchénqì xī

hooves [huːvz] NPL of **hoof**

hop [hɔp] VI 单脚跳 dānjiǎo tiào

hope [həup] I VT 希望 xīwàng II VI 盼望 pànwàng III N [U] 希望 xīwàng ▶ **I hope so/not** 希望是这样/希望不会 xīwàng shì zhèyàng/xīwàng bùhuì ▶ **to hope that...** 希望… xīwàng... ▶ **to hope to do**

sth 希望能做某事 xīwàng néng zuò mǒushì

hopefully ['həupfulɪ] ADV
▶hopefully,... 如果运气好… rúguǒ yùnqì hǎo...

hopeless ['həuplɪs] ADJ
1 [+ situation, position] 糟糕的 zāogāo de 2 (inf: useless) 无能的 wúnéng de

horizon [hə'raɪzn] N ▶the horizon 地平线 dìpíngxiàn

horizontal [hɔrɪ'zɔntl] ADJ 水平的 shuǐpíng de

horn [hɔːn] N 1 [c] [of animal] 角 jiǎo [个 gè] 2 [c] (Aut) 喇叭 lǎba [个 gè]

horoscope ['hɔrəskəup] N [c] 占星术 zhānxīngshù [种 zhǒng]

horrible ['hɔrɪbl] ADJ [+ colour, food, mess] 糟透的 zāotòu de; [+ accident, crime] 可怕的 kěpà de; [+ experience, moment, situation, dream] 令人恐惧的 lìng rén kǒngjù de

horror film N [c] 恐怖片 kǒngbù piān [部 bù]

horse [hɔːs] N [c] 马 mǎ [匹 pǐ]

horse racing N [U] 赛马 sàimǎ

hose [həuz] N [c] (also: hosepipe) 输水软管 shūshuǐ ruǎnguǎn [根 gēn]

hospital ['hɔspɪtl] N [c/U] 医院 yīyuàn [家 jiā] ▶to be in hospital or (US) in the hospital 住院 zhùyuàn

hospitality [hɔspɪ'tælɪtɪ] N [U] 好客 hàokè

host [həust] N [c] 主人 zhǔrén [位 wèi]

hostage ['hɔstɪdʒ] N [c] 人质 rénzhì [个 gè] ▶to be taken/held hostage 被绑架/扣押做人质 bèi bǎngjià/kòuyā zuò rénzhì

hostel ['hɔstl] (esp Brit) N [c] 招待所 zhāodàisuǒ [个 gè]

hostess ['həustɪs] N [c] 女主人 nǚ zhǔrén [位 wèi]

hot [hɔt] ADJ 1 [+ object] 烫的 tàng de; [+ weather, person] 热的 rè de 2 (spicy) 辣的 là de

hotel [həu'tɛl] N [c] 旅馆 lǚguǎn [个 gè] ▶to stay at a hotel 住旅馆 zhù lǚguǎn

hour ['auər] I N [c] 小时 xiǎoshí [个 gè] II hours NPL (ages) 很长时间 hěncháng shíjiān ▶the buses leave on the hour 每小时正点有一班公共汽车 měi xiǎoshí zhèngdiǎn yǒu yībān gōnggòng qìchē ▶for three/four hours 三/四个小时 sān/sìgè xiǎoshí ▶(at) 60 kilometres/miles an or per hour 每小时60公里/英里 měi xiǎoshí liùshí gōnglǐ/yīnglǐ ▶to pay sb by the hour 按小时付费给某人 àn xiǎoshí fùfèi gěi mǒurén ▶lunch hour 午餐时间 wǔcān shíjiān

house [haus] N [c] 家 jiā [个 gè] ▶at/to my house 在/到我家 zài/dào wǒjiā

housewife ['hauswaɪf] (pl housewives) N [c] 家庭主妇 jiātíng zhǔfù [个 gè]

housework ['hauswəːk] N [U] 家务劳动 jiāwù láodòng

housing estate (Brit) N [c] 住宅区 zhùzhái qū [个 gè]

hovercraft ['hɔvəkrɑːft] (pl **hovercraft**) N [c] 气垫船 qìdiàn chuán [艘 sōu]

🔵 KEYWORD

how [hau] I ADV 1 (in questions) 怎样 zěnyàng ▶**how did you do it?** 你是怎么做的？nǐ shì zěnme zuòde? ▶**how are you?** 你好吗？nǐ hǎo ma? ▶**how long have you lived here?** 你在这儿住了多久了？nǐ zài zhèr zhùle duōjiǔ le? ▶**how much milk/many people?** 有多少奶/人？yǒu duōshǎo nǎi/rén? ▶**how old are you?** 你多大了？nǐ duōdà le? ▶**how tall is he?** 他有多高？tā yǒu duō gāo? 2 (in suggestions) ▶**how about a cup of tea/a walk** etc? 来杯茶/去散步 {等} 好吗？lái bēi chá/qù sànbù {děng} hǎo ma? II CONJ 怎么 zěnme ▶**I know how you did it** 我知道你怎么做的 wǒ zhīdào nǐ zěnme zuòde ▶**to know how to do sth** 知道如何做某事 zhīdào rúhé zuò mǒushì

however [hau'ɛvə^r] ADV 1 (but) 但是 dànshì 2 (with adj, adv) 不管怎样 bùguǎn zěnyàng 3 (in questions) 究竟怎样 jiūjìng zěnyàng

hug [hʌg] I VT [+ person] 拥抱 yōngbào II N [c] 拥抱 yōngbào [个 gè] ▶**to give sb a hug** 拥抱某人 yōngbào mǒurén

huge [hjuːdʒ] ADJ 巨大的 jùdà de; [+ amount, profit, debt] 巨额的 jù'é de; [+ task] 庞大的 pángdà de

human ['hjuːmən] I ADJ 人的 rén de II N [c] (also: **human being**) 人 rén [个 gè] ▶**the human race** 人类 rénlèi ▶**human nature** 人性 rénxìng

humor ['hjuːmə^r] (US) N = **humour**

humour, (US) **humor** ['hjuːmə^r] N [U] 幽默 yōumò ▶**sense of humour** 幽默感 yōumògǎn

hundred ['hʌndrəd] I NUM 百 bǎi II **hundreds** NPL 几百 jǐbǎi ▶**a** or **one hundred books/people/dollars** 一百本书/个人/美元 yībǎiběn shū/gè rén/měiyuán

hung [hʌŋ] PT, PP of **hang**

Hungary ['hʌŋgərɪ] N 匈牙利 Xiōngyálì

hungry ['hʌŋgrɪ] ADJ 饥饿的 jī'è de ▶**to be hungry** 饿了 èle

hunt [hʌnt] I VI (for food, sport) 打猎 dǎliè II N [c] 1 (for food, sport) 狩猎 shòuliè [次 cì] 2 (for missing person) 搜寻 sōuxún [次 cì] 3 (for criminal) 追捕 zhuībǔ [次 cì]

hunting ['hʌntɪŋ] N [U] (for food, sport) 打猎 dǎliè ▶**job/house/bargain hunting** 到处找工作/住房/便宜货 dàochù zhǎo gōngzuò/zhùfáng/piányi huò

hurricane ['hʌrɪkən] N [c] 飓风 jùfēng [场 chǎng] ▶**hurricane Charley/Tessa** 查理/特萨号台风 Chálǐ/Tèsàhào táifēng

hurry ['hʌrɪ] I VI 赶紧 gǎnjǐn II N ▶**to be in a hurry (to do sth)** 急于（做某事）jí yú (zuò mǒushì) ▶**to do sth in a hurry** 匆忙地做某事 cōngmángde zuò mǒushì

▶**hurry up** VI 赶快 gǎnkuài

hurt [həːt] (pt, pp **hurt**) I VT
1 (cause pain to) 弄痛 nòngtòng
2 (injure) 使受伤 shǐ shòushāng
3 (emotionally) 使伤心 shǐ
shāngxīn II VI (be painful) 痛
tòng III ADJ 1 (injured) 受伤的
shòushāng de 2 (emotionally) 受
委屈的 shòu wěiqū de ▶**to hurt
o.s.** 伤了自己 shāngle zìjǐ ▶**I
didn't want to hurt your feelings**
我并不想伤害你的感情 wǒ bìng
bùxiǎng shānghài nǐ de gǎnqíng
▶**where does it hurt?** 哪儿疼?
nǎr téng?

husband ['hʌzbənd] N [c] 丈夫
zhàngfu [个 gè]

hut [hʌt] N [c] (shed) 木棚 mùpéng
[个 gè]

hyphen ['haɪfn] N [c] 连字符
liánzìfú [个 gè]

I [aɪ] PRON 我 wǒ

ice [aɪs] N [U] 冰 bīng; (for drink)
冰块 bīngkuài

iceberg ['aɪsbəːg] N [c] 冰山
bīngshān [座 zuò] ▶**the tip of the
iceberg** (fig) 冰山一角 bīngshān
yījiǎo

ice cream N [c/U] 冰淇淋
bīngqílín [个 gè]

ice cube N [c] 冰块 bīngkuài
[块 kuài]

ice hockey (esp Brit) N [U] 冰球
bīngqiú

Iceland ['aɪslənd] N 冰岛 Bīngdǎo

ice rink N [c] 溜冰场 liūbīngchǎng
[个 gè]

ice-skating ['aɪsskeɪtɪŋ] N [U] 溜
冰 liūbīng

icing (Culin) N [U] 糖霜

tángshuāng

icon ['aɪkɔn] N [c] (*Comput*) 图符 túfú [个 gè]

ICT (*Brit*) N ABBR (= **information and communication technology**) 通信技术 tōngxìn jìshù

ID N ABBR (= **identification**) 身份证明 shēnfèn zhèngmíng ▸ **do you have any ID?** 你有证件吗？nǐ yǒu zhèngjiàn ma?

I'd [aɪd] = **I would, I had**

idea [aɪ'dɪə] N **1** [c] (*scheme*) 主意 zhǔyì [个 gè] **2** [c] (*opinion, theory*) 看法 kànfǎ [种 zhǒng] **3** [c/U] (*notion*) 概念 gàiniàn [个 gè] ▸ **(what a) good idea!** (真是个) 好主意！(zhēnshì gè)hǎo zhǔyì! ▸ **I haven't the slightest** *or* **faintest idea** 我根本就不知道 wǒ gēnběn jiù bù zhīdào

ideal [aɪ'dɪəl] ADJ 理想的 lǐxiǎng de

identical [aɪ'dɛntɪkl] ADJ 完全相同的 wánquán xiāngtóng de ▸ **identical to** 和…完全相同 hé…wánquán xiāngtóng

identification [aɪdɛntɪfɪ'keɪʃən] N [U] (*proof of identity*) 身份证明 shēnfèn zhèngmíng

identify [aɪ'dɛntɪfaɪ] VT (*recognize*) 识别 shíbié

identity card N [c] 身份证 shēnfènzhèng [个 gè]

idiot ['ɪdɪət] N [c] 傻子 shǎzi [个 gè]

i.e. ABBR (= **id est**) 也就是 yě jiùshì

KEYWORD

if [ɪf] CONJ **1** (*conditional use*) 如果

rúguǒ ▸ **I'll go if you come with me** 如果你和我一起去的话我就去 rúguǒ nǐ hé wǒ yīqǐde huà wǒ jiù qù ▸ **if I were you** 如果我是你的话 rúguǒ wǒ shì nǐ de huà ▸ **if necessary** 如有必要 rúyǒu bìyào ▸ **if so** 如果是这样的话 rúguǒ shì zhèyàng de huà ▸ **if not** 如果不行的话 rúguǒ bùxíng de huà **2** (*whenever*) 无论何时 wúlùn héshí ▸ **if we are in Hong Kong, we always go to see her** 我们无论何时去香港，都会去看她 wǒmen wúlùn héshí qù xiānggǎng, dōuhuì qù kàntā **3** (*whether*) 是否 shìfǒu ▸ **ask him if he can come** 问他是否能来 wèn tā shìfǒu nénglái **4** (*in expressions*) ▸ **if only we had more time!** 要是我们再多点时间就好了！yàoshi wǒmen zài duōdiǎn shíjiān jiù hǎo le!

ignore [ɪg'nɔːr] VT [+ *person*] 不理 bù lǐ; [+ *advice, event*] 不顾 bù gù

I'll [aɪl] = **I will, I shall**

ill [ɪl] **I** ADJ 有病的 yǒubìng de **II the ill** NPL ▸ **the mentally/terminally ill** 精神/晚期病人 jīngshén/wǎnqī bìngrén ▸ **to fall** *or* **be taken ill** 生病 shēngbìng

单词 **ill** 和 **sick** 在语意上很相近，但使用方法略有不同。**ill** 通常不用在名词前，但可用在动词词组中，比如 **fall ill** 和 **be taken ill**。*He fell ill shortly before Christmas...One of the jury members was taken* ill. **sick** 经常用在名词前。...sick children... 在英式英语中，**ill** 比 **sick** 更为文雅和委婉。**sick** 常常指实际的身体病痛，例如晕船或呕吐。I spent the next 24 hours in bed, groaning and being sick. 美式英语中，**sick** 经常用在英国人说 **ill** 的地方。Some people get hurt in accidents or get sick.

illegal [ɪˈliːgl] ADJ 非法的 fēifǎde

illness [ˈɪlnɪs] N [C/U] 病 bìng [场 chǎng]

illusion [ɪˈluːʒən] N [C] 幻想 huànxiǎng [个 gè]

illustration [ɪləˈstreɪʃən] N [C] 插图 chātú [幅 fú]

imagination [ɪmædʒɪˈneɪʃən] N 1 [C/U] 想象力 xiǎngxiànglì [种 zhǒng] 2 [C] (mind's eye) 想象 xiǎngxiàng [个 gè]

imagine [ɪˈmædʒɪn] VT 1 (envisage) 想象 xiǎngxiàng 2 (suppose) 设想 shèxiǎng

imitate [ˈɪmɪteɪt] VT 1 (copy) 效仿 xiàofǎng 2 [+ person, sound, gesture] 模仿 mófǎng

imitation [ɪmɪˈteɪʃən] I N [C] 仿制品 fǎngzhìpǐn [件 jiàn] II ADJ 仿制的 fǎngzhì de

immediate [ɪˈmiːdɪət] ADJ 立即的 lìjí de

immediately [ɪˈmiːdɪətlɪ] I ADV (at once) 立即地 lìjí de II CONJ ▶ immediately he had said it, he regretted it 他刚一说完马上就后悔了 tā gāng yī shuōwán mǎshàng jiù hòuhuǐle

▶ **immediately before/after** 紧接着…之前/后 jǐnjiēzhe...zhīqián/hòu

immigrant [ˈɪmɪgrənt] N [C] 移民 yímín [个 gè]

immigration [ɪmɪˈgreɪʃən] I N [U] 1 (process) 移民 yímín 2 (also: **immigration control**) 移民局检查 yímínjú jiǎnchá II CPD [+ authorities, policy, controls, officer] 移民 yímín

impatient [ɪmˈpeɪʃənt] ADJ 急躁的 jízào de ▶ **to get impatient (at or with sb)** (对某事) 不耐烦 (duì mǒushì) bù nàifán

import [ɪmˈpɔːt] VT 进口 jìnkǒu

importance [ɪmˈpɔːtns] N [U] 1 (significance) 重要性 zhòngyàoxìng 2 (influence) 影响 yǐngxiǎng

important [ɪmˈpɔːtənt] ADJ 1 重要的 zhòngyào de 2 (influential) 有影响的 yǒu yǐngxiǎng de ▶ **it is important to eat sensibly** 合理进食是很重要的 hélǐ jìnshí shì hěn zhòngyào de ▶ **it's not important** 不重要的 bù zhòngyào de

impossible [ɪmˈpɒsɪbl] ADJ 不可能的 bù kěnéng de ▶ **it is impossible to understand what's going on** 不可能了解事情的进展情况 bù kěnéng liǎojiě shìqíng de jìnzhǎn qíngkuàng

impress [ɪmˈpres] VT [+ person] 给…极深的印象 gěi...jíshēn de yìnxiàng ▶ **to be impressed by or with sb/sth** 对某人/某物印象深刻 duì mǒurén/mǒuwù yìnxiàng shēnkè

impression [ɪmˈprɛʃən] N [c] 印象 yìnxiàng [个 gè] ▸**to make** or **create a good/bad impression** 留下好/不良印象 liúxià hǎo/bùliáng yìnxiàng

impressive [ɪmˈprɛsɪv] ADJ 给人深刻印象的 gěi rén shēnkè yìnxiàng de

improve [ɪmˈpruːv] I VT 改进 gǎijìn II VI [weather, situation] 改善 gǎishàn; [pupil, performance] 进步 jìnbù

improvement [ɪmˈpruːvmənt] N [c/u] 改进 gǎijìn [个 gè] ▸**improvement in** [+ person, thing] 进步 jìnbù

🔵 KEYWORD

in [ɪn] I PREP 1 在…里 zài…lǐ ▸**it's in the house/garden/box** 它在房子/花园/盒子里 tā zài fángzi/huāyuán/hézi lǐ ▸**put it in the house/garden/box** 把它放在房子/花园/盒子里 bǎ tā fàngzài fángzi/huāyuán/hézi lǐ ▸**in here/there** 在这儿/那儿 zài zhè'r/nà'r

2 (with place names) 在 zài ▸**in London/England** 在伦敦/英格兰 zài lúndūn/yīnggélán

3 (time: during) 在 zài; (within: referring to future) 在…之后 zài…zhīhòu; (referring to past) 在…之内 zài…zhīnèi ▸**in 1988/May** 在1988年/5月 zài yī jiǔ bā bā nián/wǔyuè ▸**in the morning/afternoon** 在上午/下午 zài shàngwǔ/xiàwǔ ▸**I'll see you in two weeks' time** or **in two weeks** 我两周后见你 wǒ liǎngzhōu hòu jiàn nǐ ▸**I did it in 3 hours/days** 我花了3小时/天完成 wǒ huāle sān xiǎoshí/tiān wánchéng

4 (indicating manner, style etc) 以 yǐ ▸**in pencil/ink** 用铅笔/墨水笔 yòng qiānbǐ/mòshuǐbǐ ▸**the boy in the blue shirt** 穿蓝衬衫的男孩儿 chuān lán chènshān de nánhái'r ▸**in the sun/rain** 在阳光下/雨中 zài yángguāng xià/yǔzhōng

5 (with languages) 用 yòng ▸**in English/French** 用英语/法语 yòng yīngyǔ/fǎyǔ

6 (with ratios, numbers) 每 měi ▸**one in ten people** 十分之一的人 shí fēn zhī yī de rén

7 (amongst) [+ group, collection] 在…中 zài…zhōng ▸**the best athlete in the team** 该队中最好的运动员 gāiduì zhōng zuìhǎo de yùndòngyuán

II ADV ▸**to be in** (at home, work) 在 zài ▸**to ask sb in** 把某人请到家中 bǎ mǒurén qǐngdào jiāzhōng

inch [ɪntʃ] N [c] 英寸 yīngcùn

include [ɪnˈkluːd] VT 包括 bāokuò

including [ɪnˈkluːdɪŋ] PREP 包括 bāokuò ▸**nine people were injured, including two Britons** 九个人受了伤，包括两个英国人 jiǔgè rén shòule shāng, bāokuò liǎnggè Yīngguórén

income [ˈɪnkʌm] N [c/u] 收入 shōurù [笔 bǐ]

income tax N [u] 所得税 suǒdéshuì

inconvenient [ɪnkən'viːnjənt]
ADJ [+ time, moment] 不合时宜的
bùhé shíyí de

incorrect [ɪnkə'rɛkt] ADJ 错误的
cuòwù de

increase [n 'ɪnkriːs, vb ɪn'kriːs]
I N [c] 增长 zēngzhǎng [成 chéng]
II VI 增长 zēngzhǎng **III** VT
[+ price, number, level] 提高 tígāo
▶**a 5% increase, an increase of
5%** 百分之五的增长 bǎi fēn zhī
wǔ de zēngzhǎng

incredible [ɪn'krɛdɪbl] ADJ
(amazing, wonderful) 不可思议的
bùkě sīyì de

indeed [ɪn'diːd] ADV (as a reply) 是
的 shì de ▶**yes indeed!** 的确如
此! díquè rúcǐ!

independence [ɪndɪ'pɛndns] N
[U] 独立 dúlì

independent [ɪndɪ'pɛndnt] ADJ
独立的 dúlì de

index ['ɪndɛks] (pl **indexes**) N [c]
索引 suǒyǐn [条 tiáo]

India ['ɪndɪə] N 印度 Yìndù

Indian ['ɪndɪən] **I** ADJ 印度的
Yìndù de **II** N [c] (person from India)
印度人 Yìndùrén [个 gè]

indicate ['ɪndɪkeɪt] VT **1** 表
明 biǎomíng **2** (point to) 指向
zhǐxiàng

indifferent [ɪn'dɪfrənt] ADJ **1** 没
兴趣的 méi xìngqù de **2** (mediocre)
平庸的 píngyōng de

indigestion [ɪndɪ'dʒɛstʃən] N [U]
消化不良 xiāohuà bù liáng

individual [ɪndɪ'vɪdjuəl] **I** N 个
人 gèrén **II** ADJ (personal) 个人的
gèrén de

indoor ['ɪndɔːʳ] ADJ 室内的
shìnèi de

indoors [ɪn'dɔːz] ADV 在室内
zài shì nèi

industrial [ɪn'dʌstrɪəl] ADJ 工业
的 gōngyè de; [+ accident] 因工的
yīngōng de

industrial estate (Brit) N [c] 工
业区 gōngyè qū [个 gè]

industrial park (US) N [c] 工业区
gōngyè qū [个 gè]

industry ['ɪndəstrɪ] N **1** [U]
(manufacturing) 工业 gōngyè **2** [c]
(business) 行业 hángyè [种 zhǒng]

inevitable [ɪn'ɛvɪtəbl] ADJ 不可
避免的 bùkě bìmiǎn de

infection [ɪn'fɛkʃən] N [c] 感
染 gǎnrǎn [处 chù] ▶**to have an
ear/throat infection** 耳朵/咽喉
感染 ěrduo/yānhóu gǎnrǎn

infectious [ɪn'fɛkʃəs] ADJ 传染的
chuánrǎn de

inflation [ɪn'fleɪʃən] N [U] 通货膨
胀 tōnghuò péngzhàng

influence ['ɪnfluəns] **I** N **1** [c/U]
(power) 权势 quánshì [种 zhǒng]
2 [c] (effect) 影响 yǐngxiǎng [个
gè] **II** VT 影响 yǐngxiǎng

inform [ɪn'fɔːm] VT 告诉 gàosù
▶**to inform sb that...** 告诉某人…
gàosù mǒurén…

informal [ɪn'fɔːml] ADJ
1 (relaxed) 不拘礼节的 bùjū
lǐjié de **2** [+ clothes, party] 日
常的 rìcháng de **3** [+ meeting,
discussions, agreement] 非正式的
fēizhèngshì de

information [ɪnfə'meɪʃən]
N [U] 信息 xìnxī ▶**a piece of**

information 一条信息 yītiáo xìnxi

information technology N [U] 信息技术 xìnxī jìshù

ingredient [ɪnˈgriːdɪənt] N [c] 配料 pèiliào [种 zhǒng]

inhabitant [ɪnˈhæbɪtnt] N [c] 居民 jūmín [个 gè]

inherit [ɪnˈhɛrɪt] VT 继承 jìchéng

initial [ɪˈnɪʃl] I N [c] (letter) 首字母 shǒuzìmǔ [个 gè] II **initials** NPL (of name) 首字母 shǒuzìmǔ

injection [ɪnˈdʒɛkʃən] N [c] 注射 zhùshè ▶**to give sb an injection** 给某人注射 gěi mǒurén zhùshè

injure [ˈɪndʒəʳ] VT [+ person] 伤害 shānghài ▶**he was badly injured in the attack** 他在进攻中受了重伤 tā zài jìngōng zhōng shòule zhòngshāng

injury [ˈɪndʒərɪ] N [c/u] (wound) 伤害 shānghài [个 gè] ▶**to escape without injury** 安然脱险 ānrán tuōxiǎn

ink [ɪŋk] N [c/u] 墨水 mòshuǐ [瓶 píng]

in-laws [ˈɪnlɔːz] NPL 姻亲 yīnqīn

innocent [ˈɪnəsnt] ADJ 清白的 qīngbái de

insect [ˈɪnsɛkt] N [c] 昆虫 kūnchóng [只 zhī]

insect repellent N [c/u] 杀虫剂 shāchóngjì [瓶 píng]

inside [ɪnˈsaɪd] I N 内部 nèibù II ADJ [+ wall, surface] 内部的 nèibù de III ADV 1 (go) 里面 lǐmiàn; (be) 在里面 zài lǐmiàn 2 (indoors) 在屋内 zài wū nèi IV PREP [+ place, container] 在…的里面 zài…de lǐmiàn

insist [ɪnˈsɪst] VI, VT 坚持 jiānchí ▶**to insist on sth/doing sth** 坚持要求某事/做某事 jiānchí yāoqiú mǒushì/zuò mǒushì

inspector [ɪnˈspɛktəʳ] N [c] 1 (official) 检查员 jiǎncháyuán [位 wèi] 2 (Brit) (also: **ticket inspector**) 查票员 chápiàoyuán [位 wèi]

install, instal [ɪnˈstɔːl] VT 安装 ānzhuāng

instalment, (US) **installment** [ɪnˈstɔːlmənt] N [c] 分期付款 fēnqī fùkuǎn [期 qī]

instance [ˈɪnstəns] N [c] (example) 例子 lìzi [个 gè] ▶**for instance** 例如 lìrú

instant [ˈɪnstənt] I N [c] (moment) 瞬息 shùnxī [个 gè] II ADJ 1 [+ reaction, success] 立即的 lìjí de 2 [+ coffee, soup, noodles] 速食的 sùshí de ▶**for an instant** 一瞬间 yī shùnjiān

instantly [ˈɪnstəntlɪ] ADV 立即 lìjí

instead [ɪnˈstɛd] ADV 代替 dàitì ▶**instead of** 而不是 ér bùshì

instinct [ˈɪnstɪŋkt] N [c/u] 本能 běnnéng [种 zhǒng]

instruct [ɪnˈstrʌkt] VT ▶**to instruct sb to do sth** 命令某人做某事 mìnglìng mǒurén zuò mǒushì

instruction [ɪnˈstrʌkʃən] I CPD [+ manual, leaflet] 说明 shuōmíng II **instructions** NPL 说明 shuōmíng

instructor [ɪnˈstrʌktəʳ] N [c] 教员 jiàoyuán [位 wèi]

instrument [ˈɪnstrumənt] N [c]

1 器械 qìxiè [件 jiàn] **2** (Mus) 乐器 yuèqì [件 jiàn]

insulin ['ɪnsjulɪn] N [U] 胰岛素 yídǎosù

insult [n 'ɪnsʌlt, vb ɪn'sʌlt] **I** N [C] 侮辱 wǔrǔ [个 gè] **II** VT 侮辱 wǔrǔ

insurance [ɪn'ʃuərəns] N [U] 保险 bǎoxiǎn ▶fire/life/health insurance 火/人寿/健康险 huǒ/rénshòu/jiànkāng xiǎn

insure [ɪn'ʃuəʳ] VT [+ house, car] 给…保险 gěi…bǎoxiǎn

intelligent [ɪn'tɛlɪdʒənt] ADJ 聪明的 cōngmíng de

intend [ɪn'tɛnd] VT ▶to intend to do sth 打算做某事 dǎsuàn zuò mǒushì

intense [ɪn'tɛns] ADJ [+ heat, pain] 剧烈的 jùliè de; [+ competition] 激烈的 jīliè de

intensive care N ▶to be in intensive care 接受重病特别护理 jiēshòu zhòngbìng tèbié hùlǐ

intention [ɪn'tɛnʃən] N [C/U] 打算 dǎsuàn [个 gè]

interest ['ɪntrɪst] N **1** [U/s] (in subject, idea, person) 兴趣 xìngqù **2** [c] (pastime, hobby) 爱好 àihào [个 gè] **3** [U] (on loan, savings) 利息 lìxī ▶to take an interest in sth/sb 对某事/某人感兴趣 duì mǒushì/mǒurén gǎn xìngqù

interested ['ɪntrɪstɪd] ADJ ▶to be interested (in sth/doing sth) 对（某事/做某事）有兴趣 duì (mǒushì/zuò mǒushì) yǒu xìngqù

请勿将 **interested** 和 **interesting** 混淆。如果你 **interested in** 某事，

说明你对它很感兴趣，很想了解或知道更多关于它的事情，或者想花更多的时间来做这件事。Not all of the children were interested in animals…She asked him how he became interested in politics. 如果你发现某事 **interesting**，表示它令人感兴趣，引人注意，使你乐于更多地了解这件事或者去做这件事。It must be an awfully interesting job…The interesting thing is that this is exactly the answer we got before.

interesting ['ɪntrɪstɪŋ] ADJ 有趣的 yǒuqù de

interfere [ɪntə'fɪəʳ] VI (meddle) 干涉 gānshè ▶to interfere with sth [+ plans, career, duty] 妨碍某事 fáng'ài mǒushì

interior [ɪn'tɪərɪəʳ] N [C] 内部 nèibù

intermission [ɪntə'mɪʃən] N [C] (Cine) 休息时间 xiūxi shíjiān [段 duàn]

international [ɪntə'næʃənl] ADJ 国际的 guójì de

Internet ['ɪntənɛt] N ▶the Internet 因特网 yīntèwǎng

Internet café N [C] 网吧 wǎngbā [个 gè]

interpret [ɪn'təːprɪt] VI 口译 kǒuyì

interpreter [ɪn'təːprɪtəʳ] N [C] 口译者 kǒuyìzhě [位 wèi]

interrupt [ɪntə'rʌpt] **I** VT **1** 打断 dǎduàn **2** [+ activity] 中断 zhōngduàn **II** VI (in conversation)

打岔 dǎchà

interruption [ɪntə'rʌpʃən] N [c/u] 打扰 dǎrǎo [种 zhǒng]

interval ['ɪntəvl] N [c] **1** (break, pause) 间隔 jiàngé [个 gè] **2** (Brit) (Theat, Mus, Sport) 幕间休息 mùjiān xiūxi [个 gè]

interview ['ɪntəvju:] **I** N [c/u] **1** (for job) 面试 miànshì [次 cì] **2** (Publishing, Rad, TV) 采访 cǎifǎng [次 cì] **II** vт **1** (for job) 面试 miànshì **2** (Publishing, Rad, TV) 采访 cǎifǎng ▶**to go for/have an interview** 参加面试 cānjiā miànshì

interviewer ['ɪntəvjuəʳ] N [c] 采访者 cǎifǎngzhě [位 wèi]

intimidate [ɪn'tɪmɪdeɪt] vт 恐吓 kǒnghè

into ['ɪntu] PREP 到…里面 dào…lǐmiàn ▶**come into the house/garden** 走进房子/花园里 zǒujìn fángzi/huāyuán lǐ ▶**get into the car** 进入车子 jìnrù chēzi ▶**let's go into town** 我们进城吧 wǒmen jìnchéng ba ▶**to translate Chinese into French** 把汉语翻译成法语 bǎ Hànyǔ fānyì chéng Fǎyǔ ▶**research into cancer** 对癌症的深入研究 duì áizhèng de shēnrù yánjiū ▶**I'd like to change some dollars into euros** 我想把一些美元换成欧元 wǒ xiǎng bǎ yīxiē měiyuán huànchéng ōuyuán

introduce [ɪntrə'dju:s] vт **1** (+ new idea, measure, technology) 引进 yǐnjìn **2** ▶**to introduce sb (to sb)** 给某人介绍（某人）gěi

mǒurén jièshào (mǒurén) ▶**may I introduce you (to...)?** 让我介绍你（认识…）好吗？ ràng wǒ jièshào nǐ (rènshi...) hǎo ma?

introduction [ɪntrə'dʌkʃən] N **1** [u] (of new idea, measure, technology) 引进 yǐnjìn **2** [c] (of person) 介绍 jièshào [个 gè] **3** [c] 引言 yǐnyán [个 gè]

invade [ɪn'veɪd] vт 侵略 qīnlüè

invalid ['ɪnvəlɪd] N [c] 病弱者 bìngruòzhě [个 gè]

invent [ɪn'vɛnt] vт 发明 fāmíng

invention [ɪn'vɛnʃən] N [c] 发明 fāmíng [项 xiàng]

investigate [ɪn'vɛstɪgeɪt] vт 调查 diàochá

investigation [ɪnvɛstɪ'geɪʃən] N [c/u] 调查 diàochá [项 xiàng]

invisible [ɪn'vɪzɪbl] ADJ 看不见的 kànbùjiàn de

invitation [ɪnvɪ'teɪʃən] N **1** [c] 邀请 yāoqǐng [个 gè] **2** [c] (card) 请束 qǐngjiǎn [封 fēng]

invite [ɪn'vaɪt] vт 邀请 yāoqǐng ▶**to invite sb to do sth** 邀请某人做某事 yāoqǐng mǒurén zuò mǒushì ▶**to invite sb to dinner** 请某人赴宴 qǐng mǒurén fùyàn

involve [ɪn'vɒlv] vт **1** (entail) 包含 bāohán **2** (concern, affect) 使卷入 shǐ juǎnrù ▶**to involve sb (in sth)** 使某人参与（某事）shǐ mǒurén cānyù (mǒushì)

iPod® ['aɪpɒd] N 数码随身听 shùmǎ suíshēntīng [个 gè]

Iran [ɪ'rɑ:n] N 伊朗 Yīlǎng

Iraq [ɪ'rɑ:k] N 伊拉克 Yīlākè

Iraqi [ɪ'rɑ:kɪ] **I** ADJ 伊拉克的

Yīlākè de II N [c] (*person*) 伊拉克
人 Yīlākèrén [名 míng]

Ireland ['aɪələnd] N 爱尔兰
Ài'ěrlán ▸**the Republic of Ireland**
爱尔兰共和国 Ài'ěrlán Gònghéguó

Irish ['aɪrɪʃ] I ADJ 爱尔兰的 Ài'ěrlán
de II N [U] (*language*) 爱尔兰语
Ài'ěrlányǔ III **the Irish** NPL 爱尔兰
人 Ài'ěrlánrén

Irishman ['aɪrɪʃmən] (*pl*
Irishmen) N [c] 爱尔兰男人
Ài'ěrlán nánrén [个 gè]

Irishwoman ['aɪrɪʃwumən] (*pl*
Irishwomen) N [c] 爱尔兰女人
Ài'ěrlán nǔrén [个 gè]

iron ['aɪən] I N 1 [U] (*metal*) 铁 tiě
2 [c] (*for clothes*) 熨斗 yùndǒu [个
gè] II ADJ [+ *bar, railings*] 铁的 tiě
de III VT [+ *clothes*] 熨 yùn

irresponsible [ɪrɪ'spɔnsɪbl] ADJ
[+ *person, driver*] 无责任感的 wú
zérèngǎn de; [+ *attitude, behaviour*]
不负责任的 bù fù zérèn de

irritating ['ɪrɪteɪtɪŋ] ADJ 烦人的
fánrén de

is [ɪz] VB *of* **be**

Islam ['ɪzlɑːm] N [U] 伊斯兰教
Yīsīlánjiào

Islamic [ɪz'læmɪk] ADJ [+ *law,
faith*] 伊斯兰教的 Yīsīlánjiào de;
[+ *country*] 伊斯兰的 Yīsīlán de

island ['aɪlənd] N [c] 岛 dǎo
[个 gè]

isolated ['aɪsəleɪtɪd] ADJ 1 [+ *place*]
孤零零的 gūlínglíng de 2 [+ *person*]
孤立的 gūlì de 3 [+ *incident, case,
example*] 个别的 gèbié de

Israel ['ɪzreɪl] N 以色列 Yǐsèliè

Israeli [ɪz'reɪlɪ] I ADJ 以色列的

Yǐsèliè de II N [c] (*person*) 以色列
人 Yǐsèlièrén [名 míng]

issue ['ɪʃuː] N [c] (*problem, subject*)
问题 wèntí [个 gè]

IT N ABBR (= **Information
Technology**) 信息技术 xìnxī jìshù

it [ɪt] PRON 1 (*object or animal*) 它
tā; (*referring to baby*) 他/她 tā/tā
2 (*weather, date, time*) ▸**it's raining**
正在下雨。zhèngzài xiàyǔ
3 (*impersonal*) ▸**it doesn't matter**
没关系。méiguānxi。▸**I can't
find it** 我找不到。wǒ zhǎo bù
dào ▸**what is it?** (*thing*) 是什么东
西? shì shénme dōngxi?; (*what's
the matter?*) 怎么了? zěnme le?
▸**"who is it?" — "it's me"** "是
谁?" "是我。" "shì shuí?"
"shìwǒ."

Italian [ɪ'tæljən] I ADJ 意大利
的 Yìdàlì de II N 1 [c] (*person*) 意
大利人 Yìdàlìrén [名 míng] 2 [U]
(*language*) 意大利语 Yìdàlìyǔ

Italy ['ɪtəlɪ] N 意大利 Yìdàlì

itch [ɪtʃ] VI 发痒 fāyǎng

itchy ['ɪtʃɪ] ADJ 发痒的 fāyǎng de

it'd ['ɪtd] = **it would, it had**

item ['aɪtəm] N [c] 项目 xiàngmù
[个 gè]; (*on bill*) 项 xiàng ▸**items
of clothing** 几件衣服 jǐjiàn yīfu

it'll ['ɪtl] = **it will**

its [ɪts] ADJ 1 (*of animal*) 它的 tā de
2 (*of baby*) 他/她的 tā/tā de

it's [ɪts] = **it is, it has**

itself [ɪt'sɛlf] PRON 1 (*reflexive*)
它自己 tāzìjǐ 2 (*emphatic*) 本身
běnshēn ▸**it switches itself on
automatically** 它自动接通。tā
zìdòng jiētōng ▸**I think life itself**

is a learning process 我认为生活本身是个学习的过程。 wǒ rènwéi shēnghuó běnshēn shì gè xuéxí de guòchéng. ▶by itself (*alone*) 单独地 dāndú de

I've [aɪv] = **I have**

jack [dʒæk] N [c] (*Aut*) 千斤顶 qiānjīndǐng [个 gè]

jacket ['dʒækɪt] N [c] 夹克 jiākè [件 jiàn]

jail [dʒeɪl] I N [c/u] 监狱 jiānyù [个 gè] II VT 监禁 jiānjìn

jam [dʒæm] N [c/u] (*Brit: preserve*) 果酱 guǒjiàng [瓶 píng]

janitor ['dʒænɪtər] N [c] 看门人 kānménrén [个 gè]

January ['dʒænjuərɪ] N [c/u] 一月 yīyuè; *see also* **July**

Japan [dʒə'pæn] N 日本 Rìběn

Japanese [dʒæpə'niːz] (*pl* **Japanese**) I ADJ 日本的 Rìběn de II N **1** [c] (*person*) 日本人 Rìběnrén [个 gè] **2** [u] (*language*) 日语 Rìyǔ

jar [dʒɑːr] N [c] 广口瓶 guǎngkǒupíng [个 gè]

jaw [dʒɔ:] (*Anat*) **I** N [c] 颌 hé [个 gè] **II jaws** NPL 嘴巴 zuǐba

jazz [dʒæz] N [U] (*Mus*) 爵士乐 juéshìyuè

jealous ['dʒeləs] ADJ **1** [+ *husband, wife*] 爱妒忌的 ài dùjì de **2** (*envious*) 妒忌的 dùjì de

jeans [dʒi:nz] NPL 牛仔裤 niúzǎikù ▶**a pair of jeans** 一条牛仔裤 yītiáo niúzǎikù

jelly ['dʒelɪ] N [c/U] (*US*) 果酱 guǒjiàng [瓶 píng]

jersey ['dʒə:zɪ] N [c] 针织毛衫 zhēnzhī máoshān [件 jiàn]

Jesus ['dʒi:zəs] N (*Rel*) 耶稣 Yēsū ▶**Jesus Christ** 耶稣基督 Yēsū Jīdū

jet [dʒet] N [c] (*aeroplane*) 喷气式飞机 pēnqìshì fēijī [架 jià]

jet lag N [U] 时差反应 shíchā fǎnyìng

Jew [dʒu:] N [c] 犹太人 Yóutàirén [个 gè]

jewel ['dʒu:əl] N [c] 宝石 bǎoshí [块 kuài]

jewellery, (*US*) **jewelry** ['dʒu:əlɪɪ] N [U] 首饰 shǒushì

Jewish ['dʒu:ɪʃ] ADJ 犹太的 Yóutài de

jigsaw ['dʒɪgsɔ:] N [c] (*also*: **jigsaw puzzle**) 拼图玩具 pīntú wánjù [套 tào]

job [dʒɔb] N [c] **1** (*position*) 工作 gōngzuò [份 fèn] **2** (*task*) 任务 rènwù [项 xiàng] ▶**Gladys got a job as a secretary** 格拉迪斯找到了一份秘书工作。 Gélādísī zhǎodào le yīfèn mìshū gōngzuò. ▶**a part-time/full-time job** 半职/全职工作 bànzhí/quánzhí gōngzuò

jockey ['dʒɔkɪ] N [c] (*Sport*) 赛马骑师 sàimǎ qíshī [位 wèi]

jog [dʒɔg] VI 慢跑 mànpǎo

jogging ['dʒɔgɪŋ] N [U] 慢跑 mànpǎo

join [dʒɔɪn] VT **1** [+ *club, party, army, navy, queue*] 加入 jiārù **2** [+ *person*] 会面 huìmiàn ▶**will you join us for dinner?** 你想不想和我们一起吃晚饭？ nǐ xiǎngbùxiǎng hé wǒmen yīqǐ chīwǎnfàn? ▶**join in** VI 参与 cānyù

joint [dʒɔɪnt] N [c] 关节 guānjié [个 gè]; (*Brit: Culin: of beef, lamb*) 大块肉 dàkuàiròu [块 kuài]

joke [dʒəuk] **I** N [c] 笑话 xiàohua [个 gè] **II** VI 开玩笑 kāi wánxiào ▶**you're joking** *or* **you must be joking!** (*inf*) 你在开玩笑{或}你一定在开玩笑吧！ nǐ zài kāi wánxiào {huò} nǐ yīdìng zài kāi wánxiào ba!

Jordan ['dʒɔ:dən] N 约旦 Yuēdàn

journalist ['dʒə:nəlɪst] N [c] 新闻工作者 xīnwén gōngzuòzhě [位 wèi]

journey ['dʒə:nɪ] N [c] 旅程 lǚchéng [段 duàn] ▶**a 5-hour journey** 5个小时的路程 wǔgè xiǎoshí de lùchéng ▶**to go on a journey** 去旅行 qù lǚxíng

请勿将 **journey, voyage** 和 **trip** 混淆。**journey** 是指从一地搭乘车船或飞机到另一地的过程。...a *journey of over 2000 miles*... 如果你 **journey to** 某地，你就是去那里。这是

书面的用法。*The nights became colder as they journeyed north.* **voyage** 是指从一地到另一地的长途行程，通常指乘船旅行或者太空旅行。*...the voyage to the moon in 1972...* **trip** 是指从一地到另一地的旅行过程，在目的地做短暂的停留后返回。*...a business trip to Milan...*

joy [dʒɔɪ] N [U] 快乐 kuàilè

judge [dʒʌdʒ] I N [c] 1 (*Law*) 法官 fǎguān [位 wèi] 2 (*in competition*) 裁判 cáipàn [个 gè] II VT [+ *exhibits, competition*] 评定 píngdìng

judo [ˈdʒuːdəu] N [U] 柔道 róudào

jug [dʒʌg] N [c] 壶 hú [把 bǎ]

juice [dʒuːs] N [c/U] 汁 zhī [杯 bēi]

July [dʒuːˈlaɪ] N [c/U] 七月 qīyuè
▶ **the first of July** 七月一日 qīyuè yīrì ▶ **at the beginning/end of July** 在七月初/末 zài qīyuè chū/mò ▶ **each** or **every July** 每年七月 měinián qīyuè

jump [dʒʌmp] I VI 跳 tiào II N [c] 跳 tiào ▶ **to jump over sth** 跳过某物 tiào guò mǒuwù ▶ **to jump out of a window** 从窗户跳下 cóng chuānghu tiàoxià ▶ **to jump on/off sth** 跳上/下某物 tiàoshàng/xià mǒuwù ▶ **to jump the queue** 加塞儿 jiāsāi'r

jumper [ˈdʒʌmpəʳ] N [c] (*Brit*) 毛衣 máoyī [件 jiàn]

junction [ˈdʒʌŋkʃən] (*Brit*) N [c] 交叉点 jiāochādiǎn [个 gè]

June [dʒuːn] N [c/U] 六月 liùyuè;

see also **July**

jungle [ˈdʒʌŋgl] N [c/U] 丛林 cónglín [片 piàn]

junior [ˈdʒuːnɪəʳ] ADJ 级别低的 jíbié dī de ▶ **George Bush Junior** (*US*) 小乔治•布什 xiǎo Qiáozhì•Bùshí

junior high, (*US*) **junior high school** N [c/U] 初中 chūzhōng [所 suǒ]

junior school (*Brit*) N [c/U] 小学 xiǎoxué [所 suǒ]

junk [dʒʌŋk] N [U] (*inf: rubbish*) 废旧杂物 fèijiù záwù

jury [ˈdʒuərɪ] N [c] 1 (*Law*) 陪审团 péishěntuán [个 gè] 2 (*in competition*) 评审团 píngshěn tuán [个 gè]

just [dʒʌst] I ADJ (*frm*) [+ *decision, punishment, reward*] 公平的 gōngpíng de; [+ *society, cause*] 公正的 gōngzhèng de II ADV 1 (*exactly*) 正好 zhènghǎo 2 (*merely*) 仅仅 jǐnjǐn 3 (*for emphasis*) 简直 jiǎnzhí 4 (*in instructions, requests*) 只是 zhǐshì ▶ **it's just right** 正合适 zhèng héshì ▶ **I'm just finishing this** 我马上就做完了 wǒ mǎshàng jiù zuòwán le ▶ **we were just going** 我们正要走 wǒmen zhèngyào zǒu ▶ **to have just done sth** 刚刚做完某事 gānggāng zuòwán mǒushì ▶ **just now** (*a moment ago*) 刚才 gāngcái; (*at the present time*) 现在 xiànzài ▶ **just about everything/everyone** 差不多所有东西/所有人 chàbùduō suǒyǒu dōngxi/suǒyǒu rén ▶ **just**

before/after... 就在…以前/以后 jiùzài…yǐqián/yǐhòu ▸**just enough time/money** 时间/钱正好够 shíjiān/qián zhènghǎo gòu ▸**just a minute, just one moment** (*asking someone to wait*) 等一下 děng yīxià; (*interrupting*) 慢着 mànzhe

justice ['dʒʌstɪs] N **1** [U] (*Law: system*) 司法 sīfǎ **2** [U] (*fairness*) 正义 zhèngyì

K

K ABBR **1** (*inf*) (= **thousands**) 千 qiān **2** (*Comput*) (= **kilobytes**) 千字节 qiānzìjié

kangaroo [kæŋgə'ruː] N [C] 袋鼠 dàishǔ [只 zhī]

karaoke [kɑːrə'əʊkɪ] N [U] 卡拉 OK kǎlā ōukèi

karate [kə'rɑːtɪ] N [U] 空手道 kōngshǒudào

keen [kiːn] ADJ 热衷的 rèzhōng de ▸**to be keen to do sth** 渴望做某事 kěwàng zuò mǒushì ▸**to be keen on sth** 热衷于某事 rèzhōng yú mǒushì

keep [kiːp] (*pt, pp* **kept**) VT **1** [+ *receipt, money, job*] 保留 bǎoliú **2** (*store*) 保存 bǎocún **3** (*detain*) 留liú ▸**to keep doing sth** (*repeatedly*) 总是做某事 zǒngshì zuò mǒushì;

(*continuously*) 不停做某事 bùtíng zuò mǒushì ▶**to keep sb waiting** 让某人等着 ràng mǒurén děngzhe ▶**to keep the room tidy** 保持房间整洁 bǎochí fángjiān zhěngjié ▶**to keep a promise** 履行诺言 lǚxíng nuòyán ▶**can you keep a secret?** 你能保守秘密吗? nǐ néng bǎoshǒu mìmì ma? ▶**to keep a record (of sth)** 记录(某事) jìlù (mǒushì) ▶**how are you keeping?** (*inf*) 你还好吗? nǐ hái hǎo ma?

▶ **keep away** VI ▶**to keep away (from sth)** 不接近(某处) bù jiējìn (mǒuchù)

▶ **keep off** VT FUS ▶**keep off the grass!** 请勿进入草坪! qǐng wù jìnrù cǎopíng!

▶ **keep on** VI ▶**to keep on doing sth** 继续做某事 jìxù zuò mǒushì

▶ **keep up** VI ▶**to keep up** 跟上 gēnshang ▶**to keep up with sb** (*walking, moving*) 跟上某人 gēnshàng mǒurén; (*in work*) 跟上某人 gēnshàng mǒurén

keep-fit [kiːpˈfɪt] CPD [+ *class, session, course*] 健身 jiànshēn

kept [kɛpt] PT, PP *of* **keep**

kerb, (*US*) **curb** [kəːb] N [c] 路缘 lùyuán [个 gè]

ketchup [ˈkɛtʃəp] N [U] 番茄酱 fānqiéjiàng

kettle [ˈkɛtl] N [c] 水壶 shuǐhú [把 bǎ]

key [kiː] N [c] **1** (*for lock, mechanism*) 钥匙 yàoshi [把 bǎ] **2** [*of computer, typewriter, piano*] 键 jiàn [个 gè]

keyboard [ˈkiːbɔːd] N [c] 键盘 jiànpán [个 gè]

keyhole [ˈkiːhəul] N [c] 钥匙孔 yàoshikǒng [个 gè]

kick [kɪk] **I** VT [+ *person, ball*] 踢 tī **II** N [c] 踢 tī [顿 dùn]

▶ **kick off** VI 开赛 kāisài

kick-off [ˈkɪkɔf] N [s] 开场时间 kāichǎng shíjiān

kid [kɪd] N [c] (*inf: child*) 小孩 xiǎohái [个 gè]; (*teenager*) 年轻人 niánqīngrén [个 gè] ▶**you're kidding!** 你一定是在开玩笑吧! nǐ yīdìng shì zài kāi wánxiào ba!

kidnap [ˈkɪdnæp] VT 绑架 bǎngjià

kidney [ˈkɪdnɪ] N **1** [c] (*Anat*) 肾脏 shènzàng [个 gè] **2** [c/U] (*Culin*) 腰子 yāozi [个 gè]

kill [kɪl] VT **1** [+ *person, animal, plant*] 致死 zhìsǐ **2** (*murder*) 谋杀 móushā ▶**my back's killing me** (*inf*) 我的背疼死了 wǒde bèi téngsǐ le

killer [ˈkɪlər] N [c] 凶手 xiōngshǒu [个 gè]

kilo [ˈkiːləu] N [c] 公斤 gōngjīn

kilometre, (*US*) **kilometer** [ˈkɪləmiːtər] N [c] 公里 gōnglǐ

kind [kaɪnd] **I** ADJ 友好的 yǒuhǎo de **II** N [c] (*type, sort*) 种类 zhǒnglèi [个 gè] ▶**an opportunity to meet all kinds of people** 与各种各样的人见面的机会 yǔ gèzhǒng gèyàng de rén jiànmiàn de jīhuì ▶**it was kind of them to help** 他们来帮忙真是太好了 tāmen lái bāngmáng zhēnshì tàihǎo le

kindness [ˈkaɪndnɪs] N [U] 仁慈 réncí

king [kɪŋ] N [c] 国王 guówáng [位 wèi]

kingdom ['kɪŋdəm] N [c] 王国 wángguó [个 gè]

kiss [kɪs] I N [c] 吻 wěn [个 gè] II VT 吻 wěn ▶**to give sb a kiss** 吻某人一下 wěn mǒurén yīxià
▶**to kiss sb goodbye/goodnight** 与某人吻别/吻某人一下，道晚安 yǔ mǒurén wěnbié/wěn mǒurén yīxià, dào wǎn'ān

kit [kɪt] N [u] (esp Brit: equipment) 成套用品 chéngtào yòngpǐn; (clothing) 服装 fúzhuāng

kitchen ['kɪtʃɪn] N [c] 厨房 chúfáng [个 gè]

kite [kaɪt] N [c] 风筝 fēngzhēng [个 gè]

kitten ['kɪtn] N [c] 小猫 xiǎomāo [只 zhī]

knee [niː] N [c] 膝盖 xīgài [个 gè]

kneel [niːl] (pt, pp **knelt**) VI (also: **kneel down**) 跪下 guìxià

knew [njuː] PT of **know**

knickers ['nɪkəz] (Brit) NPL 女式内裤 nǚshì nèikù ▶**a pair of knickers** 一条女式内裤 yītiáo nǚshì nèikù

knife [naɪf] (pl **knives**) N [c] 刀 dāo [把 bǎ] ▶**knife and fork** 刀叉 dāochā

knit [nɪt] VI 织 zhī

knives [naɪvz] NPL of **knife**

knob [nɔb] N [c] 球形把手 qiúxíng bǎshǒu [个 gè]

knock [nɔk] I VT (strike) 碰撞 pèngzhuàng II VI (on door, window) 敲 qiāo III N [c] 1 (blow, bump) 碰撞 pèngzhuàng [下 xià] 2 (on door)

敲门声 qiāoménshēng [声 shēng]
▶**to knock sb unconscious** [blow, blast] 把某人打昏 bǎ mǒurén dǎyūn

▶ **knock down** VT 1 (run over) 撞倒 zhuàngdǎo 2 (demolish) 拆除 chāichú

▶ **knock out** VT 1 (make unconscious) 打昏 dǎhūn 2 (Boxing) 击昏 jīhūn 3 (eliminate: in game, competition) 淘汰 táotài

▶ **knock over** VT 撞倒 zhuàngdǎo

knot [nɔt] N [c] 结 jié [个 gè] ▶**to tie a knot** 打个结 dǎ gè jié

know [nəu] (pt **knew**, pp **known**) VT 1 [+ facts, dates] 知道 zhīdào 2 [+ language] 懂 dǒng 3 [+ person, place, subject] 认识 rènshi ▶**to know that...** 知道… zhīdào…
▶**to know where/when** 知道何处/何时… zhīdào héchù/héshí…
▶**to get to know sb** 逐渐开始了解某人 zhújiàn kāishǐ liǎojiě mǒurén ▶**to know about sth** 听说过某事 tīngshuō guò mǒushì
▶**yes, I know** 对，的确如此 duì, díquè rúcǐ ▶**you never know** 很难讲 hěn nánjiǎng ▶**you know** (used for emphasis) 你得知道 nǐ děi zhīdào

knowledge ['nɔlɪdʒ] N [u] 知识 zhīshi ▶**to (the best of) my knowledge** 据我所知 jù wǒ suǒzhī

known [nəun] PP of **know**

Koran [kɔ'rɑːn] N ▶**the Koran** 《古兰经》 Gǔlánjīng

Korea [kə'rɪə] N see **North Korea**,

South Korea

Korean [kə'rɪən] **I** ADJ 朝鲜的 Cháoxiǎn de **II** N **1** (person) 朝鲜人 Cháoxiǎnrén **2** (language) 朝鲜语 Cháoxiǎnyǔ

label ['leɪbl] **I** N [c] 标签 biāoqiān [个 gè] **II** VT 用标签标明 yòng biāoqiān biāomíng

labor ['leɪbəʳ] (US) N = **labour**

laboratory [lə'bɔrətərɪ] N [c] 研 究室 yánjiūshì [个 gè]

labor union (US) N [c] 工会 gōnghuì [个 gè]

labour, (US) **labor** ['leɪbəʳ] N [U] **1** (manpower) 劳动力 láodònglì **2** ▶ **Labour** (Labour Party) 工党 Gōngdǎng ▶ **to be in labour** (Med) 处于阵痛期 chǔyú zhèntòng qī

lace [leɪs] N **1** [U] (fabric) 花边 huābiān **2** [c] [of shoe] 系带 jìdài [根 gēn]

lack [læk] **I** N [s/U] 缺乏 quēfá **II** VT [+ means, skills, experience, confidence] 缺乏 quēfá

ladder ['lædə^r] N [c] 梯子 tīzi [个 gè]

lady ['leɪdɪ] N [c] 女士 nǚshì [位 wèi] ▸**ladies and gentlemen...** 女士们，先生们… nǚshìmen, xiānshēngmen... ▸**the ladies' (Brit), the ladies' room (US)** 女厕所 nǚ cèsuǒ

lager ['lɑːgə^r] (Brit) N [c/u] 淡啤酒 dànpíjiǔ [瓶 píng]

laid [leɪd] PT, PP of **lay**

lain [leɪn] PP of **lie**

lake [leɪk] N [c] 湖 hú [个 gè]

lamb [læm] N 1 [c] (animal) 羔羊 gāoyáng [只 zhī] 2 [u] (meat) 羔羊肉 gāoyángròu

lamp [læmp] N [c] 灯 dēng [盏 zhǎn]

lamp-post ['læmppəust] (Brit) N [c] 路灯柱 lùdēngzhù [个 gè]

lampshade ['læmpʃeɪd] N [c] 灯罩 dēngzhào [个 gè]

land [lænd] N 1 [u] (area of open ground) 土地 tǔdì 2 [u] (not sea) 陆地 lùdì II vi 1 (Aviat, Space) 降落 jiàngluò 2 (from ship) 登陆 dēnglù

landing ['lændɪŋ] N [c/u] (Aviat) 降落 jiàngluò [次 cì]

landlady ['lændleɪdɪ] N [c] 女房东 nǚfángdōng [位 wèi]

landlord ['lændlɔːd] N [c] 男房东 nánfángdōng [位 wèi]

landscape ['lændskeɪp] N [c/u] 风景 fēngjǐng [道 dào]

lane [leɪn] N [c] 1 (in country) 小路 xiǎolù [条 tiáo] 2 (Aut: of road) 车道 chēdào [条 tiáo]

language ['læŋgwɪdʒ] N 1 [c] (English, Russian etc) 语言 yǔyán [种 zhǒng] 2 [u] (speech) 语言表达能力 yǔyán biǎodá nénglì

language laboratory N [c] 语言实验室 yǔyán shíyànshì [个 gè]

lap [læp] N [c] 1 (of person) 大腿的上方 dàtuǐ de shàngfāng 2 (in race) 圈 quān

laptop ['læptɔp] N [c] (also: **laptop computer**) 笔记本电脑 bǐjìběn diànnǎo [个 gè]

large [lɑːdʒ] ADJ [+ house, person] 大的 dà de; [+ number, amount] 大量的 dàliàng de

laser ['leɪzə^r] N 1 [c/u] (beam) 激光 jīguāng [束 shù] 2 [c] (machine) 激光器 jīguāngqì [台 tái]

last [lɑːst] I ADJ 1 (most recent) 最近的 zuìjìn de; [+ Monday, July, weekend etc] 上 shàng 2 (final) 最后的 zuìhòu de; (of series, row) 最后的 zuìhòu de II PRON (final one) 最后一个 zuìhòu yī gè III ADV 1 (most recently) 最近 zuìjìn 2 (at the end) 最后 zuìhòu 3 (in final position) 最后 zuìhòu IV vi (continue) 持续 chíxù ▸**last week** 上个星期 shàng gè xīngqī ▸**last night** (yesterday evening) 昨晚 zuówǎn; (during the night) 昨天夜里 zuótiān yèli ▸**the last time** (the previous time) 上一次 shàng yīcì ▸**at (long) last** (finally) 终于 zhōngyú ▸**our house is the last but one** 我们的房子是倒数第二个 wǒmen de fángzi shì dàoshǔ dì'èrgè ▸**it lasts (for) 2 hours** 持续了两个小时 chíxù le liǎnggè xiǎoshí

lastly ['lɑːstlɪ] ADV 最后 zuìhòu

late [leɪt] I ADJ **1** (*not on time*) 迟的 chí de **2** (*after the usual time*) 稍晚的 shāowǎn de II ADV **1** (*not on time*) 迟 chí **2** (*after the usual time*) 晚 wǎn ▶**we're late** 我们迟到了 wǒmen chídào le ▶**sorry I'm late** 对不起，我迟到了 duìbuqǐ, wǒ chídào le ▶**to be 10 minutes late** 迟到10分钟 chídào shí fēnzhōng ▶**in late May** 5月下旬 wǔyuè xiàxún

lately [ˈleɪtlɪ] ADV 最近 zuìjìn

later [ˈleɪtəʳ] ADV 以后 yǐhòu ▶**some time/weeks/years later** 一些时候/几个星期/几年以后 yīxiē shíhou/jǐgè xīngqī/jǐnián yǐhòu ▶**later on** 以后 yǐhòu

latest [ˈleɪtɪst] ADJ **1** [+ *book, film, news*] 最新的 zuìxīn de **2** (*most up-to-date*) 最新式的 zuì xīnshì de ▶**at the latest** 最迟 zuìchí

Latin [ˈlætɪn] N [U] 拉丁语 Lādīngyǔ

Latin America N 拉丁美洲 Lādīngměizhōu

Latin American I ADJ 拉丁美洲的 Lādīngměizhōu de II N [c] (*person*) 拉丁美洲人 Lādīngměizhōurén [个 gè]

latter [ˈlætəʳ] N ▶**the latter** 后者 hòuzhě

laugh [lɑːf] I N [c] 笑 xiào [阵 zhèn] II VI 笑 xiào ▶**laugh at** VT FUS 对…发笑 duì…fāxiào

launch [lɔːntʃ] VT **1** [+ *rocket, missile, satellite*] 发射 fāshè **2** [+ *product, publication*] 推出 tuīchū

laundry [ˈlɔːndrɪ] N [U] (*dirty washing*) 待洗的衣物 dàixǐ de yīwù; (*clean washing*) 洗好的衣物 xǐhǎo de yīwù

laundry detergent (US) N [U/c] 洗衣粉 xǐyīfěn

lavatory [ˈlævətərɪ] (Brit) N [c] 卫生间 wèishēngjiān [个 gè]

law [lɔː] N **1** [s/u] (*legal system*) 法律 fǎlù **2** [c] (*regulation*) 法规 fǎguī [条 tiáo] ▶**against the law** 违法 wéifǎ ▶**to break the law** 违法 wéifǎ ▶**by law** 依照法律 yīzhào fǎlù ▶**to study law** 学习法律 xuéxí fǎlù

lawn [lɔːn] N [c] 草坪 cǎopíng [片 piàn]

lawnmower [ˈlɔːnməuəʳ] N [c] 割草机 gēcǎojī [部 bù]

lawyer [ˈlɔːjəʳ] N [c] 律师 lùshī [位 wèi]

lay [leɪ] (pt, pp laid) I PT of **lie** II VT (*put*) 放 fàng ▶**to lay the table** 摆放餐具 bǎifàng cānjù ▶**lay down** VT (*put down*) 放下 fàngxià ▶**lay off** VT 解雇 jiěgù

layer [ˈleɪəʳ] N [c] 层 céng

layout [ˈleɪaut] N [c] 布局 bùjú [个 gè]

lazy [ˈleɪzɪ] ADJ 懒惰的 lǎnduò de

lead[1] [liːd] (pt, pp led) I N **1** [c] (*esp Brit: for dog*) 皮带 pídài [条 tiáo] **2** [c] (*Elec*) 导线 dǎoxiàn [根 gēn] II VT **1** (*guide*) 带领 dàilǐng **2** [+ *group, party, organization*] 领导 lǐngdǎo; [+ *march, demonstration, parade*] 带领 dàilǐng III VI (*in race, competition*) 领先 lǐngxiān ▶**to**

be in the lead 领先 lǐngxiān ▸**to lead the way** (*lit*) 引路 yǐnlù; (*fig*) 率先 shuàixiān

▸**lead away** VT [+ *prisoner*] 带走 dàizǒu

▸**lead to** VT FUS (*result in*) 导致 dǎozhì

lead² [lɛd] N [U] 铅 qiān

leader ['li:dəʳ] N [c] 领导人 lǐngdǎorén [位 wèi]

leaf [li:f] (*pl* **leaves**) N [c] 叶 yè [片 piàn]

leaflet ['li:flɪt] N [c] (*booklet*) 小册子 xiǎocèzi [本 běn]; (*single sheet*) 传单 chuándān [份 fèn]

league [li:g] N [c] (*Sport*) 联赛 liánsài [季 jì]

leak [li:k] I N [c] [*of liquid, gas*] 裂隙 lièxì [条 tiáo] II VI [*shoes, pipe, liquid, gas*] 漏 lòu

lean [li:n] (*pt, pp* **leaned** *or* **leant**) I VT ▸**to lean sth on/against sth** 把某物靠在某物上 bǎ mǒuwù kàozài mǒuwù shang II ADJ [+ *meat*] 瘦的 shòu de ▸**to lean against sth** [*person*] 靠在某物上 kàozài mǒuwù shàng ▸**to lean forward/back** 向前/后倾 xiàngqián/hòu qīng

▸**lean on** VT FUS 倚 yǐ

leap year N [c] 闰年 rùnnián [个 gè]

learn [lə:n] (*pt, pp* **learned** *or* **learnt**) I VT (*study*) [+ *skill*] 学 xué; [+ *poem, song*] 背 bèi II VI 学 xué ▸**to learn about sth** (*study*) 学到某物 xuédào mǒuwù ▸**to learn to do sth/how to do sth** 学做某事/怎样做某事 xuézuò mǒushì/

zěnyàng zuò mǒushì

learnt [lə:nt] PT, PP *of* **learn**

least [li:st] I ADJ (*noun*) 胝的 zuìshǎo de II ADV 1 (*adjective*) ▸**the least expensive/ attractive/interesting** 最便宜/没有魅力/没趣的 zuì piányi/méiyǒu mèilì/méi qù de 2 (*verb*) 最不 zuìbù III PRON ▸**the least** 胝 zuìshǎo ▸**at least** (*in expressions of quantity, comparisons*) 至少 zhìshǎo

leather ['lɛðəʳ] I N [U] 皮革 pígé II CPD [+ *jacket, shoes, chair*] 皮 pí

leave [li:v] (*pt, pp* **left**) I VT 1 [+ *place*] 离开 líkāi 2 [+ *school, job, group*] 放弃 fàngqì 3 (*leave behind: deliberately*) 留下 liúxià; (*accidentally*) 落 luò 4 [+ *message*] 留 liú II VI 1 (*depart*) [*person*] 离开 líkāi; [*bus, train*] 出发 chūfā 2 (*give up school*) 辍学 chuòxué; (*give up job*) 辞职 cízhí III N [U] 休假 xiūjià; (*Mil*) 假期 jiàqī ▸**to leave sth to sb** 把某物留给某人 bǎ mǒuwù liúgěi mǒurén ▸**to leave sb/sth alone** 不理会某人/某物 bù lǐhuì mǒurén/mǒuwù ▸**to leave for** [+ *destination*] 前往 qiánwǎng

▸**leave behind** VT (*forget*) 忘带 wàngdài

▸**leave on** VT [+ *light, heating*] 开着 kāizhe

▸**leave out** VT 删掉 shāndiào

leaves [li:vz] NPL *of* **leaf**

Lebanon, the Lebanon ['lɛbənən] N 黎巴嫩 Líbānèn

lecture ['lɛktʃəʳ] N [c] (*talk*) 讲

座 jiǎngzuò [个 gè] ▶to give a lecture (on sth) 作(某方面的)讲座 zuò (mǒu fāngmiàn de) jiǎngzuò

lecturer ['lɛktʃərə^r] N [c] 讲师 jiǎngshī [位 wèi]

led [lɛd] PT, PP of **lead**¹

left¹ [lɛft] I ADJ (not right) 左的 zuǒ de II N ▶the left 左侧 zuǒcè III ADV (turn, go, look) 向左 xiàngzuǒ ▶on the left 在左边 zài zuǒbiān ▶to the left 靠左边 kào zuǒbiān

left² [lɛft] I PT, PP of **leave** II ADJ ▶to be left over 剩下 shèngxià

left-hand ['lɛfthænd] ADJ [+ side, corner] 左侧的 zuǒcè de

left-handed [lɛft'hændɪd] ADJ 左撇子的 zuǒpiězi de

left-luggage [lɛft'lʌgɪdʒ] (Brit) N [U] ▶left-luggage locker 行李寄存柜 xíngli jìcún guì

leg [lɛg] N 1 [c] 腿 tuǐ [条 tiáo] 2 [c/u] 腿 tuǐ [根 gēn]

legal ['li:gl] ADJ 1 [+ system, requirement] 法律的 fǎlǜ de 2 [+ action, situation] 合法的 héfǎ de

legal holiday (US) N [c] 法定假期 fǎdìng jiàqī [个 gè]

leisure ['lɛʒə^r], US 'li:ʒə^r] N [U] 闲暇 xiánxiá

leisure centre (Brit) N [c] 娱乐中心 yúlè zhōngxīn [个 gè]

lemon ['lɛmən] N [c] 柠檬 níngméng [个 gè]

lemonade [lɛmə'neɪd] N [U] 柠檬汽水 níngméng qìshuǐ

lend [lɛnd] (pt, pp **lent**) VT 1 ▶to

lend sth to sb 把某物借给某人 bǎ mǒuwù jiègěi mǒurén 2 [bank] 贷 dài

length [lɛŋθ] N 1 [c/u] 长度 chángdù [个 gè]; [of sentence, article] 篇幅 piānfu [个 gè] 2 [c/u] (duration) 期间 qījiān [个 gè]

lens [lɛnz] N [c] [of spectacles] 镜片 jìngpiàn [片 piàn]; [of telescope, camera] 镜头 jìngtóu [个 gè]

Lent [lɛnt] N [U] 大斋节 Dàzhāijié

lent [lɛnt] PT, PP of **lend**

lentil ['lɛntɪl] N [c] 小扁豆 xiǎobiǎndòu [颗 kē]

Leo ['li:əu] N [U] (sign) 狮子座 Shīzi Zuò

leopard ['lɛpəd] N [c] 豹 bào [只 zhī]

lesbian ['lɛzbɪən] I ADJ 女同性恋的 nǚ tóngxìngliàn de II N [c] 女同性恋者 nǚ tóngxìngliànzhě [个 gè]

less [lɛs] I ADJ (noun) 更少的 gèng shǎo de II ADV 1 (adjective/adverb) 较少地 jiàoshǎo de 2 (verb) 较少 jiàoshǎo III PRON 较少的东西 jiàoshǎo de dōngxi IV PREP ▶less tax/10% discount 去掉税/10%的折扣 qùdiào shuì/bǎifēnzhīshí de zhékòu ▶less than half 不到一半 bùdào yībàn

lesson ['lɛsn] N [c] 课 kè [堂 táng]

let [lɛt] (pt, pp **let**) VT 1 ▶to let sb do sth (give permission) 允许某人做某事 yǔnxǔ mǒurén zuò mǒushì 2 ▶to let sth happen 让某事发生 ràng mǒushì fāshēng ▶to let sb know that... 告诉某人… gàosu mǒurén... 3 ▶to let sb in/out 让某人进去/出去 ràng mǒurén jìnqù/

chūqù ▶**let's go/eat** 我们走/吃吧 wǒmen zǒu/chība ▶**"to let"** "现房待租" "xiànfáng dàizhū"
▶**to let go** *(release one's grip)* 松开 sōngkāi ▶**to let sb/sth go** *(release)* 放走某人/某物 fàngzǒu mǒurén/mǒuwù
▶**let down** VT [+ *person*] 令…失望 lìng…shīwàng
▶**let in** VT 1 [+ *water, air*] 允许进来 yǔnxǔ jìnlái 2 [+ *person*] 给…开门 gěi…kāimén

letter ['lɛtər] N [c] 1 *(note)* 信 xìn [封 fēng] 2 *(of alphabet)* 字母 zìmǔ [个 gè]

letterbox ['lɛtəbɔks] *(Brit)* N [c] 信箱 xìnxiāng [个 gè]

lettuce ['lɛtɪs] N [c/u] 生菜 shēngcài [棵 kē]

level ['lɛvl] I ADJ 平的 píng de II N [c] 1 *(standard)* 水平 shuǐpíng [种 zhǒng] 2 *(height)* 水位 shuǐwèi [个 gè]

level crossing *(Brit)* N [c] 平交道口 píngjiāodàokǒu [个 gè]

lever ['li:və'], US 'lɛvə'] N [c] 杆 gǎn [根 gēn]

liar ['laɪə'] N [c] 说谎者 shuōhuǎngzhě [个 gè]

liberal ['lɪbərl] I ADJ [+ *person, attitude*] 开明的 kāimíng de II N [c] *(Pol)* ▶**Liberal** 自由党党员 Zìyóudǎng dǎngyuán [名 míng]

Libra ['li:brə] N [u] *(sign)* 天秤座 Tiānchèng Zuò

librarian [laɪ'brɛərɪən] N [c] 图书管理员 túshū guǎnlǐyuán [位 wèi]

library ['laɪbrərɪ] N [c] 图书馆 túshūguǎn [个 gè]

licence, *(US)* **license** ['laɪsns] N 1 [c] *(permit)* 许可证 xǔkězhèng [张 zhāng] 2 [c] *(also:* **driving licence)** 驾驶执照 jiàshǐ zhízhào [本 běn]

license plate *(US)* N [c] 车牌照 chēpáizhào [个 gè]

lick [lɪk] VT 舔 tiǎn

lid [lɪd] N [c] 1 *(of box, case, pan)* 盖 gài [个 gè] 2 *(eyelid)* 眼睑 yǎnjiǎn [个 gè]

lie¹ [laɪ] *(pt* **lay**, *pp* **lain)** VI *(person)* 躺 tǎng
▶**lie about** *(Brit)* VI = **lie around**
▶**lie around** VI 乱放 luànfàng
▶**lie down** VI *(person)* 躺下 tǎngxià

lie² [laɪ] I 说谎 shuōhuǎng II N [c] 谎言 huǎngyán [个 gè] ▶**to tell lies** 说谎 shuōhuǎng

life [laɪf] *(pl* **lives)** N 1 [c/u] *(living, existence)* 生命 shēngmìng [个 gè] 2 [c] *(lifespan)* 一生 yīshēng [个 gè] ▶**his personal/working life** 他的个人/工作生活 tāde gèrén/gōngzuò shēnghuó

lifeboat ['laɪfbəut] N [c] 救生船 jiùshēngchuán [艘 sōu]

life preserver [-prɪ'zə:və'] *(US)* N [c] *(lifebelt)* 救生用具 jiùshēng yòngjù [件 jiàn]; *(life jacket)* 救生衣 jiùshēngyī [件 jiàn]

lifestyle ['laɪfstaɪl] N [c/u] 生活方式 shēnghuó fāngshì [种 zhǒng]

lift [lɪft] I VT 举起 jǔqǐ II N [c] *(Brit)* 电梯 diàntī [部 bù] ▶**to give sb a lift** *(esp Brit)* 让某人搭便车 ràng mǒurén dā biànchē
▶**lift up** VT [+ *person, thing*] 举起 jǔqǐ

light [laɪt] (pt, pp **lit**) I N 1 [U] (from sun, moon, lamp, fire) 光 guāng 2 [c] (Elec, Aut) 灯 dēng [盏 zhǎn] 3 [s] (for cigarette) 打火机 dǎhuǒjī II VT [+ candle, fire, cigarette] 点燃 diǎnrán III ADJ 1 [+ colour] 淡的 dàn de 2 (not heavy) 轻的 qīng de IV **lights** NPL (also: **traffic lights**) 交通指示灯 jiāotōng zhǐshìdēng ▶**to turn** or **switch the light on/off** 开/关灯 kāi/guān dēng

light bulb N [c] 灯泡 dēngpào [个 gè]

lighter ['laɪtər] N [c] (also: **cigarette lighter**) 打火机 dǎhuǒjī [个 gè]

lighthouse ['laɪthaʊs] N [c] 灯塔 dēngtǎ [座 zuò]

lightning ['laɪtnɪŋ] N [U] 闪电 shǎndiàn

like¹ [laɪk] PREP 1 (similar to) 像 xiàng 2 (in similes) 像…一样 xiàng…yīyàng 3 (such as) 如 rú ▶**a house like ours** 像我们这样的房子 xiàng wǒmen zhèyàng de fángzi ▶**to be like sth/sb** 像某物/某人 xiàng mǒuwù/mǒurén ▶**what's he/the weather like?** 他/天气怎么样？ tā/tiānqì zěnmeyàng? ▶**to look like** [+ person] 长得像 zhǎngde xiàng; [+ thing] 类似 lèisì ▶**what does it look/sound/taste like?** 看/听/尝起来怎么样？ kàn/tīng/chángqǐlái zěnmeyàng? ▶**like this** 像这样 xiàng zhèyàng

like² [laɪk] I VT [+ person, thing] 喜欢 xǐhuan II N ▶ **his likes and dislikes** 他的好恶 tā de hàowù

▶**to like doing sth** 喜欢做某事 xǐhuān zuò mǒushì ▶**I would** or **I'd like an ice-cream/to go for a walk** 我想吃个冰激凌/去散步。 wǒxiǎng chīge bīngjílíng/qù sànbù. ▶**would you like a coffee?** 你想不想来杯咖啡？ nǐ xiǎngbùxiǎng láibēi kāfēi? ▶**if you like** (in offers, suggestions) 如果你愿意的话 rúguǒ nǐ yuànyì de huà

likely ['laɪklɪ] ADJ 很可能的 hěn kěnéng de ▶**it is likely that...** 有可能… yǒu kěnéng… ▶**to be likely to do sth** 很有可能做某事 hěnyǒu kěnéng zuò mǒushì

lime [laɪm] N [c] (fruit) 酸橙 suānchéng [个 gè]

limit ['lɪmɪt] N [c] 1 (maximum point) 限度 xiàndù [个 gè] 2 限定 xiàndìng [种 zhǒng]

limp [lɪmp] VI 跛行 bǒxíng

line [laɪn] N [c] 1 (long thin mark) 线 xiàn [条 tiáo] 2 排 pái 3 [+ of words] 行 háng 4 (Tel) 线路 xiànlù [条 tiáo] 5 (railway track) 铁路线 tiělù xiànlù [条 tiáo] ▶**hold the line please!** (Tel) 请稍等！ qǐng shāoděng! ▶**to stand** or **wait in line** 排队等候 páiduì děnghòu ▶**on the right lines** 大体正确 dàtǐ zhèngquè

linen ['lɪnɪn] I N [U] 1 (cloth) 亚麻布 yàmábù 2 (tablecloths, sheets) 亚麻制品 yàmá zhìpǐn II CPD [+ jacket, sheets] 亚麻料 yàmáliào

lining ['laɪnɪŋ] N [c/U] 衬里 chènlǐ [个 gè]

link [lɪŋk] I N [c] 1 联系 liánxì [种 zhǒng] 2 (Comput) (also: **hyperlink**)

超链接 chāoliànjiē [个 gè] II VT
1 [+ places, objects] 连接 liánjiē
2 [+ people, situations] 联系 liánxì

lion ['laɪən] N [c] 狮子 shīzi [头 tóu]

lip [lɪp] N [c] 唇 chún [个 gè]

lip-read ['lɪpriːd] VI 唇读 chúndú

lipstick ['lɪpstɪk] N [c/u] 口红 kǒuhóng [支 zhī]

liquid ['lɪkwɪd] N [c/u] 液体 yètǐ [种 zhǒng]

liquidizer ['lɪkwɪdaɪzəʳ] N [c] 榨汁机 zhàzhījī [个 gè]

liquor ['lɪkəʳ] (US) N [u] 酒 jiǔ

list [lɪst] I N [c] 单子 dānzi [个 gè] II VT 1 (record) [+ person] 列出 lièchū 2 (Comput) 列出 lièchū

listen ['lɪsn] VI 1 听 tīng; (to speaker) 听…说 tīng…shuō 2 (follow advice) 听从 tīngcóng ▶**to listen to sb** (pay attention to) 留神听某人说话 liúshén tīng mǒurén shuōhuà; (follow advice of) 听从某人 tīngcóng mǒurén ▶**to listen to sth** 听某事 tīng mǒushì

lit [lɪt] PT, PP of **light**

liter ['liːtəʳ] (US) N = **litre**

literature ['lɪtrɪtʃəʳ] N [u] 文学 wénxué

litre, (US) **liter** ['liːtəʳ] N [c] 升 shēng

litter ['lɪtəʳ] N [u] 垃圾 lājī

litter bin (Brit) N [c] 垃圾箱 lājīxiāng [个 gè]

little ['lɪtl] I ADJ 1 (small) 小的 xiǎo de 2 (young) [+ child] 小的 xiǎo de 3 (younger) ▶**little brother/sister** 弟弟/妹妹 dìdi/mèimei 4 (quantifier) ▶**to have little**

time/money 没有多少时间/金钱 méiyǒu duōshao shíjiān/jīnqián II ADV 少 shǎo ▶**a little** (small amount) 一点 yīdiǎn; (noun) 一点 yīdiǎn; (sleep, eat) 一点 yīdiǎn ▶**a little boy of 8** 一个8岁的小男孩 yīgè bāsuì de xiǎo nánhái ▶**a little bit** (adj) 有点 yǒudiǎn ▶**little by little** 逐渐地 zhújiàn de

live¹ [lɪv] I VI 1 (reside) 住 zhù 2 (lead one's life) 生活 shēnghuó II VT 1 [+ life] 过 guò ▶**live on** VT FUS [+ money] 靠…维持生活 kào…wéichí shēnghuó ▶**live together** VI 同居 tóngjū ▶**live with** VT FUS [+ partner] 与…同居 yǔ…tóngjū

live² [laɪv] I ADJ [+ animal, plant] 活的 huó de II ADV (broadcast) 实况地 shíkuàng de

lively ['laɪvlɪ] ADJ [+ person] 活泼的 huópo de; [+ place, event, discussion] 活跃的 huóyuè de

liver ['lɪvəʳ] N 1 [c] 肝脏 gānzàng [个 gè] 2 [c/u] (Culin) 肝 gān [个 gè]

lives [laɪvz] N PL of **life**

living ['lɪvɪŋ] N [u] (life) 生活 shēnghuó ▶**for a living** 作为谋生之道 zuòwéi móushēng zhīdù ▶**to earn** or **make a/one's living** 谋生 móushēng

living room N [c] 起居室 qǐjūshì [间 jiān]

load [ləud] I N [c] (thing carried) [of vehicle] 装载量 zhuāngzàiliàng [车 chē] II VT 1 (also: **load up**) [+ vehicle, ship] 装 zhuāng 2 [+ program, data] 下载 xiàzài

▶**loads of** or **a load of money/ people** (inf) 很多钱/人 hěnduō qián/rén

loaf [ləuf] (pl **loaves**) N [c] ▶**a loaf (of bread)** 一条(面包) yītiáo (miànbāo)

loan [ləun] I N [c] 贷款 dàikuǎn [笔 bǐ] II VT ▶**to loan sth (out) to sb** [+ money, thing] 把某物借给某人 bǎ mǒuwù jiègěi mǒurén

loaves [ləuvz] NPL of **loaf**

local ['ləukl] ADJ [+ council, newspaper, library] 当地的 dāngdì de; [+ residents] 本地的 běndì de

lock [lɔk] I N [c] 锁 suǒ [把 bǎ] II VT 1 锁 suǒ 2 [+ screen] 锁 suǒ ▶**lock out** VT [+ person] (deliberately) 把…锁在外面 bǎ…suǒ zài wàimian ▶**to lock o.s. out** 把自己锁在外面 bǎ zìjǐ suǒ zài wàimian ▶**lock up** VT 锁好 suǒhǎo

locker ['lɔkər] N [c] 小柜 xiǎoguì [个 gè]

lodger ['lɔdʒər] N [c] 房客 fángkè [个 gè]

loft [lɔft] N [c] (attic) 阁楼 gélóu [座 zuò]

log [lɔg] N [c] (for fuel) 木柴 mùchái [根 gēn] ▶**log in, log on** (Comput) VI 登录 dēnglù ▶**log into** (Comput) VT FUS 登入 dēngrù ▶**log out, log off** (Comput) VI 退出系统 tuìchū xìtǒng

logical ['lɔdʒɪkl] ADJ [+ argument, analysis] 逻辑的 luójí de; [+ conclusion, result] 合逻辑的 hé luójí de; [+ course of action] 合乎情理的 héhū qínglǐ de

London ['lʌndən] N 伦敦 Lúndūn

Londoner ['lʌndənər] N [c] 伦敦人 Lúndūnrén [个 gè]

lonely ['ləunlɪ] ADJ 1 [+ person] 孤独的 gūdú de 2 [+ place] 人迹罕至的 rénjì hǎn zhì de

long [lɔŋ] I ADJ 1 [+ rope, hair, table, tunnel] 长的 cháng de 2 [+ meeting, discussion, film, time] 长的 cháng de 3 [+ book, poem] 长的 cháng de II ADV (time) 长久 chángjiǔ ▶**how long is the lesson?** 这节课多长时间? zhèjiékè duōcháng shíjiān? ▶**6 metres long** 6米长 liùmǐ cháng ▶**so** or **as long as** (provided) 只要 zhǐyào ▶**long ago** 很久以前 hěnjiǔ yǐqián ▶**it won't take long** 这不需花很多时间 zhè bù xūyào huā hěnduō shíjiān ▶**a long way** 很远 hěnyuǎn

loo [lu:] (Brit: inf) N [c] 厕所 cèsuǒ [个 gè]

look [luk] I VI 1 (glance, gaze) 看 kàn 2 (search) 找 zhǎo 3 (seem, appear) 看起来 kànqǐlái II N (expression) 表情 biǎoqíng [副 fù] ▶**to look out of the window** 望向窗外 wàngxiàng chuāngwài ▶**look out!** 当心! dāngxīn! ▶**to look like sb** 长得像某人 zhǎngde xiàng mǒurén ▶**to look like sth** 看起来像某物 kànqǐlái xiàng mǒuwù ▶**it looks as if...** 看来… kànlái… ▶**to have** or **take a look at** 看一看 kànyīkàn ▶**look after** VT FUS 照顾 zhàogù

▶**look at** VT FUS 看一看 kàn yī kàn

▶**look for** VT FUS [+ *person, thing*] 寻找 xúnzhǎo

▶**look forward to** VT FUS 盼望 pànwàng ▶**to look forward to doing sth** 盼望做某事 pànwàng zuò mǒushì ▶**we look forward to hearing from you** 我们盼望收到你的回音 wǒmen pànwàng shōudào nǐde huíyīn

▶**look into** VT FUS (*investigate*) 调查 diàochá

▶**look round, look around** I VI **1** (*turn head*) 环顾 huángù **2** (*in building*) 看看 kànkan II VT FUS [+ *place, building*] 游览 yóulǎn

▶**look through** VT FUS [+ *book, magazine, papers*] 翻阅 fānyuè

▶**look up** VT [+ *information, meaning*] 查 chá

loose [luːs] ADJ **1** [+ *screw, connection, tooth*] 松动的 sōngdòng de **2** [+ *hair*] 散开的 sǎnkāi de **3** [+ *clothes, trousers*] 宽松的 kuānsōng de

lord [lɔːd] (*Brit*) (*peer*) 贵族 guìzú [位 wèi]

lorry ['lɒrɪ] (*Brit*) N [c] 卡车 kǎchē [辆 liàng]

lorry driver (*Brit*) N [c] 卡车司机 kǎchē sījī [位 wèi]

lose [luːz] (*pt, pp* lost) I VT **1** (*mislay*) 丢失 diūshī **2** (*not win*) [+ *contest, fight, argument*] 输 shū **3** (*through death*) [+ *relative, wife etc*] 失去 shīqù II VI 输 shū ▶**to lose weight** 减重 jiǎnzhòng

loss [lɒs] N [c/u] 丧失 sàngshī

[种 zhǒng]

lost [lɒst] I PT, PP *of* **lose** II ADJ [+ *object*] 丢失的 diūshī de; [+ *person, animal*] 走失的 zǒushī de ▶**to get lost** 迷路 mílù

lost and found (*US*) N = **lost property**

lost property N [u] **1** (*things*) 招领的失物 zhāolǐng de shīwù **2** (*Brit: office*) 失物招领处 shīwù zhāolǐngchù

lot [lɒt] N [c] ▶**a lot** (*many*) 许多 xǔduō; (*much*) 很多 hěnduō ▶**a lot of** 许多 xǔduō ▶**lots of** 许多 xǔduō ▶**he reads/smokes a lot** 他书读得/烟抽得很多 tā shū dúde/yān chōude hěnduō

lottery ['lɒtərɪ] N [c] 彩票 cǎipiào [张 zhāng]

loud [laʊd] I ADJ 响亮的 xiǎngliàng de II ADV (*speak*) 大声地 dàshēng de

loudly ['laʊdlɪ] ADV 大声地 dàshēng de

loudspeaker [laʊd'spiːkər] N [c] 扬声器 yángshēngqì [个 gè]

lounge [laʊndʒ] N [c] **1** (*in hotel*) 休息室 xiūxishì [间 jiān] **2** (*at airport, station*) 等候室 děnghòushì [间 jiān] **3** 起居室 qǐjūshì [间 jiān]

love [lʌv] I N [u] (*for partner, sweetheart*) 爱情 àiqíng; (*for child, pet*) 爱 ài II VT [+ *partner, child, pet*] 爱 ài; [+ *thing, food, activity*] 热爱 rè'ài ▶**to be in love (with sb)** (与某人)恋爱 (yǔ mǒurén) liàn'ài ▶**to fall in love (with sb)** 爱上(某人) àishàng (mǒurén) ▶**to make love**

做爱 zuò'ài ▶**love (from) Anne** (*on letter*) 爱你的，安妮 àinǐde，Ānní ▶**to love doing/to do sth** 喜爱做某事 xǐ'ài zuò mǒushì ▶**I'd love to come** 我非常想来 wǒ fēicháng xiǎng lái

lovely ['lʌvlɪ] (*esp Brit*) ADJ 1 [+ *place, person, music*] 漂亮的 piàoliang de 2 [+ *holiday, meal, present*] 令人愉快的 lìng rén yúkuài de；[+ *person*] 可爱的 kě'ài de

lover ['lʌvə^r] N [c] 情人 qíngrén [个 gè] ▶**a lover of art** or **an art lover** 钟爱艺术的人 zhōng'ài yìshù de rén

low [ləu] ADJ 1 [+ *wall, hill, heel*] 矮的 ǎi de 2 [+ *temperature, price, level, speed*] 低的 dī de 3 [+ *standard, quality*] 低劣的 dīliè de ▶**low in calories/salt/fat** 低卡路里/盐/脂肪 dī kǎlùlǐ/yán/zhīfáng

lower ['ləuə^r] VT (*reduce*) 降低 jiàngdī

loyal ['lɔɪəl] ADJ 忠实的 zhōngshí de

loyalty ['lɔɪəltɪ] N [u] 忠诚 zhōngchéng

luck [lʌk] N [u] 1 (*chance*) 运气 yùnqì 2 (*good fortune*) 幸运 xìngyùn ▶**good luck** 好运 hǎoyùn ▶**good luck!** or **best of luck!** 祝你好运！ zhùnǐ hǎoyùn！ ▶**bad luck** 不走运 bù zǒuyùn

luckily ['lʌkɪlɪ] ADV 幸运的是 xìngyùn de shì

lucky ['lʌkɪ] ADJ [+ *person*] 幸运的 xìngyùn de ▶**to be lucky** 走

运 zǒuyùn ▶**it is lucky that...** 侥幸的是… jiǎoxìng de shì… ▶**to have a lucky escape** 侥幸逃脱 jiǎoxìng táotuō

luggage ['lʌgɪdʒ] N [u] 行李 xíngli ▶**piece of luggage** 一件行李 yíjiàn xínglǐ

lunch [lʌntʃ] N 1 [c/u] (*meal*) 午餐 wǔcān [顿 dùn] 2 [u] (*lunchtime*) 午餐时间 wǔcān shíjiān ▶**to have lunch (with sb)** (与某人)共进午餐 (yǔ mǒurén) gòngjìn wǔcān

lung [lʌŋ] N [c] 肺 fèi [片 piàn]

Luxembourg ['lʌksəmbə:g] (*Geo*) N 卢森堡 Lúsēnbǎo

luxurious [lʌg'zjuərɪəs] ADJ 豪华的 háohuá de

luxury ['lʌkʃərɪ] I N [u] (*comfort*) 奢华 shēhuá II CPD [+ *hotel, car, goods*] 豪华 háohuá

lying ['laɪɪŋ] VB *see* **lie¹** *see* **lie²**

lyrics ['lɪrɪks] NPL 词句 cíjù

mac [mæk] (Brit: inf) N [c] 雨衣 yǔyī [件 jiàn]

machine [mə'ʃiːn] N [c] 机器 jīqì [台 tái]

machine gun N [c] 机关枪 jīguānqiāng [架 jià]

machinery [mə'ʃiːnərɪ] N [u] 机器 jīqì

mad [mæd] ADJ **1** (insane) 精神失常的 jīngshén shīcháng de **2** (inf: angry) 恼怒的 nǎonù de ▶**to go mad** 发疯 fāfēng; (get angry) 发火 fāhuǒ ▶**to be mad about** or **on sth** (inf) 狂热地爱好某物 kuángrè de àihào mǒuwù

madam ['mædəm] N 女士 nǚshì ▶**Dear Madam** 尊敬的女士 zūnjìng de nǚshì

made [meɪd] PT, PP of **make**

madness ['mædnɪs] N [u] **1** (insanity) 疯狂 fēngkuáng **2** (foolishness) 愚蠢 yúchǔn

magazine [mæɡə'ziːn] N [c] 杂志 zázhì [份 fèn]

magic ['mædʒɪk] **I** N [u] 魔法 mófǎ **II** ADJ **1** [+ formula, solution, cure] 神奇的 shénqí de **2** (supernatural) 魔法的 mófǎ de

magnet ['mæɡnɪt] N [c] 磁铁 cítiě [块 kuài]

maid [meɪd] N [c] (servant) 女仆 nǚpú [个 gè]

maiden name ['meɪdn-] N [c] 娘家姓 niángjiā xìng [个 gè]

mail [meɪl] **I** N [u] **1** ▶**the mail** 邮政 yóuzhèng **2** (letters) 邮件 yóujiàn **3** (e-mail) 电子邮件 diànzǐ yóujiàn **II** VT **1** (esp US: post) 寄出 jìchū **2** (e-mail) 发电邮给 fā diànyóu gěi ▶**by mail** 以邮寄方式 yǐ yóujì fāngshì

mailbox ['meɪlbɔks] N [c] **1** (US: for letters) 信箱 xìnxiāng [个 gè] **2** (US) 邮筒 yóutǒng [个 gè] **3** (Comput) 电子信箱 diànzǐ xìnxiāng [个 gè]

mailman ['meɪlmæn] (pl **mailmen**) (US) N [c] 邮差 yóuchāi [个 gè]

mailwoman ['meɪlwumən] (pl **mailwomen**) (US) N [c] 女邮递员 nǚ yóudìyuán [位 wèi]

main [meɪn] ADJ 主要的 zhǔyào de

main course N [c] 主菜 zhǔcài [道 dào]

mainly ['meɪnlɪ] ADV 主要地 zhǔyào de

main road N [c] 主干道 zhǔ gàndào [条 tiáo]

majesty ['mædʒɪstɪ] N (*title*) ▶**Your/His/Her Majesty** 陛下 bìxià

major ['meɪdʒəʳ] I ADJ 重要的 zhòngyào de II N [c] 1 (*Mil*) 少校 shàoxiào [位 wèi] 2 (*US*) 专业 zhuānyè [个 gè]

majority [mə'dʒɔrɪtɪ] N [s + PL VB] 大多数 dàduōshù

make [meɪk] (*pt, pp* **made**) I VT 1 [+ *object, clothes, cake*] 做 zuò; [+ *noise*] 制造 zhìzào; [+ *mistake*] 犯 fàn 2 (*manufacture*) 生产 shēngchǎn 3 (*cause to be*) ▶**to make sb sad** 使某人难过 shǐ mǒurén nánguò 4 (*force*) ▶**to make sb do sth** 促使某人做某事 cùshǐ mǒurén zuò mǒushì 5 [+ *money*] 挣 zhèng 6 (*equal*) ▶**2 and 2 make 4** 2加2等于4 èrjiā'èr děngyú sì II N [c] (*brand*) 牌子 páizi [个 gè] ▶**to make a profit/ loss** 赢利/赔钱 yínglì/péiqián ▶**what time do you make it?** 你表几点了？ nǐ biǎo jǐdiǎn le ▶**it's made (out) of glass** 是玻璃做的 shì bōli zuò de

▶ **make out** VT [+ *cheque*] 开出 kāichū

▶ **make up** VT 1 [+ *story, excuse*] 捏造 niēzào 2 (*with cosmetics*) 化妆 huàzhuāng ▶**to make up one's mind** 下定决心 xià dìng juéxīn ▶**to make o.s. up** 化妆 huàzhuāng

make-up ['meɪkʌp] N [U] (*cosmetics*) 化妆品 huàzhuāngpǐn

Malaysia [mə'leɪzɪə] N 马来西亚 Mǎláixīyà

male [meɪl] ADJ [+ *employee, child, model, friend, population*] 男的 nán de; [+ *animal, insect, plant, tree*] 雄性的 xióngxìng de

mall [mɔːl] N [c] (*also:* **shopping mall**) 大型购物中心 dàxíng gòuwù zhōngxīn [个 gè]

Malta ['mɔːltə] N 马耳他 Mǎ'ěrtā

mammal ['mæml] N [c] 哺乳动物 bǔrǔ dòngwù [个 gè]

man [mæn] (*pl* **men**) N 1 [c] (*person*) 男人 nánrén [个 gè] 2 [U] (*mankind*) 人类 rénlèi

manage ['mænɪdʒ] I VT [+ *business, shop, time, money*] 管理 guǎnlǐ II VI (*cope*) 应付 yìngfù ▶**manage to do sth** 设法做到某事 shèfǎ zuòdào mǒushì

management ['mænɪdʒmənt] N 1 [U] (*managing*) 管理 guǎnlǐ 2 [U/s] (*managers*) 管理人员 guǎnlǐ rényuán

manager ['mænɪdʒəʳ] N [c] 1 经理 jīnglǐ [位 wèi] 2 (*Sport*) 球队经理 qiúduì jīnglǐ [位 wèi]

mandarin ['mændərɪn] N 1 [U] ▶ **Mandarin (Chinese)** 普通话 Pǔtōnghuà 2 [c] (*also:* **mandarin orange**) 柑橘 gānjú [个 gè]

maniac ['meɪnɪæk] N [c] (*lunatic*) 疯子 fēngzi [个 gè]

manner ['mænəʳ] I N [s] (*way*) 方式 fāngshì II **manners** NPL 礼貌 lǐmào ▶**it's good/bad manners to arrive on time** 准时是有礼貌/无礼的表现 zhǔnshí shì yǒu lǐmào/wúlǐ de biǎoxiàn

manual ['mænjuəl] N [c] (handbook) 手册 shǒu cè [本 běn]

manufacture [mænju'fæktʃəʳ] VT 生产 shēngchǎn

manufacturer [mænju'fæktʃərəʳ] N [c] 制造商 zhìzàoshāng [个 gè]

many ['mɛnɪ] I ADJ (a lot of) 许多的 xǔduō de II PRON 许多的 xǔduō de ▸**how many** (direct question) 多少 duōshǎo ▸**twice as many (as)** (是…的)两倍 (shì…de) liǎngbèi

map [mæp] N [c] 地图 dìtú [张 zhāng]

marathon ['mærəθən] N [c] (race) 马拉松长跑 mǎlāsōng chángpǎo [次 cì]

marble ['mɑːbl] I N [u] 大理石 dàlǐshí II **marbles** NPL (game) 弹子游戏 dànzǐ yóuxì

March [mɑːtʃ] N [c/u] 三月 sānyuè; see also **July**

march [mɑːtʃ] VI 行军 xíngjūn

margarine [mɑːdʒə'riːn] N [u] 人造黄油 rénzào huángyóu

marijuana [mærɪ'wɑːnə] N [u] 大麻 dàmá

mark [mɑːk] I N [c] 1 (cross, tick) 记号 jìhao [个 gè] 2 [c] (stain) 污点 wūdiǎn [个 gè] 3 [c] (Brit: grade, score) 分数 fēnshù [个 gè] II VT 1 (indicate) [+ place] 标示 biāoshì 2 (Brit: Scol) 评分 píngfēn

market ['mɑːkɪt] N [c] 集市 jíshì [个 gè]

marketing ['mɑːkɪtɪŋ] N [u] 市场营销 shìchǎng yíngxiāo

marriage ['mærɪdʒ] N 1 [c/u] (relationship, institution) 婚姻 hūnyīn [个 gè] 2 [c] (wedding) 婚礼 hūnlǐ [场 chǎng]

married ['mærɪd] ADJ 已婚的 yǐhūn de ▸**to be married to sb** 和某人结婚 hé mǒurén jiéhūn ▸**to get married** 结婚 jiéhūn

marry ['mærɪ] VT 和…结婚 hé…jiéhūn

marvellous, (US) **marvelous** ['mɑːvləs] ADJ 极好的 jíhǎo de

masculine ['mæskjulɪn] ADJ 1 [+ characteristic, value] 男性的 nánxìng de 2 (Ling) [+ pronoun] 阳性的 yángxìng de

mashed potato [mæʃt-] N [c/u] 土豆泥 tǔdòuní [份 fèn]

mask [mɑːsk] N [c] 1 (disguise) 面罩 miànzhào [个 gè] 2 (protection) 口罩 kǒuzhào [个 gè]

mass [mæs] N [c] (large amount, number) 大量 dàliàng ▸**masses of** (inf) 大量 dàliàng

massage ['mæsɑːʒ] N [c/u] 按摩 ànmó [次 cì]

massive ['mæsɪv] ADJ [+ amount, increase] 巨大的 jùdà de; [+ explosion] 大规模的 dà guīmó de

master ['mɑːstəʳ] VT (learn) [+ skill, language] 掌握 zhǎngwò

masterpiece ['mɑːstəpiːs] N [c] 杰作 jiézuò [部 bù]

mat [mæt] N [c] 席 xí [张 zhāng]

match [mætʃ] I N 1 [c] (game) 比赛 bǐsài [场 chǎng] 2 [c] (for lighting fire) 火柴 huǒchái [根 gēn] II VI (go together) [colours, materials] 相配 xiāngpèi

mate [meɪt] N [c] (*animal*) 配偶 pèiǒu [个 gè]

material [mə'tɪərɪəl] I N 1 [c/u] (*cloth*) 衣料 yīliào [块 kuài] 2 [u] (*information, data*) 资料 zīliào II **materials** NPL (*equipment*) 用具 yòngjù

math [mæθ] (*US*) N = **maths**

mathematics [mæθə'mætɪks] (*frm*) N [u] 数学 shùxué

maths [mæθs] (*Brit*) N [u] 数学 shùxué

matter ['mætə'] I N [c] 事件 shìjiàn [个 gè] II VI (*be important*) 要紧 yàojǐn ▶**what's the matter (with...)?** (…)怎么了? (…)zěnme le? ▶**it doesn't matter** 没关系 méi guānxi

mattress ['mætrɪs] N [c] 床垫 chuángdiàn [个 gè]

maximum ['mæksɪməm] I ADJ [+ *speed, height*] 最高的 zuìgāo de; [+ *weight*] 最重的 zuìzhòng de II N [c] 最大量 zuìdàliàng

May [meɪ] N [c/u] 五月 wǔyuè; *see also* **July**

KEYWORD

may [meɪ] AUX VB 1 (*possibility*) ▶**it may rain later** 等会儿可能要下雨 děnghuǐr kěnéng yào xiàyǔ ▶**we may not be able to come** 我们可能来不了 wǒmen kěnéng lái bùliǎo ▶**he may have hurt himself** 他可能伤了自己 tā kěnéng shāngle zìjǐ 2 (*permission*) ▶**may I come in?** 我可以进来吗? wǒ kěyǐ jìnlái ma?

maybe ['meɪbiː] ADV 1 可能 kěnéng 2 (*making suggestions*) 也许 yěxǔ 3 (*estimating*) 大概 dàgài ▶**maybe so/not** 也许如此/不是 yěxǔ rúcǐ/bùshì

mayor [mɛə'] N [c] 市长 shìzhǎng [位 wèi]

me [miː] PRON 我 wǒ ▶**it's me** 是我 shì wǒ

meal [miːl] N 1 [c] (*occasion*) 一餐 yīcān [顿 dùn] 2 [c] (*food*) 膳食 shànshí [顿 dùn] ▶**to go out for a meal** 出去吃饭 chūqù chīfàn

mean [miːn] (*pt, pp* **meant**) I VT 1 (*signify*) 表示…意思 biǎoshì…yìsi 2 (*refer to*) 意指 yìzhǐ 3 (*intend*) ▶**to mean to do sth** 意欲做某事 yìyù zuò mǒushì II ADJ 1 (*not generous*) 吝啬的 lìnsè de 2 (*unkind*) 刻薄的 kèbó de ▶**what does "imperialism" mean?** "imperialism" 是什么意思? "imperialism"shì shénme yìsi? ▶**what do you mean?** 你什么意思? nǐ shénme yìsi?; *see also* **means**

meaning ['miːnɪŋ] N [c/u] 意思 yìsi [层 céng]; [*of symbol, dream, gesture*] 含义 hányì [个 gè]

means [miːnz] (*pl* **means**) N [c] (*method*) 方法 fāngfǎ [个 gè]

meant [mɛnt] PT, PP *of* **mean**

meanwhile ['miːnwaɪl] ADV 同时 tóngshí

measles ['miːzlz] N [u] 麻疹 mázhěn

measure ['mɛʒə'] VT 测量 cèliáng

measurement ['mɛʒəmənt] I N [c] (*length, width etc*) 尺寸 chǐcùn

II measurements NPL [of person] 三围 sānwéi

meat [mi:t] N [U] 肉 ròu

Mecca ['mɛkə] N 麦加 Màijiā

mechanic [mɪ'kænɪk] N [C] 机械工 jīxiègōng [位 wèi]

medal ['mɛdl] N [C] 奖章 jiǎngzhāng [枚 méi]

media ['mi:dɪə] I PL of **medium** II NPL ▶ **the media** 媒体 méitǐ

medical ['mɛdɪkl] I ADJ 医疗的 yīliáo de II N [C] (examination) 体格检查 tǐgé jiǎnchá [次 cì]

medicine ['mɛdsɪn] N 1 [U] (science) 医学 yīxué 2 [C/U] (medication) 药 yào [种 zhǒng]

Mediterranean [mɛdɪtə'reɪnɪən] N ▶ **the Mediterranean** (sea) 地中海 Dìzhōnghǎi; (region) 地中海沿岸地区 Dìzhōnghǎi yán'àn dìqū

medium ['mi:dɪəm] ADJ 1 (average) 中等的 zhōngděng de 2 (clothing size) 中码的 zhōngmǎ de

medium-sized ['mi:dɪəm'saɪzd] ADJ 中等大小的 zhōngděng dàxiǎo de

meet [mi:t] (pt, pp met) I VT 1 (accidentally) 遇见 yùjiàn; (by arrangement) 和…见面 hé…jiànmiàn 2 (for the first time) 结识 jiéshí; (be introduced to) 认识 rènshi 3 (at station, airport) 接 jiē II VI 1 (accidentally) 相遇 xiāngyù; (by arrangement) 见面 jiànmiàn 2 (for the first time) 认识 rènshi ▶ **pleased to meet you** 见到你很高兴 jiàndào nǐ hěn gāoxìng ▶ **meet up** VI 会面 huìmiàn

meeting ['mi:tɪŋ] N 1 [C] 会议 huìyì [次 cì] 2 [C] (encounter) 会面 huìmiàn [次 cì]

megabyte ['mɛgəbaɪt] N [C] 兆字节 zhàozìjié [个 gè]

melon ['mɛlən] N [C/U] 瓜 guā [个 gè]

melt [mɛlt] I VI 融化 rónghuà II VT [+ metal, ice, snow, butter, chocolate] 使融化 shǐ rónghuà

member ['mɛmbəʳ] N [C] 1 [of family, staff, public] 一员 yīyuán 2 [of club, party] 成员 chéngyuán [个 gè]

memorial [mɪ'mɔ:rɪəl] N [C] 纪念碑 jìniànbēi [座 zuò]

memorize ['mɛməraɪz] VT 记住 jìzhù

memory ['mɛmərɪ] N 1 [C/U] (ability to remember) 记忆力 jìyìlì [种 zhǒng] 2 [C] (thing remembered) 记忆 jìyì [个 gè] 3 [C/U] (Comput) 存储器 cúnchǔqì [个 gè] ▶ **to have a good/bad memory (for sth)** (对某事) 记忆力好/差 (duì mǒushì) jìyìlì hǎo/chà

men [mɛn] NPL of **man**

mend [mɛnd] VT 修理 xiūlǐ

mental ['mɛntl] ADJ [+ illness, health] 精神的 jīngshén de

mental hospital N [C] 精神病院 jīngshénbìngyuàn [个 gè]

mention ['mɛnʃən] VT 提到 tídào ▶ **don't mention it!** 不客气! bù kèqi!

menu ['mɛnju:] N [C] 1 菜单 càidān [个 gè] 2 (Comput) 选择菜单 xuǎnzé càidān [个 gè]

merry ['mɛrɪ] ADJ ▶ **Merry**

Christmas! 圣诞快乐！Shèngdàn Kuàilè!

mess [mɛs] N 1 [s/ʊ] (*untidiness*) 凌乱 língluàn 2 [s/ʊ] (*chaotic situation*) 混乱的局面 hùnluàn de júmiàn
▶ **mess about, mess around** (*inf*) VI 混日子 hùn rìzi

message ['mɛsɪdʒ] N [c] 消息 xiāoxi [条 tiáo] ▶ **to leave (sb) a message** (给某人)留个信 (gěi mǒurén)liú gè xìn

met [mɛt] PT, PP of **meet**

metal ['mɛtl] N [c/ʊ] 金属 jīnshǔ [种 zhǒng]

meter ['miːtəʳ] N [c] 1 仪表 yíbiǎo [个 gè]; (*also:* **parking meter**) 停车计时器 tíngchē jìshíqì [个 gè] 2 (*US: unit*) = **metre**

method ['mɛθəd] N [c/ʊ] 方法 fāngfǎ [种 zhǒng]

metre, (*US*) **meter** ['miːtəʳ] N [c] (*unit*) 米 mǐ

metric ['mɛtrɪk] ADJ 公制的 gōngzhì de

Mexico ['mɛksɪkəʊ] N 墨西哥 Mòxīgē

mice [maɪs] NPL of **mouse**

microchip ['maɪkrəʊtʃɪp] N [c] 集成电路块 jíchéng diànlù kuài [个 gè]

microphone ['maɪkrəfəʊn] N [c] 话筒 huàtǒng [个 gè]

microscope ['maɪkrəskəʊp] N [c] 显微镜 xiǎnwēijìng [个 gè]

microwave ['maɪkrəʊweɪv] N [c] (*also:* **microwave oven**) 微波炉 wēibōlú [个 gè]

midday [mɪd'deɪ] N [ʊ] 正午

zhèngwǔ ▶ **at midday** 在正午 zài zhèngwǔ

middle ['mɪdl] I N 1 [c] (*centre*) 中央 zhōngyāng [个 gè] 2 [s] 中 zhōng II ADJ [+ *position, event, period*] 中间的 zhōngjiān de ▶ **in the middle of the night** 在半夜 zài bànyè

middle-aged [mɪdl'eɪdʒd] ADJ 中年的 zhōngnián de

middle class ADJ (*also:* **middle-class**) 中层社会的 zhōngcéng shèhuì de

Middle East N ▶ **the Middle East** 中东 Zhōngdōng

middle name N [c] 中间名字 zhōngjiān míngzi [个 gè]

● **MIDDLE NAME**
●
● **first name** 是由父母取
● 的名字。**last name** 或
● **surname** 是家族的姓氏。
● 在说英语的国家中，名在
● 姓之前。在 **first name** 和
● **last name** 之间，还可能
● 有 **middle name**（中名），
● 这是你父母给你取的第二个
● "名"。**middle name** 通常
● 只用于正式场合，例如，选
● 课或签署文件时。

midnight ['mɪdnaɪt] N [ʊ] 半夜 bànyè ▶ **at midnight** 在午夜 zài wǔyè

midwife ['mɪdwaɪf] (*pl* **midwives**) N [c] 助产士 zhùchǎnshì [位 wèi]

might [maɪt] AUX VB (*possibility*) ▶ **I might get home late** 我可

能会晚回家 wǒ kěnéng huì wǎn huíjiā ▶**it might have been an accident** 可能是个事故 kěnéng shì gè shìgù

migraine ['mi:greɪn] N [C/U] 偏头痛 piāntóutòng [阵 zhèn]

mild [maɪld] ADJ 1 [+ *infection, illness*] 轻微的 qīngwēi de 2 [+ *climate, weather*] 温暖的 wēnnuǎn de

mile [maɪl] I N [C] 英里 yīnglǐ II **miles** NPL (*inf: a long way*) 很远的距离 hěnyuǎn de jùlí ▶**70 miles per** *or* **an hour** 每小时70英里 měi xiǎoshí qīshí yīnglǐ

military ['mɪlɪtərɪ] ADJ 军事的 jūnshì de

milk [mɪlk] N [U] 奶 nǎi

milkshake ['mɪlkʃeɪk] N [C/U] 奶昔 nǎixī [份 fèn]

millimetre, (US) **millimeter** ['mɪlɪmiːtər] N [C] 毫米 háomǐ

million ['mɪljən] I NUM 百万 bǎiwàn II **millions** NPL (*lit*) 数百万 shùbǎiwàn; (*inf: fig*) 无数 wúshù ▶**a** *or* **one million books/people/dollars** 100万本书/个人/元 yībǎiwàn běn shū/gè rén/yuán

millionaire [mɪljə'nɛər] N [C] 百万富翁 bǎiwàn fùwēng [个 gè]

mind [maɪnd] I N [C] 智力 zhìlì [种 zhǒng] II VT 1 (*Brit: look after*) [+ *child, shop*] 照看 zhàokàn 2 (*be careful of*) 当心 dāngxīn 3 (*object to*) 介意 jièyì 4 (*have a preference*) ▶**I don't mind (what/who...)** 我不在乎(什么/谁…) wǒ bù zàihu (shénme/shéi...) 5 ▶**do/would**

you mind (if...)? (如果…)你介意吗? (rúguǒ...) nǐ jièyì ma? ▶**to make up one's mind** *or* **make one's mind up** 下定决心 xiàdìng juéxīn ▶**to change one's/sb's mind** 改变主意 gǎibiàn zhǔyì ▶**I wouldn't mind a coffee** 我挺想喝杯咖啡 wǒ tǐngxiǎng hē bēi kāfēi ▶**mind the step** 小心脚下 xiǎoxīn jiǎoxià

⬤ KEYWORD

mine[1] [maɪn] PRON 我的 wǒ de ▶**this is mine** 这是我的 zhèshì wǒde ▶**these are mine** 这些是我的 zhèxiē shì wǒde

mine[2] [maɪn] N [C] 矿 kuàng [座 zuò]

mineral water [mɪnərəl-] N [U/C] 矿泉水 kuàngquánshuǐ

miniature ['mɪnətʃər] ADJ 微型的 wēixíng de

minibus ['mɪnɪbʌs] N [C] 小公共汽车 xiǎo gōnggòng qìchē [辆 liàng]

MiniDisc®, **minidisc** ['mɪnɪdɪsk] N [C] (*disc*) 迷你光碟 mínǐ guāngdié [张 zhāng]

minimum ['mɪnɪməm] I ADJ 最低的 zuìdī de II N [C] 腋量 zuìshǎoliàng

miniskirt ['mɪnɪskəːt] N [C] 超短裙 chāoduǎnqún [条 tiáo]

minister ['mɪnɪstər] N [C] 1 (*Brit*) (*Pol*) 部长 bùzhǎng [位 wèi] 2 (*Rel*) 牧师 mùshī [位 wèi]

minor ['maɪnər] ADJ [+ *repairs,*

changes] 不重要的 bù zhòngyào de; [+ injuries] 不严重的 bù yánzhòng de

minority [maɪˈnɔrɪtɪ] N 1 [s + PL VB] (of group, society) 少数 shǎoshù 2 [c] (ethnic, cultural, religious) 少数民族 shǎoshù mínzú [个 gè]

mint [mɪnt] N 1 [U] (plant) 薄荷 bòhe 2 [U] (sweet) 薄荷糖 bòhe táng

minus [ˈmaɪnəs] PREP (inf: without) 没有 méiyǒu ▶12 **minus 3** (is or equals 9) 12减3 (等于9) shí'èr jiǎn sān (děngyú jiǔ) ▶**minus 24** (degrees C/F) (temperature) 零下24(摄氏/华氏度) língxià èrshísì (shèshì/huáshì dù) ▶**B minus** (Scol) B减 bì jiǎn

minute [ˈmɪnɪt] N [c] 1 (unit) 分钟 fēnzhōng 2 一会儿 yīhuìr ▶wait or just a minute! 等一会儿! děng yīhuìr!

miracle [ˈmɪrəkl] N [c] 1 (Rel) 圣迹 shèngjì [处 chù] 2 (marvel) 奇迹 qíjì [个 gè]

mirror [ˈmɪrər] N [c] 镜子 jìngzi [面 miàn]; [in car] 后视镜 hòushìjìng [个 gè]

misbehave [mɪsbɪˈheɪv] VI 行为无礼 xíngwéi wúlǐ

miscellaneous [mɪsɪˈleɪnɪəs] ADJ 形形色色的 xíngxíng sèsè de

miserable [ˈmɪzərəbl] ADJ 1 [+ person] 痛苦的 tòngkǔ de 2 [+ weather, day] 恶劣的 èliè de

Miss [mɪs] N 1 小姐 xiǎojiě 2 (esp Brit: as form of address) 小姐 xiǎojiě ▶**Dear Miss Smith** 亲爱

的史密斯小姐 qīnài de Shǐmìsī Xiǎojiě

- **MISS, MRS, MS**

在说英语的国家中，**Mrs** (夫人) 用于已婚女士的姓名前。**Miss** (小姐) 用于未婚女士的姓名前。有些女士认为，让人们知道她是否结婚并不重要，所以往往用 **Ms** (女士) 称呼自己。与 **Mr** (先生) 类似，**Ms** 不表明任何婚姻状况。

miss [mɪs] VT 1 (fail to hit) 未击中 wèi jīzhòng 2 [+ train, bus, plane] 错过 cuòguò 3 [+ chance, opportunity] 错过 cuòguò ▶**you can't miss it** 你不会找不到 nǐ bùhuì zhǎo bùdào

missing [ˈmɪsɪŋ] ADJ [+ person] 失踪的 shīzōng de; [+ object] 丢失的 diūshī de

mist [mɪst] N [c/U] 薄雾 bówù [场 chǎng]

mistake [mɪsˈteɪk] N [c] 1 (error) 错误 cuòwù [个 gè] 2 (blunder) 过失 guòshī [个 gè] ▶**to make a mistake** 犯错 fàncuò ▶**to do sth by mistake** 误做某事 wùzuò mǒushì

mistaken [mɪsˈteɪkən] I PP of **mistake** II ADJ ▶**to be mistaken (about sth)** [person] (把某事)搞错 (bǎ mǒushì)gǎocuò

mistook [mɪsˈtuk] PT of **mistake**

misty [ˈmɪstɪ] ADJ 有雾的 yǒuwù de

misunderstand
[mɪsʌndə'stænd] (*pt, pp*
misunderstood) VT, VI 误解
wùjiě

misunderstanding
['mɪsʌndə'stændɪŋ] N [c/u] 误会
wùhuì [个 gè]

misunderstood [mɪsʌndə'stud]
PT, PP *of* **misunderstand**

mix [mɪks] I VT 混合 hùnhé II VI
(*socially*) ▸ **to mix (with sb)** (和
某人) 相处 (hé mǒurén) xiāngchǔ
III N [c] 混合 hùnhé [种 zhǒng]
▸ **to mix sth with sth** [+ *activities*]
将某物同某物混淆 jiāng mǒuwù
tóng mǒuwù hùnxiáo
▸ **mix up** VT [+ *people*] 分辨不
出 fēnbiàn bùchū; [+ *things*] 混
淆 hùnxiáo

mixed [mɪkst] ADJ 1 [+ *salad,
herbs*] 什锦的 shíjǐn de 2 [+ *group,
community*] 形形色色的 xíngxíng
sèsè de 3 [+ *school, education*] 男女
混合的 nánnǚ hùnhé de

mixture ['mɪkstʃəʳ] N [c/u] 混合
物 hùnhéwù [种 zhǒng]

mix-up ['mɪksʌp] (*inf*) N [c] 混乱
hùnluàn [种 zhǒng]

mobile phone (*Brit*) N [c] 手机
shǒujī [部 bù]

model ['mɔdl] I N [c] 1 [*of boat,
building*] 模型 móxíng [个 gè]
2 (*fashion model*) 时装模特
shízhuāng mótè [位 wèi] II ADJ
(*miniature*) ▸ **model aircraft/
train** 模型飞机/火车 móxíng
fēijī/huǒchē III VT [+ *clothes*] 展
示 zhǎnshì

modem ['məudɛm] N [c] 调制解

调器 tiáozhì jiětiáo qì [个 gè]

moderate ['mɔdərət] ADJ 中庸的
zhōngyōng de

modern ['mɔdən] ADJ 1 [+ *world,
times, society*] 现代的 xiàndài de
2 [+ *technology, design*] 新式的
xīnshì de

modern languages NPL 现代语
言 xiàndài yǔyán

modernize ['mɔdənaɪz] VT 使现
代化 shǐ xiàndàihuà

modest ['mɔdɪst] ADJ 谦虚的
qiānxū de

moisturizer ['mɔɪstʃəraɪzəʳ]
N [c/u] 保湿霜 bǎoshīshuāng
[瓶 píng]

moment ['məumənt] N 1 [c]
(*period of time*) 片刻 piànkè 2 [c]
(*point in time*) 瞬间 shùnjiān ▸ **at
the/this (present) moment** 此
刻/当前 cǐkè/dāngqián ▸ **at the
last moment** 在最后一刻 zài
zuìhòu yīkè

Monday ['mʌndɪ] N [c/u] 星期
一 xīngqīyī [个 gè]; *see also* **Tuesday**

money ['mʌnɪ] N [u] 1 (*cash*) 钱
qián 2 (*in the bank*) 存款 cúnkuǎn
3 (*currency*) 货币 huòbì ▸ **to make
money** [*person, business*] 赚钱
zhuànqián

monitor ['mɔnɪtəʳ] N [c] 显示屏
xiǎnshìpíng [个 gè]

monkey ['mʌŋkɪ] N [c] (*Zool*) 猴
hóu [只 zhī]

monotonous [mə'nɔtənəs] ADJ
[+ *life, job etc, voice, tune*] 单调的
dāndiào de

month [mʌnθ] N [c] 月 yuè
[个 gè] ▸ **every month** 每个月

měigè yuè

monthly ['mʌnθlɪ] I ADJ 每月的 měiyuè de II ADV (every month) 按月 ànyuè

monument ['mɔnjumənt] N [c] 纪念碑 jìniànbēi [座 zuò]

mood [muːd] N [c] 心情 xīnqíng [种 zhǒng] ▶to be in a good/bad/awkward mood 心情好/坏/不痛快 xīnqíng hǎo/huài/bù tòngkuài

moon [muːn] N ▶the moon 月球 yuèqiú

moonlight ['muːnlaɪt] N [U] 月光 yuèguāng

moped ['məupɛd] N [c] 机动自行车 jīdòng zìxíngchē [辆 liàng]

moral ['mɔrl] ADJ [+ issues, values] 道德的 dàodé de; [+ behaviour, person] 品行端正的 pǐnxíng duānzhèng de

KEYWORD

more [mɔː^r] I ADJ 1 更多的 gèngduō de ▶I get more money/holidays than you do 我比你有更多的钱/假期 wǒ bǐ nǐ yǒu gèngduōde qián/jiàqī 2 (additional) 再一些的 zài yīxiē de ▶would you like some more tea/peanuts? 你要再来点茶/花生吗? nǐ yào zàilái diǎn chá/huāshēng ma? ▶is there any more wine? 还有酒吗? háiyǒu jiǔ ma? ▶a few more weeks 再几个星期 zài jǐgè xīngqī

II PRON 1 (in comparisons) 更多的量 gèngduō de liàng ▶there's/there are more than I thought 比我想得更多 bǐ wǒ xiǎngde

gèngduō ▶more than 20 大于20 dàyú èrshí ▶she's got more than me 她比我得到的多 tā bǐ wǒ dédào de duō 2 (further, additional) 额外的量 éwài de liàng ▶is there/are there any more? 还有多的吗? háiyǒu duōde ma? ▶have you got any more of it/them? 你还有吗? nǐ háiyǒu ma? ▶much/many more 多得多 duōdeduō III ADV 1 (to form comparative) 更 gèng ▶more dangerous/difficult (than) (比…)更危险/难 (bǐ…)gèng wēixiǎn/nán 2 (in expressions) ▶more and more 越来越 yuèláiyuè ▶more or less (adj, adv) 差不多 chàbùduō ▶more than ever 空前的多 kōngqián de duō ▶once more 再一次 zài yīcì

morning ['mɔːnɪŋ] N [c/U] (early in the morning) 早晨 zǎochén [个 gè]; (later in the morning) 上午 shàngwǔ [个 gè] ▶good morning! 早上好! zǎoshàng hǎo! ▶at 3 o'clock/7 o'clock in the morning 凌晨3点/早上7点 língchén sāndiǎn/zǎoshàng qīdiǎn ▶this morning 今天上午 jīntiān shàngwǔ ▶on Monday morning 星期一上午 Xīngqīyī shàngwǔ

Morocco [mə'rɔkəu] N 摩洛哥 Móluògē

mortgage ['mɔːgɪdʒ] N [c] 抵押贷款 dǐyā dàikuǎn [笔 bǐ]

Moslem ['mɔzləm] ADJ, N = **Muslim**

mosque [mɔsk] N [c] 清真寺 qīngzhēnsì [座 zuò]

mosquito [mɔsˈkiːtəu] (*pl* **mosquitoes**) N [c] 蚊 wén [只 zhī]

KEYWORD

most [məust] I ADJ 1 (*almost all*) 大部分的 dàbùfen de ▶**most people** 大多数人 dàduōshù rén 2 (*in comparisons*) ▶**(the) most** 最 zuì ▶**who won the most money/prizes?** 谁赢了最多的钱/奖品? shuí yíngle zuìduō de qián/jiǎngpǐn?

II PRON 大部分 dàbùfen; (*plural*) 大多数 dàduōshù ▶**most of it/them** 它/他们的大部分 tā/tāmen de dà bùfēn ▶**I paid the most** 我付了大部分 wǒ fùle dà bùfēn ▶**to make the most of sth** 充分利用某物 chōngfèn lìyòng mǒuwù ▶**at the (very) most** 顶多 dǐngduō

III ADV (*superlative*) 1 (*with verb*) ▶**(the) most** 最 zuì ▶**what I miss (the) most is...** 我最想念的是… wǒ zuì xiǎngniàn de shì... 2 (*with adj*) ▶**the most comfortable/expensive sofa in the shop** 店里最舒服/贵的沙发 diànlǐ zuì shūfu/guì de shāfā 3 (*with adv*) ▶**most efficiently/ effectively** 最有效率/有效地 zuì yǒuxiàolǜ/yǒuxiào de ▶**most of all** 最起码的 zuì qǐmǎ de

mother [ˈmʌðər] N [c] 母亲 mǔqīn [位 wèi]

mother-in-law [ˈmʌðərɪnlɔː] (*pl* **mothers-in-law**) N [c] [*of woman*] 婆婆 pópo [位 wèi]; [*of man*] 岳母 yuèmǔ [位 wèi]

Mother's Day (*Brit*) N [c/u] 母亲节 Mǔqīn Jié [个 gè]

motivated [ˈməutɪveɪtɪd] ADJ 士气高涨的 shìqì gāozhàng de

motor [ˈməutər] N [c] 发动机 fādòngjī [个 gè]

motorbike [ˈməutəbaɪk] N [c] 摩托车 mótuōchē [辆 liàng]

motorboat [ˈməutəbəut] N [c] 摩托艇 mótuōtǐng [艘 sōu]

motorcycle [ˈməutəsaɪkl] (*frm*) N [c] 摩托车 mótuōchē [辆 liàng]

motorcyclist [ˈməutəsaɪklɪst] N [c] 摩托车手 mótuōchēshǒu [位 wèi]

motorist [ˈməutərɪst] (*esp Brit*) N [c] 开汽车的人 kāi qìchē de rén [个 gè]

motor racing (*Brit*) N [u] 赛车 sàichē

motorway [ˈməutəweɪ] (*Brit*) N [c] 高速公路 gāosù gōnglù [条 tiáo]

mountain [ˈmauntɪn] N [c] 山 shān [座 zuò]

mountain bike N [c] 山地自行车 shāndì zìxíngchē [辆 liàng]

mountainous [ˈmauntɪnəs] ADJ 多山的 duōshān de

mouse [maus] (*pl* **mice**) N [c] 1 鼠 shǔ [只 zhī] 2 (*Comput*) 鼠标 shǔbiāo [个 gè]

mouse mat [ˈmausmæt] N [c] 鼠标垫 shǔbiāo diàn [个 gè]

moustache, (*US*) **mustache** [məsˈtɑːʃ] N [c] 髭 zī [根 gēn]

mouth [mauθ] N [c] **1** 嘴 zuǐ [张 zhāng] **2** (*of river*) 河口 hékǒu [个 gè]

mouthful ['mauθful] N [c] 一 口 yīkǒu

move [mu:v] **I** VI **1** (*vehicle*) 行 进 xíngjìn; [*person, object*] 动 dòng **2** (*relocate*) 搬家 bānjiā; (*from activity*) 改换 gǎihuàn **II** VT **1** [+ *furniture, car*] 挪动 nuódòng **2** (*affect emotionally*) 感 动 gǎndòng **III** N [c] **1** 搬家 bānjiā [次 cì] **2** (*in game*) 一步 yībù ▶ **to move house/jobs/offices** 搬 家/换工作/更换办公地点 bānjiā/ huàn gōngzuò/gēnghuàn bàngōng dìdiǎn ▶ **to get a move on** (*inf*) 快 点 kuàidiǎn

▶ **move away** VI (*from town, area*) 离开 líkāi; (*from window, door*) 走 开 zǒukāi

▶ **move back** VI **1** (*return*) 回来 huílái **2** (*backwards*) 后退 hòutuì

▶ **move forward** VI [*person, troops, vehicle*] 向前移动 xiàngqián yídòng

▶ **move in** VI (*into house*) 搬入 bānrù

▶ **move into** VT FUS (*house, area*) 搬进 bānjìn

▶ **move out** VI (*of house*) 搬出去 bān chūqù

▶ **move over** VI (*to make room*) 让 开些 ràngkāixiē

movement ['mu:vmənt] N **1** [c] 团体 tuántǐ [个 gè] **2** [c] (*gesture*) 动作 dòngzuò [个 gè]

movie ['mu:vɪ] (*US*) N [c] 电影 diànyǐng [部 bù] ▶ **the movies** 电

影 diànyǐng

movie theater (*US*) N [c] 电影院 diànyǐngyuàn [个 gè]

moving ['mu:vɪŋ] ADJ **1** (*emotionally*) 动人的 dòngrén de **2** (*not static*) 活动的 huódòng de

MP N ABBR (*Brit*) (= **Member of Parliament**) 下院议员 Xiàyuàn Yìyuán

MP3 [empɪ:'θri:] N **1** (*format*) 一种 音频压缩格式 **2** (*file*) 以这种音频 压缩格式储存的声音文件

mph ABBR (= **miles per hour**) 每小 时…英里 měi xiǎoshí...yīnglǐ

Mr ['mɪstə'], (*US*) **Mr.** N ▶ **Mr Smith** 史密斯先生 Shǐmìsī xiānsheng

Mrs ['mɪsɪz], (*US*) **Mrs.** N ▶ **Mrs Smith** 史密斯太太 Shǐmìsī tàitai

Ms [mɪz], (*US*) **Ms.** N (*Miss or Mrs*) ▶ **Ms Smith** 史密斯女士 Shǐmìsī nǚshì

◯ KEYWORD

much [mʌtʃ] **I** ADJ 大量的 dàliàng de ▶ **we haven't got much time/money** 我们没有多少时 间/钱 wǒmen méiyǒu duōshǎo shíjiān/qián

II PRON 大量 dàliàng ▶ **there isn't much left** 剩下的不 多了 shèngxià de bùduō le

▶ **he doesn't do much at the weekends** 周末他不做太多事 zhōumò tā bùzuò tàiduō shì

III ADV **1** (*a great deal*) 许多 xǔduō ▶ **he hasn't changed much** 他没 变很多 tā méi biàn hěnduō ▶ "did

you like her? — "**not much**"
"你喜欢她吗？" "不太喜欢"
"nǐ xǐhuan tā ma?" "bùtài xǐhuan"
2 (*far*) …得多 …deduō ▶**I'm
much better now** 我感觉好多了
wǒ gǎnjué hǎoduō le
3 (*often*) 经常 jīngcháng ▶**do you
go out much?** 你经常出去吗？ nǐ
jīngcháng chūqù ma?

mud [mʌd] N [U] 泥 ní
muddle ['mʌdl] N [C/U] **1** [*of papers,
figures, things*] 混乱状态 hùnluàn
zhuàngtài [个 gè] **2** (*situation*) 糟
糕局面 zāogāo júmiàn [个 gè] ▶**to
be in a muddle** 一片混乱 yīpiàn
hùnluàn
muddy ['mʌdɪ] ADJ 沾满烂泥的
zhānmǎn lànní de
muesli ['mjuːzlɪ] N [U] 穆兹利，
和干水果混在一起的燕麦早餐
mug [mʌg] **I** N [C] 大杯子 dà
bēizi [个 gè] **II** VT (*rob*) 行凶抢劫
xíngxiōng qiǎngjié
mugging ['mʌgɪŋ] N [C/U] 行凶抢
劫 xíngxiōng qiǎngjié [次 cì]
multiply ['mʌltɪplaɪ] **I** VT (*Math*)
▶**to multiply sth (by sth)** （某
数）乘以某数 (mǒushù) chéngyǐ
mǒushù **II** VI (*increase*) 增加
zēngjiā
mum [mʌm] N (*Brit: inf*) 妈妈
māma
mummy ['mʌmɪ] N [C] (*Brit: inf*)
妈妈 māma [位 wèi]
murder ['məːdəʳ] **I** N [C/U] 谋
杀 móushā [个 gè] **II** VT 谋杀
móushā
murderer ['məːdərəʳ] N [C] 凶手

xiōngshǒu [个 gè]
muscle ['mʌsl] N [C/U] 肌肉 jīròu
[块 kuài]
museum [mjuːˈzɪəm] N [C] 博物
馆 bówùguǎn [个 gè]
mushroom ['mʌʃrum] N [C] 蘑菇
mógu [个 gè]
music ['mjuːzɪk] N [U] **1** 音
乐 yīnyuè **2** (*Scol, Univ*) 音乐课
yīnyuè kè
musical ['mjuːzɪkl] ADJ **1** (*related
to music*) 音乐的 yīnyuè de
2 (*musically gifted*) 有音乐天赋的
yǒu yīnyuè tiānfù de
musical instrument N [C] 乐器
yuèqì [件 jiàn]
musician [mjuːˈzɪʃən] N [C] 音乐
家 yīnyuèjiā [位 wèi]
Muslim, Moslem ['muzlɪm] **I** N
[C] 穆斯林 Mùsīlín [个 gè] **II** ADJ
穆斯林的 Mùsīlín de
must [mʌst] AUX VB **1** (*expressing
importance or necessity*) 必须 bìxū
2 (*expressing intention*) 得 děi
3 (*expressing presumption*) 一定
yīdìng **4** ▶**you must be joking** 你
准是在开玩笑 nǐ zhǔn shì zài kāi
wánxiào ▶**the doctor must allow
the patient to decide** 医生必
须让病人来决定。 yīshēng bìxū
ràng bìngrén lái juédìng. ▶**I really
must be getting back** 我真得回
去了。 wǒ zhēnděi huíqù le
mustache ['mʌstæʃ] (*US*) N =
moustache
mustard ['mʌstəd] N [U] 芥
末 jièmò
mustn't ['mʌsnt] = **must not**
my [maɪ] ADJ 我的 wǒ de

myself [maɪ'sɛlf] PRON **1** 我自己 wǒ zìjǐ **2** (*me*) 我 wǒ ▶**I hurt myself** 我伤了自己。 wǒ shāngle zìjǐ ▶**by myself** (*unaided*) 我独力地 wǒ dúlì de; (*alone*) 我独自 wǒ dúzì

mysterious [mɪs'tɪərɪəs] ADJ 神秘的 shénmì de

mystery ['mɪstərɪ] N **1** [c] (*puzzle*) 谜 mí [个 gè] **2** [c] (*story*) 推理作品 tuīlǐ zuòpǐn [部 bù]

myth [mɪθ] N [c] **1** (*legend, story*) 神话 shénhuà [个 gè] **2** (*fallacy*) 谬论 miùlùn [个 gè]

nail [neɪl] N [c] **1** [*of finger, toe*] 指甲 zhǐjiɑ [个 gè] **2** (*for hammering*) 钉子 dīngzi [个 gè]

nailfile ['neɪlfaɪl] N [c] 指甲锉 zhǐjiɑ cuò [个 gè]

nail polish N [U] 指甲油 zhǐjiɑ yóu

nail varnish (*Brit*) N = **nail polish**

naked ['neɪkɪd] ADJ 裸体的 luǒtǐ de

name [neɪm] N [c] 名字 míngzi [个 gè] ▶**what's your name?** 你叫什么名字？ nǐ jiào shénme míngzi? ▶**my name is Peter** 我叫彼得 wǒ jiào bǐdé ▶**to give one's name and address** 留下姓名和地址 liúxià xìngmíng hé dìzhǐ

nanny ['nænɪ] N [c] 保姆 bǎomǔ [个 gè]

napkin ['næpkɪn] N [c] 餐巾 cānjīn [张 zhāng]

nappy ['næpɪ] (*Brit*) N [c] 尿布 niàobù [块 kuài]

narrow ['nærəu] ADJ 窄的 zhǎi de

nasty ['nɑːstɪ] ADJ 1 [+ *taste, smell*] 恶心的 ěxīn de 2 [+ *injury, accident, disease*] 严重的 yánzhòng de

nation ['neɪʃən] N [c] 国家 guójiā [个 gè]

national ['næʃənl] I ADJ 国家的 guójiā de II N [c] 公民 gōngmín [个 gè]

national anthem N [c] 国歌 guógē [首 shǒu]

national holiday (*US*) N [c] 定假期 fǎdìng jiàqī [个 gè]

nationality [næʃə'nælɪtɪ] N [c/u] 国籍 guójí [个 gè]

national park N [c] 国家公园 guójiā gōngyuán [个 gè]

native ['neɪtɪv] ADJ [+ *country*] 本国的 běnguó de; [+ *language, tongue*] 母语的 mǔyǔ de

natural ['nætʃrəl] ADJ 1 (*normal*) 正常的 zhèngcháng de 2 [+ *material, product, food*] 天然的 tiānrán de

naturally ['nætʃrəlɪ] ADV 1 (*unsurprisingly*) 自然地 zìrán de 2 (*occur, happen*) 自然而然地 zìrán ér rán de

nature ['neɪtʃəʳ] N [u] (*also:* **Nature**) 自然界 zìránjiè

naughty ['nɔːtɪ] ADJ 淘气的 táoqì de

navy ['neɪvɪ] I N 1 ▶**the navy** (*service*) 海军 hǎijūn 2 [u] (*also:* **navy-blue**) 藏青色 zàngqīngsè

II ADJ (*also:* **navy-blue**) 藏青色的 zàngqīngsè de

near [nɪəʳ] I ADJ 近的 jìn de II ADV (*close*) 近 jìn III PREP (*also:* **near to**) 1 (*physically*) 近 jìn 2 (*just before/after*) 临近 línjìn ▶**the nearest shops are 5 km away** 最近的商店离这里有5公里远。zuìjìn de shāngdiàn lí zhèlǐ yǒu wǔ gōnglǐ yuǎn ▶**in the near future** 在不远的将来 zài bùyuǎn de jiānglái

nearby [nɪə'baɪ] I ADJ 附近的 fùjìn de II ADV 在附近 zài fùjìn

nearly ['nɪəlɪ] ADV 差不多 chà bù duō ▶**you're nearly as tall as I am** 你跟我差不多高了 nǐ gēn wǒ chàbùduō gáole ▶**nearly always** 几乎总是 jīhū zǒngshì

near-sighted [nɪə'saɪtɪd] (*US*) ADJ (*short-sighted*) 近视的 jìnshì de

neat [niːt] ADJ 1 整洁的 zhěngjié de; [+ *handwriting*] 工整的 gōngzhěng de 2 (*US: inf: great*) 绝妙的 juémiào de

neatly ['niːtlɪ] ADV 整齐地 zhěngqí de

necessarily ['nɛsɪsrɪlɪ] ADV 必然 bìrán

necessary ['nɛsɪsrɪ] ADJ 必要的 bìyào de ▶**if/when/as necessary** 如有必要/必要时/在必要处 rú yǒu bìyào/bìyào shí/zài bìyào chù

neck [nɛk] N [c] 1 (*Anat*) 颈 jǐng 2 (*of shirt, dress, jumper*) 领子 lǐngzi [个 gè]

necklace ['nɛklɪs] N [c] 项链

xiànglián [条 tiáo]

necktie ['nɛktaɪ] (US) N [C] 领带 lǐngdài [条 tiáo]

need [niːd] VT1 (require) 需要 xūyào2 (want) [+ drink, holiday, cigarette] 想要 xiǎngyào3 [+ a haircut, a bath, a wash] 得 děi ▶**to need to do sth** 必须做某事 bìxū zuò mǒushì ▶**the car needs servicing** 这辆车需要维修了 zhèliàng chē xūyào wéixiū le

needle ['niːdl] N [C]1 (for sewing) 针 zhēn [根 gēn]2 (for injections) 注射针 zhùshèzhēn [只 zhī]

negative ['nɛɡətɪv] I ADJ 1 [+ test, result] 阴性的 yīnxìng de 2 [+ person, attitude, view] 消极的 xiāojí de3 [+ answer, response] 否定的 fǒudìng de II N [C] (Ling) 否定词 fǒudìngcí [个 gè]

negotiate [nɪ'ɡəʊʃɪeɪt] VI 商讨 shāngtǎo

neighbour, (US)**neighbor** ['neɪbər] N [C] 邻居 línjū [个 gè]

neighbourhood, (US) **neighborhood** ['neɪbəhud] N [C] 地区 dìqū [个 gè]

neither ['naɪðər] I PRON (person) 两人都不 liǎngrén dōu bù; (thing) 两者都不 liǎngzhě dōu bù II CONJ ▶**I didn't move and neither did John** 我和约翰都没动 wǒ hé Yuēhàn dōu méi dòng ▶**neither do/have I** 我也不/没 wǒ yě bù/méi ▶**neither... nor...** 既不…也不… jìbù...yěbù...

neither 和 none 作代词的时候用法不同。用 **neither** 指两个人或事物，表示否定含义。*Neither had close friends at university.* **neither of** 的用法与之相同，后接代词或名词词组。*Neither of them spoke...Neither of these options is desirable.* 注意，也可以把 **neither** 用在单数可数名词之前。*Neither side can win.* **none** 可以指代三个或者三个以上的人或事物，表示否定含义。*None could afford the food.* **none of** 的用法与之相同，后接代词或名词词组。*None of them had learned anything.*

nephew ['nɛvjuː] N [C] (brother's son) 侄子 zhízi [个 gè]; (sister's son) 外甥 wàisheng [个 gè]

nerve [nəːv] N1 (Anat) 神经 shénjīng [根 gēn]2 [U] (courage) 勇气 yǒngqì ▶**to get on sb's nerves** 使某人心烦 shǐ mǒurén xīnfán

nervous ['nəːvəs] ADJ 紧张的 jǐnzhāng de ▶**to be nervous about sth/about doing sth** 对某事/做某事感到紧张不安 duì mǒushì/zuò mǒushì gǎndào jǐnzhāng bù'ān

nest [nɛst] N [C] 巢 cháo [个 gè]

net [nɛt] N1 [C] 网 wǎng [张 zhāng]2 (Comput) ▶**the Net** 网络 wǎngluò [个 gè]

Netherlands ['nɛðələndz] NPL ▶**the Netherlands** 荷兰 Hélán

network ['nɛtwəːk] N [C]1 网状系统 wǎngzhuàng xìtǒng [个 gè]

2 (*system*) 网络 wǎngluò [个 gè]

never ['nevə^r] ADV 从未 cóngwèi ▶**we never saw him again** 我们再没有见过他 wǒmen zài méiyǒu jiànguò tā

new [njuː] ADJ **1** 崭新的 zhǎnxīn de **2** [+ *product, system, method*] 新式的 xīnshì de **3** [+ *job, address, boss, president*] 新的 xīn de ▶**this concept is new to me** 我对这个概念不熟悉 wǒ duì zhège gàiniàn bù shóuxī

news [njuːz] N [U] 消息 xiāoxi ▶**a piece of news** 一条消息 yītiáo xiāoxi ▶**good/bad news** 好/坏消息 hǎo/huài xiāoxi ▶**the news** (TV, Rad) 新闻 xīnwén

newsagent ['njuːzeɪdʒənt] (*Brit*) N [c] (*also*: **newsagent's**) 报刊店 bàokāndiàn [家 jiā]

newspaper ['njuːzpeɪpə^r] N [c] 报纸 bàozhǐ [份 fèn]

New Year N [U] ▶**(the) New Year** 新年 Xīnnián ▶**in the New Year** 在新的一年中 zài xīnde yīnián zhōng ▶**Happy New Year!** 新年快乐! Xīnnián Kuàilè!

New Year's Day, (*US*) **New Year's** N [U] 元旦 Yuándàn

New Year's Eve, (*US*) **New Year's** N [U] 元旦前夜 Yuándàn qiányè

New Zealand [-'ziːlənd] I N 新西兰 Xīnxīlán II ADJ 新西兰的 Xīnxīlán de

next [nɛkst] I ADJ **1** 下一个的 xiàyīgè de **2** [+ *house, street, room*] 旁边的 pángbiān de II ADV 接下来地 jiēxiàlái de ▶**the next**

day/morning 第二天/天早晨 dì'èrtiān/tiān zǎochén ▶**the next five years/weeks will be very important** 接下来的5年/周将是至关重要的 jiēxiàlái de wǔnián/zhōu jiāngshì zhì guān zhòng yào de ▶**the next flight/prime minister** 下一次航班/下一任首相 xià yīcì hángbān/xià yīrèn shǒuxiàng ▶**next time, be a bit more careful** 下一次，要更谨慎些 xài yīcì, yào gèng jǐnshèn xiē ▶**who's next?** 下一位是谁？xià yīwèi shì shuí? ▶**the week after next** 下下个星期 xiàxiàgè xīngqī ▶**next to** (*beside*) 旁边 pángbiān

next door ADV 隔壁 gébì

NHS (*Brit*) N ABBR (= **National Health Service**) ▶**the NHS** 英国国民医疗服务制度 Yīngguó guómín yīliáo fúwù zhìdù

nice [naɪs] ADJ **1** 好的 hǎo de **2** [+ *person*] (*likeable*) 和蔼的 hé'ǎi de; (*friendly*) 友好的 yǒuhǎo de ▶**to look nice** 看上去不错 kànshàngqù bùcuò ▶**it's nice to see you** 很高兴见到你 hěn gāoxìng jiàndào nǐ

nickname ['nɪkneɪm] N [c] 绰号 chuòhào [个 gè]

niece [niːs] N [c] (*brother's daughter*) 侄女 zhínǚ [个 gè]; (*sister's daughter*) 甥女 shēngnǚ [个 gè]

Nigeria [naɪ'dʒɪərɪə] N 尼日利亚 Nírìlìyà

night [naɪt] N **1** [c/u] 黑夜 hēiyè [个 gè] **2** [c] (*evening*) 晚上 wǎnshang [个 gè] ▶**at night** 夜间 yèjiān ▶**in/during the night**

夜里 yèlǐ

nightclub ['naɪtklʌb] N [c] 夜总
会 yèzǒnghuì [个 gè]

nightie ['naɪtɪ] N [c] 睡衣 shuìyī
[件 jiàn]

nightmare ['naɪtmɛəʳ] N [c] 恶梦
èmèng [场 chǎng]

nil [nɪl] N [u] (Brit) (Sport) 零 líng
▶**they lost two nil to Italy** 他们
以0比2输给意大利队 tāmen yǐ líng
bǐ èr shūgěi yìdàlì duì 2 ▶**their
chances of survival are nil** 他们
没有幸存的可能 tāmen méiyǒu
xìngcún de kěnéng

nine [naɪn] NUM 九 jiǔ; see also
five

nineteen ['naɪn'tiːn] NUM 十九
shíjiǔ; see also **fifteen**

ninety ['naɪntɪ] NUM 九十 jiǔshí;
see also **fifty**

KEYWORD

no [nəʊ] (pl **noes**) I ADV (opposite of
"yes") 不 bù ▶"**did you see it?**" —
"**no (I didn't)**" "你看见了吗?"
"不(我没见到)" "nǐ kànjiàn le
ma?" "bù (wǒ méi jiàndào)" ▶**no
thank you, no thanks** 不用, 谢
谢你 bùyòng, xièxie nǐ
II ADJ (not any) 没有 méiyǒu ▶**I
have no milk/books** 我没有牛
奶/书 wǒ méiyǒu niúnǎi/shū ▶"**no
smoking**" "严禁吸烟" "yánjìn
xīyān" ▶**no way!** 没门儿!
méiménr!

nobody ['nəʊbədɪ] PRON 没有人
méiyǒu rén

noise [nɔɪz] N 1 [c] (sound) 响声
xiǎngshēng [阵 zhèn] 2 [u] (din) 噪
音 zàoyīn

noisy ['nɔɪzɪ] ADJ 嘈杂的 cáozá
de; [+ place] 喧闹的 xuānnào de

none [nʌn] PRON 1 (not one) 没有
一个 méiyǒu yī gè 2 (not any) 没
有一点儿 méiyǒu yīdiǎnr ▶**none
of us/them** 我们/他们谁也
没 wǒmen/tāmen shuí yě méi
▶**I've/there's none left** 我一点也
没有了/一点也没剩 wǒ yīdiǎn yě
méiyǒu le/yīdiǎn yě méi shèng

nonsense ['nɔnsəns] N [u] 胡说
八道 hú shuō bādào

non-smoking ['nɔn'sməʊkɪŋ]
ADJ 禁烟的 jìn yān de

non-stop ['nɔn'stɔp] ADV
1 (ceaselessly) 不断地 bùduàn de 2
不停地 bù tíng de

noodles ['nuːdlz] NPL 面条
miàntiáo

noon [nuːn] N [u] 中午 zhōngwǔ
▶**at noon** 中午 zhōngwǔ

no-one ['nəʊwʌn] PRON =
nobody

nor [nɔːʳ] CONJ 也不 yěbù; see also
neither

normal ['nɔːməl] ADJ 正常的
zhèngcháng de ▶**more/higher/
worse than normal** 比正常的
多/高/糟糕 bǐ zhèngchángde
duō/gāo/zāogāo

normally ['nɔːməlɪ] ADV (usually)
通常地 tōngcháng de

north [nɔːθ] I N [u/s] 北方
běifāng II ADJ 北部的 běibù de
III ADV 向北方 xiàng běifāng ▶**to
the north** 以北 yǐběi ▶**north of**

…以北 …yǐběi

North America N 北美 Běiměi

north-east[nɔːθ'iːst] I N 东北 dōngběi II ADJ 东北的 dōngběi de III ADV 向东北 xiàng dōngběi

northern['nɔːðən] ADJ 北方 的 běifāng de ▶**the northern hemisphere** 北半球 běibànqiú

Northern Ireland N 北爱尔兰 Běi'ài'ěrlán

North Korea N 朝鲜 Cháoxiǎn

North Pole N ▶**the North Pole** 北极 Běijí

north-west[nɔːθ'wɛst] I N 西 北 xīběi II ADJ 西北的 xīběi de III ADV 向西北 xiàng xīběi

Norway['nɔːweɪ] N 挪威 Nuówēi

nose[nəuz] N [c] 鼻子 bízi [个 gè]

not[nɔt] ADV 不 bù ▶**he is not or isn't here** 他不在这儿 tā bùzài zhè'er ▶**it's too late, isn't it?** 现在太晚了，不是吗？xiànzài tàiwǎn le, bùshì ma? ▶**he asked me not to do it** 他叫我不要这么做 tā jiào wǒ bùyào zhème zuò ▶**are you coming or not?** 你来不来？nǐ láibùlái? ▶**not at all** (in answer to thanks) 不客气 bù kèqi ▶**not yet/now** 还没/现在不 háiméi/xiànzài bù ▶**not really** 并不是的 bìng bùshì de

note[nəut] I N [c] 1(message) 便 条 biàntiáo [张 zhāng] 2(Brit: banknote) 纸币 zhǐbì [张 zhāng] II VT (observe) 留意 liúyì III **notes** NPL (from or for lecture) 笔记 bǐjì ▶**to make a note of sth** 记下某事 jìxià mǒushì ▶**to take notes** 记 笔记 jì bǐjì

notebook['nəutbuk] N [c] 笔记 本 bǐjìběn [个 gè]

notepad['nəutpæd] N [c] 1(pad of paper) 记事本 jìshìběn [个 gè] 2(Comput) 记事簿 jìshìbù [个 gè]

nothing['nʌθɪŋ] PRON 什么也没 有 shénme yě méiyǒu ▶**nothing new/serious/to worry about** 没有什么新的/要紧的/值得担忧 的 méiyǒu shénme xīnde/yàojǐn de/zhídé dānyōu de ▶**nothing else** 没有别的 méiyǒu biéde ▶**for nothing** 免费 miǎnfèi ▶**nothing at all** 什么也没有 shénme yě méiyǒu

notice['nəutɪs] I VT 注意到 zhùyì dào II N [c] 公告 gōnggào [个 gè] ▶**to notice that...** 注意到… zhùyì dào... ▶**to take no notice of sb/sth** 不理某人/某事 bùlǐ mǒurén/mǒushì ▶**without notice** 不事先通知 bù shìxiān tōngzhī

noticeboard['nəutɪsbɔːd] (Brit) N [c] 布告栏 bùgàolán [个 gè]

nought[nɔːt] (esp Brit) NUM 零 líng

noun[naun] N [c] 名词 míngcí [个 gè]

novel['nɔvl] N [c] 小说 xiǎoshuō [部 bù]

novelist['nɔvəlɪst] N [c] 小说家 xiǎoshuōjiā [位 wèi]

November[nəu'vɛmbər] N [c/u] 十一月 shíyīyuè [个 gè]; see also **July**

now[nau] I ADV 1 现在 xiànzài 2(these days) 如今 rújīn II CONJ ▶**now (that)** 既然 jìrán ▶**right now** 这时 zhèshí ▶**by now** 到

现在 dào xiànzài ▶**just now** 眼下 yǎnxià ▶**from now on** 从现在起 cóng xiànzài qǐ ▶**that's all for now** 就到这里 jiùdào zhèli

nowhere['nəʊwɛə^r] ADV 无处 wúchù ▶**nowhere else** 没有其他地方 méiyǒu qítā dìfang

nuclear['njuːklɪə^r] ADJ 核能的 hénéng de

nuisance['njuːsns] N ▶**to be a nuisance** [*thing*] 讨厌的东西 tǎoyàn de dōngxi

numb[nʌm] ADJ 麻木的 mámù de

number['nʌmbə^r] I N 1[c] (*Math*) 数 shù [个 gè] 2[c] (*telephone number*) 电话号码 diànhuà hàomǎ [个 gè] 3[c] (*of house, bank account, bus*) 号 hào [个 gè] 4[c/U] (*quantity*) 数量 .shùliàng II VT [+ *pages*] 给…标号码 gěi…biāo hàomǎ ▶**a number of** (*several*) 几个 ▶**a large/small number of** 大量/少数 dàliàng/shǎoshù

number plate(*Brit*) N [c] 车号牌 chēhàopái [个 gè]

nun[nʌn] N [c] 修女 xiūnǚ [名 míng]

nurse[nəːs] N [c] 护士 hùshi [位 wèi]

nursery['nəːsərɪ] N [c] 幼儿园 yòu'éryuán [个 gè]

nursery school N [c/U] 幼儿园 yòu'éryuán [个 gè]

nut[nʌt] N [c] 1(*Bot, Culin*) 坚果 jiānguǒ [枚 méi] 2(*Tech*) 螺母 luómǔ [个 gè]

nylon['naɪlɔn] N [U] 尼龙 nílóng

oak[əʊk] N 1[c] (*also:* **oak tree**) 橡树 xiàngshù [棵 kē] 2[U] (*wood*) 橡木 xiàngmù

oar[ɔː^r] N [c] 桨 jiǎng [只 zhī]

oats[əʊts] NPL 燕麦 yànmài

obedient[ə'biːdɪənt] ADJ 顺从的 shùncóng de

obey[ə'beɪ] I VT [+ *person, orders*] 听从 tīngcóng; [+ *law, regulations*] 服从 fúcóng II VI 服从 fúcóng

object[*n* 'ɔbdʒɛkt, *vb* əb'dʒɛkt] I N [c] 1(*thing*) 物体 wùtǐ [个 gè] 2(*Ling*) 宾语 bīnyǔ [个 gè] II VI 反对 fǎnduì

objection[əb'dʒɛkʃən] N [c] 异议 yìyì [个 gè]

obsess[əb'sɛs] VT 使着迷 shǐ zháomí

obsession[əb'sɛʃən] N [c] 着迷

zháomí [种 zhǒng]

obtain [əb'teɪn] VT 获得 huòdé

obvious ['ɒbvɪəs] ADJ 明显的 míngxiǎn de

obviously ['ɒbvɪəslɪ] ADV (of course) 显然地 xiǎnrán de

occasion [ə'keɪʒən] N [c] 1 (moment) 时刻 shíkè [个 gè] 2 (event, celebration) 场合 chǎnghé [种 zhǒng]

occasionally [ə'keɪʒənəlɪ] ADV 偶尔地 ǒu'ěr de

occupation [ɒkju'peɪʃən] N [c] 职业 zhíyè [种 zhǒng]

occupy ['ɒkjupaɪ] VT 1 (inhabit) [+ house, office] 占用 zhànyòng 2 ▶to be occupied [seat, place etc] 被占用 bèi zhànyòng 3 (fill) [+ time] 占用 zhànyòng

occur [ə'kəːʳ] VI 发生 fāshēng ▶to occur to sb 某人想到 mǒurén xiǎngdào

ocean ['əuʃən] N [c] 海洋 hǎiyáng [片 piàn]

o'clock [ə'klɔk] ADV ▶six o'clock 6点钟 liùdiǎnzhōng

October [ɒk'təubəʳ] N [c/u] 十月 shíyuè; see also **July**

octopus ['ɒktəpəs] N [c] 章鱼 zhāngyú [只 zhī]

odd [ɒd] ADJ 1 (strange) 奇怪的 qíguài de 2 [+ number] 奇数的 jīshù de

odour, (US) **odor** ['əudəʳ] N [c/u] 气味 qìwèi [种 zhǒng]

KEYWORD

of [ɒv, əv] PREP 1 (gen) 的 de

▶the history of China 中国历史 Zhōngguó lìshǐ ▶at the end of the street 在街的尽头 zài jiēde jìntóu ▶the city of New York 纽约城 Niǔyuēchéng 2 (expressing quantity, amount) ▶a kilo of flour 一公斤面粉 yī gōngjīn miànfěn ▶a cup of tea/vase of flowers 一杯茶/一瓶花 yìbēi chá/yìpíng huā ▶there were three of them 他们有3个 tāmen yǒu sāngè ▶an annual income of $30,000 每年3万美元 的收入 měinián sānwàn měiyuán de shōurù 3 (in dates) ▶the 5th of July 7月 5日 qīyuè wǔrì 4 (US: in times) ▶at five of three 3点差5分 sāndiǎn chà wǔfēn

KEYWORD

off [ɒf] I ADJ 1 (not turned on) 关着 的 guānzhe de 2 (cancelled) 取消的 qǔxiāo de II ADV 1 (away) ▶I must be off 我 必须得走了 wǒ bìxū děi zǒu le ▶where are you off to? 你上哪儿 去? nǐ shàng nǎr qù? 2 (not at work) ▶to have a day off (as holiday) 休假一天 xiūjià yītiān; (because ill) 休病假一天 xiūbìngjià yītiān 3 (Comm) ▶10% off 10%的折扣 bǎifēn zhī shí de zhékòu III PREP (indicating motion, removal etc) ▶to take a picture off the wall 把画像从墙上取下来 bǎ huàxiàng cóng qiáng shang qǔ xiàlái

offence, (US) **offense** [əˈfɛns] N [c] (crime) 罪行 zuìxíng [种 zhǒng]

offend [əˈfɛnd] VT (upset) 得罪 dézuì

offense [əˈfɛns] (US) N [c] = **offence**

offer [ˈɔfəʳ] I VT 1 给 gěi 2 (bid) 出价 chūjià II N [c] 1 提议 tíyì [项 xiàng] 2 (special deal) 特价 tèjià [个 gè]

office [ˈɔfɪs] N 1 [c] (room) 办公室 bàngōngshì [间 jiān] 2 [c] (department) 部门 bùmén [个 gè] 3 [c] (US: of doctor, dentist) 诊所 zhěnsuǒ [家 jiā]

office block N [c] 办公大楼 bàngōng dàlóu [座 zuò]

officer [ˈɔfɪsəʳ] N [c] 1 (Mil) 军官 jūnguān [位 wèi] 2 (also: **police officer**) 警官 jǐngguān [位 wèi]

office worker N [c] 职员 zhíyuán [个 gè]

official [əˈfɪʃl] ADJ 官方的 guānfāng de

often [ˈɔfn] ADV (frequently) 经常 jīngcháng ▶**how often do you wash the car?** 你多久洗一次车? nǐ duōjiǔ xǐ yīcì chē?

oil [ɔɪl] I N [c/u] 油 yóu [桶 tǒng] II VT [+ engine, machine] 给…加油 gěi…jiāyóu

oil rig N [c] (on land) 石油钻塔 shíyóu zuàntǎ [个 gè]; (at sea) 钻井平台 zuànjǐng píngtái [个 gè]

okay [əʊˈkeɪ] I ADJ 1 (acceptable) 可以的 kěyǐ de 2 (safe and well) 好的 hǎo de II ADV (acceptably) 不错 bùcuò III INT 1 (expressing agreement) 行 xíng 2 (in questions) 好吗 hǎo ma ▶**are you okay?** 你还好吗? nǐ hái hǎoma? ▶**it's okay with** or **by me** 这对我没问题 zhè duìwǒ méi wèntí

old [əʊld] ADJ 1 [+ person] 年老的 niánlǎo de 2 (not new, not recent) 古老的 gǔlǎo de 3 (worn out) 破旧的 pòjiù de 4 (former) 以前的 yǐqián de 5 [+ friend, enemy, rival] 老的 lǎo de ▶**how old are you?** 你多大了? nǐ duōdà le? ▶**he's 10 years old** 他10岁了 tā shísuì le ▶**older brother/sister** 哥哥/姐姐 gēge/jiějie

old age pensioner (Brit) N [c] 拿退休金的人 ná tuìxiūjīn de rén [位 wèi]

old-fashioned [ˈəʊldˈfæʃnd] ADJ [+ object, custom, idea] 老式的 lǎoshì de; [+ person] 守旧的 shǒujiù de

olive [ˈɔlɪv] N [c] 橄榄 gǎnlǎn [棵 kē]

olive oil N [u] 橄榄油 gǎnlǎnyóu

Olympic [əʊˈlɪmpɪk] I ADJ 奥林匹克的 Àolínpǐkè de II **the Olympics** NPL 奥林匹克运动会 Àolínpǐkè Yùndònghuì

omelette, (US) **omelet** [ˈɔmlɪt] N [c] 煎蛋饼 jiāndànbǐng [个 gè]

KEYWORD

on [ɔn] I PREP 1 (indicating position) 在…上 zài…shang ▶**it's on the table/wall** 它在桌上/墙上 tā zài zhuōshàng/qiángshàng ▶**the house is on the main road** 房子在主路旁 fángzi zài zhǔlù páng ▶**on the left/right** 在左边/右边 zài zuǒbiān/yòubiān ▶**on the top floor** 在顶楼 zài dǐnglóu **2**(indicating means, method, condition etc) ▶**on foot** 步行 bùxíng ▶**on the train/bus** (be, sit) 在火车/公共汽车上 zài huǒchē/gōnggòng qìchē shàng; (travel, go) 乘坐 chéngzuò ▶**on the television/radio** 在电视上/广播中 zài diànshì shàng/guǎngbō zhōng ▶**on the Internet** 在因特网上 zài Yīntèwǎng shàng ▶**to be on antibiotics** 定期服用抗生素 dìngqī fúyòng kàngshēngsù **3**(referring to time) 在 zài ▶**on Friday** 在星期五 zài xīngqīwǔ ▶**on Friday, June 20th** 在6月20日，星期五 zài liùyuè èrshí rì, xīngqīwǔ

II ADV **1**(clothes) ▶**to have one's coat on** 穿着外套 chuānzhe wàitào ▶**what's she got on?** 她穿着什么？ tā chuānzhe shénme? **2**(covering, lid etc) ▶**screw the lid on tightly** 把盖子旋紧 bǎ gàizi xuánjǐn

III ADJ **1**(turned on) 打开的 dǎkāi de

2(happening) ▶**is the meeting still on?** 会议还在进行吗？ huìyì háizài jìnxíng ma? ▶**there's a good film on at the cinema** 电影院正在上映一部好电影 diànyǐngyuàn zhèngzài shàngyìng yībù hǎo diànyǐng

once[wʌns] **I** ADV **1**(one time only) 一次 yīcì **2**(at one time) 曾经 céngjīng **3**(on one occasion) 有一次 yǒu yīcì **II** CONJ (as soon as) 一旦 yīdàn ▶**at once** (immediately) 立刻 lìkè ▶**once a** or **every month** 每月一次 měiyuè yīcì ▶**once upon a time** (in stories) 很久以前 hěnjiǔ yǐqián ▶**once in a while** 偶尔 ǒu'ěr ▶**once or twice** (a few times) 一两次 yīliǎng cì

KEYWORD

one[wʌn] **I** ADJ **1**(number) 一 yī ▶**it's one o'clock** 现在1点 xiànzài yīdiǎn ▶**one hundred/thousand children** 100/1000个孩子 yībǎi/yīqiān gè háizi

2(same) 同一的 tóngyī de ▶**shall I put it all on the one plate?** 要我把它都放在同一个盘子里吗？ yào wǒ bǎ tā dōu fàngzài tóngyīgè pánzi lǐ ma?

II PRON **1**(number) 一 yī ▶**I've already got one** 我已经有一个了 wǒ yǐjīng yǒu yīgè le ▶**one of them/of the boys** 他们中的一个/男孩中的一个 tāmen zhōng de yīgè/nánhái zhōng de yīgè ▶**one by one** 一个一个地 yīgè yīgè de **2**(with adj) 一个 yīgè ▶**I've already got a red one** 我已经有一个红的了 wǒ yǐjīng yǒu yīgè hóngde le

3(in generalizations) 人人 rénrén ▶**what can one do?** 一个人能做什么呢？ yīgèrén néng zuò shénme ne? ▶**this one** 这个

zhègè ▶**that one** 那个 nàgè
III N (*numeral*) 一 yī

 KEYWORD

oneself PRON 自己 zìjǐ ▶**to hurt
oneself** 伤了自己 shāngle zìjǐ
▶**by oneself** (*unaided*) 独力地 dúlì
de; (*alone*) 独自 dúzì

one-way ['wʌnweɪ] ADJ 1 [+ *street,
traffic*] 单行的 dānxíng de
2 [+ *ticket, trip*] 单程的 dānchéng
de

onion ['ʌnjən] N [c] 洋葱
yángcōng [个 gè]

online, on-line ['ɒnlaɪn]
(*Comput*) ADV (*on the Internet*) 网上
wǎngshang

only ['əʊnlɪ] I ADV 1 仅仅 jǐnjǐn
2 (*emphasizing insignificance*) 只
zhǐ II ADJ (*sole*) 唯一的 wéiyī de
III CONJ (*but*) 可是 kěshì ▶**I was
only joking** 我只是在开玩笑。
wǒ zhǐshì zài kāi wánxiào ▶**not
only... but (also)...** 不但…而且…
bùdàn…érqiě… ▶**an only child**
独生子女 dúshēng zǐnǚ

onto, on to ['ɒntu] PREP 到…上
dào…shàng

open ['əʊpn] I ADJ 1 [+ *door,
window*] 开着的 kāizhe de;
[+ *mouth, eyes*] 张着的 zhāngzhe
de 2 [+ *shop*] 营业的 yíngyè de
II VT [+ *container*] 打开 dǎkāi;
[+ *door, lid*] 开 kāi; [+ *letter*] 拆
开 chāikāi; [+ *book, hand, mouth,
eyes*] 开 kāi III VI 1 [*door, lid*] 开
kāi 2 [*public building*] 开门 kāimén

▶**in the open (air)** 在户外 zài
hùwài

opening hours NPL 营业时间
yíngyè shíjiān

open-minded [əʊpn'maɪndɪd]
ADJ 开明的 kāimíng de

opera ['ɒpərə] N [c] 歌剧 gējù
[部 bù]

operate ['ɒpəreɪt] I VT [+ *machine,
vehicle, system*] 操作 cāozuò II VI
1 [*machine, vehicle, system*] 工作
gōngzuò; [*company, organization*]
运作 yùnzuò 2 (*Med*) 动手术
dòngshǒushù ▶**to operate on sb**
(*Med*) 给某人动手术 gěi mǒurén
dòng shǒushù

operation [ɒpə'reɪʃən] N 1 [c]
(*procedure*) 实施步骤 shíshī
bùzhòu [个 gè] 2 [c] (*Med*) 手
术 shǒushù [次 cì] ▶**to have
an operation** (*Med*) 接受手术
jiēshòu shǒushù

operator ['ɒpəreɪtər] N [c] (*Tel*) 接
线员 jiēxiànyuán [位 wèi]

opinion [ə'pɪnjən] N [c] (*individual
view*) 观点 guāndiǎn [个 gè] ▶**in
my/her opinion** 按我的/她的意
见 àn wǒde/tāde yìjiàn

opinion poll N [c] 民意测验
mínyì cèyàn [次 cì]

opponent [ə'pəʊnənt] N [c] 对手
duìshǒu [个 gè]

opportunity [ɒpə'tjuːnɪtɪ] N
[c/u] 机会 jīhuì [个 gè] ▶**to take
the opportunity of doing sth** or
to do sth 趁机会做某事 chèn jīhuì
zuò mǒushì

oppose [ə'pəʊz] VT [+ *person, idea*]
反对 fǎnduì ▶**to be opposed to**

sth 反对某事 fǎnduì mǒushì

opposite ['ɔpəzɪt] I ADJ 1 [+ side, house] 对面的 duìmiàn de 2 [+ end, corner] 最远的 zuìyuǎn de 3 [+ meaning, direction] 相反的 xiāngfǎn de II ADV (live, work, sit) 在对面 zài duìmiàn III PREP 在…的对面 zài…de duìmiàn IV N ▶the opposite 对立面 duìlìmiàn ▶the opposite sex 异性 yìxìng

opposition [ɔpə'zɪʃən] N [U] 反对 fǎnduì

optician [ɔp'tɪʃən] N [c] 1 眼镜商 yǎnjìngshāng [个 gè] 2 (also: **optician's**) 眼镜店 yǎnjìngdiàn [家 jiā]

optimistic [ɔptɪ'mɪstɪk] ADJ 乐观的 lèguān de

option ['ɔpʃən] N [c] 1 (choice) 选择 xuǎnzé [种 zhǒng] 2 (Scol, Univ) 选修课 xuǎnxiūkè [门 mén]

or [ɔːʳ] CONJ 1 还是 háishì 2 (also: **or else**) 否则 fǒuzé

oral ['ɔːrəl] I ADJ [+ test, report] 口头的 kǒutóu de II N [c] 口试 kǒushì [次 cì]

orange ['ɔrɪndʒ] I N [c] (fruit) 柑橘 gānjú [只 zhī] II ADJ (in colour) 橙色的 chéngsè de

orange juice ['ɔrɪndʒdʒuːs] N [U] 橘子汁 júzizhī

orchard ['ɔːtʃəd] N [c] 果园 guǒyuán [个 gè]

orchestra ['ɔːkɪstrə] N [c] 管弦乐队 guǎnxián yuèduì [支 zhī]

order ['ɔːdəʳ] I N 1 (command) 命令 mìnglìng [个 gè] 2 (Comm) (in restaurant) 点菜 diǎncài [份 fèn] 3 [U] (sequence) 次序 cìxù

II VT 1 (command) 命令 mìnglìng 2 (Comm: from shop, company) 定购 dìnggòu; (in restaurant) 点菜 diǎncài III VI (in restaurant) 点菜 diǎncài ▶in alphabetical/ numerical order 按字母/数字顺序 àn zìmǔ/shùzì shùnxù ▶out of order (not working) 已坏停用 yǐhuài tíngyòng ▶in order to do sth 为了做某事 wèile zuò mǒushì ▶to order sb to do sth 命令某人做某事 mìnglìng mǒurén zuò mǒushì

ordinary ['ɔːdnrɪ] ADJ 普通的 pǔtōng de

organ ['ɔːgən] N [c] 1 (Anat) 器官 qìguān [个 gè] 2 (Mus) 管风琴 guǎnfēngqín [架 jià]

organic [ɔː'gænɪk] ADJ 1 [+ food, farming] 有机的 yǒujī de 2 [+ substance] 有机物的 yǒujīwù de

organization [ɔːgənaɪ'zeɪʃən] N [c] 组织 zǔzhī [个 gè]

organize ['ɔːgənaɪz] VT 组织 zǔzhī

original [ə'rɪdʒɪnl] ADJ 1 (first, earliest) 最初的 zuìchū de 2 (imaginative) 独创的 dúchuàng de

originally [ə'rɪdʒɪnəlɪ] ADV 起初 qǐchū

ornament ['ɔːnəmənt] N [c] 装饰物 zhuāngshìwù [件 jiàn]

orphan ['ɔːfn] N [c] 孤儿 gū'ér [个 gè]

other ['ʌðəʳ] I ADJ 1 (additional) 另外的 lìngwài de 2 (not this one) 其他的 qítā de 3 ▶the other...

(*of two things or people*) 另一… lìngyī… 4 (*apart from oneself*) 其他 qítā de II PRON 1 (*additional one, different one*) 其他 qítā 2 (*of two things or people*) ▸the other 另一个 lìng yīgè ▸the other day/week (*inf: recently*) 几天/星期前 jǐtiān/xīngqī qián

otherwise [ˈʌðəwaɪz] ADV 1 (*if not*) 否则 fǒuzé 2 (*apart from that*) 除此以外 chúcǐ yǐwài

ought [ɔːt] (*pt* ought) AUX VB 1 (*indicating advisability*) ▸you ought to see a doctor 你应该去看医生 nǐ yīnggāi qù kàn yīshēng 2 (*indicating likelihood*) ▸he ought to be there now 他现在应该到那儿了 tā xiànzài yīnggāi dào nàr le

our [ˈauəʳ] ADJ 我们的 wǒmen de

ours [auəz] PRON 我们的 wǒmen de

ourselves [auəˈsɛlvz] PRON PL 我们自己 wǒmen zìjǐ ▸we didn't hurt ourselves 我们没伤到自己 wǒmen méi shāngdào zìjǐ ▸by ourselves (*unaided*) 我们独力地 wǒmen dúlì de; (*alone*) 我们单独地 wǒmen dāndú de

○ KEYWORD

out [aut] I ADV 1 (*outside*) 在外面 zài wàimiàn ▸out here/there 这儿/那儿 zhè'r/nà'r 2 (*absent, not in*) 不在 bù zài ▸Mr Green is out at the moment 格林先生这会儿不在 Gélín xiānshēng zhèhuì'r bùzài ▸to have a day/night out 外出玩一

天/一晚 wàichū wán yītiān/yīwǎn 3 (*Sport*) ▸the ball was out 球出界了 qiú chūjiè le II ADJ ▸to be out (*out of game*) 出局的 chūjú de; (*extinguished*) [*fire, light, gas*] 熄灭的 xīmiè de III ▸ out of PREP 1 (*outside: with movement*) 出 chū; (*beyond*) 朝…外 cháo…wài ▸to go/come out of the house 从房子里走出去/来 cóng fángzi lǐ zǒu chūqù/lái 2 (*from among*) …中的 …zhōng de ▸one out of every three smokers 每3个烟民中的1个 měi sāngè yānmín zhōng de yīgè 3 (*without*) ▸to be out of milk/petrol 牛奶喝完了/汽油用完了 niúnǎi hē wán le/qìyóu yòng wán le

outdoor [autˈdɔːʳ] ADJ 1 [+ *activity*] 户外的 hùwài de 2 [+ *swimming pool, toilet*] 露天的 lùtiān de

outdoors [autˈdɔːz] ADV 在户外 zài hùwài

outing [ˈautɪŋ] N [c] 出游 chūyóu [次 cì]

outlet [ˈautlɛt] N [c] 1 (*hole, pipe*) 排放口 páifàngkǒu [个 gè] 2 (*US*) (*Elec*) 电源插座 diànyuán chāzuò [个 gè]

outline [ˈautlaɪn] N [c] 1 (*shape*) 轮廓 lúnkuò [个 gè] 2 (*brief explanation*) 概要 gàiyào [篇 piān]

outside [autˈsaɪd] I N [c] 外面 wàimiàn [个 gè]; [*of building*] 外表 wàibiǎo [个 gè] II ADJ (*exterior*) 外部的 wàibù de III ADV 1 (*be, wait*) 在外面 zài wàimiàn 2 (*go*) 向外面

xiàng wàimiàn **IV** PREP**1** [+ *place*] 在…外 zài…wài; [+ *organization*] 在…以外 zài…yǐwài**2** [+ *larger place*] 在…附近 zài…fùjìn

outskirts ['autskə:ts] NPL ▶**the outskirts** 郊区 jiāoqū ▶**on the outskirts of...** 在…的郊区 zài…de jiāoqū

outstanding [aut'stændıŋ] ADJ 杰出的 jiéchū de

oval ['əuvl] ADJ 椭圆形的 tuǒyuánxíng de

oven ['ʌvn] N [C] 烤箱 kǎoxiāng [个 gè]

KEYWORD

over ['əuvə^r] **I** ADJ (*finished*) 结束 的 jiéshù de

II PREP**1** (*more than*) 超过 chāoguò ▶**over 200 people came** 超过二百人来了 zhāoguò èrbǎirén láile

2 在…上 zài…shang; (*spanning*) 横跨 héngkuà; (*across*) 穿过 chuānguò; (*on the other side of*) 在…对面 zài…duìmiàn ▶**a bridge over the river** 横跨河流的一座桥 héngkuà héliú de yīzuò qiáo

3 (*during*) 在…期间 zài…qījiān ▶**we talked about it over dinner** 我们边吃晚饭边讨论 wǒmen biān chī wǎnfàn biān tǎolùn

4 [+ *illness, shock, trauma*] 康复 kāngfù

5 ▶**all over the town/house/ floor** 全镇/满屋子/满地 quánzhèn/mǎn wūzi/mǎndì

III ADV**1** 过 guò ▶**over here/ there** 在这里/那里 zài zhèlǐ/nàlǐ

2 (*more, above*) 超过 chāoguò ▶**people aged 65 and over** 65岁 及以上年龄的人 liùshíwǔ suì jí yǐshàng niánlíng de rén

3 (*US: again*) 再 zài

4 ▶**all over** (*everywhere*) 到处 dàochù

overcast ['əuvəkɑ:st] ADJ 多云的 duōyún de

overdose ['əuvədəus] N [C] 过量 用药 guòliàng yòngyào [剂 ji]

overseas [əuvə'si:z] ADV 向海外 xiàng hǎiwài

overtake [əuvə'teɪk] (*pt* **overtook**, *pp* **overtaken**) **I** VT (*esp Brit*) (*Aut*) 超过 chāoguò **II** VI (*esp Brit*) (*Aut*) 超车 chāochē

overtime ['əuvətaɪm] N [U] 加班 时间 jiābān shíjiān

overtook [əuvə'tuk] PT *of* **overtake**

overweight [əuvə'weɪt] ADJ 超 重的 chāozhòng de

owe [əu] VT [+ *money*] 欠 qiàn ▶**to owe sb sth** 欠某人某物 qiàn mǒurén mǒuwù

owing to ['əuıŋ-] PREP (*because of*) 因为 yīnwèi

owl [aul] N [C] 猫头鹰 māotóuyīng [只 zhī]

own [əun] **I** ADJ 自己的 zìjǐ de **II** VT [+ *house, land, car etc*] 拥有 yōngyǒu ▶**a room of my own** 我 自己的房间 wǒ zìjǐ de fángjiān ▶**on one's own** (*alone*) 独自 地 dúzì de; (*without help*) 独立 地 dúlì de

▶ **own up** vɪ (*confess*) 坦白 tǎnbái

owner ['əunəʳ] N [c] 物主 wùzhǔ [位 wèi]

oxygen ['ɔksɪdʒən] N [U] 氧气 yǎngqì

oyster ['ɔɪstəʳ] N [c] 牡蛎 mǔlì [个 gè]

ozone layer N [c] 臭氧层 chòuyǎngcéng [层 céng]

Pacific [pə'sɪfɪk] N ▶ **the Pacific (Ocean)** 太平洋 Tàipíngyáng

pack [pæk] I vᴛ 1 [+ *clothes*] 把…打包 bǎ…dǎbāo 2 [+ *suitcase, bag*] 把…装箱 bǎ…zhuāngxiāng II vɪ 打点行装 dǎdiǎn xíngzhuāng III N [*of cards*] 副 fù

▶ **pack up** vɪ (*Brit*) 打点行装 dǎdiǎn xíngzhuāng

package ['pækɪdʒ] N [c] 1 包裹 bāoguǒ [个 gè] 2 (*Comput*) 程序包 chéngxùbāo [个 gè]

packed [pækt] ADJ 拥挤的 yōngjǐ de

packet ['pækɪt] N [c] [*of cigarettes, biscuits*] 盒 hé [个 gè]; [*of crisps, sweets, seeds*] 袋 dài [个 gè]

pad [pæd] N [c] 便笺簿 biànjiānbù [个 gè]

paddle ['pædl] N [C] 1 (for canoe) 短桨 duǎnjiǎng [个 gè] 2 (US: for table tennis) 球拍 qiúpāi [只 zhī]

padlock ['pædlɔk] N [C] 挂锁 guàsuǒ [个 gè]

paedophile, (US) **pedophile** ['piːdəufaɪl] N [C] 恋童癖者 liàntóngpǐzhě [个 gè]

page [peɪdʒ] N [C] 页 yè

pain [peɪn] N [c/U] 疼痛 téngtòng [阵 zhèn] ▸to have a pain in one's chest/arm 胸痛/胳膊疼 xiōngtòng/gēbo téng ▸to be in pain 在苦恼中 zài kǔnǎo zhōng

painful ['peɪnful] ADJ [+ back, joint, swelling] 疼痛的 téngtòng de

painkiller ['peɪnkɪlər] N [C] 止痛药 zhǐtòngyào [片 piàn]

paint [peɪnt] I N [c/U] 1 (decorator's) 油漆 yóuqī [桶 tǒng] 2 (artist's) 颜料 yánliào [罐 guàn] II VT 1 [+ wall, door, house] 油漆 yóuqī 2 [+ person, object] 描绘 miáohuì 3 [+ picture, portrait] 用颜料画 yòng yánliào huà III VI (creatively) 绘画 huìhuà ▸a tin of paint 一罐颜料 yīguàn yánliào ▸to paint sth blue/white etc 把某物涂成蓝色/白色〔等〕bǎ mǒuwù túchéng lánsè/báisè 〔děng〕

paintbrush ['peɪntbrʌʃ] N [C] 1 (decorator's) 漆刷 qīshuā [个 gè] 2 (artist's) 画笔 huàbǐ [支 zhī]

painter ['peɪntər] N [C] 1 (artist) 画家 huàjiā [位 wèi] 2 (decorator) 油漆工 yóuqīgōng [个 gè]

painting ['peɪntɪŋ] N 1 [U] 绘画 huìhuà; (decorating walls, doors etc)

上油漆 shàng yóuqī 2 [C] (picture) 画 huà [幅 fú]

pair [pɛər] N [C] 1 [of shoes, gloves, socks] 双 shuāng 2 (two people) 对 duì ▸a pair of scissors 一把剪刀 yībǎ jiǎndāo ▸a pair of trousers 一条裤子 yītiáo kùzi

pajamas [pə'dʒɑːməz] (US) NPL = **pyjamas**

Pakistan [pɑːkɪ'stɑːn] N 巴基斯坦 Bājīsītǎn

Pakistani [pɑːkɪ'stɑːnɪ] I ADJ 巴基斯坦的 Bājīsītǎn de II N [C] 巴基斯坦人 Bājīsītǎn rén [个 gè]

palace ['pæləs] N [C] 宫殿 gōngdiàn [座 zuò]

pale [peɪl] ADJ 1 [+ colour] 淡的 dàn de 2 [+ skin, complexion] 白皙的 báixī de 3 (from sickness, fear) 苍白的 cāngbái de ▸pale blue/pink/green 淡蓝色/粉红色/绿色 dàn lánsè/fěnhóngsè/lùsè

Palestine ['pælɪstaɪn] N 巴勒斯坦 Bālèsītǎn

Palestinian [pælɪs'tɪnɪən] I ADJ 巴勒斯坦的 Bālèsītǎn de II N [C] 巴勒斯坦人 Bālèsītǎn rén [个 gè]

pan [pæn] N [C] (also: **saucepan**) 炖锅 dùnguō [口 kǒu]

pancake ['pænkeɪk] N [C] 薄煎饼 báo jiānbing [张 zhāng]

○ **PANCAKE**
○
○ 如果你要求英国厨师和美国
○ 厨师为你做一张 **pancake**,
○ 饼的样子决不会是一模
○ 一样。在这两个国家,
○ **pancake** 都呈扁平圆形,用

牛奶，面粉和鸡蛋打成面糊，油炸后，趁热吃。英国的饼很薄，经常卷起来，或者夹有甜味或其他口味的馅儿。很多人在 **Shrove Tuesday**（忏悔星期二）即 **Lent**（大斋节）开始前的一天吃饼，这一天就是人们熟知的 **Pancake Day**（煎饼节）。（**Lent** 是指复活节前的40天，从前基督教徒有在这段时间里斋戒的传统。）在美国，**pancake** 相对较小，较厚，通常在早餐时，就着黄油和枫糖吃。

panda ['pændə] N [c] 熊猫 xióngmāo [只 zhī]

panic ['pænɪk] I N [U] 惊恐 jīngkǒng II vi 惊慌 jīnghuāng

pants [pænts] NPL 1 (*Brit: underwear*) 内裤 nèikù 2 (*US: trousers*) 裤子 kùzi

pantyhose ['pæntɪhəʊz] (*US*) NPL 连裤袜 liánkùwà ▶ **a pair of pantyhose** 一条连裤袜 yītiáo liánkùwà

paper ['peɪpər] N 1 [U] 纸 zhǐ 2 [c] (*also*: **newspaper**) 报纸 bàozhǐ [份 fèn] ▶ **a piece of paper** (*odd bit, sheet*) 一张纸 yīzhāng zhǐ

paperback ['peɪpəbæk] N [c] 平装书 píngzhuāng shū [本 běn]

paper clip N [c] 回形针 huíxíngzhēn [枚 méi]

parachute ['pærəʃuːt] N [c] 降落伞 jiàngluòsǎn [个 gè]

parade [pə'reɪd] N [c] 游行 yóuxíng [次 cì]

paradise ['pærədaɪs] N 1 [U] (*Rel*) 天堂 tiāntáng 2 [c/U] (*fig*) 乐园 lèyuán [个 gè]

paragraph ['pærəgrɑːf] N [c] 段落 duànluò [个 gè]

parallel ['pærəlɛl] ADJ 1 平行的 píngxíng de 2 (*Comput*) 并行的 bìngxíng de

paralysed, (*US*) **paralyzed** ['pærəlaɪzd] (*Med*) ADJ 瘫痪的 tānhuàn de

paramedic [pærə'mɛdɪk] N [c] 护理人员 hùlǐ rényuán [位 wèi]

parcel ['pɑːsl] N [c] 包裹 bāoguǒ [个 gè]

pardon ['pɑːdn] N [c] ▶ **(I beg your) pardon?**, (*US*) **pardon me?** 请问您刚才说什么？ qǐngwèn nín gāngcái shuō shénme?

parent ['pɛərənt] I N [c] 1 (*father*) 父亲 fùqīn [位 wèi] 2 (*mother*) 母亲 mǔqīn [位 wèi] II **parents** NPL 父母 fùmǔ

park [pɑːk] I N [c] 公园 gōngyuán [个 gè] II vt 停放 tíngfàng III vi 停车 tíngchē

parking ['pɑːkɪŋ] N [U] 停车 tíngchē ▶ **"no parking"** "严禁停车" "yánjìn tíngchē"

parking lot (*US*) N [c] 停车场 tíngchēchǎng [个 gè]

parking meter N [c] 停车计时器 tíngchē jìshíqì [个 gè]

parking ticket N [c] 违章停车罚款单 wéizhāng tíngchē fákuǎndān [张 zhāng]

parliament ['pɑːləmənt] (*Brit*) N [c/U] 议会 yìhuì [个 gè]

parrot ['pærət] N [c] 鹦鹉 yīngwǔ

part 422

[只 zhī]

part [pɑːt] **N 1** [c/u] (*section, division*) 部分 bùfen [个 gè] **2** [c] (*of machine, vehicle*) 部件 bùjiàn [个 gè] ▶ **to take part in** (*participate in*) 参加 cānjiā
▶ **part with** VT FUS [+ *possessions*] 放弃 fàngqì; [+ *money, cash*] 花 huā

participate [pɑːˈtɪsɪpeɪt] VI 参与 cānyù ▶ **to participate in sth** [+ *activity, discussion*] 参加某事 cānjiā mǒushì

particular [pəˈtɪkjuləʳ] ADJ 特定的 tèdìng de

partly [ˈpɑːtlɪ] ADV 部分地 bùfen de

partner [ˈpɑːtnəʳ] N [c] **1** (*wife, husband, girlfriend, boyfriend*) 伴侣 bànlǚ [个 gè] **2** (*in firm*) 合伙人 héhuǒrén [个 gè] **3** (*Sport*) 搭档 dādàng [个 gè] **4** (*for cards, games*) 对家 duìjiā [个 gè] **5** (*at dance*) 舞伴 wǔbàn [个 gè]

part-time [ˈpɑːtˈtaɪm] **I** ADJ 兼职的 jiānzhí de **II** ADV (*work, study*) 部分时间地 bùfen shíjiān de

party [ˈpɑːtɪ] N [c] **1** (*Pol*) 党 dǎng [个 gè] **2** (*social event*) 聚会 jùhuì [次 cì] ▶ **birthday party** 生日聚会 shēngrì jùhuì

pass [pɑːs] **I** VT **1** (*hand*) ▶ **to pass sb sth** [+ *salt, glass, newspaper, tool*] 把某物递给某人 bǎ mǒuwù dìgěi mǒurén **2** (*go past*) 经过 jīngguò **3** [+ *exam, test*] 通过 tōngguò **II** VI **1** (*go past*) 经过 jīngguò **2** (*in exam*) 及格 jígé ▶ **to get a pass (in sth)** (*Scol, Univ*) （某考试）达到及格标准

(mǒu kǎoshì)dádào jígé biāozhǔn
▶ **pass away** VI (*die*) 去世 qùshì

passage [ˈpæsɪdʒ] N [c] 走廊 zǒuláng [条 tiáo]

passenger [ˈpæsɪndʒəʳ] N [c] 乘客 chéngkè [位 wèi]

passive [ˈpæsɪv] N [u] ▶ **the passive** (*Ling*) 被动语态 bèidòng yǔtài

passport [ˈpɑːspɔːt] N [c] 护照 hùzhào [本 běn]

password [ˈpɑːswəːd] N [c] 密码 mìmǎ [个 gè]

past [pɑːst] **I** PREP (*in front of, beyond, later than*) 过 guò **II** ADV (*by*) ▶ **to go/walk/drive past** 经/走/开过 jīng/zǒu/kāiguò **III** ADJ [+ *week, month, year*] 刚过去的 gāng guòqù de **IV** N [c] ▶ **the past** 过去 guòqù [个 gè]; (*tense*) 过去时 guòqùshí ▶ **it's past midnight** 过了午夜 guòle wǔyè ▶ **ten/(a) quarter past eight** 8点10/15分 bādiǎn shí/shíwǔ fēn ▶ **for the past few/3 days** 过去几/3天以来 guòqù jǐ/sāntiān yǐlái ▶ **the past tense** 过去时 guòqù shí ▶ **in the past** (*before now*) 在过去 zài guòqù

pasta [ˈpæstə] N [u] 意大利面食 Yìdàlì miànshí

pastry [ˈpeɪstrɪ] N **1** [u] (*dough*) 油酥面团 yóusū miàntuán **2** (*cake*) 酥皮糕点 sūpí gāodiǎn [块 kuài]

patch [pætʃ] N [c] **1** (*piece of material*) 补丁 bǔding [个 gè] **2** (*area*) 斑片 bānpiàn [块 kuài]

path [pɑːθ] N [c] (*track*) 小路 xiǎolù [条 tiáo]; (*in garden*) 小径

xiǎojìng [条 tiáo]

pathetic [pəˈθɛtɪk] ADJ (+ excuse, effort, attempt) 不足道的 bùzúdào de

patience [ˈpeɪʃns] N (U) 耐心 nàixīn

patient [ˈpeɪʃnt] I N [c] (Med) 病人 bìngrén [个 gè] II ADJ (+ person) 耐心的 nàixīn de

patrol [pəˈtrəul] VT 在…巡逻 zài…xúnluó ▶ **to be on patrol** 在巡逻中 zài xúnluó zhōng

pattern [ˈpætən] N [c] 1 花样 huāyàng [种 zhǒng] 2 (for sewing, knitting) 样式 yàngshì [个 gè]

pause [pɔːz] VI (when speaking) 停顿 tíngdùn; (when doing sth) 暂停 zàntíng

pavement [ˈpeɪvmənt] N [c] (Brit) 人行道 rénxíngdào [条 tiáo]

pay [peɪ] (pt, pp **paid**) I N [U] 工资 gōngzī II VT 1 (+ debt, bill, tax) 付 fù 2 (+ person) ▶ **to get paid** 发工资 fā gōngzī 3 ▶ **to pay sb sth** (as wage, salary, for goods, services) 付给某人某物 fùgěi mǒurén mǒuwù ▶ **how much did you pay for it?** 你买那个花了多少钱? nǐ mǎi nàgè huāle duōshǎo qián? ▶ **pay back** VT 1 (+ money, loan) 偿还 chánghuán 2 (+ person) (with money) 还给 huángěi ▶ **pay for** VT FUS 买 mǎi

payment [ˈpeɪmənt] N [c] 付款额 fùkuǎn é [笔 bǐ]

payphone [ˈpeɪfəun] N [c] 公用电话 gōngyòng diànhuà [部 bù]

PC N ABBR (= **personal computer**) 个人电脑 gèrén diànnǎo

PDA N ABBR (= **personal digital assistant**) 掌上电脑 zhǎngshàng diànnǎo

PE (Scol) N ABBR (= **physical education**) 体育 tǐyù

pea [piː] N [c] 豌豆 wāndòu [粒 lì]

peace [piːs] N [U] 1 (not war) 和平 hépíng 2 宁静 níngjìng

peaceful [ˈpiːsful] ADJ 安静的 ānjìng de

peach [piːtʃ] N [c] 桃 táo [个 gè]

peak [piːk] I N [c] 山顶 shāndǐng [个 gè] II ADJ (+ level, times) 高峰的 gāofēng de

peanut [ˈpiːnʌt] N [c] 花生 huāshēng [粒 lì]

pear [pɛəʳ] N [c] 梨 lí [个 gè]

pearl [pəːl] N [c] 珍珠 zhēnzhū [颗 kē]

pebble [ˈpɛbl] N [c] 卵石 luǎnshí [块 kuài]

peculiar [pɪˈkjuːlɪəʳ] ADJ 奇怪的 qíguài de

pedal [ˈpɛdl] N [c] 1 (on bicycle) 脚蹬子 jiǎodēngzi [个 gè] 2 (in car, on piano) 踏板 tàbǎn [个 gè]

pedestrian [pɪˈdɛstrɪən] N [c] 行人 xíngrén [个 gè]

pedestrian crossing (Brit) N [c] 人行横道 rénxíng héngdào [条 tiáo]

pedophile [ˈpiːdəufaɪl] (US) N = **paedophile**

pee [piː] (inf) VI 撒尿 sāniào

peel [piːl] I N [U] 皮 pí II VT (+ vegetables, fruit) 削 xiāo

peg [pɛg] N [c] 1 (for coat, hat, bag) 挂钉 guàdīng [枚 méi] 2 (Brit) (also: **clothes peg**) 衣夹 yījiā [个 gè]

pen [pɛn] N [c] 笔 bǐ [支 zhī];
(*also*: **fountain pen**) 自来水笔
zìláishuǐbǐ [支 zhī]; (*also*: **ballpoint
pen**) 圆珠笔 yuánzhūbǐ [支 zhī]

penalty ['pɛnltɪ] N [c] **1** 处罚
chǔfá [次 cì] **2** (*Football, Rugby*) 罚
球 fáqiú [个 gè]

pence [pɛns] (*Brit*) NPL *of* **penny**

pencil ['pɛnsl] N [c] 铅笔 qiānbǐ
[支 zhī]

pencil sharpener N [c] 铅笔刀
qiānbǐdāo [把 bǎ]

penguin ['pɛŋgwɪn] N [c] 企鹅
qǐé [只 zhī]

penicillin [pɛnɪ'sɪlɪn] N [U] 青霉
素 qīngméisù

penknife ['pɛnnaɪf] (*pl*
penknives) N [c] 小刀 xiǎodāo
[把 bǎ]

penny ['pɛnɪ] (*pl* **pennies** *or* (*Brit*)
pence) N [c] 便士 biànshì [枚 méi]

pension ['pɛnʃən] N [c] (*from state*)
养老金 yǎnglǎojīn [份 fèn]; (*from
employer*) 退休金 tuìxiūjīn [份 fèn]

pensioner ['pɛnʃənəʳ] (*Brit*) N [c]
领养老金的人 lǐng yǎnglǎojīn de
rén [个 gè]

people ['piːpl] NPL **1** 人 rén
2 (*generalizing*) 人们 rénmen ▶**old
people** 老人 lǎorén ▶**many
people** 许多人 xǔduō rén
▶**people say that...** 有人说…
yǒurén shuō…

pepper ['pɛpəʳ] N **1** [U] (*spice*) 胡椒
粉 hújiāofěn **2** [c] (*vegetable*) 胡椒
hújiāo [个 gè]

peppermint ['pɛpəmɪnt] N [c] 薄
荷糖 bòhe táng [块 kuài]

per [pəːʳ] PREP 每 měi ▶**per day**
每天 měitiān ▶**per person** 每
人 měirén ▶**per annum** 每年
měinián

per cent, percent [pə'sɛnt]
(*pl* **per cent**) N [c] 百分之…
bǎifēnzhī… ▶**by 15 per cent** 以百
分之15 yǐ bǎifēnzhī shíwǔ

perfect ['pəːfɪkt] I ADJ **1** [+ *weather,
behaviour*] 完美的 wánměi de;
[+ *sauce, skin, teeth*] 无瑕的 wúxiá
de **2** [+ *crime, solution, example*] 理
想的 lǐxiǎng de II N ▶ **the perfect
(tense)** 完成(时) wánchéng(shí)

perfectly ['pəːfɪktlɪ] ADV **1** 非常
好地 fēicháng hǎo de **2** (*honest,
reasonable, clear*) 绝对地 juéduì de

perform [pə'fɔːm] I VT 表演
biǎoyǎn II VI (*function*) [*actor,
musician, singer, dancer*] 演出
yǎnchū

performance [pə'fɔːməns] N
1 [c] (*Theat: by actor, musician,
singer, dancer*) 表演 biǎoyǎn [次
cì]; [*of play, show*] 演出 yǎnchū [场
chǎng] **2** [U] [*of employee, surgeon,
athlete, team*] 表现 biǎoxiàn

perfume ['pəːfjuːm] N **1** [c/U] 香
水 xiāngshuǐ [瓶 píng] **2** [c] 芳香
fāngxiāng [种 zhǒng]

perhaps [pə'hæps] ADV 可能
kěnéng ▶**perhaps not** 未必 wèibì

period ['pɪərɪəd] N [c] **1** (*interval,
stretch*) 周期 zhōuqī [个 gè]
2 (*time*) 时期 shíqí [段 duàn]
3 (*era*) 时代 shídài [个 gè] **4** (*esp
US: punctuation mark*) 句号 jùhào
[个 gè] **5** (*also*: **menstrual period**)
月经期 yuèjīngqī [个 gè] ▶**to have
one's period** 来例假 lái lìjià

permanent ['pə:mənənt] ADJ 持久的 chíjiǔ de; [+ *damage*] 永久的 yǒngjiǔ de; [+ *state, job, position*] 长期的 chángqī de

permission [pə'mɪʃən] N [U] **1** (*consent*) 准许 zhǔnxǔ **2** (*official authorization*) 批准 pīzhǔn

permit ['pə:mɪt] N [c] (*authorization*) 许可证 xǔkězhèng [个 gè]

persecute ['pə:sɪkju:t] VT 迫害 pòhài

person ['pə:sn] (*pl gen* **people**) N [c] 人 rén [个 gè] ▶**in person** 亲自 qīnzì ▶**first/second/third person** 第一/二/三人称 dìyī/èr/sān rénchēng

personal ['pə:snl] ADJ **1** [+ *telephone number, bodyguard*] 私人的 sīrén de; [+ *opinion, habits*] 个人的 gèrén de; [+ *care, contact, appearance, appeal*] 亲自的 qīnzì de **2** [+ *life, matter, relationship*] 私人的 sīrén de

personality [pə:sə'nælɪtɪ] N [c/U] 个性 gèxìng [种 zhǒng]

personally ['pə:snlɪ] ADV 就我个人来说 jiù wǒ gèrén láishuō

personal stereo N [c] 随身听 suíshēntīng [个 gè]

perspiration [pə:spɪ'reɪʃən] N [U] 汗 hàn

persuade [pə'sweɪd] VT ▶**to persuade sb to do sth** 劝说某人做某事 quànshuō mǒurén zuò mǒushì

pessimistic [pɛsɪ'mɪstɪk] ADJ 悲观的 bēiguān de

pest [pɛst] N [c] (*insect*) 害虫 hàichóng [只 zhī]

pester ['pɛstəʳ] VT 烦扰 fánrǎo

pet [pɛt] N [c] 宠物 chǒngwù [只 zhī]

petrol ['pɛtrəl] (*Brit*) N [U] 汽油 qìyóu

petrol station (*Brit*) N [c] 加油站 jiāyóuzhàn [个 gè]

pharmacy ['fɑ:məsɪ] N **1** [c] (*shop*) 药店 yàodiàn [家 jiā] **2** [U] (*science*) 药学 yàoxué

philosophy [fɪ'lɔsəfɪ] N [U] (*subject*) 哲学 zhéxué

phone [fəun] I N [c] 电话 diànhuà [部 bù] II VT 打电话给 dǎ diànhuà gěi III VI 打电话 dǎ diànhuà ▶**to be on the phone** (*be calling*) 在通话 ▶**by phone** 通过电话 tōngguò diànhuà
▶ **phone back** I VT 给…回电话 gěi…huí diànhuà II VI 回电 huídiàn

phone bill N [c] 话费单 huàfèi dān [张 zhāng]

phone book N [c] 电话簿 diànhuà bù [本 běn]

phone booth (*US*) N [c] 电话亭 diànhuà tíng [个 gè]

phone box (*Brit*) N [c] 电话亭 diànhuà tíng [个 gè]

phone call N [c] 电话 diànhuà [部 bù] ▶**to make a phone call** 打电话 dǎ diànhuà

phonecard ['fəunkɑ:d] N [c] 电话卡 diànhuà kǎ [张 zhāng]

phone number N [c] 电话号码 diànhuà hàomǎ [个 gè]

photo ['fəutəu] N [c] 照片 zhàopiàn [张 zhāng] ▶**to take**

a photo (of sb/sth) 给(某人/某物)拍照片 gěi(mǒurén/mǒuwù)pāi zhàopiàn

photocopier['fəutəukɔpɪər] N [c] 影印机 yǐngyìnjī [台 tái]

photocopy['fəutəukɔpɪ] I N [c] 影印本 yǐngyìnběn [个 gè] II VT [+ document, picture] 影印 yǐngyìn

photograph['fəutəɡræf] N [c] 照片 zhàopiàn [张 zhāng]

photographer[fə'tɔɡrəfər] N [c] 摄影师 shèyǐngshī [位 wèi]

photography[fə'tɔɡrəfɪ] N [U] 摄影 shèyǐng

phrase[freɪz] N [c] 1(expression) 习语 xíyǔ [个 gè] 2(in phrase book, dictionary) 短语 duǎnyǔ [个 gè]

phrase book N [c] 常用词手册 chángyòngcí shǒucè [本 běn]

physical['fɪzɪkl] ADJ 生理的 shēnglǐ de

physician[fɪ'zɪʃən] (US) N [c] 医生 yīshēng [位 wèi]

physicist['fɪzɪsɪst] N [c] 物理学家 wùlǐxué jiā [位 wèi]

physics['fɪzɪks] N [U] 物理学 wùlǐxué

physiotherapist[fɪzɪəu'θɛrəpɪst] N [c] 理疗师 lǐliáoshī [位 wèi]

physiotherapy[fɪzɪəu'θɛrəpɪ] N [U] 物理疗法 wùlǐ liáofǎ

pianist['piːənɪst] N [c] (professional) 钢琴家 gāngqínjiā [位 wèi]; (amateur) 钢琴演奏者 gāngqín yǎnzòuzhě [位 wèi]

piano[pɪ'ænəu] N [c] 钢琴 gāngqín [架 jià]

pick[pɪk] VT 1(choose) 选择 xuǎnzé 2[+ fruit, flowers] 采摘 cǎizhāi ▶**take your pick** 随意挑选 suíyì tiāoxuǎn

▶**pick out** VT (select) [+ person, thing] 挑中 tiāozhòng

▶**pick up** VT 1[+ object] (take hold of) 拿起 náqǐ; (from floor, ground) 捡起 jiǎnqǐ 2(collect) [+ person, parcel] 接 jiē

pickpocket['pɪkpɔkɪt] N [c] 扒手 páshǒu [个 gè]

picnic['pɪknɪk] N [c] (meal) 野餐 yěcān [顿 dùn]

picture['pɪktʃər] I N [c] 1(painting, drawing, print) 画 huà [幅 fú] 2(photograph) 照片 zhàopiàn [张 zhāng] 3(film, movie) 电影 diànyǐng [部 bù] II **the pictures** NPL (Brit: inf: the cinema) 电影院 diànyǐngyuàn

picture messaging[-'mɛsɪdʒɪŋ] N [U] 彩信 cǎixìn

piece[piːs] N [c] 1(fragment) 块 kuài 2 段 duàn 3 块 kuài ▶**a piece of paper** 一张纸 yīzhāng zhǐ ▶**a 10p piece** (Brit) 一枚10便士硬币 yīméi shí biànshì yìngbì

pierced[pɪəst] ADJ [+ ears, nose, lip] 穿孔的 chuānkǒng de

piercing['pɪəsɪŋ] N [c] 人体穿孔 réntǐ chuānkǒng [个 gè]

pig[pɪɡ] N [c] 猪 zhū [头 tóu]

pigeon['pɪdʒən] N [c] 鸽子 gēzi [只 zhī]

pile[paɪl] I N [c] 堆 duī [个 gè] II VT 堆起 duīqǐ ▶**piles of** or **a pile of sth** (inf) 一大堆某物 yīdàduī mǒuwù

pill[pɪl] N [c] 药丸 yàowán [粒 lì]

▶**the pill** (*contraceptive pill*) 避孕药 bìyùnyào ▶**to be on the pill** 服避孕药 fú bìyùnyào

pillow['pɪləʊ] N [c] 枕头 zhěntou [个 gè]

pilot['paɪlət] N [c] 飞行员 fēixíngyuán [个 gè]

PIN[pɪn] N ABBR (= **personal identification number**) (*also:* **PIN number**) 密码 mìmǎ

pin[pɪn] I N [c] **1**(*used in sewing*) 大头针 dàtóuzhēn [枚 méi] **2**(*badge*) 饰针 shìzhēn [枚 méi] II VT (*on wall, door, board*) 钉住 dìngzhù ▶**pins and needles** 发麻 fāmá

pinch[pɪntʃ] VT [+ *person*] 捏 niē

pine[paɪn] N **1**[c] (*also:* **pine tree**) 松树 sōngshù [棵 kē] **2**[U] (*wood*) 松木 sōngmù

pineapple['paɪnæpl] N [c] 菠萝 bōluó [个 gè]

pink[pɪŋk] I ADJ 粉红色的 fěnhóngsè de II N [c/U] 粉红色 fěnhóngsè [种 zhǒng]

pint[paɪnt] N [c] (*measure*) (*Brit: 568 cc*) 品脱 pǐntuō; (*US: 473 cc*) 品脱 pǐntuō

pipe[paɪp] N [c] **1**(*for water, gas*) 管子 guǎnzi [根 gēn] **2**(*for smoking*) 烟斗 yāndǒu [个 gè]

pirate['paɪərət] N [c] 海盗 hǎidào [个 gè]

pirated['paɪərətɪd] (*Comm*) ADJ 盗版的 dàobǎn de

Pisces['paɪsiːz] N [U] (*sign*) 双鱼座 Shuāngyú Zuò

pitch[pɪtʃ] N [c] (*Brit*) 球场 qiúchǎng [个 gè]

pity['pɪtɪ] I N [U] (*compassion*) 同情 tóngqíng **2**(*misfortune*) ▶**it is a pity that...** 真遗憾… zhēn yíhàn… II VT [+ *person*] 同情 tóngqíng ▶**what a pity!** 真可惜! zhēn kěxī!

pizza['piːtsə] N [c] 比萨饼 bǐsàbǐng [个 gè]

place[pleɪs] I N **1**[c] (*location*) 地方 dìfang [个 gè] **2**[c] 空位 kòngwèi [个 gè]; (*seat*) 座位 zuòwèi [个 gè]; (*at university, on course, on committee, in team*) 名额 míng'é [个 gè] **3**[c] (*in competition*) 名次 míngcì [个 gè] **4**(*US: inf*) ▶**some/every/no/any place** 某些/每个/没有/任何地方 mǒuxiē/měigè/méiyǒu/rènhé dìfang II VT (*put*) 放 fàng; (*classify*) ▶**in places** 有几处 yǒu jǐchù ▶**at sb's place** (*home*) 在某人的家里 zài mǒurén de jiālǐ ▶**to take sb's/sth's place** 代替某人/某物 dàitì mǒurén/mǒuwù ▶**to take place** (*happen*) 发生 fāshēng

plain[pleɪn] I ADJ (*not patterned*) 无图案花纹的 wú tú'àn huāwén de II N [c] (*area of land*) 平原 píngyuán [个 gè]

plait[plæt] I N [c] 辫子 biànzi [条 tiáo] II VT 编 biān

plan[plæn] I N [c] **1**(*scheme, project*) 计划 jìhuà [个 gè] **2**(*drawing*) 详图 xiángtú [张 zhāng] II VT 计划 jìhuà III VI (*think ahead*) 打算 dǎsuàn IV **plans** NPL (*intentions*) 计划 jìhuà ▶**to plan to do sth** 计划做某事 jìhuà zuò mǒushì

plane[pleɪn] N [c] 飞机 fēijī

[架 jià]

planet ['plænɪt] N [c] 行星
xíngxíng [个 gè]

plant [plɑ:nt] I N 1 [c] 植物 zhíwù
[株 zhū] 2 [c] (factory, power station)
工厂 gōngchǎng [个 gè] II VT 栽
种 zāizhòng

plaster ['plɑ:stə^r] N 1 [U] 灰泥
huīní 2 [c/U] (Brit) (also: **sticking
plaster**) 橡皮膏 xiàngpígāo [块
kuài] ▸**in plaster** (Brit) 打了石膏
的 dǎle shígāo de

plastic ['plæstɪk] I N [c/U] 塑料
sùliào [种 zhǒng] II ADJ [+ bucket,
chair, cup] 塑料的 sùliào de

plastic wrap (US) N [U] 保鲜膜
bǎoxiān mó

plate [pleɪt] N [c] 碟 dié [个 gè]

platform ['plætfɔ:m] N [c]
1 (stage) 平台 píngtái [个 gè]
2 (Rail) 站台 zhàntái [个 gè] ▸**the
train leaves from platform 7** 火
车从7号站台出发 huǒchē cóng
qīhào zhàntái chūfā

play [pleɪ] I N [c] 戏剧 xìjù [出
chū] II VT 1 [+ game, chess] 玩
wán; [+ football] 踢 tī; [+ cricket,
tennis] 打 dǎ 2 [+ team, opponent]
同…比赛 tóng…bǐsài 3 [+ part,
role, character] 扮演 bànyǎn
4 [+ instrument, piece of music] 演
奏 yǎnzòu 5 [+ CD, record, tape] 播
放 bōfàng III VI 1 [children] 玩耍
wánshuǎ 2 [orchestra, band] 演奏
yǎnzòu ▸**to play cards** 玩纸牌
wán zhǐpái
▸**play back** VT 回放 huífàng

player ['pleɪə^r] N [c] 1 (Sport) 选
手 xuǎnshǒu [名 míng] 2 (Mus) ▸**a**

trumpet/flute/piano player 小
号/长笛/钢琴演奏者 xiǎohào/
chángdí/gāngqín yǎnzòuzhě
[位 wèi]

playground ['pleɪgraʊnd] N [c]
(at school) 运动场 yùndòng chǎng
[个 gè]; (in park) 游戏场 yóuxì
chǎng [个 gè]

playing card ['pleɪɪŋ-] N [c] 纸牌
zhǐpái [张 zhāng]

pleasant ['plɛznt] ADJ 1 (agreeable)
令人愉快的 lìngrén yúkuài de
2 (friendly) 友善的 yǒushàn de

please [pli:z] I INT 请 qǐng II VT
(satisfy) 使高兴 shǐ gāoxìng ▸**yes,
please** 好的 hǎode

pleased [pli:zd] ADJ 开心的
kāixīn de ▸**pleased to meet
you** 见到你很高兴 jiàndào nǐ hěn
gāoxìng ▸**pleased with sth** 对某
事满意 duì mǒushì mǎnyì

pleasure ['plɛʒə^r] N 1 [U]
(happiness, satisfaction) 高兴
gāoxìng 2 [U] (fun) 享乐 xiǎnglè
▸**"it's a pleasure", "my pleasure"**
"乐意效劳""lèyì xiàoláo"

plenty ['plɛntɪ] PRON 1 (lots) 大量
dàliàng 2 (sufficient) 充足 chōngzú
▸**plenty of** [+ food, money, time] 很
多 hěnduō; [+ jobs, people, houses]
许多 xǔduō

plot [plɔt] I N 1 [c] (secret plan) ▸**a
plot (to do sth)** (做某事的) 阴谋
(zuò mǒushì de) yīnmóu [个 gè]
2 [c/U] (of story, play, film) 情节
qíngjié [个 gè] II VI (conspire) 密谋
mìmóu ▸**to plot to do sth** 密谋做
某事 mìmóu zuò mǒushì

plug [plʌg] N [c] 1 (Elec: on

appliance) 插头 chātóu [个 gè];
(*socket*) 插座 chāzuò [个 gè] **2** (*in sink, bath*) 塞子 sāizi [个 gè]
▶ **plug in** (*Elec*) VT 插上…的插头 chāshang…de chātóu

plum [plʌm] N [c](*fruit*) 梅子 méizi [颗 kē]

plumber ['plʌmə^r] N [c] 管子工 guǎnzi gōng [位 wèi]

plural ['pluərl] I ADJ 复数的 fùshù de II N [c] 复数 fùshù [个 gè]

plus [plʌs] I CONJ **1** (*added to*) 加 jiā **2** (*as well as*) 和 hé II ADV (*additionally*) 此外 cǐwài III N [c] (*inf*) ▶ **it's a plus** 这是个附加的好处 zhè shì gè fùjiā de hǎochù [个 gè] ▶ **B plus** (*Scol*) B加 bìjiā

p.m. ADV ABBR (= *post meridiem*) 下午 xiàwǔ

pneumonia [njuːˈməunɪə] N [U] 肺炎 fèiyán

pocket ['pɔkɪt] N [c] 口袋 kǒudài [个 gè]; (*fig*)

pocketbook ['pɔkɪtbuk] N [c] **1** (*US: wallet*) 皮夹 píjiā [个 gè] **2** (*US: handbag*) 手提包 shǒutíbāo [个 gè]

poem ['pəuɪm] N [c] 诗 shī [首 shǒu]

poet ['pəuɪt] N [c] 诗人 shīrén [位 wèi]

poetry ['pəuɪtrɪ] N [U] **1** (*poems*) 诗 shī **2** (*form of literature*) 诗歌 shīgē

point [pɔɪnt] I N **1** [c] (*in report, lecture, interview*) 论点 lùndiǎn [个 gè] **2** [s] (*significant part: of argument, discussion*) 要害 yàohài **3** [s] (*purpose: of action*) 目的 mùdì

4 [c] (*place*) 位置 wèizhi [个 gè] **5** [s] (*moment*) 时刻 shíkè **6** [c] (*sharp end*) 尖端 jiānduān [个 gè] **7** [c] (*in score, competition, game, sport*) 分 fēn **8** [c] (*also:* **decimal point**) 小数点 xiǎoshùdiǎn [个 gè] II VI (*with finger, stick*) 指出 zhǐchū III VT ▶ **to point sth at sb** 把某物瞄准某人 bǎ mǒuwù miáozhǔn mǒurén ▶ **there's no point (in doing that)** (那样做)毫无意义 (nàyàng zuò) háowú yìyì ▶ **two point five** (2.5) 二点五 èrdiǎnwǔ ▶ **to point at sth/sb** (*with finger, stick*) 指着某物/某人 zhǐzhe mǒuwù/mǒurén
▶ **point out** VT 指出 zhǐchū ▶ **to point out that...** 指出… zhǐchū…

pointless ['pɔɪntlɪs] ADJ 无意义的 wú yìyì de

poison ['pɔɪzn] I N [c/U] 毒药 dúyào [种 zhǒng] II VT 下毒 xiàdú

poisonous ['pɔɪznəs] ADJ (*lit*) [+ *animal, plant, fumes, chemicals*] 有毒的 yǒudú de

poker ['pəukə^r] N [U] 扑克牌 pūkèpái

Poland ['pəulənd] N 波兰 Bōlán

polar bear ['pəulə^r-] N [c] 北极熊 běijíxióng [头 tóu]

Pole [pəul] N [c] 波兰人 Bōlánrén [个 gè]

pole [pəul] N [c] **1** (*stick*) 杆 gān [根 gēn] **2** (*Geo*) 地极 dìjí [个 gè]

police [pəˈliːs] NPL **1** (*organization*) 警方 jǐngfāng **2** (*members*) 警察 jǐngchá

policeman [pəˈliːsmən] (*pl* **policemen**) N [c] 男警察 nán jǐngchá [个 gè]

police station N [C] 警察局 jǐngchá jú [个 gè]

policewoman [pəˈliːswumən] (pl **policewomen**) N [C] 女警察 nǚ jǐngchá [个 gè]

Polish [ˈpəulɪʃ] I ADJ 波兰的 Bōlán de II N [U] (language) 波兰 语 Bōlányǔ

polish [ˈpɔlɪʃ] I N [C/U] 上光 剂 shàngguāng jì [盒 hé] II VT [+ shoes] 擦亮 cāliàng; [+ furniture, floor] 上光 shàngguāng

polite [pəˈlaɪt] ADJ 有礼貌的 yǒu lǐmào de

political [pəˈlɪtɪkl] ADJ 政治的 zhèngzhì de

politician [pɔlɪˈtɪʃən] N [C] 政治 家 zhèngzhì jiā [位 wèi]

politics [ˈpɔlɪtɪks] N [U] 1 (activity) 政治 zhèngzhì 2 (subject) 政治学 zhèngzhì xué

pollute [pəˈluːt] VT 污染 wūrǎn

polluted [pəˈluːtɪd] ADJ 被污染的 bèi wūrǎn de

pollution [pəˈluːʃən] N [U] 1 (process) 污染 wūrǎn 2 (substances) 污染物 wūrǎn wù

polythene bag [ˈpɔlɪθiːn-] N [C] 聚乙烯塑料袋 jùyǐxī sùliàodài [个 gè]

pond [pɔnd] N [C] 池塘 chítáng [个 gè]

pony [ˈpəunɪ] N [C] 小马 xiǎomǎ [匹 pǐ]

ponytail [ˈpəunɪteɪl] N [C] 马尾辫 mǎwěibiàn [条 tiáo]

pool [puːl] N 1 [C] (pond) 水 塘 shuǐtáng [个 gè] 2 [C] (also:

swimming pool) 游泳池 yóuyǒngchí [个 gè] 3 [U] (game) 美 式台球 měishì táiqiú

poor [puəʳ] I ADJ 1 [+ person] 贫穷 的 pínqióng de; [+ country, area] 贫 困的 pínkùn de 2 (bad) [+ quality, performance] 低水平的 dī shuǐpíng de; [+ wages, conditions, results, attendance] 差的 chà de II NPL ▶ the poor 穷人 qióngrén ▶ poor (old) Bill 可怜的(老)比尔 kélián de (lǎo) Bǐ'ěr

pop [pɔp] N 1 [U] (Mus) 流行音乐 liúxíng yīnyuè 2 [C] (US: inf: father) 爸爸 bàba [个 gè]

popcorn [ˈpɔpkɔːn] N [U] 爆米花 bàomǐhuā

pope [pəup] N [C] 教皇 jiàohuáng [位 wèi]

popular [ˈpɔpjuləʳ] ADJ 1 [+ person, place, thing] 流行的 liúxíng de 2 [+ name, activity] 时髦的 shímáo de

population [pɔpjuˈleɪʃən] N [C] 人口 rénkǒu [个 gè]

pork [pɔːk] N [U] 猪肉 zhūròu

port [pɔːt] N 1 [C] (harbour) 港口 gǎngkǒu [个 gè] 2 [C] (town) 港市 gǎngshì [座 zuò]

portable [ˈpɔːtəbl] ADJ 便携式的 biànxiéshì de

porter [ˈpɔːtəʳ] N [C] 1 (Brit: doorkeeper) 门房 ménfáng [个 gè] 2 (US: on train) 列车员 lièchēyuán [位 wèi]

portion [ˈpɔːʃən] N [C] 份 fèn

portrait [ˈpɔːtreɪt] N [C] (picture) 画像 huàxiàng [幅 fú]

Portugal [ˈpɔːtjugəl] N 葡萄牙

Pútáoyá

Portuguese[pɔ:tju'gi:z] (pl **Portuguese**) I ADJ 葡萄牙的 Pútáoyá de II N 1[c] (person) 葡萄牙人 Pútáoyárén [个 gè] 2[U] (language) 葡萄牙语 Pútáoyáyǔ

posh[pɔʃ] (inf) ADJ [+ hotel, restaurant, car] 豪华的 háohuá de

position[pə'zɪʃən] N [c] 1 位置 wèizhi [个 gè] 2 (posture: of person's body) 姿势 zīshì [种 zhǒng]

positive['pɔzɪtɪv] ADJ 1(good) 有益的 yǒuyì de 2(affirmative) [+ test, result] 阳性的 yángxìng de 3(sure) ▶ **to be positive (about sth)** 确信 (某事) quèxìn (mǒushì)

possession[pə'zɛʃən] I N [U] 拥有 yōngyǒu II **possessions** NPL 财产 cáichǎn

possibility[pɔsɪ'bɪlɪtɪ] N [c] 1(that sth is true) 可能性 kěnéngxìng [种 zhǒng]; (of sth happening) 可能的事 kěnéng de shì [件 jiàn] 2(option) 可选性 kěxuǎnxìng [种 zhǒng]

possible['pɔsɪbl] ADJ [+ event, reaction, effect, consequence] 可能的 kěnéng de; [+ risk, danger] 潜在的 qiánzài de; [+ answer, cause, solution] 可接受的 kě jiēshòu de ▶ **it's possible (that...)** 可能 (…) kěnéng… ▶ **if possible** 如有可能 rúyǒu kěnéng ▶ **as soon as possible** 尽快 jìnkuài

possibly['pɔsɪblɪ] ADV (perhaps) 大概 dàgài

post[pəust] I N 1(Brit) ▶ **the post** (service, system) 邮政 yóuzhèng; (letters, delivery) 邮件 yóujiàn 2

[c] (pole) 柱子 zhùzi [根 gēn] 3 [c] (job) 职位 zhíwèi [个 gè] II VT (Brit) [+ letter] 邮寄 yóujì ▶ **by post** (Brit) 以邮件的方式 yǐ yóujì de fāngshì

postbox['pəustbɔks] (Brit) N [c] (in street) 邮筒 yóutǒng [个 gè]

postcard['pəustkɑ:d] N [c] 明信片 míngxìnpiàn [张 zhāng]

postcode['pəustkəud] (Brit) N [c] 邮政编码 yóuzhèng biānmǎ [个 gè]

poster['pəustər] N [c] 海报 hǎibào [张 zhāng]

postman['pəustmən] (pl **postmen**) (Brit) N [c] 邮递员 yóudìyuán [位 wèi]

post office N [c] 邮局 yóujú [个 gè]

postpone[pəus'pəun] VT 推迟 tuīchí

postwoman['pəustwumən] (pl **postwomen**) (Brit) N [c] 女邮递员 nǚ yóudìyuán [位 wèi]

pot[pɔt] N 1[c] (for cooking) 锅 guō [口 kǒu] 2[c] (also: **teapot**) 茶壶 cháhú [个 gè] 3[c] (also: **coffeepot**) 咖啡壶 kāfēihú [个 gè] 4[c] (for paint, jam, marmalade, honey) 罐 guàn [个 gè] 5[c] (also: **flowerpot**) 花盆 huāpén [个 gè]

potato[pə'teɪtəu] (pl **potatoes**) N [c/U] 马铃薯 mǎlíngshǔ [个 gè] 土豆 tǔdòu [个 gè]

potato chips (US) NPL 薯片 shǔpiàn

pottery['pɔtərɪ] N 1[U] (work, hobby) 陶艺 táoyì 2[c] (factory, workshop) 制陶厂 zhìtáo chǎng

[家 jiā]

pound [paund] N [c] 1 (*unit of money*) 镑 bàng 2 (*unit of weight*) 磅 bàng ▶a pound coin 1镑硬币 yībàng yìngbì ▶a five-pound note 5镑纸币 wǔbàng zhǐbì ▶half a pound (of sth) 半磅(某物) bànbàng (mǒuwù)

pour [pɔːʳ] VT ▶to pour sth (into/onto sth) 灌某物（到某物里/上） guàn mǒuwù (dào mǒuwù lǐ/shang) ▶it is pouring (with rain), it is pouring down 大雨如注 dàyǔ rúzhù

poverty ['pɔvətɪ] N [U] 贫穷 pínqióng

powder ['paudəʳ] N [c/U] 粉 fěn [袋 dài]

power ['pauəʳ] N [U] 1 权力 quánlì 2 (*electricity*) 电力 diànlì

powerful ['pauəful] ADJ 1 (*influential*) 有影响力的 yǒu yǐngxiǎnglì de 2 (*physically strong*) 强健的 qiángjiàn de 3 [+ engine, machine] 大功率的 dà gōnglǜ de

practical ['præktɪkl] ADJ 1 [+ difficulties, experience] 实践的 shíjiàn de 2 [+ ideas, methods, advice, suggestions] 切合实际的 qièhé shíjì de 3 [+ person, mind] 有实际经验的 yǒu shíjì jīngyàn de

practically ['præktɪklɪ] ADV 几乎 jīhū

practice ['præktɪs] I N 1 [U] (*exercise, training*) 练习 liànxí 2 [c] (*training session*) 实习 shíxí [次 cì] II VT, VI (US) = **practise** ▶in practice (*in reality*) 实际上 shíjì shàng ▶2 hours' piano practice 2小时的练琴时间 èr xiǎoshí de liànqín shíjiān

practise, (US) **practice** ['præktɪs] I VT 练习 liànxí II VI 练习 liànxí

praise [preɪz] VT 称赞 chēngzàn

pram [præm] (*Brit*) N [c] 婴儿车 yīng'érchē [辆 liàng]

prawn [prɔːn] (*Brit*) N [c] 虾 xiā [只 zhī]

pray [preɪ] VI 祷告 dǎogào

prayer [prɛəʳ] (*Rel*) N [c] (*words*) 祈祷文 qídǎowén [篇 piān]

precaution [prɪˈkɔːʃən] N [c] 预防措施 yùfáng cuòshī [项 xiàng]

precious ['prɛʃəs] ADJ [+ time, resource, memories] 宝贵的 bǎoguì de; (*financially*) 贵重的 guìzhòng de

precise [prɪˈsaɪs] ADJ 1 [+ time, nature, position, circumstances] 精确的 jīngquè de; [+ figure, definition] 准确的 zhǔnquè de; [+ explanation] 清晰的 qīngxī de 2 [+ instructions, plans] 详尽的 xiángjìn de

precisely [prɪˈsaɪslɪ] ADV (*exactly*) 确切地 quèqiè de; (*referring to time*) 正好 zhènghǎo

predict [prɪˈdɪkt] VT 预言 yùyán

prediction [prɪˈdɪkʃən] N [c] 预言 yùyán [种 zhǒng]

prefer [prɪˈfəːʳ] VT 偏爱 piān'ài ▶to prefer coffee to tea 喜欢咖啡胜于茶 xǐhuān kāfēi shèngyú chá ▶I'd prefer to go by train 我宁愿坐火车去 wǒ nìngyuàn zuò huǒchē qù

pregnant ['prɛgnənt] ADJ 怀孕的

huáiyùn de ▶**3 months pregnant** 怀孕3个月 huáiyùn sāngèyuè

prejudice ['predʒudɪs] N [c/u] 偏见 piānjiàn [个 gè]

Premier League (Brit) (Football) N ▶**the Premier League** 超级联赛 Chāojí Liánsài

preparation [prepə'reɪʃən] I N [u] 准备 zhǔnbèi II **preparations** NPL (arrangements) ▶**preparations (for sth)** (为某事)准备工作 (wèi mǒushì de) zhǔnbèi gōngzuò ▶**in preparation for sth** 为某事而准备的 wèi mǒushì ér zhǔnbèi de

prepare [prɪ'peər] I VT 准备 zhǔnbèi; [+ food, meal] 预备 yùbèi II VI ▶**to prepare (for sth)** (为某事) 做准备 (wèi mǒushì) zuò zhǔnbèi ▶**to prepare to do sth** (get ready) 准备好做某事 zhǔnbèi hǎo zuò mǒushì

prepared [prɪ'peəd] ADJ ▶**to be prepared to do sth** (willing) 有意做某事 yǒuyì zuò mǒushì ▶**prepared (for sth)** (ready) (对某事)有所准备的 (duì mǒushì) yǒu suǒ zhǔnbèi de

prescribe [prɪ'skraɪb] VT (Med) 开 kāi

prescription [prɪ'skrɪpʃən] N [c] (Med: slip of paper) 处方 chǔfāng [个 gè]; (medicine) 药方 yàofāng [个 gè]

present ['preznt] I ADJ 1 (current) 现有的 xiànyǒu de 2 (in attendance) 在场的 zàichǎng de II N 1 (not past) ▶**the present** 目前 mùqián 2 [c] (gift) 礼物 lǐwù [件 jiàn] 3 ▶**the present** (also: **present tense**) 现在时态 xiànzài shítài [个 gè] ▶**to be present at sth** 出席某事 chūxí mǒushì ▶**at present** 现在 xiànzài ▶**to give sb a present** 给某人礼物 gěi mǒurén lǐwù

president ['prezɪdənt] N [c] (Pol) 总统 zǒngtǒng [位 wèi]

press [pres] I N ▶**the press** 新闻界 xīnwén jiè II VT 1 [+ button, switch, bell] 按 àn 2 (iron) 熨平 yùnpíng ▶**to be pressed for time/money** 时间紧迫/手头紧 shíjiān jǐnpò/shǒutóu jǐn

pressure ['preʃər] N 1 [u] (physical force) 压力 yālì 2 [u] ▶**pressure (to do sth)** (做某事的)压力 (zuò mǒushì de) yālì 3 [c/u] (stress) 压力 yālì [种 zhǒng] ▶**to put pressure on sb (to do sth)** 对某人施加压力(去做某事) duì mǒurén shījiā yālì (qù zuò mǒushì)

pretend [prɪ'tend] VT ▶**to pretend to do sth/pretend that...** 假装做某事/假装… jiǎzhuāng zuò mǒushì/jiǎzhuāng…

pretty ['prɪtɪ] I ADJ 漂亮的 piàoliang de II ADV (good, happy, soon etc) 相当 xiāngdāng

prevent [prɪ'vent] VT [+ war, disease, situation] 阻止 zǔzhǐ; [+ accident, fire] 防止 fángzhǐ ▶**to prevent sb (from) doing sth** 阻止某人做某事 zǔzhǐ mǒurén zuò mǒushì ▶**to prevent sth (from) happening** 防止某事发生 fángzhǐ mǒushì fāshēng

previous ['priːvɪəs] ADJ 1 [+ marriage, relationship, experience, owner] 前的 qián de

2 [+ *chapter, week, day*] 以前的 yǐqián de

previously ['pri:vɪəslɪ] ADV 1 以前 yǐqián 2 ▶ **10 days previously** 10天前 shí tiān qián

price [praɪs] N [C/U] 价格 jiàgé [种 zhǒng]

pride [praɪd] N [U] 自豪 zìháo ▶ **to take (a) pride in sb/sth** 因某人/某事而自豪 yīn mǒurén/mǒushì ér zìháo

priest [pri:st] N [C] 神职人员 shénzhí rényuán [位 wèi]

primarily ['praɪmərɪlɪ] ADV 主要地 zhǔyào de

primary school ['praɪmərɪ-] (Brit) N [C/U] 小学 xiǎoxué [所 suǒ]

Prime Minister [praɪm-] N [C] 总理 Zǒnglǐ [位 wèi]

prince [prɪns] N [C] 王子 wángzǐ [位 wèi]

princess [prɪn'sɛs] N [C] 公主 gōngzhǔ [位 wèi]

principal ['prɪnsɪpl] I ADJ 主要的 zhǔyào de II N [C] 校长 xiàozhǎng [位 wèi]

principle ['prɪnsɪpl] N [C/U] 准则 zhǔnzé [个 gè] ▶ **in principle** (*in theory*) 原则上 yuánzé shàng

print [prɪnt] I N [C] (*photograph*) 照片 zhàopiàn [张 zhāng] II VT **1** [+ *story, article*] 出版 chūbǎn **2** (*stamp*) 印 yìn 3 (*write*) 用印刷体写 yòng yìnshuātǐ xiě 4 (*Comput*) 打印 dǎyìn
▶ **print out** VT 打印出 dǎyìn chū

printer ['prɪntər] N [C] 打印机 dǎyìnjī [台 tái]

printout ['prɪntaut] N [C] 打印输出 dǎyìn shūchū [次 cì]

priority [praɪ'ɔrɪtɪ] I N [C] (*concern*) 重点 zhòngdiǎn [个 gè] II **priorities** NPL 优先考虑的事 yōuxiān kǎolù de shì ▶ **to give priority to sth/sb** 给某事/某人以优先权 gěi mǒushì/mǒurén yǐ yōuxiān quán

prison ['prɪzn] N 1 [C/U] (*institution*) 监狱 jiānyù [个 gè] **2** [U] (*imprisonment*) 坐牢 zuòláo ▶ **in prison** 坐牢 zuòláo

prisoner ['prɪznər] N [C] 囚犯 qiúfàn [个 gè]

private ['praɪvɪt] ADJ 1 [+ *property, land, plane*] 私人的 sīrén de **2** [+ *education, housing, health care, industries*] 私有的 sīyǒu de **3** (*confidential*) 秘密的 mìmì de **4** [+ *life, thoughts, plans, affairs, belongings*] 私人的 sīrén de ▶ **in private** 私下 sīxià

prize [praɪz] N [C] 奖 jiǎng [个 gè]

prizewinner ['praɪzwɪnər] N [C] 获奖者 huòjiǎngzhě [位 wèi]

pro [prəu] PREP (*in favour of*) 赞成 zànchéng

probability [prɔbə'bɪlɪtɪ] N [C/U] ▶ **probability (of sth/that...)** (某事/…的) 可能性 (mǒushì/…de) kěnéngxìng [种 zhǒng]

probable ['prɔbəbl] ADJ 可能的 kěnéng de

probably ['prɔbəblɪ] ADV 可能 kěnéng

problem ['prɔbləm] N [C] 难题 nántí [个 gè] ▶ **what's the problem?** 有什么问题吗？ yǒu shénme wèntí ma? ▶**I had no problem finding her** 我要找她不难 wǒ yào zhǎotā bùnán ▶**no problem!** (inf) 没问题! méi wèntí!

process ['prəusɛs] I N [c] (procedure) 过程 guòchéng [个 gè] II vt (Comput) [+ data] 处理 chǔlǐ ▶**to be in the process of doing sth** 在从事某事的过程中 zài cóngshì mǒushì de guòchéng zhōng

produce [prə'dju:s] vt 1 [+ effect, result] 促成 cùchéng 2 [+ goods, commodity] 生产 shēngchǎn 3 [+ play, film, programme] 上演 shàngyǎn

producer [prə'dju:səʳ] N [c] 1 制片人 zhìpiànrén [位 wèi] 2 (of food, material: country) 产地 chǎndì [个 gè]; (company) 制造商 zhìzào shāng [个 gè]

product ['prɒdʌkt] N [c] 产品 chǎnpǐn [个 gè]

production [prə'dʌkʃən] N 1 [u] 生产 shēngchǎn; (amount produced, amount grown) 产量 chǎnliàng 2 [c] (play, show) 作品 zuòpǐn [部 bù]

profession [prə'fɛʃən] N [c] 职业 zhíyè [种 zhǒng]

professional [prə'fɛʃənl] ADJ 1 [+ photographer, musician, footballer] 职业的 zhíyè de; [+ advice, help] 专业的 zhuānyè de 2 (skilful) 专业水平的 zhuānyè shuǐpíng de

professor [prə'fɛsəʳ] N [c] 1 (Brit) 教授 jiàoshòu [位 wèi] 2 (US) 教员 jiàoyuán [位 wèi]

profit ['prɒfɪt] N [c/u] 利润

lìrùn ▶**to make a profit** 赚钱 zhuànqián

profitable ['prɒfɪtəbl] ADJ 有利润的 yǒu lìrùn de

program ['prəugræm] I N [c] 1 (also: **computer program**) 程序 chéngxù [个 gè] 2 (US) = **programme** II vt 1 (Comput) ▶**to program sth (to do sth)** 为某物编程(做某事) wèi mǒuwù biānchéng (zuò mǒushì) 2 (US) = **programme**

programme, (US) **program** ['prəugræm] I N [c] 1 (Rad, TV) 节目 jiémù [个 gè] 2 (for theatre, concert) 节目宣传册 jiémù xuānchuáncè [本 běn] 3 节目单 jiémù dān [个 gè] II vt ▶**to programme sth (to do sth)** [+ machine, system] 设定某事(做某事) shèdìng mǒushì (zuò mǒushì); see also **program**

programmer ['prəugræməʳ] (Comput) N [c] 程序员 chéngxùyuán [位 wèi]

progress ['prəugrɛs] N [u] 1 (headway) 进展 jìnzhǎn 2 (advances) 进步 jìnbù ▶**to make progress (with sth)** (对某事)取得进步 (duì mǒushì) qǔdé jìnbù

project ['prɒdʒɛkt] N [c] 工程 gōngchéng [个 gè]

promise ['prɒmɪs] I N [c] 许诺 xǔnuò [个 gè] II vi 保证 bǎozhèng III vt ▶**to promise sb sth, promise sth to sb** 保证给某人某物 bǎozhèng gěi mǒurén mǒuwù ▶**to break/keep a promise (to do sth)** 违背/遵守(做某事的)诺言 wéibèi/zūnshǒu (zuò mǒushì de) nuòyán ▶**to promise to do sth** 保证做某事 bǎozhèng zuò mǒushì

promotion [prəˈməʊʃən] N [c/u] 晋级 jìnjí [次 cì]

prompt [prɒmpt] I ADJ 1 (*on time*) 干脆的 gāncuì de 2 (*rapid*) [+ *action, response*] 迅速的 xùnsù de II N [c] (*Comput*) 提示符 tíshì fú [个 gè] ▶**at 8 o'clock prompt** 8点整 bādiǎn zhěng

pronoun [ˈprəʊnaʊn] N [c] 代词 dàicí [个 gè]

pronounce [prəˈnaʊns] VT 发音 fāyīn

pronunciation [prənʌnsɪˈeɪʃən] N [c/u] 发音 fāyīn [个 gè]

proof [pruːf] N [u] 证据 zhèngjù

proper [ˈprɒpəʳ] ADJ [+ *procedure, place, word*] 恰当的 qiàdàng de

properly [ˈprɒpəlɪ] ADV 1 充分地 chōngfèn de 2 体面地 tǐmiàn de

property [ˈprɒpətɪ] N 1 [u] (*possessions*) 财产 cáichǎn 2 [c/u] (*buildings and land*) 地产 dìchǎn [处 chù]

prostitute [ˈprɒstɪtjuːt] N [c] (*female*) 妓女 jìnǚ [个 gè] ▶**a male prostitute** 男妓 nánjì

protect [prəˈtɛkt] VT 保护 bǎohù ▶**to protect sb/sth from** or **against sth** 保护某人/某物不受某物的伤害 bǎohù mǒurén/mǒuwù bùshòu mǒuwù de shānghài

protection [prəˈtɛkʃən] N [c/u] ▶**protection (from** or **against sth)** (免受某物侵害的)保护 (miǎnshòu mǒuwù qīnhài de) bǎohù [种 zhǒng]

protest [n ˈprəʊtɛst, vb prəˈtɛst] I N [c/u] 抗议 kàngyì [个 gè] II VI ▶**to protest about/against/at sth** (*Brit*) 抗议某事 kàngyì mǒushì III VT (*US: voice opposition to*) 示威 shìwēi

Protestant [ˈprɒtɪstənt] I N [c] 新教徒 Xīnjiàotú [个 gè] II ADJ 新教的 Xīnjiào de

protester [prəˈtɛstəʳ] N [c] 抗议者 kàngyìzhě [名 míng]

proud [praʊd] ADJ 1 [+ *parents, owner*] 自豪的 zìháo de 2 (*arrogant*) 骄傲的 jiāo'ào de ▶**to be proud of sb/sth** 为某人/某事感到自豪 wèi mǒurén/mǒushì gǎndào zìháo

prove [pruːv] I VT [+ *idea, theory*] 证明 zhèngmíng II VI ▶**to prove that...** [*person*] 证明… zhèngmíng…; [*situation, experiment, calculations*] 显示… xiǎnshì… ▶**to prove sb right/wrong** 证明某人是对的/错的 zhèngmíng mǒurén shì duìde/cuòde

provide [prəˈvaɪd] VT [+ *food, money, shelter*] 供应 gōngyìng; [+ *answer, opportunity, details*] 提供 tígōng ▶**to provide sb with sth** 提供某人某物 tígōng mǒurén mǒuwù

provided (that) [prəˈvaɪdɪd-] CONJ 假如 jiǎrú

PS ABBR (= *postscript*) 附言 fùyán

psychiatrist [saɪˈkaɪətrɪst] N [c] 精神病医生 jīngshénbìng yīshēng [位 wèi]

psychological [saɪkəˈlɔdʒɪkl] ADJ

心理的 xīnlǐ de

psychologist [saɪˈkɔlədʒɪst] N [c] 心理学家 xīnlǐxué jiā [位 wèi]

psychology [saɪˈkɔlədʒɪ] N [u] 心理学 xīnlǐxué

PTO ABBR (= please turn over) 请翻过来 qǐng fān guòlái

pub [pʌb] (Brit) N [c] 酒吧 jiǔbā [个 gè]

public [ˈpʌblɪk] I ADJ 1 [+ support, opinion, interest] 公众的 gōngzhòng de 2 [+ building, service, library] 公共的 gōnggòng de 3 [+ announcement, meeting] 公开的 gōngkāi de II N [s + PL VB]
▶ **the (general) public** 民众 mínzhòng

public holiday N [c] 法定假期 fǎdìng jiàqī [个 gè]

publicity [pʌbˈlɪsɪtɪ] N [u] 1 (information, advertising) 宣传 xuānchuán 2 (attention) 关注 guānzhù

public school N [c/u] 1 (Brit: private school) 私立中学 sīlì zhōngxué [所 suǒ] 2 (US: state school) 公立学校 gōnglì xuéxiào [所 suǒ]

public transport N [u] 公共交通 gōnggòng jiāotōng

publish [ˈpʌblɪʃ] VT [+ book, magazine] 出版 chūbǎn

publisher [ˈpʌblɪʃəʳ] N [c] (company) 出版社 chūbǎnshè [家 jiā]

pudding [ˈpudɪŋ] N [c/u] (Brit: dessert in general) 甜点 tiándiǎn [份 fèn]

puddle [ˈpʌdl] N [c] 水坑

shuǐkēng [个 gè]

pull [pul] I VT 1 [+ rope, hair] 拖 tuō; [+ handle, door, cart, carriage] 拉 lā 2 [+ trigger] 扣 kòu II VI 猛拉 měnglā ▶ **to pull a muscle** 扭伤肌肉 niǔshāng jīròu ▶ **to pull sb's leg** (fig) 开某人的玩笑 kāi mǒurén de wánxiào

▶ **pull down** VT [+ building] 拆毁 chāihuǐ

▶ **pull in** VI (at the kerb) 停了下来 tíngle xiàlái

▶ **pull out** VI 1 (Aut: from kerb) 开出 kāichū; (when overtaking) 超车 chāochē 2 退出 tuìchū

▶ **pull through** VI (from illness) 恢复健康 huīfù jiànkāng; (from difficulties) 渡过难关 dùguò nánguān

▶ **pull up** I VI (stop) 停下 tíngxià II VT 1 (raise) [+ socks, trousers] 拉起 lāqǐ 2 [+ plant, weed] 拔除 báchú

pull-off [ˈpulɔf] (US) N [c] 路侧停车处 lùcè tíngchēchù [个 gè]

pullover [ˈpuləuvəʳ] N [c] 套头衫 tàotóushān [件 jiàn]

pulse [pʌls] N [c] (Anat) 脉搏 màibó [下 xià] ▶ **to take** or **feel sb's pulse** 给某人诊脉 gěi mǒurén zhěnmài

pump [pʌmp] N [c] 1 (for liquid, gas) 泵 bèng [个 gè] 2 (for getting water) 抽水机 chōushuǐjī [台 tái] 3 (for inflating sth) 打气筒 dǎqìtǒng [个 gè] ▶ **water/petrol pump** 水/油泵 shuǐ/yóubèng

▶ **pump up** VT 打气 dǎqì

punch [pʌntʃ] I N [c] 拳打

quándá [顿 dùn] **II** VT **1** (hit) 用拳打击 yòng quán dǎjī **2** [+ button, keyboard] 敲击 qiāojī **3** [+ ticket, paper] 在…上打孔 zài…shang dǎkǒng

▶ **punch in** VT 敲入 qiāorù

punctual ['pʌŋktjuəl] ADJ 准时的 zhǔnshí de

punctuation [pʌŋktjuˈeɪʃən] N [U] 标点 biāodiǎn

puncture ['pʌŋktʃə^r] **I** N [c] 刺孔 cìkǒng [个 gè] **II** VT [+ tyre, lung] 戳破 chuōpò ▶ **to have a puncture** 轮胎被扎破了 lúntāi bèi zhāpò le

punish ['pʌnɪʃ] VT 惩罚 chéngfá ▶ **to punish sb for sth/for doing sth** 因某事/做某事而惩罚某人 yīn mǒushì/zuò mǒushì ér chéngfá mǒurén

punishment ['pʌnɪʃmənt] N **1** [U] 惩罚 chéngfá **2** [c/U] (penalty) 处罚 chǔfá [次 cì]

pupil ['pjuːpl] N [c] 学生 xuéshēng [名 míng]

puppy ['pʌpɪ] N [c] 小狗 xiǎogǒu [只 zhī]

purchase ['pəːtʃɪs] (frm) VT 购买 gòumǎi

pure [pjuə^r] ADJ **1** [+ silk, gold, wool] 纯的 chún de **2** (clean) 纯净的 chúnjìng de

purple ['pəːpl] **I** ADJ 紫色的 zǐsè de **II** N [c/U] 紫色 zǐsè [种 zhǒng]

purpose ['pəːpəs] N [c] **1** [of person] 目的 mùdì [个 gè] **2** [of act, meeting, visit] 意义 yìyì [个 gè] ▶ **on purpose** 故意地 gùyì de ·

purse [pəːs] N [c] **1** (Brit: for money)

钱包 qiánbāo [个 gè] **2** (US: handbag) 手袋 shǒudài [个 gè]

push [puʃ] **I** N [c] 推 tuī **II** VT **1** [+ button] 按 àn **2** [+ car, door, person] 推 tuī **III** VI **1** (press) 按 àn **2** (shove) 推 tuī ▶ **at the push of a button** 只要按一下按钮 zhǐyào àn yīxià ànniǔ ▶ **to push one's way through the crowd** 挤过人群 jǐguò rénqún ▶ **to push sth/sb out of the way** 把某物/某人推开 bǎ mǒuwù/mǒurén tuīkāi ▶ **to push a door open/shut** 把门推开/上 bǎ mén tuīkāi/shàng ▶ **to be pushed for time/money** (inf) 赶时间/缺钱 gǎn shíjiān/quēqián ▶ **to push forward/push through the crowd** 挤向/过人群 jǐxiàng/guò rénqún

▶ **push in** VI (in queue) 插队 chāduì

▶ **push over** VT [+ person, wall, furniture] 推倒 tuīdǎo

▶ **push up** VT [+ total, prices] 提高 tígāo

pushchair ['puʃtʃeə^r] (Brit) N [c] 幼儿车 yòu'érchē [辆 liàng]

put [put] (pt, pp put) VT **1** [+ thing] 放 fàng; [+ person] (in institution) 安置 ānzhì **2** (write, type) 写 xiě ▶ **to put a lot of time/energy/effort into sth/into doing sth** 投入大量的时间/精力/努力于某事/做某事 tóurù dàliàng de shíjiān/jīnglì/nǔlì yú mǒushì/zuò mǒushì ▶ **how shall I put it?** 我该怎么说呢? wǒ gāi zěnme shuō ne? ▶ **put across, put over** VT [+ ideas, argument] 讲清 jiǎngqīng

▶ **put away** VT 把…收起 bǎ…shōuqǐ

▶ **put back** VT 1 (*replace*) 放回 fànghuí 2 [+ *watch, clock*] 倒拨 dàobō

▶ **put down** VT 1 (*on floor, table*) 放下 fàngxià 2 (*in writing*) 写下 xiěxià

▶ **put forward** VT [+ *ideas, proposal, name*] 提出 tíchū

▶ **put in** VT 1 [+ *request, complaint, application*] 提出 tíchū 2 (*install*) 安装 ānzhuāng

▶ **put off** VT (*delay*) 推迟 tuīchí; (Brit: *distract*) 使分心 shǐ fēnxīn; (*discourage*) 使失去兴趣 shǐ shīqù xìngqù ▶ **to put off doing sth** (*postpone*) 推迟做某事 tuīchí zuò mǒushì

▶ **put on** VT 1 [+ *clothes, make-up, glasses*] 穿戴 chuāndài 2 [+ *light, TV, radio, oven*] 开 kāi; [+ *CD, video*] 放 fàng ▶ **to put on weight/three kilos** etc 增重/增加了3公斤 {等} zēngzhòng/zēngjiā le sān gōngjīn {děng}

▶ **put out** VT 1 [+ *candle, cigarette*] 熄灭 xīmiè; [+ *fire, blaze*] 扑灭 pūmiè 2 (*switch off*) 关 guān 3 麻烦 máfan

▶ **put over** VT = **put across**

▶ **put through** VT (Tel) 接通 jiētōng ▶ **put me through to Miss Blair** 请帮我接布莱尔小姐 qǐng bāng wǒ jiē Bùláiěr xiǎojiě

▶ **put up** VT 1 [+ *fence, building, tent*] 建造 jiànzào; [+ *poster, sign*] 张贴 zhāngtiē 2 [+ *umbrella, hood*] 撑起 chēngqǐ 3 [+ *price, cost*] 增加 zēngjiā 4 (*accommodate*) 为…提供住宿 wèi…tígōng zhùsù ▶ **to put up one's hand** 举手 jǔshǒu

▶ **put up with** VT FUS 容忍 róngrěn

puzzle ['pʌzl] N [c] 谜 mí [个 gè]; (*toy*) 测智玩具 cèzhì wánjù [套 tào] 2 [s] (*mystery*) 谜团 mítuán

puzzled ['pʌzld] ADJ 茫然的 mángrán de

pyjamas, (US) **pajamas** [pə'dʒɑːməz] NPL 睡衣裤 shuìyīkù ▶ **a pair of pyjamas** 一套睡衣裤 yītào shuìyīkù

pylon ['paɪlən] N [c] 电缆塔 diànlǎn tǎ [个 gè]

pyramid ['pɪrəmɪd] N [c] 金字塔 jīnzì tǎ [座 zuò]

qualification [kwɔlɪfɪ'keɪʃən] N [c] 资格证明 zīgé zhèngmíng [个 gè]

qualified ['kwɔlɪfaɪd] ADJ 合格的 hégé de ▸**fully qualified** 完全合格的 wánquán hégé de

qualify ['kwɔlɪfaɪ] VI 1 (*pass examinations*) 取得资格 qǔdé zīgé 2 (*in competition*) 具备资格 jùbèi zīgé ▸**to qualify as an engineer/a nurse** *etc* 取得工程师/护士 {等}的资格 qǔdé gōngchéngshī/hùshì {děng} de zīgé

quality ['kwɔlɪtɪ] N 1 [U] (*standard*) 质量 zhìliàng 2 [c] (*characteristic: of person*) 素质 sùzhì [种 zhǒng] ▸**quality of life** 生活质量 shēnghuó zhìliàng

quantity ['kwɔntɪtɪ] N 1 [c/U] (*amount*) 数量 shùliàng 2 [U] (*volume*) 容量 róngliàng ▸**in large/small quantities** 大/少量 dà/shǎoliàng

quarantine ['kwɔrənti:n] N [U] 检疫 jiǎnyì ▸**in quarantine** 被隔离 bèi gélí

quarrel ['kwɔrəl] I N [c] 吵架 chǎojià [场 chǎng] II VI 争吵 zhēngchǎo

quarry ['kwɔrɪ] N [c] 采石场 cǎishí chǎng [座 zuò]

quarter ['kwɔːtəʳ] N [c] 四分之一 sìfēnzhīyī ▸**to cut/divide sth into quarters** 把某物切/分为4份 bǎ mǒuwù qiē/fēnwéi sìfèn ▸**a quarter of an hour** 一刻钟 yīkèzhōng ▸**it's a quarter to three** or (US) **of three** 现在是三点差一刻 xiànzài shì sāndiǎn chà yīkè ▸**it's a quarter past three** or (US) **after three** 现在是三点一刻 xiànzài shì sāndiǎn yīkè

quarter-final ['kwɔːtə'faɪnl] N [c] 四分之一决赛 sìfēnzhīyī juésài [场 chǎng]

quay [ki:] N [c] 码头 mǎtóu [个 gè]

queen [kwi:n] N [c] 1 (*monarch*) 女王 nǚwáng [位 wèi] 2 (*king's wife*) 王后 wánghòu [位 wèi]

query ['kwɪərɪ] I N [c] 疑问 yíwèn [个 gè] II VT [+ *figures, bill, expenses*] 询问 xúnwèn

question ['kwɛstʃən] I N 1 [c] (*query*) 问题 wèntí [个 gè] 2 [c] (*issue*) 议题 yìtí [项 xiàng] 3 [c] (*in written exam*) 试题 shìtí [道 dào] II VT (*interrogate*) 盘问 pánwèn

▶**to ask sb a question, to put a question to sb** 问某人一个问题，向某人提出问题 wèn mǒurén yīgè wèntí, xiàng mǒurén tíchū wèntí
▶**to be out of the question** 不可能的 bù kěnéng de

question mark N [c] 问号 wènhào [个 gè]

questionnaire [kwɛstʃə'nɛəʳ] N [c] 问卷 wènjuàn [份 fèn]

queue [kjuː] (esp Brit) I N [c] 队 dui [条 tiáo] II vɪ (also: **queue up**) 排队 páidui ▶**to queue for sth** 为某事排队 wèi mǒushì páidui

quick [kwɪk] I ADJ 1 (fast) 快的 kuài de 2 [+ look] 快速的 kuàisù de; [+ visit] 短时间的 duǎn shíjiān de 3 [+ reply, response, decision] 迅速的 xùnsùde II ADV (inf: quickly) 快地 kuài de ▶**be quick!** 快点！ kuàidiǎn!

quickly ['kwɪklɪ] ADV 1 快地 kuài de 2 迅速地 xùnsù de

quiet ['kwaɪət] ADJ 1 [+ voice, music] 悄声的 qiāoshēng de; [+ place] 安静的 ānjìng de 2 [+ person] 平静的 píngjìng de 3 (silent) ▶**to be quiet** 沉默的 chénmò de ▶**be quiet!** 请安静！ qǐng ānjìng!

quietly ['kwaɪətlɪ] ADV 1 (speak, play) 安静地 ānjìng de 2 (silently) 默默地 mòmò de

quilt [kwɪlt] N [c] 1 被子 bèizi [床 chuáng] 2 (Brit: duvet) 羽绒被 yǔróngbèi [床 chuáng]

quit [kwɪt] (pt, pp **quit** or **quitted**) I vᴛ 1 (esp US: give up) [+ habit, activity] 摆脱 bǎituō 2 (inf: leave)

[+ job] 辞去 cíqù II vɪ 1 (give up) 放弃 fàngqì 2 (resign) 辞职 cízhí

quite [kwaɪt] ADV 1 (rather) 相当 xiāngdāng 2 (completely) 十分 shífēn ▶**I see them quite a lot** 我常常见到他们 wǒ chángcháng jiàndào tāmen ▶**quite a lot of money** 很多钱 hěnduō qián ▶**quite a few** 相当多 xiāngdāng duō ▶**it's not quite finished** 像是还没结束 xiàng shì hái méi jiéshù ▶**quite (so)!** 的确（是这样）！ díquè (shì zhèyàng)! ▶**it was quite a sight** 景色十分了得 jǐngsè shífēn liǎodé

> **quite** 可用在 **a** 或 **an** 之前，后接形容词加名词结构。例如，可以说 It's quite an old car 或者 The car is quite old，以及 It was quite a warm day 或者 The day was quite warm。如前例所示，**quite** 应放在不定冠词之前。例如，不能说 It's a quite old car。**quite** 可以用来修饰形容词和副词，而且程度比 **fairly** 更强烈，但是比 **very** 弱。**quite** 暗示某事物的某种特性超出预料。Nobody here's ever heard of it but it is actually quite common。注意，不要混淆 **quite** 和 **quiet**。

quiz [kwɪz] N [c] (game) 测验 cèyàn [次 cì]

quotation [kwəʊ'teɪʃən] N [c] 1 引语 yǐnyǔ [句 jù] 2 (estimate) 报价 bàojià [个 gè]

quote [kwəʊt] **I** VT [+ *politician, author*] 引用 yǐnyòng; [+ *line*] 引述 yǐnshù **II** N [c] 引语 yǐnyǔ [句 jù] **III quotes** NPL (*inf: quotation marks*) 引号 yǐnhào ▶**in quotes** 在引号里 zài yǐnhào lǐ

r

rabbi ['ræbaɪ] N [c] 拉比(犹太教教师或法学导师)

rabbit ['ræbɪt] N [c] 兔子 tùzi [只 zhī]

rabies ['reɪbiːz] N [U] 狂犬病 kuángquǎnbìng

race [reɪs] **I** N **1** [c] (*speed contest*) 速度竞赛 sùdù jìngsài [场 chǎng] **2** [c/U] (*ethnic group*) 种族 zhǒngzú [个 gè] **II** VI 参赛 cānsài **III** VT 与…进行速度竞赛 yǔ…jìnxíng sùdù jìngsài ▶**a race against time** 抢时间 qiǎng shíjiān

race car (*US*) N = **racing car**

racecourse ['reɪskɔːs] (*Brit*) N [c] 赛马场 sàimǎchǎng [个 gè]

racehorse ['reɪshɔːs] N [c] 赛马 sàimǎ [匹 pǐ]

racetrack ['reɪstræk] N [c] (*for

cars) 赛道 sàidào [条 tiáo]; (US: for horses) 赛马场 sàimǎchǎng [个 gè]

racial ['reɪʃl] ADJ 种族的 zhǒngzú de

racing driver ['reɪsɪŋ-] (Brit) N [c] 赛车手 sàichēshǒu [位 wèi]

racism ['reɪsɪzəm] N [U] 种族歧视 zhǒngzú qíshì

racist ['reɪsɪst] I ADJ [+ policy, attack, behaviour, idea] 种族主义的 zhǒngzú zhǔyì de; [+ person, organization] 有种族偏见的 yǒu zhǒngzú piānjiàn de II N [c] 种族主义者 zhǒngzú zhǔyìzhě [个 gè]

rack [ræk] N [c] 1 (also: luggage rack) 行李架 xínglijià [个 gè] 2 (for hanging clothes, dishes) 架 jià [个 gè]

racket ['rækɪt] N [c] 球拍 qiúpāi [副 fù]

racquet ['rækɪt] N [c] 球拍 qiúpāi [副 fù]

radar ['reɪdɑːʳ] N [c/U] 雷达 léidá [个 gè]

radiation [reɪdɪ'eɪʃən] N [U] 辐射 fúshè

radiator ['reɪdɪeɪtəʳ] N [c] 暖气片 nuǎnqìpiàn [个 gè]

radio ['reɪdɪəu] N 1 [c] (receiver) 收音机 shōuyīnjī [台 tái] 2 [U] (broadcasting) 广播 guǎngbō ▶on the radio 广播中 guǎngbō zhōng

radioactive ['reɪdɪəu'æktɪv] ADJ 放射性的 fàngshèxìng de

radio station N [c] 广播电台 guǎngbō diàntái [个 gè]

RAF (Brit) N ABBR (= Royal Air Force) ▶the RAF 皇家空军

Huángjiā Kōngjūn

rag [ræg] N [c/U] 破布 pòbù [块 kuài]

rage [reɪdʒ] N [c/U] 盛怒 shèngnù [阵 zhèn]

raid [reɪd] VT [soldiers, police] 突袭 tūxí; [criminal] 袭击 xíjī

rail [reɪl] N [c] 1 (for safety on stairs) 扶手 fúshǒu [个 gè]; (on bridge, balcony) 横栏 hénglán [个 gè] 2 (for hanging clothes) 横杆 hénggān [根 gēn] 3 (for trains) 铁轨 tiěguǐ [条 tiáo] ▶by rail 乘火车 chéng huǒchē

railroad ['reɪlrəud] (US) N [c] = **railway**

railway ['reɪlweɪ] (Brit) N [c] 1 (system) 铁路 tiělù 2 (line) 铁道 tiědào [条 tiáo]

railway line (Brit) N [c] 铁路线 tiělùxiàn [条 tiáo]

railway station (Brit) N [c] 火车站 huǒchēzhàn [个 gè]

rain [reɪn] I N [U] 雨 yǔ II VI 下雨 xiàyǔ ▶in the rain 在雨中 zài yǔzhōng ▶it's raining 正在下雨 zhèngzài xiàyǔ

rainbow ['reɪnbəu] N [c] 彩虹 cǎihóng [条 tiáo]

raincoat ['reɪnkəut] N [c] 雨衣 yǔyī [件 jiàn]

rainforest ['reɪnfɔrɪst] N [c/U] 雨林 yǔlín [片 piàn]

rainy ['reɪnɪ] ADJ 多雨的 duōyǔ de

raise [reɪz] I VT 1 (lift) [+ hand, glass] 举起 jǔqǐ 2 (increase) [+ salary, rate, speed limit] 增加 zēngjiā; [+ morale, standards] 提高 tígāo 3 (rear) [+ child, family] 抚养

fǔyǎng **II** N [C] (*US: payrise*) 加薪 jiāxīn [次 cì]

rally ['rælɪ] N [C] **1** (*public meeting*) 集会 jíhuì [次 cì] **2** (*Aut*) 拉力赛 lālìsài [场 chǎng]

rambler ['ræmblə^r] N [C] (*Brit*) 漫步者 mànbùzhě [个 gè]

ramp [ræmp] N [C] 坡道 pōdào [条 tiáo]

ran [ræn] PT *of* **run**

rang [ræŋ] PT *of* **ring**

range [reɪndʒ] N [C] **1** [C] 范围 fànwéi [个 gè]; [*of subjects, possibilities*] 系列 xìliè [个 gè] **2** (*also*: **mountain range**) 山脉 shānmài [个 gè] ▶**to range from... to...** 在…到…之间 zài…dào…zhījiān

rape [reɪp] **I** N [C/U] 强奸 qiángjiān [次 cì] **II** VT 强奸 qiángjiān

rapids ['ræpɪdz] NPL 湍流 tuānliú

rare [rɛə^r] ADJ **1** 稀有的 xīyǒu de **2** [*+ steak*] 半熟的 bànshóu de

rarely ['rɛəlɪ] ADV 很少 hěnshǎo

raspberry ['rɑːzbərɪ] N [C] 山莓 shānméi [只 zhī]

rat [ræt] N [C] 田鼠 tiánshǔ [只 zhī]

rather ['rɑːðə^r] ADV 相当 xiāngdāng ▶**rather a lot** 相当多 xiāngdāng duō ▶**I would rather go than stay** 我宁愿走而不愿留下来 wǒ nìngyuàn zǒu ér bùyuàn liúxià lái ▶**I'd rather not say** 我宁可不说 wǒ nìngkě bùshuō

raw [rɔː] ADJ 生的 shēng de

raw materials NPL 原材料 yuáncáiliào

razor ['reɪzə^r] N [C] **1** (*also*: **safety razor**) 剃须刀 tìxūdāo [个 gè] **2** (*also*: **electric razor**) 电动剃须刀 diàndòng tìxūdāo [个 gè]

razor blade N [C] 剃须刀刀片 tìxūdāo dāopiàn [个 gè]

reach [riːtʃ] VT [*+ place, destination*] 到达 dàodá; [*+ conclusion, agreement, decision*] 达成 dáchéng; [*+ stage, level, age*] 达到 dádào ▶**within easy reach of...** 离…很近 lí…hěnjìn

react [riːˈækt] VI 反应 fǎnyìng

reaction [riːˈækʃən] N [C/U] 反应 fǎnyìng [种 zhǒng]

reactor [riːˈæktə^r] N [C] 反应器 fǎnyìngqì [个 gè]

read [riːd] (*pt, pp* **read** [rɛd]) **I** VI 阅读 yuèdú **II** VT **1** 读 dú **2** (*study at university*) (*Brit*) 攻读 gōngdú ▶**read through** VT **1** (*quickly*) 浏览 liúlǎn **2** (*thoroughly*) 仔细阅读 zǐxì yuèdú

reading ['riːdɪŋ] N [U] 阅读 yuèdú

ready ['rɛdɪ] ADJ 做好准备的 zuòhǎo zhǔnbèi de ▶**to get ready** 准备好 zhǔnbèi hǎo ▶**to get sb/ sth ready** 使某人/某物准备就绪 shǐ mǒurén/mǒuwù zhǔnbèi jiùxù ▶**to be ready to do sth** (*prepared*) 准备做某事 zhǔnbèi zuò mǒushì; (*willing*) 愿意做某事 yuànyì zuò mǒushì

real [rɪəl] ADJ **1** [*+ leather, gold*] 真正的 zhēnzhèng de **2** [*+ reason, interest, name*] 真实的 zhēnshí de **3** [*+ life, feeling*] 真实的 zhēnshí de

realistic [rɪəˈlɪstɪk] ADJ **1** 现实的 xiànshí de **2** (*convincing*) [*+ book,* *film, portrayal*] 逼真的 bīzhēn de

reality [riːˈælɪtɪ] N [U] (*real things*) 现实 xiànshí ▶**in reality** 事实上 shìshí shàng

realize [ˈrɪəlaɪz] VT 意识到 yìshídào ▶**to realize that...** 意识到… yìshí dào...

really [ˈrɪəlɪ] ADV **1** (*very*) ▶**really good/delighted** 真好/真高兴 zhēnhǎo/zhēn gāoxìng **2** (*genuinely*) 确实 quèshí **3** (*after negative*) 真正地 zhēnzhèng de ▶**really?** (*indicating surprise, interest*) 真的吗? zhēnde ma?

realtor [ˈrɪəltɔːʳ] (US) N [c] 房地产商 fángdìchǎn shāng [个 gè]

rear [rɪəʳ] I N [s] (*back*) 后面 hòumian II VT [+ *cattle, chickens*] (*esp Brit*) 饲养 sìyǎng

reason [ˈriːzn] N [c] 原因 yuányīn [个 gè] ▶**the reason for sth** 某事的动机 mǒushì de dòngjī ▶**the reason why** …的原因 …de yuányīn

reasonable [ˈriːznəbl] ADJ **1** [+ *person, decision*] 合情合理的 héqíng hélǐ de; [+ *number, amount*] 相当的 xiāngdāng de; [+ *price*] 合理的 hélǐ de **2** (*not bad*) 凑合的 còuhe de ▶**be reasonable!** 理智些! lǐzhì xie!

reasonably [ˈriːznəblɪ] ADV (*moderately*) 相当地 xiāngdāng de

reassure [riːəˈʃuəʳ] VT 使安心 shǐ ānxīn

receipt [rɪˈsiːt] N [c] 收据 shōujù [张 zhāng]

receive [rɪˈsiːv] VT 收到 shōudào

recent [ˈriːsnt] ADJ 最近的

zuìjìn de

recently [ˈriːsntlɪ] ADV 最近 zuìjìn ▶**until recently** 直到最近 zhídào zuìjìn

reception [rɪˈsɛpʃən] N **1** [s] (*in public building*) 接待处 jiēdàichù **2** [c] (*party*) 欢迎会 huānyínghuì [个 gè] **3** [c] (*welcome*) 反响 fǎnxiǎng [种 zhǒng]

receptionist [rɪˈsɛpʃənɪst] (*esp Brit*) N [c] 接待员 jiēdàiyuán [位 wèi]

recipe [ˈrɛsɪpɪ] (*Culin*) N [c] 食谱 shípǔ [个 gè]

recognize [ˈrɛkəgnaɪz] VT 认出 rènchū

recommend [rɛkəˈmɛnd] VT 推荐 tuījiàn

record [*n, adj* ˈrɛkɔːd, *vb* rɪˈkɔːd] I N [c] **1** (*sound-recording*) 唱片 chàngpiàn [张 zhāng] **2** (*unbeaten statistic*) 记录 jìlù [个 gè] II **records** NPL 记录 jìlù III VT (*make recording of*) 录制 lùzhì IV ADJ [+ *sales, profits, levels*] 创记录的 chuàng jìlù de ▶**in record time** 破记录地 pò jìlù de ▶**to keep a record of sth** 记录某事 jìlù mǒushì

recover [rɪˈkʌvəʳ] VI 恢复 huīfù

recovery [rɪˈkʌvərɪ] N [c/U] 康复 kāngfù

recycle [riːˈsaɪkl] VT 再生利用 zàishēng lìyòng

recycling [riːˈsaɪklɪŋ] N [U] 循环利用 xúnhuán lìyòng

red [rɛd] I ADJ **1** 红色的 hóngsè de **2** [+ *face, person*] 涨红的 zhànghóng de **3** [+ *hair*] 红褐色

的 hónghèsè de 4 [+ wine] 红的
hóng de II N [C/U] 红色 hóngsè
[种 zhǒng]

Red Cross N ▶ the Red Cross 红
十字会 Hóngshízìhuì

red-haired [rɛd'hɛəd] ADJ 红棕色
头发的 hóngzōngsè tóufa de

reduce [rɪ'djuːs] VT 减少 jiǎnshǎo
▶to reduce sth by/to 将某物
减少…/将某物减少到… jiāng
mǒuwù jiǎnshǎo…/jiāng mǒuwù
jiǎnshǎo dào…

  reduction [rɪ'dʌkʃən] N 1 [C/U]
  (decrease) 减少 jiǎnshǎo 2 [C]
  (discount) 减价 jiǎnjià [次 cì]

redundant [rɪ'dʌndnt] ADJ (Brit)
被裁员的 bèi cáiyuán de ▶to be
made redundant 被裁员 bèi
cáiyuán

refer [rɪ'fəː] VT ▶to refer sb to
[+ book] 叫某人参看 jiào mǒurén
cānkàn

  ▶ refer to VT FUS 提到 tídào

referee [rɛfə'riː] N [C] (Sport) 裁判
员 cáipànyuán [位 wèi]

reference ['rɛfrəns] N [C]
1 (mention) 提到 tídào [次 cì]
2 (for job application: letter) 证明人
zhèngmíngrén [位 wèi]

refill [riː'fɪl] VT 再装满
zàizhuāngmǎn

reflect [rɪ'flɛkt] VT [+ image] 映
出 yìngchū; [+ light, heat] 反射
fǎnshè

reflection [rɪ'flɛkʃən] N 1 [C]
(image) 影像 yǐngxiàng [个 gè] 2
[U] (thought) 沉思 chénsī

refreshing [rɪ'frɛʃɪŋ] ADJ 提神的
tíshén de

refreshments [rɪ'frɛʃmənts] NPL
饮料及小吃 yǐnliào jí xiǎochī

refrigerator [rɪ'frɪdʒəreɪtər] N [C]
冰箱 bīngxiāng [个 gè]

refugee [rɛfju'dʒiː] N [C] 难
民 nànmín [批 pī] ▶a political
refugee 政治难民 zhèngzhì
nànmín

refund [n 'riːfʌnd, vb rɪ'fʌnd] I N
[c] 退款 tuìkuǎn [笔 bǐ] II VT 偿还
chánghuán

refuse[1] [rɪ'fjuːz] VT, VI 拒绝 jùjué
▶to refuse to do sth 拒绝做某
事 jùjué zuò mǒushì ▶to refuse
sb permission 不批准某人 bù
pīzhǔn mǒurén

refuse[2] ['rɛfjuːs] N [U] 垃圾 lājī

regard [rɪ'gɑːd] I VT (consider,
view) 认为 rènwéi II N ▶to give
one's regards to 向…表示问候
xiàng…biǎoshì wènhòu

region ['riːdʒən] N [C] 区域 qūyù
[个 gè]

regional ['riːdʒənl] ADJ 地区的
dìqū de

register ['rɛdʒɪstər] N [C] 1 (at
hotel) 登记 dēngjì [个 gè] 2 (in
school) 注册 zhùcè [个 gè]

registered ['rɛdʒɪstəd] ADJ (Post)
挂号的 guàhào de

registration [rɛdʒɪs'treɪʃən] N
[C/U] [of birth, death, students] 登
记 dēngjì [个 gè]

regret [rɪ'grɛt] VT 后悔 hòuhuǐ
▶to have no regrets 没有遗憾
méiyǒu yíhàn ▶to regret that…
对…感到后悔 duì…gǎndào
hòuhuǐ

regular ['rɛgjulər] ADJ

1 [+ *breathing, intervals*] 有规律的 yǒu guīlǜ de 2 [+ *event*] 有规律的 yǒu guīlǜ de; [+ *visitor*] 经常的 jīngcháng de 3 (*normal*) 正常的 zhèngcháng de

regularly ['rɛgjuləlɪ] ADV 经常 jīngcháng

regulation [rɛgju'leɪʃən] N [c] 规章 guīzhāng [套 tào]

rehearsal [rɪ'hə:səl] N [c/U] 排练 páiliàn [次 cì]

rehearse [rɪ'hə:s] VT, VI 排练 páiliàn

reject [rɪ'dʒɛkt] VT 1 拒绝接受 jùjué jiēshòu 2 [+ *applicant, admirer*] 拒绝 jùjué

related [rɪ'leɪtɪd] ADJ [+ *people*] 有亲缘关系的 yǒu qīnyuán guānxì de ▶**to be related to sb** 和某人有关连 hé mǒurén yǒu guānlián

relation [rɪ'leɪʃən] N [c] 1 (*relative*) 亲戚 qīnqi [个 gè] 2 (*connection*) 关系 guānxì [种 zhǒng] ▶**in relation to** 与…相比 yǔ…xiāngbǐ

relationship [rɪ'leɪʃənʃɪp] N [c] 1 (*connection*) 关系 guānxì [个 gè] 2 (*rapport: between two people, countries*) 关系 guānxì [种 zhǒng] 3 (*affair*) 亲密的关系 qīnmì de guānxì [种 zhǒng] ▶**to have a good relationship** 关系亲密 guānxi qīnmì

relative ['rɛlətɪv] N [c] 亲戚 qīnqi [个 gè]

relatively ['rɛlətɪvlɪ] ADV 相对 xiāngduì

relax [rɪ'læks] VI 放松 fàngsōng

relaxation [ri:læk'seɪʃən] N [U] 消遣 xiāoqiǎn

relaxed [rɪ'lækst] ADJ 放松的 fàngsōng de; [+ *discussion, atmosphere*] 轻松的 qīngsōng de

relaxing [rɪ'læksɪŋ] ADJ 令人放松的 lìng rén fàngsōng de

release [rɪ'li:s] I N [c] 释放 shìfàng [次 cì] II VT 1 释放 shìfàng 2 [+ *record, film*] 发行 fāxíng

relevant ['rɛləvənt] ADJ 切题的 qiètí de ▶**relevant to** 和…有关的 hé…yǒuguān de

reliable [rɪ'laɪəbl] ADJ 可靠的 kěkào de; [+ *method, machine*] 可信赖的 kěxìnlài de

relief [rɪ'li:f] N [U] 如释重负 rú shì zhòng fù

relieved [rɪ'li:vd] ADJ 宽慰的 kuānwèi de ▶**to be relieved that...** 对…感到放心 duì…gǎndào fàngxīn

religion [rɪ'lɪdʒən] N 1 [U] (*belief*) 宗教信仰 zōngjiào xìnyǎng 2 [c] (*set of beliefs*) 宗教 zōngjiào [种 zhǒng]

religious [rɪ'lɪdʒəs] ADJ 1 [+ *activities, faith*] 宗教的 zōngjiào de 2 [+ *person*] 笃信宗教的 dǔxìn zōngjiào de

reluctant [rɪ'lʌktənt] ADJ 不情愿的 bùqíngyuàn de ▶**to be reluctant to do sth** 不愿做某事 bùyuàn zuò mǒushì

reluctantly [rɪ'lʌktəntlɪ] ADV 不情愿地 bùqíngyuàn de

rely on [rɪ'laɪ-] VT FUS 1 (*be dependent on*) 依赖 yīlài 2 (*trust*) 信赖 xìnlài

remain [rɪ'meɪn] VI 1 (*continue to be*) 仍然是 réngrán shì 2 (*stay*) 逗

留 dòuliú ▸to remain silent/in control 保持沉默/仍然控制局面 bǎochí chénmò/réngrán kòngzhì júmiàn

remaining [rɪˈmeɪnɪŋ] ADJ 剩下的 shèngxià de

remark [rɪˈmɑːk] N [c] (comment) 评论 pínglùn [个 gè]

remarkable [rɪˈmɑːkəbl] ADJ 不寻常的 bù xúncháng de

remarkably [rɪˈmɑːkəblɪ] ADV 极其地 jíqí de

remember [rɪˈmɛmbəʳ] VT 1 [+ person, name, event] 记住 jìzhù 2 (bring back to mind) 回想起 huíxiǎngqǐ 3 (bear in mind) 牢记 láojì ▸she remembered to do it 她记得要做某事 tā jìdé yào zuò mǒushì

remind [rɪˈmaɪnd] VT 提醒 tíxǐng ▸to remind sb to do sth 提醒某人做某事 tíxǐng mǒurén zuò mǒushì ▸to remind sb of sb/sth 使某人想起某人/某事 shǐ mǒurén xiǎngqǐ mǒurén/mǒushì

remote [rɪˈməut] ADJ 遥远的 yáoyuǎn de

remote control N [c] 遥控器 yáokòngqì [个 gè]

remove [rɪˈmuːv] VT 1 [+ object, organ] 移走 yízǒu 2 [+ clothing, bandage] 脱下 tuōxià 3 [+ stain] 清除 qīngchú

renew [rɪˈnjuː] VT [+ loan, contract] 延长 yáncháng

rent [rɛnt] I N [c/u] 租金 zūjīn [笔 bǐ] II VT 1 租用 zūyòng 2 (also: **rent out**) [+ house, room] 出租 chūzū

reorganize [riːˈɔːɡənaɪz] VT 重组 chóngzǔ

rep [rɛp] N (also: **sales rep**) 商品经销代理 shāngpǐn jīngxiāo dàilǐ [位 wèi]

repair [rɪˈpɛəʳ] I N [c/u] 修理 xiūlǐ [次 cì] II VT 1 修补 xiūbǔ 2 [+ damage] 维修 wéixiū

repay [riːˈpeɪ] (pt, pp **repaid**) VT 偿还 chánghuán

repeat [rɪˈpiːt] VT 1 重复 chóngfù 2 [+ action, mistake] 重做 chóngzuò

repeatedly [rɪˈpiːtɪdlɪ] ADV 反复地 fǎnfù de

replace [rɪˈpleɪs] VT 1 (put back) 将…放回 jiāng…fànghuí 2 (take the place of) 代替 dàitì

replay [n ˈriːpleɪ, vb riːˈpleɪ] I N [c] [of match] 重新比赛 chóngxīn bǐsài [场 chǎng] II VT [+ track, song] (on tape) 重新播放 chóngxīn bōfàng ▸to replay a match 重新比赛 chóngxīn bǐsài

reply [rɪˈplaɪ] I N [c] 回答 huídá [个 gè] II VI 答复 dáfù ▸there's no reply (Tel) 无人接听 wúrén jiētīng

report [rɪˈpɔːt] I N [c] 1 (account) 报告 bàogào [个 gè] 2 (Brit) (also: **school report**) 成绩单 chéngjìdān [份 fèn] II VT [+ theft, accident, death] 报案 bào'àn; [+ person] 告发 gàofā

report card (US) N [c] 学生成绩报告单 xuéshēng chéngjì bàogàodān [份 fèn]

reporter [rɪˈpɔːtəʳ] N [c] 记者 jìzhě [名 míng]

represent [rɛprɪ'zɛnt] VT [+ *person, nation*] 代表 dàibiǎo

representative [rɛprɪ'zɛntətɪv] N [c] 代表 dàibiǎo [个 gè]

republic [rɪ'pʌblɪk] N [c] 共和国 gònghéguó [个 gè]

reputation [rɛpju'teɪʃən] N [c] 名声 míngshēng [种 zhǒng]

request [rɪ'kwɛst] I N [c] 要求 yāoqiú [个 gè] II VT 要求 yāoqiú

require [rɪ'kwaɪəʳ] VT (*need*) 需要 xūyào ▶to be required [*approval, permission*] 必须有 bìxū yǒu

rescue ['rɛskju:] I N [c/u] 营救 yíngjiù [次 cì] II VT 解救 jiějiù

research [rɪ'sə:tʃ] N [u] 研究 yánjiū ▶to do research 从事研究 cóngshì yánjiū

resemblance [rɪ'zɛmbləns] N [c/u] 相似 xiāngsì [种 zhǒng]

reservation [rɛzə'veɪʃən] N [c] 预定 yùdìng [个 gè] ▶to make a reservation (*in hotel, restaurant, on train*) 预定 yùdìng

reservation desk (US) N [c] 预定台 yùdìngtái [个 gè]

reserve [rɪ'zə:v] VT 预定 yùdìng

reserved [rɪ'zə:vd] ADJ 1 [+ *seat*] 已预定的 yǐ yùdìng de 2 (*restrained*) 矜持的 jīnchí de

resident ['rɛzɪdənt] N [c] 居民 jūmín [位 wèi]

resign [rɪ'zaɪn] VI 辞职 cízhí

resist [rɪ'zɪst] VT [+ *temptation, urge*] 克制 kèzhì

resit [ri:'sɪt] (*Brit*) VT [+ *exam*] 补考 bǔkǎo

resolution [rɛzə'lu:ʃən] N [c/u] 决心 juéxīn [个 gè] ▶**New Year's**

resolution 新年决心 Xīnnián juéxīn

resort [rɪ'zɔ:t] N [c] (*also:* **holiday resort**) 度假胜地 dùjià shèngdì [个 gè] ▶a seaside/winter sports resort 海边/冬季运动胜地 hǎibiān/dōngjì yùndòng shèngdì ▶as a last resort 作为最后手段 zuòwéi zuìhòu shǒuduàn

resource [rɪ'zɔ:s] resources NPL 1 (*coal, iron, oil*) 资源 zīyuán 2 (*money*) 财力 cáilì ▶**natural resources** 自然资源 zìrán zīyuán

respect [rɪs'pɛkt] I N [u] 尊敬 zūnjìng II VT 尊敬 zūnjìng ▶to have respect for sb/sth 对某人/某事怀有敬意 duì mǒurén/mǒushì huáiyǒu jìngyì

respectable [rɪs'pɛktəbl] ADJ 1 [+ *area, background*] 体面的 tǐmiàn de 2 [+ *person*] 受人尊敬的 shòurén zūnjìng de

responsibility [rɪspɒnsɪ'bɪlɪtɪ] I N 1 [s] (*duty*) 职责 zhízé 2 [u] (*obligation*) 义务 yìwù II responsibilities NPL 责任 zérèn

responsible [rɪs'pɒnsɪbl] ADJ 1 (*at fault*) 负有责任的 fùyǒu zérèn de 2 (*in charge*) 负责的 fùzé de 3 (*sensible, trustworthy*) 可靠的 kěkào de

rest [rɛst] I N 1 [u] (*relaxation*) 休息 xiūxi 2 [c] (*break*) 休息 xiūxi [次 cì] 3 [s] (*remainder*) 剩余 shèngyú II VI (*relax*) 休息 xiūxi III VT [+ *eyes, legs, muscles*] 休息 xiūxi ▶to rest sth on/against sth (*lean*) 把某物靠在某物上 bǎ mǒuwù kàozài mǒuwù shàng ▸**the rest (of them)** (他们当中)其余的 (tāmen dāngzhōng)qíyú de

rest area (US) N [c] 路边服务站 lùbiān fúwùzhàn [个 gè]

restaurant ['rɛstərɔŋ] N [c] 餐馆 cānguǎn [家 jiā]

restless ['rɛstlɪs] ADJ (fidgety) 坐立不安的 zuòlì bù'ān de

restore [rɪ'stɔːʳ] VT 修复 xiūfù

restrict [rɪs'trɪkt] VT 1 [+ growth, membership, privilege] 限制 xiànzhì 2 [+ activities] 约束 yuēshù

rest room (US) N [c] 洗手间 xǐshǒujiān [个 gè]

result [rɪ'zʌlt] I N [c] [of event, action] 后果 hòuguǒ [种 zhǒng]; [of match, election, exam, competition] 结果 jiéguǒ [个 gè]; [of calculation] 答案 dá'àn [个 gè] II VI 产生 chǎnshēng ▸**to result in** 导致 dǎozhì ▸**as a result of** 由于 yóuyú ▸**to result from** 因…而产生 yīn…ér chǎnshēng

résumé ['reɪzjuːmeɪ] N [c] (US: CV) 简历 jiǎnlì [份 fèn]

retire [rɪ'taɪəʳ] VI 退休 tuìxiū

retired [rɪ'taɪəd] ADJ 退休的 tuìxiū de

retiree [rɪtaɪə'riː] (US) N [c] 领养老金的人 lǐng yǎnglǎojīn de rén [位 wèi]

retirement [rɪ'taɪəmənt] N [c/u] 退休 tuìxiū

return [rɪ'təːn] I VI 返回 fǎnhuí II VT 归还 guīhuán III N 1 [s] [of person] 返回 fǎnhuí 2 [s] [of something borrowed or stolen] 归还 guīhuán 3 [u] (Comput: key) 回车

键 huíchējiàn ▸**in return (for)** 作为(对…)的回报 zuòwéi(duì…)de huíbào ▸**many happy returns (of the day)!** 生日快乐！shēngrì kuàilè! IV CPD (Brit) [+ journey, ticket] 往返 wǎngfǎn

reunion [riː'juːnɪən] N [c] 团聚 tuánjù [次 cì]

reveal [rɪ'viːl] VT (make known) 透露 tòulù

revenge [rɪ'vɛndʒ] N [u] 复仇 fùchóu ▸**to take (one's) revenge (on sb)** (对某人)进行报复 (duì mǒurén)jìnxíng bàofù

review [rɪ'vjuː] I N [c] 评论 pínglùn [个 gè]

revise [rɪ'vaɪz] I VT (study) 复习 fùxí II VI (study) (Brit) 复习 fùxí

revision [rɪ'vɪʒən] N [u] (Brit: studying) 复习 fùxí

revolution [rɛvə'luːʃən] N 1 [c/u] (Pol) 革命 gémìng [场 chǎng] 2 [c] 变革 biàngé [场 chǎng]

reward [rɪ'wɔːd] I N [c] 奖励 jiǎnglì [种 zhǒng] II VT 奖赏 jiǎngshǎng

rewarding [rɪ'wɔːdɪŋ] ADJ 值得做的 zhídé zuò de

rewind [riː'waɪnd] (pt, pp **rewound**) VT 倒带 dàodài

rhythm ['rɪðm] N [c/u] 节奏 jiézòu [个 gè]

rib [rɪb] N [c] 肋骨 lèigǔ [根 gēn]

ribbon ['rɪbən] N [c/u] 饰带 shìdài [条 tiáo]

rice [raɪs] N [c/u] 1 (grain) 大米 dàmǐ [粒 lì] 2 (when cooked) 米饭 mǐfàn [碗 wǎn]

rich [rɪtʃ] ADJ [+ person, country] 富

有的 fùyǒu de

rid [rɪd] (pt, pp **rid**) vt ▸**to get rid of sth/sb** [+ smell, dirt, car etc] 摆脱某物/某人 bǎituō mǒuwù/mǒurén

ride [raɪd] (pt **rode**, pp **ridden** ['rɪdn]) I N [c] **1** (in car, on bicycle) 兜风 dōufēng [次 cì] **2** (on horse, bus, train) 出行 chūxíng [次 cì] II vi 骑马 qímǎ; (on bicycle) 骑车 qíchē; (in car) 乘坐 chéngzuò III vt **1** [+ horse, bicycle, motorcycle] 骑 qí **2** [+ distance] 行进 xíngjìn ▸**to give sb a ride** (US) 让某人搭车 ràng mǒurén dāchē

ridiculous [rɪ'dɪkjuləs] ADJ 荒谬的 huāngmiù de

rifle ['raɪfl] N [c] 步枪 bùqiāng [支 zhī]

right [raɪt] I ADJ **1** (not left) 右边的 yòubiān de **2** (correct) 正确的 zhèngquè de; [+ person, place, clothes] 合适的 héshì de; [+ decision, direction, time] 最适宜的 zuì shìyí de II N **1** [s] (not left) 右边 yòubiān **2** [c] (entitlement) 权利 quánlì [个 gè] III ADV **1** (correctly) 正确地 zhèngquè de **2** (properly, fairly) 恰当 qiàdàng **3** (not to/on the left) 右边地 yòubiān de IV INT 好 hǎo ▸**do you have the right time?** 你的表几点了？nǐde biǎo jǐdiǎn le? ▸**to be right** [person] 正确 zhèngquè; [answer, fact] 对 duì; [clock] 准确 zhǔnquè ▸**you did the right thing** 你做得对 nǐ zuòde duì ▸**to** or **on the right** (position) 靠{或}在右侧 kào{huò}zài yòucè ▸**to the right**

right-handed [raɪt'hændɪd] ADJ 惯用右手的 guànyòng yòushǒu de

ring [rɪŋ] (pt **rang**, pp **rung**) I N [c] (on finger) 戒指 jièzhi [枚 méi] II vi **1** [bell] 鸣响 míngxiǎng **2** [telephone] 响 xiǎng **3** (Brit) 打电话 dǎ diànhuà III vt **1** [+ bell, doorbell] 使…响 shǐ…xiǎng **2** (Brit: Tel) 给…打电话 gěi…dǎ diànhuà ▸**there was a ring at the door, the doorbell rang** 有人按门铃 yǒurén àn ménlíng ▸**to give sb a ring** (Brit: Tel) 给某人打电话 gěi mǒurén dǎ diànhuà

▸**ring back** (Brit: Tel) I vt 回电话 huí diànhuà II vi 再打电话 zài dǎ diànhuà

▸**ring up** (Brit: Tel) vt 给…打电话 gěi…dǎ diànhuà

rinse [rɪns] vt [+ dishes, clothes] 漂洗 piǎoxǐ

riot ['raɪət] I N [c] (disturbance) 暴乱 bàoluàn [次 cì] II vi 闹事 nàoshì

ripe [raɪp] ADJ 成熟的 chéngshú de

rise [raɪz] (pt **rose**, pp **risen** ['rɪzn]) I N **1** [c] (Brit: salary increase) 加薪 jiāxīn [次 cì] **2** [c] (in prices, temperature, crime rate) 上升 shàngshēng [次 cì] II vi **1** (move upwards) 上升 shàngshēng **2** [prices, numbers] 上升 shàngshēng **3** [sun, moon] 升起 shēngqǐ **4** (from chair) 起身 qǐshēn

risk [rɪsk] I N **1** [c/u] (danger) 危险 wēixiǎn [个 gè] **2** [c] (possibility, chance) 风险 fēngxiǎn [种 zhǒng]

II VT (*take the chance of*) 冒险做 màoxiǎn zuò ▸**to take a risk** 担 风险 dān fēngxiǎn ▸**to risk it** (*inf*) 冒险一试 màoxiǎn yīcì

rival ['raɪvl] **I** N [c] 竞争对手 jìngzhēng duìshǒu [个 gè] **II** ADJ [+ *teams, groups, supporters*] 对立 的 duìlì de

river ['rɪvə^r] N [c] 河 hé [条 tiáo]

river bank N [c] 河岸 hé'àn [个 gè]

road [rəud] N [c] **1** (*in country*) 公 路 gōnglù [条 tiáo] **2** (*in town*) 路 lù [条 tiáo] ▸**it takes four hours by road** 要花4小时的车程 yào huā sì xiǎoshí de chēchéng

road map N [c] 道路图 dàolùtú [张 zhāng]

road sign N [c] 交通标志 jiāotōng biāozhì [个 gè]

roast [rəust] VT 烤 kǎo

rob [rɔb] VT 抢劫 qiǎngjié ▸**to rob sb of sth** 剥夺某人的某物 bōduó mǒurén de mǒuwù

robber ['rɔbə^r] N [c] 强盗 qiángdào [个 gè]

robbery ['rɔbərɪ] N [c/u] 抢劫 qiǎngjié [次 cì]

robot ['rəubɔt] N [c] 机器人 jīqìrén [个 gè]

rock [rɔk] N **1** [c] (*boulder*) 巨石 jùshí [块 kuài] **2** [c] (*esp US: small stone*) 小石子 xiǎoshízǐ [块 kuài] **3** [u] (*Mus*) (*also*: **rock music**) 摇滚 乐 yáogǔnyuè

rocket ['rɔkɪt] N [c] **1** (*Space*) 火箭 huǒjiàn [支 zhī] **2** (*firework*) 火箭式 礼花 huǒjiànshì lǐhuā [个 gè]

rod [rɔd] N [c] **1** (*pole*) 杆 gān [根

gēn] **2** (*also*: **fishing rod**) 钓鱼竿 diàoyúgān [根 gēn]

rode [rəud] PT *of* **ride**

role [rəul] N [c] **1** (*function*) 作用 zuòyòng [个 gè] **2** (*Theat: part*) 角 色 juésè [个 gè]

roll [rəul] **I** N [c] **1** 一卷 yī juǎn [个 gè] **2** (*also*: **bread roll**) 小圆面包 xiǎoyuánmiànbāo [个 gè] **II** VT 使 滚动 shǐ gǔndòng **III** VI [*ball, stone*] 滚动 gǔndòng ▸**cheese/ham roll** 奶酪/火腿面包卷 nǎilào/huǒtuǐ miànbāojuǎn

rollerblades ['rəuləbleɪdz] NPL 直排轮溜冰鞋 zhípáilún liūbīngxié

roller coaster [-'kəustə^r] N [c] (*at funfair*) 过山车 guòshānchē [辆 liàng]

roller skates NPL 旱冰鞋 hànbīngxié

roller skating N [u] 穿旱冰鞋滑 行 chuān hànbīngxié huáxíng

Roman ['rəumən] **I** ADJ **1** (*of ancient Rome*) 古罗马的 gǔ Luómǎ de **2** (*of modern Rome*) 罗马的 Luómǎ de **II** N [c] (*in ancient Rome*) 古罗马人 gǔ Luómǎrén [个 gè]

Roman Catholic I ADJ 天主教的 Tiānzhǔjiào de **II** N [c] 天主教教徒 Tiānzhǔjiào Jiàotú [个 gè]

romance [rə'mæns] N **1** [c] (*affair*) 恋情 liànqíng [种 zhǒng] **2** [u] (*charm, excitement*) 迷人之处 mírén zhī chù

Romania [rə'meɪnɪə] N 罗马尼亚 Luómǎníyà

Romanian [rə'meɪnɪən] **I** ADJ 罗马尼亚的 Luómǎníyà de **II** N **1** [c] (*person*) 罗马尼

亚人 Luómǎníyàrén [个 gè]
2 [U] (language) 罗马尼亚语 Luómǎníyàyǔ

romantic [rə'mæntɪk] ADJ
1 [+ person] 浪漫的 làngmàn de
2 (connected with love) [+ play, story etc] 爱情的 àiqíng de **3** (charming, exciting) [+ setting, holiday, dinner etc] 浪漫的 làngmàn de

roof [ru:f] N [c] **1** [of building] 屋顶 wūdǐng [个 gè] **2** [of cave, mine, vehicle] 顶 dǐng [个 gè]

room [ru:m] N **1** [c] (in house) 室 shì [个 gè] **2** [c] (also: **bedroom**) 卧室 wòshì [个 gè] **3** [U] (space) 空间 kōngjiān ▸**single/double room** 单人/双人间 dānrén/shuāngrén jiān

root [ru:t] N [c] 根 gēn [个 gè]

rope [rəup] N [c/U] 绳子 shéngzi [根 gēn]

rose [rəuz] I PT of **rise** II N [c] (flower) 玫瑰 méigui [朵 duǒ]

rot [rɔt] I VT (cause to decay) 使腐坏 shǐ fǔhuài II VI (decay) [teeth, wood, fruit] 腐烂 fǔlàn

rotten ['rɔtn] ADJ **1** (decayed) 腐烂的 fǔlàn de **2** (inf: awful) 糟透的 zāotòu de

rough [rʌf] ADJ **1** [+ skin, surface, cloth] 粗糙的 cūcāo de **2** [+ terrain] 崎岖的 qíqū de **3** [+ sea, crossing] 波涛汹涌的 bōtāo xiōngyǒng de **4** (violent) [+ person] 粗鲁的 cūlǔ de; [+ town, area] 治安混乱的 zhì'ān hùnluàn de **5** [+ outline, plan, idea] 粗略的 cūlüè de

roughly ['rʌflɪ] ADV **1** (violently) 粗暴地 cūbào de **2** (approximately)

大约 dàyuē ▸**roughly speaking** 粗略地说 cūlüè de shuō

round [raund] I ADJ **1** (circular) 圆的 yuán de **2** (spherical) 球形的 qiúxíng de **3** [+ figure, sum] 不计尾数的 bù jì wěishù de II N [c] **1** (stage: in competition) 一轮 yī lún **2** (Golf) 一场 yī chǎng III PREP **1** (surrounding) 围绕 wéirào **2** (near) 在…附近 zài…fùjìn **3** (on or from the other side of) 绕过 ràoguò ▸**to move round the room/sail round the world** 绕房间一周/环球航行 rào fángjiān yī zhōu/huánqiú hángxíng ▸**all round** 在…周围 zài…zhōuwéi ▸**to go round (sth)** 绕过 (某物) ràoguò (mǒuwù) ▸**to go round to sb's (house)** 造访某人(的家) zàofǎng mǒurén (de jiā) ▸**all (the) year round** 一年到头 yīnián dàotóu ▸**I'll be round at 6 o'clock** 我会在6点钟到你家 wǒ huì zài liùdiǎnzhōng dào nǐjiā ▸**round about** (esp Brit: approximately) 大约 dàyuē ▸**round the clock** 连续24小时 liánxù èrshísì xiǎoshí ▸**a round of applause** 掌声雷动 zhǎngshēng léidòng ▸**round off** VT [+ meal, evening] 圆满结束 yuánmǎn jiéshù ▸**round up** VT **1** [+ cattle, sheep] 驱拢 qūlǒng **2** [+ people] 围捕 wéibǔ **3** [+ price, figure] 把…调高为整数 bǎ…tiáogāo wéi zhěngshù

roundabout ['raundəbaut] N [c] (Brit) (Aut) 环形交叉路 huánxíng jiāochālù [个 gè]

round trip I N [c] 往返旅行

往返的 wǎngfǎn de
route [ruːt] N [c] **1** (*path, journey*)
路 lù [条 tiáo] **2** (*of bus, train*) 路线
lùxiàn [条 tiáo]
routine [ruːˈtiːn] N [c/u] 例行公
事 lìxíng gōngshì [次 cì]
row¹ [rəu] I N [c] **1** 一排 yī pái **2** [*of
seats in theatre, cinema*] 一排 yī
pái II VI (*in boat*) 划船 huáchuán
III VT [+ *boat*] 划 huá ▶ **in a row**
连续 liánxù
row² [rau] N **1** [s] (*noise*) (*Brit: inf*)
吵闹声 chǎonàoshēng **2** [c] (*noisy
quarrel*) 吵架 chǎojià [场 chǎng]
rowboat [ˈrəubəut] (*US*) N [c] 划
艇 huátǐng [艘 sōu]
rowing [ˈrəuɪŋ] (*Sport*) N [u] 赛艇
运动 sàitǐng yùndòng
rowing boat (*Brit*) N [c] 划艇
huátǐng [艘 sōu]
royal [ˈrɔɪəl] ADJ 皇家的 huángjiā
de ▶ **the royal family** 王室
wángshì

- **ROYAL FAMILY**

- **royal family** （英国王室）
- 以伊丽莎白女王二世为首。
- 女王于1953年登基。她的丈
- 夫是菲利普亲王，即爱丁堡
- 公爵。他们育有四名成年
- 子女：查尔斯王子，安妮公
- 主，安德鲁王子和爱德华王
- 子。查尔斯王子，即威尔士
- 亲王是王位的继承人。他有
- 两个孩子，威廉王子和哈利
- 王子。他们的母亲是已故的
- 威尔士王妃戴安娜。

rub [rʌb] VT (*with hand, fingers*) 揉
róu; (*with cloth, substance*) 擦 cā
▶ **rub out** VT (*erase*) 擦掉 cādiào
rubber [ˈrʌbəʳ] N **1** [u] (*substance*)
橡胶 xiàngjiāo **2** [c] (*Brit*) 橡皮擦
xiàngpícā [个 gè]
rubber boot (*US*) N [c] 橡胶长
统靴 xiàngjiāo chángtǒngxuē [双
shuāng]
rubbish [ˈrʌbɪʃ] (*Brit*) I N [u]
1 (*refuse*) 垃圾 lājī **2** (*inferior
material*) 垃圾 lājī **3** (*nonsense*) 废
话 fèihuà II ADJ (*Brit: inf*) ▶ **I'm
rubbish at golf** 我高尔夫球打
得很糟糕 wǒ gāoěrfūqiú dǎde
hěn zāogāo ▶ **rubbish!** 胡说！
húshuō!
rubbish bin (*Brit*) N [c] 垃圾箱
lājīxiāng [个 gè]
rucksack [ˈrʌksæk] N [c] 背包
bèibāo [个 gè]
rude [ruːd] ADJ **1** 无礼的 wúlǐ de
2 [+ *word, joke, noise*] 粗鄙的 cūbǐ
de ▶ **to be rude to sb** 对某人无礼
duì mǒurén wúlǐ
rug [rʌg] N [c] 小地毯 xiǎodìtǎn
[块 kuài]
rugby [ˈrʌgbɪ] N [u] (*also:* **rugby
football**) 英式橄榄球 yīngshì
gǎnlǎnqiú
ruin [ˈruːɪn] I N [u] 毁坏 huǐhuài
II VT [+ *clothes, carpet*] 毁坏
huǐhuài; [+ *plans, prospects*] 葬送
zàngsòng III RUINS NPL [*of building,
castle*] 废墟 fèixū ▶ **to be in ruins**
[*building, town*] 破败不堪 pòbài
bùkān
rule [ruːl] N **1** [c] (*regulation*) 规则
guīzé [条 tiáo] **2** [c] [*of language,*

science] 规则 guīzé [条 tiáo] ▶**it's against the rules** 这是不合规定的 zhèshì bùhé guīdìng de ▶**as a rule** 通常 tōngcháng

ruler ['ru:lə'] N [c] (for measuring) 直尺 zhíchǐ [把 bǎ]

rum [rʌm] N [U] 朗姆酒 lǎngmǔjiǔ

rumour, (US) **rumor** ['ru:mə'] N [c/U] 谣言 yáoyán [个 gè]

run [rʌn] (pt **ran**, pp **run**) I N [c] 1 (as exercise, sport) 跑步 pǎobù [次 cì] 2 (Cricket, Baseball) 跑动得分 pǎodòng défēn [次 cì] II VT 1 [+ race, distance] 跑 pǎo 2 (operate) [+ business, shop, country] 经营 jīngyíng 3 [+ water, bath] 流 liú 4 [+ program, test] 进行 jìnxíng III VI 1 跑 pǎo 2 (flee) 逃跑 táopǎo 3 [bus, train] 行驶 xíngshǐ 4 (in combination) 变得 biànde ▶**to go for a run** (as exercise) 跑步锻炼 pǎobù duànliàn ▶**in the long run** 终究 zhōngjiū ▶**I'll run you to the station** 我开车送你去车站 wǒ kāichē sòng nǐ qù chēzhàn ▶**to run on** or **off petrol/batteries** 以汽油/电池为能源 yǐ qìyóu/diànchí wéi néngyuán

▶**run after** VT FUS (chase) 追赶 zhuīgǎn

▶**run away** VI (from home, situation) 出走 chūzǒu

▶**run into** VT FUS (meet) [+ person] 偶然碰见 ǒurán pèngjiàn; [+ trouble, problems] 遭遇 zāoyù

▶**run off** VI 跑掉 pǎodiào

▶**run out** VI 1 [time, money, luck] 用完 yòngwán 2 [lease, passport]

到期 dàoqī

▶**run out of** VT FUS 耗尽 hàojìn

▶**run over** VT (Aut) [+ person] 撞倒 zhuàngdǎo

rung [rʌŋ] PP of **ring**

runner ['rʌnə'] N [c] (in race) 赛跑者 sàipǎozhě [个 gè]

runner-up [rʌnər'ʌp] N [c] 亚军 yàjūn [个 gè]

running ['rʌnɪŋ] N [U] (sport) 赛跑 sàipǎo ▶**6 days running** 连续6天 liánxù liùtiān

run-up ['rʌnʌp] N ▶**the run-up to...** [+ election etc] …的前期 …de qiánqī

runway ['rʌnweɪ] N [c] 跑道 pǎodào [条 tiáo]

rush [rʌʃ] I N [s] (hurry) 匆忙 cōngmáng II VI [person] 急速前往 jísù qiánwǎng

rush hour N [c] 高峰时间 gāofēng shíjiān [段 duàn]

Russia ['rʌʃə] N 俄罗斯 Éluósī

Russian ['rʌʃən] I ADJ 俄罗斯的 Éluósī de II N 1 [c] (person) 俄罗斯人 Éluósīrén [个 gè] 2 [U] (language) 俄语 Éyǔ

rust [rʌst] N [U] 铁锈 tiěxiù

rusty ['rʌstɪ] ADJ 1 [+ surface, object] 生锈的 shēngxiù de 2 [+ skill] 荒疏的 huāngshū de

RV (US) N ABBR (= **recreational vehicle**) 娱乐车 yúlèchē

rye [raɪ] N [U] (cereal) 黑麦 hēimài

S

sack [sæk] **I** N [c] 麻袋 mádài [个 gè] **II** VT 解雇 jiěgù

sad [sæd] ADJ **1** 伤心的 shāngxīn de **2** (*distressing*) 令人悲伤的 lìngrén bēishāng de

saddle ['sædl] N [c] (*for horse*) 马鞍 mǎ'ān [副 fù]; (*on bike, motorbike*) 车座 chēzuò [个 gè]

safe [seif] **I** ADJ **1** (*not dangerous*) 安全的 ānquán de **2** (*out of danger*) 脱险的 tuōxiǎn de **3** [+ *place*] 保险的 bǎoxiǎn de **II** N [c] 保险箱 bǎoxiǎnxiāng [个 gè]

safety ['seifti] N [U] **1** 安全 ānquán **2** 平安 píng'ān

Sagittarius [sædʒɪ'tɛərɪəs] N [U] (*sign*) 人马座 Rénmǎ Zuò

said [sɛd] PT, PP *of* **say**

sail [seil] **I** N [c] 帆 fān [张 zhāng]

II VI [*ship*] 航行 hángxíng; [*passenger*] 乘船航行 chéngchuán hángxíng ▶**to go sailing** 去航行 qù hángxíng

sailing ['seɪlɪŋ] N [U] 帆船运动 fānchuán yùndòng

sailor ['seɪlər] N [c] 水手 shuǐshǒu [位 wèi]

saint [seint] N [c] 圣徒 shèngtú [个 gè]

salad ['sæləd] N [c/U] 色拉 sèlā [份 fèn]

salary ['sæləri] N [c/U] 薪水 xīnshuǐ [份 fèn]

sale [seil] **I** N **1** [s] (*selling*) 出售 chūshòu **2** [c] (*with reductions*) 贱卖 jiànmài [次 cì] **II sales** NPL (*quantity sold*) 销售量 xiāoshòuliàng ▶**to be (up) for sale** 待售 dàishòu ▶**to be on sale** (Brit) 上市 shàngshì; (US: *reduced*) 廉价出售 liánjià chūshòu

salesman ['seɪlzmən] (*pl* **salesmen**) N [c] 推销员 tuīxiāo yuán [位 wèi]

salmon ['sæmən] (*pl* **salmon**) N [c/U] 大马哈鱼 dà mǎhā yú [条 tiáo]

salon ['sælɔn] N [c] 美发廊 měifà láng [家 jiā]

salt [sɔːlt] N [U] 盐 yán

salty ['sɔːltɪ] ADJ [+ *food*] 咸的 xián de

same [seim] **I** ADJ **1** [+ *size, colour, age*] 相同的 xiāngtóng de **2** [+ *place, person, time*] 同一个的 tóngyīgè de **II** PRON ▶**the same 1** (*similar*) 一样 yīyàng **2** (*also:* **the same thing**) 同样 tóngyàng ▶**the**

same as 与…一样 yǔ…yīyàng ▶**the same book/place as** 与…一样的书/地方 yǔ…yīyàng de shū/dìfang ▶**at the same time** 同时 tóngshí

sample ['sɑ:mpl] N [c] 样品 yàngpǐn [件 jiàn] 采样 cǎiyàng [个 gè]

sand [sænd] N [U] 沙子 shāzi

sandal ['sændl] N [c] 凉鞋 liángxié [双 shuāng]

sandwich ['sændwɪtʃ] N [c] 三明治 sānmíngzhì [份 fèn] ▶**a cheese/ham/jam sandwich** 奶酪/火腿/果酱三明治 nǎilào/huǒtuǐ/guǒjiàng sānmíngzhì

sang [sæŋ] PT *of* **sing**

sanitary napkin ['sænɪtərɪ-] (*US*) N [c] 卫生巾 wèishēng jīn [块 kuài]

sanitary towel (*Brit*) N [c] 卫生巾 wèishēng jīn [块 kuài]

sank [sæŋk] PT *of* **sink**

Santa (Claus) ['sæntə('klɔːz)] N 圣诞老人 Shèngdàn Lǎorén

sardine [sɑːˈdiːn] N [c] 沙丁鱼 shādīng yú [条 tiáo]

SARS [sɑːz] N ABBR (= **severe acute respiratory syndrome**) 非典型性肺炎 fēi diǎnxíngxìng fèiyán

SAT N ABBR (*US*) (= **Scholastic Aptitude Test**) 学业能力倾向测试 Xuéyè Nénglì Qīngxiàng Cèshì

sat [sæt] PT, PP *of* **sit**

satellite ['sætəlaɪt] N 1 [c] 人造卫星 rénzào wèixīng [颗 kē] 2 [U] (*also*: **satellite television**) 卫星电视 wèixīng diànshì

satisfactory [sætɪsˈfæktərɪ] ADJ 令人满意的 lìngrén mǎnyì de

satisfied ['sætɪsfaɪd] ADJ 满足的 mǎnzú de ▶**to be satisfied with sth** 对某事满意 duì mǒushì mǎnyì

Saturday ['sætədɪ] N [c/U] 星期六 xīngqīliù [个 gè]; *see also* **Tuesday**

sauce [sɔːs] N [c/U] 酱 jiàng [种 zhǒng]

saucepan ['sɔːspən] N [c] 深平底锅 shēn píngdǐ guō [个 gè]

saucer ['sɔːsə⁽ʳ⁾] N [c] 茶杯碟 chábēi dié [个 gè]

Saudi Arabia [saudɪəˈreɪbɪə] N 沙特阿拉伯 Shātè Ālābó

sausage ['sɔsɪdʒ] N [c/U] 香肠 xiāngcháng [根 gēn]

save [seɪv] I VT 1 [+ *person*] 救 jiù 2 (*also*: **save up**) 积攒 jīzǎn 3 (*economize on*) [+ *money, time*] 节省 jiéshěng 4 (*Comput*) 存储 cúnchǔ II VI (*also*: **save up**) 积攒 jīzǎn ▶**to save sb's life** 挽救某人的生命 wǎnjiù mǒurén de shēngmìng

savings ['seɪvɪŋz] NPL (*money*) 存款 cúnkuǎn

savoury, (*US*) **savory** ['seɪvərɪ] ADJ 咸辣的 xiánlà de

saw [sɔː] (*pt* **sawed**, *pp* **sawed** *or* **sawn**) I PT *of* **see** II VT 锯 jù III N [c] 锯子 jùzi [把 bǎ]

sawn [sɔːn] PP *of* **saw**

saxophone ['sæksəfəun] N [c] 萨克斯管 sàkèsī guǎn [根 gēn]

say [seɪ] (*pt*, *pp* **said**) VT 1 说 shuō 2 [*clock, watch*] 表明 biǎomíng; [*sign*] 写着 xiězhe ▶**to say sth to**

sb 告诉某人某事 gàosù mǒurén mǒushì ▶**to say yes/no** 同意/不同意 tóngyì/bù tóngyì

scale [skeɪl] N [S] (*size, extent*) 规模 guīmó **scales** NPL 秤 chèng ▶**on a large/small scale** 以大/小规模 yǐ dà/xiǎo guīmó

scandal ['skændl] N [C] 丑闻 chǒuwén [条 tiáo]

Scandinavia [skændɪ'neɪvɪə] N 斯堪的纳维亚 Sīkāndìnàwéiyà

scanner ['skænər] N [C] (*Comput*) 扫描仪 sǎomiáo yí [台 tái]

scar [skɑː] N [C] 伤疤 shāngbā [个 gè]

scarce [skɛəs] ADJ 短缺的 duǎnquē de

scarcely ['skɛəslɪ] ADV 几乎不 jīhūbù

scare [skɛər] VT 使害怕 shǐ hàipà

scared ['skɛəd] ADJ ▶**to be scared (of sb/sth)** 害怕（某人/某物）hàipà (mǒurén/mǒuwù)

scarf [skɑːf] (*pl* **scarfs** *or* **scarves**) N [C] (*long*) 围巾 wéijīn [条 tiáo]; (*square*) 头巾 tóujīn [块 kuài]

scarves [skɑːvz] NPL *of* **scarf**

scenery ['siːnərɪ] N [U] 风景 fēngjǐng

schedule ['ʃɛdjuːl], *US* 'skɛdjuːl] N [C] **1** (*agenda*) 日程安排 rìchéng ānpái [个 gè] **2** (*US: of trains, buses*) 时间表 shíjiān biǎo [个 gè] ▶**on schedule** 准时 zhǔnshí ▶**to be ahead of/behind schedule** 提前/落后于计划 tíqián/luòhòu yú jìhuà

scheme [skiːm] N [C] (*plan*) 方案 fāng'àn [个 gè]

scholarship ['skɒləʃɪp] N [C] 奖学金 jiǎngxué jīn [项 xiàng]

school [skuːl] N **1** [C/U] (*place*) 学校 xuéxiào [所 suǒ]; (*pupils and staff*) 全体师生 quántǐ shīshēng **2** [C/U] (*US: university*) 大学 dàxué [所 suǒ] ▶**to go to school** [*child*] 上学 shàngxué ▶**to leave school** [*child*] 结束义务教育 jiéshù yìwù jiàoyù

schoolboy ['skuːlbɔɪ] N [C] 男生 nánshēng [个 gè]

schoolchildren ['skuːltʃɪldrən] NPL 学童 xuétóng

schoolgirl ['skuːlgɜːl] N [C] 女生 nǚshēng [个 gè]

science ['saɪəns] N **1** [U] (*scientific study*) 科学 kēxué **2** [C/U] (*branch of science, school subject*) 学科 xuékē [个 gè]

science fiction N [U] 科幻小说 kēhuàn xiǎoshuō

scientific [saɪən'tɪfɪk] ADJ 科学的 kēxué de

scientist ['saɪəntɪst] N [C] 科学家 kēxué jiā [位 wèi]

scissors ['sɪzəz] NPL 剪刀 jiǎndāo ▶**a pair of scissors** 一把剪刀 yībǎ jiǎndāo

scooter ['skuːtər] N [C] (*also:* **motor scooter**) 小型摩托车 xiǎoxíng mótuō chē [辆 liàng]

score [skɔː] I N [C] 比分 bǐfēn [个 gè] II VT [+ *goal, point*] 得 dé III VI (*in game, sport*) 得分 défēn

Scorpio ['skɔːpɪəʊ] N [U] (*sign*) 天蝎座 Tiānxiē Zuò

Scotch tape® (*US*) N [U] 透明胶带 tòumíng jiāodài

Scotland ['skɔtlənd] N 苏格兰 Sūgélán

Scottish ['skɔtɪʃ] ADJ 苏格兰的 Sūgélán de

scrambled egg ['skræmbld-] N [c/u] 炒鸡蛋 chǎo jīdàn [盘 pán]

scrap [skræp] VT 1 [+ car, ship] 报废 bàofèi 2 [+ project, idea, system, tax] 废弃 fèiqì

scratch [skrætʃ] I N [c] 1 (on car, furniture) 刮痕 guāhén [条 tiáo] 2 (on body) 擦伤 cāshāng [处 chù] II VT 1 (damage) 划破 huápò 2 (because of itch) 搔 sāo

scream [skri:m] VI 尖声喊叫 jiānshēng hǎnjiào

screen [skri:n] N [c] 1 (at cinema) 银幕 yínmù [个 gè] 2 (of television, computer) 屏幕 píngmù [个 gè]

screw [skru:] N [c] 螺丝 luósī [个 gè]

screwdriver ['skru:draɪvəʳ] N [c] 螺丝起子 luósīqǐzi [把 bǎ]

sculpture ['skʌlptʃəʳ] N [U] 雕塑 diāosù

sea [si:] N ▸ **the sea** 海洋 hǎiyáng ▸ **by sea** 由海路 yóu hǎilù

seafood ['si:fu:d] N [U] 海味 hǎiwèi

seagull ['si:gʌl] N [c] 海鸥 hǎi'ōu [只 zhī]

seal [si:l] N [c] 海豹 hǎibào [只 zhī]

search [sə:tʃ] I N [c] 1 (for missing person) 搜寻 sōuxún [次 cì] 2 (Comput) 检索 jiǎnsuǒ [次 cì] II VT 搜查 sōuchá

seashore ['si:ʃɔ:ʳ] N [c] 海岸 hǎi'àn [个 gè]

seasick ['si:sɪk] ADJ 晕船的 yūnchuán de ▸ **to be** or **feel seasick** 感到晕船恶心 gǎndào yūnchuán ěxīn

seaside ['si:saɪd] (Brit) N ▸ **the seaside** 海边 hǎibiān

season ['si:zn] N [c] 季节 jìjié [个 gè]

seat [si:t] N [c] 1 (chair) 椅子 yǐzi [把 bǎ]; (in car, theatre, cinema) 座 zuò [个 gè] 2 (place: in theatre, bus, train) 座位 zuòwèi [个 gè] ▸ **to take a/one's seat** 就座 jiùzuò ▸ **to be seated** (be sitting) 坐下 zuòxia

seat belt N [c] 安全带 ānquán dài [条 tiáo]

second ['sɛkənd] I ADJ 第二的 dì'èr de II ADV 第二名地 dì'èrmíng de III N [c] (unit of time) 秒 miǎo ▸ **second floor** (Brit) 三层 sáncéng; (US) 二层 èrcéng

secondary school N [c/u] 中学 zhōngxué [所 suǒ]

second-hand ['sɛkənd'hænd] ADJ 二手的 èrshǒu de

secondly ['sɛkəndlɪ] ADV 其次 qícì

secret ['si:krɪt] I ADJ 秘密的 mìmì de II N [c] 秘密 mìmì [个 gè]

secretary ['sɛkrətərɪ] N [c] 秘书 mìshū [位 wèi]

section ['sɛkʃən] N [c] 部分 bùfen [个 gè]

security [sɪ'kjuərɪtɪ] N [U] 保安措施 bǎo'ān cuòshī

see [si:] (pt **saw**, pp **seen**) VT 1 看见 kànjiàn 2 (meet) 见 jiàn 3 [+ film, play] 看 kàn 4 (notice)

意识到 yìshí dào ▶to see sb doing/do sth 看见某人做某事 kànjiàn mǒurén zuò mǒushì ▶to go and see sb 去见某人 qùjiàn mǒurén ▶see you later! 一会儿见! yīhuǐr jiàn! ▶I see 我明白 wǒ míngbai

seed [siːd] N [C/U] 籽 zǐ [粒 lì]

seem [siːm] VI 似乎 sìhū ▶it seems that... 看来…

seen [siːn] PP of **see**

seldom ['sɛldəm] ADV 不常 bùcháng

select [sɪ'lɛkt] VT 挑选 tiāoxuǎn

selection [sɪ'lɛkʃən] N [C] 供选择的范围 gōng xuǎnzéde fànwéi [个 gè]

self-confidence [sɛlf'kɔnfɪdns] N [U] 自信心 zìxìn xīn

selfish ['sɛlfɪʃ] ADJ 自私的 zìsī de

self-service [sɛlf'səːvɪs] ADJ 自助的 zìzhù de

sell [sɛl] (pt, pp sold) VT 卖 mài ▶to sell sb sth, sell sth to sb 将某物卖给某人 jiāng mǒuwù màigěi mǒurén

semi-final [sɛmɪ'faɪnl] N [C] 半决赛 bàn juésài [场 chǎng]

send [sɛnd] (pt, pp sent) VT 1 ▶to send sth (to sb) 将某物发送（给某人）jiāng mǒuwù fāsòng (gěi mǒurén) 2 [+ person] 派遣 pàiqiǎn

senior ['siːnɪər] ADJ 高级的 gāojí de

senior citizen N [C] 已届退休年龄的公民 yǐjiè tuìxiū niánlíng de gōngmín [位 wèi]

senior high, (US) **senior high school** N [C] 高中 gāozhōng

[所 suǒ]

sense [sɛns] N 1 [C] (of smell, taste) 感觉官能 gǎnjué guānnéng [种 zhǒng] 2 [U] (good sense) 明智 míngzhì 3 [C] (meaning) 释义 shìyì [个 gè]

sensible ['sɛnsɪbl] ADJ 通情达理的 tōngqíng dálǐ de; [+ decision, suggestion] 明智的 míngzhì de

sensitive ['sɛnsɪtɪv] ADJ 1 善解人意的 shànjiě rényì de 2 [+ skin] 敏感的 mǐngǎn de

sent [sɛnt] PT, PP of **send**

sentence ['sɛntns] N [C] (Ling) 句子 jùzi [个 gè]

separate [adj 'sɛprɪt, vb 'sɛpəreɪt] I ADJ [+ section, piece, pile] 分开的 fēnkāi de; [+ rooms] 单独的 dāndú de II VT (split up) 分开 fēnkāi III VI [parents, couple] 分居 fēnjū ▶to be separated [couple] 分居 fēnjū

September [sɛp'tɛmbər] N [C/U] 九月 jiǔyuè; see also **July**

serial ['sɪərɪəl] N [C] 连续剧 liánxùjù [部 bù]; (in magazine) 连载 liánzài [个 gè]

series ['sɪərɪz] (pl series) N [C] 1 一系列 yīxìliè [个 gè] 2 (on TV, radio) 系列节目 xìliè jiémù [个 gè]

serious ['sɪərɪəs] ADJ 1 严重的 yánzhòng de 2 (sincere) 当真的 dàngzhēn de; (solemn) 严肃的 yánsù de

serve [səːv] VT 1 (in shop, bar) 招待 zhāodài 2 [+ food, drink, meal] 端上 duānshang

service ['səːvɪs] N 1 [C] 服务 fúwù [项 xiàng] 2 [C] (train/bus service) 火车/公共汽车营运 huǒchē/

gōnggòng qìchē yíngyùn [种 zhǒng] **3** [c] (Rel) 仪式 yíshì [个 gè]
▶**service included/not included** 含/不含小费 hán/bùhán xiǎofèi

service charge N [c] 服务费 fúwùfèi [笔 bǐ]

service station N [c] 加油站 jiāyóu zhàn [座 zuò]

set [sɛt] (pt, pp **set**) I N **1** [c] [of cutlery, saucepans, books, keys] 套 tào **2** [c] (TV, Rad) 电视机 diànshìjī [台 tái] II ADJ [+ routine, time, price] 规定的 guīdìng de III VT **1** (put) 放 fàng **2** [+ table] 摆放 bǎifàng **3** [+ time, price, rules] 确定 quèdìng **4** [+ alarm] 设定 shèdìng; [+ heating, volume] 调整 tiáozhěng IV VI [sun] 落山 luòshān ▶**a chess set** 一副国际象棋 yīfù guójì xiàngqí
▶**set off** I VI ▶**to set off (for)** 启 程（前往）qǐchéng (qiánwǎng) II VT [+ alarm] 触发 chùfā
▶**set out** VI 出发 chūfā

settee [sɛ'tiː] N [c] 长沙发椅 cháng shāfāyǐ [个 gè]

settle ['sɛtl] VT [+ bill, account, debt] 支付 zhīfù

seven ['sɛvn] NUM 七 qī; see also **five**

seventeen [sɛvn'tiːn] NUM 十七 shíqī; see also **fifteen**

seventh ['sɛvnθ] NUM 第七 dìqī; see also **fifth**

seventy ['sɛvntɪ] NUM 七十 qīshí; see also **fifty**

several ['sɛvərl] ADJ, PRON 几 个 jǐgè

severe [sɪ'vɪəʳ] ADJ **1** [+ pain, damage, shortage] 严重的 yánzhòng de **2** [+ punishment, criticism] 严厉的 yánlì de

sew [səʊ] (pt sewed, pp sewn) VI, VT 缝 féng

sewing ['səʊɪŋ] N [U] 缝纫 féngrèn

sewn [səʊn] PP of sew

sex [sɛks] N **1** [c] (gender) 性 别 xìngbié [种 zhǒng] **2** [U] (lovemaking) 性交 xìngjiāo ▶**to have sex (with sb)** （和某人）性 交 (hé mǒurén) xìngjiāo

sexism ['sɛksɪzəm] N [U] 性别歧 视 xìngbié qíshì

sexist ['sɛksɪst] ADJ 性别歧视的 xìngbié qíshì de

sexual ['sɛksjuəl] ADJ 性的 xìng de

sexy ['sɛksɪ] ADJ 性感的 xìnggǎn de

shade [ʃeɪd] N **1** [U] 阴凉处 yīnliáng chù **2** [c] 色度 sèdù [种 zhǒng] **3** [c] (US) 遮阳窗帘 zhēyáng chuānglián [副 fù]

shadow ['ʃædəʊ] N [c] 影子 yǐngzi [个 gè]

shake [ʃeɪk] (pt shook, pp shaken ['ʃeɪkn]) I VT [+ bottle, cocktail, medicine] 摇晃 yáohuàng; [+ buildings, ground] 使震动 shǐ zhèndòng II VI [person, part of the body] 发抖 fādǒu; [building, table] 震动 zhèndòng; [ground] 震颤 zhènchàn ▶**to shake one's head** 摇头拒绝 yáotóu jùjué ▶**to shake hands (with sb)** （和某人）握手 (hé mǒurén) wòshǒu

shall [ʃæl] AUX VB **1** (indicating

future in 1st person) ▶**I shall go** 我
要走了 wǒ yào zǒule **2** *(in 1st person questions)* ▶**shall I/we open the door?** 我/我们把门打开好吗?
wǒ/wǒmen bǎ mén dǎkāi hǎoma?

shallow ['ʃæləu] ADJ 浅的 qiǎn de

shame [ʃeɪm] N [U] 耻辱 chǐrǔ
▶**it is a shame that...** …真遗憾
…zhēn yíhàn ▶**what a shame!** 太
遗憾了! tài yíhàn le!

shampoo [ʃæm'pu:] N [c/U] 洗发
液 xǐfàyè [瓶 píng]

shape [ʃeɪp] N [c] 形状
xíngzhuàng [种 zhǒng]

share [ʃɛəʳ] I N [c] **1** *(part)* 一份
yīfèn **2** *(Comm, Fin)* 股票 gǔpiào
[支 zhī] II VT **1** *[+ room, bed, taxi]* 合
用 héyòng **2** *[+ job, cooking, task]*
分担 fēndān
▶**share out** VT 平均分配 píngjūn
fēnpèi

shark [ʃɑ:k] N [c/U] 鲨鱼 shāyú
[条 tiáo]

sharp [ʃɑ:p] I ADJ **1** *[+ knife, teeth]*
锋利的 fēnglì de; *[+ point, edge]* 尖
锐的 jiānruì de; *[+ curve, bend]* 急
转的 jízhuǎn de II ADV *(precisely)*
▶**at 2 o'clock sharp** 两点整 liǎng
diǎn zhěng

shave [ʃeɪv] I VT *[+ head, legs]* 剃毛
发 tìmáofà II VI 刮脸 guāliǎn

shaving cream N [U] 剃须膏
tìxūgāo

she [ʃi:] PRON 她 tā

she'd [ʃi:d] = **she had, she would**

sheep [ʃi:p] *(pl* **sheep**) N [c] 绵羊
miányáng [只 zhī]

sheet [ʃi:t] N [c] **1** 床单 chuángdān
[床 chuáng] **2** *[of paper]* 一张

yīzhāng

shelf [ʃelf] *(pl* **shelves**) N [c]
(bookshelf) 架子 jiàzi [个 gè]; *(in cupboard)* 搁板 gēbǎn [块 kuài]

shell [ʃel] N [c] **1** 贝壳 bèiké [只
zhī] **2** *[of tortoise, snail, crab, egg, nut]* 壳 ké [个 gè]

she'll [ʃi:l] = **she will**

shellfish ['ʃelfɪʃ] *(pl* **shellfish**) I N
[c/U] 贝类海产 bèilèi hǎichǎn [种
zhǒng] II NPL *(as food)* 贝类海鲜
bèilèi hǎixiān

shelter ['ʃeltəʳ] I N [c] *(building)*
遮蔽处 zhēbìchù [个 gè] II VI 躲
避 duǒbì

shelves [ʃelvz] NPL *of* **shelf**

she's [ʃi:z] = **she is, she has**

shift [ʃɪft] VT 移动 yídòng

shin [ʃɪn] N [c] 胫部 jìngbù

shine [ʃaɪn] *(pt, pp* **shone**) VI 照
耀 zhàoyào

ship [ʃɪp] N [c] 船 chuán [艘 sōu]

shirt [ʃə:t] N [c] 衬衫 chènshān
[件 jiàn]

shiver ['ʃɪvəʳ] VI 发抖 fādǒu

shock [ʃɔk] I N **1** [c] 震骇 zhènhài
[种 zhǒng] **2** [U] *(Med)* 休克 xiūkè
3 [c] *(also:* **electric shock**) 触电
chùdiàn [次 cì] II VT 使厌恶 shǐ
yànwù

shocked [ʃɔkt] ADJ 感到不快的
gǎndào bùkuài de

shoe [ʃu:] N [c] 鞋 xié [双 shuāng]
▶**a pair of shoes** 一双鞋 yīshuāng
xié

shone [ʃɔn] PT, PP *of* **shine**

shook [ʃuk] PT *of* **shake**

shoot [ʃu:t] *(pt, pp* **shot**) I VT
(kill) 向…开枪 xiàng...kāiqiāng

II VI **1** (*with gun, bow*) ▶**to shoot (at sb/sth)** （朝某人/某物）射击 (cháo mǒurén/mǒuwù) shèjī **2** (*Football etc*) 射门 shèmén

shop [ʃɒp] **I** N [c] (*esp Brit*) 商店 shāngdiàn [家 jiā] **II** VI 购物 gòuwù ▶**to go shopping** 去买东西 qù mǎi dōngxi

shop assistant (*Brit*) N [c] 店员 diànyuán [位 wèi]

shopping [ʃɒpɪŋ] N [U] **1** (*activity*) 购物 gòuwù **2** (*goods*) 所购之物 suǒgòu zhī wù; *see also* **shop**

shopping centre, (*US*) **shopping center** N [c] 购物中心 gòuwù zhōngxīn [个 gè]

shop window N [c] 商店橱窗 shāngdiàn chúchuāng [个 gè]

shore [ʃɔːʳ] N [c] 岸 àn [个 gè]

short [ʃɔːt] **I** ADJ **1** (*in time*) 短暂的 duǎnzàn de **2** (*in length*) 短的 duǎn de **3** (*not tall*) 矮的 ǎi de **II** **shorts** NPL **1** (*short trousers*) 短裤 duǎnkù **2** (*esp US: underpants*) 男用短衬裤 nányòng duǎnchènkù ▶**a pair of shorts** 一条短裤 yītiáo duǎnkù

shortage [ʃɔːtɪdʒ] N [c/U] 短缺 duǎnquē [种 zhǒng]

shortly [ʃɔːtlɪ] ADV 马上 mǎshàng ▶**shortly after/before sth** 某事后/前不久 mǒushì hòu/qián bùjiǔ

short-sighted [ʃɔːtˈsaɪtɪd] ADJ (*Brit*) 近视的 jìnshì de

shot [ʃɒt] **I** PT, PP *of* **shoot** **II** N **1** [c] 射击 shèjī [次 cì] **2** [c] (*Football*) 射门 shèmén [次 cì] **3** [c] (*injection*) 皮下注射 píxià zhùshè [针 zhēn]

should [ʃʊd] AUX VB **1** (*indicating advisability*) ▶**I should go now** 我现在应该走了 wǒ xiànzài yīnggāi zǒule **2** (*indicating obligation*) 应当 yīngdāng **3** (*indicating likelihood*) ▶**he should be there by now/he should get there soon** 他现在该到那儿了/他该很快就到那儿了 tā xiànzài gāi dào nàrle/tā gāi hěnkuài jiù dào nàrle ▶**you should have been more careful** 你本该更加小心 nǐ běngāi gèngjiā xiǎoxīn ▶**he should have arrived by now** 他现在应该到了 tā xiànzài yīnggāi dàole

shoulder [ʃəʊldəʳ] N [c] 肩膀 jiānbǎng [个 gè]

shout [ʃaʊt] VI (*also*: **shout out**) 喊叫 hǎnjiào

show [ʃəʊ] (*pt* **showed**, *pp* **shown**) **I** N [c] **1** (*exhibition*) 展览 zhǎnlǎn [个 gè] **2** (*TV, Rad*) 节目 jiémù [个 gè] **II** VT **1** 表明 biǎomíng ▶**to show sb sth** *or* **to show sth to sb** 给某人看某物 {或} 把某物给某人看 gěi mǒurén kàn mǒuwù {huò} bǎ mǒuwù gěi mǒurén kàn **2** (*illustrate, depict*) 描述 miáoshù ▶**on show** 在展览中 zài zhǎnlǎn zhōng ▶**to show that...** 表明… biǎomíng… ▶**to show sb how to do sth** 示范某人如何做某事 shìfàn mǒurén rúhé zuò mǒushì ▶**show around** VT 带…参观 dài…cānguān

shower [ʃaʊəʳ] **I** N [c] **1** 阵雨 zhènyǔ [场 chǎng] **2** (*for washing*) 淋浴器 línyùqì [个 gè] **II** VI 洗淋浴 xǐ línyù ▶**to have** *or* **take a shower** 洗淋浴 xǐ línyù

shown [ʃəʊn] PP *of* **show**

shrank [ʃræŋk] PT *of* **shrink**

shrimp [ʃrɪmp] N [c] (*small*) 小虾 xiǎoxiā [只 zhī]; (*US: bigger*) 虾 xiā [只 zhī]

shrink [ʃrɪŋk] (*pt* **shrank**, *pp* **shrunk**) VI 缩水 suōshuǐ

shrunk [ʃrʌŋk] PP *of* **shrink**

shut [ʃʌt] (*pt, pp* **shut**) I VT 关上 guānshang; [+ *shop*] 关门 guānmén; [+ *mouth, eyes*] 闭上 bìshang II VI [*shop*] 打烊 dǎyàng III ADJ [+ *door, drawer*] 关闭的 guānbì de; [+ *shop*] 打烊的 dǎyàng de; [+ *mouth, eyes*] 闭着的 bìzhe de
▶ **shut up** VI (*inf*) 住口 zhùkǒu
▶ **shut up!** (*inf*) 闭嘴! bìzuǐ!

shuttle [ʃʌtl] N [c] (*plane, bus*) 穿梭班机/班车 chuānsuō bānjī/bānchē [架/辆 jià/liàng]

shy [ʃaɪ] ADJ 害羞的 hàixiū de

sick [sɪk] ADJ 1 (*physically*) 患病的 huànbìng de; (*mentally*) 令人讨厌的 lìngrén tǎoyàn de 2 ▶ **to be sick** (*vomit*) 呕吐 ǒutù ▶ **to feel sick** 感觉恶心 gǎnjué ěxīn

sickness [sɪknɪs] N [U] 患病 huànbìng

side [saɪd] I N [c] 1 边 biān [个 gè] 2 侧面 cèmiàn [个 gè]; [*of body*] 体侧 tǐcè [边 biān] 3 [*of paper, face, brain*] 一面 yīmiàn [个 gè]; [*of tape, record*] 面 miàn [个 gè] 4 边缘 biānyuán [个 gè] 5 [*of hill, valley*] 坡 pō [个 gè] 6 (*Brit: team*) 队 duì [支 zhī] 7 (*in conflict, contest*) 一方 yīfāng II ADJ [+ *door, entrance*] 旁边的 pángbiān de ▶ **on the other**

side of sth 在某物的另一边 zài mǒuwù de lìngyībiān

side-effect [saɪdɪfɛkt] N [c] 副作用 fù zuòyòng [个 gè]

sidewalk [saɪdwɔːk] (*US*) N [c] 人行道 rénxíngdào [条 tiáo]

sigh [saɪ] VI 叹气 tànqì

sight [saɪt] I N 1 [U] 视力 shìlì 2 [c] (*spectacle*) 景象 jǐngxiàng [种 zhǒng] II **sights** NPL ▶ **the sights** 景点 jǐngdiǎn

sightseeing [saɪtsiːɪŋ] N [U] 观光 guānguāng ▶ **to go sightseeing** 观光游览 guānguāng yóulǎn

sign [saɪn] I N 1 [c] 指示牌 zhǐshìpái [块 kuài] 2 [c] (*also:* **road sign**) 路标 lùbiāo [个 gè] 3 [c/U] (*indication, evidence*) 迹象 jìxiàng [种 zhǒng] II VT 签署 qiānshǔ ▶ **it's a good/bad sign** 这是个好/坏兆头 zhèshì gè hǎo/huài zhàotou

signal [sɪɡnl] I N [c] 1 (*to do sth*) 信号 xìnhào [个 gè] 2 (*Rail*) 信号机 xìnhàojī [部 bù] 3 (*Elec*) 信号 xìnhào [个 gè] II VI (*with gesture, sound*) ▶ **to signal (to sb)** （向某人）示意 (xiàng mǒurén) shìyì

signature [sɪɡnətʃər] N [c] 签名 qiānmíng [个 gè]

sign language N [c/U] 手语 shǒuyǔ [种 zhǒng]

signpost [saɪnpəʊst] N [c] 路标 lùbiāo [个 gè]

silence [saɪləns] N [c/U] 寂静 jìjìng [片 piàn] ▶ **in silence** 鸦雀无声 yā què wú shēng

silent [saɪlənt] ADJ [+ *person*] 沉

默的 chénmò de

silk [sɪlk] N [C/U] 丝绸 sīchóu [块 kuài]

silly ['sɪlɪ] ADJ 愚蠢的 yúchǔn de; [+ idea, object] 可笑的 kěxiào de

silver ['sɪlvər] I N [U] 银 yín II ADJ [+ spoon, necklace] 银的 yín de

SIM card ['sɪm-] N [C] 手机智能卡 shǒujī zhìnéngkǎ [张 zhāng]

similar ['sɪmɪlər] ADJ 相似的 xiāngsì de ▸ to be similar to sth 和某事物类似 hé mǒu shìwù lèisì

simple ['sɪmpl] ADJ 1 (easy) 简单的 jiǎndān de 2 [+ meal, life, cottage] 简朴的 jiǎnpǔ de

simply ['sɪmplɪ] ADV 1 (merely) 仅仅 jǐnjǐn 2 (absolutely) 完全 wánquán

since [sɪns] I ADV (from then onwards) 此后 cǐhòu II PREP 1 (from) 自⋯以来 zì...yǐlái 2 (after) 从⋯以后 cóng...yǐhòu III CONJ 1 (from when) 自从 zìcóng 2 (after) 从⋯以后 cóng...yǐhòu 3 (as) 因为 yīnwèi ▸ since then or ever since 从那时起 cóng nàshí qǐ ▸ I've been here since the end of June 我自6月底以来一直在这儿。wǒ zì liùyuè dǐ yǐlái yīzhí zài zhèr ▸ since it was Saturday, he stayed in bed an extra hour 因为是星期六，他在床上多呆了丏时。yīnwéi shì xīngqīliù,tā zài chuángshàng duō dāile yī xiǎoshí

sincere [sɪn'sɪər] ADJ 真诚的 zhēnchéng de

sincerely [sɪn'sɪəlɪ] ADV 由衷地 yóuzhōng de ▸ Yours sincerely or (US) Sincerely yours 谨上

jǐnshàng

sing [sɪŋ] (pt sang, pp sung) I VI [person] 唱歌 chànggē; [bird] 鸣叫 míng II VT [+ song] 唱 chàng

Singapore [sɪŋgə'pɔːʳ] N 新加坡 Xīnjiāpō

singer ['sɪŋəʳ] N [C] 歌手 gēshǒu [位 wèi]

singing ['sɪŋɪŋ] N [U] 唱歌 chànggē

single ['sɪŋgl] I ADJ 1 (solitary) 单个的 dāngè de 2 (unmarried) 单身的 dānshēn de II N [C] (Brit) (also: **single ticket**) 单程票 dānchéngpiào [张 zhāng]

singular ['sɪŋgjuləʳ] ADJ 单数的 dānshù de

sink [sɪŋk] (pt sank, pp sunk) I N [C] 洗涤槽 xǐdí cáo [个 gè] II VI [ship] 沉没 chénmò

sir [səʳ] N 先生 xiānsheng ▸ Dear Sir 亲爱的先生 Qīnài de Xiānsheng ▸ Dear Sir or Madam 亲爱的先生或女士 Qīnài de xiānsheng huò nǚshì

siren ['saɪərɪn] N [C] 警报器 jǐngbàoqì [个 gè]

sister ['sɪstəʳ] N [C] 姐妹 jiěmèi [对 duì]; (elder) 姐姐 jiějie [个 gè]; (younger) 妹妹 mèimei [个 gè] ▸ my brothers and sisters 我的兄弟姐妹们 wǒde xiōngdì jiěmèi men

sister-in-law ['sɪstərɪnlɔː] (pl **sisters-in-law**) N [C] (husband's sister) 姑子 gūzi [个 gè]; (wife's sister) 姨子 yízi [个 gè]; (older brother's wife) 嫂子 sǎozi [位 wèi]; (younger brother's wife) 弟媳

dìxí [个 gè]

sit [sɪt] (pt, pp **sat**) VI 1 (also: **sit down**) 坐下 zuòxià 2 (be sitting) 坐 zuò

▶ **sit down** VI 坐下 zuòxià ▶ **to be sitting down** 就座 jiùzuò

site [saɪt] N [c] (also: **website**) 网址 wǎngzhǐ [个 gè]

sitting room (Brit) N [c] 起居室 qǐjūshì [间 jiān]

situated ['sɪtjueɪtɪd] ADJ ▶ **to be situated in/on/near sth** 位于某物中/上/旁 wèiyú mǒuwù zhōng/shàng/páng

situation [sɪtju'eɪʃən] N [c] 情况 qíngkuàng [种 zhǒng]

six [sɪks] NUM 六 liù; see also **five**

sixteen [sɪks'ti:n] NUM 十六 shíliù; see also **fifteen**

sixth [sɪksθ] NUM 1 (in series) 第六 dìliù 2 (fraction) 六分之一 liùfēnzhī yī; see also **fifth**

sixty ['sɪkstɪ] NUM 六十 liùshí; see also **fifty**

size [saɪz] N 1 [c/u] [of object] 大小 dàxiǎo [种 zhǒng]; [of clothing, shoes] 尺码 chǐmǎ [个 gè] 2 [u] [of area, building, task, loss] 大 dà

▶ **what size shoes do you take?** 你穿几号的鞋？nǐ chuān jǐhào de xié?

skate [skeɪt] VI 1 (ice skate) 溜冰 liūbīng 2 (roller skate) 溜旱冰 liūhànbīng

skateboard ['skeɪtbɔːd] N [c] 滑板 huábǎn [个 gè]

skating ['skeɪtɪŋ] N [u] (ice-skating) 冰上运动 bīngshàng yùndòng; see also **skate**

skeleton ['skɛlɪtn] N [c] 骨骼 gǔgé [副 fù]

sketch [skɛtʃ] N [c] (drawing) 素描 sùmiáo [张 zhāng]

ski [ski:] VI 滑雪 huáxuě ▶ **to go skiing** 去滑雪 qù huáxuě

skiing ['ski:ɪŋ] N [u] 滑雪 huáxuě; see also **ski**

skilful, (US) **skillful** ['skɪlful] ADJ 老练的 lǎoliàn de; [+ use, choice, management] 技巧娴熟的 jìqiǎo xiánshú de

skill [skɪl] N 1 [u] (ability) 技巧 jìqiǎo 2 [c] (acquired) 技能 jìnéng [项 xiàng]

skillful ['skɪlful] (US) ADJ = **skilful**

skin [skɪn] N [c/u] 皮肤 pífū; [of animal] 皮 pí [张 zhāng]; (complexion) 肤色 fūsè [种 zhǒng]

skip [skɪp] I VT [+ lunch, lecture] 故意不做 gùyì bùzuò II N [c] (Brit: container) 无盖用以装运工地废料的废料桶

skirt [skəːt] N [c] 裙子 qúnzi [条 tiáo]

skull [skʌl] N [c] 颅骨 lúgǔ [个 gè]

sky [skaɪ] N [c/u] 天空 tiānkōng [片 piàn]

skyscraper ['skaɪskreɪpəʳ] N [c] 摩天大厦 mótiān dàshà [座 zuò]

slap [slæp] I N [c] 掌击 zhǎngjī [次 cì] II VT 掴 guó

sled [slɛd] (US) N [c] 雪橇 xuěqiāo [副 fù]

sledge [slɛdʒ] (Brit) N [c] 雪橇 xuěqiāo [副 fù]

sleep [sli:p] (pt, pp **slept**) I N 1 [u] 睡眠 shuìmián 2 [c] (nap) 睡觉 shuìjiào II VI (be asleep) 睡 shuì;

(*spend the night*) 过夜 guòyè ▶**to go to sleep** 去睡觉 qù shuìjiào
▶ **sleep with** VT FUS 和…有性关系 hé…yǒu xìngguānxì

sleeping bag ['sli:pɪŋ-] N [c] 睡袋 shuìdài [个 gè]

sleeping pill N [c] 安眠药 ānmiányào [片 piàn]

sleet [sli:t] N [U] 雨夹雪 yǔjiāxuě

sleeve [sli:v] N [c] **1** 袖子 xiùzi [个 gè] **2** (*esp Brit: of record*) 唱片套 chàngpiàn tào [个 gè]

slept [slɛpt] PT, PP of **sleep**

slice [slaɪs] N [c] 片 piàn

slide [slaɪd] (*pt, pp* **slid**) I N [c] **1** (*in playground*) 滑梯 huátī [个 gè] **2** (*Brit*) (*also*: **hair slide**) 发夹 fàjiā [个 gè] II VI ▶**to slide down/off/into sth** 滑下/离/进某物 huáxià/lí/jìn mǒuwù

slight [slaɪt] ADJ 微小的 wēixiǎo de

slightly ['slaɪtlɪ] ADV 略微地 lüèwēi de

slim [slɪm] I ADJ 苗条的 miáotiáo de II VI 节食减肥 jiéshí jiǎnféi

slip [slɪp] I VI [*person*] 滑跤 huájiāo; [*object*] 滑落 huáluò II N [c] (*mistake*) 差错 chācuò [个 gè]

slipper ['slɪpəʳ] N [c] 拖鞋 tuōxié [只 zhī]

slippery ['slɪpərɪ] ADJ 滑的 huá de

slot machine N [c] 投币机 tóubìjī [个 gè]; (*for gambling*) 吃角子老虎机 chījiǎozi lǎohǔjī [部 bù]

slow [sləu] I ADJ 慢的 màn de II ADV (*inf*) 缓慢地 huǎnmàn de ▶**my watch is 20 minutes slow**

我的表慢了20分钟 wǒde biǎo mànle èrshí fēnzhōng
▶ **slow down** VI 放松 fàngsōng

slowly ['sləulɪ] ADV 慢慢地 mànmàn de

smack [smæk] VT (*as punishment*) 打 dǎ

small [smɔ:l] ADJ **1** 小的 xiǎo de **2** (*young*) 年幼的 niányòu de **3** [+ *mistake, problem, change*] 微不足道的 wēibùzúdào de

smart [smɑ:t] ADJ **1** (*esp Brit: neat, tidy*) 漂亮的 piàoliang de **2** (*fashionable*) 时髦的 shímáo de **3** (*clever*) 聪明的 cōngmíng de

smash [smæʃ] VT 打碎 dǎsuì

smell [smɛl] (*pt, pp* **smelled** or **smelt**) I N [c] 气味 qìwèi [种 zhǒng] II VT 闻到 wéndào III VI **1** (*have unpleasant odour*) 发臭 fāchòu **2** ▶**to smell nice/ delicious/spicy etc** 闻起来香/好吃/辣{等} wén qǐlái xiāng/hǎochī/ là {děng} ▶**to smell of** 有…气味 yǒu…qìwèi

smelt [smɛlt] PT, PP of **smell**

smile [smaɪl] I N [c] 微笑 wēixiào [个 gè] II VI ▶**to smile (at sb)** (对某人)微笑 (duì mǒurén) wēixiào

smoke [sməuk] I N [U] 烟 yān II VI [*person*] 吸烟 xīyān III VT [+ *cigarette, cigar, pipe*] 抽 chōu

smoker ['sməukəʳ] N [c] 吸烟者 xīyānzhě [个 gè]

smoking ['sməukɪŋ] N [U] 吸烟 xīyān ▶**"no smoking"** "禁止吸烟" "jìnzhǐ xīyān"

smooth [smu:ð] ADJ (*not rough*)

光滑的 guānghuá de

smother ['smʌðər] VT 使窒息 shǐ zhìxī

SMS N ABBR (= **short message service**) 短信息服务 duǎn xìnxī fúwù

smuggle ['smʌgl] VT 走私 zǒusī ▶**to smuggle sth in/out** 走私进口/出口某物 zǒusī jìnkǒu/chūkǒu mǒuwù

snack [snæk] N [C] 小吃 xiǎochī [份 fèn]

snail [sneɪl] N [C] 蜗牛 wōniú [只 zhī]

snake [sneɪk] N [C] 蛇 shé [条 tiáo]

snapshot ['snæpʃɔt] N [C] 快照 kuàizhào [张 zhāng]

sneakers ['sni:kəz] (US) NPL 胶底运动鞋 jiāodǐ yùndòngxié

sneeze [sni:z] VI 打喷嚏 dǎ pēntì

snob [snɔb] (pej) N [C] 势利小人 shìlì xiǎorén [个 gè]

snooker ['snu:kər] N [U] (Sport) 英式台球 yīngshì táiqiú

snore [snɔːr] VI 打鼾 dǎhān

snow [snəʊ] I N [U] 雪 xuě II VI 下雪 xiàxuě ▶**it's snowing** 下雪了 xiàxuě le

snowball ['snəʊbɔːl] N [C] 雪球 xuěqiú [个 gè]

⬤ KEYWORD

so [səʊ] I ADV 1 (thus, likewise) 这样 zhèyàng ▶**they do so because...** 他们这样做是因为… tāmen zhèyàng zuò shì yīnwéi... ▶**if you don't want to go, say so** 如果你

不想去，就说你不想去 rúguǒ nǐ bùxiǎng qù, jiù shuō nǐ bùxiǎng qù ▶**if so** 如果这样 rúguǒ zhèyàng ▶**I hope/think so** 我希望/认为如此 wǒ xīwàng/rènwéi rúcǐ ▶**so far** 迄今为止 qìjìn wéizhǐ ▶**and so on** 等等 děngděng

2 (also) ▶**so do I/so am I** 我也一样 wǒ yě yīyàng

3 如此 rúcǐ ▶**so quickly/big (that)** 如此快/大（以至于）rúcǐ kuài/dà(yǐzhì yú)

4 (very) 非常 fēicháng ▶**so much** 那么多 nàme duō ▶**so many** 那么多 nàme duō

5 (linking events) 于是 yúshì ▶**so I was right after all** 那终究我是对的 nà zhōngjiū wǒ shì duìde

II CONJ 1 (expressing purpose) ▶**so (that)** 为的是 wèi de shì ▶**I brought it so (that) you could see it** 我带过来给你看 wǒ dàiguò lái gěi nǐ kàn

2 (expressing result) 因此 yīncǐ ▶**he didn't come so I left** 他没来，因此我走了 tā méilái, yīncǐ wǒ zǒule

soaking ['səʊkɪŋ] ADJ (also: **soaking wet**) [+ person] 湿透的 shītòu de; [+ clothes] 湿淋淋的 shīlínlín de

soap [səʊp] N [C/U] 1 肥皂 féizào [块 kuài] 2 = **soap opera**

soap opera N [C] 肥皂剧 féizào jù [部 bù]

sober ['səʊbər] ADJ 未醉的 wèizuìde

soccer ['sɔkər] N [U] 足球 zúqiú

social ['səʊʃl] ADJ 社会的 shèhuì

de 2 [+ *event, function*] 社交的 shèjiāo de

socialism ['səuʃəlɪzəm] N [U] 社会主义 shèhuì zhǔyì

socialist ['səuʃəlɪst] I ADJ 社会主义的 shèhuì zhǔyì de II N [c] 社会主义者 shèhuì zhǔyìzhě [位 wèi]

social worker N [c] 社会福利工作者 shèhuì fúlì gōngzuòzhě [位 wèi]

society [sə'saɪətɪ] N [U] 社会 shèhuì

sock [sɔk] N [c] 袜子 wàzi [双 shuāng]

socket ['sɔkɪt] N [c] (Brit) 插座 chāzuò [个 gè]

sofa ['səufə] N [c] 沙发 shāfā [个 gè]

soft [sɔft] ADJ 1 [+ *towel*] 松软的 sōngruǎn de; [+ *skin*] 柔软的 róuruǎn de 2 [+ *bed, paste*] 柔软的 róuruǎn de

soft drink N [c] 软性饮料 ruǎnxìng yǐnliào [瓶 píng]

software ['sɔftwɛəʳ] N [U] 软件 ruǎnjiàn

soil [sɔɪl] N [c/u] 土壤 tǔrǎng [种 zhǒng]

solar power N [U] 太阳能 tàiyáng néng

sold [səuld] PT, PP of **sell**

soldier ['səuldʒəʳ] N [c] 士兵 shìbīng [位 wèi]

sole [səul] N [c] 底 dǐ [个 gè]

solicitor [sə'lɪsɪtəʳ] N [c] (Brit) 律师 lǜshī [位 wèi]

solid ['sɔlɪd] ADJ 1 (not soft) 坚实的 jiānshí de 2 (not liquid) 固体的 gùtǐ de 3 [+ *gold, oak*] 纯质的 chúnzhì de

solution [sə'lu:ʃən] N [c] 解决方案 jiějué fāng'àn [个 gè]

solve [sɔlv] VT 1 [+ *mystery, case*] 破解 pòjiě 2 [+ *problem*] 解决 jiějué

○ KEYWORD

some I ADJ 1 (a little, a few) 一些 yīxiē ▸**some milk/books** 一些牛奶/书 yīxiē niúnǎi/shū 2 (certain, in contrasts) 某些 mǒuxiē ▸**some people say that...** 有些人说… yǒuxiē rén shuō... II PRON (a certain amount, certain number) 一些 yīxiē ▸**I've got some** 我有一些 wǒ yǒu yīxiē ▸**there was/were some left** 还剩下一些 hái shèngxià yīxiē ▸**some of it/them** 它的一部分/他们中的一些 tāde yī bùfen/tāmen zhōng de yīxiē

somebody ['sʌmbədɪ] PRON = **someone**

somehow ['sʌmhau] ADV 不知怎样地 bùzhī zěnyàng de

someone ['sʌmwʌn] PRON 某人 mǒurén ▸**I saw someone in the garden** 我看见花园里有人 wǒ kànjiàn huāyuán lǐ yǒurén ▸**someone else** 别人 biérén

someplace ['sʌmpleɪs] (US) ADV = **somewhere**

something ['sʌmθɪŋ] PRON 某事物 mǒushìwù ▸**something else** 其他事情 qítā shìqing ▸**would you like a sandwich or**

something? 你要来点三明治或其他什么东西吗？ nǐ yào lái diǎn sānmíngzhì huò qítā shénme dōngxi ma?

sometime ['sʌmtaɪm] ADV 某个时候 mǒugè shíhòu

请勿将 **sometimes** 和 **sometime** 混淆。**sometimes** 表示某事物只发生在某些时候，而不是总是发生。Do you visit your sister? – Sometimes... Sometimes I wish I still lived in Australia. **sometimes** 还可以表示某事物发生在特定情况下，而不是在任何情况下都会发生。Sometimes they stay for a week, sometimes just for the weekend. **sometime** 表示未来或过去某个不确定或未指明的时间。Can I come and see you sometime? ...He started his new job sometime last month.

sometimes ['sʌmtaɪmz] ADV 有时 yǒushí

somewhere ['sʌmwɛə'] ADV 在某处 zài mǒuchù ▶ **I need somewhere to live** 我需要找个地方住 wǒ xūyào zhǎogè dìfang zhù ▶ **I must have lost it somewhere** 我一定把它丢在哪儿了 wǒ yīdìng bǎ bā diūzài nǎr le ▶ **let's go somewhere quiet** 我们去个安静的地方吧 wǒmen qù gè ānjìng de dìfang ba ▶ **somewhere else** 别的地方 biéde dìfang

son [sʌn] N [c] 儿子 érzi [个 gè]

song [sɔŋ] N [c] 歌曲 gēqǔ [首 shǒu]

son-in-law ['sʌnɪnlɔː] (pl **sons-in-law**) N [c] 女婿 nǚxu [个 gè]

soon [su:n] ADV 1 (in a short time) 不久 bùjiǔ 2 (a short time later) 很快 hěnkuài 3 (early) 早 zǎo ▶ **soon afterwards** 不久后 bùjiǔ hòu ▶ **as soon as** 一…就… yī...jiù... ▶ **quite soon** 很快 hěnkuài ▶ **see you soon!** 再见！ zàijiàn!

sooner ['su:nə'] ADV ▶ **sooner or later** 迟早 chízǎo ▶ **the sooner the better** 越快越好 yuè kuài yuè hǎo

sophomore ['sɔfəmɔː'] (US) N [c] 二年级学生 èr niánjí xuéshēng [个 gè]

sore [sɔː'] ADJ 痛的 tòng de

sorry ['sɔrɪ] ADJ 懊悔的 àohuǐ de ▶ **(I'm) sorry!** (apology) 对不起！ duìbùqǐ! ▶ **sorry?** (pardon?) 请再讲一遍 qǐng zài jiǎng yībiàn ▶ **to feel sorry for sb** 对某人表示同情 duì mǒurén biǎoshì tóngqíng ▶ **to be sorry about sth** 对某事表示歉意 duì mǒushì biǎoshì qiànyì ▶ **I'm sorry to hear that...** 听到…我很伤心 tīngdào...wǒ hěn shāngxīn

sort [sɔːt] I N 1 [c] ▶ **sort (of)** 种类 zhǒnglèi [个 gè] 2 [c] (make, brand) 品牌 pǐnpái [个 gè] II VT 1 [+ papers, mail, belongings] 把…分类 bǎ...fēnlèi 2 (Comput) 整理 zhěnglǐ ▶ **sort of** (inf) 有点儿 yǒu diǎnr ▶ **all sorts of** 各种不同的 gèzhǒng bùtóng de ▶ **sort out** VT (separate) [+ problem] 解决 jiějué

sound [saund] I N [c] 声音

shēngyīn [种 zhǒng] II VI 1 [*alarm, bell*] 响 xiǎng 2 (*seem*) 听起来 tīng qǐlái ▶to make a sound 出声 chūshēng ▶that sounds like an explosion 听起来像是爆炸声的 tīngqǐlái xiàngshì bàozhàshēng de ▶that sounds like a great idea 这主意听起来妙极了 zhè zhǔyì tīngqǐlái miàojí le ▶it sounds as if... 听起来似乎… tīngqǐlái sìhū…

soup [suːp] N [C/U] 汤 tāng [份 fèn]

sour ['sauə'] ADJ 1 (*bitter-tasting*) 酸的 suān de 2 [+ *milk*] 酸的 suān de

south [sauθ] I N [s/U] 南方 nánfāng II ADJ 南部的 nánbù de III ADV 向南方 xiàng nánfāng ▶to the south 以南 yǐnán ▶south of... 在…以南 zài…yǐnán

South Africa N 南非 Nánfēi

South America N 南美洲 Nán měizhōu

south-east [sauθ'iːst] I N 东南 dōngnán II ADJ 东南的 dōngnán de III ADV 向东南 xiàng dōngnán

southern ['sʌðən] ADJ 南方的 nánfāng de ▶the southern hemisphere 南半球 nán bànqiú

South Korea N 韩国 Hánguó

South Pole N ▶the South Pole 南极 Nánjí

south-west [sauθ'wɛst] I N [s/U] 西南 xīnán II ADJ 西南的 xīnán de III ADV 向西南 xiàng xīnán

souvenir [suːvə'nɪə'] N [C] 纪念品 jìniàn pǐn [件 jiàn]

soy sauce [sɔɪ-] N [U] 酱油 jiàngyóu

space [speɪs] N 1 [C/U] (*gap, place*) 空隙 kòngxì [个 gè] 2 [U] (*beyond Earth*) 太空 tàikōng ▶to clear a space for sth 为某物腾地方 wèi mǒuwù téng dìfang

spade [speɪd] N [C] 锹 qiāo [把 bǎ]

spaghetti [spə'gɛtɪ] N [U] 意大利面 yìdàlì miàn

Spain [speɪn] N 西班牙 Xībānyá

spam [spæm] (*Comput*) N [U] 垃圾邮件 lājī yóujiàn

Spanish ['spænɪʃ] I ADJ 西班牙的 Xībānyá de II N [U] (*language*) 西班牙语 Xībānyáyǔ

spanner ['spænə'] (*Brit*) N [C] 扳钳 bānqián [个 gè]

spare [spɛə'] I ADJ 1 (*free*) 多余的 duōyú de 2 (*extra*) 备用的 bèiyòng de II N [c] = **spare part**

spare part N [C] 备件 bèijiàn [个 gè]

spare time N [U] 业余时间 yèyú shíjiān

spat [spæt] PT, PP of **spit**

speak [spiːk] (*pt* spoke, *pp* spoken) I VT [+ *language*] 讲 jiǎng II VI 讲话 jiǎnghuà ▶to speak to sb about sth 和某人谈某事 hé mǒurén tán mǒushì

special ['spɛʃl] ADJ 1 (*important*) 特别的 tèbié de 2 (*particular*) 专门的 zhuānmén de ▶we only use these plates on special occasions 我们只在特别场合才用这些碟子 wǒmen zhǐzài tèbié chǎnghé cái yòng zhèxiē diézi ▶it's nothing special 没什么特别的 méi shénme tèbié de

speciality [spɛʃɪ'ælɪtɪ], (*US*) **specialty** ['spɛʃəltɪ] N [c] (*food*) 特制品 tèzhìpǐn [种 zhǒng]; (*product*) 特产 tèchǎn [种 zhǒng]

specially ['spɛʃlɪ] ADV 专门地 zhuānmén de

specialty ['spɛʃəltɪ] (*US*) N = **speciality**

species ['spi:ʃi:z] N [c] 种 zhǒng [个 gè]

specific [spə'sɪfɪk] ADJ 1 (*fixed*) 特定的 tèdìng de 2 (*exact*) 具体的 jùtǐ de

spectacles ['spɛktəklz] NPL 眼镜 yǎnjìng

spectacular [spɛk'tækjulər] ADJ [+ *view, scenery*] 壮丽的 zhuànglìde; [+ *rise, growth*] 惊人的 jīngrénde; [+ *success, result*] 引人注目的 yǐnrén zhùmù de

spectator [spɛk'teɪtər] N [c] 观众 guānzhòng [个 gè]

speech [spi:tʃ] N [c] 演说 yǎnshuō [场 chǎng]

speed [spi:d] (*pt, pp* **sped** [spɛd]) N 1 [c/u] (*rate, promptness*) 速度 sùdù [种 zhǒng] 2 [u] (*fast movement*) 快速 kuàisù 3 [c] (*rapidity*) 迅速 xùnsù ▶**at a speed of 70km/h** 以时速70公里 yǐ shísù qīshí gōnglǐ

speed limit (*Law*) N [c] 速度极限 sùdù jíxiàn [个 gè]

spell [spɛl] (*pt, pp* **spelled** *or* **spelt**) VT 用字母拼 yòng zìmǔ pīn ▶**he can't spell** 他不会拼写 tā bùhuì pīnxiě

spelling ['spɛlɪŋ] N [c] (*of word*) 拼法 pīnfǎ [种 zhǒng] ▶**spelling mistake** 拼写错误 pīnxiě cuòwù

spelt [spɛlt] PT, PP *of* **spell**

spend [spɛnd] (*pt, pp* **spent**) VT 1 [+ *money*] 花费 huāfèi 2 [+ *time, life*] 度过 dùguò ▶**to spend time/energy on sth** 在某事上花时间/精力 zài mǒushì shàng huā shíjiān/jīnglì ▶**to spend time/energy doing sth** 花时间/精力做某事 huā shíjiān/jīnglì zuò mǒushì ▶**to spend the night in a hotel** 在旅馆度过一晚 zài lǚguǎn dùguò yīwǎn

spent [spɛnt] PT, PP *of* **spend**

spicy ['spaɪsɪ] ADJ 辛辣的 xīnlà de

spider ['spaɪdər] N [c] 蜘蛛 zhīzhū [只 zhī] ▶**spider's web** 蜘蛛网 zhīzhū wǎng

spill [spɪl] (*pt, pp* **spilt** *or* **spilled**) I VT 使溢出 shǐ yìchū II VI 溢出 yìchū ▶**to spill sth on/over sth** 将某物洒在某物上 jiāng mǒuwù sǎzài mǒuwù shàng

spinach ['spɪnɪtʃ] N [u] 菠菜 bōcài

spine [spaɪn] N [c] 脊柱 jǐzhù [根 gēn]

spit [spɪt] (*pt, pp* **spat**) I N [u] (*saliva*) 唾液 tuòyè II VI 吐唾液 tǔ tuòyè

spite [spaɪt] N [u] 恶意 èyì ▶**in spite of** 尽管 jǐnguǎn

splendid ['splɛndɪd] ADJ (*excellent*) 极好的 jíhǎo de

split [splɪt] (*pt, pp* **split**) VT 1 (*divide*) 把…划分 bǎ…huàfēn 2 [+ *work, profits*] 平分 píngfēn ▶**split up** VI 分手 fēnshǒu

spoil [spɔɪl] (*pt, pp* **spoiled** *or*

spoilt) VT 1 (*damage*) 损害 sǔnhài 2 [+ *child*] 溺爱 nì'ài

spoilt [spɔɪlt] I PT, PP of **spoil** II ADJ 宠坏的 chǒnghuài de

spoke [spəuk] PT of **speak**

spoken ['spəukn] PP of **speak**

spokesman ['spəuksmən] (*pl* **spokesmen**) N [c] 男发言人 nán fāyánrén [位 wèi]

spokeswoman ['spəukswumən] (*pl* **spokeswomen**) N [c] 女发言人 nǚ fāyánrén [位 wèi]

sponge [spʌndʒ] N [U] 海绵 hǎimián

spoon [spu:n] N [c] 匙 chí [把 bǎ]

sport [spɔ:t] N 1 [c] (*particular game*) 运动 yùndòng [项 xiàng] 2 [U] (*generally*) 体育 tǐyù

sportswear ['spɔ:tswɛər] N [U] 运动服 yùndòngfú

spot [spɔt] N [c] 1 (*mark*) 斑点 bāndiǎn [个 gè] 2 (*dot*) 点 diǎn [个 gè] 3 (*pimple*) 疵点 cídiǎn [个 gè] ▶ **on the spot** (*in that place*) 在现场 zài xiànchǎng; (*immediately*) 当场 dāngchǎng

sprain [spreɪn] VT ▶ **to sprain one's ankle/wrist** 扭伤脚踝/手腕 niǔshāng jiǎohuái/shǒuwàn

spray [spreɪ] VT 1 [+ *liquid*] 喷 pēn 2 [+ *crops*] 向…喷杀虫剂 xiàng…pēn shāchóng jì

spread [sprɛd] (*pt, pp* **spread**) VT 1 ▶ **to spread sth on/over** 把某物摊在…上 bǎ mǒuwù tānzài…shang 2 [+ *disease*] 传播 chuánbō

spreadsheet ['sprɛdʃi:t] N [c] 电子表格 diànzǐ biǎogé [份 fèn]

spring [sprɪŋ] N 1 [c/U] (*season*) 春季 chūnjì [个 gè] 2 [c] (*wire coil*) 弹簧 tánhuáng [个 gè] ▶ **in (the) spring** 在春季 zài chūnjì

spy [spaɪ] N [c] 间谍 jiàndié [个 gè]

spying ['spaɪɪŋ] N [U] 当间谍 dāng jiàndié

square [skwɛər] I N [c] 1 正方形 zhèngfāng xíng [个 gè] 2 (*in town*) 广场 guǎngchǎng [个 gè] 3 (*Math*) 平方 píngfāng [个 gè] II ADJ 正方形的 zhèngfāng xíng de ▶ **2 square metres** 2平方米 èr píngfāngmǐ

squash [skwɔʃ] I N [U] (*Sport*) 壁球 bìqiú II VT 把…压碎 bǎ…yāsuì

squeeze [skwi:z] VT 用力捏 yònglì niē

stab [stæb] VT 刺 cì

stable ['steɪbl] I ADJ 稳定的 wěndìng de II N [c] 马厩 mǎjiù [个 gè]

stadium ['steɪdɪəm] (*pl* **stadia** ['steɪdɪə] *or* **stadiums**) N [c] 体育场 tǐyùchǎng [个 gè]

staff [stɑ:f] N [c] 职员 zhíyuán [名 míng]

stage [steɪdʒ] N [c] 1 (*in theatre*) 舞台 wǔtái [个 gè] 2 (*platform*) 平台 píngtái [个 gè] ▶ **in the early/final stages** 在早/晚期 zài zǎo/wǎnqī

stain [steɪn] I N [c] 污迹 wūjì [处 chù] II VT 沾污 zhānwū

stainless steel ['steɪnlɪs-] N [U] 不锈钢 bùxiù gāng

stair [stɛər] I N [c] (*step*) 梯级 tījí [层 céng] II **stairs** NPL (*flight of steps*) 楼梯 lóutī

stall [stɔːl] N [c] 货摊 huòtān [个 gè]

stamp [stæmp] I N [c] **1** 邮票 yóupiào [枚 méi] **2** (in passport) 章 zhāng [个 gè] II VT [+ passport, visa] 盖章于 gàizhāng yú

stand [stænd] (pt, pp **stood**) I VI **1** (be upright) 站立 zhànlì **2** (rise) 站起来 zhàn qǐlái **3** ▶ **to stand aside/back** 让开/退后 ràngkāi/ tuìhòu II VT ▶ **I can't stand him/it** 我无法容忍他/它 wǒ wúfǎ róngrěn tā/tā

▶ **stand for** VT FUS [abbreviation] 代表 dàibiǎo

▶ **stand out** VI 醒目 xǐngmù

▶ **stand up** VI (rise) 起立 qǐlì

standard [ˈstændəd] I N [c] **1** (level) 水平 shuǐpíng [种 zhǒng] **2** (norm, criterion) 标准 biāozhǔn [个 gè] II ADJ **1** [+ size] 普通的 pǔtōng de **2** [+ procedure, practice] 标准的 biāozhǔn de **3** [+ model, feature] 规范的 guīfàn de

stank [stæŋk] PT of **stink**

star [stɑːʳ] N [c] **1** 星 xīng [颗 kē] **2** (celebrity) 明星 míngxīng [个 gè] ▶ **a 4-star hotel** 4星级旅馆 sì xīngjí lǚguǎn

stare [steəʳ] VI ▶ **to stare (at sb/ sth)** 盯着 (某人/某物) dīngzhe (mǒurén/mǒuwù)

start [stɑːt] I N [c] 开始 kāishǐ [个 gè] II VT **1** (begin) 开始 kāishǐ **2** [+ business] 创建 chuàngjiàn **3** [+ engine, car] 启动 qǐdòng III VI (begin) 开始 kāishǐ ▶ **to start doing** or **to do sth** 开始做某事 kāishǐ zuò mǒushì

▶ **start on** VT FUS 开始 kāishǐ

▶ **start over** (US) VI, VT 重新开始 chóngxīn kāishǐ

▶ **start up** VT 创办 chuàngbàn

starter [ˈstɑːtəʳ] N [c] (Brit) 开胃菜 kāiwèi cài [道 dào]

starve [stɑːv] VI **1** (be very hungry) 挨饿 áiè **2** (die from hunger) 饿死 èsǐ ▶ **I'm starving** 我饿极了 wǒ è jí le

state [steɪt] I N [c] **1** (condition) 状态 zhuàngtài [种 zhǒng] **2** [c] (country) 国家 guójiā [个 gè] **3** [c] (part of country) 州 zhōu [个 gè] II **the States** NPL (inf) 美国 Měiguó ▶ **state of affairs** 事态 shìtài

statement [ˈsteɪtmənt] N [c] 声明 shēngmíng [个 gè]

station [ˈsteɪʃən] N [c] **1** (railway station) 车站 chēzhàn [个 gè] **2** (on radio) 电台 diàntái [个 gè]

statue [ˈstætjuː] N [c] 塑像 sùxiàng [尊 zūn]

stay [steɪ] I N [c] 逗留 dòuliú [次 cì] II VI **1** (in place, position) 呆 dāi **2** (in town, hotel, someone's house) 逗留 dòuliú **3** (in state, situation) 保持 bǎochí III VT ▶ **to stay the night** 过夜 guòyè ▶ **to stay with sb** 在某人家暂住 zài mǒurén jiā zànzhù

▶ **stay in** VI 呆在家里 dāizài jiālǐ

▶ **stay up** VI 不去睡 bùqùshuì

steady [ˈstedɪ] ADJ **1** [+ progress, increase, fall] 稳定的 wěndìng de **2** [+ job, income] 固定的 gùdìng de

steak [steɪk] N [c/u] 牛排 niúpái [份 fèn]

steal [sti:l] (pt **stole**, pp **stolen**) I VT 偷窃 tōuqiè II VI 行窃 xíngqiè ▶he stole it from me 他 从我这里把它偷走了 tā cóng wǒ zhèlǐ bǎ tā tōuzǒu le

steam [sti:m] I N [U] 蒸汽 zhēngqì II VT 蒸 zhēng

steel [sti:l] I N [U] 钢铁 gāngtiě II CPD 钢制 gāngzhì

steep [sti:p] ADJ 陡的 dǒu de

steering wheel N [C] 方向盘 fāngxiàng pán [个 gè]

step [stɛp] I N 1 [C] (stage) 阶段 jiēduàn 2 [C] (of stairs) 梯 级 tījí [层 céng] II VI ▶to step forward/backward etc 向前/后 {等}迈步 xiàngqián/hòu {děng} màibù
▶ step aside = step down
▶ step down, step aside VI 辞 职 cízhí

stepbrother ['stɛpbrʌðə'] N [c] (with shared father) 异母兄弟 yìmǔ xiōngdì [个 gè]; (with shared mother) 异父兄弟 yìfù xiōngdì [个 gè]

stepdaughter ['stɛpdɔ:tə'] N [c] 继女 jìnǚ [个 gè]

stepfather ['stɛpfɑ:ðə'] N [c] 继 父 jìfù [位 wèi]

stepmother ['stɛpmʌðə'] N [c] 继母 jìmǔ [位 wèi]

stepsister ['stɛpsɪstə'] N [c] (with shared father) 异母姐妹 yìmǔ jiěmèi [个 gè]; (with shared mother) 异父姐妹 yìfù jiěmèi [个 gè]

stepson ['stɛpsʌn] N [c] 继子 jìzǐ [个 gè]

stereo ['stɛrɪəu] N [c] 立体声装置

lìtǐ shēng zhuāngzhì [套 tào]

sterling ['stə:lɪŋ] N [U] 英国货 币 Yīngguó huòbì ▶one pound sterling 一英镑 yī yīngbàng

stew [stju:] N [c/u] 炖的食物 dùn de shíwù [种 zhǒng]

stewardess ['stjuədɛs] N [c] 女 乘务员 nǚ chéngwù yuán [位 wèi]

stick [stɪk] (pt, pp **stuck**) I N [c] 1 (of wood) 枯枝 kūzhī [根 gēn] 2 (walking stick) 拐杖 guǎizhàng [根 gēn] II VT ▶to stick sth on or to sth (with glue etc) 将某物粘贴 在某物上 jiāng mǒuwù zhāntiē zài mǒuwù shang
▶ stick out VI 伸出 shēnchū

sticker ['stɪkə'] N [c] 不干胶标签 bù gānjiāo biāoqiān [个 gè]

sticky ['stɪkɪ] ADJ 1 [+ substance] 黏的 nián de 2 [+ tape, paper] 黏性 的 niánxìng de

stiff [stɪf] I ADJ 1 [+ person] 酸痛的 suāntòng de; [+ neck, arm etc] 僵 硬的 jiāngyìng de 2 [+ competition] 激烈的 jīliè de II ADV ▶to be bored/scared stiff 讨厌/害怕极 了 tǎoyàn/hàipà jíle

still [stɪl] I ADJ 1 [+ person, hands] 不动的 bùdòng de 2 (Brit: not fizzy) 无气泡的 wú qìpào de II ADV 1 (up to the present) 仍然 réngrán 2 (even) 更 gèng 3 (yet) 还 hái 4 (nonetheless) 尽管如此 jǐnguǎn rúcǐ ▶to stand/keep still 站着别 动/别动 zhànzhe biédòng/biédòng
▶he still hasn't arrived 他还没到 tā hái méi dào

sting [stɪŋ] (pt, pp **stung**) I N [c] 刺 cì [根 gēn] II VT 刺 cì

stink [stɪŋk] (*pt* **stank**, *pp* **stunk**)
I N [c] 恶臭 èchòu [种 zhǒng] II VI
发臭 fāchòu

stir [stəːʳ] VT 搅动 jiǎodòng

stitch [stɪtʃ] N [c] (*Med*) 缝针
féngzhēn [枚 méi]

stock [stɔk] N [c] 供应物
gōngyìng wù [种 zhǒng]
▶ **stock up** VI ▶ **to stock up** (**on**
or **with sth**) 储备（某物）chǔbèi
(mǒuwù)

stock exchange N [c] 股票交易
所 gǔpiào jiāoyì suǒ [个 gè]

stocking [stɔkɪŋ] N [c] 长统袜
chángtǒng wà [双 shuāng]

stole [stəul] PT *of* **steal**

stolen [stəuln] PP *of* **steal**

stomach [stʌmək] N [c] 1 (*organ*)
胃 wèi [个 gè] 2 (*abdomen*) 腹部
fùbù [个 gè]

stomach ache N [c/u] 胃痛
wèitòng [阵 zhèn]

stone [stəun] N 1 [u] 石头 shítou
2 [c] (*pebble*) 石子 shízǐ [块 kuài]

stood [stud] PT, PP *of* **stand**

stop [stɔp] I VT 1 停止 tíngzhǐ
2 (*prevent*) 阻止 zǔzhǐ II VI
1 [*person, vehicle*] 停下来 tíng
xiàlái 2 [*rain, noise, activity*] 停
tíng III N [c] (*for bus, train*) 车
站 chēzhàn [个 gè] ▶ **to stop**
doing sth 停止做某事 tíngzhǐ
zuò mǒushì ▶ **to stop sb (from)**
doing sth 阻止某人做某事 zǔzhǐ
mǒurén zuò mǒushì ▶ **stop it!** 住
手！zhùshǒu!

stoplight [stɔplaɪt] (*US*) N [c] (*in*
road) 交通信号灯 jiāotōng xìnhào
dēng [个 gè]

store [stɔːʳ] I N [c] 1 (*Brit: large*
shop) 大商店 dà shāngdiàn [家
jiā] 2 (*US: shop*) 店铺 diànpù [家
jiā] II VT 1 [+ *provisions, information*]
存放 cúnfàng 2 [*computer, brain*]
[+ *information*] 存储 cúnchǔ

storey, (*US*) **story** [stɔːrɪ] N [c]
层 céng

storm [stɔːm] N [c] 暴风雨
bàofēngyǔ [场 chǎng]

stormy [stɔːmɪ] ADJ 有暴风雨的
yǒu bàofēngyǔ de

story [stɔːrɪ] N [c] 1 (*account*) 描
述 miáoshù [种 zhǒng] 2 (*tale*) 故
事 gùshì [个 gè] 3 (*in newspaper, on*
news broadcast) 报道 bàodào [条
tiáo] 4 (*US: of building*) = **storey**

stove [stəuv] N [c] 炉子 lúzi
[个 gè]

straight [streɪt] I ADJ 1 笔直
的 bǐzhí de 2 [+ *hair*] 直的 zhí de
II ADV 1 (*walk, stand, look*) 直 zhí
2 (*immediately*) 直接地 zhíjiē de

straightforward [streɪtfɔːwəd]
ADJ 简单的 jiǎndān de

strain [streɪn] I N 1 [c/u] (*pressure*)
负担 fùdān [个 gè] 2 [c/u] ▶ **back/**
muscle strain 背部/肌肉扭伤
bèibù/jīròu niǔshāng [处 chù] II VT
[+ *back, muscle*] 扭伤 niǔshāng

strange [streɪndʒ] ADJ 1 (*odd*)
奇怪的 qíguài de 2 (*unfamiliar*)
[+ *person, place*] 陌生的 mòshēng
de

stranger [streɪndʒəʳ] N [c] 陌生
人 mòshēng rén [个 gè]

strap [stræp] N [c] [*of watch, bag*]
带 dài [根 gēn]

straw [strɔː] N 1 [u] 稻草 dàocǎo

2 [c] (*drinking straw*) 吸管 xīguǎn [根 gēn]

strawberry ['strɔːbərɪ] N [c] 草莓 cǎoméi [个 gè]

stream [striːm] N [c] 溪流 xīliú [条 tiáo]

street [striːt] N [c] 街道 jiēdào [条 tiáo]

streetcar ['striːtkɑːʳ] (*US*) N [c] 有轨电车 yǒuguǐ diànchē [部 bù]

strength [strεŋθ] N **1** [u] 力气 lìqì **2** [u] (*of object, material*) 强度 qiángdù

stress [strεs] I N [c/u] 压力 yālì [个 gè] II VT [+ *point, importance*] 强调 qiángdiào

stressful ['strεsful] ADJ 紧张的 jǐnzhāng de

stretch [strεtʃ] I VI 伸懒腰 shēn lǎnyāo II VT [+ *arm, leg*] 伸直 shēnzhí
▸ **stretch out** VT [+ *arm, leg*] 伸出 shēnchū

strict [strɪkt] ADJ **1** [+ *rule, instruction*] 严格的 yángé de **2** [+ *person*] 严厉的 yánlì de

strike [straɪk] (*pt, pp* **struck**) I N [c] 罢工 bàgōng [场 chǎng] II VI **1** 罢工 bàgōng **2** [*clock*] 报时 bàoshí ▸ **to be on strike** 在罢工 zài bàgōng

striker ['straɪkəʳ] N [c] **1** (*person on strike*) 罢工者 bàgōng zhě [名 míng] **2** (*Football*) 前锋 qiánfēng [个 gè]

string [strɪŋ] (*pt, pp* **strung**) N **1** [c/u] 细绳 xìshéng [根 gēn] **2** [c] (*on guitar, violin*) 弦 xián [根 gēn]

strip [strɪp] I N [c] (*of paper, cloth*)

狭条 xiátiáo [条 tiáo] II VI (*undress*) 脱光衣服 tuōguāng yīfu; (*as entertainer*) 表演脱衣舞 biǎoyǎn tuōyī wǔ

stripe [straɪp] N [c] 条纹 tiáowén [个 gè]

striped [straɪpt] ADJ 有条纹的 yǒu tiáowén de

stroke [strəuk] I N [c] (*Med*) 中风 zhòngfēng [次 cì] II VT [+ *person, animal*] 抚摸 fǔmō

stroller ['strəuləʳ] (*US*) N [c] 婴儿小推车 yīng'ér xiǎo tuīchē [辆 liàng]

strong [strɔŋ] ADJ **1** [+ *person, arms, grip*] 有力的 yǒulì de **2** [+ *object, material*] 牢固的 láogù de **3** [+ *wind, current*] 强劲的 qiángjìng de

struck [strʌk] PT, PP *of* **strike**

struggle ['strʌgl] VI **1** (*try hard*) 尽力 jìnlì **2** (*fight*) 搏斗 bódòu

stubborn ['stʌbən] ADJ 偏强的 juéjiàng de

stuck [stʌk] I PT, PP *of* **stick** II ADJ ▸ **to be stuck** [*object*] 卡住 qiǎzhù; [*person*] 陷于 xiànyú

student ['stjuːdənt] N [c] **1** (*at university*) 大学生 dà xuéshēng [名 míng] **2** (*at school*) 中学生 zhōng xuéshēng [名 míng] ▸ **a law/medical student** 一名法律/医学学生 yīmíng fǎlù/yīxué xuéshēng

studio ['stjuːdɪəu] N [c] **1** (*TV, Rad, Mus*) 摄影室 shèyǐng shì [个 gè] **2** [*of artist*] 画室 huàshì [个 gè]

study ['stʌdɪ] I N [c] (*room*) 书房 shūfáng [间 jiān] II VT [+ *subject*]

攻读 gōngdú III VI 学习 xuéxí

stuff [stʌf] I N [U] 1(*things*) 物品 wùpǐn 2(*substance*) 东西 dōngxi II VT [+ *peppers, mushrooms*] 给…装馅 gěi…zhuāngxiàn; [+ *chicken, turkey*] 把填料塞入 bǎ tiánliào sāirù

stuffy ['stʌfɪ] ADJ 闷热的 mēnrè de

stung [stʌŋ] PT, PP *of* **sting**

stunk [stʌŋk] PP *of* **stink**

stunning ['stʌnɪŋ] ADJ 1(*impressive*) 惊人的 jīngrén de 2(*beautiful*) 极漂亮的 jí piàoliàng de

stupid ['stjuːpɪd] ADJ 1 笨的 bèn de 2 [+ *question, idea, mistake*] 愚蠢的 yúchǔn de

style [staɪl] N 1[c] (*type*) 方式 fāngshì [种 zhǒng] 2[U] (*elegance*) 风度 fēngdù 3[c/U] (*design*) 样式 yàngshì [种 zhǒng]

subject ['sʌbdʒɪkt] N [c] 1(*matter*) 主题 zhǔtí [个 gè] 2(*Scol*) 科目 kēmù [个 gè] 3(*Gram*) 主语 zhǔyǔ [个 gè]

submarine [sʌbmə'riːn] N [c] 潜水艇 qiánshuǐtǐng [艘 sōu]

substance ['sʌbstəns] N [c] 物质 wùzhì [种 zhǒng]

substitute ['sʌbstɪtjuːt] I N [c] 1(*person*) 代替者 dàitì zhě [位 wèi] 2(*thing*) 代用品 dàiyòngpǐn [件 jiàn] II VT ▶ **to substitute sth (for sth)** 用某物代替（某物）yòng mǒuwù dàitì (mǒuwù)

subtitles ['sʌbtaɪtlz] NPL 字幕 zìmù

subtract [səb'trækt] VT ▶ **to**

subtract sth (from sth) （从某数中）减去某数 (cóng mǒushù zhōng) jiǎnqù mǒushù

suburb ['sʌbəːb] N [c] 郊区 jiāoqū [个 gè]

subway ['sʌbweɪ] N [c] (*US: underground railway*) 地铁 dìtiě [条 tiáo]

succeed [sək'siːd] VI 成功 chénggōng ▶ **to succeed in doing sth** 成功地做某事 chénggōng de zuò mǒushì

success [sək'sɛs] N [U/c] 成功 chénggōng ▶ **without success** 一无所成 yī wú suǒ chéng

successful [sək'sɛsful] ADJ 成功的 chénggōng de

successfully [sək'sɛsfəlɪ] ADV 成功地 chénggōng de

such [sʌtʃ] ADJ 1(*of this kind*) 此类的 cǐlèi de 2(*so much*) 这等 zhèděng ▶ **such a lot of** 那么多 nàme duō ▶ **such as** (*like*) 像 xiàng

suck [sʌk] VT 含在嘴里舔吃 hánzài zuǐlǐ tiǎnchī

sudden ['sʌdn] ADJ 意外的 yìwài de

suddenly ['sʌdnlɪ] ADV 突然 tūrán

suede [sweɪd] N [U] 仿麂皮 fǎng jǐpí

suffer ['sʌfəʳ] VI 1(*due to pain, illness, poverty*) 受损失 shòu sǔnshī 2(*be badly affected*) 受苦难 shòu kǔnàn

sugar ['ʃugəʳ] N [U/c] 糖 táng [勺 sháo]

suggest [sə'dʒɛst] VT 建议 jiànyì

▶**to suggest that...** (*propose*) 建议… jiànyì…

suggestion [sə'dʒɛstʃən] N [c] 建议 jiànyì [条 tiáo] ▶**to make a suggestion** 提建议 tí jiànyì

suicide ['suːsaɪd] N [c/u] 自杀 zìshā ▶**a suicide bomber** 人肉炸弹 rénròu zhàdàn ▶**to commit suicide** 自杀 zìshā

suit [suːt] I N [c] 西装 xīzhuāng [套 tào] II VT 1 (*be convenient, appropriate*) 对…合适 duì…héshì 2 [*colour, clothes*] 适合 shìhé

suitable ['suːtəbl] ADJ 1 [+ *time, place*] 合适的 héshì de 2 [+ *person, clothes*] 适合的 shìhé de

suitcase ['suːtkeɪs] N [c] 手提箱 shǒutíxiāng [个 gè]

sum [sʌm] N [c] 1 (*amount*) 数额 shù'é [笔 bǐ] 2 (*calculation*) 算术题 suànshù tí [道 dào] ▶**to do a sum** 算算术 suàn suànshù
▶**sum up** VI 总结 zǒngjié

summarize ['sʌməraɪz] VT 概括 gàikuò

summary ['sʌmərɪ] N [c] 摘要 zhāiyào [个 gè]

summer ['sʌmə'] N [c/u] 夏季 xiàjì [个 gè] ▶**in (the) summer** 在夏季 zài xiàjì

summit ['sʌmɪt] N [c] 峰顶 fēngdǐng [个 gè]

sun [sʌn] N 1 [s/c] (*in the sky*) 太阳 tàiyáng [轮 lún] 2 [u] (*heat*) 太阳的光和热 tàiyáng de guāng hé rè; (*light*) 阳光 yángguāng

sunbathe ['sʌnbeɪð] VI 晒日光浴 shài rìguāngyù

sunburn ['sʌnbəːn] N [u] 晒斑 shàibān

sunburnt ['sʌnbəːnt] ADJ = **sunburned**

sunburned ['sʌnbəːnd], **sunburnt** ADJ 晒伤的 shàishāng de

Sunday ['sʌndɪ] N [c/u] 星期天 xīngqītiān [个 gè]; *see also* **Tuesday**

sung [sʌŋ] PP *of* **sing**

sunglasses ['sʌnglɑːsɪz] NPL 墨镜 mòjìng

sunk [sʌŋk] PP *of* **sink**

sunny ['sʌnɪ] ADJ 晴朗的 qínglǎng de ▶**it is sunny** 天气晴朗 tiānqì qínglǎng

sunrise ['sʌnraɪz] N [u] 拂晓 fúxiǎo

sunscreen ['sʌnskriːn] N [c/u] 遮光屏 zhēguāng píng [个 gè]

sunset ['sʌnsɛt] N 1 [u] (*time*) 傍晚 bàngwǎn 2 [c] (*sky*) 日落 rìluò [次 cì]

sunshine ['sʌnʃaɪn] N [u] 阳光 yángguāng

suntan ['sʌntæn] I N [c] 晒黑 shàihēi [处 chù] II CPD [+ *lotion, cream*] 防晒 fángshài

super ['suːpə'] (*Brit: inf*) ADJ 极好的 jíhǎo de

supermarket ['suːpəmɑːkɪt] N [u] 超级市场 chāojí shìchǎng

supervise ['suːpəvaɪz] VT 监督 jiāndū

supper ['sʌpə'] N [c/u] 1 (*early evening*) 晚餐 wǎncān [顿 dùn] 2 (*late evening*) 夜宵 yèxiāo [顿 dùn]

supply [sə'plaɪ] I VT 提供 tígōng

II N [C/U] 供应量 gōngyìng liàng ▸**to supply sb/sth with sth** 为某人/某物提供某物 wèi mǒurén/mǒuwù tígōng mǒuwù

support [sə'pɔːt] VT 1 (*morally*) 支持 zhīchí 2 (*financially*) 供养 gōngyǎng 3 [+ *football team*] 支持 zhīchí

supporter [sə'pɔːtə'] N [C] 支持者 zhīchí zhě [个 gè]

suppose [sə'pəuz] VT 认为 rènwéi ▸**I suppose** 我想 wǒ xiǎng ▸**I suppose so/not** 我看是/不是这样 wǒ kàn shì/bùshì zhèyàng ▸**he's supposed to be an expert** 人们以为他是个专家 rénmen yǐwéi tā shì gè zhuānjiā

supposing [sə'pəuzɪŋ] CONJ 假使 jiǎshǐ

sure [ʃuə'] ADJ 1 有把握的 yǒu bǎwò de 2 ▸**to be sure to do sth** (*certain*) 肯定做某事 kěndìng zuò mǒushì ▸**to make sure that...** (*take action*) 保证… bǎozhèng…; (*check*) 查明… chámíng… ▸**sure!** (*inf: of course*) 当然了！dāngrán le! ▸**I'm sure of it** 我确信 wǒ quèxìn ▸**I'm not sure how/why/when** 我不能肯定如何/为什么/什么时候 wǒ bùnéng kěndìng rúhé/wèishénme/shénme shíhou

surf [sə:f] I N [U] 拍岸的浪花 pāi'àn de lànghuā II VT ▸**to surf the Internet** 网上冲浪 wǎngshang chōnglàng ▸**to go surfing** 去冲浪 qù chōnglàng

surface ['sə:fɪs] N 1 [C] (*of object*) 表面 biǎomiàn [个 gè] 2 [C] (*top layer*) 表层 biǎocéng [个 gè]

▸**on the surface** 在表面上 zài biǎomiàn shàng

surfboard ['sə:fbɔːd] N [C] 冲浪板 chōnglàng bǎn [块 kuài]

surgeon ['sə:dʒən] N [C] 外科医师 wàikē yīshī [位 wèi]

surgery ['sə:dʒərɪ] N 1 [U] (*treatment*) 外科手术 wàikē shǒushù 2 [C] (*Brit: room*) 诊所 zhěnsuǒ [家 jiā]

surname ['sə:neɪm] N [C] 姓 xìng [个 gè]

surprise [sə'praɪz] I N 1 [C] (*unexpected event*) 意想不到的事物 yìxiǎng bùdào de shìwù [个 gè] 2 [U] (*astonishment*) 诧异 chàyì II VT 使感到意外 shǐ gǎndào yìwài ▸**to my (great) surprise** 使我（很）惊奇的是 shǐ wǒ (hěn) jīngqí de shì

surprised [sə'praɪzd] ADJ 惊讶的 jīngyà de

surprising [sə'praɪzɪŋ] ADJ 出人意外的 chūrén yìwài de

surrender [sə'rɛndə'] VI 投降 tóuxiáng

surround [sə'raund] VT 包围 bāowéi

surroundings [sə'raundɪŋz] NPL 环境 huánjìng

survey ['sə:veɪ] N [C] 民意测验 mínyì cèyàn [项 xiàng]

survive [sə'vaɪv] VI 幸存 xìngcún

survivor [sə'vaɪvə'] N [C] 幸存者 xìngcúnzhě [个 gè]

suspect [n 'sʌspɛkt, vb səs'pɛkt] I N [C] 嫌疑犯 xiányí fàn [个 gè] II VT 1 [+ *person*] 怀疑 huáiyí 2 [+ *sb's motives*] 质疑 zhìyí

3 (think) 猜想 cāixiǎng ▶to suspect that... 怀疑… huáiyí…

suspense [səs'pɛns] N [U] 焦虑 jiāolǜ

suspicious [səs'pɪʃəs] ADJ [+ circumstances, death, package] 可疑的 kěyí de ▶to be suspicious of or about sb/sth 对某人/某事起疑心 duì mǒurén/mǒushì qǐ yíxīn

swallow ['swɔləu] VT 吞下 tūnxià

swam [swæm] PT of **swim**

swan [swɔn] N [c] 天鹅 tiān'é [只 zhī]

swap [swɔp] VT ▶to swap sth (for) (exchange for) (以某物) 作交换 (yǐ mǒuwù) zuò jiāohuàn; (replace with) 以…替代某物 yǐ…tìdài mǒuwù ▶to swap places (with sb) (与某人) 换位子 (yǔ mǒurén) huàn wèizi

swear word [swɛəʳ-] N [c] 骂人的话 màrén de huà [句 jù]

sweat [swɛt] VI 出汗 chūhàn

sweater ['swɛtəʳ] N [c] 毛衣 máoyī [件 jiàn]

sweatshirt ['swɛtʃəːt] N [c] 棉毛衫 miánmáoshān [件 jiàn]

Sweden ['swiːdn] N 瑞典 Ruìdiǎn

sweep [swiːp] (pt, pp **swept**) VT 扫 sǎo

sweet [swiːt] I N (Brit) 1 [c] (chocolate, mint) 糖果 tángguǒ [颗 kē] 2 [c/u] (pudding) 甜点 tiándiǎn [份 fèn] II ADJ 1 (sugary) 甜的 tián de 2 可爱的 kě'ài de ▶sweet and sour 糖醋 tángcù

swept [swɛpt] PT, PP of **sweep**

swerve [swəːv] VI 突然转向 tūrán zhuǎnxiàng

swim [swɪm] (pt **swam**, pp **swum**) I VI 1 [person, animal] 游水 yóushuǐ 2 (as sport) 游泳 yóuyǒng II VT [+ distance] 游 yóu III N [c] ▶to go for a swim 去游泳 qù yóuyǒng [次 cì] ▶to go swimming 去游泳 qù yóuyǒng

swimming ['swɪmɪŋ] N [U] 游泳 yóuyǒng

swimming pool N [c] 游泳池 yóuyǒng chí [个 gè]

swimsuit ['swɪmsuːt] N [c] 游泳衣 yóuyǒng yī [套 tào]

swing [swɪŋ] (pt, pp **swung**) I N [c] 秋千 qiūqiān [副 fù] II VT [+ arms, legs] 摆动 bǎidòng III VI 1 [pendulum] 晃动 huàngdòng 2 [door] 转动 zhuǎndòng

switch [swɪtʃ] I N [c] 开关 kāiguān [个 gè] II VT (change) 改变 gǎibiàn
▶ **switch off** VT 关掉 guāndiào
▶ **switch on** VT [+ light, engine, radio] 开启 kāiqǐ

Switzerland ['swɪtsələnd] N 瑞士 Ruìshì

swollen ['swəulən] ADJ 肿胀的 zhǒngzhàng de

swop [swɔp] N, VT = **swap**

sword [sɔːd] N [c] 剑 jiàn [把 bǎ]

swum [swʌm] PP of **swim**

swung [swʌŋ] PT, PP of **swing**

syllabus ['sɪləbəs] (esp Brit) N [c] 教学大纲 jiàoxué dàgāng [个 gè]

symbol ['sɪmbl] N [c] 1 (sign) 象征 xiàngzhēng [种 zhǒng] 2 (Math, Chem) 符号 fúhào [个 gè]

sympathetic [sɪmpə'θɛtɪk] ADJ 有同情心的 yǒu tóngqíngxīn de

sympathy ['sɪmpəθɪ] N [U] 同情心 tóngqíng xīn

syringe [sɪ'rɪndʒ] N [C] 注射器 zhùshè qì [支 zhī]

system ['sɪstəm] N [C] 1 (organization, set) 系统 xìtǒng [个 gè] 2 (method) 方法 fāngfǎ [种 zhǒng]

table ['teɪbl] N [C] 桌子 zhuōzi [张 zhāng] ▶ **to lay** or **set the table** 摆餐桌 bǎi cānzhuō

tablecloth ['teɪblklɔθ] N [C] 桌布 zhuōbù [块 kuài]

tablespoon ['teɪblspuːn] N [C] 餐匙 cānchí [把 bǎ]

tablet ['tæblɪt] N [C] 药片 yàopiàn [片 piàn]

table tennis N [U] 乒乓球 pīngpāngqiú

tact [tækt] N [U] 机智 jīzhì

tactful ['tæktful] ADJ 老练的 lǎoliàn de

tactics ['tæktɪks] NPL 策略 cèlüè

tadpole ['tædpəul] N [C] 蝌蚪 kēdǒu [只 zhī]

taffy ['tæfɪ] (US) N [U] 太妃糖 tàifēitáng

tag [tæg] N [c] **1** (*label*) 标签 biāoqiān [个 gè] **2** (*electronic*) 标签 biāoqiān [个 gè]

tail [teɪl] N [c] 尾巴 wěiba [条 tiáo] ►**"heads or tails?" — "tails"** "正面还是背面？" "背面" "zhèngmiàn háishì bèimiàn?" "bèimiàn"

tailor ['teɪləʳ] N [c] 裁缝 cáiféng [个 gè]

take [teɪk] (*pt* **took**, *pp* **taken**) VT **1** [+ *holiday, vacation*] 度 dù; [+ *shower, bath*] 洗 xǐ **2** (*take hold of*) 拿 ná **3** (*steal*) 偷走 tōuzǒu **4** (*accompany*) 送 sòng **5** (*carry, bring*) 携带 xiédài **6** [+ *road*] 走 zǒu **7** [+ *bus, train*] 乘坐 chéngzuò **8** [+ *size*] 穿 chuān **9** [+ *time*] 花费 huāfèi **10** [+ *exam, test*] 参加 cānjiā **11** [+ *drug, pill*] 服用 fúyòng ►**don't forget to take your umbrella** 别忘了带雨伞。 bié wàngle dài yǔsǎn
►**take apart** VT (*dismantle*) [+ *bicycle, radio, machine*] 拆开 chāikāi
►**take away** VT **1** (*remove*) 拿走 názǒu **2** (*carry off*) 带走 dàizǒu
►**take back** VT [+ *goods*] 退回 tuìhuí
►**take down** VT (*write down*) 记录 jìlù
►**take off** I VI 起飞 qǐfēi II VT [+ *clothes, glasses, make-up*] 脱下 tuōxià
►**take out** VT [+ *person*] 邀请 yāoqǐng
►**take up** VT **1** [+ *hobby, sport*] 开始 kāishǐ **2** [+ *time, space*] 占用 zhànyòng

takeaway ['teɪkəweɪ] (*Brit*) [c] **1** (*shop, restaurant*) 外卖店 wàimàidiàn [家 jiā] **2** (*food*) 外卖 wàimài [个 gè]

taken ['teɪkən] PP *of* **take**

takeoff ['teɪkɔf] N [c] 起飞 qǐfēi [次 cì]

takeout ['teɪkaut] (*US*) N [c] **1** (*shop, restaurant*) 外卖店 wàimàidiàn [家 jiā] **2** (*food*) 外卖 wàimài [个 gè]

tale [teɪl] N [c] 故事 gùshì [个 gè]

talent ['tælnt] N [c/u] 才能 cáinéng [种 zhǒng]

talented ['tæləntɪd] ADJ 有才能 的 yǒu cáinéng de

talk [tɔːk] I N **1** [c] (*prepared speech*) 讲话 jiǎnghuà [次 cì] **2** [u] (*gossip*) 谣言 yáoyán **3** [c] (*discussion*) 交谈 jiāotán [次 cì] II VI **1** (*speak*) 说话 shuōhuà **2** (*chat*) 聊 liáo ►**to talk to** *or* **with sb** 跟某人谈话 gēn mǒurén tánhuà ►**to talk about sth** 谈论某事 tánlùn mǒushì
►**talk over, talk through** VT 仔细商讨 zǐxì shāngtǎo

talkative ['tɔːkətɪv] ADJ 健谈的 jiàntán de

talk show N [c] (*US*) 脱口秀 tuōkǒuxiù [个 gè]

tall [tɔːl] ADJ 高的 gāo de ►**he's 6 feet tall** 他6英尺高 tā liù yīngchǐ gāo

tame [teɪm] ADJ 驯服的 xùnfú de

tampon ['tæmpɔn] N [c] 月经棉栓 yuèjīng miánshuān [个 gè]

tan [tæn] N [c] 晒黑的肤色 shàihēi de fūsè [种 zhǒng]

tangerine [tændʒə'riːn] N [c] 红橘 hóngjú [个 gè]

tank [tæŋk] N [c] **1** (Mil) 坦克 tǎnkè [部 bù] **2** (for petrol, water) 箱 xiāng [个 gè]

tanker ['tæŋkəʳ] N [c] **1** (ship) 油轮 yóulún [艘 sōu] **2** (truck) 油罐车 yóuguànchē [辆 liàng]

tanned [tænd] ADJ 晒黑的 shàihēi de

tap [tæp] N [c] (esp Brit) 龙头 lóngtóu [个 gè]

tap-dancing ['tæpdɑːnsɪŋ] N [U] 踢踏舞 tītàwǔ

tape [teɪp] I N **1** [c] (cassette) 磁带 cídài [盘 pán] **2** [U] (adhesive) 胶带 jiāodài II VT **1** (record) 录制 lùzhì **2** (attach) 贴 tiē

tape measure N [c] 卷尺 juǎnchǐ [把 bǎ]

tape recorder N [c] 录音机 lùyīnjī [台 tái]

tar [tɑː] N [U] 沥青 lìqīng

target ['tɑːgɪt] N [c] **1** (of missile) 目标 mùbiāo [个 gè] **2** (aim) 目标 mùbiāo [个 gè]

tart [tɑːt] N [c] 果馅饼 guǒxiànbǐng [个 gè]

tartan ['tɑːtn] I N [c/U] 苏格兰方格呢 Sūgélán fānggéní [块 kuài] II ADJ [+ rug, scarf etc] 苏格兰方格的 Sūgélán fānggé de

● **TARTAN**

● 是一种有图案的厚羊毛布
● 料，其图案是由不同宽度
● 和颜色的直线条垂直交叉
● 组成。**tartan** 用来做 **kilt**
● 一一种苏格兰成年男子和
● 男孩子在正式场合穿的特
● 别的短裙。这种布料起源
● 于 **Highlands** （苏格兰高
● 地）一即苏格兰群山连绵的西
● 北部。在那里，**tartan** 被作
● 为反抗英国王室的标志，并
● 因此在1747年至1782年期间
● 被禁用。不同的颜色和图案
● 代表着苏格兰的不同地区。

task [tɑːsk] N [c] 任务 rènwù [项 xiàng]

taste [teɪst] I N **1** [c] (flavour) 味道 wèidao [种 zhǒng] **2** [c] (sample) 尝试 chángshì [次 cì] **3** [U] (choice, liking) 品位 pǐnwèi II VI ▶ **to taste of/like sth** 有/像某物的味道 yǒu/xiàng mǒuwù de wèidao

tasty ['teɪstɪ] ADJ 味美的 wèiměi de

tattoo [tə'tuː] N [c] 纹身 wénshēn [个 gè]

taught [tɔːt] PT, PP of **teach**

Taurus ['tɔːrəs] N [U] 金牛座 JīnniúZuò

tax [tæks] N [c/U] 税 shuì [种 zhǒng]

taxi ['tæksɪ] N [c] 出租车 chūzūchē [辆 liàng]

taxi rank (Brit) N [c] 出租车候客站 chūzūchē hòukèzhàn [个 gè]

taxi stand (US) N [c] 出租车候客站 chūzūchē hòukèzhàn [个 gè]

TB N ABBR (= **tuberculosis**) 肺结核 fèijiéhé

tea [tiː] N [c/U] **1** (drink) 茶 chá [杯 bēi] **2** (dried leaves) 茶叶 cháyè [片

piàn] **3** (Brit: evening meal) 晚饭 wǎnfàn [顿 dùn]

○ **TEA**
○
○ 英国人和美国人喝的茶大多
○ 是红茶。通常茶里要加牛
○ 奶，可能还加糖，当然也可
○ 以在茶里只放几片柠檬。花
○ 草茶 (**herbal tea**)，如薄荷
○ 或甘菊茶，正风行起来。**tea**
○ 还可以指下午小餐，通常有
○ 三明治，蛋糕，还有茶。在英
○ 国的一些地方，**tea** 还可以
○ 指晚上的正餐。

teach [tiːtʃ] (pt, pp **taught**) **I** VT
1 ▶ to teach sb sth, teach sth to sb 教某人某事，将某事教给某人 jiāo mǒurén mǒushì, jiāng mǒushì jiāogěi mǒurén **2** [+ pupils, subject] 教 jiāo **II** VI (be a teacher) 教书 jiāoshū ▶ to teach sb to do sth/how to do sth 教某人做某事/怎样做某事 jiāo mǒurén zuò mǒushì/zěnyàng zuò mǒushì

teacher ['tiːtʃə'] N [c] 教师 jiàoshī [位 wèi]

team [tiːm] N [c] **1** (of people, experts, horses) 组 zǔ [个 gè] **2** (Sport) 队 duì [个 gè]

teapot ['tiːpɔt] N [c] 茶壶 cháhú [个 gè]

tear¹ [tɛə'] (pt **tore**, pp **torn**) **I** N [c] (rip, hole) 裂口 lièkǒu [个 gè] **II** VT 撕裂 sīliè
▶ tear up VT 撕毁 sīhuǐ

tear² [tɪə'] N [c] (when crying) 眼泪 yǎnlèi [滴 dī] ▶ to burst into tears 哭起来 kū qǐlái

tease [tiːz] VT 逗弄 dòunong

teaspoon ['tiːspuːn] N [c] 茶匙 cháchí [把 bǎ]

teatime ['tiːtaɪm] (Brit) N [U] 茶点时间 chádiǎn shíjiān

tea towel (Brit) N [c] 擦拭布 cāshìbù [块 kuài]

technical ['tɛknɪkl] ADJ **1** [+ problems, advances] 技术的 jìshù de **2** [+ terms, language] 专业的 zhuānyè de

technician [tɛk'nɪʃən] N [c] 技师 jìshī [位 wèi]

technological [tɛknə'lɔdʒɪkl] ADJ 工艺的 gōngyì de

technology [tɛk'nɔlədʒɪ] N [c/U] 工艺学 gōngyìxué [门 mén]

teddy (bear) ['tɛdɪ(-)] N [c] 玩具熊 wánjùxióng [只 zhī]

teenage ['tiːneɪdʒ] ADJ 十几岁的 shíjǐsuì de

teenager ['tiːneɪdʒə'] N [c] 青少年 qīngshàonián [个 gè]

tee-shirt ['tiːʃəːt] N = **T-shirt**

teeth [tiːθ] NPL of **tooth**

telephone ['tɛlɪfəun] N [c] 电话 diànhuà [部 bù]

telephone book, telephone directory N [c] 电话簿 diànhuàbù [个 gè]

telescope ['tɛlɪskəup] N [c] 望远镜 wàngyuǎnjìng [架 jià]

television ['tɛlɪvɪʒən] N **1** [c] (also: **television set**) 电视机 diànshìjī [台 tái] **2** [U] (system) 电视 diànshì

tell [tɛl] (pt, pp **told**) VT **1** (inform) ▶ to tell sb sth 告诉某人某事 gàosù mǒurén mǒushì **2** [+ story, joke] 讲 jiǎng ▸**to tell sb to do sth** 指示某人做某事 zhǐshì mǒurén zuò mǒushì ▸**to tell sb that...** 告诉某人说… gàosù mǒurén shuō…

▸**tell off** VT ▸**to tell sb off** 斥责某人 chìzé mǒurén

teller ['tɛlə'] (US) N [C] (in bank) 出纳员 chūnàyuán [个 gè]

telly ['tɛlɪ] (Brit: inf) N [C/U] 电视 diànshì [台 tái]

temper ['tɛmpə'] N [C/U] 脾气 píqì [种 zhǒng] ▸**to lose one's temper** 发怒 fānù

temperature ['tɛmprətʃə'] N 1 [C/U] (of place) 气温 qìwēn 2 [U] (of person) 体温 tǐwēn ▸**to have or be running a temperature** 发烧 fāshāo

temple ['tɛmpl] N [C] 庙宇 miàoyǔ [座 zuò]

temporary ['tɛmpərərɪ] ADJ 临时的 línshí de

temptation [tɛmp'teɪʃən] N [C/U] 诱惑 yòuhuò [种 zhǒng]

tempting ['tɛmptɪŋ] ADJ 诱人的 yòurén de

ten [tɛn] NUM 十 shí

tend [tɛnd] VI ▸**to tend to do sth** 倾向于做某事 qīngxiàng yú zuò mǒushì

tennis ['tɛnɪs] N [U] 网球运动 wǎngqiú yùndòng

tennis court N [C] 网球场 wǎngqiúchǎng [个 gè]

tennis player N [C] 网球手 wǎngqiúshǒu [位 wèi]

tense [tɛns] I ADJ 紧张的 jǐnzhāng de II N [C] (Ling) 时态 shítài [种 zhǒng]

tension ['tɛnʃən] N 1 [C/U] (of situation) 紧张的局势 jǐnzhāng de júshì [个 gè] 2 [U] (of person) 焦虑 jiāolù

tent [tɛnt] N [C] 帐篷 zhàngpeng [顶 dǐng]

tenth [tɛnθ] NUM 1 (in series) 第十 dì shí 2 (fraction) 十分之一 shífēn zhī yī; see also **fifth**

term [tə:m] N [C] 学期 xuéqī [个 gè] ▸**in the short/long term** 短/长期 duǎn/chángqī ▸**to be on good terms with sb** 与某人关系好 yǔ mǒurén guānxi hǎo

terminal ['tə:mɪnl] I ADJ 晚期的 wǎnqī de II N [C] 1 (Comput) 终端 zhōngduān [个 gè] 2 (at airport) 终点站 zhōngdiǎnzhàn [个 gè]

terminally ['tə:mɪnlɪ] ADV ▸**terminally ill** 病入膏肓的 bìng rù gāo huāng de

terrace ['tɛrəs] N [C] 1 (Brit: row of houses) 成排的房屋 chéngpái de fángwū [排 pái] 2 (patio) 平台 píngtái [个 gè]

terraced ['tɛrəst] ADJ [+ house] 成排的 chéngpái de

terrible ['tɛrɪbl] ADJ 1 [+ accident, winter] 可怕的 kěpà de 2 (very poor) 糟糕的 zāogāo de 3 糟透的 zāotòu de

terribly ['tɛrɪblɪ] ADV 1 (very) 非常 fēicháng 2 (very badly) 差劲地 chàjìn de

terrific [tə'rɪfɪk] ADJ 1 [+ amount, thunderstorm, speed] 惊人的 jīngrén de 2 [+ time, party, idea] 极好的 jíhǎo de

terrified ['tɛrɪfaɪd] ADJ 吓坏的 xiàhuài de

terror ['tɛrəʳ] N [U] 恐惧 kǒngjù

terrorism ['tɛrərɪzəm] N [U] 恐怖主义 kǒngbù zhǔyì

terrorist ['tɛrərɪst] I N [c] 恐怖分子 kǒngbù fènzǐ [个 gè] II ADJ 恐怖分子的 kǒngbù fènzǐ de

test [tɛst] I N [c] 1 (*trial, check*) 试验 shìyàn [次 cì] 2 (*Med*) 检验 jiǎnyàn [次 cì] 3 (*Scol*) 测验 cèyàn [个 gè] 4 (*also*: **driving test**) 驾驶考试 jiàshǐ kǎoshì [次 cì] II VT 1 (*try out*) 试验 shìyàn 2 (*Scol*) 测试 cèshì

test tube N [c] 试管 shìguǎn [根 gēn]

text [tɛkst] I N 1 [U] (*written material*) 正文 zhèngwén 2 [c] (*book*) 课本 kèběn [本 běn] 3 [c] (*also*: **text message**) 手机短信 shǒujī duǎnxìn [条 tiáo] II VT (*on mobile phone*) 发短消息 fā duǎnxiāoxi

textbook ['tɛkstbuk] N [c] 课本 kèběn [本 běn]

text message N [c] 短信 duǎnxìn [条 tiáo]

than [ðæn, ðən] PREP (*in comparisons*) 比 bǐ ▶**it's smaller than a matchbox** 它比一个火柴盒还小 tā bǐ yīgè huǒcháihé hái xiǎo ▶**more/less than Paul** 比保罗多/少 bǐ Bǎoluó duō/shǎo ▶**more than 20** 多于20 duōyú èrshí ▶**she's older than you think** 她比你想的年纪要大 tā bǐ nǐ xiǎngde niánjì yào dà

thank [θæŋk] VT [+ *person*] 感谢 gǎnxiè ▶**thank you (very much)** (非常)感谢你 (fēicháng) gǎnxiè nǐ ▶**no, thank you** 不,谢谢 bù, xièxie ▶**to thank sb for (doing) sth** 感谢某人(做)某事 gǎnxiè mǒurén (zuò) mǒushì

thanks [θæŋks] I NPL 感谢 gǎnxiè II INT 谢谢 xièxie ▶**many thanks, thanks a lot** 多谢 duōxiè ▶**no, thanks** 不了,谢谢 bùle, xièxie ▶**thanks to sb/sth** 多亏某人/某事 duōkuī mǒurén/mǒushì

Thanksgiving (Day) ['θæŋksɡɪvɪŋ(-)] (*US*) N [c/u] 感恩节 Gǎn'ēnjié [个 gè]

KEYWORD

that [ðæt] (*demonstrative adj, pron: pl* those) I ADJ 那 nà ▶**that man/woman/book** 那个男人/女人/那本书 nàgè nánrén/nǚrén/nàběnshū ▶**that one** 那一个 nàyīgè II PRON 1 (*demonstrative*) 那 nà ▶**who's/what's that?** 那是谁/那是什么? nàshì shuí/nàshì shénme? ▶**is that you?** 是你吗? shì nǐ ma? ▶**that's my house** 那是我的房子 nàshì wǒde fángzi 2 (*relative*) …的 …de ▶**the man that I saw** 我见过的那个男的 wǒ jiànguò de nàgè nánde ▶**the woman that you spoke to** 和你说过话的那个女的 hé nǐ shuōguò huà de nàgè nǚde III CONJ 引导宾语从句的关系代词 ▶**he thought that I was ill** 他以为我病了 tā yǐwéi wǒ bìngle

IV ADV (*so*) 如此 rúcǐ ▶**that much/bad/high** 如此多/糟糕/高 rúcǐ duō/zāogāo/gāo

 KEYWORD

the [ðiː, ðə] DEF ART **1** 定冠词，用于指代已知的人或物 ▶**the man/girl/house/book** 男人/女孩/房子/书 nánrén/nǚhái/fángzi/shū ▶**the men/women/houses/books** 男人/女孩/房子/书 nánrén/nǚhái/fángzi/shū ▶**the best solution** 最好的解决方案 zuìhǎo de jiějué fāng'àn **2** (*in dates, decades*) 表示具体时间 ▶**the fifth of March** 3月5日 sānyuè wǔrì ▶**the nineties** 90年代 jiǔshí niándài **3** (*in titles*) 用于称谓中 ▶**Elizabeth the First** 伊丽莎白一世 Yīlìshābái Yīshì

theatre, (*US*) **theater** [ˈθɪətəʳ] N **1** [c] (*building*) 剧院 jùyuàn [座 zuò] **2** [c] (*Med*) (*also*: **operating theatre**) 手术室 shǒushùshì [间 jiān] **3** [c] (*US*) (*also*: **movie theater**) 电影院 diànyǐngyuàn [家 jiā]

theft [θɛft] N [c/u] 盗窃 dàoqiè [次 cì]

their [ðɛəʳ] ADJ **1** (*of men, boys, mixed group*) 他们的 tāmen de; (*of women, girls*) 她们的 tāmen de; (*of things, animals*) 它们的 tāmen de **2** (*his or her*) 他/她的 tā/tā de

theirs [ðɛəz] PRON (*of men, boys,*

mixed group) 他们的 tāmen de; (*of women, girls*) 她们的 tāmen de; (*of animals*) 它们的 tāmen de ▶**a friend of theirs** 他们/她们的一个朋友 tāmen/tāmen de yīgè péngyou

them [ðɛm, ðəm] PRON (*plural referring to men, boys, mixed group*) 他们 tāmen; (*referring to women, girls*) 她们 tāmen; (*referring to things and animals*) 它们 tāmen

theme park N [c] 主题公园 zhǔtí gōngyuán [座 zuò]

themselves [ðəmˈsɛlvz] PL PRON **1** (*referring to men, boys, mixed group*) 他们自己 tāmen zìjǐ; (*referring to girls, women*) 她们自己 tāmen zìjǐ; (*referring to animals*) 它们自己 tāmen zìjǐ **2** (*emphatic: referring to men, boys, mixed group*) 他们本人 tāmen běnrén; (: *referring to women, girls*) 她们本人 tāmen běnrén ▶**they all enjoyed themselves** 他们/她们都玩得很开心。 tāmen/tāmen dōu wánde hěn kāixīn ▶**by themselves** (*unaided*) 他/她们独立地 tā/tāmen dúlì de; (*alone*) 他/她们独自地 tā/tāmen dúzì de

then [ðɛn] ADV **1** (*at that time: past*) 当时 dāngshí; (*future*) 那时 nàshí **2** (*after that*) 之后 zhīhòu ▶**by then** 到那时 dào nàshí ▶**before then** 在那之前 zài nà zhīqián ▶**until then** 直到那时 zhídào nàshí ▶**since then** 自从那时 zìcóng nàshí ▶**well/OK then** 好吧 hǎoba

there [ðɛəʳ] ADV 那儿 nàr

▶**they've lived there for 30 years** 他们在那儿住了30年 tāmen zài nàr zhùle sánshí nián ▶**is Shirley there please?** (*on telephone*) 请问雪莉在吗? qǐngwèn Xuělì zàima? ▶**it's over there** 在那边 zài nàbiān ▶**there he is!** 他在那儿呐! tā zài nàr ne! ▶**there you are** (*offering something*) 给你 gěinǐ ▶**there is/there are** 有 yǒu ▶**there has been an accident** 发生了一个事故 fāshēng le yīgè shìgù

therefore [ˈðɛəfɔːʳ] ADV 因此 yīncǐ

there's [ðɛəz] = **there is, there has**

thermometer [θəˈmɒmɪtəʳ] N [C] 温度计 wēndùjì [个 gè]

these [ðiːz] I PL ADJ (*demonstrative*) 这些 zhèxiē II PL PRON 这些 zhèxiē ▶**these days** 目前 mùqián

they [ðeɪ] PL PRON 1 (*referring to men, boys, mixed group*) 他们 tāmen; (*referring to women, girls*) 她们 tāmen; (*referring to animals, things*) 它们 tāmen 2 (*in generalizations*) 人们 rénmen

they'd [ðeɪd] = **they had, they would**

they'll [ðeɪl] = **they shall, they will**

they're [ðɛəʳ] = **they are**

they've [ðeɪv] = **they have**

thick [θɪk] ADJ 1 [+ *slice, line, book, clothes*] 厚的 hòu de 2 [+ *sauce, mud, fog*] 浓的 nóng de ▶**it's 20 cm thick** 有20厘米粗 yǒu èrshí límǐ cū

thief [θiːf] (*pl* **thieves** [θiːvz]) N [C] 贼 zéi [个 gè]

thigh [θaɪ] N [C] 大腿 dàtuǐ [条 tiáo]

thin [θɪn] ADJ 1 [+ *slice, line, book, material*] 薄的 báo de 2 [+ *person, animal*] 瘦的 shòu de

thing [θɪŋ] I N [C] 1 事 shì [件 jiàn] 2 (*physical object*) 物品 wùpǐn [件 jiàn] II **things** NPL 1 (*belongings*) 东西 dōngxi 2 (*in general*) 情形 qíngxíng ▶**a strange thing happened** 发生了一件很奇怪的事。fāshēng le yījiàn hěn qíguài de shì ▶**how are things going?** 情形如何? qíngxíng rúhé?

think [θɪŋk] (*pt, pp* **thought**) I VI 1 (*reflect*) 思考 sīkǎo 2 (*reason*) 想 xiǎng II VT 1 (*be of the opinion, believe*) 认为 rènwéi 2 (*believe*) 以为 yǐwéi ▶**what do you think of...?** 你认为…怎么样? nǐ rènwéi…zěnmeyàng? ▶**to think about sth/sb** 想着某事物/某人 xiǎngzhe mǒu shìwù/mǒurén ▶**to think of doing sth** 考虑做某事 kǎolǜ zuò mǒushì ▶**I think so/not** 我想是/不是的 wǒ xiǎng shì/bùshì de ▶**think over** VT [+ *offer, suggestion*] 仔细考虑 zǐxì kǎolǜ

third [θəːd] NUM 1 (*in series*) 第三 dì sān 2 (*fraction*) 三份 sānfèn ▶**a third of** 三分之一 sān fēn zhī yī; *see also* **fifth**

thirdly [ˈθəːdlɪ] ADV 第三 dì sān

Third World I N ▶**the Third World** 第三世界 Dì Sān Shìjiè II ADJ [+ *country, debt*] 第三世界的

Dì Sān Shìjiè de

thirst [θə:st] N [C/U] 口渴 kǒukě [阵 zhèn]

thirsty ['θə:stɪ] ADJ 渴的 kě de

thirteen [θə:'ti:n] NUM 十三 shísān; see also **fifteen**

thirteenth [θə:'ti:nθ] NUM 第十三 dì shísān; see also **fifth**

thirty ['θə:tɪ] NUM 三十 sānshí; see also **fifty**

KEYWORD

this [ðɪs] (pl these) I ADJ
1 (demonstrative) 这 zhè ▶this man 这个男人 zhègè nánrén ▶this house 这座房子 zhèzuò fángzi ▶this one is better than that one 这个比那个好 zhègè bǐ nàgè hǎo
2 (with days, months, years) 这个 zhège ▶this Sunday/month/year 这个星期天/月/今年 zhègè xīngqītiān/yuè/jīnnián
II PRON 这个 zhège ▶who's/what's this? 这是谁/什么？ zhèshì shuí/shénme? ▶this is Janet (in introduction) 这是珍妮特 zhèshì Zhēnnítè; (on telephone) 我是珍妮特 wǒshì Zhēnnítè ▶like this 像这个一样的 xiàng zhègè yīyàng de
III ADV (demonstrative) ▶this much/high/long 这么多/高/长 zhème duō/gāo/cháng

thorn [θɔ:n] N [C] 刺 cì [根 gēn]

thorough ['θʌrə] ADJ 1 [+ search, investigation] 彻底的 chèdǐ de 2 (methodical) [+ person] 细致的 xìzhì de

those [ðəuz] I PL ADJ 那些 nàxiē II PL PRON 那些 nàxiē ▶those people/books 那些人/书 nàxiē rén/shū ▶are those yours? 那些是你的吗？ nàxiē shì nǐde ma?

though [ðəu] I CONJ (although) 虽然 suīrán II ADV 但是 dànshì ▶even though 尽管 jǐnguǎn

thought [θɔ:t] I PT, PP of **think** II N [C] 想法 xiǎngfǎ [个 gè]

thoughtful ['θɔ:tful] ADJ 1 (deep in thought) 深思的 shēnsī de 2 (considerate) 体贴的 tǐtiē de

thoughtless ['θɔ:tlɪs] ADJ [+ behaviour, words, person] 不体贴的 bù tǐtiē de

thousand ['θauzənd] NUM ▶a or one thousand 一千 yī qiān ▶thousands of 许许多多 xǔ xǔ duō duō

thread [θrɛd] N [C/U] 线 xiàn [根 gēn]

threat [θrɛt] N [C/U] 威胁 wēixié [个 gè]

threaten ['θrɛtn] VT 1 (make a threat against) [+ person] 威胁 wēixié 2 (endanger) [+ life, livelihood] 使受到威胁 shǐ shòudào wēixié

three [θri:] NUM 三 sān; see also **five**

three-quarters [θri:'kwɔ:təz] I NPL 四分之三 sìfēn zhī sān II ADV ▶three-quarters full/empty 四分之三满/空 sìfēn zhīsān mǎn/kōng III PRON 四分之三 sìfēn zhī sān ▶three-quarters

of an hour 45分钟 sìshíwǔ fēnzhōng

threw [θruː] PT of **throw**

thriller ['θrɪləʳ] N [c] 惊险 jīngxiǎn [场 chǎng]

thrilling ['θrɪlɪŋ] ADJ 令人兴奋的 lìng rén xīngfèn de

throat [θrəut] N [c] 1 (gullet) 咽喉 yānhóu [个 gè] 2 (neck) 脖子 bózi [个 gè] ▸**to have a sore throat** 嗓子疼 sǎngzi téng

through [θruː] I PREP 1 [+ place] 穿过 chuānguò 2 (throughout) [+ time] 整个 zhěnggè 3 (coming from the other side of) 穿过 chuānguò II ADJ [+ ticket, train] 直达的 zhídá de ▸**(from) Monday through Friday** (US) (从)周一到周五 (cóng) zhōuyī dào zhōuwǔ

throughout [θruː'aut] PREP 1 [+ place] 遍及 biànjí 2 [+ time] 贯穿 guànchuān

throw [θrəu] (pt threw, pp thrown [θrəun]) VT 1 (toss) [+ stone, ball] 丢 diū 2 [+ person] 抛 pāo
▸ **throw away** VT 1 [+ rubbish] 扔掉 rēngdiào 2 [+ opportunity] 错过 cuòguò
▸ **throw out** VT 1 [+ rubbish] 扔掉 rēngdiào 2 (from team, organization) 赶走 gǎnzǒu
▸ **throw up** (inf) VI (vomit) 呕吐 ǒutù

thru [θruː] (US) = **through**

thumb [θʌm] N [c] 大拇指 dàmǔzhǐ

thumbtack ['θʌmtæk] (US) N [c] 图钉 túdīng [颗 kē]

thunder ['θʌndəʳ] N [U] 雷 léi

thunderstorm ['θʌndəstɔːm] N [c] 雷雨 léiyǔ [阵 zhèn]

Thursday ['θəːzdɪ] N [c/U] 星期四 xīngqīsì [个 gè]; see also **Tuesday**

tick [tɪk] I N [c] (esp Brit: mark) 勾号 gōuhào [个 gè] II VI (clock, watch) 嘀嗒作响 dīdā zuòxiǎng III VT (esp Brit) [+ item on list] 打勾 dǎgōu
▸ **tick off** VT (esp Brit) [+ item on list] 打勾 dǎgōu

ticket ['tɪkɪt] N [c] (for public transport, theatre, raffle) 票 piào [张 zhāng] 2 [c] (also: **parking ticket**) 违章停车罚单 wéizhāng tíngchē fádān [张 zhāng]

ticket inspector N [c] 查票员 chápiàoyuán [位 wèi]

ticket office N [c] 售票处 shòupiàochù [个 gè]

tickle ['tɪkl] VT 挠 náo

tide [taɪd] N [c] 潮汐 cháoxī
▸**high/low tide** 涨/落潮 zhǎng/luò cháo

tidy ['taɪdɪ] I ADJ 整洁的 zhěngjié de II VT (also: **tidy up**) 整理 zhěnglǐ
▸ **tidy up** VT, VI 整理 zhěnglǐ

tie [taɪ] I N [c] 1 (clothing) 领带 lǐngdài [条 tiáo] 2 (Sport) 淘汰赛 táotàisài [局 jú] 3 (draw: in competition) 平局 píngjú [个 gè] II VT (also: **tie up**) 扎 zā
▸ **tie up** VT 1 [+ parcel] 捆绑 kǔnbǎng 2 [+ dog] 拴 shuān 3 [+ person] 捆绑 kǔnbǎng

tiger ['taɪgəʳ] N [c] 老虎 lǎohǔ [只 zhī]

tight [taɪt] I ADJ 1 [+ shoes, clothes]

紧身的 jǐnshēn de **2** (strict)
[+ budget, schedule] 紧张的
jǐnzhāng de; [+ security, controls]
严格的 yángé de **II** ADV (hold,
squeeze, shut) 紧紧地 jǐnjǐn de

tightly ['taɪtlɪ] ADV 紧紧地
jǐnjǐn de

tights [taɪts] (Brit) NPL 连裤袜
liánkùwà

tile [taɪl] N [c] **1** (on roof) 瓦 wǎ [片
piàn] **2** (on floor, wall) 砖 zhuān
[块 kuài]

till [tɪl] **I** N [c] (Brit) 收银台
shōuyíntái [个 gè] **II** PREP, CONJ
= **until**

timber ['tɪmbə^r] (Brit) N [U] 木
料 mùliào

time [taɪm] N **1** [U] 时间 shíjiān **2**
[U] (period) 时候 shíhou **3** [s] (by
clock) 时间 shíjiān **4** [c] (occasion)
次 cì ▶**to have a good/bad time**
度过一段愉快/不愉快的时光
dùguò yīduàn yúkuài/bù yúkuài
de shíguāng ▶**to spend one's
time doing sth** 花时间做某事 huā
shíjiān zuò mǒushì ▶**three times
a day** 一日三次 yīrì sāncì ▶**all
the time** 总是 zǒngshì ▶**at the
same time** (simultaneously) 同时
tóngshí ▶**at times** (sometimes) 有
时 yǒushí ▶**in time (for)** 正好赶
上 (…) zhènghǎo gǎnshàng (…)
▶**in a week's/month's time** 一
周/月以后 yīzhōu/yuè yǐhòu ▶**on
time** 准时 zhǔnshí ▶**5 times 5
is 25** 5乘5等于25 wǔ chéng wǔ
děngyú èrshíwǔ ▶**what time is
it?, what's the time?** 几点了？
jǐdiǎn le? ▶**time off** 休假 xiūjià

timetable ['taɪmteɪbl] N [c]
1 (Brit) (Rail etc) 时刻表 shíkèbiǎo
[个 gè] **2** (Brit) (Scol) 课程表
kèchéngbiǎo [个 gè] **3** (programme
of events) 计划表 jìhuàbiǎo [个 gè]

tin [tɪn] N **1** [U] (metal) 锡 xī **2** [c]
(Brit: can) 罐 guàn [个 gè] **3** [c]
(container: for biscuits, tobacco)
听 tīng

tin opener [-əupnə^r] (Brit) N [c]
开罐器 kāiguànqì [个 gè]

tiny ['taɪnɪ] ADJ 极小的 jíxiǎo de

tip [tɪp] **I** N [c] **1** (of branch,
paintbrush) 顶端 dǐngduān [个
gè] **2** (to waiter) 小费 xiǎofèi [笔
bǐ] **3** (Brit: for rubbish) 弃置场
qìzhìchǎng [个 gè] **4** (advice) 提
示 tíshì [个 gè] **II** VT **1** [+ waiter]
给…小费 gěi…xiǎofèi **2** (pour) 倒
出 dàochū

tiptoe ['tɪptəu] VI 踮着脚走
diǎnzhe jiǎo zǒu ▶**on tiptoe** 踮着
脚走 diǎnzhe jiǎo zǒu

tire ['taɪə^r] N (US) = **tyre**

tired ['taɪəd] ADJ 累的 lèi de ▶**to
be tired of (doing) sth** 厌倦于
(做) 某事 yànjuàn yú (zuò) mǒushì

tiring ['taɪərɪŋ] ADJ 令人疲劳的
lìng rén píláo de

tissue ['tɪʃuː] N [c] (paper
handkerchief) 纸巾 zhǐjīn [张 zhāng]

title ['taɪtl] N **1** [c] (of book, play) 标
题 biāotí [个 gè] **2** [c] (Sport) 冠军
guànjūn [个 gè]

⬤ KEYWORD

to [tuː, tə] **I** PREP **1** (direction)
到 dào ▶**to France/London/**

school/the station 去法国/伦敦/学校/车站 qù Fǎguó/Lúndūn/xuéxiào/chēzhàn

2 (*as far as*) ▸ **from here to London** 从这儿到伦敦 cóng zhèr dào Lúndūn

3 (*position*) 向 xiàng ▸ **to the left/right** 向左/右 xiàng zuǒ/yòu

4 (*in time expressions*) ▸ **it's five/ten/a quarter to five** 差5分/10分/一刻5点 chà wǔfēn/shífēn/yīkè wǔ diǎn

5 (*for, of*) 的 de ▸ **a letter to his wife** 给他妻子的丁信 gěi tā qīzi de yīfēng xìn

6 (*indirect object*) ▸ **to give sth to sb** 给某人某物 gěi mǒurén mǒuwù ▸ **to talk to sb** 对某人说 duì mǒurén shuō ▸ **a danger to sb** 对某人的危险 duì mǒurén de wēixiǎn

7 (*towards*) ▸ **to be friendly/kind/loyal to sb** 对某人友好/仁慈/忠实 duì mǒurén yǒuhǎo/réncí/zhōngshí

8 (*in relation to*) ▸ **30 miles to the gallon** 每加仑可行30英里 měi jiālún kě xíng sānshí yīnglǐ ▸ **three goals to two** 3比2 sān bǐ èr

9 (*purpose, result*) ▸ **to come to sb's aid** 来帮某人的忙 lái bāng mǒurén de máng

10 (*indicating range, extent*) ▸ **from... to...** 从…到… cóng...dào... ▸ **from May to September** 从5月到9月 cóng wǔyuè dào jiǔyuè

II WITH VERB **1** (*simple infinitive*) 与

原形动词一起构成动词不定式 ▸ **to go/eat** 走/吃 zǒu/chī

2 (*with vb omitted*) 用来代替动词不定式或不定式短语,避免重复 ▸ **I don't want to** 我不想

3 (*in order to*) 为了 wèile ▸ **I did it to help you** 我这么做是为了帮你 wǒ zhème zuò shì wèile bāngnǐ

4 (*equivalent to relative clause*) 用作定语 ▸ **I have things to do** 我有事要做 wǒ yǒushì yào zuò

5 (*after adjective etc*) 用于某些动词, 名词, 形容词后构成不定式 ▸ **to be ready to go** 准备走 zhǔnbèi zǒu ▸ **too old/young to do sth** 年纪太大/太小以至于不能做某事 niánjì tàidà/tàixiǎo yǐzhì yú bùnéng zuò mǒushì ▸ **to and fro** 来来回回地 lái lái huí huí de

toast [təʊst] N **1** [U] (*Culin*) 烤面包 kǎomiànbāo **2** [c] (*drink*) 祝酒 zhùjiǔ [次 cì] ▸ **a piece** *or* **slice of toast** 一片烤面包 yīpiàn kǎo miànbāo ▸ **to drink a toast to sb** 为某人干杯 wèi mǒurén gānbēi

toaster ['təʊstə'] N [c] 烤面包机 kǎo miànbāo jī [台 tái]

tobacco [tə'bækəʊ] N [U] 烟草 yāncǎo

tobacconist's (shop) [tə'bækənɪsts-] N [c] 烟草店 yāncǎodiàn [家 jiā]

today [tə'deɪ] **I** ADV 今天 jīntiān **II** N [U] 今天 jīntiān ▸ **what day is it today?** 今天星期几? jīntiān xīngqījǐ? ▸ **today is the 4th of March** 今天是3月4日 jīntiān shì sānyuè sìrì

toddler ['tɒdləʳ] N [C] 学步的小孩 xuébù de xiǎohái [个 gè]

toe [təu] N [C] 1 [of foot] 脚趾 jiǎozhǐ [个 gè] 2 [of shoe, sock] 脚趾处 jiǎozhǐchù [个 gè] ▶**big/little toe** 大/小脚趾 dà/xiǎo jiǎozhǐ

toffee ['tɒfɪ] N 1 [U] (Brit: substance) 太妃糖 tàifēitáng 2 [C] (sweet) 乳脂糖 rǔzhītáng [颗 kē]

together [tə'geðəʳ] ADV 1 (with each other) 一起 yīqǐ 2 (at the same time) 同时 tóngshí 3 (combined) 加起来 jiā qǐlái ▶**together with** 连同 liántóng

toilet ['tɔɪlət] N [C] 1 (apparatus) 抽水马桶 chōushuǐ mǎtǒng [个 gè] 2 (Brit: room) 卫生间 wèishēngjiān [个 gè] ▶**to go to the toilet** (esp Brit) 上厕所 shàng cèsuǒ

toilet paper N [U] 卫生纸 wèishēngzhǐ

toiletries ['tɔɪlətrɪz] NPL 卫生用品 wèishēng yòngpǐn

toilet roll N [C/U] 卫生卷纸 wèishēng juǎnzhǐ [卷 juǎn]

told [təuld] PT, PP of **tell**

toll [təul] N [C] (on road, bridge) 通行费 tōngxíngfèi [笔 bǐ]

tomato [tə'mɑːtəu] (pl **tomatoes**) N [C/U] 西红柿 xīhóngshì [个 gè]

tomorrow [tə'mɔrəu] I ADV 明天 míngtiān II N [U] 明天 míngtiān ▶**the day after tomorrow** 后天 hòutiān ▶**tomorrow morning** 明天早晨 míngtiān zǎochén

ton [tʌn] N [C] 1 (Brit) 英吨 yīngdūn 2 (US) (also: **short ton**) 美吨 měidūn 3 (metric ton) 公吨 gōngdūn

tongue [tʌŋ] N [C] (Anat) 舌头 shétou [个 gè]

tonic ['tɒnɪk] N [U] (also: **tonic water**) 奎宁水 kuíníngshuǐ

tonight [tə'naɪt] ADV N [U] 今晚 jīnwǎn

tonsil ['tɒnsl] N [C] 扁桃体 biǎntáotǐ [个 gè]

tonsillitis [tɒnsɪ'laɪtɪs] N [U] 扁桃腺炎 biǎntáoxiànyán

too [tuː] ADV 1 (excessively) 太 tài 2 (also) 也 yě ▶**you're from Brooklyn? Me too!** 你从布鲁克林来？我也是！nǐ cóng Bùlǔkèlín lái? Wǒ yěshì!

took [tuk] PT of **take**

tool [tuːl] N [C] 用具 yòngjù [种 zhǒng]

tooth [tuːθ] N [C] (pl **teeth**) 牙齿 yáchǐ [颗 kē]

toothache ['tuːθeɪk] N [C/U] 牙痛 yátòng [阵 zhèn] ▶**to have toothache** 牙痛 yátòng

toothbrush ['tuːθbrʌʃ] N [C] 牙刷 yáshuā [把 bǎ]

toothpaste ['tuːθpeɪst] N [C/U] 牙膏 yágāo [管 guǎn]

top [tɒp] I N 1 [C] [of mountain, building, tree, stairs] 顶部 dǐngbù [个 gè] 2 [C] [of page] 顶端 dǐngduān [个 gè] 3 [C] [of surface, table] 表面 biǎomiàn [个 gè] 4 [C] (lid: of box, jar, bottle) 盖子 gàizi [个 gè] 5 [C] (blouse) 上衣 shàngyī [件 jiàn] II ADJ 1 [+ shelf, step, storey, marks] 最高的 zuìgāo de 2 [+ executive, golfer] 顶级的 dǐngjí de ▶**at the top of the stairs/**

page/street 在楼梯/页面的顶端/街道的尽头 de dǐngduān/jiēdào de jìntóu ▶**to be** or **come top** 独占鳌头 dúzhàn áotóu

topic['tɒpɪk] N [c] 话题 huàtí [个 gè]

torch[tɔːtʃ] N [c] (Brit) 手电筒 shǒudiàntǒng [个 gè]

tore[tɔːr] PT of **tear**[1]

torn[tɔːn] PP of **tear**[1]

tortoise['tɔːtəs] N [c] 乌龟 wūguī [只 zhī]

torture['tɔːtʃər] I N [U] 酷刑 kùxíng II VT 对…施以酷刑 duì…shīyǐ kùxíng

total['təutl] I ADJ 总的 zǒng de II N [c] 总数 zǒngshù [个 gè] ▶**in total** 总共 zǒnggòng

totally['təutəlɪ] ADV 1 (agree, destroy) 完全地 wánquán de 2 (different, new) 绝对地 juéduì de

touch[tʌtʃ] I N [c] (contact) 触摸 chùmō [次 cì] II VT 1 (with hand, foot) 触摸 chùmō 2 (move: emotionally) 感动 gǎndòng III VI (be in contact) 接触 jiēchù ▶**to get in touch with sb** 与某人联系 yǔ mǒurén liánxì ▶**to lose touch (with sb)** (与某人) 失去联系 (yǔ mǒurén) shīqù liánxì

tough[tʌf] ADJ 1 (strong, hard-wearing) [+ material] 坚韧的 jiānrèn de 2 [+ meat] 老的 lǎo de 3 (physically) 强壮的 qiángzhuàng de 4 (rough) 无法无天的 wú fǎ wú tiān de

tour['tuər] I N [c] 1 (journey) 旅行 lǚxíng [次 cì] 2 [of town, factory, museum] 观光 guānguāng [次 cì] 3 (by pop group, sports team) 巡回表演 xúnhuí biǎoyǎn [个 gè] II VT [+ country, city] 观光 guānguāng ▶**to go on a tour of** [+ region] 去…旅行 qù…lǚxíng

tourism['tuərɪzm] N [U] 旅游业 lǚyóuyè

tourist['tuərɪst] I N [c] 游客 yóukè [位 wèi] II CPD [+ season, attraction] 旅游 lǚyóu

tow[təu] VT [+ vehicle, trailer] 拖 tuō ▶**tow away** VT [+ vehicle] 拖走 tuōzǒu

toward(s)[tə'wɔːd(z)] PREP 1 (in direction of) 朝着 cháozhe 2 (with regard to) 对于 duìyú 3 (near) 接近 jiējìn

towel['tauəl] N [c] 毛巾 máojīn [条 tiáo]

tower['tauər] N [c] 塔 tǎ [座 zuò]

tower block (Brit) N [c] 高楼大厦 gāolóu dàshà [座 zuò]

town[taun] N [c] 城镇 chéngzhèn [个 gè]

town hall (Brit) N [c] 市政厅 shìzhèngtīng [个 gè]

tow truck (US) N [c] 拖车 tuōchē [部 bù]

toy[tɔɪ] I N [c] 玩具 wánjù [个 gè] II CPD [+ train, car] 玩具 wánjù

trace[treɪs] N [c] 痕迹 hénjì [个 gè]; [of person] 踪迹 zōngjì [个 gè]

track[træk] N [c] 1 (path) 小径 xiǎojìng [条 tiáo] 2 (Rail) 轨道 guǐdào [条 tiáo] 3 (on tape, record) 曲目 qǔmù [个 gè]

tracksuit['træksuːt] (Brit) N [c]

运动服 yùndòngfú [套 tào]

tractor ['træktə'] N [c] 拖拉机 tuōlājī [部 bù]

trade [treɪd] I N 1 [U] (buying and selling) 贸易 màoyì 2 [c] (skill, job) 谋生之道 móushēng zhī dào [种 zhǒng] II VT (exchange) ▸ **to trade sth (for sth)** (esp US) 用某物交换(某物) yòng mǒuwù jiāohuàn (mǒuwù)

trademark ['treɪdmɑːk] N [c] 商标 shāngbiāo [个 gè]

trade union (esp Brit) N [c] 工会 gōnghuì [个 gè]

tradition [trə'dɪʃən] N [c/u] 传统 chuántǒng [个 gè]

traditional [trə'dɪʃənl] ADJ 传统的 chuántǒng de

traffic ['træfɪk] N [U] 交通 jiāotōng

traffic circle (US) N [c] 转盘 zhuànpán [个 gè]

traffic jam N [c] 交通阻塞 jiāotōng zǔsè [阵 zhèn]

traffic lights NPL 红绿灯 hónglùdēng

traffic warden (esp Brit) N [c] 交通管理员 jiāotōng guǎnlǐyuán [位 wèi]

tragedy ['trædʒɪdɪ] N [c/u] 1 (disaster) 极大的不幸 jídà de bùxìng [个 gè] 2 (Theat) 悲剧 bēijù [个 gè]

tragic ['trædʒɪk] ADJ 悲惨的 bēicǎn de

trailer ['treɪlə'] N [c] 1 (Aut) 拖车 tuōchē [部 bù] 2 (US: caravan) 房式拖车 fángshì tuōchē [辆 liàng]

train [treɪn] I N [c] (Rail) 火车 huǒchē [辆 liàng] II VT 1 (teach skills to) 培训 péixùn 2 [+ athlete] 培养 péiyǎng III VI 1 (learn a skill) 受训练 shòu xùnliàn 2 (Sport) 锻炼 duànliàn

trained [treɪnd] ADJ 经专门训练的 jīng zhuānmén xùnliàn de

trainee [treɪ'niː] N [c] 1 (apprentice) 受训者 shòuxùnzhě [位 wèi] 2 (in office, management job) 实习生 shíxíshēng [个 gè]

trainer ['treɪnə'] N [c] 1 (Sport) 教练 jiàoliàn [ ] 2 (Brit: shoe) 运动鞋 yùndòngxié [双 shuāng]

training ['treɪnɪŋ] N [U] 1 (for occupation) 培训 péixùn 2 (Sport) 训练 xùnliàn

training course N [c] 培训班 péixùnbān [个 gè]

tram [træm] (Brit) N [c] (also: **tramcar**) 有轨电车 yǒuguǐ diànchē [辆 liàng]

tramp [træmp] N [c] 流浪者 liúlàngzhě [个 gè]

trampoline ['træmpəliːn] N [c] 蹦床 bèngchuáng [个 gè]

transfer ['trænsfə'] N 1 [c/u] [of money, documents] 转移 zhuǎnyí [次 cì] 2 [c] (Sport) 转会 zhuǎnhuì [次 cì]

transit ['trænzɪt] N 1 ▸ **in transit** (people) 在途中 zài túzhōng 2 [U] (US) 运输 yùnshū

translate [trænz'leɪt] VT 翻译 fānyì

translation [trænz'leɪʃən] N 1 [c] (text) 译文 yìwén [篇 piān] 2 [U] (act of translating) 翻译 fānyì

translator [trænz'leɪtə'] N [c] 译

者 yìzhě [个 gè]

transparent [træns'pærnt] ADJ
透明的 tòumíng de

transplant [vb træns'plɑ:nt, n
'trænsplɑ:nt] **I** VT (Med) 移植
yízhí **II** N [c/U] (Med: operation) 移
植 yízhí [次 cì]

transport [n 'trænspɔ:t, vb
træns'pɔ:t] **I** N [U] 交通工
具 jiāotōng gōngjù **II** VT 运送
yùnsòng ▸ **public transport** (esp
Brit) 公共交通 gōnggòng
jiāotōng

transportation ['trænspɔ:'teɪʃən]
N [U] (US: transport) 运输 yùnshū

trap [træp] **I** N [c] 陷阱 xiànjǐng
[个 gè] **II** VT **1** [+ animal] 诱捕
yòubǔ **2** (in building) 困住 kùnzhù

trash [træʃ] N [U] (US) 废物 fèiwù

trash can (US) N [c] 垃圾桶
lājītǒng [个 gè]

travel ['trævl] **I** N [U] (travelling)
旅行 lǚxíng **II** VI 前往 qiánwǎng
III VT [+ distance] 走过 zǒuguò

travel agency N [c] 旅行社
lǚxíngshè [个 gè]

travel agent N [c] **1** (shop, office)
旅行中介 lǚxíng zhōngjiè [个 gè]
2 (person) 旅行代理人 lǚxíng
dàilǐrén [个 gè]

traveller, (US) **traveler** ['trævlə']
N [c] 旅行者 lǚxíngzhě [位 wèi]

traveller's cheque, (US)
traveler's check N [c] 旅行支票
lǚxíng zhīpiào [张 zhāng]

travelling, (US) **traveling**
['trævlɪŋ] N [U] 行程 xíngchéng

travel sickness N [U] 晕车/船/机
症 yùnchē/chuán/jī zhèng

tray [treɪ] N [c] 托盘 tuōpán
[个 gè]

treasure ['trɛʒə'] N [U] 宝藏
bǎozàng

treat [tri:t] VT **1** (behave towards)
[+ person, object] 对待 duìdài
2 (Med) [+ patient, illness] 医
治 yīzhì

treatment ['tri:tmənt] N [c/U]
(Med) 治疗 zhìliáo [次 cì]

treble ['trɛbl] VI 增至三倍 zēng
zhì sānbèi

tree [tri:] N [c] 树 shù [棵 kē]

tremble ['trɛmbl] VI (with fear,
cold) 战栗 zhànlì

tremendous [trɪ'mɛndəs] ADJ
1 (enormous) 极大的 jídà de
2 (excellent) 极棒的 jíbàng de

trend [trɛnd] N [c] **1** (tendency) 趋
势 qūshì [种 zhǒng] **2** (fashion) 潮
流 cháoliú [个 gè]

trendy ['trɛndɪ] (inf) ADJ 时髦的
shímáo de

trial ['traɪəl] N [c/U] (Law) 审理
shěnlǐ [次 cì] ▸ **on trial** (Law) 受
审 shòushěn; (on approval) 试
验 shìyàn

triangle ['traɪæŋgl] N [c] (Math)
三角 sānjiǎo [个 gè]

tribe [traɪb] N [c] 部落 bùluò
[个 gè]

trick [trɪk] **I** N [c] **1** (by conjuror) 戏
法 xìfǎ [个 gè] **2** (deception) 伎俩
jìliǎng [个 gè] **II** VT (deceive) 耍花
招 shuǎ huāzhāo

tricky ['trɪkɪ] ADJ 棘手的 jíshǒu
de

tricycle ['traɪsɪkl] N [c] 三轮车
sānlúnchē [辆 liàng]

trip [trɪp] I N [c] 1 (*journey*) 出行 chūxíng [次 cì] 2 (*outing*) 外出 wàichū [次 cì] II VI (*also*: **trip up**) 绊倒 bàndǎo ▸ **to go on a trip** 外出旅行 wàichū lǚxíng

triple ['trɪpl] I ADJ 三部分的 sān bùfen de II VI 三倍于 sānbèi yú

triplets ['trɪplɪts] NPL 三胞胎 sānbāotāi

triumph ['traɪʌmf] N [c] 巨大的成功 jùdà de chénggōng [个 gè]

trivial ['trɪvɪəl] ADJ 琐碎的 suǒsuì de

trolley ['trɔlɪ] N [c] 1 (*Brit*) 手推车 shǒutuīchē [辆 liàng] 2 (*US: vehicle*) 电车 diànchē [辆 liàng]

trombone [trɔm'bəun] N [c] 长号 chánghào [只 zhī]

troop [tru:p] I N [c] [*of people, animals*] 群 qún II **troops** N [c] PL (*Mil*) 部队 bùduì [支 zhī]

trophy ['trəufɪ] N [c] 奖品 jiǎngpǐn [个 gè]

tropical ['trɔpɪkl] ADJ 热带的 rèdài de

trouble ['trʌbl] N 1 [c/u] (*difficulties, bother, effort*) 麻烦 máfan [个 gè] 2 [s] (*problem*) 问题 wèntí 3 [u] (*unrest*) 骚乱 sāoluàn ▸ **to be in trouble** (*with police, authorities*) 惹麻烦 rě máfan ▸ **the trouble is...** 问题是… wèntí shì... ▸ **stomach/back trouble** 胃部/背部毛病 wèibù/bèibù máobìng

trousers ['trauzəz] (*Brit*) NPL 裤子 kùzi ▸ **a pair of trousers** 一条裤子 yītiáo kùzi

trout [traut] N [c/u] 鳟鱼 zūnyú

[条 tiáo]

truck [trʌk] N [c] 卡车 kǎchē [辆 liàng]

truck driver N [c] 卡车司机 kǎchē sījī [位 wèi]

true [tru:] ADJ 真实的 zhēnshí de

truly ['tru:lɪ] ADV (*genuinely*) 确实地 quèshí de ▸ **yours truly** (*in letter*) 您忠诚的 nín zhōngchéng de

trumpet ['trʌmpɪt] N [c] 小号 xiǎohào [把 bǎ]

trunk [trʌŋk] I N [c] 1 [*of tree*] 树干 shùgàn [个 gè] 2 [*of elephant*] 象鼻 xiàngbí [个 gè] 3 (*US: of car*) 后备箱 hòubèixiāng [个 gè] II **trunks** NPL (*also*: **swimming trunks**) 游泳裤 yóuyǒngkù

trust [trʌst] VT 信任 xìnrèn

truth [tru:θ] N [u] 事实 shìshí

try [traɪ] I N [c] 尝试 chángshì [个 gè] II VT (*attempt*) 试 shì III VI (*make effort*) 努力 nǔlì ▸ **to try to do sth, try doing sth** 尽力做某事 jìnlì zuò mǒushì

▸ **try on** VT 试穿 shìchuān

▸ **try out** VT 试验 shìyàn

T-shirt ['ti:ʃə:t] N [c] 短袖衫 duǎnxiùshān [件 jiàn]

tub [tʌb] N [c] 1 (*container*) 缸 gāng [个 gè] 2 (*US*) 浴缸 yùgāng [个 gè]

tube [tju:b] N 1 [c] (*pipe*) 管子 guǎnzi [根 gēn] 2 (*container*) 筒 tǒng [个 gè] 3 (*Brit*) ▸ **the tube** (*underground*) 地铁 dìtiě

tuberculosis [tjubə:kju'ləusɪs] N [u] 肺结核 fèijiéhé

Tuesday ['tju:zdɪ] N [c/u] 星

期二 xīngqī'èr [个 gè] ▸**it is Tuesday 23rd March** 今天是3月23号，星期二 jīntiān shì sānyuè èrshísān hào, xīngqī'èr ▸**on Tuesday** 在星期二 zài xīngqī'èr ▸**on Tuesdays** 每个星期二 měigè xīngqī'èr ▸**every Tuesday** 每逢星期二 měiféng xīngqī'èr ▸**last/next Tuesday** 上个/下个星期二 shànggè/xiàgè xīngqī'èr ▸**Tuesday morning/afternoon/ evening** 星期二早晨/下午/晚上 xīngqī'èr zǎochén/xiàwǔ/wǎnshàng

tuition [tjuːˈɪʃən] N [U] **1** 教学 jiàoxué **2** (fees) 学费 xuéfèi

tumble dryer (Brit) N [c] 滚筒干衣机 gǔntǒng gānyījī [台 tái]

tummy [ˈtʌmɪ] (inf) N [c] 肚子 dùzi [个 gè]

tuna [ˈtjuːnə] N [c/u] (also: **tuna fish**) 金枪鱼 jīnqiāngyú [条 tiáo]

tune [tjuːn] N [c] 曲调 qǔdiào [个 gè]

Tunisia [tjuːˈnɪzɪə] N 突尼斯 Tūnísī

tunnel [ˈtʌnl] N [c] 隧道 suìdào [条 tiáo]

Turk [təːk] N [c] 土耳其人 Tǔ'ěrqírén [个 gè]

Turkey [ˈtəːkɪ] N 土耳其 Tǔ'ěrqí

turkey [ˈtəːkɪ] N **1** [c] (bird) 火鸡 huǒjī [只 zhī] **2** [U] (meat) 火鸡肉 huǒjī ròu

Turkish [ˈtəːkɪʃ] I ADJ 土耳其的 Tǔ'ěrqí de II N [U] (language) 土耳其语 Tǔ'ěrqíyǔ

turn [təːn] I N [c] (in game, queue, series) 机会 jīhuì [个 gè] II VT **1** [+ part of body] 转动 zhuàndòng **2** [+ object] 调转 diàozhuǎn **3** [+ handle, key] 转动 zhuàndòng **4** [+ page] 翻 fān III VI **1** (rotate) [object, wheel] 旋转 xuánzhuǎn **2** (change direction) [person] 转身 zhuǎnshēn **3** [vehicle] 转向 zhuǎnxiàng ▸**it's my turn to...** 轮到我做… lúndào wǒ zuò... ▸**to take turns** or **to take it in turns (to do sth)** 轮流做（某事）lúnliú zuò (mǒushì)

▸ **turn around** VI = **turn round**

▸ **turn back** VI 往回走 wǎnghuí zǒu

▸ **turn down** VT [+ heat, sound] 调低 tiáodī

▸ **turn into** VT FUS 变成 biànchéng

▸ **turn off** VT **1** [+ light, radio, tap] 关 guān **2** [+ engine] 关掉 guāndiào

▸ **turn on** VT [+ light, radio, tap] 打开 dǎkāi

▸ **turn out** VT [+ light, gas] 关掉 guāndiào ▸**to turn out to be** (prove to be) 原来是 yuánlái shì

▸ **turn round, turn around** VI [person, vehicle] 调转 diàozhuǎn

▸ **turn up** I VI **1** [person] 露面 lòumiàn **2** [lost object] 出现 chūxiàn II VT [+ radio, heater] 开大 kāidà

turning [ˈtəːnɪŋ] N [c] (in road) 拐弯 guǎiwān [个 gè]

turn signal (US) N [U] 指示器 zhǐshìqì

turquoise [ˈtəːkwɔɪz] ADJ [+ colour] 青绿色的 qīnglǜsè de

turtle ['tə:tl] (Brit) N [C] 龟 guī [只 zhī]

tutor ['tju:təʳ] N [C] **1** (Brit) (Scol) 助教 zhùjiào [位 wèi] **2** (private tutor) 家庭教师 jiātíng jiàoshī [位 wèi]

tuxedo [tʌk'si:dəu] (US) N [C] 男式晚礼服 nánshì wǎnlǐfú [件 jiàn]

TV N ABBR (= television) 电视 diànshì

tweezers ['twi:zəz] NPL 镊子 nièzi ▶a pair of tweezers 一把镊子 yībǎ nièzi

twelfth [twɛlfθ] NUM (in series) 第十二 dì shí'èr; see also **fifth**

twelve [twɛlv] NUM 十二 shí'èr ▶at twelve (o'clock) (midday) 中午12点 zhōngwǔ shí'èr diǎn; (midnight) 凌晨零点 língchén língdiǎn; see also **five**

twentieth ['twɛntɪɪθ] NUM 第二十 dì èrshí

twenty ['twɛntɪ] NUM 二十 èrshí ▶twenty-one 二十一 èrshíyī; see also **fifty**

twice [twaɪs] ADV 两次 liǎngcì ▶twice as much/long as 多/长至两倍 duō/chángzhì liǎngbèi

twin [twɪn] I ADJ [+ sister, brother] 孪生的 luánshēng de II N [C] **1** (person) 双胞胎 shuāngbāotāi [对 duì] **2** (also: **twin room**) 双人房 shuāngrénfáng [间 jiān]

twist [twɪst] VT **1** (turn) 扭 niǔ **2** [+ ankle] 扭伤 niǔshāng

two [tu:] NUM 二 èr; see also **five**

two-percent milk [tu:pə'sɛnt-] (US) N [U] 半脱脂奶 bàn tuōzhīnǎi

type [taɪp] I N **1** [C] (sort, kind) 类型 lèixíng [种 zhǒng] **2** [U] (Typ) 字体 zìtǐ II VT, VI 打字 dǎzì ▶ **type into** VT 录入 lùrù

typewriter ['taɪpraɪtəʳ] N [C] 打字机 dǎzìjī [台 tái]

typical ['tɪpɪkl] ADJ 典型的 diǎnxíng de

tyre, (US) **tire** ['taɪəʳ] N [C] 轮胎 lúntāi [个 gè]

UFO N ABBR (= **unidentified flying object**) 不明飞行物 bùmíng fēixíngwù

ugly [ˈʌɡlɪ] ADJ 丑陋的 chǒulòu de

UK N ABBR (= **United Kingdom**) ▶**the UK** 大不列颠及北爱尔兰联合王国 Dàbùlièdiān jí Běi'ài'ěrlán Liánhéwángguó

ulcer [ˈʌlsəʳ] N [c] 溃疡 kuìyáng [处 chù]

umbrella [ʌmˈbrɛlə] N [c] 伞 sǎn [把 bǎ]

umpire [ˈʌmpaɪəʳ] N [c] (Tennis, Cricket) 裁判员 cáipànyuán [位 wèi]

UN N ABBR (= **United Nations**) ▶**the UN** 联合国 Liánhéguó

unable [ʌnˈeɪbl] ADJ ▶**to be unable to do sth** 不能做某事 bùnéng zuò mǒushì

unanimous [juːˈnænɪməs] ADJ 一致同意的 yīzhì tóngyì de

unavoidable [ʌnəˈvɔɪdəbl] ADJ 不可避免的 bùkě bìmiǎn de

unbearable [ʌnˈbɛərəbl] ADJ 难以忍受的 nányǐ rěnshòu de

uncertain [ʌnˈsəːtn] ADJ 不确定的 bù quèdìng de ▶**to be uncertain about sth** 对某事心无定数 duì mǒushì xīn wú dìng shù

uncle [ˈʌŋkl] N [c] (father's older brother) 伯父 bófù [位 wèi]; (father's younger brother) 叔父 shūfù [位 wèi]; (father's sister's husband) 姑父 gūfù [位 wèi]; (mother's brother) 舅父 jiùfù [位 wèi]; (mother's sister's husband) 姨父 jífù [位 wèi]

uncomfortable [ʌnˈkʌmfətəbl] ADJ [+ person] 不舒服的 bù shūfu de; [+ chair, room, journey] 不舒适的 bù shūshì de

unconscious [ʌnˈkɔnʃəs] ADJ 失去知觉的 shīqù zhījué de

under [ˈʌndəʳ] I PREP 1 (beneath) 在…下面 zài…xiàmian 2 (less than) [+ age, price] 不到 bùdào II ADV 1 (go, fly) 从下面 cóng xiàmian 2 (in age, price etc) 以下 yǐxià

underground [ˈʌndəɡraund] I N ▶**the underground** (Brit: railway) 地铁 dìtiě II ADJ 地下的 dìxià de

underline [ʌndəˈlaɪn] (Brit) VT 在…下面划线 zài…xiàmian huàxiàn

underneath [ʌndəˈniːθ] I ADV 在下面 zài xiàmian II PREP 1 在…下面 zài…xiàmian 2 (fig) 在…背后

zài...bèihòu

underpants [ˈʌndəpænts] NPL
内裤 nèikù

underpass [ˈʌndəpɑːs] N [c] 地下
通道 dìxià tōngdào [条 tiáo]

undershirt [ˈʌndəʃəːt] (US) N [c]
贴身内衣 tiēshēn nèiyī [件 jiàn]

understand [ʌndəˈstænd] (pt, pp
understood) VT 明白 míngbai;
[+ foreign language] 懂 dǒng

understanding [ʌndəˈstændɪŋ]
ADJ 通情达理的 tōngqíng dálǐ de

understood [ʌndəˈstud] PT, PP of
understand

underwater [ˈʌndəˈwɔːtəʳ] ADV
在水下 zài shuǐxià

underwear [ˈʌndəwɛəʳ] N [U] 内
衣 nèiyī

undo [ʌnˈduː] (pt **undid**, pp
undone) VT 解开 jiěkāi

undress [ʌnˈdrɛs] VI 脱衣服
tuō yīfu

uneasy [ʌnˈiːzɪ] ADJ 不安的 bùˈān
de ▸ **to be uneasy about sth** 为
某事忧虑 wèi mǒushì yōulǜ

unemployed [ʌnɪmˈplɔɪd] I ADJ
失业的 shīyè de II NPL ▸ **the
unemployed** 失业者 shīyèzhě

unemployment [ʌnɪmˈplɔɪmənt]
N [U] 失业 shīyè

unexpected [ʌnɪksˈpɛktɪd] ADJ
意外的 yìwài de

unexpectedly [ʌnɪksˈpɛktɪdlɪ]
ADV 意外地 yìwài de

unfair [ʌnˈfɛəʳ] ADJ 不公平的 bù
gōngpíng de

unfamiliar [ʌnfəˈmɪlɪəʳ] ADJ 陌
生的 mòshēng de

unfashionable [ʌnˈfæʃnəbl] ADJ

过时的 guòshí de

unfit [ʌnˈfɪt] ADJ 不太健康的 bù
tài jiànkāng de

unfold [ʌnˈfəuld] VT 展开 zhǎnkāi

unforgettable [ʌnfəˈgɛtəbl] ADJ
难忘的 nánwàng de

unfortunately [ʌnˈfɔːtʃənətlɪ]
ADV 可惜 kěxī

unfriendly [ʌnˈfrɛndlɪ] ADJ 不友
善的 bù yǒushàn de

unhappy [ʌnˈhæpɪ] ADJ 愁苦的
chóukǔ de

unhealthy [ʌnˈhɛlθɪ] ADJ
1 [+ person] 身体不佳的 shēntǐ
bùjiā de **2** [+ place, diet, lifestyle] 不
利于健康的 bù lìyú jiànkāng de

uniform [ˈjuːnɪfɔːm] N [c/U] 制服
zhìfú [套 tào]

uninhabited [ʌnɪnˈhæbɪtɪd] ADJ
无人居住的 wúrén jūzhù de

union [ˈjuːnjən] N [c] (also: **trade
union**) 工会 gōnghuì [个 gè]

Union Jack N [c] 英国国旗
Yīngguó guóqí [面 miàn]

unique [juːˈniːk] ADJ 罕有的
hǎnyǒu de

unit [ˈjuːnɪt] N [c] **1** (single whole)
单位 dānwèi [个 gè] **2** (group,
centre) 小组 xiǎozǔ [个 gè] **3** (in
course book) 单元 dānyuán [个 gè]

United Kingdom N ▸ **the United
Kingdom** 大不列颠及北爱尔兰联
合王国 Dàbùlièdiān Jí Běiˈàiěrˈlán
Liánhéwángguó

United Nations N ▸ **the United
Nations** 联合国 Liánhéguó

United States (of America)
N ▸ **the United States (of
America)** 美利坚合众国 Měilijiān

Hézhòngguó

universe ['juːnɪvəːs] N [c] 宇宙 yǔzhòu [个 gè]

university [juːnɪ'vəːsɪtɪ] I N [c/u] 大学 dàxué [所 suǒ] ▶**to go to university** 上大学 shàng dàxué II CPD [+ student, professor, education, year] 大学 dàxué

unkind [ʌn'kaɪnd] ADJ 刻薄的 kèbó de

unknown [ʌn'nəun] ADJ **1** [+ fact, number] 未知的 wèizhī de **2** [+ writer, artist] 名不见经传的 míng bù jiàn jīngzhuàn de

unleaded [ʌn'lɛdɪd] I ADJ 无铅 的 wúqiān de II N [u] 无铅燃料 wúqiān ránliào

unless [ʌn'lɛs] CONJ 除非 chúfēi

unlikely [ʌn'laɪklɪ] ADJ 未必会发 生的 wèibì huì fāshēng de ▶**he is unlikely to win** 他获胜的希望不 大 tā huòshèng de xīwàng bùdà

unload [ʌn'ləud] VT **1** [+ objects] 卸 xiè **2** [+ car, lorry] 从…上卸货 cóng…shang xièhuò

unlock [ʌn'lɔk] VT 开 kāi

unlucky [ʌn'lʌkɪ] ADJ **1** [+ person] 不幸的 bùxìng de **2** [+ object, number] 不吉利的 bù jílì de

unmarried [ʌn'mærɪd] ADJ 未婚 的 wèihūn de

unnatural [ʌn'nætʃrəl] ADJ 反常 的 fǎncháng de

unnecessary [ʌn'nɛsəsərɪ] ADJ 不必要的 bù bìyào de

unpack [ʌn'pæk] I VI 开包 kāibāo II VT [+ suitcase, bag] 打开…取出 东西 dǎkāi…qǔchū dōngxi

unpleasant [ʌn'plɛznt] ADJ 使

人不愉快的 shǐ rén bù yúkuài de; [+ person, manner] 令人讨厌的 lìng rén tǎoyàn de

unplug [ʌn'plʌg] VT 拔去…的插 头 báqù…de chātóu

unpopular [ʌn'pɔpjulər] ADJ 不 受欢迎的 bù shòu huānyíng de

unrealistic ['ʌnrɪə'lɪstɪk] ADJ 不 切实际的 bù qiè shíjì de ▶**it is unrealistic to expect that...** 指 望…是不切实际的 zhǐwàng…shì bùqiè shíjì de

unreasonable [ʌn'riːznəbl] ADJ 无理的 wúlǐ de

unreliable [ʌnrɪ'laɪəbl] ADJ **1** [+ person, firm] 不可信赖的 bù kě xìnlài de **2** [+ machine, method] 不 可靠的 bù kěkào de

unroll [ʌn'rəul] VT 展开 zhǎnkāi

unscrew [ʌn'skruː] VT 旋开 xuánkāi

unsuccessful [ʌnsək'sɛsful] ADJ **1** [+ attempt, application] 失败的 shībài de **2** [+ person, applicant] 不 成功的 bù chénggōng de

unsuitable [ʌn'suːtəbl] ADJ **1** [+ place, time, clothes] 不适宜 的 bù shìyí de **2** [+ candidate, applicant] 不合适的 bù héshì de ▶**to be unsuitable for sth/for doing sth** 不适于某事/做某事 bù shìyú mǒushì/zuò mǒushì

untidy [ʌn'taɪdɪ] ADJ **1** [+ room] 不 整洁的 bù zhěngjié de **2** [+ person, appearance] 邋遢的 lātā de

until [ən'tɪl] I PREP 直到…时 zhídào…shí II CONJ 到…为止 dào…wéizhǐ ▶**until now** 直到现 在 zhídào xiànzài ▶**until then** 届

时 jiéshí

unusual [ʌnˈjuːʒʊəl] ADJ 不寻常的 bù xúncháng de

unwilling [ʌnˈwɪlɪŋ] ADJ ▶ **to be unwilling to do sth** 不愿做某事 bùyuàn zuò mǒushì

unwrap [ʌnˈræp] VT 打开…的包装 dǎkāi…de bāozhuāng

KEYWORD

up [ʌp] I PREP 1 (*to higher point on*) 沿…向上 yán…xiàngshàng ▶ **he went up the stairs/the hill/the ladder** 他上了楼/山/梯子 tā shàngle lóu/shān/tīzi
2 (*along*) 沿着 yánzhe
3 (*at higher point on*) 在…高处 zài…gāochù; [+ *road*] 在…高远处 zài…gāoyuǎnchù ▶ **they live further up the street** 他们住在这条街那边儿 tāmen zhùzài zhètiáo jiē nàbiānr
II ADV 1 (*towards higher point*) 往上 wǎngshàng ▶ **the lift only goes up to the 12th floor** 电梯只到12层楼以上 diàntī zhǐdào shí'èr céng lóu yǐshàng
2 (*at higher point*) 高高地 gāogāo de ▶ **up here/there** 这/那上面 zhè/nà shàngmiàn
3 ▶ **to be up** (*be out of bed*) 起床 qǐchuáng
4 (*to/in the north*) 在/向北方 zài/xiàng běifāng ▶ **he often comes up to Scotland** 他常北上去苏格兰 tā cháng běishàng qù Sūgélán
5 (*approaching*) ▶ **to go/come/run up (to sb)** (朝某人)走去/过来/跑去 (cháo mǒurén) zǒuqù/guòlái/pǎoqù
6 ▶ **up to** (*as far as*) 直到 zhídào; (*in approximations*) 多达 duōdá ▶ **I can spend up to £100** 我可以花到100英镑 wǒ kěyǐ huādào yībǎi yīngbàng
7 ▶ **up to** *or* **until** 直到 zhídào ▶ **I'll be here up to** *or* **until 5.30 pm** 我会一直呆到下午5点30分 wǒ huì yīzhí dāidào xiàwǔ wǔdiǎn sānshífēn ▶ **up to now** 直到现在 zhídào xiànzài
8 ▶ **it is up to you** (*to decide*) 随便你 (决定) suíbiàn nǐ (juédìng)
9 ▶ **to feel up to sth/to doing sth** 感到能胜任某事/感到有力气做某事 gǎndào néng shèngrèn mǒushì/gǎndào yǒu lìqì zuò mǒushì

update [*vb* ʌpˈdeɪt, *n* ˈʌpdeɪt] I VT 更新 gēngxīn II N [c] 最新信息 zuìxīn xìnxī [条 tiáo]

uphill [ˈʌpˈhɪl] ADV (*walk, push*) 往坡上 wǎng pōshang

upright [ˈʌpraɪt] ADV (*sit, stand*) 挺直地 tǐngzhí de

upset [ʌpˈsɛt] (*pt, pp* **upset**) I VT [+ *person*] 使苦恼 shǐ kǔnǎo II ADJ 1 (*unhappy*) 心烦意乱的 xīnfán yìluàn de 2 [+ *stomach*] 不服服的 bù shūfu de ▶ **to be upset about sth** 为某事感到烦恼 wèi mǒushì gǎndào fánnǎo

upside down [ʌpsaɪd-] ADV 上下颠倒地 shàngxià diāndǎo de

upstairs [ʌpˈstɛəz] ADV 1 (*be*) 在楼上 zài lóushang 2 (*go*) 往楼上

wǎng lóushang

up-to-date [ˈʌptəˈdeɪt] ADJ 最新的 zuìxīn de

upwards [ˈʌpwədz] ADV 向上 xiàngshàng

urgent [ˈəːdʒənt] ADJ 紧急的 jǐnjí de

US N ABBR (= **United States**) ▶**the US** 美国 Měiguó

us [ʌs] PRON 我们 wǒmen

USA N ABBR (= **United States of America**) ▶**the USA** 美国 Měiguó

use [n juːs, vb juːz] I N [c/u] (purpose) 用途 yòngtú [种 zhǒng] II VT 1 [+ object, tool] 使用 shǐyòng 2 [+ word, phrase] 应用 yìngyòng ▶**to make use of sth** 利用某物 lìyòng mǒuwù ▶**it's no use** 没用的 méiyòng de ▶**it's no use arguing/crying** etc 吵/哭 {等}是没用的 chǎo/kū {děng} shì méiyòng de ▶**to be no use (to sb)** (对某人)毫无用处 (duì mǒurén) háowú yòngchù ▶**she used to do it** 她过去是这么做的 tā guòqù shì zhème zuò de ▶**I didn't use to** or I **used not to worry so much** 我过去不这么焦虑 wǒ guòqù bù zhème jiāolǜ ▶**to be used to sth/to doing sth** 习惯于某事/做某事 xíguàn yú mǒushì/zuò mǒushì ▶**to get used to sth/to doing sth** 开始习惯于某事/做某事 kāishǐ xíguàn yú mǒushì/zuò mǒushì ▶ **use up** VT 用完 yòngwán

useful [ˈjuːsful] ADJ 有用的 yǒuyòng de ▶**to be useful for sth/doing sth** 对某事/做某事有帮助的 duì mǒushì/zuò mǒushì yǒu bāngzhù de

useless [ˈjuːslɪs] ADJ (pointless) 徒劳的 túláo de

user [ˈjuːzər] N [c] 使用者 shǐyòngzhě [位 wèi]

user-friendly [ˈjuːzəˈfrɛndlɪ] ADJ 易于使用的 yìyú shǐyòng de

usual [ˈjuːʒuəl] ADJ 惯常的 guàncháng de ▶**as usual** 像往常一样 xiàng wǎngcháng yīyàng ▶**warmer/colder than usual** 比平常暖和/冷 bǐ píngcháng nuǎnhe/lěng

usually [ˈjuːʒuəlɪ] ADV 通常地 tōngcháng de

V

vacancy ['veɪkənsɪ] N [c] (*job*) 空缺 kòngquē [个 gè]; (*hotel room*) 空房 kòngfáng [间 jiān] ▶ **"no vacancies"** "客满" "kèmǎn"

vacant ['veɪkənt] ADJ 空着的 kòngzhe de

vacation [və'keɪʃən] N [c] (*esp US*) 休假 xiūjià [次 cì] ▶ **to take a vacation** 休假 xiūjià ▶ **to be/go on vacation** 在/去度假 zài/qù dùjià

vaccinate ['væksɪneɪt] VT ▶ **to vaccinate sb (against sth)** 给某人接种疫苗(预防某疾病) gěi mǒurén jiēzhòng yìmiáo (yùfáng mǒu jíbìng)

vacuum cleaner N [c] (*also:* **vacuum**) 真空吸尘器 zhēnkōng xīchénqì [台 tái]

vague [veɪg] ADJ 不清楚的 bù qīngchǔ de

vain [veɪn] ADJ (+ *person*) 自负的 zìfù de ▶ **in vain** 徒然 túrán

Valentine's Day ['væləntaɪnz-] N [c/u] 情人节 Qíngrénjié [个 gè]

valid ['vælɪd] ADJ 有效的 yǒuxiào de

valley ['vælɪ] N [c] 山谷 shāngǔ [个 gè]

valuable ['væljuəbl] ADJ 贵重的 guìzhòng de

value ['vælju:] N 1 [c/u] (*financial worth*) 价值 jiàzhí [种 zhǒng] 2 [u] (*worth in relation to price*) 价格 jiàgé

van [væn] N [c] (*Aut*) 厢式运货车 xiāngshì yùnhuòchē [辆 liàng]

vandalism ['vændəlɪzəm] N [u] 蓄意破坏公物的行为 xùyì pòhuài gōngwù de xíngwéi

vandalize ['vændəlaɪz] VT 肆意毁坏 sìyì huǐhuài

vanish ['vænɪʃ] VI 消失 xiāoshī

variety [və'raɪətɪ] N 1 [u] (*diversity*) 多样性 duōyàngxìng 2 [s] (*range: of objects*) 若干 ruògān

various ['vɛərɪəs] ADJ 不同的 bùtóng de

vary ['vɛərɪ] I VT (*make changes to*) 更改 gēnggǎi II VI (*be different*) 有差异 yǒu chāyì

vase [vɑ:z, US veɪs] N [c] 花瓶 huāpíng [个 gè]

VCR N ABBR (= **video cassette recorder**) 录像机 lùxiàngjī

VDT (*US*) N ABBR (= **visual display terminal**) 视频显示装置 shìpín xiǎnshì zhuāngzhì

VDU (*Brit*) N ABBR (= **visual display unit**) 视频显示装置 shìpín xiǎnshì zhuāngzhì

veal [viːl] N [U] 小牛肉 xiǎoniúròu

vegan ['viːgən] N [c] 纯素食主义者 chún sùshí zhǔyìzhě [个 gè]

vegetable ['vɛdʒtəbl] N [c] 蔬菜 shūcài [种 zhǒng]

vegetarian [vɛdʒɪ'tɛərɪən] I N [c] 素食者 sùshízhě [个 gè] II ADJ [+ *diet, restaurant etc*] 素的 sù de

vehicle ['viːɪkl] N [c] 机动车 jīdòngchē [辆 liàng]

vein [veɪn] N [c] 静脉 jìngmài [条 tiáo]

velvet ['vɛlvɪt] N [c/U] 天鹅绒 tiān'éróng [块 kuài]

vending machine ['vɛndɪŋ-] N [c] 自动售货机 zìdòng shòuhuòjī [部 bù]

verb [vəːb] N [c] 动词 dòngcí [个 gè]

versus ['vəːsəs] PREP 对 duì

vertical ['vəːtɪkl] ADJ 垂直的 chuízhí de

very ['vɛrɪ] ADV 1 很 hěn 2 ▶ the **very end/beginning** 最终/一开始 zuìzhōng/yī kāishǐ ▶ **very much so** 确实如此 quèshí rúcǐ ▶ **very little** 极少的 jíshǎo de ▶ **there isn't very much (of...)** (…)不太多了 (…)bùtài duōle

vest [vɛst] N [c] 1 (*Brit: underwear*) 汗衫 hànshān [件 jiàn] 2 (*US: waistcoat*) 马甲 mǎjiǎ [件 jiàn]

vet [vɛt] N [c] (*esp Brit: veterinary surgeon*) 兽医 shòuyī [个 gè]

veterinarian [vɛtrɪ'nɛərɪən] (*US*)

N [c] 兽医 shòuyī [个 gè]

via ['vaɪə] PREP 经由 jīngyóu

vicar ['vɪkər] N [c] 教区牧师 jiàoqū mùshī [位 wèi]

vicious ['vɪʃəs] ADJ 1 [+ *attack, blow*] 剧烈的 jùliè de 2 [+ *person, dog*] 凶残的 xiōngcán de

victim ['vɪktɪm] N [c] 受害者 shòuhàizhě [个 gè] ▶ **to be the victim of** 成为…的受害者 chéngwéi...de shòuhàizhě

victory ['vɪktərɪ] N [c/U] 胜利 shènglì [次 cì]

video ['vɪdɪəʊ] I N 1 [c] (*film*) 录像 lùxiàng [段 duàn] 2 [U] (*system*) 录像 lùxiàng 3 [c] (*cassette*) 录像带 lùxiàngdài [盘 pán] 4 [c] (*esp Brit: machine*) 录像机 lùxiàngjī [台 tái] II VT (*esp Brit*) 录下 lùxià

video camera N [c] 摄像机 shèxiàngjī [台 tái]

video game N [c] 电子游戏 diànzǐ yóuxì [种 zhǒng]

video recorder N [c] 录像机 lùxiàngjī [台 tái]

Vietnam ['vjɛt'næm] N 越南 Yuènán

Vietnamese [vjɛtnə'miːz] (*pl* **Vietnamese**) I ADJ 越南的 Yuènán de II N 1 [c] (*person*) 越南人 Yuènánrén [个 gè] 2 [U] (*language*) 越南语 Yuènányǔ

view [vjuː] N [c] 1 景色 jǐngsè [道 dào] 2 (*opinion*) 看法 kànfǎ [种 zhǒng]

village ['vɪlɪdʒ] N [c] 村庄 cūnzhuāng [个 gè]

vine [vaɪn] N [c] 葡萄藤

pútáoténg [条 tiáo]

vinegar ['vɪnɪgəʳ] N [c/u] 醋 cù [瓶 píng]

vineyard ['vɪnjɑːd] N [c] 葡萄园 pútáoyuán [座 zuò]

violence ['vaɪələns] N [u] 暴力 bàolì

violent ['vaɪələnt] ADJ 暴力的 bàolì de

violin [vaɪə'lɪn] N [c] 小提琴 xiǎotíqín [把 bǎ]

violinist [vaɪə'lɪnɪst] N [c] 小提琴手 xiǎotíqínshǒu [个 gè]

virgin ['vəːdʒɪn] N [c] 处女 chǔnǚ [个 gè]

Virgo ['vəːgəu] N [u] (sign) 处女座 Chǔnǚ Zuò

virus ['vaɪərəs] (Med, Comput) N [c] 病毒 bìngdú [种 zhǒng]

visa ['viːzə] N [c] 签证 qiānzhèng [个 gè]

visit ['vɪzɪt] I N [c] 1 (to person) 拜访 bàifǎng [次 cì] 2 (to place) 访问 fǎngwèn [次 cì] II VT 1 [+ person] 拜访 bàifǎng 2 [+ place] 游览 yóulǎn
▸ **visit with** (US) VT FUS 拜访 bàifǎng

visitor ['vɪzɪtəʳ] N [c] 1 (to city, country) 游客 yóukè [位 wèi] 2 (to person, house) 来客 láikè [位 wèi]

visual ['vɪzjuəl] ADJ 视觉的 shìjué de

vital ['vaɪtl] ADJ 至关重要的 zhìguān zhòngyào de

vitamin ['vɪtəmɪn, US 'vaɪtəmɪn] N [c] 维生素 wéishēngsù [种 zhǒng]

vivid ['vɪvɪd] ADJ 1 生动的

shēngdòng de 2 [+ colour, light] 鲜艳的 xiānyàn de

vocabulary [vəu'kæbjulərɪ] N 1 [c/u] [of person] 词汇量 cíhuìliàng 2 [c] [of language] 词汇 cíhuì [个 gè]

vodka ['vɔdkə] N [c/u] 伏特加酒 fútèjiā jiǔ [瓶 píng]

voice [vɔɪs] N [c] 嗓音 sǎngyīn [种 zhǒng]

voice mail N [u] 语音留言 yǔyīn liúyán

volcano [vɔl'keɪnəu] (pl **volcanoes**) N [c] 火山 huǒshān [座 zuò]

volleyball ['vɔlɪbɔːl] N [u] 排球 páiqiú

volume ['vɔljuːm] N [u] 音量 yīnliàng ▸ **volume one/two** [of book] 第一／二册 dìyī/èrcè

voluntary ['vɔləntərɪ] ADJ 1 (not compulsory) 自愿的 zìyuàn de 2 [+ work, worker] 志愿的 zhìyuàn de

volunteer [vɔlən'tɪəʳ] N [c] (unpaid worker) 志愿者 zhìyuànzhě [个 gè] ▸ **to volunteer to do sth** 自愿做某事 zìyuàn zuò mǒushì

vomit ['vɔmɪt] I N [u] 呕吐物 ǒutùwù II VT 吐 tù III VI 呕吐 ǒutù

vote [vəut] I N [c] 选票 xuǎnpiào [张 zhāng] II VI 投票 tóupiào ▸ **to take a vote on sth** 就某事进行表决 jiù mǒushì jìnxíng biǎojué ▸ **to vote for sb** 投某人票 tóu mǒurén piào ▸ **to vote for/against sth** 投票支持／反对某事 tóupiào zhīchí/

fǎnduì mǒushì

voucher ['vautʃər] N [c] 代金券 dàijīnquàn [张 zhāng]

vowel ['vauəl] N [c] 元音 yuányīn [个 gè]

wage [weɪdʒ] N [c] (also: **wages**) 工资 gōngzī [份 fèn]

waist [weɪst] N [c] 1 腰 yāo [个 gè] 2 [of clothing] 腰身 yāoshēn [个 gè]

waistcoat ['weɪskəut] (Brit) N [c] 马甲 mǎjiǎ [件 jiàn]

wait [weɪt] I vi 等待 děngdài II N [c] (interval) 等待时间 děngdài shíjiān [段 duàn] ▶**to wait for sb/sth** 等候某人/某物 děnghòu mǒurén/mǒuwù ▶**wait a minute!** 等一下! děngyīxià! ▶**to keep sb waiting** 让某人等着 ràng mǒurén děngzhe

waiter ['weɪtər] N [c] 男服务员 nán fúwùyuán [位 wèi]

waiting list ['weɪtɪŋ-] N [c] 等候者名单 děnghòuzhě míngdān

[个 gè]

waiting room ['weɪtɪŋ-] N [c] 等候室 děnghòushì [间 jiān]

waitress ['weɪtrɪs] N [c] 女服务员 nǚ fúwùyuán [位 wèi]

wake [weɪk] (*pt* **woke** *or* **waked**, *pp* **woken** *or* **waked**)
▶ **wake up I** VT 唤醒 huànxǐng **II** VI 醒来 xǐnglái

Wales [weɪlz] N 威尔士 Wēi'ěrshì
▶ **the Prince of Wales** 威尔士王子 Wēi'ěrshì Wángzǐ

walk [wɔːk] **I** N [c] 散步 sànbù [次 cì] **II** VI 走 zǒu **III** VT [+ *distance*] 走 zǒu ▶ **it's 10 minutes' walk from here** 从这儿走有10分钟的路程 cóng zhèr zǒu yǒu shífēnzhōng de lùchéng ▶ **to go for a walk** 去散步 qù sànbù

walking ['wɔːkɪŋ] N [u] 步行 bùxíng

wall [wɔːl] N [c] **1** (*of building, room*) 墙 qiáng [堵 dǔ] **2** (*around garden, field*) 围墙 wéiqiáng [圈 quān]

wallet ['wɒlɪt] N [c] 钱包 qiánbāo [个 gè]

wallpaper ['wɔːlpeɪpər] N [c/u] 墙纸 qiángzhǐ [张 zhāng]

walnut ['wɔːlnʌt] N [c] (*nut*) 核桃 hétao [个 gè]

wander ['wɒndər] VI 漫游 mànyóu

want [wɒnt] VT **1** (*wish for*) 想要 xiǎngyào **2** (*inf: need*) 需要 xūyào ▶ **to want to do sth** 想要做某事 xiǎngyào zuò mǒushì ▶ **to want sb to do sth** 希望某人做某事 xīwàng mǒurén zuò mǒushì

war [wɔːr] N [c/u] 战争 zhànzhēng

[场 chǎng]

wardrobe ['wɔːdrəub] N [c] 衣橱 yīchú [个 gè]

warehouse ['wɛəhaus] N [c] 仓库 cāngkù [间 jiān]

warm [wɔːm] ADJ **1** [+ *meal, soup, water*] 温热的 wēnrè de; [+ *day, weather*] 暖和的 nuǎnhe de **2** [+ *clothes, blankets*] 保暖的 bǎonuǎn de **3** [+ *applause, welcome*] 热情的 rèqíng de ▶ **it's warm** 天很暖和 tiān hěn nuǎnhe ▶ **are you warm enough?** 你觉得够暖和吗？ nǐ juéde gòu nuǎnhe ma ▶ **warm up I** VI [*athlete, pianist*] 热身 rèshēn **II** VT [+ *food*] 加热 jiārè

warn [wɔːn] VT ▶ **to warn sb that** 警告某人… jǐnggào mǒurén… ▶ **to warn sb not to do sth** 告诫某人不要做某事 gàojiè mǒurén bùyào zuò mǒushì

warning ['wɔːnɪŋ] N **1** [c] (*action, words, sign*) 警告 jǐnggào [个 gè] **2** [c/u] (*notice*) 预兆 yùzhào [个 gè]

was [wɒz] PT *of* **be**

wash [wɒʃ] **I** VT 洗 xǐ **II** VI [*person*] 洗净 xǐjìng ▶ **to wash one's face/hands/hair** 洗脸/手/头发 xǐliǎn/shǒu/tóufa ▶ **to have a wash** 洗一下 xǐyīxià
▶ **wash up** VI **1** (*Brit: wash dishes*) 洗餐具 xǐ cānjù **2** (*US: have a wash*) 洗一洗 xǐyīxǐ

washbasin ['wɒʃbeɪsn] N [c] 脸盆 liǎnpén [个 gè]

washcloth ['wɒʃklɔθ] (*US*) N [c] 毛巾 máojīn [条 tiáo]

washing ['wɒʃɪŋ] N [u] **1** (*dirty*) 待

洗衣物 dàixǐ yīwù **2** (clean) 洗好的衣物 xǐhǎo de yīwù ▶**to do the washing** 洗衣服 xǐ yīfu

washing machine N [c] 洗衣机 xǐyījī [台 tái]

washing powder (Brit) N [c/u] 洗衣粉 xǐyīfěn [袋 dài]

wasn't ['wɒznt] = **was not**

wasp [wɒsp] N [c] 黄蜂 huángfēng [只 zhī]

waste [weɪst] I N **1** [s/u] [of resources, food, money] 浪费 làngfèi **2** [u] (rubbish) 废料 fèiliào II VT [+ money, energy, time] 浪费 làngfèi; [+ opportunity] 失去 shīqù ▶**it's a waste of time** 这是浪费时间 zhèshì làngfèi shíjiān

wastepaper basket ['weɪstpeɪpə-] (Brit) N [c] 废纸篓 fèizhǐlǒu [个 gè]

watch [wɒtʃ] I N [c] 手表 shǒubiǎo [块 kuài] II VT **1** (look at) 注视 zhùshì; [+ match, programme, TV] 看 kàn **2** (pay attention to) 关注 guānzhù III VI 注视 zhùshì ▶**to watch sb do/doing sth** 看着某人做某事 kànzhe mǒurén zuò mǒushì
▶**watch out** VI 提防 dīfang
▶**watch out!** (inf) 小心！xiǎoxīn!

water ['wɔːtər] I N [u] 水 shuǐ II VT [+ plant] 给…浇水 gěi…jiāoshuǐ ▶**a drink of water** 一杯水 yībēishuǐ

waterfall ['wɔːtəfɔːl] N [c] 瀑布 pùbù [条 tiáo]

watermelon ['wɔːtəmɛlən] N [c] 西瓜 xīguā [个 gè]

waterproof ['wɔːtəpruːf] ADJ 防

水的 fángshuǐ de

water-skiing ['wɔːtəskiːɪŋ] N [u] ▶**to go water-skiing** 去滑水 qùhuáshuǐ

wave [weɪv] I N [c] **1** (of hand) 挥动 huīdòng [下 xià] **2** (on water) 波浪 bōlàng [个 gè] II VI 挥手示意 huīshǒu shìyì III VT [+ hand] 挥 huī ▶**to wave goodbye to sb, wave sb goodbye** 向某人挥手告别 xiàng mǒurén huīshǒu gàobié

wax [wæks] N [u] 蜡 là

way [weɪ] I N **1** [c] (route) 路 lù [条 tiáo] **2** [s] (distance) 距离 jùlí **3** [c] (direction) 方向 fāngxiàng [个 gè] **4** [c] (manner) 方式 fāngshì [种 zhǒng] **5** [c] (method) 方法 fāngfǎ [个 gè] II **ways** NPL (habits) 习俗 xísú ▶**"which way?" — "this way"** "往哪边？" "这边" "wǎng nǎbiān?" "zhèbiān" ▶**on the way** 在路上 zài lùshàng ▶**it's a long way away** 离这儿很远 lí zhèr hěnyuǎn ▶**to lose one's way** 迷路 mílù ▶**the way back** 回去的路 huíqù de lù ▶**to give way** (break, collapse) 倒塌 dǎotā ▶**the wrong way round** (Brit) 刚好相反 gānghǎo xiāngfǎn ▶**in a way** 在某种程度上 zài mǒuzhǒng chéngdù shàng ▶**by the way...** 顺便提一下… shùnbiàn tíyíxià… ▶**"way in"** (Brit) "入口" "rùkǒu" ▶**"way out"** (Brit) "出口" "chūkǒu" ▶**way of life** 生活方式 shēnghuó fāngshì ▶**do it this way** 这么做 zhème zuò

we [wiː] PL PRON 我们 wǒmen

weak [wiːk] ADJ **1** 虚弱的 xūruò

de 2 [+ *tea, coffee, substance*] 淡的 dàn de

wealthy ['wεlθɪ] ADJ 富有的 fùyǒu de

weapon ['wεpən] N [c] 武器 wǔqì [种 zhǒng]

wear [wεər] (*pt* **wore**, *pp* **worn**) VT 穿着 chuānzhe; [+ *spectacles, jewellery*] 戴着 dàizhe ►**I can't decide what to wear** 我拿不定主意该穿什么 wǒ nábùdìng zhǔyì gāi chuān shénme
►**wear out** VI 耗尽 hàojìn

weather ['wεðər] N [U] 天气 tiānqì ►**what's the weather like?** 天气怎么样? tiānqì zěnmeyàng?

weather forecast N [c] 天气预报 tiānqì yùbào [个 gè]

web [wεb] N [c] ►**the Web** 互联网 hùliánwǎng [个 gè] ►**on the Web** 在互联网上 zài hùliánwǎng shàng

web page N [c] 网页 wǎngyè [个 gè]

website ['wεbsaɪt] N [c] 网址 wǎngzhǐ [个 gè]

we'd [wiːd] = **we had, we would**

wedding ['wεdɪŋ] N [c] 婚礼 hūnlǐ [场 chǎng]

Wednesday ['wεdnzdɪ] N [c/U] 星期三 xīngqīsān [个 gè]; *see also* **Tuesday**

week [wiːk] N [c] 星期 xīngqī [个 gè] ►**this/next/last week** 本/下/上周 běn/xià/shàngzhōu ►**once/twice a week** 一周一次/两次 yìzhōu yīcì/liǎngcì

weekday ['wiːkdeɪ] N [c] 工作日

gōngzuòrì [个 gè] ►**on weekdays** 在工作日 zài gōngzuòrì

weekend [wiːk'εnd] N [c] 周末 zhōumò [个 gè] ►**at the weekend** 在周末 zài zhōumò ►**this/next/last weekend** 这个周末/下周末/上周末 zhègè zhōumò/xiàzhōu mò/shàngzhōu mò

weigh [weɪ] I VT 称…的重量 chēng…de zhòngliàng II VI ►**she weighs 50kg** 她的体重为50公斤 tāde tǐzhòng wéi wǔshí gōngjīn

weight [weɪt] I N [U] 重量 zhòngliàng II **weights** NPL (*in gym*) 举重器械 jǔzhòng qìxiè ►**to lose weight** 体重减轻 tǐzhòng jiǎnqīng

welcome ['wεlkəm] I N [c] 欢迎 huānyíng II VT 欢迎 huānyíng ►**welcome to Beijing!** 欢迎到北京来! huānyíng dào Běijīng lái! ►**"thank you" — "you're welcome!"** "谢谢你。" "别客气!" "xièxie nǐ" "bié kèqi!" ►**to give sb a warm welcome** 热烈欢迎某人 rèliè huānyíng mǒurén

well [wεl] I N [c] 井 jǐng [口 kǒu] II ADV 1 (*to a high standard*) 好 hǎo 2 (*completely*) 充分地 chōngfèn de III ADJ (*healthy*) 身体好的 shēntǐ hǎo de IV INT 唔 ńg ►**to do well** [*person*] 做得好 zuòde hǎo; [*business*] 进展顺利 jìnzhǎn shùlì ►**well done!** 棒极了! bàngjí le! ►**as well** (*in addition*) 也 yě ►**I don't feel well** 我觉得不舒服 wǒ juéde bù shūfu ►**get well soon!** 早日康复! zǎorì kāngfù! ►**well,**

as I was saying... 那么，像我
刚才所说的… nàme, xiàng wǒ
gāngcái suǒshuō de...

we'll [wiːl] = **we will, we shall**

well-known ['wɛl'nəun] ADJ
[+ person] 有名的 yǒumíng de;
[+ fact, brand] 众所周知的 zhòng
suǒ zhōu zhī de

well-off ['wɛl'ɔf] ADJ 富裕的
fùyù de

Welsh [wɛlʃ] I ADJ 威尔士的
Wēi'ěrshì de II N [U] (language) 威
尔士语 Wēi'ěrshìyǔ III NPL ▶the
Welsh 威尔士人 Wēi'ěrshìrén

went [wɛnt] PT of **go**

were [wəːʳ] PT of **be**

we're [wɪəʳ] = **we are**

weren't [wəːnt] = **were not**

west [wɛst] I N 1 [U/s] (direction)
西方 xīfāng 2 ▶the West (Pol) 西
方国家 xīfāng guójiā II ADJ 西部
的 xībù de III ADV 向西 xiàng xī
▶west of ⋯以西 ...yǐxī

western ['wɛstən] I ADJ (Geo) 西
部的 xībù de II N [C] 西部影片
xībù yǐngpiàn [部 bù]

West Indian I ADJ 西印度群岛的
Xīyìndù Qúndǎo de II N [C] 西印
度群岛人 Xīyìndù Qúndǎorén
[个 gè]

West Indies [-'ɪndɪz] NPL ▶the
West Indies 西印度群岛 Xīyìndù
Qúndǎo

wet [wɛt] ADJ 1 [+ person, clothes]
湿的 shī de; [+ paint, cement,
glue] 未干的 wèigān de 2 (rainy)
[+ weather, day] 多雨的 duōyǔ de
▶to get wet 弄湿 nòngshī

we've [wiːv] = **we have**

whale [weɪl] N [C] 鲸 jīng [头 tóu]

◯ KEYWORD

what [wɔt] I PRON 1 什么 shénme
▶**what is happening?** 发生了什
么事？fāshēng le shénme shì?
▶**what is it?** 那是什么？nàshì
shénme? ▶**what are you doing?**
你在干什么？nǐ zài gànshénme?
▶**what did you say?** 你说什么？
níshuō shénme?
2 (in indirect questions/speech
subject, object) 什么 shénme ▶**do
you know what's happening?**
你知道发生了什么事吗？nǐ
zhīdào fāshēng le shénme shì
ma?
3 (relative) 所…的 suǒ...de ▶**I
saw what was on the table** 我
看见了桌上的东西 wǒ kànjiàn le
zhuōshàng de dōngxi
II ADJ 1 什么 shénme ▶**what
time is it?** 几点了？jǐdiǎn le?
▶**what size is this shirt?** 这件衬
衫是几码的？zhèjiàn chènshān
shì jǐmǎ de?
2 (in exclamations) 多么 duōme
▶**what a mess!** 真是一团糟！
zhēnshì yītuán zāo! ▶**what a
lovely day!** 多么好的天气啊！
duōme hǎo de tiānqì a!
III INT 什么 shénme ▶**what,
no coffee!** 什么，没咖啡了！
shénme, méi kāfēi le!

whatever [wɔt'ɛvəʳ] I ADV
(whatsoever) 任何 rènhé II PRON
▶**do whatever is necessary/you**

want 做任何必要的/你想做的事情 zuò rènhé bìyào de/nǐ xiǎngzuò de shìqíng

wheat [wiːt] N [U] 小麦 xiǎomài

wheel [wiːl] N [c] **1** 轮 lún [个 gè] **2** (*also*: **steering wheel**) 方向盘 fāngxiàngpán [个 gè]

wheelchair [ˈwiːltʃɛəʳ] N [c] 轮椅 lúnyǐ [部 bù]

KEYWORD

when [wɛn] I ADV (*interrogative*) 什么时候 shénme shíhou ▶**when did it happen?** 什么时候发生的? shénme shíhou fāshēng de? II PRON (*relative*) ▶**the day when** 当⋯的那一天 dāng...de nà yī tiān III CONJ (*in time clauses*) 当⋯时 dāng...shí ▶**be careful when you cross the road** 过马路时要当心 guò mǎlù shí yào dāngxīn ▶**she was reading when I came in** 当我进来时她正在阅读 dāng wǒ jìnlái shí tā zhèngzài yuèdú ▶**I know when it happened** 我知道什么时候发生的 wǒ zhīdào shénme shíhou fāshēng de

where [wɛəʳ] I ADV (*in or to what place*) 在哪里 zài nǎlǐ II CONJ (*the place in which*) 哪里 nǎli ▶**where are you from?** 你是哪里人? nǐ shì nǎlǐ rén?

whether [ˈwɛðəʳ] CONJ 是否 shìfǒu ▶**I don't know whether to accept or not** 我不知道是接受还是不接受 wǒ bù zhīdào shì jiēshòu

háishì bù jiēshòu

KEYWORD

which [wɪtʃ] I ADJ **1** (*interrogative singular*) 哪个 nǎge; (*plural*) 哪些 nǎxiē ▶**which picture do you want?** 你要哪幅画? nǐ yào nǎfú huà? ▶**which one/ones?** 哪个/些? nǎgè/xiē? **2** (*in indirect questions/speech singular*) 哪个 nǎge; (*plural*) 哪些 nǎxiē ▶**he asked which book I wanted** 他问我要哪本书 tā wènwǒ yào nǎběn shū II PRON **1** (*interrogative subject, object*) 哪个 nǎge ▶**which of these is yours?** 这些中的哪个是你的? zhèxiē zhōng de nǎgè shì nǐde? **2** (*in indirect questions/speech subject, object*) 哪个 nǎge ▶**ask him which of the models is the best** 问他哪种型号是最好的 wèn tā nǎzhǒng xínghào shì zuìhǎo de **3** (*relative subject, object*) ⋯的那个⋯ ...de nàge... ▶**the shot which you heard/which killed him** 你听到的那一枪/杀死他的那一枪 nǐ tīngdào de nàyīqiāng/shāsǐ tā de nàyīqiāng

while [waɪl] I N [s] 一会儿 yīhuìr II CONJ **1** (*during the time that*) 在⋯时 zài...shí **2** (*although*) 虽然 suīrán ▶**While I'm very fond of him, I don't actually want to marry him.** 虽然我很喜欢他，但我真的不想嫁给他。 suīrán wǒ hěn xǐhuān tā, dàn wǒ zhēnde bùxiǎng jiàgěi tā. ▶**for a while** 有一会儿 yǒu yīhuǐr

whisky, (US) **whiskey** ['wɪskɪ] N [c/U] 威士忌酒 wēishìjì jiǔ [瓶 píng]

whisper ['wɪspər] VI 低语 dīyǔ

whistle ['wɪsl] I VI 吹口哨 chuī kǒushào II N [c] **1** (device) 哨子 shàozi [个 gè] **2** (sound) 口哨声 kǒushàoshēng [声 shēng]

white [waɪt] I ADJ **1** 雪白的 xuěbái de; [+ wine] 白的 bái de **2** [+ coffee] 加奶的 jiā nǎi de **3** [+ person] 白种人的 báizhǒngrén de II N [U] (colour) 白色 báisè

⬤ KEYWORD

who [hu:] PRON **1** 谁 shéi ▶**who is it?** 是谁? shì shuí? ▶**who did you discuss it with?** 你和谁讨论了? nǐ hé shuí tǎolùn le? **2** (in indirect questions/speech subject, object, after preposition) 谁 shéi ▶**I told her who I was** 我告诉了她我是谁 wǒ gàosù le tā wǒ shì shuí ▶**I don't know who he gave it to** 我不知道他把它给了谁 wǒ bù zhīdào tā bǎ tā gěile shuí **3** (relative subject, object) …的那个… …de nàge… ▶**the girl who came in** 进来的那个女孩 jìnlai de nàge nǚhái ▶**the man who we met in Sydney** 我们在悉尼遇到的那个男子 wǒmen zài Xīní yùdào de nàge nánzǐ

whole [həʊl] I ADJ 整个的 zhěnggè de II N **1** [c] (entirety) 整体 zhěngtǐ [个 gè] **2** ▶**the whole of sth** 某物的全部 mǒuwù de quánbù [个 gè] ▶**the whole (of the) time** 所有的时间 suǒyǒu de shíjiān ▶**on the whole** 大体上 dàtǐ shàng

whom [hu:m] (frm) PRON **1** (interrogative) 谁 shéi **2** (relative) 所…的那个… suǒ…de nàge… ▶**the man whom I saw/to whom I spoke** 我见到的/我跟他说话的那个男的 wǒ jiàndào de/wǒ gēn tā shuō guò huà de nàge nánde

whose [hu:z] I ADJ **1** (interrogative) 谁的 shéi de **2** (relative) …的 …de II PRON 谁的 shéi de ▶**whose is this?** 这是谁的? zhè shì shéi de? ▶**whose book is this/coats are these?** 这本书是谁的/这些外套是谁的? zhèběnshū shì shuíde/zhèxiē wàitào shì shuíde? ▶**the woman whose car was stolen** 汽车给偷走的那个女的 qìchē gěi tōuzǒu de nàgè nǚde

⬤ KEYWORD

why [waɪ] I ADV 为什么 wèishénme ▶**why is he always late?** 为什么他总是迟到? wèishénme tā zǒngshì chídào? ▶**why not?** 为什么不呢? wèishénme bù ne? ▶**I don't know why** 我不知道为什么 wǒ bù zhīdào wèishénme II CONJ 为什么 wèishénme ▶**I wonder why he said that** 我想知道他为什么那么说 wǒxiǎng zhīdào tā wèishénme nàme shuō

▶**the reason why he did it** 他那么做的原因 tā nàme zuò de yuányīn

wicked ['wɪkɪd] ADJ (evil) [+ person] 邪恶的 xié'è de; [+ act, crime] 罪恶的 zuì'è de

wide [waɪd] I ADJ 1 宽的 kuān de 2 [+ range, variety, publicity, choice] 广泛的 guǎngfàn de II ADV ▶**to open sth wide** 张大某物 zhāngdà mǒuwù

widow ['wɪdəu] N [c] 寡妇 guǎfù [个 gè]

widower ['wɪdəuəʳ] N [c] 鳏夫 guānfū [个 gè]

width [wɪdθ] N [c/u] 宽度 kuāndù [个 gè]

wife [waɪf] (pl **wives**) N [c] 妻子 qīzi [个 gè]

wild [waɪld] ADJ 1 野生的 yěshēng de 2 [+ person, behaviour] 狂野的 kuángyě de

wildlife ['waɪldlaɪf] N [u] 野生动物 yěshēng dòngwù

⬤ KEYWORD

will [wɪl] I AUX VB 1 ▶**I will call you tonight** 我今晚会给你打电话的 wǒ jīnwǎn huì gěi nǐ dǎ diànhuà de ▶**what will you do next?** 下面你要做什么？xiàmiàn nǐ yào zuò shénme?
2 (in conjectures, predictions) 该是 gāishì ▶**he'll be there by now** 他现在该到了 tā xiànzài gāidào le
3 (in commands, requests, offers) ▶**will you be quiet!** 你安静点！

nǐ ānjìng diǎn!
II N 1 (volition) 意志 yìzhì ▶**against his will** 违背他的意愿 wéibèi tāde yìyuàn
2 (testament) 遗嘱 yízhǔ [个 gè] ▶**to make a will** 立遗嘱 lì yízhǔ

willing ['wɪlɪŋ] ADJ ▶**to be willing to do sth** 愿意做某事 yuànyì zuò mǒushì

win [wɪn] (pt, pp **won**) I N [c] 胜利 shènglì [个 gè] II VT 1 在…中获胜 zài…zhōng huòshèng 2 [+ prize, medal] 赢得 yíngdé III VI 获胜 huòshèng

wind [wɪnd] N [c/u] 风 fēng [阵 zhèn]

window ['wɪndəu] N [c] 1 窗户 chuānghu [扇 shàn]; (in shop) 橱窗 chúchuāng [个 gè]; (in car, train) 窗 chuāng [个 gè] 2 (Comput) 视窗 shìchuāng [个 gè]

windscreen ['wɪndskri:n] (Brit) N [c] 挡风玻璃 dǎngfēng bōlí [块 kuài]

windshield ['wɪndʃi:ld] (US) N [c] 挡风玻璃 dǎngfēng bōlí [块 kuài]

windsurfing ['wɪndsə:fɪŋ] N [u] 帆板运动 fānbǎn yùndòng

windy ['wɪndɪ] ADJ [+ weather, day] 有风的 yǒufēng de ▶**it's windy** 今天风很大 jīntiān fēng hěndà

wine [waɪn] N [c/u] 葡萄酒 pútáojiǔ [瓶 píng]

wing [wɪŋ] N [c] 1 翅膀 chìbǎng [个 gè]; [of aeroplane] 机翼 jīyì [个 gè] 2 [of building] 侧楼 cèlóu [座 zuò]

wink [wɪŋk] VI [person] 眨眼

zhǎyǎn ▶**to give sb a wink, wink at sb** 向某人眨了眨眼 xiàng mǒurén zhǎlezhǎ yǎn

winner [ˈwɪnər] N [c] 获胜者 huòshèngzhě [位 wèi]

winter [ˈwɪntər] I N [c/u] 冬季 dōngjì [个 gè] II vi 过冬 guòdōng ▶**in (the) winter** 在冬季 zài dōngjì

wipe [waɪp] vt (dry, clean) 擦 cā ▶**to wipe one's nose** 擦鼻子 cā bízi
▶**wipe up** vt 把…擦干净 bǎ…cā gānjìng

wire [ˈwaɪər] N [c] (Elec: uninsulated) 电线 diànxiàn [根 gēn]; (insulated) 电缆 diànlǎn [条 tiáo]

wise [waɪz] ADJ 睿智的 ruìzhì de

wish [wɪʃ] I N [c] 愿望 yuànwàng [个 gè] II vt 但愿 dànyuàn ▶**best wishes** 良好的祝愿 liánghǎo de zhùyuàn ▶**with best wishes** 祝好 zhùhǎo ▶**give her my best wishes** 代我向她致意 dài wǒ xiàng tā zhìyì ▶**to wish to do sth** 想要做某事 xiǎngyào zuò mǒushì

◯ KEYWORD

with [wɪð, wɪθ] PREP **1** 和…在一起 hé…zài yīqǐ ▶**I was with him** 我和他在一起 wǒ hé tā zài yīqǐ ▶**I'll be with you in a minute** 请稍等 qǐng shāoděng ▶**we stayed with friends** 我们和朋友们呆在一起 wǒmen hé péngyǒumen dāizài yīqǐ
2 (indicating feature, possession) 有 yǒu ▶**the man with the grey hat/blue eyes** 戴着灰帽子/有蓝眼睛的男人 dàizhe huī màozi/yǒu lán yǎnjīng de nánrén
3 (indicating means, substance) 用 yòng ▶**to walk with a stick** 拄着拐杖走 zhǔzhe guǎizhàng zǒu ▶**to fill sth with water** 在某物里装满水 zài mǒuwù lǐ zhuāngmǎn shuǐ
4 (indicating cause) ▶**red with anger** 气得涨红了脸 qìde zhànghóngle liǎn

without [wɪˈðaut] PREP 没有 méiyǒu ▶**without a coat** 未穿外套 wèichuān wàitào ▶**without speaking** 不曾说话 bùcéng shuōhuà

witness [ˈwɪtnɪs] N [c] (gen, also in court) 目击者 mùjīzhě [位 wèi]

witty [ˈwɪtɪ] ADJ 诙谐的 huīxié de

wives [waɪvz] NPL of **wife**

woke [wəuk] PT of **wake**

woken [ˈwəukn] PP of **wake**

wolf [wulf] (pl **wolves** [wulvz]) N [c] 狼 láng [条 tiáo]

woman [ˈwumən] (pl **women**) N [c] 妇女 fùnǚ [位 wèi]

won [wʌn] PT, PP of **win**

wonder [ˈwʌndər] I vt ▶**to wonder whether/why etc** 想知道是否/为什么{等} xiǎng zhīdào shìfǒu/wèishénme {děng} II vi 感到奇怪 gǎndào qíguài

wonderful [ˈwʌndəful] ADJ 绝妙的 juémiào de

won't [wəunt] = **will not**

wood [wud] N **1** [u] 木材 mùcái **2** [c] (forest) 树林 shùlín [棵 kē]

wool [wul] N [U] 羊毛 yángmáo

word [wəːd] N 1 [c] 词 cí [个 gè] 2 [s] (*promise*) 诺言 nuòyán ▶**what's the word for "pen" in French?** "钢笔" 这个词在法语里怎么说? "gāngbǐ"zhègè cí zài Fǎyǔ lǐ zěnme shuō? ▶**in other words** 换句话说 huàn jù huà shuō

word processing [-'prəusɛsɪŋ] N [U] 文字处理 wénzì chǔlǐ

word processor [-prəusɛsəʳ] N [c] (*machine*) 文字处理器 wénzì chǔlǐqì [个 gè]

wore [wɔːʳ] PT *of* **wear**

work [wəːk] I N 1 [U] (*tasks, duties*) 事情 shìqing 2 [U] (*job*) 工作 gōngzuò II VI 1 (*have job, do tasks*) 工作 gōngzuò 2 (*function*) 运行 yùnxíng 3 (*be successful*) [*idea, method*] 起作用 qǐ zuòyong ▶**to go to work** 去上班 qù shàngbān ▶**to be out of work** 失业 shīyè ▶**to work hard** 努力工作 nǔlì gōngzuò
▶ **work out** I VI (*Sport*) 锻炼 duànliàn II VT [+ *answer, solution*] 努力找出 nǔlì zhǎochū; [+ *plan, details*] 制订出 zhìdìng chū

worker ['wəːkəʳ] N [c] 工人 gōngrén [位 wèi] ▶**a hard/good worker** 工作努力/良好的人 gōngzuò nǔlì/liánghǎo de rén

work experience N [U] 工作经历 gōngzuò jīnglì

workstation ['wəːksteɪʃən] N [c] 1 (*desk*) 工作台 gōngzuòtái [个 gè] 2 (*computer*) 工作站 gōngzuòzhàn [个 gè]

world [wəːld] I N ▶**the world** 世界 shìjiè II CPD [+ *champion, record, power, authority*] 世界 shìjiè; [+ *tour*] 环球 huánqiú ▶**all over the world** 全世界 quán shìjiè

World-Wide Web [wəːld'waɪd-] N ▶**the World-Wide Web** 万维网 Wànwéiwǎng

worn [wɔːn] PP *of* **wear**

worried ['wʌrɪd] ADJ 闷闷不乐的 mènmèn bù lè de ▶**to be worried about sth/sb** 担心某事/某人 dānxīn mǒushì/mǒurén

worry ['wʌrɪ] I N 1 [U] (*feeling of anxiety*) 忧虑 yōulù 2 [c] (*cause of anxiety*) 担心 dānxīn [种 zhǒng] II VT 使担心 shǐ dānxīn III VI 担心 dānxīn

worse [wəːs] I ADJ 更坏的 gènghuài de II ADV (*comparative of badly*) 更糟地 gèngzāo de ▶**to get worse** 逐渐恶化 zhújiàn èhuà

worst [wəːst] I ADJ 最坏的 zuì huài de II ADV (*superlative of badly*) 最糟地 zuì zāo de III N [s/U] 最坏的事 zuì huài de shì ▶**at worst** 在最坏的情况下 zài zuìhuài de qíngkuàng xià

worth [wəːθ] I N [U] 价值 jiàzhí II ADJ ▶**to be worth £50** 值 50英镑 zhí wǔshí yīngbàng ▶**it's worth it** 这是值得的 zhèshì zhídé de ▶**400 dollars' worth of damage** 价值400美元的损失 jiàzhí sìbǎi měiyuán de sǔnshī ▶**it would be (well) worth doing...** (很)值得做… (hěn) zhídé zuò...

● KEYWORD

would [wud] AUX VB 1 ▶ **I would love to go to Italy** 我很愿意去意大利 wǒ hěn yuànyì qù Yìdàlì ▶ **I'm sure he wouldn't do that** 我确定他不会那么做的 wǒ quèdìng tā bùhuì nàme zuòde **2** (in offers, invitations, requests) ▶ **would you like a biscuit?** 你要来块饼干吗? nǐ yào lái kuài bǐnggān ma? ▶ **would you ask him to come in?** 你要叫他进来吗? nǐ yào jiàotā jìnlai ma? **3** (be willing to) ▶ **she wouldn't help me** 她不愿意帮助我 tā bù yuànyì bāngzhù wǒ **4** (in indirect speech) ▶ **he said he would be at home later** 他说他晚点儿会在家的 tā shuō tā wǎndiǎnr huì zàijiā de

wouldn't ['wudnt] = **would not**

wrap [ræp] VT (cover) 包 bāo ▶ **wrap up** VT (pack) 包起来 bāo qǐlái

wrapping paper ['ræpɪŋ-] N [U] (gift wrap) 包装纸 bāozhuāngzhǐ

wreck [rɛk] I N [c] **1** (wreckage: of vehicle, ship) 残骸 cánhái [个 gè] **2** (US: accident) 事故 shìgù [次 cì] II VT [+ car, building] 摧毁 cuīhuǐ

wrestling ['rɛslɪŋ] N [U] 摔跤 shuāijiāo

wrinkled ['rɪŋkld] ADJ 布满皱纹的 bùmǎn zhòuwén de

wrist [rɪst] N [c] 手腕 shǒuwàn

[个 gè]

write [raɪt] (pt **wrote**, pp **written**) I VT **1** [+ address, number] 写下 xiěxià **2** [+ letter, note] 写 xiě **3** [+ novel, music] 创作 chuàngzuò **4** [+ cheque, receipt, prescription] 开 kāi II VI 写字 xiězì ▶ **to write to sb** 写信给某人 xiěxìn gěi mǒurén ▶ **write down** VT 记下 jìxià

writer ['raɪtə'] N [c] 作家 zuòjiā [位 wèi]

writing ['raɪtɪŋ] N [U] **1** (sth written) 文字 wénzì **2** (handwriting) 笔迹 bǐjì ▶ **in writing** 以书面形式 yǐ shūmiàn xíngshì

written ['rɪtn] PP of **write**

wrong [rɔŋ] I ADJ **1** [+ person, equipment, kind, job] 不合适的 bù héshì de **2** [+ answer, information, report] 错误的 cuòwù de **3** (morally bad) 不道德的 bù dàodé de II ADV (incorrectly) 错误地 cuòwù de ▶ **to be wrong** [answer] 是错的 shì cuòde; [person] 弄错的 ▶ **what's wrong?** 出了什么事? chūle shénme shì? ▶ **what's wrong with you?** 你怎么了? nǐ zěnme le? ▶ **to go wrong** [plan] 失败 shībài; [machine] 发生故障 fāshēng gùzhàng

wrote [rəut] PT of **write**

WWW (Comput) N ABBR (= World-Wide Web) 万维网 Wànwéiwǎng

Xmas ['ɛksməs] N ABBR (=
 Christmas) 圣诞节 Shèngdànjié
X-ray ['ɛksreɪ] I N [c] (*photo*) X光
 照片 X guāng zhàopiàn [张 zhāng]
 II VT 用X光检查 yòng X guāng
 jiǎnchá ▶**to have an X-ray** 做
 一次X光检查 zuò yīcì X guāng
 jiǎnchá

yacht [jɔt] N [c] **1** (*sailing boat*) 帆
 船 fānchuán [艘 sōu] **2** (*luxury craft*)
 游艇 yóutǐng [艘 sōu]
yard [jɑːd] N [c] (*US: garden*) 庭院
 tíngyuàn [座 zuò]
yawn [jɔːn] I VI 打呵欠 dǎ hēqiàn
 II N [c] 呵欠 hēqiàn [个 gè]
year [jɪərʲ] N [c] **1** 年 nián **2** (*Scol,
 Univ*) 学年 xuénián [个 gè]
 ▶**every year** 每年 měinián ▶**this
 year** 今年 jīnnián ▶**last year**
 去年 qùnián ▶**a** *or* **per year** 每
 年 měinián ▶**we lived there for
 years** 我们住在那儿有好多年了
 wǒmen zhùzài nàr yǒu hǎoduō
 nián le
yellow ['jɛləu] I ADJ 黄色的
 huángsè de II N [c/U] 黄色
 huángsè [种 zhǒng]

yes [jɛs] I ADV 是的 shìde II N [c] (*answer*) 是 shì

yesterday ['jɛstədɪ] I ADV 昨天 zuótiān II N [U] 昨天 zuótiān ▶**the day before yesterday** 前天 qiántiān

yet [jɛt] I ADV (*up to now: with negative*) 还 hái; (*in questions*) 已经 yǐjīng II CONJ 然而 rán'ér ▶**they haven't finished yet** 他们还没完工。 tāmen hái méi wángōng ▶**yet again** 又一次 yòu yīcì

yog(h)urt ['jəugət] N [c/U] 酸奶 suānnǎi [瓶 píng]

you [juː] PRON 1 (*singular*) 你 nǐ; (*plural*) 你们 nǐmen 2 任何人 rènhérén ▶**you never know** 谁知道 shuí zhīdào

young [jʌŋ] ADJ 幼小的 yòuxiǎo de ▶**my younger brother/sister** 我的弟弟/妹妹 wǒde dìdi/mèimei

your [jɔːʳ] ADJ (*of one person*) 你的 nǐ de; (*of more than one person*) 你们的 nǐmen de

yours [jɔːz] PRON (*of one person*) 你的 nǐ de; (*of more than one person*) 你们的 nǐmen de ▶**is this yours?** 这是你/你们的吗？ zhèshì nǐ/nǐmen de ma? ▶**yours sincerely/faithfully** 你真挚的/忠实的 nǐ zhēnzhì de/zhōngshí de

yourself [jɔːˈsɛlf] PRON 1 你自己 nǐzìjǐ 2 (*you*) 你 nǐ ▶**by yourself** (*unaided*) 独立地 dúlì de; (*alone*) 独自地 dúzì de

yourselves [jɔːˈsɛlvz] PL PRON 1 你们自己 nǐmen zìjǐ 2 (*you*) 你们 nǐmen ▶**by yourselves** (*unaided*)

独力地 dúlì de; (*alone*) 独自地 dúzì de

youth club N [c] 青年俱乐部 qīngnián jùlèbù [个 gè]

youth hostel N [c] 青年招待所 qīngnián zhāodàisuǒ [个 gè]

Z

zebra crossing ['ziːbrə-] (*Brit*) N
[c] 斑马线 bānmǎxiàn [条 tiáo]
zero ['zɪərəu] (*pl* **zero** *or* **zeroes**)
N **1** [U/c] (*number*) 零 líng [个 gè]
2 [U] (*nothing*) 没有 méiyǒu ▶ **5**
degrees below zero 零下5度
língxià wǔdù
zip [zɪp] N [c] (*Brit: fastener*) 拉链
lāliàn [条 tiáo]
zip code (*US*) N [c] 邮政编码
yóuzhèng biānmǎ [个 gè]
zipper ['zɪpər] (*US*) N [c] 拉链
lāliàn [条 tiáo]
zone [zəun] N [c] (*area*) 地带 dìdài
[个 gè]
zoo [zuː] (*pl* **zoos**) N [c] 动物园
dòngwùyuán [个 gè]
zucchini [zuːˈkiːnɪ] (*pl* **zucchini** *or*
zucchinis) (*US*) N [c/U] 绿皮密生

Chinese in Action

GREETINGS

▼ MEETING PEOPLE

● It is very important to use the appropriate form of greeting in China. As with other cultures, the way that you greet somebody will depend on whether you know them or whether they are a stranger. The most common greeting is:

> 你好 (nǐ hǎo), or
> 您好 (nín hǎo)

● The form 您好 (nín hǎo) is more formal and should be used when you want to show particular respect.

● Chinese people show great respect for the wisdom and experience of their elders. The senior people present will usually initiate the greetings, and you should greet the oldest, most senior person before any others.

▼ SOME TYPICAL GREETINGS

你好! (nǐ hǎo)	*Hello!*
嗨! (hāi)	*Hi!*
喂! (wèi)	*Hello! (usually on the phone)*
早上好! (zǎoshang hǎo)	*Good morning!*
早! (zǎo)	*Morning!*
最近身体怎么样? (zuìjìn shēntǐ zěnmeyàng)	
	How have you been?
还不错, 谢谢 (hái bùcuò, xièxie)	
	Fine, thanks.
好久不见! 最近还好吗? (hǎojiǔ bù jiàn! zuìjìn hái hǎo ma?)	
	Long time no see! How are you doing?
很好, 谢谢, 你怎么样? (hěn hǎo, xièxie, nǐ zěnmeyàng)	
	Very well, thank you, and you?
挺好的, 多谢。(tǐng hǎo de, duōxiè)	
	Fine, thanks.
棒极了! (bàng jí le)	*Great!*
一般。(yībān)	*So-so.*

▼ CHINESE NAMES

● Chinese family names are placed first, followed by the given name. For instance, in the name "Zhao Li," "Zhao" is the family name, "Li" the given name. Family names usually consist of one syllable, whereas given names can have either one or two syllables.

● Chinese people call their close friends and family members by their given names. For example, "Ma Wenli" may be addressed by close friends as "Wenli."

GREETINGS

- In formal situations you should address Chinese people by their family name or full name and the appropriate courtesy title. Unlike English, professional, social, and family titles always follow the name:

  Mr. Liu would be 刘先生 (Liú xiānsheng)
  Mr. Li Nan 李楠先生 (Lǐ Nán xiānsheng)
  Mrs. Liu 刘夫人 (Liú fūrén)
  Miss Liu 刘小姐 (Liú xiǎojiě)
  Ms. Liu 刘女士 (Liú nǚshì)
  Dr. Ma would be 马医生 (Mǎ yīshēng)
  Professor Xu would be 徐教授 (Xú jiàoshòu)

- Chinese people will often address people by their surname followed by their job title, for example

  叶主任 (Yè zhǔrèn)   Director Ye
  林老师 (Lín lǎoshī)   Teacher Lin

- Most Chinese women continue using their maiden names even after marriage, but they may indicate their marital status by using 太太 (tàitai) or 夫人 (fūrén) with their maiden name.

- 小姐 (xiǎojiě) is a polite and common form of address for a woman. An older woman can be addressed as 大姐 (dàjiě).

- If you want to address a group of people formally – for example, at a meeting – you say 女士们先生们 (nǚshìmen xiānshengmen) meaning 'Ladies and Gentlemen' (or just 女士们 ('Ladies') or 先生们 ('Gentlemen') if the group is not mixed).

- When you are not sure about someone's name or title, you should address him or her as 先生 (xiānsheng) (Sir) or 女士 (nǚshì) (Madam) or 小姐 (xiǎojiě) (Miss).

▼ INTRODUCTIONS

让我把你介绍给我的朋友们。(ràng wǒ bǎ nǐ jièshào gěi wǒ de péngyoumen) *Let me introduce you to my friends.*

我想让你认识一下我的丈夫。(wǒ xiǎng ràng nǐ rènshi yīxià wǒ de zhàngfu) *I'd like you to meet my husband.*

请允许我介绍一下到场的嘉宾。(qǐng yǔnxǔ wǒ jièshào yīxià dàochǎng de jiābīn) *Please allow me to introduce these distinguished guests.*

这是珍妮特。(zhè shì Zhēnnítè) *This is Janet.*

In response:

很高兴见到您。(hěn gāoxìng jiàndào nín) *Pleased to meet you.*

嗨，你好。(hāi, nǐ hǎo) *Hi, how are you doing?*

GREETINGS

您好。(nín hǎo) *How do you do?*

- If you want to attract the attention of someone you do not know – for example, in the street or in a shop – you say 劳驾 (láojià).

▼ PARTING

- The most common way to say goodbye to someone is 再见 (zàijiàn). Other alternatives are 回见 (huíjiàn) and 再会 (zàihuì).

再见！(zàijiàn) *Goodbye!*
再会！(zàihuì) *Bye!*
7点见。(qīdiǎn jiàn) *See you at seven.*
晚安！(wǎn'ān) *Good night!*
明天见！(míngtiān jiàn) *See you tomorrow!*
星期一见！(xīngqīyī jiàn) *See you on Monday!*
"回见！" "好，再会" (huíjiàn – hǎo, zàihuì) *'See you later.' – 'Okay, bye.'*

▼ BUSINESS CARDS

- Business/name cards are frequently used in business circles in China and will almost always be exchanged when meeting someone for the first time on business.

- Cards should be held in both hands when they are being offered or received. When receiving another person's card, you should take the time to look at it attentively before putting it away.

寰宇进出口有限责任公司

王长海　　总经理

地址：北京市和平路15号
邮编：100082
电话：+8610 64446666
传真：+8610 64446688
E-mail: wangchanghai@huanyu.com

Huan Yu Import & Export Co. Ltd.

Wang Changhai　　General Manager

Address: No. 15 Heping Road, Beijing, China
Zip Code: 100082
Tel.: +8610 64446666
Fax: +8610 64446688
E-mail: wangchanghai@huanyu.com

TELEPHONE

▼ MAKING A PHONE CALL

- When Chinese people make a phone call, they ask for the person they wish to speak to by name. It is not the Chinese caller's habit to give their own name first when making or receiving a call.

- When answering the telephone the standard response upon picking up the receiver is 喂 (wèi).

- When giving telephone numbers, Chinese speakers normally read out the numbers one by one so that:

  020 7900 0283 would be read:

  零二零 七九零零 零二八三
  líng'èrlíng qījiǔlínglíng líng'èrbāsān

- When making a phone call, you might want to say:

  喂？(wèi) *Hello?*
  请问…在吗？(qǐngwèn…zài ma) *Could I speak to … please?*
  是…吗？(shì…ma) *Is that …?*
  我怎么拨外线电话？(wǒ zěnme bō wàixiàn diànhuà) *How do I make an outside call?*
  …的区号是多少？(…de qūhào shì duōshao) *What is the code for … ?*
  我5分钟后打回来。(wǒ wǔ fēnzhōng hòu dǎ huílái) *I'll call back in 5 minutes.*
  他回来时，可否让他给我回电话？(tā huílái shí, kěfǒu ràng tā gěi wǒ huí diànhuà)
  Could you ask him to call me when he gets back?
  对不起，我拨错号了。(duìbuqǐ,wǒ bōcuò hào le) *Sorry, I must have dialled the wrong number.*
  电话掉线了。(diànhuà diàoxiàn le) *We were cut off.*
  线路很不清楚。(xiànlù hěn bù qīngchu) *This is a very bad line.*

- You might hear:

  请讲。(qǐng jiǎng) *Speaking.*
  请问您是哪位？(qǐngwèn nín shì nǎ wèi) *Who's speaking?*
  请问您找哪位？(qǐngwèn nín zhǎo nǎ wèi) *Who would you like to speak to?*
  请别挂断。(qǐng bié guàduàn) *Please hold (the line).*
  没人接听。(méi rén jiētīng) *There's no reply.*
  电话占线。(diànhuà zhànxiàn) *The line is engaged (Brit) or busy (US).*
  请问您是哪位？(qǐngwèn nín shì nǎ wèi) *Who shall I say is calling?*
  您要留言吗？(nín yào liúyán ma) *Would you like to leave a message?*

TELEPHONE

▼ AN EXAMPLE CONVERSATION

您好，这里是北京饭店。
Hello, Beijing Hotel.

请转二零一六房间分机，我找张先生。
Please could you put me through to room number 2016? I'd like to speak to Mr. Zhang.

好的，请稍等。
Hold on one moment, please.

他不在，您能帮我给他捎个话吗？
He doesn't seem to be in at the moment. Can I leave a message?

当然可以。
Of course.

请让他给约翰·史密斯回电话，电话号码是零零四四二零七三零六三八九二。
Could you ask him to call John Smith back? The phone number is 00442073063892.

好的。
Okay.

▼ USEFUL TELEPHONE VOCABULARY

打电话 (dǎ diànhuà) *make a phone call*
电话号码 (diànhuà hàomǎ) *phone number*
分机号码 (fēnjī hàomǎ) *extension number*
市话 (shìhuà) *local call*
长途电话 (chángtú diànhuà) *national call*
国际长途电话 (guójì chángtú diànhuà) *international call*

CHINESE IN ACTION

▼ **PERSONAL LETTERS**

● **Starting and ending a personal letter**

Opening lines:
亲爱的妈妈: *Dear Mum*
小强: *Dear Xiao Qiang*

Closing lines:
祝身体健康! *Take care!*
祝万事如意! *All the best*

● **Sample letter**

> *i* Note the use of a colon after the recipient's name.

婷婷:

　　好久没给你写信了。近来还好吗？最近工作忙吗？你是否还在上夜校？

　　我工作还很忙，天天加班。但老板对我很好，晚上经常开车顺路送我回家。过两天公司放假，准备和同事一起去旅游。

　　先写到这儿吧，有空给你打电话。

　　祝
万事如意!

　　　　　　　　　　　　　毛毛
　　　　　　　　　　2007年2月4日

> *i* The date should be written after your signature.

● **Useful expressions**

真高兴收到你的来信。 *It was lovely to hear from you.*
对不起, 没能及时给你回信, 只因… *Sorry I didn't reply sooner but …*
代我向…问好。 *Give my regards to …*
东东谨祝一切安好。 *Dong Dong sends his best wishes.*
盼早日回信。 *Looking forward to hearing from you.*

CORRESPONDENCE

▼ FORMAL LETTERS

● Starting and ending a formal letter

Opening lines:
致启者: Dear Sir or Madam
致有关人: To whom it may concern

Closing lines:
敬上 Regards
此致 敬礼! Yours sincerely

● Sample letter

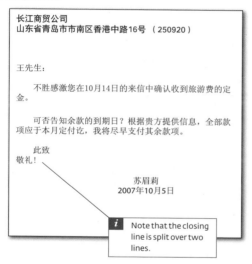

长江商贸公司
山东省青岛市市南区香港中路16号 （250920）

王先生：

　　不胜感激您在10月14日的来信中确认收到旅游费的定金。

　　可否告知余款的到期日？根据贵方提供信息，全部款项应于本月定付讫，我将尽早支付其余款项。

　　此致
敬礼!

苏眉莉
2007年10月5日

> **i** Note that the closing line is split over two lines.

● Useful expressions

现答复您…的来信。*In reply to your letter of …*
有关… *With reference to …*
收到您…来信不胜感激。*Thank you for your letter of …*
我们荣幸地通知您… *We are pleased to inform you that …*
我们很遗憾地通知您… *We regret to inform you that …*
为…致信给您。*I am writing to you to …*
如需详情，尽请与我联系。*If you require any further information, please do not hesitate to contact me.*
切盼回复。*I look forward to hearing from you.*

CORRESPONDENCE

▼ ADDRESSING AN ENVELOPE IN CHINESE

● You should start in the upper left hand corner with the addressee's post code. The address is written in the middle of the envelope, followed by the name of the addressee.

● Note that the address is written in the order:
> province, city
> street, house number
> addressee's name

● The sender's address and name, followed by their postcode, should be written in the lower right hand corner of the envelope.

● **Sample envelope**

> **i** Addressee's postcode

310000

浙江 杭州
定安路99号3幢1单元201室
张鹏收

北京长安路37号 王露
100018

> **i** Sender's address, name and postcode

CORRESPONDENCE

▼ E-MAIL

- E-mail is becoming very popular in China, but it is important to check that the person you are writing to actually uses it. Many Chinese executives and officials have an e-mail address but do not check their mail very regularly.

- Business e-mails should be brief but not too familiar or chatty.

- **Sample e-mail**

◀	▶▶	✎	📥	✉
回复	转发	写信	收件箱	收信

收件人：lili@cmail.com.cn

抄送：

主题：拓展产品系列讨论会

王经理：

　　根据近期的市场调研，我公司的彩电产品系列目前有些滞后于市场的发展需要，为提高企业竞争力，建议召开一次讨论会，共同商讨、制定相应措施。

　　会议时间暂定为2007年6月2日星期三下午2:00，地点在公司二楼小会议室。请通知相关人员准时参加。

　　如有问题，请尽早回复。

　　此致

敬礼!

　　　　　　　　　　　　　　　　　张 力

收件人：	To:
抄送：	Cc:
主题：	Subject:

NUMBERS

▼ CARDINAL NUMBERS

0	零 (líng)	24	二十四 (èrshísì)
1	一 (yī)	25	二十五 (èrshíwǔ)
2	二 (èr)	30	三十 (sānshí)
3	三 (sān)	31	三十一 (sānshíyī)
4	四 (sì)	40	四十 (sìshí)
5	五 (wǔ)	50	五十 (wǔshí)
6	六 (liù)	60	六十 (liùshí)
7	七 (qī)	70	七十 (qīshí)
8	八 (bā)	80	八十 (bāshí)
9	九 (jiǔ)	90	九十 (jiǔshí)
10	十 (shí)	100	一百 (yībǎi)
11	十一 (shíyī)	101	一百零一
12	十二 (shí'èr)		(yībǎi líng yī)
13	十三 (shísān)	212	二百一十二
14	十四 (shísì)		(èrbǎi yīshí'èr)
15	十五 (shíwǔ)	1,000	一千 (yīqiān)
16	十六 (shíliù)	1,001	一千零一
17	十七 (shíqī)		(yīqiān líng yī)
18	十八 (shíbā)	2,500	二千五百
19	十九 (shíjiǔ)		(èrqiān wǔbǎi)
20	二十 (èrshí)	100,000	十万 (shíwàn)
21	二十一 (èrshíyī)	1,000,000	一百万 (yībǎi wàn)
22	二十二 (èrshí'èr)	1,000,000,000	十亿 (shíyì)
23	二十三 (èrshísān)		

▼ ORDINAL NUMBERS

1st	第一 (dì-yī)	15th	第十五 (dì-shíwǔ)
2nd	第二 (dì-èr)	20th	第二十 (dì-èrshí)
3rd	第三 (dì-sān)	50th	第五十 (dì-wǔshí)
4th	第四 (dì-sì)	100th	第一百 (dì-yībǎi)
5th	第五 (dì-wǔ)	101st	第一百零一
6th	第六 (dì-liù)		(dì-yībǎi líng yī)
7th	第七 (dì-qī)	110th	第一百一十
8th	第八 (dì-bā)		(dì yībǎi yīshí)
9th	第九 (dì-jiǔ)	1,000th	第一千 (dì-yīqián)
10th	第十 (dì-shí)		

▼ FRACTIONS AND PERCENTAGES

½	二分之一 (èr fēn zhī yī)	0.5	零点五 (líng diǎn wǔ)
⅓	三分之一 (sān fēn zhī yī)	3.5	三点五 (sān diǎn wǔ)
¼	四分之一 (sì fēn zhī yī)	6.89	六点八九 (liù diǎn bājiǔ)
⅔	三分之二 (sān fēn zhī èr)	10%	百分之十 (bǎi fēn zhī shí)
		100%	百分之百 (bǎi fēn zhī bǎi)

DATE

▼ DAYS OF THE WEEK

星期一 (xīngqīyī)	Monday
星期二 (xīngqī'èr)	Tuesday
星期三 (xīngqīsān)	Wednesday
星期四 (xīngqīsì)	Thursday
星期五 (xīngqīwǔ)	Friday
星期六 (xīngqīliù)	Saturday
星期日 (xīngqīrì)	Sunday

▼ MONTHS OF THE YEAR

一月 (yīyuè)	January
二月 (èryuè)	February
三月 (sānyuè)	March
四月 (sìyuè)	April
五月 (wǔyuè)	May
六月 (liùyuè)	June
七月 (qīyuè)	July
八月 (bāyuè)	August
九月 (jiǔyuè)	September
十月 (shíyuè)	October
十一月 (shíyīyuè)	November
十二月 (shí'èryuè)	December

▼ TALKING ABOUT THE DATE

今天几号？	What's the date today?
今天星期几？	What day is it today?
今天是2004年1月20日。	It's the 20th of January 2004.
在20日	on 20th
1月1日	the first of January
在2月	in February
在2005年	in 2005
在十九世纪	in the nineteenth century
在九十年代	in the nineties

▼ WHEN?

今天	today
昨天	yesterday
明天	tomorrow
前天	the day before yesterday
后天	the day after tomorrow
昨天上午/下午/晚上	yesterday morning/afternoon/evening
明天上午/下午/晚上	tomorrow morning/afternoon/evening
第二天	the next day
每个星期六	every Saturday
下周日	next Sunday
上周二	last Tuesday

TIME

▼ **WHAT TIME IS IT?**

几点了? (jǐ diǎn le?)

1点
(yī diǎn)

1点15分 / 1点一刻
(yī diǎn shíwǔ fēn / yī diǎn yīkè)

1点25分
(yī diǎn èrshíwǔ fēn)

1点30分 / 1点半
(yī diǎn sānshí fēn / yī diǎn bàn)

1点45分 / 2点差一刻
(yī diǎn sìshíwǔ fēn / liǎng diǎn chà yī kè)

1点50分 / 2点差10分
(yī diǎn wǔshí fēn / liǎng diǎn chà shí fēn)

上午9点 / 晚上9点
(shàngwǔ jiǔ diǎn / wǎnshang jiǔ diǎn)

中午12点 / 凌晨零点
(zhōngwǔ shí'èr diǎn / língchén líng diǎn)

▼ **USEFUL EXPRESSIONS**

几点开始? What time does it start?
20分钟后 in twenty minutes
大约在8点钟 at around eight o'clock
上午 in the morning
下午 in the afternoon
傍晚 in the evening

English in Action

▼ 姓名和称谓

姓名

在说英语的国家中，姓名是由父母取的 *first name* （名字）和父母双方或一方的 *surname* （姓氏）组成。*forename* 即 *first name*。

> **i** 许多人还有 *middle name* （中名）。*middle name* 也是由父母取的，通常用缩略形式，而不用全称。*middle name* 用缩略形式在美国尤为常见：*John F Kennedy*。
> *Christian name* （教名）是指基督徒给孩子取的名字。

姓名缩写

initials （姓名缩写）是由某人的 *first name, middle name* 和 *surname* 的第一个字母的大写形式组成。例如，如果某人的全名是 *Elizabeth Margaret White*，她的姓名缩写即为 *EMW*。在某些商务和银行业环境中，她可以自称或被称为：*E.M.White*。
作者的姓名通常用 *initials*：*J.K. Rowling, E.M. Forster*。

先生、夫人等

如果某人不是你的朋友，你可以用头衔加姓氏礼貌地称呼他。*Mr* （先生）用于男士的姓氏前。已婚女士被称为 *Mrs* （夫人），未婚女士使用 *Miss* （小姐）或 *Ms* （女士）。

> *Mr Nichols can see you now.* （用于办公室会话）

人们有时也用这种比较礼貌的方式称呼比自己年长的人。

> *We'd better let Mrs Townsend know.*
> *Perhaps you should invite Mr Thomson as well.*

> **i** 过去，已婚的女性总是改用夫姓。如今，一些女性婚后仍延用自己的姓氏。如果不清楚一位女士是否已婚，可使用称呼 *Ms*。一些较年轻的女性更倾向于使用 *Ms*，而不是 *Mrs* 或 *Miss*，但是较年长的女性则不喜欢使用 *Ms* 这一称呼。

知名人士

一般只用姓氏来称呼作家、作曲家、艺术家和其他知名人士。

> *the works of Shakespeare*
> *the paintings of Van Gogh*

昵称

人们常用 *nickname*，名字的非正式形式，来称呼他人，在会话中更是如此。许多名字都有约定俗成的简短形式。例如，如果某人的名字是 *James*，人们可以称他为 *Jamie, Jim* 或 *Jimmy*。

▼ 称呼他人

称呼不认识的人

- 如果你想引起某个不认识的人的注意 —— 比如，在大街上或在商店里 —— 通常说 *Excuse me*。

    Excuse me. You've dropped your scarf.
    Excuse me. I think I'm next.

- 在现代英语中，*Mr*，*Mrs*，*Miss* 和 *Ms* 作为头衔，只用在姓氏前，而不能单独使用。*gentleman* 或 *lady*，*sir* 或 *madam* 也都不能单独用来称呼不认识的人。*sir* 或 *madam* 通常是商店中的工作人员用于招呼顾客时才用的礼貌性称呼。

> **ℹ** 在正式的场合称呼一群人 —— 例如，开会时 —— 可用 *ladies and gentlemen*。如果是性别单一的一群人，可以只称呼 *ladies* 或 *gentlemen*。
> *Good evening, ladies and gentlemen.*

称呼认识的人

- 如果你知道对方的姓氏，你可用头衔（通常是 *Mr*，*Mrs* 或 *Miss*）加姓氏称呼他们。这种用法相当正式。初次见面，或在电话中与你不认识的人交谈时，你会使用这种称呼方式。

    Thank you, Mr Jones.
    Goodbye, Dr Kirk

- 在英国、美国、澳大利亚等国的工作场所中，人们通常直呼名字，甚至对老板也是如此。在学校里，学生通常用 *Mr*，*Mrs* 或 *Miss* 加上姓氏称呼老师。在许多日常会话中，除非你想特别指明说话的对象，否则根本不用提及对方的姓名。

    What do you think, John?
    Are you going to the meeting with the new Finance Director?

> ⚠ 在 *Mr*，*Mrs* 和 *Miss* 后，只能加姓氏，而绝对不能加名。

ENGLISH IN ACTION

▼ 问候

与人打招呼

● 与人打招呼通常用 hello。这个词既非太正式，又不会太随便，适用于大多数场合。在 hello 的后面，通常加上对方的名字或寒暄的话。

> 'Hello, Tina.' — 'Hello. How are you today?'
> Hello, John. Had a good day?

● hi 或 hiya 是更为随便的问候方式，在年轻人中以及美式英语中尤为常用。

> Hiya, Tommy. How are you doing?

● 若要以正式方式问候他人，所用的词要视一天里的具体时间而定。

中午12点钟之前说 good morning。

> Good morning, Mr Wright. How are you today?

中午12点钟和6点钟之间说 good afternoon，6点之后人们说 good evening。

> Good afternoon. Could I speak to Ms Duff, please?
> Good evening. I'd like a table for four, please.

在拨打正式电话，以及与政府官员、商界人士等会面时，通常使用这些问候形式。

> ⚠ 只有晚间与人告别，或当自己或他人上床睡觉之前，才能说 good night。它不能用来问候别人。
> good day 在英式英语中是一种已经过时，并且相当正式的说法，但在美式英语和澳大利亚英语中仍较为常见。

● 如果某人说 How are you?，你可以简单地回答 Very well, thank you. 或 Fine, thanks.。你也可以礼貌地反问一声 How are you?，或更随便些 And you?。

> 'Hello, John. How are you?' — 'Fine, thanks, Mark. And you?'

● 在见面问候或告别时显得热情而有礼貌，人们有时说 Nice to see you.。

> 'Hello, it's nice to see you again. How are you?' – 'Nice to see you too, Mr Bates.'

特别的日子

● 在某人的生日见到其人时，可以说 *Happy Birthday!* 或 *Many happy returns!*。

● 在圣诞节见到别人时，可以说 *Merry Christmas!* 或 *Happy Christmas!*。

● 在新年，你可以祝愿人们 *Happy New Year!*。

分别

● 与人分别时，说 *goodbye*。这种表达方式有点正式。

> *'Goodbye, John,' Miss Saunders said.*

● *bye* 是更常用的告别方式，而且比较随便。

> *See you about seven. Bye.*

● *bye-bye* 的语气更加随便，它用于关系密切的亲戚和朋友之间，以及向小孩子道别时。

> *Bye-bye, dear. See you tomorrow.*

---

i　道晚安时，可以用 *goodnight* 或 *night*。
> *Well, I must be going. Night, John.*
> *I'm off to bed. Goodnight, everyone.*

● 如果你认为很快能再次见到对方，可以说。　*See you later.*

> *'See you later.' – 'Okay, bye.'*
> *See you on Monday.*

● 许多讲美式英语的人会用 *have a nice day* 向他们不太熟识的人道别。例如，在商店或酒店中工作的人员会对顾客这样说。

⚠ 在现代英语中，*good morning*，*good afternoon* 和 *good evening* 不用于告别。

---

i　在正式场合，比如商务会议，人们通常用握手以示问候或道别。在不太正式的场合下表示问候或道别时，男士们也会握手，或者，互相轻拍后背或肩膀，而女士们则常常亲吻女性或男性亲友。在问候或道别时，你也可以只用上述表达方式而不使用任何肢体动作，如握手、拍肩或是亲吻。

ENGLISH IN ACTION

ENGLISH IN ACTION

▼ 自我介绍和介绍他人

自我介绍

● 与陌生人初次见面，在自我介绍时，可以告诉对方你的姓名或介绍你是谁。你需要先说 hello 或其他客套的话。

> *'Hello. I'm Harry,' said the boy.*
> *'I don't think we've met, have we? Are you visiting?' – 'Yes, I'm Peter Taylor.'*

● 如果想显得正式些，则说 *May I introduce myself?*。

> *May I introduce myself? I'm Dr Anderson.*

> *i* 初次见面说 How do you do?，是一种极为正式，并且已经过时的表达方式。正确的回答也应是 How do you do?。
> *'I'm Nigel Jessop. How do you do?' – 'How do you do? I'm Alison Vere.'*

介绍他人

● 在介绍从未谋面的人相互认识时，说 *This is ...*。介绍时，使用何种姓名形式可以视场合的正式程度而定（见第2页）。

> *This is Shirley , Mr McKay. Shirley, this is Mr McKay.*

● 如果需要正式些，则说 *I'd like to introduce ...*。

> *Mr Anderson, I'd like to introduce my wife.*

● 比较随意的介绍某人的方式是 *I don't think you know ..., do you?*。

> *'I don't think you know Ann, do you?' – 'No, I don't think we've met. How are you?'*

> ⚠ 用手指指着别人介绍是很无礼的行为。但是，可以用手指指着物品或指示方向。

对介绍的应答

● 当你被介绍给对方后，你们双方都互道 hello。

> *'Francis, this is James.' – 'Hello, Francis. How are you?'*

● 如果双方都很年轻，而且不是在很正式的场合，可以说 hi。

> *'Jan, this is my boyfriend Jeff.' – 'Hi, Jeff.'*

▼ 邀请

邀请某人做某事

● 通常，礼貌地邀请某人做事，应说 Would you like to …?。

> *Would you like to come to my party on Saturday?*
> *Well, would you like to comment on that, Tessa?* (在会议或讨论中)

● 另一种礼貌的邀请形式是，祈使句与 please 连用。这种形式多由处于主导位置的一方使用。

> *Please help yourself to a drink.*
> *Sit down, please.*

● 也可用 How would you like to …? 或 Why don't you …? 间接地邀请某人，或用以 how about 开头的问句邀请。

> *How would you like to come and work for me?*
> *Why don't you come to the States with us in November?*
> *How about coming to stay for a few days?*
> *How about some lunch?*

i	如果应邀到某人家中做客，通常要带小礼物，比如鲜花或蛋糕。如被邀请就餐，大多数人会顺便带一瓶酒。主人通常会当面打开礼物。

回应邀请

● 如果接受邀请，就说 thank you。如果更加随便的话，就说声 thanks。

> *'You could borrow our tent if you'd like.' – 'Thank you. I'll come round and pick it up some time.'*

也可加一句 Yes, I'd love to. 或 I'd like that very much.。

> *'Won't you join me for lunch?' – 'Thanks, I'd like that very much.'*

● 如果拒绝邀请，不愿拜访某人或随某人去某地，则说 I'm sorry, I can't.。如果想解释原因，则用 I'm afraid … 或 I'd like to but …，再加上原因。

> *'Can you come and spend the day with me on Sunday?' – 'Oh, I'm sorry. I can't.'*
> *'We're having a party on Saturday. Can you come?' – 'I'm afraid I'm busy.'*
> *'Would you like to stay for dinner?' – 'I'd like to but I can't tonight.'*

ENGLISH IN ACTION

▼ 感谢他人

表示感谢

● 如果别人刚刚为你做了某事，或送给你某物，表示感谢的常用方式是说 thank you，或更随意地说声 thanks。

> 'Don't worry. I've given you a good reference.' – 'Thank you, Mr Dillon.'
> 'There's your receipt.' – 'Thanks.' (在商店)

● 人们常常加上 very much 以加强语气。

> 'Here you are.' – 'Thank you very much.'

你也可以说 Thanks a lot.（但不能说 Thank you a lot. 或 Thanks lots.）。

> 'I'll ring you tomorrow morning.' – 'OK. Thanks a lot.'

● 如果需要解释为何感谢对方，则说 Thank you for ... 或 Thanks for ...。

> Thank you for the earrings, Dad.
> Thanks for helping out.

在信中感谢某人（见第13页），一般都说 Thank you for ...。

> Dear Madam, Thank you for your letter of 5 June.

在正式的商务信函中，可以用 I am grateful for ...。

> I am grateful for your prompt reply to my request.

如果是给朋友的信，则用 Thanks for ...。

> Thanks for writing.

> ℹ️ 你会听到一些讲英式英语的人说 cheers 或 ta 表示感谢，这是非正式的表达方式。

如果某人请你吃东西，表示拒绝时，可以说 No, thank you. 或 No, thanks.（不能只说 Thank you.）。

> 'Would you like a coffee?' – 'No, thank you.'

如何回答感谢

● 如果某人因你帮忙而表示感谢，则应回答 That's all right. 或 That's OK.。

> 'Thank you, Charles.' – 'That's all right, David.'

如果想显得既礼貌又友好，可以说 It's a pleasure. 或 Pleasure.。

> 'Thank you very much for talking to us about your research.' – 'It's a pleasure.'

ENGLISH IN ACTION

▼ 道歉

致歉

● 如果打扰了某人或麻烦了某人，有多种道歉方式。最常用的是 sorry 或 I'm sorry。

> *'Stop that, you're giving me a headache.' – 'Sorry.'*
> *Sorry I'm late.*

可以在 I'm sorry 中加上副词 very, so, terribly 或 extremely，加强语势。

> *I'm very sorry if I worried you.*
> *I'm terribly sorry but I have to leave.*

> **i** 当不小心做了某事，例如踩了某人的脚，可以说 sorry 或 I'm sorry。讲美式英语的人则说 excuse me。

● 当打搅了某人或打断了某人的工作时，用 Excuse me, I'm sorry to disturb you.。这是礼貌的道歉方式。

> *Excuse me for disturbing you at home.*
> *I'm sorry to disturb you but I need your signature.*

● 如果想请某人让一下路，或想同陌生人讲话时，可以用 excuse me。一些说美式英语的人则会说 pardon me。

> *Excuse me, but is there a good restaurant near here?*
> *Excuse me, do you mind if I squeeze past you?*
> *Pardon me, Sergeant. I wonder if you'd do me a favor?*(美)

● 如果因需要做某事而不得不离开片刻，例如在商务环境中，或与不太熟识的人在一起时，也可以说 Excuse me。

> *Excuse me for a moment. I have to make a telephone call.*

> **i** 如果做了令人尴尬或失礼的事时，譬如打饱嗝、打嗝、打喷嚏或吃东西时发出声音，应该道歉。人们通常会说 excuse me 或 I beg your pardon。

接受道歉

● 接受道歉通常有固定的表达形式，例如 That's okay., Don't worry about it., 或 It doesn't matter.。

> *'I'm sorry.' – 'That's okay.'*
> *'I apologize for what I said.' – 'Don't worry about it.'*
> *'I'm sorry to ring so late.' – 'I'm still up. It doesn't matter.'*

▼ 写信该如何开头和结尾

给公司或组织机构的信件

称谓

Dear Sir
Dear Madam
Dear Sir or Madam
Dear Sirs(英)/*Gentlemen*(美)

结束语

Yours faithfully(英)
Yours truly(美)

如果是非常正式的信件，或不知道收信人的姓名，对男士用 *Dear Sir*，对女士则用 *Dear Madam*。如果不确定收信人的性别，写 *Dear Sir or Madam* 是最保险的。如果是写给公司而不是个人时，在英式英语中用 *Dear Sirs*，在美式英语中用 *Gentlemen*。

写给已知姓名的个人正式信件

称谓

Dear Ms Roberts
Dear Dr Jones
Dear Professor Honeyford

结束语

Yours sincerely(英)
Sincerely yours/Yours truly(美)

结尾可用下列表达方式，显得不那么正式：

Yours
Kind regards
(With) best wishes

给朋友或熟人的信件

称谓

Dear Jeremy
Dear Aunt Jane
Dear Granny
Hi Josh

结束语

All the best
Love (from)
Lots of love (from)
All my love

男士给男士写信时，不常用 *Love*，*All my love* 和 *Lots of love*，而多用 *Yours*，*Best wishes* 或 *All the best* 一类的表达方式。

电子邮件

尽管有时也需要用电子邮件发送正式信函，但是，当人们写电子邮件时，普遍比写信要随意。信件的开头和结尾方式同样适用于电子邮件。

> *i* 人们在给关系亲密的朋友或男/女朋友写信或电子邮件时，往往在落款后加几个
> X。X代表吻。

▼ 英国地址

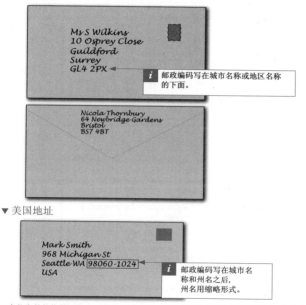

> Ms S Wilkins
> 10 Osprey Close
> Guildford
> Surrey
> GL4 2PX

> *i* 邮政编码写在城市名称或地区名称
> 的下面。

> Nicola Thornbury
> 64 Newbridge Gardens
> Bristol
> BS7 4BT

▼ 美国地址

> Mark Smith
> 968 Michigan St
> Seattle WA 98060-1024
> USA

> *i* 邮政编码写在城市名
> 称和州名之后，
> 州名用缩略形式。

● 寄往海外的信件通常要写发件人的地址。发件人的地址写在信封的背面，并在地
址前加注 sender 或 from。

● 称呼通常由收信人的头衔、名字的首字母及姓氏组成：

> *Ms S Wilkins*
> *Dr. P Smith*

● 如果是非正式书信，可以只写收信人的名和姓：

> *Sarah Wilkins*

● 如果收信人是已婚的夫妇，通常只写男方名字的首字母：

> *Mr and Mrs G T Black*

ENGLISH IN ACTION

11

▼ 给朋友的电子邮件

| ◀ reply | ▶▶ forward | ✎ compose | 📥 inbox | 📨 get mail |

To:	gemma@net.co.uk
From:	gordon@onemo.net
Subject:	Concert next week
cc:	
bcc:	

> ℹ 电子邮件(gemma@net.co.uk)的英文读法为:
> gemma **at** net **dot** co **dot** uk

Hi Gemma

I've just bought the new album by 'The Roads', and it's brilliant!
I've got a spare ticket to a concert they're giving in Edinburgh
next Wednesday evening, so I hope you can make it.

See you soon!

Gordon

▼ 商业电子信函

| ◀ reply | ▶▶ forward | ✎ compose | 📥 inbox | 📨 get mail |

| To:kevin.morrison@unt.com |
| From:charles.stimpson@unt.com |
| Subject:Budget meeting |
| cc: |
| bcc: |

Following on from our phone conversation this
morning, the Budget meeting will now be held on
Wednesday at 10 a.m. in the South Meeting Room. I
hope that you can attend.

Charles

ENGLISH IN ACTION

重点词组

To	收件人	Send	发送
From	发件人	Forward	转发
Subject	主题	Reply	答复发件人
Cc	抄送	Compose	撰写
Bcc	密件抄送	Delete	删除
Attachment	附件		

信件和电话

▼ 感谢信（英式）

41 Mallard Crescent
Leeds
LS6 9BR

► 2 January 2006

> ℹ 在非正式信件中，地址和日期写在右上角，或只写日期。参见第24页日期的写法。

Dear Tom and Lucy

Thank you for the lovely Christmas presents you sent me. The scarf is beautiful and the book is just what I wanted. As you know, J K Rowling is my favourite author.

I hear you're off to Spain soon. I'm so envious! I haven't got any holidays planned, but I'm going to London next weekend to see my aunt and uncle.

Thanks again for the presents, and have a great time in Spain. Don't forget to send me a postcard!

Lots of love

Carolyn

ENGLISH IN ACTION

重点词组

可以用下列方式开头：
It was lovely to hear from you.
Thanks for your letter.
Sorry I haven't written sooner.
It was great to see you last weekend/week/Monday.

可以用下列方式结尾：
Write soon.
Look forward to seeing you soon.
Give my regards to Sally.
Julia sends you a big hug.

▼ 给笔友的信

14 Glebe Avenue
Bristol
BR6 7AL

14 August 2007

Dear Xiao Ming

I'm so excited to have a Chinese pen pal! I'm hoping to learn lots about your country and the way you live from your letters.

I thought I would start by telling you a few things about myself. I'm 14 years old and live with my mum and dad and my little sister, Jenny, in a city in the south of England. Our house has three bedrooms and a big garden. We have two cats who are quite old now and sleep all the time. My best friend, Jack, lives next door.

My school isn't far from the house, so I can walk there when it isn't raining. My favourite subjects are languages and geography. I'd like to learn to speak a few words in Chinese. Can you teach me something?

What sorts of things do you like doing in your spare time? I like playing on the computer and watching football. Mum says I should get more exercise!

Please write back soon and tell me all about yourself and your family. I can't wait to hear from you!

All the best

Nick

ENGLISH IN ACTION

● 重点词组

I'm hoping to …
… a few things about myself/you …
What sorts of things … ?
I can't wait to hear from you

1386 Pine Boulevard
Los Angeles, California
20015

May 25, 2007

> i 以英式风格写信的人，在*Dear...*后面
> 加逗号或不加任何标点。以美式风格
> 写信的人，则在*Dear...*后面加冒号。
> 参见第2页有关姓名和头衔的内容。

Dear Julia:
How are things? I'm sorry I haven't written earlier but I've been so busy moving into my new apartment.

It's my birthday on June 14 and I'm having a party to celebrate. Can you come? It starts at 7 p.m. and will probably end around midnight. There'll be food but please bring a bottle! If you'd like to stay the night, I have plenty of room and it will give us a chance to catch up on each other's news.

I hope you'll be able to come and look forward to hearing from you soon.

Love

Marie

▼ 酒店预订函(英式)

26 Guanghua Road
Chaoyang District
Beijing 100027
China

Mrs Elaine Hudson
Manager
Poppywell Cottage
Devon
DV3 9SP

23rd June 2007

Dear Mrs Hudson

> i 在商务信函的右上角，写上发信人自
> 己的地址，但不要写发信人的姓名。
> 日期紧接在收信人地址的下一行。在
> 信纸的左上角，通常在日期的下一
> 行，写上收信人的姓名和／或职务头
> 衔。如果使用带信头的信纸，日期写
> 在收信人地址的上一行上或下一行，
> 或写在信纸的右上角。参见第24页有
> 关日期的写法。

My sister stayed with you last year and has recommended your guest house very highly.

I would like to reserve a room for one week from 18th–24th August. I would be very grateful if you would let me know how much this would be for two adults and two children and whether you have a room free between these dates.

Yours sincerely
Ming Li

▼ 投诉信（美式）

323 Florida Grove Rd
Hopelawn
New Jersey
NJ 08851

Railroad Inc.
43 Abbeyhill Drive
Hopelawn
New Jersey
NJ 08952

July 27, 2007

Dear Sir or Madam:

I traveled from Atlantic City to New York on one of your trains last Friday July 20 and am writing to let you know that I am very dissatisfied with the service you are providing.

The train was not only one hour late leaving Atlantic City it lost a further 30 minutes en route. The heating did not appear to be working and there was no restaurant car. I feel that your customers are paying very high prices for tickets to travel on your trains but are receiving a very unsatisfactory level of service. I have been very reluctant to take my car into the city and have no wish to add to the general congestion and pollution but you can be sure that I will be driving from now on.

Yours truly

Michael Pentangeli

ENGLISH IN ACTION

▼ 打电话

接通

● 下列表达可以帮助你找到正确的电话号码:

What is the dialling code for Liverpool? (英式)
What is the area code for Los Angeles? (美式)
What is the number for directory enquiries? (英式)
What is the number for directory assistance? (美式)
I want to make a reverse-charge call to London. (英式)
I want to make a collect call to London. (美式)
How do I get an outside line?

开始通话

接听电话

● 接听电话时,通常先说 *hello*,或使用比较正式的问候方式(参见第4页)。如果当时你在工作,可以给出自己的姓名,所在部门或公司的名称,或给出电话号码或分机号码。参见第21页,如何报电话号码。

Hello?
Hello, Li Xin speaking.
Good morning, Lotus Blossom Hotel. Can I help you?
Eight six nine two three five seven. Hello?

如何问候接听电话的人

● 当对方接听电话并致以问候后,打电话的人通常也要问候对方,然后说 *It's ...* 或 *This is ...* 以表明自己的身份。

Oh, hello. It's Mei Rong here.
Hello. This is Rong.

结束通话

● 可以用第5页中任何一种告别方式结束通话。也可以说 *Speak to you soon.* 或 *Thanks for ringing.*。

在办公室

要求接通某人

● 如果你知道联络对方的姓名或分机号码,或想转接到某个特定部门,可以使用下列的短语。

Hello. Could I speak to Susan, please?
Hello. Is Paul there, please?
Could you put me through to Dr Henderson, please?
Can I have extension 5443, please?

● 如果你认为自己知道接听电话的人是谁,则可以问 *Is that ...?*。

如果正是其人，对方则回答 Speaking.。

'Hello. Is that Emma?' – 'Speaking.'

接线员或秘书可能会说…

●如果是与接线员或秘书通话，他们可能会使用以下表达方式：

Who shall I say is calling?

Hold the line, please.

Hold on, I'll see if she's in.

I'll just get him.

One moment, please.

I'm putting you through now.

Dr Jackson is on another line. Do you want to hold?

There's no reply.

I'm sorry. Mr Green isn't here at the moment.

Would you like to leave a message?

留言

●如果想找的人不在，你可以留言，告知晚些时候会再打，或者让别人转告，请他回电话：

Could I leave a message, please?

I'll call back in half an hour.

Would you ask him to call me when he gets back?

通话故障

●如果无法接通想拨打的号码，可以用下列惯用语解释问题所在：

I can't get through.

Their phone is out of order.

I can't get a signal here.

I must have dialled the wrong number.

We were cut off.

●也有可能无法听清对方的话：

We've got a crossed line.

This is a very bad line.

The line is breaking up.

录音留言

●录音留言在英国和美国非常普遍，在大型公司或组织里就更加常见。无人接听电话时就会听到：

Your call is in a queue and will be answered shortly.

All our operatives (美) are busy at the moment. Please hold the line.

Please replace the handset and try again.

The number you are calling is engaged (英)/busy (美). Please try again later.

信件和电话

The number you have dialled has not been recognized.
Please hold the line while we try to connect you.

● 人们通常也会在家中的电话答录机上录下个人留言，以下是告知拨打电话的人何时开始录音的标准方式：

Please speak after the tone (英)/*beep* (美).

▼ 手机短信

随着手机的出现，一种新的短信"语言"诞生了，并且因其迅捷、有趣，尤其受到年轻人的青睐。它的特点是，根据类似的发音，采用简短的拼写方式：例如，*U* 代表 *you*，*R* 代表 *are*，*d8* 代表 *date* 以及 *2nite* 代表 *tonight*。新的表达方式总是不断地出现。

2 = to
2DAY = today
2MORO = tomorrow
2NITE = tonight
2U = to you
4 = for
B = be
B4 = before
COZ = because
CU = see you
D8 = date
EZ = easy
GR8 = great
H8 = hate
L8R = later
LOL = laugh out loud/lots of love
LV = love
M8 = mate
MSG = message
NE = any
NE1 = anyone
OIC = oh I see
PLS = please
PPL = people
R = are
RN = right now
RU = are you
RUOK = are you OK?
S/O = someone
S/TH = something

SUM1 = someone
THX = thanks
TTFN = ta ta *or* bye for now
TTYL = talk to you later
TXT = text
U = you
V = very
WAN2 = want to
WIV = with
XLNT = excellent
WKND = weekend
W/O = without
WUD = what are you doing?
Y = why
YR = your

THX 4 THE MSG.
XLNT NEWS! CU AT
THE WKND THEN.
LOL JAMES

数字

▼ 基数

下列的数字称作基数。根据此表，你可以知道如何构成其他数字。数字可用作形容词（用于名词前，有时也称作限定词）或代词（用于代替名词）。

0	nought(英)/naught(美), zero, nothing, oh	100	one hundred/a hundred
1	one	101	one hundred and one/
2	two		a hundred and one
3	three	102	one hundred and two/
4	four		a hundred and two
5	five	110	one hundred and ten/
6	six		a hundred and ten
7	seven	120	one hundred and twenty/
8	eight		a hundred and twenty
9	nine	200	two hundred
10	ten	300	three hundred
11	eleven	400	four hundred
12	twelve	500	five hundred
13	thirteen	1000	one thousand/
14	fourteen		a thousand
15	fifteen	1001	one thousand and one/
16	sixteen		a thousand and one
17	seventeen	1010	one thousand and ten/
18	eighteen		a thousand and ten
19	nineteen	1100	one thousand one hundred
20	twenty	1200	one thousand two hundred
21	twenty-one	1500	one thousand five hundred
22	twenty-two	2000	two thousand
23	twenty-three	5000	five thousand
24	twenty-four	10,000	ten thousand
25	twenty-five	20,000	twenty thousand
26	twenty-six	100,000	one hundred thousand/
27	twenty-seven		a hundred thousand
28	twenty-eight	150,000	one hundred and fifty thousand/
29	twenty-nine		a hundred and fifty thousand
30	thirty	1,000,000	one million/a million
40	forty	2,000,000	two million
50	fifty	1,000,000,000	one billion/a billion
60	sixty		
70	seventy		
80	eighty		
90	ninety		

▼ 重点短语

She's fifteen (years old).

on page two hundred and fifty-six

two plus seven are nine

eight minus two are six

hundreds of years

the two women

all five candidates

two small children

Fifteen people were missing.

Five of the children came with their father.

in fives

They sold the house for £150,000.

数字

- one 作为数字用在名词前，强调只有一个事物，或用于表示表达的精确性。当谈论一个团体中的特定一员时也用 one。否则，就用 a。

  There was only one gate into the palace.
  One member said that he would never vote for such a proposal.
  A car came slowly up the road.

- 数字0有如下几种表达方式：

  在温度、税率、利率中，用 zero
  It was fourteen below zero when they woke up.

  在小数点前，用 nought(英式)/naught(美式)
  nought point eight nine (0.89)

  表示计算，在口语中用 nothing
  five minus five is nothing

  当一个一个地报数字，或在小数点后时，用 oh 或字母 o
  point oh eight nine (.089)

  在体育比分中，用 nil
  England beat Germany one-nil.

- 介于999和100的数字通常用阿拉伯数字表示。当朗读或写成单词时，在英式英语中，百位数和十位数之间用 and 连接，而在美式英语中，省略 and。

  261 →   *two hundred and sixty-one* (英)
                two hundred sixty-one (美)

- 介于1000 和 9999 之间的数字，逗号通常放在第1个数字后：1,526

- 有时以空格代替逗号：15 000 1 986 000

- 当大于 9999 的数字写成阿拉伯数字时，通常在右起第3位数字前加逗号，在右起第6位数字前加逗号，依次类推，从而把数字分成3个数字一组的几组：15,000 1,986,000

---

i **欲知更多?**

报电话号码时，要单独报出每个数字

    0171 447 3352
    🔊 *oh one seven one four four seven three three five two*

当重复数字时，英国人用单词 "double"，美国人直接重复数字

    0171 447 3352
    🔊 *oh one seven one double four seven double three five two* (英)
    zero one seven one four four seven there three five two (美)

ENGLISH IN ACTION

数字

▼ 序数词

序数词用于表明某物在一个系列或序列中所处的位置，可以用作形容词(用于名词前，the 或 her一类的限定词之后)、代词(代替名词)，或副词(在谈论赛跑或其他比赛时，与某些动词连用，比如come 或 finish)。大多数分数的分母用序数词表示。

1st	first	26th	twenty-sixth
2nd	second	27th	twenty-seventh
3rd	third	28th	twenty-eighth
4th	fourth	29th	twenty-ninth
5th	fifth	30th	thirtieth
6th	sixth	31st	thirty-first
7th	seventh	32nd	thirty-second
8th	eighth	40th	fortieth
9th	ninth	41st	forty-first
10th	tenth	42nd	forty-second
11th	eleventh	50th	fiftieth
12th	twelfth	60th	sixtieth
13th	thirteenth	70th	seventieth
14th	fourteenth	80th	eightieth
15th	fifteenth	90th	ninetieth
16th	sixteenth	100th	hundredth
17th	seventeenth	101st	hundred and first
18th	eighteenth	102nd	hundred and second
19th	nineteenth	103rd	hundred and third
20th	twentieth	110th	hundred and tenth
21st	twenty-first	200th	two hundredth
22nd	twenty-second	1000th	thousandth
23rd	twenty-third	2000th	two thousandth
24th	twenty-fourth	10,000th	ten thousandth
25th	twenty-fifth	1,000,000th	millionth
	1,000,000,000th	billionth	

We live on the fourth floor.
in the twelfth century
on her twenty-first birthday
The first two years have been very successful.
An Italian came second.
I was the first to arrive.
the third of a series of documentaries

● 如上表所示，序数词常用缩略形式表示，1加 st 为 first，2加 nd 为 second，3加 rd 为 third, fourth 到 ninth 分别用相应的基数词加 th 表示 —— 例如，6th。这些缩写形式在日期中尤为常用。

星期和日期

▼ 星期

Monday	星期一	Saturday	星期六
Tuesday	星期二	Sunday	星期日
Wednesday	星期三		
Thursday	星期四		
Friday	星期五		

What day <u>is it</u> today? <u>It's</u> Thursday.
Why didn't you come to the meeting <u>on</u> Wednesday?
I'm usually here <u>on</u> Mondays and Fridays.
Deliveries <u>usually</u> arrive <u>on a</u> Thursday.
The attack took place <u>last</u> Thursday.
Talks are likely to start <u>next</u> Tuesday.
We meet here <u>every</u> Saturday morning.
I'll be away <u>from</u> Monday <u>to</u> Friday.
I'll need an answer <u>by</u> Monday.
We're having a party on <u>the last</u> Sunday <u>in</u> May.

▼ 月份

January	一月	July	七月
February	二月	August	八月
March	三月	September	九月
April	四月	October	十月
May	五月	November	十一月
June	六月	December	十二月

● 月份前用介词 in。

It always snows <u>in</u> January.
I flew to London <u>in early</u> March.
It happened <u>in late</u> May, and the apple trees were in bloom.
He spent two weeks with us <u>in July</u> 1993.

⚠ next（下一个）或 last（上一个）加月份，前面不用介词 in。
　　Staff were on strike <u>last</u> June.
　　I don't know where I'll be <u>next</u> November.

● 某月中的具体日子前用介词 on。

His exhibition opens <u>on 5 February</u>（英）/February 5（美）.
The trial will begin <u>on August the twenty-second</u>.

> **i** 在英国，一学年分为三个 terms（学期），夏季有长假期，圣诞节和复活节各有一个
> 较短的假期。在美国，一学年分为两个 semesters（学期），十月、四月以及圣诞节
> 和复活节都会放假。

▼ 季节

Spring	春季	Autumn (英)/Fall (美)	秋季
Summer	夏季	Winter	冬季

- 季节前的介词用 in。

    In winter the nights are extremely cold.
    It's nice to get away in the spring.
    We met again in the spring of 1977.

> ⚠ next (下一个) 或 last (上一个) 加上季节, 前面不用介词 in。
> *The final report is due out next autumn (英)/fall (美).*
> *I was supposed to go last summer.*

▼ 日期的写法

- 书写日期有几种不同的方式:

13 September	*September 13*
13th September	*September 13th*

- 上面的例子是书信中日期的书写方式。美国人通常把月份放在最前面。

- 若想给出年份, 则将年份放在最后。如果将日放在月后, 则用逗号将年份与日期分开。

    13th September 2004 (in a letter)
    My date of birth is 13 September 1957.
    I was born on September 13th, 1957.

- 也可按如下所示的方式, 将日期完全用数字表达。数字形式常常用于信或表格的上部。在英国, 日放在最前面。

    13/9/57 或 *13.9.57*

- 在美国, 月份放在日之前。

    9/13/57 或 *9.13.57*

▼ 日期的读法

- 即使日期是用基数词表示, 也要读作序数词。

    September 13 读作 *September the thirteenth* (英)

- 若月放在表示日的数字之后, 月份前要加介词 of。

    13 September 读作 *the thirteenth of September*

> ℹ 在以上两种情况下, 美国人通常都读作 September thirteenth。

- 若所指的月份很明确, 就可省略月份。

  'What's the date today?' – 'It's the twelfth.'

▼ 年的读法

- 读年份时一般分成两部分。例如:

  1957 读作 *nineteen fifty-seven*
  1860 读作 *eighteen sixty*

  以"20-"开头的年份 —— 例如, 2003 和 2010 —— 可以读作 *two thousand and ...*。例如:

  2003 读作 *two thousand and three*
  2010 读作 *two thousand and ten*

  以"20-"开头的年份也可以分成两部分读, 例如:

  2020 可读作 *twenty twenty*
  2004 可读作 *twenty oh four*

- 以"-00"结尾的年份, 可将第二部分读作 *hundred*。例如:

  1900 读作 *nineteen hundred*

  人们常常写 the year 2000, 而不是仅仅写成 2000。人们通常将其读作 *the year two thousand*。

- 以"01-09"结尾的年份有两种读法。例如:

  1807 可读作 *eighteen oh seven* 或 *eighteen hundred and seven*。

▼ 年代和世纪

- 1970 –1979 可以读作 *the nineteen seventies*, 或非正式的读法为 *the seventies*。

  the 1960s 读作 *the (nineteen) sixties*
  the 1970s 读作 *the (nineteen) seventies*

- 说到 20 世纪的年代时, 不必指出世纪。例如, 1920s 可以读作 *the twenties*。它可以写作 the '20s, the 20s 或 the Twenties。

⚠ 1400 –1499 称作 the fifteenth century (15世纪), 而不是 "the fourteenth century" (14世纪)。这非常合逻辑, 因为 1 世纪是指从 1年 —— 公元纪年的开始 —— 到 99年。我们现在正处于 21 世纪 (2000–2099)。

- 世纪还可以写作序数词, 例如, the 20th century。

时间

▼ 几点了？

It's one o'clock

It's a quarter past one (英)
It's a quarter after one (美)
It's one fifteen

It's half past one (英)
It's half after one (美)
It's one thirty

It's a quarter to two (英)
It's a quarter of two (美)
It's one forty-five

Its twenty-five past one (英)
It's twenty-five after one (美)
It's one twenty-five

It's ten to two (英)
It's ten of two (美)
It's one fifty

It's 13 minutes to two (英)
It's 13 minutes of two (美)
It's one forty-seven

⚠ o'clock 只用在表示整点的时间后。例如，可以说 five o'clock，但不能说 "ten past five o'clock" 或 " a quarter past five o'clock"。
- 可以用 minutes 表示5分钟以内的时间，或精确地表示时间。
  It was twenty-four minutes past ten.
  We left home at exactly five minutes to ten.

- 从以上例子可知，可以用小时加过了多少分钟来表示时间。
  7.35 可以读作 *seven thirty-five* 或 *twenty-five minutes to eight*。

- 在整点后未必一定用 o'clock。人们常常只用数字。
  I used to get up every morning at six.

- 如果过整点的分钟数小于10，许多人在分钟数前用 o，读作 oh。例如：
  10.07 可以读作 *ten oh seven* 或 *ten seven*。

时间

注意, 在写时间时, 英国人在小时后加圆点, 譬如: 10.07。而美国人多用冒号: 7:35。

● 若所指的钟点很明确, 在介词 past 或 to 之后不必加钟点。

> 'What time is it?' – 'Twenty-five past.'
>
> 'What time does the train leave?' – 'I think it's at quarter to.'

问时间	回答
What time is it?	It's nearly ten past twelve. (英)
	It's nearly ten after twelve. (美)
What's the time now?	It's three o'clock exactly.
What time do you make it?	I make it four twenty-seven.
Do you have the time (on you)?	Yes, it's half past nine.
Can you tell me the time?	Yes, it's nearly quarter to eight.

相关用语

Mary left at three and caught the bus.

The students must leave their rooms by nine o'clock this morning.

He was home by six for dinner.

She was busy until three o'clock, when she had to meet her parents.

I've been awake since four.

Did you see the eleven o'clock news?

`04:00`		`16:00`
four in the morning		four in the afternoon
4 a.m.		4 p.m.

`09:00`		`21:00`
nine in the morning		nine in the evening
9 a.m.		9 p.m.

`12:00`	
twelve in the morning	midday
12 a.m.	noon

● 可以加 a.m. (代表 ante meridiem, 拉丁语, 表示 "中午之前") 表示午夜到中午之间的时间。同样, p.m. (代表 post meridiem, 表示 "中午之后") 表示中午到午夜之间的时间。这些缩写通常不用于对话中, 而且从不与 o'clock 连用。

> *The doors will be opened at 10 a.m.*
>
> *He finally got home at 11.30 p.m., having set out at 6 a.m.*